Instructor's Resource Manual

THE MAKING OF THE WEST

PEOPLES AND CULTURES

THIRD EDITION

MALIA B. FORMES
Western Kentucky University

DAKOTA HAMILTON
Humboldt State University

PAUL A. TOWNEND
University of North Carolina Wilmington

BEDFORD/ST. MARTIN'S   Boston ◆ New York

2 1 0 9 8
e d c b a

For information, write: Bedford/St. Martin's, 75 Arlington Street, Boston, MA 02116 (617-399-4000)

ISBN-10: 0–312–46521–1
ISBN-13: 978–0–312–46521–6

Preface

This instructor's manual draws on our experiences as classroom teachers. All of us have used *The Making of the West: Peoples and Cultures* in our classrooms, and we have brought our experience with the Western Civilization course and with this textbook to revising this manual for the third edition. There are a number of exciting changes to this edition of *The Making of the West*, and these changes have been incorporated into the instructor's material presented here and on the book's companion Web site (**bedfordstmartins.com/hunt**). We discuss these new features in the following sections, but the strong integrative approach of the first two editions of the textbook remains integral to our vision. We all have been pleased with the success in using this approach in our classrooms, and we hope you will too.

Changes to This Manual

We have revised this manual not only to reflect changes in *The Making of the West* but also to make the manual easier to use and more specific in its suggestions. The most significant change is the tighter integration between the textbook, this manual, and the student online study guide. Each chapter now includes the new opening *Focus Question* from the textbook. The manual's chapter summaries have been revised into precise *Annotated Chapter Outlines* with specific references to textbook page numbers. Recommendations for *Lecture Strategies* and *Class Discussion Starters* have been separated into two distinct sections. The sections previously entitled *Historical Skills* have been replaced by discrete sections that include *Reviewing the Text, Discussing the Documents, Working with Visual Sources*, and *Mapping Exercises*, all referencing material in the textbook and all providing model answers with specific page numbers from the text. Also new are suggestions for in-class assignments and presentations and for essay questions. Finally, this new edition has a section in each chapter for users of the companion reader, *Sources of* THE MAKING OF THE WEST, edited by Katharine J. Lualdi. The nature and purpose of all resources in this manual, old and new, are described below.

Chapter Resources

Five to eight *Main Chapter Topics* open each chapter of this manual. These topics are broad enough for quick referencing and offer good starting points for lecture and discussion. These topics are followed by the textbook chapters' new *Focus Question* and one or two possible answers provided to help you and your students identify the central developments that will make each chapter and period a coherent whole and that connect the peoples, places, and historical events featured. The *Annotated Chapter Outline* articulates the main events and themes of each heading and subheading within the chapter. Following the outlines, three to five suggestions for *Lecture Strategies* incorporate political, social, economic, and cultural themes. *Class Discussion Starters* utilize both primary documents and secondary materials to provide ideas for engaging students in discussions. *Reviewing the Text* sections provide model answers to the new questions featured at the end of each textbook chapter—the review questions that also appear at the close of each major section of the chapter—and the Making Connections questions. These questions also appear in the student Online Study Guide without model answers. The new *Discussing the Documents* sections in the manual provide instructors with the questions from the student Online Study Guide along with model answers, as well as additional original questions for discussing the book's primary documents in class. Each chapter also has a section For Users of *Sources of The Making of the West* providing discussion questions for connecting two of the documents in each chapter of the reader with the textbook. *Working with Visual Sources* references visual activities and features in the textbook and that students can access in the Online Study Guide and provides model answers not available to students. The *Mapping Exercises* sections contain ideas for working with all of the textbook's major maps in the classroom. *In-Class Assignments and Presentation Topics* sections provide specific ideas for piquing students' interest and generating useful discussions or for in-class assignments. Finally, the section on *Additional Resources* contains relevant literature and film for formulating lecture ideas and/or for students who want to read further and, where applicable, a list of other Bedford/St. Martin's titles and supplementary resources relevant to the chapter.

Appendix Essays: Enhancing the Western Civilization Classroom

For instructors who may wish to try something new in the classroom, these essays offer ways to change the dynamic of their courses. First-time instructors may find these short tutorials helpful to refer to as they experiment with different teaching techniques throughout the semester. The essays include:

- "What Is 'The West'?," by Michael D. Richards (Sweet Briar College)
- "Active Learning Strategies for the Western Civilization Classroom," by Dakota Hamilton (Humboldt State University)
- "Working Primary Sources into the Western Civilization Syllabus," by Katharine J. Lualdi (University of Southern Maine)
- "Visual Literacy: The Image in the Western Civilization Classroom," by Paul R. Deslandes (Texas Tech University)
- "Literature and the Western Civilization Classroom," by Michael D. Richards (Sweet Briar College)

Supplements Available with *The Making of the West: Peoples and Cultures*, Third Edition

This *Instructor's Resource Manual* serves as the keystone to the comprehensive collection of supplements available for *The Making of the West: Peoples and Cultures*, Third Edition. Each chapter of this manual closes with a list of the specific components relevant to that chapter.

For Instructors

Print Resources

Transparencies A set of over 200 full-color acetate transparencies for *The Making of the West* includes all full-sized maps and many images and figures from the text.

New Media Resources

Using the Bedford Series in History and Culture with The Making of the West at bedfordstmartins.com/using series. This short online guide provides practical suggestions for using the volumes in the Bedford Series in History and Culture in conjunction with *The Making of the West*. This reference supplies connections between textbook themes and each series book and provides ideas for classroom discussions. The guide supplies not only connections between the text and the supplements but also ideas for starting discussions focused on a single primary-source volume.

NEW HistoryClass. Bedford/St. Martin's online learning space for history gives you the right tools and the rich content to create your course, your way. An interactive e-book and e-reader enable you to easily assign relevant textbook sections and primary documents. Access to the acclaimed content library, Make History, provides unlimited access to thousands of maps, images, documents, and Web links. The tried-and-true content of the Online Study Guide offers a range of activities to help students access their progress, study more effectively, and improve their critical thinking skills. Customize provided content and mix in your own with ease—everything in HistoryClass is integrated to work together in the same space.

Instructor's Resource CD-ROM. This disc provides instructors with ready-made and customizable *PowerPoint* multimedia presentations built around chapter outlines, maps, figures, and selected images from the textbook. The disc also contains images in jpeg format and outline maps in PDF format for quizzing or handouts.

Computerized Test Bank—by Joseph Coohill, Pennsylvania State University at New Kensington, Malia B. Formes, Western Kentucky University, Frances Mitilineos, Loyola University Chicago, and Paul A. Townend, University of North Carolina-Wilmington, available on CD-ROM. This fully updated test bank offers over 80 exercises per chapter, including multiple-choice, identification, source analysis, relationship and causation questions, and full-length essay questions. Instructors can customize quizzes and edit both questions and answers, as well as export them to a variety of formats, including WebCT and Blackboard. The disc includes answer keys and essay outlines.

Book Companion Site at bedfordstmartins.com/hunt. The companion Web site gathers all the electronic resources for *The Making of the West*, including the Online Study Guide and related Quiz Gradebook, at a single Web address, providing convenient links to lecture, assignment, and research materials as well as PowerPoint chapter outlines and the digital libraries at Make History.

NEW Make History at bedfordstmartins.com/makehistory. Comprising the content of our five acclaimed online libraries—Map Central, the Image Library, DocLinks, HistoryLinks, and PlaceLinks, *Make History* provides one-stop access to relevant digital content including maps, images, documents, and Web links. Students and instructors alike can search this free, easy-to-use database by keyword, topic, date, or specific chapter of *The Making of the West* and can download the content they find. Instructors can also create collections of content and post them to the Web to share with students.

Content for Course Management Systems. A variety of student and instructor resources developed for this textbook area ready for use in course management systems such as Blackboard, WebCT, and other platforms. This e-content includes nearly all of the offerings from the book's *Online Study Guide* as well as the book's test bank.

Videos and Multimedia. A wide assortment of videos and multimedia CD-ROMs on various topics in European history is available to qualified adopters.

For Students

Print Resources

Sources of THE MAKING OF THE WEST, Third Edition—Volumes I (to 1740) and II (since 1500)—by Katharine J. Lualdi, University of Southern Maine. This companion sourcebook provides written and visual sources to accompany each chapter of *The Making of the*

West. Political, social, and cultural documents offer a variety of perspectives that complement the textbook and encourage students to make connections between narrative history and primary sources. Short chapter summaries and document headnotes contextualize the wide array of sources and perspectives represented, while discussion questions guide students' reading and promote historical thinking skills. The third edition features five or more written documents per chapter and one-third more visual sources. Available free when packaged with the text and now available in the e-book (see above).

NEW Trade Books. Titles published by sister companies Farrar, Straus and Giroux; Henry Holt and Company; Hill and Wang; Picador; and St. Martin's Press are available at a 50 percent discount when packaged with Bedford/St. Martin's textbooks. For more information, visit **bedfordstmartins.com/tradeup**.

NEW The Bedford Glossary for European History. This handy supplement for the survey course gives students historically contextualized definitions for hundreds of terms—from Abbasids to Zionism—that students encounter in lectures, reading, and exams. Available free when packaged with the text.

Bedford Series in History and Culture. Over 100 titles in this highly praised series combine first-rate scholarship, historical narrative, and important primary documents for undergraduate courses. Each book is brief, inexpensive, and focused on a specific topic or period. Package discounts are available.

Online Study Guide at bedfordstmartins.com/hunt. The popular Online Study Guide for *The Making of the West* is a free and uniquely personalized learning tool to help students master themes and information in the textbook and improve their historical skills. Assessment quizzes let students evaluate their comprehension and provide them with customized plans for further study through a variety of activities. Instructors can monitor student progress through the online Quiz Gradebook or receive e-mail updates.

Online Reference and Research Aids at bedfordstmartins.com/hunt. Provides links to history-related databases, indexes, and journals, plus contact information for state, provincial, local, and professional history organizations.

The Bedford Research Room at bedfordstmartins.com/hunt. The Research Room, drawn from Mike Palmquist's *The Bedford Researcher*, offers a wealth of resources—including interactive tutorials, research activities, student writing samples, and links to hundreds of other places online—to support students in courses across the disciplines. The site also offers instructors a library of helpful instructional tools.

Make History. Comprising the content of our five acclaimed online libraries—Map Central, the Image Library, DocLinks, HistoryLinks, and PlaceLinks, *Make History* provides one-stop access to relevant digital content including maps, images, documents, and Web links. Students and instructors alike can search this free, easy-to-use database by keyword, topic, date, or specific chapter of *The Making of the West* and can download the content they find.

The St. Martin's Tutorial on Avoiding Plagiarism. This online tutorial reviews the consequences of plagiarism and explains what sources to acknowledge, how to keep good notes, how to organize research, and how to integrate sources appropriately. The tutorial includes exercises to help students practice integrating sources and recognize acceptable summaries.

Diana Hacker's Research and Documentation Online. This Web site provides clear advice on how to integrate primary and secondary sources into research papers, how to cite sources correctly, and how to format in MLA, APA, *Chicago*, or CBE style.

The Bedford Bibliographer at bedfordstmartins.com/hunt. *The Bedford Bibliographer*, a simple but powerful Web-based tool, assists students with the process of collecting sources and generates bibliographies in four commonly used documentation styles.

A Student's Online Guide to History Reference Sources. This Web site, by Jules Benjamin, provides links to history-related databases, indexes, and journals, plus contact information for state, provincial, local, and professional history organizations.

We are grateful for the suggestions that we received from instructors using *The Making of the West.* We trust that the changes stemming from this feedback will make this material even more useful to instructors.

Contents

The Beginnings of Human Society

TO C. 4000 B.C.E.

PROLOGUE RESOURCES

Main Chapter Topics

1. Prehistoric human societies existed at the mercy of the environment and the constant search for food. By cooperating in hunting and gathering, members of Paleolithic societies ensured their survival.

2. With the discovery of agriculture and the domestication of animals, the Neolithic Revolution (10,000–4000 B.C.E.) marked the human transition from a nomadic existence as hunter-gatherer to a more settled lifestyle. It also led to an increasingly gender-based division of labor and the emergence of social hierarchy. By 6500 B.C.E., the invention of irrigation facilitated the establishment of settled agricultural communities in the Fertile Crescent.

Focus Question

What were the most significant changes in human beings' lives during the Stone Age?

1. The invention of agriculture and the domestication of plants provided human beings with more plentiful, better-quality food, shelter, and clothing. A more secure way of life, which led to greater material abundance, more specialized occupations, and the growth of population, improved people's lives.

2. Losses included increased inequality associated with social stratification and the development of patriarchy, increased warfare, and the disease contracted from larger populations living in close proximity to domesticated animals.

Annotated Chapter Outline

I. The Paleolithic Age, 200,000–10,000 B.C.E.

A. The Life of Hunter-Gatherers, pp. P-5–P-6

1. The earliest known fossil remains of humans were found in Africa and date to around 160,000 years ago.
2. Between 50,000 and 45,000 years ago, a change in weather patterns motivated the descendents of these earliest humans to migrate from Africa into Asia and Europe.
3. Hunter-gatherers lived in groups of twenty to thirty people who constantly roamed in search of food.
4. Women, whose mobility was limited by the need to carry and nurse infants, usually stayed near the camp and gathered edible plants, fruits, and nuts.
5. Men did most of the hunting of large animals, which took them far from their camps.
6. Because the work of everyone was crucial in hunting and gathering food, these societies were probably egalitarian.

B. Technology, Trade, Religion, and Hierarchy, pp. P-6–P-8

1. Technological innovation helped Paleolithic people increase their chances for survival.
2. One of the most important innovations was the control of fire, which helped people stay warm in cold climates and allowed them to cook indigestible wild plants, turning the plants into edible and nutritious food.
3. Long-distance trade began in the Stone Age as different bands of hunter-gatherers

exchanged items such as blades, jewelry, flint, and seashells.

4. Archaeological discoveries, including cave paintings and burial sites, suggest that Paleolithic hunter-gatherers developed religious beliefs.
5. Religious belief is further evidenced by "Venus figurines," statuettes of women with extra-large breasts, abdomens, buttocks, and thighs, which were possibly related to rituals of fertility and birth.
6. In addition to suggesting that people had some notions about an afterlife, the items that were buried with the dead indicate a degree of social hierarchy.

II. The Neolithic Age, 10,000–4000 B.C.E.

A. The Neolithic Revolution, pp. P-8–P-10

1. It is uncertain how humans learned to sow and harvest crops, but we do know the practice began in a part of southwestern Asia known as the Fertile Crescent—a region that stretches in an arc between modern Israel and southern Iraq.
2. Climatic changes around ten to twelve thousand years ago promoted the growth of wild grains, which provided a ready food supply for hunter-gatherers in the region.
3. Over time, humans would have learned to plant part of the seeds garnered from one crop to produce another.
4. During this period, people also learned to herd and breed animals.
5. Unlike Africa, the large mammals in the Fertile Crescent were easily domesticated, starting with sheep that were used as a source of meat around 8500 B.C.E.

B. Neolithic Origins of Modern Life and War, p. P-10

1. The development of agriculture and herding replaced hunting and gathering for some humans, and laid the foundations for our modern way of life.
2. In order to cultivate crops, people began to settle in permanent communities.
3. Parents began to have more children because agriculture required a great deal of labor and could support a larger population.
4. Living in such close proximity with animals, however, introduced epidemic diseases to humans.
5. Neolithic peoples gradually spread the knowledge of agriculture and the domestication of animals beyond the Fertile Crescent.
6. By 4000 B.C.E., this knowledge extended throughout Europe.

C. Daily Life in the Neolithic Village of Çatalhöyük, pp. P-10–P-14

1. Some of the most intriguing evidence of the changes in human life that took place during the Neolithic period is found in the village of Çatalhöyük in modern Turkey.
2. By 6500 B.C.E., farmers had erected a settlement of rectangular mud-brick houses that housed a population of perhaps six thousand at its height.
3. The villagers planted a variety of crops and diverted water from a nearby river to increase their harvests.
4. They also pastured domestic animals and by this time were using the animals' hides and milk in addition to their meat.
5. Because the community had enough surplus of food to feed itself without everyone having to work in the fields, some people began to develop crafts as a full-time occupation.
6. Some of these craft specialists made jewelry from lead and copper, and it is possible that they knew how to smelt metal from ore.
7. These people traded with other communities, exchanging obsidian from a nearby volcano for flint and seashells.
8. Shrines and burial sites were decorated with religious images that suggest a fascination with the secrets of life and fertility.
9. Some form of social hierarchy was most likely used because the need to plan irrigation and regulate the exchange of goods between farmers and crafts producers required leaders with more authority than those in hunter-gathering societies.

D. Gender Inequality in the Neolithic Age, pp. P-14–P-15

1. By the late Neolithic period, new developments in herding and agriculture were probably responsible for the disappearance of the equality between men and women that existed in Paleolithic societies.
2. The plow appeared after 4000 B.C.E. and was operated by men because it required more physical strength than digging with sticks and hoes.
3. Larger herds became more common and needed to be moved farther away from the

community because they constantly required new land to graze.

4. Men, who did not have to nurse children, probably tended these herds.
5. Because women had to bear and raise more children to support agriculture, they were increasingly tied to the central settlement where they performed new labor-intensive tasks such as turning milk into cheese and spinning wool.
6. The predominance of men in agriculture in the late Neolithic period combined with women's lessened mobility apparently led to women's loss of equality with men.

Lecture Strategies

1. The Paleolithic Age is by far the longest period in human history, yet there are no written records from this era. Stress the length of this period as compared to the much shorter Neolithic Age and the relatively recent origins of recorded history. Such perspective may provide students with a sense of wonder at the longevity of Paleolithic society and an appreciation for the interdisciplinary nature of research on early humans, in which contributions by archaeologists, anthropologists, biologists, and art historians are all important.

2. What was revolutionary about the Neolithic Revolution? Many people associate the term "revolution" with immediate, political upheaval. Applying the word to developments that occurred over thousands of years may be novel for some students. Encourage them to think about what makes something revolutionary. Must it be launched deliberately? Does revolution require leaders with well-defined goals? Does it have to happen quickly? Does revolution lead to permanent changes? Which was more revolutionary—inventing agriculture and domesticating animals, or the consequences of these innovations for subsequent human history?

3. Compare and contrast the Paleolithic and Neolithic Ages. Was there more continuity or change between the two periods? Securing food, a gendered division of labor, trade, and religious beliefs characterized both eras. Were the types of food, work, trade, and religion substantially different after the Neolithic Revolution? Did agriculture and the domestication of animals change all aspects of human society?

Class Discussion Starters

1. The need to rely on archaeological evidence when studying the pre-historical Paleolithic and Neolithic periods is obvious. Discuss the limitations and benefits of using archaeological evidence—tool types, materials, remnants of burial sites, artwork—to reconstruct early human societies. What do these reveal about the human relationship with the environment? Slides of the cave paintings of Lascaux, of the various Venus figurines, and of the early settlement at Çatalhöyük could facilitate discussion. Especially problematic is the frequent ascription of religious meaning or ritual use to representative artwork or to items for which no practical function is immediately apparent. Why do archaeologists and historians frequently resort to such identifications? For an introduction to archaeological methods aimed at the general reader, see Jane McIntosh, *The Practical Archaeologist: How We Know What We Know about the Past* (London: Paul Press, 1986).

2. Another common approach to deciphering prehistoric human societies is drawing conclusions based on parallels with anthropological studies of extant (though rapidly disappearing) Stone Age tribes, such as those of the Amazon basin or New Guinea. How valid are such comparisons? What biases might modern observers bring to their accounts of primitive peoples? Are some aspects of human organization less susceptible to the influence of modern civilization than others, and thus might they serve as better indicators of what early human societies might have been like?

3. Did the benefits outweigh the losses of the Neolithic Revolution? Discuss the ways in which people's lives improved due to better, more reliable food sources and contrast these advantages with increased warfare and social inequality.

4. How did the Neolithic Revolution pave the way for the development of civilization? Discuss the ways in which permanent settlements, material surpluses, and increased division of labor were prerequisites for the development of states and systems of writing.

Reviewing the Text

Review Questions

1. What were the most important activities, skills, and beliefs that helped Paleolithic hunt-gatherers survive?
[model answer] *They invented new forms of tools, weapons, and jewelry. They learned how to create sharper edges and points in stone, bone, or wood to create better tools and weapons. They banded together in groups of about twenty to thirty. They shared their food and other resources with each other. Men did most of the hunting, women bore and cared for children, and children gathered plans, fruits, and nuts. Their societies were egalitarian, meaning that all adults enjoyed a general equality in decision making. Their early religious beliefs emphasized fertility and birth. In an age in which the average life*

expectancy was from twenty-five to thirty years, reproduction was a particularly important part of their rituals and iconography. One example of the emphasize on fertility is the prehistoric Venus figurine depicted on p. P-7.

2. What were the consequences of the Neolithic Revolutions for people's lives?
[model answer] *1. Permanent settlements supported larger, more prosperous populations than those of hunter-gatherer communities: People lived in huts constructed of mud brick and made pottery they used as containers. A massive defensive wall enclosed Jericho, showing that the inhabitants feared attack by outsiders seeking their resources.*
2. Expansion in religious expression: Hunter-gatherers buried their dead with grave goods but in permanent settlements, such as Jericho and Çatalhöyük, villagers built shrines and created wall paintings and buried their dead beneath the floors of their houses.
3. Surplus economy: The Neolithic Revolution created a surplus of goods and a division of labor in Çatalhöyük, which led to the production of specialized crafts in metalwork and textiles that were exchanged through trade.
4. Increased knowledge and technology: Neolithic peoples transformed their environment through agriculture, herding, diverting of streams, and cutting down of forests. Their understanding of crop planting and processing of food they had raised into such products as bread and cheese increased over time. Metalworkers at Çatalhöyük may have experimented with smelting metal from ore.

Making Connections

1. Explain whether you think human life was more stressful in the Paleolithic period or the Neolithic period.
[model answer] It might be thought that life in the Paleolithic period was less stressful because things were simple and basic, but the constant search for food would have made survival uncertain. Life was probably less stressful in the Neolithic Age because the introduction of animal husbandry and crop cultivation made the food supply more secure.

2. What do you believe were the most important differences and similarities between Stone Age life and modern life? Why?
[model answer] The most striking difference is probably that Stone Age peoples lived in small groups numbering between twenty and thirty members, whereas people today tend to live on their own or within relatively small family groups. For Stone Age peoples, survival required that the entire community work together. To some extent, this is still the case today, as both members of any modern couple must work to maintain their household.

Discussing the Documents

Questions from Online Study Guide with Model Answers

New Sources, New Perspectives: Daily Bread, Damaged Bones, and Cracked Teeth (p. P-12)

1. What was wrong with the toe bones that researchers found in Syria? What might have caused these bone deformities?
[model answer] *The ends of the bones of the big toes were flatter and broader than what is considered normal today. These bone deformities were probably caused by being bent in the same position for long periods. The only posture that could create such severe bending is kneeling.*

2. Why do researchers assume that the bending position has something to do with agriculture? What other sources might they use to confirm this hypothesis?
[model answer] *Researchers assume that this position is related to agriculture because Neolithic people spent most of their time growing and preparing food. Artwork and sculptures from the same region and period showing people kneeling to grind grain are also used to confirm the information provided by skeletons.*

3. What do the discoveries of these bones tell us about agricultural production and the division of labor by gender for Neolithic people?
[model answer] *These discoveries tell us that Neolithic people endured a fair amount of physical discomfort to produce their food supply. The fact that both men and women engaged in the production of flour for bread indicates that no gender division of this labor was possible or desired. This might imply that the society considered men and women's work equally valuable and thus had a social organization less dominated by men than in societies where tasks were divided according to gender.*

Other Questions for Discussing These Documents in Class

New Sources, New Perspectives: Daily Bread, Damaged Bones, and Cracked Teeth (p. P-12)

1. How did scientific research by biological anthropologists and osteological archaeologists contribute to historians' understanding of the consequences of the development of agriculture?
2. How have later paintings and sculptures from the region influenced historians' conclusions?

Working with Visual Sources

For this exercise, please refer to the Bison Painting in the Cave at Lascaux on p. P-7 of the textbook or to the image on the book companion site's Online Study Guide under the "Visual Activity" for the Prologue.

Students viewing the image at the Online Study Guide are asked two questions about the image. The questions and model answers (not made available to students) are below. Project this image, available on the Instructor's Resources CD-ROM, in class or ask students to look at the image in their textbooks and answer the questions.

1. What can these cave paintings tell us about prehistoric times?
[model answer] *These paintings show that large animals were an important part of life in prehistoric times. Although it is unclear how important the particular animals depicted on these caves were for hunting, they at least had some sort of significance that caused them to be painted so often. These paintings also show that prehistoric humans were capable of abstract thought.*

2. Why is it impossible to understand the intended meaning of these images?
[model answer] *These images were created in prehistoric times, meaning that they were produced before there were any written or historical records. We have no description from that time of what the people who made these images thought or intended.*

Mapping Exercises

Map Activity from OSG—Model Answer for Map Activity #2

For this activity, please refer to the map on p. P-9. Students are asked these questions:

Where are the earliest agricultural sites concentrated?
[model answer] *The earliest agricultural sites, which date between 10,000 and 6500 B.C.E., were concentrated mostly in the Fertile Crescent—a strip of land that winds between modern Israel, through Syria, and then toward southern Iraq. A few settlements were also located in Greece as well as one on the southern shore of the Caspian Sea.*

In which direction did the knowledge of agriculture spread between 6500 B.C.E. and 4000 B.C.E.?
[model answer] *From its origins in the Fertile Crescent, the knowledge of agriculture spread mostly westward into Europe, arriving in central Europe between 6500 B.C.E. and 5000 B.C.E. By 4000 B.C.E., it had spread as far west as the British Isles, and into parts of Africa.*

Where were the first agricultural sites in Africa?
[model answer] *Agricultural sites dating between 6500 B.C.E. and 5000 B.C.E. have been found in the region of the lower Nile river valley. Between 5000 B.C.E. and 4000 B.C.E. agriculture developed further up the Nile and in upland regions to the west in north-central Africa.*

Map 1: The Development of Agriculture, p. P-9

Have students scrutinize the location and spread of early agricultural sites. What geophysical features do most sites have in common? How do the locations of earlier sites and later ones differ? What might explain these differences? What might account for the presence of later agricultural sites in what is now the middle of the Sahara desert?

In-Class Assignments and Presentation Topics

1. Consider the types of evidence researchers examine in order to learn about human societies before the advent of written language. How should we balance the insights provided by scholars working in different fields such as archaeology, biology, and art history? What are the benefits and limitations of the types of evidence considered in the "New Sources, New Perspectives" selection on Daily Bread, Damaged Bones, and Cracked Teeth (p. P-12)?

2. Discuss the significance of categorizing the Paleolithic (Old Stone) and Neolithic (New Stone) Ages according to the technology the people used. How useful is it to define a society by its use of particular tools? How does this method of categorization relate to the importance of archaeology in learning about early human societies? Were Neolithic societies more "advanced" than Paleolithic societies?

Essay Questions

1. Compare and contrast the Paleolithic Age with the Neolithic Age. In what ways did the Neolithic Revolution transform people's lives? What stayed the same? Were people's lives easier or harder after the Neolithic Revolution?

2. What was the Neolithic Revolution? Describe the main developments associated with it and explain why historians believe these developments were revolutionary.

Other Bedford/ St. Martin's Resources for the Prologue

The following resources are available to accompany the Prologue. Please refer to the Preface of this manual for detailed descriptions of all the ancillaries.

For Instructors

Transparencies

The following map and images from the Prologue are available as full-color acetates.

- Map P.1: The Development of Agriculture, p. P-9
- Bison Painting in the Cave at Lascaux, p. P-7
- Prehistoric Venus Figurine, p. P-7

Instructor's Resources CD-ROM

The following map and image from the Prologue, as well as a chapter outline, are available on disc in both PowerPoint and jpeg formats.

- Map P.1: The Development of Agriculture, p. P-9
- Bison Painting in the Cave at Lascaux, p. P-7

For Students

Study Guides

The Online Study Guide at **bedfordstmartins.com/hunt** helps students synthesize the material they have learned as well as practice the skills historians use to make sense of the past. The following Map, Visual, and Document activities are available for the Prologue.

Map Activity

- Map P.1: The Development of Agriculture, p. P-9

Visual Activity

- Bison Painting in the Cave at Lascaux, p. P-7

Reading Historical Documents

- New Sources, New Perspectives: Daily Bread, Damaged Bones, and Cracked Teeth, p. P-12

CHAPTER

1

Early Western Civilization

4000–1000 B.C.E.

CHAPTER RESOURCES

Main Chapter Topics

1. The term *Western civilization* is not as simple as it may seem. The word *civilization* has lost its precision, and western civilization began not in Europe but in Africa and Asia. Moreover, these earliest civilizations borrowed from one another and later societies borrowed from the earlier ones. Western civilization has never been isolated from other parts of the globe; rather, its pattern is to incorporate the ideas, arts, and technologies of other peoples and regions.

2. Mesopotamia contained the West's first large-scale civilization. Mesopotamians developed the wheel, the earliest writing system (cuneiform), complex mathematics, bronze, and the first empire (Akkad). Its numerous city-states, ruled by monarchs who claimed a divine connection, often warred with each other for control of territory and resources.

3. The West's second great civilization arose when Upper and Lower Egypt unified around 3000 B.C.E. Unlike Mesopotamia, Egypt enjoyed long periods of relatively isolated and peaceful development and was thus remarkably stable. Its society, which adhered to the principle of *maat* (the harmonious ordering of the world), was headed by a king (called pharaoh in the New Kingdom) who was considered to be the human incarnation of a god. The Egyptians' belief in an afterlife is manifest in their magnificent tombs and pyramids, built to house their mummified dead. From 3000 to about 1100 B.C.E., Egyptian history was divided into three long periods of unification (Old, Middle, and New kingdoms), broken by two periods of internal revolts, foreign invasions, and the irregular flooding of the Nile.

4. The first Mediterranean civilizations emerged around 2000 B.C.E. The Cretan (or Minoan) culture was prosperous, peaceful, and centered on palace complexes that controlled religious, economic, and political life. Minoan arts and writing influenced those of Mycenaean Greece, but the militaristic and independent Greek settlements had a distinct culture of their own. Mycenaean Greece was destroyed by civil war following an earthquake. During that same period, from 1200 to 1000 B.C.E., many Mediterranean and Near Eastern societies were stricken by a series of catastrophes, including invasions by the mysterious Sea Peoples, invasions by the Philistines, and internal turmoil. The cumulative effect of these events plunged the region into a widespread Dark Age.

Focus Question

What changes did Western civilization bring to human life?

1. Compare and contrast the ancient Mesopotamians and Egyptians. Both civilizations arose in fertile river valleys and developed complex systems of centralized authority, stratified social hierarchies, polytheistic religion, and justice. The main environmental difference was that the Tigris and Euphrates rivers flooded more irregularly and violently than the Nile. As a consequence, Mesopotamia experienced more political instability and fragmentation, and Mesopotamian culture and religion stressed insecurity. Humans had only limited influence over the awesome and arbitrary power of the gods, and immortality was possible only through achievements in this life. In Egypt, by contrast, the regular, gentle flooding of the Nile and the greater isolation of the country from outside invaders promoted long periods of unified leadership under a single kingdom. Egyptian culture and religion promoted order and stability (maat), a slightly higher status for women, and a fully developed sense of an afterlife.

2. Compare and contrast the Minoans and Mycenaeans. Both developed maritime civilizations that depended on trade and Mediterranean polyculture,

with the Mycenaeans based on mainland Greece and the Minoans on the island of Crete. Traditionally, Minoans have been regarded as the earliest Greeks to develop civilization, although linguistic evidence is inconclusive about whether or not the Minoans were related to the Mycenaean Greeks. The Mycenaeans lived in separate city-states that were often at war with each other, while the absence of fortifications at Minoan settlements has led some scholars to suspect that they had a peaceful society. Some researchers have also suggested that Minoan women possessed higher social status than women in the more patriarchal Mycenaean society. By 1400 B.C.E., however, the Mycenaeans had taken over Crete.

3. Cultural diversity and contact among different societies characterized the period of early Western civilization. Trade and warfare provided the most important means of cross-cultural contact and innovation, although ultimately warfare proved destructive for the early civilizations of Anatolia, Crete, and Greece. Language, writing, literature, and art were all borrowed, often by conquerors. For example, the Akkadians adopted and spread the culture of the Sumerians, the Minoan Linear B script was used to write Mycenaean Greek, and the alphabet developed by Canaanites became the basis of subsequent Greek and Roman writing.

Annotated Chapter Outline

I. The Controversial Concept of Western Civilization

A. Defining Western Civilization, pp. 4–6

1. Civilization is a complex level of human activity and interaction characterized by political states with authority based in cities, according to traditional historical definitions.
2. Humans all over the world chose to develop civilization that generates surplus resources through diverse economies, establishes strong social hierarchies and local identities, and develops knowledge of written language.
3. Civilization is a global and persistent phenomenon but its boundaries tend to change in terms of geography and particular ideas and practices, depending on the time period considered.
4. Western civilization is not a simple list of characteristics, nor is it separate from the rest of the world; study of its history is what reveals its nature and value.

B. Locating Early Western Civilization, pp. 6–7

1. Based on traditional definition, Western civilization's foundations lie in Mesopotamia 4000–3000 B.C.E. and in Egypt beginning around 3050 B.C.E.
2. These older civilizations influenced later civilizations and their views on religion, war, status, and technology.
3. Every civilization has established some sort of social hierarchy, possibly as a result of human nature.
4. Cultural interaction, provoked by international trade and war, prompted much of civilization's evolution.

II. Mesopotamia, Home of the First Civilization, 4000–1000 B.C.E.

A. Cities and Society, 4000–2350 B.C.E., pp. 7–12

1. The earliest cities developed in Mesopotamia when its inhabitants figured out how to raise crops on the fertile but arid land along the Tigris and Euphrates rivers.
2. Mesopotamians irrigated their farmlands by building canals.
3. To maintain this intricate system, they needed a high level of social organization.
4. The Mesopotamians developed the city-state in which an urban center exercised political and economic control over the surrounding countryside.
5. In these cities, residents built large temple-towers, called ziggurats, dedicated to their deities whom they believed controlled their fortunes.
6. Mesopotamians lived in hierarchical societies with kings at the top, followed by priests and priestesses, common people, and slaves at the bottom.
7. Most slaves lacked almost all legal rights.
8. Kings lived in elaborate, urban palaces where they ruled with a council of advisors.
9. The king acknowledged the gods as his rulers, and was expected to rule justly and firmly to maintain divine goodwill for his people and protect them from attacks by outside forces.
10. Sumerian city dwellers first invented a form of writing—a script called cuneiform—in order to keep track of taxes and financial transactions.
11. Although professional scribes first used writing primarily for accounting purposes, it also became useful for recording

religious beliefs and traditional stories, making written literature an important cultural element in human civilization for the first time.

12. Priests and priestesses enjoyed high status because they used divination—observing and interpreting signs, star patterns, and dreams—to discover how the people should please the gods.

B. Metals, the Akkadian Empire, and the Ur III Dynasty, c. 2350–c. 2000 B.C.E., pp. 12–13

1. Bronze Age metallurgy indirectly led to the creation of the first empire.
2. Bronze was used to create new luxury goods, tools, and weapons.
3. Metal goods—especially lavishly adorned weapons—became status symbols, displaying the wealth and the power of the male hunter and warrior.
4. Thus the nature of wealth, once measured only in foodstuffs, land, and animals, came to include metal goods.
5. The new emphasis on metal goods led monarchs to crave lands rich in the ores needed to create them.
6. About 2350 B.C.E., King Sargon of Akkad began acquiring access to these ores through force rather than trade.
7. The Akkadians conquered territory and city-states southeast to the Persian Gulf and northwest through Syria to the Mediterranean.
8. Although acquiring land was the primary goal, conquest also encouraged cultural interaction between peoples, spreading Mesopotamian literature, religion, and culture into a larger geographic area.
9. The Akkadian Empire fell about 2200 B.C.E., prey to civil war or possibly invasion.
10. Akkadian poetry explained both the rise and fall of the empire as the will of the gods, reflecting the precarious nature of human life in the face of divine power.

C. Assyrian, Babylonian, and Canaanite Achievements, 2000–1000 B.C.E., pp. 13–16

1. Two kingdoms, Assyria and Babylonia, appeared in the second millennium B.C.E. to fill the power vacuum left by the fall of the Akkadian empire.
2. Innovations in Assyria and Babylonia in the areas of commerce, law, and learning left lasting influences on Western civilizations: Assyrians became the leading traders of the ancient Near East, and their economy was based on private enterprise rather than on the exclusive royal control over collection and redistribution of goods.
3. With the growth of private commerce, the need to guarantee fairness and reliability in business dealings also increased.
4. As part of the king's responsibility to protect his subjects, King Hammurabi of Babylon (r. 1792–1750 B.C.E.) created a code of laws that recorded the king's decisions in crimes and commercial disputes.
5. This code aimed to protect less-powerful members of society even as it strictly divided Babylonian society into categories of free persons, commoners, and slaves.
6. Most of the laws expressed the king's view of justice and, in everyday practice, the people assembled in courts to determine most cases by their own judgment.
7. The archeological remains of Mesopotamian cities show evidence of an active urban culture, including recreation, such as taverns and public parks, and sophisticated learning, especially in mathematics and astronomy.
8. The Canaanite society in the region on the eastern coast of the Mediterranean made innovations in writing and business that still influence Western civilization today.
9. The city-states of Canaan grew rich through trade and commerce with many different cultures.
10. The Canaanite alphabet, in which a single letter stood for only one sound in the language, developed around 1600 B.C.E.
11. This alphabet proved more efficient and adaptable than pictographic writing, such as the cuneiform and hieroglyphic scripts, and it became the basis for Greek, Roman, and modern alphabets.

III. Egypt, the First Unified Country, 3050–1000 B.C.E.

A. From Egypt Unification to the Old Kingdom, 3050–2190 B.C.E., pp. 16–20

1. Civilization in ancient Egypt revolved around the Nile River and the fertility that its annual flood provided to the surrounding farmland.
2. Egypt's location on the Nile River delta supported seaborne trade to Mediterranean ports, and the deserts on the east and west sides of the river protected Egypt from invasion.

3. King Narmer, a powerful monarch who claimed to reign with divine authority, united Egypt into a single, centralized kingdom about 3100–3000 B.C.E.
4. Contact with the Nubians to the south may have influenced Egyptian political and social organization.
5. Egyptians may have learned about writing through contact with Sumerians and developed their pictographic script, called hieroglyphs.
6. Religion played a central role in the lives of all Egyptians.
7. The divine power of the king depended on his possessing *maat*, the truth or divine justice that kept the forces of nature in balance—particularly the annual flooding of the Nile.
8. A strong belief in an afterlife is revealed in Egyptian tombs, which were elaborate.
9. Several Egyptian kings displayed their power and wealth by erecting huge pyramids at the center of building complexes, which contained tombs used for royal funerals and religious ceremonies.
10. In the Egyptians' highly structured social hierarchy, men and women maintained a remarkably equal degree of legal rights.
11. Egyptian art and literature from this period displayed interest in maintaining proper relations with the gods and instructing high officials in appropriate behavior.

B. The Middle and New Kingdoms in Egypt, 2061–1081 B.C.E., pp. 20–23

1. When climatic changes altered the usual flood pattern of the Nile, the divine authority of the monarch eroded and civil war destroyed the unity of the Old Kingdom.
2. A period of instability, known as the First Intermediate Period (2181–2050 B.C.E.), ripped apart the Kingdom of Two Lands until the kings gradually reunited Egypt into what is known as the Middle Kingdom (2050–1786 B.C.E.).
3. The restored central authority of the monarchy pushed the boundaries of Egypt farther south and expanded trade with other lands.
4. The unity of the Middle Kingdom lasted less than three centuries.
5. The Second Intermediate Period (1786–1567 B.C.E.) opened when Egypt succumbed to invasions by the Hyksos.
6. The Hyksos, Semitic peoples from the Syria-Palestine region, introduced bronze making, hump-backed cattle, horses, war chariots, and olive trees.
7. After nearly two hundred years, kings from Thebes once again united Egypt into the New Kingdom (1567–1085 B.C.E.).
8. These kings earned the title "warrior pharaoh" because of their use of foreign wars and diplomacy to promote Egypt's interests.
9. As in the past, both slaves and free workers performed labor on mammoth royal tombs, temples, and palaces.
10. Religion retained its central place in New Kingdom society.
11. Theban pharaohs promoted the cult of their god Amen-Re until he overshadowed other gods.
12. In everyday life, however, ordinary people devoted their attentions to deities outside the royal cults.

IV. The Hittites, Minoans, and Mycenaeans, 2200–1000 B.C.E.

A. The Hittites, 1750–1200 B.C.E., pp. 24–25

1. The Hittites became the most powerful society of central Anatolia about 1750 B.C.E.
2. Their rise to power depended in part on the fertility of their homeland between the Black and Caspian seas, and on their skills in war, trade, and diplomacy.
3. The Hittites spoke an Indo-European language, belonging to the linguistic group that would eventually populate most of Europe.
4. Much like Egyptian kings, Hittite rulers held an exalted religious status and felt responsible for maintaining divine goodwill toward their subjects.
5. Hittite kings maintained their rule through alliances with noble families.
6. When unity with noble families was strong, they launched ambitious military campaigns, even conquering Babylon in 1595 B.C.E.
7. Their economic strength depended on controlling long-distance trade routes and raw materials, especially metals.
8. At the battle of Kadesh in 1274 B.C.E., the Hittites fought the Egyptians, who were also expanding their territory, but the conflict ended in a stalemate.
9. This stalemate ended sixteen years later when the Hittite king negotiated a truce

with the Egyptian pharaoh because of the growing threat from the Assyrians.

10. Thirteen years later, the Hittites and Egyptians sealed their alliance with a marriage.
11. This treaty, which survives in both Hittite and Egyptian languages, is a landmark in the history of international diplomacy.

B. The Minoans, 2200–1400 B.C.E., pp. 25–27

1. On the island of Crete, the flourishing and creative Minoan civilization developed elaborate architecture and an extensive trade system with the ancient Near East.
2. By 2200 B.C.E., the inhabitants of Crete lived in a palace society where the general population clustered around the sprawling homes of their rulers that formed the focal point of civil and religious activities.
3. Minoan rulers served as both chiefs and priests.
4. Minoans also developed their own script, called Linear A, and advanced their agriculture by diversifying crops into grains, olives, and grapes.
5. This system, known as Mediterranean polyculture, not only optimized a farmer's labor by spreading it out into different seasons, it also provided a better diet and stimulated population growth.
6. The economic surplus allowed specialized artisans to produce goods, such as storage jars, clothes, or lamps, which they traded for food.
7. The huge storage areas uncovered in the ruins of Cretan palaces indicate that rulers controlled the distribution of goods.
8. Individuals gave over the products of their labor to the local authority, which redistributed the goods to the general population.
9. Many aspects of Minoan culture remain tantalizingly unknown to modern scholars, some of whom have speculated about whether or not their language was related to Greek, whether the lack of defensive walls signifies an absence of warfare, and whether the depiction of female figures in Minoan art reflects the domination of women in Minoan society.

C. The Mycenaeans, 1800–1000 B.C.E., pp. 27–28

1. The Mycenaeans, the first mainland civilization in Greece, emerged at the hilltop site of Mycenae on the Peloponnese peninsula in southern Greece.
2. These coastal settlements depended on the sea for food and trade, fiercely competing with one another for control of natural resources and territory.
3. Palace records reveal that rulers tightly controlled the distribution of goods to the community.
4. The Mycenaeans had much in common with the Minoans, with whom they frequently interacted, first through trade then later by conquest.
5. The Mycenaean burial chamber, called a *tholos*, reveals architectural patterns and goods derived from Minoan culture.
6. Linear B tablets found in Minoan palaces reveal that the Mycenaeans eventually took control of Crete about 1400 B.C.E.
7. Linear B is a script based on Linear A but used to record Greek.
8. Mycenaean men placed an extremely high value on warfare.
9. Their most important divinities were gods of war, and men were often buried with their weapons and armor.

D. The Period of Calamities, 1200–1000 B.C.E., pp. 28–30

1. Prior to 1200 B.C.E., a state of relative equilibrium existed among the various civilizations of the Mediterranean and Near Eastern world.
2. This began to unravel between 1200 and 1000 B.C.E. as a series of foreign invasions, civil wars, and natural disasters affected every state in the region.
3. Egyptian and Hittite records refer to Sea Peoples who raided their kingdoms.
4. They were probably a mixture of mercenary soldiers who had deserted their rulers and professional raiders who attacked these kingdoms in waves and set in motion a chain reaction as those persons displaced by the invasions in turn invaded other territories.
5. The economic disruption that these raids caused contributed to the fall of the Hittite kingdom about 1200 B.C.E. and severely weakened Egypt.
6. The Mycenaean civilization in Greece was also affected by this period of calamity, but its problems were homegrown.
7. Major earthquakes combined with the near-constant warfare between jealous

local rulers proved to be too great a burden for the palaces' redistributive economies.
8. Many Mycenaeans took to the road and resettled elsewhere, essentially putting an end to the palace-based society.

Lecture Strategies

1. Egypt is referred to as an empire only with the emergence of the New Kingdom. Discuss what is meant by the term and how it applies to the New Kingdom (as opposed to the Old and Middle kingdoms). What distinguishes an empire? What are some of the problems typical of an empire? How does Egypt's empire compare to the Hittite Empire? Discussion of empire can be a running theme throughout the course; it would therefore be appropriate to foreshadow successive empires such as Greece and Rome.

2. Mesopotamian, Egyptian, Hittite, and (perhaps) Cretan women enjoyed a higher status and greater legal rights than many western women would in later periods. Even the mythical women of Bronze Age Greece—Helen, Penelope, Clytemnestra—were represented as possessing more freedom than women had in later Greece with the exception of Spartan women. Are there features of dynastic, centralized monarchies and redistributive economies that might have benefited women's social and legal standing? Why were mythical women depicted as possessing more freedom and power than ordinary Greek women? What sort of lessons for Greek women were embedded within these stories? In addition to the ample sources listed in the chapter bibliography, see Robin Gay, *Women in Ancient Egypt* (Cambridge, MA: Harvard University Press, 1993); Barbara Lesko, "Women of Ancient Egypt and Western Asia" and Marion Katz, "Daughters of Demeter: Women in Ancient Greece," in *Becoming Visible: Women in European History*, 3rd ed., R. Bridenthal, S. Stuard, and M. Kooz, eds. (Boston: Houghton Mifflin, 1998). Both articles have current and solid bibliographies.

3. The environment determined much of the development of western cultures. Compare the topography, climate, and available natural resources of Mesopotamia, Egypt, the eastern Mediterranean coast, Crete, and mainland Greece with their social, political, and economic development. How central a role do the students believe was played by the environment? How did it affect intercultural contacts, economic prosperity, political organization, or artistic production? Is the role of the environment overemphasized? Especially when they must introduce a large volume of material in a compressed fashion, instructors often use broad-brush presentations of societies and assign to them a national character. (An exaggerated example might be that the rocky and mountainous internal terrain of Greece led to the individualistic, freedom-loving character of the ancient Greeks.) To what extent are generalizing schemas necessary in historical surveys? Conversely, what are the pitfalls of such depictions? These questions can help sensitize students to both the utility and the inadequacies of boiling down societies to their essential historical features and contributions.

4. Mesopotamian empires marked the appearance of the form of political organization that would typify much of the premodern west. Discuss the factors that led to their emergence. How did such empires function? What were the political, economic, and social consequences of empire? How was imperial power maintained, and what led to its loss? G. Stein and M. S. Rothman, eds., *Chiefdoms and Early States in the Near East: The Organizational Dynamics of Complexity* (Madison: University of Wisconsin Press, 1994) investigates the growth of political centralization in the early Mesopotamian city-states. Guillermo Algaze, *The Uruk World System: The Dynamics of Expansion of Early Mesopotamian Civilization* (Chicago: University of Chicago Press, 1993) argues that economic exploitation of peripheral areas was a key component of Sumer's rise. For a general history of political and social organization in Mesopotamia, see Amelie Kurht, *The Ancient Near East* (New York and London: Routledge, 1997).

Class Discussion Starters

1. Investigate with students the ingredients commonly thought essential for the emergence of civilization (urban settlements, religious cults, writing, diversified agriculture, organized political structures, etc.). Generate a list of justifications for the inclusion of each item on the "civilization list." Are some items more crucial than others? Have students identify additional factors, perhaps intangible, that they believe also qualify as building blocks for civilization. One could also review the items characteristic of earlier human groupings, such as cooperation in obtaining food, toolmaking, and the division of labor. Are these exclusively human traits? Do they define society, if not civilization? This question also makes a convenient jumping-off point for an analysis of the very concept of civilization. (See "Terms of History: Civilization," p. 6.)

2. Have students discuss Terms of History: Civilization, p. 6. Comparison of the definitions given, including Random House dictionary's third definition ("any type of culture, society, etc., of a specific place, time, or group"), could generate a lively debate about what students understand the essential components of civilization (or "Civilization" or "a civilization") to be

or what they should be. But instructors might also encounter some resistance or confusion from students upon even raising the question, especially in a highly diversified classroom.

You might ask whether the group can agree on a level of technological or artisanal achievement that should form the entry point for civilization. Or is the term more appropriately used in connection with moral, religious, or ethical content? Does the absence of war qualify a society as civilized? Or is conflict an inevitable concomitant to a civilized state? At what point does a society achieve civilization: when its elites attain the hallmarks of civilization, or when those hallmarks are more uniformly available to the populace at large?

3. The way in which rulers and their achievements were depicted reveals much about the nature of power and authority throughout history. King Hammurabi is depicted in an ancient carving receiving the laws from the god Shamash (the artifact is now in the Louvre). Not only was Hatshepsut regularly depicted as male, she also had the glories of her reign carved on obelisks erected throughout Egypt. Ramesses II had the treaty he negotiated with the Hyksos chiseled onto a public wall. The unusual depiction of Amunhotep IV (Akenaten) probably signaled that he was breaking away from the past. A discussion of how these representations both reflect and feed into concepts of power and authority would pave the way for further discussions on the subject in later chapters.

4. Discuss the probable historical constants in the lives and work of ordinary people during this period. How were the lives of peasants, urban laborers, and slaves in Mesopotamia, Egypt, and/or Bronze Age Greece alike or dissimilar? This approach can lead to the subject of history viewed from the bottom up, rather than from the top down, as well as introducing the role of technology as an agent of historical change. Useful studies (among many) of daily life include: Rosalie David, *The Pyramid Builders of Ancient Egypt*, 2nd ed. (New York and London: Routledge, 1996); and C. Snell, *Life in the Ancient Near East, 3100–332 B.C.* (New Haven, CT: Yale University Press, 1997). For women's work, often considered even more timeless than men's, see Elizabeth Wayland Barbara, *Women's Work: The First 20,000 Years* (New York: W. W. Norton, 1994).

5. The widespread crisis of 1200 to 1000 B.C.E. remains among the most absorbing puzzles of ancient history. Discuss the varying theories for the collapse and weigh their merits with the class. Major positions on the debate include N. K. Sanders, *The Sea Peoples*, rev. ed. (London: Thames & Hudson, 1985); and Eliezer D. Oren, *The Sea Peoples and Their World: A Reassessment* (Philadelphia: University of Pennsylvania Museum, 2000). Central older theories are contained in Colin Renfrew, "Systems Collapse As Social Transformation," in *Transformations: Mathematical Approaches to Culture Change*, C. Renfrew and K. I. Cooke, eds. (San Diego: Academic Press, 1979), pp. 481–506; and in Emily Vermeule, "The Fall of the Mycenaean Empire," *Archaeology* (1960): 66–75. Chapter 4 of Nancy Demand, *A History of Ancient Greece* (New York: McGraw-Hill, 1996) gives a quick introduction to the competing theories. For a more detailed synthesis, see Robert Drews, *The End of the Bronze Age: Changes in Warfare and Catastrophe ca. 1200 B.C.* (Princeton: Princeton University Press, 1993).

Reviewing the Text

Review Questions

1. What are the challenges of defining Western civilization?

[model answer] *It is difficult to identify precisely the sets of ideas and customs that make up the culture of a particular civilization. For example, while contemporary definitions of Western civilization are most often rooted in the Judeo-Christian concept of monotheism, ancient societies, such as Mesopotamia, Egypt, and Greece, all believed in polytheism. It is hard to locate Western civilization geographically. Did it spread from Mesopotamia to Egypt to Greece? Many non-western ancient societies, such as those in India, China, and the Americas had comparably complex societies to those in Mesopotamia and Egypt, yet they are not considered "western."*

2. How did life change for people in Mesopotamia when they began to live in cities?

[model answer] *The emergence of cities depended on the development of farming. Once Mesopotamian farmers produced food surpluses, the population grew and people began to inhabit urban centers that exercised political and economic control over the surrounding countryside. This arrangement is known as a city-state. Cities were crowded, and rich and poor alike could become ill from the water supply, which was often contaminated by sewage because there was no system of waste disposal. Urban development led to the creation of bureaucracy and a clearly defined social hierarchy. While kings and royal families were the highest-ranking people, slaves were at the bottom of the social ladder. Kings, who were expected to ensure justice by pleasing the gods, lived in luxurious palaces, while slaves were almost wholly dependent on other people. The development of writing systems allowed for both record-keeping and the ability to record myths. Religion was at the heart of Mesopotamian civilization, and people believed that the gods determined the conditions of their lives.*

3. How did religion guide people's lives in ancient Egypt?
[model answer] *Prosperity and safety depended on the king's observations of rituals. In Egypt, the pharaoh was considered a god in human form, though the man himself was mortal; on his summoning, the divine power made the Nile flood. The failure of the Nile to flood could cause the failure of royal power, as could a king's personal desire for religious reform. The Hittite king served as the high-priest of the Hittites' storm god, and had to maintain strict ritual purity to cultivate divine goodwill toward subjects. Because of their strong belief in an afterlife, all Egyptians spent as much as they could afford on tombs for themselves and their family, and for the construction and decoration of temples dedicated to their gods. Egyptians' religious lives enhanced their desire for increased wealth and resources through conquest.*

4. How did war determine the fates of the early civilization of Anatolia, Crete, and Greece?
[model answer] *In Anatolia, aggressive rulers used warfare to expand their control over long-distance trade routes in order to obtain raw materials, especially metals. However, beginning in 1190 B.C.E., seafaring raiders wiped out the Hittite kingdom and cut off its trade routes. The warlike spirit of Mycenaean culture probably contributed to the destruction of the Mycenaeans as much as or more so than actual Sea Peoples' invasions. After conquering the Minoans based in Crete, the Greek-speaking Mycenaeans were in almost constant internal turmoil. Civil war, as well as natural disasters such as earthquakes, led to the loss of power among Mycenaean rulers as the redistributive economy collapsed.*

Making Connections

1. Compare and contrast the environmental factors affecting the emergence of the world's first civilizations in Mesopotamia and Egypt.
[model answer] *Both Mesopotamia and Egypt had fairly reliable access to water. The Tigris and Euphrates rivers flooded irregularly, necessitating the development of irrigation techniques, which required a high population density and organizational and bureaucratic institutions, or cities. The Nile River, however, flooded regularly and did not require the development of irrigation techniques. As a consequence, cities in Egypt developed more slowly. Deserts bordered the fertile areas of both Mesopotamia and Egypt and provided some limited degree of defense.*

2. What were the advantages and disadvantages of living in a unified country under a single central authority compared to living in a region with separate city-states?
[model answer] *People in unified countries enjoyed advanced technologies, elaborate architecture, striking art, a taste for luxury items, and extensive trade networks. Two disadvantages were the ongoing warfare and the generally harsh punishments that rulers meted out to those that broke the laws.*

Discussing the Documents

Questions from Online Study Guide with Model Answers

Hammurabi's Laws for Physicians (p. 15)

1. Laws are often a useful type of historical document because they can tell us much about daily life in past societies. What do these laws tell us about Mesopotamian society?
[model answer] *The Mesopotamians had made important advances in medicine and even practiced surgery. By the time of Hammurabi (1792–1750 B.C.E.), Mesopotamians had a monetary economy in which currency, rather than usable goods, was the medium of exchange. There was also a marked social hierarchy.*

2. What do these laws reveal about the social hierarchy of Mesopotamia?
[model answer] *The value of a person depended on his or her social rank, with "freemen" on the top, "commoners" in the middle, and slaves at the bottom. Slaves were the property of their owners, and when a slave was injured it was the owner who was compensated.*

Declaring Innocence on Judgment Day in Ancient Egypt (p. 22)

1. What does this excerpt tell us about Egyptian religious beliefs?
[model answer] *The long list of deities mentioned shows that Egyptian religion was polytheistic with a complex array of gods. The Egyptians believed in an afterlife in which an individual was judged for his or her actions on Earth.*

2. What does this document tell us about an Egyptian sense of morality?
[model answer] *Egyptian morals entailed treating others, even animals, fairly and justly. Egyptians were also expected to respect religious property and to lead a sexually pure existence.*

Other Questions for Discussing These Documents in Class

Terms of History: Civilization (p. 6)

1. How closely does our modern usage of the word *civilization* relate to the meaning of the ancient Roman word *civilis*?

2. The word *civilization* is often used to convey a sense of "comparative superiority." Explain what this means.

Hammurabi's Laws for Physicians (p. 15)

1. Describe the legal principle of equivalent punishment as it relates to Hammurabi's collection of laws.

2. What does this document reveal about the social structure of ancient Mesopotamia?

Declaring Innocence on Judgment Day in Ancient Egypt (p. 22)

1. Why do you suppose the Egyptians practiced "negative confession," where the dead listed not their accomplishments but the evil acts that they had not committed over the course of their lives?

Comparison Questions

1. Explain how *Hammurabi's Laws for Physicians* in Mesopotamia and *Declaring Innocence on Judgment Day in Ancient Egypt* illustrate definitions of *civilization*.

2. Compare and contrast the notions of judgment in Hammurabi's laws and the Egyptian *Book of the Dead*.

For Users of *Sources of The Making of the West*

The following documents are available in Chapter 1 of the companion sourcebook by Katharine J. Lualdi, University of Southern Maine.

1. Defining Humanity: *Epic of Gilgamesh* (c. 2000 B.C.E.)
2. Establishing Law and Justice: King Hammurabi, *The Code of Hammurabi* (Early Eighteenth Century B.C.E.)
3. Exploring New Lands: *The Story of Sinuhe* (Late Nineteenth Century B.C.E.)
4. Writing Experiences: *Egyptian Scribal Exercise Book* (Twelfth Century B.C.E.)
5. Allying for Peace: *The "Eternal Treaty" between the Egyptians and Hittites* (c. 1259 B.C.E.)

Discussion Ideas for Sources of The Making of the West, *Chapter 1*

1. *The Code of Hammurabi* provides insight into many facets of Mesopotamian society in the early eighteenth century B.C.E. Discuss how the code illustrates social hierarchy and gender inequality in Babylonian civilization and relate this to the broader pattern of increased social stratification and patriarchy after the Neolithic Revolution. The code proclaims to uphold "the principles of truth and equity," through such practices as equivalent punishment, yet by modern standards the document is far from egalitarian. A discussion of the distinction between equity and equality could prepare students for related topics in later chapters. It could also serve to introduce the class to thinking about the past on its own terms and not imposing present-day values and expectations.

2. The development of writing is one of the characteristics of the first civilizations. How does the *Egyptian Scribal Exercise Book* reflect the importance of written language? What other characteristics of civilization does it reveal? Students might consider both the existence of the physical text itself and its content glorifying the high status of scribes. How does the account of different Egyptian professions compare with what students have read about Babylonian professions (including that of physicians)? If there were a *Sumerian Scribal Exercise Book*, would its content and tone likely be similar to this Egyptian document? Does the document reflect any ideas that are unique to Western civilization?

Working with Visual Sources

For this exercise, please refer to The Ziggurat of Ur in Sumer on p. 9 of the textbook or to the image on the book companion site's Online Study Guide under the "Visual Activity" for Chapter 1.

Students viewing the image in the Online Study Guide are asked two questions about the image. The questions and model answers (not made available to students) are below. Project this image, available on the Instructor's Resources CD-ROM, in class or ask students to look at the image in their textbooks and answer the questions.

1. What evidence is there of a hierarchical organization of society?
[model answer] *At the top of this box are the king and the social elite, possibly priests and aristocrats. On the bottom are laborers and possibly slaves. The king and the elite are seated, while everyone else is standing. The king is seated higher and portrayed as being larger than the rest.*

2. What does this scene tell us about Sumerian life?
[model answer] *This scene shows the majority of Sumerians working in agriculture, raising crops and animals. The product of their work was used to support the king, priests, and aristocracy who were at the top of the hierarchy. This shows that there was a division of labor and a distinct hierarchy.*

Mapping Exercises

Map Activity from OSG—Model Answer for Map Activity #2

For this activity, please refer to the map on p. 23. Students are asked these questions:

Where was Greek civilization concentrated about 1500 B.C.E.?
[model answer] *The Minoan civilization was centered on the island of Crete, while the Mycenaean civilization was on the Peloponnese peninsula, the southern tip of mainland Greece, and scattered throughout the islands of the Aegean Sea.*

Using what you have read in the text, which geographical factors motivated the Greeks to settle in these places, and how did it affect the character of their civilization?
[model answer] *The Greek mainland was mountainous and did not have the same types of river plains that fostered the development of civilization in Mesopotamia and Egypt, although Crete did have some fertile plains. The irregular coastline of Greece and its many islands, however, were favorable for harbors and sailing. This feature prompted the Greeks to settle near the sea and become dependent upon it for food and trade. Because the Greeks were a seagoing people, they made regular contact with other Mediterranean civilizations, which brought outside influences into their culture.*

Map 1.1: The Ancient Near East, 4000–3000 B.C.E., p. 8

Where is Egypt located in relation to the Fertile Crescent? How did the location of Kadesh contribute to its becoming the site of battle between the Egyptians and the Hittites?

Map 1.2: Ancient Egypt, p. 17

Consider the expansion of Egyptian territory over time. Which areas were ruled by the Old Kingdom? Where did the Middle and New Kingdoms expand? What was the principal route into and out of Egypt? What prevented the ancient Egyptians from expanding to the east and west of the Nile valley?

Map 1.3: Greece and the Aegean Sea, 1500 B.C.E., p. 23

Locate the centers of Minoan and Mycenaean civilization. How did Crete's location contribute to the Minoans' initial independence of the Mycenaeans and the island's relative insulation from later Greek history?

Mapping the West: The Period of Calamities, 1200–1000 B.C.E., p. 30

Trace the paths of the Sea Peoples' invasions. What was their presumed point of origin? Based on what you know about their destinations, what might have led them to target such locations? How would their movements have affected trade and commerce in the Mediterranean and Near East?

In-Class Assignments and Presentation Topics

1. The widely used *Epic of Gilgamesh* provides a highly engaging and accessible entry to a time and place that seems highly remote to most students. Good papers or presentations can be elicited by asking students to read for a very specific end. For example, gender roles and relations, or attitudes toward sexuality can be explored by examining the characters of Ishtar, the harlot, and the tavern maid, and their interactions with male characters. Students could investigate the relationship of humans to the environment as embodied in the presentation of Enkidu as wild man or the episode of the flood. Parallels with stories in the Hebrew Bible (introduced in Chapter 2) may also interest students, most obviously of the flood (and of Utnapishtim with Noah). Serpents play decisive roles in each work as well, with regard to the Plant of Life for Gilgamesh and the Tree of Life for Adam and Eve.

2. Many facets of Mesopotamian or Egyptian daily life can be approached via a reading of translations of cuneiform tablets or the personal poetry of ancient Egypt, some of which is presented from a female viewpoint. Many collections of Egyptian poems are included in the anthologies of Egyptian poetry in the chapter bibliography. An interesting selection is the "Collection of Contracts from Mesopotamia, 2300–428 B.C.E." at the site. For a glimpse into personal lives, see the collection of translated business and personal cuneiform letters by Leo Oppenheim, *Letters from Mesopotamia* (Chicago: University of Chicago Press, 1987).

3. The proliferation of high-quality, academically solid visual resources for this period on the Internet can be mined by students to re-create daily life, to create their own travel guides for ancient visitors to ancient sites, and to aid in further research.

4. The Indiana Jones films and their many offspring capitalized on the perennial romance of the archaeologist's profession. Students may be interested in the real-life explorations of Knossos, Mycenae, and Troy. Investigations of the findings as they relate to the historical sources can lead students to consider the

complementary roles of archaeological and textual analysis in the reconstruction of ancient history. Students can also evaluate how the preconceptions of archaeologists such as Arthur Evans and Heinrich Schliemann may have distorted their interpretations of their findings. A good place to start is William Biers, *The Archaeology of Greece*, 2nd ed. (Ithaca, NY: Cornell University Press, 1996), with specialized bibliographies for individual periods and sites. Also see Arthur Evans, *The Palace of Minos*, 4 vols. (London: Macmillan, 1964 [originally published 1921–1935]); and William A. McDonald and Carol G. Thomas, *Progress into the Past: The Rediscovery of Mycenaean Civilization*, 2nd ed. (Bloomington: Indiana University Press, 1990). A basic work on the general subject is Paul MacKendrick, *The Greek Stones Speak* (New York: W. W. Norton, 1962). For an ancient Greek's comments on the Greek "sights," consult J. G. Frazer, *Pausanias's Description of Greece*, 6 vols. (New York: Macmillan, 1965 [originally published 1898]).

Essay Questions

1. Discuss the foundations of Western civilization. Which geographical areas were initially defined as being part of the West? What are the characteristics of civilization in general? What were some of the characteristics of early Western civilization? Why is the idea of civilization a controversial one?

2. Civilizations such as those of the ancient Mesopotamians and Egyptians were concerned with order and stability. Discuss how this concern is evident in the documents "Hammurabi's Laws for Physicians" and "Declaring Innocence on Judgment Day in Ancient Egypt."

3. Scholars disagree about the origins of patriarchal institutions in the west. The debate over the causes of women's (greater or lesser) exclusion from positions of political, legal, and economic authority in ancient societies has continued for many years. Compare and contrast the status of women in Mesopotamia, Egypt, Minoan Crete, and Mycenae. If the instructor wishes students to consult outside sources, a central, if controversial, place to begin is Gerda Lerner, *Creation of Patriarchy* (Oxford: Oxford University Press, 1987). For an opposing opinion, see Cynthia Eller, *The Myth of Matriarchal Prehistory* (Boston: Beacon, 2000). Collections of articles that focus on deciphering gender roles and relationships based on prehistoric archaeology include *Engendering Archaeology*, Joan M. Gero and Margaret W. Conkey, eds. (Oxford: Blackwell, 1991); *Reader in Gender Archaeology*, Kelley Hays-Gilpin and David S. Whitley, eds. (New York and London: Routledge, 1998); and *Reading the Body: Representation and Remains in the Archaeological Record*, Alison E. Rautman, ed. (Philadelphia: University of Pennsylvania Press, 2000).

4. New Kingdom Egypt witnessed the reigns of several fascinating and famous pharaohs, any of whom could serve as the focus for a more general investigation of the period. Students could focus on Ramesses II ("the Great," r. 1304–1238 B.C.E.), among the most powerful of all pharaohs, who left an impressive military, architectural, and personal history. Many believe it was during his pharaonate that the Hebrews left Egypt under Moses. Or students could investigate the experimental reign of Amunhotep IV (Akhenaten, r. 1379–1362 B.C.E.) and his wife Queen Nefertiti, under whom not only religion but also Egyptian art changed profoundly. Students could also explore the controversy over whether or not Nefertiti became co-ruler with her husband, Amunhotep IV (Akhenaten). Hatshepsut (r. 1498–1483 B.C.E.) does, of course, garner much attention as the only female pharaoh. An absorbing and well-illustrated popular introduction to all the pharaohs is Peter Clayton, *Chronicle of the Pharaohs* (London: Thames and Hudson, 1994). Studies of individual pharaohs include Joyce Tyldesley's biographies of *Hatshepsut: The Female Pharaoh* (New York: Viking Penguin, 1996) and *Ramesses: Egypt's Greatest Pharaoh* (London: Viking, 2000); Bernadette Menu, *Ramesses II: Greatest of the Pharaohs* (New York: Harry Abrams, 1999); Donald Redford, *Akhenaten: The Heretic King* (Princeton: Princeton University Press, 1987); and Eric Hornung, *Akhenaten and the Religion of Light* (Ithaca, NY: Cornell University, 1999). Primary sources include Sir Alan Gardiner, *The Kadesh Inscriptions of Ramesses II* (Oxford: Oxford University Press, 1960) and *The Amarna Letters*, William Moran, trans. (Baltimore: Johns Hopkins University Press, 1992), both good for investigating Egyptian interactions with foreign powers. For an analysis of Egyptian diplomacy from a modern, political perspective, see Raymond Cohen and Raymond Westbrook, eds., *Amarna Diplomacy: The Beginning of International Relations* (Baltimore: Johns Hopkins University Press, 1999).

Additional Resources: Literature

Dalley, Stephanie, and C. J. Fordyce, trans. and eds., *Myths from Mesopotamia: Creation, the Flood, Gilgamesh, and Others*. 1998.

Foster, John L., *Hymns, Prayers, and Songs: An Anthology of Ancient Egyptian Lyric Poetry*. 1996.

Lichtheim, Miriam, *Ancient Egyptian Literature*, 3 vols. 1973–1980.

Richardson, M. E. J., *Hammurabi's Laws: Text, Translation and Glossary*. 2000.

Sandars, N. K., trans., *The Epic of Gilgamesh*. 1960.

Simpson, William Kelly, ed., *The Literature of Ancient Egypt: An Anthology of Stories, Instructions, and Poetry*, 3rd ed. 2003.

Singer, Itamar, *Writings from the Ancient World: Hittite Prayers*. 2002.

Additional Resources: Film and Video

Egypt's Golden Empire (2002) (PBS: VHS/DVD, 180 min.) This excellent three-part series focuses on the period between 1570 B.C.E. and 1070 B.C.E. and covers the reigns of Ahmose, Hatshepsut, Amunhotep III, Akenaton, Tutankhamon, and Ramesses the Great.

OTHER BEDFORD/ST. MARTIN'S RESOURCES FOR CHAPTER 1

The following resources are available to accompany Chapter 1. Please refer to the Preface of this manual for detailed descriptions of all the ancillaries.

For Instructors

Transparencies

The following maps and images from Chapter 1 are available as full-color acetates.

- Map 1.1: The Ancient Near East, c. 4000–3000 B.C.E.
- Map 1.2: Ancient Egypt
- Map 1.3: Greece and the Aegean Sea, c. 1500 B.C.E.
- Mapping the West: The Period of Calamities, c. 1200–1000 B.C.E.
- The "Standard of Ur" of Sumer, p. 9
- Egyptian Hieroglyphs, p. 18

Instructor's Resources CD-ROM

The following maps and image from Chapter 1, as well as a chapter outline, are available on disc in both PowerPoint and jpeg formats.

- Map 1.1: The Ancient Near East, 4000–3000 B.C.E.
- Map 1.2: Ancient Egypt
- Map 1.3: Greece and the Aegean Sea, 1500 B.C.E.
- Mapping the West: The Period of Calamities, 1200–1000 B.C.E.
- The "Standard of Ur" of Sumer, p. 9

For Students

Study Guides

The Online Study Guide at **bedfordstmartins.com/hunt** helps students synthesize the material they have learned as well as practice the skills historians use to make sense of the past. The following Map, Visual, and Document activities are available for Chapter 1.

Map Activity

- Map 1.3: Greece and the Aegean Sea, 1500 B.C.E.

Visual Activity

- The "Standard of Ur" of Sumer, p. 9

Reading Historical Documents

- Hammurabi's Laws for Physicians, p. 15
- Declaring Innocence on Judgment Day in Ancient Egypt, p. 22

CHAPTER

2

The Near East and the Emergence of Greece

1000–500 B.C.E.

CHAPTER RESOURCES

Main Chapter Topics

1. The invasions by the Sea Peoples and concurrent disasters (1200–1000 B.C.E.) completely destroyed many Bronze Age settlements and left Egypt permanently weakened. When civilizations reemerged by the first millennium B.C.E., the competitive and militaristic Mesopotamian city-states returned to their old patterns of empire building, while the first participatory governments emerged in archaic Greece.

2. The Neo-Assyrian, then Neo-Babylonian, and then Persian empires, dominated Near Eastern history of the period. The Persian Empire, established by Cyrus the Great, was the largest the west had yet produced. (In the fifth century B.C.E., the Persians would threaten to absorb the independent Greek city-states, which confronted their opponent in the later Persian wars.)

3. Scarce natural resources led the Greeks to establish colonies and trade networks throughout the Mediterranean and Black Sea. Rivalries between Greek city-states were common. Nonetheless, a common language, religion, cult centers, artistic conventions, and the Olympic Games (begun in 776 B.C.E.) created a pan-Hellenic sense of "Greek" identity and solidarity.

4. In the eastern Mediterranean the Hebrews briefly established an independent monarchy under Saul, David, and Solomon. Their monotheism developed fully, and their scriptural corpus of the Torah and the prophetic books were set down in writing. Their religion and law served to sustain Jewish identity throughout the frequent periods of diaspora that characterized their subsequent history.

5. The Greeks reacquired literacy when they adapted the Phoenician (Canaanite) alphabet. Among the literary masterpieces of the era were the lyric poems of Sappho and the epics of Homer. Homer's depiction of warriors in the Trojan War in *The Iliad* vividly explores the nature of *aretê* ("excellence") embodied in Achilles and his enemy Hector and captures the essence of ideal Greek manhood that inspired future leaders including Alexander the Great. Hesiod's *Theogony* recounts the genealogy of the gods, their suffering, and their concern for justice among humankind.

6. The political organization of the Greek city-states varied, ranging from tyranny in Corinth, to military oligarchy in Sparta, to nearly complete democracy of male citizens in Athens. But whatever their political structure, city-states shared a concept of citizenship in the polis. Citizen women enjoyed various protections but were barred from direct political participation. Even slaves, who were prevalent throughout the Greek world, were denied legal protections.

7. Sparta's nearly totalitarian regime, based on strict subordination of the individual to the state and the subjugation of *Helots*—slaves who performed all manual labor—earned the polis its reputation for repression and made it the premier military force of archaic Greece. In contrast, Athens worked out a functioning democratic government. Solon and Cleisthenes reformed economic, political, and judicial laws to bring Athens closest to extending equal legal and political rights to all male citizens, regardless of class.

8. The dualism of the Zoroastrians of Persia and the monotheism of the Hebrews changed the religious composition of the west, and the rationalism of the pre-Socratic Greek thinkers offered a logical, empirical view of nature and the cosmos.

Focus Question

How did the social and political organization that Greece developed differ from those of the Near East?

1. Recovery from the Dark Age came sooner to Mesopotamia than to Greece, and the Neo-Assyrians and Neo-Babylonians showed continuity with earlier

monarchical, polytheistic empires in the region. The Persian Empire continued this tradition, permitting a great deal of regional autonomy under satraps and promoting the worship of traditional Babylonian deities. The period of decline persisted a couple of centuries longer for the Greeks, but ongoing trade and cross-cultural contact with Near Eastern peoples fostered eventual recovery and in substantially different form from the earlier Minoan and Mycenaean periods. Most notably, these new "Archaic Age" Greeks developed a notion of citizenship that eventually, in Athens, became democratic, and they began to use reason and logic rather than myth and religion to explain natural phenomena.

2. Greece's geography, as a land of peninsulas and islands, distinguished it from the territories of the Near East, fostered its prosperity in seaborne trade and "colonization," and helped to shape its unique social and political organization. The Greeks remained politically divided into separate city-states, yet they possessed a common language and culture, worshipped the same gods, and developed a sense of collective identity that transcended the independence of each polis. The city-states experimented with a variety of political models, including tyranny, oligarchy, and democracy, yet they all shared a concept of citizenship unique in the ancient world that involved some sharing of power in even the most autocratic of tyrannies.

3. In contrast to the powerful empires of the Near East and the autonomous city-states of Greece, both of which were polytheistic, the Hebrews made their most influential contribution to Western civilization through their unique religious ideas. Monotheism and the importance of scripture eventually proved influential in the development of Christianity and Islam, as well as Judaism. Despite the brevity and relative fragility of Hebrew political independence, Hebrew religion became as influential in the Western tradition as the political ideas and rationalism of the Greeks.

Annotated Chapter Outline

I. From Dark Age to Empire in the Near East, 1000–500 B.C.E.

A. The New Empire of Assyria, 900–600 B.C.E., pp. 35–36

1. After the violence of the Dark Age of 1200–1000 B.C.E., several large empires emerged in succession.
2. By 900 B.C.E., a new and powerful Assyrian kingdom had risen in Mesopotamia.
3. Using highly trained infantrymen, these Neo-Assyrians subjugated neighboring territories to bring in revenue to supplement their domestic economy, which was based on agriculture and trade.
4. Neo-Assyrian kings treated conquered peoples brutally and maintained order by instilling fear.
5. They removed many conquered peoples from their homelands to work on building projects in Assyria.
6. Neo-Assyrian administration and literature reflected a passion for war, hunting, and practical technology.
7. The Neo-Assyrians exhibited a fondness for monumental architecture and built huge temples to their gods.
8. The harshness of their rule led to numerous rebellions.
9. In 612 B.C.E., the Medes (an Iranian people) and the Chaldeans (a Semitic people) joined forces to overthrow the Neo-Assyrian Empire.

B. The Neo-Babylonian Empire, 600–539 B.C.E., pp. 36–37

1. Because they led the defeat of the Neo-Assyrians, the Chaldeans took the largest share of the conquered territory and established the short-lived Neo-Babylonian Empire.
2. The Neo-Babylonian Empire, with its lavish architecture, was Babylon's most powerful until it fell to the Persians in 539 B.C.E.
3. The Chaldeans adopted many aspects of Babylonian culture: they preserved the Near-Eastern tradition of wisdom literature in prose and poetry that taught morality and proper behavior, and ancient literature, including the *Epic of Gilgamesh.*
4. The Chaldeans also made advances in astronomy by using a mixture of science and religion to interpret natural phenomena, a practice that would greatly influence Greek scientists.

C. The Persian Empire, 557–500 B.C.E., pp. 37–39

1. The great general and diplomat Cyrus (r. 557–530 B.C.E.), using a combination of military strength and religious tolerance, founded the next great empire in the Near East.
2. Persian kings ruled as autocrats and, because they saw themselves as superior to all other humans, they emphasized the distance between the king and his subjects through magnificent displays of wealth, ritual, and harsh punishments of wrongdoers.

3. Persian kings seldom interfered with their subjects as long as they remained peaceful.
4. They kept their empire running smoothly by depending on satraps, provincial governors who ruled enormous territories with little interference from the king.
5. Persian kings declared themselves to be agents to the Persian god, Ahura Mazda.
6. Their religion, Zoroastrianism, centered on Ahura Mazda and believed that the world was an arena for the battle between good (truth) and evil (lies).
7. This dualistic doctrine, which promised salvation to those who chose to live on the side of truth and damnation to those electing the way of the lie, would influence Western religions.

D. The Hebrews, Origins to 539 B.C.E., pp. 39–42

1. Developing over a long period of time and reflecting the influences from their polytheistic neighbors, the Hebrews' new kind of religion worshiped a single deity, which made a formal covenant, or agreement, to protect his followers if they worship only him and live by his laws.
2. This tradition later provided the foundation for Christianity and Islam.
3. Hebrew sacred scripture—the Pentateuch or Torah—set forth the religious and moral code as part of their covenant with their god.
4. Although its content is similar to that of Mesopotamian law codes, the Hebrew code applied equally to all persons, regardless of social class.
5. According to the Bible, the patriarch Abraham left Mesopotamia, migrated to Canaan, and led a semi-nomadic existence until the Hebrews migrated into Palestine and eventually Egypt, where they became enslaved.
6. The Hebrew deity, Yahweh, through Moses, led the Hebrews out of bondage and back to Canaan and established his covenant with them through the Ten Commandments about 1250 B.C.E.
7. The Hebrew nation, previously a loosely organized band of tribes, became a national monarchy under Saul and his successors David (r. 1010–970 B.C.E.) and Solomon (r. 961–922 B.C.E.).
8. Solomon built the premier Jewish religious monument, the temple in Jerusalem.
9. After Solomon's death, the monarchy split into two kingdoms: Israel to the north and Judah to the south.
10. In 597 B.C.E., the Babylonians conquered Jerusalem and deported the Jews from their homeland, an event the Jews lamented as "the Exile," which left a mark on Hebrew history and teachings.
11. Jewish prophets taught apocalypticism, which predicted the end of this world and salvation for the Jews if they observed divine law strictly.
12. Despite the Diaspora ("dispersion of the population"), after which many Jews did not return to their homeland, these laws and teachings helped Jews maintain their identity and beliefs even while living in foreign lands.
13. The center of Judaism became preservation and understanding of a sacred text: the Torah (the first five books of the Hebrew Bible) to which were eventually added the books of the prophets, psalms, and other writings.
14. This focus on monotheism, ethical behavior, and scripture set important religious precedents that endure to this day in Western culture.

II. Remaking Greek Civilization, 1000–750 B.C.E.

A. The Greek Dark Age, 1000–750 B.C.E., pp. 42–45

1. After the fall of Mycenaean civilization, Greek society endured poverty and depopulation.
2. During the Dark Age, Greeks lost their knowledge of writing and created no great works of art or architecture.
3. Less land was cultivated, and farming continued on a subsistence level.
4. As herding became more common than farming, the population became more nomadic.
5. Trade endured and, through contact with the Phoenicians—seafaring traders from Canaan—the Greeks again learned to write by adapting the Phoenician alphabet to the Greek language.
6. Exposure to Near Eastern art and luxury items from Egypt and Syria encouraged artistic development. Most important, trade brought iron metallurgy.
7. Cheaper and stronger than bronze, iron was the metal of choice for agricultural tools, swords, and spear points.

8. Sharp and durable iron farming tools increased food production, leading to population growth.
9. During the Dark Age, many men and women competed for social status and leadership through individual excellence (aretê).
10. Men achieved aretê through prowess in war and persuasiveness in speech, whereas women demonstrated aretê through the savvy management of their households.
11. The theme of individual excellence was prominent in the works of the Greek poet Homer who described the exploits of the Greeks during the Trojan War in *The Iliad*, and recounted the ten-year journey of the legendary Greek hero Odysseus in *The Odyssey*.

B. The Values of the Olympic Games, pp. 45–46

1. The most vivid evidence for the rebirth of Greek society was the founding of the Olympic Games in 776 B.C.E., which took place every four years as part of a religious festival held at Olympia in honor of the greatest of Greek gods, Zeus.
2. Athletes competed in games that emphasized military skills, such as running, wrestling, jumping, throwing and, later, horse and chariot races.
3. Although women were banned, they did have their own separate Olympic festival on a different date in honor of the goddess Hera.
4. The Olympic Games glorified individual excellence.
5. They were a step toward a new kind of collective Greek identity not wholly defined by the individual or the local community in that they welcomed any socially elite Greek male competitor and any male spectator.
6. The Greek city-states, which were often at war with each other, placed such a high value on these games that they called a truce for several weeks during each Olympiad to allow athletes and spectators to travel safely.

C. Homer, Hesiod, and Divine Justice in Greek Myth, pp. 46–47

1. Greek myths described the activities of gods and goddesses and their relationships with humans.
2. Homer's poems revealed that the gods interacted with human beings, but their interactions were not always just.
3. The works of the poet Hesiod, by contrast, emphasized justice as a force in the universe, which contributed to Greece's emerging social and political structures.
4. Hesiod's works carried the message that existence, even for the gods, was full of struggle, sorrow, and violence.
5. In his *Theogony* (Genealogy of the Gods), Hesiod describes the birth of the gods from the union of primeval Chaos and Earth.
6. His poems gave justice a central importance and stressed the high priority that the gods, especially Zeus, placed on it.
7. Hesiod felt that social elites who failed to live up to the ideal created tension between themselves and the peasants.
8. This feeling that commoners deserved fair treatment from the elites encouraged the movement toward a new form of political organization.

III. The Creation of the Greek Polis, 750–500 B.C.E.

A. The Physical Environment of the Greek City-State, pp. 47–48

1. During the Archaic Age (750–500 B.C.E.), Greeks organized into a new form of independent city-state called the *polis*.
2. Greeks used citizenship as the defining characteristic of their city-states.
3. Although the political systems of the city-states varied, Greek citizens usually governed themselves.
4. The Greek homeland lay in and around the Aegean Sea, part of the Mediterranean dotted with numerous islands, with the southern Balkan Peninsula on the west and the coast of Anatolia (Ionia) on the east.
5. Although language and religion united the Greek peoples, the mountains, islands, and Ionian territories isolated the city-states, which did not merge into a single, centralized nation.
6. Greek geographic characteristics also restricted large-scale agriculture, which in turn limited the size of each city-state's population.
7. Most Greeks never traveled far from home because overland transport was slow and rudimentary.
8. The most plentiful resource was timber for building houses and ships, although some deposits of metal ore, clay for pottery and sculpture, and stone for special buildings and works of art were also available.
9. Barley, wine grapes, and olives were the most important crops.

10. People raised pigs, sheep, goats, and chickens, but level terrain that was needed for raising horses and cattle was scarce.

B. Trade and "Colonization," 800–580 B.C.E., pp. 48–51

1. The geography of Greece made sea travel convenient even though sailing carried the risk of encountering pirates or weathering storms.
2. The search for more land and resources led the Greeks to establish new settlements throughout the Mediterranean.
3. They were not alone in this expansion; many peoples, such as the Phoenicians, established new settlements.
4. The Phoenician settlement—Carthage—in North Africa became a Mediterranean power in its own right.
5. Greek traders often remained abroad for long periods of time, establishing permanent settlements and spreading their culture.
6. Usually only males traveled, finding wives in areas where they settled.
7. By 580 B.C.E., Greeks had settled in present-day Spain, southern France, southern Italy, and Sicily, North Africa, and the Black Sea coast.
8. Their settlements in southern Italy and Sicily became so large that the region was called Magna Graecia, or "Great Greece."
9. Greek settlements in the east were fewer, possibly because monarchies in the area restricted immigration.
10. Still, they established eastern trading stations, and their contact with Near Eastern cultures influenced Greek art and architecture.
11. Although historians have long referred to these settlements as "colonies," few were colonies in the modern sense of being established and administered by governments.
12. Rather, enterprising men founded most "colonies" with little state involvement.
13. City-states often claimed settlements as "colonies" once they prospered.

C. Citizenship and Freedom in the Greek City-State, pp. 51–57

1. Greeks believed in religious reciprocity—that humans must honor the gods in order to receive blessings from them.
2. By the same token, Greeks avoided acts, such as violating oaths, that might offend a deity and bring punishment.
3. Homicide led to a ritual contamination, or *miasma*, of the murderer and all those around him or her.
4. Religious practice centered around community rituals, such as sacrifices and festivals that maintained the gods' goodwill toward the city-state.
5. To organize politics, Greeks devised the concept of citizenship.
6. Greek citizenship meant equal treatment under the law regardless of social status, although women had fewer rights than men.
7. The most dramatic element of citizenship in many city-states was that all free adult male citizens shared in governance by participating in assemblies.
8. The degree of power-sharing varied from polis to polis.
9. Some were ruled by tyrants, some by oligarchies, some by direct democracy, but all acknowledged citizenship and the rights it bestowed.
10. Historians long theorized that the extension of political rights was related to the "hoplite revolution."
11. Hoplites were infantrymen who paid for their own weapons and armor.
12. The theory states that because iron made weapons more affordable, the growing number of hoplites who defended the community demanded equal political rights.
13. The theory does not, however, explain how political rights were won by men too poor to equip themselves as hoplites.
14. Poor men may have been granted political rights because of their nonmilitary, but essential, labor; or tyrants may have granted them rights in order to marshal political support; or historians may have underestimated the importance of poor men who fought as "light troops" in support of the hoplites.
15. Whatever the reason, the unprecedented extension of political rights to poor men constituted the most innovative feature of Archaic Age society.
16. Slaves, whose numbers grew during this period, were excluded from citizenship.
17. Some slaves gained their freedom and blended into the noncitizen population (*metics*), but no one is known to have called for the abolition of slavery.
18. By managing all household concerns, women enabled male relatives to participate in politics.

19. Although excluded from politics, some women performed important religious duties, which gave them freedom of movement and elevated social status.
20. Marriages were arranged, and brides brought a dowry to the marriage, which the husband was legally bound to preserve and return in case of divorce.

IV. New Directions for the Polis, 750–500 B.C.E.

A. Oligarchy in Sparta, 700–500 B.C.E., pp. 57–60

1. Sparta was ruled by an oligarchy consisting of a small group of men.
2. The Spartans had three ruling bodies: two military leaders called kings who served as head of the government, a council of twenty-eight elders, and five elected magistrates called *ephors*.
3. All free, adult Spartan men, known as "the Alike," were part of an assembly with limited powers whose purpose was to approve legislation.
4. Military readiness was the primary concern in Sparta, and their economy depended completely on a large population of enslaved Greeks called Helots who were usually captives from neighboring regions, especially Messenia.
5. By 700 B.C.E., the Helots outnumbered their masters, who constantly feared rebellion.
6. Therefore, every year, the ephors formally declared war on the Helots, which allowed Spartans to kill them without the risk of offending the gods.
7. Helots were forced to endure public humiliation and wear distinctive caps to signal their inferiority.
8. Helots performed all nonmilitary labor, which allowed male citizens opportunity for full-time, lifelong training for war.
9. At age seven, boys moved to communal barracks and lived there until they turned thirty, an arrangement designed to make a boy loyal to his fellow men, not his biological family.
10. Harsh conditions and training cultivated strength, cunning, courage, and disregard of pain.
11. Those who could not endure were denied Alike status.
12. An older man often chose an adolescent for a relationship that combined mentoring and sexual relations and was intended to strengthen personal loyalty among soldiers.
13. Spartan women were known for their relative liberty, could own property, and were expected to bear healthy children.
14. Sparta's population was never large, and men became legally required to marry to produce enough children to replace the men killed in battle.

B. Tyranny in Corinth, 657–585 B.C.E., pp. 60–62

1. In city-states where competition between members of the social elite for political power was especially bitter, a single family might suppress its rivals and establish itself as a tyranny.
2. Greek tyrants were not necessarily brutal, ruthless leaders; some were benevolent.
3. They typically secured power by improving the economic lot of the masses and maintaining the appearance of consulting them in political decisions.
4. Tyrants usually preserved the existing laws and political institutions of the city-state.
5. In Corinth, in 657 B.C.E., the family of Cypselus rebelled against a harsh oligarchy and marshaled popular support for Cypselus's sole rule by promoting the economic interests of poorer citizens.
6. The reign of Cypselus ushered in a period of economic expansion and prosperity.
7. His son took over in 625 B.C.E. and continued his father's policy of economic expansion by founding colonies and pursuing commercial contacts with Egypt.
8. He lost popular support because he ruled harshly, and his heir and successor was overthrown.

C. Democracy in Athens, 632–500 B.C.E., pp. 62–64

1. In Athens the economy improved rapidly during 800–700 B.C.E. and the population expanded at a phenomenal rate.
2. Good farmland and opportunities for seaborne trade allowed many families to achieve a modest prosperity.
3. By the seventh century B.C.E., Athens created an assembly where all free adult male citizens helped decide the community's affairs and elect magistrates called *archons*.
4. Only the elite were archons; because they possessed no income, poor men could not afford to serve.

5. Around 621 B.C.E., an economic crisis drove Athens to empower Draco to revise and clarify the laws, but Draco's laws were insupportably harsh.
6. By 600 B.C.E., citizens were deeply in debt and were being sold into slavery, and in 594 B.C.E. Athens appointed Solon to avert a civil war.
7. Solon ended the sale of citizens for debt and freed enslaved debtors.
8. He cancelled the debts of the poor but did not redistribute the lands of the rich.
9. Solon reformed politics by dividing citizens into four groups according to wealth.
10. The richer the man, the higher the governmental office he could hold.
11. Laborers, at the lowest rank, were not eligible for any position but upward mobility was now possible.
12. Solon also created a Council of Four Hundred, who made the assembly more efficient by setting its agenda.
13. Solon's judicial reforms granted male citizens the right to bring charges on behalf of victims and to appeal cases to the assembly.
14. To balance these democratic reforms, he granted broader powers to the elite Areopagus Council, which judged the most serious cases.
15. Solon extended power to all citizens and made the laws apply equally to all free Athenian men.
16. In 546 B.C.E., Peisistratus interrupted democracy by establishing himself tyrant.
17. His son Hippias ruled so harshly that in 510 B.C.E. his rivals called on Sparta to liberate Athens from tyranny.
18. In 508 B.C.E., the Athenians elected Cleisthenes, "the Father of Athenian Democracy," to expand the reforms that had begun under Solon.
19. Cleisthenes increased the size of the council to five hundred and divided the city-state into constituent units called *demes*.
20. Each deme chose council members in proportion to its population.
21. Also, candidates for public office had to be spread widely throughout the demes, thus balancing power between the urban center and the surrounding country villages.

D. New Ways of Thought and Expression, 630–500 B.C.E., pp. 64–65

1. During the Archaic Age, intellectuals and artists began to expand upon ideas and techniques learned from Near Eastern cultures.
2. Painting and sculpture became more vivid and realistic, and lyric poetry expressing individual feelings became popular.
3. Sappho of Lesbos was famous for her love poems, while Archilochus of Paros wrote on soldiering, friends lost at sea, and love gone astray.
4. Philosophy and science were led by the pre-Socratic philosophers who devised new explanations of the human world and its relation to the gods and goddesses.
5. Thales and Anaximander from Ionia began to theorize that the universe was based on laws of nature rather than on the unpredictable behavior of the gods as described in myths.
6. Believing that the universe was neither random nor arbitrary, they named it *cosmos*, meaning ordered and beautiful.
7. Pythagoras taught that patterns and relationships of numbers explained the entire world, began the systematic study of mathematics, and described the numerical aspects of musical harmony.
8. These thinkers emphasized rationalism—the notion that one should support an argument through the use of evidence and logic rather than through the authority of established belief.
9. The new belief that humans were not merely subject to the whims of the gods gave people hope that they could improve their lives through hard work.

Lecture Strategies

1. A central theme in Greek history is the participation of citizens in the political life of the polis under the rule of law. To what extent was equality achieved, and at what costs? These questions can be explored through a comparison of Sparta and Athens, the two city-states for which by far the most information has survived. Were the Spartans with their identical social standing as citizen-warriors more equal than the obviously class-stratified society of Athens? Did the women of Sparta really enjoy a more equal status with men than the quite secluded middle- and upper-class

Athenian women? Do the students agree with the sentiment that, in a democracy, the citizen is the slave of the polis? Discussions of Athenian developments are found in Nicholas Jones, *Ancient Greece: State and Society* (Upper Saddle River, NJ: Prentice Hall, 1997), which, despite its title, focuses primarily on Athens; the more detailed Charles Hignett, *A History of the Athenian Constitution to the End of the Fifth Century B.C.E.* (Oxford: Clarendon, 1952); and for citizen involvement in the functioning of democracy, R. Sinclair, *Democracy and Participation in Athens* (Cambridge, UK: Cambridge University Press, 1988). For Sparta, consult P. Cartledge, *Sparta and Laconia: A Regional History, 1300–362 B.C.E.* (New York and London: Routledge, 1979); and A. Powell, *Classical Sparta: Techniques Behind Her Success* (Norman, OK: University of Oklahoma Press, 1988).

2. The text suggests that the emergence of a middle class in Athens was an essential ingredient in the development of its democratic institutions. Similarly, economic crisis provided the impetus for the early democratic reforms of Draco and Solon. What is the role of economic prosperity in the formation of participatory government? Contrast Athenian democracy with the empires of the Near East or the pharaonic dynasties of Egypt, both vastly more prosperous and powerful than archaic Greece. Did the nondistributive nature of the Greek economies entail an individual initiative that the subject peoples of Egypt or the Near Eastern empires lacked? Was minimal social welfare more precarious to sustain in the Greek city-states than in a redistributive economy? For the development of Greek democracy, see Victor Hanson, *The Other Greeks: The Family Farm and the Agrarian Roots of Western Civilization* (New York: Free Press, 1995), which considers the role of the independent hoplite-farmer. Also see Chester Starr, *Economic and Social Growth of Early Greece, 800–500 B.C.E.* (Oxford: Oxford University Press, 1977).

3. By the time of the Persian Wars, the Persians represented the threatening "other" to the Greeks, who characterized them as "barbarians." However, the Persian Empire and its rulers were widely admired in the ancient world. For example, the Hebrew Bible describes Cyrus the Great as the "anointed" of God (Isaiah II, 45:1–3). Review the generally tolerant and sophisticated policies that the Persian leaders exercised in order to maintain their vast empire (the Romans would later follow similar practices in the administration of their own subject territories). The discussion can introduce the topics of European/Near Eastern cultural and political rivalries and interpenetration that would be important in subsequent eras (during the Persian Wars, the Hellenistic and Roman eras, medieval Christianity and Islam, and so on). The class can also address the issue of cultural vilification that often accompanies war. For further information on Persia, see J. M. Cook, *The Persian Empire* (New York: Schocken, 1987).

4. Athenians possessed a reputation for litigiousness as great as that of modern Americans. Outline the central role that juries played in the civic life of this polis. Remember, serving on juries was one of the main political duties (and privileges) of every male citizen, including those who were poor. Personal reputation and rhetorical skill often played crucial roles in determining the outcome of a trial. In which ways did trials operate in this city-state where, for men at least, there was very little distinction to be made between the "public" and "private" realms? How did the emphasis on public speaking contribute to one's public career? How did reputation affect daily life in this face-to-face community, especially regarding gender roles? Many illuminating studies, often influenced by anthropology, have recently appeared: David Cohen, *Law, Violence, and Community in Classical Athens* (Cambridge, UK: Cambridge University Press, 1995); S. Todd, *The Shape of Athenian Law* (Oxford: Oxford University Press, 1993); also, the collected articles in P. Cartledge, P. Miller, and S. Todd, eds., *Nomos: Essays in Athenian Law, Politics, and Society* (Cambridge, UK: Cambridge University Press, 1990), especially R. Osborne, "Vexatious Litigation in Classical Athens."

5. Given the emphasis on personal liberty in Greek history and writings, the phenomenon of tyrannies may seem strange. However, the inefficiencies of democracy may at times have made tyranny seem attractive, especially in periods of crisis. Explore the episodes of tyrannical rule in the archaic city-states, considering why some (those of Cypselas and Peisistratus, for example) succeeded, while others (Cylon, Hippias) failed. What were the broader political and social realities that surrounded each episode? A standard study of Greek tyranny remains A. Andrewes, *The Greek Tyrants* (New York: Harper & Row, 1956). See also James McGrew, *Tyranny and Political Culture in Ancient Greece* (Ithaca, NY: Cornell University Press, 1993).

Class Discussion Starters

1. The scriptural tradition and laws of the Hebrews served not only to articulate their religious teachings but also to cement their identity as a scattered people nearly always under the political domination of others. Discuss the ways in which the stories contained in the Hebrew Bible serve this function throughout their history of diaspora.

2. The emergence of hoplite warfare marked a significant transformation in the history of military tactics. Discuss the personal stake Greeks had in military prowess, as it was revealed in the elite martial

culture of Homer's *The Iliad*. Contrast the individualistic exploits of the Homeric heroes with the coordinated group effort required of hoplites. This idea can be impressed on students by having them (if they are willing) recreate a hoplite phalanx formation. Also, compare the expense involved in chariot-based warfare to the relatively minimal equipment of hoplite infantry. Then debate both the merits and inadequacies of the "hoplite theory" of the origins of democracy. The class could also explore the hoplite as the ideal Spartan citizen. Useful details on military techniques can be found in Victor Hanson, ed., *Hoplites: The Classical Greek Battle Experience* (London and New York: Routledge, 1998); *The Western Way of War: Infantry Battle in Classical Greece*, 2nd ed. (Berkeley and Los Angeles: University of California Press, 2000); and J. F. Lazenby, *The Spartan Army* (Chicago: University of Chicago Press, 1985). For a sociohistorical perspective on Greek warfare, see John Rich and Graham Shiply, eds., *War and Society in the Greek World* (London and New York: Routledge, 1995).

3. Persian Zoroastrianism centered on dualism and on the role of free will in human salvation, concepts that continue to dominate western religious thought. Discuss these concepts as they appear in Zoroastrianism and then ask the students to comment on how they might relate to: earlier religious traditions encompassed by the Egyptian Book of the Dead and the Ten Commandments in Exodus; later religious developments; and western intellectual traditions in general. Mary Boyce provides a general introduction in *A History of Zoroastrianism: The Early Period* (Leiden: Brill, 1996). Translated primary sources can be found in the section on Persian Religion in the *Internet Ancient History Sourcebook: Ancient Near East*.

4. Painted vases, a major Athenian product, often featured vivid scenes from daily life. A slide or PowerPoint presentation could launch a discussion about virtually any aspect of this broad topic, or furnish the basis for an in-class writing assignment. Excellent collections are reproduced in John Boardman's *Athenian Black Figure Vases* (Oxford: Oxford University Press, 1974) and *Athenian Red Figure Vases* (Oxford: Oxford University Press, 1975).

5. The Homeric epics provide an inexhaustible supply of information about many facets of archaic Greek culture and society, as well as a reflection of its semi-mythical Mycenaean past. Selected passages from *The Iliad* and *The Odyssey* can serve as a basis for lectures on notions of masculinity and military virtue, the lives of women (mortal and immortal) and the family, religious beliefs of the early Greeks, inter-Hellenic conflict and cooperation in the face of a common adversary, relations between social classes, and the complicated Greek attitude toward the non-Greek (the "other," in this case, the Trojans). More specifically, the figure of Hector serves as an example of the warrior tempered by civilization, Nestor as the perfect heroic figure, Penelope as the epitome of constancy and faithfulness, and so on. See Robert Fagles, trans., *The Iliad* (New York: Penguin, 1990) and *The Odyssey* (New York: Penguin, 1996).

Reviewing the Text

Review Question

1. In what ways was religion important in the Near East from c. 1000 B.C.E. to c. 500 B.C.E.?
[model answer] *Religious beliefs reflected major cultural values of Near Eastern societies and provided moral and ethical codes that reinforced social order and collective identity. The monumental temples and religious beliefs of the Neo-Assyrians glorified the warfare that was crucial to the consolidation of the Neo-Assyrian Empire. The Chaldeans blended the teachings about morality and proper behavior of their ancient wisdom literature with scientific observations of celestial phenomena into beliefs that gods communicated their will to humans. Under the Persians, such standards for behavior, and a belief that gods could be a force for good or for evil, evolved into a strong moral code important to Persian kings' authority. Claiming to be agents of the supreme god of good, Persian kings used religious beliefs to reinforce their authority as divine rulers. Influenced by these ideas and experiences that encouraged their adoption of a belief in a single god, the Hebrews developed a strong moral code that defined their collective society and gave them a cultural strength to survive as a people without a homeland state to provide a basis for their shared cultural identity.*

2. What factors proved most important in the Greek recovery from the troubles of the Dark Age?
[model answer] *During the two and a half centuries of the Greek Dark Age, trade with other civilizations, never completely cut off, yielded economic and cultural recovery. Abroad, the Greeks learned how to smelt iron ore. Iron enabled them to produce better and cheaper agricultural tools, which improved the food supply dramatically, and that in turn allowed the decimated population to expand. Elite Greeks produced food surpluses to trade for foreign luxury goods. Contact with civilizations from the Near East and Egypt contributed significantly to Greek social and cultural recovery. Greek art was influenced by art of the Near East, reviving the depiction of humans and animals. Writing, which had disappeared in Greece, was relearned from the Phoenicians around 800 B.C.E., and was adapted to the Greek language. This allowed Greek literature to be recorded, which helped to shape the values and structure of the reviving Greek civilization.*

3. How did the physical, social, and intellectual conditions of life in the Archaic Age promote the emergence of the Greek city-state?
[model answer] *The mountainous geography of Greece, which limited interaction among population centers, isolated its communities and fostered their independent development. With the fall of Mycenaean civilization, the cities of Greece lacked a strong central authority, and communities developed concepts of governance and citizenship that grew from the traditions of small community life in which all men contributed to decision making for local affairs. An idea of citizenship that entailed shared responsibilities of power and justice in political and legal equality (primarily for male citizens) became the foundation of political community in Greek city-states. Competition among cities for the region's growing trade fostered the development of competitive cultural values that reinforced the cities' individual identities. It is considered possible that this competition between Greek cities as independent polities also encouraged recognition of even the poor as citizens because their contributions as troops were important for the communities' defense.*

4. What were the main differences among the various forms of government in the Greek city-states?
[model answer] *City-states developed three basic forms of government. All were societies based on citizenship but with differing bases of political authority. Democracies permitted all male citizens to participate in government, the only form of Greek government with genuine political power sharing. In oligarchies, a small number of male citizens dominated policymaking. In tyrannies, a single family came to dominate politics, with its leader assuming control as an individual.*

Making Connections

1. What characteristics made the Greek city-state a different form of political and social organization from that in Near Eastern city-states?
[model answer] *The most radical difference was the Greeks' belief in the equality of citizens as the basis of social organization. For those who were citizens, this diminished the hierarchical nature of the social structure. Many near eastern societies were empires, geographically larger than Greek city-states, with a central authority connecting the larger realm. In their independence from each other, the city-states remained much smaller political entities.*

2. How were the ideas of the Ionian philosophers different from mythic traditions?
[model answer] *Ionian philosophers sought to explain natural phenomena through reason, rejecting the idea that deities created and controlled the natural world. Because the universe was ordered, they believed, it could be understood through tangible evidence. Their pursuit of reasons and evidence, which came to be called rationalism, laid the foundation for scientific thought.*

Discussing the Documents

Homer's Vision of Justice in the Polis (p. 46)

1. What were some of the activities described in the polis at peace?
[model answer] *There were weddings, singing, and dancing. There were also public disputes in the agora.*

2. How does this description show the division of male and female roles in the polis?
[model answer] *It is clear that men participated in the polis's politics, whereas women stayed at home. Homer writes that "the women lingered smilingly on their doorsteps . . . their husbands had gone off as a group to the polis's gathering place."*

Cyrene Records Its Foundation as a Greek Colony (p. 52)

1. Who was sent to the new colony, and under what terms and conditions were they sent?
[model answer] *One adult son from each household was sent. Only free males were sent; women and slaves were not. Those ordered to the colony faced the death penalty and the confiscation of their property if they did not go; so did their families if they harbored them. If they were unable to establish a successful colony in Cyrene after five years, they would be allowed to return home without any penalty.*

2. Most Greek colonies began as trading outposts founded by independent entrepreneurs without any official state involvement. What was the role of the Theran state in founding this colony, and what might its motives have been?
[model answer] *The Theran state ordered its citizens to send adult males to Cyrene and threatened those who refused with the death penalty. Its motive was most likely to relieve the state of its excess population.*

Contrasting Views: Persians Debate Democracy, Oligarchy, and Monarchy (p. 58)

1. Why did Otanes believe that democracy would be the best type of government?
[model answer] *Otanes believed that the equality of democracy would encourage accountability, which would prevent the abuses that a monarch might be tempted to commit. In protecting and expressing his power, a monarch becomes arbitrary, jealous, abusive, and self-serving. Community rule, on the other hand, serves all its participants.*

2. Why did Megabyzus advocate oligarchy?
[Model answer] *Megabyzus believed that the leaders of an oligarchy, who would be "a group of the best men," would be better able to rule intelligently because they had more access to knowledge and training than the people as a mass.*

3. Why did Darius prefer monarchy?
[Model answer] *Darius believed that monarchy would provide society with the absolute best leadership, "the one best man." With either oligarchy or democracy, shared power could foster jealousy, hatred, and competition to dominate. That pursuit of power would then become more important to its participants than caring for common interests.*

Other Questions for Discussing the Documents in Class

Homer's Vision of Justice in the Polis (p. 46)

1. How does Homer describe the wedding celebrations? Who are the participants? Is it significant that part of the celebrations take place in public?
2. How does Homer describe the dispute at the agora? Who are the participants? What is the significance of it occurring in a public place?
3. Compare and contrast these two examples of communal life in the polis.

Cyrene Records Its Foundation as a Greek Colony (p. 52)

1. What does this document suggest about Greek attitudes towards equality and fairness? Are these concepts identical?
2. What is the relationship between those who stayed at home in Greece and those who settled in North Africa?

Contrasting Views: Persians Debate Democracy, Oligarchy, and Monarchy (p. 58)

1. On what point does Otanes agree with Megabyzus?
2. Are there any points of agreement among all three authors?
3. Which of the three points of view is stated most persuasively and why?

Comparative Questions

1. What insight do these documents provide into Greek politics in the Archaic Age?
2. According to these documents, what was the role of citizenship?

For Users of *Sources of The Making of the West*

The following documents are available in Chapter 2 of the companion sourcebook by Katharine J. Lualdi, University of Southern Maine.

1. Empires and Divine Right: *Inscription Honor Cyrus, King of Persia* (r. 557–530 B.C.E.)
2. Monotheism and Mosaic Law: *The Book of Exodus, Chapters 19–20* (c. tenth–sixth centuries B.C.E.)
3. Two Visions of the City-State: Tyrtaeus of Sparta and Solon of Athens, *Poems* (seventh–sixth centuries B.C.E.)
4. Greek Colonization: Herodotus, *The Foundation of Cyrene* (late seventh century B.C.E.)
5. A Woman's Voice: *The Poems of Sappho of Lesbos* (sixth century B.C.E.)

Discussion Ideas for Sources of The Making of the West, *Chapter 2*

1. Although other Near Eastern states, such as the empire of the Persians, surpassed Israel and Judah in political power and longevity, the Hebrews have had a lasting impact on Western civilization through their religion. What is the relationship between the development of monotheism and the Jewish Diaspora? How did Judaism help the Hebrews endure even when they were dispersed from their homeland? How did the Covenant at Sinai in The Book of Exodus help unify and strengthen Jewish society? How might the focus on scripture have contributed to the influence of Judaism on later Christianity and Islam? Why might Judaism have had a greater long-term influence on Western civilization than Zoroastrianism?
2. Sparta and Athens are often contrasted as two of the most distinctive Greek city-states. How do the visions of Tyrtaeus of Sparta and Solon of Athens compare and contrast? Are there similarities between Spartan warriors and Athenian citizens? What do the two authors have to say about honor? What is Solon's vision of citizenship and freedom? How does Solon characterize the relationship between gods and humans? What insight does Tyrtaeus's poem provide into Spartan communal life and the relationship between older and younger warriors? How does this compare with Solon's regrets about "war that kills so many beautiful youths"?

Working with Visual Sources

For this exercise, please see The Great King of Persia on p. 37 of the textbook or view the image on the book companion site's Online Study Guide under the

"Visual Activity" for Chapter 2. Students viewing the image at the Online Study Guide are asked three questions about the image. The questions and model answers (not made available to students) are below. Project this image, available on the Instructor's Resources CD-ROM, in class or ask students to look at the image in their textbooks and answer the questions.

1. According to the caption in the textbook, size was used to indicate the greater importance of the king and his son. Which other features were used to stress the importance of the king?
[model answer] *The king is seated while everyone else is standing. His beard, along with that of his son, is longer than everyone else's.*

2. Judging from the postures of the figure and the objects they are holding, what seems to be going on in this picture?
[model answer] *This appears to be the king's throne room, where his son and perhaps another advisor (the man holding what appears to be rope) attend him. Soldiers guard him. It looks as if the man approaching him is coming to ask him for something or perhaps has been called before him for some reason. The man approaches respectfully, with his stick lowered, his body inclined forward, and his hand to his mouth.*

3. If this sculpture were located in a waiting room for petitioners, what function might it serve? What about if it were located in the king's private chambers? In the guard's quarters?
[model answer] *If it was in the waiting room, it might have been designed to prepare petitioners for their audience with the king, reminding them of the proper posture to adopt when greeting him. If it was in the king's private quarters, he might have had it commissioned to celebrate or commemorate his power and dignity. If it was in the guards' quarters, it might have been designed to reinforce their feelings of loyalty toward the king and their desire to protect him.*

For this exercise, please see Limestone Statue of Kaemheset, Old Kingdom Egypt, c. 2400 B.C.E. and Marble Statue of Croesus, Archaic Age Greece, c. 530–520 B.C.E., on p. 50 of the textbook or view the images on the book companion site's Online Study Guide under the "Visual Activity: Seeing History" for Chapter 2.

Students viewing the image at the Online Study Guide are asked two questions about the images. The questions and model answers (not made available to students) are below. Project these images, available on the Instructor's Resources CD-ROM, in class or ask students to look at the images in their textbooks and answer the questions.

1. What do you think Egyptian and Greek artists were expressing by using this style?
[model answer] *The erect posture and calm, forward-facing expressions of the figures project order, stability, and power. These were all virtues in Egyptian culture and Greek artists may have found this style appealing in an era of recovery following the upheaval of the Dark Age.*

2. What do you think could have been the reasons for placing statues inside or outside of tombs and for portraying their subjects clothed or nude?
[model answer] *Statues placed outside of tombs might have served as monuments to the deceased, while those placed inside tombs were probably intended for more religious purposes. In the Egyptian tradition, they played a role in the passage to the afterlife. Nude subjects may have been more idealized, rejoicing in the perfection of the human body. Clothed statues may have been intended as more realistic portraiture, or the clothing may have signified the subject's social status.*

Mapping Exercises

Map Activity from OSG—Model Answers for Map Activity #2

For this activity, please refer to the map on p. 48. Students are asked these questions:

By 500 B.C.E., where could Greek settlers be found outside their homeland?
[model answer] *Greeks could be found on the west coast of Anatolia, along the coast of the Black Sea, and on the coasts of southern France, southern Italy, and Sicily. They had also established a few settlements in Spain and on the north coast of Africa, particularly in Egypt.*

Other than the Greeks, which civilizations controlled large portions of the Mediterranean coastline?
[model answer] *The Persian Empire controlled most of the eastern Mediterranean coastline. The Phoenicians had settled most of the north coast of Africa and controlled much of the southern coast of Spain. Egypt still maintained its ports in the Nile Delta region.*

Which peoples did Greek settlers or colonists come into contact with?
[model answer] *The Greeks would have been in contact with the Celts of France and Spain, and the Scythians and Samaritans along the Black Sea. They would have also interacted with the Phoenicians, Egyptians, and Persians along the coast of North Africa.*

Map 2.1, Expansion of the Neo-Assyrian Empire, c. 900–650 B.C.E., p. 35

Along which rivers and seas did the Neo-Assyrians expand? How does the territory of the Neo-Assyrian

Empire compare with that of the Neolithic Fertile Crescent discussed in the Prologue?

Map 2.2, Expansion of the Persian Empire, c. 550–490 B.C.E., p. 38

How do the borders of the Persian Empire compare with those of the Neo-Assyrians in Map 2.1? Which territories did the Persians claim that the Neo-Assyrians had not?

Map 2.3, Dark Age Greece, p. 43

Which part of Dark Age Greece had the most city-states?

Map 2.4, Archaic Greece, 750–500 B.C.E., p. 48

How do the boundaries of Archaic Greece compare with those of Dark Age Greece in Map 2.3? Ask students to locate Athens, Sparta, and Corinth.

Map 2.5: Phoenician and Greek Expansion, 750–500 B.C.E., p. 49

How did the sea facilitate expansion while simultaneously limiting the territory targeted for colonization? Why did expansion occur to the west and north, rather than south and east? What do the distances between their mother city-states and the locations of these colonies say about the availability of free land and the maritime technology and skills of the Greeks?

Mapping the West: Mediterranean Civilizations, c. 500 B.C.E., p. 66

This map provides a striking visual contrast between the relative sizes of Greece and the Persian Empire. Have students note all the civilizations that the Persian Empire encompassed under one central authority, compared with the often-squabbling and tiny Greek city-states. What does this comparison tell them about the resources, wealth, and manpower at Persia's disposal in the upcoming Persian Wars between the empire and a pan-Hellenic force? What added information might it lend to their understanding of the power of the Greeks' belief that they constituted a bastion of liberty against the "tyranny of eastern despotism"?

In-Class Assignments and Presentation Topics

1. The contrast between Athens and Sparta often fascinates students, especially the lifestyle of Sparta. Have students explore in a class presentation the fundamental distinctions and similarities of these rivals by comparing the reforms attributed to Lycurgus and Solon. The content of their reforms can be found in their biographies in Plutarch's *Parallel Lives*. Solon provides additional information in some of his poems; translations are contained in David Mulroy, *Early Greek Lyric Poetry* (Ann Arbor: University of Michigan Press, 1992).

2. Athens and Sparta differed radically from each other both socially and politically. A comparison between the cultures from an Athenian or Spartan perspective would be revealing of both societies. Students can assume a variety of roles—warrior, aristocrat, peasant, woman, slave—and compare them to their respective counterparts.

3. Have students track down a Greek god or goddess they can personally identify with. Have them briefly describe their particular god and discuss what their choice says about themselves. To ensure that students read beyond the obvious twelve Olympic gods, it may be necessary to restrict their selections to lesser figures. See J. E. Zimmerman, *Dictionary of Classical Mythology* (New York: Bantam Books, 1964; rpt. 1983).

4. Have the students explore the emergence of Greek individualism as expressed in archaic lyric poems. How do they represent the "public" topics of military valor, arranged marriages, religious rituals, or civic service in politics? Conversely, what range of emotions and personal topics do they discuss? Popular choices include Archilocus of Paros, whose poems were banned as subversive in Sparta, and Sappho, for a woman's point of view. Theognis, Alcaeus, and Tyrtaeus say many interesting things as well. Students could also compare the Greek lyrics with the personal poetry from ancient Egypt. Good collections of translations from the Greek are Andrew Miller, *Greek Lyric* (Indianapolis: Hackett, 1996); and Barbara Fowler, *Archaic Greek Poetry* (Madison: University of Wisconsin Press, 1992).

5. Students can approach the life of an independent, middle-class farmer as embodied in *Hesiod's Works and Days: A Translation and Commentary for the Social Sciences*, D. W. Hardy and W. C. Neale, trans. and eds. (Berkeley and Los Angeles: University of California Press, 1996). Further background information can be obtained from Alison Burford, *Land and Labor in the Greek World* (Baltimore: Johns Hopkins University Press, 1993). This collection of aphorisms and "commonsense" reflections on women, hired hands, sibling rivalry, and the corruption of those in political authority reveals a society far from that embodied in the Homeric epics. What constitutes a successful life, according to the speaker?

Essay Questions

1. The question of the origins of Greek civilization has recently generated considerable and heated

scholarly debate. The study that sparked the controversy was Martin Bernal's *Black Athena: The Afroasiatic Roots of Classical Civilization*, vols. 1 and 2 (New Brunswick, NJ: Rutgers University Press, 1987 and 1991). Among the numerous responses to it is Mary Lefkowicz's pointed *Not Out of Africa: How Afrocentrism Became an Excuse to Teach Myth as History* (New York: Basic Books, 1996). Have students explore the merits of the argument on both sides. This topic provides a good introduction to historiography and revisionism in history.

2. Greek sexuality is another controversial topic that has generated numerous analyses from a wide variety of methodological perspectives. In addition to the works listed in the chapter bibliography, see J. J. Winkler, *The Constraints of Desire: The Anthropology of Sex and Gender in Ancient Greece* (New York and London: Routledge, 1989); David Cohen, *Law, Sexuality, and Society: The Enforcement of Morals in Classical Athens* (Cambridge, UK: Cambridge University Press, 1992); David Halperin and John Winkler, eds., *Before Sexuality: The Construction of Erotic Experience in the Ancient Greek World* (Princeton: Princeton University Press, 1990); and K. J. Dover, *Greek Homosexuality* (Cambridge, MA: Harvard University Press, 1978; rpt. 1989). A unique examination of the metaphors Greeks used for the female body is Paige DuBois, *Sowing the Body: Psychoanalysis and Ancient Representations of Women* (Chicago: University of Chicago Press, 1988).

3. The Greek mystery religions, such as the cult of Demeter at Eleusis and the cult of Orpheus, provide an interesting contrast to the more well-known, official state cults of deities like Athena and Zeus. They also shed light on the religious role of Greek women. See E. R. Dodds, *The Greeks and the Irrational* (Berkeley: University of California Press, 1951). Two examinations by leading authorities are W. K. C. Guthrie, *Orpheus and Greek Religion: A Study of the Orphic Movement* (Princeton: Princeton University Press, 1993); and Walter Burkert, *Ancient Mystery Cults* (Cambridge, MA: Harvard University Press, 1987). See also Marvin W. Meyer, *The Ancient Mysteries: A Sourcebook of Sacred Texts* (Philadelphia: University of Pennsylvania Press, 1999); and Thomas Carpenter and Christopher Faraone, eds., *Masks of Dionysus* (Ithaca, NY: Cornell University Press, 1993). For information on sanctuaries and oracles, see Matthew Dillon, *Pilgrims and Pilgrimage in Ancient Greece* (London and New York: Routledge, 1997).

Additional Resources: Literature

Barnes, Jonathan, ed. and trans., *Early Greek Philosophy*. 1987.

Campbell, David A., trans., *Greek Lyric*, 5 vols. 1982–1993.

Fagles, Robert, trans., *The Odyssey*. 1999.

Fitzgerald, Robert, trans., *The Iliad*. 1989.

Greene, David, trans., *The History: Herodotus*. 1988.

M. L. West, trans., *Hesiod's Theogony, Works, and Days*. 1999.

Lieber, David L., ed., *Etz Hayim: Torah and Commentary*. 2001.

Malandra, William W., *An Introduction to Ancient Iranian Religion: Readings from the Avesta and the Achaemenid Inscriptions*. 1983.

Additional Resources: Film and Video

In Search of the Trojan War (1985) (DVD, 360 min.) An Emmy-nominated, six-part series hosted by documentary host Michael Wood, who traces the archaeological search for proof of Homer's account of the Trojan War.

OTHER BEDFORD/ST. MARTIN'S RESOURCES FOR CHAPTER 2

The following resources are available to accompany Chapter 2. Please refer to the Preface of this manual for detailed descriptions of all the ancillaries.

For Instructors

Transparencies

The following maps and images from Chapter 2 are available as full-color acetates.

- Map 2.1: Expansion of the Neo-Assyrian Empire, c. 900–650 B.C.E.
- Map 2.2: Expansion of the Persian Empire, c. 550–490 B.C.E.
- Map 2.3: Dark Age Greece
- Map 2.4: Archaic Greece, c. 750–500 B.C.E.
- Map 2.5: Phoenician and Greek Expansion, c. 750–500 B.C.E.
- Mapping the West: Mediterranean Civilizations, c. 500 B.C.E.
- The Great King of Persia, p. 37
- Athletic Competition, p. 45

Instructor's Resources CD-ROM

The following maps and images from Chapter 2, as well as a chapter outline, are available on disc in both PowerPoint and jpeg formats.

- Map 2.1: Expansion of the Neo-Assyrian Empire, c. 900–650 B.C.E.
- Map 2.2: Expansion of the Persian Empire, c. 550–490 B.C.E.

- Map 2.3: Dark Age Greece
- Map 2.4: Archaic Greece, 750–500 B.C.E.
- Map 2.5: Phoenician and Greek Expansion, 750–500 B.C.E.
- Mapping the West: Mediterranean Civilizations, c. 500 B.C.E.
- The Great King of Persia, p. 37
- Limestone Statue of Kaemheset, Old Kingdom Egypt, c. 2400 B.C.E., p. 50
- Marble Statue of Croesus, Archaic Age Greece, c. 530–520 B.C.E., p. 50

For Students

Study Guides

The Online Study Guide at **bedfordstmartins.com/hunt** helps students synthesize the material they have learned as well as to practice the skills historians use to make sense of the past. The following Map, Visual, and Document activities are available for Chapter 2.

Map Activity

- Map 2.4: Archaic Greece, 750–500 B.C.E.

Visual Activity

- The Great King of Persia, p. 37
- Limestone Statue of Kaemheset, Old Kingdom Egypt, c. 2400 B.C.E., p. 50
- Marble Statue of Croesus, Archaic Age Greece, c. 530–520 B.C.E., p. 50

Reading Historical Documents

- Homer's Vision of Justice in the Polis, p. 46
- Cyrene Records Its Foundations as a Greek Colony, p. 52
- Contrasting Views: Persians Debate Democracy, Oligarchy, and Monarchy, p. 58

CHAPTER

3

The Greek Golden Age

C. 500–400 B.C.E.

CHAPTER RESOURCES

Main Chapter Topics

1. Persian invasions of the Greek mainland galvanized the independent Greek city-states into a unified resistance and moved them toward the Golden Age of Greece. Because more of the art, literature, architecture, and other surviving products of the Golden Age have come down to us from Athens, discussion of the Golden Age is mostly a discussion of Athens.

2. Athens took full advantage of its naval leadership in the Persian Wars by establishing an Aegean Empire and political primacy in mainland Greece. The political institutions of Athens, in particular its direct democracy, are the most important and enduring legacies of Greece's Golden Age.

3. Greek art was intimately connected to the rituals of civic and religious life, epitomized by the Parthenon and its frieze and sculpture. Art, architecture, and theater were public affairs paid for by the wealthy and with the dues of the Delian League.

4. Greek women did not participate in politics, yet they were active and essential members of the city-state's domestic and religious life.

5. Although generally respectful of religious traditions, Greek philosophers, scientists, historians, and playwrights pioneered intellectual options that did not depend on accepted ideas or the caprices of the gods but rather on investigation of ethics and assumptions, logic and observation, consideration of cultural differences, political analysis, and the exploration of moral dilemmas and responsibilities.

6. The Peloponnesian War (431–404 B.C.E.) between Athens and Sparta ended the Golden Age by depleting the military and economic strength of Athens.

Focus Question

Did war bring more benefit or more harm—politically, socially, and intellectually—to Golden Age Athens?

1. The Persian Wars and the Peloponnesian War frame the achievements of Golden Age Athens. Facing a common, external threat, the Greeks allied in the Hellenic League in order to defeat the invading Persians. Once their victory was assured, competition among the Greek city-states resumed, with Sparta dominating the new Peloponnesian League and Athens controlling the rival Delian League, which became a de facto Athenian Empire, enriching the polis and financing its Golden Age. Conflict among the Greeks continued throughout the middle decades of the fifth century, during the period that Athens achieved its greatest innovations in democracy, philosophy, and the arts. The ongoing competition among cities culminated in the destructive Peloponnesian War between Athens and Sparta in which Athens was defeated, its experiment in radical democracy collapsing in tyranny and civil war. Initially, war against the Persians had served as a spur to creativity and prosperity, but by century's end the protracted Peloponnesian War ended Greece's Golden Age.

2. The radical democracy and cultural flowering of Athens were products of historical circumstances, forged in the context of war, imperialism, and political expediency. Tribute paid by Delian League members underwrote such symbols of the Golden Age as the Parthenon, financed the expansion of Athens's navy, and paid for Athenian oarsmen who gained influence in their city's widening democracy. These relatively poor citizen men sought equality before the law and direct political participation in the polis. Elite citizen leaders, such as Pericles, spearheaded such reforms, in part to win popular support for themselves. At the same time

as participation by citizen men expanded and the scope of their powers increased, Athenian citizenship was restricted and actually became more difficult to obtain. Metics and enslaved people, despite their large numbers, were denied citizenship and political rights, and citizen women lacked many of the rights of their male counterparts. The reinforcing of such social boundaries between men and women and between citizens and noncitizens may have assuaged popular anxiety over the pace of change in Athens, including the development of rationalism and the challenges it posed to traditional beliefs in education and philosophy.

Annotated Chapter Outline

I. **Wars between Persia and Greece, 499–479 B.C.E.**

A. **From the Ionian Revolt to the Battle of Marathon, 499–490 B.C.E., p. 71**

1. In 499 B.C.E., when the Greeks of Ionia revolted against their Persian rulers, Athens took the side of the Ionians.
2. The Persians felt that the Athenians had betrayed their agreement of 507 B.C.E. when Athens had asked for Persia's help against Sparta.
3. Under King Darius I (r. 522–486 B.C.E.), the Persians sent forces in 490 B.C.E. to take control of Athens, but were unexpectedly turned back after a furious battle near the village of Marathon.
4. The Athenian army won the battle by sending its heavily armed and armored infantry (hoplites) against the more lightly armed Persians.
5. The surviving Persians departed. Athenian confidence soared: they had single-handedly defeated the most powerful empire with the largest army in the ancient Near East.
6. The Marathon victory positioned the city-state to take a leading role in the political and cultural life of Greece.

B. **The Great Persian Invasion, 480–479 B.C.E., pp. 72–74**

1. Ten years after the battle of Marathon, Darius's son Xerxes I (r. 486–465 B.C.E.) led a huge Persian army into Greece.
2. In response, thirty-one Greek city-states banded together into what is now known as the Hellenic League.
3. The Hellenic League was led by Sparta, which was chosen because of its military reputation.
4. In 480 B.C.E., at Thermopylae, the Persian army defeated the Spartans and then marched south to burn Athens.
5. Notwithstanding, the Greek navy under the leadership of Athenian Themistocles defeated the Persian navy at Salamis.
6. Spartan-led infantry then defeated the remaining Persian forces in 479 B.C.E.
7. Social elites, hoplites, and poor men who rowed the warships all participated in the campaigns.
8. The Hellenic League's victory was, therefore, not just a military success; it was a remarkable act of dedication to independence and political freedom that cut across social and economic lines and briefly overcame centuries of hostility among the city-states of Greece.

II. **Athenian Confidence in the Golden Age, 478–431 B.C.E.**

A. **The Establishment of the Athenian Empire, pp. 74–75**

1. After working together to defeat the Persians, both Sparta and Athens formed separate alliances with other city-states to strengthen their positions against each other.
2. Sparta, with its superior infantry, led the Peloponnesian League; whereas Athens, with its superior navy, led the Delian League.
3. Although both leagues held assemblies in which each participating city-state had a role in determining policy, in reality Sparta and Athens approved all decisions in their respective leagues.
4. The Delian League's city-states were obliged to pay for the league's warships, which were increasingly built and manned by Athenians, thus giving Athens overwhelming power over other league members.
5. In this way, an originally democratic alliance swiftly became an empire.
6. Athens lost some of its popularity but grew rich and prosperous from its share of spoils taken from conquered Persian outposts and dues paid by Delian League members.
7. Athenians answered criticism by pointing out their success in driving the Persians from the Aegean Sea and protecting Greece from the Persian interference.

B. **Radical Democracy and Pericles' Leadership, 461–431 B.C.E., pp. 75–77**

1. In the 460s and 450s B.C.E., Athenian reformers created a radical democracy that balanced direct democracy with leadership by elite citizens.
2. Reforms began when the relatively poor oarsmen who powered the triremes (Greek warships) demanded changes in the handling of criminal cases and civil suits.
3. By 460 B.C.E., the judicial power of the elites was reduced: cases would now be decided by juries who were chosen by lottery, paid a stipend, and given a secret ballot.
4. Term limits, pay for most members of the Council of Five Hundred, and open investigation and punishment of corruption followed.
5. Nevertheless, the generals—the ten highest officials—were elected and unpaid, which effectively restricted generalships to elites.
6. Once a year, all male citizens could vote to ostracize one official from the city for being a danger to democracy.
7. The great orator Pericles (c. 495–429 B.C.E.) became the most influential general in Athens by persuading the assembly to pass legislation that supported reforms important to the poor.
8. Pericles' most important democratic reform was paying men who served in public office and on juries, making it possible for poor men to serve.
9. Pericles also limited Athenian citizenship to children of Athenian-born parents, whereas previously only a child's father had to be Athenian. This act increased the status of Athenian women.
10. Pericles also recommended frequent military campaigns against the Peloponnesian League.
11. These frequent campaigns helped improve the lives of the oarsmen, but ended after the Persians slaughtered thousands of Athenians in a naval battle over Egypt.
12. In 446 B.C.E., Pericles signed a peace treaty with Sparta in order to freeze the balance of power and preserve Athenian control of the Delian League.

C. **The Urban Landscape, pp. 77–80**

1. The wealth that Athens accumulated during the Greek Golden Age of Pericles' rule flowed mainly into public building projects, art, and festivals rather than to private luxuries.
2. Generals who led successful military campaigns used their wealth to fortify and beautify the city with landscaping, exercise tracks, and stoas—large open buildings that provided shade and important places of public gathering.
3. Out of their own personal wealth, citizens also paid for major public expenses because there were no direct taxes.
4. In 447 B.C.E., Pericles used public funds to erect the foremost symbol of the Greek Golden Age—a gateway and enormous marble temple known as the Parthenon.
5. Like all Greek temples, the Parthenon was meant to house its deity (in this case Athena), not to serve as a gathering place for worshippers.
6. The Parthenon's massive size and sculpted frieze of gods and citizens reflected the confidence of Golden Age Athenians who felt a new and unique sense of closeness to the gods.
7. Athenians' confidence showed in their sculpture, which depicted figures in a variety of dynamic, energetic poses, instead of statues with stiff postures.

III. **Tradition and Innovation in Athens's Golden Age**

A. **Religious Tradition in a Period of Change, pp. 80–82**

1. Greek religion was a combination of public cults—collective worship of a particular god or goddess—and more personal hero and mystery cults, each with its own prayers and rituals.
2. Golden Age Athens held more festivals than any other city-state; nearly half the days of the year included one.
3. The biggest public festivals featured parades, athletic competitions, and performing arts spectacles.
4. The feasting that followed the sacrifice of a large animal provided occasions for the community to assemble and reaffirm its ties to the divine world and to feast on the roasted meat of the sacrificed animal.
5. For poor people, the free meat at festivals was possibly the only meat they ever got.
6. Greeks also sought personal relations with the gods through hero cults, which performed rituals at the tombs of famous men and women who were thought to

possess powers that would benefit the living.

7. The secret ceremonies of mystery cults—the most famous being that of Demeter and her daughter Persephone—offered worshipers hope of blessings in this life and in the afterlife.
8. Mystery cults and other ceremonials demonstrate the importance of religious traditions for Athenians.

B. Women, Slaves, and Metics, pp. 82–86

1. Excluded from politics, upper-class Athenian women gained respect and status through family and religious life.
2. Poor women worked, often as small-scale merchants and craft producers.
3. The primary role for all Greek women was childbearing—men were expected to respect and support their wives.
4. Laws protected a woman's dowry and allowed her to inherit land; however, if a man's only heir was a daughter, the law required his closest male relative to marry her and produce sons so that her inheritance would go to a male heir.
5. Sparta did not have such laws; the renowned scholar Aristotle claimed that 40 percent of Sparta's property was owned by women.
6. To preserve her reputation and ensure the paternity of her children, an upper-class woman was expected to avoid close contact with men other than family members or close friends.
7. Bearing male children brought women special honor, since sons could represent their parents in court, support them in their old age, and protect them in a city with no regular police force.
8. A small number of women, known as companions or *hetairas*, however, could maintain a high level of independence, but they lacked the respectability reserved for wives and mothers.
9. Typically well-educated, companions conversed freely with Athenian men at dinner parties called symposia and sometimes sold sexual favors at a high price.
10. Slaves continued to play a crucial role in Athens's economy and commercial growth increased demand for them.
11. In Pericles' time, slaves numbered about two-fifths of the total population.
12. The economic and cultural vitality of Athens also attracted many *metics* (foreigners granted permanent residency) from all areas surrounding the Mediterranean.
13. Metics contributed greatly to the city's prosperity and were expected to pay taxes and serve in the military, but they nonetheless had an inferior social and legal status.

C. Innovations in Education and Philosophy, pp. 86–92

1. Education and philosophy provided the most heated tension between innovation and tradition in Golden Age Athens.
2. Athenian education was customarily a private matter that stressed the importance of maintaining traditional ways.
3. Formal education for boys came from private teachers to whom well-to-do families sent their sons to learn reading, writing, music, and athletics.
4. Boys also trained for athletics and military service in gymnasia.
5. Young girls from wealthy families were instructed at home by educated slaves who taught reading, writing, and arithmetic—skills needed for managing a household.
6. Poor girls and boys received no formal education, but learned a trade and perhaps gained some literacy by assisting their parents at work or by serving as apprentices.
7. Young men from prosperous families learned about public life by observing their elders and sometimes by attaching themselves to an older mentor.
8. Sex between mentors and young students was accepted in elite circles in many city-states, including Athens, Sparta, and Thebes; other city-states banned the practice believing that it indicated a man's inability to control his desires.
9. As democracy became more radical, persuasive speech became a highly valued skill, and sophists came to Athens to teach public speaking to the rich.
10. These sophists also challenged traditional beliefs. Protagoras, for example, stated that there was no absolute reality and no absolute truth; rather, individual humans judged and defined the world around them subjectively.
11. Many fifth-century B.C.E. philosophers, not just the sophists, offended religious

traditionalists by questioning the existence of the gods and supernatural phenomena.
12. Sophists threatened Athenian democracy, since only wealthy men could afford training in public argumentation.
13. Socrates (469–399 B.C.E.) taught that virtue and happiness came through a life of just behavior rather than through wealth or public success.
14. Socrates upset Athenians because he often made them feel dumb and undermined their ethical beliefs.
15. Herodotus and Thucydides invented history writing, basing their accounts on reliable evidence and critical thinking.
16. Herodotus's *Histories* described the Persian wars as a clash between the east and west; Thucydides's *History of the Peloponnesian War* stated that power politics—not divine intervention—was history's primary force.
17. In medicine, Hippocrates challenged traditional practices by teaching that careful observation of patients and the nature of the human body were more important than magic or ritual.

D. The Development of Greek Tragedy, pp. 92–95

1. During three-day festivals honoring the god Dionysus, elaborate publicly funded plays were staged in large outdoor theaters in Athens.
2. Written in verse and solemn language, tragic dramas dealt with stories about the interaction between gods and humans.
3. Three male actors performed all the speaking roles while a chorus of fifteen performed songs and dances in the orchestra (the circular area in front of the stage).
4. Actors playing the lead roles, called the protagonists, competed for the designation of best actor.
5. Most playwrights were elite men, the three most famous being Aeschylus (525–456 B.C.E.), Sophocles (c. 496–406 B.C.E.), and Euripides (c. 485–406 B.C.E.). Prize-winning playwrights achieved high prestige.
6. The tragedies that befell the play's characters illuminated the problems that error, ignorance, and hubris, or violent arrogance, posed to Athenian democratic society.
7. Thus, tragedies were both entertaining and educational, presenting moral issues that reminded citizens of their obligations to the city-state.

E. The Development of Greek Comedy, pp. 95–96

1. Like tragedies, Greek comedies were written in verse and performed outdoors during festivals honoring Dionysus.
2. Comic playwrights competed for the prize of best comedy by creating poetry, raising constant jokes and puns, and making frank, often brutal, commentary on public policy and politicians.
3. Emerging about the same time as radical democracy, this remarkably free form of public criticism helped keep public figures from becoming too arrogant or aloof.
4. The plays of Aristophanes (c. 455–385 B.C.E.) became famous for parodying political figures.
5. His play *Lysistrata* was remarkable for portraying women who acted bravely and aggressively against men who threatened traditional family life.

IV. The End of the Golden Age, 431–403 B.C.E.

A. The Peloponnesian War, 431–404 B.C.E., pp. 97–99

1. Athenian aggression against Spartan allies Corinth and Megara brought an end to a 446 B.C.E. treaty between the two city-states and triggered the Peloponnesian War.
2. When Sparta demanded that Athens ease restrictions on its allies, the Athenian assembly (under the leadership of Pericles) refused to compromise.
3. The Spartans launched the first attack by invading Athenian territory.
4. Pericles devised a strategy of naval raids on Spartan territory and avoided land battles with Sparta's superior infantry.
5. This strategy might have worked if Pericles had not died in 429 B.C.E., when a plague struck Athens.
6. The Athenians embarked on an aggressive and ultimately disastrous military plan that included the invasion of Sparta's ally, Sicily, where the Athenian navy was devastated.
7. In the aftermath of this defeat, the Athenian commander Alcibiades was deposed, leading to his desertion to Sparta.
8. In 413 B.C.E., Sparta began a deadly campaign in the Athenian countryside,

destroying its agriculture and crippling its mining industry.

9. After seven more years of fighting, with financial aid from its former enemy—Persia—Sparta built a strong navy that finally forced Athens to surrender in 404 B.C.E.

B. Athens Humbled: Tyranny and Civil War, 404–403 B.C.E., p. 99

1. The victorious Spartans installed an antidemocratic oligarchy in Athens that consisted of a small group of elite Athenians who brutally repressed any democratic opposition.
2. Known as the Thirty Tyrants, this oligarchic regime ruled for eight months in 404–403 B.C.E.
3. The competing ambitions of its members weakened the tyrants, however, and gave a democratic resistance movement the opportunity it needed to finally expel them.
4. The restored democracy immediately proclaimed a truce and granted the first known amnesty in Western history, forbidding retribution against the tyrants.
5. After nearly thirty years of war, the devastated economy and weakened military signaled the end to the innovative Golden Age of Athens.

Lecture Strategies

1. The concept of radical democracy best expressed the politics of fifth-century Athens. But this democracy was not without its flaws. One approach to introducing students to Athenian political life is to ask them to identify who was omitted from of the Athenian polity and to explore why. What were the rules of Athenian democracy? Who established these rules? Additional discussion may come from comparing the participatory style of Athenian democracy to the representative forms of government currently practiced. A good introduction to this topic is Thomas R. Martin, *Ancient Greece: From Prehistoric to Hellenistic Times* (Princeton: Princeton University Press, 1996).

2. It is important to talk about political concepts and the outstanding contributions of Athenians to art, architecture, and drama in the Golden Age, but students will probably also wish to know more about how ordinary Athenians lived. A good overview for nonspecialists can be found in Sir Peter Hall, *Cities in Civilization* (New York: Pantheon Books, 1998), chapter 2, "The Fountainhead: Athens 500–400 B.C.E." A far more detailed and authoritative study can be found in James Davidson, *Courtesans and Fishcakes: The Consuming Passions of Classical Athens* (New York: St. Martin's, 1998). Also very readable is Robert Flacelière, *Daily Life in Greece at the Time of Pericles* (London: Weidenfeld and Nicolson, 1965).

3. Two wars bracket Greece's Golden Age: the Persian Wars (499–479 B.C.E.) and the Peloponnesian War (431–404 B.C.E.). In his history of the Peloponnesian War, Thucydides attributed the war to Athenian hubris and Sparta's fear of Athenian power. Although not all scholars would endorse Thucydides' interpretation, this explanation can still be useful in discussing the end of the Golden Age and the rise of Sparta. Donald Kagan's essay "The Peloponnesian War, 431–404 B.C.E." in his book *On the Origins of War and Preservation of Peace* (New York: Doubleday, 1995), pp. 15–74, provides a helpful reflection on how and why the war occurred and how it changed Greece forever.

Class Discussion Starters

1. Pericles' *Funeral Oration*, as recorded by Thucydides in about 429 B.C.E., is remarkably revealing of not only Athens but also more modern democracies. Ostensibly praising those who had died in the early campaigns of the Peloponnesian War, Pericles uses the opportunity to justify the war and prepare the citizens for more casualties. While the document is rhetorically brilliant, it has a classic tragic feel to it. Pericles, and indeed all of Athens, suffers from that tragic flaw, hubris. It is particularly illuminating to first trace where in the text Pericles exaggerates Athenian virtues and ambitions. Is Athens really that noble, or is the situation more gray than sharply black or white? Is there a modern equivalent to Athens? Can a reflection of the United States be found in this document?

2. What did women do on a day-to-day basis? What ideas prevailed about marriage and childcare? How did expectations for husbands and wives compare? What role did women play in religion? Why were female characters so often used in Greek drama and comedy to discuss difficult issues? Ask students to discuss these questions in light of the text in Contrasting Views: The Nature of Women and Marriage (pp. 84–85). Useful sources include Mary R. Lefkowitz and Maureen B. Fant, eds., *Women in Greece and Rome*, 2nd ed. (Baltimore: Johns Hopkins University Press, 1992), which has short selections from documents illustrating the place of women in everyday life; the first four chapters of Elaine Fantham, et al.,

Women in the Classical World: Image and Text (New York: Oxford University Press, 1994), which offer lively accounts and contemporary images of the roles of Greek women during this period; and essays by Sarah Pomeroy: "Women and the City of Athens," "Private Life in Classical Athens," and "Images of Women in the Literature of Classical Athens" in her very accessible *Goddesses, Whores, Wives, and Slaves in Classical Antiquity* (New York: Schocken Books, 1975). See also the broader context provided by the discussion of family life in Sarah B. Pomeroy's *Families in Classical and Hellenistic Greece: Representation and Realities* (New York: Oxford University Press, 1997).

3. Slides of the Parthenon, its frieze, and its statues are an engaging way to introduce students to contributions of fifth-century Athens to public architecture. Ask students to identify ways in which Athenian art and architecture were used to inspire civic loyalty and other, similarly uplifting emotions. What were the connections between Greek architecture and politics? What is the role and function of public architecture in a democracy? Ask students to compare their reactions to contemporary public buildings with their reaction to the Parthenon.

4. Compare the photograph of the Acropolis of Athens (p. 79) and the Theater of Dionysus at Athens (p. 94) with Map 3.2 of Fifth-Century B.C.E. Athens (p. 78). What does the arrangement of buildings suggest about Athenian attitudes toward religion, the theater, and politics? Why is the acropolis separate from the agora? Why is the theater near the Parthenon? What does the existence of so many public spaces and buildings reveal about Athenian social life? How might this relate to Athenian democracy? Is your understanding of the map enhanced by viewing the photograph that shows the higher elevation of the acropolis relative the rest of the city?

Reviewing the Text

Review Questions

1. How did the Greeks overcome the challenges presented by the Persian invasions?
[model answer] *Innovative strategies, including a military alliance, and the talents of Spartan generals combined with a broad-based dedication to the ideal of political freedom in the defeat of the Persian Empire: Judging independence of action less important than the preservation of political freedom, thirty-one independent city-states allied in the Hellenic League creating a new unified force. Without that unity each city-state would undoubtedly have been defeated separately. The same determination encouraged men of all social levels in the city-states to participate in their defense. The League's generals relied on innovative strategies to defeat the Persians' superior numbers.*

2. What factors produced political change in fifth-century B.C.E. Athens?
[model answer] *Rivalry for power among the city-states contributed to the expansion of Athens's influence and control over other city-states. Also, investments in Athens's naval force, to secure that power, fostered an expansion of democracy within the city-state by providing opportunity to more poor citizens. As the democratic base expanded, leaders became more responsive to ordinary men's demands in order to win their votes for elective offices. The resulting "radical democracy" gave political power to all male citizens through participation in both the Assembly and the court system.*

3. How did new ways of thinking in the Golden Age change traditional ways of life?
[model answer] *Increasing prosperity fostered the emergence of new educational institutions as citizens had the money to pay for better education for their children. Educated men, called Sophists, offered classes to train young men in the knowledge and political skills needed for success in pubic life. They introduced ideas of moral relativism and persuasive argument that threatened traditional beliefs about morality and religion. The reasoning through logic and evidence that they and other philosophers advocated also encouraged the development of historical writing and new forms of art and architecture, including the use of theater as a form of social commentary.*

4. What factors determined the course of the Peloponnesian War?
[model answer] *A four-year epidemic of plague undermined the disciplined defensive strategy that might have won the Peloponnesian war for Athens. Following that, Athens's leaders changed tactics and pursued more aggressive strategies. These did bring victories, but ultimately the Assembly made decisions to reject peace and pursue the total defeat of Sparta. This gave Sparta the time and opportunity to enlist naval aid from Persia and defeat Athens.*

Making Connections

1. What were the most significant differences between Archaic Age Greece and Golden Age Greece?
[model answer] *Greece's Golden Age brought an expansion of democracy and increased wealth from overseas trade. Philosophical ideas that emerged from Archaic Age Greece encouraged innovations in education and thought that increased scientific understanding, particularly through new beliefs in the value of using reason and evidence to determine understanding of*

phenomena, and produced innovations in art, architecture, and theater.

2. For what sorts of things did Greeks of the Golden Age spend public funds? Why did they believe these things were worth the expense?
[model answer] *Citizens of Athens chose to finance construction of public buildings, art, and competitive theater festivals. Such monumental public works were used to demonstrate Athenians' relations with the gods, symbolizing their gratitude for the evident favor in which the gods held the city. They also funded salaries for government service so that men of lower than elite status could serve as officials and jurors. This expanded the scope of democracy and insured a broader support within the population for the government and a stronger state.*

Discussing the Documents

Questions from Online Study Guide with Model Answers

Athenian Regulations for a Rebellious Ally (p. 88)

1. What did the Chalcidians and Athenians swear to each other?
[model answer] *The Athenians promised not to destroy the city of Chalcis, harm its citizens, or their property without a trial. The Chalcidians swore not to rebel against Athens, to pay tribute to Athens, and to support the Athenians in war.*

2. Who held the advantage in this agreement?
[model answer] *Athens held the advantage. It only swore not to harm Chalcis and the Chalcidians without due process, while the Chalcidians swore to send soldiers and money to Athens.*

Sophists Arguing Both Sides of a Case (p. 90)

1. How does this document reflect Protagoras's denial of an absolute standard of truth?
[model answer] *This passage shows that any event has both bad and good results, depending on where one stood. For example, milk is a good thing because it maintains strong bones and healthy teeth, but it is a bad thing if one is allergic to it. Therefore, milk can be both good and bad.*

2. Why might ideas like this be controversial in Athens during the fifth century?
[model answer] *By denying absolute truths, Protagoras and people who thought like him, could conclude that human institutions and values were only matters of convention and not products of nature or an absolute reality. This meant that Athenian traditions and laws were subjective and arbitrary.*

Contrasting Views: The Nature of Women and Marriage (pp. 84–85)

1. What evidence and arguments for differing natures for men and women do these documents offer?
[model answer] *The differences in men's and women's "bodies and spirits"—their physical and emotional differences—demonstrated that the gods gave men natures more suited to work outdoors and gave women natures more suited to indoor work. Further evidence, according to Socrates, was shown in the successful partnerships these complementary roles provided in creating households and families. Euripides believed that women's greater honesty, management skills, and holiness were also proven by their behavior.*

2. Do you think Athenian women would have found these arguments convincing? Why or why not?
[model answer] *Women whose lives fit the Greek model of the ideal of marriage and family would likely have found the agency they held within their role persuasive that the differences are valid. But a woman who did not have a place as wife and mother might be less convinced that such was the only appropriate role for her in society.*

Other Questions for Discussing These Documents in Class

Pericles Addresses the Athenians in the First Year of the Peloponnesian War (431–430 B.C.E.) (p. 84)

1. Why does Pericles equate excellence for women with widowhood? What does this suggest about the role of war in Golden Age Athens? Must warriors be exclusively male? What implications does military service have for active citizenship in Athenian democracy?

2. Why is being worthy of little comment, whether in Pericles's "short piece of advice" or by men in general, considered to be virtuous for women?

Melanippe Explains Why Men's Criticism of Women is Baseless, Late Fifth Century B.C.E. (p. 84)

1. Why does Melanippe believe that women's greatest role is religious rather than domestic?

2. What characteristics would Melanippe likely apply to a "bad woman"?

Socrates Discusses Gender Roles in Marriage, Late Fifth Century B.C.E. (pp. 84–85)

1. How does Socrates portray the relationship between a husband and wife?

2. In what ways were the roles of husbands and wives complementary, if not equal?

Greek Marriage Contract from Egypt (311–310 B.C.E.) (p. 85)

What does the marriage contract suggest about the relationship between daughters and their parents? Do sons appear to have the same relationship with their fathers and mothers?

Athenian Regulations for a Rebellious Ally (p. 88)

1. What insight do the Athenian Regulations for a Rebellious Ally provide into the relationship between Athens and Chalcis? Why were the terms not the same for both sides? Why would the Chalcidians agree to these regulations?

2. How does this document illustrate Athenian imperialism?

Sophists Arguing Both Sides of a Case (p. 90)

1. Are the double arguments of the Sophists logical? Are they convincing?

2. How do the arguments promote the idea of moral relativism? Why would some people object to these arguments?

Comparative Questions

1. How does Socrates' vision of marriage compare with that described in the Greek marriage contract?

2. What is the significance in Socrates naming only the husband, Ischomachus, and not Ischomachus's wife, while the marriage contract names both spouses, Heraclides and Demetria?

3. Would Melanippe have agreed or disagreed with the ideas presented in the other documents?

4. How does the relationship between Athens and Chalcis compare with that of husbands and wives detailed in the documents on the Nature of Women and Marriage?

For Users of *Sources of The Making of the West*

The following documents are available in Chapter 3 of the companion sourcebook by Katharine J. Lualdi, University of Southern Maine.

1. The Golden Age of Athens: Thucydides, *The Funeral Oration of Pericles* (429 B.C.E.)
2. The Emergence of Philosophy: Plato, *The Apology of Socrates* (399 B.C.E.)
3. The Advance of Science: Hippocrates of Cos, *On the Sacred Disease* (400 B.C.E.)
4. In Defense of Manly Honor: Euphiletus, *A Husband Speaks in His Own Defense* (c. 400 B.C.E.)
5. The Geography of Daily Life: *Overhead Views of a House in Olynthos* (c. 432 B.C.E.)
6. Protesting War, Performing Satire: Aristophanes, *Lysistrata* (411 B.C.E.)

Discussion Ideas for Sources of The Making of the West, *Chapter 3*

1. The Greek Golden Age took place during a century dominated by warfare. To what degree did war foster the creative achievements of the era, and to what degree was conflict with Persia and among the Greek city-states harmful? Consider *The Funeral Oration of Pericles.* How did the circumstances of the Peloponnesian War contribute to Pericles' leadership and the creation of radical democracy in Athens? How does Thucydides' account illustrate Pericles' skill as a public speaker?

2. Aristophanes criticizes the Peloponnesian War in *Lysistrata*, yet one might argue that the Golden Age public theatre it exemplifies owed its existence to a broader cultural flowering that occurred within the context of war. Why might Aristophanes have chosen to present an anti-war play as comedy rather than as tragedy? Do the farcical elements of the plot and the focus on female characters strengthen or weaken the play's ability to persuade its audience? Both Aristophanes and Pericles seem to elevate Athenian women. Aristophanes makes them protagonists in his play, and *The Making of the West* text discusses Pericles' role in enhancing women's importance through changes in citizenship requirements. What were the motives of the two men? To what degree were they concerned with the status of women in Greek society? Consider what *Lysistrata* and *The Funeral Oration* actually have to say about women.

Working with Visual Sources

For this exercise, please refer to the Vase Painting of a Woman Buying Shoes on p. 83 of the textbook or view the image on the book companion site's Online Study Guide under the "Visual Activity" for Chapter 3.

Students viewing the image at the Online Study Guide are asked three questions about the image. The questions and model answers (not made available to students) are below. Project this image, available on the Instructor's Resources CD-ROM, in class or ask students to look at the image in their textbooks and answer the questions.

1. Which gestures, postures, and activities represented on the vase tell us that it is a picture of humans and not gods?

[model answer] *The figures seem to be working with their hands and everyday objects. Gods were not usually represented performing labor or visiting shops.*

2. What does the image on this vase tell us about certain women's activities outside the home?
[model answer] *Because the woman is being fitted for a pair of custom-made shoes, we can assume that she is from an upper-class family. In city-states such as Athens, upper-class women had restricted access to public life but could be accompanied in public by a husband or male relative who supervised the woman's interactions with other men. Such supervision was not expected or required when women met other women.*

3. As this vase indicates, the Greeks incorporated scenes from everyday life in their artwork, rather than focusing exclusively on the gods. Why do you think the Greeks chose to include scenes from everyday life in their artwork?
[model answer] *As with the frieze of the Parthenon where humans mixed with the gods, this vase demonstrates that the Greeks believed it was important to represent themselves engaged in the tasks of everyday life. This tendency may have indicated that, unlike societies in which such scenes were uncommon, the Greeks felt themselves to be in control of their world. Victories against the Persian forces at battles like the one at Marathon, the enormous wealth of Athens, and a burgeoning intellectual life were all aspects of life that gave Athenians confidence in their ability to accomplish great things.*

Mapping Exercises

Map Activity from OSG—Model Answers for Map Activity #2

For this activity, please refer to the map on p. 97. Students are asked these questions:

Which was more powerful on land, the Delian League's forces represented by Athens, or the Peloponnesian League's forces represented by Sparta? Which was more powerful on water? What evidence led you to your conclusions?
[model answer] *The Peloponnesian League represented by Sparta was more powerful on land because of its superiority in hoplites and cavalry. The Delian League represented by Athens was more powerful on the water because of its larger number of triremes or warships.*

Judging from the type of military it had, would you expect many of the cities belonging to the Delian League to be on the coast or inland? Where would you expect many of the cities belonging to the Peloponnesian League to be located?
[model answer] *Because of the high number of triremes the Delian League possessed, I would expect many of the Delian League's cities to be located by water. I would expect many of the cities belonging to the Peloponnesian League to be located inland due to the high number of foot soldiers and cavalry.*

Map 3.1, The Persian Wars, 499–479 B.C.E., p. 72

Ask students to locate and identify the following: Athens, Sparta, Marathon (King Darius's invasion), Themopylae, Salamis, and Plataea (King Xerxes' invasion). After the various sites have been located and identified, ask students to use this information in comparing and contrasting the invasions of Darius and of Xerxes. What can we see from the map that we might not notice in a written account?

Map 3.2, Fifth-Century B.C.E. Athens, p. 78

Ask students to locate and identify the following: the agora, Painted Stoa, acropolis, Parthenon, and Theater of Dionysus. In addition to referring to the relevant illustrations in the text "The Acropolis of Athens" (p. 79); "Scene from the Parthenon Frieze," (p. 80); and "Theater of Dionysus at Athens," (p. 94), what do the various sites suggest about public life in Athens during this period?

Map 3.3, The Peloponnesian War, 431–404 B.C.E., p. 97

Ask students to locate the territories that were allied with Athens and those that were allied with Sparta. Note that the Delian League areas were located between Sparta and its ally Macedonia. What strategic implications did this create? Why did the Athenians decide to expand the war and attack Sparta's ally Syracuse? Might this have been an effort to deflect the Spartans away from the Greek peninsula and minimize the impact of their alliance with Macedonia? How did the expansion of the war to Sicily and to the western coast of Anatolia affect Sparta's military tactics, which were traditionally based on the prowess of its land army, as compared with Athens's naval strategies?

Mapping the West: Greece, Europe, and The Mediterranean, 400 B.C.E., p. 100

Ask students to examine the map and to reflect on where Greece is in the Mediterranean and also on what lies to the north and west of Greece (ask them to examine the inset map carefully and note the location of Macedonia). Students should compare this map to Mapping the West: Mediterranean Civilizations, c. 500 B.C.E. (p. 66) and note changes, not only for the Greek city-states but for other major centers of civilization as well.

In-Class Assignments and Presentation Topics

1. Greek plays can form the basis of multiple assignments. One such assignment might be to have students read one of Sophocles' Theban plays. *Sophocles: The Three Theban Plays,* Robert Fagles, trans. (New York: Penguin Books, 1984, and later printings) is readily available. Many students will already be familiar with King Oedipus or Antigone. Both tragedies explore the twin themes of aretê and hubris. The tension between aretê and hubris is one of the underlying motifs of Sophocles' plays: while Oedipus and Antigone strive for aretê, both unwittingly succumb to hubris. Students can write an essay on the tension between these themes in Athens's Golden Age, making reference where appropriate to material from the play assigned. Many of the surviving Greek plays are also available on video. Keeping with Sophocles, the director Don Taylor produced all three of the Theban plays in 1984, with Michael Pennington as Oedipus, John Shrapnel as Creon, and Juliet Stevenson as Antigone. These would be appropriate for student review assignments. Or Taylor's Oedipus could be contrasted to Tyrone Guthrie's 1957 production of the play in which he keeps to performance conventions of Greek tragedy. The director Peter Hall has also produced filmed stage productions of *The Oresteia* (1983) and these would also be suitable for developing student assignments.

2. Greeks in the Golden Age were fascinated by the tension between aretê and hubris, not only in theater but also in the political struggle between Athens and Sparta. Was Athens's commitment to aretê ultimately an example of hubris? Did Athens fall victim to pride? In exploring the Greeks' fascination with aretê and hubris, students might be asked to analyze what these two words reveal about the ideals of Greece's Golden Age. Additionally, students might comment on analogous situations in the contemporary period.

3. Milan Kundera once observed that if "you scratch a European you will find a Greek." This is true, especially in the sense that western thought is indelibly marked by Greece's Golden Age. Discuss this notion in class, with special reference to Socrates, Thucydides, Hippocrates, and Sophocles. Ask students to write an essay using one of these four historical figures as a means of commenting on connections between the Golden Age of Greece and Western civilization.

4. Have students explore and then debate the complexities involved in the trial of Socrates. A mock trial can be set up where students are divided between the defense and prosecution. Some students can even be assigned specific roles to play, such as that of Socrates and his three principal accusers: Meletus, Anytus, and Lycon. Was Socrates justly charged and sentenced to death or was it a gross miscarriage of justice? Students will have to wrestle with contemporary Greek standards, which often clash with more modern sensibilities. See I. F. Stone, *The Trial of Socrates* (New York: Anchor Books, 1989).

Essay Questions

1. Men, not women, tell us what we know of Greek women. But even though we do not know exactly what Greek women thought, we do know that such women as Clytemnestra, Medea, Melanippe, Helen, Penelope, and Antigone commanded the respect of all Greeks. Have students write an essay or do a report in class on celebrated women in Greek mythology and theater, analyzing their authority, persona, and special powers. A good resource would be Mary R. Lefkowitz, *Women in Greek Myth* (Baltimore: Johns Hopkins University Press, 1986). Another useful resource is an essay by Sarah Pomeroy, "Images of Women in the Literature of Classical Athens," in her book *Goddesses, Whores, Wives, and Slaves in Classical Antiquity* (New York: Schocken Books, 1975).

2. The city-state of Sparta is often contrasted with Athens. Ask students to do a research project on political arrangements, social life, and values in fifth-century B.C.E. Sparta. Another possibility would be for students to debate the merits of Spartan and Athenian approaches to life. In addition to the sources listed in the chapter bibliography, Anton Powell, *Athens and Sparta: Constructing Greek Political and Social History, 478–371 B.C.E.* (Portland, OR: Areopagitica, 1988) is a good introduction. Paul Cartledge, *Sparta and Lakonia: A Regional History Thirteen Hundred to Three Sixty-Two B.C.E.* (New York: Routledge, 1979) will be helpful for students comparing Sparta and Athens.

3. Classical Greece is particularly well known for its beautiful vases, and this despite the fact that such pottery was viewed as utilitarian rather than works of high art. Have students research red figure pottery, answering questions such as: Why were stories about both ordinary life and the exploits of the gods depicted on vases? What do such stories tell us about everyday life in Greece? What do the shapes of vessels tell us about their use? And why did potters compete among themselves for workmanship?

4. The Persian and Peloponnesian Wars dominated fifth-century Greece, yet their outcomes had very different implications for political and cultural life in the city states, particularly Athens. Compare and contrast the two wars. In your answer consider the causes and consequences of each conflict, the different military strategies and techniques, and explain why

Athens was unable to replicate its earlier success against the Persians and therefore lost the later war against the Spartans.

Additional Resources: Literature

Fagles, Robert, trans., *Sophocles: The Three Theban Plays*. 2000.

Henderson, Jeffrey, trans., *Aristophanes: Acharnians, Lysistrata, Clouds*. 1997.

Hughes, Ted, trans., *Aeschylus: The Oresteia*. 2000.

Strassler, Robert B., ed., *The Landmark Thucydides: A Comprehensive Guide to the Peloponnesian War*. 1996.

Vellacott, Philip, trans., *Euripides: Medea and Other Plays*. 1963.

Additional Resources: Film and Video

Mystery of the Parthenon (2001) (VHS, 52 min.) This excellent documentary describes the building of the Parthenon. The Athenians lacked sophisticated tools or machinery, and yet constructed one of the most magnificent temples of the ancient world.

OTHER BEDFORD/ST. MARTIN'S RESOURCES FOR CHAPTER 3

The following resources are available to accompany Chapter 3. Please refer to the Preface of this manual for detailed descriptions of all the ancillaries.

For Instructors

Transparencies

The following maps and image from Chapter 3 are available as full-color acetates.

- Map 3.1: The Persian Wars, 499–479 B.C.E.
- Map 3.2: Fifth-Century B.C.E. Athens
- Map 3.3: The Peloponnesian War, 431–404 B.C.E.
- Mapping the West: Greece, Europe, and the Mediterranean, c. 400 B.C.E.
- A Persian Royal Guard, p. 73
- Vase Painting of a Woman Buying Shoes, p. 83

Instructor's Resources CD-ROM

The following maps and image from Chapter 3, as well as a chapter outline, are available on disc in both PowerPoint and jpeg formats.

- Map 3.1: Persian Wars, 499–479 B.C.E.
- Map 3.2: Fifth-Century B.C.E. Athens
- Map 3.3: The Peloponnesian War, 431–404 B.C.E.
- Mapping the West: Greece, Europe, and the Mediterranean, 400 B.C.E.
- Vase Painting of a Woman Buying Shoes, p. 83

For Students

Study Guides

The Online Study Guide at **bedfordstmartins.com/hunt** helps students synthesize the material they have learned as well as practice the skills historians use to make sense of the past. The following Map, Visual, and Document activities are available for Chapter 3.

Map Activity

- Map 3.3: The Peloponnesian War, 431–404 B.C.E.

Visual Activity

- Vase Painting of a Woman Buying Shoes, p. 83

Reading Historical Documents

- Contrasting Views: The Nature of Women and Marriage, p. 84
- Athenian Regulations for a Rebellious Ally, p. 88
- Sophists Argue Both Sides of a Case, p. 90

CHAPTER

4

From the Classical Hellenistic World

400–30 B.C.E.

CHAPTER RESOURCES

Main Chapter Topics

1. Rather than creating a lasting peace, the end of the Peloponnesian War (431–404 B.C.E.) led to the decline of the independent Greek polis. Military rivals Athens, Thebes, and Sparta vied for control of the weakened mainland Greece and independence of the city-states was doomed.

2. The execution of Socrates disenchanted Plato with Athenian democracy, leading him to philosophical contributions to ethics, government, and metaphysics. Aristotle's pragmatism showed in his systemization of logical arguments based on observable evidence and his wide-ranging investigations.

3. Debilitated Greece was vulnerable to its historically weaker northern neighbor, Macedonia. Although held in contempt by southern Greeks, King Philip II and his son Alexander the Great saw themselves as the saviors of Greek culture and guaranteed its dissemination and ascendancy throughout the Mediterranean world, especially after Alexander's conquest of the Persian Empire.

4. Alexander's empire did not outlast him. Upon his death, his generals split the territory into three Hellenistic kingdoms, ruled by the Antigonid, Seleucid, and Ptolemaic dynasties. The successor kings governed through personal rule and were assisted by an elite class of administrators composed of Greek and Macedonian immigrants and local nobles.

5. Elite language and culture were Greek, yet extensive fusions with indigenous culture produced a vigorous combination of eastern and Greek elements. Cultural contacts inspired a more personal and emotive artistic style, especially in sculpture, whereas intellectual exchanges stimulated advances in science, particularly in the areas of geometry and mathematics.

6. The new philosophical schools of the time reflected political and social disorder and the waning of democracy. Focus shifted away from the metaphysical inquiries of Plato and scientific analyses of Aristotle to the more introverted approaches of the Epicureans, Stoics, Cynics, and Skeptics, all of whom tried to outline a program for the best manner in which to live daily life and achieve inner peace in turbulent times.

7. The Hellenistic Greeks adopted mystery cults of foreign deities (such as Isis), healing cults (such as that of Asclepius), the cults of Hellenized foreign gods (such as Serapis), and ruler cults. At the same time, many Jews emigrated from their homeland and established themselves in Hellenized cities like Alexandria and in Greece itself.

Focus Question

What were the major political and cultural changes in the Hellenistic Age?

1. The Classical Age of Greece gave way to the Hellenistic World because King Philip II of Macedonia, and later his son Alexander the Great, exploited discord among the Greek city-states and built an empire based in the eastern Mediterranean. The imperial form of government imposed by the Macedonians eclipsed the citizenship-based governments of Classical Greece, and monarchy once again became the dominant political model in the Mediterranean. Monarchy persisted even after the death of Alexander and the fragmentation of his empire into the three Hellenistic kingdoms founded by Antigonus, Seleucus, and Ptolemy.

2. A combination of tolerance for many local practices and the spread of Greek language and culture throughout Alexander's empire facilitated Macedonian authority over such far-flung territories. The use of Koine, or the simplified form of the Greek language,

spread throughout Alexander's empire and fostered the creation of a shared, international Hellenistic (or Greek-like) culture. This cross-cultural interaction between Europe, Asia, and Egypt greatly enriched the later Romans and subsequently influenced Western civilization.

3. Political and cultural ideas changed in response to the failure of the Classical Greek city-states to preserve their complete independence; the upheaval and uncertainty associated with Alexander's brief but spectacular conquests; and the subsequent establishment of the Hellenistic kingdoms. Greek philosophers such as Plato and Aristotle criticized democracy as an imperfect form of government in its empowerment of the uneducated and the unwise. Later Hellenistic thinkers such as the Epicureans, Stoics, Skeptics, and Cynics rejected the absolute ideals and communal civic engagement of the classical Greeks, formulating philosophies based on uncertainty, relativism, and a retreat into private, individualized behavior.

Annotated Chapter Outline

I. Classical Greece after the Peloponnesian War, 400–350 B.C.E.

A. Restoring Daily Life in Athens, pp. 105–106

1. After the thirty-year Peloponnesian War ended the Athenian Golden Age, the devastated city-state began economic recovery.
2. Country people left their ruined homes to live in the city.
3. When their husbands and brothers did not return from battle, many women were forced to find work outside the home selling bread or clothing.
4. Private business owners rejuvenated the economy by engaging in trade and selling manufactured goods out of their homes or from small shops.
5. As prosperity returned, men began to join women in weaving cloth, and a few women established careers in the arts, which led to limited relaxation of gender-defined occupations.
6. In 393 B.C.E., the rebuilding of the Long Walls, which lined the route that connected the port to the city's center, provided protection for traders and encouraged the reconstruction of the navy.
7. Although daily life had been restored, most Athenian families earned only enough to clothe their families and survive on a meager diet.

B. The Execution of Socrates, 399 B.C.E., pp.106–107

1. The bitterness that remained after their defeat by Sparta and the brutal reign of the Thirty Tyrants led the Athenians to seek out someone to blame for the loss of divine favor they had apparently enjoyed during the Golden Age.
2. The amnesty, however, prevented direct retribution against the Thirty Tyrants.
3. Socrates became a target because many felt that his philosophy had corrupted his student Critias, who was one of the most violent members of the Thirty Tyrants.
4. Socrates was charged with impiety—behavior that angered the gods—and was tried before a jury of 501 male citizens chosen by lottery.
5. The accusers charged Socrates with not believing in the gods, introducing new divinities, and luring young men away from Athenian moral traditions.
6. Instead of refuting the charges, Socrates announced his intention to carry on his work.
7. The jurors narrowly voted to convict.
8. The prosecutors proposed death, assuming that the defendant would, as was usual, ask for exile.
9. Instead, Socrates argued that he deserved a reward, not a punishment, and only after his friends persuaded him, he proposed a fine.
10. The jury chose death. Drinking poison made from hemlock, Socrates accepted execution calmly, saying "no evil can befall a good man either in life or in death."
11. Many Athenians soon came to regret the execution of Socrates as a tragic mistake and a severe blow to their city-state's reputation.

C. The Philosophy of Plato, pp. 107–108

1. The death of Socrates caused his most famous student, Plato (429–347 B.C.E.), to turn against democracy.
2. Plato tried to turn Dionysius, tyrant of Syracuse, into a model ruler.
3. Having failed, Plato decided that politics could not solve the problems created by war and revenge.
4. He instead devoted himself to a life of private contemplation of the nature of reality.
5. In Athens, about 386 B.C.E., Plato established the Academy, a philosophical

school that attracted numerous students, including Aristotle (384–322 B.C.E.).
6. Plato recorded his ideas in dialogue form to induce reflection.
7. His own reflections convinced him that moral qualities in their ultimate reality are universal and absolute, not relative.
8. Plato placed these absolutes in a higher metaphysical ("beyond the physical") realm and called them "Forms."
9. He argued that humans could not directly experience the absolute reality of goodness or justice because earthly circumstances render absolutes relative.
10. Through their senses, humans experienced only dim and imperfect manifestations of these realities.
11. Plato also developed a dualistic model of humanity, stating that humans possessed immortal souls housed in mortal bodies.
12. In his dialogue *The Republic*, Plato wrote that the ideal government would be an enlightened oligarchy.
13. Its highest class consisted of the "guardians," educated in mathematics, astronomy, and metaphysics, who ruled as philosopher-kings.
14. Next came the "auxiliaries," who defended the community, and at the bottom were the "producers" who made the objects the community needed.
15. Women and men were equal, but neither men nor women could possess private property or nuclear families; children were raised communally.
16. Plato did not think this society was possible, but he believed that an ideal would guide people to live justly.

D. Aristotle, Scientist and Philosopher, pp. 108–110

1. Aristotle came to study at Plato's academy at age seventeen.
2. After Plato's death, Aristotle became an itinerant scholar and served as tutor to the young Alexander the Great.
3. He then returned to Athens to found his own school, the Lyceum (later the Peripatetic School).
4. Aristotle emphasized scientific investigation of the natural world and developed a rigorous system of logic.
5. He based his ideas in common sense and observations, an approach he believed to be the most compatible with natural sciences such as biology and zoology.
6. He denied the existence of Plato's Forms and a reality beyond the world of the senses.
7. Like Plato, Aristotle criticized democracy because it placed government in the hands of the uneducated masses.
8. He also reaffirmed the inferiority of slaves to free people and of women to men.
9. In the field of ethics, Aristotle argued that people should use their intellect to reach the "mean," a balance between totally suppressing desires and recklessly indulging them.
10. Insisting that the life of the mind and the experience of the real world were inseparable, Aristotle's ideal ethical system had to address moral situations that people experienced.

E. Greek Political Disunity, p. 110

1. During the fifty years following the Peloponnesian War, Sparta, Athens, and Thebes all struggled with each other for control of Greece.
2. The Spartans led the way in provoking warfare, pursuing aggressive policies that forced other city-states to forge temporary alliances in mutual defense.
3. Sparta countered these alliances by entering into an agreement with Greece' s long-time enemy, Persia—a blatant renunciation of its traditional claim to defend Greek freedom.
4. In 386 B.C.E., Sparta signed the so-called King's Peace, which gave the Persians the right to control the Greek city-states of Anatolia in exchange for the Spartans' right to pursue their own interests in Greece without Persian interference.
5. The Athenians successfully fought back with a rejuvenated navy and a new kind of foot soldier, called a *peltast*, which gave their ground forces more tactical mobility and flexibility.
6. By 377 B.C.E., Athens had once again become the leader of a naval alliance of Greek city-states.
7. Both Sparta and Athens were, however, eventually overshadowed by the growing power of Thebes.
8. The Theban army won a decisive victory over an invading Spartan army in 371 B.C.E.
9. It then invaded the Spartan homeland and forever destroyed the Spartan fighting power by granting freedom to many Spartan helots (slaves).

10. Athens then forged an alliance with Sparta—its greatest enemy—revealing the magnitude of the perceived Theban threat.
11. The combined Athenian and Spartan army met the Theban forces at the battle of Mantinea in 362 B.C.E., where Thebes was victorious, but lost its best general in battle.
12. The battle of Mantinea left the city-states in impotent disunity.
13. Every attempt by a major Greek city-state to win control over mainland Greece during this period failed.
14. The futile fighting among the Greeks left them gravely susceptible to a rising power to the north, the kingdom of Macedonia.

II. The Rise of Macedonia, 359–323 B.C.E.

A. The Roots of Macedonian Power, pp. 110–111

1. Macedonian kings needed the support of their most powerful nobles in order to govern effectively.
2. These nobles were their social equals and headed large bands of followers.
3. The monarchs of Macedonia accepted that their people had freedom of speech to address them with advice and complaints.
4. To demonstrate their prowess, kings participated in the favorite pastimes of the male nobles (fighting, hunting, and drinking), while queens achieved influence because they came from the most powerful families of the realm.
5. Macedonians also had great ethnic pride, viewing themselves as Greek by blood and yet superior to the Greeks, whom they looked down upon for their soft and easy lives.
6. Greeks of the city-states looked down upon Macedonians as barbarians from an insignificant land.
7. Although they spoke similar languages and many Macedonian nobles learned to speak Greek, mutual contempt led to great hostility between the Macedonians and the Greeks.

B. The Rule of Philip II, 359–336 B.C.E., pp. 111–112

1. After a long history of disunity, the Macedonian kingdom was unified by Philip II.
2. To seize power, Philip took advantage of a military defeat in 359 B.C.E. at the hands of the neighboring Illyrians, who had slaughtered Philip's predecessor and four thousand troops.
3. Charismatic and clever, Philip persuaded the nobles to support him while he reorganized the army.
4. He used phalanxes of soldiers armed with long spears and taught them to move in formation.
5. These phalanxes Philip combined with cavalry that made first strikes against enemy infantry and protected the flanks of the phalanxes.
6. Philip's new army crushed the Illyrians and defeated his rivals for the kingship.
7. By the late 340s B.C.E., Philip had used diplomacy, bribery, and military action to persuade or coerce most of northern Greece to follow his lead in foreign policy.
8. His ambition was to lead a combined Macedonian and Greek army against the Persian Empire.
9. Unwilling to join Philip, Athens and Thebes headed an alliance of southern Greek city-states against him but, after Philip won a decisive battle at Chaeronea in Boeotia in 338 B.C.E., the Greek city-states lost their independence in international politics.
10. The city-states did, however, retain their internal freedom and remained the basic social and economic units of Greece.

C. The Rule of Alexander the Great, 336–323 B.C.E., pp. 112–115

1. Alexander ascended to the throne when a Macedonian assassin killed his father in 336 B.C.E.
2. Once king, Alexander immediately murdered his potential rivals and attacked Macedonia's enemies.
3. To demonstrate the price of disloyalty, in 335 B.C.E. Alexander destroyed Thebes for rebelling.
4. In 334 B.C.E., Alexander led a united Macedonian and Greek army against Persia, conquering all the lands from Turkey to Egypt to Uzbekistan.
5. His astonishing successes earned him the title "the Great," and his exploits on and off the battlefield won him a heroic reputation.
6. Alexander's brilliance and physical courage inspired a reckless bravery in his men, and he gave away virtually all his land and property to create new landowners who would furnish still more troops.

7. Alexander modeled himself on Achilles and kept a copy of *The Iliad* under his pillow.
8. Many conquered peoples esteemed Alexander for his honor, demonstrated by his respectful treatment of the women of the defeated Persian court.
9. Absolute monarch of a vast empire, Alexander proclaimed his desire to be honored as a god.
10. Most Greeks honored this striking announcement because his unprecedented feats appeared to exceed the bounds of human possibility.
11. Although his soldiers mutinied during a campaign to conquer India and forced him to return to Persia, Alexander *had* changed the Mediterranean world.
12. He established colonies of Greeks and Macedonians throughout the ancient Near East—including Alexandria in Egypt, which became a famous center for science, philosophy, and art.
13. By including non-Macedonians in his administration at peacekeeping outposts, Alexander brought the worlds of Greece and the ancient Near East into closer contact than ever before.
14. His unexpected death in 323 B.C.E. brought about the close of the Classical Age.

III. The Hellenistic Kingdoms, 323–30 B.C.E.

A. Creating New Kingdoms, pp. 115–116

1. When Alexander died without an heir in 323 B.C.E., Antigonus (382–310 B.C.E.), Seleucus (358–281 B.C.E.), and Ptolemy (367–282 B.C.E.) seized power and divided his kingdom among them (having murdered Alexander's wife, son, and mother).
2. Antigonus took Anatolia, Macedonia, and Greece; Seleucus took Babylonia and the East as far as India; and Ptolemy took Egypt.
3. These successor kings had no legitimate, dynastic claims; they ruled by "personal monarchy," transforming themselves into kings through military power, prestige, and ambition.
4. At first they struggled with each other to enlarge their kingdoms, but by the third century B.C.E., they had reached a balance of power.
5. The Antigonids had been reduced to a kingdom in Macedonia, but they also controlled mainland Greece.
6. The Seleucids ruled Syria and Mesopotamia, having been forced to give up their easternmost territory to the Indian king Chandragupta (r. 323–299 B.C.E.) and most of Persia to the Parthians.
7. The Ptolemies retained control of Egypt.
8. The balance of power was relative, and frequent struggles over border areas left room for the establishment of smaller, independent kingdoms.
9. The most famous of these independent kingdoms was the Attalid kingdom in western Anatolia and its capital city of Pergamum.

B. The Structure of Hellenistic Kingdoms, pp. 116–118

1. Hellenistic kings often built up legitimate regimes by incorporating local traditions into their administration.
2. The survival of rulers' dynasties ultimately rested on their personal ability and their power.
3. As foreign kings ruling over indigenous peoples, the Hellenistic kings needed strong armies, administrations, and a cooperative elite.
4. The royal armies and navies required vast revenues for artillery and warships, expensive military technology, increasing numbers of mercenaries, and land for grants promised to military men.
5. To collect the necessary funds, urban administrations staffed by immigrant Greeks and Macedonians kept order for the king and collected taxes to be sent to the royal treasury.
6. Following Alexander's example, however, the Seleucids and Ptolemies also employed non-Greeks in mid- and lower-level administrative positions that called for more interaction with the native peoples.
7. Locals aspiring to a government career improved their chances by learning Greek.
8. Non-Greeks tended to live in separate communities, and only Greeks and Macedonians had access to the highest ranks of royal society.
9. Administrators were to maintain order and direct the tax system.
10. Cities were the economic and social hubs of the Hellenistic kingdoms, and new cities were adorned with features of Classical Greek city-states, such as gymnasia and theaters.

11. The kings knew they needed the urban elites' cooperation to control their vast kingdoms in peace and maintain a steady flow of tax revenues.
12. To flatter and honor elites, the kings used the royal administrative system to give them rewards for loyal service.
13. Hellenistic kings also supported immigration to cities to build support for their policies.
14. Jews in particular emigrated from their homeland into Anatolia, Greece, and Egypt.
15. In the most important Hellenistic city, Alexandria, Jews became an influential minority.

C. The Layers of Hellenistic Society, pp. 118–120

1. Hellenistic society was divided into a distinct hierarchy.
2. The royal household occupied the top of the hierarchy, followed by Greek and Macedonian elites, then the indigenous urban elites.
3. Large groups of small merchants, artisans, and laborers occupied the bottom.
4. Slaves were excluded from the normal bounds of society, but their labor remained important to Hellenistic kingdoms.
5. The majority of people continued to live in small villages in the countryside, working the land to produce enough food to support the urban populations.
6. Most lived on the edge of subsistence, surviving on inadequate diets of grain and vegetables.
7. In the Seleucid and Ptolemaic kingdoms, much of the rural population lived as dependent tenant farmers working the king's estates.
8. Known as "peoples," these workers were not slaves, but had little chance of advancing their position or ever acquiring their own land.
9. Women held varying levels of social and political status, depending on their background.
10. Hellenistic queens could obtain great wealth and influence, and the occasional exceptional woman might be rewarded with a position in her community's government.
11. Most women, however, remained under the legal control of men.
12. Possessing the most power and influence in Hellenistic society, the wealthy showed signs of increasing philanthropy toward the less fortunate.
13. The Seleucid queen Laodice gave a ten-year endowment to fund dowries for needy girls in the city of Iasus.
14. By donating funds that provided for schools, temples, free grain, doctors, and relief from disasters, the wealthy followed the example of royalty, increasing their honor and prestige.
15. Philanthropy became necessary to the poor masses that no longer had a political voice to demand reforms.

D. The End of the Hellenistic Kingdoms, p. 120

1. Squabbles between Greek city-states prompted repeated Roman intervention in attempts to maintain peace, which in turn led to wars in which the Antigonid kingdom fell to Rome.
2. Although the Seleucid and Ptolemaic kingdoms remained independent until the first century B.C.E., internal uprisings and external threats left them weak and divided.
3. The Seleucid kingdom fell to Rome in 64 B.C.E., followed by the Ptolemaic kingdom in Egypt thirty-four years later when the Egyptian queen Cleopatra chose the losing side in the Roman civil war between Mark Antony and the future emperor Augustus.
4. In this way, Rome became heir to all the Hellenistic kingdoms.

IV. Hellenistic Culture

A. The Arts under Royal Patronage, pp. 120–122

1. The Hellenistic kings spent money on a vast scale to support scholarship and the arts; they increased the international reputation of their courts by having famous thinkers, poets, and artists produce works under their patronage.
2. The Ptolemaic kings led this trend, building a library at Alexandria that held 500,000 books.
3. They also established the first scholarly research institute, called the Museum, a building in which the king's scholars dined together and produced encyclopedias of knowledge, such as *On the Rivers of Europe* by Callimachus.
4. Writers and artists avoided subjects that criticized public policy or political topics.

5. Rather, artistic expression tended to emphasize private, personal emotions.
6. The new poetry demanded great intellectual effort as well as emotional engagement from the audience, and could not be understood without an education in literature.
7. In an increasingly urban society, Theocritus was the first Greek poet to describe a contrast between town and country in pastoral poems.
8. His *Idylls* idealized the countryside as a place of peace and harmony.
9. Some Hellenistic women composed short poems called epigrams that expressed personal feelings, especially intense expressions of love.
10. Theater moved away from politics and focused on individual emotion and the often humorous experiences of daily life, as seen in comedies by Menander.
11. Sculptors also worked to present emotions and depicted widely varied subjects vividly and realistically.
12. The new styles and subjects, in particular the female nude, pleased the kings and wealthy elites who paid the artists' commissions.

B. Philosophy for a New Age, pp. 122–126

1. In the Hellenistic period, people sought personal tranquility amid the monarchs' restless and threatening forces.
2. Hellenistic philosophers moved away from metaphysics and toward materialism—a doctrine asserting that only things made of matter truly existed.
3. Hellenistic philosophies were divided into three related areas: *logic*, the process for discovering truth; *physics*, the fundamental truth about the nature of existence; and *ethics*, the means whereby humans should achieve happiness through logic and physics.
4. The two most influential schools of thought—Epicureanism and Stoicism—reached a wide audience because their doctrines applied to all of society, including women and slaves.
5. Epicureanism, named for its founder, Epicurus (341–271 B.C.E.), taught that matter consisted of microscopic atoms in random movement and that all human knowledge was derived from experience and perception.
6. Epicurus recommended withdrawal from society to avoid turbulent emotions.
7. Stoicism was based on the belief that fate controlled life, but that humans should still make pursuit of virtue their goal—particularly endurance, self-control, good sense, courage, justice, and temperance.
8. Some Stoics advocated equal rights for women and proposed unisex clothing to reduce distinctions between men and women.
9. Two of the most radical new philosophies were Skepticism, which asserted that the contradictory nature of the human senses prevented certain knowledge about anything; and Cynicism, which rejected every convention of ordinary life and argued that individuals should aim for complete self-sufficiency.
10. The most famous Cynic was Diogenes, who reportedly lived in a large storage jar.

C. Scientific Innovation, pp. 126–127

1. Science became separate from philosophy.
2. Science benefited from the exploits of Alexander the Great and the patronage of kings who brought the best scientists together at Alexandria.
3. Geometry and mathematics advanced under Euclid, who analyzed two- and three-dimensional space, and Archimedes, who determined the approximate value of pi.
4. Early in the third century B.C.E., Aristarchus of Samos became the first to argue that earth revolved around the sun.
5. Later scholars rejected his theory because he had assumed a circular rather than elliptical orbit for earth, a mistake that threw off his calculations of celestial movement.
6. Eratosthenes of Cyrene (275–194 B.C.E.) pioneered mathematical geography, calculating the circumference of earth on the basis of the shadows cast by widely separated but identically tall objects.
7. Scientific discoveries such as pneumatics and steam pressure rarely resulted in applied technology except for obvious military uses: for example, catapults and wheeled siege towers.
8. A notable exception was the Pharos, a three-hundred-foot-high lighthouse at Alexandria with mirrored panels that reflected the light of a bonfire to passing ships.

9. Around 325 B.C.E., Hellenistic medical researchers discovered the value of measuring the pulse in diagnosing illness and studied anatomy by dissecting cadavers.
10. Hellenistic medical knowledge grew with increased cultural contacts and the royal support given to research, but was limited by the inability to measure minute quantities or observe phenomena invisible to the naked eye.
11. Through experimentation, however, Hellenistic researchers helped advance Western scientific thought toward the essential step of reconciling theory with observed data.

D. Cultural and Religious Transformations, pp. 127–129

1. The explosion in the use of the Greek language in the form called *koine* (meaning "shared" or "common") reflects the emergence of an international culture based on Greek models.
2. Religious practices in particular became diverse, since cults that previously held only local significance could spread throughout the Mediterranean world.
3. Their followers adopted new beliefs that matched their old assumptions about how to remedy the unpredictable nature of human life.
4. Some worshipers appealed directly to gods Luck and Chance.
5. Others joined ruler cults, expressing gratitude and flattery to rulers in hope of obtaining royal favors.
6. Various populations established ruler cults in recognition of great benefactors.
7. Other cults sought cures for physical ills from healing divinities such as Asclepius, a god thought to miraculously cure worshipers who visited his shrines.
8. The mystery cult for the Egyptian goddess Isis achieved enormous popularity among Greeks and, later, Romans.
9. Isis was beloved as a goddess who cared for human welfare in life and in death.
10. Even some Jews who held onto their ritual practices and monotheism began to use the Greek language and move to Hellenistic cities; and some Jewish priests supported Greek rule.
11. In the second century B.C.E., internal dissension among the Jews erupted over the amount of Greek influence that was compatible with traditional Judaism.
12. When the Seleucid king Antiochus IV (r. 175–163 B.C.E.) converted the main Jewish temple in Jerusalem into a Greek temple and outlawed the practice of Jewish religious rites, Judah the Maccabee led a popular revolt.
13. After twenty-five years of war against the Seleucids, the Jews eventually won independence and rededicated the temple for worship of their god, Yahweh.

Lecture Strategies

1. The career of Philip II of Macedonia was nearly as surprising as that of his celebrated son, yet receives far less attention. Review the diplomatic, personal, and military tactics that paved the way for, and must have created a lasting impression on, Alexander. Compare the tactics and achievements and ask the class to identify those features of Philip's program that have the clearest parallels in Alexander's career and campaigns. What could Alexander have learned from his father about military strategy; "public relations" with his troops, allies, and enemies; and building and maintaining a strong personal image? For the background on Philip's reign, see E. Borza, *In the Shadow of Olympus: The Emergence of Macedon* (Princeton: Princeton University Press, 1990); on the character of his rule, see J. R. Ellis, *Philip II and Macedonian Imperialism* (London: Thames and Hudson, 1986).

2. In the Hellenistic Age, many things that had formerly given individuals a sense of identity and purpose in life (such as citizenship in the polis or belief in traditional religion) were eroded by foreign domination, the aftermath of war, and the rise of philosophical rationalism. Might Alexander have seemed to many to be a divinely appointed savior sent to restore order? In which ways was his proclaimed mission to create a "brotherhood of all mankind" a message particularly well-suited for his age? Was his being Macedonian, rather than Greek, an advantage in achieving his goals? On the superhuman persona of Alexander, see A. F. Steward, *Faces of Power: Alexander's Image and Hellenistic Politics* (Berkeley: University of California Press, 1993).

3. Of the post-Alexandrine dynasties, the Ptolemaic kingdom endured the longest. Explore the reasons for this longevity by discussing its location in Egypt and the Ptolemies' adoption of Egyptian practices. How did the latter contribute to the status of several of their queens, most famously Arsinoe II and Cleopatra? Discuss Ptolemaic patronage of culture,

especially the building of the lighthouse of Pharos and the great library (the Museum) at Alexandria. Were they trying to transform Alexandria into a "new Athens"? For a recent general introduction, see Gunther Hoelbl, *A History of the Ptolemaic Empire* (New York and London: Routledge, 2000). Other good overviews are Naphtali Lewis, *Greeks in Ptolemaic Egypt* (Oxford: Clarendon, 1986); and Alan K. Bowman, *Egypt After the Pharaohs, 332 B.C.–A.D. 642*, 2nd ed. (Berkeley: University of California Press, 1996). The culture of Alexandria is explored from a variety of perspectives and disciplines in the collected articles in *Alexandria and Alexandrianism* (papers delivered at a symposium organized by the J. Paul Getty Museum in 1993; Malibu, 1996).

Class Discussion Starters

1. The Hellenistic era has often been labeled as "decadent." Ask students what reasons they can provide for and/or against that label. Compare the culture and the artistic production of the cosmopolitan, dynastic Hellenistic kingdoms with those of the small-scale, independent city-states of Classical Greece. Why were the latter frequently believed to embody the pinnacle of Western civilization? One of the best ways to make this comparison is through a survey of Hellenistic art. Background and illustrations can be found in two excellent overviews: Christine Havelock, *Hellenistic Art* (New York: W. W. Norton, 1981); and J. J. Pollitt, *Art in the Hellenistic Age* (Cambridge, UK: Cambridge University Press, 1986). See also J. Onians, *Art and Thought in the Hellenistic Age: The Greek World View, 350–50 B.C.E.* (London, 1979); A. F. Stewart, *Art, Desire, and the Body in Ancient Greece* (Cambridge, UK: Cambridge University Press, 1997); and B. Brown, *Anticlassicism in Greek Sculpture of the Fourth Century B.C.E.* (New York, New York University Press, 1973).

2. Despite the shift in the visual arts to a more emotive, realistic style, a greater diversity of subjects, and increased private patronage, monumental public sculpture programs still appeared. An outstanding example is the Telephos frieze from the great altar of Zeus at Pergamum. This work was commissioned by Eumenes II, monarch of the small, autonomous kingdom that existed alongside its much larger Seleucid neighbor. Use slides to discuss the altar's iconographic program. What political messages did the king hope to convey? Compare it to the Parthenon frieze. What similarities in subject and treatment do the students perceive? How do their styles reflect the eras in which they were composed? Does the difference between the political regimes that commissioned them (one a democracy, the other a monarchy) seem evident? See Nancy De Grummond, ed., *From Pergamon to Sperlonga: Sculpture and Context* (Berkeley and Los Angeles: University of California Press, 2000); and Elisabeth Rohde, *The Altar of Pergamon* (Germany, Berlin State Museum, 1983).

3. Women in the Hellenistic Age played a more prominent political role than they had in earlier Greek history. This topic can be explored by examining women's roles in the royal household of Philip II (his wives Olympias and Cleopatra), in Alexander's political dealings with conquered peoples (his selection of Ada to be satrap of Caria), and in the Ptolemaic dynasty (Arsinoe II, Cleopatra VII). Which features of dynastic monarchy, as opposed to the Greek participatory governments dominated by male citizens, might account for women's more prominent role? Also consider the political uses of marriage, such as Philip II's polygamy or Alexander's policies for his soldiers. Would the influence of Near Eastern cultures in the Hellenistic world in part account for these practices? On women in Macedonia, see Elizabeth Carney, "Women and Basileia: Legitimacy and Female Political Action in Macedonia," *Classical Journal* 90 (1995): 367–91; and "The Politics of Polygamy: Olympias, Alexander, and the Murder of Philip," *Historia* 41 (1992): 167–89. For the Ptolemies, see Sarah Pomeroy, *Women in Hellenistic Egypt: From Alexander to Cleopatra* (New York: Schocken Books, 1984).

4. Alexander had a penchant for founding cities; in fact, such foundations constituted a key means by which Greek culture was spread. Cities, with their large immigrant populations, also served as the setting of social, intellectual, and cultural cross-fertilization. Review the founding of some of Alexander's "Alexandrias," and discuss with the class ways in which urban planning was central to Hellenistic culture. How did the Hellenistic city differ—politically, architecturally, socially, and economically—from the Greek polis? A large amount of literature on this topic includes the standard work of J. B. Ward-Perkins, *Cities of Ancient Greece and Italy: Urban Planning in Classical Antiquity* (New York: George Braziller, 1974). More recent works include E. J. Owens, *The City in the Greek and Roman World* (New York and London: Routledge, 1990); and R. Tomlinson, *From Mycenae to Constantinople: The Evolution of the Ancient City* (New York and London: Routledge, 1992).

Reviewing the Text

Review Questions

1. How did daily life, philosophy, and the political situation change in Greece during the period 400–350 B.C.E.?

[model answer] *Continuing competition for power after the Peloponnesian War undermined Greek independence and changed daily life. Loss of prosperity with the economic and social disruptions that resulted from the raids and deaths of warfare altered household structures and economies. Widows moved their families into relatives' homes, creating larger households and increased pressures to support them. Many turned to household manufacturing to produce income in these changed circumstances. Philosophers disillusioned by events rejected the relativism of the Sophists, for a belief in the universality of ethical principles in which philosophy would serve as a guide for life. Aristotle rejected democracy, believing it did not provide rule by the most educated and moderate. Ultimately, the constant state of war left the Greek city-states vulnerable to external threats.*

2. What were the accomplishments of Alexander the Great and what was their effect, both for the ancient world and for later Western civilization?
[model answer] *He avenged Greece's defeat by the Persian Empire, developed military technology, and forged an empire larger than any previous entity, through the near east from Greece and Egypt to what is now Afghanistan and Uzbekistan. He initiated cultural connections through this vast region that expanded trade and knowledge. The legacy of cultural interaction forged long-standing ties through the region. He also introduced the concept of the possibility of great empires, ruled from a central authority and unifying far-flung regions.*

3. What were the political and social structures of the new Hellenistic kingdoms?
[model answer] *Society combined Greek and local traditions. But the use of Greeks as officials and administrators in the structure of power in local governments produced strong hierarchical political and social structures in these societies.*

4. How did the political changes of the Hellenistic period affect art, science, and religion?
[model answer] *Royal patronage shaped artistic expression, limiting artists' sense of freedom, but royal wealth did enable the development of major centers of art and science. Art and literature focused more on personal life and avoided political ideas that might have offended royal supporters. Philosophers also looked inward, rather than examine questions of state policy, where the individual had no control. Known as materialism, this philosophical perspective focused on exploring logic and the nature of existence as paths to human well-being. Stimulated by the scientific discoveries of Alexander's expeditions and royal support, science came into its own as a field of inquiry, with major advances in astronomy and mathematics as well as technology and medicine. Religious cults combined Greek and near eastern beliefs, seeking ways to remedy the troubles of human lives. Many focused on the belief that kings were representatives of the gods on Earth, which fostered the idea that a god could be present on Earth as a savior to humanity.*

Making Connections

1. What made ancient people see Alexander as "great"? Would he be regarded as "great" in today's world?
[model answer] *The accomplishments of Alexander the Great went far beyond what any previous leader had envisioned or attempted. The success of his monumental actions gave him the stature that is acknowledged in his title. Today, however, his ambitions might more likely be regarded as arrogance and megalomania in their lack of regard for the rights of nation states and their inhabitants.*

2. What are the advantages and disadvantages of governmental support of the arts and sciences? Compare such support in the Hellenistic kingdoms to that in the United States today (e.g., through the National Endowment for the Humanities, National Endowment for the Arts, and the National Science Foundation).
[model answer] *One advantage is that publicly funded art and science is more accessible to the people at large. These programs also provide funding to creative and imaginative people, who might not otherwise be able to pursue their projects, and demonstrate that the United States, like ancient Greece, values art and scientific discovery and believes that people have a right to enjoy and benefit from them. One of the disadvantages is that art and scientific discovery can be controversial. Some people may appreciate the work of a particular artist (indeed, they may even be offended), or they may object to certain kinds of scientific research.*

Discussing the Documents

Questions from Online Study Guide with Model Answers

Aristotle on the Nature of the Greek Polis (p. 109)

1. According to Aristotle, why do people form political entities such as city-states?
[model answer] *Aristotle argues that natural necessity brings things into partnerships where one cannot live without the other. An example of this is the male and female of an animal species, which cannot reproduce without one another. Similar partnerships for mutual benefit occur in the household, the village (which is a partnership of several households), and, at the highest level, the polis (which is a partnership of several villages). Thus, just as humans by nature have partners of the opposite sex to reproduce, so too do they live by nature in a city-state.*

2. How do Aristotle's explanations of human society differ from earlier explanations?
[model answer] *Aristotle bases his arguments on nature rather than theology or mythology. The gods did*

not ordain that society should be the way it is; rather, nature did.

Epigrams by Women Poets (p. 122)

1. What do the Epigrams by Women Poets suggest about Hellenistic attitudes toward death?
[model answer] *The poets believed that death was determined by one's fate and was not something to be welcomed; it entailed a loss of earthly delights.*

2. What do the Epigrams by Women Poets suggest about Hellenistic attitudes toward private life and emotion?
[model answer] *The poets saw life as pleasurable and the joining of men and women and their sexual passions as one of its greatest pleasures.*

New Sources, New Perspectives: Papyrus Discoveries and Menander's Comedies (p. 124)

1. What makes situational comedy so appealing?
[model answer] *Sitcoms deal with issues familiar to people in their daily lives, situations with which many people can identify. Sitcoms bring humor to circumstances that can involve some of the difficulties and frustrations of daily existence. Acknowledging them and the possibility that others experience similar issues and revealing their humorous aspects, perhaps makes the vagaries of daily life more bearable.*

1. Why would Greeks living in the fourth century B.C.E. prefer situational comedy to political satire or darker forms of humor?
[model answer] *The nature of monarchical rule that discouraged political expression in philosophy and art undoubtedly also discouraged political expression in daily life. Comedies fit more appropriately into a social culture that was focused more on private life than on a political life to which most people had little access. Ordinary citizens could relate to the stories in comedies.*

Other Questions for Discussing These Documents in Class

Aristotle on the Nature of the Greek Polis (p. 109)

1. Discuss Aristotle's concept of "nature." What is its relation to the Greek polis?

2. Aristotle states that "necessity" pairs or brings together elements that will not survive without the other. These partnerships are based on the idea that some people are naturally servants and others are naturally masters. What examples does he provide of such partnerships?

3. Since Aristotle stresses that these partnerships are rooted in nature, how might critics argue against his political model?

Epigrams by Women Poets (p. 122)

1. Why might female poets have turned their talents toward the composition of epigrams?

2. What specific passages in the epigrams convey the depth of human emotion?

3. What was the subject matter of the epigrams?

New Sources, New Perspectives: Papyrus Discoveries and Menander's Comedies (p. 124)

1. If Menander was an acclaimed playwright, why haven't more copies of his plays survived?

2. What role have historians, literary scholars, and archaeologists played in making use of these papyrus discoveries?

3. What is papyrus, what challenges does ancient papyrus present to scholars, and how did these fragments survive to the present day?

4. How might the subject of Menander's plays relate to their discovery on papyrus texts discarded as garbage or wrapped around mummies?

Comparative Questions

1. What do the epigrams and the New Comedy suggest about the importance of literature in the life of the Greek polis?

2. Which of the three types of writing—political treatise, poetry, or comedy—do you believe provides historians with the most extensive information about ancient Greece?

For Users of *Sources of The Making of the West*

The following documents are available in Chapter 4 of the companion sourcebook by Katharine J. Lualdi, University of Southern Maine.

1. The Conquest of New Lands: Arrian, *The Campaigns of Alexander the Great* (Fourth Century B.C.E.)
2. Imperial Bureaucracy: Zeno, Egyptian Official, *Records* (259–250 B.C.E.)
3. Everyday Life: *Funerary Inscriptions and Epitaphs* (Fifth–First Centuries B.C.E.)
4. In Pursuit of Happiness: Epicurus, *Letter to a Friend* (Late Third Century B.C.E.)
5. Exacting Science: Eratosthenes, *Measurement of the Earth* (Third Century B.C.E.) and *Modern Diagram of Eratosthenes' Measurement*

Discussion Ideas for Sources of The Making of the West, *Chapter 4*

1. How does Alexander the Great appeal to his Macedonian troops in his speech in The Conquest of New Lands? What does he claim that he and his father Philip have done for them? Are his assertions persuasive? What insight does the speech offer into the nature of Alexander's leadership? What relationship does Alexander claim to have with his men? Does he sound autocratic? How did the soldiers respond to the speech? How reliable do you think Arrian of Nicomedia's account is? Are there sections of the passage that are more credible than others?

2. Ask students to describe Eratosthenes' method for measuring the circumference of the earth. How did Eratosthenes' background as a geographer and mathematician influence his work? What does Eratosthenes' research and career illustrate about scientific innovation in the Hellenistic Age?

Working with Visual Sources

For this exercise, please refer to Dying Barbarians on p. 121 of the textbook or view the image on the book companion site's Online Study Guide under the "Visual Activity" for Chapter 4.

Students viewing the image at the Online Study Guide are asked three questions of the image. The questions and model answers (not made available to students) are below. Project this image, available on the Instructor's Resources CD-ROM, in class or ask students to look at the image in their textbooks and answer the questions.

1. Hellenistic sculptors sought to capture emotions in their work. Which emotions does this sculpture convey?
[model answer] *The fallen woman in this sculpture conveys a sense of sadness and defeat, while her husband, poised for death, stands with a defiant sense of pride and bravery.*

2. According to the textbook caption, the male figure has just killed the female figure, his wife, in order to prevent their being captured by the enemy. Might this artist's rendition of a murder-suicide have promoted criticism of the conquerors' tactics?
[model answer] *It was common in the Hellenistic world to take conquered peoples as slaves. These slaves were then given the opportunity to buy their freedom. The fact that this was a common practice implies that the sculpture was not meant to criticize the conquerors, but rather to reflect the despair of the couple in light of the complete defeat of the Gauls. Stressing the noble bravery of the vanquished also increased the glory of the victor.*

3. What effect does including a female figure have on this sculpture that is meant to commemorate a battle?
[model answer] *Although women in the Hellenistic kingdoms enjoyed greater freedom than women in classical Athens, this sculpture underscores the preeminence of the man in the marital relationship: the female figure is passive compared to the male, she is on a lower level and, while he looks up, she collapses downward. The sculpture does convey a strong sense of the couple's loyalty and togetherness, but nothing gives us the sense that the wife is the warrior's equal, especially given that his defeat in battle and wounded sense of pride necessitate her death at his hand instead of the option of life as his enemies' slave.*

Mapping Exercises

Map Activity from OSG—model answers for Map Activity #2

For this activity, please refer to the map on p. 114. Students are asked these questions:

Which directions did Alexander take during his conquests, and how were his conquests limited?
[model answer] *Starting from Macedonia, Alexander went south as far as Egypt, and then east as far as northern India where a mutiny forced him to turn back in 326 B.C.E. Alexander was limited in Egypt by the Sahara desert, and never penetrated into the Arabian desert.*

As a result of Alexander's conquests, which cultures mixed?
[model answer] *The Greek culture of Alexander's homeland mingled with Egyptian culture and with the cultures of the Near East, including the Persians. Some of the cultures surrounding northern India also mixed with the Greeks.*

Map 4.1: Expansion of Macedonia under Philip II, 359–336 B.C.E., p. 112

How did the geography of Greece influence the expansion of the Macedonians toward the south and the east, but not toward the north or the west? What role did geography play in Athens, rather than Sparta, leading a coalition against the Macedonians at the Battle of Chaeronea?

Map 4.2: Conquests of Alexander the Great, 336–323 B.C.E., p. 114

Using the scale, calculate the approximate distances that Alexander and his men covered between campaigns and compare these with the dates of their military engagements. What do these calculations tell students about the pace of Alexander's progress? About his effectiveness in motivating his troops? Ask students to identify the locations of the various "Alexandrias" founded by Alexander and comment on their placement, in light of how he related to the indigenous populations and the rulers of various conquered provinces. What might account for his choice to not found cities in some places?

Map 4.3 Hellenistic Kingdoms, 240 B.C.E., p. 116

How did geography contribute to the breakup of Alexander's empire after his death? Why might the Seleucid kingdom have given up its claim to Parthia and Bactria? What means of transportation could account for the scattered locations of the independent Greek states?

Mapping the West: Roman Takeover of the Hellenistic World, to 30 B.C.E., p. 130

Note the strategic position of Rome in the Mediterranean region. Compare this map to Map 4.2. Where did Alexander's conquests end? How did his conquests facilitate Roman development and expansion? How might the concentration of much of the Hellenistic world into fairly expansive, but consolidated kingdoms have simplified Roman conquests to the east? Ask students to evaluate the extent to which a highly developed, international community that spoke the same language (Greek) may have contributed to the foundations of Roman administration of its eastern provinces. How might this situation have been different if Alexander's empire had remained intact?

In-Class Assignments and Presentation Topics

1. Ask students to investigate the responses of Plato and Aristotle to the failure of Athenian democracy by comparing selected passages from *The Republic* and *Politics*. Do they blame the structure of democratic government or human nature? What alternatives do they offer to democracy? What do they feel are the government's responsibilities to the people? What obligations must the people in turn fulfill?

2. The identity of those responsible for Philip II's murder remains a mystery. Students may want to attempt to solve it by comparing different historical versions of the event and weighing the evidence. See Plutarch, "Life of Alexander," 9.3–12; Arrian, *Anabasis*; and Aristotle, *Politics*, 5.1311.a25–1311.b3. Ask students whether they believe Alexander was in any way implicated in the affair. How convincing is the argument that Alexander's mother Olympias was behind the deed? Was the assassination the result of a conspiracy or did Pausanias act alone?

3. Have students reconstruct the "myth" of Alexander that had begun to disseminate during his lifetime, based on a reading of Plutarch's "Life" or Arrian's *Anabasis*. Among the questions they could address are: How did Alexander self-consciously cultivate this image? Did his tactics change depending on whether he was interacting with allies, followers, or enemies? What was Alexander's ostensible ideal? How did he try to live up to it? How had he been prepared for his position? Do students believe his persona was all artifice or a projection of his true personality? How laudable was Alexander's "mission"? Did he achieve it, and if so, how and at what cost? If not, why not? Did the benefits to the subjects of his conquered territories outweigh the loss of their autonomy? Ask students to identify and evaluate a few of the episodes that contributed to the legend of Alexander during his lifetime (nearly every recorded episode might qualify). A few choices are: his destruction of Thebes, sparing only the city's temples and the descendants of Pindar; the Gordian knot; the taming of his horse Bucephalus; his restoration of Cyrus's tomb at Pasargadae; and his return of Poros's kingdom after the latter surrendered to him. For sources, see *Alexander the Great: Translation of the Extant Historians*, C. A. Robinson, ed. (Golden, CO: Ares, 1998).

4. Students could also approach the previous topic from the viewpoint of modern scholarship. Ask students to read one of the myriad, recent biographies of Alexander and present a summary report of the book to the class. This assignment could lead to a discussion about the reasons for Alexander's enduring popularity and about why such divergent portraits of him have emerged. The following are among the better studies of Alexander to appear recently and all arrive at notably different conclusions about the man. Michael Wood, *In the Footsteps of Alexander the Great* (Berkeley and Los Angeles: University of California Press, 1997) is a discussion of Alexander's life and achievements formulated in the context of the author's personal retracing of the 22,000-mile route of Alexander's conquests. N. G. L. G. Hammond, *The Genius of Alexander the Great* (Chapel Hill: University of North Carolina Press, 1998) is a decidedly laudatory portrayal. Peter Green, *Alexander of Macedon, 356–323 B.C.E.: A Historical Biography* (Berkeley and Los Angeles: University of California Press, 1992) is written by a professor of classics who is also a published novelist. For some notable fictional accounts of Alexander the Great and the successor kingdoms, see Mary Renault's trilogy *Fire from Heaven*, *The Persian Boy*, and *Funeral Games* (New York: Pantheon, respectively, 1969, 1972, 1981; all three are in Vintage reprints, 2002).

5. Have students read one of the plays of Menander and discuss the elements of the central plot and stock characters. How does the play compare with romantic comedies of today? What accounts for the shift away from the lofty meditations on human fate and the political critiques that formed the subject matter of earlier drama? What might this shift indicate about the audience? The complete plays have been translated by David Sclavitt in *Menander* (Philadelphia: University of Pennsylvania Press, 1998), and include *The Grouch (Dyskolos)*, *Desperately Seeking Justice*, and *The Girl from Samos*.

6. With their almost gleefully irreverent disregard for social conventions, the Cynics are easily the most entertaining of all the philosophical schools to spring up in the Hellenistic world. Outline their principles. Does a serious message lie behind their unorthodox behavior or were they only trying to shock people? Why were they able to thrive when Socrates' less extreme message resulted in his condemnation? What were they reacting against? Unlike the schools of Plato and Aristotle, some of these new schools admitted women and even slaves into their circles. What accounts for this difference? Have students read "The Cynic" in Lucan's *Dialogues*, vol. 8, M. D. MacLeod, trans. Loeb Classical Library (Cambridge, MA: Harvard University Press, 1967). The brief biography of the female Cynic Hipparchia by Diogenes Laertes ("Life of Hipparchia," in *Lives and Ideas of Eminent Philosophers*, vol. 6, pp. 96–98, Celia Luschnig, trans.) is at the Diotima Web site. Diogenes Laertes also has information on the Cynic Antisthenes, a pupil of Socrates, and Diogenes of Sinope.

Essay Questions

1. Remarkable discoveries characterized Hellenistic science, especially among the scholars who gathered at Alexandria. Many of these breakthroughs would be lost to the west for centuries, only to be rediscovered during the Renaissance or later. Students can explore the world of Hellenistic science in George Sarton, *Hellenistic Science and Culture in the Last Three Centuries* B.C.E. (New York and London: Dover, 1993); see also the chapters on Hellenistic science in Peter Green, *Alexander to Actium: The Historical Evolution of the Hellenistic Age* (Berkeley and Los Angeles: University of California Press, 1993); and David Lindberg, *The Beginnings of Western Science* (Chicago: University of Chicago Press, 1992).

2. The innovations in military technology and strategy of Philip II and Alexander have generated a substantial amount of scholarship. Philip's substitution of the sarissa transformed hoplite warfare and helped bring about its demise by opening up the possibility of military service to more men. Philip also pioneered the use of siege engines, which for the first time rendered heavily fortified cities vulnerable to foreign attack, and escalated the financial costs of war considerably. Standard works on the topic remain F. E. Adcock, *The Greek and Macedonian Art of War* (Berkeley: University of California Press, 1967); D. W. Engels, *Alexander the Great and the Logistics of the Macedonian Army* (Berkeley: University of California Press, 1978); and N. G. Hammond and G. T. Griffith, *A History of Macedonia*, vol. 2 (New York: Oxford University Press, 1979), 405–49. Among more recent works, see the section on Macedonian expansion in Victor Hanson, *The Wars of the Ancient Greeks and Their Invention of Western Military Culture* (London: Cassell, 1999).

3. Students could assess the extent to which Hellenistic culture constituted a truly "international" culture by investigating its manifestation in divergent parts of Alexander's empire and in the successor kingdoms. This topic would also permit students to examine the extent to which indigenous cultures influenced the shape of the imported Greek culture. Starting points for research include P. Bernard, "An Ancient Greek City in Central Asia (Ai Khanoum)," *Scientific American*, vol. 246, no. 1 (1982): 148–59; P. Bilde, et al., *Aspects of Hellenism in Italy: Towards a Cultural Unity?* (Copenhagen: Museum Tusculanus Press, 1993); F. L. Holt, *Alexander the Great and Bactria* (Leiden: Brill, 1988); and the older but informative G. N. Banerjee, *Hellenism in Ancient India* (Calcutta, 1920). For various aspects of Hellenistic culture, see the articles in Peter Green, ed., *Hellenistic History and Culture* (Berkeley and Los Angeles: University of California Press, 1993).

Additional Resources: Literature

Allen, Reginald, trans., *Plato: Euthyphro, Apology, Crito, Meno, Gorgias, Menexenus*. 1989.

Connor, Robert, trans., *Greek Orations: 4th Century* B.C.*: Lysias, Isocrates, Demosthenes, Aeschines, Hyperides and Letter of Philip*. 1987.

Cornford, Francis, trans., *Plato: Republic*. 1988.

Inwood, Brad, and Gerson, L.P., eds., *Hellenistic Philosophy: Introductory Readings*. 1997.

McKeon, Richard, ed., *The Basic Works of Aristotle*. 2001.

Page, D. L., ed., *Corinna*. 1953.

Page, D. L., and Gow, A. S. F., eds., *The Greek Anthology, The Garland of Philip, and Some Contemporary Epigrams*. 1968.

Thomas, I., trans., *Greek Mathematical Works*, 2 vols. 1953.

Verity, Anthony, trans., *Theocritus: Idylls*. 2003.

Walten, Michael, trans., *Six Greek Comedies*. 2002.

Additional Resources: Film and Video

In the Footsteps of Alexander the Great (1998) (DVD 240 minutes in 4 parts). Series hosted by Michael Wood, who retraces Alexander the Great's journey across sixteen countries.

Other Bedford/St. Martin's Resources for Chapter 4

The following resources are available to accompany Chapter 4. Please refer to the Preface of this manual for detailed descriptions of all the ancillaries.

For Instructors

Transparencies

The following maps and image from Chapter 4 are available as full-color acetates.

- Map 4.1: Expansion of Macedonia under Philip II, 359–336 B.C.E.
- Map 4.2: Conquests of Alexander the Great, 336–323 B.C.E.
- Map 4.3: Hellenistic Kingdoms, 240 B.C.E.
- Mapping the West: Roman Takeover of the Hellenistic World, to 30 B.C.E.
- Emotion in Hellenistic Sculpture, p. 118
- Dying Barbarians, p. 121

Instructor's Resources CD-ROM

The following maps and image from Chapter 4, as well as a chapter outline, are available on disc in both PowerPoint and jpeg formats.

- Map 4.1: Expansion of Macedonia under Philip II, 359–336 B.C.E.
- Map 4.2: Conquests of Alexander the Great, 336–323 B.C.E.
- Map 4.3: Hellenistic Kingdoms, 240 B.C.E.
- Mapping the West: Roman Takeover of the Hellenistic World, to 30 B.C.E.
- Dying Barbarians, p. 121

For Students

Study Guides

The Online Study Guide at **bedfordstmartins.com/hunt** helps students synthesize the material they have learned as well as practice the skills historians use to make sense of the past. The following Map, Visual, and Document activities are available for Chapter 4.

Map Activity

- Map 4.2: Conquests of Alexander the Great, 336–323 B.C.E.

Visual Activity

- Dying Barbarians, p. 121

Reading Historical Documents

- Aristotle on the Nature of the Greek Polis, p. 109
- Epigrams by Women Poets, p. 122
- New Sources, New Perspectives: Papyrus Discoveries and Menander's Comedies

CHAPTER

5

The Rise of Rome

753–44 B.C.E.

CHAPTER RESOURCES

Main Chapter Topics

1. From about 753 to 44 B.C.E., Rome developed from humble beginnings into the dominant power of its day. It incorporated much of Europe, northern Africa, Egypt, and the eastern Mediterranean within a single state system that was sustained for centuries and that left its traces in the history of all modern Western societies.

2. Rome's social structure included class divisions and a patron–client system of benefits and obligations, whereas traditional morality emphasized virtue, fidelity, and devotion to the common good above personal interest.

3. Rome expanded its territory through conquest and alliances, incorporating former enemies into the state and its army and sharing with them the rewards of further expansion; this trend toward inclusiveness extended even to slaves who, once freed, became citizens.

4. Cross-cultural influences came to Rome via its central and accessible location on the Italian peninsula and in the Mediterranean Sea and new arts, ideas, and traditions were introduced into a relatively open and tolerant Roman system. Conquest extended the reach of influences even farther.

5. Rome's republic was shaped by the struggle of the orders—social and political strife between the patricians and the plebeians. Over time, the plebeians gained political and legal ground largely through a series of strikes in which they withdrew from the army, while shrewd patricians made concessions to stave off more severe consequences for the community.

6. Rome's territorial conquests were beneficial to many, but also crippled the economy, bankrupting farmer-soldiers, straining food supplies, and increasing the numbers of urban poor, which resulted in new political tensions.

7. Over time, ambition for personal power and wealth overrode traditional values and reduced the republic to a factionalized, sometimes violent state vulnerable to civil war and political upheaval at the mercy of autocratic generals and their client armies.

Focus Question

How did traditional Roman values affect the rise and the downfall of the Roman republic?

1. Roman moral values such as *virtus* (courage, strength, loyalty) and *fides* (faithfulness) shaped such institutions as the patron–client system, the family, education, and religion. The Roman belief in service to the community, public status, and shared decision making contributed to the development of the republic and its imperialist expansion. The Romans believed that values should drive politics and that they had a divine destiny to build an empire built on the rule of law.

2. As the empire grew, it altered the balance of many of the traditional Roman values and posed major challenges to the republican form of government. By the third and second centuries B.C.E., near-constant war disrupted the traditional agrarian economy of Rome, undermining the status of free but poor Romans and creating a large, volatile urban population that played an increasing role in politics.

3. During the era of the Late Republic, a series of powerful, ambitious men well-versed in traditional Roman practices and beliefs rose to prominence, introducing a system of factional politics that undermined the institutions of the republic and transformed such traditional values as virtus and fides. Individual strength and achievement became more

important than service to the community or the state, and the support of client armies and the urban poor transformed earlier notions of shared decision making, weakening the influence of such republican institutions as the Senate and the Ladder of Offices.

Annotated Chapter Outline

I. **Roman Social and Religious Traditions**

A. **Roman Moral Values, pp. 134–136**

1. Roman values and morals were the foundation of their social and religious institutions.
2. Romans believed their values had been handed down from ancient times and called them *mos maiorum*, or "the way of the ancestors."
3. Moral values of virtue, courage, faithfulness, and respect known as *virtus* defined how a person interacted with others.
4. Those who possessed *fides*, or faithfulness, conducted themselves properly by keeping their obligations, showing proper respect to the gods and their elders, and exercising self-control, earned status and the respect of others.
5. Men earned status through election to high public office and public recognition of their contributions to the common good, while women earned status through bearing children and teaching them moral and social values.
6. Because it was believed that the aristocrats, or those of high birth, automatically deserved respect and authority, Romans expected their elites to live up to the highest standards of Roman values.
7. Over time, however, wealth rather than birth and high morals came to convey social status.

B. **The Patron–Client System, p. 136**

1. Roman laws and traditions built their society around the patron–client system that defined the obligations of relationships between people of different social status.
2. A patron, a man of superior status, provided his clients with "benefits" such as legal or political support, career advancement, gifts, or loans.
3. In return, clients owed "duties," which could include gathering votes in their patrons' campaigns for public office and lending their patrons money to support public works or dowries.
4. Patrons expected clients to accompany them to the forum daily and signal their social success by gathering at their homes.
5. These mutual obligations were passed on to succeeding generations, reinforcing faithful maintenance of patron–client relationships as the way to achieve social stability.

C. **The Roman Family, pp. 136–138**

1. The Roman family was the foundation of Roman society because it taught values and determined the ownership of property.
2. Men and women shared the duty of teaching values to their children, but *patria potestas* ("power of the father") gave a father ownership, if he cared to exercise it, of all property accumulated by children or slaves as long as he lived.
3. Fathers also held legal power of life and death over their households, a right rarely exercised, except perhaps in instances of infant exposure.
4. Patria potestas did not give husbands legal power over their wives, however, because the wife remained under her father's power until he died, whereupon she was free of such control.
5. Most upper-class women managed to maintain a relative degree of independence and were allowed to own and manage property.
6. They also exercised informal political influence by expressing their opinions to their husbands.
7. Women often contributed to the family financially, with some owning businesses and many poorer women producing and selling small goods.

D. **Education for Public Life, p. 138**

1. The goal of education was the teaching of traditional values, language, and literature.
2. Only wealthy families could afford to hire teachers, and, because Romans regarded Greek literature as the world's best, some parents purchased literate Greek slaves to teach their children.
3. Although both boys and girls learned to read, other aspects of education were divided along gender lines.
4. Girls learned literature and music, how to make educated conversation at dinner parties, and especially how to teach social and moral values to their children.

5. Boys were trained physically for military fighting, but primarily they learned the skill of rhetoric or persuasive public speaking that was essential to a successful political career.
6. Many boys learned these skills by accompanying their father or another family member to hear the speeches of famous orators such as Cicero.

E. Public and Private Religion, pp. 138–139

1. Rome's three chief gods—Jupiter, Juno, and Minerva—shared Rome's most revered temple at the top of the Capitoline.
2. Roman gods were believed to protect the city in times of war and preserve agricultural prosperity.
3. Other cults had special guardian powers; for example, the shrine of Vesta housed an eternal flame symbolizing the permanence of the Roman state.
4. The Vestal Virgins, who were six unmarried women sworn to thirty years of chastity at a young age, tended the shrine, making sure the flame never burned out.
5. Religious rites were also part of family life: most private homes maintained a shrine to house the spirits of the household and the spirits of ancestors.
6. Many Roman religious rituals and public celebrations were meant to promote the health and stability of the community.
7. Although Romans associated religion with national security and prosperity more than with individual morality, some of their gods were personified moral qualities such as piety and virtue.
8. Before undertaking any important enterprise Romans performed a ritual called "taking the auspices" in which they would consult the gods by interpreting such things as the behavior of sacred birds or the appearance of thunder and lightning.
9. The *pontifex maximus* (supreme priest) served as the head of state religion and the ultimate authority on religious matters affecting government.

II. From Monarchy to Republic

A. Roman Society under the Kings, 753–509 B.C.E., pp. 139–142

1. Although little direct evidence exists about the founding of Rome, legend reports that it was ruled by a series of kings.
2. These kings created the Senate, a body of advisers from the city's leading men, and laid the foundations for Rome's growth by assimilating outsiders and granting citizenship to freed slaves.
3. During the first 250 years of monarchy, Rome underwent tremendous expansion of both population and territory, gaining control of some three hundred square miles of surrounding land that could support a population of thirty to forty thousand.
4. The city's advantageous location and fertile soil contributed to its prosperity.
5. Roman culture gained from contact with other cultures neighboring this expanded area, especially the Greeks, who had long had settlements in southern Italy.
6. Cross-cultural influences also came from the Etruscans, an independent people living in the hills and plains to the north of Rome.
7. Romans used what appealed to them in other cultures, and made revisions to fit their own ideas, values, and circumstances.

B. The Early Roman Republic, 509–287 B.C.E., pp. 142–145

1. According to legend, the republic was formed in reaction to the tyrannical behavior of Rome's kings in 509 B.C.E.
2. To prevent rule by one man or family, power was distributed more widely among elected officials.
3. The first two hundred years of the republic were marked by strife between about 130 elite families (the *patricians*) and the rest of the population (the *plebeians*), and were known as "the struggle of the orders," during which the plebeians struggled to improve their political, social, and economic position.
4. By withholding military service the plebeians won several concessions, the most important of which was the Twelve Tables, Rome's first written laws and a symbol of Roman commitment to justice for all citizens.
5. The highest political offices were still available primarily to the patricians and were attained by holding a series of administrative positions that ended with the consulship, Rome's highest public office.
6. Eventually, the plebeians managed to counter patrician dominance with the formation of a panel of tribunes who guarded their interests, and the passage of

a law requiring at least one consul to be a plebeian.

7. Laws were passed in a complex system of assemblies that voted in groups, so that even though the poor did not have access to higher offices because they had no salary, they had at least some level of participation in public affairs.
8. The Romans developed a sophisticated system of civil law that regulated disputes over property and personal interests that became the core of many Western legal codes.

III. Roman Imperialism and Its Consequences

A. Expansion in Italy, 500–220 B.C.E., pp. 145–146

1. The Romans defeated the Etruscans and the Greeks in southern Italy, controlling the Italian peninsula by 220 B.C.E.
2. Romans sometimes enslaved defeated peoples and seized large parcels of land.
3. On the other hand, the Romans granted citizenship to many other defeated enemies or made lasting alliances in exchange for rendering military aid in future wars.
4. Because allies then received a share of the spoils from the next war, Rome cleverly turned former adversaries into partners.
5. The Romans built roads and established colonies of citizens throughout the peninsula.
6. Latin began to replace other languages in Italy, and the roads built to connect the Roman colonies helped create a more unified culture.
7. The wealth resulting from the expansion attracted many people to Rome to take advantage of its amenities, such as aqueducts that provided fresh running water to the city, and construction projects that created jobs.
8. With the new agricultural lands and plunder from campaigns, patricians and plebeians acquired great wealth and merged to form one elite class.

B. Wars with Carthage and in the East, 264–121 B.C.E., pp. 146–149

1. After the Gauls sacked Rome in 387 B.C.E., the Romans' fear of foreign invasions intensified, and they began to see the expanding empire of Carthage in North Africa as a threat.
2. Moreover, Carthage's trade routes and fertile agricultural lands made it an enticing prize.
3. The three Punic Wars—all won by Rome—proved the Romans' willingness to sacrifice lives, expend huge sums, and fight as long as necessary to win.
4. The First Punic War, in which the Romans first learned naval warfare, made Sicily Rome's first province, a foreign territory ruled and taxed by Roman officials, and emboldened Rome to seize the nearby islands of Sardinia and Corsica.
5. Rome issued an ultimatum to Carthage against future expansion, prompting the great Carthaginian general Hannibal to invade Italy.
6. Despite Hannibal's years of ravaging Italy, the Romans won the Second Punic War by invading the Carthaginian homeland in North Africa.
7. Following this victory, the Roman Senate imposed harsh fines and penalties on Carthage and took their territory in Spain.
8. The Third Punic War began when the Carthaginians retaliated against the aggressive Numidian king, a Roman ally.
9. This time the Romans razed Carthage and seized its entire empire.
10. Roman territory now included Spain, North Africa, Macedonia, Greece, and parts of Asia Minor.

C. Greek Influence on Roman Literature and the Arts, pp. 149–150

1. Roman expansion encouraged cross-cultural contact.
2. In fact, many early Latin authors were not from Rome, and their work reflected a mingling of the familiar with the foreign—particularly with the Greeks, from whom they borrowed models of literature and art.
3. Although some writers such as Cato—whose histories of Rome helped make Latin the language of prose—worried that Greek influence would weaken Roman manhood, most works still reflected traditional Roman values.
4. Later Roman writers, such as Lucretius (94–55 B.C.E.) and Catullus (84–54 B.C.E.), were inspired by the content and style of Greek literature.
5. Cicero wrote many works that adapted Hellenic philosophy, especially Stoicism, to Roman life, creating the doctrine of *humanitas*.
6. The ideals of humanitas based the value of human life on generous and honest treatment of others and commitment to a

morality that applied to all people regardless of their differences.

7. In art, Romans adapted the realism used by Hellenistic sculptors to individual portrait sculptures, making it a point not to hide unflattering features.
8. Portraits of women were in general more idealized, perhaps to reflect the goal of bliss in family life, while those of men showed the toll of age and effort to emphasize how hard they worked in serving the republic.

D. Stresses on Republican Society, pp. 150–152

1. The wars of expansion of the third and second centuries B.C.E. caused great stresses on small rural farmers by disrupting traditional agricultural life.
2. Farmers were not only the backbone of the Roman economy but also the primary source for soldiers.
3. The Punic Wars and numerous military interventions in Macedonia and Greece called for prolonged campaigns abroad that took farmers away from their fields and families.
4. While farmers were away fighting and dying, their families and hired hands often faced starvation.
5. With a surging growth in the number of young people, many homeless relocated to Rome to look for menial work.
6. This influx of desperate people heightened tension in the city, and by the second century B.C.E., Rome had to import grain to feed its swollen population.
7. By contrast, Rome's elite reaped substantial rewards from the wars and used their gains to enrich their families and fund large public building projects.
8. By absorbing small, bankrupt farms and illegally seizing public land in defeated territories, rich landowners formed *latifundia*, giant estates worked by slaves and free laborers.
9. Provincial officials who ruled by martial law could use their power to squeeze even more money, property, and service from the population they governed.
10. They faced no punishment because members of the Senate excused one another's crimes.
11. Growing wealth helped the elites control most of Rome's offices, but it also strained the traditional Roman values of upright-ness and moderation.
12. For many, money had become more important than working for the public good.

IV. Upheaval in the Late Republic

A. The Gracchus Brothers and Factional Politics, 133–121 B.C.E., pp. 152–153

1. When Tiberius and Gaius Gracchus tried to use their power as tribunes to help the farmers, some members of the elite placed personal interests ahead of the community and resorted to murder.
2. The upper-class Gracchus brothers asked that the rich make concessions to aid the poor and strengthen the state.
3. When opponents blocked him, Tiberius overrode the Senate by having the Plebeian Assembly pass laws that would redistribute public land to landless Romans.
4. Tiberius went against Roman tradition and ran for reelection as tribune.
5. His senatorial opponents responded by clubbing him and several of his followers to death.
6. When Gaius Gracchus became tribune ten years later, he pushed for subsidized grain prices and jobs funded through public works projects.
7. In addition, he proposed that courts try provincial governors (all from the Senate class) for corruption, with juries drawn from the *equites*, or equestrian class, of wealthy businessmen.
8. The Senate countered by authorizing the consuls to use whatever force was necessary to "defend the republic"—in other words, to kill Gaius.
9. Gaius killed himself, and hundreds of his followers were killed by the senators.
10. These violent deaths made murder a political tactic and polarized the elites into two factions: the *populares* (for the people) and the elitist *optimates* ("the best").
11. These factions persisted as a source of friction and violence until the end of the first century B.C.E.

B. Marius and the Origin of Client Armies, 107–100 B.C.E., p. 153

1. A new kind of leader emerged in response to the disarray of the elite and constant military threats: equestrian men who relied on fame, fortune, and the ability to lead a loyal army of clients to win their way to the consulship.
2. The first of these so-called new men was Gaius Marius (157–86 B.C.E.), who

capitalized on his military achievements to win an unprecedented six terms as consul.

3. Marius was opposed by the optimates, who saw him as an outsider and a threat because most of his support came from the common people.
4. Marius's military reforms that allowed men who owned virtually nothing the chance to better their lot by serving in the army created an army that behaved like its general's clients—far more loyal to its patron-general than to the state.
5. As other commanders after Marius used client armies to advance their own political careers rather than the interests of Rome, the disintegration of the republic accelerated.

C. Sulla and Civil War, 91–78 B.C.E., pp. 153–155

1. In the early first century B.C.E. Rome rejected its Italian allies' demands for citizenship, beginning a four-year-long Social War (from *socius*, meaning "ally").
2. Although the Roman army won the bloody war against the confederacy of Italian allies, the Romans granted the allies citizenship, allowing all freeborn peoples of Italy south of the Po River to vote in the Roman assemblies.
3. The success of general Lucius Cornelius Sulla in the Social War won him election as consul in 88 B.C.E.
4. In the same year, Sulla was granted the command of an army against the rebellious king Mithridates VI in Asia Minor.
5. Sulla's rival Marius had the command transferred to him by plebiscite.
6. Furious, Sulla marched his client army against Rome itself—an outrage against all Roman values.
7. All his officers except one deserted him in disgust, but his common soldiers remained loyal.
8. Sulla killed or exiled his opponents and then left to defeat Mithridates.
9. While Sulla stripped Asia Minor bare, Marius and his friends embarked on their own reign of terror in Rome.
10. In 83 B.C.E., Sulla returned to Rome, and civil war ensued.
11. Sulla was victorious and resorted to proscription to eliminate his opponents, posting lists of his enemies to be hunted down and executed.
12. The Senate appointed him dictator, a traditionally temporary office for times of emergency that Sulla held indefinitely, and he used his position to reorganize the government in the interest of the optimates.
13. His bloody career underlined the changes in Roman society: war now served to acquire fortunes rather than to defend the community; the patron–client system led poor soldiers to feel more loyalty to their commanders than to their republic; and the ambitious desired power and wealth for their own sake, which overshadowed any concern for public service.

D. The Republic's Downfall, 83–44 B.C.E., pp. 155–159

1. After the reign of Sulla, other great military generals dominated the final years of the republic.
2. The young Gnaeus Pompey (106–48 B.C.E.) gathered a private army to fight for Sulla and achieved remarkable success.
3. In 71 B.C.E., Pompey seized the glory when his army defeated the massive slave rebellion led by Spartacus.
4. Elected consul, he gained tremendous popularity by eliminating pirates in the Mediterranean who had been threatening the supply of imported grain, and by expanding Rome's territory in the east by seizing Syria.
5. Pompey endangered his position, however, by ignoring the tradition of consulting the Senate on policies for conquered territories.
6. Pompey's enemies in Rome tried to undermine him by proclaiming concern about the desperate living conditions of the urban poor.
7. Pompey responded by forming an informal alliance called the First Triumvirate with two previous political rivals, Crassus and Julius Caesar.
8. The alliance between Pompey and Caesar was cemented by the marriage of Caesar's daughter Julia to Pompey.
9. One year after allying with Pompey, Caesar won election as a consul and began to build a client army in Gaul.
10. Caesar's military prowess and success at plundering central and northern Gaul won him great devotion from his soldiers and great dread from his political enemies in Rome.

11. Following the deaths of Crassus in battle and Caesar's daughter in childbirth, the alliance between Caesar and Pompey ended, and they went to war.
12. Caesar led his army against Rome after Pompey was appointed sole consul.
13. Popular support for Caesar forced Pompey, and most senators, to flee Rome; Caesar's army followed Pompey to Spain and then to Greece, defeated his armies and won a decisive battle at Pharsalus in 48 B.C.E.
14. Pompey fled to Egypt and was murdered by ministers of the boy-pharaoh Ptolemy.
15. After defeating the final holdouts from the civil war, Caesar took over as sole ruler of the Roman Empire, appointing himself dictator in 48 B.C.E.
16. He established policies that endeared him to most of the common people but outraged the optimates.
17. A band of optimate senators stabbed Caesar to death on March 15, 44 B.C.E.
18. Although his murderers saw themselves as liberators, the common people were furious with the murderers of their hero and benefactor.
19. The damage to the traditional political systems of the republic was never repaired.

Lecture Strategies

1. Rome's relationship to Classical Greece was one of reverent, but not slavish or uncritical, imitation. A revealing approach to the Roman republic could examine the role of Classical Greek traditions in Roman social, cultural, religious, and political life. In what ways did Rome absorb these traditions into its own system? In which forms did they survive? In what ways did these Greek traditions transform Roman society?

2. The central Roman value of virtue, which encompassed uprightness, faithfulness, respect, and an adherence to tradition, was gradually subordinated to a lust for power and wealth among social elites. But the hierarchical organization of society and an emphasis on social status as the measure of personal worth underlay the system throughout this transformation. In what ways might one view the crumbling of the republic as less a negation of traditional values than a playing out of inherent contradictions? See the sections on the republic in Paul Veyne, *Bread and Circuses*, Brian Pearce, trans. (New York: Penguin, 1990). This analysis can fuel an examination of the causes of Roman social unrest, as well as the methods used to combat it.

3. Rome's expansionist foreign policy carried dramatic consequences for the city, its population, and other territories already within its domain. Because war and conquest were so central to Roman politics, students may be interested to learn how Roman foreign policy was related to domestic policy. What factors propelled Rome's expansion? What were the effects of that expansion on Roman life? What political alternatives existed at various points in Roman republican history in regard to foreign policy and the cultivation and distribution of resources? What factors influenced the decisions that were ultimately made? An introduction to the topic can be found in Elizabeth Rawson, "The Expansion of Rome," in *The Roman World*, John Boardman, et al., eds. (Oxford: Oxford University Press, 1986).

Class Discussion Starters

1. Geographically, Rome was particularly well situated for prominence in the ancient world. While examining maps of Italy and the Mediterranean in conjunction with an identification of Rome's chief rivals, discuss the factors that may have motivated, assisted, or inhibited Roman expansion. Such a discussion can incorporate economic considerations, military strategy, and political maneuvering. For an overview, see Chapter 3 of Lesley Adkins and Roy A. Adkins, *Handbook to Life in Ancient Rome* (Oxford: Oxford University Press, 1994).

2. The family was, of course, the institution to which most Romans were most immediately subordinated. An examination of the familial structure and its workings can serve as a good introduction to the daily life of average Romans. In what ways did the Roman family reinforce the broader social order? Such a discussion could involve both the internal familial functions, such as instilling education and values in children, and societal functions, including property distribution and social status. Useful information can be found in Jane F. Gardner, *Women in Roman Law and Society* (Bloomington: Indiana University Press, 1986); and Richard P. Saller, *Patriarchy, Property, and Death in the Roman Family* (Cambridge, UK: Cambridge University Press, 1994). An excellent and wide-ranging selection of excerpted primary sources for all aspects of Roman social history can be found in Jo-Ann Shelton, *As the Romans Did: A Sourcebook in Roman Social History* (Oxford: Oxford University Press, 1988).

3. Rome's devotion to a stable, social hierarchy in which all citizens knew and respected their proper roles entailed vastly different prescriptions for men

and women. An examination of the differences in male and female roles and virtues as embodied in education, politics, morality, and so on, can help highlight some of the assumptions on which Roman society was based. The legends of the early Roman city and of the formation of the Roman republic can provide illuminating starting points. This discussion can also include an examination of the role of women in Roman politics. See the story of Lucretia in Livy, *The Early History of Rome*, A. de Sélincourt, trans. (New York: Penguin, 1960). On women in politics, see Richard Bauman, *Women and Politics in Ancient Rome* (London and New York: Routledge, 1992).

4. Compare and contrast the empire of Alexander the Great and the empire built by the Romans. Students might consider such factors as the territorial extent of each empire, the role of ambitious "great men" such as Alexander and Julius Caesar, and the significance of Roman institutions that contributed to ongoing rule.

Reviewing the Text

Review Questions

1. What common themes underlay Roman values? How did Romans' behavior reflect those values?
[model answer] *The values of* virtus *and* fides, *loyalty and duty, formed the foundation of a social structure in which patron–client relationships knit social classes together in reciprocal relationships structured by benefits and duties. Status, authority, and ultimately political power, were based on the respect one earned through loyalty, faithfulness, and associated moral behavior. The social structure, from the family through the offices of the political system, reflected the hierarchy of relationships created by these values.*

2. How and why did the Roman republic develop its complicated political and judicial systems?
[model answer] *Rome's political and judicial systems developed out of conflicts over power. Initially, patricians overthrew the monarchy in response to its abuses and created a system based on values of duty and hierarchy, in which loyal service provided entry to a hierarchy of public offices. Initially, patricians (the elite) monopolized these offices, but the much larger groups of plebeians in the population forced the creation of new political offices and opening of others to give them a voice in political decision making. The result was a complex multitiered system of public offices in three assemblies and a jury system that gave political power to both major groups in society.*

3. What advantages and disadvantages did Rome's victories over foreign peoples create for both rich and poor Romans?
[model answer] *Rome's war campaigns and victories provided opportunities for high-level army and administrative personnel to benefit from plunder by gaining access to new agricultural lands. The need for additional troops in warfare also opened up new opportunities for some to work their way up through the military to better positions in society. However, many of the poor suffered because of the wars. The requirements for long military service took farmers away from their land, decreasing their ability to maintain their farms. Some lost their lands, which were taken up in large holdings by the wealthy. A growing population of landless poor left the countryside for the cities, where they often struggled to survive.*

4. What factors generated the conflicts that caused the republic's downfall?
[model answer] *After the founding of the Roman republic in 509 B.C.E., the two "orders"—the elite patricians and the masses of plebian citizens—struggled for dominance in social and economic matters. Patricians monopolized political offices and banned intermarriage between the orders. Plebeians, who were sometimes wealthy citizens, periodically pressured the patricians for more rights and improved conditions by withdrawing from the city and refusing to perform military service. The patricians, composed of only about 130 families, could not survive without plebeians in the army. Over time the plebeians attained a series of reforms and written laws granting greater equality and social mobility. These reforms included the earliest written code of Roman law, the Twelve Tables. Later the tribunes were created: ten annually elected plebeians empowered to stop actions that would harm plebeians or their property. By 367 B.C.E., an additional law required that at least one of the two consuls, the highest officials of Rome, be a plebeian. And in 287 B.C.E. the Plebeian Assembly, originally the counter-measure to the powerful patrician Centuriate Assembly, won the right to make laws legally binding to all Romans.*

Making Connections

1. How do the political and social values of the Roman republic compare to those of the Greek city-state in the Classical Age?
[model answer] *Roman political and social divisions were institutionalized in a way that they were not in classical Greece. Patricians were at the top, equestrians in the middle, and plebeians at the bottom of society, and a person's political and legal rights depended upon his or her class. There was the shared value of putting the common good over personal interests, but virtue, acting in good faith, and fidelity, fulfilling one's obligations at all costs, were more Roman values than Greek ones.*

2. What were the positive and the negative consequences of war for the Roman republic?
[model answer] *Many people suffered hardship during the Punic Wars (264–146 B.C.E.) and the conquest of Macedonia and Greece. Farmers were kept away from home for long periods of time during their obligatory military service, and many lost their farms and became destitute because they were unable to cultivate their land. With less production, food prices soared, forcing the poor into low-paying jobs and even prostitution. This caused economic and political tension, especially in urban areas. While the poor got poorer, the rich got richer, buying up farms and enjoying the spoils of military conquests.*

Discussing the Documents

Questions from Online Study Guide with Model Answers

The Rape and Suicide of Lucretia (p. 144)

1. What does the document reveal about female virtue and courage in Rome?
[model answer] *Motivated by honor and the virtues she would represent to other women, Lucretia submits to her own destruction. Her courageous attempt to refuse the advances of Sextus Tarquinius, her confession to her family, and eventual suicide, reflect the high value placed on virtuous behavior and living in an honest and honorable way. Her insistence that her husband and his friend avenge her defilement demonstrates her belief that the importance of honor extends to her family, and the reasons for her own death demonstrate her belief in the importance to society of living honorably.*

2. How might the attack on Lucretia and her response justify the decision by the Roman elite to expel the monarchy?
[model answer] *Sextus Tarquinius uses his power to violate the honor of both an individual and a family, disregarding a central moral value of Roman society. He abused not only Lucretia, but also one of the most important political and social values on which society was based. By selfishly using his power for his own benefit, he violated the terms of protection and duty on which the legitimacy of his rule depended.*

Polybius on Roman Military Discipline (p. 154)

1. What qualities were emphasized in the Roman army?
[model answer] *Above all, Roman soldiers were expected to obey orders. Centurions were not to be bold and take risks, but were to be "steady and solid." Soldiers were expected to hold their positions in battle, even when it cost them their lives.*

2. How do these military values reflect traditional Roman values?
[model answer] *Romans were driven by virtue, which stressed meeting one's obligations. If one failed to meet one's obligations, one risked offending the community and the gods. Consequently, a soldier who fell asleep at his post or deserted his post in battle had more to fear from his comrades and family than the enemy.*

Contrasting Views: What Was Julius Caesar Like? (pp. 156–157)

1. What characteristics made Julius Caesar such a remarkable individual?
[model answer] *Caesar seems to have had a strong self-confidence, but also an equally strong sense of virtue. His quick and clever mind and engaging personality, accompanied by dedication to his tasks and a strong sense of appropriate justice, drew others to him and won their confidence.*

2. How and why do an individual's personal characteristics matter for political success?
[model answer] *Good leadership can result from both intelligence and charisma. An ability to communicate ideas and win others' trust and loyalty can be as important as the decisions one makes in winning political support.*

Other Questions for Discussing These Documents in Class

The Rape and Suicide of Lucretia (p. 144)

1. How do the feminine ideals of virtue and courage embodied by Lucretia compare with the masculine virtues suggested by Lucius Junius Brutus?

2. Is it significant that tyrannical royal privilege, in the form of the assault by Sextus Tarquinius, was directed at a woman rather than a man? How might the story differ if Sextus Tarquinius had attacked Lucretia's husband instead?

Polybius on Roman Military Discipline (p. 154)

1. What qualities should Roman centurions possess and why?

2. How did the disgrace, associated with injury or death, influence the behavior of Roman centurions?

Contrasting Views: What Was Julius Caesar Like? (pp. 156–157)

1. How does the portrait Julius Caesar created explaining why he fought the civil war compare with the assessment of the man made by his biographer Suetonius?

2. How did Cicero's assessment of Caesar change between January and March of 49 B.C.E.?

3. Why might Caesar have forgiven Catallus for mocking him? How does his attitude toward the poet compare with his treatment of others, as described in the Contrasting Views documents?

4. Which of the Contrasting Views accounts of Julius Caesar gives you the fullest understanding of what the man was like?

5. What was Julius Caesar's most important quality as a military leader?

6. What characteristics of Julius Caesar reflected traditional Roman values?

Comparative Questions

1. Did Julius Caesar live up to the ideals of Roman masculinity as described by Livy in the Rape and Suicide of Lucretia and by Polybius on Roman Military Discipline?

2. Based on these documents, what role did violence and the military play in the development of Roman ideals of virtuous conduct?

For Users of *Sources of The Making of the West*

The following documents are available in Chapter 5 of the companion sourcebook by Katharine J. Lualdi, University of Southern Maine.

1. Formalizing Roman Law: *The Twelve Tables* (451–449 B.C.E.)
2. Artistic Influences: *Etruscan Statuette of a Rider* (c. 434–400 B.C.E.) and *Roman Bust of Lucius Junius Brutus* (c. 300 B.C.E.)
3. Status and Discrimination: *Roman Women Demonstrate against the Oppian Law* (195 B.C.E.)
4. "Cultivating Justice and Piety": Cicero, *On the Commonwealth* (54 B.C.E.)
5. Failure and Factionalism: *The Gracchan Reforms* (133 B.C.E.)
6. Towards Empire: Julius Caesar, *The Gallic War* (52 B.C.E.)

Discussion Ideas for Sources of The Making of the West, *Chapter 5*

1. What traditional Roman values and customs are apparent in *The Twelve Tables*? How does the code illustrate Roman belief in the importance of law, tradition, and communal values? What examples are there of *fides* (faithfulness)? Of *patria potestas* (father's power)? What rights did Roman women possess?

2. What insight does Cicero provide into Roman values? More specifically, what should be the proper relationship between moral standards and public service? What should be the purpose of dictatorship in a time of political instability? How does this document reflect Cicero's belief in *humanitas* (humaneness)? In what ways might Cicero's use of a dream involving Punic War heroes assist him in persuading his readers?

Working with Visual Sources

For this exercise, please refer to Aqueduct at Nîmes in France on p. 146 of the textbook or view the image on the book companion site's Online Study Guide under the "Visual Activity" for Chapter 5.

Students viewing the image at the Online Study Guide are asked three questions of the image. The questions and model answers (not made available to students) are below. Project this image, available on the Instructor's Resources CD-ROM, in class or ask students to look at the image in their textbooks and answer the questions.

1. Describe the aqueduct. What are the characteristics of its design?
[model answer] *The aqueduct is symmetrical, with large arches set at even intervals in two large rows, one on top of the other, and a third smaller row of arches on top. The curve of the arches is complemented by the straight lines separating one level from the other. The aqueduct is made of stones that appear to be regularly and evenly shaped.*

2. The height and length of the aqueduct created a steady flow of water. Did the aqueduct also have political purposes?
[model answer] *The height and length of the aqueduct make it an imposing structure, one that towers over the landscape. To create such an enormous structure was to make a statement about the power of Rome, which "towered" over the entire Mediterranean.*

3. When the Romans designed the aqueduct, they were influenced not only by the needs of transporting water, but also by characteristics of their culture. How does the design of the aqueduct reflect Roman values?
[model answer] *In addition to the symbolic importance of the imposing size of the structure, the design of the aqueduct, with its straight lines and symmetrical arches, emphasizes order and regularity. The stones bring a sense of permanence. Its presence alone is a reminder of the Roman value of public service, of supporting the res publica, "the people's matter"—in this case, a water supply.*

Mapping Exercises

Map Activity from OSG—Model Answers for Map Activity #2

For this activity, please refer to the map on p. 147. Students are asked these questions:

What territories did Rome control by time Julius Caesar died in 44 B.C.E.?
[model answer] *Rome controlled the entire Italian peninsula and the islands of the Mediterranean, Spain and Gaul, much of North Africa, Greece and Macedonia, a large portion of Asia Minor, and Syria.*

What are some of the events that prompted Roman expansion outside the Italian peninsula?
[model answer] *Perhaps the most important events in Roman expansion were the three Punic Wars fought between 264 and 146 B.C.E. These wars added most of Spain, northern Italy, Illyria, Greece, Macedonia, and North Africa to the Roman Empire. The gift of the kingdom of Pergamum also added to Rome's territory. The campaigns by Caesar who conquered Gaul and Pompey who conquered Syria extended Rome's empire still further.*

Map 5.1: Ancient Italy, 500 B.C.E., p. 140

Ask students to consider the location of Rome in regard to the geographical and cultural layout of the Italian peninsula. Which natural and cultural resources surrounded Rome in all directions? How might these considerations have factored into Rome's course of early expansion?

Map 5.2: The City of Rome during the Republic, p. 143

Ask students to compare this map of Rome with Map 3.2 of fifth-century Athens. In what ways was Rome's forum similar to Athens's agora? What structures are located in or near the forum, and what does this suggest about their significance? Note Rome's location on the Tiber River, the network of roads leading into the city, and the defensive walls surrounding it.

Map 5.3: Roman Expansion, 500–44 B.C.E., p. 147

Consider Rome's position in relation to both the Mediterranean and Europe. What strategic interests fueled the course of its expansion? What were Rome's vulnerabilities, and how did Rome account for them? Ask students to locate Rome's major rivals and discuss the geographical and strategic considerations each had to face.

Mapping the West: The Roman World at the End of the Republic, 44 B.C.E., p. 160

The Mediterranean Sea served as a highway linking Roman territories. Ask students to consider which geographical features fostered the growth of the Roman Empire and which ones served as barriers against further Roman expansion. How do the boundaries of the Roman world compare with those of the Hellenistic world depicted in Map 4.3?

In-Class Assignments and Presentation Topics

1. Ask students to write an essay on the phenomenon of the Roman "new man." One of the major characteristics of this development was the open encouragement of popular armies to be loyal to their commanders rather than to the ideals of the republic. Which factors gave rise to this phenomenon? What were its effects on Roman political life? What were the defining characteristics of these new notable Romans, compared with the notable figures of the past? An exceptionally useful source is the Roman historian Appian's *The Civil Wars*, particularly the first book.

2. Have students read the biographies of Tiberius and Gaius Gracchus and compare their lives and politics with those of Julius Caesar. In what ways were they similar, especially in their policies affecting ordinary Romans? Also, compare their fellow elites' reactions to their policies. What factors made the Senate, ostensibly a popular organization designed to protect against tyranny, less popular than these "populist tyrants"? The biographies are found in Plutarch, *Lives of the Noble Greeks and Romans*: "Gaius Gracchus," pp. iii–ix; "Tiberius Gracchus," pp. viii.7–ix.5, xiv.1–2; "Julius Caesar," pp. lvii, lxiii–lxvii.

3. The notion of absolute patriarchal authority was the central tenet of family life. And yet the Roman republic was distrustful of such centralized, tyrannical authority in politics. Ask students to report on the tension caused by basing a republic adverse to unchecked power on a familial structure that demanded such power. How might this system have fed into Rome's political system? Did it contribute to the fall of the republic? Why or why not?

4. The Punic Wars were among the most important and influential events in the history of the republic's foreign conquests. What were the motivating factors in these conflicts? In what ways did they shape or transform Rome militarily? What were some of the economic consequences? This topic can involve discussion of the taxation of Sicily, the command of trade routes, the development of the navy, the strains the

wars placed on the Roman economy, and the means employed by Roman leaders to finance their efforts. For a general history of the wars, see Polybius's *Histories*. For a more detailed look at the financing of the war and related issues, see Livy's *History*.

5. On a more lighthearted note, you might have students discuss the portrayal of the late republic in such major Hollywood epics as *Spartacus* (1960), which deals with notions of slavery, freedom, the erosion of republican Rome, the spread of senatorial corruption, and the power of the "new man." Examine how well students can separate the fictionalized elements from history and how movements of the late 1950s and early 1960s, like the civil rights movement, fed into the production. Brent Shaw wrote a wonderful introduction to Spartacus and the Roman slave wars in his Bedford History and Culture Series book, *Spartacus and the Slave Wars* (Boston: Bedford/St. Martin's, 2000). For a historical discussion of the events portrayed in the film, see Keith Bradley, *Slavery and Rebellion in the Roman World, 140 B.C.E.–70 B.C.E.* (Bloomington: Indiana University Press, 1989). As for the fictionalized elements or the portrayal of overall themes, an interesting discussion could involve the implicit comparison of Rome to the United States in such Hollywood films, including the values and morals represented.

Essay Questions

1. Although slavery was a fact of life throughout the Roman republic, it was a far more fluid condition than its modern variations, such as that in the antebellum American South. Have students write or report on the nature of slavery in the republic. What did it mean to be a slave? They might consider how Roman expansionist policies contributed to the creation of a slave state, not only through the conquest of other peoples, but also through the transformation of small, failing farms into estates for wealthy elites. A good place to begin is Keith Bradley, *Slavery and Society at Rome* (Cambridge, UK: Cambridge University Press, 1994).

2. Have students research and report on the struggle of the orders. What interests did each side of the struggle pursue? In which values were those competing interests rooted? What measures were taken in advance of each faction's interests? In what ways were the political maneuverings of this struggle related to the overtly violent struggle for political power by a small number of individuals during the late republic? For excerpts from primary sources, see the numerous sections indexed under "plebeians" and "patricians" in Naphtali Lewis and Meyer Reinhold, eds., *Roman Civilization, Sourcebook 1: The Republic* (New York: Harper & Row, 1966). On the general class structure of the republic, see chapters 1 and 10 in Jo-Ann Shelton, *As the Romans Did: A Sourcebook in Roman Social History* (Oxford: Oxford University Press, 1988). On the nature of this struggle under the Gracchus brothers, see chapters 44 and 45 in Nels M. Bailkey, ed., *Readings in Ancient History: Thought and Experience from Gilgamesh to St. Augustine*, 5th ed. (Lexington, MA: D. C. Heath, 1996).

Additional Resources: Literature

Grant, Michael, trans., *Selected Works by Marcus Tullius Cicero*. 1960.

de Selincourt, Aubrey, trans., *Livy: The Early History of Rome*. 2002.

———. *The War with Hannibal by Livy*. 1965.

Latham, R. E., trans., *Lucretius: On the Nature of the Universe*. 1994.

Walton, J. Michael, ed., *Four Roman Comedies by Plautus and Terence*. 2003.

Waterfield, Robin, trans., *Roman Lives: A Selection of Eight Roman Lives by Plutarch*. 2000.

Additional Resources: Film and Video

Spartacus (1960) (VHS/DVD, 3 hrs., 16 min.). This lavishly produced film tells the story of the slave rebellion led by Spartacus against the Romans in 71 B.C.E. It nicely captures the feel of the period and the kind of political intrigues that were so much a part of the late republic.

Other Bedford/St. Martin's Resources for Chapter 5

The following resources are available to accompany Chapter 5. Please refer to the Preface of this manual for detailed descriptions of all the ancillaries.

For Instructors

Transparencies

The following maps and image from Chapter 5 are available as full-color acetates.

- Map 5.1: Ancient Italy, 500 B.C.E.
- Map 5.2: The City of Rome during the Republic
- Map 5.3: Roman Expansion, 500–44 B.C.E.
- Mapping the West: The Roman World at the End of the Republic, 44 B.C.E.

- Wolf Suckling Romulus and Remus, p. 132
- Aqueduct at Nîmes in France, p. 146

Instructor's Resources CD-ROM

The following maps and image from Chapter 5, as well as a chapter outline, are available on disc in both PowerPoint and jpeg formats.

- Map 5.1: Ancient Italy, 500 B.C.E.
- Map 5.2: The City of Rome during the Republic
- Map 5.3: Roman Expansion, 500–44 B.C.E.
- Mapping the West: The Roman World at the End of the Republic, 44 B.C.E.
- Aqueduct at Nîmes in France, p. 146

Using the Bedford Series with The Making of the West

Available in print as well as online at **bedfordstmartins.com/oconnor,** this guide by Maura O'Connor, University of Cincinnati, offers practical suggestions for using *Spartacus and the Slave Wars* by Brent D. Shaw, in conjunction with chapters 5 and 6 of the textbook.

For Students

Study Guides

The Online Study Guide at **bedfordstmartins.com/hunt** helps students synthesize the material they have learned as well as practice the skills historians use to make sense of the past. The following Map, Visual, and Document activities are available for Chapter 5.

Map Activity

- Map 5.3: Roman Expansion, 500–44 B.C.E.

Visual Activity

- Aqueduct at Nîmes in France, p. 146

Reading Historical Documents

- The Rape and Suicide of Lucretia, p. 144
- Polybius on Roman Military Discipline, p. 154
- Contrasting Views: What Was Julius Caesar Like? pp. 156–57

CHAPTER

6

The Roman Empire

44 B.C.E.– 284 C.E.

CHAPTER RESOURCES

Main Chapter Topics

1. In 27 B.C.E., Octavian announced the restoration of the republic, but, with the Senate's cooperation, established himself as sole ruler of the principate. Titled "Augustus" and "princeps," he retained the Senate, consuls, courts, and other republican trappings to make his monarchy palatable to the Roman people.

2. Rome grew into the western world's most populous city where most inhabitants lived in crowded and dirty dwellings; new official forces and policies were designed to maintain order; and emperors provided expansive public amenities.

3. Imperial power depended on the loyalty of the army. Further, military operations continued to drive the economy. For a time, foreign conquests provided new revenue and slaves, but also required heavy expenditures. As time went on, defensive requirements increasingly strained the Roman economy.

4. Roman culture altered under imperial rule, reaching its literary peak in the first two centuries C.E. Lavish and violent spectacles such as gladiatorial combats were the focus of popular culture.

5. The first two centuries of the empire were relatively stable, with few major military conflicts and a strong economy. Increasingly, however, enemies and subjects on the imperial periphery exploited Roman weaknesses.

6. In the easternmost portion of the Roman Empire, political pressures and cultural and religious disputes among Jews moved them toward rebellion at the same time that Jesus of Nazareth's teachings produced Christianity. The new religion spread westward and its followers suffered persecution, yet were still able to build institutional structures that coped with questions of doctrine and conduct.

7. In the third century C.E., economic instability, attacks from abroad, and natural disasters brought the empire to a crisis that would only resolve itself with yet another profound political and religious transformation.

Focus Question

How did Augustus's "restored republic" successfully keep the Pax Romana for more than two centuries, and why did it fail in the third century?

1. Augustus achieved a remarkable degree of stability and prosperity in the Roman world. He was enormously successful in "inventing tradition" to justify as the restoration of the republic what was essentially a new, imperial, and monarchical form of government. He retained institutions such as the Senate, the consuls, and the courts, and he made his authority palatable by taking the title *princeps*, or first man among equals. Augustus also created a direct relationship between himself and ordinary people, extending to politics a paternalistic patron–client system in which he took personal responsibility for the well-being of non-elites, for example, by providing grain to poor urban inhabitants. In addition, the Augustan principate derived strength and legitimacy from its systems of law and citizenship, which were applied equitably, if not equally, throughout the empire. These policies encouraged local elites in the provinces to accommodate with Roman rule and facilitated the process of Romanization, particularly as the Romans showed tolerance for other cultural traditions, such as those of the Greeks in the former Hellenistic provinces to the east. These Roman practices, along with the empire's considerable size, fostered peace and a flourishing economy.

2. Roman institutions such as the law and the army were strong and flexible, yet much depended on

the man who was princep. As the historian Tacitus observed, emperors resembled the weather, and people had "to wait for bad ones to pass and hope for good ones to appear." Although the empire successfully endured a number of "bad" leaders early on, such as Caligula and Nero, by the third century structural problems within the empire, such as inflation and the difficulty of defending a vast frontier, made the perils of weak leadership more disastrous. The lack of a clearly institutionalized method of succession exacerbated this problem, as succession was not strictly dynastic, and the praetorian guard played a decisive role in choosing the next emperor. This "militarization" of the succession process was decidedly "unrepublican" and served to strengthen the power of brute force over that of rule of law.

3. In some ways, the qualities that fueled the Pax Romana led to its ultimate collapse in the third century. The context for the patron–client relationship between princeps and their followers, the role of the army, the empire's borders, and new religious beliefs, such as Christianity, all changed over time. As imperial conquest and expansion were replaced by the goal of maintaining existing frontiers, the military became increasingly expensive and difficult to fund. This resulted in growing financial pressures, including rampant inflation, by the time of the Severan emperors. Leaders also faced growing demands from their client soldiers and hungry urban populations dependent upon subsidized grain. At the same time, Christianity spread across the empire and seemed to pose an increasing threat to traditional Roman values of order, stability, and tradition. By the end of the third century, the republican-like features of Augustus's princeps had been eclipsed by the imperatives of an empire under pressure.

Annotated Chapter Outline

I. Creating the Pax Romana

A. From Republic to Principate, 44–27 B.C.E., p. 165

1. After the assassination of Caesar, Octavian, Antony, and a third general named Lepidus formed the Second Triumvirate to eliminate Caesar's assassins and their supporters using proscription.
2. Eventually, however, Antony and Octavian forced Lepidus into retirement and then turned on each other.
3. Rallying the support of Caesar's troops with promises of a share in the dead general's wealth, Octavian marched on Rome and forced the Senate to declare him consul.
4. To marshal support, Octavian skillfully used the Romans' fear of foreigners by claiming that Antony planned to make his lover, the Egyptian queen Cleopatra VII, their ruler.
5. At the naval battle of Actium in 31 B.C.E. Octavian defeated Antony and Cleopatra's forces; Antony and Cleopatra fled to Egypt, where they committed suicide together rather than be taken captive.

B. Augustus's "Restoration of the Republic," 27 B.C.E–14 C.E., pp. 165–167

1. After his victory, Octavian distributed land to his army veterans and established Roman colonies in the provinces, declaring the republic restored in 27 B.C.E.
2. Recognizing Octavian's power, the Senate granted him extraordinary powers and the honorary title *Augustus*, meaning "divinely favored."
3. Augustus shrewdly brought peace to Rome by maintaining a façade of republican continuity.
4. His new system of government was called the *principate* after the time-honored title Augustus took for himself, *princeps*, meaning "first man."
5. Augustus left republican institutions intact: the Senate met, the assemblies gathered, consuls and tribunes were elected, and Augustus himself lived and dressed like a republican citizen of old.
6. In actuality, Augustus possessed sole authority by controlling the army and treasury.
7. He turned the army into a professional force, increased its loyalty to him, and stationed permanent troops, the praetorian guard, in Rome for the first time.
8. Augustus cultivated his image as a stern but caring "father of his country" in slogans and images on coins and with splendid building projects that honored his victory and the new era of peace.
9. The huge Forum of Augustus, which contained sculptures of Roman heroes and provided public space for religious rituals and ceremonies, was dedicated in 2 B.C.E.
10. The profound changes brought about by his reign and his ability to promote himself worked within the boundaries of Roman traditions, bringing stability and order to Rome.

C. Augustan Rome, pp. 167–172

1. Life in Rome under Augustus's rule, as in all ancient cities, was marked by overcrowding, poor sanitation, and dangerous conditions.
2. Most urban residents lived in cramped apartment houses called "islands" that were poorly built and often in danger of collapse.
3. Public sanitation was a major problem because no system for the sanitary disposal of waste existed.
4. Everyone used the public baths to stay clean, but this custom also facilitated the spread of communicable diseases.
5. Augustus addressed some problems by creating a public fire department and police force.
6. As Rome's foremost patron, he also used his own fortune to pay for imported grain to feed thousands of poor citizens.
7. Because some members of the upper classes spent more money on luxuries and careers than on raising families, Augustus passed laws encouraging large families.
8. Nonetheless, over the coming centuries, many of the old elite families died out.
9. Roman slaves worked in a variety of conditions, ranging from grim work in the fields or mines to household work in the homes of the wealthy.
10. Slaves could sometimes earn their own money and purchase their freedom or even their own slaves.
11. Because Rome granted citizenship to freed slaves, some could hope to increase their fortune and move up the social scale.
12. Public entertainment, headed by violent gladiatorial shows where men (and sometimes women) put on extravagant displays of violent hand-to-hand combat, became extremely popular during the principate.
13. These productions became a way for emperors to display their wealth and power; onlookers could also take advantage of the gatherings to voice their wishes to the emperor in attendance.

D. Imperial Education, Literature, and Art, pp. 172–174

1. During Augustus's rule, education continued in its traditional forms, but oratory, literature, and sculpture were now used for legitimizing and supporting the new principate.
2. Oratory, the art of public speaking, was a skill still limited to the wealthy and ceased to be important for open debates or criticism of policy decisions; instead, it was used to argue legal cases and to lavish praise on the emperor.
3. Because Latin literature flourished during the reign of Augustus, modern critics have identified the era as a "golden age."
4. During this period Virgil wrote his epic poem *The Aeneid*, which celebrates Augustus while gently offering a critique about the price paid in freedom for such success.
5. The poet Ovid (43 B.C.E–17 C.E.), whose *Art of Love* and *Love Affairs* mocked the emperor's moral legislation, was tolerated by Augustus; but in 8 B.C.E., when Ovid became embroiled in a scandal with Augustus's daughter, the emperor banished him from Rome.
6. Sculpture, too, reflected the emperor's deliberate presentation of himself as serene and dignified, and was closer to the idealized style of the Classical period than to the realistic Hellenistic style of portraits popular during the republic.

II. Maintaining the Pax Romana

A. Making Monarchy Permanent, 14–180 C.E., pp. 174–176

1. To avoid a struggle over power when he died, Augustus established a pattern for succession by choosing and training an heir with the Senate's blessing.
2. Lacking a son of his own, Augustus adopted the general Tiberius (42 B.C.E.–37 C.E.) who possessed the respect and support of the army.
3. Like Augustus, Tiberius (r. 14–37 C.E.) maintained the façade of republican government during his rule.
4. His last years, however, were spent away from Rome, opening the door for abuses by subordinates; he also failed to prepare a suitable heir.
5. As his successor, Tiberius chose Augustus's great-grandson Gaius (r. 37–41 C.E.), also known as Caligula.
6. Cruel and violent, Caligula overspent the treasury on personal whims and often engaged in outrageous behavior.
7. His abuses led to his assassination in 41 C.E.

8. With the support of the praetorian guard, Claudius (r. 41–54 C.E.) became the next appointed emperor.
9. Claudius established important precedents by enrolling men from the provinces in the Senate and employing freed slaves as administrators—his actions helped to keep the peace in Rome's far-flung territories and guaranteed loyalty within the government.
10. Nero (r. 54–68 C.E.), Claudius's sixteen-year-old successor, spent outrageous sums on extravagant public festivals and building projects.
11. In 69 C.E., rebellious commanders overthrew his regime, and Nero committed suicide.
12. This year became known as the "Year of the Four Emperors," a year of civil war eventually won by Vespasian (r. 69–79 C.E.).
13. By forcing the Senate to recognize his authority and encouraging emperor worship in the provinces, Vespasian established his family, the Flavians, as the new dynasty.
14. His successors, Titus (r. 79–81 C.E.) and Domitian (r. 81–96 C.E.), further restored imperial prestige and engaged in campaigns on the frontiers.
15. Titus captured Jerusalem in 70 C.E. and finished Rome's Coliseum, a state-of-the-art amphitheater for public entertainments.
16. Domitian balanced the budget and led the army north against the growing threat from aggressive tribes, but his arrogance bred resentment in the Senate, leading to his murder in 96 C.E.
17. Fortunately for Rome, the next five emperors—Nerva (r. 96–98 C.E.), Trajan (r. 98–117 C.E.), Hadrian (r. 117–138 C.E.), Antoninus Pius (r. 138–161 C.E.), and Marcus Aurelius (r. 161–180 C.E.)—succeeded each other peacefully, and though often engaged in wars in the provinces, these five "good emperors" reigned for nearly one hundred years without civil war.

B. Life in the Roman Golden Age, 96–180 C.E., pp. 176–181

1. During the prosperous Golden Age of the five good emperors, Rome's theoretical military goal remained expansion, but military activity focused on defense and maintaining order.
2. Roman legions stationed in the provinces maintained peace, which allowed long-distance trade to operate smoothly.
3. Noncitizens who served in the army picked up many Roman customs and earned citizenship upon discharge.
4. Because maintenance of the army and its loyalty depended on providing regular pay and bonuses to the soldiers, the lack of new conquests posed a revenue problem.
5. Most provincial taxes were spent in the provinces.
6. Senatorial and equestrian governors with small staffs ran the provinces, which eventually numbered about forty.
7. Taxes on agricultural land in the provinces provided most of the funds for government and army operations.
8. If there was a shortfall in taxes, these officials had to make up the difference from their own pockets.
9. Life in the provinces comprised widely diverse languages, customs, and religions.
10. Roman rulers largely tolerated these differences as long as peace and social order were maintained.
11. New communities grew up around the settlements of army veterans, which spread Roman laws, customs, and the Latin language across Western Europe.
12. In the East, where Greek and Near Eastern cultures had flourished for thousands of years, Romanization had less of an impact, but the Roman system of government was widely accepted.
13. The continued vitality of Greek culture and language contributed to a flourishing of literature, including works by Lucian (117–180), who composed satirical dialogues, and Plutarch (50–120), who wrote *Parallel Lives*, biographies of Greek and Roman men.
14. Tacitus (56–120) composed his *Annals* as a biting narrative of the Julio-Claudians, while the poet Juvenal (c. 65–130) skewered pretentious Romans and grasping provincials.
15. Apuleius (125–170) entertained readers with his lusty novel *The Golden Ass*.
16. Roman society remained strictly hierarchical and made legal distinctions between the orders: those outside the small circle of "better people" were

subject to harsher penalties than elites for the same crimes.

17. A healthy population was a concern; medical practices of the time could do little to promote healthy births and reduce infant mortality.
18. Childbearing became an important social duty to the Romans, so both public and private sources worked to encourage childbearing and to support or even adopt orphaned children.

III. The Emergence of Christianity

A. Jesus and His Teachings, pp. 181–182

1. Discontented with foreign rule, many Jews of the time adopted apocalyptic ideas, believing that a Messiah would come to Earth and reward the righteous while punishing the wicked.
2. Originating as a sect within Judaism based on the teachings of Jesus of Nazareth, Christianity grew into a new religion whose followers proclaimed Jesus as the Messiah.
3. The teachings of Jesus, written down by others in what would become the New Testament Gospels, stressed God's love for humanity and the need for humans to love one another, and taught that God's kingdom in heaven was open to all believers regardless of social status or apparent sinfulness.
4. The Roman governor saw the public ministry of Jesus as a threat to peace and had him crucified in Jerusalem in 30. His followers continued to spread his teachings.
5. Paul of Tarsus, a former persecutor of Christians, converted after a vision and helped establish Christianity as separate from Judaism by allowing converts to dispense with Jewish rites and dietary laws.
6. Paul traveled throughout the Mediterranean world, preaching the divinity of Jesus and salvation through faith. Paul stressed ethical behavior, sexual morality, and rejection of polytheism (the worship of more than one god).
7. Although Paul believed that only men should teach the new religion, early Christians were less patriarchal: for example, a businesswoman named Lydia founded the congregation in Philippi in Greece.
8. Jesus's disciples gravitated to towns and cities to preach and they established many small urban congregations.
9. In 66, a disastrous Jewish revolt was crushed by the future emperor Titus, who destroyed the Jerusalem temple and sold most of the city's population into slavery.
10. The loss of the Jewish ritual center deepened the divide between Judaism and Christianity.

B. Growth of a New Religion, pp. 182–185

1. Christianity faced several obstacles—most notably ignorance of and disdain for their "superstition," and opposition from Roman officials, who viewed Christians' refusal to participate in the imperial cult as disloyal, even treasonous.
2. Most Romans felt that tolerating this new faith would offend the gods, and so Christians became targets to blame for public disasters, such as the fire in Rome during Nero's reign in 64.
3. They were sometimes punished so cruelly that some Romans became sympathetic to them.
4. The heroism of martyrs who died for their beliefs inspired believers to persevere, and Tertullian called their blood "the seed of the Church."
5. Christians had to resolve differences in beliefs and create an organization to settle questions about how they should live.
6. The appointment of bishops to direct conduct and to differentiate between true belief (orthodoxy) and false belief (heresy) aroused some controversy, but it was the early church's most important institutional development.
7. Bishops were held to be part of an apostolic succession; that is, Jesus's apostles appointed successors who received from them the powers they had been granted by Jesus, and the line of succession led down to the bishops.
8. Women in the church were shut out of the leadership.
9. By choosing lives of celibacy, however, some women rejected the traditional roles of wives and mothers and achieved a measure of independence and authority.

C. Competing Beliefs, pp. 185–188

1. Christianity shared beliefs with polytheistic cults and philosophies that provided comfort and guidance to people trying to survive the harshness of ancient life.
2. Polytheism, sometimes called paganism, never constituted a unified religion and permitted people to worship and seek

the favor of many divinities rather than just one.

3. The popular cult of the Egyptian goddess Isis offered a personal religious experience that demanded a moral way of life.
4. Images of Isis often appeared in art as a mother nursing her son, and her followers believed Isis promised them the chance for life after death.
5. The mystery cult of Mithras also enjoyed great popularity throughout the empire, although little information about it has survived to this day.
6. Stoic philosophy guided the lives of many Romans; stoics believed in a life of self-discipline and duty.
7. Plotinus's (205–270) philosophy of Neoplatonism, so named because it developed out of Plato's philosophy, influenced many Christians; it promoted the rejection of physical life in order to focus on spiritual purity and union with God.

IV. The Third-Century Crisis

A. Defending the Frontiers, pp.188–190

1. Emperors had fended off invaders since the first century, but these invaders' experience fighting Roman armies made them increasingly dangerous.
2. In addition, a resurgent Persian threat under the Sassanid kings forced the emperors to move troops to the east at the expense of defending the north.
3. Emperors hired skilled Germanic warriors as auxiliary soldiers for the Roman army and settled them on the edges of the empire as buffers against other invaders.
4. The huge amount of supplies needed to maintain an army engaged in constant fighting on the frontiers seriously strained the imperial treasury, and as successful conquests dwindled, the army that had once enriched Rome became the empire's chief expense.
5. In addition, inflation had driven up prices and was exacerbated when some emperors devalued coinage by putting less silver in each coin, a vain attempt to cut costs that set the stage for the full financial collapse of the empire.

B. The Severan Emperors and Catastrophe, pp. 190–191

1. The reign of Septimius Severus (r. 193–211) fatally drained the treasury, while his sons' murderous rivalry and reckless spending destroyed the government's stability.
2. Because inflation had devalued the soldiers' wages, Severus spent large sums of money to improve their conditions, which further increased inflation.
3. Severus's son Caracalla (r. 211–217), who came to the throne after he murdered his brother, also increased the soldiers' pay and funded lavish building projects, putting enormous pressure on provincial officials to collect the necessary taxes.
4. Caracalla tried to expand the tax base by granting Roman citizenship to every free person in imperial territory, but this policy failed to solve the budget crisis.
5. His death opened a half-century of civil war that, compounded by natural disasters, fragmented the principate.
6. Near anarchy ensued as leaders of client armies struggled with one another to become emperor, and the dire economic situation took a tremendous toll on the population, which began to decline.
7. Foreign enemies benefited from the chaos as the frontier areas became vulnerable to raids, and bands of robbers became common in the border regions.
8. Rome's lowest point came in 260 when the Persian king Shapur I defeated and captured the Roman emperor Valerian (r. 253–260).
9. To polytheists, the troubles seemed to be connected to the presence of the Christians, who became the victims of organized and violent persecutions.
10. These persecutions failed to stop the crisis, however, and a new form of authoritarian leadership emerged to restore the fragmented principate.

Lecture Strategies

1. The Augustan era, in which Rome's political sphere was transformed definitively from republic to empire, provides an interesting study in the methods used to placate a public and consolidate and win support for a new political order. For example, Augustus was a shrewd propagandist and solidified his power in many cases by referring to the restoration of the republic while in fact strengthening his own position as sole ruler. Ask students to identify the different forms this propaganda assumed in the Augustan era. Why was it so important that Augustus shape the transformation in this way? After so many years of

one-man or three-man rule in the late republic, why was it still necessary for Augustus to advertise his power in terms of old republican values? How did this propaganda coincide with other major innovations of the period, such as the inheritance tax or the development of a police force? In what ways were social allegiances realigned throughout this process? See Paul Veyne, *Bread and Circuses: Historical Sociology and Political Pluralism*, Brian Pearce, trans. (New York: Penguin, 1990). For a broader look at imperial propaganda, see Chapter 30 of Sir Ronald Syme, *The Augustan Aristocracy* (Oxford: Clarendon, 1986).

2. An examination of urban life in the early empire, particularly in Rome, can introduce students to the everyday lives of ordinary Romans. A discussion of Roman urban life could include an examination of the layout and structure of apartment dwellings; the local economy, employment, and consumer markets; the cultural aspects of cosmopolitan living; the functions of the public baths and other public amenities; and the measures used to remedy the growing problems of the tightly concentrated population, such as subsidized food, the development of a police force, and building specifications. What types of inequalities were present in urban living, and in what ways were the social welfare measures implemented to deal with them? In which ways was the city stratified? An excellent source is Dave Favro, *The Urban Image of Augustan Rome* (Cambridge, UK: Cambridge University Press, 1996).

3. A prerequisite to power throughout the first few centuries of the Roman Empire was the emperor's tight relationship with the military. When the loyalty and confidence of the army waned, an emperor found himself in a weakened position and was frequently killed. With tight control of the military, however, an emperor's position was relatively secure. In what ways does this feature of Roman imperial politics denote a sort of continuity from the late republic? Which factors influenced the prominence of the army? What effect did its prominence have on Roman society? What does this tell us about the underlying nature of Roman politics? See J. B. Campbell, *The Emperor and the Roman Army: 31 B.C.E.–235 C.E.* (Oxford: Clarendon, 1984); and Ramsay MacMullen, *Corruption and the Decline of Rome* (New Haven, CT: Yale University Press, 1998).

4. Even though Christianity's message resonated with a great number of people throughout this tumultuous period, first among Jews in the east and then gradually among Gentiles in the west, this dissemination was also greatly aided by its position within the Roman Empire. For instance, the communication and travel infrastructure of Rome facilitated the spread of this new religion. What effects did this feature have on the Christian message, as related by the Gospels and the teachings of Paul of Tarsus? What factors shaped the various audiences' receptivity? How did the new religion's coming of age within Rome affect its early development? For instance, the development of Christian institutions, such as the hierarchical organization of bishops to decide orthodoxy, could be seen as a reflection of the Roman political and social structure. You can also relate these developments to the overall climate of the period as it affected Christians, leading to their persecution. See Harry Y. Gamble, *Books and Readers in the Early Christian Church* (New Haven, CT: Yale University Press, 1995); and Ramsay MacMullen, *Christianizing the Roman Empire, A.D. 100–400* (New Haven, CT: Yale University Press, 1994).

Class Discussion Starters

1. Discuss family life in the Roman Empire. In what ways did it represent continuity with republican norms? In what ways did family life change under the empire? In particular, you could examine Augustus's legislation on marriage, adultery, and sexuality. Which social, political, and economic conditions necessitated these legal changes? For example, you could examine the structure of the economy and how it related to the demand for increased population, the perceived importance of extending the lineage, particularly of upper-class families, and how the transmission of familial property related to the laws against adultery. Which moral issues were involved in the decision to enact this legislation? What were its effects? How did these changes affect women? Several good sources for these issues include Jane F. Gardner, *Family and Familia in Roman Law and Life* (Oxford: Oxford University Press, 1998); Beryl Rawson, ed., *The Family in Ancient Rome: New Perspectives* (Ithaca, NY: Cornell University Press, 1986); and Chapter 11 of Elaine Fantham, et al., *Women in the Classical World: Image and Text* (Oxford: Oxford University Press, 1994).

2. Roman culture during this period was marked by extreme violence, particularly in its popular entertainment, such as the gladiatorial contests. Discuss the social, political, and cultural functions of this sanctioned violence. What purposes did it serve? Why were the emperors so supportive of it? Because Roman emperors could exhibit their greatness and generosity through these circuses, what can we determine about the culture of violence that surrounded imperial Rome? Also, discuss the social interchange at these events that presented the opportunity for a degree of communication between the populace and its rulers. Could these events be viewed in part as an outlet for the pervasive violent currents that had wrought so much havoc in the late republic? What do these factors

tell us about the cultural and political climate of the period? Two excellent books on gladiators and the games are Roland Auguet, *Cruelty and Civilization: The Roman Games* (New York and London: Routledge, 1994); and Carlin Barton, *The Sorrows of Ancient Romans* (Princeton: Princeton University Press, 1993). See also Chapter 4, section 9, of Paul Veyne, *Bread and Circuses*, cited in "Lecture Strategies" number 1. Clips from films such as *Ben Hur* (1959), *Spartacus* (1960), and *Gladiator* (2000) could be used to illustrate the gladiatorial games.

3. Roman art in the imperial period connotes an interesting shift in substance and form. With tighter control at the very top of the social hierarchy, the reflection of imperial values through art became more necessary in order to project the proper image of imperial power. In sculpture, for example, rugged realism gave way to glorified idealism. Students may be interested in the ways that the demands of politics influenced artistic expression. This idea can be related to the vigorous promotion—both in Rome and in the provinces—of the worship of the emperor as a living deity. Have the class discuss the ways in which imperial values were brought to bear in art. See J. Lendon, *Empire of Honour* (Oxford: Clarendon, 1997). In addition, see the images online of Augustan-era art and architecture at Augustus: Images of Power, maintained by the Classics Department of the University of Virginia.

4. The development of Roman law is important not only for its central place in Roman social life, but also for its effect on subsequent western legal systems. In particular, the notion of intent as the decisive factor in settling disputes, rather than the "mere" facts, represents a profound alteration in legal concepts of guilt and justice. What effect did this new idea have on the development of the legal system? For example, how did the work of legal practitioners and their place in society change? What advantages and disadvantages did this focus on intent have on ordinary citizens? For a brief overview of this period of Roman legal development, see Chapter 2 of Peter Stein, *Roman Law in European History* (Cambridge, UK: Cambridge University Press, 1999); and Olga Tellegen-Couperus, *A Short History of Roman Law* (New York: Routledge, 1993).

5. The development of Christianity was one of the most influential landmarks of Western history. A discussion of the conditions that gave rise to this new force can therefore provide valuable insights into the social, cultural, and political climate of the post-classical world. What conditions helped spur the development of this new religion? How did Jesus's message fit into the context of the contemporary struggle between Jews and Romans? In what ways are the Jewish traditions from which Jesus's teaching had sprung related to its subsequent development in Christianity? See Martin Goodman, ed., *Jews in a Graeco-Roman World* (Oxford: Clarendon, 1998); and Robert Louis Wilken, *The Christians as the Romans Saw Them* (New Haven, CT: Yale University Press, 1984).

Reviewing the Text

Review Questions

1. How did the peace gained through Augustus's "restoration of the republic" affect Romans' lives?
[model answer] *Augustus's peace ended civil conflict in Roman society, but government reforms limited freedom of expression. Political discussions, literature, art, and public entertainments were heavily censored to contain only expressions that legitimized the new political system. The changes brought stability and economic prosperity to society although Rome and other cities became very densely populated and experienced the associated issues of poverty and poor sanitation. Augustus's new systems for public safety and welfare also contributed to the increase of stability in society.*

2. In the early Roman empire, what was life like in the cities and in the country for the elite and for ordinary people?
[model answer] *The cities offered luxury and entertainment for the wealthy. The elite benefited from better access to good housing, food, and fresh water, which they shared with the poor; however, they also suffered from the infectious diseases and overcrowded urban environment that the poor were forced to tolerate. Slaves, especially those working in agriculture or manufacturing, lived the most difficult lives among the Romans.*

3. Which factors supported the growth of Christianity, and which opposed it?
[model answer] *Christianity's message of salvation and the bonds of community it fostered encouraged its spread, while the persecution of government and society worked to discourage its growth. Jesus's message that all true believers would enter the kingdom of heaven gave hope to people whose lives were difficult. It gave believers a sense of mission and fostered bonds of community with others who believed. Its growth was further strengthened by the establishment of a hierarchical organization headed by bishops who defined doctrine and encouraged institutional stability. Threats of punishment and death by Roman officials and the ostracism of fellow citizens would have limited the appeal of Christianity.*

4. What were the causes and the effects of the Roman crisis in the third century C.E.?
[model answer] *By the mid-third century inflation, increased costs of supporting the army, the devaluation of the imperial coinage, irresponsible spending, and*

political instability combined to create a financial crisis for the Roman Empire. Inflation and a lack of new imperial conquests had reduced the tax revenues and strained imperial finances. Consequently, the value of soldiers' incomes decreased dramatically, just as the need for fit and loyal troops increased in order to fend off hostile invaders along the borders to the north and east. In order to retain the army's support, the Severan emperors gave them substantial pay raises in addition to the traditional gifts of extra money expected of imperial patrons, despite the pressure this placed on the relatively stagnant economy. Inflation increased further when some emperors tried to cut costs by debasing the imperial coinage, causing merchants to raise prices in order to make up for the loss. Emperor Caracalla tried to fix the budget in 212 C.E. by extending Roman citizenship dramatically to increase inheritance-tax revenues, but his extravagant spending soon wrecked the imperial budget again and paved the way for ruinous inflation in the coming decades. Growing political strife and intermittent civil war also contributed to the growing financial problems of the empire and disturbed the regular patterns of life and trade. The financial system of Rome fully collapsed in the 250s and 260s C.E.

Making Connections

1. What were the similarities and differences between the crisis in the first century B.C.E. that undermined the republic and the crisis in the third century C.E. that undermined the principate?
[model answer] *Although there were serious power struggles among some of the military generals, the Roman republic in the first century B.C.E. was essentially prosperous and strong internally. By the third century C.E., however, Rome was suffering economic instability largely because of overexpenditure by the military, attacks from abroad, and natural disasters. There was also a crisis in leadership as several successive emperors were assassinated.*

2. If you had been a first-century Roman emperor under the principate, what would you have done about the Christians and why? What if you had been a third-century emperor?
[model answer] *Most people today would probably have extended some degree of toleration to the Christians in the first century on the grounds that this might have warded off the religious conflicts that occurred later in the third century. For instance, Christians might have been allowed freedom of worship on the payment of a special tax. Some aspects of Christianity might have been incorporated into traditional Roman religious practices, given the similarities between them. This would have been in keeping with Roman policies in other parts of the empire.*

Discussing the Documents

Questions from Online Study Guide with Model Answers

Augustus, Res Gestae *(My Accomplishments) (p. 168)*

1. How does Augustus legitimize his authority in this document?
[model answer] *Augustus claims that he liberated the people at his own expense from the "tyranny of faction" and that his powers and titles were granted to him by the Senate and other public assemblies. He claims that he remained faithful to the ways of the ancestors (mos majorum) and that he possessed "no more power than the others who were my colleagues in each magistracy." Thus he did not break with any tradition, but was upholding traditional Roman values.*

2. Judging from this document and what you have read in the text, what was Augustus's strategy for maintaining his authority?
[model answer] *Augustus was the absolute ruler of Rome, but he disguised his rule behind the illusion that he was upholding the political traditions of the republic. He emphasized his many honors but claimed that they were granted to him by the traditional institutions of the republic as a reward for his accomplishments. He claims that he did not seek any honors, refusing the dictatorship when it was offered to him, but he says he was doing his duty as a Roman to protect the republic.*

The Scene at a Roman Bath (p. 170)

1. What does this document say about the density of the population of Rome?
[model answer] *Because Seneca says he lived on the second floor of a bath house, this suggests that apartments were difficult to come by and that the population must have been rather dense. On the street he can hear voices of unrelated professions and hobbies: the ballplayer, sausage seller, and armpit plucker, for instance. The passage also suggests that those engaged in service professions such as the masseuse had a steady stream of middle-class clients.*

2. Seneca is not the only person being assaulted in Rome. In your text, what does Seneca's contemporary Juvenal say about second-floor inhabitants? What do these two accounts say about life in Rome?
[model answer] *Being on the ground was probably more dangerous than being on the second floor. Juvenal describes how people walking on the street may be hit by flying debris from second-floor apartments. Augustus tried to impose a height limit of seventy feet on buildings to prevent the structures from collapsing on people*

below. Romans were constantly exposed to the dangers of living in a dense city.

Contrasting Views: Christians in the Empire: Conspirators or Faithful Subjects? (pp. 186–187)

1. Do you think that Pliny's procedure in dealing with the accused Christians respected the Roman legal principle of equity? Explain.
[model answer] *Pliny required the accused to prove their own innocence by worshipping Roman gods. This violated the principle of equity that required an accuser to provide proof of a person's guilt.*

2. How should a society treat a minority of its members whose presence severely disturbs the majority?
[model answer] *A society can punish, expel, or kill individuals and groups who do not conform and are disruptive. Or it can work to develop an understanding of the values and perspectives of the group in question and to negotiate a viable place for its members within society. The possibilities would depend on the nature of the "disturbance" and the ways in which it violated the parameters of society.*

Other Questions for Discussing These Documents in Class

Augustus, Res Gestae *(My Accomplishments) (p. 168)*

1. What examples did Augustus provide to justify his rule?
2. Ask students to consider the kinds of things valued by both Augustus and Roman citizens.
3. In what ways does the *Res Gestae* resemble an obituary?

The Scene at a Roman Bath (p. 170)

1. What insight does Seneca provide into the physical experience of living in a typical Roman city?
2. What types of people does Seneca describe?
3. What is Seneca's attitude toward the people he describes?

Contrasting Views: Christians in the Empire: Conspirators or Faithful Subjects? (pp. 186–187)

1. In Tertullian's Defense of his Fellow Christians, what is the distinction between praying for the safety of the emperors and praying to them?
2. What examples does Tertullian provide of Christians' loyalty to the empire?
3. What tactics did Pliny employ against the Christians in Bithynia?
4. How does the author of the first document justify the refusal of Christians to worship the emperor?
5. How does the author of the first document depict those who oppose Christians?
6. How did Trajan respond to Pliny's inquiry, and what does this exchange say about the Roman persecution of Christians in general?

Comparative Questions

1. Compare and contrast the types of leadership described by Augustus in *Res Gestae* and by Trajan in his reply to Pliny. What were the principal challenges each emperor faced? In what ways were their approaches similar? How did they differ?
2. Tertullian denies that Christians disrupted public order. Can the same be said of the Romans described by Seneca?
3. Is there any common ground between Tertullian on the one hand and Pliny and Trajan on the other? Could the Christians and the Roman officials reach a compromise on the status of Christians in the empire?

For Users of *Sources of The Making of the West*

The following documents are available in Chapter 6 of the companion sourcebook by Katharine J. Lualdi, University of Southern Maine.

1. In Defense of Roman Authority and Order: *Imperial Edicts for the Government of Cyrene* (7 B.C.E.)
2. An Urban Empire: *Notices and Graffiti Describe Life in Pompeii* (First Century C.E.)
3. New Influences to the North: Tacitus, *Germania* (c. 98 C.E.)
4. Persecuting a New Religion: *Interrogation of Christians* (180 C.E.)
5. Revolt in the Colonies: Flavius Josephus, *The Jewish War* (70 C.E.)

Discussion Ideas for Sources of The Making of the West, *Chapter 6*

1. The eruption of Mount Vesuvius that buried Pompeii in ash preserved the city at a single moment in its history and has provided later scholars with a rich source of material about daily life in the Roman Empire. Notices and graffiti that would ordinarily have been lost provide historians with a useful window into the past. Based on these writings, describe Roman politics and society. What role did people play in government? What social groups and occupations

existed? What information is there about men and women and their relations? How do these brief, public jottings compare with Seneca's letter describing *The Scene at a Roman Bath*? Consider both the content of the two readings and the authors' intent.

2. *Germania* by Tacitus is the most important source about Germanic peoples in Roman times. What kinds of information does the text provide? How does Tacitus describe politics and society among the early Germans? What was their government like? Were they urbanized, as the Romans were? What does Tacitus say about men and women and marriage? What were his motivations in writing? How credible is he, writing as an outsider? Although both *Germania* and the graffiti at Pompeii are valuable sources about life in the West during the first century, the texts and the people they describe differ substantially. Discuss some of these differences, including the authorship, purpose, and tone of the writings.

Working with Visual Sources

For this exercise, please refer to Marble Statue of Augustus from Prima Porta on p. 173 and Catacomb Painting of Christ as the Good Shepherd on p. 183 of the textbook or view the images on the book companion site's Online Study Guide under the "Visual Activity" for Chapter 6.

Students viewing the images at the Online Study Guide are asked three questions of the images. The questions and model answers (not made available to students) are below. Project these images, available on the Instructor's Resources CD-ROM, in class or ask students to look at the images in their textbooks and answer the questions.

1. How are the statue and painting similar? What are the significant symbols reflected in each artistic rendition?
[model answer] *Both show an individual man surrounded by symbols that explain his role as leader. Augustus's breastplate is decorated with a battle scene, symbolizing both peace and his military power; his bare feet indicate that he is near-divine, and the Cupid also emphasizes this by signaling his dynasty's succession from the goddess Venus. Jesus carries an injured sheep, representing the human flock he has come to save, and he carries milk and honey, symbolizing the bounty of the Promised Land.*

2. To whom would the statue of Augustus have appealed most, and why? To whom would the painting of Jesus have appealed most, and why?
[model answer] *The statue of Augustus would have appealed to those respectful of his military might and grateful for the peace, both internal and external, that he had fostered, especially because there had been civil turmoil before his establishment of the principate. The painting of Jesus would have appealed to those seeking spiritual guidance and the promise of life after death. A deity possessing the compassion of a shepherd caring for his flock and the keys to the heavenly kingdom could have attracted the admiration and fidelity of disillusioned Roman citizens.*

3. As suggested by the statue and the painting, to what extent did Christian values clash with Roman values, and to what extent did they correspond?
[model answer] *Both the statue and the painting reflect a desire to follow and believe in a strong man capable of improving society and the lot of individual lives. However, whereas Augustus was depicted as a towering conqueror, Jesus was depicted as a gentle caregiver.*

Mapping Exercises

Map Activity from OSG—Model Answers for Map Activity #2

For this activity, please refer to the map on p. 192. Students are asked these questions:

From which directions did raids on the Roman Empire come during the late third century C.E.?
[model answer] *Raids came primarily from the northern frontier and along the southern coast of the Black Sea. However, a few raids came from the southern edges of the empire in North Africa and Egypt and from the Sasanid Empire to the east.*

What commodities did these raids threaten?
[model answer] *The northern part of the empire supplied wine and some slaves, while the southern part of the empire supplied grain, olive oil, and slaves.*

Map 6.1: The Expansion of the Roman Empire, 30 B.C.E.–117 C.E., p. 176

Augustus's conquest of Egypt and the subsequent conquest of Mesopotamia gave Rome ample breathing room around the entire Mediterranean Sea. This period represented the height of Rome's territorial dominion. How did the Mediterranean Sea facilitate Rome's expansion? What kept Rome from spreading beyond the regions shown?

Map 6.2: Natural Features and Languages of the Roman World, p. 178

What were the two principal languages of the Roman world? Which language was more important in the administration of law? Which areas of the empire were associated with the production of particular crops? Which parts of the empire were the most urbanized?

Map 6.3: Christian Populations in the Late Third Century C.E., p. 184

Have students identify and consider the varying geographic proliferation of Christian peoples in the Roman Empire. Which factors may have contributed to these variations? Why might the new religion have become popular in some areas and not in others?

Mapping the West: The Roman Empire in Crisis, 284 C.E., p. 192

Where was the Roman Empire under attack from outsiders? Was there a relationship between established trade routes and the routes taken by outside raiders? Can you determine from the map the relative importance of sea routes as opposed to land routes?

In-Class Assignments and Presentation Topics

1. Have students read Augustus's *Res Gestae* and write an essay comparing Augustus's reign as it is portrayed by Augustus himself with the assessment that students can surmise by a close reading of the text. The point of this exercise is to get students to develop skills in analyzing primary sources critically and identify biases and euphemisms.

2. The legal institution of the orders is an important event in the development of the Roman legal system. Have students write briefly on the effects this policy had on the social hierarchy. Of particular interest are the clues the policy provides regarding Roman notions of justice. What does this development reveal about expectations of behavior and the value of individuals in Roman society?

3. Have students give a class presentation discussing the extent to which the Roman economy was dependent on the military. In particular, ask them to analyze the effects of relying on military conquest as a basis for revenue. How did this reliance place stress on public expenditures? What constraints did a heavily militarized system place on the society? More broadly, how might this economic foundation of conquest and slavery have affected the culture at large?

4. Ask students to compare and contrast the two major philosophical systems that emerged in this period: Stoicism and Neoplatonism. In which Roman and Greek traditions were these philosophies steeped? What were their similarities and differences? In what ways did they influence Christian theology and philosophy? See Martin L. Clarke, *The Roman Mind: Studies in the History of Thought from Cicero to Marcus Aurelius* (New York: W. W. Norton, 1968).

5. Have students watch a film dealing with the Roman Empire, perhaps *Ben Hur* (1959), *Gladiator* (2000), or parts of (or all of) *I, Claudius* (1976). Students should consider issues of historical accuracy in their essay: Are the characters, both real and imaginary, appropriately drawn? Has the filmmaker gotten the plot, whether historically or fictionally based, correct? What about the setting? Students should also consider the larger question of whether such films should be historically accurate. This essay assignment could be the basis of an online and/or in-class discussion.

Essay Questions

1. Compare and contrast the character studies made by Tacitus (55–117 C.E.) in *The Annals* and by Suetonius (69–140 C.E.) in *The Lives of the Caesars, of Tiberius, Claudius, and Nero*. How similar is their approach? Do they have any bias? What is Suetonius's approach to the other emperors?

2. An examination of the changing face of Roman literature during the imperial period can provide a useful glimpse into the relationship between politics and culture. Have students research and write on the substantive and formal changes in literature in Roman imperial society. Students can also incorporate the effects of literacy patterns on literature. A useful source on imperial-era literature is John Wight Duff, *Literary History of Rome from the Origins to the Close of the Golden Age* (London: Ernest Benn, 1953). On the effects of literacy patterns, see Chapter 7 of William V. Harris, *Ancient Literacy* (Cambridge, MA: Harvard University Press, 1989).

3. Pagan Roman and Christian belief systems differed markedly in their conceptions of the status of women and of female virtue. Have students report on the contrasting views of women's autonomy and sexuality. Of particular interest is the relationship between sex and freedom for both systems. In each system, how did sex relate to the control of women and toward what specific ends? Which assumptions about gender and sex were shared by both systems? What do these ideas tell us about the underlying social structures of the period? Two invaluable sources are Aline Rousselle, *Porneia: On Desire and the Body in Antiquity* (Cambridge, MA: Blackwell, 1983); and Peter Brown, *The Body and Society: Men, Women, and Sexual Renunciation in Early Christianity* (New York: Columbia University Press, 1988).

Additional Resources: Literature

Arrowsmith, William, trans., *Petronius: The Satyricon.* 1990.
Graves, Robert, trans., *Suetonius: The Twelve Caesars.* 2003.
Green, Peter, trans., *Ovid:. The Erotic Poems The Amores, The Art of Love, Cures for Love, On Facial Treatment for Ladies.* 1983.
Hays, Gregory, trans., *Marcus Aurelius: Meditations.* 2003.
Mandelbaum, Allen, trans., *The Aeneid of Virgil.* 1981.
Martin, Charles, trans., *Ovid: Metamorphoses.* 2003.
Radice, Betty, trans., *The Letters of the Younger Pliny.* 1976.
Wellesley, Kenneth, trans., *Tacitus: The Histories.* 1972.

Additional Resources: Film and Video

Quo Vadis? (1951) (VHS, 171 min.). The conflicts between the Roman Empire and the new religion of Christianity are played out between a slave girl and a Roman officer during the reign of Nero.

Ben Hur (1959) (VHS/DVD, 212 min.). This dramatization of Civil War General Lew Wallace's 1880 novel about the struggles faced by a Jewish aristocrat in the Roman Empire in the first century is the best of the three adaptations that were made. Although the plot is fictional, the period has been fairly accurately recreated. The film is most famous for the magnificent chariot race scene.

Fall of the Roman Empire (1964) (VHS/DVD, 153 min.). Although based on Edward Gibbon's monumental history of Rome, the film focuses mainly on the period surrounding the death of Emperor Marcus Aurelius and the succession of his unbalanced son, Marcus Aurelius Commodus Antoninus.

I, Claudius (1975) (VHS/DVD, 740 min.). Robert Graves's novel has been dramatized in thirteen episodes of about fifty-five minutes each. It is an excellent and lucid account of the Roman emperors of the first century, beginning with Augustus and ending with Claudius.

Jesus of Nazareth (1977) (VHS/DVD, 382 min.). This film is Franco Zeffirelli's lavish miniseries about the life and death of Jesus.

Gladiator (2000) (VHS/DVD, 155 min.). Set in the second century, a Roman general is falsely accused of treason and made a slave. Trained to be a gladiator, he waits for an opportunity to avenge himself on the emperor. This film is good at recreating life, especially the gladiatorial games, during the Roman Empire.

Empires: Peter and Paul (2003) (DVD, 194 min.). This PBS documentary focuses on Peter and Paul and their influence on the early years of Christianity.

Other Bedford/St. Martin's Resources for Chapter 6

The following resources are available to accompany Chapter 6. Please refer to the Preface of this manual for detailed descriptions of all the ancillaries.

For Instructors

Transparencies

The following maps and images from Chapter 6 are available as full-color acetates.

- Map 6.1: The Expansion of the Roman Empire, 30 B.C.E.–117 C.E.
- Map 6.2: Natural Features and Languages of the Roman World
- Map 6.3: Christian Populations in the Late Third Century C.E.
- Mapping the West: The Roman Empire in Crisis, 284 C.E.
- Literacy and Social Status, p. 172
- Marble Statue of Augustus from Prima Porta, p. 173

Instructor's Resources CD-ROM

The following maps and image from Chapter 6, as well as a chapter outline, are available on disc in both PowerPoint and jpeg formats.

- Map 6.1: The Expansion of the Roman Empire, 30 B.C.E.–117 C.E.
- Map 6.2: Natural Features and Languages of the Roman World
- Map 6.3: Christian Populations in the Late Third Century C.E.
- Mapping the West: The Roman Empire in Crisis, 284 C.E.
- Marble Statue of Augustus from Prima Porta, p. 173

Using the Bedford Series with The Making of the West

Available in print as well as online at **bedfordstmartins.com/oconnor,** this guide by Maura O'Connor, University of Cincinnati, offers practical suggestions for using *Spartacus and the Slave Wars* by Brent D. Shaw, in conjunction with chapters 5 and 6 of the textbook.

For Students

Study Guides

The Online Study Guide at **bedfordstmartins.com/hunt** helps students synthesize the material they have learned as well as practice the skills historians use to make sense of the past. The following Map, Visual, and Document activities are available for Chapter 6.

Map Activity

- Mapping the West: The Roman Empire in Crisis, 284 C.E., p. 192

Visual Activity

- Marble Statue of Augustus from Prima Porta, p. 173
- Catacomb Painting of Christ as the Good Shepherd, p. 183

Reading Historical Documents

- Augustus, *Res Gestae* (My Accomplishments), p. 168
- The Scene at a Roman Bath, p. 170
- Contrasting Views: Christians in the Empire: Conspirators or Faithful Subjects? p. 186

CHAPTER

7

The Transformation of the Roman Empire

284–600 C.E.

CHAPTER RESOURCES

Main Chapter Topics

1. In an attempt to halt the damage caused by the late imperial period civil wars, Diocletian (r. 284–305) created the authoritarian dominate. His creation of the tetrarchy divided the empire into two eastern and two western administrative sections. Although abandoned by his successors, the tetrarchy prefigured the final split between the Latin west and the Greek east.

2. Constantine (r. 306–337) converted to Christianity and passed the Edict of Milan, which granted religious freedom throughout the empire in 313. Augustine, bishop of Hippo (354–430), laid much of the doctrinal groundwork for the newly recognized faith in his influential writings. Still, Christians divided over Arianism, Monophysitism, Nestorianism, and Donatism. In response, the councils of Nicaea (325) and Chalcedon (451) met to distinguish orthodoxy from heresy.

3. Christianity developed an administrative hierarchy modeled on the Roman imperial bureaucracy. The bishop of Rome claimed preeminence among bishops as the apostolic successor of Peter, but he was recognized as pope only in the west. Ascetic monasticism attracted Christians who wished to withdraw from the world and devote themselves to contemplation. Monasticism, at first eremitical, became cenobitical under Pachomius in Upper Egypt. Basil "the Great" of Caesarea (330–379) in the east and Benedict of Nursia (c. 480–553) in the west developed different regulations for monastic life—some service-oriented and some contemplative.

4. The flight of multiethnic tribes was set in motion by the westward migrations of the Huns beginning in the 370s. Unable to accommodate the influx, the eastern empire drove those fleeing into the west. In 410, the Visigoths sacked the city of Rome. Afterward, they and the tribes that followed established their own kingdoms within the old borders of the empire, gradually replacing imperial government while replicating many of its features—especially Roman law. By the time Theodoric (r. 493–526) established his Ostrogothic kingdom in Italy, there would never again be an officially recognized western Roman emperor.

5. The Germanic kingdom of the Franks (Francia) proved the most enduring. The Frankish king Clovis (r. 485–511) rejected Arianism in favor of Orthodox Christianity, strengthening his relations with the western church. Under his descendants, the Merovingians, the Frankish kingdom became the largest in western Europe, occupying an area that became most of modern France.

6. In the west, cities and the infrastructure decayed. Meanwhile, wealthy provincials withdrew to rural Roman villas, which were usually self-sufficient and fortified, and served as centers of civilization and learning, thus preserving the written legacy of classical antiquity. In the east, multilingual, multiethnic urban centers flourished.

7. The Byzantine Empire combined a Greek-speaking culture with a determination to be the preserver of Rome's imperial greatness, which it retained until its capture by the Ottoman Turks in 1453.

8. The Byzantine emperor Justinian (r. 527–565) briefly reclaimed western Roman territory, launched a monumental building program, and systematized Roman law. The enormous cost of the wars and the escalating taxes required to cover these conflicts drained the east of resources. In the west, the ravages of the Gothic wars destroyed much of the remnants of the ancient Roman infrastructure.

Focus Question

What were the most important sources of unity and of division in the Roman Empire from the reign of Diocletian to the reign of Justinian, and why?

1. Paradoxically, Christianity became the single most important source both of unity and division. Tension between Christianity and traditional Roman polytheism was a source of discord, particularly early in the period. Diocletian launched the Great Persecution in an unsuccessful attempt to weaken Christianity, thereby strengthening the empire and his own rule. Polytheism persisted, particularly among elites. Divisions among Christians were also intense, as "heretical" creeds such as Arianism, Monophysitism, Nestorianism, and Donatism challenged Christian orthodoxy over matters of theology, ritual, and church/state relations. Gradually, the emperors embraced Christianity. In the early fourth century, Constantine converted and implemented a policy of religious freedom with the Edict of Milan. Theodosius I established Christianity as the state religion of the Roman Empire in 391, and by the time of Justinian, those who deviated from the increasingly established orthodox beliefs faced official persecution. Ironically, as division between east and west solidified, and the Roman Empire in the west gave way to non-Roman kingdoms, Christianity flourished. For example, successors to the Romans such as Clovis, king of the Franks, converted from Arianism to Christianity. The Christian church also inherited the institutional legacy of the Roman Empire, including geographical designations such as dioceses, which had been created by the anti-Christian Diocletian, as part of his effort to strengthen the empire two centuries earlier.

2. After Christianity, the influx of "Germanic" immigrants from north and east of the Danube and Rhine rivers was the most powerful and paradoxical source of division and unity. Initially, the Romans had admired some aspects of the so-called "barbarian" peoples on their frontiers, and over the centuries they had recruited them as soldiers and permitted their families to settle within the empire. By the late fourth century, however, these peoples had become a growing, disruptive force in the Roman world. Following the "barbarian" victory at the battle of Adrianople in 378, the emperor Theodosius I was forced to accommodate with the newcomers, creating a new precedent by allowing them to establish their own kingdom within Roman borders. In an effort to relieve the eastern part of the empire from increasing incursions of migrants, the emperors in Constantinople paid the invading Central Asian Huns to spare their lands, pushing the invaders, and those fleeing them, further to the west. Germanic groups such as the Visigoths, Vandals, Anglo-Saxons, Ostrogoths, and Franks eclipsed what was left of the Italian-based half of the empire and established multiple new kingdoms. Although they have frequently been regarded as destroyers of the Roman Empire in the west, in fact they embraced many of its legacies, including Christianity and Roman law, which have served as unifying elements in subsequent western civilization.

Annotated Chapter Outline

I. **Reorganizing the Empire, 284–395**

  A. **From Reform to Fragmentation, pp. 197–200**

    1. In order to make imperial strength more visible and thus more effective, Diocletian (r. 284–305) imposed the most autocratic system of rule in Roman history.
    2. Called the *dominate* from the Latin word *dominus* meaning "master," his regime did away with any pretense of shared authority between the emperor and the elites that was characteristic of the principate.
    3. Over time, emperors demonstrated their superior status by ceremony at court and by special clothing that made it clear that ordinary citizens were their subjects.
    4. The emperors of the dominate used strict laws and often brutal punishments to solve the previous century's civil disorder.
    5. To combat the threat of fragmentation, Diocletian divided the empire into four administrative districts, two in the west and two in the east, each with its own capital city and military force.
    6. He established a tetrarchy ("rule by four") by appointing three other "partners" to join him in governing the districts.
    7. Despite this attempt to eliminate internal conflict, Diocletian's successor, Constantine (r. 306–337), had to fight a long civil war to establish his position as emperor.
    8. Fearing disloyal partners, Constantine abolished the tetrarchy.
    9. He refounded the ancient city of Byzantium as Constantinople in 324 with the intention of making it into the "new Rome."
    10. Finally, he designated his three sons as joint heirs to his throne.
    11. However, their bloody rivalry began a long process that ended with the empire split in two—east and west—in 395, with a separate emperor ruling each half.

12. The eastern emperors inherited Constantinople, and in the west the emperor made Ravenna the permanent capital because it had its own port and was more easily defended than Rome.

B. The High Cost of Rescuing the Empire, pp. 200–202

1. In order to rescue the empire, Diocletian needed vast revenues, particularly to support the large army.
2. Diocletian meant to improve the financial situation by restricting "unjust" commerce and exacting more taxes from the populace.
3. Trying to curb rapid inflation, in 301 Diocletian imposed an elaborate system of wage and price controls called the Edict on Maximum Prices, which was completely ineffective because merchants refused to cooperate and government officials could not enforce it.
4. Desperate to control the people liable for taxes, Diocletian imposed oppressive restrictions, making many occupations compulsory and hereditary, thus eliminating hope for social mobility.
5. *Coloni*, tenant farmers who had traditionally been free to move from farm to farm, were increasingly tied to a particular plot of land; bakers and soldiers also found themselves and their descendants tied to their occupations.
6. Hit especially hard were the propertied urban classes, who served as municipal officials (curials) and were made to spend their own money to pay for shortfalls in tax collection so that public service often led to financial ruin.
7. Criminals were sentenced to curial offices as punishment, and elites sought exemption from public service through connections to the emperor, positions in the army or church, or through bribery—while some simply fled.
8. The erosion of traditional Roman values of public service and the financial burden placed on the rural population led to increased friction between government and populace, especially in the west.

C. The Emperors and Official Religion, pp. 202–204

1. Believing that Rome's problems were caused by the gods' anger at the Christians who rejected them, Diocletian launched a massive attack against Christians in 303 called the Great Persecution.
2. He seized their property, expelled them from his administration, tore down churches, and executed them for refusing to participate in official religious rituals.
3. Ironically, the gruesome public execution of Christian martyrs, which persisted in the east for a decade, not only failed to eradicate Christianity but also aroused sympathy from some of their polytheist neighbors.
4. The Great Persecution ended dramatically when Constantine converted to the new faith, after experiencing a vision that promised him support in battle from the Christian God.
5. When he subsequently won the crucial battle of the Milvian Bridge in 312, he declared himself a Christian.
6. Constantine did not make Christianity the official religion; instead, in the Edict of Milan in 313, he decreed religious toleration for all faiths.
7. He returned Christian property seized under the Great Persecution and compensated polytheists who had bought the confiscated property.
8. He recognized the Lord's Day as a holy occasion and legal holiday each week, but he called it "Sunday" which honored both new and old divinities.
9. Although a Christian, Constantine also continued to hold the traditional office of pontifex maximus to honor his non-Christian subjects who still greatly outnumbered Christians.

II. Christianizing the Empire, 312–c. 540

A. Changing Religious Beliefs, pp. 204–209

1. Polytheists and Christians did share some beliefs, but there was no quick and easy transition to a Christian empire.
2. Polytheists and Christians debated passionately about whether there was one God or many and what kind of interest he or she or they took in the human world.
3. The emperor Julian (r. 361–363) tried to restore the traditional gods and impose his intellectual sect of polytheism as the official religion.
4. In reaction, subsequent Christian emperors began slowly removing polytheism's official privileges.
5. Eventually Christianity was made the state religion by the emperor Theodosius (r. 379–395), who banned polytheist sacrifices, denied positions in the

administration to polytheists, and ordered all polytheist temples closed.

6. Despite these bans, many temples and non-Christian schools such as Plato's Academy remained open.
7. Judaism continued to endure, and important works of religious scholarship—the Midrash and the Palestinian and Babylonian Talmuds—laid the foundation for later Jewish life and practice.
8. Christianity's official status attracted new followers. For example, Christian soldiers no longer faced a conflict between serving Christ and serving a polytheist emperor and government.
9. Many people found Christianity's strong sense of community and its emphasis on charitable works appealing.
10. Women were excluded from the church's hierarchy, but they could earn status by giving their property to the congregation or renouncing marriage to dedicate their lives to Christ.
11. The establishment of Christianity in the Roman Empire depended largely on its success in constructing a formal leadership through a hierarchy of male bishops.
12. Bishops held the right to ordain priests and control their congregations' finances, and came to replace curials as the emperor's partners in local rule.
13. The bishops of Rome claimed apostolic succession from the Apostle Peter to whom Jesus had given special authority. They were the most powerful bishops in the western empire and took the title *pope*, from the Greek word for "father."

B. Establishing Christian Orthodoxy, pp. 209–212

1. As Christianity flourished, the church hierarchy sought a uniform doctrine to maintain authority and ensure the congregations' spiritual purity.
2. Christians disagreed about what constituted orthodoxy (official doctrine proclaimed by the councils of bishops) and heresy (private beliefs at odds with the official creed).
3. One of the most significant dissenters was Arius of Alexandria (c. 260–336), who proclaimed that Jesus was not identical in nature to God, a view that implied that Christian monotheism was not absolute.
4. Arianism found widespread support because it simplified the nature of the Trinity—Father, Son, and Holy Spirit.
5. In 325, Constantine convened 220 bishops at the Council of Nicaea to debate Arianism.
6. The council voted to banish Arius and declared that the Father and Son were "of one substance," but Arianism persisted under Constantine II (r. 337–361), whose missionaries converted many tribal peoples on the far borders of the empire.
7. Monophysites ("single-nature believers") believed that Jesus's nature was primarily divine not human and established independent churches.
8. Followers of Nestorius, the bishop of Constantinople in 428, believed that Jesus had been born human and given his divine nature later.
9. Donatism began when the North African priest Donatus refused to readmit to the church Christians who had cooperated with imperial authorities to avoid martyrdom during the Great Persecution.
10. In 451, the Council of Chalcedon tried again to establish a uniform orthodoxy; they failed in the east but produced important doctrines followed in the west.
11. Augustine (354–430), the bishop of Hippo in North Africa, became the most influential thinker in establishing church orthodoxy. His writings supported secular law and social institutions because they sought to prevent anarchy and moral corruption in a fallen world of imperfect humans.
12. Augustine also believed humans should strive for asceticism, the practice of denying themselves pleasures, because human passions, particularly sexual desire, destroyed harmony with God.
13. Virginity and sexual renunciation, even in marriage, became a sign of such high virtue that by the fourth century congregations began to demand that bishops and priests be celibate.

C. The Emergence of Christian Monks, pp. 212–214

1. Although Christianity became legally and socially acceptable, some men and women chose to withdraw from everyday society to live solitary lives of asceticism, imitating Jesus's suffering.
2. Known as monasticism, this movement eventually led monks to form communities for mutual support in the pursuit of holiness.
3. Once persecution ended, living as a monk became a way for a Christian to emulate

the sacrifice of Christ in a "living martyrdom."

4. Monasticism provided an opportunity to achieve excellence and recognition, which was a traditional ideal in the ancient Western world.
5. Christians believed that extremely holy ascetics could provide protection and healing after their deaths. Relics of these saints, such as body parts or pieces of clothing, became treasured as sacred.
6. Some monasteries strove for complete self-sufficiency; others offered charitable services to the community at large, including the foundation of the first hospitals such as those established by Basil of Caesarea (c. 330–379).
7. The most isolationist and ascetic monasticism developed in the eastern empire, while in the west, Benedict of Nursia (c. 480–553) developed the milder Benedictine Rule, which prescribed daily routines of prayer, scriptural readings, and manual labor.
8. People joined monasteries for social as well as theological reasons.
9. Occasionally, parents sent their babies to be raised in the monasteries—a practice called *oblation*, the offering of a holy gift—because they were either unable to care for them or were fulfilling pious vows.
10. The church hierarchy resented monasteries' independence and renown because financial contributions began to go to monasteries rather than to local churches; also, monks earned their holy status through their own actions rather than by having it bestowed on them by church officials.

III. Non-Roman Kingdoms in the West, c. 370–550s

A. Non-Roman Migrations, pp. 215–219

1. Fourth-century emperors continued to encourage the migration of non-Roman peoples into the Roman Empire, recruiting their men to serve in the Roman army.
2. By the later fourth century, floods of non-Roman men, women, and children left their homelands to settle in Roman territory.
3. Individual clans were based on kinship; these clans were grouped into loosely based multiethnic coalitions called tribes that anyone could join.
4. Assemblies of free male warriors governed the tribes, which were prone to internal conflict and violent feuds.
5. Mass migrations began in earnest when the Huns invaded eastern Europe, particularly under the ambitious leadership of Attila (r. c. 440–453).
6. The experience of the Visigoths typified that of the refugee tribes. Fleeing the Huns, the Visigoths requested asylum from the eastern emperor in return for military service.
7. When greedy Roman officials mistreated the Visigoths, they rebelled and defeated the army.
8. After the death of emperor Theodosius, who had granted the Visigoths permission to establish an independent kingdom, the eastern emperors threatened war, so the Visigoths moved west and sacked Rome in 410.
9. The weak western government reluctantly let them settle in southwestern Gaul, where they organized into a kingdom and expanded into Spain.
10. Concessions to the Visigoths encouraged other tribes to use force to gain territory and independence, as did the Vandals in North Africa and the Anglo-Saxons in Britain.
11. In the west, Theodoric led the Ostrogoths who were in the imperial military service to usurp control from Odoacer, the viceroy ruling in the west, and to rule from the capital at Ravenna.
12. Theodoric, an Arian Christian, left many Roman institutions intact and appropriated the traditions of the Roman past to stabilize his own rule.
13. Finally, the Franks transformed Roman Gaul into Francia when their king, Clovis (r. 485–511), overthrew the Visigothic king with help from the eastern emperor. His Merovingian dynasty lasted longer than any of the other western kingdoms, forging a bond between non-Roman military prowess and Roman traditions.

B. Mixing Traditions, pp. 219–221

1. The non-Roman kingdoms adopted many aspects of Roman law codes to maintain a sense of justice and order.
2. The Visigothic kings were the first to adopt a written code of law; it was composed in Latin and made compensation the primary method for resolving disputes.
3. The Frankish king Clovis also wrote laws in Latin for the Merovingian kingdom, formalizing a system of fines for criminals,

including the *wergild*, the payment that a murderer had to pay his victim's kin as compensation for his crime and to limit vendettas.

4. The waves of migration and frequent raids further weakened the West's economy, quickening the shift of economic activity away from the cities and toward the countryside.
5. Preferring self-sufficiency and isolation, wealthy Romans built sprawling estates that were fortified and staffed by tenants who were bound to the land like slaves, a development accelerated by the disrepair of Roman roads and bridges.
6. As the vestiges of provincial government disappeared, these self-sufficient nobles no longer needed to contribute service or taxes to a central authority, and some became astonishingly rich and independent.

IV. The Roman Empire in the East, c. 500–565

A. Imperial Society in the East, pp. 222–223

1. Historians refer to the eastern empire after 600 as the Byzantine Empire because the old name for Constantinople was Byzantium.
2. By the early sixth century, the eastern empire had achieved great authority and wealth.
3. Trade routes and agriculture helped keep the markets of its large cities flourishing, and elites spent freely on imported luxury goods.
4. In keeping with Roman tradition, the eastern emperors sponsored religious festivals and public entertainment, such as the popular chariot races, to enhance their image.
5. The eastern emperors considered themselves the preservers of Roman tradition and tried to minimize the influence of the "barbaric" migrant peoples.
6. Despite reverence for "Romanness," the eastern empire was widely diverse with many different ethnicities, languages, and competing theologies.
7. Women in the eastern empire lived more like the women of classical Greece than Roman women, supporting their households, having minimal legal rights, and avoiding unnecessary contact with men outside their family circle.
8. Women of the imperial family could achieve exceptional power. For example, Theodora, who married the emperor Justinian, constantly influenced and advised him.
9. Christianity made divorce difficult to obtain. In addition, remarriage by widows was frowned upon, and harsher penalties for sexual offenses became common.
10. Governments in the eastern empire aggravated social divisions because officials demanded bribes or "fees" to perform their services, something the elite could accommodate with cash or connections.
11. Poor people could not afford to pay hefty amounts, so emperors resorted to fixing limits on the bribes officials could demand.

B. The Reign of Justinian, 527–565, pp. 223–225

1. Justinian (r. 527– 565) launched ambitious expeditions over several decades to reclaim the west and restore the old Roman Empire.
2. With enormous effort and expense, his generals reoccupied Italy, parts of southern Spain, and North Africa.
3. Although the empire was temporarily reunited, the lengthy wars destroyed the west's infrastructure and the east's economy.
4. The already overburdened population was taxed so heavily that the countryside became plagued by constant banditry, and many people poured into the cities seeking relief and protection.
5. Justinian's unpopular taxes led to the Nika Riot in 532, which left much of Constantinople in ruins.
6. To make matters worse, in the 540s an epidemic killed a third of the empire's inhabitants, creating a shortfall of army recruits and reducing tax revenues.
7. To create stability, Justinian instituted a building program that demonstrated his overpowering supremacy and religiosity. The most spectacular of these projects was the reconstruction of the Church of the Holy Wisdom (Hagia Sophia).
8. Justinian's increased autocracy eroded the autonomy of the empire's cities, as imperial officials took control of the provinces away from local elites.
9. To solidify authority, Justinian unified all the laws of the empire in the monumental *Codex*, completed in 534.
10. To expedite legal cases, his scholars also condensed the millions of regulations of the *Codex* into the *Digest* in 533.

11. Justinian's laws outlawed male homosexual relations for the first time in Roman history.
12. Justinian tried unsuccessfully to compel religious unity, but the eastern and western churches embarked firmly on the diverging courses that would result in formal schism five hundred years later.

C. Preserving Classical Traditions, pp. 225–227

1. The Christianization of the empire endangered the survival of classical Latin and Greek literature as polytheistic art and literature was viewed as subversive. As Christian writings became the most important literature of the age, classical texts fell into neglect.
2. Latin and Greek scholarship survived in the east, however, because elite Christians seeking plum government jobs had to be fluent in Latin and Greek, so elite education adhered to the Roman tradition of studying Greek and Latin classics.
3. Moreover, classical rhetoric got a new lease on life as the best method for presenting Christian theology.
4. The Christian writer Ambrose, the bishop of Milan from 374 to 397, imitated the style of the great Roman orator Cicero in his description of Christian ethics.
5. The patriarch Jerome was another admirer of Cicero.
6. Saints' lives were modeled on ancient traditions of laudatory biography, and many Christian artists incorporated polytheistic symbols and imagery in their paintings and mosaics.
7. The works of the Christian theologian John Philoponus (c. 490–570), who led the Neoplatonist school in Alexandria, demonstrated the possibilities when the classical past was used for inspiration in forward-looking Christian scholarship.
8. The growth of Christian literature generated the technological innovation of the codex, which was a book with bound pages, a great improvement over cumbersome and easily damaged papyrus scrolls.
9. Dangers to classical learning remained, however, most vividly demonstrated by the closing of Plato's school, the Academy, in 530 after many of its scholars emigrated to Persia to escape the harsh restrictions placed on polytheists and the loss of support from the Athenian elite.

Lecture Strategies

1. A perennially fascinating topic for students is: What really caused the decline and fall of the Roman Empire? Outlining the numerous scholarly (and less scholarly) theories that have been advanced frequently leads to lively discussions about their relative merits and the dangers of oversimplification when debating historical causality. If you lack the time to read all of Gibbon's classic, you can start with Donald Kagan, ed., *The End of the Roman Empire: Decline or Transformation?*, 3rd ed. (Lexington, MA: D. C. Heath, 1992), which offers a first-rate selection of competing viewpoints taken from the works of leading scholars, including Gibbon. For passages from relevant primary sources, refer to the Internet Ancient History Sourcebook. Other excellent studies, among the myriad that discuss this topic, are Peter Brown, *The World of Late Antiquity* (London: Thames & Hudson, 1971), which views the era as one characterized by Christianity's rise rather than Rome's fall. Arther Ferrill, *The Fall of the Roman Empire* (London: Thames & Hudson, 1988), treats the fall largely as a result of military factors. There is also a highly informative set of essays in Part 1 of *Debating the Middle Ages: Issues and Readings*, Lester Little and Barbara Rosenwein, eds. (Malden, MA: Blackwell, 1998), including Chris Wickham's "The Fall of Rome Will Not Take Place."

2. Students often hold the misconception that most early Christians faced persecution and eventual death in the arena at the hands of Romans. You can illuminate the complexity of the development of Christianity during these centuries by stressing the range of Roman responses—both official and unofficial—to Christianity and the ways in which Christianity coexisted with the polytheistic religions of the late Roman Empire. Ramsey Macmullen, *Christianity and Paganism in the Fourth to Eighth Centuries* (New Haven, CT: Yale University Press, 1999), is a good place to begin. For a detailed presentation of the beliefs of ordinary pagans and Christians, see Robin Lane Fox's massive *Pagans and Christians* (New York: Alfred A. Knopf, 1989), which forms an interesting contrast to E. R. Dodds, *Pagan and Christian in an Age of Anxiety: Some Aspects of Religious Experience from Marcus Aurelius to Constantine*, rpt. (Cambridge: Cambridge University Press, 1990). A short treatment that argues for the distinctly Christian character of martyrdom is G. W. Bosersock, *Martyrdom and Rome* (Cambridge: Cambridge University Press, 1995).

3. Theodoric was perhaps the most accomplished of the early Germanic leaders ruling in western Europe. A discussion of his reign can illuminate the difficulties connected with the establishment of Germanic states in the post-imperial west and the

ways in which some Germanic rulers set out to assimilate and utilize the accomplishments of their Roman heritage. A solid treatment, with excellent discussion of diplomatic policy, is John Moorhead, *Theodoric in Italy* (Oxford: Oxford University Press, 1993). Primary sources containing remarks on Theodoric are the *History of the Goths* by Jordanes and the letters of Sidonius Apollinaris. A standard history of the Goths is Herwig Wolfram, *The History of the Goths* (Berkeley: University of California Press, 1990). Theodoric patronized some of the leading intellectuals of his time, including Boethius and Cassiodorus.

Class Discussion Starters

1. The transformations that occurred during the late empire occasioned drastic measures in the realms of administration, law, finances, and the military. Ask students to assess the effectiveness of Diocletian's reforms and their impact on the empire. See G. H. Stevenson, *Roman Provincial Administration* (Oxford: Oxford University Press, 1975 [originally published 1939]). Stephen Williams's biography *Diocletian and the Roman Recovery* (New York and London: Routledge, 1996) argues for the overall success of Diocletian's policies. For the establishment and political history of the tetrarchy, see Simon Corcoran, *The Empire of the Tetrarchs: Imperial Pronouncements and Government, A.D. 284–324* (Oxford: Oxford University Press, 1996). The overviews provided by A. H. M. Jones, *The Later Roman Empire 284–602: A Social, Economic, and Administrative Survey* (Norman: University of Oklahoma Press, 1964) and Averil Cameron, *The Later Roman Empire, A.D. 284–430* (Cambridge, MA: Harvard University Press, 1993) place Diocletian's policies in their broader historical context.

2. The legalization of Christianity generated the problem of defining exactly what constituted its religious orthodoxy. In the process, many conflicting opinions on fundamental questions of faith were declared heresy. Students may be interested to learn more about the wide diversity of beliefs that fell within the purview of Christianity and about the attempts to establish orthodox doctrine in the early church councils. Discussion should also include why such doctrines were perceived as being destructive. Useful introductions to the intricacies of the early doctrinal dispute include Stuart G. Hall, *Doctrine and Practice in the Early Church* (Grand Rapids, MI: William Eerdmans, 1992); *Encyclopedia of Early Christianity*, E. Ferguson, M. P. McHugh, and F. W. Norris, eds., 2nd ed. (New York: Garland, 1998); and *Encyclopedia of the Early Church*, A. Di Berardino, ed. (Oxford: Oxford University Press, 1992). Two general surveys of early church history that contain helpful sections on the role of the councils and the content of various early heresies are Henry Chadwick, *The Early Church* (New York: Viking Penguin, 1993); and W. H. C. Frend, *The Rise of Christianity* (Minneapolis: Augsburg Fortress Publications, 1984). Primary-source selections online can be found at the Internet Medieval Sourcebook.

3. Augustine's impact on the development not only of Christianity but also on western thought in general is profound. Discussion of his life can serve to introduce many central themes in the history of late antiquity. The classic biography of Augustine is Peter Brown's *Augustine of Hippo*, rpt. (Berkeley: University of California Press, 2000), which can be read in conjunction with a well-received study by Gary Wills, *Saint Augustine* (New York: Penguin, 1999). For an introduction to Augustine's ideas, see Eugene Portalie, *A Guide to the Thought of Saint Augustine* (Washington, DC: Regnery, 1960); and Robert Markus, *Saeculum: History and Society in the Theology of Saint Augustine* (Cambridge: Cambridge University Press, 1970). Finally, consult the helpful resources available at James O'Donnell's Late Antiquity site at <http://ccat.sas.upenn.edu/jod/augustine.html>.

4. Monasticism, while not invented in the west, became the preeminent expression of ideal Christianity in western Europe during the early Middle Ages. Have students discuss the appeal of monasticism and the reasons for conflict between monastic orders and bishops. Explore the development of monasticism in general in the fundamental work by David Knowles, *Christian Monasticism* (New York: McGraw-Hill, 1969). For a recent study focused on the early medieval period, see Marilyn Dunn, *The Emergence of Monasticism: From the Desert Fathers to the Early Middle Ages* (Malden, MA: Blackwell, 2001). See also the materials available on the Internet Medieval Sourcebook on the Benedictine movement, including the complete text of Benedict's rule and Gregory the Great's biography of Benedict. For the participation of women in early western monasticism, see Susanna Elm, *Virgins of God: The Making of Asceticism* (Oxford: Oxford University Press, 1994).

Reviewing the Text

Review Questions

1. How did Diocletian's policies end the third-century crisis, and why did they fail to work in the long run?
[model answer] *Diocletian ended the crisis by asserting his authority with more absolute power than Rome had*

previously experienced. But his extreme policies had a divisive impact politically, economically, and socially, and he failed to forge a sense of unity within the empire or create true prosperity. By assuming absolute authority as the "dominate" and using it to enforce harsh punishments and penalties for violations of order in society, Diocletian restored social order, but unequal punishments served to deepen divisions between common people and the wealthy. Politically, he reorganized government by dividing the territory into four administrative districts and splitting civil and military authority. But this did not eliminate rivalries for power. Taxes were increased and wages and price controls imposed to provide the army with the funding needed to enforce Diocletian's policies and manage the far-flung empire. The wealthy were required to finance public needs within their communities, a financial stress that broke down long-standing traditions of public service.

2. How did Christianity both unite and divide the Roman Empire?
[model answer] *Christianity created social disruption from its inception, as people blamed the failures of Roman society on the defection of increasing numbers from the traditional gods. Once the emperor converted, however, the new religion attracted many with its promise of salvation as well as the social security of belonging to the emperor's religion. Christianity fostered a sense of social solidarity in the shared identity of its believers and drew the poor to its rank through traditions of charity, uniting different levels of society. As the church developed a centralized authority, it encouraged uniformity in beliefs and practices that further strengthened a sense of social unity.*

3. How did the barbarian migrations and invasions change the Roman Empire and Roman society?
[model answer] *Barbarian invasions increased the cultural and political divide between the eastern and western regions of the Roman Empire. Their presence in the western region violently disrupted the political and social order and economic systems of Roman society. Imperial government was replaced with regional kingdoms that restructured the political order and forged new ethnic identities. Cultural practices developed that combined Roman ways with those of the newcomers. Power became more localized and the economy became localized as well, as infrastructure deteriorated without centralized control, and wealth became centered in the estates of elites and their surrounding supporters. The eastern empire remained more stable, as Justinian kept invaders at bay.*

4. What policies did Justinian undertake to try to restore and strengthen the Roman Empire?
[model answer] *Justinian waged war against the barbarians to try and reunite the Roman Empire. To strengthen the unity in the east, he developed a legal code and instituted religious reforms. Central to his efforts was the strengthening of central authority as the source of his decision-making. He codified laws and promoted religious purity to foster unity and encourage divine support.*

Making Connections

1. What were the main similarities and differences between the political reality and the political appearance of the principate and the dominate?
[model answer] *Augustus called himself princeps, which harkened back to the days of the republic. He held no more formal authority than any other leader and guided Rome solely by virtue of the respect and moral authority he merited. In practice, however, Augustus created a hereditary monarchy masked by republican traditions and emblems. Diocletian, however, did not attempt to cloak his authority in republican trappings, but rather called himself dominus, or master, making clear his imperial authority.*

2. What were the main similarities and differences between traditional Roman religion and Christianity as official state religions?
[model answer] *Both Roman religion and Christianity tried to impose their beliefs on others, and they often harshly repressed dissenting views. Both believed in the concepts of sacrifice and eternal life. Religious figures in both religious traditions often played prominent secular roles in society and government. Although the local traditions of conquered peoples were often assimilated into Roman practices, aiding in the acceptance of Roman religion, local customs were not incorporated into Christianity as frequently. Sacrifices were often literal in traditional Roman religion, whereas the sacrifice of the central Christian service was metaphorical. Women sometimes had official, leading roles in Roman religion, but they were edged out of similar leadership positions in Christianity.*

Discussing the Documents

Questions from Online Study Guide with Model Answers

Diocletian's Edict on Maximum Prices and Wages (p. 201)

1. To what does Diocletian attribute the rise in prices?
[model answer] *The soldiers' need for food and supplies presented an opportunity for suppliers to raise prices to*

amounts that Justinian believed were unwarranted and a product of the opportunism of the merchants rather than reasonable supply and demand.

2. What insight does the information on wages for workers provide into the social stratification of the period? What was the apparent relationship between a worker's skill and his or her economic status?
[model answer] *Education and skill were valued and rewarded with higher economic status. A skilled carpenter was paid more than a laborer. A teacher of higher academics received higher wages than a teacher with general elementary knowledge.*

3. What reasons can you suggest for the higher price of beer from Gaul as opposed to beer from Egypt?
[model answer] *Beer from Gaul was likely to have been a superior product and preferred by social elites over beer from Egypt.*

The Edict of Milan on Religious Liberty (p. 203)

1. What might Constantine and Licinius have gained by granting religious liberty? To what degree might internal security have been a priority?
[model answer] *They hoped to gain the favor of all gods that could be in a position to influence the fate of the empire. What they were likely to gain in society was the end of tensions and conflicts among people with different religious beliefs. "Public tranquility" was clearly a goal, and increasing social stability would have been important to strengthening society in general.*

2. Is there a difference between proclaiming religious liberty as opposed to religious toleration?
[model answer] *Religious liberty implies that no single religion is favored by political authorities; religious toleration would suggest that there is an "official" religion and, while people are allowed to worship as they please, there are advantages to being a member of the official faith.*

3. How might Constantine's personal religious beliefs have influenced the edict?
[model answer] *Since Constantine had recently converted to Christianity, he certainly would have believed that Christians should be able to follow their faith unhindered. But beyond that, the proclamation of freedom to worship also would have secured for him the political support of Christians in the empire.*

New Sources, New Perspectives: Was There a Decline and Fall of the Roman Empire? (p. 218)

1. What is the difference between seeing works of art as evidence for history and as sources of beauty? What are the advantages and disadvantages of each approach?
[model answer] *Art as valuable historical evidence conveys a sense of cultural values and beliefs, as well as cultural practices. That perspective necessarily locates the art in the context of its time and place, which then become more important aspects in interpreting it than the aesthetic elements. Appreciating art as a source of beauty is an individual judgment based on personal aesthetics. Beauty, unless it is being assessed in relation to its importance to the historical role of the object, is not necessarily relevant to what art provides as a source of evidence.*

2. How do people determine whether art is "superior" or "inferior"? Are such judgments important to make?
[model answer] *The quality of art is relative to the cultural context in which it was created or that is judging it. It could be useful to know whether a work of art was considered "superior" within its own historical context in order to best understand what it reveals about the society in which it was created.*

Other Questions for Discussing These Documents in Class

New Sources, New Perspectives: Was There a Decline and Fall of the Roman Empire? (p. 218)

1. Ask students whether they agree with the text's statement that Gibbon "lived to regret his choice of a title because his work continued telling the empire's story far beyond A.D. 476" (and, in fact, he ended with the conquest of Constantinople in 1453). In what ways might Gibbon's title be considered apt? Can the students suggest other phrases to encapsulate the changes that the Roman Empire experienced during the time period covered in this chapter?

2. To what extent did the Germanic migration to and domination of the former imperial territory in the west signal a "transformation" as opposed to the creation of something entirely new?

3. Ask students to explain how the eagle pins worn by Goths illustrate the transformation, rather than the decline and fall, of the Roman Empire.

Comparative Questions

1. Although they deal with very different topics, both Diocletian's and Constantine's documents are imperial edicts. What insight do they provide into official imperial style?

2. How would you compare the insights yielded by written texts, such as the edicts, to those gleaned from artistic evidence, such as the Gothic pins and brooches?

For Users of *Sources of The Making of the West*

The following documents are available in Chapter 7 of the companion sourcebook by Katharine J. Lualdi, University of Southern Maine.

1. The Establishment of Roman Christian Doctrine: Arius, *Letter to Alexander, Bishop of Alexandria* (c. 320 C.E.) and *The Nicene Creed* (325 C.E.)
2. Polytheism versus Christianity: Quintas Aurelius Symmachus and St. Ambrose: *The Altar of Victory Sparks a Religious Debate* (384 C.E.)
3. The Development of Monasticism: St. Jerome, *Letter 107* (403 C.E.)
4. Germanic Law in the Roman Empire: *The Burgundian Code* (c. 475–525 C.E.)
5. Emergence of Byzantium: Procopius, *Secret History* (550 C.E.)

Discussion Ideas for Sources of The Making of the West, *Chapter 7*

1. What reasons does Quintas Aurelius Symmachus give for restoring the Altar of Victory? How does his attitude towards Roman history and tradition compare with that of Roman elites in preceding centuries? How does St. Ambrose's reply illustrate the growing influence and orthodoxy of Christianity? Historians often focus on those developments that will become influential in later periods, consequently much emphasis has been placed on the Christianization of the Roman Empire. How does the debate between Symmachus and St. Ambrose illustrate the relationship between polytheism and Christianity as it appeared in the 380s?

2. How does Procopius describe the Emperor Justinian and the Empress Theodora? Is his account credible? How does it compare with the description in your textbook? In what ways might Justinian and Theodora's power and success have contributed to Procopius's critical account? Consideration of this document might lead the class into a broader discussion of how their understanding of primary sources is enhanced by prior study of secondary sources such as the textbook.

Working with Visual Sources

For this exercise, please refer to Jesus as Sun God on p. 208 of the textbook or view the image on the book companion site's Online Study Guide under the "Visual Activity" for Chapter 7.

Students viewing the image at the Online Study Guide are asked four questions of the image. The questions and model answers (not made available to students) are below. Project this image, available on the Instructor's Resources CD-ROM, in class or ask students to look at the image in their textbooks and answer the questions.

1. How does this mosaic portray Jesus?
[model answer] *The mosaic portrays Jesus as a chariot driver. Rays of light, a halo of sorts, shine around his head. This Christian mosaic reflects the traditional depiction of the Greek sun god, Apollo.*

2. This representation of Jesus uses symbolism associated with the god Apollo, whose chariot, as it moved through the sky, was believed to be the sun. Why did the artist choose to use polytheistic symbolism?
[model answer] *Most likely, the artist was not saying that Jesus was Apollo or that the movement of the sun in the sky was due to Jesus's driving a chariot; instead, he or she might have been emphasizing Jesus's divine role as the "light" of the world with the use of symbols polytheists would recognize.*

3. What does this mid-third-century image of Jesus tell us about the status of Christianity in the empire?
[model answer] *This image tells us that Christianity was in the process of absorbing images and symbols of the old religions—the chariot, for instance—into its own symbolic and representational repertoire, such as the sunbeams in the shape of the cross. The absorption of polytheistic themes probably indicates that Christianity was attracting more followers, and the use of polytheistic symbolism might have helped make Jesus more familiar and comfortable to recently converted Christians or to devout polytheists.*

4. Why might this image be particularly appealing in a burial chamber?
[model answer] *The association of Jesus with the sun might suggest an association with heaven, the Christian paradise. Since many ancient religions believed that the dead needed help to arrive in the afterlife, this image of Jesus may suggest the deceased's belief that Jesus would "drive" him or her to heaven in his chariot. Also, the rising of the sun could be a metaphor for the resurrection of the dead.*

For this exercise, please refer to Seeing History: Adam and Eve on the Sarcophagus of Junius Bassus, 359 C.E. on p. 207 of the textbook or to the image on the book companion site's Online Study Guide under the "Visual Activity: Seeing History" for Chapter 7.

Students viewing the image at the Online Study Guide are asked two questions about the image. The questions and model answers (not made available to students) are below. Project this image, available on the Instructor's Resources CD-ROM, in class or ask students to look at the image in their textbooks and answer the questions.

1. How does this sculpture portray Adam and Eve?
[model answer] *Adam and Eve stand with their bodies turned slightly away from each other, covering their*

nakedness, while a serpent is coiled around the tree between them. The couple appears shamed and humiliated; therefore, the sarcophagus illustrates the point in the Old Testament text after they have succumbed to Satan's temptation, disobeyed God, and fallen from grace in the Garden of Eden.

2. What does this sarcophagus suggest about the place of Christianity in Roman society at the time of Junius Bassus?
[model answer] *The scene is restricted entirely to Biblical imagery, framed by classical architectural features. There are no polytheistic elements, as in earlier works of Christian art. This suggests that Christianity has established a firm hold as the religion of elite Romans like Junius Bassus who were prosperous enough to afford such funerary art. The strict adherence of the scene to the Old Testament account underscores the centrality of the Bible within Christian tradition.*

Mapping Exercises

Mapping Activity from OSG—Model Answer for Map Activity #2

For this activity, please refer to the map on p. 220. Students are asked these questions:

How was the Roman world divided up in 526?
[model answer] *The former Roman Empire was divided between the East, which became the Byzantine Empire, and the West, which was further divided into several smaller kingdoms.*

The eastern empire created a more centralized, authoritarian political system. Why would such a political system have been difficult to establish in the West?
[model answer] *The unified political geography and the absence of rivals in the eastern empire made it possible for the Byzantine emperors to create a highly centralized, authoritarian political system. Fragmentation in the West left each king vulnerable to competition from, or invasion by, other kings; thus, it was almost impossible for western kings to establish the type of authority exhibited by the Byzantine emperors.*

Map 7.1: Diocletian's Reorganization of 293, p. 199

Have students identify the four districts and twelve dioceses of Diocletian's reorganized empire. Why might Diocletian have chosen to create the particular four districts that he did? What relationship do these political borders have to those of earlier periods, such as the Hellenistic age and the time of the Roman republic?

Map 7.2: The Spread of Christianity, 300–600, p. 209

Ask students which factors helped to account for the spread of Christianity to the farthest reaches of the Roman Empire. Have students locate the geographical distribution of monasteries. What conclusions can they draw from the concentrations of monastic centers in the British Isles? Gaul? Portions of North Africa? The Near East? Asia Minor?

Map 7.3: Migrations and Invasions of the Fourth and Fifth Centuries, p. 216

Discuss the general direction of the movements of the groups represented on this map. Why did these peoples focus on the western, rather than the eastern, portion of the empire? Which kinds of information are obscured by the presentation of large waves of migration and invasion that occurred over two centuries in a static format, such as a map? Why are virtually no battles represented? Which groups covered the most ground? What do students know about the lifestyles of these groups?

Map 7.4: Peoples and Kingdoms of the Roman World, 526, p. 220

Ask students to identify the most politically and ethnically diverse regions of the Roman world. Is there a connection between the ethnic diversity and political fragmentation of Western Europe? How does the division between east and west compare to the earlier division between the Greek and Roman spheres of influence in the Mediterranean?

Mapping the West: Western Europe and the Eastern Roman Empire, 600, p. 228

Have students identify the key cities and their locations that Justinian controlled after his reunification of the empire. Which areas remained independent of imperial control? Did these areas pose a threat? Which historical factors were present in 600 that prevented the continued existence of the reunited empire after Justinian's death? Given the conditions in Rome and western Europe in 600, what, if anything, did Justinian's military conquests achieve?

In-Class Assignments and Presentation Topics

1. Students can explore the impact of developing Christianity on the roles and lives of women in late antiquity. Pertinent primary-source selections from the Bible and early church fathers on the "nature" of women are gathered in Alcuin Blamires, ed., *Women Defamed and Women Defended: An Anthology of Medieval Texts* (Oxford: Oxford University Press, 1992). The diversity of female responses to Christianity is evident from an analysis of the texts that concentrate on individual

women's lives; among the most moving is the "Passion of St. Perpetua," notable also for containing a first-person account of her imprisonment leading up to her martyrdom. Other excellent texts are the travelogue to the Holy Land of the pilgrim Egeria and the life of St. Macrina. Background information can be found in Gillian Clark, *Women in Late Antiquity: Pagan and Christian Lifestyles* (New York: Oxford University Press, 1993).

2. Have students form groups and assign each group a multiethnic tribe to research. Then each group should present its findings to the class on its tribe's history and what can be discerned from archaeological remains. Good choices include the Vandals, Goths, Saxons, Lombards, and early Franks. The sometimes legendary histories of many of these tribes were chronicled by contemporary Christian writers. See, for example, Paul the Deacon (History of the Lombards), Jordanes (History of the Goths), Gregory of Tours (History of the Franks), and Isidore of Seville (on the Visigoths). In addition to the works cited in the chapter bibliography, students can consult the following studies for additional information: E. A. Thompson, *Romans and Barbarians* (Madison: University of Wisconsin Press, 1982); M. Todd, et al., *The Early Germans* (Malden, MA: Blackwell, 1992); N. Christie, *The Lombards* (Malden, MA: Blackwell, 1995); and Alberto Ferreiro, ed., *The Visigoths: Studies in Culture and Society* (Leiden: Brill, 1999).

3. Have the class debate the nature of Constantine's conversion to Christianity: Was it prompted by true religious devotion or political expediency? Samuel Lieu and Dominic Montserrat, eds., *From Constantine to Julian: Pagan and Byzantine Views, A Source History* (New York and London: Routledge, 1996), considers Constantine's reign from the perspective of non-Christian sources. H. A. Drake, *Constantine and the Bishops: The Politics of Intolerance* (Baltimore: Johns Hopkins University Press, 2000), discusses the political motives behind Constantine's religious policies. Constantine's conversion could also be compared to the conversion of the Frankish leader Clovis, two accounts of which are located in the Internet Medieval Sourcebook.

4. It is difficult to resist the attraction of the history of Theodora and Justinian. Have the class compare Procopius's characterizations of them in *The Buildings* and the *Wars* to the lurid version he presents in the *Secret History*. For more in-depth information, students may want to investigate the standard study by Robert Browning, *Justinian and Theodora* (London: Thames & Hudson, 1987). For an analysis of Procopius's works, see Averil Cameron, *Procopius and the Sixth Century* (New York and London: Routledge, 1996).

5. Representing a far-flung portion of the empire that was never fully romanized, the British Isles may be of interest to students for more reasons than merely the Arthur legend. What special problems did the British Isles present to the Romans? This subject is well-documented on the Internet, and many primary sources are available there. Standard studies for Roman Britain include Peter Salway, *Roman Britain* (Oxford: Oxford University Press, 1993); and P. H. Blair, *Roman Britain and Early England, 55* B.C. *to* A.D. *871* (New York: W. W. Norton, 1978).

6. Students can increase their knowledge about Roman attitudes toward Germanic and other barbarians, and about the Romans' views of themselves, by analyzing Roman commentaries on the peoples who lived on the edges or beyond their empire. Tacitus's *Germania,* which can be found in Patrick Geary, *Readings in Medieval History*, 2nd ed. (Peterborough, Ont.: Broadview, 1998), gives students a glimpse of a Roman's assessment of the Germanic peoples as a whole, even though Tacitus describes individual tribal groups. Attila and the Huns also form an excellent subject for this kind of assignment.

7. Have students research the Roman military in late antiquity—its major battles and the conditions on the frontiers. A broad survey of tactics is contained in Edward Luttwak, *Grand Strategy of the Roman Empire* (Baltimore: Johns Hopkins University Press, 1990). Michael Dodgeon and Samuel Lieu, eds., *Roman Eastern Frontier and the Persian Wars, 226–323* (New York and London: Routledge, 1994), provides a documentary history of battles on the eastern border of the empire. Thomas Burns, *Barbarians within the Gates of Rome: A Study of the Roman Military Policy and the Barbarians, ca. 375–425* (Bloomington: Indiana University Press, 1994), discusses the use of Germanic troops within the Roman army.

Essay Questions

1. Students may want to consider the slow decline of urbanism in the western empire and the shift of the imperial capital to Constantinople in the east. John R. Curran, *Pagan City and Christian Capital: Rome in the Fourth Century* (Oxford: Oxford University Press, 2000), explores the emergence of Rome's rise as the center of western Christendom even as it lost its status as center of the Roman Empire. J. Rich, *The City in Late Antiquity* (London and New York: Routledge, 1996), combines historical and archaeological perspectives to examine the decline of urbanism in some parts of the empire after the third century and its survival in other regions. N. Christie and S. Losebly, eds., *Towns in Transition: Urban Evolution in Late Antiquity and the Early Middle Ages* (Burlington, VT: Ashgate, 1996), examines the ongoing vigor of some urban centers but argues they ultimately lost their Roman character.

2. Late-antiquity Jews occupied a problematic position within the Roman Empire because they were accorded a status that differed from other non-Roman

religions. Students can investigate primary-source documents in Margaret H. Williams, *The Jews Among the Greeks and the Romans: A Diasporan Sourcebook* (Baltimore: Johns Hopkins University Press, 1998). The legal status of Jews in the empire is considered in Alfredo Mordechai Rabello, *The Jews in the Roman Empire: Legal Problems, from Herod to Justinian* (Burlington, VT: Ashgate, 2000). See also Louis H. Feldman, *Jew and Gentile in the Ancient World: Attitudes and Interactions from Alexander to Justinian* (Princeton: Princeton University Press, 1993). An online collection of primary sources and links can be found at the Internet Jewish History Sourcebook.

3. The history of magic long predates the witch crazes of the early modern era. An influential survey of the subject found in Valerie Flint, *The Rise of Magic in Early Medieval Europe* (Princeton: Princeton University Press, 1994), argues that the necromantic traditions of late antiquity became assimilated into the beliefs of early medieval Christianity. J. Gager, *Curse Tablets and Binding Spells from the Ancient World* (Oxford: Oxford University Press, 1999), examines the history of magical incantations in antiquity. For an overview of magical beliefs and practices in the Byzantine Empire from the fourth century until the Ottoman conquest, see Henry P. Maguire, ed., *Byzantine Magic* (Washington, DC: Dumbarton Oaks, 1995).

Additional Resources: Literature

Chadwick, Henry, trans., *Augustine: Confessions*. 1991.
Cruse, C.F., trans., *Eusebius' Ecclesiastical History*. 1998.
Dods, Marcus, trans., *Augustine: City of God*. 1994.
Whiston, William, trans., *The Works of Josephus*. 1980.
Williamson, G.A., trans., *Procopius: The Secret History*. 1982.

Additional Resources: Film and Video

OTHER BEDFORD/ST. MARTIN'S RESOURCES FOR CHAPTER 7

The following resources are available to accompany Chapter 7. Please refer to the Preface of this manual for detailed descriptions of all the ancillaries.

For Instructors

Transparencies

The following maps and images from Chapter 7 are available as full-color acetates.

- Map 7.1: Diocletian's Reorganization of 293
- Map 7.2: The Spread of Christianity, 300–600
- Map 7.3: Migrations and Invasions of the Fourth and Fifth Centuries
- Map 7.4: Peoples and Kingdoms of the Roman World, 526
- Mapping the West: Western Europe and the Eastern Roman Empire, 600
- Jesus as Sun God, p. 208
- The Soaring Architecture of Hagia Sophia, p. 226

Instructor's Resources CD-ROM

The following maps and image from Chapter 7, as well as a chapter outline, are available on disc in both PowerPoint and jpeg formats.

- Map 7.1: Diocletian's Reorganization of 293
- Map 7.2: The Spread of Christianity, 300–600
- Map 7.3: Migrations and Invasions of the Fourth and Fifth Centuries
- Map 7.4: Peoples and Kingdoms of the Roman World, 526
- Mapping the West: Western Europe and the Eastern Roman Empire, 600
- Jesus as Sun God, p. 208

For Students

Study Guides

The Online Study Guide at **bedfordstmartins.com/hunt** helps students synthesize the material they have learned as well as practice the skills historians use to make sense of the past. The following Map, Visual, and Document activities are available for Chapter 7.

Map Activity

- Map 7.4: Peoples and Kingdoms of the Roman World, 526, p. 220

Visual Activity

- Jesus as Sun God, p. 208
- Seeing History: Adam and Eve on the Sarcophagus of Junius Bassus, 359 C.E., p. 207

Reading Historical Documents

- Diocletian's Edict on Maximum Prices and Wages, p. 201
- The Edict of Milan on Religious Liberty, p. 203
- New Sources, New Perspectives: Was There a Decline and Fall of the Roman Empire? p. 218

CHAPTER

8

Islam, Byzantium, and the West

600–750

Chapter Resources

Main Chapter Topics

1. Adaptation and transformation characterized the western world during the seventh and eighth centuries, a period that marked the end of antiquity and the beginning of the Middle Ages.

2. Islam, a new monotheistic faith founded by the Meccan prophet Muhammad (c. 570–632), arose in the Arabian Desert and unified the Bedouin tribes of the region. Its clear teachings (set down in the Qur'an) and emphasis on individual devotion won converts and displaced polytheism.

3. In the century after Muhammad's death, Muslim armies under the Umayyad caliphs took the Near East and northern Africa from the Byzantine Empire. The ummah was triumphant, but in 656 the caliph Uthman was murdered by soldiers who were hoping to replace him with Ali, a son-in-law of Muhammad. Civil war followed until Ali's death in 661. Those loyal to the Umayyads were called Sunni; followers of Ali were called Shi'ite.

4. Despite the short-lived gains of Justinian, the Byzantine Empire was soon losing territory. By 750, new invasions by Lombards, Slavs, Avars, and Bulgars had diminished its power and robbed it of the Balkans; it then entered a period in which life centered on rural estates instead of urban centers. New opposition to the veneration of icons led to an imperial policy of iconoclasm (prohibition of icons) imposed on the Byzantine Empire from 726 to 843. Wars with the Sasanids regained previously lost territory in the Near East and Egypt, but left both sides exhausted.

5. In western Europe, many Germanic tribes moved from Arian to Orthodox Christianity. Roman and non-Roman traditions mingled in Visigothic Spain and Lombard Italy, where the ancient institutions remained especially vigorous. The most powerful of the Christianized Germanic peoples were the Merovingian Franks who would dominate western Europe for several centuries.

6. Irish monks and Roman missionaries reintroduced Christianity to Anglo-Saxon England. England effectively elected the Roman over the Irish church when it accepted the Roman date of Easter at the Synod of Whitby (664). Roman customs and learning were reintroduced at Christian schools, but the English, unique among European kingdoms of that time, also developed a flourishing vernacular language used in literature, preaching, and law.

7. Under Pope Gregory the Great (r. 590–604), the Roman papacy laid the foundations of its future political power in Europe. Moreover, the Roman church broke with the Byzantine church over clerical celibacy and Lenten fasting. Iconoclasm in the eastern church further exacerbated the rift. Gradually, the popes came to represent the only political power in Italy other than the Lombards.

8. In Byzantium, Islam, and western Europe, warfare led to the flattening of social hierarchies and the replacement of secular political authority and classical learning with religiously allied leadership and education.

Focus Question

What three cultures took the place of the Roman Empire, and to what extent did each of them draw on and reject Roman traditions?

1. The Byzantines, Arab Muslims, and western Europeans were heirs of the Romans. Because each of these cultures came to occupy territory that had been part of the earlier Roman Empire, they were able to draw upon Hellenistic and Roman traditions. To varying degrees, all three were influenced by Roman

administrative practices, and they all embraced forms of monotheism with Roman-era roots. The Byzantine Empire was the most direct heir of Roman administration and law in the east, but the administrative structure and legal foundations of the western church were also derived from that of the Roman Empire. Even the Arab Muslims drew upon Roman precedent as they built their own empire, preserving conquered cities, hiring local civil servants, and tolerating the religions of "peoples of the book." Christianity, which had become the faith of the Romans, prevailed in both halves of the former empire, and the Islamic religion of the Arabs drew upon Roman-era Jewish and Christian roots. In contrast with the Romans, however, all of the new cultures linked religion and politics much more closely together, and they rejected the republican political traditions of Roman antiquity.

2. Conquest and warfare played a role in which each culture embraced Roman traditions. The uncertainty and instability resulting from war may have contributed to the rejection of representative political institutions and the increasing association between politics and religion, and Byzantine emperors and western kings sought to bolster their authority through religious means. The connection between politics and religion was most pronounced among the Arab Muslims, whose political and religious institutions were inseparable, and whose belief in religious jihad fueled military conquest. Warfare also contributed to the decline of cities in both halves of the old Roman Empire, particularly the west where the urban culture of the Romans virtually disappeared. The Arab Muslim invasions of territories that had previously been part of the Roman Empire drew them into contact with Roman traditions. Similarly, warfare in the Balkans led to the increasing separation of the eastern and western halves of the former Roman Empire. This resulted in the decline of Latin as a language of the Byzantine Empire and the expansion of the religious and political autonomy of the popes in Rome. Men such as Pope Gregory forged relations with the new Germanic kingdoms of western Europe, who were themselves heirs of Roman traditions, including Christianity.

Annotated Chapter Outline

I. Islam: A New Religion and a New Empire

A. Nomads and City Dwellers, pp. 232–233

1. Islam began as a religion of city dwellers, but grew to include the loosely organized Bedouin tribal society populating the Arabian Peninsula.
2. Bedouins formed few cities and had little political organization. Accustomed to desert life, they herded sheep or camels and traded or raided for other goods.
3. This tribal, nomadic way of life produced a profound oral culture.
4. Mecca, a major desert oasis near the Red Sea, played an important religious role because it contained a shrine of many idols, the Ka'ba, that served as a sacred place where war and violence were prohibited.
5. The tribe that controlled the shrine, the Quraysh, benefited by taxing pilgrims who journeyed there and selling them food and drink.
6. These pilgrims, safe from violence on these sacred grounds, bartered in safety and peace.

B. The Prophet Muhammad and the Faith of Islam, pp. 233–234

1. Muhammad (c. 570–632) was born in Mecca, orphaned early, and raised under the care of his uncle, a leader of the Quraysh tribe.
2. He became a trader and married Khadija, a rich widow.
3. Muhammad often spent days away from home in a nearby cave in prayer and contemplation.
4. Beginning in 610, Muhammad heard a voice and had a vision that summoned him to worship Allah, the God of the Jews and Christians. (Allah means "the God" in Arabic.) He accepted the call as coming from God.
5. Over the next years he received messages that he understood to be divine revelation. At first committed to memory and transmitted orally, the messages were recorded and became the holy book of Islam, the Qur'an, which means "recitation."
6. For Muslims, the Qur'an came to be the basis of history, prophecy, and the legal and moral code by which men and women should live.
7. It emphasizes the nuclear family as the basic unit of Muslim society.
8. For its adherents, Islam replaces the protection and particularism of the tribe with an identity as part of the *ummah*, or community of believers, which was like a supertribe that shared a belief in one God and a specific set of religious practices.

9. Because Muslims have no priests, liturgy, or intermediaries between humans and God, Islam depends entirely on individual faith and adherence to the Qur'an.

C. Growth of Islam, c. 610–632, pp. 234–236

1. Muhammad found his first converts in his wife Khadija and his friends and family.
2. His insistence that all polytheistic cults be abolished polarized Meccan society, however, and he decided to find a place more receptive to his message.
3. In 622, Muhammad made the Hijra, or emigration, to the city of Medina, an event that marks year one on the Muslim calendar.
4. At Medina, Muhammad found followers willing to listen to his message and make him the leader of their community.
5. Muhammad's political position in Medina set the pattern by which Islamic society would come to be governed—rather than adding a church to political institutions, politics and religion were identical.
6. In 624, Muhammad led an ambush on a Meccan caravan at the battle of Badr, where he and his followers killed forty-nine of the Meccans, took numerous prisoners, and confiscated much booty. This event transformed traditional Bedouin plundering into the Muslim virtue of jihad (literally meaning "striving" or "holy war").
7. The victory enabled Muhammad to gain new adherents and to consolidate his power in Medina.
8. Suspecting that Jews, who had failed to convert to Islam, were supporting hostile tribes, Muhammad had the Jews of Medina expelled, executed, or enslaved.
9. He also instituted new practices that defined Islam as a unique religion (which eventually came to be called the Five Pillars of Islam). These practices included the *zakat*, a tax on possessions to be used for alms, the fast of Ramadan during the ninth month of the Islamic year, and the hajj, a yearly pilgrimage to Mecca.
10. During the *salat*, formal worship that was to be performed at least three times a day, Muslims could include the *shahadah*, or profession of faith.
11. Muhammad also had Muslims at prayer physically turn away from Jerusalem, the center of Jewish worship, and toward Mecca and the Ka'ba instead.
12. In 630 Muhammad and thousands of followers marched into Mecca and took over the city.
13. Islam's prestige now convinced many to convert, and by the time of his death two years later, Muhammad had united many Arab-speaking tribes.
14. Islam improved the status of women. Infanticide was prohibited, and although polygyny was still practiced, men were obliged to treat all their wives equally, giving each a dowry and certain inheritance rights.
15. By the eighth century, however, women began to pray apart from the men, and their condition reverted to patriarchal restriction.
16. Arab men continued to be warriors but now as Muslims carrying out God's injunction to strive against unbelievers—a form of jihad.

D. The Caliphs, Muhammad's Successors, 632–750, pp. 236–237

1. Muhammad's reorganization of Arab society resulted in a formidable military force, which his successors, the caliphs, used to attack the Roman and Persian worlds.
2. To the east, they defeated the Sasanid Empire, capturing its capital of Ctesiphon in 637 and taking all of Persia by 651.
3. During the late seventh and early eighth centuries, Muslim forces controlled territory from Spain to India.
4. The Arabs owed their success to the weakened state of the Persian and Byzantine empires, which were exhausted from fighting one another.
5. When Muhammad unexpectedly died of an illness in 632, a crisis of succession followed.
6. The first caliphs came from the circle of men close to Muhammad who had accompanied him on the Hijra.
7. The first two caliphs from the Umayyad family ruled peacefully, but the third, Uthman (r. 644–656), a son-in-law to Muhammad, aroused discontent and was accused of favoritism in his distribution of offices and revenues.
8. His opponents supported his rival, Ali, also a son-in-law of Muhammad and a member of the Hashim clan. After a group of soldiers murdered Uthman, civil war broke out between the two factions.

9. Although Ali was killed by one of his own followers in 661, and the Umayyad caliphs remained in power until 750, the faction supporting Ali, the *Shi'at Ali* or *Shi'ites*, continued to shun the caliphs, who were supported by "mainstream" Muslims, the Sunni.
10. Shi'ites awaited the arrival of the true leader, the imam, whom they believed would come only from the house of Ali.
11. The Muslims borrowed the institutions of those they conquered, issuing coins and hiring Byzantines and Persians to serve in their administrations.
12. By imposing Arabic as the language of government, they brought together areas that had not yet been linguistically united.

E. Peace and Prosperity in Islamic Lands, pp. 237–238

1. Ironically, Islamic warriors brought peace and prosperity to the territory they conquered. They regarded Christians and Jews as other "people of the book" and allowed them to work and worship as they pleased, as long as they paid a special tax.
2. Muslim scholars began writing down the formerly oral Arabic literature, determining the definitive version of the Qur'an and compiling pious narratives about Muhammad (called *hadith* literature).
3. Arab calligraphy became an art, and a literate class created new forms of prose writing (including official documents) in Arabic on subjects from hunting to ruling.
4. The caliphs found written poetry an important medium for propaganda, and their patronage helped poets reach a wider audience.
5. Poets used clever language and satire that evoked courage and piety.
6. Some poetry described erotic love, a topic that scandalized conservative Muslims but reflected the diverse and prosperous urban society of the Umayyad period.
7. By the close of the Umayyad period in 750, Islamic civilization was multiethnic, urban, and sophisticated.

II. Byzantium: A Christian Empire under Siege

A. Wars on the Frontiers, c. 570–750, pp. 239–240

1. From the last third of the sixth century, Byzantium was almost constantly at war.
2. The first major challenge came from the Sasanid Empire of Persia, which began to focus its attention on the western half of Mesopotamia near the Byzantine border, collecting land taxes and turning Persia into a major trading center.
3. The Sasanid king Chosroes II (r. 591–628) invaded the Byzantine Empire in 603, conquering Jerusalem and Egypt by 620, territory that Byzantium gained back in 627 under the emperor Heraclius.
4. War between the Persians and Byzantium made both empires vulnerable to invading forces.
5. Byzantium was faced with the migrations of the Germanic Lombards, who took much of southern Italy, and the Slavs, who conducted raids on the Balkan countryside and attacked eastern cities with the help of the Avars.
6. In addition, the Bulgar defeat of the Byzantine army in 681 forced the emperor to recognize an independent Bulgar state in the Balkans.
7. Once lost by the Byzantine Empire, these territories no longer served as a major link between the East and West: Avar and Slavic control of the Balkans cut off trade and travel, and the Bulgar state threw a political barrier across the Danube, widening the already growing cultural gap between the two regions.
8. Very little communication between the east and west took place in the seventh century; Byzantine scholars no longer learned Latin, and they lost interest in the history of the West.

B. From an Urban to a Rural Way of Life, pp. 240–242

1. By the eighth century, the Byzantine Empire was quite small. Conquered Byzantine subjects in Egypt and Syria lived under Arab rule, but their daily lives remained essentially unchanged.
2. Although they paid a special tax, non-Muslims could practice their religions in peace and were permitted to keep and farm their land.
3. The most radical transformation for Byzantines occurred not in the territories lost, but in the shrunken empire itself. Under the pressure of constant invasions, towns that once served as bustling trade hubs or centers of imperial administration vanished or were transformed.
4. Warfare reduced some cities to rubble, and, once cities were rebuilt, the limited resources available went to constructing

defensive city walls or large churches, rather than to the public baths or marketplaces that formerly served as centers of public life.

5. The focus of daily life shifted to the church and the home.
6. The skills and institutions of urban workers helped keep some cities, particularly Constantinople, active as centers of manufacturing and long-distance trade through their production and distribution of luxury items like fine silk textiles.
7. Consequently, agriculture became the main focus of economic and social life.
8. Unlike in the west, where a rich and powerful elite controlled the agricultural economy, in the east free and semi-free peasants dominated, growing food, herding cattle, and tending to small vineyards, interacting primarily with their families or nearby monasteries.
9. Drawing upon Roman legal traditions, Byzantine law promoted the nuclear family by limiting divorce and punishing marital infidelity. While abortion and incest were banned, women and men were given equal power over their children.

C. New Military and Cultural Forms, pp. 242–243

1. With rural life taking precedence economically and socially, it is not surprising that military, political, and cultural changes accompanied the transformation of the countryside.
2. Seeking a comparable land force, the imperial government encouraged the development of a middle class of farmer-soldiers.
3. Promises of land and low taxes attracted men without property to serve in the military, where they fought side by side with landowning farmers who provided their own weapons and horses.
4. To counter frontier attacks in the seventh century, the empire was divided into military districts called *themes*; all civil matters in each district were put into the hands of a single general called a *strategos* (plural *strategoi*), who also served as regional tax collector.
5. Cultural changes in the eighth century led parents to provide their children with a religious education, rather than a classical one.
6. Teachers at rural elementary schools used the Book of Psalms as their primer, while saints' lives and devotional texts became the main subjects for study.
7. Secular, classical learning remained out of favor throughout the seventh and eighth centuries.

D. Religion, Politics, and Iconoclasm, pp. 243–245

1. Because the spiritual and secular realms were considered inseparable, bishops functioned as both state administrators in their cities and as religious leaders; likewise, the emperor served as head of both church and state.
2. The emperor appointed the chief religious official, the patriarch of Constantinople; formulated Christian doctrine; and convened church councils.
3. The patriarch of Constantinople and the other patriarchs were at the head of a three-tier system of church officials: they appointed the metropolitans (bishops who headed an entire province), who in turn appointed the bishops, who held authority over dioceses.
4. Although in theory monasteries were under the control of the local bishop, they often exercised enormous power and independence.
5. The most important and controversial issue facing the eighth-century Byzantine church was the use of icons, images of holy people that were believed to possess holy powers. Many Byzantine Christians made icons the focus of their religious devotion, believing that they physically manifested the holy persons they depicted.
6. Others, including soldiers, abhorred icons and pointed to the Islamic prohibition of such images as one of the reasons for the Arabs' military success.
7. The issue became a test of authority for Byzantine emperors; because icons served as intermediaries between worshipers and God, they undermined the emperor's exclusive place in the divine and temporal order. Above all, the emperors opposed icons because their soldiers did, and they needed the support of the troops.
8. The controversy climaxed in 726 under Emperor Leo III the Isaurian (r. 717–741).
9. Following a defeat of Arabs who were besieging Constantinople, officers in the

imperial court tore down the golden icon of Christ at the palace in Constantinople and replaced it with a cross.

10. In protest, a crowd of women went on a furious rampage in support of icons, prompting Leo to ban all icons and order them to be destroyed, beginning the period of iconoclasm (literally, "icon-smashing"). This ban forced changes in private worship, since many people now had to destroy their personal icons or worship in secret.
11. Iconoclasm also prompted attacks on monasteries, where many collections of holy images were destroyed, vast properties were confiscated, and intractable monks were forced to marry. In this way, iconoclasm strengthened imperial authority by destroying communities that might otherwise have been centers of resistance to imperialism.
12. Reorganized and reoriented, the Byzantine rulers were better able to meet the Arab onslaught.

III. Western Europe: A Medley of Kingdoms

A. Frankish Kingdoms with Roman Roots, pp. 246–248

1. During the sixth century, the Franks established themselves as the dominant power in Roman Gaul.
2. Their kings, the Merovingians, founded their kingdom on territory still dotted with Roman villas and farmlands and lined with Roman roads.
3. Yet, old Roman cities were losing their commercial and cultural vitality due to depopulation, and gradually the surrounding forests and pastureland reflected the farming and village settlement patterns of the Franks.
4. Although slaves still worked the estates of wealthy landowners and some free peasants cultivated their own small plots, most people lived as semi-free peasants settled on small holdings, called *manses*, which included a house, small garden, and cultivatable land.
5. These peasants—some of whom were descendants of the Roman *coloni*, some the descendants of slaves, and some of Frankish origin—owed dues and labor to a landowner in exchange for living on and working the land.
6. Aristocrats lived in small villages surrounded by huts of peasants, shepherds, and artisans. This early medieval village was intensely localized and clustered around a protector, either a rich man or a saint's relics (bones, teeth, hair, or clothes).
7. The belief in the power of a saint's relics to protect and heal led to a new relationship between the living and the dead. Whereas in the classical world, the dead were banished from the presence of the living, in the medieval world, the holy dead held a place of high esteem.

B. Economic Activity in a Peasant Society, pp. 248–250

1. In peasant society, most people lived on the edge of survival. From the fifth to the eighth centuries, a dramatic drop in the mean temperature in Europe reduced the yield of crops, leading to shortages and famine.
2. The agricultural system at best produced a tenuous living: the traditional light wooden plows of the Mediterranean worked poorly in the heavy, wet soil in the north of the Frankish kingdom.
3. The upper class of landowning warriors and churchmen lived off the work of peasants, and when occasional surpluses became available, they were traded through a gift economy: booty was seized, tributes demanded, and wealth hoarded, all to be redistributed to friends and dependents.
4. Those in power amassed great wealth in their treasuries and storehouses, which added to their prestige, and religious people and monasteries benefited from generous gifts.
5. Some people continued to engage in long-distance trade, exchanging slaves, furs, and honey from the west for the luxuries and manufactured goods, such as silks and papyrus, from the east.
6. Jews were integrated into all areas of life in Europe. Some Jews were rich landowners, while others were independent peasants.
7. Some lived in towns with a small Jewish quarter, but most lived on the land like their Christian neighbors.
8. Women were not as noticeably set apart from men in the Merovingian period as they had been in Roman times. Women received dowries and could inherit property; a few were independent entrepreneurs as well.

C. The Powerful in Merovingian Society, pp. 250–253

1. In Merovingian society, monarchs and aristocrats held power through hereditary wealth, status, and political influence.
2. Many aristocrats lived in leisurely abundance, the men spending their time honing their skills as warriors and developing the virtues necessary for leading armed men.
3. The production of children was the focus of marriage because heirs were crucial to the survival of aristocratic power and property.
4. Formal marriage was expensive, although there were less formal, less costly types of marriage.
5. By the seventh century, aristocrats abandoned classical texts and focused on giving their children a Christian education.
6. Bishops, generally aristocrats, ranked among the most powerful men of the time. Some, like Gregory of Tours, considered themselves to be protectors of their citizens, and all were expected to be the moral supervisors of priests.
7. Aristocratic families determined whom their daughters would marry because marriages bound together whole extended families.
8. Wives controlled their dowries and could sell, give away, or rent out their property if they were widowed and without children.
9. Some men made gifts or bequests of land to their wives or daughters, granting many aristocratic women enormous wealth.
10. Although legally controlled by their husbands, Merovingian women could exert control over their children and property or run their own lives (and others') by ruling convents as abbesses.
11. Unattached aristocratic women were rare and therefore valuable.
12. The Merovingian kings bolstered their power by allying themselves with the local lay aristocrats. They drew their power from plunder, the tax system, public lands, and legal fines; much of this system was based on the remaining framework of the Roman administration.
13. The king's courts functioned as schools for aristocratic sons, thus strengthening the bond between the monarchy and the aristocracy. Kings also sent officials—counts and dukes—to rule in their name in various regions.
14. Because the king acted as arbitrator for competing aristocratic interests, obtaining royal favor was crucial to receiving prominent appointments and land gifts.
15. The power of the kings conferred great authority on their chief court official, the mayor of the palace.
16. In time, one mayoral family, the Carolingians, would replace the Merovingian dynasty.

D. Christianity and Classical Culture in the British Isles, pp. 253–255

1. After the Anglo-Saxon invasions, England settled into a mosaic of about a dozen kingdoms ruled by separate kings.
2. Irish monks, converted by St. Patrick in the fifth century, introduced their form of Christianity to northern England. These Irish monasteries were organized around traditional rural clans, and typically were communities of blood relatives, servants, slaves, monks, and nuns.
3. Bishops were often under the authority of abbots since monasteries, rather than cities, were the centers of population settlement.
4. In southern England, Christianity was introduced by the missionaries of Pope Gregory the Great (r. 590–604).
5. Under the leadership of Augustine (not the same Augustine as the bishop of Hippo), these missionaries brought Roman practices that were at odds with Irish Christianity.
6. Stressing loyalty to the pope and a hierarchy of bishops rather than abbots, they divided England into dioceses headed by an archbishop and bishops.
7. The Roman and Irish churches disagreed on the correct date of Easter, a dispute resolved in 664 when Oswy, king of Northumbria, organized the Synod of Whitby. Oswy and his churchmen, convinced that Rome possessed the authority of St. Peter, chose the Roman calculation for the date of Easter, paving the way for Roman Christianity in England.
8. Rome was also esteemed by many English churchmen because it was a center of knowledge and holy objects.
9. Benedict Biscop (c. 630–690), a founder of two monasteries, traveled to Rome and brought back relics as well as many precious books that he used to establish a monastic library.

10. Christianity and its dependence on written texts transformed the previously oral cultures of England and Ireland, and during the seventh and eighth centuries Irish and English monasteries became centers of literature and learning.
11. Archbishop Theodore (r. 669–690) founded a school at Canterbury where texts of the classical past as well as Christian works were the objects of study.
12. Nonetheless, the vigorous Anglo-Saxon oral tradition was only partly superceded, and much of it was adapted to Christian culture.
13. Bede (673–735), another important scholar, encouraged Christian priests to use Anglo-Saxon to instruct the faithful. Anglo-Saxon also became a written language, unlike vernacular languages elsewhere in Europe, which were rarely written.
14. Despite the vitality of local culture, after the Synod of Whitby, the English church was tied to the Church of Rome.

E. Unity in Spain, Division in Italy, pp. 255–256

1. In Spain, the Visigothic king Leovigild (r. 569–586) established rule by military might, but as an Arian he lacked the support of the local elite.
2. Leovigild's son Reccared converted to Roman Christianity in 587, and at the Third Council of Toledo, most of the Arian bishops also converted. Afterward, bishops and kings in Spain cooperated in an unprecedented way.
3. Kings gave the churchmen the freedom to establish their own hierarchy, and the bishops in turn supported the Visigothic king, who ruled as a minister to the Christian people.
4. Bishops anointed the king in a ritual that paralleled the ordination of priests, and rebellion against the king was considered equal to rebellion against Christ.
5. This practice, together with the military support of the great landowners, helped centralize the power of the Visigoths. As a result, the Arabs, who arrived in 711, had only to defeat a single army and kill the king to conquer all of Visigothic Spain.
6. In Italy the Lombard king faced a hostile papacy and fiercely independent dukes.
7. Because of the uneven conversion of the Lombards to Roman Christianity, the Lombard kings never received strong support from churchmen.
8. Yet, through military power and the maintenance of Roman institutions, the Lombards kept their royal authority.
9. They assigned dukes to rule the stronger cities and established a royal capital at Pavia, where the kings built churches and monasteries, maintained defensive walls, and minted coins.
10. Lombard territory was never fully united. As soon as the Lombards began to make serious headway against the duchies of Spoleto and Benevento, the pope, fearing for his own position, called on the Franks for help.

F. Political Tensions and the Power of the Pope, p. 256

1. By 600, the pope was both ruler and subordinate.
2. Pope Gregory the Great (r. 590–604) laid many of the foundations for the papacy's later temporal and spiritual ascendancy.
3. He wielded great secular authority by organizing the defenses of Rome and paying for its army, hearing court cases, making treaties, and providing welfare services.
4. As a spiritual leader, Gregory sent missionaries to England; maintained close ties with churchmen in Spain, who were converting the Visigoths to Catholic Christianity; and wrote many spiritual works and biblical commentaries.
5. Gregory's handbook for the clergy, *Pastoral Rule*, encouraged practical reforms within the church and promoted clerical celibacy.
6. Yet the popes were also bishops of the Roman Empire, which was ruled by the eastern emperor in Constantinople. In the seventh century, however, the emperor's authority on religious matters began to unravel.
7. Justinian II convened a council in 691 that determined rules for the church.
8. Pope Sergius I (r. 681 or 689–701) rejected the rules because they permitted priestly marriages and prohibited fasting on Saturdays in Lent.
9. Outraged, Justinian tried to arrest the pope, but Italian armies sided with the pope against the emperor.
10. The rift widened in the early eighth century when Emperor Leo III tried to increase taxes on papal property.

11. In addition, Leo's ban on icons went against papal tolerance of relics and sacred images.
12. These tensions were accompanied by increasing friction between the papacy and the Lombards; Pope Zachary (r. 741–752) sought an ally in the Franks to the north by sanctioning the deposition of the last Merovingian king and backing his replacement, the first Carolingian king, Pippin III the Short (r. 751–768).
13. In 753, Pope Stephen II (r. 752–757) called on Pippin to march into Italy to fight the Lombards, and so events in Rome came to have a profound effect on the Frankish kingdom as well as Italy.

Lecture Strategies

1. The success of Islam depended in part on its simplicity of teachings, its appealing message, and its compatibility with Bedouin life. Explore the world into which Muhammad was born and the reasons for Islam's spectacular expansion in its first century. Hugh Kennedy provides a general introduction in *The Prophet and the Age of the Caliphates: The Islamic Near East from the Sixth to the Eleventh Century* (White Plains, NY: Longman, 1989). On the code of honor in Bedouin societies, see Frank Henderson Stewart, *Honor* (Chicago: University of Chicago Press, 1994). Patricia Crone, *Meccan Trade and the Rise of Islam* (Princeton: Princeton University Press, 1986) discusses the economic world of Mecca during Islam's early years.

2. The Byzantine Empire's transformation and internal struggles demonstrate how precarious these centuries were even for a region usually thought to have escaped the "dark ages" of the west. In particular, the controversy over icons highlights the tenuous peace in the area. Good guides to this period of Byzantine history include Mark Whittow, *The Making of Byzantium, 600–1025* (Berkeley: University of California Press, 1996); and John Julius Norwich, *Byzantium: The Early Centuries* (New York: Knopf, 1989). For a focused study on the role of icons in Byzantine history, see Kenneth Parry, *Depicting the Word: Byzantine Iconophile Thought of the Eighth and Ninth Centuries* (Boston: Brill, 1996).

3. Outline the particular advantages that the Merovingians enjoyed during this period and the legacy they developed for subsequent Carolingian rulers. An excellent introduction is Patrick Geary, *Before France and Germany: The Creation and Transformation of the Merovingian World* (Oxford: Oxford University Press, 1990). For a treatment that combats the common assessment of the Merovingians as quintessential barbarians, see Ian Wood, The *Merovingian Kingdoms, 450–751* (White Plains, NY: Longman, 1994).

4. Gregory the Great's pontificate was one of the most influential in history and set the course for an independent western Christendom. Explore his policies on both secular and ecclesiastical matters and the historical circumstances that might have influenced the increasing politicization of the papacy. Would it have been possible for the pope to have remained an exclusively, or even predominantly, spiritual authority during the early Middle Ages? The best fundamental biography is J. Richards, *Consul of God: The Life and Times of Gregory the Great* (New York and London: Routledge, 1980). For an investigation of his religious thought, see Carole Straw, *Gregory the Great: Perfection in Imperfection*, rprt. (Berkeley: University of California Press, 1991).

Class Discussion Starters

1. Have students discuss the terms "Dark Ages" and "Middle Ages." What are the origins of these terms? Are they at all useful, or should historians abandon them? What characteristics of the period following the fall of the Roman Empire in the west led some scholars to adopt such terminology?

2. Compare and contrast the challenges faced by the three principal heirs of Rome: the Byzantine Empire, the Muslim Arabs, and the western European kingdoms. Did all three experience the post-Roman era as one of decline?

3. War is often a catalyst for broader political and social changes. Discuss the impact of warfare on the Byzantine Empire, the Muslim Arabs, and the western Europeans between 600 and 750. Students might divide into groups, each one responsible for reporting back to the rest of the class on a different society.

4. Ask students to discuss the development of Sunni and Shi'ite branches of Islam. How did disagreement over who should succeed Muhammad lead to the division of Muslims? The establishment of the Umayyads and the fragmentation of Islam in its first century can be investigated in Bernard Lewis, ed., *Islam: From the Prophet Muhammad to the Capture of Constantinople*, vol. 1 (Oxford: Oxford University Press, 1987); and P. Holt and Bernard Lewis, eds., *Cambridge History of Islam*, vol. 1a (Cambridge: Cambridge University Press, 1978).

Reviewing the Text

Review Questions

1. How and why did the Muslims conquer so many lands in the period 632–750?

[model answer] *By his death in 632, Muhammad had, through persuasion, negotiation, and force, united much of the population of the Arabian Peninsula in Islam. Among these early converts were many Bedouin tribes, who began to turn their warrior culture to advancing the cause of Islam. As they united in Islam, the Bedouins took warrior skills, developed through generations of intertribal fighting, and turned them outward. The passion of their religious beliefs in what they believed to be the ultimate true faith fired their unity and determination to bring in unbelievers. Conquests came rapidly because some regions, such as the Byzantine and Sasanid states, were weakened from their own wars. Oppressed Christians and Jews in those and other regions welcomed the new Muslim overlords, who were more accepting of religious differences, and provided support in those areas for the new rulers.*

2. What stresses did the Byzantine Empire endure in the seventh and eighth centuries, and how was iconoclasm a response to those stresses?
[model answer] *Constant warfare resulting from invasions into Byzantium in the late sixth and seventh centuries undermined the integrity of its cities and the regional economy and cut the empire off culturally from the west. The region shifted from an urban-centered society to a rural-based society, which altered traditional hierarchies of authority. In these more uncertain times, religion began to assume greater importance than secular knowledge. Many people, particularly men serving the army who experienced the defeats of battle and the emperor who depended on those troops, began to question why God seemed to have turned away from the empire. Arabs, whose new religion of Islam forbade the worship of graven images, were repeatedly victorious. One cultural change that emerged from this was a belief that the worship of icons would alienate God. This iconoclasm became official policy as the emperor sought to regain favor and also to appease military troops.*

3. What were the similarities and differences among the kingdoms that emerged in western Europe, and how did their histories combine and diverge?
[model answer] *Political power and social relations in the countries that emerged from the western Roman Empire were structured by kin networks, church patronage, royal courts, and wealth. Daily life and government reflected a legacy of Roman traditions mixed with the ways of local peoples and the influences of the growing power of Christianity. Though Christianity was the dominant religious practice through the region, its expression varied: Irish worship was structured by its traditions of clan organization; the English church more strongly reflected the hierarchical traditions of Rome; Frankish Christianity revered Saints as agents of God's work. Spain retained stronger ties to Roman culture and strong connections between rulers of church leaders. In Italy, long-standing rivalries between secular leaders and the church created much weaker ties between church and state. In all, power was held by monarchs and aristocrats, who included religious leaders. In the Merovingian kingdoms, power gradually merged into three centers and then a single ruler, which strengthened power. A similar centralization of power in Spain led to its defeat as the invading Arabs' victory was accomplished by killing the king.*

Making Connections

1. What were the similarities and the differences in political organization in the Islamic, Byzantine, and western European worlds in the seventh century?
[model answer] *In Byzantium and the Islamic kingdom, power was centralized in a single leader and capital city, while western Europe was divided among regional powers, some controlling larger territories, such as England or the three Frankish kingdoms, while others held smaller territories, such as the kingdoms of Italy, though the tendency was toward the merging of larger regions under a central authority. In all three regions, secular and religious leaders shared political power. In Byzantium and western Europe, religious and political leadership shared power through their influence over each other and mutual need for support. In the Islamic world, religious beliefs place authority in a combined religious and political leader, the caliph.*

2. Compare and contrast the role of religion in the Islamic, Byzantine, and western European societies in the seventh century.
[model answer] *Religion was a central factor in daily and political life in all three regions. It influenced the social hierarchy and provided access to political power. In the Islamic world, it was the source of political authority and, as Islamic conquests spread, religion became a source of shared cultural identity among diverse groups of people. Although all were predominantly Christian cultures, the kingdoms of Byzantium and western Europe interpreted religious doctrines in different ways, which contributed to their development of difference cultural identities. However, all shared with Islam the same religious roots of monotheism and shared religious origins.*

Discussing the Documents

Questions from Online Study Guide with Model Answers

The Fatihah of the Qur'an (p. 234)

1. What, besides his oneness, does the Fatihah emphasize about God?
[model answer] *The Fatihah presents God as compassionate and caring, and as both the source and ultimate judge of human life.*

2. How does the Muslim idea of God compare to Jewish and Christian ideas of God?

[model answer] *All three are very similar in their views of God as the creator of life and judge of human behavior, as well as a God of compassion for those in need.*

On Holy Images (p. 245)

1. How does John of Damascus justify the worship of icons?
[model answer] *John of Damascus believes that God became visible so humans could view him in the flesh and that in such incarnations, as are represented by icons, the physical representations take on the spiritual quality of God and become a union with him. Without such visible icons it would not be possible to represent God, who is a spirit. Therefore, worshipping icons is the same a worshipping God.*

2. How does John distinguish between God and the images depicted in icons?
[model answer] *God is a spirit with no body and no visible form. Icons are representations of that essence and become its embodiment in a visible form that humans can recognize.*

3. How does John compare the relationship of among the Trinity (God, Christ, and the Holy Spirit) to the relationship between God and an icon?
[model answer] *An icon is not God, nor his spirit, but a representation of his flesh in the same way that the Son of God became flesh so that humans could recognize and understand his presence. Icons are a means provided by God for humans to connect with the divine in the same way as the Trinity provides this connection.*

New Sources, New Perspectives: Anthropology, Archaeology, and Changing Notions of Ethnicity (p. 249)

1. The society of the United States has been called a melting pot. In what ways might the same be said about European societies?
[model answer] *Modern European societies were certainly melting pots in their emergence as distinct societies through the early Middle Ages. Roman culture mixed with existing regional cultures, which then blended with traditions of the invaders who spread through the Roman Empire. Trade networks also spread cultural views and practices. The societies that emerged in western Europe blended the traditions of various ethnic groups into what evolved as distinctive national cultures by the modern era.*

2. How do common myths nourish contemporary notions of ethnicity?
[model answer] *Beliefs that certain cultural practices or views are a result of biologically determined character and abilities foster views that some ethnicities are inherently inferior or indelibly exhibit a particular cultural trait. Such beliefs lead to emphasis on the differences among groups of people and also can deny the possibilities for cultural change within an ethnic group. If change in cultural practices and beliefs within a group is not recognized, then groups risk losing ethnic identity in the view of others if these certain attached traits do change.*

Other Questions for Discussing These Documents in Class

The Fatihah of the Qur'an (p. 234)

1. The Qur'an is a compilation of the messages Muhammad received during his life from the archangel Gabriel. Ask students to consider how God is described in the text and compare it to the way God is portrayed in the Old Testament and the New Testament.

2. The relatively short phrases emphasize the poetic nature of the Qur'an, but what other reasons were there for brevity? For example, Muslims were expected to memorize as much of the Qur'an as possible, and keeping passages brief aided that task. Simplistic verses were also appropriate for uncomplicated messages about God's love.

On Holy Images (p. 245)

1. Ask students to explain how John of Damascus justified the use of icons.

2. Why might the popes in Rome have supported icons although the Byzantine emperors came to oppose them?

New Sources, New Perspectives: Anthropology, Archaeology, and Changing Notions of Ethnicity (p. 249)

1. Have students explain how scholars' understanding of ethnicity has changed.

2. How have newer, cultural notions of ethnicity affected historians' interpretations of the early medieval period in Europe?

Comparative Questions

1. Do ethnicity and religion have anything in common? For example, if ethnicity is cultural, and therefore can be acquired or shed, can the same be said of adherence to Christianity or Islam?

2. Compare and contrast the Fatihah of the Qur'an and John of Damascus's discussion of holy images. In what ways is God similar in both texts? What differences are there? Do the similarities indicate that Muslims would share John's views about icons?

For Users of *Sources of The Making of the West*

The following documents are available in Chapter 8 of the companion sourcebook by Katharine J. Lualdi, University of Southern Maine.

1. The Foundations of Islam: *Qur'an*, Suras 1, 53, 98 (c. 610–632)
2. Jihad and Jizya: *Islamic Terms of Peace* (633–643)
3. Byzantine Life: *The Life of St. Theodore of Sykeon* (Early Seventh Century)
4. A Noblewoman's Life: *The Life of Lady Balthild, Queen of the Franks* (Late Seventh Century)
5. Roman Christian Missions: Pope Gregory the Great, *Letters* (598–601)

Discussion Ideas for Sources of The Making of the West, *Chapter 8*

1. Christianity and Islam are both proselytizing religions. What strategies did leaders of each pursue to encourage new adherents, and how did each respond to members of other faiths? Considering Jihad and Jizya: Islamic Terms of Peace, how did Muslim leaders treat Jews and Christians in their territories? What reasons did these Muslim leaders have for accommodating with the "peoples of the book"? Were their motives primarily religious, political, or financial? How could Muslims reconcile their belief that Allah is the one true God with their policies of toleration? How do the letters dictating terms of peace characterize Allah? What purpose might the authors have hoped to serve by describing God in this manner?

2. How do the letters of Pope Gregory compare with those of the Arab officials? Was Gregory, like the Arabs, willing to tolerate the continued practice of religions other than his own? Why might Gregory have decided that the church should accommodate with local practices? How do Gregory's letters, written to a bishop and an abbot, compare with those written by Muslim officials to the people they have conquered? What impact would the relative size of the non-Christian community have on Gregory's policies? For example, is accommodation necessary because the pagan population was in the majority? How would this situation compare with that in the Arab world where non-Muslims were a minority?

Working with Visual Sources

For this exercise, please refer to Mosaic at Santo Stefano Rotondo on page 257 of the textbook or view the image on the book companion site's Online Study Guide under the "Visual Activity" for Chapter 8.

Students viewing the image at the Online Study Guide are asked three questions of the image. The questions and model answers (not made available to students) are below. Project this image, available on the Instructor's Resources CD-ROM, in class or ask students to look at the image in their textbooks and answer the questions.

1. What is depicted in this mosaic?
[model answer] *The mosaic depicts a cross topped with the head of Jesus, surrounded by a round border. On either side of the cross are two Roman martyrs, Primus and Felician. They are wearing floor-length robes and each carries a scroll and has a halo.*

2. Why did Pope Theodore want to depict Primus and Felician?
[model answer] *Pope Theodore had moved the relics of the two martyrs to this church in Santo Stefano. He had them depicted in the mosaic to remind local churchgoers that the relics provided special protection to the church and its faithful. Expensive and beautiful mosaics, like this one, that incorporate styles and materials frequently used by Byzantine artists, helped to emphasize the wealth and status of the pope.*

3. Judging from this mosaic, why might the popes be opposed to iconoclasm?
[model answer] *The figures of the martyrs and the face of Jesus provide familiar and accessible focuses for worship; for many churchgoers, the image of their God and those of other protective entities such as the martyrs are more comprehensible and comforting than abstract symbols of an abstract force. Associating holy powers with specific individuals provided a focus for worship and a foundation for faith. Iconoclasm took away that focus by forbidding all images of saints, martyrs, or God that might have threatened the fidelity of some Christians and the longevity of the Catholic Church.*

For this exercise, please refer to Seeing History: Persian Silver Coin (minted 606) and Umayyad Silver Dirham (minted 696/697) on page 239 of the textbook or view the images on the book companion site's Online Study Guide under the "Visual Activity: Seeing History" for Chapter 8.

Students viewing the images at the Online Study Guide are asked two questions about the images. The questions and model answers (not made available to students) are below. Project these images, available on the Instructor's Resources CD-ROM, in class or ask students to look at the images in their textbooks and answer the questions.

1. Which elements on the Arabic coin show Persian influence and which are distinctively Arabic?
[model answer] *The Arabic coin borrows from the earlier Persian model by including a portrait of a*

Sasanid ruler and depictions of crescents and stars. Arabic elements include the name of the Ummayad provincial governor and the inscription mentioning Allah.

2. What does this suggest about the relationship between the Islamic world and the Persian Empire they conquered?
[model answer] *Although the Arabs conquered the Persians militarily, they accommodated with their culture, borrowing certain elements. They retained the portrait of a Persian Sasanid leader and adopted the imagery of the crescents and stars, while adding the Muslim Arabic text. The Ummayads' depiction of a human form, despite the prohibition of such images by other Muslims, suggests their flexibility in assimilating Persian traditions and building upon them to claim legitimacy as new rulers in the area of modern Iraq and Iran.*

Mapping Exercises

Map Activity from OSG—Model Answer for Map Activity #2

For this activity, please refer to the map on page 258. Students are asked these questions:

How was the former Roman Empire divided up in 750?
[model answer] *The most significant division was the Umayyad caliphate, which encompassed Persia, Arabia, Syria, North Africa, and Spain. The Byzantine Empire by this time had been reduced to Anatolia, Greece, parts of mainland Italy, and the islands of Sicily and Sardinia. The Frankish kingdom was also a major power, holding most of Gaul and parts of western Germany.*

Why did the pope, isolated in Rome, look northward to the Franks for protection against the Lombards?
[model answer] *The pope was engaged in conflicts with the Byzantine emperor over issues such as increasing taxes, priestly marriage, and the worship of icons, and realized that the attention of Constantinople was focused eastward toward the Arab threat. Because the Franks were relatively near, and because they shared a common border with the Lombards, the pope correctly assumed that the Franks would be interested in defeating the Lombards militarily.*

Map 8.1: Expansion of Islam to 750, p. 236

Have students identify the regions that were acquired by the Muslims during the first great wave of Islamic expansion. How might control of these areas have aided in the further conquest of new territories? What can students surmise about the effectiveness of the Arabic language and Islam as unifying forces across such a great geographical expanse, much of it consisting of mountainous, desert terrain?

Map 8.2: Byzantine and Sasanid Empires, c. 600, p. 241

Which of the two empires appears larger and why? How did the location of the Arabs facilitate their invasion of each empire?

Map 8.3, Diagram of the City of Ephesus, p. 242

Discuss the transformation of the city reflected in this map. Ask students to contrast the nature of the central sites of the ancient city (such as the agora and embolos) with those of the medieval city. What do they reveal about the quality of urban life in the earlier period? Its institutions? Occupations? How cosmopolitan do the students judge ancient Ephesus to have been? What might account for the adaptation of older structures for new uses, such as transforming ancient baths into medieval residences? Compare this map to the map of Tours, c. 600 (page 248).

Map 8.4: The Merovingian Kingdoms in the Seventh Century, p. 247

Ask students to identify the three principal Merovingian kingdoms. How might their locations account for the fact that Aquitaine and the tributary regions were governed differently? Given the territorial extent of the kingdoms, what reasons might kings have had for traveling continuously and not settling in a capital city?

Mapping the West: Europe and the Mediterranean, c. 750, p. 258

Ask students how this map reflects the changed balance of power that characterized the west during this period. Which portions of the former Roman Empire were now under Byzantine control? Under Islamic control? How might Islamic hegemony over so extensive a portion of the formerly great ancient empires of Rome, Persia, and Alexander have affected the preservation of the learning and cultures of the past in these areas?

In-Class Assignments and Presentation Topics

1. Ask students to recreate the debate surrounding icons in the Byzantine Empire, using relevant primary sources to enumerate the arguments on both sides of the issue. John of Damascus's statements in defense of icons and the decrees of the Iconoclast

Council of Constantinople (754) are available in the "Byzantium" section of the Internet Medieval Sourcebook.

2. In early medieval Islamic societies, both Jews and Christians enjoyed religious toleration as "peoples of the book." Ask students to discuss the relationship of Islam to its sibling monotheistic religions, Judaism and Christianity, as presented in the Qur'an. Several translations of the complete text are available in the Internet Islamic History Sourcebook.

3. The status of women and the role of the family in early Islam can be explored through numerous primary texts and Web sites. For a scholarly discussion, students can also consult Leila Ahmed, *Women and Gender in Islam: Historical Roots of a Modern Debate* (New Haven, CT: Yale University Press, 1992), which, among other topics, discusses the influence of Bedouin societal norms and practices on the dynamics of gender roles within Islam.

4. The Merovingians, with their long-haired kings, possessed an often brutal and highly colorful history that students may want to explore. Ask them to recreate that history by reading *Gregory of Tours, History of the Franks.*

5. One of the most influential legacies of ancient Rome for the Germanic societies that superseded it was its law. Numerous Germanic kings issued their own codes in imitation of the ancient compilations. These laws, many of which survive, can help students reconstruct the norms and values of the early medieval Germanic kingdoms. The Lombard codifications are translated, with commentary, in Katherine Fischer Drew, *The Lombard Laws* (Philadelphia: University of Pennsylvania Press, 1973).

6. The Christianization of western Europe occurred over a long period of time and, in the process, its new converts transformed the religion. Ask students to discuss the impact that the norms of Germanic warrior culture had on the Christian faith (and vice versa) as Germanic peoples abandoned their traditional polytheism for the new religion. Excellent sources for this question are the histories of the various Germanic groups that were written by contemporary churchmen (but remind students of the point of view from which these works were produced). Relevant portions of Bede's *Ecclesiastical History*, Jordanes's *History of the Goths*, and Gregory of Tours's *History of the Franks* are contained in *Readings in Medieval History*, Patrick Geary, ed., 2nd ed. (Peterborough, Ont.: Broadview Press, 1997).

Essay Questions

1. Students interested in military history might want to investigate the reorganization of the Byzantine military during this troubled period in its history. See the studies by J. F. Haldon, *Recruitment and Conscription in the Byzantine Army c. 550–950: A Study on the Origins of the Stratiotika Ktemata* (Vienna, 1979); and W. E. Kaegi, *Byzantine Military Unrest, 471–843: An Interpretation* (Amsterdam: A. M. Hakkert, 1981).

2. Abbesses and elite women frequently occupied influential positions in the Christianized Germanic kingdoms of western Europe. Among the numerous books on this subject are Suzanne Wemple, *Women in Frankish Society: Marriage and the Cloister, 500 to 900* (Philadelphia: University of Pennsylvania Press, 1981); Dick Harrison, *The Age of Abbesses and Queens: Gender and Political Culture in Early Medieval Europe* (Lund, Sweden: Nordic Academic Press, 1998); and Jo Ann McNamara, John Halborg, and Gordon Whatley, eds., *Sainted Women of the Dark Ages* (Durham, NC: Duke University Press, 1992).

3. Religious practices, such as the veneration of relics, of early medieval Christianity often seem quite superstitious and alien to students. An excellent, short introduction to the role saints occupied in early Christendom is Peter Brown, *The Cult of the Saints: Its Rise and Function in Latin Christianity* (Chicago: University of Chicago Press, 1981). On relics, see Patrick Geary, *Living with the Dead in the Middle Ages* (Ithaca, NY: Cornell University Press, 1995). For comparisons of similar practices in a slightly later period, students can consult Lester Little, *Benedictine Maledictions: Liturgical Cursing in Romanesque France* (Ithaca, NY: Cornell University Press, 1994); and Patrick Geary, *Sacra Furta: Thefts of Relics in the Central Middle Ages* (Princeton: Princeton University Press, 1990).

Additional Resources: Literature

Dawood, N. J., trans., *The Koran*. 1990.
Guillaume, A., trans., *The Life of Muhammad*. 1955.
Sherley-Price, Leo, trans., *Bede: The Eccelsiastical History of the English Peoples*. 1991.
Thorpe, Lewis, trans., *Gregory of Tours: The History of the Franks*. 1983.

Additional Resources: Film and Video

OTHER BEDFORD/ST. MARTIN'S RESOURCES FOR CHAPTER 8

The following resources are available to accompany Chapter 8. Please refer to the Preface of this manual for detailed descriptions of all the ancillaries.

For Instructors

Transparencies

The following maps and image from Chapter 8 are available as full-color acetates.

- Map 8.1: Expansion of Islam to 750
- Map 8.2: Byzantine and Sasanid Empires, c. 600
- Map 8.3: Diagram of the City of Ephesus
- Map 8.4: The Merovingian Kingdoms in the Seventh Century
- Mapping the West: Europe and the Mediterranean, c. 750
- Icon of the Virgin and Child, p. 244
- Mosaic at Santo Stefano Rotondo, p. 257

Instructor's Resources CD-ROM

The following maps and image from Chapter 8, as well as a chapter outline, are available on disc in both PowerPoint and jpeg formats.

- Map 8.1: Expansion of Islam to 750
- Map 8.2: Byzantine and Sasanid Empires, c. 600
- Map 8.3: Diagram of the City of Ephesus
- Map 8.4: The Merovingian Kingdoms in the Seventh Century
- Mapping the West: Europe and the Mediterranean, c. 750
- Mosaic at Santo Stefano Rotondo, p. 257

For Students

Study Guides

The Online Study Guide at **bedfordstmartins.com/hunt** helps students synthesize the material they have learned as well as practice the skills historians use to make sense of the past. The following Map, Visual, and Document activities are available for Chapter 8.

Map Activity

- Mapping the West: Europe and the Mediterranean, c. 750, p. 258

Visual Activity

- Mosaic at Santo Stefano Rotondo, p. 257

Reading Historical Documents

- The Fatihah of the Qur'an, page 234
- On Holy Images, page 245
- New Sources, New Perspectives: Anthropology, Archaeology, and Changing Notions of Ethnicity, p. 249

CHAPTER

9

Emperors, Caliphs, and Local Lords

750–1050

Chapter Resources

Main Chapter Topics

1. From 850 to 1050, the Byzantine, Islamic, and western Christian worlds experienced the rise of powerful, but short-lived empires that were quickly supplanted by the dispersal of power under the control of numerous local rulers. In all three regions, new military elites also arose. Despite these stressful times, each realm witnessed a corresponding period of artistic and intellectual renaissance.

2. After a century of defensive warfare against the Muslims, the Byzantine Empire went on the offensive (c. 850) and recovered some of the territory it had lost. These victories led to a revival of court life during the Macedonian renaissance (c. 870–1025).

3. The new states of Bulgaria, Serbia, and Kievan Russia emerged from the Slavic polities established from 850 to 950 and were heavily influenced by Byzantine religion and culture.

4. Civil war in the Islamic world ended the Umayyad caliphate in 750, which was succeeded by the Abbasid caliphate based in Baghdad. Islamic political and religious unity splintered into regional Islamic states during the ninth century. These states remained united by commerce and the Arabic language. The entire Islamic world experienced an artistic and scientific renaissance from about 790 to 1050.

5. In France, the Carolingian mayors of the palace deposed the Merovingian kings (c. 750). The military conquests of Charlemagne (r. 768–814) created the largest empire since the fragmentation of the western Roman Empire in the fifth century.

6. Hoping to combine Germanic and Roman strengths in a new Christian empire, Charlemagne imitated ancient imperial practices by conducting a building campaign at his capital of Aachen, standardizing weights and measures, promoting education, and improving communication and law enforcement throughout his realm. Pope Leo III endorsed his efforts on Christmas day, 800, crowning him "Emperor and Augustus" in Rome. This action marked a definitive papal swing away from the Byzantine emperor and toward the west.

7. The gains of the Carolingians were largely lost in the chaos of intrafamilial struggles that followed under Charlemagne's successors (814–911). This conflict resulted in the three-part division of the empire with the Treaty of Verdun (843), which roughly defined the divisions of modern Europe.

8. As the Carolingian Empire disintegrated, foreigners invaded: Vikings from the north, Muslims from the south, and Magyars from the east. Vikings eventually settled in the Danelaw in England, halted by King Alfred the Great (r. 871–899). In France, they settled in Normandy after the conversion of their leader, Rollo, to Christianity in 911. During that same period, Muslims began to conquer Sicily. The Magyars were defeated in 955 at Lechfeld by the German king Otto I (r. 936–973).

Focus Question

What forces led to the dissolution—or weakening—of centralized governments in the period 750–1050, and what institutions took their place?

1. In the eighth century, Arab Muslim invaders challenged both the Byzantine empire and the kingdoms of western Europe. While the Muslims established long-lasting societies in the Middle East, North Africa, and Spain, Frankish and Byzantine leaders turned their military victories against the invaders into stronger, more centralized governments. Charlemagne, descendant of Charles Martel, the Frankish leader who

had defeated Muslims from al-Andalus in 732, built upon his predecessors' military victories to create the largest western European empire since the Romans. Similarly, Byzantine emperors capitalized on their victories over Muslim attackers in Asia Minor, going on the offensive in the second half of the ninth century. The subsequent relative prosperity of both the Byzantine and Carolingian empires supported cultural renaissances which rivaled that of the Islamic world in the same period. In each region, military success translated into cultural flowering.

2. Over the long run, however, forces of localism and regional fragmentation prevailed in all three areas. In the Byzantine Empire, the booty and new lands obtained through military victories fueled the emergence of the *dynatoi* as new, local elites whose power competed with the centralized authority of the emperors in Constantinople. The Islamic and western European realms experienced even greater fragmentation. Regional lords challenged the power of the Abbasid caliphs, establishing autonomous territories in al-Andalus and the Fatimid caliphate. Divisions within Islam between Sunnis and Shi'ites, as well as ethnic differences, reinforced the fragmentation. In western Europe, the unity of Charlemagne proved short-lived in the wake of regional differences and the emergence of local leaders such as the castellans who provided more immediate, localized defense against groups such as the Vikings and who exercised effective leadership based on personal bonds.

Annotated Chapter Outline

I. The Emperor and Local Elites in the Byzantine Empire

A. Imperial Power, pp. 262–264

1. Around 850, the Byzantines stopped merely defending their territory and began advancing on the Islamic Empire, reclaiming much of the territory lost one hundred years earlier.
2. These victories gave new prestige to the army and imperial court, and emperors collected revenues from vast imperial estates along with taxes and services in lieu of taxes from the general population.
3. Emperors exchanged ambassadors with other rulers and held elaborate ceremonies to receive and entertain foreign diplomats. These ceremonies were meant to demonstrate the sacred power of imperial majesty.
4. The emperor's great wealth was accumulated from a prosperous agricultural economy organized for trade.
5. Markets organized by entrepreneurs attracted foreign merchants and a steady stream of commodities that ensured imperial revenues.
6. Because trade was intermingled with foreign policy, the Byzantine government considered trade a political as well as an economic matter.
7. Emperors therefore offered privileges, such as reduced customs dues and free lodging, to certain foreign traders such as Venetians and Syrians.

B. The Macedonian Renaissance, c. 870–c. 1025, pp. 264–266

1. With the empire regaining its military strength and the court remembering Byzantium's past glory, the Byzantine emperors revived classical intellectual pursuits.
2. Icons were restored permanently in 843, and the scholarly elite were encouraged to thrive once again.
3. Basil I (r. 867–886) from Macedonia founded the imperial dynasty of the period known as the Macedonian renaissance ("rebirth") (c. 870–c. 1025).
4. Centered in Constantinople, the renaissance of the study of classics was advanced by intellectual elite who had continued to study classics over the preceding century despite the trend toward a religious education.
5. New artistic works flourished under the sponsorship of emperors and members of the imperial court who served as patrons to writers, philosophers, and historians.
6. Scholars wrote summaries of classical literature and copied manuscripts of religious texts.
7. The clearest evidence of the integration of classical and Christian traditions is found in painted illustrations (called illuminations) in hand-copied manuscripts. Artists made their illustrations comprehensible by blending classical models with Christian subjects.

C. The *Dynatoi*: A New Landowning Elite, p. 266

1. Alongside the scholarly and artistic elite in Byzantium, a new elite group formed in the countryside that was made up of powerful military families called *dynatoi*

who had enriched themselves with booty and new lands taken during the wars of the tenth century.

2. Although they usually exercised power locally, they competed with imperial power and at times even occupied the imperial throne, as was the case with Nicephorus Phocas II, who was declared emperor by his armies and ruled Constantinople (963–969) until rival dynatoi brought him down.
3. The dynatoi took over entire villages and used peasant labor for their advantage.
4. In this way, the social hierarchy resembled that of western Europe, where land owned by aristocrats was farmed by peasants whose tax and service obligations bound them to the land they cultivated.

D. In Byzantium's Shadow: Bulgaria, Serbia, Russia, pp. 266–268

1. The shape of modern eastern Europe was created during the period 850–950.
2. Slavic settlements dotted the region from the Danube River south to Greece and north to the Black Sea.
3. Under Khagan Krum (r. c. 803–814), the Bulgars ruled over a large realm of Slavic peoples, but they faced campaigns by Emperor Nicephorus I (r. 802–811) to reclaim former Byzantine regions.
4. Nicephorus waged war against the Slavs of Greece and established a new Christian diocese in their territory, organizing it into a *theme* and settling Christians there to counter Slavic paganism.
5. Nicephorus again attacked the Bulgars but was killed by Khagan Krum.
6. After a truce established in 816, a period of intermittent skirmishes and wars followed until Emperor Basil II ("the Bulgar-Slayer" [r. 976–1025]) began a slow and methodical conquest that reclaimed the region for Byzantium and forced the Bulgarian ruler to accept Christianity.
7. The Byzantines also supported the new Serbian state, which opposed the Bulgars.
8. In 863, two brothers—Cyril and Methodius—went as missionaries to the Slavs and devised the first alphabet for the Slavic language.
9. In Russia, the Vikings (who penetrated from the north by the ninth century) blended into the larger Slavic population.
10. One of the Viking chiefs, Oleg, controlled southwestern Russia, and his tribal association formed the nucleus of Kievan Russia.
11. Around 905, Oleg marched to Constantinople, forcing the Byzantines to open their empire to Russian trade in exchange for peace.
12. Russian ties to Byzantium were further strengthened when Vladimir (r. c. 980–1015), grand prince of Kiev and Russia, adopted Byzantine Christianity and married the emperor's sister Anna. Vladimir's conversion made Russia heir to Byzantine culture and religion, but set it apart from Roman Catholic western Europe.
13. Still, Russian rulers like Prince Iaroslav the Wise (r. 1019–1054), via marriages and intellectual development, connected Russia with the classical past.
14. The contentious heirs of Iaroslav embroiled Kievan Russia in civil wars.
15. Geographically at the crossroads between the Islamic east and the Christian west, Russia was enriched by many traditions but remained vulnerable to military pressures.

II. The Caliphate and Its Fragmentation

A. The Abbasid Caliphate, 750–c. 950, pp. 268–269

1. In 750, a civil war ousted the Umayyads and established the new Abbasid caliphate to rule over Islam.
2. The Abbasids had formed an uneasy coalition with the Shi'ites and non-Arabs, who had been excluded from the Umayyad government.
3. The Abbasids shifted the location of its capital away from Damascus—with its Roman traditions—and established a new capital at Baghdad, near the Sasanid capital of Ctesiphon.
4. The Abbasid caliphs adopted Sasanid court ceremonies and made their administration more centralized; they controlled the appointment of regional governors and increased their staffs.
5. The Abbasid caliph Harun al-Rashid (r. 786–809) ruled over a splendid and flourishing empire.
6. The Abbasid rule fell into decline after Harun's death, however, because its tax base was inadequate to support a huge army and a complex civil administration.
7. Governors of regions such as Syria and Egypt often refused to remit tax revenue,

and ex-soldiers—seeking higher salaries and supporting different caliphs—fought for power in savage civil wars.

8. During the tenth century, the caliphs became figureheads and independent rulers took over various Islamic regions.
9. Many of these new rulers came to depend on armies of Mamluks: Turkish slaves or freedmen trained as professional, mounted soldiers.
10. Mamluks were well paid, allowing them to maintain their own horses and arms, and their prestige gained them high positions at the courts of regional rulers.

B. Regional Diversity in Islamic Lands, pp. 269–270

1. The Islamic world was vulnerable to fragmentation because it was based on the conquest of diverse regions. Muslims were of different ethnicities, practiced different customs, and identified with different areas.
2. By the tenth and eleventh centuries, Islamic states were built on local traditions and local rulers, while the split between Sunnis and Shi'ites still polarized Muslims.
3. In 909, one group of Shi'ites in North Africa, the Fatimids, built a Muslim state ruling Tunisia and by 969 declared themselves rulers of Egypt.
4. For two hundred years, the Fatimid dynasty controlled North Africa, Arabia, and even Syria for a time.
5. Sunni Muslims ruled al-Andalus, Islamic Spain's central and southern heart, after the Umayyad Abd al-Rahman fled to Morocco (756) during the Abbasid revolution, gathered an army, and invaded Spain.
6. Victorious, he took the secular title *emir* ("commander") and fixed his capital at Córdoba.
7. The Spanish emirate ruled over a broad range of peoples that included Jews and Christians, who were allowed to worship and live according to their own laws.
8. Abd al-Rahman III (r. 912–961) took the title caliph ("successor") and granted all religious groups freedom and equal opportunity in the civil service.
9. He also made diplomatic contacts with Byzantine and European rulers.
10. Nevertheless, like western Europe and Byzantium, the Spanish emirate fell victim to internal fragmentation after 1031, when rulers of the small independent regions called *taifas* took power.

C. Unity of Commerce and Language, pp. 270–271

1. Despite their diversity, the regions of Islam maintained a measure of unity via trade networks and language.
2. Arabic, the language of the Qur'an, was used in both commerce and government.
3. Although every region had its own political and commercial systems, borders remained open; there were few obstacles to travel and trade.
4. These open borders extended to non-Muslims as well. For example, the Tustari brothers, Jewish merchants from southern Iran, established a flourishing textile business between Iran and Egypt.
5. The Tustaris' commercial success helped them achieve high status in Jewish society and afforded them contacts with Muslim rulers.
6. Converting to Islam, a son of one of the brothers became *vizier* ("chief minister") to the Fatimids in Egypt.
7. Islamic society supported networks more vast than those represented by the Tustari brothers.
8. Muslim merchants engaged in trade with England, Timbuktu, central Africa, and Russia.

D. The Islamic Renaissance, c. 790–1050, pp. 271–272

1. The dissolution of the caliphate multiplied the centers of learning and intellectual productivity, allowing the Islamic renaissance to flourish throughout the Islamic world.
2. This renaissance was particularly strong in court centers such as Córdoba, where tenth-century caliphs sponsored scholars, poets, and artists.
3. As early as the eighth century, the Abbasid caliphs also endowed research libraries and set up centers where scholars read, translated, and commented on classics from Persia, India, and Greece.
4. Others excelled in mathematics: Al-Khwarizmi wrote a well-known book on equations (c. 825) that became the basis for modern algebra; another scholar used Indian numerals to arrive at the concept of zero.

5. These concepts were introduced into western Europe four centuries later and known as "Arabic" numerals.
6. The new independent Islamic rulers also supported science.
7. Ibn Sina (980–1037), known in the west as Avicenna, wrote books on logic, the natural sciences, and physics. His *Canon of Medicine* systematized earlier treatises and reconciled them with his own experience as a physician.
8. Long before there were universities in the west, institutions of higher learning existed in the Islamic world. Each madrasa ("school") was within or attached to a mosque.
9. Professors led classes on interpreting the Qur'an and other literary and legal texts. The students (who were all men) paid a fee for learning, but there were also scholarship students.
10. In Byzantium and the west, scholars wrote on expensive parchment that kept manuscripts in the hands of the very rich.
11. In Islam, however, the use of cheaper paper, made from materials such as rags and vegetable fibers, made the writings of the intellectual elite widely available.

III. The Creation and Division of a New European Empire

A. The Rise of the Carolingians, pp. 272–273

1. The Carolingians came to power by monopolizing the position of palace mayor under the Merovingian kings.
2. Charles Martel, palace mayor from 714 to 741, gained renown for defeating an invading army of Muslims from al-Andalus in 732. His name is used to refer to the dynasty (*Carolus* is Latin for "Charles").
3. Martel spent most of his time fighting other aristocrats trying for independent lordships.
4. Martel and his family turned aristocratic factions against one another and allied themselves with influential religious and political institutions, gaining the loyalty of both lay and clerical aristocrats.
5. In 751, Pippin III (d. 768), Charles Martel's son, deposed the last Merovingian king, took the throne himself, and persuaded Pope Zachary to legitimize his actions.
6. The Carolingians returned the favor by supporting the pope against the Lombards a few years later.
7. Pippin campaigned against the Lombard king until 756, when the Donation of Pippin made peace between the papacy and the Lombards.
8. The papacy regained control of cities that had been ruled by the Lombards, and the Roman pope's rule over the "republic of St. Peter" tied Italy to the policies of the pope and the Frankish kings, rather than to those of the Byzantine emperors.
9. The Carolingian partnership with the Roman church was expressed through the ceremony of anointment, during which bishops put holy oil on the foreheads of the Carolingian kings.

B. Charlemagne and His Kingdom, 768–814, pp. 273–275

1. The most famous Carolingian king was Charles the Great, called Charlemagne (r. 768–814).
2. Although sometimes brutal, he supported scholarly enterprises and won many wars intended to reunite Europe.
3. Charlemagne invaded Italy and seized the crown of the Lombard kings in 774.
4. Then he began a long war in the north with the Saxons, finally seizing their territory and converting them at sword point to Christianity.
5. Charlemagne also campaigned successfully against the Avars to the southeast.
6. He met with less success against the Arabs to the southwest, although he did establish a military buffer zone, or march, between al-Andalus and his own realm.
7. By the 790s, a realm the size of Charlemagne's had not been seen since the Roman Empire.
8. Charlemagne began to follow the old Roman model by sponsoring building programs, standardizing weights and measures, and serving as an intellectual and artistic patron.
9. He built a capital city at Aachen, where he copied many classical architectural elements from Byzantine Ravenna.
10. To discourage corruption, Charlemagne appointed special officials called *missi dominici* ("those sent out by the lord king") to oversee his regional governors, the counts.
11. Around the mid 750s, papal officials forged a document called the Donation of Constantine that declared the pope heir of

the Emperor Constantine's secular powers and territory.

12. This claim increased tensions between the Carolingians and the pope and the eastern emperor at Constantinople, which led to a precarious balance among the three powers.
13. In 799, however, Pope Leo III (r. 795–816) tipped the balance when he fled Rome under accusations of adultery and perjury to seek protection from Charlemagne.
14. Charlemagne sent him back to Rome under royal protection. In return, Leo, supported by all the clergy and nobles, crowned Charlemagne emperor and acclaimed him as "Augustus" on Christmas day, 800.
15. Although Charlemagne was greatly displeased by the pope playing "emperor maker," he later chose a title that implied he was indeed God's chosen emperor of the Roman Empire.

C. The Carolingian Renaissance, c. 790–c. 900, pp. 275–277

1. Beginning in the 790s, and continuing for about a century, the Carolingians supported a revival of learning designed to enhance their status, educate their officials, reform the liturgy, and purify Christianity.
2. Scholars studied and worked to create accurate texts of everything they read, from Roman imperial writers, such as Suetonius and Virgil, to the works of church fathers.
3. The English scholar Alcuin (c. 732–804) brought Anglo-Saxon scholarship to the court at Aachen, where he became Charlemagne's chief adviser.
4. Alcuin wrote letters on the king's behalf, counseled him on policy, and tutored members of the king's household, including the women.
5. Charlemagne entrusted him with improving an edition of the Vulgate (the Latin Bible).
6. Charlemagne ordered the cathedrals and monasteries to teach reading and writing to all who wanted to learn, and some churchmen expressed hope that schools for children would be established in even the smallest villages.
7. Although this dream was never realized, it indicates that, at the same time the Islamic world was organizing the madrasa system of schools, the Carolingians were thinking about the importance of education for more than just a small number of elites.
8. Like the Byzantines, Carolingian artists illuminated texts modeled after early images.
9. Long after the Carolingian dynasty had ended, their mode of inquiry and scholastic endeavors continued in monastic schools for generations.
10. The invention of standardized, easily read handwriting, the Caroline minuscule, made manuscript study easier for future scholars.

D. Charlemagne's Successors, 814–911, pp. 277–278

1. Charlemagne's son and successor, Louis the Pious (r. 814–840), was also crowned emperor by the pope; as his name implies, he took his role as Christian emperor seriously.
2. Louis brought the monastic reformer Benedict of Aniane to court and in 817 issued a capitulary (a summary of a royal decision) that imposed a uniform way of life on all monasteries of the empire, based on the rule of St. Benedict.
3. His first wife, Ermengard, was crowned empress by the pope in 816. In 817, their first son, Lothar, was given the title emperor and made co-ruler with Louis.
4. By making his other two sons sub-kings under imperial authority, Louis hoped to satisfy all three sons and thus prevent the splintering of his empire.
5. When Ermengard died, Louis married Judith, and their son, later known as "Charles the Bald," was born in 823.
6. Jealous of this fourth heir, the sons of Ermengard rebelled, starting a series of struggles that continued after Louis's death in 840.
7. In 843, the Treaty of Verdun divided the empire among the three surviving brothers (one of Ermengard's sons had died). This arrangement roughly defined the future political divisions of western Europe.
8. Charles the Bald (r. 843–877) received the western third (present-day France); Louis the German (r. 843–876) received the eastern third (present-day Germany); the "Middle Kingdom" was given to Lothar (r. 840–876), along with the imperial title.
9. Parts of the Middle Kingdom were absorbed by France and Germany; the remainder eventually formed the modern

states of the Netherlands, Belgium, Luxembourg, Switzerland, and Italy.

10. The success of Charlemagne's empire had been supported by the loyalty of a small group of privileged aristocrats, laymen and churchmen alike, with lands and offices across the realm. Their loyalty was based on shared values, friendship, expectation of gain, and formal ties of vassalage and fealty.
11. Once the empire had been divided into three realms and the borders fixed, the aristocrats lost their expectations of new lands and offices.
12. They put down roots in particular regions and began to gather their own followings.
13. Powerful local traditions, such as different languages, also undermined imperial unity.

E. Land and Power, pp. 278–279

1. Carolingian wealth originally came from land and plunder.
2. After the spoils of war ceased, the Carolingians still had access to money and goods through trade, as the Carolingian economy intermingled with that of the Abassids.
3. With the decline of the Abassids, their far-flung trade network was disrupted, which weakened the Carolingians.
4. Land was the most important source of wealth and power. Carolingian aristocrats held many estates scattered throughout the Frankish Empire that were reorganized into productive units that modern historians call "manors."
5. A typical manor consisted of arable fields, vineyards, meadows where animals could roam, and woodland, all scattered about the countryside rather than in a compact unit.
6. These manorial estates were worked by peasant families, each having their own manse—small holdings that contained a house, garden, and small pieces of arable land. Peasant families were also expected to work the demesne—the very large manse of the manor's lord.
7. Unlike slaves, peasant families could neither be separated involuntarily nor be displaced from their manses, making them the precursors to the nuclear family.
8. Out of these manors came the most productive agricultural technique of the time: the three-field system. In this system, two-thirds of the arable land was farmed simultaneously: one field with winter wheat, one field with summer crops, and the third field left fallow.
9. The sown fields and the fallow field were rotated so that the use of each field repeated only every three years. This rotation produced larger yields than the two-field system that used only half of the land at a time.
10. All peasants owed dues and services to their manor's lord, whether lay or clerical, that varied by individual arrangement.
11. Peasant men spent most of their time working in the fields; women were often to be found at the lord's house in the *gynaeceum* (women's workshop), where they wove cloth and sewed garments, or served as cooks or sculleries in the kitchen.
12. Although the Carolingians, like other lords, benefited from their extensive estates, surpluses were rare.
13. When the king's lands were divided up in the partitioning of the empire and in new invasions, Carolingian dependence on manors scattered throughout the kingdom became a cause of weakness.

F. Viking, Muslim, and Magyar Invasions, c. 790–955, pp. 279–282

1. Like the Roman emperors they emulated, Carolingian kings faced outside threats at their borders: Vikings to the north, Muslims to the south, and Magyars to the east.
2. At about the same time they were moving into Russia, the Vikings from Scandinavia moved westward, traveling in independent bands and often as families.
3. Both merchants and pirates, Vikings followed a chief in search of profit, prestige, and land. By the mid-eighth century, Vikings settled in northeast England, later called the *Danelaw*.
4. In southern England, King Alfred the Great (r. 871–899) bought time and peace by paying a tribute to the Vikings, later called the *Danegeld*, which would became the basis of a lucrative tax system. In 878, Alfred stopped the payments and led a victorious army against the Vikings.
5. On the continent, after 850, Viking attacks became well-organized expeditions for regional control.
6. Rollo, the leader of a contingent of Vikings in France, accepted Christianity in 911 and

gained control of a part of France that took the name Normandy ("land of the northmen").

7. At the same time, Carolingian and English missionaries were moving into Scandinavia.
8. Once converted, Danish kings created the kingdom of Denmark.
9. By about 1000, the Danes had extended their control to parts of Sweden, Norway, and even, under King Cnut (r. 1017–1035), to England.
10. Also, in the ninth century, Muslims began a slow conquest of Sicily (827), eventually establishing independent rule.
11. Muslim pirates set up bases on islands in the Mediterranean from whence they could rob, take prisoners, collect ransom, and selectively support the feuds of their Christian neighbors.
12. Another group—the Magyars—arrived in the west around 899. They drove a wedge between the Slavs near the Frankish kingdom to the west and those near the Byzantine Empire to the east.
13. From their bases in present-day Hungary, the Magyars also raided far to the west, attacking Germany and Italy between 899 and 955.
14. The German king Otto I (r. 936–973) defeated a Magyar army at the battle of Lechfeld in 955, after which the raids subsided. Historians today, however, believe that the containment of the Magyars was due to their transformation from nomads to farmers.
15. The Viking, Muslim, and Magyar invasions were in some ways a continuation of the invasions that had beset the Roman Empire in the fourth and fifth centuries; they were also the last attacks against western Europe from outsiders.
16. The Vikings and Magyars show a similar pattern in which raiders and migrants were gradually absorbed into European society.

IV. After the Carolingians: The Emergence of Local Rule

A. Public Power and Private Relationships, pp. 282–285

1. Personal loyalty was the key to ruling. Carolingian kings relied on their *fideles* ("faithful men"; "vassals"), who received a share of the revenues of their administrative districts as well as fiefs ("land grants").
2. These fiefs were intended to be temporary rewards for service but by the end of the ninth century fiefs could be passed on to heirs.
3. More and more warriors were drawn into these personal networks of vassals. A typical warrior had several vassals while being himself a vassal to a higher lord.
4. Monasteries had vassals to fight for them while their abbots might be vassals to the king or another powerful lord.
5. Kings' vassals mustered troops, collected taxes, and administered justice.
6. In return, vassals looked to their lords for protection and hoped to receive fiefs in return for loyal service.
7. At the bottom of the social scale were the peasants who made up the majority of the population.
8. As local rulers gathered power, peasants became their dependents, not as vassals but as serfs. Serfdom was an inherited rather than voluntary dependency.
9. In general, the three-field system and heavy plows pulled by horses raised the standard of living for most peasants.
10. Some landlords lightened the dues and services owed by peasants to allow them to drain marshes and cut down forests for new lands. Other landlords converted dues and labor services into cash payments, which remained fixed despite inflation, an advantage for peasants.
11. By the tenth century, many peasants lived in rural villages and began to develop a sense of community with the church as the focal point for local activity. Villagers shared oxen or horses, and their sense of common purpose sometimes encouraged them to seek privileges as a group.
12. The status of peasants varied from region to region and some peasants had to work the land on more than one estate, owing service to more than one lord.
13. Landlords built large castles and imposed wider powers of the ban—that is, holding the right to collect taxes, hear court cases, levy fines, and muster men for defense.
14. In southern France, counts and other princes, known as "castellans" because they controlled castles, subjected everyone near their castle to their ban.
15. In northern France, princes gained control of many castles and so dominated much broader regions.

16. Peasants owed dues for protection whether or not they worked a castellan's lands.
17. Castellans formed relationships with other large landowners, supported local monasteries, and appointed local priests.

B. Warriors and Warfare, pp. 285–286

1. Although warriors were differentiated by rank (kings, counts, and dukes at the top; castellans and ordinary knights ranging farther down the scale), all shared a common way of life.
2. Knights and their lords fought on horseback wearing metal armor and helmets. Such armament and the adoption of horseshoes and stirrups constituted a military revolution because they allowed knights to fight better, travel farther, and use heavier weapons than ever before.
3. Lords and their vassals often lived, ate, hunted, and fought together. They also competed against one another in military games.
4. Unmarried knights who lived with their lords were called youths no matter what their age. Their perpetual status as bachelors reflected a change in families and inheritance.
5. Before about 1000, families divided their estates among all their children. French families, however, began to leave the entire inheritance to a single male heir in order to prevent fragmentation of their large estates and the power and wealth that accompanied them. This system is generally referred to as "primogeniture."
6. Fathers passed down to these sons not only manors, but titles, castles, and authority of the ban.
7. This system left many younger sons without an inheritance and therefore without the prospect of marriage and family. Instead, the younger sons lived at court as "youths" or joined the clergy.
8. Primogeniture generally bypassed daughters, therefore a major source of power was denied to most women.
9. Widows and daughters in families that had no sons could inherit property.
10. Aristocratic wives could also act as "lords" of estates while their husbands were at war.

C. Efforts to Contain Violence, pp. 286–287

1. In the long run, war was bad for warriors and their lords, devastating cities and the countryside.
2. Bishops worried about the dangers to church property, and peasants cried out against destruction of crops.
3. Sentiment against violence was united in a movement called the Peace of God, which began in the south of France and had spread widely by 1050.
4. At local meetings of bishops, counts, lords, and sometimes lower-class men and women, provisions of peace were set forth that limited violence against peasants and the theft of property under the threat of excommunication.
5. A second set of agreements, the Truce of God, soon supplemented the Peace of God to limit conflict between armed men: fighting between warriors was prohibited on days of religious significance, including every Thursday, Friday, Saturday, and Sunday.
6. Local knights and nobles swore to enforce the truce and fight against any who broke it.
7. Other attempts to limit violence took place at assemblies where lords and vassals mediated wars and feuds.
8. In other cases, monks and laymen would try to reach compromises that would leave the honor of each disputant intact.

D. Political Communities in Italy, England, and France, pp. 287–289

1. In Italy, cities remained the primary centers of power as great landlords established their seats there rather than in the countryside.
2. The cities remained places for important marketplaces. Peasants sold their surplus goods there, artisans and merchants produced their wares, and foreign traders came to offer their merchandise.
3. More than anyplace else, the noble rich in Italian cities depended on cash; both servile and free tenants paid their rents in currency.
4. Family organization also differed slightly in Italy. Rather than being patrilineal, families organized themselves into an economic corporation of sorts in which all male members shared profits of the family's inheritance and all women were excluded.
5. Early Italian businesses and banks would be based on this model.
6. In England, where King Alfred ("the Great") of Wessex (r. 871–899) was facing

Viking invasions, the monarchy developed new mechanisms of royal government.

7. Alfred instituted military reforms funded by taxes on peasant holdings, and divided the army into two parts: one to defend fortifications (*burhs*), the other to serve as a mobile force.
8. Beginning a program of religious reform, he brought scholars to his court to write and educate others. Under Alfred's guidance, many Latin religious texts were translated into the vernacular language: Anglo-Saxon (Old English).
9. Although Latin remained the language of scholarship in the rest of Europe during the ninth and tenth centuries, the Anglo-Saxon language came to be used for both administration and literature in England.
10. Alfred's campaigns and those of his successors rolled back Danish (Viking) rule in England.
11. As peace returned, administrative districts called "shires" and "hundreds" were established throughout England for judicial and taxation purposes.
12. Alfred's grandson Edgar (r. 957–975) further strengthened royal power by being the sworn lord of all the great men of the kingdom, by directing the military, and by controlling appointments to the English church.
13. The king's control was still tenuous, however, because most royal officials were great landowners who supported the king only when it served their interests.
14. At the beginning of the eleventh century, the Danes invaded England, and the Danish king Cnut (Canute [r. 1017–1035]) seized the throne. He nonetheless kept many English institutions intact.
15. French kings had a harder time coping with invasions because their realm was much larger than England.
16. At the end of the tenth century, dukes, counts, and important bishops elected a new king, Hugh Capet (r. 987–996), to prevent civil war.
17. The power of these new Capetian kings was generally limited to the territory around Paris with independent castellans controlling nearby areas.
18. Yet, because they were anointed kings and represented the idea of unity inherited from Charlemagne, their prestige was enormous.
19. Most of the counts, at least in northern France, became the king's vassals, promising not to harm him.

E. Emperors and Kings in Central and Eastern Europe, pp. 289–291

1. In Germany, five duchies (regions dominated by dukes) emerged in the late Carolingian period, each much larger than the counties and castellanies of France.
2. With the death in 911 of the last Carolingian king, the dukes elected one among them to replace him.
3. As Magyar invasions increased, the dukes gave the royal title to the duke of Saxony, Henry I (r. 919–936), who set up fortifications and reorganized the army that contributed to a defeat of a Magyar army in 933.
4. His son Otto I earned even greater prestige by taking the Lombard crown (951) and defeating the Magyars (955). Otto's victories raised the German's expectations for land and booty, but his successors, the Ottonian dynasty, could not always provide the expected gifts.
5. Younger royal sons led revolts against the Ottonian kings, often with the support of the aristocracy.
6. Believing that the well-being of the church depended on them, the Ottonians gave bishops the power of the ban and allowed them to collect revenues and call men to arms. Bishops became royal officials, while also carrying out their pastoral and religious duties.
7. German kings claimed the right to appoint bishops, even the pope, and to "invest" them with their office through a special ceremony.
8. The Ottonians also encouraged scholarly pursuits, such as the study of classical rhetoric and debate.
9. The kings of Germany faced opposition from powerful dukes and princes who refused to be royal vassals because vassalage was considered beneath the dignity of free men.
10. The successors of the Ottonians—the Salians—relied on ministerials, men who were legally serfs but collected taxes, administered justice, and fought on horseback.
11. Further east, the Czechs converted under the rule of Václav (r. 920–929) who

became duke of Bohemia, remaining within the German sphere.

12. In 966, Mieszko I (r. 963–992), the leader of the Poles, accepted Christian baptism to forestall a German attack, and he skillfully claimed allegiance to a number of German princes as they suited his needs. In 991, Mieszko placed his realm under the protection of the pope.
13. His son Boleslaw the Brave (r. 992–1025) greatly expanded Poland's boundaries and, in 1000, received a royal crown with papal blessing.
14. In the region now known as Hungary, the Magyars settled and became landowners.
15. At the end of the tenth century, Stephen I (r. 997–1038) accepted Christianity and in turn German knights and monks helped him to consolidate his power.
16. The economic basis for the power of central European rulers gradually shifted from slave raids to agriculture, encouraging a proliferation of regional centers of power that challenged monarchical rule.
17. From the eleventh century onward, all the medieval Slavic states would face a constant problem of internal division.

Lecture Strategies

1. The scholars of the Islamic renaissance produced an impressive legacy for the development of western science because they were responsible for transmitting much of the knowledge of classical antiquity and also for generating important scientific discoveries. A survey of this topic can be found in C. A. Qadir, *Philosophy and Science in the Islamic World: From Origins to the Present Day* (New York and London: Routledge, 1988). For more in-depth information, the essays in *Religion, Learning, and Science in the Abbasid Period*, J. D. Latham, R. B. Serjeant, and M. J. L. Young, eds. (Cambridge: Cambridge University Press, 1990) cover the gamut of Islamic philosophy and science during that period, and include a survey of the classical Greek works that were translated into Arabic.

2. The Byzantine Empire faced attack throughout most of its history, yet managed to maintain its independence until the end of the Middle Ages. Trace the details and successes of Byzantine military strategy and organization and determine the social or political consequences of features such as the dynatoi. Warren Treadgold, *Byzantium and Its Army, 284–1081* (Stanford, CA: Stanford University, 1995) covers the organization and functioning of the themes; and John Haldon, *Warfare, State, and Society in the Byzantine World* (London: UCL Press, 1999) provides a general overview. Eric McGeer, *Sowing the Dragon's Teeth: Byzantine Warfare in the Tenth Century* (Washington, DC: Dumbarton Oaks, 1995) contains the texts of two Byzantine military treatises on tactics used against Muslim forces, the *Praecepta Militaria* by Nikephoros Phokas, and the *Taktika* by Nikephoros Ouranos.

3. The achievements of Charlemagne's reign and the Carolingian renaissance are sometimes credited with bringing Europe out of the early Middle Ages. Present the innovations of the period and the extent to which they imitated Roman imperial precedents. A recent collection that evaluates the Carolingian renaissance in political theory, education, art, and music, in addition to literary production, is Rosamond McKitterick, ed., *Carolingian Culture: Emulation and Innovation* (Cambridge: Cambridge University Press, 1994). On the Carolingian education initiative, see Bernhard Bischoff and Michael M. Gorman, *Manuscripts and Libraries in the Age of Charlemagne* (Cambridge: Cambridge University Press, 1994). On the spread of literacy in the Carolingian world beyond the clergy and monasteries, see Rosamond McKitterick, *The Carolingians and the Written Word* (Cambridge: Cambridge University Press, 1989). John Beckwith, *Early Medieval Art: Carolingian, Ottonian, Romanesque*, rpt. (London: Thames & Hudson, 1988), contains information and illustrations for artistic production. For primary sources, refer to Paul Edward Dutton, *Carolingian Civilization: A Reader* (Peterborough, Ont.: Broadview, 1993). For the broader political and historical context of Charlemagne's reign, see E. James, *The Origins of France: From Clovis to the Capetians, 500–1000* (New York: St. Martin's, 1982).

Class Discussion Starters

1. Scholars continue to question the existence of feudalism. Have students discuss the text in "Terms of History: Feudalism" (p. 283), as well as the sections on "Land and Power" (p. 278) and "After the Carolingians: The Emergence of Local Rule" (p. 282). Ask them to debate the strengths and weaknesses of the term "feudalism" as a description of this medieval way of life. One of the most influential studies arguing against the existence of ninth- or tenth-century feudalism is Susan Reynolds, *Fiefs and Vassals: The Medieval Evidence Reinterpreted* (Oxford: Oxford University Press, 1996). Another overview of the scholarly debate is contained in Part 2 of *Debating the Middle Ages: Issues and Readings*, Lester Little and Barbara Rosenwein, eds. (Malden, MA: Blackwell, 1998), particularly the introduction and Elizabeth Brown's "Feudalism: The Tyranny of a Construct."

2. The apocalyptic predictions made during the first millennium were hardly less dire than those made for the second. Have students discuss medieval millenarianism, perhaps comparing it to how the coming of the year 2000 was anticipated in our own time. How did events such as invasions by Vikings, Muslims, and Magyars influence attitudes toward the coming of the year 1000? See Richard Landes, "Lest the Millennium Be Fulfilled: Apocalyptic Expectations and the Pattern of Western Chronography, 100–800 C.E.," in Werner Verbeke, Daniel Verhulst, and Andries Welkenhysen, eds., *The Use and Abuse of Eschatology in the Middle Ages* (Leuven University Press, 1988), pp. 137–211. For the lack of impact the millennium made on the minds of Anglo-Saxon England, see Zacharias Thundy, *Millennium: Apocalypse, Antichrist, and Old English Monsters c. 1000 A.D.* (Notre Dame, IN: Cross Cultural Publications, 1998). For a history of medieval millenarianism, which covers this period, see Bernard McGinn, *Visions of the End: Apocalyptic Traditions in the Middle Ages* (New York: Columbia University Press, 1998); and for millenarian traditions beginning in the new millennium, see Norman Cohn, *The Pursuit of the Millennium* (Oxford: Oxford University Press, 1990).

3. Medieval Spain under Muslim rule represented one of the most diverse and vibrant cultures in the west, described by the term *convivencia*—the coexistence of Jews, Christians, and Muslims under the Muslim caliphs of Córdoba. Provide students with additional background information to discuss this development. Recent studies of the intermingling of the three religions include Mark D. Meyerson and Edward D. English, eds., *Christians, Muslims, and Jews in Medieval and Early Modern Spain: Interaction and Cultural Change* (Notre Dame, IN: University of Notre Dame Press, 1999); and Roger Collins, *Early Medieval Spain: Unity in Diversity, 400–1000*, 2nd ed. (New York: St. Martin's, 1995). David Wasserstein, *The Caliphate in the West: An Islamic Political Institution in the Iberian Peninsula* (Oxford: Clarendon, 1993), examines the establishment of Muslim authority in early medieval Spain. Vivian B. Mann and Thomas F. Glick, eds., *Convivencia: Jews, Muslims, and Christians in Medieval Spain* (New York: Braziller, 1992) is the catalog of an exhibition at the Jewish Museum in New York, featuring images of objects that reflect the cultural and intellectual flourishing of the age.

4. The Christianization and emergence of the eastern Slavic states is a topic of particular interest in light of recent historical events. Have students discuss this process, contrasting developments among the eastern Slavs with those who were influenced by Roman Christianity further to the west. A standard introduction to Kievan Russia is George Vernadsky, *Kievan Russia* (New Haven, CT: Yale University Press, 1973). For the process of Christianization of the Slavic peoples, see Boris Gasparov and Olga Raevsky-Hughes, eds., *Slavic Cultures in the Middle Ages*, vol. 1 of *Christianity and the Eastern Slavs* (Berkeley: University of California Press, 1993).

Reviewing the Text

Review Questions

1. What were the effects of expansion on the power of the Byzantine emperor?
[model answer] *Military victories over new territories brought prestige and wealth to the imperial court, which enhanced the power of the emperor both within the empire and other kingdoms of the region. Outside the capital, especially in border regions distant from the center, the wealth of victory fostered the emergence of a military elite, the* dynatoi, *who gained power locally, enough that some families became strong enough to take over the imperial throne.*

2. What forces fragmented the Islamic world in the tenth and eleventh centuries, and what forces held it together?
[model answer] *The initial fragmentation Islam experienced was the division into Sunni and Shi'ite sects in the dispute over the succession. As the empire grew, its vast expanse required a large army and increasingly complex civil service to administer. The costs of empire came to exceed its revenues and the caliphs' ability to provide for local needs. By the tenth century, caliphs had become central figureheads more than actual powers, and Islamic rule was divided among local independent Islamic rulers. The Islamic world was composed of many diverse ethnicities to begin with, so the practice of differing cultural customs in different areas contributed to the fragmentation. Nonetheless, peoples throughout the Islamic world experienced a sense of cultural unity in their devotion to the Qur'an, their language, and the trade networks across open borders that connected them.*

3. What were the strengths and weaknesses of Carolingian institutions of government, warfare, and defense?
[model answer] *Partnership with the Roman church provided support that contributed to the Carolingians' ability to expand into and hold territories. Warfare itself was profitable and as long as the realm was expanding, revenues from new takings of wealth helped to support the Carolingian dynasty. The loyalty of aristocrats across the realm, who shared in the goals and values of Charlemagne and gained opportunities and wealth from the expansion, helped forge and stabilize the kingdom. Carolingian support of scholarship strengthened the realm also. The weakness of the kingdom, as in other*

empires, was its size. Opportunity and wealth were no longer available for loyal supporters, and regional leaders cultivated their independent strength within their own lands. Heirs to the throne divided the empire in 843.

4. After the dissolution of the Carolingian Empire, what political systems developed in western, northern, eastern, and central Europe, and how did these systems differ from one another?
[model answer] *With the breakup of the Carolingian Empire, the French kings had more prestige than power and represented the idea of French unity more than they determined it. Political control was centered in the territorial lords who dominated the countryside through their feudal relationships with vassals and retainers. Christian monarchies emerged to the east, aligned with the Roman church. Compared to France, rule was more centralized in the large territories of Germany, Poland, Hungary and Bohemia, with the German king and the Catholic church influencing regional power. In Italy, great lords built their centers of power in the cities, creating a decentralized political structure. In England, the Anglo-Saxon king Alfred consolidated power in a centralized monarchy that, as in France, worked with the support of Lords who were great landowners.*

Making Connections

1. How were the Byzantine, Islamic, and European economies similar? How did they differ? How did these economies interact?
[model answer] *Land was the main source of wealth for the Byzantine, Islamic, and European economies. All knew of and used money (coins) for local and long-distance trade, though long-distance commerce was far more important and widespread in the Islamic world than elsewhere. Byzantine control over commerce, centered at Constantinople, was unmatched elsewhere. There were interactions between these economies. Scandinavia was the hinge between the silver of the Islamic world and western Europe, while Venice served as the intermediary between Byzantine products and those of Europe.*

2. Compare the effects of the barbarian invasions into the Roman Empire with the effects of the Viking, Muslim and Magyar invasions into Carolingian Europe.
[model answer] *The barbarian invasions into the Roman Empire ended with the creation of many new kingdoms. In 899, the Magyars invaded an area along the Danube (today's Hungary) and divided the Slavs in Carolingian Europe, forcing those in the Frankish kingdom to come under the rule of Germany, and those on the Byzantine side (Serbs, Bulgarians, and Russians) to be absorbed by Byzantium. The invaders who stayed were absorbed into the Roman Catholic culture of western Europe. The Viking invasions led to settlements in Normandy and Danelaw (in England). Scandinavia itself was also converted to Roman Catholicism c. 1000.*

Discussing the Documents

Questions from Online Study Guide with Model Answers

The Book of the Prefect (p. 265)

1. Who was the source of the law, and for what reason was it given?
[model answer] *God was the source of law, which he established to establish equity among humans to prevent them from abusing each other, and to prohibit the strong from hurting the weak.*

2. Why was it important that a notary be well educated and of good character?
[model answer] *A notary must be well educated to insure that he correctly understands and interprets law, and of good character to prevent the possibility of his acting in a corrupt manner in interpreting and implementing the law.*

When She Approached (p. 272)

1. How does this poem characterize family relationships?
[model answer] *The poem portrays a sense of love and attachment within the family, suggesting that family relationships provide important emotional connections.*

2. Comment on the relationship between political changes and cultural changes.
[model answer] *The poem suggests that in order to accommodate the new political circumstances, existing cultural values and practices were being challenged and altered.*

Contrasting Views: Charlemagne: Roman Emperor, Father of Europe, or the Chief Bishop? (p. 276)

1. According to the documents, what were Charlemagne's strengths as a leader?
[model answer] *Charlemagne is commended for his patience and steadfast leadership. He appears pious and respectful of God and his emissary the Pope, although in his welcome of the Pope he demonstrates his skills as a diplomat and politician as much as he is demonstrates piety. He is portrayed as having a strong sense of justice.*

2. Which of the three documents portrays Charlemagne in the most flattering light, and why?
[model answer] *Einhard's assessment of Charlemagne's treatment of his brother and responsibilities in his family*

is more flattering of the king as a human and leader than the more obsequious diplomat in the poem or the rather manipulative power described by Notker the Stammerer.

3. How does Notker the Stammerer's biography of Charlemagne compare with that of Einhard's? Which of the two is more believable, and why?
[model answer] *Notker the Stammerer's description suggests that Charles had a semi-divine ability to wreak justice by causing things to happen, such as the bishop's illness. The description of Charles's character offered by Einhard, which includes a suggestion of questionable motives in putting aside his first marriage, is more believable because it sketches him in his daily concerns and possible faults as well as describing his larger feats.*

Other Questions for Discussing These Documents in Class

The Book of the Prefect (p. 265)

1. What are the similarities and differences in the rules governing notaries and jewelers?
2. How were Byzantine authorities able to enforce the regulations in *The Book of the Prefect*?

When She Approached (p. 272)

1. What does the poem suggest about cultural values in Muslim Spain?
2. Why would the *taifa* leader patronize a poet who dramatized his sorrow at leaving his family to find employment at the *taifa*'s court?

Contrasting Views: Charlemagne: Roman Emperor, Father of Europe, or the Chief Bishop? (p. 276)

1. Which of the three documents presents the most believable portrait of Charlemagne, and why?
2. Taken altogether, do the documents stress Charlemagne's religious or political aspects?

Comparative Questions

1. Considering *The Book of the Prefect, When She Approached*, and the views of Charlemagne, how would you assess the significance of personal relationships in this period?
2. Which leader seems to assert the greater power over his people, the Byzantine emperor or Charlemagne?
3. Do any of the authors criticize Charlemagne? Is there anything in their accounts that causes you to have a negative view of Charlemagne?

For Users of *Sources of The Making of the West*

The following documents are available in Chapter 9 of the companion sourcebook by Katharine J. Lualdi, University of Southern Maine.

1. The Rule of Charlemagne: *General Capitulary for the* Missi (802)
2. Resistance from Constantinople: Liutprand of Cremona, *Report to Otto I* (968)
3. The Macedonian Renaissance: *Veroli Casket* (c. 1000)
4. A New Islamic Dynasty: Ahmad al-Ya'qūbī, *Kitāb al-buldān* (Ninth Century)
5. Advances in Medicine: Abū Bakr Muhammad ibn Zakarīyū Al-rāzī, *A Treatise on the Small-Pox and Measles* (c. 910)
6. The Faithful Vassal: Fulbert of Chartres, *Letter to William of Aquitaine* (1020)

Discussion Ideas for Sources of the Making of the West, *Chapter 9*

1. What insight does *A Treatise on the Small-Pox and Measles* provide into the Muslim world of the tenth century? How does the document illustrate the Islamic renaissance? What information does it provide about Muslim attitudes toward science and reason? What does Al-rāzī's explanation suggest about the state of scientific understanding of smallpox at the time? What does his treatise reveal about the relationship between science and religion in his society?
2. What insight does the *Letter to William of Aquitaine* by Fulbert of Chartres provide into feudal relations in post-Carolingian Europe? Why did William seek the assistance of the bishop in his conflict with his vassals? Why were so many of the obligations stated in negative terms? The duties of lords and vassals are mutual, but are they equal? How does the "Terms of History: Feudalism" discussion in the textbook influence your analysis of this document?

Working with Visual Sources

For this exercise, please refer to The Crowning of Constantine Porphyrogenitos on p. 264 of the textbook or view the image on the book companion site's Online Study Guide under the "Visual Activity" for Chapter 9.

Students viewing the image at the Online Study Guide are asked three questions of the image. The questions and model answers (not made available to students) are below. Project this image, available on the Instructor's Resources CD-ROM, in class or ask students to look at the image in their textbooks and answer the questions.

1. By depicting Christ crowning the emperor, what message did the artist seek to convey regarding the source of the emperor's power?
[model answer] *The artist shows that Christ is the ultimate source of the emperor's power, and therefore Constantine Porphyrogenitos ruled by the will of God. Significantly, no earthly representative of the Christian church is depicted, thereby minimizing any rival authority possessed by Byzantine bishops.*

2. Note the relative flatness of the image and the lack of perspective and background for the figures. What might have been the artist's intention in depicting Christ and the emperor in this manner?
[model answer] *The artist was interested in depicting hierarchy and symbolism and was less concerned with providing a naturalistic, three-dimensional image.*

3. Why is Christ elevated above the emperor?
[model answer] *Christ's higher elevation depicts symbolically his superiority to the emperor. He is the source of Constantine Porphyrogenitos's power; therefore, he is shown higher. The artist may also have been invoking imagery of heaven as being on a higher plane than earth.*

Mapping Exercises

Map Activity from OSG—Model Answer for Map Activity #2

For this activity please refer to the map on p. 292. Students are asked these questions:

How was Europe and the Mediterranean divided among the "three heirs" of the Roman Empire (western Europe, the Byzantine Empire, and the Muslim world) around 1050?
[model answer] *Various Islamic caliphates and emirates controlled the eastern Mediterranean, North Africa, and a large portion of Spain. The Byzantine Empire ruled Anatolia, Greece, and southern Italy, but was also culturally influential in Kievan Russia, which had adopted Byzantine Christianity. Western Europe was divided into several smaller kingdoms, the most important of which were France, England, and the Holy Roman Empire.*

Based on what you know about the decentralization of power, in what ways is the depiction of the distribution of power in Europe and the Mediterranean around 1050 on this map deceptive?
[model answer] *The large territorial units do not accurately reflect the distribution of power in Europe c. 1050. The depiction of large political territories of the west is misleading because each was plagued by widespread, internal fragmentation. In Europe, local power was held by princes, dukes, counts, and castellans, whose loyalty to the king was largely voluntary and based on a reciprocal relationship. In the Byzantine Empire, the strategoi wielded a great deal of control as wealthy landowners. With the dissolution of the caliphate, the Islamic territory was likewise divided among regional leaders.*

Map 9.1: The Expansion of Byzantium, 860–1025, p. 263

Ask students to name the principal cities of the Byzantine Empire. How does the expansion of Byzantium in this period compare with its earlier borders at the time of Emperor Justinian? (See Mapping the West: Western Europe and the Eastern Roman Empire, 600 C.E., p. 228.) Which neighbors existed in 860 who had not been present in 600?

Map 9.2: Islamic States, c. 1000, p. 269

Ask students to identify the regions that border the edges of Muslim-controlled territories. What advantages in the region (such as control over much of the Mediterranean) did the various Islamic powers enjoy?

Map 9.3: Expansion of the Carolingian Empire under Charlemagne, p. 275

How far do Charlemagne's conquests replicate the constitution of the ancient Roman Empire in the west? Which forces might have prevented him from enlarging his subject territory even further? Which portions of western Europe lay outside his control? Which groups dominated those areas?

Map 9.4: Muslim, Viking, and Magyar Invasions of the Ninth and Tenth Centuries, p. 281

Discuss the range and impact of this series of invasions that struck western Europe from all sides at roughly the same time. What negative consequences might have resulted? How did these contribute to the rise of the new warrior class? The transformation of agricultural society? The fragmentation of political authority in the west? What possible positive effects might these invasions have occasioned, even if unintended?

Mapping the West: Europe and the Mediterranean, c. 1050, p. 292

What were the internal weaknesses of these apparently balanced geographic powers? How many smaller territories can students identify that would emerge as powers in their own right? Do students note the presence of numerous urban centers throughout the region, not merely along the Mediterranean? What might the increased number of cities indicate and imply for the future development of the region?

In-Class Assignments and Presentation Topics

1. The Vikings rival the crusades and the Black Death in popularity as a topic. Have students explore Viking history and culture (and perhaps dispel a few myths about them). Although recorded at a later date, the sagas form a powerful literary tradition and serve as an entertaining introduction to many of the norms and practices of Nordic cultures. Students interested in Viking women can read Jenny Jochen, *Women in Old Norse Society* (Ithaca, NY: Cornell University Press, 1995). An introduction to Viking interactions with Europe is P. H. Sawyer, *Kings and Vikings: Scandinavia and Europe, A.D. 700–1100* (New York: Barnes & Noble, 1994). The treasures found at the Sutton Hoo burial site in East Anglia, England, well illustrate the culture reflected in this literature.

2. Students can investigate the Islamic world of the Abbasid caliphate, which they probably know only from the fame of *The Thousand and One Nights* (also known as *The Arabian Nights*). See Guy LeStrange, *Baghdad During the Abbasid Caliphate: From Contemporary Arabic and Persian Sources* (Westport, CT: Greenwood, 1983).

3. Einhard's biography of Charlemagne makes entertaining reading for students, in large part because of the author's lively and opinionated remarks on his subject. If students read the biography in conjunction with Charlemagne's letters and capitularies, they can begin to piece together this renowned leader's achievements, motivations, and impact on western European history. Students can also compare the versions of Charlemagne that emerge from two different biographies (Einhard's and Notker the Stammerer's) in *Two Lives of Charlemagne* (New York: Viking Penguin, 1976). For a reassessment of Charlemagne's reign and the "Pirenne thesis," based on archaeological evidence, see Richard Hodges and David Whitehouse, *Mohammad, Charlemagne, and the Origins of Europe* (Ithaca, NY: Cornell University Press, 1983).

4. Have students research the daily lives of "those who worked." Useful introductions to the topic of peasant life include: J. A. Raftis, ed., *Pathways to Medieval Peasants* (Toronto: University of Toronto Press, 1981); David Herlihy, *Medieval Households* (Cambridge, MA: Harvard University Press, 1990); Barbara Hanawalt, *The Ties that Bound: Peasant Families in Medieval England* (Oxford: Oxford University Press, 1988); and George Duby's important *Early Growth of the European Economy: Warriors and Peasants from the Seventh to the Twelfth Centuries* (Ithaca, NY: Cornell University Press, 1990). For an interesting perspective on medieval childhood, see John Boswell, *The Kindness of Strangers: The Abandonment of Children in Western Europe from Late Antiquity to the Renaissance* (New York: Pantheon Books, 1989).

5. Even though they may strike students as rather "low-tech," the technological innovations of this period (such as the three-field system, the adoption of the horse as a draft and military animal, the heavy plow, and the stirrup) precipitated wide-ranging transformations in western European life. Have students research and report on the various facets of this technological revolution. The classic text is Lynn White, *Medieval Technology and Social Change* (Oxford: Oxford University Press, 1962). Other useful studies include R. H. C. Davis, *The Medieval Warhorse* (London: Thames & Hudson, 1989); and, on changes in construction, John Kenyon, *Medieval Fortifications* (New York: St. Martin's, 1990). For military innovations, see the video *NOVA: Secrets of Lost Empires II: Medieval Siege*, where modern scholars and craftsmen build a trebuchet using the same technology available two thousand years ago.

6. Ask students to explore the flowering of the Macedonian renaissance. *The Suda*, an encyclopedic compendium of knowledge dating from the late tenth century, provides a fascinating entry into the intellectual world of the Macedonian renaissance.

7. Many notable "national" epics were composed in these centuries. These texts can be mined for numerous topics, such as notions of warfare, masculinity, the "other," and kingship. See Seamus Heaney, *Beowulf: A New Verse Translation* (New York: Farrar, Straus, & Giroux, 2000). Two scholarly studies that consider the history behind these epics are Peter Haidu, *The Subject of Violence: The Song of Roland and the Birth of the State* (Bloomington: Indiana University Press, 1993); and R. Fletcher, *The Quest for El Cid* (Oxford: Oxford University Press, 1991).

Essay Questions

1. Islamic law forms an excellent source for information about Muslim society. For an introduction, see Ann K. S. Lambton, *State and Government in Medieval Islam: An Introduction to the Study of Islamic Political Theory: The Jurists* (Oxford: Oxford University Press, 1981); and the collected essays in Muhammad Khalid Masud and Brinkley Messick, eds., *Islamic Legal Interpretation: Muftis and Their Fatwas* (Cambridge, MA:

Harvard University Press, 1996). For the status of women under medieval Islamic law, see Nikki R. Keddie and Beth Baron, eds., *Women in Middle Eastern History: Shifting Boundaries in Sex and Gender* (New Haven, CT: Yale University Press, 1993).

2. Byzantine civilization during the Macedonian renaissance has received a fair amount of scholarly attention in the past few years. Students might find it intriguing to compare the culture of the Greek east to that of the post-Carolingian west. A survey of social groups in Byzantine society is presented in the articles assembled in Guglielmo Cavallo, ed., *The Byzantines* (Chicago: University of Chicago Press, 1992), which discuss all social strata and many occupations. Each selection contains a useful bibliography for further research. A standard historical overview of the period is Mark Whittow, *The Making of Byzantium, 600–1025* (Berkeley: University of California Press, 1996). A stimulating group of essays that explores gender roles and identity in Byzantium is Liz James, ed., *Women, Men and Eunuchs: Gender in Byzantium* (New York and London: Routledge, 1997). Serious bibliographic researchers should access the online library catalog of Dumbarton Oaks, the foremost center for Byzantine studies in the United States.

3. The status and lives of women in the west changed with the emergence of regional centers of power, economic transformation, and the Carolingian renaissance. A good overview can be found in the collected essays of David Herlihy in *Women, Family, and Society in Medieval Europe* (New York: Berghahn Books, 1995); and his short introduction to women's work, *Opera Muliebria* (Burr Ridge, IL: McGraw-Hill, 1991). For royal women, see P. Stafford, *Queens, Concubines, Dowagers: The King's Wife in the Early Middle Ages* (Athens, GA: University of Georgia Press, 1983). Women in Carolingian France are discussed in Suzanne Wemple, *Women in Frankish Society: Marriage and Cloister, 500–900* (Philadelphia: University of Pennsylvania Press, 1981). For an intriguing series of essays on women and religious life in the period, see Jane Tebbits Schulenberg, *Forgetful of Their Sex: Female Sanctity and Society, ca. 500–1100* (Chicago: University of Chicago Press, 1997). The advice of Dhuoda to her son is translated in Carol Neel, trans., *Handbook for William: A Carolingian Woman's Counsel for Her Son* (Washington, DC: Catholic University of America Press, 1999).

4. The cultural differences between Islamic and western European countries during this period are striking. With Córdoba as a reference point, students should make comparisons between it and an English and Carolingian "city." Where would they have preferred to live and why? Compare Islamic and western Europe medical theories and practices. Which are nearest to modern medicine?

Additional Resources: Literature

Chickering, Howell D., *Beowulf: A Dual-Language Edition*. 1977.
Haddawy, Husain, trans., *The Arabian Nights*. 1990.
Harrison, Robert, trans., *The Song of Roland*. 2002.
Neel, Carol, trans., *Handbook for William: A Carolingian Woman's Counsel for Her Son by Dhuoda*. 1991.
Thorpe, Lewis, trans., *Two Lives of Charlemagne*. 1969.

Additional Resources: Film and Video

NOVA: Secrets of Lost Empires II: Medieval Siege (2000) (DVD and VHS, 60 minutes). In this documentary, modern scholars and craftsmen build a trebuchet using the same technology available two thousand years ago.

OTHER BEDFORD/ST. MARTIN'S RESOURCES FOR CHAPTER 9

The following resources are available to accompany Chapter 9. Please refer to the Preface of this manual for detailed descriptions of all the ancillaries.

For Instructors

Transparencies

The following maps and images from Chapter 9 are available as full-color acetates.

- Map 9.1: The Expansion of Byzantium, 860–1025
- Map 9.2: Islamic States, c. 1000
- Map 9.3: Expansion of the Carolingian Empire under Charlemagne
- Map 9.4: Muslim, Viking, and Magyar Invasions of the Ninth and Tenth Centuries
- Mapping the West: Europe and the Mediterranean, c. 1050
- The Crowning of Constantine Porphyrogenitos, p. 264
- The Macedonian Renaissance, p. 266

Instructor's Resources CD-ROM

The following maps and image from Chapter 9, as well as a chapter outline, are available on disc in both PowerPoint and jpeg formats.

- Map 9.1: The Expansion of Byzantium, 860–1025
- Map 9.2: Islamic States, c. 1000
- Map 9.3: Expansion of the Carolingian Empire under Charlemagne
- Map 9.4: Muslim, Viking, and Magyar Invasions of the Ninth and Tenth Centuries
- Mapping the West: Europe and the Mediterranean, c. 1050
- The Crowning of Constantine Porphyrogenitos, p. 264

For Students

Study Guides

The Online Study Guide at **bedfordstmartins.com/hunt** helps students synthesize the material they have learned as well as practice the skills historians use to make sense of the past. The following Map, Visual, and Document activities are available for Chapter 9.

Map Activity

- Mapping the West: Europe and the Mediterranean, c. 1050, p. 292

Visual Activity

- The Crowning of Constantine Porphyrogenitos, p. 264

Reading Historical Documents

- The Book of the Prefect, p. 265
- When She Approached, p. 272
- Contrasting Views: Charlemagne: Roman Emperor, Father of Europe, or the Chief Bishop? pp. 276–277

CHAPTER

10

Merchants and Kings, Popes and Crusaders

1050–1150

Chapter Resources

Main Chapter Topics

1. The new profit-based economy in Europe gave rise to social, cultural, and political changes; cities were structured around and rebuilt for commerce, extensive international trade, money for trade and exchange; and advances in technology increased production and further altered social relationships.

2. The wealth and power of the church prompted calls from within it for reform and inspired new monastic movements. Reformers altered the level and nature of church involvement in everyday life. Popes and others called for the abolition of simony (purchase of church offices) and clerical marriage.

3. In the name of reform, the church—especially the papacy—extended and increased its power and took on the character of a political monarchy, raising armies and institutionalizing its authority as it vied with secular rulers for control of Europe.

4. This rivalry was epitomized by the Investiture Conflict, in which pope Gregory VII and emperor Henry IV contended for the right to appoint men to high church offices. In this intense political battle, the emperor outmaneuvered the pope temporarily, but the overall dynamics of the conflict consolidated church supremacy and shifted imperial power into the hands of German princes.

5. In 1095, Pope Urban II proclaimed the First Crusade, calling on Christians to expel the Muslims from the Holy Land. This call stirred a combination of piety and bigotry, greed and self-sacrifice. During the First Crusade, followers of Peter the Hermit slaughtered Jews who were living peacefully in Europe. In the Near East, the crusaders defeated the Muslims at Jerusalem and established crusader states. By the end of the thirteenth century, however, these crusader states fell permanently to the Muslims. The main, lasting impact of the crusades on the west was on its imagination.

6. Monarchs in Europe set about consolidating their rule. In the Byzantine Empire, the arrival of the Seljuk Turks brought a new dynasty and a call for military aid from the west, but the emperors eventually gained prestige and military might by making concessions to the nobility. In England, the Norman Conquest brought English society into the purview of continental politics and William the Conqueror became the most powerful monarch in Europe, establishing a regime that combined Norman and Anglo-Saxon traditions of government and law. Meanwhile, King Louis VI and Abbot Suger of Saint-Denis laid the groundwork for the gradual extension of royal power in France. Emperors in Germany and Italy faced some of the most serious challenges as the outcome of the Investiture Conflict and rivalry with German princes and Italian cities compelled them to search for new sources of imperial power.

Focus Question

How did the commercial revolution affect religion and politics?

1. The commercial revolution fueled many of the major political, social, and cultural developments of the twelfth century. The new money economy, the growth of cities, and the emergence of a prosperous merchant class brought both benefits and losses for Europeans. Monarchies underwent revival, sustained in part by new forms of wealth. In England and France in particular, the new commercial economy afforded kings new sources of revenue, and hence of power. Similarly, town dwellers in regions such as Italy and Flanders secured political autonomy in exchange for

financial patronage of local rulers. Peasants achieved greater productivity, obtained access to markets, and gained increased personal freedom, but these gains were offset by new cash obligations to their landlords. Jews were prominent among the new urban, entrepreneurial classes, but they lacked the same political rights as Christians. As a consequence, they became vulnerable to vicious pogroms during the Crusades. While the Crusades further stimulated trade and reflected growing European prosperity, confidence, and power, they also manifested violence, imperialism, and persecution both within Europe and in the Middle East.

2. As the most powerful institution in the West, inextricably linked to politics, the church was the focal point for many of the economically based developments and their consequences. The church was an early and important beneficiary of the new prosperity. Popes in particular gained wealth and power through such means as their patronage of the prosperous Benedictine monastery at Cluny; and under leaders such as Leo IX and Gregory VII, a papal monarchy had developed. The amassing of such wealth and power promoted a movement for reform manifested in the Investiture Conflict, the Crusades, and the creation of new monastic orders emphasizing poverty and austerity.

Annotated Chapter Outline

I. **The Commercial Revolution**

A. **Fairs, Towns, and Cities, pp. 296–299**

1. The centers of the new economy developed around castles and monasteries where great lords encouraged peasants to cultivate new land and convert services and dues to cash payments.
2. The use of cash fostered the development of local markets where lords could sell surpluses and buy luxury goods from traders and craftspeople.
3. The local markets and markets outside old city walls attracted traders and craftspeople to settle there and gradually grew into substantial towns and cities.
4. The cities that arose around trade lay principally along trade routes and especially along major waterways.
5. Most long-distance traders were Jews and Italians.
6. Urban commerce in Italy had never quite ceased, nor had Italian contacts with the east been severed.
7. Jews, many of whom had been driven off their lands in northern Europe when lords reorganized the countryside, turned to commerce full time.
8. Most towns grew haphazardly and were crowded.
9. Almost all medieval cities contained a marketplace, a castle, and several churches.
10. To accommodate a growing population, long narrow houses were built in some cities to maximize living space.
11. Usually constructed on a wood frame filled with wattle and daub (twigs covered with clay), these buildings were set perpendicular to the main streets and housed businesses on the lower floor and residences on the upper floor.
12. Livestock was housed in enclosures at the rear of these dwellings, as urban inhabitants perpetuated the rural practice of living off food they raised themselves.
13. A building boom began in the tenth century and accelerated through the thirteenth century.
14. Specialized buildings for trade, government, and charity were built, as were numerous defensive walls within which lay a network of narrow streets.
15. New bridges and country roads linked the urban markets, which made overland transport possible.
16. Commercial centers grew fastest along key waterways such as the Mediterranean coast, the Baltic Sea, the English Channel, and the Rhine, Po, and Rhône rivers.

B. **Organizing Crafts and Commerce, pp. 299–301**

1. Although not mechanized, medieval industries were highly organized through guilds.
2. Urban guilds were originally religious and charitable associations of people in the same line of trade, but by the second half of the twelfth century, they became professional corporations defined by statutes and rules covering issues like dues, working hours, and production standards.
3. Within each guild existed a hierarchy: young apprentices learning the trade were at the bottom, journeymen and journeywomen were in the middle, and the accomplished masters were at the top.
4. The journeymen and journeywomen, who were relatively free and independent day laborers working for wages, marked an important stage in the economic history of the west because, for the first time, many

workers were neither slaves nor dependents.

5. Journeywomen were invariably paid less than men.
6. The masters controlled almost all the offices and policies of the guild.
7. The ancestors of modern capitalism may be seen in the development of new kinds of business arrangements, including partnerships, contracts, and large-scale productive enterprises.
8. Partnerships brought individuals together to pool their resources and fund larger ventures. Italians, especially extended families, developed a partnership for commerce by sea called the *compagnia*, in which some partners invested money and other partners undertook the actual voyages in hopes of making a profit.
9. Contracts also began to be used for sales, exchanges, and loans.
10. The church banned usury (charging interest on loans); interest was therefore often disguised as a "late payment" penalty.
11. The use of loans to finance businesses signaled a changed attitude toward credit: risk was acceptable if it brought profit.
12. Because contracts and partnerships could finance large-scale enterprises, light industry began to develop in the eleventh century.
13. Cloth began to be produced on a larger scale using water mills, and new deep-mining technology combined with improved forging techniques made iron practical for use in agricultural tools and plows.
14. Iron tools made farming more productive, which in turn fed the commercial revolution.

C. Communes: Self-Government for the Towns, p. 301

1. Townspeople—a group that included tradespeople, artisans, innkeepers, and money changers—did not fit into the old, medieval social groups: those who fought, prayed, or labored.
2. Townspeople lived in close quarters and shared mutual interests in reliable coinage, laws that facilitated commerce, freedom from service and dues, and liberty to buy and sell as the market dictated.
3. To townspeople, freedom meant having their own officials and law courts, and they petitioned their rulers—bishops, kings, counts, castellans—for the right to govern themselves.
4. Communes were town institutions of self-government. They consisted of sworn associations of citizens that formed a legal corporate body.
5. Communes were most common in Italy, France, and Flanders.
6. In Milan in 1097, for example, after a series of armed clashes, the townspeople transferred authority from the archbishop and the clergy to a government headed by the city's leading men who called themselves "consuls," a title that recalled the republican government of ancient Rome.
7. Outside Italy, movements took place within the framework of larger kingdoms.
8. William Clito, ruler of Flanders (in present-day Belgium), lifted certain tolls and taxes and granted his citizens their own laws and courts and the right to mint coins in return for their recognition of his claim to the region.
9. While creating new forms of business and political associations, urban men and women achieved a measure of self-rule.

D. The Commercial Revolution in the Countryside, pp. 301–302

1. By 1150, rural life was increasingly organized around the marketplace, bringing new opportunities and obligations to both peasants and lords.
2. Lords hired trained, literate agents to administer their estates, calculate profits and losses, and make marketing decisions.
3. Aristocrats continued to base their power on displays of wealth and generosity but, by the late twelfth century, some townsmen could boast fortunes that rivaled those of the great landholders.
4. Many aristocrats, whose honor and authority was still tied to personal generosity, patronage, and displays of wealth, went into debt as their spending exceeded their income.
5. As the lords' need for wealth grew, peasants became more involved in the commercial economy.
6. The population grew, creating greater demand for food and farmland.
7. Lords offered privileges to peasants who would plow or drain these marginal lands, such as the rights to settle the land they reclaimed or lighter monetary dues.

8. In places like Flanders, which was a natural meeting point for traders from England and France, monasteries sponsored drainage projects and built canals to link cities with agricultural regions.
9. Overpopulation strained the old manse organization to the breaking point.
10. In the twelfth century, up to twenty peasant families might live on what had been originally the manse of a single family.
11. Peasants and lords turned services and dues into money rents paid annually, which gave peasants greater control of their land, allowing them to sell their plots or pass them on to their children.
12. Peasants, notwithstanding, had to either pay higher taxes for these privileges or join together to buy their collective liberty at a high price.
13. By joining together, peasants gained a new sense of identity and solidarity.
14. The new money economy that came with the commercial revolution gave greater access to markets, greater productivity, and increased personal freedom for peasants, all of which was offset by greater cash obligations: they ate better, but they had to spend more.

II. **Church Reform**

A. **Beginnings of Reform, pp. 303–305**

1. The Benedictine monastery of Cluny, which had been founded by the duke and duchess of Aquitaine (910), was one of the earliest centers of monastic reform.
2. The abbots of Cluny pushed for reform by encouraging clerical celibacy and better treatment of the poor; soon, other monasteries followed their example.
3. By the eleventh century, the Cluniacs had linked their reform programs to the papacy.
4. In Germany and Italy, a small group of clerics and monks attacked practices that violated canon law (the laws decreed at church councils and by bishops and popes).
5. They were particularly concerned with clerical marriage and simony (paying to get a church office).
6. Emperor Henry III (r. 1039–1056) supported the reformers and refused to accept money or gifts in return for church appointments.
7. Henry also appointed Pope Leo IX (r. 1049–1054) following a disputed election (1046) in which three men were claiming the papacy.
8. During his short reign, Leo expanded the pope's role and changed the Catholic Church.
9. He insisted on being elected by the clergy and people of Rome and made unprecedented journeys into Germany and France to hold church councils.
10. Leo sponsored the creation of a canon law textbook—the *Collection in 74 Titles*—which emphasized the pope's power and the accountability of the clergy to his authority.
11. In 1054, Leo sent Humbert of Silva Candida to Constantinople to argue against the patriarch of Constantinople on behalf of the pope's new, lofty claims.
12. Humbert and the patriarch each excommunicated the other, which precipitated the Great Schism: the Roman Catholic and Greek Orthodox churches were now largely separate.
13. The papacy intervened in many worldly matters such as supporting Christians in northern Spain who were pursuing the *reconquista* ("reconquest") of Muslim Spain.

B. **The Gregorian Reform and the Investiture Conflict, 1073–1122, pp. 305–307**

1. Eleventh-century papal reform is most closely associated with Pope Gregory VII (r. 1073–1085) and his famous clash with Emperor Henry IV (r. 1056–1106).
2. Gregory believed that the emperor was a layman with no right to interfere in church matters.
3. Henry IV believed that his duties included the welfare of church and state; he and his bishops were therefore the church's rightful leaders.
4. In 1075, Gregory prohibited lay investiture, the practice of laymen (like Henry) appointing bishops and presenting them with their symbols of office.
5. Henry defied this order and invested the archbishop of Milan.
6. Gregory excommunicated Henry and gave the people in his kingdom permission to rebel against him.
7. Under threat of rebellion by the German princes, Henry met the pope at Canossa (1077) and stood as a penitent outside the fortress where the pope was staying.

8. Because no priest could refuse absolution to a penitent, Gregory was forced to lift his excommunication, yet this solved nothing.
9. Civil war broke out when the princes elected an antiking (a king chosen illegally) and Henry and his supporters elected an antipope.
10. The conflict was finally resolved with the Concordat of Worms of 1122.
11. This compromise relied on an important distinction between the spiritual and secular parts of the investiture ritual.
12. Under the concordat, the symbols of the church office (the ring and the staff) would be given to the bishop by a churchman, then the emperor or his representative would touch the bishop with a scepter symbolizing the land and other possessions that came with the office.
13. In the end, secular rulers continued to play a role in the appointment of churchmen, but few still claimed that the king was head of the church.
14. The conflict strengthened the papacy and shattered the balance of power between political and ecclesiastical powers in Germany and Italy.
15. German princes consolidated their lands at the expense of royal power.

C. The Sweep of Reform, pp. 307–309

1. Christians had always believed that the sacraments were God's way of infusing everyday existence with grace, but Christians were unsure about how they worked, how many there were, or even what their significance was.
2. In the eleventh century, the church began to emphasize the importance of the sacraments and the role of the priest in administering them.
3. For instance, after the Gregorian reforms, the clergy began stressing the sanctity of marriage and, for the first time, marriage became a ceremony performed by a priest.
4. The clergy prohibited marriage between couples as distant as seventh cousins, which had the potential for disrupting aristocrats' control over family alliances.
5. Reformers above all stressed the special importance of the Eucharist, or Holy Communion.
6. Emphasis on this sacrament set priests apart from the laity; reformers taught that no layman or any woman could perform anything equal to the Eucharist and that it was the key to salvation.
7. The church began enforcing the celibacy of priests, and in 1123 the pope proclaimed all clerical marriages invalid.
8. The policy of clerical celibacy broke with traditional local practices in many places and exacerbated the schism with the Eastern Orthodox Church, which did not practice celibacy.
9. Gratian's *Harmony of Discordant Canons* (later revised and expanded to the *Decretum*) gathered thousands of passages from the decrees of popes and councils and writings of the church fathers.
10. When he uncovered any discord in his sources, Gratian imposed "harmony" by arguing that the contradictory passages dealt with different situations.
11. Gratian's work clarified and organized church laws (canon law) and rules. At the same time, the papal curia ("government") began to resemble a court of law with its own collection agency.
12. The pope, with his bureaucracy, law courts, and financial apparatus, had become a monarch.

D. New Monastic Orders of Poverty, pp. 309–311

1. In the twelfth century, the lifestyle associated with the opulence of Benedictine monasteries was seen as greed.
2. To emphasize poverty as a key element of religious life, Bruno of Cologne founded the Carthusian monastic order.
3. This order consisted of monasteries limited to twelve monks (the number of Christ's apostles) who took vows of silence and lived in seclusion in small, individual huts.
4. The Burgundian Cistercian order grew more rapidly than the Carthusian.
5. Governed by simplicity above all, Cistercians did not dye their robes, which earned them their nickname "white monks."
6. Under the guidance of St. Bernard (c. 1090–1153), the Cistercian order grew from the founding of its first monastery at Cîteaux in France (1098) to more than three hundred monasteries established throughout Europe by the mid-twelfth century.
7. Many cloistered nuns also adopted Cistercian customs.

8. Cistercian churches reflected the order's emphasis on poverty. They were small and standardized, constructed of undecorated stone. Wall paintings and sculpture were prohibited.
9. Each monastic enclave possessed highly organized farms and grazing lands called granges.
10. Cistercian monks dedicated themselves to private prayer, contemplation, and monastic administration.
11. Cistercian spirituality emphasized intense, personal emotion, the humanity of Christ, and the Virgin Mary.
12. All Cistercian churches were dedicated to the Virgin Mary, but none displayed the holy relics common in other churches.
13. The monks spent much of their time managing the monastery's estates and tending flocks of sheep, both of which, by the end of the twelfth century, yielded substantial profits.
14. Although they were founded in reaction to the wealth of the commercial revolution, the Cistercians became part of it.

III. The Crusades

A. Calling the Crusade, pp. 311–313

1. The First Crusade was called in response to the Byzantine emperor's request for help against a new wave of Muslim invasions by the Seljuk Turks.
2. In 1071, the Byzantine emperor Romanus IV met the Seljuk Turks with a mercenary army at Manzikert.
3. There he was defeated and captured, ending Byzantine domination in eastern Turkey.
4. In 1095, emperor Alexius I appealed to Pope Urban II in hope of receiving new mercenary troops for his army.
5. Urban chose to interpret the request differently; at the Council of Clermont, he called upon an excited throng of people to take up arms and wrest the Holy Land away from "the wicked race."
6. Urban's call gave the papacy a new role in military matters.
7. Both men and women, rich and poor, young and old participated in the crusade for a variety of reasons that ranged from sincere piety to a desire for wealth.

B. The First Crusade, pp. 313–316

1. The armies were not an organized military force but a series of separate militias, each following a different commander and often speaking different languages.
2. One band, not commissioned by the pope, consisted of commoners led by Peter the Hermit called the "People's (or Peasants') Crusade."
3. On its way to the Holy Land, the band made a deliberate detour to attack Jews living peacefully in Germany, who were now perceived as infidels.
4. Most of the participants in the People's Crusade met their deaths in Asia Minor.
5. The conquest of the Holy Land was facilitated by Muslim disunity.
6. After seizing Antioch (1098) and killing every Turk in the city, the crusaders went on to take Jerusalem (1099).

C. The Crusader States, pp. 316–317

1. The victorious leaders of the First Crusade organized crusader states that were treated as lordships, in which leaders granted fiefs to their vassals.
2. After many of the European crusaders returned home, the rulers who remained learned to coexist and trade with the indigenous peoples.
3. Mostly, however, they focused on military matters, recruiting knights from Europe.
4. A new group, the Knights Templar, whose name comes from their living quarters in the area near the former Jewish Temple at Jerusalem, devoted themselves to warfare.
5. Their missions included protecting pilgrimage routes from Palestine to Jerusalem, manning town garrisons of the crusader states, and transporting money from Europe to the Holy Land.
6. This last mission led to tremendous wealth for the Templars and a system of "branch" banks across Europe.

D. The Disastrous Second Crusade, p. 317

1. Crusader states began to decline shortly thereafter as the Turks began a counteroffensive.
2. The fall of Edessa in 1144 launched the ineffectual Second Crusade.
3. Ruling monarchs became involved with the cause: Louis VII of France and Emperor Conrad III in Germany, as well as St. Bernard.
4. The Germans, at the prompting of Alfonso VI of Castile, turned their interest eastward for a *reconquista* of Spain.
5. A lack of any clear or coordinated plan kept the French and German groups from

working together, and both were badly hurt by Turkish attacks.

6. When the leaders finally met at Acre and agreed to attack Muslim-controlled Damascus, they encountered a stiff defense and abandoned the attack after five days, ending the crusade.
7. In the wake of this defeat, Louis VII divorced his wife, Eleanor of Aquitaine, who then married Henry, count of Anjou and duke of Normandy, and set in motion a series of events with far-reaching consequences when Henry became king of England.

E. The Long-Term Impact of the Crusades, pp. 317–319

1. The success of the First Crusade was limited.
2. Although numerous new crusades were called, and eight major ones were fought between 1096 and the late thirteenth century, the Holy Land fell to the Muslims permanently in 1291.
3. The crusades inspired later expeditions such as Columbus's in 1492.
4. While the crusades stimulated trade, the commercial revolution would have happened without them.
5. The impact of the crusades on the west was mainly on its imagination.
6. The crusades worsened Islamic disunity, although they did not cause it.
7. Before the crusades, the split between Shi'ite and Sunni Muslims was more serious in many ways than the rift between Muslims and Christians.
8. The brutal conquest of Jerusalem shocked and dismayed Muslims.

IV. The Revival of Monarchies

A. Reconstructing the Empire at Byzantium, p. 319

1. The Byzantine Empire had begun to recover from the defeat at Manzikert by 1081.
2. Under attack from all sides and facing internal discontent, Emperor Alexius I (r. 1081–1118) managed to stave off defeat by turning his enemies against one another.
3. To wage all the wars he had to fight, Alexius relied more on mercenaries and allied dynatoi armed and mounted like European knights and accompanied by their own troops.
4. In return for their services, he gave these nobles lifetime possession of large estates and their dependent peasants.
5. This arrangement satisfied the provincial nobles and grants of offices appeased the urban elite.
6. Alexius's Comnenian dynasty (1081–1185) continued to exercise a measure of authority via these concessions to the nobility.

B. England under Norman Rule, pp. 319–321

1. Twelfth-century kings of England were the most powerful monarchs in Europe because they ruled their kingdom by right of conquest.
2. When the Anglo-Saxon king Edward the Confessor (r. 1042–1066) died childless in 1066, three men contended for the throne: Harold, earl of Wessex; Harald Hardrada, king of Norway; and William, duke of Normandy.
3. Edward had named Harold as successor on his deathbed but, after Harold's coronation, William (1027–1087) prepared for battle.
4. By appealing to the pope, William received the banner of St. Peter as a sign of God's approval, and invaded England.
5. King Harold defeated Harald Hardrada at Stamford Bridge in the north of England, and then marched his army to meet William in the south just one week later.
6. The two evenly matched armies clashed at Hastings on October 14, 1066, and, at the end of the day, Harold was dead and William was king of England.
7. As a result of the conquest, an estimated one out of five persons in England died, and William supplanted the Saxon aristocracy with families from the continent.
8. The Normans retained many Anglo-Saxon institutions, such as writs to communicate the king's orders.
9. The Norman kings also imitated continental arrangements, setting up a political hierarchy dominated by the king and his castles.
10. Because England was the king's by conquest, he was free to divide its land as he pleased, primarily to his barons and family members, who became his vassals.
11. In 1086 William ordered a survey and census of England, which was called

Domesday. It was the most extensive inventory of land, livestock, taxes, and population that had ever been compiled in Europe.

12. The Norman Conquest tied England to the languages, politics, institutions, and culture of the continent.
13. The barons of England also kept their great estates in Normandy and elsewhere and, in fact, many English kings spent more time on the continent than they did in England.

C. Praising the King of France, pp. 321–322

1. Although the twelfth-century kings of France governed little more than the area surrounding Paris known as the Île-de-France, they also took part in the monarchical revival.
2. Louis VI the Fat (r. 1108–1137) was a tireless defender of royal power, whose efforts were recorded by his close adviser, Suger (1081–1152), the abbot of Saint-Denis.
3. In Louis's biography, written by Suger, the king was portrayed as a pious hero with feudal rights over the French nobles and as a defender of the church and the poor.
4. According to Suger, Louis waged war to keep God's peace but respected the preeminence of the papacy in religious matters.
5. Louis made the most of the king's right to call upon his vassals to aid him in times of war and to collect many dues and taxes—especially the latter.
6. The king also drew revenues from the thriving commercial city of Paris, and royal officials (called "provosts") enforced his royal laws and collected taxes.
7. With money and land, Louis VI could dispense the favors and give the gifts that built up his prestige and power.
8. Together, Louis and Suger created the territorial core and royal ideal of the future French monarchy.

D. Surviving as Emperor, pp. 322–323

1. Henry IV, emperor and king of both Germany and Italy, was a powerful ruler commanding important resources of church and state.
2. Henry IV's son, Henry V, faced new challenges following the Investiture Conflict and its resolution with the Concordat of Worms in 1122.
3. Although the Concordat of Worms left the king with considerable power within the church to "invest" bishops with property, the agreement said nothing about the ruler's relationship with the German princes or Italian cities.
4. Henry V and his successor Lothar III both died childless, leaving the princes to elect Conrad III.
5. Conrad's nephew Frederick Barbarossa would seek new sources of imperial power in the future.

Lecture Strategies

1. The commercial economy in western Europe was one of the most influential developments of medieval history, but is taken for granted today. Students might find it interesting to see how this system affected those who lived during its early stages. By which mechanisms did the commercial economy develop? Who were its primary champions and opponents? Why? How did it affect social relationships? Demographics? Urbanism? Daily life? How did it affect the political order? A handful of classic studies on this topic include Henri Pirenne, *Economic and Social History of Medieval Europe* (New York: Harcourt Brace Jovanovich, 1933). Chapter 1 details the revival of commerce, the growth of European cities, and the role of the crusades in economic growth; Chapter 4 outlines the emerging role of money. One of the best general overviews is Georges Duby, *The Early Growth of the European Economy: Warriors and Peasants from the Seventh to the Twelfth Century* (Ithaca, NY: Cornell University Press, 1978), which includes a discussion of the general social context as the economy emerged from the feudal period.

2. Another development of eleventh- and twelfth-century western Europe that would have a crucial, lasting impact on Europe was the centralization of authority in the western kingdoms. An overview will provide a useful understanding of the basis of the modern state system. For a look at the general features of state building in the medieval west, see Joseph Reese Stayer, *On the Medieval Origins of the Modern State* (Princeton, NJ: Princeton University Press, 1970), which is an outstanding short overview of the development of national political institutions during this period. For more detailed studies of particular national systems and their development, see H. G. Richardson and G. O. Sayles, *The Governance of Medieval England from the Conquest to Magna Carta* (Edinburgh: Edinburgh University Press, 1963); and Alfred Haverkamp, *Medieval Germany, 1056–1276*, H. Braum and R. Mortimer, trans. (Oxford: Oxford

University Press, 1992). Compare and contrast the development of centralized royal authority in these countries. What are the factors that influenced the pace and extent of consolidation? How did the rulers of these countries confront these considerations?

3. The crusades were among the most dramatic and harrowing events of the Middle Ages, characterized by brutal warfare, ugly racial and religious bigotry, and military expansionism. Examine the crusades from varying perspectives: religious, social, cultural, economic, and political. How did the crusading spirit fit contemporary Christian beliefs? What motives, emotions, and incentives did the pope offer the people to induce them to join the crusades? What might have been some of the pope's ulterior motives? How did the crusades fit into the political climate of western Europe at that time? How did the crusades affect relations between the west and Byzantium? Between the west and Muslims? What, if anything, can explain the behavior of the crusaders toward the Jews? What were some of the economic and cultural outcomes of the crusades? For a good overview, see Jonathan Riley Smith, *The First Crusade and the Idea of Crusading* (Philadelphia: University of Pennsylvania Press, 1986); and Thomas F. Madden, *A Concise History of the Crusades* (Lanham, MD: Rowman & Littlefield, 1999). For the contribution of the crusades to the cross-cultural contact and mutual enrichment of both Muslim and Christian societies, see Bernard Lewis, *The Muslim Discovery of Europe* (New York: W. W. Norton, 1982); and M. R. Menocal, *The Arabic Role in Medieval Literacy* (Philadelphia: University of Pennsylvania Press, 1990).

Class Discussion Starters

1. The increasing hostility in church–state relations during this period crystallized in the Investiture Conflict. The growing ambitions and territorial and jurisdictional claims of the emperor and the pope revealed the growing chasm in what was once a much more harmonious relationship. What might have given rise to this hostility? In discussing the Investiture Conflict, have students compare the behaviors of Henry and Gregory. How did they each appeal to the people for recognition of their authority? What rhetorical and propagandistic devices did they use? Who actually "won" the Investiture Conflict? What does all this tell us about the underlying nature of people's notions of authority at the time? See Gerd Tellenbach, *Church, State, and Christian Society at the Time of the Investiture Conflict* (Oxford: Blackwell, 1940), which is an older but excellent overview that includes much useful discussion of religious worldviews, conceptions of freedom, and notions of hierarchy. Also see Brian Tierney, *The Crisis of Church and State, 1050–1300* (Englewood Cliffs, NJ: Prentice Hall, 1964), a good introduction to vital documents.

2. The reform movement within the church reflects problems that some perceived in the church, aggravated by the church's interaction with a rapidly changing social reality. Ask students to discuss how the church reacted to the reform movements. In which ways were the calls for reform accommodated? Modified? Ignored? What was the basis for the criticisms? How did this movement fit into the growing church–state conflict? What were some of the differences in the responses of various monastic orders and the papacy? An excellent source is I. S. Robinson, *The Papacy, 1073–1198: Continuity and Innovation* (Cambridge, UK: Cambridge University Press, 1990). Also see Gerd Tellenbach, *The Church in Western Europe from the Tenth to the Twelfth Century* (Cambridge, UK: Cambridge University Press, 1993), which details the Catholic Church's religious, social, and political development through the reform movement and into the high Middle Ages.

3. Ask students to discuss how the Norman Conquest transformed the face of England and set the country on its course to rapid, royal consolidation. Normans shrewdly integrated their own practices and institutions with those already in place in Anglo-Saxon England. What paths did the Normans take in solidifying their conquest? How effective were they? What were the reactions of the various groups within England? See R. Allen Brown, *The Normans* (Rochester, NY: Boydell & Brewer, 1994).

4. Discuss the relationship between the crusade against Muslims in the Holy Land, the *reconquista* in Spain, and the pogrom against Jews in the Rhineland. How were these events related? How might the crusaders have reconciled their violent acts with the moral teachings of Christianity? What role did church institutions such as the papacy play in these events? In addition to religious faith, what may have motivated the crusaders? Have students consider the Contrasting Views documents on the First Crusade as part of their discussion.

Reviewing the Text

Review Questions

1. What new institutions resulted from the commercial revolution?
[model answer] *New financial and business institutions developed during the commercial revolution, as cities became centers of production and trade as well as religion and politics. Permanent commercial centers emerged in existing cities alongside castles and monasteries. The*

business of production was organized and regulated through guilds of craftsmen and a system of wage labor developed. New business institutions grew as people pooled resources and cooperated to increase business and profitability. Business partnerships and the creation of contracts for sales, exchanges, and loans restructured commerce and its financial arrangements. A new town institution, the commune, developed to encompass the new relationships that grew in the commercial revolution.

2. What were the causes and consequences of the Gregorian reform?
[model answer] *The reforms grew out of conflicts over who would have ultimate power and authority in church matters—a king in his own country or the Pope in Rome over church officials in all countries. It ended with a compromise that in effect diminished the authority of kings in church matters, giving the Pope increased access to power in all kingdoms through his control over church appointments. The emperor could no longer act as head of the church, which empowered local lords in Germany and Italy to act more independently. Reforms concerning the sacraments increased church involvement in people's daily lives and, along with the requirement of celibacy for priests, served to reinforce the special role of priests in society.*

3. How and why was the First Crusade a success, and how and why was it a failure?
[model answer] *The First Crusade achieved its goal of capturing Jerusalem and established Christian Crusader states in the region. From the perspective of Byzantine Emperor Alexius, it failed to restore the territory to his empire, as control remained in the hands of crusaders. And though the region was now nominally Christian, in reality the population remained a mix of faiths.*

4. Which ruler—Alexius, William the Conqueror, or Louis VI—was the strongest, which the feeblest, and why?
[model answer] *William the Conqueror seems to have been the most powerful and Louis VI the weakest. William's strength began with his military defeat of the English people and the military power he was able to command. Retaining personal control of large amounts of English land and granting control of much of the rest to a small number of loyal followers from the continent enhanced his power. He seems to have dictated the structure and terms of power more clearly than Alexius or Louis VI. Alexius maintained his power in part by granting concessions to other nobility, which diluted his own power to some extent. Louis VI's kingdom was less centralized than the others' and local lords held greater independent powers than in England. Louis was more a lord of lords than the lord of the land, able to solicit the respect and loyalty of his territorial lords more when it suited their own ends than as a result of his own political power.*

Making Connections

1. What were the similarities and what were the differences between the powers wielded by the Carolingian kings and those wielded by twelfth-century rulers?
[model answer] *Both Carolingian kings and twelfth-century rulers relied on vassals to administer their territories while retaining highly developed personal powers, but they differed in that twelfth-century rulers controlled much smaller territories than Carolingian kings and had a more adversarial relationship with the papacy. And while Carolingian kings largely depended on the wealth from their estates and warfare to support themselves, twelfth-century rulers collected taxes, took in dues from their vassals, and benefited (through taxes on commerce) from the rise of cities and the expansion of trade.*

2. How may the First Crusade be understood as a consequence of the Gregorian reform?
[model answer] *Both Carolingian kings and twelfth-century rulers relied on vassals to administer their territories while retaining highly developed personal powers, but they differed in that twelfth-century rulers controlled much smaller territories than Carolingian kings and had a more adversarial relationship with the papacy. And while Carolingian kings largely depended on the wealth from their estates and warfare to support themselves, twelfth-century rulers collected taxes, took in dues from their vassals, and benefited (through taxes on commerce) from the rise of cities and the expansion of trade.*

Discussing the Documents

Questions from Online Study Guide with Model Answers

A Byzantine View of Papal Primacy (p. 305)

1. What position does Nicetas take on the issue of papal primacy?
[model answer] *Nicetas sees the church in Rome as the first among equals, and, in his role as leader of the church in Rome, the Pope as the primary bishop, but not, as he says, the "Prince" or ruler over all other bishops.*

2. How does Nicetas justify the separation of the Byzantine church from the Roman church?
[model answer] *The Roman church does not include representatives of the Byzantine church in its councils or decision-making. Nicetas believes the Byzantine church is justified in separating itself from the dictates of the Roman church that the Byzantine church did not have a role in formulating or approving.*

Penance for the Invaders (1070) (p. 322)

1. What does the document reveal about the role of the church in overseeing penance?
[model answer] *Penance is an institution through which the church enforces elements of moral order, and it appears that the church has authority even over the king's men to enforce its decisions on this.*

2. What does the practice of penance suggest about the nature of sin?
[model answer] *The practice suggests that sin can be redeemed by actions taken after the act. Sins are not permanent if they are recognized and accounted for by penitential actions.*

Contrasting Views: The First Crusade (pp. 314–315)

1. What commonalities, if any, do you detect between the religious ideas of the crusaders and those whom they attacked?
[model answer] *All share a belief in Jerusalem as a holy place. The documents discuss the importance of prayer for Jews and Muslims in appealing to God and for Christians and Jews a belief that God can make decisions that influence the course of events—e.g., providing good weather and ample provisions, or responding to repentance and prayer with assistance.*

2. What were the similarities and what were the differences in the experiences of the Jews in Rhineland cities and the Arabs in Jerusalem?
[model answer] *Both were attacked, but many Jews found sympathy and help with their local Bishops. Both experienced death, the destruction of their religious property, and the plunder of valuable possessions.*

3. What were the motives of the crusaders?
[model answer] *In this document, the crusaders appear to be motivated by a sense of destiny, the fulfillment of the prophecy of David, and the importance of acknowledging and saving for Christianity the place in which Christ lived.*

New Sources, New Perspectives: The Cairo Geniza (p. 318)

1. What do the documents in the geniza tell us about Muslim as well as Jewish life in medieval Cairo?
[model answer] *The documents contain small details of daily life that can reveal cultural values, practices, and issues of concern to average people. The excerpt discussing debt indicated that Muslims likely held social power over Jewish residents, and that Jews had a strong sense of community among themselves within the greater Arab world.*

2. What new questions might historians explore with the geniza documents?
[model answer] *These documents could be used to explore social relations and power among groups of citizens and the role of women and the power they held in society, as well as details of daily life concerning people's occupations and activities, their cultural values, educational institutions, social structure, and much more.*

Other Questions for Discussing These Documents in Class

A Byzantine View of Papal Primacy (p. 305)

1. Ask students to analyze the central issue of Nicetas's argument, that there is a difference between the office of bishop of Rome and the officeholder. How was Nicetas able to recognize the primacy of the one but not the other?

2. In what ways does Nicetas have a moderate view of the question of papal primacy?

Penance for the Invaders (1070) (p. 322)

1. What does the document suggest about the relationship between sin and penance?

2. How did the church reconcile Christian prohibitions on violence with the realities of medieval warfare?

Contrasting Views: The First Crusade (pp. 314–315)

1. Which of the three accounts presents the fullest account, including points of view of the most participants?

2. Describe the most important insights contained in each document.

Comparative Questions

1. Collectively, what do all of the documents suggest about the role of violence in the Middle Ages?

2. Describe the relationship between religion and violence in medieval culture.

3. What was the relationship between papal claims to power, the invasion of England, and the crusades?

For Users of *Sources of The Making of the West*

The following documents are available in Chapter 10 of the companion sourcebook by Katharine J. Lualdi, University of Southern Maine.

1. Medieval Cities: *Urban Charters of Jaca, Spain* (c. 1077) and *Lorris, France* (1155)
2. Sources of the Investiture Conflict: *Emperor Henry IV and Pope Gregory VII* (1076)
3. Calling the First Crusade: *Pope Urban II* (1095)
4. Arab Response to the First Crusade: *Ibn al-Athīr* (1097–1099)
5. The Power of William I: *The Anglo-Saxon Chronicle* (1085–1086)

Discussion Ideas for **Sources of the Making of the West,** *Chapter 10*

1. Ask students to compare and contrast the urban charters of Jaca, Spain and Lorris, France. What do the two documents suggest about the relationship between cities, kings, and the church? What were the objectives of Sancho I and Louis VII in granting these charters? How did they reconcile the granting of rights to the cities with their own power as leaders? What do these charters illustrate about the commercial revolution and its consequences?

2. Ask students to consider the sources of the Investiture Conflict. What was the central issue about which Emperor Henry IV and Pope Gregory VII disagreed? Why was the struggle seen as part of a larger movement of church reform? What quotations in their letters illustrate the two men's appeals to religious forms of authority to support their respective positions? The class might also want to compare the Investiture Conflict with the issues raised by the document on the Byzantine view of papal primacy.

Working with Visual Sources

For this exercise, please refer to Bayeux "Tapestry" on p. 321 of the textbook or view the image on the book companion site's Online Study Guide under the "Visual Activity" for Chapter 10.

Students viewing the image at the Online Study Guide are asked three questions of the image. The questions and model answers (not made available to students) are below. Project this image, available on the Instructor's Resources CD-ROM, in class or ask students to look at the image in their textbooks and answer the questions.

1. In this segment of the "tapestry," which is actually 231 feet long and 20 inches wide over all, the embroidery presents us with Norman knights on horseback, an English warrior with battle-ax, and a lower border of Norman archers. Who seems to be winning this battle? Why do you think this?
[model answer] *The Norman knights on horseback seem to be winning this battle. Mounted on their horses, they are charging toward the English warriors with their weapons ready to strike. The English are poised for battle with shields, sword, and battle-ax raised, but seem to be falling back.*

2. According to historical accounts of the Battle of Hastings, English troops were worn down primarily by Norman archers. Look at the relationship between the Norman archers and the Norman knights in the embroidery. Which group seems to be playing a more decisive role in this victory?
[model answer] *In the tapestry, the knights seem to be playing a more decisive role in the victory. They are confronting the English warriors head on and are the same size as the English warriors, while the archers, relegated to a lower plane of the scene, are much smaller.*

3. Why might this segment of the tapestry depict the knights playing a more important role and displaying more bravery than the archers?
[model answer] *The tapestry is 231 feet long and 20 inches wide and only a small portion is included in the reproduction shown in the textbook, so we do not really know what stage of the battle is being presented here. Even so, the archers who were the decisive troops of this particular battle are small figures relegated to the lower border, and the knights are clearly the main subject of the tapestry. A reasonable explanation is that because the archers' arrows flew a hundred yards or more, these soldiers would not have been in the heart of the battle or in much hand-to-hand combat, so perhaps the artist was trying to illustrate the archers' relative distance. Another reasonable explanation is that the artist minimized the remarkable role of the archers—mere commoners—in order to depict the powerful and wealthy Norman knights as the decisive force in the battle.*

Mapping Exercises

Map Activity from OSG—Model Answer for Map Activity #2

For this activity please refer to the map on p. 324. Students are asked these questions:

What were the three main religions of the Mediterranean world in this period? Does the absence of Judaism from the map mean that there were no Jews in the regions depicted?
[model answer] *Catholic Christianity, Eastern Orthodox Christianity, and Islam were the main religions. The map depicts only the dominant religions in each area. Minority religions such as Judaism do not appear, although their absence from the map does not mean that Jews were nonexistent.*

In what areas did Christians and Muslims coexist?
[model answer] *Muslims and Catholic Christians were located in western Europe in parts of what is today Spain and Portugal. In the eastern Mediterranean, Muslims and Catholic Christians lived in the areas where crusader states had been established. Muslims also coexisted with Eastern Orthodox Christians in Asia Minor, where the Seljuk Dominions came into contact with the Byzantine Empire.*

Map 10.1: Medieval Trade Routes in the Eleventh and Twelfth Centuries, p. 298

This map gives students a glimpse of the "global economy" of the day and can thus be useful in discerning some general patterns that have survived or have been abandoned in the years since in the development of the modern global economy. Have students identify major regional specialization and routes of trade. How might such production and trade patterns affect rulers and their policies, as well as the social and economic development of the societies?

Map 10.2: The First Crusade, 1096–1099, p. 312

This map identifies the geographical disparities within Europe at the launching of the First Crusade. In light of the contemporary political situation, with the Investiture Controversy still fairly recent, what advantages might the pope have seen in launching a crusade against non-Christians outside of Europe and building sentiment against such "outsiders"? How might such activities have contributed to the slaughtering of the Jews inside Europe by the crusaders?

Mapping the West: Major Religions in the West, c. 1150, p. 324

Ask students to identify the three main religious regions of the Mediterranean world. What historical developments account for the areas in Spain and the Near East where two or more religions were influential? What does this map suggest about the Jewish population of Europe?

In-Class Assignments and Presentation Topics

1. Have students write a short essay on the causes and consequences of the movement to centralize church authority. Which conditions within the church and the broader society gave rise to this movement? What form did this development take? How was it related to the church's broader political, religious, and economic ambitions? This could include a discussion of the militarization of the church and what it meant for religious life and for western society. For an overview, see I. S. Robinson, *The Papacy, 1073–1198: Continuity and Innovation* (Cambridge, UK: Cambridge University Press, 1990). See also Colin Morris, *The Papal Monarchy: The Western Church from 1050 to 1250* (Oxford: Clarendon, 1989), a sweeping study of the church's political development and centralization, its economic dealings, territorial expansion, and governmental structure.

2. Using "Four Accounts of the Crusades," in Patrick Geary, ed., *Readings in Medieval History*, 2nd ed. (Peterborough, Ont.: Broadview Press, 1997), have students write a concise history of the crusades drawing on the western Christian, Byzantine, Jewish, and Muslim accounts. The purpose of this exercise is to teach students how to use primary sources; identify biases, inaccuracies, and differing perspectives; and construct a sensible history of their own using disparate available data. In addition, such an exercise will instruct students about the degree to which history is not simply one person's version of what occurred but a historian's or contemporary's own perspectives embedded in his or her writing.

3. Ask students to deliver a presentation on the role of technological development in the eleventh and twelfth centuries. This presentation should include some of the major causes and consequences of technological innovation. What effects did technological change have on social relations, the economy, and so on? An excellent study of the role of technological development in economic growth and commercialization is Frances Gies and Joseph Gies, *Cathedral, Forge, and Waterwheel: Technology and Invention in the Middle Ages* (New York: HarperCollins, 1994), which includes a useful section on Asian contributions to western medieval technological development.

4. Students may be curious about what life was like for ordinary persons during this period of dramatic transformation. Assign a short writing assignment on the social history of the period. Students could approach the topic from a variety of angles. There are several useful sources for such an assignment: Robert Fossier, *Peasant Life in the Medieval West* (Columbia: University of South Carolina Press, 1988); David Herlihy, *Medieval Households* (Cambridge, MA: Harvard University Press, 1985), which includes excellent discussions of marriage patterns, family size, sexual relations, and emotional life; and Georges Duby, ed., and Arthur Goldhammer, trans., *A History of Private Life*, vol. 2, *Revelations of the Medieval World* (Cambridge, MA: Harvard University Press, 1988), which features an interesting assessment of the concept and nature of private life.

Essay Questions

1. Ask students to research and report on the changing role and status of women in the medieval west. There are a variety of possibilities for such a paper, and a wealth of excellent sources from which to draw ideas and perspectives. Christiane Klapisch-Zuber, ed., *A History of Women*, vol. 2, *Silences of the Middle Ages* (Cambridge, MA: Harvard University Press, 1992) includes excellent essays on various topics related to women in the Middle Ages. Emilie Amt, ed., *Women's Lives in Medieval Europe: A Sourcebook* (New York: Routledge, 1993) is a collection of primary sources that is valuable for its particular focus on legal developments and legacies that shaped women's lives. Another good collection of essays appears in Patricia H. Labalme, ed., *Beyond Their Sex: Learned Women of the European Past* (New York: New York University Press, 1980). A related reading that may be of use to students is Caroline Bynum, *Jesus as Mother: Studies in the Spirituality of the High Middle Ages* (Berkeley: University of California Press, 1982). Bynum interestingly frames key social and religious institutions and practices that, she argues, manifest an increasing feminized character, and discusses the effects it had on social life.

2. Have students give a detailed analysis of family and social life. How were social and familial relations configured? How did daily life differ among peasants, laborers, merchants, and royalty? See Georges Duby, ed., *A History of Private Life*, vol. 2, *Revelations of the Medieval World*, Arthur Goldhammer, trans. (Cambridge, MA: Harvard University Press, 1988); Robert Fossier, *Peasant Life in the Medieval West* (Columbia: University of South Carolina Press, 1988); Michel Mollat, *The Poor in the Middle Ages: An Essay in Social History*, Arthur Goldhammer, trans. (New Haven, CT: Yale University Press, 1986); David Herlihy, *Medieval Households* (Cambridge, MA: Harvard University Press, 1985); and Frances Gies and Joseph Gies, *Marriage and Family in the Middle Ages* (New York: HarperCollins, 1989).

Additional Resources: Literature

Atherton, Mark, ed., *Selected Writings: Hildegard of Bingen*. 2001.

Cusimano, Richard C., trans., *Abbot Suger: The Deeds of Louis the Fat*. 1992.

Peter, Edward, ed., *The First Crusade: The Chronicle of Fulcher of Chartres and Other Source Materials*. 1998.

Sewter, E. R., trans., *The Alexiad of Anna Comnena*. 1979.

Terry, Patricia, trans., *The Song of Roland*. 1992.

Thompson, Augustine, trans., *Gratian: The Treatise on Laws*. 1993.

Additional Resources: Film and Video

The Crusades: Crescent and the Cross (2005) (DVD, 180 min.). Originally aired on the History Channel, this documentary includes dramatic reenactments.

OTHER BEDFORD/ST. MARTIN'S RESOURCES FOR CHAPTER 10

The following resources are available to accompany Chapter 10. Please refer to the Preface of this manual for detailed descriptions of all the ancillaries.

For Instructors

Transparencies

The following maps and images from Chapter 10 are available as full-color acetates.

- Map 10.1: Medieval Trade Routes in the Eleventh and Twelfth Centuries
- Map 10.2: The First Crusade, 1096–1099
- Mapping the West: Major Religions in the West, c. 1150
- Figure 10.1 Floor Plan of a Cistercian Monastery, p. 310
- Bayeux "Tapestry," p. 321

Instructor's Resources CD-ROM

The following maps and image from Chapter 10, as well as a chapter outline, are available on disc in both PowerPoint and jpeg formats.

- Map 10.1: Medieval Trade Routes in the Eleventh and Twelfth Centuries
- Map 10.2: The First Crusade, 1096–1099
- Mapping the West: Major Religions in the West, c. 1150
- Bayeux "Tapestry," p. 321

Using the Bedford Series with The Making of the West

Available in print as well as online at **bedfordstmartins.com/oconnor,** this guide by Maura O'Connor, University of Cincinnati, offers practical suggestions for using *Power and the Holy in the Age of the Investiture Conflict: A Brief History with Documents* by Maureen C. Miller, in conjunction with Chapter 10 of the textbook.

For Students

Study Guides

The Online Study Guide at **bedfordstmartins.com/hunt** helps students synthesize the material they have learned as well as practice the skills historians use to make sense of the past. The following Map, Visual, and Document activities are available for Chapter 10.

Map Activity

- Mapping the West: Major Religions in the West, c. 1150, p. 324

Visual Activity

- Bayeux "Tapestry," p. 321

Reading Historical Documents

- A Byzantine View of Papal Primacy, p. 305
- Contrasting Views: The First Crusade, pp. 314–315
- New Sources, New Perspectives: The Cairo Geniza, p. 318
- Penances for the Invaders (1070), p. 322

CHAPTER

11

The Flowering of the Middle Ages

1150–1215

CHAPTER RESOURCES

Main Chapter Topics

1. The cultural, economic, technological, and intellectual developments of the twelfth century transformed human affairs in western Europe, affecting everything from the everyday patterns of life to the conception of humankind's position in the universe. These changes, in turn, altered the political divisions of Europe and initiated a movement toward a new social order characterized by nationalist sentiment and pride.

2. The western European kingdoms underwent rapid and significant institutionalization and bureaucratization to solidify royal authority and stabilize their societies. The pace and extent of these transformations varied due to local political conditions; it was most pronounced in England, whereas the eastern European countries slowly fragmented and drifted into instability, further weakening their positions.

3. In some cases, this institutionalization and extension of royal authority met with considerable opposition. In England, leading barons rebelled against the irresponsible use of authority by King John (r. 1199–1216), forcing him to sign Magna Carta in 1215. This document for the first time placed formal restrictions on the extent of royal power and established legal guarantees of the rights of free men, setting a precedent for later democratic, constitutional governments.

4. Prosperous courts patronized troubadour poetry in vernacular language rather than in clerical Latin. These poems transmitted values and ideals that emphasized the importance of women and proper conduct by men toward them. Chivalry instituted new codes of behavior for the upper classes that included the courtly behavior celebrated in troubadour poetry and added a code of conduct for the battlefield, a code that distinguished the knightly class from the mercenaries who were replacing them.

5. The accelerating commercial economy produced new patterns of daily life, as more persons from the countryside moved into the cities, furthering the division of labor between societal groups. New industry gave rise to hierarchical guilds in which children first served apprenticeships for their future occupations; then worked for wages as journeymen; and finally earned the rank of master—all coordinated by guild officers.

6. Universities began as guilds of teaching masters but came to include students and schools as well. Universities in different cities excelled in particular branches of learning—law at Bologna, medicine at Montpellier, and so on.

7. The era witnessed the emergence of several new religious movements. Some of these, such as the Franciscans, were able to win recognition by the church as monastic orders, whereas others—Albigensians or Cathars and Waldensians—were charged with heresy by a church now organized enough to define and attack heretics.

8. The rise of nationalism and the increasingly strict nature of Christian identity generated bitterness against the "others" of western European societies. Jews would be particularly singled out for both social and physical harsh persecution.

Focus Question

What tied together the cultural and political achievements of the late twelfth century?

State-building, religious fervor, and the growth of a vernacular high culture linked political and cultural achievements of the late twelfth century.

1. Western European leaders moved away from personal forms of authority dependent upon kinship

and vassalage. They expanded, centralized, and institutionalized their power, developing professional bureaucracies and systems of law. This process was most fully realized in England, where kings of the Angevin dynasty used the power of common law to unify their territory. The French monarchs, notably Philip Augustus, augmented their power through conquest of territory, principally that held in continental Europe by the English kings. In central and eastern Europe, leaders met with less success in consolidating their power. Emperor Frederick Barbarossa faced challenges from German princes, Italian cities, and the papacy. Further east, the Hungarian kingdom, Kiev, and the Byzantine Empire became weaker and more fragmented.

2. Aristocrats countered the growing power of monarchs in a variety of ways, some of which fueled cultural developments and the growth of national sentiments. In England, barons forced King John to acknowledge their rights in Magna Carta. In continental Europe, vernacular forms of high culture, such as the songs of the troubadours and the literature of the epic and romance, stimulated national feelings and expressed the distinctively aristocratic theme of courtly love.

3. Other examples of the cultural flowering of the period included new forms of theological learning, principally those based on logic, religious fervor and persecution; the rise of universities; and the emergence of Gothic architecture. Religious fervor had its foundations in the universities, where new forms of questioning, such as that of Peter Abelard in *Sic et Non*, stimulated a range of new religious expressions. Some, such as those of the Albigensians and Waldensians, would be defined by the church as heretical, while others such as the Franciscans and Dominicans achieved official sanction. Crusades against the Albigensians, non-Christians in northern Europe, and Muslims in Spain all strengthened existing political authorities, as well as enforcing the power of the church. For example, the French monarchy consolidated its power in southern France, German princes extended their influence into the Baltic, and the kingdom of Castile expanded as a result of the *Reconquista*.

Annotated Chapter Outline

I. New Schools and Churches

A. The New Learning and the Rise of the University, pp. 328–332

1. Since the Carolingian period, schools connected to monasteries and cathedrals had been the training ground of monks and priests.
2. By the end of the eleventh century, the best schools were in the larger cities such as Reims, Paris, Montpellier, and Bologna.
3. Because schools had traditionally trained clergymen, the male students (there were no female students) were considered clerics whether or not they had been ordained.
4. Using the common language of Latin, students could drift from place to place to schools throughout Europe, wherever a noted master was teaching.
5. Students sought training in the seven liberal arts, which consisted of the trivium (grammar, rhetoric, and logic) and the quadrivium (arithmetic, geometry, music theory, and astronomy).
6. Logic excited the most interest because medieval scholars were convinced that it could clarify every issue—even questions about the nature of God.
7. After studying the liberal arts, students went on to study medicine, theology, or law.
8. Three figures typify the scholars of the period: Abelard, Heloise, and Peter the Chanter.
9. Born into a family of lesser French nobility, Peter Abelard (1079–1142) studied in Paris under William of Champeaux and began to attract students of his own.
10. Around 1122 or 1123, he prepared *Sic et Non*, a textbook for his students that arranged opposing theological arguments on 156 subjects side by side, incorporating passages from the Bible, church fathers, and papal letters.
11. Laying out authoritative texts in this manner was not new, but Abelard's calling attention to contradicting statements was.
12. Abelard's fame as a teacher brought him a new student, Heloise (c. 1100–c. 1163/1164), the niece of a Parisian cleric named Fulbert and one of the few learned women of her time.
13. Abelard and Heloise soon became secret lovers and, when Heloise became pregnant, they married secretly to protect Abelard's career; because of the new emphasis placed on clerical celibacy, the marriage would have compromised Abelard's prospects.
14. Suspecting foul play, Fulbert paid a servant to castrate Abelard.

15. Soon after, the two entered separate monasteries but maintained a correspondence.
16. Heloise was a successful abbess, but felt great loss at being separated from Abelard.
17. Abelard also suffered, but his greatest loss came with the attack on his intellect: the Council of Soissons, in 1121, condemned Abelard's book on the Trinity and forced him to burn it.
18. Peter the Chanter, like Abelard, came from the petty nobility. He studied in Reims and became "Chanter" of Notre Dame in Paris in 1183.
19. Like all masters, Peter gave lectures. Lectures consisted of a recitation of a passage from an important text followed by explanation and commentary.
20. Peter also "disputed" the texts, drawing upon the logic of Aristotle to describe other explanations and refute them.
21. Peter commented on all books of the Bible, unlike most theology masters who concentrated on the psalms and New Testament.
22. Peter was particularly interested in exploring social issues and the sacrament of penance.
23. Inspired by Peter, his followers preached in and around Paris.
24. Guilds of masters and students (Latin, *universitas*) also developed at the beginning of the thirteenth century, where each guild was connected to the masters' schools so that eventually the term *university* applied to the guild *and* the school.
25. The universities regulated such issues as student housing, discipline, and scholastic proficiency; the masters' behavior and lectures; and the standards required for students to become masters.
26. The curriculum of each university differed in content and duration, attracting students who wished to study that particular university's specialty, such as law or liberal arts.
27. With few exceptions, both masters and students were considered clerics, a condition that barred women from joining and made university men subject to church courts rather than to the secular jurisdiction of towns.
28. The special privileges of universities made them virtually self-governing corporations, sometimes leading to friction with their respective towns.
29. Still, many towns relied on the influx of students and masters to patronize local businesses, and so the two usually learned to negotiate for their mutual benefit.

B. Architectural Style: From Romanesque to Gothic, pp. 332–336

1. Eleventh-century Benedictine monasteries like Cluny were built or sometimes rebuilt in the Romanesque style.
2. Most Romanesque churches had massive stone walls and brightly decorated interiors.
3. The various parts of the church, designed in the shapes of cubes, cones, and cylinders, were distinct units with inventive sculptural reliefs enlivening their pristine geometrical forms.
4. In Romanesque churches, with the stone walls and cavernous choirs, prayer took a musical form called plainchant or Gregorian chant.
5. Plainchants consisted of melodies sung in unison without accompaniment, ranging from simple to highly ornate.
6. By the twelfth century, a large repertoire existed; the Gregorian chants had been transmitted orally but were eventually recorded in written notation.
7. Elaborate reliquaries and altars gilded in gold and silver, and decorated with precious gems and pearls, were considered the appropriate accoutrements of worship.
8. Monks and priests, benefiting from the gift economy, offered prayers to God in the most splendid of settings.
9. Gothic architecture began around 1135 and reflected the self-confidence and the wealth of the cities.
10. Usually taking form as a cathedral, these Gothic churches became the religious, social, and commercial focal points of many cities.
11. The Gothic movement also extended into other art forms, including sculpture and painting.
12. Gothic style appealed to both human logic and reason and a sense of the divine.
13. Beginning with the remodeling of the church of Saint-Denis by Abbot Suger, this style, which melded royal and ecclesiastical interests and ideals, spread from France throughout Europe.
14. Gothic techniques included ribbed vaulting, which gave a sense of precision and order; the pointed arch, which produced a feeling of soaring height; and

flying buttresses, which took the weight of the vault off the walls, permitting large areas to be cut away and filled with stained-glass windows.

II. Governments as Institutions

A. England: Unity through Common Law, pp. 336–340

1. By the mid-twelfth century, England's government was the most institutionalized administration in Europe.
2. When William the Conqueror's son Henry I (r. 1100–1135) died without a male heir, a civil war ensued.
3. One side supported Henry's daughter Matilda.
4. The other side supported Stephen of Blois (r. 1135–1154) who was the son of Henry's sister Adela.
5. Not wanting to be ruled by a woman, many were delighted to see Stephen take the throne.
6. The war weakened King Stephen's authority, and the English barons and high churchman used it to their advantage to gain new privileges.
7. Stephen was eventually forced to name Matilda's son Henry as his successor.
8. Henry II (r. 1154–1189) immediately quelled the barons and also imposed monarchical power by expanding his system of courts.
9. Royal justices made regular trips called "eyres" to every locality in England.
10. Certain crimes—murder, arson, rape—were declared violations of the "king's peace," no matter in what jurisdiction they were committed.
11. The royal justices also heard civil cases, such as disputes over inheritance or dowries between free men and women (persons of the knightly class or above).
12. In this way, the Angevin kings made local affairs royal business and united the kingdom under a system of common law.
13. The English monarchy used records to further institutionalize royal power.
14. Henry faced stiff opposition from the church, which had a separate system of justice and refused to submit to the royal courts.
15. The conflict over royal jurisdiction between Henry and his archbishop Thomas Becket became the greatest battle between church and state in the twelfth century.
16. Becket was martyred when Henry's henchmen murdered him in his own cathedral, and public outcry compelled Henry to do public penance.
17. In the end, both church and royal courts expanded to deal with the growing litigiousness of society.
18. Henry exerted power in England through his royal courts while relying upon war and negotiation to maintain his power in France, where he was technically a vassal of the French king.
19. Henry faced rebellions begun by his own sons with help from the king of France throughout his life.
20. Under Henry and his sons Richard I (r. 1189–1199) and John (r. 1199–1216), the monarchy grew rich from court fees, royal estates, taxes from the cities, and customary feudal dues called "reliefs" and "aids."
21. Richard I is remembered as an "absentee" king because he left England for the Third Crusade the same year he was crowned and was captured and held for ransom while returning home; but this proved the efficiency of the royal administration, which continued to operate in his absence.
22. The rule of Richard's brother John was compromised by his need to maintain control over his holdings in France.
23. When the French king Philip II (r. 1180–1223) confiscated John's northern French territories, John had to increase taxes and dues to pay for an army to fight Philip.
24. Nonetheless, John's army was defeated in 1214 at the battle of Bouvines, after which the English barons rebelled against him.
25. At Runnymede in June 1215, John signed Magna Carta ("Great Charter") that defined the "customary" obligations and rights of the nobility.
26. Magna Carta forbade the king from breaking these customs without consulting his barons and ordered him to uphold the customs and rights held in common by all free men, essentially implying that the king was not above the law.

B. France: Consolidation and Conquest, pp. 340–341

1. Ironically, the weakness of the French monarchy led to its expansion.
2. In 1180, the French crown passed to fourteen-year-old Philip II.
3. When Philip ascended to the throne, the royal domain was limited to the

Île-de-France. The king of England held Anjou, Normandy, and Aquitaine.

4. In the 1190s, Philip wrested territory from Flanders; he then seized Normandy, Anjou, and other territory from King John in 1204.
5. Such acts earned him the nickname Philip Augustus.
6. Philip confirmed this triumph by winning the decisive battle of Bouvines (1214), becoming the richest and most powerful ruler in France.
7. Using officers who carried out their tasks in accordance with Norman customs, Philip managed to maintain a tight hold on Normandy and received homage and fealty from most of the Norman aristocracy.
8. To govern his new territories, Philip instituted new forms of administration by employing royal officials who kept important accounts and files in permanent repositories.
9. Previously, royal arrangements had been committed to memory and any written decrees had been kept by the recipient rather than the king.
10. Like the English monarchs, Philip relied on members of the lesser nobility—educated knights and clerics—for his administrative staff.
11. They served as officers of his court, oversaw the king's estates, and collected his taxes. These officials made the king's power felt locally as never before.

C. Germany: The Revived Monarchy of Frederick Barbarossa, pp. 341–346

1. The Investiture Conflict started a civil war between the imperial party, led by the Staufer, or Hohenstaufen, clan and the papal party led by the Welfs.
2. By 1152, all parties longed for peace and elected as king Frederick I (r. 1152–1190), called Barbarossa, whose mother was a Welf and whose father was a Staufer.
3. In order to maintain their loyalty, Frederick handed out duchies and privileges to the German princes, demanding in return that they acknowledge him formally and publicly as their lord.
4. By using the lord–vassal relationship, Frederick placated the princes and gave himself a free hand to rule, but the princes still prevented him from consolidating his power.
5. In 1157, a letter from Pope Hadrian IV (r. 1154–1159) reopened the Investiture Conflict by implying that Frederick was the pope's vassal.
6. Frederick invaded Italy and gained control of the northern cities (1158).
7. When he tried to consolidate his power in Italy as a "universal" emperor, he failed to recognize the importance of local pride and traditions.
8. His appointment of arrogant and abusive magistrates called *podestà* to administer the cities aroused local resentment.
9. By 1167, the northern cities had joined with Pope Alexander III (r. 1159–1181) to form the Lombard League, which defeated Frederick at the battle of Legnano (1176) and forced him to withdraw most of his forces from Italy.
10. Ironically, Frederick based his rule in Germany on the increasingly outmoded personal ties of lord and vassal at precisely the time when rulers elsewhere were relying more on salaried officials.
11. Frederick faced problems in Germany, especially with the powerful Henry the Lion (c. 1130–1195), who controlled Saxony and Bavaria.
12. Henry invested bishops, collected dues from vast estates, and exercised judicial power.
13. Threatened by Henry's growing power, Frederick called Henry to the king's court in 1179 for violating the peace.
14. When Henry did not appear, Frederick charged him with violating his duty as vassal, confiscated his holdings, and, in 1180, drove him out of Germany.
15. Because Frederick had relied on support from the other princes to enforce his decree against Henry, he felt compelled to divide Henry's lands among them.

D. Eastern Europe and Byzantium: Fragmenting Realms, p. 346

1. In contrast to western Europe, the characteristic pattern in the east was for states to form under the leadership of one great ruler and then fragment under his successors.
2. For example, in Hungary King Béla III (r. 1172–1196) built a state that appeared similar to western kingdoms, but his governmental institutions failed to endure in the decades that followed his rule, which

were marked by wars between his sons and by the division of monarchical holdings among aristocrats.
3. Russia experienced a similar cycle, as the fighting between the sons of Grand Prince Vsevolod III (r. 1176–1212) began to erode the authority of the nucleus state of Suzdal.
4. Although it was a consolidated, bureaucratic state, Byzantium also began to weaken in the mid-twelfth century.
5. Traders from the west, especially Venetians, began to dominate Byzantium's commerce, and civil servants were bypassed so that relatives of the emperor and the military elite could be appointed to administrative positions.
6. As Byzantine rule became more personal and western rule became more bureaucratic, the two gradually became more similar.

III. The Growth of a Vernacular High Culture

A. The Troubadours: Poets of Love and Play, pp. 347–348

1. Duke William IX of Aquitaine (r. 1071–1126), the grandfather of Eleanor, wrote lyric poems in Occitan, the vernacular language of southern France, that were perhaps inspired by love poetry in Arabic and Hebrew from al-Andalus.
2. It became a model for troubadours, male and female lyric poets who dazzled their audiences with original rhymes and varied meters.
3. Most of their poems resembled Latin religious poetry of the same time period, indicating that the vernacular and Latin religious cultures overlapped.
4. The troubadours' most common topic, love, echoed the twelfth-century church's emphasis on the emotional relationship between God and humans.
5. The key to troubadour verse is the idea of *cortesia* ("courtesy"): the refinement of individuals living at court and their struggle to achieve an ideal of virtue.
6. Troubadours sang about love for an unattainable lady, sexual conquests, equality between lovers, and love as the source of virtue.
7. Overall, courtly literature recognized and praised the power of women, making the genre popular among aristocratic women, many of whom were patrons of the troubadours.
8. The image of powerful women was not merely a literary device, however; southern France had many powerful female lords who owned property, led vassals into battle, and entered into political alliances.
9. From southern France, love poetry spread to Italy, northern France, England, and Germany.
10. Eventually, similar poetry appeared in these regions in other vernacular languages.

B. The Literature of Epic and Romance, pp. 348–349

1. Although not as common as love poetry, long narrative poems that glorified heroism on the battlefield, called *chansons de geste* ("epics"), were another popular form of vernacular literature.
2. These poems followed a long, oral tradition and, like the poetry of troubadours, implied a code of behavior for aristocrats.
3. By the end of the twelfth century, nobles and knights had begun to merge into one class, threatened from below by the growing wealth of merchants and from above by the growing power of kings.
4. Knights, losing their military importance to mercenary infantrymen, desired a code of conduct that would set them apart and provide solidarity and a knightly ethos.
5. Epic poems featured protagonists who longed for battle, examined themes and moral issues that made war both tragic and inevitable, and explored contradictory values and loyalties.
6. Other long poems, called romances, explored the relationships between men and women.
7. These poetic forms reached the height of their popularity in the late twelfth and early thirteenth centuries.
8. The legend of King Arthur inspired the writings of Chrétien de Troyes (c. 1150–1190).
9. Chrétien's Lancelot was the ideal chivalric knight—a great warrior—but he was also chivalrous, following the ideals of refinement, fair play, piety, and loyalty.
10. Whether actual knights lived up to this ideal is uncertain, but they most likely saw themselves as conforming to a code of knightly chivalry.

IV. Religious Fervor and Crusade

A. New Religious Orders in the Cities, pp. 349–351

1. During the twelfth century, a new religious fervor both embraced urban life and offered new forms of religious expression when many were criticizing the existing church as too wealthy, impersonal, and spiritually superficial.
2. St. Francis (c. 1182–1226) founded the most famous orthodox religious movement.
3. Born into the family of a wealthy cloth merchant in Assisi, Italy, Francis renounced his family's wealth and lived in extreme poverty.
4. Francis attracted numerous followers, leading the pope to recognize the Brothers (friars) of St. Francis as an official religious order.
5. The Franciscans lived in urban areas where they spent their time preaching, ministering to lepers, and performing manual labor.
6. In 1212, an eighteen-year-old noble-woman, Clare, formed the Order of the Sisters of St. Francis, which worked alongside the friars until the church had them cloistered under the Benedictine rule.
7. Women also formed new lay sisterhoods, such as the pious communities in northern Europe called the Beguines.
8. The Beguines lived without formal vows or rules, chose to be celibate, and earned their living by weaving cloth or tending the sick and elderly.
9. In addition to orthodox religious movements, ideas circulated that contradicted church doctrine and authority; consequently they were labeled heresies.
10. The most visible heretics were the dualists who saw the world as torn between good and evil forces and believed the devil had created the material world.
11. Like some orthodox movements of the past, they rejected sex and wealth, but they did so to an extreme, challenging the value of church authority.
12. The church condemned other groups as heretical because they allowed lay members to preach, threatening the established church hierarchy.
13. For instance, in southeastern France in the 1170s, a merchant named Waldo sold all his belongings, vowed a life of poverty, and preached the Gospel in the vernacular in the streets of Lyon.
14. Scandalized, the church denounced, excommunicated, and expelled Waldo and his followers, the Waldensians, from Lyon.

B. Disastrous Crusades to the Holy Land, pp. 351–353

1. Following the crushing defeat of the crusaders in the Second Crusade, the Third Crusade (1189–1192) aimed to take control of Jerusalem from Saladin (1138–1193), who ruled over all of Egypt and Syria by 1186.
2. Called by the pope and led by Emperor Frederick Barbarossa, Philip II of France, Leopold of Austria, and Richard I of England, the Third Crusade was hampered by political tensions between the rulers of Europe and Byzantium and accomplished little.
3. In 1202, the Fourth Crusade was called.
4. The crusading army could not afford to pay the Venetians who were supplying the ships to the Holy Land.
5. The Venetians persuaded the crusaders to pay for the fleet by attacking the Christian city of Zara, Venice's competitor in the Adriatic.
6. The Venetians then persuaded the crusaders to join them in attacking another commercial rival: Constantinople.
7. After a long siege, the crusaders brutally sacked the city—raping, killing, plundering, and ransacking it for treasure and relics.
8. Even though the pope decried the attack, he ordered the crusaders to remain there for a year to consolidate their gains.
9. Choosing Baldwin of Flanders as the new Byzantine emperor, the crusaders and the Venetians parceled out the empire among themselves.
10. Although popes continued to call for crusades to the Holy Land until the mid-fifteenth century, the Fourth Crusade marked the last major mobilization of men and leaders.
11. New values placed greater emphasis on the interior pilgrimage of the soul and on rulers who remained in their native countries to care for their people.

C. Victorious Crusades in Europe and on Its Frontiers, pp. 353–355

1. In addition to crusades to the Holy Lands, wars were waged against perceived infidels in Europe.
2. During the second half of the twelfth century, Christian Spain achieved a political configuration that would endure for centuries: Aragon in the east, Castile in the middle, and Portugal in the southwest.
3. The leaders of these kingdoms competed against each other for territory, but all sought to gain an advantage over the Muslims to the south.
4. The Spanish Muslims failed to unite against this threat.
5. Moreover, a new group of Berber Muslims from North Africa declared a holy war against the Muslims of al-Andalus.
6. During the 1140s, the kings of Portugal, Castile, and Aragon sent victorious armies against Muslim cities.
7. Then, in 1212, the kings of Castile and Aragon won a decisive victory over the Almohades at Las Navas de Tolosa.
8. By the twelfth century, the partly pagan, mostly Slavic-speaking inhabitants of the eastern Baltic region were added to the papacy's list of infidels marked for a crusade and either conversion or extermination.
9. The Danish king Valdemar I (r. 1157–1182) and Henry the Lion of Saxony led the first phase of the Northern Crusades, carrying out uncoordinated attacks on the Slavs but managing to bring the region under their control.
10. The Slavic princes typically surrendered, converted, and then had their lands restored to them after they had become vassals of the Christian rulers.
11. Although they suffered from the attacks, Slavs found it advantageous to convert to Christianity for religious and commercial purposes.
12. The Northern Crusades led to the permanent settlement of German speakers in the Baltic region, forming an enduring relationship between northern Europe and its neighbors to the south and west.
13. Baltic peoples, now surrounded by churches and monasteries, gradually adopted institutions of western Europe such as cities, guilds, universities, castles, and manors.
14. Only the Lithuanians successfully resisted western aggression and Christianity.
15. The first crusade to be launched within Europe itself started with papal missions, led by the Dominicans.
16. The Dominican order was founded by Saint Dominic (1170–1221), whose followers, like the Franciscans, rejected the wealth of the official church and instead went about on foot, preaching and begging.
17. Sometimes, the church resorted to force in its campaigns against heretics.
18. In 1208, the murder of a papal legate in southern France prompted the pope to demand that northern princes invade Languedoc and wrest control from the heretics.
19. This Albigensian Crusade (1209–1229) marked the first time a pope granted warriors fighting in Christian Europe the same spiritual benefits offered to crusaders in the Holy Land.
20. This crusade had both political and religious dimensions, pitting southern French princes against northern leaders who wanted to demonstrate their piety and win new possessions.
21. In 1229, after twenty years of fighting, the Capetian kings of France took over the crusade and brought Languedoc under the control of the French crown.

Lecture Strategies

1. Present the ways the church reacted to the changing face of western culture in the twelfth and early thirteenth centuries. Which policies did it implement? Why? How did the church's crusades—both inside and outside Europe—affect the church and European society? Why was the movement to weed out heresies so vociferous? Why were some dissident orders eventually integrated into the church? Some excellent introductory sources for this discussion are Colin Morris, *The Papal Monarchy: The Western Church from 1050 to 1250* (Oxford: Clarendon, 1989); and I. S. Robinson, *The Papacy, 1073–1198: Continuity and Innovation* (Cambridge, UK: Cambridge University Press, 1990).

2. Universities as cohesive institutions grew to prominence during this period, giving a geographical center to the flourishing scholastic movement and the developing intellectual culture generally. What role did the universities play in shaping the development of knowledge and learning? Which residual functions

did the universities serve? How did they interact within their communities and contribute to the economy? How might such interaction have affected the universities? See John Baldwin, *The Scholastic Culture of the Middle Ages, 1000–1300* (Lexington, MA: D. C. Heath, 1971), which analyzes the broader development of scholasticism; and Hilde de Ridder-Symoens, ed., *A History of the University in Europe*, vol. 1, *Universities in the Middle Ages* (Cambridge, UK: Cambridge University Press, 1992), an outstanding and comprehensive study of the topic.

3. Students may be interested in the extent to which there existed a "global economy" of sorts as far back as the twelfth century. Trace the role of international commerce and economic development on the political, cultural, and social development of Europe. How did this pattern emerge? By which mechanisms did it function? How did it affect the nature of work? Demographics? Social interaction? Class development? A classic study is Georges Duby, *The Early Growth of the European Economy: Warriors and Peasants from the Seventh to the Twelfth Century* (Ithaca, NY: Cornell University Press, 1978), which includes a discussion of the development of bourgeois freedom, local legal systems, the effects of monetary circulation, and international trade. See also Robert S. Lopez and Irvin W. Raymond, *Medieval Trade in the Mediterranean World* (New York: Columbia University Press, 1990), a good outline of the medieval global economy, its trade practices and mechanisms, and the development of commercial contracts and international markets.

4. The monastic movements of the high Middle Ages were an integral component of European spiritual and cultural life, providing an alternative to the norms of everyday work and religion. What was the nature of these alternatives as embodied in the different recognized orders of the time? Why were these movements able to integrate their practices into the Catholic orthodoxy? What was their appeal? What were their economic contributions? How did they encourage and propel cultural enrichment? For a general overview, see C. H. Lawrence, *Medieval Monasticism: Forms of Religious Life in Western Europe in the Middle Ages* (New York: Longman, 1988). Chapters 1 and 2 of Lester K. Little, *Religious Poverty and the Profit Economy in Medieval Europe* (Ithaca, NY: Cornell University Press, 1978) discuss the transformation from a gift economy to a profit economy and its effects on people's social relations and religious thought. The book also contains interesting discussions of reactions that the religious had to commercial urbanism; monks, hermits, major orders, and heretical sects; and monasteries and their economic contributions. Finally, Part 1 of John Moorman, *A History of the Franciscan Order from Its Origins to the Year 1517* (Oxford: Clarendon, 1968) considers Francis and the development of the Franciscan order during his lifetime.

Class Discussion Starters

1. Students would benefit greatly from an in-depth discussion of Magna Carta, a central document in the history of constitutional government that has particular relevance to the United States. Which major factors led to the drafting and signing of Magna Carta? Which interests represented the groups involved? How are these interests reflected in the document? Was it a comprehensive assurance of civil liberties? Why or why not? What were its strengths and weaknesses? J. C. Holt, *Magna Carta*, 2nd ed. (Cambridge, UK: Cambridge University Press, 1982) is one of the best-known studies of the history, context, significance, and range of this document. (The text of Magna Carta is reprinted at the back of this manual, in Appendix 4.)

2. This period had a substantial impact on women, their work, their positions in society, and their relationships. Discuss how all these things changed during the twelfth and thirteenth centuries. Which factors contributed to these changes? How did the commercial development of the economy affect women? Did the trends toward nationalism or concurrent campaigns against outsiders have any implications for women's status in society? Numerous sources are available for detailed discussions of these topics. See Christiane Klapisch-Zuber, ed., *A History of Women*, vol. 2, *Silences of the Middle Ages* (Cambridge, MA: Harvard University Press, 1992); and Emilie Amt, ed., *Women's Lives in Medieval Europe: A Sourcebook* (New York: Routledge, 1993). These books contain revealing readings on the development of women's status, the former through contemporary essays and the latter through primary sources. For the changing economic roles of women, see Barbara Hanawalt, ed., *Women and Work in Pre-Industrial Europe* (Bloomington: Indiana University Press, 1986), which contains descriptions of and discusses on women in diverse occupations.

3. The antiheretical campaigns within the church were among the most startling events of this period. Why was the church so threatened by these movements? Which alternatives did the heretical movements propose? What impact did the social context of the individual movements have on the church's decision to uproot them? What differentiated these movements from other religious dissidents who were accepted by the church? See Edward Peters, ed., *Heresy and Authority in Medieval Europe* (Philadelphia: University of Pennsylvania Press, 1980).

4. The high Middle Ages was a period of fantastic technological progress that contributed greatly to the flourishing of culture and economic production.

Students' appreciation of the revolutionary character of the period can be greatly enhanced by a discussion of the manner in which technological change came about, as well as its effects on society. How did technology alter the nature of work? How did it affect the relationship between human beings and their environment? See Frances Gies and Joseph Gies, *Cathedral, Forge, and Waterwheel: Technology and Invention in the Middle Ages* (New York: HarperCollins, 1994). Another excellent study is Jean Gimpel, *The Medieval Machine: The Industrial Revolution in the Middle Ages* (New York: Holt, Rinehart & Winston, 1976). Gimpel's book centers on the role of technological development in the production of energy, agriculture, and the movement into industrial production with some discussion of its effects on environmental and labor conditions.

Reviewing the Text

Review Questions

1. What was new about learning in schools and the architecture of church buildings in the twelfth and early thirteenth centuries?
[model answer] *Schools grew from institutions for preparing monks and priests, to sources of knowledge for all men interested in becoming scholars as well as institutions for training professionals in medicine and law, as well as the clergy. The seven liberal arts became the focus of education, with logic at the center, and were seen as the means to order and answer all issues. By the thirteenth century, teachers, known as masters, organized universities as centers of education. New churches in the Gothic style were built in cities; they had pointed arches that appealed to the desire to become closer to the divine. Architectural innovations of arches and buttresses created soaring spaces.*

2. What new sources and institutions of power became available to rulers in the second half of the twelfth century?
[model answer] *Government bureaucracies of hired educated men administered the business of European kingdoms. As with the royal courts in England that traveled throughout the realm, such systems extended the government presence and authority over all. In England, the government was strengthened by a system of common laws that codified the king's authority and fostered stability. The French king used alliances among regional lords to augment his power and consolidate a kingdom. In a similar manner, the German king Frederick I created a system of vassalage by bargaining with local princes for their support in exchange for certain rights and territory. This provided a source of power, but it also placed constraints on his authority.*

3. How did the idea of crusade change from the time of the original expedition to the Holy Land?
[model answer] *Intense religiosity in the twelfth century fueled crusades that went beyond the idea of saving the Holy Land. The focus of the crusades spread from the Holy Land to other regions within and surrounding Europe. Also, particularly in the Fourth Crusade, the prospect of profit and securing trade motivated the zeal of some crusaders.*

Making Connections

1. What were the chief differences that separated the ideals of the religious life in the period 1150–1215 from those of the period 1050–1150?
[model answer] *In the later period, many more people pursued the religious life, even though the cloistered life was repudiated and life in the world embraced. Heresy was also a new concern in the later period, and new doctrines were condemned as heretical.*

2. How was the gift economy associated with Romanesque architecture and the money economy with the Gothic style?
[model answer] *Heavy and serious, Romanesque churches were designed to house prayer that was offered as a gift to God. Gothic churches were designed to lead worshippers to knowledge of God, perhaps more an acquisition rather than a gift. The gift economy structured exchanges for mutual benefit while the money economy provided a product or service for a fee.*

Discussing the Documents

Questions from Online Study Guide with Model Answers

Frederick I's Reply to the Romans (p. 344)

1. Why did the Romans want to give Frederick the crown, and on what did they base their authority to do so?
[model answer] *The city governors cited Rome's ancient status as the center of the empire as the source of their authority to grant the crown and also undoubtedly recognized the political advantage that would be theirs if the city rather than the crown was seen as the ultimate source of the emperor's power and authority.*

2. On what grounds does Frederick deny the right of the Romans to give him the crown?
[model answer] *Frederick maintains that Rome's role as the center of the empire is in the past and its attributes long since passed on to other centers of authority. It is vested in the rule of the Franks, he says.*

The Children's Crusade (1212) (p. 355)

1. What motivated the children who joined the crusade?
[model answer] *The young people responded to Nicolas's claim that he was divinely protected and inspired; both the claim and their response reflected the intense religiosity and importance of religion in the era.*

2. Why did the chronicler conclude that the Children's Crusade had "issued from the deception of the devil"?
[model answer] *The journey was obviously inspired by the devil as evidenced in the dire consequences: the young people failed their mission, were enslaved, and worse.*

3. Might one argue that all of the crusades "issued from the deception of the devil"?
[model answer] *In the same light as the failure of the children's crusade, the failures of many of the crusades could be blamed retrospectively as the work of the devil. While God may have inspired some, which with his blessing met with some success, the crusades that failed would not have been his work, but rather tricks of the devil.*

Contrasting Views: Magna Carta (pp. 342–343)

1. From the clauses of Magna Carta that say what will henceforth *not* be done, speculate about what the king *had been* doing.
[model answer] *The Magna Carta indicated that many civil liberties were regularly ignored by the king. He had restricted the power and activities of the church and in many ways—taking property and belongings (i.e., the government's/crown's) for his own use or enrichment—acted arbitrarily in honoring individuals' rights. The provision that forbids exacting vassalage payments indicates that he also imposed monetary obligations without the consent or counsel of those who would be obligated to pay.*

2. How did the barons of 1242 use Magna Carta as a symbol of liberty?
[model answer] *The barons point out that since the king had not lived up to the terms to which he agreed in the Magna Carta, they were justified in refusing him further aid. The provisions to which he had agreed in the document gave them the liberty to refuse him further support.*

Other Questions for Discussing These Documents in Class

Frederick I's Reply to the Romans (p. 344)

1. According to Bishop Otto of Freising's account, how did Frederick justify his claim to be the rightful heir of the Roman Empire to the citizens of the city of Rome?

2. How persuasive do you find Frederick to be?

3. How were the Romans likely to receive Frederick's statement? Students might consider specific quotations such as "insipid and swollen pride."

Contrasting Views: Magna Carta (p. 355)

1. What was the goal of the barons in forcing King John to sign Magna Carta?

2. Why has the document become a symbol of liberty?

3. How do the three provisions that were dropped from later versions of the charter (i.e., those marked with asterisks) differ from those that were retained in the definitive 1225 version of the document?

Comparative Questions

1. Based on these documents, how would you compare Frederick and John as monarchs?

2. Both Frederick's reply to the Romans and the assessment of the Children's Crusade were recorded by chroniclers. What similarities and differences do you see in the style of the documents? Which chronicler seems to be further removed from the event he describes?

For Users of *Sources of The Making of the West*

The following documents are available in Chapter 11 of the companion sourcebook by Katharine J. Lualdi, University of Southern Maine.

1. Scholarly Pursuits and Youthful Frolics: *Medieval University Life* (Twelfth–Early Thirteenth Centuries)
2. Gothic Architecture: Abbot Suger, *The Abbey Church of St.-Denis* (1144)
3. Courtly Love: Chrétien de Troyes, *Erec and Enide* (c. 1170)
4. Franciscan Piety: St. Francis and St. Clare of Assisi, *Selected Writings* (Thirteenth Century)
5. The Sack of Constantinople: *Account of Niketas Choniates* (1204)

Discussion Ideas for Sources of The Making of the West, *Chapter 11*

1. Ask students to consider the nature of medieval university life and the relationship between universities, the church, and kings. What sorts of privileges did King Frederick I and King Philip II grant?

What motivations might they have had for doing so? What role did religion play in their explanations for granting these privileges? Is it significant that they were cast as privileges and not as rights? What do the poems suggest about the activities and concerns of university students? Do these documents provide much insight into the academic side of university life? How does medieval university life compare with university life in our time?

2. Ask students to consider the nature of Gothic architecture. According to Abbot Suger, what were the characteristics of Gothic architecture? How does his account compare with the information about Gothic cathedrals in the textbook feature Seeing History: "Romanesque versus Gothic: The View Down the Nave"? How does Suger's account enhance your understanding of the motivation behind the Gothic style? What role does Suger attribute to divine inspiration in the reconstruction of the abbey of St. Denis?

Working with Visual Sources

For this exercise, please refer to The Murder of Thomas Becket on p. 339 of the textbook or view the image on the book companion site's Online Study Guide under the "Visual Activity" for Chapter 11.

Students viewing the image at the Online Study Guide are asked two questions about the image. The questions and model answers (not made available to students) are below. Project this image, available on the Instructor's Resources CD-ROM, in class or ask students to look at the image in their textbooks and answer the questions.

1. How does this image contribute to Becket's image as a martyr?
[model answer] *Becket is shown being murdered from behind as he is kneeling in front of an altar. He is unarmed and his posture suggests that he is submitting to his fate. This image emphasizes that he was a clergyman (by his tonsured haircut and his bishop's staff) and that he died while performing his duties inside a church.*

2. What does this image show about the different types of power that the church and the state had in medieval England?
[model answer] *The state had military power and could use force against dissenters. However, this could turn against the state when it misused force. The church had a type of moral authority that could trump the power of the state. The state could not harm a clergyman inside a church without there being any consequences.*

For this exercise, please refer to Seeing History: "Romanesque versus Gothic Architecture: The View Down the Nave," Saint-Savin-sur-Gartempe (begun 1095) and Bourges (begun 1195) on p. 335 of the textbook or view the images on the book companion site's Online Study Guide under the "Visual Activity: Seeing History" for Chapter 11.

Students viewing the images at the Online Study Guide are asked two questions about the images. The questions and model answers (not made available to students) are below. Project these images, available on the Instructor's Resources CD-ROM, in class or ask students to look at the images in their textbooks and answer the questions.

1. Describe the main architectural features of Saint-Savin-sur-Gartempe. How do they compare with those of Bourges?
[model answer] *Saint-Savin-sur-Gartempe is characterized by a round, barrel-vaulted ceiling, heavy pillars, and a dark interior decorated with colorful paintings on the ceiling. By contrast, characteristics of Bourges include pointed arches, ribbed vaulting, and stained-glass windows admitting light.*

2. Based on these two photographs, what are the main differences between Romanesque and Gothic architecture?
[model answer] *Romanesque interiors were dark and solid with rounded ceilings, reflecting solidity and solemnity. Flying buttresses carried the weight of Gothic cathedrals to the exterior, permitting the soaring height, ribbed vaulting, pointed arches, and many stained-glass windows characteristic of the style. As a result, Gothic cathedrals were lofty and serene.*

Mapping Exercises

Map Activity from OSG—Model Answer for Map Activity #2

For this activity please refer to the map on p. 324. Students are asked these questions:

Which territories were held by Henry II of England, and in what capacity?
[model answer] *Henry II held England, Scotland, Wales, parts of Ireland, and parts of France. Territories in Scotland, Wales, and Ireland were Henry's by conquest but were held as fiefs by Henry's vassals. Henry held France as a fief of the French king, making him the French king's vassal.*

How does this map help explain why it was worthwhile for Frederick to make claims on Italy?
[model answer] *Located on the Mediterranean Sea, with access to trade from North Africa, Greece, Byzantium, and beyond, Italy was a commercial hub. Italian cities maintained flourishing businesses. Such wealth would have been enticing to any ruler, especially one based in Swabia, as Frederick was.*

How does this map help explain why neither Henry II nor Frederick was able to retain full control over all of the territories that made up their realms?
[model answer] *The scope of these territories, combined with conflicting and overlapping claims of ownership and control, made it difficult for these rulers to maintain their territory. Logistically, Henry had to hold on to territory on two sides of the English Channel, while Frederick's empire was enormous. Also, both Henry and Frederick demanded the loyalty of peoples who shared different cultures and traditions; their expectations of unity and fidelity may have been unrealistic.*

Map 11.1: Europe in the Age of Henry II and Frederick Barbarossa, 1150–1190, p. 338

Have students identify the various domains and what their relationships were to the rulers of western Europe at the time. How did France fit into these relationships? How might a French ruler in this situation endeavor to secure his own autonomy?

Map 11.2: Crusades and Anti-Heretic Campaigns, 1150–1204, p. 352

This map details the emergence of a profoundly changed Europe and is based on cultural and political patterns that would have a tremendous influence on the development of modern Europe. How might the emerging social conditions within the western European nations have contributed to the zeal for aggressive expansion at this time?

Map 11.3: The Reconquista, 1150–1212, p. 354

Have students identify the principal political territories in the Iberian Peninsula. How did the geographical location of Castile contribute to its expansion, relative to the other territories, during the Reconquista?

Mapping the West: Europe and Byzantium, c. 1215, p. 356

How does the Byzantine Empire compare in size with the western European territories and the Islamic areas? What does this suggest about its relative power at the time? How do the crusader states compare in size with the Islamic territories? What does this reveal about the relative influence of the two in the Holy Land?

In-Class Assignments and Presentation Topics

1. The development of chivalry and courtly love is among the most celebrated features of medieval lore. The precise nature of these trends and ideas embodies a rich and complex mixture of romantic idealism, conceptions of nobility and proper behavior, ideals of love and honor, and an emerging consciousness of the roles of men and women. Have students write a short essay on courtly love and chivalry from any of these perspectives, illustrating the factors that helped bring these to life and made them so popular. Why were these ethical codes, transmitted through poetry, stories, and norms of behavior, so important at the time? A good starting place is Andreas Capellanus, *The Art of Courtly Love*, John Jay Parry, trans. (New York: Columbia University Press, 1960), a veritable handbook of love among the noble classes, with a vivid portrayal of life in a medieval French court. Georges Duby's *The Chivalrous Society*, C. Postan, trans. (Berkeley: University of California Press, 1977) is an excellent overview of chivalric development in its social context. See also Roger Boase, *The Origin and Meaning of Courtly Love: A Critical Study of European Scholarship* (Manchester, UK: Manchester University Press, 1977). A good collection of troubadour songs is James L. Wilhelm, ed., *Lyrics of the Middle Ages: An Anthology* (New York: Garland, 1990).

2. Have students investigate the development of the international Gothic style and its spread throughout medieval Europe. Few movements in history have so skillfully combined engineering prowess, artistic expression, and intellectual content. There are extensive visual and textual resources available on the Internet. Also of interest is David Macaulay's *Cathedral* (New York: Houghton Mifflin, 1985), available on video, which demonstrates the construction of the Gothic cathedral Notre Dame de Beaulieu.

3. Have students write an essay on the Third or Fourth Crusade. What were the stated objectives of these crusades? To what extent were these objectives achieved? Why? How did the internal dynamics of the crusading armies affect not only the outcome of the crusades, but also the character of western Europe? How did the crusades change relations with Byzantium and the Islamic countries? What role did the crusader states play in the Third and Fourth Crusades? Good introductory materials include Malcolm Cameron Lyons, *Saladin: The Politics of the Holy War* (Cambridge, UK: Cambridge University Press, 1997); and Donald E. Queller and Thomas F. Madden, *The Fourth Crusade: The Capture of Constantinople* (Philadelphia: University of Pennsylvania Press, 1999).

Essay Questions

1. Assign a research paper on the institutionalization of national governments in this period. What was the general effect of this trend across Europe? How

precisely was this movement carried out in England? Germany? France? What accounted for the different levels and paces of bureaucratization? For the general trends and a precise overview across Europe, see Joseph Reese Stayer, *On the Medieval Origins of the Modern State* (Princeton: Princeton University Press, 1970), a concise overview. For more detailed studies of individual governments, see H. G. Richardson and G. O. Sayles, *The Governance of Medieval England from the Conquest to Magna Carta* (Edinburgh: Edinburgh University Press, 1989); Benjamin Arnold, *Princes and Territories in Medieval Germany* (New York: Cambridge University Press, 1991); and John W. Baldwin, *The Government of Philip Augustus: Foundations of French Royal Power in the High Middle Ages* (Berkeley: University of California Press, 1986).

2. Students today may not be aware of how profoundly revolutionary the introduction of logic as the central tenet of human beliefs was when it resurfaced in Europe in the twelfth century. Ask them to write a research paper on the topic discussing how logic emerged and how it transformed western philosophical systems. See Michael T. Clanchy, *Abelard: A Medieval Life* (Oxford: Blackwell, 1997), a wide-ranging source that discusses Abelard's role as scholar, teacher, logician, theologian, and heretic, along with an extensive discussion of the social context. Also see Richard William Southern, *Scholastic Humanism and the Unification of Western Europe*, vol. 1, *Foundations* (Oxford: Blackwell, 1994), an essential text on the broader, revolutionary aspects of the scholastic movement.

Additional Resources: Literature

Goldin, Frederick, ed., *Lyrics of the Troubadours and Trouvères: Original Texts, with Translations*. 1973.

Meirow, C. C., trans., *Otto of Freising: The Deeds of Frederick Barbarossa*. 1990.

Parry, John Jay, trans., *Andreas Capellanus: The Art of Courtly Love*. 1960.

Radice, Betty, trans., *The Letters of Abelard and Heloise*. 1998.

Raffel, Burton, trans., *Chrétien de Troyes, Yvain: The Knight of the Lion*. 1987.

Wilhelm, James L., trans., *Lyrics of the Middle Ages: An Anthology*. 1990.

Additional Resources: Film and Video

Becket (1964; Peter Glenville, dir.; with Peter O'Toole and Richard Burton). This excellent film charts the stormy relationship between King Henry II and his archbishop of Canterbury, highlighting the growing tensions between church and state during the Middle Ages.

The Lion in Winter (1968; Anthony Harvey, dir.; with Peter O'Toole and Katharine Hepburn). This excellent film nicely captures the tumultuous relationship between Henry II and his wife, Eleanor of Aquitaine, as they and their surviving three sons fight over the succession.

Cadfael (1990s; VHS/DVD). Ellis Peters's mystery novels about Brother Cadfael, a twelfth-century monk in Shrewsbury, England, are dramatized in thirteen fifty-minute, self-contained episodes. The episodes, especially the later ones, are historically accurate in their settings, and details about everyday life in the Middle Ages have been interwoven seamlessly into the plots.

OTHER BEDFORD/ST. MARTIN'S RESOURCES FOR CHAPTER 11

The following resources are available to accompany Chapter 11. Please refer to the Preface of this manual for detailed descriptions of all the ancillaries.

For Instructors

Transparencies

The following maps and images from Chapter 11 are available as full-color acetates.

- Map 11.1: Europe in the Age of Henry II and Frederick Barbarossa, 1150–1190
- Map 11.2: Crusades and Anti-Heretic Campaigns, 1150–1204
- Map 11.3: The Reconquista, 1150–1212
- Mapping the West: Europe and Byzantium, c. 1215
- The Murder of Thomas Becket, p. 339
- Frederick Barbarossa, p. 341

Instructor's Resources CD-ROM

The following maps and image from Chapter 11 as well as a chapter outline, are available on disc in both PowerPoint and jpeg formats.

- Map 11.1: Europe in the Age of Henry II and Frederick Barbarossa, 1150–1190
- Map 11.2: Crusades and Anti-Heretic Campaigns, 1150–1204
- Map 11.3: The Reconquista, 1150–1212
- Mapping the West: Europe and Byzantium, c. 1215
- The Murder of Thomas Becket, p. 339

For Students

Study Guides

The Online Study Guide at **bedfordstmartins.com/hunt** helps students synthesize the material they have learned as well as practice the skills historians use to make sense of the past. The following Map, Visual, and Document activities are available for Chapter 11.

Map Activity

- Map 11.1: Europe in the Age of Henry II and Frederick Barbarossa, 1150–1190

Visual Activity

- The Murder of Thomas Becket, p. 339
- Saint-Savin-sur-Gartempe (begun 1095), p. 335
- Bourges (begun 1195), p. 335

Reading Historical Documents

- Frederick I's Reply to the Romans, p. 344
- The Children's Crusade (1212), p. 355
- Contrasting Views: Magna Carta, pp. 342–343

CHAPTER

12

The Medieval Search for Order

1215–1340

Chapter Resources

Main Chapter Topics

1. Under Pope Innocent III (r. 1198–1216), the Roman church continued its mission of reforming society by refocusing on both clergy and laity. The Fourth Lateran Council (1215) undertook the harmonious unification of all Christendom through the systematization of Christian ritual, law, and practice. The council also called for the extirpation of heretics. They and other marginal groups endured systematic exclusion and persecution.

2. The church integrated scholasticism into the defense of doctrines and dogmas, particularly through the work of Thomas Aquinas (c. 1225–1274). In turn, scholasticism influenced, directly or indirectly, new vernacular expressions of faith and philosophy, manifest in such works as the *Divine Comedy* of Dante Alighieri (1265–1321).

3. The arts flourished. Literature was produced in vernacular languages, rather than just Latin, which was increasingly reserved for scholarship and the church. Gothic architecture was refined, reflecting the integration of reason and faith to which scholastic philosophy aspired, while musical notation was improved to record duration of notes to better indicate rhythm.

4. Despite the church's attempts to promote unity, Christendom continued to splinter into regional factions as secular polities developed into nation-states, such as those of England and France. The emergence of parliaments and the continued institutionalization of royal authority reorganized western Europe and renewed conflict between church and state.

5. The disempowerment of the church relative to the nation-state was highlighted by the conflict between France's King Philip IV the Fair (r. 1285–1314) and Pope Boniface VIII (r. 1294–1303). Boniface's concessions to Philip and Edward I of England and the following Avignon Papacy in France marked the end of papal dominance in the west.

6. While the centralized nation-states ascended, Italy and Germany remained divided by internal factions and small but independent states. Spain, meanwhile, was divided along religious lines with Muslims and Christians vying for power. The fragmentation of eastern European countries left them vulnerable to attack by invading Mongols.

7. Invasions by the Mongols overran the eastern periphery of Christendom but also bridged the gap between the west and China for the first time in history, opening a new era of intercultural exchange that included vast new trade routes, and forming an integrated, Eurasian economy.

Focus Question

In what areas of life did thirteenth-century Europeans try to impose order, and how successful were these attempts?

1. Inspired by their Christian faith, thirteenth-century Europeans at all levels of society sought order and unity in a world they believed God had created. In religious, intellectual, and political areas of life, people sought to create a Medieval Synthesis balancing order and harmony. The attempt was most successful in intellectual and artistic life, as exemplified by scholasticism (particularly the work of Thomas Aquinas), Gothic Art, and new achievements in literature and music.

2. Efforts to achieve balance in political and religious affairs proved to be less successful by the end of the thirteenth century. Although the church, specifically the papacy, sought to regulate all aspects of life through such means as the Fourth Lateran Council, by

the end of the century monarchs such as Philip the Fair were asserting their autonomy from the pope and their authority over the church within their own kingdoms. Increasingly, religious and secular power competed with one another more often than they cooperated, and institutions claiming universal authority, namely the papacy and the empire, clashed. Other attempts to impose religious order, such as through the Inquisition and the persecution of Jews, contradicted the promise of harmony and rationalism embodied by scholasticism.

3. In terms of politics, the birth of representative institutions such as the Cortes, Estates-General, and Parliament seemed to promise a balance between monarchs, lords and bishops, and townspeople. In practice, however, kings wielded decisive power and did not always apply it effectively as exemplified by their inept response to the Great Famine in northern Europe. In central and eastern Europe, attempts to forge strong central authorities faltered as the Holy Roman Empire became increasingly fragmented and the Mongols attacked Russia, Poland, and Hungary.

Annotated Chapter Outline

I. The Church's Mission

A. Innocent III and the Fourth Lateran Council, pp. 360–362

1. Pope Innocent III (r. 1198–1216) was the first pope to be trained at the city schools, studying theology at Paris and law at Bologna.
2. In 1215, he convened the Fourth Lateran Council with legislation aimed at increasing the authority of the church over the clergy and the laity.
3. The canons concerning the sacraments, particularly the Eucharist and marriage, changed the lives of laypeople the most.
4. The Council claimed broader church jurisdiction over marriages and emphasized that only priests could transform the bread and wine of the Eucharist into the actual body and blood of Christ.
5. The Council also required Jews to wear some outward sign of their religion, such as a badge or special clothing.
6. Lastly, the Fourth Lateran Council directed secular authorities to rid their lands of heretics; rulers were threatened with excommunication and loss of land and vassals if they failed to do so.

B. The Inquisition, p. 362

1. The Fourth Lateran Council's longest decree blasted heretics, and rulers took heed.
2. An *inquisition* was a method long used to summon people and discover facts or uncover crimes.
3. Church-appointed inquisitors now rounded up people suspected of heresy for interrogation.
4. First, inquisitors called the people of a district to a "preaching," and promised clemency to those who confessed their heresy promptly.
5. Then, at a general inquest, each man and woman was questioned about what he or she knew about heresy.
6. Those who quickly recanted, or were unaware that their beliefs were heresies, were given lenient penalties, but those who refused to repent were viewed as threats to the salvation of others and punished severely.
7. During the thirteenth century, long-term imprisonment became a tool for repressing heresy, even if the heretic confessed, and for further interrogation concerning other supposed heretics and heretic plots.

C. Lay Piety, pp. 362–365

1. Dominican and Franciscan friars took on the mission to regulate and Christianize lay behavior.
2. Large numbers of friars and others trained in the universities took to the road and preached to townsfolk.
3. People flocked to hear preachers in order to know how the Christian message and church doctrine applied to their daily lives.
4. Some laypeople tied their lives to the friars by becoming tertiaries.
5. They adopted some of the practices of the friars but continued to live secular lives.
6. Many thirteenth-century women sought outlets for their intense piety.
7. Some continued living as wives and mothers while punctuating their days and weeks with religious devotion; others sought lives of quiet activity through the mysticism of the Beguines or practiced charity and service through the mendicant orders.

D. Jews and Lepers as Outcasts, pp. 365–367

1. Jews had been perceived as aliens and lived under legal restrictions ever since the Roman Empire became Christian.
2. Forced off their lands in the eleventh century, many Jews had moved to the cities.
3. As guilds tightened their control over the crafts, they forbade Jews from joining.
4. Thus, many Jews were compelled to live as moneylenders.
5. Many European lords claimed Jews as their serfs and the Jews' property as their own, and kings such as Henry II and Philip Augustus imposed arbitrary taxes and confiscated Jewish property to benefit the royal treasuries.
6. At times, those who borrowed money from Jewish moneylenders eradicated their debts by attacking or stirring up resentment toward the Jews.
7. Attacks against Jews also grew out of a new teaching about the Mass.
8. According to this doctrine, once the priest blessed the wine and bread at Mass, Christ himself, wounded and bleeding, lay upon the altar.
9. Christians' anxieties about this transformation seem to be behind the circulation of morbid stories about Jews reenacting the Crucifixion of Jesus by ritually sacrificing Christian children.
10. This preposterous charge, called "blood libel" by historians, led to massacres of Jews in England, France, Spain, and Germany.
11. Lepers also played a role in medieval society.
12. They were not allowed to live in society because of their contagious and disfiguring disease, so they lived in isolated houses set up for charitable reasons and segregation purposes.
13. Some lepers were formally expelled from the community in a ceremony that was meant to signify burial.

II. The Medieval Synthesis

A. Scholasticism: Harmonizing Faith and Reason, pp. 367–369

1. Scholasticism was the logical method of inquiry and exposition used to sum up and reconcile all knowledge.
2. Scholastics were confident that logical reasoning could unite knowledge obtained through the senses with knowledge based in faith.
3. Scholastics worked to attune Aristotle's pagan philosophy to Christian faith.
4. St. Thomas Aquinas (c. 1225–1274) was the most famous scholastic.
5. In 1273, he published the *Summa Theologiae*, which explored in great depth all important topics, both human and divine.
6. Thomas addressed both sides of each question and concluded his discussion of the issue with a decisive position and a refutation of opposing views.
7. The effort to unite the secular and the sacred continued for another generation after Thomas, but fissures appeared in the beginning of the fourteenth century, as in the *summa* of John Duns Scotus (c. 1266–1308).
8. Duns Scotus found the world and God to be less compatible: he believed illumination came not as a matter of course, but only when God chose to intervene.
9. Even among scholastics, unity was elusive, and later thinkers argued that reason alone could not find truth.

B. New Syntheses in Writing and Music, pp. 369–370

1. Thirteenth-century writers and musicians also explored the relationship between the secular and sacred worlds.
2. Dante Alighieri (1265–1321) harmonized the scholastic universe with the mysteries of faith and the poetry of love in the *Commedia* (*Divine Comedy*).
3. The poem describes Dante's journey through hell and purgatory to paradise—an allegory about the soul's search for direction and understanding.
4. Dante followed a guide representing reason through hell and purgatory, but followed new guides representing earthly love and divine love through paradise.
5. Dante wrote the *Commedia* in the language used by everyday Florentines, which so elevated the dialect that it provided the basis of modern Italian.
6. Musicians, too, developed new forms that bridged the secular and the sacred.
7. The most distinctive musical form of the thirteenth century, the motet, consisted of two or more melodies performed at once (a type of music called polyphony).

8. A typical motet had two or three melodies, the lowest being from a liturgical chant melody and the others being sung in Latin or French or both.
9. Latin texts were typically sacred, while French texts were typically secular.
10. The basis of modern musical notation came from a marking system established by Franco of Cologne.

C. Gothic Art, pp. 370–372

1. Gothic architecture began around 1135 with the remodeling of the church of Saint-Denis by Abbot Suger, and spread from France throughout Europe.
2. The pointed arches and flying buttresses supported large windows, making stained glass an important new art form.
3. "Stained" glass is not exactly an accurate description; glass workers added chemicals to the sand before heating, blowing, and flattening the glass to create the colors.
4. The enormous size of these windows allowed complicated themes to be expressed in a graphic way through the colored glass.
5. The Gothic movement also extended into sculpture and painting.
6. Sculpted in the round, Gothic figures moved and interacted with one another.
7. In painting, Giotto (1266–1337) experimented with the illusion of depth, and his figures express a range of emotion.
8. By blending religious meanings with human forms, Giotto found another way to bring together the natural and divine realms.
9. Gothic style appeared in paintings as a decorative motif and manuscript illuminations featured stained-glass windows as background themes.

III. The Politics of Control

A. The Weakening of the Empire, pp. 373–375

1. During the thirteenth century, the clash between popes and emperors had roots in Frederick Barbarossa's failure to control northern Italy, which was crucial to emperors for symbolic and economic reasons.
2. Barbarossa's son Henry VI (r. 1190–1197) and his grandson Frederick II (r. 1212–1250), who had inherited Sicily from his mother, labored without success to grasp Italy, and a series of popes excommunicated Frederick II several times.
3. With the *Constitutions of Melfi* in 1231, Frederick set up a government of salaried officials and royal courts in Sicily that gave him greater control and profits there.
4. In 1232, Frederick II freed himself from the obstruction of the princes in Germany with his "Statute in Favor of the Princes," which allowed the princes to turn their regions into virtually independent states.
5. These concessions to the German princes left German regions divided until the nineteenth century.
6. Ironically, it was at the German monarchy's low point that the term "Holy Roman Empire" was coined.
7. In 1273, the princes bestowed the meaningless honorific "Holy Roman Emperor" on Rudolph (r. 1273–1291) of the Habsburg family.
8. The papacy denied the island of Sicily to Frederick's heirs by calling other rulers to take over.
9. This tactic led to competing claims between Aragon and the house of Anjou, causing a war that impoverished the area.
10. Moreover, the popes drew criticism for using religion as a political tool.

B. Louis IX and a New Ideal of Kingship, pp. 375–376

1. The more successful rulers of Europe were those content with smaller, more manageable kingdoms.
2. In France, the new ideal of the "stay-at-home" monarch started with Louis IX (r. 1226–1270).
3. Louis was revered as administrator, judge, and "just father" of his people.
4. Through his administrators, he vigorously imposed his laws and justice over much of France.
5. During his reign, the parlement of Paris, the royal court of justice, became permanently housed in Paris and staffed by professional judges.
6. Louis was content with his large inherited kingdom, preferring peace to expansion.
7. While respectful of the church, Louis maintained the dignity of the king and his rights.
8. In his view, royal and ecclesiastical power were to work side by side, neither one subservient to the other.

9. Although Louis did not advocate violence against Jews, his hatred of them was well known.
10. He sometimes subjected Jews to arrest and canceled debts owed to them.
11. In 1297, Louis was canonized, winning great prestige for the French monarchy.

C. The Birth of Representative Institutions, pp. 376–377

1. In the thirteenth century, to enlist more broadly based support, monarchs across Europe summoned parliaments.
2. These representative bodies grew out of ad hoc advisory sessions held by kings with their nobles and the clergy.
3. Gradually, these sessions became formal meetings of the kings' chief councils including representatives of all three orders—clergy, nobles, and commoners.
4. As townspeople came to participate regularly, kings began to depend on them; in this way, commoners were integrated into the work of the government.
5. In Spain, the *cortes* of Castile-León were among the earliest assemblies and the first to include townsmen.
6. At Oxford in 1258, the barons, unhappy over Henry III's (r. 1216–1272) wars and debts, forced the king to dismiss his foreign advisers and rule with the advice of a Council of Fifteen chosen jointly by the barons and the king.
7. This new arrangement foundered, however, leading to civil war in 1264.
8. At the battle of Lewes, Simon de Montfort (c. 1208–1265) captured the king and became England's de facto ruler.
9. Simon called a parliament in 1265, summoning townspeople as well as clergy and noblemen.
10. Even though Henry's son Edward I (r. 1272–1308) quickly reclaimed the crown, the idea of representative government that included commoners had arrived.

D. The Weakening of the Papacy, pp. 377–379

1. In France, representative government originated in the conflict between Pope Boniface VIII (r. 1294–1303) and King Philip IV (r. 1285–1314).
2. Boniface claimed that only the pope could authorize the taxation of clerics, and he called on the clergy to disobey any royal orders demanding taxes.
3. In response, Philip forbade the export of precious metals, jewels, and money from France.
4. The loss of revenue forced Boniface to concede that kings could be authorized to tax the clergy in emergencies.
5. In 1301, Philip tested Boniface by arresting the bishop of Pamiers for slandering the king, and Boniface reacted angrily.
6. In 1302, Philip convened representatives of the clergy, nobles, and townspeople in Paris to justify and propagandize his position. (This new assembly was the ancestor of the Estates-General, the French equivalent of a parliament.)
7. Boniface's reply, the bull *Unam Sanctam*, insisted that for salvation, every human creature is subject to the pope.
8. In 1303, Philip ordered his agents to invade Boniface's palace in Anagni, capture the pope, bring him to France, and try him—but the people of Anagni thwarted the attempt.
9. Boniface died shortly thereafter, however, and the next two popes hastily pardoned Philip.
10. The plight of Boniface revealed that claims to universal authority were losing weight in the face of tightly controlled national states.
11. In 1309, the papacy fled civil disorder in Rome and settled at Avignon, a city very close to and greatly influenced by France, and remained there until 1378.
12. The Avignon popes, many of them French, established a sober and efficient organization that gave the papacy more say than ever before in the appointment of churchmen, even as they slowly let go of the idea of leading all of Christendom.

E. The Rise of the *Signori*, pp. 379–380

1. During the thirteenth century, new groups called the *popolo* ("people") attempted to take over control of the communes.
2. Armed and militant, the popolo demanded a voice in city government, particularly in matters of taxation.
3. In some cities, nobles overcame and dissolved the popolo, while in others the popolo squeezed the nobles out of the government.
4. The constant feuding and compromising between the factions made many Italian cities centers of civil discord.

5. Thus weakened, the cities were prey to great regional nobles who, siding with one faction or another, often made themselves *signori* (singular *signore*, meaning "lord") of the cities.
6. Typically, signori kept the peace at the price of repression, replacing the commune with a government dominated by one powerful family.

F. The Mongol Takeover, p. 380

1. The fragmentation of political power left eastern Europe and Russia vulnerable to invasions from Asia.
2. Mongol invasions began at the start of the thirteenth century on the northern border of China under the leadership of Chingiz (or Genghis) Khan (c. 1162–1227), and in the 1230s, the attacks spread to areas in Russia, Poland, and Hungary.
3. Only the death of the Mongols' leader, the Great Khan (Chingiz's son, Ogodei, 1186–1241), prevented an attack on Germany.
4. By the 1250s, the Mongols had taken Iran, Iraq, and Syria.
5. The Mongols ruled longest in Russia, where they captured Kiev in 1240 and ruled from the mouth of the Volga River for about two hundred years.
6. The Mongol Empire in Russia, later called the Golden Horde, adopted much of the local government apparatus.
7. The Mongols opened China to Europeans for the first time.
8. Some missionaries, diplomats, and merchants traveled over land or sea to China, the most famous being Marco Polo (1254–1324).
9. Merchant activity in China paved the way for missionaries, such as the Franciscan John of Monte Corvino in 1289.
10. Thus, the Mongols threw open new routes to the east that helped bring the two halves of the known world together; this in turn began the search for exotic goods and missionary opportunities that would lead to a new world, the Americas.

G. The Great Famine, pp. 380–382

1. Natural disasters and political ineptitude brought on the Great Famine of 1315–1322 in northern Europe.
2. Heavy rains destroyed crops, farm animals died, and scarcity drove up the price of food, all of which led to hunger, disease, and death.
3. Peasants and poor urban dwellers were hardest hit, while some wealthy lords, churches, monasteries, and merchants profited from the new high prices they could charge.
4. Both urban and rural areas lost 5 to 10 percent of their populations, which led to a loss of manpower and decreased productivity.
5. The famine was regarded as God's punishment for humanity's sins, and the clergy responded with prayers and calls for people to do penance.
6. Practical responses included the giving out of food by charitable monasteries, attempts by kings to control high interest rates on loans, migration of peasants eastward to Poland, and charitable policies of towns.
7. Social causes of the Great Famine included the exponential growth in population during the tenth to twelfth centuries. Even a small crop failure would have disrupted the system of distribution, but in the case of the Great Famine, the consequences were devastating.
8. Political causes of the disaster included warfare, which ruined crops, diverted manpower and resources, and disrupted the economy.
9. Political leaders exacerbated the misery of the famine by imposing heavy taxes and requisitioning grain to support their troops.
10. Merchants and peasants resisted, and in France people attacked royal castles and officials and turned against Jews and lepers.

Lecture Strategies

1. Innocent III's pontificate represented the apex of papal authority in the medieval west. His ambitious program for the renewal of western Christendom, much of it included in the decrees of the Fourth Lateran Council, addressed all facets of society. Even though he was not the first pope to assert such power, in many ways he was the most effective in having his message heeded. Discuss the factors that may have enabled him to succeed where earlier and later popes failed. A comprehensive collection of essays that examines many facets of Innocent's pontificate and its historical context is John C. Moore et al., eds., *Pope Innocent III and His World* (Aldershot, UK: Ashgate,

1999). For a recent biography that stresses the political and legal dimensions of Innocent's career, see Jane Sayers, *Innocent III: Leader of Europe, 1198–1216* (Harlow, UK: Addison-Wesley Longman, 1993). An older collection of short essays that debates the merits of Innocent's papacy is James Powell, ed., *Innocent III: Vicar of Christ or Lord of the World?* 2nd ed. (Washington, DC: Catholic University of America, 1994). Key primary sources can be found in Brian Tierney, ed., *The Crisis of Church and State: 1050–1300*, rpt. (Toronto: University of Toronto Press, 1994).

2. France's early cohesion into a nation-state and Germany's fragmentation form an interesting contrast in the political fates of two important regions. What were the political and social conditions in each that contributed to their differing political outcomes? Besides the biographies of Louis IX and Frederick II listed in the chapter bibliography, the essays in William Tronzo, ed., *Intellectual Life at the Court of Frederick II Hohenstaufen* (New Haven, CT: Yale University Press, 1998) are useful for researching Germany. For an innovative analysis of how the symbolism of medieval French monarchy contributed to the growing sense of French nationalism, see Colette Beaune, *The Birth of an Ideology: Myths and Symbols of Nation in Late-Medieval France* (Berkeley: University of California Press, 1991).

3. During this period, popular governments emerged in the west for the first time since the end of the Roman republic. Examine this trend and the reasons for the rise of the Italian communal city-states, including growing internationalism, commercialism, and the spread of secular education. Good introductions are provided by Daniel Waley, *The Italian City-Republics* (Harlow, UK: Addison-Wesley Longman, 1988); and Giovanni Tobacco, *The Struggle for Power in Medieval Italy* (New Haven, CT: Yale University Press, 1990). For a detailed account of culture, society, and economic life in late-medieval Italy, see John Larner, *Italy in the Age of Dante and Petrarch, 1216–1380* (White Plains, NY: Longman, 1980). A 1995 collection of essays highlighting the various dimensions of state-building in Italy, including legal and fiscal aspects, is Julius Kirshner, ed., *The Origins of the State in Italy, 1300–1600* (Chicago: University of Chicago Press, 1995).

Class Discussion Starters

1. As European contact with the rest of the world increased and nation-states centralized, the social marginalization of certain groups within Europe was also on the rise. Heretics, Jews, and prostitutes all became the focus of exclusionary legislation, official prosecution, and even mob violence. Discuss with students how these phenomena might be related. Two highly influential studies on the topic are Norman Cohn, *Europe's Inner Demons: The Demonization of Christians in Medieval Christendom*, rev. ed. (Chicago: University of Chicago Press), and R. I. Moore, *The Formation of a Persecuting Society* (Oxford: Blackwell, 1990). Several excellent studies supplement them, particularly David Nirenberg, *Communities of Violence: Persecution of Minorities in the Middle Ages* (Princeton: Princeton University Press, 1996), which concentrates on France and Spain.

2. Scholars have often viewed the tall Gothic cathedrals as architectural manifestations of the intellectual search for harmony that was expressed philosophically in scholasticism. Debate the merits of this interpretation. A beautifully written, highly personal version of this approach can be found in Henry Adams, *Mont Saint Michel and Chartres*, rpt. ed. (Princeton: Princeton University Press, 1981). A modern assessment of how the innovations of Gothic art were perceived in the high Middle Ages is Michael Camille, *Gothic Art: Glorious Visions* (New York: Harry N. Abrams, 1996). For information on the construction techniques used in building the cathedrals, see John Fitchen, *The Construction of the Gothic Cathedrals* (Chicago: University of Chicago Press, 1981).

3. Magna Carta and the nascent national parliaments can be viewed as precursors of modern western political ideals and institutions. Discuss the development of the division of power between king and parliament and its contemporary analogues in the doctrines of the separation of powers and of individual rights. How did these institutions serve to balance the array of political interests present in western European societies? What were their shortcomings as "representative" institutions? The development of constitutional government in medieval England has received much attention. Two important works are H. G. Richardson and G. O. Sayles, *The English Parliament in the Middle Ages* (Rio Grande, OH: Hambledon Press, 1981); and J. R. Lander, *The Limitations of English Monarchy in the Later Middle Ages* (Toronto: University of Toronto Press, 1989). For France, see Joseph Strayer, *The Reign of Philip the Fair* (Princeton: Princeton University Press, 1980); and John Baldwin, *The Government of Philip Augustus: Foundations of French Royal Power in the Middle Ages* (Berkeley: University of California Press, 1991). For Spain, see Joseph O'Callaghan, *The Cortes of Castile-León, 1188–1350* (Philadelphia: University of Pennsylvania Press, 1989). For Germany, see Benjamin Arnold, *Princes and Territories in Medieval Germany* (Cambridge, UK: Cambridge University Press, 1991). On developments in medieval political theory and their importance for succeeding centuries, see Brian Tierney, *Religion, Law, and the Growth of Constitutional Thought, 1150–1650* (Cambridge, UK: Cambridge

University Press, 1982); and James Blythe, *Ideal Government and the Mixed Constitution in the Middle Ages* (Princeton: Princeton University Press, 1992).

4. The rise of the Cathar heresy signaled spreading discontent with the Catholic church at the height of its greatest power under Innocent III. Discuss the content of this heresy, its similarity to earlier heretical movements such as Manichaeanism, and the church's often highly repressive moves to contain it, including crusade and inquisitorial prosecution. In addition to Ladurie's *Montaillou*, see Michael Costen, *The Cathars and the Albigensian Crusade* (Manchester: Manchester University Press, 1997). A standard overview of medieval heresy is Malcolm Lambert, *Medieval Heresy: Popular Movements from Bogomil to Hus* (New York: Holmes & Meier, 1977).

Reviewing the Text

Review Questions

1. How did people respond to the teachings and laws of the church in the early thirteenth century?
[model answer] *Thirteenth-century Europeans were highly concerned with piety and with understanding how to live their lives in a religious manner; they sought to find order and harmony in life and the church seemed to offer the rules that might provide it. So they listened to the priests and preachers and shaped their behavior to church teachings. Many who had the means dedicated themselves to religious lives, either by joining religious orders or by tying themselves to the church as tertiaries, or they placed religious behavior and concerns at the center of their daily activities. Others led religious lives by attending church and looking to church teachings to determine appropriate behavior in various circumstances but did not place religion at the center of their lives.*

2. How did artists, musicians, and scholastics try to link this world with the divine?
[model answer] *Scholarship and the arts sought to express the connection between the divine and the daily world, to demonstrate the ways in which divine laws and order underscored the realities of life. Scholars worked to show that the knowledge of the senses and reason was compatible with the knowledge provided through religious faith. They applied logic and reason to religious teachings to justify that many daily activities were expressions of divine order. Artists and writers also worked to express the connections between the divine and the worldly, depicting and exploring religious subject matter.*

3. How did the search for order result in cooperation—and confrontation—between the secular rulers of the period 1215–1340 and other institutions, such as the church and the towns?
[model answer] *The attempt to order large territories into one entity, e.g., Italy and Germany into one empire, was frustrated by the magnitude of the task, but also by conflict with the church for political control of the region. The kings in Spain, England, and France ordered their countries through cooperation, organizing their rules by gathering local leaders as supporters in what came to be the representative institutions of parliaments. At times, as in France, this brought secular authorities into conflict with church authorities. Conflict in Italian states centered around contests for control between local lords and the people.*

Making Connections

1. Why was Innocent III more successful than Boniface VIII in carrying out his objectives?
[model answer] *Through the laws of the Fourth Lateran Council, Innocent III created a sense of order for people in their lives; this order seemed to fit with the needs of the day. Boniface's approach to controlling and maintaining church power was confrontational in its challenge to secular rulers, and his efforts to extend papal control brought accusations that he used religion as a political tool. Boniface seems to have made secular rulers feel threatened in their control over their territories in a period when these rulers were increasing and consolidating their powers. In that way, the circumstances of the times also contributed to Boniface's greater difficulties.*

2. What impact did the Mongol invasions have on the medieval economy?
[model answer] *By opening routes to China, the Mongol invasion introduced new trade opportunities to the European economy and an interest in seeking out others that stimulated greater economic activity.*

Discussing the Documents

Questions from Online Study Guide with Model Answers

The Debate between Reason and the Lover (p. 369)

1. How is this section of the poem a kind of *sic et non*?
[model answer] *Reason and the Lover both describe characteristic ways in which love can affect humans. Reason provides the "non," viewing love as false emotions and driven by lust; the Lover provides the "sic" of love as a force for good in human life.*

2. How does Reason's idea of love in this poem compare with that of Duke William IX of Aquitaine in Chapter 11 (p. 347)?

[model answer] *Both Reason and William IX seem to view love as an essential element to the fullness of life. As a lover, William will die if his love is not returned, and Reason says that having it is more important than living a moral life.*

Ausculta Fili *(Listen, Beloved Son) (p. 379)*

1. What purpose did it serve for Pope Boniface VIII to portray himself as King Philip's father and the church as "holy mother?"
[model answer] *The Pope states that Philip should conduct himself as a son to parents, which would require his respect for the Pope and church and place them as authority figures over Philip. The Pope reminds Philip that this is the relationship created by God for humans who wish to remain within his favor and grace.*

2. By the time of Pope Boniface VIII, political leadership in Europe had become increasingly institutionalized and bureaucratized. How does the *Ausculta Fili* letter fit into this historical trend?
[model answer] *The Ausculta places the church—and Pope—at the head of the hierarchy of authority created in institutions and bureaucracies to manage secular power. As those political institutions developed, it was necessary for the Pope to articulate the place of the church within (i.e., at the top of) them to secure the role of the church in the power structure. The church has also developed a hierarchy of power, as he mentions "the ecclesiastical hierarchy," which emerged in the same era and of the same impulses as the secular hierarchy to centralize and organize systems for creating order in society and structures of control.*

New Sources, New Perspectives: The Peasants of Montaillou (pp. 364–365)

1. In what ways are modern court cases like Fournier's Inquisition register? In what ways are they unlike such a source? Could you use modern court cases to reconstruct the life of a community?
[model answer] *As with Fournier's register, modern court cases can expose details of individuals' lives and feelings and require testimony concerning past events, sometimes years in the past. People who are accused are also testifying in fear of the outcome. But much detail that goes beyond the actual focus of the case in a modern court is ruled out as not relevant, so a major difference is that today witnesses may not be required to answer some questions that might provide the kinds of incidental details that Fournier elicited.*

2. What are the advantages and the pitfalls of using a source such as the register for historical research?
[model answer] *As the text notes, the information in the register is both selective (in terms of the subjects covered by the religious focus of the questions and also respondents' desires to save themselves) and subject to the vagaries of memory (as they discuss events that took place many years in the past). Perhaps the most significant disadvantage is that the words of the sources are translated by individuals who were most likely quite biased in their perspective. The advantages of the register lie in the details it conveys about the peasant's daily life, a type of information for which there are few written sources.*

3. Do you think that Raimond might have made up his testimony? Why or why not?
[model answer] *Raimond might have made up his testimony if he had a grudge (as did the priest mentioned in the discussion) against the individual whose statements he is recounting. Perhaps if he was an Albigensian himself, he might have made it up to mock the inquisitors by comparing humans to a mule or to deflect inquiry against himself.*

4. What does this testimony suggest about the impact of church doctrines in the French countryside?
[model answer] *Raimond's testimony suggests that Christian church doctrines had not fully penetrated the small villages of the countryside. Although the older man's perspective indicates an awareness of questions of the soul and afterlife—issues that are addressed by church doctrine—it also indicates that church perspectives have not been accepted. The remoteness of the villages in the French countryside probably minimized the impact of church doctrine upon the people there.*

Other Questions for Discussing These Documents in Class

The Debate between Reason and the Lover (p. 369)

1. Jean de Meun's portion of the *Roman de la Rose (Romance of the Rose)* explores a philosophical consideration of love, as this passage demonstrates. What is the writer's definition of reason and love?

2. How do women fit into this picture? How does Meun view the affection of women?

3. How "reasonable" is Reason's response to the Lover?

Ausculta Fili (Listen, Beloved Son) (p. 379)

1. How did Boniface justify his superiority over Philip the Fair? What does he claim is his source of authority?

2. Why might Boniface have chosen to communicate through such a personal letter, addressing Philip as a "beloved son"?

3. What about the letter would Philip find infuriating?

New Sources, New Perspectives: The Peasants of Montaillou (pp. 364–365)

1. Why do existing sources make it difficult to know what medieval peasants thought?

2. What kinds of information were recorded in the Inquisition records of Bishop Fournier of Pamiers about the villagers of Montaillou and their religious beliefs?

3. What are some of the shortcomings of using a document such as Fournier's register?

Comparative Questions

1. How does the concept of love in The Debate between Reason and the Lover compare with the notion of love implied in Boniface's letter to his "beloved son" Philip?

2. Which argument seems to be the more reasonable, that of Reason in *Roman de la Rose* or that of Boniface in *Ausculta Fili*?

For Users of *Sources of The Making of the West*

The following documents are available in Chapter 12 of the companion sourcebook by Katharine J. Lualdi, University of Southern Maine.

1. A Female Mystic: *Letters and Poems of Hadewijch of Brabant* (1220–1240)
2. The Rise of Anti-Semitism: Thomas of Monmouth, *The Life and Martyrdom of St. William of Norwich* (c. 1173)
3. Imagining Hell: Dante Alighieri, *Divine Comedy* (c. 1313–1321)
4. Bureaucratic Institutions: *Summons of Representatives of Shires and Towns to Parliament* (1295) and *Rolls of Parliament, Petitions and Answers* (1290–1305)
5. A Mongol's View: Guyuk Khan, *Letter to Pope Innocent IV* (1246)

Discussion Ideas for Sources of the Making of the West, *Chapter 12*

1. The letters and poems of Hadewijch of Brabant illustrate the growth of lay piety, specifically that of women, in thirteenth-century Europe. In what ways might her writings be seen as a search for religious order and harmony? How does she describe her relationship with God? What is the relationship between faith and reason in her work? How might the church have responded to her ideas about love and passion?

2. Dante Alighieri's *Divine Comedy* shares certain features with Hadewijch of Brabant's letters and poems. What are they? In what ways does his work illustrate a search for order, harmonizing reason with faith and love? How does Dante describe Hell? Does the poem reveal anything about God? What purpose is served by including so many characters from classical mythology and history?

Working with Visual Sources

For this exercise, please refer to Louis IX and Blanche of Castile on p. 375 of the textbook or view the image on the book companion site's Online Study Guide under the "Visual Activity" for Chapter 12.

Students viewing the image at the Online Study Guide are asked three questions of the image. The questions and model answers (not made available to students) are below. Project this image, available on the Instructor's Resources CD-ROM, in class or ask students to look at the image in their textbooks and answer the questions.

1. What artistic style influenced the way in which Louis IX and Blanche of Castile were depicted? How can you tell?
[model answer] *The artist was working in the Gothic style, which emphasized movement and naturalism, often portraying subjects in three dimensions. Louis IX and his mother are portrayed as three-dimensional figures, as shown by the way the folds of their robes flow over the curve of their bodies. The monarchs are also depicted in movement and clearly in conversation with each other.*

2. Portrayals of royalty often show them with the symbol of their power. What symbols of Louis's and Blanche's power are depicted in this miniature? By looking at the figures, can you tell who rules?
[model answer] *The artist has placed Louis and his mother on thrones, clearly indicating their royal status. Both are wearing ornate crowns and they are dressed in fine fabrics—Blanche's mantel is lined in ermine, a symbol of purity, and Louis's luxurious cloak is fastened with a large jeweled broach. Louis, however, is clearly the primary ruler because he holds a scepter and an orb, typical symbols of regal authority.*

3. Compare this miniature of a French monarch of the thirteenth century to the miniature of Frederick Barbarossa, a German monarch of the twelfth century, on p. 341 in Chapter 11. Were there different notions of hierarchy and monarchy in Germany and France?

[model answer] *Since Frederick meant to end the civil strife between the Welf and Staufer factions in Germany, it is significant that the artist portrayed him as the sire of sons, the first of many patriarchs in a successful dynasty. Louis, on the other hand, is depicted as a young boy with his mother, Blanche of Castile, who could boast of royal lineage. The miniature of Frederick also asserts the traditional imperial might and the commanding force of the emperor: Frederick, in the lower action scene, embarks on the Third Crusade, unabashedly felling the forests of Hungary on his mission to spread Christianity and expand the influence and treasury of Germany. Unlike the empire, France of the thirteenth century was a small, more united polity, a budding national state, and Louis as its king is portrayed as a sedate ruler, introspective even, a man content with his regal status and his monarchical holdings, a fact confirmed by his willingness to keep the peace with England and make concessions to Henry III.*

Mapping Exercises

Map Activity from OSG—Model Answer for Map Activity #2

For this activity please refer to the map on p. 324. Students are asked these questions:

How did the Iberian peninsula change over the course of the thirteenth century, and what possible effects did these changes have?
[model answer] *During the thirteenth century, the reconquista led to the expansion of Christian kingdoms, leaving only one small area in the south under Muslim control. This would have great consequences on the Muslim populations who lived there, as well the Jews who were generally well treated under Muslim rule. Territorial expansion also afforded Christian kingdoms, notably Castile, greater access to sea trade via the Mediterranean Sea and the Atlantic Ocean.*

How does the geographical relationship between the Papal States and France and England explain the pope's loss of influence in these countries?
[model answer] *The Papal States are much smaller than either France or England, and they are separated from these countries by long distances. When the monarchs of France and England consolidated their control over their kingdoms, they had less need for papal alliances. They preferred to keep the revenues that could be gained from taxing the clergy and deal with religious dissenters in their own way. The relatively limited military resources of the Papal States combined with their distance from France and England made it difficult for popes to insist on these countries' allegiances.*

Map 12.1: Europe in the Time of Frederick II, r. 1212–1250, p. 374

What made the Italian peninsula such a coveted area? Why would the papacy have felt consistently threatened by foreign powers? Ask students to identify the territorial anomalies on this map, given the general trend toward the consolidation of regions under the control of a handful of major political powers.

Map 12.2: France under Louis IX, r. 1226–1270, p. 376

Ask students to identify the two main regions within Louis IX's kingdom. How did Louis's holdings compare with those of the French monarch in the late twelfth century as depicted in Map 11.1: Europe in the Age of Henry II and Frederick Barbarossa, 1150–1190, p. 338? What does the growth of the French king's territory suggest about his power, particularly in comparison with the power of the English kings?

Map 12.3: The Mongol Invasions to 1259, p. 381

Have students identify the Mongols' routes of conquest in the order in which they occurred. What are the implications of the fact that this process, which integrated disparate cultures and tied economies together, was achieved by violent conquest? How might this conquest have influenced cultural exchange and notions of collective identities?

Mapping the West: Europe, c. 1340, p. 383

Ask students to see how many individual nation-states and other political entities they can identify on this map. What was the likely impact of the increased number of relatively small, politically autonomous states for the economic reality of the medieval west? What was its likely effect on political ideologies and foreign political relations? What was the significance of western empires, such as the Holy Roman and Byzantine empires, when comparing their relatively modest geographical dimensions to the former Roman, Persian, or Carolingian empires?

In-Class Assignments and Presentation Topics

1. The late-thirteenth to early-fourteenth centuries were a time of great international travelers, some of whose accounts still survive. An examination

of the insights and prejudices these writers express can help students to appreciate just how international the world was and also to discern the dynamics of cultural confrontations that occurred, even when travelers explored regions dominated by their own religious and political traditions. Wonderful paper or presentation topics can be based on the observations of Ibn Battuta (a Muslim) concerning his travels in Africa, and on those of Marco Polo (an Italian) concerning China. Recent editions of their works are *Ibn Battuta in Black Africa* (Williston, VT: Markus Wiener, 1994) and *The Travels of Marco Polo* (London: Wordsworth, 1997). Students can also compare these two authors with the twelfth-century Jewish travel writer, Benjamin of Tudela, whose journeys are discussed in *The World of Benjamin of Tudela: A Medieval Mediterranean Travelogue* (Madison, NJ: Fairleigh Dickinson University Press, 1995).

2. The Inquisition usually generates great interest among students. Have them outline the inquisitorial procedures that they find in the Inquisition Manual of Bernard Gui, available with additional primary sources in the Internet Medieval Sourcebook. You can also ask students to reconstruct the historical events that lay behind the records of an Inquisition trial, such as that of Beatrice de Planissoles. The transcripts of that investigation are reproduced in Patrick Geary, *Readings in Medieval History*, 2nd ed. (Peterborough, ON: Broadview, 1997).

3. Despite highly challenging content, the writings of Thomas Aquinas can lead students to confront the power and limits of applying logic to theological questions. What do the documents reveal about the state of empirical inquiry in the west? The parameters of the questions that scholastics asked? The ability of the church to adapt to new intellectual paradigms? The section on "Intellectual Life" of the Internet Medieval Sourcebook gives excerpts from Aquinas's works, as well as from those of earlier philosophers, which students can access and use for comparative essays.

4. The propaganda war between Philip the Fair and Boniface VIII dramatically illustrates how tensions between church and state came to a head at the turn of the fourteenth century. Students can trace the escalation of the conflict by investigating the alternating claims to universal authority and accusations launched by the two; students should also consider the role that public opinion played in the outcome of the conflict. Key primary sources and secondary commentaries are contained in Charles Wood, ed., *Philip the Fair and Boniface VIII: State vs. Papacy*, 2nd ed. (Melbourne, FL: Krieger, 1976).

5. Despite its magnificent poetry and biting commentary on contemporary events, Dante's *Divine Comedy* is a difficult text for the uninitiated to comprehend. However, with a little guidance, students often find the landscape of the Inferno to be fascinating, especially because they can read the poem in two excellent translations: John D. Sinclair (Oxford: Oxford University Press, 1990); and Robert Pinsky (New York: Farrar, Straus & Giroux, 1994).

Essay Questions

1. Have students investigate the cultural history of the Mongols, the creation of the Yuan Mongol dynasty in China, or the rule of the Golden Horde. Were they, in fact, savage nomadic horsemen, as they are often depicted in the popular imagination? In which ways did they adapt to the societies of their subject territories? What were their contacts like with the powers of the west? The earliest major Mongolian source is Paul Kahn's translation of the thirteenth century's *Secret History of the Mongols* (Boston: Cheng & Tsui, 1999). A good, general introduction is David Morgan, *The Mongols* (Oxford: Blackwell, 1986). Two scholarly biographies of the most famous of the Mongol rulers are: Morris Rossabi, *Khubilai Khan: His Life and Times* (Berkeley: University of California, 1988); and Paul Ratchnevsky, *Genghis Khan: His Life and Legacy* (Oxford: Blackwell, 1993). For Mongolian conquest and imperial rule, see John Joseph Saunders, *The History of the Mongol Conquests*, rpt. (Philadelphia: University of Pennsylvania Press, 2001); and Charles J. Halperin, *Russia and the Golden Horde: The Mongol Impact on Medieval Russian History* (Bloomington: Indiana University Press, 1987).

2. The cult of the Virgin Mary and the celebration of the lady in the courtly love tradition signaled new ways of conceptualizing female nature and the status of women. Ask students to explore how such changes were manifested in the devotional practices of high medieval Christianity in the west. The works of Caroline Bynum are central to any exploration of this topic, especially *Holy Feast and Holy Fast: The Religious Significance of Food to Medieval Women* (Berkeley: University of California Press, 1987); and *Jesus as Mother: Studies in the Spirituality of the High Middle Ages* (Berkeley: University of California Press, 1982). A different perspective on female devotional practices and food is presented in Rudolph Bell, *Holy Anorexia* (Chicago: University of Chicago Press, 1985). On women and mysticism, see the essays in Ulrike Wiethaus, ed., *Maps of Flesh and Light: The Religious Experience of Medieval Women Mystics* (Syracuse, NY: Syracuse University Press, 1993).

3. The study of medieval women has generated a corresponding and growing interest in changing

definitions of masculinity in the high Middle Ages, especially as it relates to the development of courtly romance and troubadour poetry. A fundamental source for a range of perspectives on the topic is Clare Lees, ed., *Medieval Masculinities: Regarding Men in the Middle Ages* (Minneapolis: University of Minnesota Press, 1994). See also Jeffrey Jerome Cohen and Bonnie Wheeler, eds., *Becoming Male in the Middle Ages* (New York: Garland, 1997).

4. The opening of trade routes and the push to missionize the east indicate that cross-cultural contacts were occurring at a rapid rate during this period. Students might want to investigate the international economy and this world of exploration that occurred before the more well-known "Age of Exploration." A substantial collection of primary documents is Robert Lopez and Irving Raymond, eds., *Medieval Trade in the Mediterranean World* (New York: Columbia University Press, 1990). A broad perspective of cross-cultural interactions prior to Columbus is Jerry Bentley, *Old World Encounters: Cross-Cultural Contacts and Exchanges in Pre-Modern Times* (Oxford: Oxford University Press, 1993).

5. A wealth of information is available on everyday life for the Medieval period, and students can be asked to research any number of subjects, including food, armory, clothing, medicine, children, music, and so on. Students can present their findings in class, thus collectively forming a picture of what life, in all of its varieties, was like in the thirteenth and early fourteenth centuries. Students can begin with the work of Joseph and Frances Gies, who have published widely on the Middle Ages.

Additional Resources: Literature

Horgen, Frances, trans., *Guillaume De Lorris and Jean De Meun: The Romance of the Rose*. 1999.
Latham, Ronald, trans., *The Travels of Marco Polo*. 1958.
Matarasso, Pauline Maud, ed., *The Quest of the Holy Grail*. 1969.
Shaw, M. R. B., trans., *Jean de Joinville and Geoffroy de Villehardouin: Chronicles of the Crusade*. 1963.
Singleton, Charles S., trans., *The Divine Comedy*. 1970.

Additional Resources: Film and Video

Robin Hood (1991; John Irvin, dir.; with Patrick Bergen and Uma Thurman). This version is a largely faithful retelling of the Robin Hood story in a fairly accurate setting.

Braveheart (1995; Mel Gibson, dir.; with Mel Gibson and Sophie Marceau). This film is a somewhat inaccurate depiction of the life of thirteenth-century Scotsman, William Wallace.

Other Bedford/St. Martin's Resources for Chapter 12

The following resources are available to accompany Chapter 12. Please refer to the Preface of this manual for detailed descriptions of all the ancillaries.

For Instructors

Transparencies

The following maps and image from Chapter 12 are available as full-color acetates.

- Map 12.1: Europe in the Time of Frederick II, r. 1212–1250
- Map 12.2: France under Louis IX, r. 1226–1270
- Map 12.3: The Mongol Invasions to 1259
- Mapping the West: Europe, c. 1340
- Sentences Imposed by an Inquisitor, 1308–1323, p. 363
- Louis IX and Blanche of Castile, p. 375

Instructor's Resources CD-ROM

The following maps and image from Chapter 12, as well as a chapter outline, are available on disc in both PowerPoint and jpeg formats.

- Map 12.1: Europe in the Time of Frederick II, r. 1212–1250
- Map 12.2: France under Louis IX, r. 1226–1270
- Map 12.3: The Mongol Invasions to 1259
- Mapping the West: Europe, c. 1340
- Louis IX and Blanche of Castile, p. 375

For Students

Study Guides

The Online Study Guide at **bedfordstmartins.com/hunt** helps students synthesize the material they have learned as well as practice the skills historians use to make sense of the past. The following Map, Visual, and Document activities are available for Chapter 12.

Map Activity

- Map 12.1: Europe in the Time of Frederick II, r. 1212–1250

Visual Activity

- Louis IX and Blanche of Castile, p. 375

Reading Historical Documents

- The Debate between Reason and the Lover, p. 369
- New Sources, New Perspectives: The Peasants of Montaillou, pp. 364–365

CHAPTER

13

Crisis and Renaissance

1340–1492

Chapter Resources

Main Chapter Topics

1. The loss of up to a half of the population of Europe during the Black Death altered the dynamics of feudalism and decreased overall production, but increased individual wealth and the demand for luxury goods. As grain prices fell, farmers diversified their crops, which resulted in a better overall diet for Europeans. The Black Death also fueled further persecution of the Jews.

2. The Hundred Years' War caused widespread destruction in France and Burgundy, but it also created a new sense of nationalism and accelerated changes in the nature of warfare with the advent of cannons and the use of mercenaries. France and Burgundy emerged at the end of the war as powerful rivals, while England entered into civil war at home.

3. The Ottoman Empire continued to expand and captured Constantinople in 1453.

4. The Avignon papacy extended its powers and curia, but the Great Schism split the papacy between Avignon and Rome from 1378 to 1415. Popular religious groups, such as the Lollards and Hussites (or Taborites), questioned the conduct of the church hierarchy, the validity of church teachings, and the nature of the church itself.

5. The tragedies of the latter Middle Ages were shaken off as the Renaissance ("rebirth") of European civilization produced a revolution in art and learning in Italy that spread to other countries. The humanist movement embodied a renewed interest in classical antiquity and was central to the Renaissance. Man now became "the measure of all things."

6. Vernacular literature, produced by middle-class writers for an educated laity, became popular. There was a parallel revival in classical literature.

7. The status of artists changed; they were no longer viewed as mere artisans. Artists idealized the human form and introduced visual perspective into their work. Architects imposed order on space, and composers found new ways to express emotion through polyphonic music.

8. Renaissance society in Florence was stratified: the "little people," or small shopkeepers and artisans, made up 60 percent of the population, whereas "fat people," wealthier merchants and tradesmen, made up 30 percent. The elites of Florence—bankers and extremely wealthy merchants—controlled the government.

9. Burgundy consisted of French, German, and Dutch territories and was held together for much of the fifteenth century by two able dukes. It was a center of Renaissance culture, but it declined when Charles the Bold (1433–1477) was killed in battle. Louis XI seized Burgundian land and further expanded French territory when he inherited Anjou. England grew economically strong in the fifteenth century despite a civil war known as the Wars of the Roses.

Focus Question

How were the crises of the fourteenth and fifteenth centuries and the Renaissance related?

1. By disrupting existing patterns of life, the various crises created opportunities for new developments, such as the revival of classical culture that brought forth new forms of music and art in the Renaissance. The Black Death had the largest impact on the lives of Europeans, killing perhaps as many as 60 percent of the population in some areas and utterly transforming the social and economic landscape of communities. However, for survivors there were new opportunities in the form of improved agriculture, more diversified economies, and greater prosperity,

including better wages and living standards. This new prosperity helped fuel such developments as the founding of new universities and the amassing of wealth among urban elites. The Renaissance flourished in both environments. Universities became centers of humanist learning, and wealthy city dwellers, along with monarchs and popes, became important patrons of Renaissance art, architecture, and music.

2. Although the frequent warfare of the fourteenth and fifteenth centuries proved destructive for its victims, in the longer term such conflict strengthened the political power of the victors, contributing to the growth of modern, centralizing states. For example, France benefited from its ultimate victory in the Hundred Years' War, English kings further consolidated their power following the Wars of the Roses, and the Spanish monarchy emerged as one of the strongest in Europe following the union of Castile and Aragon and the expulsion of Muslims from Granada. Victory in warfare also benefited many rulers, such as the kings of France and the dukes of Burgundy, who became important patrons of the northern Renaissance. Similarly, contact between Venice and the Ottomans, who had defeated the Byzantines, stimulated the development of the Renaissance in these areas.

3. Upheaval in the church, combined with the horrors of the Black Death and the dislocation of the Hundred Years' War, stimulated important changes in European religious life and contributed to political developments as well. The devastation caused by the plague prompted spiritual uncertainty among many, while during the Great Schism competition among the rival popes weakened the prestige of the papacy. Both developments undermined the authority of the church and stimulated new religious movements such as those of the Lollards and the Hussites. Both groups were important precursors of the sixteenth-century Reformation, and the Hussites had a significant political impact in Bohemia, where their movement became a national revolt of Czechs against Germans. Similarly, by forcing the leaders of Europe to take sides over which pope to support, the Great Schism undermined the political unity of the church and enhanced the opportunities of kings to lay claim to the church in their own countries, as when Louis XI established Gallicanism in France.

Annotated Chapter Outline

I. **Crisis: Disease, War, and Schism**

A. **The Black Death, 1346–1353, pp. 388–391**

1. The Black Death, as named by historians, was probably caused by the bacterium *Yersinia pestis*, and it decimated the population wherever it struck and wreaked havoc on social and economic structures.
2. This "pestilential disease" began in 1346 near the Black and Caspian seas.
3. The plague traveled westward, carried to Europe by fleas that lived on rats that came to seaports on merchant ships.
4. By 1348, the plague had spread to Aragon, all of Italy, the Balkans, and most of France before creeping north into Germany, England, and Scandinavia, and finally reaching Russia by 1351.
5. Recurring every ten to twelve years throughout the fourteenth century, the plague continued at longer intervals until the eighteenth century.
6. Conservative estimates put the death toll in Europe between one-third and one-half of the population, although the effects of the plague were oddly localized.
7. Part of what made the disease so devastating was that it occurred in the wake of local famines.
8. Some cities responded to the Black Death with decrees limiting travel and effectively setting up citywide quarantines.
9. Other cities instituted stricter sanitary laws, especially in regard to butchers and retailers of meat.
10. Some believed the plague was God's way of punishing a sinful world and sought to save themselves through repentance.
11. Bands of men and women called flagellants appeared and publicly whipped themselves until blood flowed.
12. In some communities, the religious fervor sparked by flagellants led to violence against Jews.
13. Anti-Semitic persecutions spread through central and western Europe, destroying many Jewish communities.
14. To escape the slaughter, many German Jews fled to Poland, where the incidence of the plague was low and where the authorities welcomed Jews as productive taxpayers.
15. A theme of art, literature, and performance that grew out of the preoccupation with death was called the Dance of Death and featured skeletal figures and people processing to their graves.
16. Preachers talked about the death theme, poets wrote dialogues about it, and life-sized paintings mirrored this journey toward death.
17. At the same time it was causing a bleak view of the world, the Black Death brought opportunity for its survivors.

18. Fewer people meant less demand for food, and thus less land was needed for farming.
19. Peasants and landlords diversified agriculture to compensate for the lower demand, turning to stockbreeding and barley cultivation, which, along with more money to spend, improved the average diet.
20. The decline in population meant less competition for employment and allowed workers to demand higher wages, resulting in a better standard of living.
21. These periods of epidemic were generally followed by a slight jump in birthrate, due most likely to better employment opportunities as well as greater frequency of marriage and at younger ages.
22. The Black Death also altered patterns of education; donors who wanted to be known as patrons of education founded local colleges and universities, enabling the post-plague generation to be educated nearer to home.

B. The Hundred Years' War, 1337–1453, pp. 391–396

1. In 1337, French king Philip VI confiscated Guyenne, the area around Bordeaux, which was a part of the continent still held by the English monarchs.
2. Edward III of England countered by claiming the French throne, leading to more than a century of intermittent conflict.
3. The Hundred Years' War took place in four phases.
4. The first three phases were characterized by weakening French power, a stronger England, and creation of a new kingdom, Burgundy, that was initially allied with England.
5. The fourth phase of the war began when young King Henry V of England (r. 1413–1422) invaded and inflicted a crushing defeat of the French at Agincourt (1415) but saw the English slowly driven out of France until they only held Calais.
6. This turnaround in the tide of war was due largely to a sixteen-year-old peasant girl who was inspired by visions in which God told her to fight against the English.
7. Joan of Arc fought courageously in the successful battle of Orléans, and convinced the dauphin to travel to the cathedral in Reims to be anointed and crowned King Charles VII.
8. In 1431, in a failed attempt to take Paris, Joan was captured, turned over to the English, and burned at the stake after being tried as a witch.
9. Both England and France drew other countries into the war by hiring foreign mercenaries and by the economic effects of various export and import interdependencies.
10. As a result of the war and a strategic marriage, the duchy of Burgundy absorbed the Low Countries and became a powerful independent state commanding the wealth of the Flemish cities.
11. This period saw a shift from the chivalry of the medieval nobility as the leaders in battle to more modern warfare via mercenaries, or hired soldiers.
12. Lulls in the war made way for marauding bands of soldiers (Free Companies) to ravage the French countryside, terrorizing peasants and extracting "protection" money from them.
13. Foot soldiers and archers became more important than swordsmen as the French mastered the crossbow as a weapon and the English employed longbows that sent volleys of arrows.
14. Gunpowder, forged cannons, and handguns also made their appearance on the battlefields during this era.
15. Given the changes in the conduct of war and the formation of armies, Charles VII established a standing French army, financed with higher taxes and royal judicial claims so that, by 1500, the French monarchy would emerge as one of the leading powers of Europe.
16. Widespread resentment among the common people of France and England, who paid ever higher taxes to support the Hundred Years' War, fueled popular uprisings, which contributed to further political and social disorder.
17. Uprisings took place in Flanders in 1338, where the citizens, whose livelihood depended on English wool, rebelled against their count's pro-French policy.
18. In 1358, a revolt broke out in Paris, led by Etienne Marcel, in which the townspeople, unhappy with heavy taxes and the incompetence of the warrior nobility, sought greater political influence, but in the end the rebels were savagely killed in battles or executed.
19. In that same year in the countryside, peasants revolted against the nobility in

a movement its opponents called the Jacquerie, with both sides guilty of brutal atrocities.

20. In England, the passage of a poll tax by Parliament in 1377 to pay for the war triggered a peasant revolt known as Wat Tyler's Rebellion, and rebels from outlying areas joined urban workers in London.
21. Although the rebellion was put down, its leaders, who were later executed, set in motion the end of serfdom through their radical demands.

C. The Ottoman Conquest of Constantinople, 1453, pp. 396–397

1. In the east, the Ottoman dynasty became a formidable force in Anatolia and the Balkans.
2. Under Murat I (r. 1360–1389), the Ottomans reduced the Byzantine Empire to Constantinople and vassal-state status.
3. In the Balkans, the Ottomans allied with the Bulgarians and even some Serbian princes to win the Battle of Kosovo in 1389, destroying the last organized Christian resistance.
4. Sultan Mehmed II (r. 1451–1481) decided to take the city of Constantinople itself, all that remained of the Byzantine Empire.
5. Mehmed II prepared for the conquest by building a fortress near the city, and then he launched an attack by land and sea in March 1453.
6. After a three-month siege, cannons broke through the city walls of Constantinople and the attackers plundered the city and killed the emperor.
7. Mehmed saw himself as a Muslim Roman emperor and turned most Byzantine churches, including the Hagia Sophia, into mosques.
8. The Ottoman sultans, as central monarchs, maintained a highly disciplined military force that supervised the local administrators, built a system of roads to make trade easier and more profitable, and embarked on an ambitious program of expansion and conquest.
9. By 1500, the Ottoman Empire expanded to cover not only the Balkans and Anatolia, but Serbia, Athens and the Peloponnese, and Bosnia.

D. The Great Schism, 1378–1417, pp. 397–401

1. War, disease, and crises in the church caused by papal scandal greatly affected Europeans' spiritual life.
2. Moving the papacy from Rome to Avignon in 1309 caused an outcry, especially among Italians.
3. Critics of the papacy, such as Marsilius of Padua and William of Ockham, believed that Christians themselves—the congregation of the faithful, both laity and clergy—formed the Church and held its power.
4. Ockham rejected Thomas Aquinas's Aristotelian philosophy and argued that universal concepts existed only as mere representations in the mind and that observation and human reason were limited means to understanding the universe and knowing God.
5. His insistences that simple explanations were superior to complex ones became known as Ockham's razor.
6. The Great Schism began when Pope Gregory XI (r. 1371–1378) moved the papacy from Avignon back to Rome.
7. After his death in 1378, when cardinals met to elect a new pope, a riotous crowd clamored for election of a Roman.
8. Hoping to gain important posts in the papal government, the cardinals chose an Italian, Urban VI.
9. Once pope, Urban immediately sought to limit the power of the cardinals, who, in response, elected another pope, Clement VII, who returned the papal court to Avignon.
10. Urban and Clement each excommunicated the other, commencing the Great Schism in 1378.
11. Political divisions in Europe perpetuated the schism: France immediately recognized Clement as pope, as did rulers in Burgundy, Scotland, and Castile.
12. Meanwhile, England professed allegiance to Urban, as did the rulers of Poland, Hungary, and most of the Holy Roman Empire.
13. Each of the popes in Rome and Avignon excommunicated the Christians in Europe who allied with the other pope.
14. Given the state of confusion in Christendom, many intellectuals argued that the crisis justified calling a council to represent the faithful, even though doing so meant going against canon law and papal authority.
15. Cardinals loyal to neither pope met in 1409 at the Council of Pisa, the first attempt to resolve the schism.

16. The council then deposed both popes and elected a new pontiff, but both Urban and Clement refused to acknowledge the council's authority, meaning that Europe found itself with *three* popes.
17. Successor to the newest pope, Pope John XXIII, convened a church council at Constance in 1414.
18. The cardinals, bishops, and theologians at the meeting deposed John XXIII and the Avignon pope, and the Roman pope, Gregory XII, accepted the council's authority and resigned in 1415.
19. The rulers in the rest of Christendom recognized the council's appointee, Martin V, as the new, and only, pope.
20. The Great Schism, along with the miseries of the plague and wars, caused spiritual anxiety among ordinary Christians.
21. The pious sought to ensure their salvation through plenary indulgence (full forgiveness of sin) for those who made pilgrimages to designated holy places, and to reduce the amount of time in purgatory by purchasing indulgences or earning them by certain devout acts.
22. Devotion in the home also grew, enhanced by portable images of Mary and the life and passion of Christ, as well as purchase of Books of Hours that contained specific prayers for specific days.
23. Religious anxiety, intellectual dissent, and social unrest threatened church unity.
24. In England, a powerful anticlerical movement known as the Lollards developed from the teachings of John Wycliffe (c. 1330–1384), an Oxford professor.
25. Wycliffe's ideas advanced his belief that the community of believers, and not the clerical hierarchy, constituted the true church.
26. Wycliffe emphasized Bible reading and individual conscience as the path to salvation.
27. The Lollards came to challenge social inequality of every sort.
28. The most serious challenge to clerical authority in the fourteenth century originated in Bohemia.
29. Jan Hus (d. 1415) led a reform party that focused its discontent on the issue of the laity's receiving both the bread and the wine at Mass.
30. The reformers hoped to achieve a level of equality with the clergy, for whom the chalice of wine was traditionally reserved.
31. Although Hus was guaranteed protection by Emperor Sigismund, he was burned at the stake as a heretic at the Council of Constance, which set off a national revolution.
32. The Hussites gathered at Mount Tabor in southern Bohemia and renamed themselves the Taborites.
33. They modeled themselves after the first Christians of the New Testament, practicing communal ownership of goods and restructuring their community according to Biblical injunctions, which included giving some political rights to women.
34. The Hussites eventually won the right to receive both the bread and the wine at Mass, a practice that continued until the sixteenth century.

II. The Renaissance: New Forms of Thought and Expression

A. Renaissance Humanism, pp. 401–403

1. Three delegates at the Council of Constance—Cincius Romanus, Poggius Bracciolini, and Bartholemeus Montepolitianus—went to the library of a monastery in the town of St. Gall in order to "rescue" classical Latin texts.
2. Although these men were working for the pope, they were admirers of the ancients.
3. Humanism was a movement to revive classical Latin, and later Greek, as well as the sensibilities that accompanied the language.
4. Humanism began in the Italian city-states, and the humanists drew parallels between themselves and the scholars of the city-states in the ancient world.
5. Humanism was a way to confront the crises of the fourteenth through sixteenth centuries.
6. Humanists wrote poetry, history, moral philosophy, and grammar, all based on classical models, especially those of Cicero.
7. Most humanists combined sincere Christian piety with a new appreciation of the pagan past.
8. Francesco Petrarch, who was the first humanist, was much influenced by the Great Schism and coined the phrase "Babylonian captivity" to describe it.
9. Petrarch is best known for his poems dedicated to Laura and for his book *On the Solitary Life*, in which he claimed that the solitude required for reading the classics

was similar to the solitude required by those who devoted their lives to God.

10. Lauro Quirini was a less famous but more representative humanist who wrote disparagingly of the Turks and their capture of Constantinople.
11. Giovanni Pico della Mirandola was a flamboyant humanist who believed that Jewish mystical writings supported Christian scriptures, but the church found some of his views to be heretical.
12. Pico's *Oration on the Dignity of Man* summed up the humanist view that humanity's potential to become either a boor or an angel was infinite.
13. Christine de Pisan was a humanist writer and courtier who wrote poems inspired by classical models in order to support herself, her mother, and her children after she was widowed.
14. Although her patrons included the Duke of Burgundy and an English earl, she admired Joan of Arc and lamented the violence of the Hundred Years' War.

B. The Arts, pp. 403–408

1. Architects and artists also admired ancient Athens and Rome, but they modified classical models and melded them with medieval artistic traditions.
2. Renaissance artists and musicians worked for patrons, who included churchmen, secular rulers, and republican governments.
3. In contrast to medieval cities that had grown without planning, Renaissance cities were re-imagined by architects, such as Leon Battista Alberti, as places of order and harmony containing both public and private spaces.
4. Renaissance architectural features included piazzas (open public squares), porticos (covered walkways of columns), and regular geographical forms inspired by classical buildings.
5. Examples of Renaissance architecture include Duke Federico's palace at Urbino, designed by Luciano Laurana, and Alberti's new façade for Santa Maria Novella in Florence.
6. The sculptor Lorenzo Ghiberti melded classical and medieval elements in his design for bronze doors for a baptistery in Florence. Depicting the Old Testament story of the sacrifice of Isaac by Abraham, the sculpture of Isaac was modeled on classical nudes, while Abraham and the quatrefoil frame were drawn from medieval models. Cast in a single piece, the bronze doors also reflected new technology.
7. Renaissance artists also drew upon the ancient world for subject matter, such as in Sandro Botticelli's *The Birth of Venus.*
8. Renaissance painters perfected perspective, the illusion of three-dimensional space.
9. Some practitioners of perspective, such as Leonardo da Vinci, were military engineers as well as artists, and the introduction of long-range weaponry such as cannons occurred at the same time as the perfection of perspective in painting.
10. Although Ghiberti, Botticelli, and Da Vinci were all Italian artists, a northern Renaissance was also taking place among artists such as the Dutch painter Jan van Eyck. Important sponsors of the northern Renaissance included the courts of France and Burgundy.
11. Renaissance portraiture, such as that by van Eyck, emphasized the individuality and dignity of the subject.
12. Renaissance rulers spent as much as six percent of their annual revenue to support musicians and composers.
13. Music added glamour and glory to the courts and reputations of patrons.
14. Music was appreciated for its ability to express the innermost feelings of the individual.
15. Patrons included the Avignon popes, the duke of Ferrara, his daughter Isabella d'Este, and her husband, the duke of Mantua.
16. Composers included Josquin Desprez, who was the duke of Ferrara's chaplain; Tromboncino, who was Isabella's favorite; and Johannes Ockehem, who was chaplain to three French kings.
17. As a major sponsor of music, the church needed choirs of singers, and many composers got their start as choir boys.
18. The Great Schism encouraged more musical production as rival popes sought to outdo each other.
19. Renaissance musicians such as Josquin Desprez found new ways to compose expressive music by juxtaposing images of classical mythology with Christian liturgy to convey personal emotion.

III. Consolidating Power

A. New Political Formations in Eastern Europe, pp. 409–410

1. In the eastern half of the Holy Roman Empire, Bohemia gained new status under

King Vladislav Jagiello, who built his palace using Renaissance architectural elements, the first of such buildings north of the Alps.

2. Bohemia experienced religious and political crisis as the nobility, both Hussite and Catholic, clashed, and most of Europe considered Bohemia a heretic state.
3. Further north, cities, rather than the landed nobility, held power.
4. The most successful alliance of cities was the Hanseatic League, a loose federation of mainly north-German cities formed to protect their mutual interests in defense, trade, and art.
5. The Hanseatic League linked the Baltic coast with Russia, Norway, the British Isles, France, and the cities of Italy.
6. In the fifteenth century, the Hanseatic League confronted new rivals and began a long, slow decline.
7. Two new monarchies emerged in Poland and Lithuania.
8. Formed in the tenth century, by 1300 Poland had begun to recover from the devastating Mongol invasions. The kingdom expanded demographically and economically, in part due to the migration of Jewish and German settlers who helped build towns such as Cracow.
9. Lithuania was the only major holdout from Christianity in Eastern Europe, until it expanded into southern Russia and its Grand Dukes flirted with both Roman Catholic and Orthodox Christianity.
10. Poland and Lithuania were united following the 1386 marriage of Lithuanian Grand Duke Jogailo and Polish Queen Jadwiga. Jogailo was subsequently elected by the Polish nobility as King Wladyslaw II Jagiello. He became a Catholic and promised to convert Lithuania. The union of Poland and Lithuania lasted until 1772.

B. Powerful States in Western Europe, pp. 410–411

1. The kingdoms of France, England, Spain, and the duchy of Burgundy dominated fifteenth-century western Europe, although Burgundy had disappeared by the end of the century.
2. The kingdom of Spain was created by the 1469 marriage of Isabella of Castile and Ferdinand of Aragon.
3. Castile was more powerful than Aragon, and Navarre was a pawn between the two.
4. Isabella and Ferdinand ruled jointly over their separate dominions, but they consolidated their central power through taxation, bureaucracy, a compliant cortes, and ideology that glorified monarchy.
5. Marriage between the duke of Burgundy and the heiress of Flanders created the duchy of Burgundy.
6. Between 1384 and 1476 Burgundy filled the territorial gap between France and Germany, controlling a patchwork of provinces and regions inhabited by French, Dutch, and German-speaking subjects.
7. Unlike France, England, and Spain, Burgundy was an artificial creation whose coherence depended upon the skillful exercise of statecraft by its dukes, such as Philip the Good and his son Charles the Bold. Both men cultivated a personal relationship with their subjects and developed a "theatre" state of performance rituals in which the Burgundian dynasty provided the link among the diverse territories.
8. When Charles the Bold died without heirs, France and the Holy Roman Empire divided up the duchy, with the Low Countries going to the empire and France taking the rest.
9. Recovering quickly from its victory in the Hundred Years' War, the French kingdom grew larger and more powerful under Louis XI.
10. After the Anjou dynasty died out, France virtually doubled its territories as Louis inherited southern France and took over much of the former duchy of Burgundy.
11. Louis XI strengthened his power as king by imposing new taxes, maintaining western Europe's first standing army, and dispensing with meetings of the Estates-General.
12. The king also obtained virtual control of the church in France with the 1438 Pragmatic Sanction of Bourges. This established Gallicanism, or the control by French kings of ecclesiastical revenues and appointments of French bishops.
13. In England, Henry Tudor became King Henry VII following his victory in the Wars of the Roses, which were intermittent civil wars that primarily affected soldiers and the nobility.
14. The English economy continued to grow, especially the woolen cloth industry.

15. London merchants, the nobility, gentry, and yeomanry (free farmers) were the chief beneficiaries of economic prosperity.
16. Tudor monarchs took advantage of this prosperity to bolster their treasury and their power.

C. Republics, pp. 411–413

1. Although most of Europe was dominated by monarchical power, there were three important republics: Switzerland, Venice, and Florence.
2. All three prided themselves on traditions of self-rule, but all three were dominated by elites, or even by one family.
3. By the end of the fourteenth century, the Swiss Confederation had developed out of an alliance among the cities of the alpine region of the Holy Roman Empire.
4. Originally their purpose was to keep the peace, but they pledged to aid one another against the Holy Roman Emperor.
5. Wealthy merchants and tradesmen, rather than the landed nobility, dominated the Swiss Confederation, although ordinary people had some political importance in rural communes.
6. The Swiss were known for their independent stance against the emperor, their republican freedom, and the hiring out of poor foot soldiers as mercenaries to kings elsewhere in Europe.
7. Venice became the center of an extensive empire, with merchant ships crossing the Mediterranean and a navy of over 3,000 vessels.
8. In the fifteenth century, Venice began to conquer land in northern Italy and came up against the equally powerful city-state of Milan.
9. With the 1454 Peace of Lodi, Venice and Milan ended their struggle for control of the eastern part of northern Italy.
10. The Peace of Lodi was signed the year after the Ottoman conquest of Constantinople, and Venice wanted to end its conflict with Milan so it could direct its energies against the Turks. However, the Venetians also traded with the Ottomans, and the two powers influenced each other's art and culture.
11. Venice was ruled by a Great Council dominated by the city's most important families. The Great Council elected the doge, who was the leading magistrate.
12. The ordinary people of Venice never revolted against their government, as did the popolo of other Italian cities. Venice's location on water may have been a factor in this, as much central planning was required to maintain the city's buildings and services.
13. The conquest of Padua in 1405 transformed Venetian culture, bringing humanism and Renaissance art to the city.
14. The style of the Venetian Renaissance remained distinctive, however, as Venice had long been influenced by Byzantine art. Characteristic features included strong colors, intense lighting, and sensuous use of paint.
15. Florence was also a republic, but its society and political life were turbulent as political factions and social classes competed for power.
16. The Ciompi Revolt of 1378, named after wool workers, was the most important of these civil uprisings. Following the revolt, the ciompi won the right to form a guild, and power was redistributed in the city.
17. By the 1390s, the upper classes were again monopolizing government, and by 1434 the Medici family became the dominant power.
18. Cosimo de' Medici (1384–1464) founded his political power on the wealth of the Medici bank.
19. Cosimo's grandson Lorenzo "the Magnificent" took power in 1467 and bolstered the regime's legitimacy through his patronage of the humanities and the arts, possibly encouraging the young artist Michelangelo.
20. The Medicis made many enemies and were driven from power several times, but in 1530 the Florentine republic fell for good as the Medicis took power again, declaring themselves dukes of Florence.

D. The Tools of Power, pp. 413–414

1. In 1427, in Florence, then the center of Renaissance culture, the government compiled a comprehensive tax record of city households.
2. Completed in 1430, this census provided important details about social relations and demographics.
3. Florentines recognized class divisions, referring to the "little people" (workers, artisans, and small merchants: about 60 percent of the population) and the

"fat people" (wealthier merchants and other professionals: about 30 percent of the population).

4. At the bottom of the hierarchy were slaves and servants, mostly women from the surrounding countryside employed in domestic service.
5. At the top, a tiny 1 percent of patricians, bankers, and wool merchants controlled a quarter of the city's wealth.
6. Most Florentines lived in households of six or more, although the family unit itself—whether nuclear or extended—varied depending on wealth.
7. Extended families and higher numbers of children were the norm in families of rich patricians and landowning peasants in the countryside.
8. Middle- and upper-class families hired wet nurses to breast-feed their infants.
9. Poor families sometimes could not afford to raise their children and abandoned them to strangers or public charity.
10. Leaders of fifteenth-century states used the full force of their new powers against internal and external enemies.
11. In Spain, Ferdinand and Isabella began a systematic persecution of Jews and *conversos*, Jewish people who had converted to Christianity following vicious attacks on Jews in 1391.
12. *Conversos* had taken advantage of opportunities reserved for educated Christians, and many had risen to high positions, which bred resentment. Their commitment to Christianity was also questioned.
13. Persecution of *conversos* was justified by branding them heretics and traitors.
14. Isabella and Ferdinand set up the Inquisition in Spain to persecute *conversos*. In addition, they decreed in 1492 that all Jews in Spain must convert or leave the country.
15. The monarchs pursued similar policies against Muslims, conquering that same year the last Islamic stronghold at Granada. In 1502 all Muslims were required to adopt Christianity or leave the kingdom.

Lecture Strategies

1. To help students understand the impact and implications of the Black Death in the fourteenth century, discuss the changes that would be placed on contemporary society, especially their university town, if the student population rose constantly. Rents would increase, competition for housing would become fierce, employment would be difficult to find, and special payments or bribes might be required to obtain a job or apartment. Then ask students to work through the same scenario with the student population plummeting by 50 percent within a few years. Question how they might react to widespread death if they did not know its cause. Reactions might include a rise in spirituality or an urge to live for today. Next, apply all these scenarios to the fourteenth century. David Herlihy, *The Black Death and the Transformation of the West* (Cambridge, MA: Harvard University Press, 1997) is by far the best short and readable work for students on the subject.

2. A lecture on the disease itself is also effective. The plague came in three related strains: the bubonic, pneumonic, and septicemic. The bacteria reproduced in the digestive tract of fleas living on black rats. Fleas are animal-specific, but when the preferred host is unavailable, they will bite another host, such as humans. When they bite, they first regurgitate into the bloodstream, depositing the bacteria. The pneumonic plague was transmitted via air (pneumos) if one coughed or sneezed. Little is known about the septicemic (blood-transmitted) strain because victims died within a few hours of contraction. Read Robert S. Gottfried, *The Black Death: Natural and Human Disaster in Medieval Europe* (New York: Free Press, 1985). The results of recent DNA research should be included in any discussion of the plague. Geneticist Dr. Stephen O'Brien of the National Institutes of Health in Washington, D.C., convincingly argues that a mutated gene, CCR5, known colloquially as Delta 32, determined whether someone became infected. Interestingly, Delta 32 seems to play a similar role with HIV. The results of his work are available on PBS video *Secrets of the Dead: Mystery of the Black Death*.

3. With the Hundred Years' War and the emergence of the plague, people of the fourteenth century were constantly surrounded by death. For a look at the various issues related to death in the Middle Ages, see Christopher Daniell, *Death and Burial in Medieval England* (London and New York: Routledge, 1997); and Rosemary Horrox, "Purgatory, Prayer and Plague: 1150–1380" and Philip Morgan "Of Worms and War: 1380–1558," in Peter C. Jupp and Calre Gittings, eds., *Death in England: An Illustrated History* (Manchester: Manchester University Press, 1999; rpt., New Brunswick, NJ: Rutgers University Press, 2000).

4. Compare the elaborate ceremonies surrounding fifteenth-century monarchs and their families. Emphasizing the divine nature of kingship, these ceremonies were also an immediate and tangible display of

secular power and authority. Burgundy was accounted the most sophisticated court in Europe, and France and England vied to compete on the same level. For royal ceremony in Burgundy, see Peter Arnade, *Realms of Ritual: Burgundian Ceremony and Civic Life in Late Medieval Ghent* (Ithaca, NY: Cornell University Press, 1996); Rolf Strom-Olsen, "Dynastic Ritual and Politics in Early Modern Burgundy: The Baptism of Charles V," in *Past and Present*, no. 175 (2002), pp. 34–64; Edward A. Tabri, "The Funeral of Duke Philip the Good," in *Essays in History*, vol. 33 (1990–1991) (http://www.lib.virginia.edu/journals/EH/EH33/tabri33.html); and Christine Weightman, *Margaret of York: Duchess of Burgundy, 1446–1503* (Stroud, UK: Alan Sutton, 1989 [rpt., Palgrave Macmillan, 1993]). For French coronation ceremonies, see Richard A. Jackson, *Vive le Roi! A History of the French Coronation from Charles V to Charles X* (Chapel Hill: University of North Carolina Press, 1984). For English ceremony and ritual in general, see Brian R. Price, "The Manner and Form of the Coronation of the Kings and Queens of England," *Archeologia*, vol. 57, Part 1 (1996). For Henry VII's coronation, see William Jerdan, ed., *The Rutland Papers* (The Camden Society, 1842, series I, vol. 21 [rpt., New York: AMS Press, 1968]). For further information on royal ceremonies, see biographies of individual monarchs and their consorts.

Class Discussion Starters

1. Each social and political group of the fourteenth century attempted to defend and advance its position during a climate of change and realignment. Divide the class into groups representing peasants, urban workers, artisans, merchants, aristocracy, clergy, and monarchy. Ask each group to develop an argument for its defense and advancement. What do the people want? Why should they get it? Who is disadvantaged by their advancement? What leverage do they possess? What power should they have? Why? What power are they willing to concede? Why? Have them read George Huppert, *After the Black Death: A Social History of Early Modern Europe*, 2nd ed. (Bloomington: Indiana University Press, 1998).

2. The larger towns and cities of Europe during the fourteenth and fifteenth centuries often purchased their independence from feudal aristocrats; yet, as soon as they did so, the wealthy merchants who had supplied the money began acting like aristocrats. Discuss what provided status in medieval society. The class might begin by discussing what provides status in contemporary American society. Read Sylvia Thrupp, *The Merchant Class of Medieval London, 1300–1500* (Ann Arbor, MI: University of Michigan Press, 1989); and Paul Fussell, *Class* (New York: Summit Books, 1983).

3. Slides of Gothic and Renaissance architecture, especially churches, are readily available. Comparing the architecture of a Gothic cathedral and a Renaissance church to classical Greek or Roman architecture dramatically illustrates the idea of a rebirth. To be fair, one should point out that the comparison should be between Italian Gothic and Italian Renaissance, not northern Italian Gothic and Italian Renaissance. This comparison can be made with slides of any of the late-medieval Italian palaces. The best way to have students analyze a Renaissance building is to have them study it level by level. The classical features will then be readily apparent.

4. To study Renaissance art and skill, perception, and value of art, have students read and discuss Michael Baxandall, *Painting and Experience in Fifteenth-Century Italy*, 2nd ed. (Oxford: Oxford University Press, 1988).

5. For the origins of humanism, students could read and discuss Nicholas Mann, "The Origins of Humanism" and Michael D. Reeve, "Classical Scholarship," in Jill Kraye, ed., *The Cambridge Companion to Renaissance Humanism* (Cambridge, UK: Cambridge University Press, 1996, 1997, 1998). This entire book would also be useful for more advanced studies of humanism.

Reviewing the Text

Review Questions

1. What crises did Europeans confront in the fourteenth and fifteenth centuries, and how did they handle them?
[model answer] *Disease and warfare disrupted the European world in the fourteenth and fifteenth centuries. A plague called the Black Death swept Europe in the mid-fourteenth century, killing a third or more of the population. Cities were quarantined and religious fervor increased. The population loss stimulated changes in the agricultural economy and opened opportunities to workers for better employment and wages, which resulted in an improved standard of living and an increase in the birth rate. War between England and France for more than one hundred years and by the Ottoman Turks against the Byzantine Empire restructured power relations in Europe. The French and English kings hired mercenary armies to fight the battles, changing the nature of warfare; the French king established a permanent standing army. Ottoman expansion after their defeat of Constantinople was accomplished through the centralized control of the sultans and a highly trained military force. A schism in the church contributed to the social anxiety of late fourteenth-century Europe, prompting new forms of devotion and new heretical movements.*

2. How and why did Renaissance humanists, artists, and musicians revive classical traditions?
[model answer] *The crises of the era stimulated a renewed interest in the knowledge, values, and arts of the classical past, eras of Greek and Roman history, perhaps because they suggested a time of greater order and harmony, but also because the growing prosperity of the era and expansion of education encouraged new attention to scholarship and the arts. Writers and artists revived and expanded on classical literature in a movement called humanism. Architects and artists also contributed to this renaissance with work inspired by classical traditions to develop new styles of expression.*

3. How did the monarchs and republics of the fifteenth centuries use (and abuse) their newly consolidated powers?
[model answer] *As their control of government and their territories strengthened, European monarchs used their power and wealth to fund elaborate court functions that demonstrated and reinforced the legitimacy and strength of their courts. A part of this includes providing support for scholarship and the arts. They promoted industry and commerce to strengthen their realms economically. New taxes were imposed to support such activities. And some, particularly the monarchs of Spain, chose to foster the strength of their nations through Christianity by expelling the heretical minority, Jews, converted Jews, and Muslims.*

Making Connections

1. How did the rulers of the fourteenth century make use of the forms and styles of the Renaissance?
[model answer] *Fourteenth-century rulers used the enriched art and architecture of the Renaissance to enhance the pomp and ceremonial display of their courts as symbols of their power. They patronized poets, writers, and musicians whose works provided court entertainments, contributed to nobles' prestige, and expressed patriotism. Kings commissioned portraits of themselves as expressions of their stature. Renaissance principles of architecture and city planning contributed to developing greater order and harmony in public spaces, such as markets, gathering places, and public buildings.*

2. On what values did the Renaissance humanists and artists agree?
[model answer] *Renaissance humanists expressed values of religious piety in art, music, and writing, but they also demonstrated a respect for human individuality. They emulated the literature and teaching of the classical era because they valued the knowledge that stemmed from that era. Order and harmony took on importance in their contemporary era of crises, and they turned to classical forms to capture those values in their modern society.*

Discussing the Documents

Questions from Online Study Guide with Model Answers

Wat Tyler's Rebellion (1381), p. 398

1. Describe how Wat Tyler's Rebellion began.
[model answer] *Wat Tyler's Rebellion began when a group of men, led by Wat Tyler, converged on London and demanded that the King put an end to unjust taxes.*

2. How would you assess the motives of the rebels?
[model answer] *The actions of the rebels seem to have been motivated by the unfair treatment of the peasant class in England in the late fourteenth century. The peasants were taken advantage of by the tax-collectors who sought to collect as much money as possible in order to serve their own personal interests.*

Giovanni Pico della Mirandola, Oration on the Dignity of Man *(p. 404)*

1. In what ways does Pico's oration embody humanist ideals?
[model answer] *Pico expresses a sense of the individualism that characterized humanism when he described humans as "constrained by no limits" and able to use "free will" to shape their own lives. He also notes the centrality of religion because he states that humans were created to provide someone to admire and love the work of God.*

2. What insight does the oration provide into the relationship between religion and secularism during the Renaissance?
[model answer] *God is the source of humanity, but has left to humans the secular decisions concerning the nature and activities of their own lives. This suggests a divide between religion and secularism in society in terms of the ultimate authority determining the perspectives and actions of humans.*

Contrasting Views: Joan of Arc: Who was "the Maid"? (pp. 394–395)

1. Given the norms of the time, in what ways was Joan ordinary?
[model answer] *The testimony of a fellow villager presents Joan as a normal young woman who lived with and worked alongside her family just as others in her village. She worked in the fields and at women's domestic tasks and joined in fun with other young people. The only action by which she singled herself out as other than normal was in attending church more willingly than other young folks. However, the fear she expressed concerning the first time she heard the voice indicates that she probably did not perceive herself as other than ordinary in her religiosity.*

2. How fixed were male and female roles in fifteenth-century France?
[model answer] *These three documents describe a society that to some degree accepted women's participation in men's roles. Joan helps in what was presumably men's work of plowing and tending animals and ultimately is accepted in the very male role of leading a force of soldiers. These sources don't indicate whether men ever stepped into women's roles.*

Other Questions for Discussing These Documents in Class

Giovanni Pico della Mirandola, Oration on the Dignity of Man *(p. 404)*

1. According to this document, what is the fundamental nature of humankind?
2. What role, if any, does religion play in this understanding of human nature?

Contrasting Views: Joan of Arc: Who was "the Maid"? (pp. 394–395)

1. Which of the three descriptions of Joan was provided by someone who seems to have known her best?
2. Which of the three descriptions best captures the Joan of Arc who led the French to victory at the Battle of Orléans?
3. Is there anything in Joan's background that accounts for her rise to prominence?

Comparative Questions

1. In what ways might Joan of Arc and the participants in Wat Tyler's Rebellion be seen as embodying the view of human nature as described in the *Oration on the Dignity of Man*?
2. In what ways might Joan of Arc, the English rebels, and Giovanni Pico della Mirandola all be regarded as rebels who challenged traditional forms of authority?

For Users of *Sources of The Making of the West*

The following documents are available in Chapter 13 of the companion sourcebook by Katharine J. Lualdi, University of Southern Maine.

1. Demographic Catastrophe: *The Black Death* (Fourteenth Century)
2. Crisis and Change: Thomas Walsingham: *Peasant Rebels in London* (1381)
3. The Great Schism: Catherine of Siena, *Letters* (1376–1377) and Councils of Pisa and Constance, *Decrees* (1409–1417)
4. Satirizing the Church: Geoffrey Chaucer, *The Pardoner's Prologue* (1387–1400)
5. Extolling Humanism: Giovanni Rucellai and Leonardo Bruni, *Florence in the Quattrocento* (1427 and 1457)
6. Women's Place in Renaissance Italy: *Letters from a Widow and Matriarch of a Great Family* (1450–1465)

Discussion Ideas for Sources of The Making of the West, *Chapter 13*

1. According to Giovanni Rucellai and Leonardo Bruni's writings in *Florence in the Quattrocento*, what made life in Renaissance Italy so wonderful? In what ways do these two men reflect the ideals of humanism as discussed in *The Making of the West* text? To what extent do you think their writings reflect an ideal rather than the reality of fourteenth-century Florentine life?
2. Some scholars have argued that the benefits of the Renaissance were disproportionately enjoyed by male elites, and they have questioned whether or not there was a Renaissance for women and people of the lower social orders. Based on the *Letters from a Widow and Matriarch of a Great Family*, how would you assess the place of women in the Italian Renaissance? What seem to be Alessandra's principal concerns? How do these compare with those of Giovanni Rucellai and Leonardo Bruni? What insight does Alessandra provide into Florentine politics and social structure? Does the fact that Alessandra's writings consisted of private letters to her son, while Rucellai and Bruni's words were intended for a public audience influence your assessment of the documents?

Working with Visual Sources

For this exercise, please refer to Book of Hours on p. 400 of the textbook or view the image on the book companion site's Online Study Guide under the "Visual Activity" for Chapter 13.

Students viewing the image at the Online Study Guide are asked three questions of the image. The questions and model answers (not made available to students) are below. Project this image, available on the Instructor's Resources CD-ROM, in class or ask students to look at the image in their textbooks and answer the questions.

1. What does this picture portray?
[model answer] *This picture shows an agricultural scene in the foreground, while in the background stand a fortified castle and a large Gothic church. Five peasants are working in the fields. Three men are swinging scythes*

to harvest hay, and two women are raking the hay into stacks.

2. What does this illustration reveal about gender roles?
[model answer] *This illustration shows members of the peasant class. It is clear that both sexes take part in manual labor, at least in agriculture. However, there does appear to be a division of labor because the men, wielding scythes, are engaged in the more strenuous and probably more hazardous activity.*

3. Given the hardships that peasants faced in the fourteenth century, is this depiction of peasant life realistic?
[model answer] *The peasants in the illustration are genteel and well dressed, and they appear to be working very gracefully at their tasks. However, the realities of life for fourteenth-century peasants would have included backbreaking work, poor harvests, famine, unsanitary conditions, and the devastation of intermittent wars. This illustration idealizes medieval peasants because it shows these five men and women, and the land they are working, as free of hardship.*

Mapping Exercises

Map 13.1: The Hundred Years' War, 1337–1453, p. 393

In northern Europe, France barely exists in the early fourteenth century but, by the end of the Hundred Years' War, France expands to become a huge and dominant player in European affairs.

Map 13.2: Ottoman Expansion in the Fourteenth and Fifteenth Centuries, p. 397

In the Balkans, the Ottoman Empire is expanding rapidly into Europe, surrounding the remnants of the Byzantine Empire and threatening to overrun Christianity.

Mapping the West: Europe c. 1492, p. 415

Identify the major states of Europe and compare them to those depicted in Mapping the West: Europe, c. 1340 in chapter 12 (p. 383). How did the political boundaries change? Is the size of a country always a reflection of its power?

In-Class Assignments and Presentation Topics

1. Have students log on to one of the major medieval Web sites, such as the Internet Medieval Sourcebook, and evaluate the primary documents available for the period. Students should address the types of information that might be gleaned from them.

2. Assign small groups of students to research different classes in medieval society, such as peasants, merchants, aristocracy, clergy, and even the monarchy. Then, have them devise a justification for the existence of their class in society, the power they hold, and why they should be given greater rights or income within society.

3. Examine the illustrations of Joan of Arc (p. 392) and the Duke of Berry's Book of Hours (p. 400). Both are manuscript illuminations. Do they have anything else in common? How does the image of Joan compare with that of men and women in the Book of Hours? The Duke's book presents an idealized vision. Can the same be said of the portrait of Joan? How would you assess the purpose of each illustration?

4. The progress of the Renaissance is especially apparent in the three sculptures of David by three different artists: Donatello (c. 1430), Verrochio (1465), and Michelangelo (c. 1501–1504). Ask students to first briefly explain what the story of David and Goliath is all about. What is most important in the story? Next, have them describe Donatello's *David*. What is emphasized in his work? Then have students compare Verrochio's version of *David* to Donatello's. How are the statues similar? How do they differ? Finally, have students compare Michelangelo's *David* with the other two. What physical changes have taken place? How do those changes reflect the intellectual changes of the Renaissance? Students should understand that in the story, David overcomes the giant Goliath through inner, spiritual strength. This central idea is captured in Donatello's earlier version of *David*. Over time, however, the physical attributes of David came to equal his spiritual strength, until they are represented equally in Michelangelo's version. The physicality of Michelangelo's *David* is in itself a reflection of inner spirituality.

5. Ask students whom they would want to interview if they could travel back to the Renaissance. Ask them to explain their choice and elaborate on the questions they would like to ask their person. Or, whom would students like to be if they could travel back to the Renaissance? Again, ask them to explain their choice.

6. Renaissance paintings were often rich in symbolic references that most persons today would not notice or be able to interpret. Without reference to textbooks or the Internet, ask students to consider Jan van Eyck's *The Arnolfini Marriage*. Ask them to try and explain every single item in the painting, from the bed to the dog at their feet. Also ask students to explain the posture of the couple.

7. Ask students to choose the Renaissance artist they would most like to capture their likeness in a portrait. Which medium would they want their chosen artist to use? Which criteria did they use to select their artist? To get students to think beyond the most commonly known artists, exclude Michelangelo, Da Vinci, and Raphael.

Essay Questions

1. Ask students to write an essay or present a report answering the following question: If you were a wealthy merchant from Baghdad visiting Europe in 1385, what would be most noticeable and distinctive? Then, turn the scenario around: What would be most noticeable and distinctive to a wealthy European merchant visiting Baghdad or Córdoba? Students should discuss the physical world as well as attitudes.

2. Ask students to write an essay or present a report on the following question: If this chapter is about the collapse of medieval order, what "order" collapsed?

3. Ask students to read Christine de Pisan's *The Book of the City of Ladies*. What is her "defense" of medieval women? Based on that defense, how were women perceived by medieval society? Describe Pisan's ideal woman. Would she have been very much like a modern woman of today? Would Pisan be satisfied with what women have achieved today?

4. If Europe was such a backwater provincial area of the world in 1300, what changes enabled Europeans to begin to discover and then dominate much of the world by 1500?

5. The Renaissance is sometimes presented as an artistic movement that had little influence on the lives of most people in Europe. By 1500, however, the Renaissance impacted nearly everyone in Europe in some way. Explain why this was the case.

6. What were the roles of art and material goods during the Renaissance? The best book on the subject is Lisa Jardine, *Worldly Goods: A New History of the Renaissance* (New York: W. W. Norton, 1996).

Additional Resources: Literature

Brereton, Geoffrey, trans., *Jean Froissart: Chronicles.* 1979.

Bondanella, Julia Conaway and Peter Bondanella, trans., *Giorgi Vasari: The Lives of the Artists.* 1998.

Caponigri, A. Robert, trans., *Giovanni Pico della Mirandola: Oration on the Dignity of Man.* 1996.

Castiglione, Baldassare. *The Book of the Courtier.* 1528.

Connell, William J., trans., *The Prince by Niccolò Machiavelli with Related Documents.* 2005.

McWilliam, G. H., trans., *Giovanni Boccacio: The Decameron.* 2003.

Quillen, Carol, trans., *Petrarch's Secret.* 2003.

Additional Resources: Film and Video

The Return of Martin Guerre (1982; DVD, 123 min.). Gerard Depardieu stars in this film about a soldier who returns from war and assumes the identity of a fellow fighter. Based on a true event, it nicely captures peasant life in sixteenth-century France. The film is in French with English subtitles.

The Name of the Rose (1986; Jean-Jacques Annaud, dir.; with Sean Connery and Christian Slater). A medieval monk applies deductive reasoning to solve a series of murders within a monastery. The film is remarkably accurate in its details both large and small, but especially in its depiction of medieval tensions between faith and reason.

The Anchoress (1993; VHS/DVD, 91 min.). A young woman who commits herself to the life of an anchoress must deal with the conflicting influences and ambitions of the local priest, a local administrative officer, and her mother. The story is based on the letters of a fourteenth-century anchoress and care has been taken to re-create life in the countryside in medieval England.

Messenger: The Story of Joan of Arc (1999; DVD, 158 min.). A dark and somewhat speculative account of Joan of Arc, this film captures the dirt, grime, and extreme religiosity and intrigue of the period.

Joan of Arc (1999; DVD, 3 hrs.). This miniseries closely follows the traditional story of Joan of Arc. Careful attention has been paid to the minutiae of medieval life.

The Agony and the Ecstasy (1965; VHS, 140 min.). The painting of the Sistine Chapel's ceiling serves as the backdrop for the war of wills fought between Pope Julius II and Michelangelo in this lavish production.

Mad Love (2001; DVD, 118 min.) This is a lavish dramatization of the life of Juana la Loca, a daughter of Ferdinand of Aragon and Isabella of Castile, who became queen of Castile on her mother's death. She supposedly became unbalanced upon the death of her handsome and powerful husband, Philip the Fair of Burgundy, and was placed in confinement by her father, who assumed control of the Castilian crown. The storyline has been enhanced, but the main events are depicted accurately enough. Spanish with English and French subtitles.

Empires: The Medici: Godfathers of the Renaissance (2004; VHS/DVD, 4 hrs.). This excellent four-part series explores the Medici family's rise to power in

Florence. Special emphasis is placed on their artistic patronage, which contributed to the flourishing of the Renaissance.

OTHER BEDFORD/ST. MARTIN'S RESOURCES FOR CHAPTER 13

The following resources are available to accompany Chapter 13. Please refer to the Preface of this manual for detailed descriptions of all the ancillaries.

For Instructors

Transparencies

The following maps and images from Chapter 13 are available as full-color acetates.

- Map 13.1: The Hundred Years' War, 1337–1453
- Map 13.2: Ottoman Expansion in the Fourteenth and Fifteenth Centuries
- Mapping the West: Europe c. 1492
- Book of Hours, p. 400
- Joan of Arc, c. 1420, p. 392

Instructor's Resources CD-ROM

The following maps and image from Chapter 13, as well as a chapter outline, are available on disc in both PowerPoint and jpeg formats.

- Map 13.1: The Hundred Years' War, 1337–1453
- Map 13.2: Ottoman Expansion in the Fourteenth and Fifteenth Centuries
- Mapping the West: Europe c. 1492
- Book of Hours, p. 400

Using the Bedford Series with The Making of the West

Available in print as well as online at **bedfordstmartins.com/usingseries,** this guide offers practical suggestions for using John Aberth, *The Black Death: The Great Mortality of 1348–1350: A Brief History with Documents*; and Carol Quillen, Petrarch's *The Secret* in conjunction with chapters 13 and 14 of the textbook.

For Students

Study Guides

The Online Study Guide at **bedfordstmartins.com/hunt** helps students synthesize the material they have learned as well as practice the skills historians use to make sense of the past. The following Map, Visual, and Document activities are available for Chapter 13.

Map Activity

- Map 13.3: Europe c. 1492

Visual Activity

- Book of Hours, p. 400

Reading Historical Documents

- Wat Tyler's Rebellion (1381), p. 398
- Giovanni Pico della Mirandola, *Oration on the Dignity of Man*, p. 404
- Contrasting Views: Joan of Arc: Who Was "the Maid"? pp. 394–395

CHAPTER

14

Global Encounters and Religious Reforms

1492–1560

CHAPTER RESOURCES

Main Chapter Topics

1. The Portuguese were the first to undertake long-distance voyages of exploration. They rounded the Cape of Good Hope and settled forts along the African, Sri Lankan, and Indian coasts. Columbus persuaded the Spanish that a new route to India lay across the Atlantic. He discovered the Bahamas instead, and Spain began a long exploitation of the native population and sugarcane industry. Spain soon conquered the Aztecs, Incans, and Mayans, and took advantage of the precious metals found in Mexico and Bolivia. Other countries explored North America, but did not establish permanent communities there until the seventeenth century. The slave trade began to be concentrated in West Africa.

2. The established church was unable to meet the needs of individuals and society in the sixteenth century because of internal corruption. Focus on money, sale of indulgences, overemphasis on veneration of relics, nepotism, simony, and lack of clerical professionalism and integrity weakened the church at a time when socioeconomic and political changes caused a great demand for explanation and consolation.

3. Christian humanists believed that the corruption of the church and the ignorance of the people could be ameliorated through education. Men such as Desiderius Erasmus (c. 1466–1536) and Thomas More (1478–1535) encouraged reform within the Catholic church.

4. When Martin Luther (1483–1546) made public his complaints concerning the church in 1517, the church's hierarchy underestimated Luther as a mere discipline problem, whereas the people saw an opportunity to break free of Rome's monetary demands and other deficiencies.

5. Luther's break from the Catholic church encouraged other reformers to take stands on their beliefs, creating multiple strains of Protestantism, such as Calvinism and Anabaptism.

6. Frustration with the dire socioeconomic conditions common in the sixteenth century merged with the calls for church reform to produce social unrest, rebellion, and severe retaliation by the governments of Europe. Politics and religion became virtually inseparable as Catholic regimes faced Protestant opposition, secular leaders sought ways of controlling religion within their borders, and Catholic states clashed with Protestant ones.

Focus Question

Why did Christian unity break up in Europe just when Europeans began to expand their influence overseas in dramatic fashion?

1. The Reformation permanently fragmented western Christianity, and religious confrontations between Catholics and Protestants complicated political rivalries within and between states. Catholic leaders in France and the Holy Roman Empire faced challenges by Protestants, while the rulers of some states, most notably England, became Protestant and severed their countries' loyalty to the papacy.

2. The first western European kingdoms to expand overseas, Portugal and Spain, were motivated by the desire to expand Roman Catholic Christianity, as well as by other goals such as the pursuit of gold, personal glory, and the ambition to chart the unknown. New religious orders such as the Jesuits were a product of the Catholic renewal that is sometimes termed the Catholic Reformation or the Counter-Reformation. This order, founded by the Spaniard Ignatius of Loyola, became an important element in overseas territories, where Jesuits played a

central role in attempts to convert indigenous peoples in the Americas and Asia. While some missionaries, such as Jesuits in Brazil, brought a repressive and coercive message, other Catholics such as the Dominican Bartolomé de Las Casas were among the strongest voices to condemn the brutal aspects of colonialism, including slavery.

3. As the Europeans involved in overseas colonization expanded to include the English and the Dutch, they exported their own, Protestant varieties of Christianity, extending the divisions within Christendom around the globe. Monarchs enhanced the power of their states by claiming overseas colonies, enriching their treasuries through colonial trade, including slavery, and by asserting pre-eminent authority over religion within their countries and their empires. This pattern included both Protestant states such as England, where the monarch became "Defender of the Faith," and Catholic states such as France, where kings, not the papacy, dominated the Gallican church. Competition between states and empires was cultural as well as political because of the rivalry between Catholics and Protestants.

Annotated Chapter Outline

I. **Widening Horizons**

A. **Portuguese Explorations, pp. 420–421**

1. In 1433, Portugal began systematic exploration of the western coast of Africa.
2. Using technologies such as the lateen sail, new types of ships, better charts and instruments, and financed by the Portuguese monarchy, the explorers were motivated by a crusading zeal against Muslims and legend of a mysterious Christian kingdom established by Prester John.
3. The Portuguese hoped to bypass the Ottoman Turks' overland routes and reach the spice-producing lands of South and Southeast Asia.
4. In 1499, Vasco da Gama led a Portuguese fleet around the southern tip of Africa and reached Calicut, India, the center of the spice trade.
5. Returning to Lisbon, da Gama brought along Chinese porcelain, which sparked a porcelain mania and the import of more than 70 million pieces of porcelain, which still is called "china."
6. By 1517, a chain of Portuguese forts dotted the Indian Ocean, reaching from Mozambique to Malacca (modern Malaysia).

B. **The Voyages of Columbus, pp. 421–423**

1. Born in Genoa, Christopher Columbus (1451–1506) gained valuable experience serving in Portuguese voyages down the West African coast and then settled in Spain.
2. Inspired by *The Travels of Marco Polo,* Columbus proposed to sail west to find a new route to Asia's gold and spices.
3. Columbus found patrons in Isabella of Castile and Ferdinand of Aragon.
4. In August 1492, with three ships and about ninety men, Columbus set sail with a contract to assert Castilian sovereignty over any new land and peoples and to share any profits with the crown.
5. Reaching what is today the Bahamas, Columbus explored the Caribbean islands and encountered the peaceful Arawaks, who were impressed by the Europeans' military technology and their appearance.
6. Trusting natives notwithstanding, the Europeans' agenda was to find gold, subjugate the natives, and propagate Christianity.
7. Columbus's second voyage in 1493 found no gold mines or spices and switched to kidnapping slaves, who were exported to Spain.
8. The Spanish monarchs, eager for riches, sent officials and priests to the Americas (named after the Italian explorer Amerigo Vespucci).
9. Columbus's career illustrated the changing balance between the Mediterranean and the Atlantic.
10. After the voyages of Christopher Columbus, Portugal's interests clashed with those of Spain.
11. Mediated by Pope Alexander VI, the 1494 Treaty of Tordesillas divided the Atlantic world between the two monarchies, reserving the West African coast and the route to India for Portugal, and the oceans and lands to the west for Spain.
12. Unintentionally, this agreement also allowed Portugal to claim Brazil in 1500.

C. **A New Era in Slavery, pp. 423–425**

1. Although slavery had existed since antiquity, the European voyages of discovery expanded the economic scale of slave labor and attached race and color to slavery.

2. During the Renaissance, nearly all slaves arrived in the Mediterranean ports of Barcelona, Marseille, Venice, and Genoa.
3. Some were captured in war or piracy; others (black Africans) were sold by African and Bedouin traders to Christian buyers.
4. In western Asia, impoverished families sold children into slavery, and many in the Balkans became slaves following the devastation of the Ottoman invasions.
5. Slaves served as domestic servants in leading Mediterranean cities, as galley slaves in naval fleets, and as agricultural laborers.
6. In the Ottoman army, slaves even formed an important elite contingent.
7. After the Portuguese voyages, Africans increasingly filled the ranks of slaves. When traders exploited warfare in West Africa, the Portuguese trade in "pieces" (as slaves were called) drew criticism at home from some conscientious clergy.
8. However, slavery's critics could not deny the enormous profits brought in by the slave trade.
9. Most slaves worked in the sugar plantations in the Portuguese Atlantic islands and in Brazil.
10. Some worked as domestic servants in Portugal, where Africans constituted 3 percent of the population in the sixteenth century.
11. An institution of exploitation, slavery would truly begin to flourish in the Americas.

D. Conquering the New World, pp. 425–426

1. In 1500, the native peoples of the Americas were divided into many different societies, with the Aztec and Inca civilizations of the Mexican and Peruvian highlands being the most organized.
2. Spanish explorers Hernán Cortés (c. 1485–1547) and Francisco Pizarro (c. 1475–1541) organized gold-seeking expeditions from a base in the Caribbean.
3. With the assistance of native peoples who had been subjugated by the Aztecs, Cortés captured the Aztec capital of Tenochtitlán in 1519, adding Mexico (then called New Spain) to the Spanish empire of King Charles V.
4. In the south, Pizarro exploited civil war between Incan kings to seize the Peruvian highlands.
5. Spain's American empire extended from Mexico to Chile, making it the largest in the world at that time.
6. The Spaniards also subdued the Mayas on the Yucatan peninsula and discovered silver mines in what is today Bolivia.
7. Not to be outdone, other Europeans joined in the scramble for gold and riches.
8. The French began to search for a "northwest passage" to China and wanted to establish settlements in what would become Canada.
9. Because of harsh winters and native hostilities, however, permanent European settlements in Canada and the present-day United States would not succeed until the seventeenth century.
10. The discovery of the Americas initiated a huge global movement of people, animals, plants, manufactured goods, and precious metals.
11. This exchange between "worlds" also brought diseases from Europe that wiped out the indigenous populations of the Caribbean Islands within fifty years of Columbus's first landing.

II. The Protestant Reformation

A. The Invention of Printing, pp. 426–427

1. The invention of movable type allowed printers to produce books and pamphlets on a scale and at a cost never before possible.
2. Durable metal molds for each letter of the alphabet were set in a frame and used to cast multiple copies of a page when pressed against a sheet of paper.
3. Paper mills in Italy were producing paper that was much cheaper than parchment.
4. Movable type took bookmaking out of the hands of human copyists, allowing entire manuscripts to be printed with only a small amount of human labor.
5. In 1467, two German printers established the first press in Rome and produced 12,000 volumes in five years.
6. Frankfurt-am-Main in Germany became an international meeting place for printers and booksellers in the 1490s, attracting an elite audience.
7. One of the treasures to come out of this time was the Gutenberg Bible, of which only 185 were printed and which today can be found in only the greatest library collections.
8. Mechanical printing created a wider community of scholars, increasing the

speed at which knowledge could be transmitted and encouraging the free expression and exchange of ideas.
9. The advent of printing was so important that it brought about a communications revolution.
10. Its disruptive potential did not go unnoticed by political and religious authorities who quickly instituted censorship regulations.

B. Popular Piety and Christian Humanism, pp. 427–429

1. During this time, even though most people in Europe believed devoutly, the clergy seemed increasingly incapable of meeting the spiritual needs of the people.
2. In this environment, popular forms of piety took hold as urban merchants and artisans yearned for priests to preach edifying sermons, conscientiously administer the sacraments, and lead moral lives.
3. Through scholarship and social reform, Christian humanists sought to adapt the ethical ideals of classical antiquity to a Christian society.
4. Christian humanists such as Desiderius Erasmus (c. 1466–1536) and Thomas More (1478–1535) emphasized Christian piety as defining true virtue.
5. Erasmus used his sharp wit to criticize the corruption of the clergy and the bloody ambitions of the Christian princes.
6. Erasmus believed that education could reform individuals and society.
7. He dreamed of a unified, peaceful Christendom where learning would eclipse ignorance and charity, and good works would be valued over religious ceremonies devoid of meaning.
8. Erasmus wrote *Handbook of the Militant Christian* (1503) and *The Praise of Folly* (1509). In the latter work he satirized his contemporaries' love of power and wealth.
9. A man of peace, Erasmus chose Christian unity over division as the Reformation swept Europe.
10. He pleased neither the Protestants nor the Catholics entirely and ended his career isolated from both.
11. The Englishman Thomas More, to whom Erasmus dedicated *The Praise of Folly*, became Henry VIII's lord chancellor in 1529, but he retired in 1532 in protest of Henry VIII's break with the Roman Catholic Church and his control of the clergy.
12. More's best-known work, *Utopia* (1516), was inspired by the voyages of discovery.
13. Describing an imaginary land, the book was a critique of More's own society.
14. The inhabitants of Utopia are equally dedicated to hard work and education, and do not suffer from crime, starvation, or poverty.
15. More believed that politics, property, and war created human misery.

C. Martin Luther and the Holy Roman Empire, pp. 429–432

1. Martin Luther, a young German friar tormented by his own religious anxieties, triggered the first major religious reform.
2. After abandoning the law for a monastery, Luther found little consolation in the sacraments.
3. His sense of sinfulness and fear of damnation despite frequent penance deepened his unease with the church.
4. Sent to study theology, Luther experienced grace and insight into salvation, realizing that faith alone saved him from sin.
5. While he was working out his personal search for salvation, Luther became disgusted with a priest named Johann Tetzel who arrived in Wittenberg to sell indulgences—substitutes for the spiritual activities of prayer and pilgrimage—which Luther saw as a corrupt practice.
6. In 1517, Luther posted ninety-five theses—propositions for academic debate—that questioned the sale of indulgences and church offices.
7. Printed and spread rapidly, Luther's theses released a torrent of pent-up resentment among the laity, many of whom shared Luther's position.
8. In *Freedom of a Christian*, Luther distinguished between teachings from the Gospels and invented church doctrines and laws, arguing that faith could be developed "by Scripture alone."
9. He further argued that sinners were saved "by faith alone" rather than by good works.
10. Finally, he argued that a "priesthood of all believers" should replace professional clerics.
11. In *To the Nobility of the German Nation*, Luther appealed to nationalism, calling on

German princes to defend their nation from corrupt Italians in Rome.

12. In *On the Babylonian Captivity of the Church,* he condemned the papacy as the Antichrist.
13. The church misjudged Luther's influence when they ordered him to keep quiet.
14. In 1521, Luther defended his faith before Charles V (r. 1520–1558) at the Imperial Diet of Worms, but was spared from the potential consequences of his actions because he enjoyed the protection of Frederick the Wise, the elector of Saxony.
15. The early Reformation was essentially an urban movement, and anti-Roman evangelicals included German princes, city officials, professors, priests, and laypeople.

D. Huldrych Zwingli and John Calvin, pp. 432–433

1. In 1520, the chief preacher in Zurich, Huldrych Zwingli (1484–1531), openly declared himself a reformer and attacked the corruption of the ecclesiastical hierarchy and church rules such as fasting and clerical celibacy.
2. Under Zwingli's leadership, Zurich became the center of the Swiss reform movement.
3. Because Zwingli and Luther differed on some points of doctrine—most notably about the nature of the Eucharist—Zwingli developed a reform movement independent from that of Luther.
4. Luther believed that Christ was both truly and symbolically present in the bread and wine of this sacrament, whereas Zwingli believed that the Eucharist was only a symbol of Christ's union with believers.
5. Troubled by these theological differences, evangelical princes and magistrates assembled the major reformers at Marburg in central Germany in 1529.
6. Several days of intense discussions resolved some of the doctrinal differences, but Luther and Zwingli did not agree on the Eucharist; therefore, the German and Swiss movements continued along divergent paths.
7. John Calvin (1509–1564), a Frenchman who studied law, led another reform movement that took hold in France and Switzerland.
8. Influenced by the humanists, Calvin gradually abandoned the Catholic church.
9. The Reformation found many adherents in France, culminating in the Affair of the Placards in 1534 when church doors were posted with broadsheets denouncing the Mass.
10. This affair provoked a national crackdown on Protestants, and Calvin fled abroad.
11. He stopped in Geneva, which had renounced its allegiance to its Catholic bishop, and there took up leadership of the Genevan reform party.
12. After triumphing in 1541 over the old Genevan families who opposed his regime, Calvin made Geneva a tightly disciplined Christian republic.
13. Calvin's 1536 publication *The Institutes of the Christian Religion* made him the first reformer to organize reformist doctrines, organization, history, and practices in a logical and systematic way.
14. Calvin developed his own doctrine of predestination, according to which God had predestined every human to either salvation or damnation before the creation of the world.
15. Fusing society and church into a "Reformed church," Calvin created a theocracy in Geneva.
16. Intolerant of dissenters and advocating rigorous discipline, Calvin made Geneva the new center of the Reformation, the city in which missionaries trained and from which books of Calvinist doctrine were exported.
17. Calvin's ideas spread throughout much of Europe and even to New England, his "Reformed Church" becoming the prevailing form of Protestantism in many countries.

E. The Anglican Church in England, pp. 433–434

1. In England, the reform originated with the king rather than with men trained as clergy.
2. Despite a tradition of religious dissent in England dating back to Wycliff, Protestantism gained few adherents there in the 1520s.
3. King Henry VIII broke with the Roman Catholic Church and founded the Anglican Church.
4. Initially Henry had opposed the Reformation and had been granted the title "Defender of the Faith" by the pope.
5. Henry needed a male heir and wanted to marry Anne Boleyn. In order to do so, he sought to have his marriage to Catherine

of Aragon invalidated by the pope, but the pope refused.

6. As a result, Henry chose two Protestants for important positions—Thomas Cromwell as chancellor and Thomas Cranmer as archbishop of Canterbury.
7. Under their leadership, Parliament passed acts severing ties between the English church and Rome.
8. The Act of Supremacy of 1534 made Henry head of the Anglican church.
9. Other legislation recognized his marriage to Anne and invalidated claim to the throne by Mary, who was his daughter by Catherine.
10. The crown also confiscated and sold the property of monasteries.
11. Henry later divorced Anne, with whom he had a daughter, the future Elizabeth I. He married four more times and had one son, Edward.
12. By the time of Henry's death in 1547, the principle of royal supremacy in religious matters was firmly established in England.

III. Reshaping Society through Religion

A. Protestant Challenges to the Social Order, pp. 435–437

1. The message of Christian freedom proclaimed by Luther resonated with the oppressed, and popular demand pressured many local officials to appoint new clerics committed to reform.
2. In 1525, many peasants who resented the church's greed, led by former priest Thomas Muntzer, rebelled in a massive rural uprising in southern and central Germany that was brutally suppressed by the Catholic and Protestant princes.
3. Luther did not agree with Muntzer's mixing of religion and social protest, and so he sided with the princes and city officials who turned against the rebels.
4. By the end of the year, the princes and their armies had killed, injured, or imprisoned more than 100,000 rebels.
5. Because of its conservative political philosophy and dependence on the protection of the established political authority, the Lutheran church lost supporters in rural areas and became an increasingly urban phenomenon.
6. Emerging as champions of an orderly religious reform, many German princes who had suppressed the peasant revolt confronted Emperor Charles V, who supported Rome.
7. In 1529, Charles declared Catholicism the empire's only legitimate faith.
8. The Lutheran German princes protested and thus came to be called Protestants.
9. The fragmentation of the Holy Roman Empire increased as people supported their prince over the Catholic orthodoxy of the Emperor.
10. In Zurich, while Zwingli was challenging the Roman church, some laypeople secretly pursued their own religious path.
11. Believing that only adults possessed the reason and free will to choose Christ, these men and women believed that the baptizing of infants was invalid and called for the rebaptizing of adults; they came to be called Anabaptists, which literally means "rebaptizers."
12. Even though Zwingli condemned this movement, it spread quickly through southern Germany.
13. One group of Anabaptists seized control of the city of Münster in 1534, believing that the end of the world was near.
14. They abolished private property in imitation of the early Christian church and dissolved traditional marriages, allowing men to have multiple wives.
15. Besieged by a combined Protestant and Catholic army in 1535, the city fell and the leaders of the Anabaptists were killed.
16. Nonetheless, the Anabaptist movement survived in northwestern Europe under the Dutch reformer Menno Simons (1469–1561), whose followers were eventually called Mennonites.

B. New Forms of Discipline, pp. 437–438

1. A new urban, middle-class culture in Protestant Europe urged greater religious conformity and stricter moral behavior.
2. The Latin Bible—the Vulgate—was the only Bible authorized by the Catholic church.
3. As reformers turned to the Scriptures, vernacular translations of the Bible appeared, making it more accessible to the laity.
4. Bible reading became a common pastime within the family, especially in places where the Bible occupied a central place in the family's history.
5. Catholic German Bibles soon appeared, giving the Catholic laity access to the

scriptures, a sharp departure from medieval church practices.

6. Not all Catholic authorities welcomed translations: England's church hierarchy reacted swiftly against English-speaking Bibles and burned William Tyndale at the stake as a heretic for his translation.
7. The attitude against the English Bible changed when Henry VIII broke with Rome and adopted the Reformation.
8. Secular governments began to take over public charity in the early sixteenth century.
9. The new Protestant work ethic linked hard work and prosperity with piety and consequently equated laziness and poverty with a lack of moral worth.
10. The Reformation led to restructuring relief for the poor, with officials appointed by magistrates to head urban agencies that certified the genuine poor and distributed welfare funds.
11. Protestants championed the end of clerical celibacy and embraced marriage.
12. Protestants, in their quest for order and discipline in worship and in society, reaffirmed the ideal of the patriarchal family.
13. Common-law marriages were suppressed, marriages had to be registered by both a government official and clergy, and marriages required parental consent.
14. Early in the Reformation years, Protestant women attained greater marital equality than those of subsequent generations.

C. Catholic Renewal, pp. 438–440

1. Many Catholics had called for reform before Martin Luther, but the papacy had failed to respond.
2. Under Pope Paul III (r. 1534–1549), the Catholic church finally pursued reform, a movement sometimes called the Catholic Reformation.
3. Pope Paul III convened the Council of Trent, which met sporadically from 1545 to 1563 and reached conclusions that would revitalize Catholicism for the following two centuries.
4. The council reasserted clerical supremacy over the laity, required bishops to reside in their dioceses, and ordered the establishment of seminaries to train priests in each diocese.
5. The council also reaffirmed the doctrine of transubstantiation, that the bread of communion truly becomes the body of Christ, thus firmly rejecting the Protestant position on the Eucharist.
6. It stipulated that all weddings take place in a church and be registered with the clergy.
7. Finally, the council rejected the Protestants' permitting of divorce.
8. The council's proclamations made permanent the divisions between the Catholics and Protestants and ended all hope for reconciliation.
9. The Catholic Reformation also prompted the formation of new religious orders, the most important being the Society of Jesus (the Jesuits), who became the papacy's most vigorous defenders.
10. Established by a Spanish nobleman, Ignatius of Loyola (1491–1556), the order was recognized by the church in 1540.
11. Young men were attracted by Ignatius's austerity and piety and, by the time of Ignatius's death, Europe had more than one thousand Jesuits who established hundreds of colleges throughout Catholic Europe.
12. In addition, Jesuit missionaries would help spread Roman Catholicism to Africans, Asians, and Native Americans.
13. To win new souls to replace those lost to Protestantism, and to convince Catholics and Protestants that the Catholic church enjoyed divine favor, Catholic missionaries traveled throughout the globe.
14. Different missionaries, however, brought differing messages to indigenous peoples.
15. To some, Catholicism offered reason and faith; to others, it was a repressive and coercive alien religion.
16. Some missionaries converted indigenous populations by force, despite criticism.
17. After an initial period of relatively little discrimination, the Catholic church began to adopt strict rules biased by color in Spanish America.
18. In 1555, it forbade holy orders to Indians, mestizos (mixed European-Indians), mulattoes (mixed European-Africans), Muslims' descendants, and Jews.
19. The Portuguese, however, were more willing to train Africans and Asians as missionaries.
20. Under Portuguese protection, Jesuit missionaries preached the Gospel to elite Confucian scholars in China and to the samurai (the warrior aristocracy) in Japan.

21. Because European missionaries admired Chinese and Japanese civilizations, they relied on sermons rather than force to win converts.
22. The Jesuit Francis Xavier pioneered missionary work in India and Japan, paving the way for future missionary success in Asia.

IV. A Struggle for Mastery

A. The High Renaissance Court, pp. 441–442

1. A stabilizing center of the politics of dynasty and religion was the royal court, which was used to instill loyalty in nobles and awe in subjects.
2. The court was the royal household, which included a community of servants, noble attendants, officials, artists, and soldiers.
3. Court officials performed a myriad of other tasks.
4. Renaissance culture was promoted by the political elite.
5. The French court of Francis I (r. 1515–1547) became the largest in Europe, numbering 1,622 members, excluding nonofficial courtiers.
6. Courts were mobile at the time, and entourages of animals, people, furniture, and documents moved among a king's many palaces.
7. Hunting and other warlike recreations were a passion for the men of the court.
8. The literature of the time reveals much about this court culture.
9. Two writers, Ludovico Ariosto (1474–1533) and Baldassare Castiglione (1478–1529) composed works that glorified this extravagant court culture.
10. Ariosto's epic poem, *Orlando Furioso*, was modeled after Greek and Roman poetry and portrayed court culture as the highest synthesis of Christian and classical values; it tells a tale of combat and valor in the tradition of the medieval chivalric romance.
11. Castiglione's equally popular *The Courtier* represented court culture as a perfect synthesis of military virtues and literary and artistic cultivation.
12. In *The Courtier*, a man is defined by his refined language, dignified demeanor, and service to his prince and his lady.
13. Princes, on the other hand, could not always afford to be polite, but had to maintain a firm grip on power in order to benefit their subjects.

B. Dynastic Wars, pp. 442–444

1. French claims to Italian lands triggered wars between France and Spain for control of the continent.
2. Most battles between the Valois and Habsburgs were fought in Italy and the Low Countries.
3. The Italian Wars (1494–1559) between the French Valois dynasty, led by Francis I, and the Habsburg dynasty, led by Charles V, eventually involved most Christian monarchs and the Ottoman sultan.
4. The Italian states fought for their independence, the Protestant princes of Germany used the conflict as leverage to obtain privileges from the emperor, and the Ottoman Turks saw the conflict as an opportunity for territorial expansion.
5. Under Sultan Suleiman I "the Magnificent" (r. 1520–1566), the Ottoman Empire reached the height of its power, defeating Christian forces in Hungary and laying siege to Vienna.
6. Desperate to overcome the forces of Charles V, which had seized the French city of Nice and were campaigning to capture Tunis on the North African coast, Francis I formed an alliance with the Turks.
7. The alliance between a Christian king and the Muslim sultan shocked many Christians and, although it was brief, the alliance demonstrated that religion was but one of many factors in power politics.
8. In 1525, the Spanish at Pavia captured Francis I.
9. Francis was detained in Spain until he renounced his claims to Italy; but he immediately resumed making these claims when he returned to France.
10. In 1527, in retaliation for a papal alliance with France, Charles's troops, many of whom were German Protestant mercenaries, sacked Rome.
11. Protestants and Catholics alike saw this as a punishment from God, prompting the Catholic church to turn toward reform.
12. The Italian Wars dragged on through the 1540s, ending only when the French king, too bankrupt to keep fighting, acknowledged defeat by signing the Treaty of Cateau-Cambrésis in 1559.

C. Financing War, pp. 444–445

1. Western armies grew and armed themselves with new, more effective weapons.

2. This trend was costly, as were new defensive measures.
3. Because royal revenues could not keep up with war expenditures, the government devalued its coinage, which caused rapid inflation.
4. Charles V boasted the largest army in Europe, but was sinking ever deeper into debt, as was his opponent Francis I.
5. The European monarchs raised taxes, sold offices, and even confiscated property and goods to pay for their costly wars.
6. When these efforts proved insufficient, both the Valois and Habsburg monarchs looked to their leading bankers for loans, but these loans carried high interest rates.
7. The German Fugger Bank was the largest in sixteenth-century Europe.
8. Begun by Jakob Fugger (1459–1525), it built an international financial empire that helped make kings.
9. As personal banker to Charles's grandfather (Maximilian I) and the Habsburg dynasty, the Fugger family reaped handsome profits from the war.
10. In 1519, Fugger assembled a consortium to secure the election of Charles V as Holy Roman Emperor, tightening the alliance between the bank and the imperial office.
11. Between 1527 and 1547, the bank's assets more than doubled, the majority of which were loans to the Habsburgs.
12. Charles, however, barely managed to stay one step ahead of his creditors, and his successor in Spain eventually lost control of state finances.
13. The cycle of war and debt continued for years, draining the French and Spanish treasuries and forcing the monarchs to end sixty years of warfare with the Treaty of Cateau-Cambrésis in 1559.

D. Divided Realms, pp. 445–446

1. Throughout Europe, rulers viewed religious discord as a threat to the stability of their realms.
2. In France, the Calvinist movement grew steadily.
3. Francis I and his successor Henry II maintained a balance between the Catholics and Huguenots, but after 1560 France plunged into decades of savage religious wars.
4. English Protestants had been relatively few until the reign of Henry VIII (r. 1509–1547).
5. During the brief reigns of Edward VI (r. 1547–1553) and Mary (r. 1553–1558), official religious policies oscillated between Protestantism and Catholicism.
6. Under Elizabeth I, Anglicanism was restored and came to define the English nation.
7. In Scotland, as Protestantism gained adherents, powerful noble clans directly challenged the devoutly Catholic monarchy.
8. John Knox (1514–1572), a prominent Scottish reformer, published a diatribe against Mary Tudor and Mary of Guise of the ruling Tudor family who had allied themselves with France through Mary Tudor's marriage to Francis, heir to the French throne.
9. In 1560, the Protestants seized control of the Scottish parliament and queen regent Mary of Guise (d. 1560), a Catholic, fled to England.
10. Parliament installed Mary's infant son James as king and turned toward the Calvinist version of the Reformation, which would set up potential conflict with England and its Anglican Church.
11. In Germany in 1531, Protestant princes formed the Schmalkaldic League, which assailed the Catholic emperor Charles V, the bishops, and a few remaining Catholic princes.
12. In 1541, Charles convened the Imperial Diet at Regensburg, attempting to mediate between Protestants and Catholics, but negotiations broke down rapidly.
13. With French neutrality and papal support, Charles went to war with the Schmalkaldic League.
14. When Charles defeated the league in 1547 and captured the Lutheran princes, he restored Catholics' right to worship in Protestant lands while at the same time permitting Lutherans to keep their own rites.
15. Protestants opposed Charles's declaration, and the Protestant princes, now led by Duke Maurice of Saxony, once more raised arms against Charles and sent the surprised and bankrupt emperor fleeing to Italy where, in 1555, he agreed to the Peace of Augsburg.
16. The settlement recognized the Evangelical (Lutheran) church and allowed the German princes—whether Catholic or Protestant—to determine the religion for their lands.
17. The agreement omitted other groups, such as the Calvinists and Anabaptists, which would lead to conflict in the future.

18. An exhausted and disappointed Emperor Charles V resigned his many thrones, splitting the kingdom between his son Philip II and his brother Ferdinand, and retired to a monastery in southern Spain to seek salvation.

Lecture Strategies

1. Exploration can be approached in several ways. One effective method is to go review everything students already know about exploration and piece those facts together with a few that they may not be aware of to develop a picture of why Europeans began to explore. These additional issues include: the rediscovery of classical geography texts and world maps; the use of the printing press for dissemination of information; the impending and eventual fall of Constantinople to the Ottomans and the continual threat to the west by the Turks; the growth of capitalism; the rise of the middle class; the merging of Atlantic and Mediterranean ship technology; and the creation of a superpower through the marriage of Ferdinand and Isabella.

2. Why was Portugal the first nation in Europe to begin exploration? The answer is the same as the real-estate answer to why a house sells: location, location, location. Present all the relevant aspects of Portugal's location, such as its position far from the Ottoman Empire; close to the African coast; at the point of contact between the Mediterranean and Atlantic (convenient for the merger of the two technologies and navigational knowledge); next to larger, more powerful neighbors; and the way it juts out into the water like a peninsula.

3. Trace the relationship between religion and the state in Reformation-era Europe. Compare and contrast the motives of leaders such as the kings of France, Spain, and England and the princes of the Holy Roman Empire. What methods did they use to secure religious authority, and therefore political power, in their realms? Compare and contrast different experiences of the Reformation, such as England, where the monarch took the lead, and the Holy Roman Empire, where the actions of ordinary people were ultimately suppressed in the Peasants' War. Consider how the political resolution by the Peace of Augsburg of the religious wars in the Holy Roman Empire favored princes, rather than the people, and excluded non-Lutheran varieties of Protestantism. What does this suggest about the relative importance of power politics and religious freedom as the Reformation proceeded?

Class Discussion Starters

1. How could the Catholic church be forced to reform its ways from within? Could a reformation have taken place internally as had happened many times over the centuries of the church?

2. Discuss the differences in the Protestant beliefs, including views on communion and church governance. There are three different positions on communion: (a) the bread is the spiritual and physical body of Christ (Catholic and Lutheran beliefs); (b) the bread is the spiritual body of Christ (Calvinist belief); and (c) the bread is symbolic of the body of Christ (Anabaptist belief). Governance also has three different forms: (a) the clergy have the authority (Episcopal form); (b) an elected council has the authority (Presbyterian form); and (c) the entire membership holds the authority (Congregational form).

3. Why did the Protestant movement fracture into so many separate sects? Some of the fractures resulted from differing religious beliefs, such as those on communion, but regional and national differences also had an impact. Students might discuss how easy it is to find fault with the existing system, but how difficult it is to agree on a replacement.

4. Discuss the expansion of Europeans' knowledge of the world. Ask students to consider the two world maps depicted in the Seeing History feature on p. 424. Which of the voyages of exploration described in the text contributed the most to the changing understanding of world geography?

Reviewing the Text

Review Questions

1. Which European countries led the way in maritime exploration and what were their motives?
[model answer] *Portugal and Spain led the maritime explorations that took Europeans to what they came to call the Americas. They were motivated by a desire to discover new routes to expand trade activities and then by the prospect of new riches in trade goods and precious metals once new lands were discovered. The passionately Catholic Spaniards also added to these goals the desire to spread Christianity.*

2. How did Luther, Zwingli, Calvin, and Henry VIII challenge the Roman Catholic Church?
[model answer] *Luther, Zwingli, Calvin and Henry VIII challenged the authority of the church and in consequence church control over society. Luther placed the authority of religion in the words of the Bible rather than in the dictates of church officials, encouraging the faithful to read and interpret the word of God for themselves. He directly denounced the corruption he saw in the church hierarchy. Zwingli also attacked the corruption of church officials and the interpretation of aspects of doctrine. And Calvin, too, questioned fundamental Catholic teachings, and his doctrine of*

predestination eliminated the role of Catholic priests as agents of redemption. While the three clergymen questioned church doctrine, Henry VIII questioned the political authority of the church and severed ties with the Catholic church when the Pope refused to support his goals. At the heart of the matter was whether church or crown had ultimate authority in religious matters in England. Henry created the Anglican church to place the church under the political authority of the crown.

3. How did the forces for radical change unleashed by the Protestant Reformation interact with the urge for social order and stability?
[model answer] *The new religious ideas of Protestantism provided vehicles for the unrest and protest of the discontent in society, but also spoke of conformity and moral behavior. This resonated with desires for order and stability in society. Protestants fostered development of a new work ethic that encouraged discipline and promoted the family as a sacred institution and important source of order.*

4. How did religious divisions complicate the efforts of rulers to maintain political stability and build stronger states?
[model answer] *In a world where the authority of secular leaders and church leaders had long been entwined, linking religious values to state values, division in the church threatened to bring division in society. New religious ideas sometimes empowered local dissent and violent protest movements, threatening social order and control. Religious differences influenced loyalties and fostered factions, which also led to violence. Such religious conflict undermined stability in France for forty years. Similarly in England, Scotland, and Germany, religious politics were at the center of loyalty to the crown and the battles fought to secure it. Overall, as religious divisions challenged political authority and undermined unity, rulers fought to restore order to their societies.*

Making Connections

1. Why was Charles V ultimately unable to prevent religious division in his lands?
[model answer] *The Protestant princes who brought religious disunity to Charles V's lands controlled lands that were the chief source of the empire's wealth. Charles V's initial victories against them were undermined by lack of support from the Pope, who feared growing secular power, his debts from decades of war with France, and ultimately, by the traditions of independence that structured the states of Germany. The empire was never a highly centralized power, and local princes accustomed to certain freedoms in ruling their states fought back, forcing Charles to compromise and accept religious division.*

2. How did the different religious groups respond to the opportunity presented by the printing press?
[model answer] *The printing press provided a new weapon for religious reformers, such as Luther and Calvin. They printed copies of their writings and broadsides declaring their objections to Catholic practice to spread their ideas. The circulation of these copies enabled their words to travel much farther and faster than they otherwise would have. Protestants encouraged individual reading of the Bible, and the printing press made that possible as well and at a scale not previously known. The Bible appeared in Catholic and Protestant versions and in translations in common languages.*

Discussing the Documents

Questions from Online Study Guide with Model Answers

Columbus Describes His First Voyage (1493), p. 423

1. What personal motivations does Columbus describe in his interaction with the Native Americans he encountered?
[model answer] *Columbus was looking to the future and was motivated to establish a relationship with the people he encountered that would lead to their providing resources in great quantity. He refers to "such things as they possess in abundance" that Spain "greatly needed," and does not detail what the resources are, though he mentions that they have gold and cotton to trade. His motivations in the moment are to develop good relations and encourage the "Indians" to convert to Christianity in order to secure their loyalty and access to whatever valuable resources they possessed for Spain's monarchs.*

2. What possibilities for Europeans does Columbus describe in the lands he encountered?
[model answer] *He envisions that these new lands will become Christian and be willing to establish substantial trade relations with Spain. He implies that the islands contain significant quantities of resources that would be useful to the Spanish.*

Ordinances for Calvinist Churches (1547), p. 433

1. Judging from these regulations, what sorts of behavior were of greatest concern to the Calvinist leaders?
[model answer] *Calvinist leaders sought to eliminate sources of social disorder, such as drunkenness and partying (immoral songs and dances). They wished to suppress excessive profit making and gambling, both of which could contribute to individual debt, which in turn could also compromise social order. Concern for social order is also apparent in restrictions on times of worship;*

unsupervised worship could foster inappropriate ideas and beliefs. Blasphemy would have been a direct challenge to the authority of God and religion.

2. What insight do the regulations provide into the relationship between church and state in Geneva?
[model answer] *There does not appear to be a line between religious and secular behavior if the church can regulate behavior through the imposition of fines for violations, control interest rates and public entertainments, and punish drunkenness.*

Contrasting Views: Martin Luther: Holy Man or Heretic? p. 431

1. Why did Johannes Cochlaeus condemn Martin Luther? How did he construct a negative image of Luther?
[model answer] *Cochlaeus presented Luther as a rebel and troublemaker by associating him with radicals and a historical troublemaker. His negative image begins with the association with sin made in his choice of seven heads. The labels he chose also suggest anti-Catholic sentiments.*

2. Evaluate the visual representations of Luther as a godly man. Which one is more effective?
[model answer] *The effectiveness of the visual representations depends on the perspective of the viewer. From the present-day perspective, or perhaps that of a more educated individual in the sixteenth century, the association of Luther with the traditional symbols of sanctity in the woodcut "Luther as a Monk" is a more positive image. The representation of Luther and Leviathan, however, might hold more emotional power and dramatic appeal to a less literate peasant of the sixteenth century whose world view still included elements of superstition and who would be drawn to the powerful imagery.*

Other Questions for Discussing These Documents in Class

Columbus Describes His First Voyage (1493), p. 423

1. How does Columbus view the Indians? How does he assess his own conduct toward them?
2. What do you make of Columbus taking some Indians by force in order for them to learn his language? Why was it not an equal priority for the Europeans to learn the Indians' language?
3. What can you glean from Columbus's account about how the Indians might have regarded the Spaniards?

Ordinances for Calvinist Churches (1547), p. 433

1. What do the activities regulated by the ordinances have in common?
2. Based on these regulations, would you expect Geneva to be a particularly unruly or a particularly strict community?

Contrasting Views: Martin Luther: Holy Man or Heretic? p. 431

1. What reasons would the artists have for focusing on Martin Luther rather than on the movement he started?
2. Which of the three images is the easiest to interpret, and why?

Comparative Questions

1. Based on these documents and images, how would you describe the role of religion in the late fifteenth and sixteenth centuries?
2. Considering Columbus's first voyage and the Geneva ordinances, how would you assess the relationship between religion and politics in this period?

For Users of *Sources of The Making of the West*

The following documents are available in Chapter 14 of the companion sourcebook by Katharine J. Lualdi, University of Southern Maine.

1. Worlds Collide: Bernal Díaz del Castillo, *The True History of the Conquest of New Spain* (c. 1567)
2. Illustrating a Native Perspective: *Lienzo de Tlaxcala* (c. 1560)
3. Defending Native Humanity: Bartolomé de Las Casas, *In Defense of the Indians* (c. 1548–1550)
4. Scripture and Salvation: Martin Luther, *Freedom of a Christian* (1520)
5. Reforming Christianity: John Calvin, *Articles Concerning Predestination* and *The Necessity of Reforming the Church* (c. 1560 and 1543)

Discussion Ideas for Sources of The Making of the West, *Chapter 14*

1. The Europeans came as conquerors to the New World. What evidence of this motivation does Bernal Díaz del Castillo provide in his account of the Spaniards' arrival at the Aztec capital of Tenochtitlán? How would you characterize the interaction between the Aztec leader Moctezuma and the leader of the Spanish expedition, Hernan Cortés? In what ways did Cortés signal his belief in his superiority? What role

did religion play in the exchange between the two men? Although Díaz provides a critical perspective on Cortés, in what ways is his ability to present an entirely objective account of the encounter limited?

2. The ideas of Martin Luther had radical implications for politics as well as religion. Which aspects of his *Freedom of a Christian* challenge Catholic authority? What does Luther mean by freedom? Did he advocate political freedom? If so, why did he eventually condemn the Peasants' Revolt described in *The Making of the West* chapter? How does Luther's Protestant vision of Christianity's basic elements compare with that of Catholicism as expressed by Hernan Cortés in Díaz's work?

Working with Visual Sources

For this exercise, please refer to Albrecht Dürer, *The Knight, Death, and the Devil* on p. 428 of the textbook or view the image on the book companion site's Online Study Guide under the "Visual Activity" for Chapter 14.

Students viewing the image at the Online Study Guide are asked three questions about the image. The questions and model answers (not made available to students) are below. Project this image, available on the Instructor's Resources CD-ROM, in class or ask students to look at the image in their textbooks and answer the questions.

1. What does this engraving depict?
[model answer] *The engraving shows an armor-clad, solemn-faced knight riding on horseback through a desolate forest; in the background rises a castle, or perhaps a cathedral. A dog accompanies him, his horse's stride is steady and majestic, and he is armed with a mighty lance and a fearsome sword; he seems a formidable opponent. But even so, he is confronted by a devil wielding a pike and a second, mounted demonic figure holding an hourglass.*

2. Which figure in this illustration is meant to represent death?
[model answer] *The demonic figure on horseback with the hourglass is meant to represent death. The shifting sands of the hourglass symbolize the passage of time. Traditionally, death comes to an individual when his or her "sands of time" run out.*

3. How might this engraving support Erasmus's argument that greed and the lust for power served as obstacles to true religious faith?
[model answer] *Regardless of the religious conflicts caused by the Reformation, all Christians believed that the reward for true religious faith and a righteous Christian life was the everlasting salvation of heaven. If the knight were interpreted as a pious and devoted Christian traveling through the desolate and dangerous wasteland that is life, beset by demons of worldly temptation and always facing the inevitability of his own death, then the castle in the background might be construed as eternal salvation, the knight's ultimate destination. To stay true to his goal and not be unnecessarily waylaid in his journey toward salvation, the knight must not be distracted by temptations confronting him along the way because they are only obstacles to his attaining true religious faith and, therefore, salvation.*

For this exercise, please refer to Seeing History: Expanding Geographic Knowledge: World Maps in an Age of Exploration on p. 424 of the textbook or view the images on the book companion site's Online Study Guide under the "Visual Activity: Seeing History" for Chapter 14.

Students viewing the images at the Online Study Guide are asked two questions about the images. The questions and model answers (not made available to students) are below. Project these images, available on the Instructor's Resources CD-ROM, in class or ask students to look at the images in their textbooks and answer the questions.

1. Which sections of the maps are most detailed and accurate?
[model answer] *The most detailed and accurate sections are those about which Europeans had the most extensive first-hand knowledge, namely Europe, the Mediterranean, and the west coast of Africa. Because the Europeans had not yet sailed into the Indian Ocean or across the Atlantic, they did not have an accurate understanding of the geography of those regions.*

2. Although it differs considerably from modern depictions of the age of exploration, why is Martellus's map useful to historians?
[model answer] *Precisely because Martellus's depictions of the Americas and the Indian Ocean are inaccurate, they provide evidence that Europeans had not explored these areas. The map is also a good source of western attitudes and assumptions about world geography prior to the late fifteenth- and sixteenth-century voyages of discovery. Martellus helps to explain why Columbus and Magellan set out on westward voyages in anticipation of reaching Asia.*

Mapping Exercises

Map Activity from Online Study Guide—Model Answers for Map Activity #2

For this activity, please refer to Mapping the West: Reformation Europe, c. 1560 on p. 447. Students are asked these questions:

Which countries were affected by the Protestant Reformation c. 1560 and which were not?
[model answer] *England, Scotland, Norway, Sweden, and Denmark were predominantly Protestant by 1560 as were much of the northeastern part of the Holy Roman Empire and the northern part of the Swiss Confederation. Protestantism was also growing in Poland and parts of Hungary, and had made inroads into Bohemia. Spain and the Italian states were untouched by the Protestant Reformation as was much of the southern and central region of the Holy Roman Empire. Most of France was also unaffected, although large parts of the south and east were influenced by Calvinism.*

Judging from the map, which other areas of Europe do you believe had the potential for conflict over the question of religion?
[model answer] *England, although mostly Anglican, contained scattered pockets where Calvinist influences were strong and it was also bordered by largely Catholic Ireland. Likewise, although France was mostly Catholic, large areas, especially in the south, were strongly influenced by Calvinism, making a future struggle over religion likely. Finally, eastern Europe possessed a large mixed area; inhabitants of Austria, Hungary, Poland, Bohemia, and Lithuania could suffer religious strife as demographics shifted and established authorities exerted more spiritual control.*

Map 14.1: Early Voyages of World Exploration, p. 422

Ask students to identify the principal routes of the voyages of discovery and speculate as to why the first expeditions were along the west coast of Africa while later ones concentrated on sailing westward across the Atlantic.

Map 14.2: Spanish and Portuguese Colonies in the Americas, 1492–1560, p. 425

How did the fact that the Europeans arrived by sea influence their choice of territories to colonize? How did the Treaty of Tordesillas influence the colonization of South America?

Map 14.3: The Peasants' War of 1525, p. 435

Ask students to locate the centers of the uprising. How involved were cities in the revolt? What factors might explain the role of cities in what has been characterized as a peasants' rebellion?

Map 14.4: Habsburg-Valois-Ottoman Wars, 1494–1559, p. 442

How did the relative geographical locations of Spain, France, the Holy Roman Empire, and the Ottoman Empire influence the motivations behind the conflict and the areas in which it was fought?

Mapping the West: Reformation Europe, c. 1560, p. 447

Why did the spread of Protestantism dissipate by 1560? How did the existing balance affect politics? How did politics affect the religious balance?

In-Class Assignments and Presentation Topics

1. Why did Europeans begin to explore in the fifteenth century rather than in the fourteenth century? Include technological, economic, and political motivations.
2. How did the invention of the printing press affect religion, politics, university study, humanism, and overall knowledge? Which occupations were most affected by the printing press? Least affected?
3. Assign some students to read David Herlihy, *Women, Family and Society in Medieval Europe* (New York: Berghahn Books, 1995); and have other students read Roland Bainton, *Women of the Reformation in Germany and Italy* (Boston: Beacon, 1974). Then ask students to make presentations on the roles of women in the periods.
4. William J. Bouwsma, *John Calvin: A Sixteenth-Century Portrait* (Oxford: Oxford University Press, 1988) makes a strong case for Calvin as a person torn between the Middle Ages and the modern era. Students examining this topic can better understand the dramatic changes that were taking place.
5. Assign to small groups of students different Christian denominations, such as Catholic, Lutheran, Calvinist, Anabaptist, or Anglican. Ask each group to present the major principles on which their assigned religion is based and to argue why that religion is the correct or best religion.
6. Discuss with the class or ask students to write about which came first: the Protestant Reformation or the Catholic Reformation. As they examine this question, they should see that the early Protestant reformers were originally Catholic reformers. Additionally, you might ask students to explain why the Catholic church did not reform until after the 1550s, and why it did so at that time.

Essay Questions

1. Ask students to write an essay answering the following question: If an explorer traveled to South

America (or to India) in the fifteenth century, what differences would be most noticeable between the new land and Europe? Students should include in their essay the differences in geography, plant and animal life, and human society, as well as all inanimate objects, such as clothing, houses, farming, industry, and political structures.

2. Have students write an essay on whether and how the Reformation did or did not improve the lives of Europeans. Richard Marius, *Martin Luther: The Christian Between God and Death* (Cambridge, MA: Belknap, 1999) is a good starting point. Marius believes that Luther's Reformation caused terrible devastation that might have been avoided.

3. Assign an essay on whether the Reformation was more medieval or Renaissance. In some ways, the Reformation was medieval, such as in its total reliance on God and God's power to save one's soul, while in other ways the Reformation was Renaissance, such as in its emphasis on education and the power of education to change people's lives. Start by having the class read William J. Bouwsma, *John Calvin: A Sixteenth-Century Portrait* (Oxford: Oxford University Press, 1988).

4. Have students write an essay on how the Reformation affected women in Europe. The following will help students with this assignment: Olwen Hufton, *The Prospect Before Her: A History of Women in Western Europe* (New York: Alfred A. Knopf, 1998); and Elisja Schulte van Kessel, "Virgins and Mothers Between Heaven and Earth," in Natalie Zemon Davis and Arlette Farge, eds., *A History of Women in the West*, vol. 3, *Renaissance and Enlightenment Paradoxes* (Cambridge, MA: Belknap, 1993). Hufton makes a case for the continued opportunities in convents, while van Kessel makes an equally strong case for the deterioration of opportunities for women in Reformation Europe.

5. Assign students an essay in which they support or oppose a move to call the first half of the sixteenth century the "Age of Charles V." Have students begin by reading Roland Bainton, *The Reformation of the Sixteenth Century* (Boston: Beacon Press, 1952 [rpt. 1985]); W. S. Maltby, *Reign of Charles V* (New York: Palgrave Macmillan, 2002); W. P. Blockmans and P. Blockmans, trans., *Emperor Charles V* (Oxford: Oxford University Press, 2002); and I. van den Hoven-Vardon, *Renaissance Monarchy: The Reigns of Henry VIII, Francis I, and Charles V* (Oxford: Oxford University Press, 2002).

6. England's Reformation was different from Europe's Reformation because it was sparked by Henry VIII's desire for a divorce and his need for a male heir. Ask students to write an essay in which they examine the degree to which the English Reformation was a government-led movement. Begin by looking at J. J. Scarisbrick, *The Reformation of the English People* (Oxford: Blackwell, 1984 [rpt. 1985]); C. Haigh, ed., *The English Reformation Revised* (Cambridge, UK: Cambridge University Press, 1987); D. MacCulloch, *Suffolk and the Tudors: Politics and Religion in an English County 1500–1600* (Oxford: Oxford University Press, 1986); and M. C. McClendon, *The Quiet Reformation* (Stanford: Stanford University Press, 1999).

Additional Resources: Literature

Bull, George, trans., *Conte Castiglione Baldassare: The Book of the Courtier*. 1976.

Dolan, John P., ed., *The Essential Erasmus*. 1964.

Sacks, David Harris, ed., *Utopia by Sir Thomas More*. 1999.

Waldman, Guido, trans., *Ludovico Ariosto: Orlando Furioso*. 1999.

Additional Resources: Film and Video

A Man for All Seasons (1999; Fred Zinnermann, dir.; with Paul Scofield and Robert Shaw, 120 min.). Although it captures the setting of the English Tudor period well, this film romanticizes Sir Thomas More and the events of the last years of his life.

Anne of a Thousand Days (1969; Charles Jarrott, dir.; with Richard Burton and Genevieve Bujold). This film, rich in atmospheric detail, traces the stormy relationship between King Henry VIII and his second wife, Anne Boleyn.

1492: Conquest of Paradise (1992; VHS, 145 min.). This film is a largely accurate retelling of Christopher Columbus's discovery of the New World.

Lady Jane (1985; Trevor Nunn, dir.; with Helena Bonham Carter). This film nicely captures the feel of the English Tudor period. Some events are accurately depicted, such as the physical beatings to which Jane Grey was subjected, but the love story between Jane and her husband (John Dudley) and their sympathy for the poor are pure fantasy.

Luther (2003; Eric Till, dir.; with Joseph Fiennes, 121 min.). This film is about Martin Luther and the Protestant Reformation. Although events are confused chronologically, the film does capture the atmosphere of the period.

The Six Wives of Henry VIII (1970; VHS/DVD, approx. 9 hrs.). Each 90-minute episode takes as its subject one of Henry VIII's six wives. Although some of the material is dated in places—especially the sixth episode on Katherine Parr—this series remains the best film drama to date of Henry VIII and his wives. The costumes of the main characters have been carefully researched and accurately reproduced.

OTHER BEDFORD/ST. MARTIN'S RESOURCES FOR CHAPTER 14

The following resources are available to accompany Chapter 14. Please refer to the Preface of this manual for detailed descriptions of all the ancillaries.

For Instructors

Transparencies

The following maps and images from Chapter 14 are available as full-color acetates.

- Map 14.1: Early Voyages of World Exploration
- Map 14.2: Spanish and Portuguese Colonies in the Americas, 1492–1560
- Map 14.3: The Peasants' War of 1525
- Map 14.4: Habsburg-Valois-Ottoman Wars, 1494–1559
- Mapping the West: Reformation Europe, c. 1560
- Albrecht Dürer, *The Knight, Death, and the Devil*, p. 428
- Luther as Monk, p. 431

Instructor's Resources CD-ROM

The following maps and image from Chapter 14, as well as a chapter outline, are available on disc in both PowerPoint and jpeg formats.

- Map 14.1: Early Voyages of World Exploration
- Map 14.2: Spanish and Portuguese Colonies in the Americas, 1492–1560
- Map 14.3: The Peasants' War of 1525
- Map 14.4: Habsburg-Valois-Ottoman Wars, 1494–1559
- Mapping the West: Reformation Europe, c. 1560
- Albrecht Dürer, *The Knight, Death, and the Devil*, p. 428

Using the Bedford Series with The Making of the West

Available in print as well as online at **bedfordstmartins.com/usingseries**, this guide offers practical suggestions for using *Utopia by Sir Thomas More*, edited with an introduction by David Harris Sacks; *The Prince*, by Niccolò Machiavelli, edited by William J. Connell; *Christopher Columbus and the Enterprise of the Indies*, edited by Geoffrey Symcox and Blair Sullivan; *Victors and Vanquished: Spanish and Nahua Views of the Conquest of Mexico*, edited with an introduction by Stuart B. Schwartz, in conjunction with Chapter 14 of the textbook; and *The Trial of Mary Queen of Scots: A Brief History with Documents* by Jayne Elizabeth Lewis in conjunction with chapters 14 and 15 of the textbook.

For Students

Study Guides

The Online Study Guide at **bedfordstmartins.com/hunt** helps students synthesize the material they have learned as well as practice the skills historians use to make sense of the past. The following Map, Visual, and Document activities are available for Chapter 14.

Map Activity

- Mapping the West: Reformation Europe, c. 1560

Visual Activity

- Albrecht Dürer, *The Knight, Death, and the Devil*, p. 428
- World Map by Henricus Martellus, 1489, p. 424
- World Map by Abraham Ortelius, 1570, p. 424

Reading Historical Documents

- Columbus Describes His First Voyage (1493), p. 423
- Ordinances for Calvinist Churches (1547), p. 433
- Contrasting Views: Martin Luther: Holy Man or Heretic? p. 431

CHAPTER

15

Wars of Religion and the Clash of Worldviews

1560–1648

Chapter Resources

Main Chapter Topics

1. The Peace of Augsburg (1555) officially recognized Lutheranism within the Holy Roman Empire but did not recognize Calvinism. Nonetheless, Calvinism expanded rapidly after 1560, not only altering the religious balance of power in Europe, but also producing political repercussions—including civil war and revolt—in the Netherlands, France, Scotland, and other parts of Europe.

2. Philip II of Spain, the most powerful monarch of his time, did not succeed in his quest to restore Catholic unity in Europe nor in his efforts to destroy political enemies in France, the Netherlands, and England. England and the Netherlands emerged from the conflict as great European powers in economic and military terms.

3. The Thirty Years' War, the last and most deadly of the wars of religion, began in 1618. By its end in 1648, much of central Europe lay in ruins and the balance of power had shifted away from the Habsburgs—the monarchs of Spain and Austria—toward France, England, and the Dutch Republic. The war's large armies necessitated bureaucracy and powerful centralized states.

4. The Thirty Years' War exacerbated the economic crisis already under way in Europe. Famine and disease also contributed to the suffering. The war shifted the economic balance of power; as the war ended, northwestern Europe began to dominate international trade, but the Spanish and Portuguese retained preeminence in the New World.

5. Even as religious wars raged, thinkers posited nonreligious theories of political authority and scientific explanations for natural phenomena. In this revolution, the Dutch Republic, England, and, to a lesser extent, France led the way. Nevertheless, many still believed in magic and witchcraft and accepted supernatural explanations for natural phenomena.

6. The scientific revolution overturned the theories of Ptolemy and Aristotle, which had passed unquestioned for centuries. More important, however, was the early-seventeenth-century insistence on deductive and inductive scientific investigation that created the basis for rapid expansion of knowledge.

Focus Question

What were the long-term political, economic, and intellectual consequences of the conflicts over religious beliefs?

1. The Thirty Years' War devastated central Europe where it was fought, and permanently altered European politics, contributing to the shift in power from southern and eastern Europe toward the northwest. The conflict was the bloodiest, but also the last, of the wars of religion in Europe. Its resolution by the Peace of Westphalia inaugurated a new diplomatic pattern whereby wars were settled by meetings involving all the combatants, a practice that has continued to the present. The outcome of the war also altered the political balance of power as the Holy Roman Empire declined relative to France, which surpassed Spain to become the strongest state in continental Europe; and Sweden emerged as the dominant state in northern Europe. Meanwhile, the English benefited from having stayed out of the war, avoiding its expense and destruction.

2. The crisis precipitated by the wars of religion, the climatic change produced by the Little Ice Age, and the economic recession of the early seventeenth century prompted some Europeans to seek new, nonreligious sources of authority. The development of

new ideas in the arts, politics, and philosophy led to the creation of a secular worldview based upon new scientific methods of research and reasoning. For example, Henry IV brought the French wars of religion to an end by placing the order and security of the state above matters of faith. In so doing, his actions were justified by the writings of Jean Bodin, who advocated strong monarchical power as the best means of maintaining order. In the arts, theater flourished, as exemplified by the works of William Shakespeare, which reflected timely concerns over the nature of power and the crisis of authority. Mannerism and the baroque, as well as opera, also possessed a new, theatrical style that emphasized emotion. In the natural sciences, empiricism, heliocentrism, and the grand synthesis of the laws of movement developed by Isaac Newton offered a new, rational vision of the universe that did not depend upon faith in God.

3. Despite the breakthroughs in secular thinking, European culture and society remained complex and sometimes contradictory. Leading scientists also practiced alchemy and astrology, and a witch craze swept across Europe, targeting the most vulnerable and marginal women in society. Inequality, oppression, and persecution persisted and even expanded in certain areas. Religious authorities, notably the Catholic church, opposed the new scientific thinking and brought men such as Galileo Galilei before the Inquisition. Slavery expanded in the colonies of the New World, and serfdom intensified in eastern Europe, most notably in Muscovy. This accelerated the divergence in the experiences of eastern and western Europeans, a pattern that would last through the twentieth century.

Annotated Chapter Outline

I. Religious Conflicts Threaten State Power, 1560–1618

A. French Wars of Religion, 1562–1598, pp. 452–455

1. Following the Peace of Augsburg in 1555 Calvinism began to make inroads into France, where noble converts provided military protection for the newly established Huguenot church.
2. The situation became volatile after King Henry II was accidentally killed in a jousting match in 1559, leaving the throne to his fifteen-year-old son Francis.
3. Francis died soon after and ten-year-old Charles IX became king with his Florentine mother Catherine de Medici as regent.
4. In 1562, a series of wars began in which two factions—the Catholics, led by the Guise family, and the Protestant Huguenots, led by the Bourbon family—struggled for control and influence over the French throne tenuously held by the Catholic Valois family.
5. Catherine sought to play the Guise and Bourbon families against each other, but tensions continued, coming to a head in August 1572. In a wave of violence known as the St. Bartholomew's Day Massacre, three thousand Huguenots were murdered in Paris, and ten thousand died in the provinces in the six weeks that followed.
6. This persecution led Huguenots to justify resistance by claiming that the Valois had violated a contract between ruler and ruled—an argument based on constitutionalism.
7. The wars did not end until Henry of Navarre, head of the Bourbon faction, became king of France in 1589.
8. To put an end to the fighting, Henry IV, as he was now known, converted to Catholicism and issued the Edict of Nantes, which allowed the Huguenots to worship freely in specified towns and maintain their own troops, fortresses, and courts.
9. Henry IV reestablished monarchical authority by creating a new bureaucracy staffed by members of a new social elite, the "nobility of the robe," meant to act as a counterweight to the ancient nobility.
10. Henry IV was assassinated in 1610.

B. Challenges to Spain's Authority, pp. 455–458

1. At the time of his accession, Philip II of Spain (r. 1556–1598) controlled the western Habsburg lands in Spain and the Netherlands as well as the Spanish colonies in the Americas, making him the most powerful ruler in Europe.
2. He made it his mission in life to restore Catholic unity to Europe and drive back the Muslims.
3. In 1571, Philip defeated the Ottoman Turks in the Battle of Lepanto, which gave him control of the Mediterranean.
4. He also expelled the Moriscos, converts to Catholicism who practiced Islam in secret and rebelled when they lost hope of Turkish assistance.

5. When Calvinists in the Netherlands attacked Catholic churches in 1566, Philip sent an army that sacked Antwerp in 1576, an atrocity known as the Spanish Fury.
6. The Spanish Fury so shocked the largely Catholic southern provinces that they joined forces with the largely Protestant northern provinces to expel the Spanish.
7. Whereas the southern provinces eventually returned to Spain, the northern provinces became the Dutch Republic, a federation controlled by the wealthiest families of each province.
8. The economy of the Dutch Republic—based on shipping, commerce, and manufacturing—prospered, and Amsterdam became the main European money market for two centuries.
9. The Dutch Republic tolerated religious diversity and became a haven for persecuted peoples, such as Jews who had been expelled from Spain and who helped to make the republic a leading intellectual and scientific center in the seventeenth and eighteenth centuries.

C. Elizabeth I's Defense of English Protestantism, pp. 458–459

1. When Elizabeth I (r. 1558–1603) succeeded her Catholic sister Mary as queen of England, she brought Protestantism back to England but refused to bow to Calvinist Puritans who wanted all traces of Catholicism removed from the ritual and governance of the Church of England.
2. Puritans, who were strict Calvinists, gained influence in English society and tried to have theaters and Sunday fairs closed down.
3. In addition to internal tensions, Elizabeth faced foreign intrigues.
4. In 1588, she beheaded her Catholic cousin, Mary, Queen of Scots, who was next in line for the English throne, when Mary offered Philip II of Spain her right to the Scottish throne.
5. Frustrated for political and religious reasons, Philip sent his armada into the English Channel in 1588 to fight the English navy.
6. When the Spanish Armada was virtually wiped out by the English navy, Spain suffered a severe psychological blow.
7. Triumphant, Elizabeth I consolidated her control as queen and left her successor, James I (r. 1603–1625), king of Scotland and England, a kingdom of expanding international importance.

D. The Clash of Faiths and Empires in Eastern Europe, pp. 459–460

1. The Battle of Lepanto was a setback for the Ottoman Turks but only a temporary one.
2. Two years later—in 1573—they seized the island of Cyprus from the Venetians.
3. The Ottoman Empire controlled the Balkans, where they allowed Orthodox Christians and Jews to practice their religions rather than forcing them to convert to Islam.
4. Both Christians and Jews therefore had no reason to rebel.
5. Orthodox Christians were also officially protected in Russian lands by the Muscovite tsars.
6. Tsar Ivan IV (r. 1533–1584), named "the Terrible" for his ruthlessness, cruelty, and unpredictable fits of rage, brought the entire Volga valley under his control, expanded eastward into Siberia, and attempted to seize lands in the west to gain access to the Baltic Sea.
7. Ivan's drive west was blocked by Sweden and Poland-Lithuania.
8. Poland-Lithuania maintained peace between the Catholic majority and Protestant nobles because its monarch had limited powers and was required to practice religious toleration.
9. During the chaotic Time of Troubles that followed Ivan's death, the king of Poland-Lithuania tried to seize the Russian throne for his son, but was defeated in 1613.
10. A Russian nobleman, Michael Romanov (r. 1613–1645) established a new dynasty that resumed state building.

II. The Thirty Years' War, 1618–1648

A. Origins and Course of the War, pp. 460–462

1. The fighting that devastated central Europe had its origins in a combination of political weakness, ethnic competition, and religious conflict.
2. In 1617, Catholic Habsburg heir Archduke Ferdinand became king of Bohemia and curtailed Protestants' religious freedom.
3. The Czechs, the region's largest ethnic group, began an anti-Habsburg, anti-Catholic resistance, called the "defenestration of Prague."
4. When the unpopular king was elected emperor of the Holy Roman Empire

(as Ferdinand II, r. 1619–1637), the Bohemian resistance deposed him and chose a new Calvinist king.
5. Imperial armies defeated the Czechs at the Battle of White Mountain.
6. Ferdinand bought the services of Albrecht von Wallenstein (a Protestant Czech) to raise a mercenary army that plundered much of Protestant Germany with the emperor's approval.
7. In response to Wallenstein, King Christian IV of Denmark (r. 1596–1648) invaded northern Germany to protect Protestants and to extend his own influence.
8. Wallenstein defeated Christian IV, giving Ferdinand II reign over Denmark and the Protestants there.
9. Ferdinand II issued the Edict of Restitution in 1629, which outlawed Calvinism in the empire and reclaimed Catholic church property confiscated by Lutherans.
10. King Gustavus Adolphus of Sweden entered the war to protect Protestant interests (and Sweden's trade in northern Europe).
11. Catholic France subsidized Sweden, glad to help any enemy of the Habsburgs.
12. Gustavus Adolphus triumphed and occupied the Catholic parts of southern Germany until his death in 1632 when he was killed at the battle of Lützen.
13. In 1635, France entered the conflict openly by declaring war on Spain.
14. Religion took a back seat as Catholic France and Catholic Spain fought for dominance of Europe.
15. By the early 1640s, exhaustion and internal conflicts brought all sides to the negotiating table.

B. The Effects of Constant Fighting, pp. 462–463

1. Ordinary people suffered horrors during the Thirty Years' War, as army after army plundered and destroyed cities and rural villages alike.
2. Peasant revolts and plague outbreaks added to the chaos.
3. When warring governments neglected to pay their armies, soldiers then turned on the local population, looting, pillaging, raping, torturing, and murdering large numbers of civilians.
4. The difficult economic conditions many people faced made it easier for rulers to recruit their own subjects into these armies, although mercenary armies still predominated.

C. The Peace of Westphalia, 1648, pp. 463–465

1. The Peace of Westphalia was the first time that all warring parties had been present during settlement negotiations and all agreed to a common treaty.
2. This model is still used today.
3. France and Sweden gained the most from this treaty.
4. France acquired parts of Alsace and replaced Spain as the most powerful country in continental Europe, while Sweden acquired several northern territories from the Holy Roman Empire.
5. The Habsburgs lost the most.
6. The Dutch obtained their independence from Spain, and each German ruler gained the right to choose his state's religion and more autonomy from the Holy Roman Emperor.
7. Within the Holy Roman Empire, Lutheranism would henceforth dominate in the north, Calvinism in the area of the Rhine River, and Catholicism in the south.
8. The Thirty Years' War changed the political landscape of Europe forever.
9. From this time onward, wars would be fought over political and economic problems not religious ones.
10. States enlarged bureaucracies to raise the taxes necessary to support larger armies and lavish courts.
11. All ranks of society bitterly resented escalating demands for taxes, and some ordinary people resisted by forming makeshift armies to battle royal forces.
12. As bureaucracies grew, monarchs started to rely on officials who took the role of modern prime ministers to manage and advise on affairs of state.
13. The chief minister of France, Cardinal Richelieu, proclaimed that the state's interest was above all else (the principle of *raison d'état*, or reason of state).
14. To mitigate the growth of the state, monarchs cultivated an image of power, requiring courtiers to follow precise rituals in splendid settings designed to showcase the vigor and prestige of the monarchy.

III. Economic Crisis and Realignment

A. From Growth to Recession, pp. 465–467

1. In the second half of the sixteenth century, population growth coincided with an influx of precious metals from the

Americas into western Europe, resulting in dramatic inflation; in the early seventeenth century, however, a recession spread slowly across Europe.

2. Both foreign trade and the population of Europe declined, in part because of the Thirty Years' War.
3. The import of precious metals declined after 1625, largely because Native Americans who worked in Spanish colonial mines died off.
4. Textile production declined as well due to a shrinking labor force and a decrease in demand.
5. Grain prices fell as the population dropped, and many farmers used their land for pasture or vineyards.
6. With the exception of the Dutch Republic, and to a lesser extent, England, western Europe entered a period of economic decline.
7. The Dutch fared better than most due to a growing population and innovative agricultural practices.
8. Vulnerable populations succumbed to epidemic diseases and to famines caused by bad harvests due to climatic changes.

B. Consequences for Daily Life, pp. 467–469

1. Food shortages were devastating, especially because most of the population depended on grain for survival.
2. From 1594 to 1597, famine caused people across Europe to revolt in protest.
3. Many people ended up as vagabonds and bandits.
4. Malnutrition made Europe's population less resistant to diseases such as typhus, influenza, and, most feared of all, plague.
5. The economic crisis heightened the contrast between rich and poor.
6. Depending on where they lived in the seventeenth century, the peasantry either became better off due to increased landholdings and selling on the market, or continued to experience incredibly hard times, losing land and working for others at low wages.
7. Women were especially vulnerable to bad economic cycles because many job opportunities were restricted to men, and some who found jobs as servants were not allowed to leave them.
8. Uncertain economic times led many to postpone marriage and have fewer children, especially the poor.
9. Infant mortality remained high, and about half of the children died before age twenty.
10. Childbirth carried great risks for women, about 10 percent of whom died in the process.
11. Couples in all ranks of society began marrying later and limiting family size in the seventeenth century.

C. The Economic Balance of Power, pp. 469–471

1. The crisis of the seventeenth century led to a shift in the balance of power in Europe.
2. The long-standing superiority of the Mediterranean economies of Italy and Spain came to an end.
3. The northwestern countries of England, the Dutch Republic, and France became the new economic leaders.
4. However, the difference between north and south in western Europe was soon overshadowed by the difference between east and west, as nobles east of the Elbe River increased their hold over the peasantry at the same time that peasants in western Europe were gaining greater autonomy.
5. Eastern European economies depended exclusively on increased agricultural production, whereas those of western Europe also expanded their trade with the new world.
6. In Muscovy, peasants were forced into serfdom by the Code of Laws in 1649.
7. Because of Spain's and Portugal's hold on South America, the English, French, and Dutch turned to North America and the Caribbean.
8. The English encouraged settlement in their colonies and attempted to convert to Christianity those native peoples whom they had not previously driven out through violent tactics.
9. Religious groups on the margins of English society, such as the Pilgrims and Puritans, established new communities in North America, laying the foundations of representative government there.
10. French settlements in Canada were limited, but fur traders pushed into the Great Lakes region to find beaver pelts that became fashionable.
11. Both England and France also gained control of territory in the Caribbean, where they cultivated tobacco and sugarcane.

IV. The Rise of Secular and Scientific Worldviews

A. The Arts in an Age of Crisis, pp. 471–472

1. Traditional beliefs were increasingly challenged during the late sixteenth and early seventeenth centuries.
2. The plays of William Shakespeare reflected the anxieties of the period and, in particular, debates concerning the nature of power and the crisis of authority.
3. Plays such as *Hamlet* (1601), *King Lear* (1605), and *Macbeth* (1606) particularly dramatize the uncertainty and chaos resulting from misappropriated or misused authority.
4. These plays also link family relationships to questions about the legitimacy of government, paralleling the situations of real-life monarchs such as Elizabeth I.
5. In painting, a style called mannerism used distorted perspective and bizarre effects to emphasize a theme, such as religious intensity.
6. The most famous mannerist painter is El Greco.
7. The baroque style (noted for its almost theatrical use of curves, exaggerated lighting, intense emotions, and release from restraint) broke with the Renaissance focus on perspective and harmony.
8. The baroque style glorified the Catholic religion and the power of monarchy in the Habsburgs' Catholic territories.
9. Opera, a new musical form that grew up parallel to the baroque style of the visual arts, combined music, drama, dance, and scenery in a grand sensuous display.
10. It was often designed to be performed for aristocratic and royal audiences.
11. Claudio Monteverdi (1567–1643), an innovative composer of opera, contributed to the development of both opera and the orchestra, and composed music for specific instruments as well as voices.

B. The Natural Law of Politics, pp. 472–474

1. The conflicts over religion led some to develop a new set of principles upon which to base the authority of the state.
2. French essayist Michel de Montaigne revived the ancient doctrine of skepticism and argued that total certainty, in religion or in any other matter, was never attainable, and he emphasized through essays the need for tolerance and open-mindedness.
3. This viewpoint implied that religions were not worth fighting over.
4. The French lawyer Jean Bodin promoted order as the most important quality for a state, and argued that only a strong monarch could ensure order.
5. These ideas helped lay the foundation for absolutism, the idea that the monarch should be the sole and uncontested source of power.
6. Dutch jurist Hugo Grotius argued that natural law, not religious authority, should govern politics.
7. Natural law was designed to defend natural rights, which included the right to life, body, freedom, and honor, and Grotius said that it was the duty of government to uphold these rights.
8. Grotius argued that torture, widespread during this time, infringed upon natural rights.
9. All of these thinkers helped develop a more secular political theory in which authority was no longer based on religion.

C. The Scientific Revolution, pp. 474–478

1. By the early seventeenth century, a new scientific method based on systematic experiments and rational deduction was established.
2. Previously, astronomy was based on Aristotle and Ptolemy, who had argued that the perfect planets revolved in perfect crystal spheres around the corrupted Earth.
3. Nicolaus Copernicus began this revolution in astronomy by arguing that Earth and the other planets revolved around the sun.
4. Tycho Brahe rejected this heliocentrist model, but his discovery of a new star in 1572 challenged the Aristotelian notion that the heavens were perfect and unchanging.
5. Brahe's assistant, Johannes Kepler, continued Brahe's observations of planetary movement and adopted the Copernican view.
6. He provided mathematical proof for a heliocentric model and discovered that planetary motion was elliptical not circular.
7. Galileo Galilei provided further evidence for heliocentrism and, using a telescope of his own design, discovered four moons around Jupiter, the phases of Venus, sunspots, and hills on the moon, all of

which proved that the heavens were no more perfect than Earth.
8. Better understanding of anatomy and pharmacology advanced medicine: the human body, like the universe, was now to be understood through experiment and rational deduction.
9. Sir Francis Bacon championed inductive reasoning through observation and experimental research, and René Descartes promoted deductive reasoning from self-evident principles.
10. Scientific research and economic growth would come to be centered in the northern Protestant countries, where it was less constrained by church control.
11. Building upon the earlier work of scientists, Sir Isaac Newton finally synthesized astronomy and physics with his law of universal gravitation.
12. Far from seeing religion and science in conflict, Newton hoped that his discovery of universal laws would help demonstrate the existence of God and an orderly and rational creation.

D. Magic and Witchcraft, pp. 478–479

1. Despite the new emphasis on clear reasoning, observation, and independence from past authority, science had not yet become separate from magic.
2. Many of the great scientists of the day also practiced alchemy and astrology.
3. At a time when most people believed in astrology, magical healing, prophesy, and ghosts, it is not surprising that many people also believed in witchcraft, including magistrates such as Jean Bodin.
4. Belief in witches was not new, but the official persecution of witches was.
5. In a time of economic crisis, plague, constant warfare, and religious differences, witchcraft trials provided an outlet for social anxiety that was legitimated by state power.
6. Witch trials peaked in Catholic and Protestant Europe between 1560 and 1640, ironically during the same time breakthroughs of the new science occurred.
7. Women accounted for an estimated 80 percent of accused witches.
8. Targets were usually those who lived on the margins of society and were believed to harbor vengeful sentiments against those who were better off.
9. Witchcraft trials declined when scientific thinking raised doubts about the quality of evidence being used in court and when the educated classes began to see witchcraft as nothing more than peasant superstition.

Lecture Strategies

1. The latter half of the sixteenth century includes the Catholic or Counter-Reformation, the spread of Calvinism, the French Wars of Religion, and the Dutch revolt. What makes this period both dynamic and brutal are the ways in which strong defenses of religious ideas intertwine with more mundane political and economic motives. To expose your students to the importance of this material, examine the impact of Calvinism on politics in this period, particularly the idea of the right to resist tyrants. This idea could be presented in the abstract initially, but then placed in the context of either the French Wars of Religion or the Dutch revolt. Even though religious motives are important in this era, it is also worth reminding students that political considerations, personal or family ambitions, and the like remain important factors.

On the idea of the right to resist tyrants, see Chapter 6, section 5 (pp. 153–162) of Perez Zagorin, *Rebels and Rulers, 1500–1660*, vol. 1, *Society, States, and Early Modern Revolution: Agrarian and Urban Rebellions* (Cambridge, UK: Cambridge University Press, 1982); and Chapter 12 of H. G. Koenigsberger and George L. Mosse, *Europe in the Sixteenth Century* (London: Longman, 1968). Zagorin and Koenigsberger and Mosse cover many other topics in a clear and dependable way.

For the French Wars of Religion, in addition to titles cited in the bibliography for Chapter 15 of *The Making of the West*, see Chapter 1 of Robin Briggs, *Early Modern France, 1560–1715* (Oxford: Oxford University Press, 1977) for a competent survey. See also Bernard Chevalier, "France from Charles VII to Henry IV," in Thomas A. Brady, Jr., Heiko A. Oberman, and James D. Tracy, eds., *Handbook of European History, 1400–1600: Late Middle Ages, Renaissance, and Reformation: Structures and Assertions* (Grand Rapids, MI: William B. Eerdmans, 1996), for a good survey with an extensive bibliography.

For the Dutch revolt, Jonathan Israel's book is excellent (see chapter bibliography). Other good discussions include the essay by J. W. Smit, "The Netherlands Revolution," pp. 19–54, in Robert Forster and Jack P. Greene, eds., *Preconditions of Revolution in Early Modern Europe* (Baltimore, MD: Johns Hopkins University Press, 1970); and Chapter 11 in Perez Zagorin, *Rebels and Rulers, 1500–1660: Provincial Rebellion, Revolutionary Civil Wars, 1560–1660*, vol. 2 (Cambridge, UK: Cambridge University Press, 1982). A far more detailed discussion by an expert on the period is

Geoffrey Parker, *The Dutch Revolt*, rev. ed. (New York: Viking Penguin, 1989).

2. Philip II is a central and somewhat tragic figure in the latter part of the sixteenth century. His own story is certainly worth reviewing and in the process it is possible to comment on major developments throughout western Europe and in the New World. Henry Kammen's biography, cited in the chapter bibliography, is superb. A survey of Spain in the sixteenth century, also by Henry Kammen, "The Habsburg Lands: Iberia," in *Handbook of European History, 1400–1600*, is cited in suggestion 1. Appended to the essay is an extensive bibliography. Also useful is Chapter 11 of H. G. Koenigsberger and George L. Mosse, *Europe in the Sixteenth Century* (cited in suggestion 1). More detailed coverage may be found in H. G. Koenigsberger, *The Habsburgs and Europe, 1516–1660* (Ithaca, NY: Cornell University Press, 1971).

An exciting focus for a discussion of Philip II and events in western Europe during his reign is the Spanish Armada of 1588 (there were additional armadas). In addition to Garrett Mattingly's highly readable account (cited in the chapter bibliography), several studies were published during the four hundredth anniversary in 1988. One that presents the Armada from the Spanish perspective is Felipe Fernandez-Armesto, *The Spanish Armada: The Experience of War in 1588* (Oxford: Oxford University Press, 1988). Colin Martin and Geoffrey Parker, *The Spanish Armada* (New York: W. W. Norton, 1988) is an evenhanded presentation of the event.

3. Organize a lecture around Tsar Ivan IV (the Terrible). He is a fascinating character in his own right, and his reign offers a good point at which to introduce the Russian Empire into the analysis of western civilization. His reign—that of Boris Godunov, the "Time of Troubles," and the founding of the Romanov dynasty—would make an interesting session and a vivid contrast to the stories of rulers in western Europe.

Two essays—Nancy Shields Kollmann, "Muscovite Russia, 1450–1598," and Hans-Joachim Torke, "From Muscovy Toward St. Petersburg, 1598–1689"—furnish essential background and interpretation. They are both part of Gregory L. Freeze, ed., *Russia: A History* (Oxford: Oxford University Press, 1997). See also Part One of W. Bruce Lincoln, *The Romanovs: Autocrats of All the Russias* (New York: Dial Press, 1981) for good coverage of the first Romanovs. The essay by Michael Cherniavsky, "Ivan the Terrible as Renaissance Prince," *Slavic Review*, vol. 27 (1968), pp. 195–211, presents Ivan as a person of considerable learning and sophistication, an important point to make in view of his later bizarre behavior. *The Modern Encyclopedia of Russian and Soviet History* is an excellent source for dependable articles on people, events, and institutions from Russian history (Gulf Breeze, FL: Academic International Press, 1976). Note that as of volume 56, the encyclopedia was retitled *The Modern Encyclopedia of Russian, Soviet, and Eurasian History*. Finally, students should see at least a few scenes from Sergei Eisenstein's masterpiece, *Ivan the Terrible* (New York: Janus Films, 184 min.), parts 1 (1944) and 2 (1946). Although Eisenstein's film says as much about the times in which it was made (Stalin's Russia) as about Ivan's time, it offers an intriguing interpretation of Ivan as an individual. It is also a landmark film in the history of cinema (the script and a good deal of background information are available in an edition published by Simon & Schuster, New York, 1970).

4. The Thirty Years' War is a short title for a series of complicated, interlocking events of high drama and great significance in European history. Students will probably find a detailed discussion of battles and alliances confusing. You may wish to present an outline using the phases mentioned in the text and stressing the mixture of religious, political, and other motives. There are, of course, dramatic events beginning with the defenestration of Prague. (And here you may wish to mention the next defenestration of Prague, which took place 330 years later in 1948, when the foreign minister of Czechoslovakia, Jan Masaryk, either jumped or was thrown out of the window of his office; this event was part of the Communist takeover of Czechoslovakia that year.) The period also provides fascinating historical figures, such as Gustavus Adolphus and Richelieu, and many stories of atrocities and great suffering. This point would also be a good time to review the Peace of Westphalia and to assess the relative strength of the various European powers.

The Treaty of Westphalia (or Peace of Westphalia) is readily available online. A book that takes a topical approach to war in this period (chapters include "The Changing Art of War," "Recruitment," and "Life and Death in the Armies") is Frank Tallett, *War and Society in Early-Modern Europe, 1495–1715* (London: Routledge, 1992). E. Neville Williams, ed., *Facts on File Dictionary of European History, 1485–1789* (New York: Facts on File, 1980), may be of some use as well.

Class Discussion Starters

1. Elizabeth I of England continues to fascinate and intrigue students. How was she able not only to succeed in ruling England for decades, but also to succeed brilliantly? How much did she contribute to England's rise to great power status by the end of the sixteenth century? What was she like as an individual? What was it like to live in Elizabethan England?

Two good introductory studies are Susan Watkins, *The Public and Private Worlds of Elizabeth I* (New York: Thames and Hudson, 1998); and Geoffrey

Reagan, *Elizabeth I* (New York: Cambridge University Press, 1988). A readable book that presents Elizabeth and her England is Peter Brimacombe, *All the Queen's Men: Elizabeth I and the English Renaissance* (New York: St. Martin's Press, 2000). An excellent but long biography is that of Wallace T. MacCaffrey, *Elizabeth I: War and Politics, 1588–1603* (Princeton: Princeton University Press, 1992). Finally, students would enjoy viewing *Elizabeth* (New York: PolyGram Video, 1999, 124 min.), with Cate Blanchett as Elizabeth. Whether you screen some or all of the film, it could furnish the basis for a discussion of what Elizabeth was like as a person and what England was like as a country. It would also be necessary, of course, to discuss the problems and possibilities of presenting history in feature films. (Students who cannot get enough of Elizabeth I will also enjoy *Elizabeth R*, with Glenda Jackson in the lead role [CBS Fox Video, 1995, six videocassettes, 90 min. per segment, also available on DVD].)

2. The three major figures of the early scientific revolution are Francis Bacon, René Descartes, and Galileo Galilei. Each man has been the object of a good deal of attention in the past decade and the subject of excellent, readable books. Their life histories and major ideas make for interesting comparisons, which students could discuss, and they each offer important insights into the broader circumstances of their time.

Dava Sobel, a talented writer about science and technology, recently published *Galileo's Daughter: A Historical Memoir of Science, Faith, and Love* (New York: Walker & Co., 1999), a book based on more than a hundred letters from Galileo's oldest daughter, a nun, to her father. In addition, Michael Sharratt wrote *Galileo: Decisive Innovator* (Cambridge, UK: Cambridge University Press, 1996). Two outstanding reference works are Peter K. MacHamer, ed., *The Cambridge Companion to Galileo* (Cambridge, UK: Cambridge University Press, 1998); and Maurice A. Finocchiaro, ed., *The Galileo Affair: A Documentary History* (Berkeley: University of California Press, 1989).

It is difficult to discuss Francis Bacon without also mentioning René Descartes, but to deal with Bacon, Descartes, and Galileo may make for an overcrowded session. Although reviewing Bacon's and Descartes's contributions to the scientific method may be more practical, doing so omits Bacon's career as a courtier (a point of comparison with Galileo and an opening for a discussion of early-seventeenth-century England). On Bacon, in addition to the book by Perez Zagorin, there is a recent biography by Lisa Jardine and Alan Steward, *Hostage to Fortune: The Troubled Life of Francis Bacon* (New York: Hill & Wang, 1999). See also Markku Peltonen, ed., *The Cambridge Companion to Bacon* (Cambridge, UK: Cambridge University Press, 1996). For Descartes, see John Cottingham, ed., *The Cambridge Companion to Descartes* (Cambridge, UK: Cambridge University Press, 1992). Also by Cottingham, who has turned studying Descartes into a cottage industry, are *A Descartes Dictionary* (Oxford: Blackwell Reference, 1993); and *Descartes* (Oxford: Oxford University Press, 1998), a collection of articles. Finally, two good biographies are Stephen Gaukroger, *Descartes: An Intellectual Biography* (Oxford: Oxford University Press, 1995); and Genevieve Rodis-Lewis, *Descartes: His Life and Thought* (Ithaca, NY: Cornell University Press, 1999).

3. Many of Shakespeare's plays, especially his history plays, reveal much about how the English interpreted and related history to contemporary events and circumstances. Some possible topics for discussion include the relationship between church and state in late-sixteenth-century England, the evolving concept of "commonweal" and "commonwealth," the limits and responsibilities of monarchical authority, traditional versus "modern" views on warfare, and gender relationships. All of Shakespeare's plays are available in Bedford/St. Martin's editions, which include critical essays with each text. Also see Russ McDonald, *The Bedford Companion to Shakespeare: An Introduction with Documents* (Boston: Bedford/St. Martin, 2001). Also, some relatively recent and notable film productions of many of Shakespeare's plays, including *Henry V* and *Hamlet* with Kenneth Branagh, *King Lear* with Ian Holm, and *Richard III* with Ian McKellan, might be the basis of further discussion.

4. The development of the French state in the first half of the seventeenth century is a process worth discussing in some detail. During this period, the theory and practice of absolutism began to take shape. Although Louis XIV took developments much further, it is worthwhile tracing what one scholar calls "the birth of absolutism" in this period.

The major figure in the development of the French state is Cardinal Richelieu, one of the all-time great practitioners of politics. For two good biographies, consult Anthony Levi, *Cardinal Richelieu and the Making of France* (New York: Carroll & Graf, 2000); and Joseph Bergin, *The Rise of Richelieu* (New Haven, CT: Yale University Press, 1991). A good biography of Louis XIII is A. Lloyd Moote, *Louis XIII, The Just* (Berkeley: University of California Press, 1989). In addition to Robin Briggs (cited in suggestion 1), see Yves-Marie Berce, *The Birth of Absolutism: A History of France, 1598–1661* (New York: St. Martin's Press, 1996). James B. Collins, *The State in Early Modern France* (New York: Cambridge University Press, 1995) continues the story all the way to 1789.

5. Isaac Newton is the central figure of the latter part of the scientific revolution and should receive top billing in any discussion of the breakthroughs associated with that movement. Yet, as Lisa Jardine shows in *Ingenious Pursuits: Building the Scientific Revolution*

(New York: Nan A. Talese, 1999), ingenious devices often lie behind the theory, observations, and mathematics associated with scientific discovery. Jardine provides a context for Newton by portraying a world in which there are increasingly accurate clocks, improvements in microscopes and telescopes, navigational advances, attempts to chemically analyze unknown substances, and other developments that advanced theory and made possible practical applications. Newton should probably receive the lion's share of attention in any lecture or discussion, but it would also be useful to introduce someone like Robert Boyle whose basic contributions to chemistry depended in large part on the equipment created and made by Robert Hooke, an important scientist in his own right. Jardine is also useful in demonstrating that most scientists in the seventeenth century, even Newton, were very much a part of their times. See also Edward G. Ruestow, *The Microscope in the Dutch Republic* (Cambridge, UK: Cambridge University Press, 1996).

For more on Newton, see Richard S. Westfall, *The Life of Isaac Newton* (Cambridge, UK: Cambridge University Press, 1993); Michael White, *Isaac Newton: The Last Sorcerer* (Reading, MA: Addison-Wesley, 1997); and I. Bernard Cohen and Richard S. Westfall, eds., *Newton: Texts, Background, Commentaries* (New York: W. W. Norton, 1996).

Reviewing the Text

Review Questions

1. How did state power depend on religious unity at the end of the sixteenth century and the start of the seventeenth?
[model answer] *Religion had been deeply entwined with political rule for centuries. A ruler's contract with citizens included his responsibility to uphold the "true religion." Religious beliefs fostered powerful loyalties, so religious division easily translated into political conflict. But the conflicts that emerged threatened to undermine the strength of the European nations. France and the Netherlands ultimately placed state strength over religious conformity by the end of the sixteenth century by instituting religious toleration. In Spain and England, religion remained a national force, determined by the preference of the crown, in Spain for Catholicism, in England for Anglican Protestantism, and as such, religious unity contributed to the strength of state power. Religious disunity in Spain's empire, however, undermined Spain's ability to retain control of the Netherlands. In the Ottoman realm and eastern Europe, religious toleration strengthened states by ensuring peace; religious conflict was disruptive to social order and state building. Where monarchs, church, and citizenry were in agreement, religious unity could contribute to state power, but it was no longer essential.*

2. Why did the war fought over religious differences result in stronger states?
[model answer] *The Thirty Years' War made it clear that state interests had become far more important than religious concerns, as governments worked to maintain armies and retain territory. The costs and logistics of war required new systems for taxes and bureaucracies of management. Developing these increased the centralization and strength of state authority.*

3. What were some of the consequences of economic recession in the early 1600s?
[model answer] *Economic decline was compounded by years of poor harvests, which were followed by famine and disease. These conditions contributed to large-scale uprisings and revolts in some places. In other places, many responded to famine by migrating in search of better opportunity, creating a significant homeless population. The crisis widened the gap between rich and poor and constrained women's opportunities. In the long term, patterns of family changed, as marriages were postponed until people were older, resulting in families with fewer children. The shifting economic balance among states triggered by the recession favored northwestern European countries that were well positioned for the growing Atlantic trade. England, the Dutch Republic, and France began to assume dominance in commerce.*

4. How did belief in witchcraft and the rising prestige of scientific method coexist?
[model answer] *Magic and science had long been associated as two forms of intellectual pursuit. So even as scientific understanding grew, many still believed in alchemy, astrology, and other elements of what was called "natural magic." Witchcraft fell within this line of thought as a "black magic." Science was still a long way from explaining everything and, especially in times of social stress, the search to explain a crisis readily turned to blaming unknown forces.*

Making Connections

1. How did the balance of power shift in Europe between 1560 and 1648? What were the main reasons for the shift?
[model answer] *Economic power shifted from Spain, Portugal, and the Mediterranean world to the nations of northwestern Europe, as commerce with the Americas became a significant force in European state building. Initially strengthened by the precious metals mined in Latin America, Spain lost power when those financial resources declined. England, France, and the Netherlands positioned in ideal geographic locations for developing*

trade across the Atlantic strengthened their economic power. England especially was well positioned, having been more sheltered from the ravages of the Thirty Years' War.

2. Relate the new developments in the arts and sciences to the political and economic changes of this period of crisis.
[model answer] *The decline in the attachment of religious authority to public policy fostered growing interest in searching out nonreligious explanations for political authority and natural phenomena. Thinkers who felt less constrained by the potential censorship or persecution of the church were more willing to look beyond previously accepted explanations and, in fact, sought explanations that were based in the verifiable evidence of the natural world. Secular subjects and secular values became more common themes in the arts. Theater explored topics of current concern related to politics and social issues. The dramatic religious emotionality of mannerism and baroque art reflected reformation Catholicism.*

Discussing the Documents

Questions from Online Study Guide with Model Answers

The Horrors of the Thirty Years' War, p. 462

1. How does Hans Grimmelshausen characterize the violence of the Thirty Year's War?
[model answer] *He characterizes the violence as senseless and gratuitous, apparently enacted without clear reason. It is also incredibly cruel and destructive.*

2. What does Hans Grimmelshausen's attitude toward religious war in general seem to be, and how is this reflected in the ultimate outcome of the Thirty Years' War?
[model answer] *He is condemning of the activities of the war and implies that the religious causes and goals had little relevance to peasants' daily life. The peasants had as little ability to resist or influence the soldiers' presence and actions as they did the ultimate division of lands and religion among political powers.*

Sentence Pronounced Against Galileo (1663), p. 477

1. What does the sentence against Galileo reveal about the relationship between the Roman Catholic Church and the Scientific Revolution?
[model answer] *The church clearly felt threatened by ideas of science, recognizing that these ideas had the potential to undermine and contradict church teachings. The sentence expresses the church belief that the scientific perspectives are erroneous as well as being heresy.*

2. What reasons may the church have had for taking the particular actions that the inquisitors outlined in their sentence?
[model answer] *By offering to absolve Galileo if he would recant, the church would have avoided potential public resistance against the church if they persecuted or executed him, while at the same time gaining a public acknowledgment that his statements were false, thus preserving belief in church doctrine. It was also important to prevent his book from being read and to keep others from understanding the reason and sense of Galileo's conclusions.*

New Sources, New Perspectives: Tree Rings and the Little Ice Age, pp. 466–467

1. What were the historical consequences of global cooling in the seventeenth century?
[model answer] *The weather changes disrupted transportation networks and reduced crop yields. Two consequences were famines and population loss.*

2. Why would trees be especially vulnerable sources of information about climate?
[model answer] *Tree rings reflect the amount of growth a tree experiences each year. The amount of growth is determined by warmth, moisture, and the length of the growing season, so smaller rings would indicate colder or drier years or years with shorter frost-free times. This is especially useful because trees provide a record of many years in succession and can document long-term trends in climate change.*

Other Questions for Discussing These Documents in Class

The Horrors of the Thirty Years' War, p. 462

1. What does Grimmelshausen's work suggest about the experience of the Thirty Years' War for ordinary men and women?

2. What may have been Grimmelshausen's objective in turning his firsthand experiences into a novel? Would this passage be much different if he were writing an autobiographical account instead?

Sentence Pronounced Against Galileo (1663), p. 477

1. Why were Galileo's ideas considered heresy by the Roman Catholic Church?

2. What does the sentence pronounced by the Inquisition suggest about European life in the early seventeenth century?

New Sources, New Perspectives: Tree Rings and the Little Ice Age, pp. 466–467

1. What impact did global cooling have on Europeans in the seventeenth century?

2. How does the evidence of the Little Ice Age compare with the usual sources of information historians draw upon?

Comparative Questions

1. Considering the effects of the Thirty Years' War, the Inquisition against Galileo, and the Little Ice Age, how would you characterize life in seventeenth-century Europe?

2. Who seems to have been more powerless and why: Galileo in the hands of the Inquisition or the peasants described by Grimmelshausen?

For Users of *Sources of The Making of the West*

The following documents are available in Chapter 15 of the companion sourcebook by Katharine J. Lualdi, University of Southern Maine.

1. Legislating Tolerance: Henry IV, *Edict of Nantes* (1598)
2. Barbarians All: Michel de Montaigne, *Of Cannibals* (1580s)
3. The Scientific Challenge: Galileo, *Letter to the Grand Duchess Christina* (1615)
4. The Persecution of Witches: *The Trial of Suzanne Gaudry* (1652)
5. Commercial Endeavors: David Pieterzen DeVries, *Voyages from Holland to America* (1655)

Discussion Ideas for Sources of The Making of the West, *Chapter 15*

1. The religious divisions precipitated by the Reformation led to devastating wars of religion across Europe. With the Edict of Nantes in 1598, Henry IV brought civil war between Catholics and Protestant Huguenots in France to an end. Based on the text of the document, what were Henry's primary motivations in issuing the edict? Were Catholics and Protestants treated equally? What is the difference between religious toleration and religious freedom? Did the edict bring religious freedom to France?

2. The persecution of witches in sixteenth- and seventeenth-century Europe was one of many responses to the crises of the era. Ironically, however, trials such as that of Suzanne Gaudry coincided with the Scientific Revolution. In what ways did Gaudry's trial reflect the anxieties of the age? What factors led to her being accused of witchcraft? Why did she confess and then recant? In what ways did the court proceedings reflect new scientific thinking about the evidence?

Working with Visual Sources

For this exercise, please refer to Queen Elizabeth I of England on p. 458 of the textbook or view the image on the book companion site's Online Study Guide under the "Visual Activity" for Chapter 15.

Students viewing the image at the Online Study Guide are asked two questions about the image. The questions and model answers (not made available to students) are below. Project this image, available on the Instructor's Resources CD-ROM, in class or ask students to look at the image in their textbooks and answer the questions.

1. How does this picture emphasize the link between church and state in Elizabethan England?
[model answer] *The fact that a prayerbook shows the monarch praying shows a unity between religion and the state. There are several royal emblems here, such as the sword, the scepter, and the crown. The crown is placed higher than the prayerbook, symbolizing the fact that the state was above the church.*

2. What type of image of the monarchy does this picture present?
[model answer] *This picture shows the queen as a pious person. She is dressed in rich clothing, and surrounded by symbols of power.*

For this exercise, please refer to Seeing History: Religious Differences in Painting of the Baroque Period: Rubens and Rembrandt on p. 473 of the textbook or view the images on the book companion site's Online Study Guide under the "Visual Activity: Seeing History" for Chapter 15.

Students viewing the image at the Online Study Guide are asked two questions about the images. The questions and model answers (not made available to students) are below. Project these images, available on the Instructor's Resources CD-ROM, in class or ask students to look at the images in their textbooks and answer the questions.

1. How do the portraits of Bathsheba by Rubens and Rembrandt differ?
[model answer] *Rubens depicts Bathsheba before she receives the letter of summons from King David, showing her as an object of beauty and desire, as David would have seen her. Rembrandt, in contrast, shows Bathsheba's sadness after the letter has arrived and she has read it. Rembrandt's image is also more focused on Bathsheba, with fewer background elements and a darker setting.*

2. How do these differences reflect a contrast between Catholic and Protestant artistic styles?
[model answer] *Rembrandt focuses on Bathsheba's inward emotion in a way that reflects the Protestant concern with the individual and her relationship to God. Rubens's image is lighter and more theatrical with*

typical baroque elements such as the curves visible in the fabric on the chair and the draperies.

Mapping Exercises

Map Activity from OSG—Model Answers for Map Activity #2

For this activity, please refer to Map 15.2, The Empire of Philip II, r. 1556–1598 on p. 456. Students are asked these questions:

What was the extent of Philip II's empire?
[model answer] *Philip controlled much of the western Mediterranean. He ruled Spain and Portugal, southern Italy and parts of the North African coastline. He also ruled much of the eastern, southern, and northwestern parts of the Holy Roman Empire. In addition, he had several colonies in North and South America, on the east and west coasts of Africa, in India, and in Asia.*

How did the geographical extent of the Spanish territories influence Spain's political interests?
[model answer] *Spain had the largest empire in the world at the time of Philip II, with territories widely dispersed in the Americas and Europe, as well as along the coasts of Africa, India, and east Asia. During the period that Spain controlled Portugal, competition between those two powers for overseas territories was held in check. Meanwhile, Spanish Habsburg possessions in Italy and the Netherlands drew the Spaniards into conflicts with the Dutch and with the Austrian Habsburgs in the Holy Roman Empire. Spain also clashed with rival maritime power England, as illustrated on the map by the symbol showing where the English defeated the Spanish Armada.*

Map 15.1: Protestant Churches in France, 1562, p. 453

In which parts of France were the largest concentrations of Huguenots? The Protestant Bourbons came from Navarre. Would you expect to see many Protestants in this part of France?

Map 15.2: The Empire of Philip II, r. 1556–1598, p. 456

Ask students to review Philip's possessions, both in Europe and in other parts of the world. What does the map suggest about Philip's difficulties in accomplishing his goals? Remind students of the differences in opinions and understandings between the Dutch and Philip and then ask them to consider how serious these kinds of problems might be in other parts of Philip's empire.

Map 15.3: The Thirty Years' War and the Peace of Westphalia, 1648, p. 463

According to the invasion route arrows on the map, which regions of Europe were most involved in the war? Ask students to identify the location of principal battles and to find Westphalia, where the peace was settled. Based on where the depicted battles took place, which areas were most devastated by the fighting?

Map 15.4: European Colonization of the Americas, c. 1640, p. 470

Ask students to identify principal areas that were colonized and the European countries that claimed them. Based on the specific American territories occupied by certain European states, can you tell which European countries were the first to send expeditions and which Europeans arrived later?

Mapping the West: The Religious Divisions of Europe, c. 1648, p. 480

Ask students to compare this map to Map 15.3, The Thirty Years' War and the Peace of Westphalia, 1648 (p. 463). Which religions gained from the fighting in the Thirty Years' War? Which religions were not affected by the fighting? For which religions might the Thirty Years' War present a mixed picture of wins and losses?

In-Class Assignments and Presentation Topics

1. Assign students an essay on Henry IV of France as a leader. Emphasize that the essay is not to be a capsule biography of Henry, but an assessment of those characteristics that allowed him to lead effectively both before and after he became king. As preparation for the essay, ask the class to list and discuss characteristics they believe contributed to effective leadership. Even though the focus should be as much as possible on leadership in the late sixteenth century, some reference to the present will be unavoidable and probably useful.

2. Was the defeat of the Spanish Armada in 1588 a turning point in history? Ask students to write a counterfactual essay arguing that the Spanish Armada was successful. Then, what happened? Why? Help students understand that this exercise is more than creative writing. They must have, for example, some basis for deciding that Philip would or would not have proceeded to invade England, or for deciding that Henry would or would not eventually become king of France.

3. Set up a discussion of motives in the Thirty Years' War. Each student or small group of students is assigned a country or an individual to investigate before the discussion. In the first part of the discussion, students should represent the country or individual. In the second part of the discussion, students should attempt to survey the Thirty Years' War as a whole in terms of motive and try to reach a conclusion about the decline of organized religion as a reason for war.

4. Ask students to pretend they are living in 1648 and represent one country at the court of another. They are to report on the host country and compare it to the country they are representing. For the essay, students should use maps and the terms of the Peace of Westphalia as well as information from *The Making of the West* and class discussions.

Essay Questions

1. What did it take to be a scientist in the early seventeenth century? Ask students to do a research project on Galileo's career as a scientist. They should pay particular attention to the sources of his funding and to the politics, including church politics, of doing science. The sources listed in the chapter bibliography and in suggestion 2 of "Class Discussion Starters" are good starting points.

2. Divide students into three or four groups and assign each group a country. Each group then investigates trials for witchcraft in that country and produces a fifteen-minute courtroom drama, which they perform before the rest of the class. Use Alan C. Kors and Edward Peters, *Witchcraft in Europe, 1100–1700: A Documentary History* (Philadelphia: University of Pennsylvania Press, 1972); and Brian P. Levack, *The Witch-Hunt in Early Modern Europe* (London: Longman, 1987) as starting points.

3. In reference to questions 1 and 2 here, students may want to investigate notable astrologers of the period, such as Dr. John Dee at the English court, and Nostradamus at the French court. How and for whom did these men divine the future? What differentiated their activities from witchcraft? See Gerald Suster, *John Dee* (Berkley, CA: North Atlantic Books, 2003); Benjamin Woolley, *The Queen's Conjurer: The Science and Magic of Dr. John Dee, Advisor to Queen Elizabeth I* (New York: Henry Holt & Co., 2001); and Damon Wilson, *The Mammoth Book of Nostradamus and Other Prophets* (London: Robinson Publishers, 1999).

Additional Resources: Literature

Grossman Edith, trans., *Miguel de Cervantes: Don Quixote*. 2003.

Screech, M. A. trans., *Michel de Montaigne: The Complete Essays*. 1993.

Wells, Stanley et al., eds., *William Shakespeare: The Complete Works*. 1999.

Additional Resources: Film and Video

Elizabeth R (1971; VHS, DVD, 9 hrs.). This series of six episodes of approximately 90 minutes each chronicles the major events of Elizabeth I's life including her establishment on the throne of England, the marriage negotiations with the Duc d'Alencon, the execution of Mary, Queen of Scots, and the Spanish Armada. Although made in 1971, the series remains the best film drama to date of Elizabeth's life. The queen's gowns are stunningly re-created from surviving portraits.

Mary, Queen of Scotland (1971; Charles Jarrott, dir.; with Vanessa Redgrave). Although inaccurate on some details, the film does accurately reflect the queen's strained relations with the Scottish nobles, the Protestant John Knox, and her reprobate husband, Henry Darnley.

La Reine Margot (1994; DVD, 144 min.). This dramatization of Alexandre Dumas's novel about Marguerite de Valois includes her marriage to Henri of Navarre and the Massacre of St. Bartholomew's Day in 1572. Although the plot has been embellished, it is a largely accurate retelling of those events. Care has been lavished on costumes and settings. The film is in French with English subtitles.

Dangerous Beauty (1998; VHS/DVD, 112 min.). This film is set in sixteenth-century Venice and focuses on the life of a prominent courtesan. The film nicely captures the culture of the period, especially religious sensibilities and the restrictions placed on women. Care has been taken to re-create accurate costumes and settings. The film is in English and French, with subtitles.

Shakespeare in Love (1998; John Madden, dir.; with Gwyneth Paltrow and Joseph Fiennes). Because so little is actually known about Shakespeare's early years as a playwright, this fictional account seems plausible, even if it is also unlikely. Great care has been lavished to get the costuming and setting right.

Elizabeth (1998; Shekhar Kapur, dir.; with Cate Blanchett and Joseph Fiennes). Although the plot is extremely garbled, Blanchett's likeness to known portraits of Elizabeth is striking, and suggests what the queen might have looked like in the flesh.

Galileo's Battle for the Heavens (2002; VHS, 2 hrs.). Dava Sobel's novel, *Galileo's Daughter*, is the basis for this dramatized biography of Galileo. The film uses the letters Galileo wrote to his illegitimate daughter to explore his life and work.

Elizabeth (2003; DVD, 197 min.). This excellent series, presented by the Tudor historian David Starkey, traces Elizabeth's life up to her accession using archival material and reenactments.

In Search of Shakespeare (2004; VHS/DVD, 4 hrs.). Michael Wood provides a historical context for William Shakespeare's plays by tracking down the playwright in the historical records and in the places he visited. Although a bit breathless in his enthusiasm, Wood does an excellent job of piecing together what is known about the playwright's life in this four-part series.

Other Bedford/St. Martin's Resources for Chapter 15

The following resources are available to accompany Chapter 15. Please refer to the Preface of this manual for detailed descriptions of all the ancillaries.

For Instructors

Transparencies

The following maps and images from Chapter 15 are available as full-color acetates.

- Map 15.1: Protestant Churches in France, 1562
- Map 15.2: The Empire of Philip II, r. 1556–1598
- Map 15.3: The Thirty Years' War and the Peace of Westphalia, 1648
- Map 15.4: European Colonization of the Americas, c. 1640
- Mapping the West: The Religious Divisions of Europe, c. 1648
- Queen Elizabeth I of England, p. 458
- The Life of the Poor, p. 468

Instructor's Resources CD-ROM

The following maps and image from Chapter 15, as well as a chapter outline, are available on disc in both PowerPoint and jpeg formats.

- Map 15.1: Protestant Churches in France, 1562
- Map 15.2: The Empire of Philip II, r. 1556–1598
- Map 15.3: The Thirty Years' War and the Peace of Westphalia, 1648
- Map 15.4: European Colonization of the Americas, c. 1640
- Mapping the West: The Religious Divisions of Europe, c. 1648
- Queen Elizabeth I of England, p. 458

Using the Bedford Series with The Making of the West

Available in print as well as online at **bedfordstmartins.com/usingseries,** this guide offers practical suggestions for using Peter C. Mancall, *Envisioning America: English Plans for the Colonization of North America, 1580–1640,* Sir Walter Raleigh's *The Discovery of Guiana,* edited by Benjamin Schmidt, Jayne Elizabeth Lewis, *The Trial of Mary Queen of Scots,* and Allan Greer, *The Jesuit Relations,* in conjunction with chapters 15 and 16 of the textbook.

For Students

Study Guides

The Online Study Guide at **bedfordstmartins.com/hunt** helps students synthesize the material they have learned as well as practice the skills historians use to make sense of the past. The following Map, Visual, and Document activities are available for Chapter 15.

Map Activity

- Map 15.2: The Empire of Phillip II, r. 1556–1598

Visual Activity

- Queen Elizabeth I of England, p. 458
- Peter Paul Rubens, *Bathsheba at the Fountain,* c. 1635, p. 473
- Rembrandt van Rijn, *Bathsheba at Her Bath,* 1654, p. 473

Reading Historical Documents

- The Horrors of the Thirty Years' War, p. 462
- Sentence Pronounced against Galileo, p. 477
- New Sources, New Perspectives: Tree Rings and the Little Ice Age, p. 466

CHAPTER

16

State Building and the Search for Order

1648–1690

CHAPTER RESOURCES

Main Chapter Topics

1. Louis XIV personified the idea of absolutism. Louis established his personal rule by manipulating courtiers, employing middle-class officials, creating Europe's largest army, associating the monarchy with advances in the arts and "new science," engaging in military campaigns to expand French power and influence, and dealing ruthlessly with any opposition.

2. Central and eastern European rulers followed Louis XIV's model of absolutism. The ruler of Brandenburg-Prussia worked to rebuild after the Thirty Years' War and unite far-flung territories; the Austrian Habsburgs fought off the Ottoman Turks and governed many ethnic and religious groups; and the Russian tsars controlled a large but poor empire through enserfment of the peasants.

3. English kings failed to establish absolutism. Rather, political and social upheaval between 1642 and 1660, and again in 1688 to 1689, strengthened the constitutional position of an elected parliament. The revolution of 1688 led to the legal guarantee of parliamentary government.

4. The Dutch Republic also founded a strong constitutional system. After William and Mary came to the English throne, the Netherlands joined England to block Louis XIV's efforts to dominate Europe. The Dutch economy, learning, and arts flourished together.

5. Still shaken by the upheavals of the wars of religion, Europeans sought new bases for authority in politics, science, and the arts. Although seeking greater freedom, they labored to balance freedom with order. The new worldview emphasized order and regularity, while slavery became an established aspect of the emerging Atlantic system.

Focus Question

What were the most important differences between absolutism and constitutionalism, and how did they establish order?

1. Absolutism emphasized a top-down understanding of political authority. The monarch, who ruled by divine right, was envisioned as the father of his people, or, in keeping with new scientific ideas, the "sun" around which the political system orbited. While the power of absolute monarchs was often limited in practical terms, by promoting court culture, bureaucracy, ruthless centralized authority, and the monarch's supreme status in relation to the law, absolute rulers attained a great deal of political power. Constitutional systems limited the monarch's power and insisted that monarchs govern within established law, with the understanding that political authority was derived, in theory, from the consent of the governed. Government was a kind of contract.

2. Practically speaking, monarchial authority in constitutional systems was limited by assemblies of elite, wealthy, propertied men, who were often aristocrats. While constitutionalism triumphed in Britain and among the Dutch, ultimately the absolutist system appealed directly to the ambitions and anxieties of most European monarchs of the era, and was more widely endorsed and imitated.

Annotated Chapter Outline

I. Louis XIV: Absolutism and Its Limits

A. The Fronde, 1648–1653, pp. 485–486

1. Louis XIV came to the throne in 1643 at the age of five.
2. His mother, Anne of Austria, and her advisor, Cardinal Mazarin, ruled in Louis's name.

3. To raise money for the Thirty Years' War, Mazarin sold new offices, raised taxes, and forced creditors to lend money to the government.
4. In 1648, a coalition of his opponents demanded that the parlements (high courts) have the right to approve new taxes.
5. When Mazarin refused and arrested the leaders of these parlements, a series of revolts, known as the Fronde, broke out, which at one time or another involved nearly every social group in France.
6. Nobles wanted to reacquire the power and local influence they had lost after the religious wars ended in 1598. The middle and lower classes opposed the government's repeated tax increases.
7. Throughout France there was fighting among armies raised by diverse social and political groups.
8. Louis and his mother were forced to flee Paris, and Mazarin and Anne agreed to compromise with the parlements.
9. The monarchy survived the rebellions, but they had a lasting influence on the young king who later enacted politics to prevent any such revolts.

B. Court Culture as an Element of Absolutism, pp. 486–489

1. Mazarin died in 1661 and twenty-two-year-old Louis XIV decided to conduct the government himself without appointing a first minister.
2. Louis's first priority was controlling the nobility, which still possessed local armies and a great deal of local power and autonomy.
3. Using a double-edged policy of bestowing honors and offices and threatening disfavor or punishment, Louis brought the nobility under control by requiring their attendance at his court.
4. Away from the court, however, local nobles still held considerable power, and royal officials learned to compromise with them.
5. Life at court required careful attention, and the tiniest lapse in etiquette could lead to ruin. In this way, Louis made himself the center of French power and culture.
6. Louis also used the arts to glorify his image, having artists represent him as Apollo, the Sun King, a Roman emperor, and a great military leader.
7. Artists, writers, and composers were employed and protected by the government to produce works that celebrated the monarchy.
8. Louis also used massive public works projects and, in particular, the enlargement of the Palace of Versailles, to manifest and increase his prestige. Versailles, which housed fifteen thousand people, represented Louis XIV's success in controlling the French nobility and dominating European affairs.

C. Enforcing Religious Orthodoxy, p. 489

1. Louis justified his actions by referring to the doctrine of divine right, which argued that kings were ordained by God to rule and had a duty to instruct their subjects in religion much like a father would his family.
2. Louis believed that the defense of orthodox Catholicism was one of his most important tasks as king.
3. Louis first took action against the Jansenists, who, although Catholic, resembled the Protestants in their emphasis on God's grace and original sin and in their austere religious practices that were similar to the English Puritans.
4. Because Jansenists considered individual conscience to be more important than obeying church authority, Louis enforced decrees against Jansenists and closed their churches starting around 1660.
5. In 1685, Louis revoked the Edict of Nantes, thereby depriving Huguenots of their rights.
6. Louis wanted to convert the Huguenots to Catholicism, but instead many Huguenots emigrated from France to Protestant countries, whose citizens were shocked by the French king's actions.

D. Extending State Authority at Home and Abroad, pp. 489–492

1. Louis expanded the royal bureaucracy to consolidate his authority and run his kingdom more efficiently.
2. Louis used his appointed officials, rather than those who owned their offices, to collect taxes, to finance public works, to provision the army, to gather information regarding his subjects, and to subordinate local interests to royal will.
3. His most important minister was Jean-Baptiste Colbert, who became head of royal finances and helped Louis develop

mercantilism, meaning that the government intervened wherever possible to increase national wealth.

4. Mercantilism called for government participation in all aspects of the economy. The French royal government established overseas trading companies, granted monopolies to manufacturers, regulated production of virtually all French products, and imposed high tariffs on foreign goods to encourage French industry. The result was an expanded bureaucracy.
5. Mercantilist policy also called for expanding colonial control in New France.
6. Also, desiring to establish French dominance in Europe, Louis increased the size of the army and was continually at war with other European powers between 1667 and 1713.
7. Even though Louis ultimately lost nearly all the territory he had won, France's many military victories conferred glory upon the French monarchy.
8. Absolutism and war fed each other, as Louis's bureaucracy found new ways to raise money to support the army, and military success justified further expansion of state power.
9. At the same time, however, these wars also eroded the state's resources and hindered administrative and legal reforms such as eliminating the buying and selling of offices and lowering taxes.
10. Ordinary people paid the price for Louis's policies, paying higher taxes, serving in the military, quartering soldiers, and facing extortion when food supplies fell short.

II. Absolutism in Central and Eastern Europe

A. Brandenburg-Prussia: Militaristic Absolutism, pp. 493–494

1. Frederick William of Hohenzollern, the Great Elector of Brandenburg-Prussia, welded the scattered lands that composed his territory into an absolutist state.
2. Pressed by the expense of fighting the Thirty Years' War and then reconstructing his territory after it, Frederick William struck a deal with the nobility, known as Junkers, to ensure a dependable income from the collection of taxes.
3. In exchange for allowing him to collect taxes, he granted the Junkers complete control over their enserfed peasants and exempted the Junkers themselves from taxation.
4. A Calvinist, Frederick William avoided the display of wealth and luxury of the French court, and used this tax revenue to create an efficient bureaucracy and enlarge the Prussian army to almost four times its original size.
5. His army mirrored the rigid domination of the nobility over the peasantry—nobles were officers, peasants the troops—in a militaristic society in which the army always had priority.
6. He rebuffed Louis XIV by welcoming twenty thousand French Huguenots to resettle in Brandenburg-Prussia after the revocation of the Edict of Nantes.
7. He was so successful that, in 1701, his son Frederick I persuaded the Holy Roman Emperor to grant him the title "king in Prussia."

B. An Uneasy Balance: Austrian Habsburgs and Ottoman Turks, pp. 494–495

1. To unite territories of different ethnicities, religions, and languages, Holy Roman Emperor Leopold I (r. 1658–1705) developed an absolutist government that chipped away at local powers, expanded the bureaucracy, and replaced the mercenaries hired to fight in the Thirty Years' War with a well-disciplined, permanent standing army.
2. In Bohemia, Leopold replaced the nobility who had revolted against Austrian authority in 1618 with a new multiethnic aristocracy composed of German-speaking, Catholic Czechs, Germans, Italians, and even Irish who were loyal to the emperor.
3. Austria fought the Ottoman Turks for more than 150 years. In 1683, the Turks made it as far as Vienna, but with the help of the Polish cavalry Leopold repelled the siege. In the Treaty of Karlowitz, the Turks surrendered Hungary to Leopold in 1699.
4. To tighten his control over devastated Hungary, Leopold revived the parliamentary diet, which was dominated by pro-Habsburg Hungarian nobles who buttressed the dynasty until its fall in 1918.
5. Leopold engaged in public building projects to root out any remaining Turkish influence and assert Austrian superiority with the flamboyant Austrian baroque style.

6. The Ottoman Turks also consolidated state power through a combination of settlement and military control.
7. They settled hundreds of thousands of Turkish families in the Balkans.
8. Rather than suppress peasant armies, the Ottoman state hired them as mercenaries.
9. To avoid a revolt by the elites, Ottoman leaders played them off each other.
10. Although weak in western eyes, the Ottomans still posed a massive threat to Europe's southeast borders.

C. Russia: Setting the Foundations of Bureaucratic Absolutism, pp. 496–497

1. Like their European counterparts, the Russian tsars wanted absolute power. In 1648, Tsar Alexei (r. 1645–1676) set off a rebellion by attempting to change the administrative structure of the state.
2. He responded to the rebellion by convoking the Assembly of the Land, which consisted of noble delegates from the provinces, and issuing a law code that assigned all subjects to a hereditary class.
3. Slaves and free peasants were merged into a serf class, while nobles had to give absolute loyalty to the tsar and were required to serve in the military.
4. In 1667, Stenka Razin led a peasant rebellion that promised freedom from serfdom.
5. Razin was captured four years later, and thousands of his followers met grisly deaths, but his memory lived on in folk songs and legends.
6. To extend his power and emulate his western rivals, Alexei increased the size of his army to more than six times its original size, and imposed control over state policy and the Russian Orthodox church.
7. A state-dominated church meant the obliteration of the Old Believers, who often chose martyrdom rather than adopt Russian Orthodox practices.
8. The Assembly of the Land never met again after 1653, whereas the state bureaucracy continued to expand and intervene more and more in daily life.
9. Alexei encouraged western culture even while some Russians remained suspicious of foreign influences.

D. Poland-Lithuania Overwhelmed, p. 497

1. Poland-Lithuania did not merely reject the absolutist model. Through decades of war, the monarchy weakened while its nobles became virtually autonomous warlords.
2. In 1648 in Ukraine, runaway peasants and poor nobles, known as Cossacks, formed bands and revolted against the king in an uprising known as the Deluge.
3. In 1654, the Cossacks offered Ukraine to the Russian tsar, provoking a Russo-Polish war that ended with the tsar annexing eastern Ukraine and Kiev in 1667.
4. Neighboring powers also took advantage of Poland-Lithuania's weakness and sent armies to seize territory.
5. The fighting destroyed many towns and a third of the Polish population.
6. Amidst the chaos, the country abandoned its policy of religious toleration of Jews and Protestants.
7. Tens of thousands of Jews were slaughtered, and surviving Jews moved from towns to *shtetls* (Jewish villages).
8. The Poland-Lithuania commonwealth elected Jan Sobieski to be king (r. 1674–1696); he attempted to rebuild the monarchy on the absolutist model but was unsuccessful.

III. Constitutionalism in England

A. England Turned Upside Down, 1642–1660, pp. 498–502

1. Charles I (r. 1625–1649) wanted to establish absolutism in England, but wealthy English landowners had long participated in government through Parliament and expected to be consulted on royal policy.
2. In 1629, when Parliament wanted Charles to agree to the Petition of Right (a promise not to levy taxes without Parliament's consent), he closed Parliament for eleven years.
3. He irritated Puritans by favoring Anglican rituals similar to Catholic rites. With Charles's support, Archbishop Laud tried to impose the Anglican liturgy on Presbyterian Scots, and the Scots invaded the north of England in 1640, forcing Charles to summon Parliament to levy new taxes.
4. Moderate elements within Parliament voted to undo some of the king's less-popular measures. Charles attempted to arrest them and, when opposition arose, he left London to raise an army.
5. The English civil war began in 1642. Charles's army, known as the Cavaliers,

found their support in northern and western England.

6. The Parliamentary forces, known as the Roundheads, had their stronghold in the areas surrounding and including Longon. The Puritan Roundheads were led by Oliver Cromwell.
7. In 1646, Cromwell's New Model Army defeated the royalists.
8. Parliament then split into moderate Presbyterians and radical Independents.
9. The Presbyterians made up the majority, but the Independents controlled the army and used it to purge the Presbyterians from Parliament. The remaining members were known as the Rump Parliament.
10. Other religious and political dissenters included the Levellers, the Baptists, and the Quakers. Many new sects emphasized women's spiritual equality.
11. In 1648, the Rump Parliament found Charles I guilty of trying to create "an unlimited and tyrannical power." On January 30, 1649, he was beheaded.
12. The Rump Parliament then abolished the monarchy and formed a republic led by Oliver Cromwell, who tolerated no opposition.
13. He conquered Scotland again and brutally subdued Ireland, waged war on the Dutch, and, in 1651, enacted the first Navigation Act to protect English commerce.
14. But Cromwell alienated supporters with higher taxes than those imposed by the monarchy and with harsh tactics against dissent.
15. In 1653, Cromwell abolished the Parliament and named himself Lord Protector.
16. In 1660, two years after Cromwell's death, a newly elected Parliament called Charles II, the son of the beheaded king, to the throne.

B. The Glorious Revolution of 1688, pp. 502–504

1. Although most English welcomed the monarchy back in 1660, many soon came to fear that Charles II wished to establish absolutism on the French model.
2. In 1670, Charles secretly agreed to convert to Catholicism in exchange for money from Louis XIV to fight the Dutch.
3. Although Charles never pronounced himself a Catholic, he did ease restrictions on Catholics and Protestant dissenters, thereby coming into conflict with a Parliament intent on supporting the Church of England.
4. In 1673, Parliament passed the Test Act, which required government officials to pledge allegiance to the Church of England.
5. In 1678, Parliament tried to deny the throne to any Roman Catholic because they did not want the king's brother and heir James, a Catholic convert, to inherit the throne.
6. Charles did not allow this law to pass, splitting Parliament into two factions: Tories, who supported a strong, hereditary monarchy and the Anglican church; and Whigs, who supported a strong Parliament and toleration for non-Anglicans.
7. James II succeeded his brother as king and pursued absolutist and pro-Catholic policies.
8. When his wife gave birth to a son that ensured a Catholic heir to the throne, the Whigs and Tories in Parliament united and offered the throne to James's older Protestant daughter Mary and her husband, the Dutch ruler William, prince of Orange.
9. In the Glorious Revolution, so-called because it was effected with relatively little bloodshed, James fled to France, and William and Mary granted a bill of rights that confirmed Parliament's rights in government.
10. The propertied classes that controlled Parliament now focused on consolidating their power and preventing any future popular turmoil.

C. Social Contract Theory: Hobbes and Locke, pp. 504–505

1. Thomas Hobbes (1588–1679) was an English royalist who believed that human beings were essentially self-centered and focused on survival. He outlined his thoughts in *Leviathan* (1651) and made his case by appealing to science instead of religion.
2. Hobbes believed that only a strong authority (either a king or a parliament) could assure stability and force people to follow the laws.
3. To obtain this strong authority, people had to voluntarily give up some personal liberty. Royalists opposed Hobbes because his ideas emphasized a social contract—instead of divine right—between ruler

and ruled, whereas Parliamentarians objected to his emphasis on absolute authority.
4. John Locke (1632–1704) also believed in a social contract between ruler and ruled, but Locke had a more optimistic view of human nature.
5. He believed that human beings were essentially good and peaceful and that the purpose of government was to protect life, liberty, and property.
6. If government failed in this task, or overstepped its bounds, the people had a right to resist.
7. He articulated his anti-authoritarian position in *Two Treatises of Government* (1690).
8. In *Essay Concerning Human Understanding* (1690), Locke stated that each human was born with a mind that was a tabula rasa (blank slate).
9. All knowledge came from sensory experience, not from anything innate, and education shaped personality by channeling sensory experience.
10. These views indicated that "all men are created equal." Locke's views helped justify the Glorious Revolution and, in later centuries, the American Revolution, equal rights for women, and the abolition of slavery.

IV. Outposts of Constitutionalism

A. The Dutch Republic, pp. 505–507

1. By 1648, when it gained formal independence from Spain, the Dutch Republic was a decentralized constitutional state.
2. Rich merchants, called regents, controlled local affairs and represented their provinces at the Estates General, which controlled foreign policy and appointed a stadholder, an executive officer who was responsible for defense and represented the state at ceremonial functions.
3. The Dutch Republic encouraged trade by importing products from all over the world, becoming Europe's finance capital.
4. Dutch citizens became the most prosperous and best-educated middle class in Europe and supported the visual arts.
5. Their relative wealth decreased the need for women to work outside the home, and the Dutch made the family household the source of society's morality. The clear division of gender roles within the Dutch family would later become prevalent elsewhere in Europe and the United States.
6. The high levels of urbanization and literacy created a large readership, and Dutch tolerance led to a freedom of publishing unknown elsewhere in Europe.
7. By the late seventeenth century, the cost of repeated wars with England at sea and France on land contributed to a relative decline, and French influence became more prominent in Dutch intellectual and artistic life.

B. Freedom and Slavery in the New World, p. 508

1. After the Spanish and Portuguese demonstrated that using black Africans as slave labor in their colonies was profitable, the French and English purchased and brought African slaves to their Caribbean colonies.
2. The highest church and government officials in Catholic and Protestant countries condoned the slave trade.
3. The English instituted a slave code in Barbados in 1661 that stripped Africans of their legal rights and made slavery an inherited status.
4. In 1685, Louis XIV of France similarly regulated Africans through a "black code."
5. By 1700, private companies transported 36,000 Africans a year to the New World.
6. At the same time, English settlers in North America had representative legislatures that gave colonial elites control over local matters.
7. Plentiful land made it possible for ordinary immigrants to become landowners and elites.
8. Native Americans lost their lives and their homelands as they succumbed to disease and European conquest.
9. In their attempts to disqualify them from the benefits of constitutionalism, Europeans alternately portrayed Native Americans as villainous heathens or as "noble savages" doomed to extinction.

V. The Search for Order in Elite and Popular Culture

A. Freedom and Constraint in the Arts and Sciences, pp. 509–512

1. Artists, writers, and architects grappled with issues of faith, reason, and authority.
2. John Milton wrote about the benefits and dangers of individual liberty for human beings.

3. The two dominant artistic styles of the era—baroque and classical—approached the individual differently.
4. The baroque was favored by the Catholic church and patronized by Habsburg rulers because the emotional response it evoked proved to be especially suitable for inspiring awe in public displays of faith and of the power of the monarch and the Catholic church.
5. Gian Lorenzo Bernini, the pope's official artist, used architecture and sculpture to express the combination of religious and political purposes in baroque art.
6. The Habsburgs' enemy, Louis XIV, rejected the baroque in favor of the classical, which reflected the ideals of antiquity, order, and harmony and was exemplified by the paintings of Nicolas Poussin and Claude Lorrain.
7. Classicism placed the important individual firmly at the intersection of straight lines.
8. Women artists such as Merian excelled in documenting the natural world in vibrant still lifes and botanical paintings.
9. Even amid the religious controversies associated with the scientific revolution, many rulers supported scientific exploration and experimentation.
10. Frederick William of Brandenburg-Prussia funded agricultural experiments.
11. Colbert of France founded the Royal Academy of Sciences in 1666, which funded scientists studying alchemical experiments and mechanical devices.
12. The Royal Society of London encouraged investigative activity through observation and experimentation.

B. Women and Manners, pp. 512–514

1. Nobles developed individual self-discipline in the court, where they distinguished themselves from other groups in society through their dress, behavior, and activities.
2. Noblemen, like noblewomen, learned the art of pleasing to gain favor with the king.
3. The plays of Molière reassured aristocrats that this part of their identity was inimitable, yet also implied that the middle class could learn manners, too.
4. Treatises on etiquette were published.
5. Elite women gained access to intellectual life through the salon, an informal gathering presided over by a socially eminent woman in her home.
6. Salons encouraged conversations about love, philosophy, and literature, providing authors with an audience for their ideas.
7. Some women also wrote; they were especially successful with a new literary genre, the novel.
8. Aphra Behn, one of the first professional women writers, was a novelist who wrote the best seller *Oroonoko*.
9. As women became more important in taste, literature, and manners, they stirred the fear and resentment of many clergy, scientists, scholars, and playwrights, who warned of the dangers of their influence over men and ridiculed their literary and social ambitions.

C. Reforming Popular Culture, pp. 514–515

1. New developments in science, the arts, literature, and manners did not touch the majority of Europe's population who were illiterate peasants.
2. Protestant and Catholic churches extended their campaigns that had begun in the sixteenth century to root out "pagan" practices, reaching much of rural Europe in the seventeenth century.
3. Royal officials worked with clergy to impose orthodox religious practices and to suppress activities they deemed incompatible with Christian doctrine and standards of behavior, such as maypoles, animal sacrifices, and praying to the moon.
4. In both Protestant and Catholic countries, the campaign against superstition helped to extend state power.
5. At the same time, attitudes toward the poor changed: previously, poverty had been a Christian virtue and support of the poor a key part of Christian charity. Now the poor were seen as dangerous, lazy, and immoral.
6. Local governments and organizations tried to reform the poor and to separate them from society by advocating discipline and putting them in hospitals built on government order.
7. Villagers and townspeople often countered this attempt at separation by pushing back with their own values and maintaining their own forms of village justice and punishment.
8. Many religious festivals took on popular interpretation as villagers converted to

Catholicism while keeping their own prior identities in the ways they celebrated the festivals.

Lecture Strategies

1. How did Louis make himself into the indispensable center of the French political system? Include as much as possible the means by which the monarch's authority and preeminence was demonstrated through art, architecture, court ritual, and public performance. What did he hope to accomplish through this and other means? This would be a good point at which to discuss Versailles, which became something like a giant stage for Louis's long-running play. Who else contributed to Louis's system? How important were they, whether prominent individuals like Colbert, or groups of people like the intendants? How might we assess Louis's efforts? Point out the ways that, even in an absolutist state, the monarch's power was limited or focused narrowly on the challenge of maintaining authority.

In addition to the sources listed in the chapter bibliography, William Beik, *Louis XIV and Absolutism: A Brief Study with Documents* (Boston: Bedford/St. Martin's, 1999) presents a detailed look in a book that is slightly over two hundred pages long. Robin Briggs, *Early Modern France, 1560–1715* (Oxford: Oxford University Press, 1977) offers a good overview; and David J. Sturdy, *Louis XIV* (New York: St. Martin's Press, 1998) is also a useful source. Of tremendous interest to students, and a lively read, is Joan DeJean's take on the rise of French culture on the global stage in connection with the reign of Louis XIV, in *The Essence of Style: How the French Invented High Fashion, Fine Food, Chic Cafes, Style, Sophistication, and Glamour* (New York: Free Press, 2005). Finally, Robert W. Berger, *A Royal Passion: Louis XIV as Patron of Architecture* (Cambridge, UK: Cambridge University Press, 1994) includes a wealth of information on Louis's many construction projects.

2. Although seventeenth-century Russia offers many points of contrast with western Europe, it too attempted to create an autocratic political system in which the tsar was all-powerful. Perhaps the most important point is that the consolidation of serfdom not only allowed the aristocracy and the monarch to live in great luxury, it also enabled them to mobilize the relatively scarce resources of Russia and eventually to make it into one of the great European powers. The startling contrast between aristocratic and peasant life may be best illustrated by the Russian case.

The reign of Tsar Alexei is important for the law code of 1649; for the attempts to reform the Russian Orthodox church, which gave rise to the Old Believers; and for the rebellion led by Stenka Razin. In all these instances, the state became more powerful. However, it all fell apart after Alexei died. During the interim between Alexei and Peter, Peter's older half sister, Sophie, was regent. Sophie was an interesting figure in her own right and worth spending time on. Overall, the tensions inherent in attempting to improve one's own very traditional society via imitation and cultural borrowing is a great theme for students to be exposed to.

In addition to the books listed in the chapter bibliography, Part 1 of W. Bruce Lincoln's *The Romanovs: Autocrats of All the Russias* (New York: Dial Press, 1981) has an excellent discussion of the Romanov tsars in the seventeenth century. Chapter 3, by Hans-Joachim Torke, "From Muscovy toward St. Petersburg, 1598–1689," in Gregory L. Freeze, ed., *Russia: A History* (Oxford: Oxford University Press, 1997) is a good survey. Richard S. Hellie, ed. and trans., *Muscovite Law Code (Ulozhenie) of 1649*, vol. 1 (Irvine: University of California Press, 1988) makes available this seminal document. Paul Avrich, *Russian Rebels, 1600–1800* (New York: Schocken Books, 1972) contains a good account of Stenka Razin's rebellion. Finally, Lindsay Hughes, *Sophia: Regent of Russia, 1657–1704* (New Haven, CT: Yale University Press, 1990) is the definitive biography.

3. Students should understand the events of both the English civil war and the Glorious Revolution. Much of what occurred during the American Revolution had its roots in seventeenth-century England. At the same time, it is important not to present a view of these events that suggests that they are inevitable steps along the way to democratic politics. The undemocratic aspects of Parliament and the continuing importance of aristocratic and royal influence should be stressed. A distinction should also be made between these events and those of the French Revolution in the following century. The situation in England, which involved both political and religious issues, led to some highly radical doctrines by such groups as the Levellers and the Diggers, but most English revolutionaries wanted to defend property rights and the political privileges of Parliament, the aristocracy, and the established Church, even if they sought reforms. It may also be worthwhile to compare the revolution of 1688 with the civil war and subsequent events of the 1640s and to ask why England of 1688 did not take the same path as England of the 1640s. Events in eighteenth-century France began with a discussion about revising political arrangements but quickly moved in more radical directions, particularly on religious and economic questions as the radicals gained power.

Many books about the events of the 1640s and 1650s are available. A good overview of the entire period is Wilfrid R. Prest, *Albion Ascendant: English History, 1660–1815* (Oxford: Oxford University Press, 1998). For a somewhat more controversial but interesting take on much of the same period, Jonathan Scott's *England's Troubles: Seventeenth Century English Political Instability in European Context* (Cambridge, UK: Cambridge University Press, 2000) provides a broad perspective. Ann Hughes, *The Causes of the English Civil War* (New York: St. Martin's Press, 1999) is a good discussion of the important question of how the civil war began. Conrad Russell, in *The Fall of the British Monarchies, 1637–1642* (Oxford: Clarendon Press, 1991), downplays political conflict and restricts the revolutionary period to the late 1630s and early 1640s. He also stresses the extent to which the English revolution was a British problem. David Underdown, *A Freeborn People: Politics and the Nation in Seventeenth-Century England* (Oxford: Clarendon Press, 1996) offers a modified Marxist overview. Michael Walzer, *The Revolution of the Saints: A Study in the Origins of Radical Politics* (New York: Atheneum, 1975) is an important study of seventeenth-century Puritanism as a factor in revolutionary politics. A scholarly study of the revolution can be found in W. A. Speck, *Reluctant Revolutionaries: Englishmen and the Revolution of 1688* (New York: Oxford University Press, 1988). Ronald Hutton's collection of essays on Stuart Britain, *Debates in Stuart History* (New York: Palgrave Press, 2004) offers an engaging and extremely well-informed take on a range of subjects, from the Civil War to Oliver Cromwell to the reign and character of Charles II, and provides an excellent overview of changing perspectives on these events.

On Oliver Cromwell, the central figure of the English civil war, see Peter Gaunt, *Oliver Cromwell* (Oxford: Blackwell, 1995). John Dunn, *The Political Thought of John Locke* (Cambridge, UK: Cambridge University Press, 1969) presents a careful study of *The Two Treatises of Government* and other political writings by Locke.

4. Despite the upheavals caused by civil war and revolution, the seventeenth century proved to be a period of liberation for many Englishwomen. With their men away fighting in the civil war, or in exile during the Commonwealth, women assumed the management of households and businesses both small and large. They petitioned Parliament, sometimes directly, for the restoration of confiscated property, and joined nonconformist religious sects that encouraged political action as an extension of their religious beliefs. Many Englishwomen also took up the pen for public as well as private reflection and testimony. Lucy Hutchinson's memoir, excerpted in the text (see Contrasting Views, pp. 500–501), provides students with a concrete example of this kind of writing. Nor were women silenced after the restoration. As a consequence, a remarkable amount of primary material concerning Englishwomen survives from the seventeenth century. A good deal of this material has been published, and it reveals women's experiences in vivid detail. An in-depth exploration of this subject would help right the balance of a period that is often weighted toward men's experiences. See Antonia Fraser, *The Weaker Vessel* (New York: Alfred A. Knopf, 1984); Mary Prior, ed., *Women in English Society 1500–1800* (London: Methuen, 1985); Patricia Crawford, *Women and Religion in England 1500–1720* (London: Routledge, 1993 [rpt. 1996]); Ann Laurence, *Women in England 1500–1760* (New York: St. Martin's Press, 1994); and Sara Mendelson and Patricia Crawford, *Women in Early Modern England, 1550–1720* (Oxford: Oxford University Press, 1998). Some of the printed primary material from the period could be assigned to students in order to provide a common text for class discussion. See Elspeth Graham et al., eds., *Her Own Life: Autobiographical Writings by Seventeenth-Century Englishwomen* (London: Routledge, 1989 [rpt. 1992]); D. J. H. Clifford, ed., *The Diaries of Lady Anne Clifford* (Stroud, Gloucestershire: Alan Sutton, 1990 [rpt. 2003]); James Fitzmaurice et al., eds., *Major Women Writers of Seventeenth-Century England* (Ann Arbor: University of Michigan Press, 1997); Sylvia Brown, ed., *Women's Writing in Stuart England: The Mothers' Legacies of Dorothy Leigh, Elizabeth Joscelin, and Elizabeth Richardson* (Stroud, Gloucestershire: Sutton Publishing, 1999 [rpt. 2000]); and Patricia Crawford and Laura Gowing, eds., *Women's Worlds in Seventeenth-Century England: A Sourcebook* (London: Routledge, 2000).

5. The Netherlands in the seventeenth century managed not only to establish an unusual constitutional system of government, but also created a vibrant and relatively tolerant urban culture. For a brief moment, it was the European center of art, finance, and commerce. What did Dutch society look like? How far down the social hierarchy did the prosperous, comfortable way of life extend?

Depending on your level of comfort with art history, you might find it relatively easy to discuss Dutch society and economics in terms of paintings. In addition to the books by Schama and Israel listed in the chapter bibliography, see Paul Zumthor, *Daily Life in Rembrandt's Holland* (Stanford, CA: Stanford University Press, 1994); Michael North, *Art and Commerce in the Dutch Golden Age: A Social History of Seventeenth-Century Netherlandish Painting* (New Haven, CT: Yale University Press, 1997); and Mariet Westermann, *A Worldly Art: The Dutch Republic, 1585–1718* (New York: Harry Abrams, 1996). A useful overview of the history of this period is J. L. Price, *The Dutch Republic in the Seventeenth Century* (New York: St. Martin's Press, 1999). Another, more specialized title is Mike Dash, *Tulipomania: The Story of the World's Most Coveted Flower and the Extraordinary Passions It Aroused* (New York: Crown Publishers, 2000). If you are looking for a workable historical novel that raises many interesting issues about art, gender, and bourgeois culture, you might make good use of Tracy

Chevalier's *The Girl with the Pearl Earring* (New York: Plume, 1999).

6. It can be valuable to offer students an understanding of how daily life was different from today for various social classes, and for men or women. A great deal of information on how life was lived and what constituted proper behavior is given in the books listed in suggestion 4. Notions of masculine honor and aristocratic dueling traditions can also be explored, particularly in connection with the conventions and expectations of court culture. In addition to the pioneering work of Norbert Elias cited in the chapter bibliography, there is the somewhat spotty book by Roger Chartier, ed., *A History of Private Life,* vol. 3, *Passions of the Renaissance* (Cambridge, MA: Belknap Press, 1989), which is organized thematically and is chronologically wide-ranging. Anna Bryson, *From Courtesy to Civility: Changing Codes of Conduct in Early Modern England* (Oxford: Clarendon Press, 1998) offers a great deal of information and an extensive bibliography. Also useful are the overview and first two essays in Part 1 of Marilyn J. Boxer and Jean H. Quataert, eds., *Connecting Spheres: Women in the Western World, 1500 to the Present* (New York: Oxford University Press, 1987). Food was also wrapped up in issues relating to social class and manners. There are many good Internet sites on the history of food, but see also C. Anne Wilson, ed., *Banquetting Stuffe* (Edinburgh: Edinburgh University Press, 1991); Peter Brears, *Food and Cooking in Seventeenth-Century Britain: History and Recipes* (London: English Heritage, 1985); and Gilly Lehmann, *The British Housewife: Cookery-books, Cooking and Society in 18th-century Britain,* Author's draft of Part I: *Cookery Books and Cookery Before 1700,* http://www.kal69.dial.pipex.com/shop/pp./048frame.htm (accessed Dec. 21, 2007).

Class Discussion Starters

1. In discussing Louis XIV and absolutism in France, challenge students to imagine why the aristocracy did not more effectively resist the monarchy's innovations in government. In what specific ways were aristocratic privileges challenged? To whom was the business of running the country increasingly entrusted? How were the advantages of the aristocracy enhanced in certain ways by Louis? It would be helpful to make use of Marie de Sévigné's letter describing life at Versailles, and to have students list the various attractions and opportunities afforded by court culture.

2. Explore with students the dynamic in Russia and Alexei's westernizing efforts. What was the appeal of French culture in particular, and why make a priority of introducing foreign entertainment and fashion? In what ways did western "science" and technological progress make western cultural values more appealing? What is the connection between a "modern" military and western-style dress and fashion? It would also be valuable, in connection with the Old Believers, to discuss the reasons why many resisted change, innovation, and foreign influence.

3. Explore with students why Hobbes's *Leviathan* may have been appealing to English men and women at mid-century. In what ways could it be used to justify the power of someone like Oliver Cromwell? Explore the different implications of seeing the political world as Hobbes did, or as Locke did. Why were issues of sovereignty, particularly the tensions between Parliamentary and monarchial authority, so hard to resolve in Great Britain? One useful approach to the 1641–1660 and 1688–1691 disturbances in England is to review with students the way the conflict looked different from Scottish, Irish, and English perspectives. Why were many in Scotland and Ireland more willing to compromise with Charles I in 1649? Why did the Irish tend to support James II? Why was Jacobinism so much stronger in Scotland? Whatever answers students work their way toward, they will see the importance of perspective in interpreting the same set of historical facts.

4. A discussion of the consequences of the revolution for women can also be broadened to include issues of class raised by the Levellers and other socially radical groups associated with the revolution. How were these outcomes different from what either Puritan radicals or Parliamentary reformers of 1640 might have wanted? A discussion exploring these developments can underscore the difficulty of controlling or limiting the social consequences of political disturbances, a pattern that can be returned to when later revolutions are examined.

5. Begin a discussion by asking students what place on the map of seventeenth-century western Europe would they have found most appealing to live in and why; use this to bring up the advantages of the Dutch system and its appeal to many "modern" notions of toleration, freedom, and other benefits. What were the attractions of the Dutch way of life and the Dutch political system to outsiders? Where would the "odds" have been best for living a good life (if you can agree on what that means!)? What were the relative advantages and disadvantages of aristocratic life in Eastern Europe? Great Britain? France? Why did European monarchs tend to imitate the French model?

6. The popular cultivation of manners as a way to reestablish order and define the social hierarchy is an interesting topic that could easily be connected to present-day concerns about behavior in social situations. How are college and high school behaviors different? Why do manners and customs change?

How do we learn what social rules are, and how did seventeenth-century people do so? Why was proper behavior so important at court in particular? Why were books on manners so popular in this society?

Reviewing the Text

Review Questions

1. How "absolute" was the power of Louis XIV?
[model answer] • ***Theoretically, Louis ruled alone, but he depended on a growing bureaucracy:*** *Local officials, taxpayers, creditors who provided loans, and nobles at court all limited his actual ability to control the state.*
• ***Louis was the center of French government and court culture:*** *Ruling without a first minister, Louis lessened threats to his power by domesticating warrior nobles; he enticed nobles with gifts, honors, and the threat of losing his favor. Public works projects and funding of the arts and sciences proclaimed his wealth, style, and wisdom to all subjects.*
• ***Louis ruled by divine right:*** *Considering it a king's duty to instruct his subjects in the true religion, Louis staunchly defended the institution of the Catholic Church. He revoked the Edict of Nantes in 1685, and eliminated the rights of Calvinists and Huguenots.*
• ***Military bureaucracy extended state authority:*** *Louis XIV's bureaucracy strengthened the military by expanding state control over military financing, conscription, and supply. The army's growth and success in war justified the expansion of state power.*

2. Why did absolutism flourish everywhere in eastern Europe except Poland-Lithuania?
[model answer] • ***Absolutism succeeded when leaders controlled, accommodated, or pacified the nobility:*** *Leaders in Brandenburg-Prussia offered nobles more money or pacified them with more independence, military power, or bureaucratic positions. In Austria, the Holy Roman Emperor created a new noble class that spoke German, professed Catholicism, and would be loyal to the Austrian dynasty. Ottoman sultans stayed in power by playing elites off one another as they vied for political power. In Russia, the tsar controlled his nobles by creating a new class of chattel-serfs in exchange for their obedience.*
• ***Military strength bolstered absolutism:*** *In countries where absolutism succeeded, a political leader increased power by maintaining control over the military. Military successes contributed to the personal prestige of the monarch, and the military could be used both to promote territorial expansion and to overawe potential aristocratic opponents of centralized authority.*
• ***In Poland-Lithuania a weak monarchy combined with a powerful nobility to create chaos:*** *Poland-Lithuania's nobles became autonomous warlords and, despite brief attempts to rebuild the monarchy, nobles dominated parliament. Each noble held absolute veto power, and this system both deadlocked parliamentary government and took away any remaining power the monarchy had.*

3. What differences over religion and politics caused the conflict between king and Parliament in England?
[model answer] • ***Authority to raise taxes and pass laws:*** *Because England had no single constitutional document, a variety of laws, judicial decisions, charters, petitions, and customary procedures regulated relations between the king and Parliament. Common disagreements arose over the king's levying of taxes and the passing of laws without Parliament's consent, which resulted in civil war. Ultimately, the dispute was theoretical. Could monarchs act outside the law, and could their will be substituted for that of Parliament as they saw fit?*
• ***Power to call Parliament into session:*** *Until the 1689 Bill of Rights mandated regular meetings and royal–parliamentary cooperation, a king's only weapon against a rebellious Parliament was to not call Parliament into session, or to disband an unruly assembly.*
• ***Puritan/Anglican/Catholic conflict over royal authority to impose religious beliefs:*** *While English Puritans agitated for the removal of any vestiges of Catholicism from the Anglican church, kings usually moved in the opposite direction because of their personal religious beliefs, their Catholic spouses, or their desires to make alliances with Catholic monarchs. The monarchy remained committed to a church structure that could be controlled from the top down, through Bishops appointed by the monarch and accountable to him or her. Puritans sought a less hierarchical, more locally accountable church. Parliament viewed the royal imposition of religious beliefs as just another form of royal control and attempted to limit kings' actions.*

4. Why did constitutionalism thrive in the Dutch Republic and the British North American colonies, even as their participation in the slave trade grew?
[model answer] • ***Slave trade profits allowed constitutional governments to remain independent and to oppose absolutism:*** *The Dutch Republic and England led the coalition that blocked Louis XIV's efforts to dominate continental Europe. Both were oriented toward overseas commerce, a major part of which was the Atlantic trade in African slaves. The British North American colonies also developed a constitutional government while using African slaves as a major labor force.*
• ***Political and religious authorities condoned expanding the slave trade:*** *The governments of constitutional monarchies and republics alike encouraged trafficking in African slaves, often by private companies. The highest church and government authorities in Catholic and Protestant countries condoned or at least tolerated the expanding slave trade.*

• ***Appeal of slavery to all countries:*** *Slavery enabled European nations to set up large-scale farming operations in their colonies and to produce desirable products such as sugar for consumption in the home country. In general, slavery succeeded because it provided a much needed labor force, which in turn increased profits for planters, merchants, and, under mercantilism and prevailing customs practices, governments.*

5. How did elite and popular culture become more separate in the seventeenth century?
[model answer] • **Increased literacy in the noble and middle classes distinguished them from illiterate peasants:** *Literacy reflected the value of new scientific ideas, literature, and artistic and cultural developments. Peasant culture focused on work, communal forms of entertainment, and religion.*
• ***Importance of manners:*** *For nobles and the middle classes, manners became a form of self-discipline. Nobles' behavior at court became the basis for their class identity. The middle classes believed that manners equated incorrect behavior with dirt and rusticity; those who did not know how to behave were peasants. Such beliefs helped the middle class to differentiate themselves from their social inferiors.*
• ***Elites tried to change popular religious practice:*** *Both Protestant and Catholic reform movements pushed to remove festive (or pagan) communal elements of religion that interfered with sober religious observance.*
• ***New elite attitude toward poverty:*** *Though previously linked with charity and virtue in Christianity, the upper classes began to see the poor as dangerous, deceitful, and lacking character. By the mid-seventeenth century, officials turned hospitals into houses of confinement for beggars and prostitutes. The elites wanted to separate the poor from society to change them, or at least keep them from contaminating others.*

Making Connections

1. What accounts for the success of absolutism in some parts of Europe and its failure in others?
[model answer] *Absolutism relied to a great extent on the personality of monarchs, so one factor was the charisma and character of the monarchs who attempted to strengthen royal rule. A still more critical factor, as the failure of absolutism in England and Poland both demonstrate, is the relative power of the gentry and aristocracy and their determination to control and mediate political power through assemblies and legislatures. In England in particular, the outcome of military conflict between closely matched royal and parliamentary armies was, in the long run, decisive.*

2. How did religious differences in the late seventeenth century still cause political conflict?
[model answer] *Although the Thirty Years' War demonstrated that religion had to be separated out of international politics, religious conflict nevertheless remained a domestic issue, and this was especially true for England. The English civil war (1642–1646) and the Glorious Revolution (1688) were, to a large extent, conflicts over religion.*

3. Why was the search for order a major theme in science, politics, and the arts during this period?
[model answer] *To a certain extent, new ideas and innovations in these areas can be related to fear and a loss of certainty. Every aspect of life seemed chaotic after the Thirty Years' War, and artists and intellectuals sought to make sense of the changing world. Hobbes and Locke sought a political philosophy rooted in nature, whereas scientists like Newton attempted to explain the workings of the universe and to connect scientific observation to theological questions. Artists were employed to emphasize the power, authority, and, significantly, control of the Catholic church and absolutist states like France.*

Discussing the Documents

Questions from Online Study Guide with Model Answers

Marie de Sévigné, Letter Describing the French Court (1675), p. 487

1. What is Sévigné's attitude toward court life?
[model answer] *Sévigné says that the entertainments are boring because there are so many of them. There are "pleasures" at Versailles, but court life can be surprising and disturbing as well.*

2. What does Sévigné's letter reveal about Louis's mistress, Madame de Montespan?
[model answer] *Sévigné had a nickname for her (Quantova). Montespan had seven children by Louis and was the subject of a great deal of "fuss" at court. Despite her triumphant attitude, Sévigné found her to be sad.*

John Milton, Defense of Freedom of the Press (1644), p. 511

1. How does John Milton depict books in this passage?
[model answer] *Milton describes books as living things, and an "image of God." Because they contain knowledge that lasts past the lifetime of individuals, they are immortal. They are also essential to civilization because a "rejected truth" is impossible to recover, which makes "whole nations fare the worse."*

2. Why is freedom of the press essential for maintaining virtue, even when published books are immoral?

[model answer] *According to Milton, there is no virtue in never facing vice "with all her baits and seeming pleasures." Virtue comes with facing vice and resisting it; "that which purifies us is trial, and trial is by what is contrary." If all vice were to be eliminated, then virtue would no longer exist.*

Contrasting Views: The English Civil War (pp. 500–501)

1. Why would both the king and the parliamentary leaders find the Levellers' views disturbing?
[model answer] *The document offers obvious challenges to royal authority in its assertion of parliamentary supremacy and the fundamental right of Parliament to call all other government officials to account—the issue of the accountability of the king's servants and ministers to Parliament was a crucial issue in the buildup to war. At the same time, parliamentarians also had grounds for concern. The document called for a new, fairer system for choosing representatives and insisted that the people (not the Parliament, dominated as it was by the wealthy and aristocrats) had sovereignty over their elected representatives.*

2. Why did Hobbes's arguments about political authority upset supporters of both monarchy and Parliament?
[model answer] *Both the Parliament and the king believed in a well-ordered state and in their interpretation of the existing political system. The notion that politics was made (and unmade?) by men acting to protect and promote their interests was fundamentally disturbing to monarch and parliamentarian alike. The document is ambivalent about the nature of the sovereign power the people would resolve to constitute—it may be either an individual or a parliament, according to this excerpt. But in either case its power should be absolute and sufficient to "overawe" potential resistance. Neither patriarchal nor parliamentary models for politics had much room for Hobbes's vision of government as a contract to preserve civilization from endless war and associated destruction and instability.*

Other Questions for Discussing These Documents in Class

Marie de Sévigné, Letter Describing the French Court (1675), p. 487

1. Use Sévigné's comments about boredom to discuss the relationship between too much luxury and pleasure and boredom. Can people become overstimulated? (You might bring video games into the conversation!) What are some of the possible social consequences of boredom?

2. Does Sévigné's letter reveal much about the power and influence of women at the court? Was court life a good venue for women to exercise power?

John Milton, Defense of Freedom of the Press (1644), p. 511

1. Have students work through the specific reasons Milton gives against censorship. Why is it a mistake for states to do so, even given that the written word is powerful?

2. Short of licensing laws, against which Milton protests here, how can governments combat or control the circulation of "dangerous" ideas? Does Milton offer any suggestions or insight?

Contrasting Views: The English Civil War, pp. 500–501

1. To what extent do the critiques by the Levellers and Lucy Hutchinson of existing political authorities reflect class tensions? What do they reveal about what the civil war may have been about for those involved in fighting it?

2. Discuss the difficulties inherent in moving forward after "successful" revolutions. If political authority was successfully located in Parliament, as the Levellers demanded, what would Lucy Hutchinson and those who thought like her expect from that institution? Are those views reconcilable with Hobbes? Was the revolution about political structures, the misbehavior of the King and court, or the rights of subjects?

Comparative Questions

1. Use the documents to reflect on the getting and keeping of political power in this period. Why was Louis in France able to assert control of his aristocracy and his people, and what caused the monarchy to be more vulnerable in Britain?

2. Review the visions of ideal political authority described or touched on in the documents. How should governments act, and how should they be controlled? What is appealing to students about all of them? What is worrisome about them?

For Users of *Sources of The Making of the West*

The following documents are available in Chapter 16 of the companion sourcebook by Katharine J. Lualdi, University of Southern Maine.

1. Civil War and Social Contract: Thomas Hobbes, *Leviathan* (1651)

2. The Consent of the Governed: John Locke, *The Second Treatise of Government* (1690)
3. Opposing Serfdom: Ludwig Fabritius, *The Revolt of Stenka Razin* (1670)
4. Fighting for Empire: *A True and Exact Relation of the Raising of the Siege of Vienna* (1683)
5. In Search of the Northwest Passage: Jacques Marquette, *Exploring the Mississippi* (1673)

Discussion Ideas for Sources of The Making of the West, *Chapter 16*

1. Working with *Leviathan* and *The Second Treatise*, have students consider the context in which both texts were written. In what ways might the chaos of the English civil war and the execution of Charles I influenced the political thought of Hobbes? For Locke, how were the ongoing tensions between king and Parliament relevant to his arguments? Why were both men so concerned about the relationship between government and the interests and consent of the governed?

2. Use *The Revolt of Stenka Razin* and *A True and Exact Relation* to generate a discussion about military conflict and violence in this period. What inspires the officers and soldiers in these accounts to fight and die? Does religion seem to be the strongest motivation in the battle for Vienna, or are other motivations at work as well? Make sure you discuss the French presence in the Ottoman army and what it might reveal about the dynastic dimension to the conflict. What does *The Revolt* reveal about the nature of military loyalty and the fragility of authority? You might explore, in light of the text, why the army may have been unreliable in such a conflict and what that reveals about the actual power of absolutist states of the era.

3. Discuss how *Exploring the Mississippi* contributes to our understanding of the way Europeans saw frontier territories and unexplored regions. What motivations do students believe (in light of the document) were most important?

Working with Visual Sources

For this exercise, please refer to A Typical Dutch Scene from Daily Life on p. 507 of the textbook or view the image on the book companion site's Online Study Guide under the "Visual Activity" for Chapter 16.

Students viewing the image at the Online Study Guide are asked three questions about the image. The questions and model answers (not made available to students) are below. Project this image, available on the Instructor's Resources CD-ROM, in class or ask students to look at the image in their textbooks and answer the questions.

1. Who are the people in this painting and what are they doing?
[model answer] *The people in the painting are the baker Arent Oostwaard and his wife. They are putting baked goods on a tray.*

2. What are the people in this painting wearing and what moods do their facial expressions and body postures suggest?
[model answer] *Arent Oostwaard and his wife are wearing modest and clean clothing. Their expressions are calm and smiling, and their postures appear relaxed and active.*

3. What does this painting tell us about Dutch attitudes toward daily life?
[model answer] *The attitude of Dutch painter Jan Steen as revealed in* The Baker Arent Oostwaard and His Wife *presents daily life as industrious but happy and relaxed. The painting hints that ordinary people are in charge of their own lives by presenting the baker and his wife in respectable clothing, making bread, and happy.*

Mapping Exercises

Map Activity from Online Study Guide—Model Answer for Map Activity #2

For this activity, please refer to Map 16.3: Dutch Commerce in the Seventeenth Century on p. 506. Students are asked these questions:

Where were some of the places that the Dutch Republic had commercial contact with?
[model answer] *The Dutch Republic traded with other parts of Europe, with North and South America, and with Africa. It also had ports in India and in southeast Asia, and traded with China and Japan.*

Where did the Dutch control territory, and how were these possessions important for trade?
[model answer] *The Dutch controlled territory in the New Netherlands of North America and more extensive territory in South America (Dutch Brazil and Guiana), important for the sugar and tobacco trades. They also had a provisioning station at Cape Town and forts on the coast of West Africa involved in the slave trade and in India, important for the cloth trade. Extensive territories in the islands of the Indian Ocean (Ceylon, Java, Macassar) were involved in the spice trade and in trade with China.*

Map 16.1: Louis XIV's Acquisitions, 1668–1697, p. 492

Ask students to examine the map and consider what goals Louis may have had in the various campaigns.

Why were the Spanish Netherlands and the lands of the Holy Roman Empire tempting to Louis?

Map 16.2: State Building in Central and Eastern Europe, 1648–1699, p. 494

How would the expansion of Austrian Habsburg territories to the east change the nature of that empire? (Discuss with students the ethnic composition of the empire's population, both in the older segment and in the newer territories.) The Austrian Habsburgs acquired vast new territories outside the boundaries of the Holy Roman Empire. What changes did this foreshadow for the position of the Austrian Habsburgs within the Holy Roman Empire? Finally, ask students to speculate about Brandenburg-Prussia's next moves within the Holy Roman Empire, based on the geographical nature of the state.

Map 16.3: Dutch Commerce in the Seventeenth Century, p. 506

Ask the students to identify zones of Dutch commercial activity (in the Atlantic, the Baltic, and the Indian/Pacific Ocean areas). How did goods move within these zones? Make lists of what was traded within each zone. What role did places like Cape Town and Amsterdam play in the commercial patterns that the Dutch developed? What information would you need, besides what the map provides, to get a sense of the relative importance of the various trades the Dutch participated in?

Mapping the West: Europe at the End of the Seventeenth Century, p. 516

Ask students to rank the European powers as military powers, as economic powers, and as centers of intellectual and cultural life. Then ask students to justify their rankings. Would any of the European powers occupy the same position on all three lists? Which state was "strongest" overall and why? Ask students what other kinds of information they would like to have available for constructing the lists.

In-Class Assignments and Presentation Topics

1. Assign students to read William Beik, *Louis XIV and Absolutism: A Brief Study with Documents* (Boston: Bedford/St. Martin's, 1999) and have them write an essay on Louis's understanding of absolutism as a political system. What did he believe were its uses? How did he set about constructing it? Did he see it as the means to other goals or as an end in itself? It would probably be helpful to discuss absolutism and touch on Louis's version in a preliminary way. You may wish to limit the number of questions students pursue in their essays. For example, the last question will raise several different issues and may well be enough to serve as the basis for a short essay. Consult Beik's book, which contains a fine list of questions following the primary source documents, for additional ideas about assignments.

2. Students should enjoy doing presentations on individuals, groups, and events in the English civil war. Possible topics might include the Levellers, Ranters, Quakers, and other dissenting religious groups of the period; Charles I, Charles II, or James II; Oliver Cromwell, William Laude, or the Irish clan chief Owen Roe O'Neill. This assignment will work better if the class spends a session outlining the major events, people, and some of the more important interpretations of the English civil war before they present their reports. Students should prepare their reports before this session, and use the review as a way of checking their understanding of the material and clarifying points that are not yet clear. Encourage them to bring in documents, illustrations, and other material that will help their audience grasp the information in the reports more quickly.

3. Select four paintings by Jan Vermeer and make reproductions of them readily available (you might use links to established Web sites). Students are to choose one and write informally about what the painting tells them about life during the seventeenth century in the Netherlands. Stress that the essay is not intended to be written from the perspective of art history; comments about Vermeer's blues or yellows are not what you are looking for. Although students may wish to read about the paintings they have chosen, the essays should be based mostly on what each student learns about seventeenth-century life in the Netherlands.

4. Ask students to consider the connections between manners and social hierarchy. Are manners primarily a way of distinguishing one group from another? Students should choose a seventeenth-century example and a twenty-first-century example and explain how they perceive each. Let them know that the examples may be seen in different ways. Using a handkerchief in the seventeenth century, for example, set one apart from most other people. Using a Blackberry or an iPhone in a restaurant in the twenty-first century may likewise be connected to social hierarchy.

Essay Questions

1. Historical fiction is often much maligned by historians. It is certainly difficult to do well, but when

good writing is combined with historical accuracy, such fiction can be a wonderful entrée into the study of history. Four recent novels deal with paintings and other aspects of the Netherlands in the seventeenth century. Provide students with a brief synopsis of each novel and with a short bibliography of readings they may use in ascertaining the skill of a particular novelist in making use of historical fact (draw from the chapter bibliography and from "Lecture Strategies," number 4). The novels are Tracy Chevalier, *Girl with a Pearl Earring* (New York: Dutton, 1999); Deborah Moggach, *Tulip Fever* (New York: Delacorte Press, 2000); Susan Vreeland, *Girl in Hyacinth Blue* (Denver, CO: MacMurray & Beck, 1999); and Katherine Weber, *The Music Lesson* (New York: Picador USA, 2000). The novels by Chevalier and Moggach are set in the seventeenth century, Vreeland's book tells the story of a fictitious Vermeer across time, and Weber deals with a real Vermeer in a twentieth-century setting. Vreeland and especially Weber may move further away from the seventeenth century than is useful, so some care should be taken in setting up the assignment.

2. Ask students to investigate England, France, and the Dutch Republic in the 1670s and 1680s in order to decide in which country they would most like to have lived and in which country they would least like to have lived. It might be helpful to have a discussion beforehand about criteria. For example, is political stability the main criterion, or should it be economic development, social opportunity, or cultural and intellectual vitality? You may have some success creating characters with brief biographies and assigning them to the students in order to attune them to the period's gender, class, and race dynamics—for example, a bookseller, a Catholic merchant, a recently freed slave, or an extremely talented musician. This research project may be done by individuals or by groups. It may result in a traditional essay, some type of statistical or visual presentation, or perhaps a combination of all three. Another related assignment is to divide the class into three real-estate companies, which then make presentations on the country they believe provides the best way of life in the late seventeenth century. Each company would organize itself into those who did the basic research, those who wrote the copy or created the presentations, and those who actually made the pitch. Each member of the company would be required to write a short essay commenting on the experience.

Additional Resources: Literature

Cobb, Walter J., trans., *Madame de Lafayette: The Princesse de Cleves*. 1992.

Frame, Donald M., trans., *Tartuffe and Other Plays by Molière*. 1967.

Leonard, John, ed., *John Milton: Paradise Lost*. 2003.

Tuck, Richard, ed., *Hobbes: Leviathan*. 1991.

Montgomery, George R., trans., *Gottfried Wilhelm Leibniz: Discourse on Metaphysics and the Monadology*. 1992.

Shapiro, Ian, ed., *Two Treatises of Government and a Letter Concerning Toleration by John Locke*. 2003.

Additional Resources: Film and Video

Restoration (1994; VHS/DVD, 118 min.). The court of Charles II of England serves as a backdrop to this film. Although the plot is fiction, some historical events are chronicled, such as the Great Plague of 1665. The film is strong on such details as setting and costuming, and especially strong on seventeenth-century science and medicine.

The Last King (2004; DVD, 188 min.). Although the events of Charles II's life and reign are compressed, this film provides an excellent and largely accurate account of the English king. The contradictions in the king's character have been nicely captured, and care has been lavished on costuming and sets.

OTHER BEDFORD/ST. MARTIN'S RESOURCES FOR CHAPTER 16

The following resources are available to accompany Chapter 16. Please refer to the Preface of this manual for detailed descriptions of all the ancillaries.

For Instructors

Transparencies

The following maps and images from Chapter 16 are available as full-color acetates.

- Map 16.1: Louis XIV's Acquisitions, 1668–1697
- Map 16.2: State Building in Central and Eastern Europe, 1648–1699
- Map 16.3: Dutch Commerce in the Seventeenth Century
- Mapping the West: Europe at the End of the Seventeenth Century
- A Typical Dutch Scene from Daily Life, p. 507
- Gian Lorenzo Bernini, *Ecstasy of St. Teresa of Ávila* (c. 1650), p. 509

Instructor's Resources CD-ROM

The following maps and image from Chapter 16, as well as a chapter outline, are available on disc in both PowerPoint and jpeg formats.

- Map 16.1: Louis XIV's Acquisitions, 1668–1697
- Map 16.2: State Building in Central and Eastern Europe, 1648–1699
- Map 16.3: Dutch Commerce in the Seventeenth Century
- Mapping the West: Europe at the End of the Seventeenth Century
- A Typical Dutch Scene from Daily Life, p. 507

Using the Bedford Series with The Making of the West

Available in print as well as online at **bedfordstmartins.com/usingseries,** this guide offers practical suggestions for using Allan Greer, *The Jesuit Relations*, William Beik, *Louis XIV and Absolutism* and Steven C. A. Pincus, *England's Glorius Revolution, 1688–1989* in conjunction with Chapter 16 of the textbook.

For Students

Study Guides

The Online Study Guide at **bedfordstmartins.com/hunt** helps students synthesize the material they have learned as well as practice the skills historians use to make sense of the past. The following Map, Visual, and Document activities are available for Chapter 16.

Map Activity

- Mapping the West: Europe at the End of the Seventeenth Century

Visual Activity

- A Typical Dutch Scene from Daily Life, p. 506

Reading Historical Documents

- Marie de Sévigné, Letter Describing the French Court (1675), p. 487
- John Milton, Defense of Freedom of the Press (1644), p. 511
- Contrasting Views: The English Civil War, pp. 500–501

CHAPTER

17

The Atlantic System and Its Consequences

1690–1740

CHAPTER RESOURCES

Main Chapter Topics

1. An Atlantic system involving the exchange of manufactured goods, slaves, and plantation commodities such as coffee, sugar, cotton, and tobacco linked western Europe, the western coast of Africa, and the Western Hemisphere together in a commercial network. It created a powerful impetus for economic expansion in the first half of the eighteenth century.

2. The growth in commerce and population helped to create new social and cultural patterns, most readily visible in the cities of western Europe. A more literate public demonstrated interest in concerts, novels, and the often-critical views of writers and artists, and broadened the audience for, and range of, artistic production.

3. The new balance of power that emerged after Louis XIV's death (1715) resulted in greater stability for European states, less frequent and ruinous wars, and increased opportunity to expand control both at home and in the colonies.

4. Within the new balance of power, Russia and Prussia emerged as claimants to the status of great powers, Sweden and the Dutch Republic lost ground and could no longer be considered great powers, and Poland-Lithuania began a gradual weakening process that led to its disappearance by the end of the eighteenth century. Successful mobilization of political and military resources produced great-power status, while failure to mobilize adequate resources led to decline relative to the great powers.

5. The European Enlightenment owed its origins and development—at least in part—to the new balance of power and economic expansion. It emphasized a secular, scientific, critical, but also optimistic, attitude as it began to gain momentum in the 1730s and 1740s. It also stimulated debate concerning the condition of women and their place in society.

6. Europe crossed a major threshold in the first half of the eighteenth century, moving from an economy governed by scarcity to one that promised increasing growth and improvement.

Focus Question

What were the most important consequences of the growth of the Atlantic system?

1. The Atlantic system, which grew up rapidly around the trade generated by the plantation economies of the Americas, had a number of significant consequences. The system produced tremendous wealth for plantation owners and many merchants and greater prosperity for many others in the west, particularly the growing urban middle class. A consumer society developed in the west, as new products such as sugar and tobacco were integrated into daily life and as incomes rose for the middle class. Cultural and artistic changes also flowed from the growing influence of the middle class.

2. The need for labor in the Atlantic marketplace fueled migrations to the cities in northwestern Europe and the colonies, and also spawned the development of the slave system. Slavery ultimately came to provide the labor force for the plantation system, and millions of black Africans were taken out of Africa and sent to the plantations of the Americas, where they labored under brutal and exploitative conditions that became increasingly systematically oppressive.

Annotated Chapter Outline

I. **The Atlantic System and the World Economy**
   A. **Slavery and the Atlantic System, pp. 521–526**
      1. Eighteenth-century European trade in the Atlantic expanded rapidly and became

more interconnected. Large European-owned plantations turned out staple crops such as sugar, tobacco, and coffee that could produce fabulous wealth and were farmed by slave labor.

2. State-chartered private companies from several European states exported slaves from the West African coast to the plantations in Brazil, the Caribbean, and the North American mainland. Staggering numbers of slaves crossed the Atlantic in increasing numbers, peaking in the 1780s but continuing through the middle of the nineteenth century. More than 11 million Africans were brought to the Americas as slaves.
3. The black population of the Americas was highest in areas where large plantations were most common. Blacks outnumbered whites by wide margins in the Caribbean and parts of British North America.
4. Slaves, bought from other Africans who acquired them through warfare or kidnapping, were treated cruelly on the three-month journey across the Atlantic. As many as one-fourth died on the way.
5. In the Americas, slaves were subject to degrading treatment and oppressive working conditions. Slaves in sugar-growing areas worked hardest, died in huge numbers, and had to be replaced. In North America, slave populations grew naturally.
6. Slaves resisted their condition in a variety of ways. Masters feared slave conspiracies and revolts, although these were uncommon. Slaves were controlled by beatings, whippings, and repressive laws.
7. The plantation system altered consumption patterns and led to high demand in Europe for tobacco and sugar.
8. Although some Europeans condemned slavery and Christianity preached spiritual equality, over the course of the eighteenth century Europeans came to see Africans as racially inferior. The belief that Africans were meant to be slaves coexisted with growing talk of liberty and rights.

B. World Trade and Settlement, pp. 526–528

1. The Atlantic system helped extend European trade relations across the globe and led to the seizure of territory and the establishment of new settlements.
2. Densest settlements were established in the Americas. France, Spain, Britain, and Portugal competed for territory.
3. Local economies shaped diverse colonial social relations. In Spanish and Portuguese settlements, sexual contact with native populations led to racially diverse populations. Intermarriage aided the spread of Christianity in Spanish colonies.
4. More men than women emigrated from Europe, although the imbalance was reduced in the eighteenth century. Female emigrants faced risk of disease, illegitimate pregnancy, and forced marriages.
5. Government-sponsored piracy was common in the sixteenth and seventeenth centuries. Later in the 1600s independent pirates or buccaneers became common, especially in the Caribbean, despite efforts by governments to eliminate them.
6. White settlement in Africa and Asia remained small scale. Africa remained largely unexplored, and by 1720 the European presence in China was restricted to a small number of merchants in Guangzhou. In the East Indies, large Dutch coffee plantations were established in Java.
7. By the 1740s France and England were rivals with India for controlling the spice, cotton, and silk trades. Both countries expanded their influence as India's Muslim rulers lost control to local leaders.
8. Europeans found eastern religious practices exotic and interesting, but deemed the east to be culturally inferior.

C. The Birth of Consumer Society, pp. 528–529

1. Population growth in Europe, approximately 20 percent between 1700 and 1750, fueled demand for foreign goods. Declining death rates, due to improvement in the climate, better agricultural techniques, and the disappearance of the plague after the 1720s, led to a population explosion that was most noticeable in cities.
2. The combined effects of economic expansion and population growth brought about a consumer revolution. Imports soared and items such as tea, tobacco, chocolate, and coffee became virtual necessities, and coffeehouses spread throughout Europe.
3. A new economic dynamic developed as ordinary people gained more disposable income, which caused an increase in the demand for consumer goods. Rising demand created jobs and increased purchasing power, and many English authors began to portray humans as

consuming animals with boundless appetites.

4. "Consumerism" was opposed by many thinkers, but this did not slow its growth. The consumer revolution was uneven and spread from cities to the countryside, from England to the Continent, and from western to eastern Europe.

II. New Social and Cultural Patterns

A. Agricultural Revolution, pp. 529–531

1. An agricultural revolution was pioneered by the Flemish and Dutch in the 1600s, but matured in Britain in the eighteenth century and then spread throughout Europe. Farmers increased the amount of land under cultivation; consolidated plots into larger, more efficient units; practiced crop rotation and fodder production; and began to selectively breed their better-fed livestock. Food prices fell, and production increased dramatically.
2. Bigger landowners benefited most and increased their holdings by "enclosing" common land and putting pressure on small farmers and villagers to sell land and give up grazing rights. Class structures in England became more hierarchical, marked by big landlords, enterprising tenant farmers, and poor agricultural laborers.
3. New farming techniques spread slowly across western Europe, and subsistence agriculture remained dominant. Outside of the highly urbanized Low Countries, most Europeans remained in the countryside on the margins of the new market economy.
4. In eastern Europe, conditions for peasants often worsened where landlords attempted to improve and expand their holdings. Serfdom, marked by compulsory labor services, was widespread among the peasantry and differed little from slavery.

B. Social Life in the Cities, pp. 531–534

1. From 1650–1750, migration from the countryside increased the population of cities over ten thousand by 44 percent. Urbanization increased most rapidly in northwestern Europe, matching the level of urbanization previously found in the Italian states and the Iberian Peninsula. Eastern Europe was less urban than western, and in 1750 London became the largest European city with 675,000 inhabitants.
2. Landed nobles were at the top of the social system. They often lived extravagantly in cities, employed large numbers of servants and artisans, and held key positions in political systems.
3. The middle class, composed of urban officials, merchants, professionals, and landowners, developed a distinctive way of life.
4. Below the middle class, artisans and shopkeepers, organized in professional guilds, worked with journeymen, apprentices, servants, and laborers. The unemployed poor survived on charity and intermittent work. Women married to artisans and shopkeepers often ran both businesses and families. Predominantly female domestic servants were increasingly common in large cities.
5. Social status was readily apparent, and living conditions varied widely according to social class. Occupations and social class were apparent from dress.
6. Social differences were reflected in literacy rates, which were higher among the upper classes. Literacy among the lower classes was more common in Protestant countries. Despite some improvements, most peasants remained illiterate and primary schooling was inadequate almost everywhere. There were no national systems of control or supervision of primary education.
7. Growing middle-class literacy contributed to the development of a new, literate public in cities. Books and periodicals became more common from the 1690s, beginning in Britain and the Dutch Republic. In England magazines were established and many provincial newspapers, often read in coffeehouses, were published by 1720. Newspapers developed more slowly on the continent.

C. New Tastes in the Arts, pp. 534–536

1. The new literate public also interested itself in painting and concerts and patronized new writers and artists, who now had new sources of income beyond the church, rulers, and courtiers. The audience for the arts expanded, leading to the appearance of new forms of political and social criticism.
2. Rococo painting, best exemplified by the work of Antoine Watteau (1684–1721) and François Boucher (1703–1770), challenged baroque and classical schools.

Like baroque, rococo emphasized irregularity and asymmetry, but was more subtle and intimate. The decorative rococo style was reflective of the sensibilities of the middle-class public.

3. Public concerts were first performed in England in the 1670s and became more frequent from the 1690s. Opera houses and city concert halls spread. The growth of a public that supported music allowed composers to work for a broader audience, although court and church patrons still commissioned much of the music in the eighteenth century.
4. The German composer George Frideric Handel (1685–1759) was among the first to grasp the new directions in music. Handel introduced the oratorio, which combined the drama of opera with the majesty of religious and ceremonial music and featured the chorus over the soloists. His oratorio *Messiah* (1741) reflected his personal piety but also his ability to capture the enthusiasm of music's new public.
5. An unprecedented explosion of novels also captured the imagination of the public, and new writers and booksellers appeared to meet the new demand for books. Women figured prominently in this development, as characters and novelists. Novelists such as Eliza Haywood (1693?–1756) and Daniel Defoe (1660–1731) depicted changing social circumstances and the challenges they presented to men and women.

D. Religious Revivals, p. 536

1. Most of Europe remained devoutly religious.
2. In Protestant Europe, Pietism rocked the complacency of the established churches. Pietists wanted a more deeply emotional, even ecstatic religion, and their emphasis on intense religious practice and reading the Bible contributed to the increase in literacy. Pietism was strongest in Prussia.
3. In Catholic France, Quietism and Jansenism had a common emphasis on mystical union with God and simple but intense devotional practice.
4. Jansenism took a revivalist turn in the 1720s. Adherents resisted government attempts to control the movement, and Jansenists became more politically active in opposition to crown policies after mid-century.

III. Consolidation of the European State System

A. French Absolutism Thwarted, pp. 536–538

1. When Louis XIV died at age 76 in 1715, many of his accomplishments had already begun to unravel. Despite high taxes, wars had exhausted his treasury.
2. William III, prince of Orange and King of England and Scotland (r. 1689–1702) forged an alliance including Britain, the Dutch Republic, Sweden, Austria, and Spain, which fought Louis to a stalemate in the Nine Years' War (1689–1697).
3. The War of Spanish Succession, which lasted from 1701–1713, began when the Spanish king Charles II died without an heir and a relative of Louis XIV was named as his successor.
4. In order to prevent the union of France and Spain, several other powers united against France and eventually forced it to accept disadvantageous terms in the Peace of Utrecht of 1713–1714.
5. Louis's second grandson was recognized as king of Spain, but he had to renounce any future claim to the French crown, thereby preventing the union of the two kingdoms. Spain surrendered valuable territories in Italy and the Netherlands and ceded Gibraltar to Britain.
6. At home Louis XIV's absolutism fostered resentment from the nobility, and after his death the regents for his five-year-old great-grandson and successor, Louis XV (r. 1715–1774), tried to give the nobility and parlements a greater say in political affairs.
7. His regents also experimented with financial reforms, such as the creation of a state bank, which collapsed a few months later.
8. France did benefit from peace. Large projects for canal and road construction contributed to a prolonged period of prosperity.

B. British Rise and Dutch Decline, pp. 538–540

1. Relations between England, Scotland, and Ireland were complicated by the problem of succession. With the death of William and Mary, the English crown passed to Mary's sister Anne, who died in 1714 without an heir.
2. To ensure the throne remained under Protestant control, Parliament provided for the elector of Hanover, a Protestant great-grandson of James I, to become King George I (r. 1714–1727).

3. Many in Scotland and Ireland supported the claims of James II and, after his death in 1701, those of his son James Edward. Fear of "Jacobitism" led Scottish Protestants to agree to an Act of Union in 1707, which abolished the separate Scottish Parliament and reaffirmed the Hanoverian succession.
4. A Jacobite rebellion in Scotland failed in 1715, but Jacobitism remained a threat through the 1740s.
5. Ireland, 90 percent Catholic, was the site of conflict between James II and William III in 1689 until James fled to France. Catholics forfeited land to Protestants, and the Protestant-controlled Irish Parliament passed a series of laws severely restricting political, economic, and religious rights of Catholics. Impoverished Catholic Ireland was treated as a colony.
6. In Great Britain, the constitutional system provided for the monarch to rule with Parliament. Parliament was dominated by the Whig party. Government was dominated by a few hundred families of the landed gentry.
7. George I and George II (r. 1727–1760) relied heavily on Sir Robert Walpole (1676–1745), who strengthened the power of Parliament through his use of patronage and became the first "prime minister" responsible for guiding legislation through the House of Commons. In the long run, the patronage system used by Walpole and his successors alienated the Tories, London's middle class, and Britain's North American colonies.
8. Partisan differences between Whigs, who supported the Hanoverian succession and the rights of dissenting Protestants, and the Tories, who supported the Stuart line and the Anglican church, did not hamper Great Britain's growing power. Great Britain became a great power during this period by virtue of its navy and the successful establishment in 1694 of the Bank of England, which strengthened the government's ability to finance wars.
9. During this period the Dutch Republic lost much of its influence in international politics as it lost much of its share in Baltic trade and its control of India, Ceylon, and Java.

C. **Russia's Emergence as a Major Power, pp. 540–544**

1. In Russia, Peter the Great's (r. 1689–1725) attempt to transform Russia into a "westernized" absolutist state ignited enduring controversy.
2. Peter recruited foreigners to Russia to build scientific academies and technical schools, and forced the nobility to adopt western language, culture, and manners.
3. In 1703 he began construction of St. Petersburg, a new capital on the Baltic coast symbolizing Russia's opening to the west; St. Petersburg represented a decisive break with Russia's past.
4. Peter insisted on more public roles for traditionally denigrated women.
5. Peter's reforms affected only the Russian elites. The masses paid for the innovations and construction with new taxes. Serfs remained completely dominated by the aristocracy.
6. Government and finance were organized along western models and the Russian army was expanded and modernized.
7. Peter was ruthless, torturing and executing thousands who opposed him. He arrested his own son, Alexei, who died in prison.
8. Through the Table of Ranks established in 1722 he made the social and economic privileges the nobles enjoyed depend on their service to the crown.
9. His establishment in 1721 of the Holy Synod, a bureaucracy of laymen under his supervision, brought the Russian Orthodox church under royal control.
10. Sweden had dominated the Baltic region since the Thirty Years' War, but lost its preeminence in 1700 when Peter joined an anti-Swedish coalition with Denmark, Saxony, and Poland.
11. Charles XII of Sweden (r. 1697–1718) was initially successful against the coalition, but suffered a critical defeat in Russia at the battle of Poltava (1709) and died in battle in 1718.
12. After the Treaty of Nystad (1721) Sweden ceded its Baltic provinces to Russia and its territories on the north German coast to Prussia and its allied German states.
13. An aristocratic reaction against the incessant demands for the war swept away Swedish absolutism.
14. In Prussia King Frederick William I (r. 1713–1740) drew upon all state resources to support his army, which was the best equipped and best trained in Europe.
15. Prussia sat on the sidelines during the War of Polish Succession (1733–1735), which

pitted France, Spain, and Sardinia against Russia and Austria.

16. After being driven out by the Russians, the French agreed to accept the Austrian candidate in exchange for the province of Lorraine.
17. Austria remained busy with the Turks on its southeastern border. In 1699 Austria forced the Turks to recognize its rule over all of Hungary, and it occupied Belgrade in 1717.
18. In the 1730s the Turks retook Belgrade, while a Hungarian army forced many political concessions from its Austrian rulers.

D. The Power of Diplomacy and the Importance of Population, pp. 544–546

1. No single power emerged from the wars of the first half of the eighteenth century as clearly superior to the others, and the idea of maintaining a balance of power guided both military and diplomatic maneuvering.
2. The diplomatic service developed an elaborate set of regular features, first in France and then in other European states.
3. Despite the increase in professional diplomacy, rulers still engaged in spying and secret diplomacy.
4. The diplomatic system in the early eighteenth century proved successful enough to ensure that nations followed the model of the Peace of Westphalia (1648): in the midst of every crisis and war, the great powers would convene and work out a written agreement detailing the requirements for peace.
5. Because each state's strength depended largely on the size of its army, the growth and health of the population became an increasing concern of government.
6. William Petty's *Political Arithmetick* (1690) used statistical estimates of human capital, such as population and wages, to determine Britain's national wealth.
7. In 1727, Frederick William I of Prussia founded two university chairs to encourage population studies.
8. Population statistics were used to explain the environmental causes of disease, and air quality became one of the key determinants of whether a place was considered healthy or unhealthy.
9. Cities were the unhealthiest places to live because of poor sanitation and high population density.
10. Data gathered by medical geographers led local governments to undertake drainage and sanitation measures, which helped to lower death rates.
11. Hospitals evolved from charities concerned with moral worthiness into medical institutions that defined patients by their diseases.
12. Physicians changed the practice of diagnosis by using specialized Latin terms for illnesses and performed postmortem dissections to gain better knowledge of anatomy and disease. The gap between patients and medical experts increased.
13. Despite these changes, medical care remained something of a free-for-all. No clear line separated the few trained physicians from quacks.
14. Many treatments were ineffective or dangerous, and hardly any infectious diseases could be cured.
15. Smallpox inoculation was introduced to Europe from the Middle East in the early eighteenth century, thanks largely to the efforts of Lady Mary Wortley Montagu (1689–1762). Inoculation spread more widely after 1796 when a milder serum was developed.
16. The unsanitary conditions of urban life—overcrowded housing with poor ventilation, poor sanitation, and contaminated water sources—contributed to the spread of many diseases.
17. Public bathhouses disappeared from cities as they became associated with epidemic illnesses, and fear of the effects of contact with water even caused avoidance of private bathing. Physicians taught that bathing was hazardous.

IV. The Birth of the Enlightenment

A. Popularization of Science and Challenges to Religion, pp. 546–549

1. The writers of the Enlightenment glorified the geniuses of the new science and championed the scientific method as the solution for social problems.
2. Works such as Bernard de Fontenelle's *Conversations on the Plurality of Worlds* (1686) made the Copernican heliocentric view of the universe accessible to the literate public.
3. By 1700, mathematics and science became fashionable in high society.
4. Science offered a model for all forms of knowledge. As the prestige of science

increased, some developed a skeptical attitude toward enforced religious conformity.

5. From the safety of the Dutch Republic, Pierre Bayle (1647–1706), a Huguenot refugee from Louis XIV's persecutions, issued a series of books and essays that insisted that even religion must meet the test of reasonableness and urged religious toleration. Bayle's *Historical and Critical Dictionary* (1697) became a model of critical thought in the west.
6. Biblical authority was subjected to historical criticism. Discoveries in geology and investigations into miracles, comets, and oracles led to a call for the use of reason to combat superstition and prejudice.
7. Traditionalists held that human beings were incapable of subjecting everything to reason, especially in the religious realm.
8. Authorities found religious skepticism unsettling because it threatened to undermine state power. The French government took the lead in suppressing outspoken works, but censorship whetted the public appetite for forbidden books.
9. The middle class Frenchman Voltaire (François-Marie Arouet, 1694–1778) was inspired by Bayle, and became famous despite official persecution for his attacks on Catholic bigotry and the rigidities of the French government.
10. Voltaire also popularized Newtonian science with his *Elements of the Philosophy of Newton* (1738). He became internationally famous.

B. Travel Literature and the Challenge to Custom and Tradition, p. 549

1. Expanding knowledge of the world outside Europe allowed increasing numbers of travel writers to contrast and criticize their home societies.
2. Visitors to new colonies sought "the state of nature" among "noble savages," although they often misinterpreted what they observed.
3. In China, travelers found prosperity and an ancient civilization.
4. The basic lesson of travel literature in the 1700s was that customs varied and were relative to place.
5. A fictional travel account by the high-ranking French judge Montesquieu, entitled *Persian Letters* (1721), satirized European institutions and suggested that France and Persia were similarly despotic. The influential *The Spirit of the Laws* (1748), inspired by Montesquieu's own travels to England, compared the governments of England and France.

C. Raising the Woman Question, pp. 549–550

1. Women writers used the language of tyranny and freedom to argue for a change in their status. Feminist ideas were presented systematically for the first time during the Enlightenment and represented a fundamental challenge to traditional societies.
2. Mary Astell's (1666–1731) successful book *A Serious Proposal to the Ladies* (1694), advocated the founding of a private women's college to remedy women's lack of education.
3. Later works, such as *Reflections upon Marriage* (1706), criticized the unequal relationship between the sexes in marriage.
4. Astell inspired other women, such as Elizabeth Singer Rowe, to write in a similar vein.
5. Most male writers stuck to the traditional view of women—that they were less reasonable than men and did not need a systematic education.
6. Over the course of the eighteenth century, *Ovism*, the anti-Aristotelian belief that women's eggs were essential in making new humans, was advanced by scientists and physicians.
7. Debates about women's nature and appropriate social roles were an important part of Enlightenment discourse.

Lecture Strategies

1. Instructors may approach the large and fascinating topic of the Atlantic system from different vantage points. One such starting point is the Caribbean sugarcane plantation. A look at the Caribbean sugarcane plantation might first involve a discussion of the growing of the sugarcane, then the process of refining sugar, and finally, the system by which the end product—refined sugar—was exported to England. It could also include an examination of the lives of the planters. A good source to consult for a closer look at the lives of the planters and the production of sugar is Richard S. Dunn, *Sugar and Slaves: The Rise of the Planter Class in the English West Indies, 1624–1713* (Chapel Hill: University of North Carolina Press, 1972); see particularly chapters 6 and 8. Dunn's book also offers a detailed examination of slavery as it was practiced on sugarcane

plantations (Chapter 7). Slavery, of course, differed from crop to crop as well as from region to region, so that generalizations must be made with care. Sidney W. Mintz, *Sweetness and Power: The Place of Sugar in Modern History* (New York: Viking Penguin, 1985) is a classic study of sugar, capitalism, and power. Its range is wider than Dunn's book, but Chapter 2, "Production," will be helpful in discussing the production of sugar.

2. A closer examination of the practical workings of the emerging British political system under Walpole can help students develop a more nuanced understanding of the complexities of constitutionalism as it existed in the early eighteenth century. Be sure to emphasize that the English Bill of Rights, in practice, dealt with the political rights of Parliament in constitutional relationship to the monarchy. The Hanovarian Succession was important both because it was aimed at heading off Jacobitism and because it emphasized the authority of Parliament to make and unmake the monarchy. For additional information, look to Nicholas Rogers's *Whigs and Cities: Popular Politics in the Age of Walpole and Pitt* (Oxford: Oxford University Press, 1989), which explores the connections between popular and elite politics. The most significant study of Walpole's rule can be found in H. T. Dickenson's *Walpole and the Whig Supremacy* (London: English Universities Press, 1973).

3. The divergent careers of Johann Sebastian Bach and George Frideric Handel offer opportunities for an exploration of the disparate worlds of music in the early eighteenth century. These explorations can open up discussions of religion, commerce, urban developments, and leisure activity. Some knowledge and feeling for the music of the times would be an advantage, but not a necessity. Playing recorded compositions by these composers is highly recommended. For Bach, a good place to start is Denis Arnold, *Bach* (Oxford and New York: Oxford University Press, 1983), a brief biography in the *Past Masters* series. Jan Chiappusso, *Bach's World* (Bloomington: Indiana University Press, 1968) is a useful book. Other possibilities include the recent, full-length biography by Christoph Wolff, *Johann Sebastian Bach: The Learned Musician* (New York: W. W. Norton, 2000); and Wolff's revised and enlarged edition of Hans T. David and Arthur Mendel, *The Bach Reader: A Life of Johann Sebastian Bach in Letters and Documents* (New York: W. W. Norton, 1966 [rev. ed., 1998]). See also a review of Wolff's biography that serves as a good introduction to major issues connected with Bach's life: Robert L. Marshall, "In Search of Bach," *The New York Review of Books* 47.10 (June 15, 2000), 47–51. For Handel, one might begin with Dean Winton, *The New Grove Handel* (New York: W. W. Norton, 1982), a short biography; or H. C. Robbins Landon, *Handel and His World* (Boston: Little, Brown, 1984). Other possibilities include Paul Henry Lang, *George Frideric Handel* (New York: W. W. Norton, 1966), a comprehensive biography; and Otto Erich Deutsch, *Handel: A Documentary Biography* (New York: DaCapo Press, 1974).

4. Just as Louis XIV was the dominant personality of the latter part of the seventeenth century, Peter the Great was the larger-than-life figure for the first part of the eighteenth century. Almost single-handedly, Peter made the Russian Empire one of the major powers of Europe and created in St. Petersburg a new city destined to play an extraordinary role in Russian history over the following four centuries. An excellent overview of Peter's career can be found in Chapter 4 of W. Bruce Lincoln, *The Romanovs: Autocrats of All the Russias* (New York: Dial Press, 1981). Chapter 5 deals with the planning and construction of St. Petersburg. M. S. Anderson, *Peter the Great*, 2nd ed. (New York: Longman, 1995) is an excellent short biography. The best book on Peter and his Russia is Lindsey Hughes, *Russia in the Age of Peter the Great* (New Haven: Yale University Press, 1998). It is divided by topics, of which probably the most interesting are "Peter's People" (Chapter 6), "St. Petersburg and the Arts" (Chapter 7), and "Peter: Man, Mind, and Methods" (Chapter 11).

5. Historiography can be a daunting topic, but developments in Atlantic world scholarship and the emergence of a new historical field lend themselves to some exploration with students and offer opportunities to discuss the limitations and challenges of historical scholarship. Highlight the transnational, bottom-up nature of most Atlantic world scholarship, as well as the difficulties and challenges faced by scholars in stepping outside of "national" stories and research, to come to terms with regional developments. Explain how topics such as migrations (willing and unwilling), trading networks, religious revivals, and the spread of new patterns of consumption are all impossible to come to terms with in relation to national histories, and how the structure of history as an academic discipline has responded to the challenge of explaining the Atlantic system. It may be useful to send students to (or show in class) some relevant Web sites to emphasize the connections, such as Harvard University's International Seminar of the History of the Atlantic World at http://www.fas.harvard.edu/~atlantic/. Reflections on the growth of Atlantic world history as a field for teaching and scholarship are widely available; include Bernard Bailyn's reflective (if too Anglo-centric) *Atlantic History: Concepts and Contours* (Cambridge, MA: Harvard University Press, 2005) and Alison Games's recent "Atlantic History: Definitions, Challenges, and Opportunities," *American Historical Review* 111, no. 3 (June 2006), 741–757. Students might also be exposed to critiques of Atlantic history such as the one advanced by Peter Coclanis in "*Drang Nach Osten*: Bernard Bailyn,

The World-Island, and the Idea of Atlantic History," *Journal of World History* 13, no. 1 (Spring 2002), 169–182.

6. Voltaire is probably the best-known literary figure of the Enlightenment, and his career encompassed many of the different facets of that movement. A particularly fascinating account of the young Voltaire is found in the first chapter of Peter Gay, *Voltaire's Politics: The Poet as a Realist* (Princeton, NJ: Princeton University Press, 1959). Theodore Besterman's biography, listed in the chapter bibliography, should also be consulted. A good overview of the early Enlightenment may be found in Leonard Krieger, *Kings and Philosophers, 1689–1989* (New York: W. W. Norton, 1970). Part 1 of Krieger's book also contains a good discussion of the political and military history of the period from 1690 to 1740.

Class Discussion Starters

1. The new items of consumption—sugar, coffee, and tea—and the ways in which these staples changed urban social and cultural life can be the subject of an interesting class session. Besides looking at historical patterns, one might refer to present-day habits and institutions connected with these items. Sidney Mintz's *Sweetness and Power* contains a chapter on the widespread consumption of tea, coffee, and chocolate. Mark Pendergrast offers an informative if somewhat breezy book on coffee, *Uncommon Grounds: The History of Coffee and How It Transformed Our World* (New York: Basic Books, 1999). Consult Chapter 1 for an overview of the history of the spread of coffee drinking. Chapter 10 of Wilfrid R. Prest, *Albion Ascendant: English History, 1660–1815* (New York: Oxford University Press, 1998) places consumption of coffee, chocolate, and tea in the first half of the eighteenth century in a British context. Prest's book is part of J. M. Roberts, ed., series *The Short Oxford History of the Modern World.*

2. In conjunction with suggestion number 1 above, you may also want to consider the wide-ranging consequences of the explosion of the alcohol trade as a vital dimension of Atlantic commerce. Exploring the far-reaching social and cultural transformations of alcohol and firearms on native cultures is always worthwhile, but the introduction of cheap rum, gin, and market-produced whiskeys throughout the Atlantic world changed patterns of consumption everywhere. Students are always alert to how changed circumstances affect alcohol consumption and are often thoughtful about the social consequences of increased/transformed patterns of drinking. For some thought-provoking history on these developments, which might work as class reading in whole or in part, see Jessica Warner, *Craze: Gin and Debauchery in the Age of Reason* (New York: Four Walls Eight Windows, 2002), or Frederick Smith's *Caribbean Rum: A Social and Economic History* (Gainesville, FL: University of Florida Press, 2005).

3. In his many careers and his novels, Daniel Defoe offers interesting approaches to social and cultural patterns in England of the late seventeenth and early eighteenth centuries. Most students will already know or be familiar with the plot of Robinson Crusoe even if they have not read the book. The novel can be used to introduce a variety of pertinent themes: capitalism, colonialism, and racism, among others. A good place to begin is Peter Earle's interesting and informative *The World of Defoe* (London: Weidenfeld & Nicolson, 1976), particularly parts 3 and 4, which discuss society and the economy in England and the life cycle of the individual. Paula Backscheider offers a comprehensive investigation of Defoe's stranger-than-fiction life in *Daniel Defoe: His Life* (Baltimore, MD: Johns Hopkins University Press, 1989). John J. Richetti, *Daniel Defoe* (Boston: Twayne Publishers, 1987) is a useful, brief biography and analysis of Defoe's major works. Finally, Max Byrd, ed., *Daniel Defoe: A Collection of Critical Essays* (Englewood Cliffs, NJ: Prentice Hall, 1976) and Frank H. Ellis, ed., *Twentieth-Century Interpretations of Robinson Crusoe: A Collection of Critical Essays* (Englewood Cliffs, NJ: Prentice Hall, 1969) are both good introductions to literary criticism of Defoe and his most famous novel.

4. Peter the Great's campaign of westernization can be used as a jumping off point for a discussion about the challenges leaders faced in reforming established identities with "foreign" ideas. Students could list specific reforms initiated by Peter, and the carrot-and-stick methods used by Peter to create elite support for his efforts. What is the relationship between altering fashions, dress, and entertainment, and changing who a people fundamentally are? Do students sympathize with Peter's goals? Why did groups like the Old Believers resist change? The resources listed in lecture strategy number 4 above will be useful for informing the discussion.

Reviewing the Text

Review Questions

1. How is consumerism related to slavery in the early eighteenth century?
[model answer] • ***Consumption of commodities like coffee, tea, and chocolate increased as nations formed new economic links:*** *The Atlantic system bound together the economies of western European countries: Europeans bought slaves in western Africa, transported and sold them in colonies in North and South America and*

the Caribbean, bought commodities produced on the plantations there, and then sold the goods in European ports.

• ***Growth of international trade created a new consumer society:*** *The Atlantic system, combined with population growth, increased international trade. This altered the consumption patterns of ordinary people. Worldwide colonization, powered by slavery, produced new supplies of goods. Goods were available more cheaply, and what had previously been luxuries for a small portion of the population became necessities to the majority. The increasing wealth of the upper and middle non-noble classes kept the demand for luxuries strong.*

2. How were new social trends reflected in cultural life in the late 1600s and early 1700s?

[model answer] • ***English peasantry disappeared as a result of the "enclosure movement":*** *Wealthy British landowners pressured small farmers and villagers to sell their land or give up common lands as part of the agricultural movement toward large, centralized farms, thus eliminating community grazing rights. In the interest of greater agricultural efficiency and production for the marketplace, the English countryside was ultimately restructured into a more hierarchical society of big landlords, tenant farmers, and poor agricultural laborers.*

• ***Urban populations skyrocketed:*** *Poor peasants, forced out of communal farming, flocked to the cities. Between 1650 and 1750, cities with at least ten thousand inhabitants increased in population by 44 percent.*

• ***Condition of peasants worsened in eastern Europe:*** *To produce more grain for the Baltic market, aristocratic landowners in Prussia, Poland, and parts of Russia opened up more land for cultivation. Landlords increased their serfs' compulsory labor services, and began to manage their estates directly. Serfs in some places hardly differed from slaves, with the landowners running their estates like plantations.*

• ***Distinctive urban culture:*** *The lower classes made up the majority of urban residents, but a small middle class developed a distinct identity and created a new urban culture. Literacy increased in cities and a literate public emerged with a desire for affordable books, magazines, and arts. The opportunity to produce work for a paying audience liberated authors, artists, and composers, who no longer depended on royal patronage.*

• ***Religious revival:*** *Both Protestantism and Catholicism were invigorated by unorthodox reform movements. Protestant Pietism, strongest among Lutherans in Prussia, emphasized mysticism, scripture reading, and intense catechetical instruction. Quietism and Jansenism among Catholics were controversial movements that eventually were condemned by the Pope, but which also gained enthusiastic adherents, particularly in France.*

3. What events and developments led to greater stability and less warfare in the European state system?

[model answer] • ***Warfare between 1690–1740 changed nations' military, economic, and commercial positions, and, by weakening France, helped to keep the peace:*** *France's power was checked after 1715, and peace allowed domestic and colonial trade to boom. Britain emerged an economically strong naval power, gained a stronger hold on Scotland and Ireland, and became "Great Britain" as its empire increased. The Dutch shifted focus to international long-distance trade and finance, and their power declined after 1700.*

• ***Russia westernized:*** *Russian tsars transformed public life and established a new, absolutist state based on a western model. Peter I reorganized government finances and the military, forced nobles into state and military service, placed himself at the head of the Russian Orthodox church, founded schools and the Russian Academy of Sciences, and demanded western styles of dress be worn at court. Russia emerged as a European power.*

• ***Poland-Lithuania weakened:*** *When Russia became the leading power in the Baltic, it turned its attention to eastern Europe. Poland-Lithuania became a battleground of European powers after 1733, but Russia emerged as a powerful state capable of controlling its neighbors.*

• ***A new diplomacy:*** *The Utrecht Peace committed European nations to maintaining a balance of power. Because no single, superior power emerged from the wars, nations worked to maintain peace through equilibrium. Along with diplomacy, this equilibrium was maintained militarily through leagues, coalitions, and huge armies.*

• ***Nations studied their populations to improve their positions in the global balance:*** *Because each nation's strength depended on the size of its army, the growth and health of the population increasingly concerned governments. These internal concerns made states less willing to engage in wars.*

4. What were the major issues in the early decades of the Enlightenment?

[model answer] • ***Science and the scientific method:*** *By 1700, mathematics and science had become fashionable pastimes for the upper classes. Science was felt to offer a model for all forms of knowledge and an approach for testing all forms of understanding.*

• ***Interest in science contributed to a skeptical attitude toward religion and superstition:*** *Some Enlightenment authors doubted the need for religious conformity, especially when it led to religious persecution. Authors demanded that faith meet tests of reason. To combat superstition and prejudice, Enlightenment thinkers urged the use of reason in the investigation of witches, comets, miracles, and oracles.*

• ***Reason-based skepticism contributed to criticism of state authority and society:*** *In France, authors criticized the government by praising constitutional and religiously tolerant aspects of the British government. A mix of increased travel and colonization and a rise in literacy led* *to the popularization of travel literature, which either described faraway places, or framed criticism of the author's homeland.*

• ***New thinking on the role of women:*** *A few male authors considered the role and position of women in a society a measure of the freedom it gave its citizens in general. They wrote against tyranny, servitude, and supported the "state of nature" of equality among humans. Women also became more literate and wrote books advocating increased education and equality for women that were publicly successful.*

Making Connections

1. How did the rise of slavery and the plantation system change European politics and society?
[model answer] *It soon became apparent to European countries that colonization, and the new products that came with it, was more profitable than mining for precious metals. European countries competed with each other, issuing state charters for the founding of colonies. A growing European market for plantation goods, such as sugar, tobacco, and coffee, all produced by cheap slave labor, changed European consumption habits. Smoking became widespread, and coffeehouses, where people could meet socially and discuss business and politics, became popular.*

2. Why was the Enlightenment born just at the moment the Atlantic system took shape?
[model answer] *The optimism generated by rapid economic and territorial expansion, the emergence of a new consumer society, and the stabilization of the European state system all generated optimism about the future. This optimism, in turn, stimulated a renewed interest in ideas, especially in the area of science. Skepticism, which was an integral part of scientific inquiry, was quickly extended to other areas, including religion. At the same time, people became more familiar with foreign cultures and ideas through the trade and exchanges that were part of the Atlantic system, and travel writing that was part of Enlightenment discourse found an interested audience.*

3. What were the major differences between the wars of the first half of the eighteenth century and those of the seventeenth century? (Refer to Chapters 15 and 16.)
[model answer] *Religion had been a major factor in the wars of the seventeenth century. By the first half of the eighteenth century, nations went to war mainly for political and territorial reasons, often formulated in relationship to the dynastic concerns of monarchies. Although the cost of warfare increased dramatically, the battles tended to be localized; they did not encompass huge areas of conflict and the countryside was not ravaged in the way it had been in the Thirty Years' War. Nations during the eighteenth century also formed alliances to balance the perceived power and ambitions of countries outside the alliances. By then, diplomatic services had also developed regular procedures, which aided the negotiation of international differences.*

Discussing the Documents

Questions from Online Study Guide with Model Answers

The Social Effects of Growing Consumption, p. 530

1. How does Defoe suggest the new economy is affecting relations between "Tradesmen" and "Gentlemen?"
[model answer] *The line between tradesmen and gentlemen, according to Defoe, needed to be broken down as commerce and industry produced more and more prosperity for tradesmen. Although gentlemen continued to look down on tradesmen, the wealth of tradesmen had increased to the extent that they were wealthier than gentlemen. The availability of new products and an increase in consumption, meanwhile, was contributing to the decline of aristocratic fortunes.*

2. What advice does Defoe offer the English aristocracy?
[model answer] *Defoe suggests that intermarriage to combine the families of the gentry and tradesmen will allow many aristocrats to retrieve "decay'd" family fortunes. Aristocrats should get over their contempt for merchants and tradesmen and recognize that without the infusion of wealth they can offer, many families will die out. Aristocratic sons should marry the daughters of tradesmen.*

Voltaire, Letters Concerning the English Nation *(1733), p. 548*

1. How does Voltaire respond to those who might fear that philosophy is a danger to religious faith?
[model answer] *Voltaire says that even Christian philosophers knew that faith and reason were two different matters and that philosophers would never form a religious sect because their writings were not meant for everyone. Too few people read, and of those who did too few read philosophy. Past philosophers like Montaigne, Bayle, or Spinoza created less of a stir than religious divines did. Philosophy did not reach a wide enough audience to challenge the status quo.*

2. Does Voltaire's opinion of humanity as seen in this excerpt seem to be optimistic or pessimistic?
[model answer] *Voltaire estimates that the vast majority of humanity is illiterate and incapable of understanding much more than the ambition of religious divines. Those*

who are literate would sooner amuse themselves with romance novels than read anything philosophical. Voltaire pessimistically estimates that the thinking portion of humanity is infinitesimal.

New Sources, New Perspectives: Oral History and the Life of Slaves, pp. 524–525

1. What did the runaway slaves mentioned in these accounts aim to accomplish when they attacked plantations?
[model answer] *Slaves sometimes sought revenge against masters and overseers, especially when they were guilty of harsh treatment. After the attacks, whatever goods remaining on the plantations were taken by slaves. Slave oral histories suggest that tools were especially targeted. Slaves may also have been seeking food.*

2. Why would runaway slaves make an agreement with the Dutch colonial officials to return future runaways?
[model answer] *The documents indicate that slaveholders were determined to retrieve runaways and to punish runaways when they could be found. Such agreements may have preserved, at least for a time, the freedom of earlier runaways. In this case, the development of constructive relations with plantation communities provided benefits to growing slave communities, including eventual recognition of their independence. They also allowed slaves access to trade or goods that they needed to stay alive and to sustain existing runaway communities as they developed.*

3. Can oral histories recorded in the twentieth century be considered accurate versions of events that took place in the eighteenth century? How can they be tested?
[model answer] *Oral histories often contain useful information about how a community perceives its own past, and they may also contain useful information about what actually happened, even at some distance in time. Oral history is most effective when it can be tested against contemporary written accounts, in this case, records left by plantation societies, and against what evidence archeologists and other kinds of overlapping evidence reveal.*

Other Questions for Discussing These Documents in Class

The Social Effects of Growing Consumption

1. Does Defoe seem to believe that life is improving? For whom, and how?
2. What is happening to existing class structures, according to Defoe, in connection with growing commercialization? What consequences does he foresee?

Voltaire, Letters Concerning the English Nation *(1733)*

1. Is Voltaire's defense of free thought cynical of religiously based criticism? What view does it offer of the common people?
2. What kind of debates does Voltaire suggest are most dangerous?

New Sources, New Perspectives: Oral History and the Life of Slaves

1. What patterns of resistance and rebellion do the short narratives presented show? How organized were the runaways?
2. Why were slave revolts and reprisals for them so brutal?

Comparative Questions

1. How do all of these documents add to your understanding of the broad trends in social change in this period? How did established patterns of relationship (between masters and slaves; between the aristocracy and the rest of society; between church and state) fare under new pressures?
2. What do Defoe's description of trends in his society, Voltaire's *Letters*, and the documents on slave revolts together say about the relationship of eighteenth-century people to established authority? Can you connect what you see here to Enlightenment principles about reason and challenges to the conventional ways of doing things?

For Users of *Sources of The Making of the West*

The following documents are available in Chapter 17 of the companion sourcebook by Katharine J. Lualdi, University of Southern Maine.

1. Captivity and Enslavement: Olaudah Equiano, *The Interesting Narrative of the Life of Olaudah Equiano Written by Himself* (1789)
2. A "Sober and Wholesome Drink": *"A Brief Description of the Excellent Vertues of that Sober and Wholesome Drink, called Coffee"* (1674)
3. In Defense of Military Action: Tsar Peter I, *Letter to His Son, Alexei* (October 11, 1715) and *Alexei's Response* (October 31, 1715)
4. Challenging Absolutism: Montesquieu, *Persian Letters: Letter 37* (1721)
5. Questioning Women's Submission: Mary Astell, *Reflections upon Marriage* (1706)

Discussion Ideas for Sources of The Making of the West, *Chapter 17*

1. Why, according to *A Brief Description...*, is coffee better than alcohol? What are the specific benefits the author wants consumers to associate with the drink? What does the document tell you about how demand was created for new products?

2. Atlantic world dynamics contributed to the rethinking of gender and racial relations, particularly as notions of freedom and liberty were discussed by Enlightenment thinkers. What appears to have been most unacceptable about the lot of slaves (Equiano's *The Interesting Narrative*) and women (Astell's *Reflection upon Marriage*)?

3. The correspondence between Peter the Great and his son Alexei is very sad and very human. What does it reveal about the nature of absolutism and the demands such a regime placed on monarchs? Were there disadvantages to the state due to the absolutist system's dependence on a monarch's personality and temperament? Feel free to incorporate observations from Montesquieu about Louis XIV.

Working with Visual Sources

For this exercise, please refer to The Exotic as Consumer Item: *Africa* on p. 529 of the textbook or view the image on the book companion site's Online Study Guide under the "Visual Activity" for Chapter 17.

Students viewing the image at the Online Study Guide are asked two questions about the image. The questions and model answers (not made available to students) are below. Project this image, available on the Instructor's Resources CD-ROM, in class or ask students to look at the image in their textbooks and answer the questions.

1. What does this image tell us about eighteenth-century Europeans' perceptions of Africans and the African continent?
[model answer] *Among the many ways to interpret a painting, no one particular reading is necessarily the "correct" one. The first thing this image tells us is that Europeans' perceptions of Africa and Africans was not gained first-hand but depended on the accounts of travelers, writers, and artists such as Carriera. Second, it is reasonable to think that the symbolism and imagery used by Carriera corresponded to a general idea of Africa that her audience would recognize. Carriera sought to portray Africa as a strange and exciting continent, full of wealth but not without a certain element of danger. Africa's exoticism is apparent from her feathered and jeweled turban and brightly colored garment, while her precious necklaces and earrings evoke its riches. The wriggling snakes, clutched in her left hand, might symbolize the perils that await the unwary foreign visitor to that continent.*

2. What impression of Africa do you think the artist wished to convey to her audience?
[model answer] *Overall, the image is attractive and emphatically feminine: Africa is beautiful and beautifully dressed—a far cry from a brutalized victim of slavery and racism. Carriera has also chosen to highlight her subject's sexuality: the string of red beads moves down toward her breasts, her lips are parted, her cheeks are flushed pink, and her neck and ears are decorated. The snakes in her hand suggest male sexuality, as might the scorpion. At the same time Carriera creates an impression of innocence. Pearls were a symbol of virginity, and Africa's turban is white, the color of purity. Moreover, covering the hair was a sign of female modesty. And while snakes suggest male sexuality, the snakes here are held harmlessly in Africa's hand, and the scorpion is an ornament that is chained to her necklace. Carriera seems to be an advocate of Africa, having given her both attractiveness and self-control.*

Mapping Exercises

Map Activity from OSG—Model Answers for Map Activity #2

For this activity, please refer to Map 17.1: European Trade Patterns, c. 1740 on p. 522. Students are asked these questions:

What territories were primarily involved as exporters and importers in the slave trade at this time?
[model answer] *During this period slaves were mainly being imported into the Spanish and Portuguese colonies in Central and South America, although small French and Dutch colonies in these regions also imported slaves. Slaves were exported primarily from the west coast of Africa, but some were also exported from Portuguese territories on the east coast of Africa as well.*

What products did Europeans import from colonies in the Americas?
[model answer] *Europeans imported precious metals from Central and South America. From the West Indies they imported sugar, and from the colonies in North America they imported timber, fish, and tobacco.*

Describe how the triangular trade network worked in the Atlantic system.
[model answer] *The triangular trade system was a network in which Europe, Africa, and the Americas were joined together in an interconnected economic relationship. Africa and the Americas both provided markets for manufactured goods from Europe. Africa provided slaves, which were brought to the Americas, where their labor*

produced the raw materials that were sent back to Europe to make more manufactured goods. Thus Europe depended on Africa and America both as markets for the goods it produced and for the labor and raw materials needed to produce them.

Map 17.1: European Trade Patterns, c. 1740, p. 522

What goods went out of Europe? How might the need for trade goods have stimulated the economies of Europe? What obvious challenge did westerners face in their trade with Asia? What was the triangular trade?

Map 17.2, Europe, c. 1715, p. 537

Why did France prefer to cede vast territories in Canada rather than its relatively small island possessions in the Caribbean? What was important about the Mediterranean outposts, particularly Gibraltar, that Great Britain gained from Spain?

Map 17.3: Russia and Sweden after the Great Northern War, 1721, p. 543

Notice where the decisive battle of Poltova occurred. What does this tell you about the scale of the war? What two countries expanded as a result of the war? What do the locations of Russian territorial gains suggest about the importance of securing access to the Baltic Sea?

Mapping the West: Europe in 1740, p. 531

Ask students to discuss what "decline" meant to Spain, the Dutch Republic, Poland-Lithuania, and Sweden. How would they rank the five major powers of Great Britain, France, Austria, Prussia, and Russia? Why would they rank them this way? Ask students to review the map on p. 516 and comment on the differences between Europe in 1740 and Europe at the end of the seventeenth century. Which differences do they regard as the most significant? Why?

In-Class Assignments and Presentation Topics

1. Using the material in Chapter 17, including Figure 17.1 (p. 521) and Figure 17.2 (p. 523) and relevant illustrations, break the class into three groups. Have each group explain the slave trade from a different perspective including: (1) a London merchant involved in all aspects of Atlantic trade; (2) a sugar plantation owner with five hundred slaves; and (3) a first-generation slave on a Brazilian sugar plantation contemplating running away. You might have the students conduct "modern" investigative television or radio interviews of spokesmen for each group.

2. Ask students to compare and contrast the agricultural practices of western Europe with those of eastern Europe and the New World. Have the class discuss the social and economic implications of these practices. Make use of Figures 17.1 and 17.2 and other relevant features in the chapter.

3. Ask students what city life was like in the early eighteenth century. In an essay, have students describe it as fully as possible, including the physical layout, the different groups inhabiting the city, new items of consumption, and opportunities for cultural and leisure activities.

4. Ask students to analyze the reasons for the rise of the British and the decline of the Dutch in a brief essay. Which reasons are the most persuasive, and why? Students may need to do additional reading for this assignment. In addition to a selection from Prest's *Albion Ascendant* (see "Lecture Strategies," number 2), have the class read an excerpt from Jonathan Israel, *The Dutch Republic: Its Rise, Greatness, and Fall: 1477–1806* (Oxford: Clarendon Press, 1995).

5. In a presentation, have students evaluate Peter the Great's efforts to transform Russia into a modern European state. The discussion should particularly include whether the price paid by Russian society was worth the result. What reforms generated the most resistance? Ask students to use relevant maps and illustrations as part of their presentations.

Essay Questions

1. Have students write an essay or present a report on the world of one of the following: Johann Sebastian Bach, George Frideric Handel, Antoine Watteau, François Boucher, Daniel Defoe, Pierre Bayle, Eliza Haywood, or Voltaire. For Bach and Handel, see "Lecture Strategies," number 4. For Watteau and Boucher, begin with H. W. Janson and Anthony F. Janson, *History of Art*, 5th ed. (New York: Harry N. Abrams, 1999 [rev. ed.]). For Voltaire, see the bibliographical suggestions for "Lecture Strategies," number 6. For general background on challenges faced by Eliza Haywood and English women, see Ann Laurence, *Women in England 1500–1760* (New York: St. Martin's Press, 1994); and Sara Mendelson and Patricia Crawford, *Women in Early Modern England, 1550–1720* (Oxford: Oxford University Press, 1998). Also, for Voltaire and Pierre Bayle, see Peter Gay's important book on the Enlightenment, *The Enlightenment: An Interpretation*, vol. 1,

The Rise of Modern Paganism (New York: Alfred A. Knopf, 1967), with its remarkable bibliography.

2. Ask students to do a research project on Peter the Great's grand tour of western Europe in 1697–1698. They should choose one of the locations Peter visited and report on what he experienced and learned there. In addition, as a follow-up to Peter's visit, students can write a commentary on what Peter might have wanted to know about that location's politics, economy, and society. See the bibliographical suggestions in "Lecture Strategies," number 4. Students will require additional help with bibliography. For the Netherlands and for Britain, see the books listed in "In-Class Assignments and Presentation Topics," number 4; and in "Lecture Strategies," number 3. For the Austrian Empire, see Robert J. W. Evans, *The Making of the Habsburg Empire, 1550–1700* (Oxford: Clarendon Press, 1979); and Robert A. Kann, *A History of the Habsburg Monarchy, 1526–1918* (Berkeley: University of California Press, 1974).

Additional Resources: Literature

Allen, Robert J., ed., *Addison and Steele: Selections from the Tatler and the Spectator*. 1997.

Caretta, Vincent, ed., *The Interesting Narrative of the Life of Olaudah Equiano and Other Writings: Revised Edition*. 2003.

Betts, C. J., trans., *Persian Letters by Charles Louis de Secondat Montesquieu*. 1977.

Defoe, Daniel, *Moll Flanders*. 1722.

Defoe, Daniel, *Robinson Crusoe*. 1719.

de Fontenelle, Bernard le Bovier, *Conversations on the Plurality of Worlds*. 1990.

Hill, Bridget, ed., *The First English Feminist: Reflections upon Marriage and Other Writings by Mary Astell*. 1986.

Moseley, C. W., ed., *Travels of Sir John Mandeville by John Mandeville*. 1984.

Oakleaf, David, ed., *Eliza Haywood: Love in Excess*. 2000.

Scholar, Angela, trans., *Abbé Prévost: Manon Lescaut*. 2004.

Additional Resources: Film and Video

Longitude (2000; VHS/DVD, 200 min.). This film retells the true story of eighteenth-century clockmaker John Harrison's search for a way to determine longitude. The film reflects Harrison's frustration, which was as much with the English naval authorities as it was with himself. Care has been taken to re-create the period accurately.

Other Bedford/St. Martin's Resources for Chapter 17

The following resources are available to accompany Chapter 17. Please refer to the Preface of this manual for detailed descriptions of all the ancillaries.

For Instructors

Transparencies

The following maps and image from Chapter 17 are available as full-color acetates.

- Map 17.1: European Trade Patterns, c. 1740
- Map 17.2: Europe, c. 1715
- Map 17.3: Russia and Sweden after the Great Northern War, 1721
- Mapping the West: Europe in 1740
- The Exotic as Consumer Item: *Africa*, p. 529
- Peter the Great Modernizes Russia, p. 541

Instructor's Resources CD-ROM

The following maps and image from Chapter 17, as well as a chapter outline, are available on disc in both PowerPoint and jpeg formats.

- Map 17.1: European Trade Patterns, c. 1740
- Map 17.2: Europe, c. 1715
- Map 17.3: Russia and Sweden after the Great Northern War, 1721
- Mapping the West: Europe in 1740
- The Exotic as Consumer Item: *Africa*, p. 529

Using the Bedford Series with The Making of the West

Available in print as well as online at **bedfordstmartin.com/usingseries,** this guide offers practical suggestions for using *The Jesuit Relations: Natives and Missionaries in Seventeenth-Century North America*, edited with an Introduction by Allan Greer, in conjunction with chapters 16 and 17 of the textbook, *Crosscurrents in the Black Atlantic, 1770-1965*, by David Northrup, in conjunction with chapters 17 and 20 of the textbook, *Slavery, Freedom, and the Law in the Atlantic* World, by Sue Peabody and Keila Grinberg, and Margaret C. Jacob, *The Enlightenment: A Brief History with Documents*, in conjunction with chapters 17 and 18 of the textbook.

For Students

Study Guides

The Online Study Guide at **bedfordstmartins.com/hunt** helps students synthesize the material they have learned as well as practice the skills historians use to make sense of the past. The following Map, Visual, and Document activities are available for Chapter 17.

Map Activity

- Map 17.1: European Trade Patterns, c. 1740

Visual Activity

- The Exotic as Consumer Item: *Africa,* p. 529

Reading Historical Documents

- The Social Effects of Growing Consumption, p. 530
- Voltaire, *Letters Concerning the English Nation* (1733), p. 548
- New Sources, New Perspectives: Oral History and the Lives of Slaves, pp. 524–525

CHAPTER

18

The Promise of Enlightenment

1740–1789

CHAPTER RESOURCES

Main Chapter Topics

1. The philosophes, the most influential figures in the Enlightenment, were private intellectuals dedicated to solving the real problems of the world.

2. Most of the philosophes subscribed to the idea that humans could, through the use of reason, understand and improve society and politics. Most also saw organized religion as an obstacle to human progress and reasonable reform.

3. The success of religious revival in the middle decades of the century and the growing popularity of Romanticism in the arts demonstrate that many westerners felt that reason alone could not answer many of life's most profound questions.

4. Many nobles concentrated on reasserting their privileges and resisting radical social and political changes associated with the Enlightenment, although in some parts of the west the aristocracy began intermarrying with the middle class. A large number of the expanding middle classes enthusiastically participated in the Enlightenment as a means of both demonstrating their position in society and bringing about change and reform. In general, the lower classes, buffeted by economic change, and particularly the rise in prices, had little to do with the Enlightenment and maintained a separate popular culture with its own entertainments.

5. Taken together, the War of the Austrian Succession and the Seven Years' War confirmed Prussia's status as a great power and reinforced Britain's standing as the leading colonial power at the expense of the French Empire.

6. In addition to traditional forms of popular discontent, governments now had to respond to a broad and informed public opinion, one of the most important results of the Enlightenment. That result had consequences for public order and the ability of states to control the public, particularly in the case of British North America.

Focus Question

How did the Enlightenment influence Western politics, culture, and society?

1. Broadly—in fact, for many historians and philosophers, the changes in the West were so significant that they actually constitute the beginning of the modern era. In part because its influential philosophes were so determined to engage in broad social criticism, to encourage the development of politics in new directions, and to argue for the widespread incorporation of reason as the principal guide for political and social organization, the Enlightenment was no mere intellectual movement. By providing an alternative rationale for social organization from religious or even absolutist ones, the philosophes offered to the emerging middle class, reform-minded aristocrats, and also to "Enlightened" monarchs such as Catherine the Great of Russia, Gustavus III of Sweden, and Joseph II of Austria , a set of principles for guiding public action.

2. Of course, philosophes and other "practitioners" of Enlightenment values disagreed about where reason might lead politically and socially, so Enlightenment values and priorities were highly variable. Enlightened monarchs in particular sought to use the new ideas to continue to build popular support for their own power and aspirations. The writings of Enlightenment thinkers nevertheless put on the table fundamental issues of profound importance to the development of the West, including church-state relations, the rights of women and slaves, and the limits of reason.

Annotated Chapter Outline

I. The Enlightenment at Its Height

A. Men and Women of the Republic of Letters, pp. 556–558

1. The Enlightenment was a cosmopolitan movement found everywhere in the west.
2. Although the Enlightenment was centered in France, philosophes believed that they were part of a "republic of letters," which transcended political boundaries.
3. They believed in the importance of reason, reform, and freedom.
4. The philosophes believed in the eradication of superstition and bigotry; religious fanaticism; and the application of reason to social issues and problems.
5. Philosophes believed that the spread of knowledge, through projects such as the *Encyclopedia* and the expansion of "natural rights" such as intellectual freedom, freedom of the press, and religion, would produce progress.
6. Most philosophes came from the upper classes and, except in rare cases, they were men. Universities in France, dominated by the Catholic clergy, were unreceptive to Enlightenment ideas.
7. Enlightenment ideas spread through books, pamphlets, letters, and salons hosted by middle-class and aristocratic women.

B. Conflicts with Church and State, pp. 558–560

1. Whereas most influential Europeans believed that religion was necessary for a good society and government, changes in attitude toward God and religion began to emerge in the eighteenth century.
2. Both deism (the belief that God existed, but did not intervene in earthly affairs) and atheism (the belief that God did not exist) emerged as alternatives to the traditional belief that God constantly intervened in all aspects of human affairs.
3. Deists such as the philosophe Voltaire attacked most of the claims of organized Christianity, asserting that religion was the prime source of fanaticism and brutality among humans.
4. Opposition to religious intolerance led Voltaire and others to attack the close ties between the church and the state as well as certain practices, such as torture, practiced by governments.
5. Philosophes also attacked both church and state for policies of colonization and for condoning slavery, although both continued.
6. Enlightenment writers had conflicting views of natives. Some found them innocent and primitive; to others they seemed untrustworthy and savage. Views of Africans could be especially negative.
7. Enlightenment belief in natural rights helped fuel the antislavery movement, which organized political campaigns against slavery in Britain, France, and the United States. Abolitionists began to petition for an end to slavery and the slave trade.
8. Enlightenment thinkers usually advocated reform over revolution. They regarded the people as ignorant, violent, and prone to superstition, and pinned their hopes on educated elites and enlightened rulers.

C. The Individual and Society, pp. 560–564

1. The Enlightenment contributed to a profound transformation of attention away from theological and religious questions and toward the secular study of society. Religion remained important, but Enlightenment thinkers argued that religion was essentially a private issue, a question of individual conscience.
2. Many historians and philosophers consider the Enlightenment to be the origin of modernity. The philosophes argued that reason rather than religion should direct social and political life.
3. At the same time, however, the philosophes disagreed about what reason revealed.
4. The modern discipline of economics took shape around questions about free markets raised by the Scottish philosopher Adam Smith.
5. Smith rejected mercantilism and argued that in an economy left to follow its own natural laws and free of government intervention, individual interests would be harmonized with those of society as a whole, leading to increased wealth for society and individual improvement.
6. Another philosophe, Jean-Jacques Rousseau, was less certain that individual interests and the welfare of the people as a whole could be reconciled. He believed

that science and the arts raised artificial barriers between people and their natural state. He advocated a simple, rural life over urban society.

7. In works such as *The New Heloise* (1761) and *Émile* (1762) Rousseau explored the need for persons to deny their individual desires in order to become part of society.
8. In *The Social Contract* (1762), Rousseau argued that people contracting with each other to surrender their individual interests to the "general will" (the good of the community) could be a source of universal morality and freedom.
9. Rousseau's arguments, which implied that people would be more free and moral under a republican form of government with direct democracy, threatened the legitimacy of eighteenth-century governments and became a kind of political bible for the French revolutionaries of 1789.
10. Rousseau's political vision attacked property rights and made no provision for preserving individual freedoms. Rousseau argued that people could be forced to be free by the terms of the social contract.

D. Spreading the Enlightenment, pp. 564–566

1. The Enlightenment flourished in places with an educated middle class and was thus centered in London, Amsterdam, and Paris.
2. In those countries where constitutionalism and the guarantee of individual rights were most advanced (such as Adam Smith's England), Enlightenment thinkers tended to focus on economics, philosophy, and history.
3. In countries with few middle-class citizens (such as Spain), it was easier for governments to censor Enlightenment writings.
4. France was the Enlightenment hotspot because the monarchy alternated between encouraging and harshly criticizing the new thinking. Most French Enlightenment thinkers were subjected to arrest, exile, and imprisonment, but became cultural heroes.
5. France had few guarantees of freedom but enjoyed higher levels of prosperity and cultural development than most European countries. The government controlled publishing, but not as tightly as did Spain or Russia.
6. From the 1760s on, the French government tended to ignore, rather than censor, the flood of philosophical treatises, as well as pornographic books and pamphlets that were undermining the authority of the monarchy.
7. In the German states, on the other hand, intellectuals tended to avoid direct confrontation with the government.
8. Thinkers such as Gotthold Lessing and Moses Mendelssohn promoted religious toleration, whereas Immanuel Kant laid the foundation for modern philosophy with his 1781 work, *The Critique of Pure Reason,* which argued that reason alone could not answer all philosophical questions.

E. The Limits of Reason: Roots of Romanticism and Religious Revival, pp. 566–567

1. A new artistic movement known as romanticism emphasized individual genius, emotion, and the joys of nature—aspects of life that could come into conflict with reason.
2. The limitations of reason were popularized widely in a 1774 novel by Johann Wolfgang von Goethe, *The Sorrows of Young Werther*, in which unrequited love leads a rational young man to suicide.
3. Religious revivals also underlined the limits of reason.
4. Pietism continued to spread in the German states, while the British North American colonies experienced a "Great Awakening."
5. Israel ben Eliezer invented a new form of popular prayer for Jews that was meant to allow the supernatural to speak through the body of the person who prayed.
6. Followers of ben Eliezer, known as the Hasidim, often expressed their devotion through music, dance, and prayer, and spread these practices throughout Poland and Lithuania.
7. In Great Britain, John Wesley founded Methodism, which emphasized self-discipline and a methodical approach to religion.
8. Like ben Eliezer and the Pietists, the popular itinerant preacher Wesley believed in an intensely personal and emotional faith, as well as hard work, thrift, and abstinence.

II. Society and Culture in an Age of Enlightenment

A. The Nobility's Reassertion of Privilege, pp. 567–568

1. Although the standard of living of nobles (perhaps 3 percent of the European population) varied, the wealthiest European nobles lived a lavish and luxurious lifestyle.
2. Due to the commercialization of agriculture and inflation, and their increasingly expensive lifestyles, nobles sought to generate as much revenue as possible from their traditional privileges.
3. In countries such as France, "seigneurial dues" were added to the peasants' financial burden, which also included government taxes, custom duties, and the tithe (one-tenth of the crop paid to the church).
4. Nobles also protected exclusive rights, such as their right to hunt game.
5. Despite Enlightenment writers' criticism of aristocratic privilege, nobles maintained their marks of distinction.
6. Their dress, their exclusive right to wear a sword, their own pews in church, and their private quarters in the university all signified their superiority over other social groups.
7. In many countries, most nobles cared little about Enlightenment ideas, but in France, Great Britain, and the western German states, nobles were more receptive.
8. Nobles in western Europe sometimes married into middle-class families and formed a new mixed elite.

B. The Middle Class and the Making of a New Elite, pp. 568–571

1. The Enlightenment offered the middle class an intellectual and cultural route to self-improvement.
2. These individuals occupied the middle position on the social ladder; most lived in cities and worked as doctors, lawyers, or government officials, or earned a living through investment in trade, land, or manufacturing.
3. The urban middle class (or bourgeoisie) grew steadily in western Europe in the eighteenth century.
4. Nobles and members of the middle class mingled in salons, Masonic lodges, and learned societies.
5. Masonic lodges promoted Enlightenment ideals and encouraged equality among their members (known as "freemasons").
6. Enlightenment ideas were also disseminated through learned societies, in which nobles and middle-class persons met to discuss new scientific innovations or practical social reform.
7. The intermingled elite of nobles and middle-class people also shared tastes in travel, architecture, and the arts.
8. Travel to Italy among youths from both social groups inspired interest in a neoclassical style, which began pushing aside baroque and rococo styles.
9. The new emphasis on emotion and family inspired a growing taste for moralistic family scenes in paintings that evoked moral issues through the depiction of everyday life, and appealed to the middle class.
10. Music was also affected by the rise of a new mixed elite, as it became more accessible to listeners and as professional orchestras in large concert halls began developing a repertoire of "classics," pieces performed repeatedly for paying audiences.
11. A growing literate public led to a frenzied increase in publication.
12. Lending libraries, as well as newspapers, proliferated.
13. Women read as much as men, and a new genre of children's literature emerged.

C. Life on the Margins, pp. 571–573

1. Despite booming foreign trade, increased food production, and rising wages in many trades, at least 10 percent of Europe's urban population depended on some form of charity.
2. Periodic food shortages and inflation caused economic difficulty for day laborers in the cities and peasants with small land holdings.
3. The growing number of poor overwhelmed local governments.
4. Workhouses in which the poor could be confined became more expensive to run; governments therefore developed new institutions to confine beggars and vagabonds that combined workshop, hospital, and prison.
5. Both nobles and middle class feared the increase in rural banditry and crimes against property that accompanied the growing numbers of the poor.

6. Although literacy had increased among the lower classes in western Europe, many still could not read.
7. While the nobles and middle classes attended concerts and art exhibitions, peasants attended fairs and festivals, and workers relaxed in cafés or gambled at bullbaiting, bearbaiting, dogfighting, and cockfighting matches.
8. Sexual behavior also changed, as out-of-wedlock births among the urban lower classes soared in the eighteenth century.
9. Foundling hospitals were established to care for a growing number of abandoned babies; other women attempted abortion or infanticide.
10. Reformers criticized existing laws against fornication and infanticide, but not harsh punishments against male homosexuals (or "sodomites"), which could include imprisonment or execution.
11. The Enlightenment also sparked a new view of parents' value and expectations of children who were no longer considered miniature adults or little sinners in need of harsh discipline.

III. State Power in an Era of Reform

A. War and Diplomacy, pp. 573–576

1. In contrast to the earlier religious wars that had killed thousands of civilians, wars in the eighteenth century were fought by increasingly large professional armies.
2. Military strategy became more cautious, but wars continued to break out as the balance of power became unstable.
3. In the War of the Austrian Succession (1740–1748), Prussia and France fought Austria and Great Britain on the occasion of Maria Theresa's ascension to the imperial throne.
4. Overseas, France and Great Britain fought for dominance in India and North America.
5. The peace treaty of 1748 established Maria Theresa as empress, but did not resolve the conflict between Britain and France.
6. In 1756, a reversal of alliances—with Prussia and Great Britain allied against Austria, France, Russia, and Sweden—laid the foundation for the Seven Years' War (1756–1763).
7. This war began when Prussia invaded Austria's ally Saxony and soon spread around the globe (in North America, this conflict was called the French and Indian War).
8. Despite nearly losing, the withdrawal of Russia from the conflict allowed Prussia to emerge from the war a great power.
9. The militarization of Prussian society (through widespread noble participation in the military and the "canton system" that trained peasants and kept them on reserve) created one of the largest armies Europe had ever seen.
10. In 1772, Prussia became even stronger when Frederick the Great proposed that Poland-Lithuania, a large but weak state, be divided among Austria, Russia, and Prussia.
11. The Polish-Lithuanian commonwealth effectively disappeared.

B. State-Sponsored Reform, pp. 576–577

1. In the aftermath of the Seven Years' War, Enlightened absolutists attempted to make increased taxes more acceptable by proposing social reforms designed to bring about greater equality and efficiency in justice and administration.
2. In Austria and Prussia, monarchs insisted on greater attention to merit, hard work, and professionalism in the government bureaucracy.
3. Frederick II of Prussia instituted a uniform civil justice system, Joseph II of Austria ordered the compilation of a uniform law code, and Catherine II of Russia drew up a document called the *Instruction* that represented her hopes for legal reform.
4. Rulers used Enlightenment criticism of organized religion to gain greater control over church affairs.
5. Catholic Spain, France, and Portugal expelled the Jesuits, the major Catholic teaching order that maintained close ties to the papacy.
6. Enlightened absolutists also desired greater control over education: Joseph II issued a General School Ordinance in 1774 that ordered state subsidies for state-regulated, local schools; the Prussian school code of 1763 required all children between age five and thirteen to attend school; Catherine II also tried to expand education.
7. Many rulers favored religious toleration, but Joseph II went farthest, granting freedom of religion in 1781 to Protestants, Orthodox Christians, and Jews.
8. In 1787, Louis XVI restored the civil rights of Protestants but still banned them from holding public office, Catholics in Great

Britain were prohibited from worshipping freely or sitting in Parliament, and in most European states rights and opportunities available to the Jews were limited.

C. **Limits of Reform, pp. 577–578**

1. Groups threatened by reforms resisted government policy.
2. Joseph II abolished the personal aspects of serfdom in 1781; he also removed the tithe to the church, shifted more tax burden to the nobles, and converted peasants' labor obligations into cash payments. These reforms were met with furious resistance from the nobility.
3. When Joseph II died in 1790, his brother Leopold II was forced to revoke most of them.
4. Reforms in Prussia and France also met with resistance.
5. In France, the physiocrats, a group of economists, urged the deregulation of the grain trade to encourage productivity and the abolition of the guilds because they prevented free entry into the trades.
6. In 1763, the French government abolished price controls on grain, but was forced to reinstate them following a famine in 1770.
7. Louis XV also wanted to decrease the power of the parlements, or high courts. When, in 1771, the government ruled that judges no longer owned their offices, they responded with charges of tyranny.
8. In 1774, Louis XVI restored the old parlements.
9. Louis XVI chose as his chief minister the reforming Jacques Turgot (a contributor to the *Encyclopedia*) who deregulated the grain trade, suppressed the guilds, converted peasants' forced labor into a cash tax payable by landowners, and reduced court expenses.
10. He also began to introduce a system of elected local assemblies.
11. Widespread resistance led by parlements and courtiers, as well as riots sparked by rising grain prices, forced the king to abandon his minister and his reforms.
12. Enlightenment-era reforms often raised unrealistic hopes in France.

IV. **Rebellions against State Power**

A. **Food Riots and Peasant Uprisings, pp. 578–580**

1. Population growth, inflation, and the extension of the market system placed added pressure on the eighteenth-century poor.
2. Citizens believed it was the government's responsibility to ensure they had enough food, and often rioted when they felt abandoned or threatened by the government.
3. The food supply in particular became a focus of political and social conflict as the government's desire to increase production by deregulating the grain trade came in conflict with traditional belief in a "just price" for food.
4. Poor farmers, agricultural workers, and city wage workers rioted to enforce the sale of grain or flour at a "just" price; the riots were often led by women who could not feed their children.
5. One of the most turbulent riots of the last half of the eighteenth century was the 1775 Flour War in France, prompted by a price increase caused by the 1774 deregulation of the grain trade.
6. In Russia, frustrations with serfdom provoked the 1773 Pugachev rebellion.
7. Emelian Pugachev, positioning himself as a "redeemer tsar," claimed he would save the people from oppression.
8. The government finally captured and executed Pugachev, but only after the rebels had attacked and slain numerous noble families.

B. **Public Opinion and Political Opposition, pp. 580–581**

1. The rise of public opinion as a force independent of court society caused enduring changes in European politics.
2. This public opinion, expressed in the parlements of France, as well as in salons, Masonic lodges, newspapers, and pamphlets all over Europe, increasingly demanded broader political participation, basing its demand on the Enlightenment idea of individual rights.
3. Monarchs such as Gustavus III of Sweden also appealed to public opinion in order to gain support for reforms.
4. Public opinion could be mobilized to challenge a government, as the Wilkes affair in Great Britain demonstrated.
5. John Wilkes, who was a member of Parliament, attacked the government in his newspaper and was arrested.
6. Parliament denied Wilkes his rightful seat when he was reelected, and a major

campaign in favor of Parliamentary reform was ignited.

7. The devastation caused by the 1780 Gordon riots, which were organized by anti-Catholic crusader Lord George Gordon to protest limited toleration for Catholics, also demonstrated the new power of public opinion to make its voice heard on political matters.

C. **Revolution in North America, pp. 581–583**

1. In Great Britain's North American colonies, the public increasingly came to consider the British government corrupt and despotic.
2. Reformers argued that the British government, by not allowing them representation in Parliament, did not recognize their traditional British liberties.
3. The economies of the America colonies and their populations flourished between 1750 and 1776. At the end of the Seven Years' War, when the British Parliament introduced new taxes to the colonies, those taxes were met with violent rioting.
4. These taxes were repealed, but the 1773 tax on tea revived opposition that culminated in the Boston Tea Party.
5. The First Continental Congress convened in 1774 and unsuccessfully petitioned the crown for redress.
6. In 1775, the Second Continental Congress organized an army with George Washington at its head.
7. The colonies declared their independence in 1776 in the Declaration of Independence, which was written in the language of the Enlightenment.
8. The war with its American colonies led Britain into war with France, Spain, and the Dutch Republic and produced a worldwide conflict. With foreign support, the colonies achieved their independence in 1783.
9. In a radical departure from European models, in 1787 the newly independent states created a republic with a two-house legislature, an indirectly elected president, and an independent judiciary.
10. Although women and slaves were excluded from political participation, the U.S. Constitution specified that the government drew its authority from the people.
11. A 1791 Bill of Rights outlined essential individual rights that the government could never overturn.
12. Interest in the new American republic was greatest in France.

Lecture Strategies

1. How the Enlightenment actually operated is a highly important topic. One way to approach it is by examining a list of the different venues of the Enlightenment:

- encyclopedias and dictionaries;
- short stories and novels;
- pamphlets;
- newspapers, journals;
- almanacs, books on etiquette, books on how to write letters;
- coffeehouses, reading rooms, lending libraries, booksellers;
- salons, scientific societies, academies;
- letters and conversation;
- theater and opera; and
- engravings and other works of art.

Examples of some of these could be provided for the class, or students could be assigned to report on various venues. Students should also be encouraged to discuss how opinion is formed and information exchanged today: How much is new? How much has been discarded? How much from the past is still utilized?

Some resources are mentioned below in the segments dealing with Voltaire and Jefferson. Other possibilities include Thomas Munck, *The Enlightenment: A Comparative Social History, 1721–1794* (London: Arnold, 2000), which includes an extensive bibliography; Sarah Maza, *Private Lives and Public Affairs: The Causes Célèbres of Prerevolutionary France* (Berkeley: University of California Press, 1993); Robert Darnton, *The Business of the Enlightenment: A Publishing History of the Encyclopedia, 1775–1800* (Cambridge, MA: Belknap Press, 1979) and his *The Forbidden Best-Sellers of Pre-Revolutionary France* (New York: W. W. Norton, 1995); and Dena Goodman, *The Republic of Letters: A Cultural History of the French Enlightenment* (Ithaca, NY: Cornell University Press, 1994).

2. Catherine the Great is a fascinating historical figure. A consideration of her life and reign opens up many possibilities, including an examination of the attempt in Russia to construct an effective central government (which could easily become a comparative examination by bringing in the efforts made in Prussia, France, or Austria); the problems encountered during rapid social change (which would involve a discussion of the causes of the Pugachev rebellion); the nature of serfdom in Russia; and, of course, the extent of Catherine's commitment to the Enlightenment.

A useful overview of Catherine's career can be found in Part 2 of Bruce Lincoln, *The Romanovs: Autocrats of All the Russias* (New York: Dial Press, 1981). The best biography of Catherine is by Isabel de Madariaga, *Catherine the Great: A Short History* (New Haven, CT: Yale University Press, 1990). De Madariaga is also the author of a comprehensive study, *Russia in the Age of Catherine the Great* (New Haven, CT: Yale University Press, 1981). Part 1 of Gregory L. Freeze, *From Supplication to Revolution: A Documentary Social History of Imperial Russia* (New York and Oxford: Oxford University Press, 1988) contains a wonderful selection of documents on the nobility, the peasantry, the bureaucracy, and women, among other groups. Other documents, including Catherine's Nakaz or Instruction, Pugachev's "Emancipation Decree," and Catherine's Charter to the Nobility, can be found in Basil Dmytryshyn, ed., *Imperial Russia: A Source Book, 1700–1917*, 3rd ed. (Fort Worth, TX: Holt, Rinehart & Winston, 1990). Two outstanding essays are available on the causes and the course of the Pugachev rebellion: Paul Avrich, *Russian Rebels, 1600–1800* (New York: Schocken Books, 1972), Part 4; and Marc Raeff's essay in Robert Forster and Jack P. Greene, eds., *Preconditions of Revolution in Early Modern Europe* (Baltimore: Johns Hopkins University Press, 1970).

3. Frederick II of Prussia is an equally fascinating historical figure and perhaps of greater overall importance than Catherine. Moreover, the particular challenges Prussia faced in these years can provide insight into future events involving Germany. In any case, his life and career might serve as the basis for lectures and discussion on the topics of enlightened despotism, Frederick's relationship with Voltaire, and Prussia and great-power politics at the end of the eighteenth century. Chapter 2 of Holger H. Herwig, *Hammer or Anvil: Modern Germany 1648–Present* (Lexington, MA: D. C. Heath, 1994) is an excellent overview, placing Frederick and Prussia in the context of mid- to late-eighteenth-century Europe. Biographies include Theodore Schieder and Sabina Berkeley, *Frederick the Great* (New York: Longman, 1999), a good introduction; and the recent publication, Giles MacDonogh, *Frederick the Great: A Life in Deed and Letters* (New York: St. Martin's Press, 2000), where the emphasis is on intellectual matters, particularly Frederick's love-hate relationship with Voltaire. Two older studies worth consulting are Sidney B. Fay and Klaus Epstein, *The Rise of Brandenburg-Prussia to 1786* (Malabar, FL: R. E. Krieger, 1981); and Hans Rosenberg's classic study of the Prussian royal bureaucracy, *Bureaucracy, Aristocracy, and Autocracy: The Prussian Experience, 1660–1815* (Cambridge, MA: Harvard University Press, 1958). Finally, for Frederick or Catherine, Marc Raeff, *The Well-Ordered Police State: Social and Institutional Change Through Law in the Germanies and Russia, 1600–1800* (New Haven, CT: Yale University Press, 1983) is useful. This book is not about the police state as we have come to know it in the twentieth century, but rather, as the subtitle indicates, about earlier efforts to regulate various aspects of citizens' lives in an attempt to improve them.

4. The art of William Hogarth, both as a mass-produced "marketing" phenomenon and as visual image, and indeed Hogarth's own career and biography, offers invaluable windows into eighteenth-century anxieties about urbanization, the rise of middle-class values and sensibilities, and the sometimes critical relationship between the social classes. Of particular interest are Hogarth's images of "Gin Lane" and "Beer Street," which are entertaining for students but which also illustrate concerns about changing tastes, the urban poor, alcohol, and the cash economy. Similar concerns can be found in "Four Times of the Day," his series of images of London in various states of disarray. "Rake's Progress," as with many of his other images, can be read as criticism of a corrupt aristocratic elite, but there are attacks on all social groups to the extent that it is clear he saw "corruption" as a cross-class phenomenon. Images of Hogarth's prints abound on the Internet. Scholarly appreciations of his art and career are widely available—background reading for lecturers can be found in Jenny Uglow's extensive and context-rich *Hogarth: A Life and a World*, 2nd ed. (London: Farrar, Straus, and Giroux, 2002). See also David Bindman, *Hogarth and His Times: Serious Comedy* (Berkeley, CA: University of California Press, 1997). A much briefer overview is Matthew Craske, *William Hogarth* (Princeton, NJ: Princeton University Press, 2000).

5. Tracking the progress of a religious reform movement like Methodism and the associated "Great Awakening" of the middle decades of the eighteenth century offers a very effective way of demonstrating how Atlantic world dynamics actually worked in practice and serves to flesh out what the text has to say about popular movements and the emotional turn in religious practice. Methodism is especially effective as a focus because Wesley's biography, from his conservative Anglican upbringing to his participation in the Georgia mission, and his disillusionment and eventual inspirational exposure to Moravian pietism, offers an excellent opportunity to personalize the abstract circulations of goods, people, and ideas around the Atlantic world. The Great Awakening itself also offers opportunities for discussing dynamics of race, gender, and the "mass marketing" of ideologies that were appealing to the new, literate middle class. Frank Lambert's work (most recently, *Inventing the Great Awakening* [Princeton, NJ: Princeton University Press, 2001]) is sensitive to Atlantic world scholarship, the complexities of historical interpretations of religious

revivals of the period, and the interrelationship between cultural, religious, and economic activity. Mark Knoll's *The Rise of Evangelicalism: The Age of Edwards, Whitefield, and the Wesleys* (Downer's Grove, IL: Intervarsity Press, 2003) is authoritative on the religious dimension and conscious of the diversity of the early evangelical movement of which Wesley was a critical part. In general, it is important to find a way to personalize the possibilities that the Atlantic World opened up for many, without romanticizing the disruptions and challenges of the emerging new patterns of race relations, migration, emigration, work, and domestic life.

Class Discussion Starters

1. Voltaire is one of the most interesting and broadly representative of the philosophes. Over his long career, he used various methods to reach the public and the powerful. *Candide*, a short and entertaining satire, exemplified one approach. Students might read the entire text or only a selection. Alternatively, selections from Voltaire's *Philosophical Dictionary* might be used as a basis for discussion, or you can use selections from both *Candide* and *Philosophical Dictionary*. Discussions of Voltaire's satire on optimism, his emphasis on the importance of a realistic approach and hard work, and other aspects of his views might best be understood when prefaced by introductory comments on his life and career.

Daniel Gordon's translation of *Candide* features such an introduction and useful documentary material (Boston: Bedford/St. Martin's, 1999). Another useful edition is that by Robert M. Adams (New York: W. W. Norton, 1966). The edition of Voltaire's *Philosophical Dictionary* by Peter Gay is highly recommended (New York: Harcourt Brace & World, 1962). See Chapter 1 in Peter Gay, *The Party of Humanity: Essays in the French Enlightenment* (New York: W. W. Norton, 1971 [originally published in 1959]) for an excellent introduction to Voltaire and his *Philosophical Dictionary*. Other useful books include Peter Gay, *Voltaire's Politics: The Poet as Realist* (New York: Vintage Books, 1965 [originally published in 1959]); William F. Bottiglia, ed., *Voltaire: A Collection of Critical Essays* (Englewood Cliffs, NJ: Prentice Hall, 1968), which includes several useful short essays; Hadyn Trevor Mason, *Voltaire: A Biography* (Baltimore: Johns Hopkins University Press, 1981), a dependable short biography; and Theodore Besterman, *Voltaire*, 3rd ed. (Chicago: University of Chicago Press, 1976), a comprehensive study.

2. Because Thomas Jefferson is someone with whom most students are familiar, his career is useful as a good illustration of where Enlightenment thought might take a practical politician. Querying number eleven, "Aborigines," from Jefferson's *Notes on the State of Virginia*, which is concerned in large part with his investigation of Indian burial mounds, should provoke a discussion about how the Enlightenment functioned. Ask students to consider how Jefferson's investigation reflects the methods of the Enlightenment. Effective visual presentations might be built around Jefferson's plans for the University of Virginia, his main residence of Monticello, or his summer home in Poplar Forest.

A comprehensive biography of Jefferson is Willard Sterne Randall, *Thomas Jefferson: A Life* (New York: Henry Holt, 1993). Ken Burns's video portrait *Thomas Jefferson* (Alexandria, VA: PBS Video, 1997) at three hours is too long to be shown in one class period, but selections from it would be useful to a consideration of Jefferson as a participant in the Enlightenment. It can be put on reserve for students to watch, or perhaps be shown outside of class if students are interested. *Notes on the State of Virginia* is available in an edition published by Viking Penguin Books (New York, 1998). It is also included in the Library of America edition of *Jefferson's Writings* (New York, 1984). Jefferson in Paris is the subject of Howard Crosby Rice, *Thomas Jefferson's Paris* (Princeton, NJ: Princeton University Press, 1976). Pauline Maier provides a good discussion of Jefferson's role in writing the Declaration of Independence in *American Scripture: Making the Declaration of Independence* (New York: Alfred A. Knopf, 1997). See also Garry Wills, *Inventing America: Jefferson's Declaration of Independence* (Garden City, NY: Doubleday, 1978). In a time when Jefferson's attitude toward slavery, his relationship with Sally Hemings, and his treatment of native Americans have been the subjects of searching critiques, Joseph J. Ellis offers a helpful examination of Jefferson's character in *American Sphinx: The Character of Thomas Jefferson* (New York: Alfred A. Knopf, 1997). Also useful in this regard is Jan Lewis and Peter S. Onuf, eds., *Sally Hemings & Thomas Jefferson: History, Memory, and Civil Culture* (Charlottesville: University of Virginia Press, 1999). Finally, S. Allen Chambers, *Poplar Forest and Thomas Jefferson* (Forest, VA: The Corporation for Jefferson's Poplar Forest, 1993) is a fascinating, detailed architectural history of Jefferson's summer home in central Virginia.

3. Mozart's career as a child prodigy and a phenomenally gifted composer continues to fascinate students. He exemplifies the artist caught in a changing world where patronage was still important but opportunities to reach a wider public were also present. Mozart's life also offers the possibility of examining changes in society when new groups arise to challenge the dominance of the aristocracy.

Amadeus, or at least a portion of the film (Burbank, CA: Warner Home Video, 1997), is a good place to start. Can this silly person be the musical genius we all associate with neoclassicism? Was competition between composers really so fierce? What does the relationship between Mozart and Salieri tell us about neoclassicism? Is there a bit of the romantic in the brooding, passionate Salieri? Is the relationship a metaphor for a struggle between good and evil? Two short biographies are available: Peter Gay, *Mozart* (New York: Lipper/Viking Books, 1999); and John Rosselli, *The Life of Mozart* (Cambridge and New York: Cambridge University Press, 1998). Howard Gardner takes a different approach in *Extraordinary Minds: Portraits of Four Exceptional Individuals and an Examination of Our Own Extraordinariness* (New York: Basic Books, 1997). Other useful titles include H. C. Robbins Landon, ed., *The Mozart Compendium* (New York: Schirmer Books, 1990); and the rather lengthy study by Daniel Heartz, *Haydn, Mozart, and the Viennese School, 1740–1780* (New York: W. W. Norton, 1995).

4. Protests in western Europe in the last half of the eighteenth century can form the basis for interesting class meetings in which participants discuss the social structure of France and England, popular protest movements, the role of the Enlightenment, and the validity of using a Marxist approach to these questions. Two English historians stand out for their contributions to debates about popular protest in this period. One is E. P. Thompson, whose major book, *The Making of the English Working Class* (New York: Random House, 1963), is a classic. Although it is long, it is well worth reading. Two articles provide many of Thompson's insights, although without the wealth of detail: "The Moral Economy of the English Crowd of the Eighteenth Century," *Past and Present* 50 (May 1971), 76–136; and "Eighteenth-Century English Society: Class Struggle Without a Class?" *Social History* 3.2 (May 1978), 137–165. The other English historian is George Rude, whose best-known book is *The Crowd in History: A Study of Popular Disturbances in France and England, 1730–1848* (New York: John Wiley & Sons, 1964). Also useful are his *Paris and London in the Eighteenth Century: Studies in Popular Protest* (New York: Viking Press, 1970); and *Hanoverian London, 1714–1808* (Berkeley and Los Angeles: University of California Press, 1971). Finally, Jack A. Goldstone, *Revolution and Rebellion in the Early Modern World* (Berkeley and Los Angeles: University of California Press, 1991) discusses eighteenth-century France from a demographic and economic point of view and tries to locate the causes of the crisis that becomes the French Revolution. It is not an entirely convincing argument, but the reader learns an enormous amount. Goldstone also provides an extensive bibliography.

5. The essence of the Enlightenment was social criticism within a framework of critical communication. Begin a class by asking students to identify a social problem and to compose a paragraph convincing an audience of peers that the problem is significant. Then the students should write a paragraph or two suggesting a solution. The "problems" and "solutions" should be shared and debate/discussion encouraged. It can be pointed out that this sort of exchange and the belief in the value of discussion and rational argument were at the core of what philosophes did. It will no doubt also be clear to students that reason did not always lead people to the same conclusions. The same exercise can be done orally in a "salon-like" setting, perhaps with a designated "host/hostess" to frame and modulate discussion. Students can be asked to comment on the relationship between wit/style and reason in persuading people to consider a given problem or its solution.

Reviewing the Text

Review Questions

1. What were the major differences between the Enlightenment in France, Great Britain, and the German states?

[model answer] • ***The Enlightenment was distinctly cosmopolitan; most philosophes thought of themselves as part of an international "republic of letters" united by shared ideals:*** *The epicenter of the Enlightenment, which flourished best where there was an educated, middle-class audience for its ideas, was formed by the triangle of London, Paris, and Amsterdam, and diffused outward to eastern and southern Europe.*

• ***In France, particularly in Paris, Enlightenment-era critics of church and state often suffered harassment and persecution:*** *The Catholic Church and royal authorities attempted to control publication and circulation of books and ideas that were thought to be subversive. But sufficient freedom, prosperity, and cultural development existed for ideas to thrive despite this, and Enlightenment thinkers became cultural heroes. Enlightenment thought helped to weaken the monarchy.*

• ***In Great Britain, where there was more freedom, Enlightenment ideas circulated freely and the movement had less of an "edge":*** *London was a center of Enlightenment thinking, however, and in Scotland universities were important centers of Enlightenment thought. Prosperity and literacy in Britain were avid consumers of Enlightenment literature.*

• ***German Enlightenment thinkers were less likely to engage in confrontation with authorities:*** *There was little freedom across Germany, particularly in Prussia. Universities were also centers of Enlightenment thought in parts of Germany, and the work of Gotthold Lessing and Immanuel Kant strongly promoted reason and toleration.*

2. What were the major differences in the impact of the Enlightenment on nobles, middle classes, and lower classes?

[model answer] • ***Nobles typically resisted Enlightenment ideas; those in nations with a large middle class sometimes embraced change and participated in reform:*** *In eastern Europe, royal laws delineated and protected nobles' rights and exempted them from some legal and financial responsibilities. In France, Britain, and western Germany, the nobility was more open to new ideas due to interactions with the middle class and Enlightenment authors.*

• ***New Enlightenment venues offered more class equality and served to transmit middle-class sensibilities:*** *In western Europe, middle-class professionals and nobles mingled in salons, Masonic lodges, and local learned societies. These organizations often functioned as mini-constitutional democracies in which all members voted and could serve as officers.*

• ***Urban lower classes grew increasingly literate and participated in their own social activities:*** *Literacy enabled the poor to engage in some of the shared ideas of the Enlightenment, but the urban culture for the poor involved more traditional public entertainments such as fairs, taverns, and gambling organized around animal fights.*

3. What prompted enlightened absolutists to undertake reforms in the second half of the eighteenth century?
[model answer] *Two major European wars had resulted from instability in Europe's balance of power. In the aftermath, involved nations needed money to fund growing armies, to organize navies, and to counter inflation. The modernization of government, including legal, judicial and penal reform to unify law codes and dispose of torture, the development of state-run educational systems, and the control of the church, which would result in religious toleration, all made tax increases more palatable to the population.*

4. Why did public opinion become a new factor in politics in the second half of the eighteenth century?
[model answer] • ***The spread of literacy and Enlightenment ideals and reforms informed common persons about government's activities:*** *Ideals of constitutionalism and equality encouraged the populace to care about political decisions, and to feel that they should have a means to express their opinions. Newspapers began to cover daily political affairs, and the public learned the basics of political life despite their limited participation in most countries. The spread of literacy, as well as the proliferation of venues for social interaction, encouraged the spread of information.*

• ***Access to information facilitated public riots and revolutions and also provided the opportunity to shape public opinion:*** *Riots occurred in opposition to governmental policies in the seventeenth and early eighteenth centuries. Newspapers and pamphlets, however, provided an alternative means to protest political and economic situations. Recognizing and using the power of print, monarchs and parliaments appealed to the public to gather support for their reforms or to condemn rebellious ideas.*

Making Connections

1. Why would rulers feel ambivalent about the Enlightenment, supporting reform on the one hand, while clamping down on political dissidents on the other hand?
[model answer] *Some of the absolutist rulers of this period, such as Catherine the Great of Russia, Frederick II (the Great) of Prussia, and Joseph II of Austria, wanted to be perceived as modern and progressive. Although they were interested in reform to at least some degree, and embraced Enlightenment ideas they deemed useful in that regard, they rejected anything that had the potential to threaten their personal power and authority. So, while Catherine, Frederick, and Joseph were interested in education, and instituted education reform in their countries, they (or their successor in Joseph's case) backed down on other reforms that were opposed by their powerful nobility, such as legal reform in Russia, serf reform in Habsburg territories, and agricultural reform in Prussia.*

2. Which major developments in this period ran counter to the influence of the Enlightenment?
[model answer] *Although absolutist rulers were "enlightened despots," military aggression (in the form of the War of the Austrian Succession [1740–1748] and the Seven Years' War [1756–1763]), rather than reasoned negotiation, continued to be the means by which international disputes were settled. The nobility across Europe also continued to insist on their traditional rights and privileges, at the expense of those at the bottom of the socioeconomic hierarchy. Slavery continued to run counter to Enlightenment ideas amid calls for its abolition. Excessive reliance on reason also began to wear thin, and this discontent fed into a new movement—romanticism—which emphasized individual genius, deep emotion, and the joys of nature. Reaction to the Enlightenment also took the form of religious revival. The Pietists in Germany, revivalists in the United States, and Methodists in England all put pressure on the Enlightenment ideal of a society governed by reason.*

3. In what ways had politics changed, and in what ways did it remain the same during the Enlightenment?
[model answer] *The Enlightenment was an elite movement that had little resonance for most ordinary people. Enlightenment thinkers attempted to convince elites to adopt new ideas, however, and they also made an effort to make political processes more subject to the weight of "public opinion," which became increasingly*

important to effective governance. The notions of the philosophes also placed traditional ideas about church-state relations under pressure, and endorsed a model of more secular governance that had considerable influence. Many Enlightenment-era monarchs, notably Catherine II of Russia, Joseph II of Austria, and Frederick II of Prussia, seeking to increase the credibility of their regimes or their ability to gain advantages over rival states, adopted aspects of Enlightenment political thought and Enlightenment-inspired administrative and legal reform. Such reforms prompted resistance, however, and reforming leaders sought ultimately to enhance their power and influence over traditional elites first and foremost.

Discussing the Documents

Questions from Online Study Guide with Model Answers

Denis Diderot, "Encyclopedia" (1755), p. 559

1. According to Diderot, what are the best sources of information? What provides the best "rules" to people?
[model answer] *Diderot, with his fellow philosophes, saw human reason and critical engagement with ideas and opinions as the best source of information. He envisioned the Encyclopedia as a clearinghouse for daring, forthright thinking that could "ride roughshod over all these ancient puerilities" and prejudices. In all of this, nature, rather than classical ideas, offered the best "rules" for people to follow in constructing society.*

2. What are the problems, from Diderot's point of view, with the past? How has society changed, and how and why has it improved?
[model answer] *In the past, people lacked intellectual courage and daring, and simply passed on old ideas that were not rooted in reason without subjecting them to rigorous interrogation. Diderot's age is intellectually daring and determined to restore "liberty" to the arts and sciences. His is a "reasoning age."*

Thomas Jefferson, Declaration of Independence (July 4, 1776), p. 582

1. In which ways is this document a product of the Enlightenment?
[model answer] *The Declaration of Independence justifies the actions of the revolutionaries with an appeal to the laws of nature rather than on tradition or religion. It claims that governments are "instituted among Men, deriving their just powers from the consent of the governed." It also states that a "respect to the opinions of mankind" requires them to declare the reasons why they are separating from their sovereign. The secular justification of the American Revolution, the idea that government derives from the governed, and the value of public opinion were all derived from the Enlightenment.*

2. How does this document go beyond what original Enlightenment thinkers advocated?
[model answer] *Most Enlightenment thinkers did not believe that revolution was the best way to bring about reform. They typically did not trust the people of the lower classes, whom they viewed as superstitious, ignorant, and violent, and would not have approved placing the government in their hands. Enlightenment thinkers generally believed that published criticism was the best way of bringing about change.*

Contrasting Views: Women and the Enlightenment, pp. 562–563

1. Why would women in the eighteenth century read Rousseau with such interest and even enthusiasm?
[model answer] *Rousseau's work was interesting and appealing to women in part because he used female characters in* Émile *to address a range of issues that mattered to women—education, child rearing, and family life. In the excerpt here, he is sympathetic to the difficult role in which society placed women. He ascribed to women a critical role in shaping the future and in educating, influencing, and forming men.*

2. Why does Madame de Beaumer address herself to male readers if the *Journal des Dames* is intended for women?
[model answer] *The* Journal des Dames *certainly addressed issues of interest to women, but it also sought to present a female perspective to men and to influence their treatment of women. In her editorial, Beaumer urges men to respect women and to give them greater opportunities. It is necessary, she suggests, for young women to know history and to have "striking images" presented to them that "will guide them toward virtue."*

3. Why would Macaulay focus so much of her analysis on Rousseau? Why does she not just ignore him?
[model answer] *Rousseau was a crucial figure of the Enlightenment, and his reputation was considerable. Because the Enlightenment encouraged thinkers to challenge each other's ideas, it was natural for Macaulay to challenge Rousseau's perspective on women. His writing, as she suggests, is popular, influential, and appealing, even while it offers, from her point of view, a corrupted understanding of the natural position of women.*

4. Was the Enlightenment intended only for men?
[model answer] *Each of these authors suggests that it was not. Education of all human beings, and opportunities for them to develop and cultivate their reason, were vitally important. For Rousseau, this required that women be trained for their proper role in life—to fulfill the taxing*

duties of motherhood and the formation of male character, although women were "rationally" destined to serve and strengthen men, who were stronger intellectually. For Beaumer and Macaulay, the potential of women to develop intellectually was limited by prejudice and the nature of female education. Properly raised and directed toward developing their reason and cultivating historical and practical knowledge, women could join men in benefiting from Enlightenment progress.

Other Questions for Discussing These Documents in Class

Denis Diderot, "Encyclopedia" (1755)

1. How does Diderot describe his own time? What does he understand to be different or significant about his era?

2. What will govern this new age, and what is its relationship to tradition? If Diderot is describing the "Enlightenment" as he defines "Encyclopedia," why do you suppose it was an attractive idea to many and a repellent or dangerous one to others?

Thomas Jefferson, Declaration of Independence (July 4, 1776)

1. Students can be asked to identify the Enlightenment ideas encapsulated in the Declaration of Independence.

2. According to Jefferson, what rights and responsibilities do citizens have? What is the relationship between citizens and their governments?

Contrasting Views: Women and the Enlightenment

1. Discuss with students the disagreements present in these documents about the proper role of women in society. How does Macauley in particular attack Rousseau's opinions about the nature of women?

2. How does the specific question of education and the formation of the female intellect figure in the understanding of women presented by Rousseau, Beaumer, and Macauley? Outline with students the positions of the authors.

Comparative Questions

1. Are there common characteristics among these documents describing the principles that ought to govern political and social relationships?

2. What do these documents have to say about the individual and his or her relationship to society? What role should individuals as such play in promoting social change or ordering human communities?

For Users of *Sources of The Making of the West*

The following documents are available in Chapter 18 of the companion sourcebook by Katharine J. Lualdi, University of Southern Maine.

1. Spreading Enlightenment: Marie-Thérèse Geoffrin and M. d'Alembert, *The Salon of Madame Geoffrin* (1765)
2. An Enlightened Worker: Jacques-Louis Ménétra, *Journal of My Life* (1764–1802)
3. Reforming the Law: Cesare Beccaria, *On Crimes and Punishments* (1764)
4. Reforming Commerce: Adam Smith, *An Inquiry into the Nature and Causes of the Wealth of Nations* (1776)
5. Enlightened Monarchy: Frederick II, *Political Testament* (1752)

Discussion Ideas for Sources of The Making of the West, *Chapter 18*

1. Discuss what character traits made Mme. Geoffrin an ideal salon hostess. How might a woman like her serve to advance Enlightenment ideas? Does her letter to the King of Poland demonstrate any sense of inferiority?

2. In what sense are Ménétra's criticisms of the Catholic church and Beccaria's of the law similar? How do they see legal and religious authority?

3. Discuss the ways in which Smith argues that individually rational economic behaviors produce better social results. What are the disadvantages to society of failing to act rationally in economic matters?

4. In considering Frederick II's arguments for monarchy, discuss what, in this document, he bases his arguments on. What principles should govern a monarch's actions, and why? What limitations on "reason" and what compromises with public opinion should a monarch be willing to make?

5. Considering the documents as a whole, discuss the ways in which Enlightenment thought represented a threat to established ways of doing things.

6. Note the way much of this material discusses ordinary people and established custom. Do any of these documents reflect arrogance, elitism, or contempt for either?

Working with Visual Sources

For this exercise, please refer to Jean-Baptiste Greuze, *Broken Eggs* (1756) on p. 570 of the textbook or view the image on the book companion site's Online Study Guide under the "Visual Activity" for Chapter 18.

Students viewing the image at the Online Study Guide are asked two questions about the image. The questions and model answers (not made available to students) are below. Project this image, available on the Instructor's Resources CD-ROM, in class or ask students to look at the image in their textbooks and answer the questions.

1. What changes in artistic taste does this painting represent?
[model answer] *During the eighteenth century, a new emphasis focused on emotion and family life, especially among the middle class, which was becoming increasingly active in the art world. This view was a change from the intimate sensuality of rococo and the monumental baroque style.*

2. What are some of the social changes of the time that might have influenced this painting?
[model answer] *Sexual behavior was changing during this time, as out-of-wedlock births rose to 20 percent from 5 percent the century before. Increased mobility among villagers would also have allowed a man to avoid responsibility for impregnating a woman. This man is obviously just being confronted and, if the child is his, he has clearly been away for an extended period of time.*

Mapping Exercises

Map Activity from OSG—Model Answers for Map Activity #2

For this activity, please refer to Map 18.2: The Seven Years' War, 1756–1763 on p. 575. Students are asked these questions:

What were the two main alliances during the Seven Years' War?
[model answer] *The two main alliances were between France, Spain, Austria, Hungary, Russia, and Sweden on one side, and Prussia, Portugal, and Great Britain on the other.*

What were the main theaters of fighting during the Seven Years' War?
[model answer] *During the Seven Years' War, fighting in Europe was mainly conducted in the German and Austrian territories of central Europe. However, hostilities also happened in Portugal and in European colonies in North America, the West Indies, and India. These remote battles suggest that colonial interests had become a factor in European power politics.*

Map 18.1: War of the Austrian Succession, 1740–1748, p. 574

Using the map, have students consider the war aims of the belligerents. The map reveals where fighting occurred; what does this tell students about the nature of such conflicts? What issues did the conflict leave unresolved? Students should discuss Britain's interest in weakening France, particularly by preventing French control of the Austrian Netherlands, and the ongoing tensions between Austria and Prussia over their relative influence among the German states. The location of much of the fighting outside of the territory of the main belligerents is worth noting in relation to the ability of smaller states to avoid the consequences of conflict between the larger powers.

Map 18.2: The Seven Years' War, 1756–1763, p. 575

Comparing this map to Map 18.1, in what ways was the Seven Years' War different from the War of Austrian Succession? How was conflict changing? It is well worth having students note the significance of balance-of-power politics in terms of the willingness of countries to choose new allies. The expanding scale of war with the involvement of more European states, particularly Russia, and the growing importance of non-European theaters are important to point out.

Mapping the West: Europe and the World, c. 1780, p. 583

Ask students to compare this map with the map of Europe in 1740 (Mapping the West, page 551). What reasons can they suggest for changing the focus from Europe to the world? Ask students to keep in mind the locations and results of the Seven Years' War and the American War for Independence as they think about this question.

Among the reasons that might be cited: the Seven Years' War was a world war with important ramifications beyond Europe. Among other results, the French were ousted from Canada and India, and the British Empire took the lead in imperial affairs. Also, the American War for Independence led to the creation of the United States of America, with both short-term and long-term implications. The European situation had also changed in various respects, but the major powers remained the same as they were in 1740.

In-Class Assignments and Presentation Topics

1. Ask students to reflect on the kinds of activities that preoccupied a philosophe. They should be asked to try to make some general statements about what philosophes did, what they believed in, and which changes they wanted to make. These statements

should be based on the activities and characteristics of particular individuals. For example, Denis Diderot's work as editor of the *Encyclopedia* can be seen as an attempt to collect useful knowledge about various topics, as an example of the collective work many philosophes engaged in, and as an indication of the value philosophes placed on education. Remind students that the philosophes differed from one another. For example, while most were vitally interested in improving government, their ideas about this topic varied widely. A variation on this assignment is to ask students to write essays or give reports on particular philosophes, emphasizing the extent to which a particular philosophe was a representative figure.

2. Provide students with the list of the different venues of the Enlightenment (see "Lecture Strategies," number 1) and ask them to reflect on why and how one or more venues may have been useful in spreading ideas of the Enlightenment. This topic would work well as an in-class writing assignment if, after the class had discussed the means for acquainting people with Enlightenment ideas, each student was asked to write more expansively on one of the venues. A variation on this topic would be to ask students to write an essay on how they currently learn about the world around them (the Internet, TV, conversations with friends, and so on) and what venue is particularly influential as they form opinions about current issues. Which venue or venues are most like Enlightenment models? Which are least like them? Which would a philosophe prefer? Why? Emphasize the importance of networks of collaboration and communication in spreading Enlightenment ideas.

3. Using the visual material available in Chapter 18 (see the suggestions on p. 570 for *Broken Eggs*), students could be asked to write about morality and sexuality in the eighteenth century, including new ideas about marriage and about raising children. Ask students to reflect on the differences caused by factors such as gender and social groups.

4. The War of the Austrian Succession and the Seven Years' War, taken together, produced significant changes in the European balance of power. Ask students to write an essay discussing how these wars affected the relative standing of one of the following major powers: Austria, France, Great Britain, Prussia, or Russia.

5. Rousseau's ideas on education, especially as they are represented in *Émile* and elsewhere in his writings, conflict with his treatment of his own children and his relationships with their mothers. Ask students to explore this issue, keeping in mind such questions as whether his behavior or personality traits can be reconciled with his writings. Is it important that we be able to do so?

Essay Questions

1. For Voltaire and many others, the enlightened despot offered the best opportunity for the Enlightenment to fulfill its various goals. An enlightened despot would have both the intelligence to see the benefits the Enlightenment could provide and the power to bring those benefits into being. In effect, they offered a fast track for reform. Students could be asked to choose an enlightened despot from the following list and identify and investigate a specific issue that especially concerned that ruler, for example, religious freedom, freedom of the press, economic reform, education reform, or women's issues. Students should not merely describe the enlightened despot's thoughts on the particular subject, but also to evaluate that person's treatment of the issue. To what extent was the ruler "enlightened" as opposed to "despotic"?

- Catherine II
- Frederick II
- Maria Theresa
- Joseph II
- Louis XVI

Suggested readings for Catherine II and Frederick II have already been listed in "Lecture Strategies," numbers 2 and 3, respectively. For Joseph II and Maria Theresa, see Charles Ingrao, *The Habsburg Monarchy 1618–1815* (Cambridge: Cambridge University Press, 1994). For Maria Theresa, see C. A. Macartney, *Maria Theresa and the House of Austria* (Mystic, CT: Verry, 1969). For Joseph II, see T. C. W. Blanning, *Joseph II and Enlightened Despotism* (London: Longman, 1970). For Louis XVI, see John Hardman, *Louis XVI* (New Haven, CT: Yale University Press, 1993).

2. The use of images to supplement text has had a long tradition in Europe but it became far more widespread during the eighteenth century. Students can be assigned research projects on some of the more popular illustrators from the period, such as William Hogarth (discussed in Lecture Strategy number 4), James Gillray, or Thomas Rowlandson; or even on a particular series, such as Hogarth's *The Rake's Progress* (1733–1734) or *Marriage à la Mode* (1743). Another possibility is to review the literature on the impact of satirical prints and political caricatures. Students might begin by reading chapters 2 and 3 in Thomas Munck, *The Enlightenment: A Comparative Social History, 1721–1794* (London: Arnold, 2000). These chapters take up traditional popular and elite culture along with what the author calls "broadening the horizon," a variety of cultural changes. From there, students might go to Ronald Paulson, *Hogarth*, 3 vols. (New Brunswick, NJ: Rutgers University Press, 1991–1993); or the other sources mentioned in Lecture Strategy

number 4. Less information is available on Gillray and Rowlandson. For Gillray, see Draper Hill, *Mr. Gillray the Caricaturist* (Greenwich, CT: Phaidon, 1965). For Rowlandson, see the ubiquitous Ronald Paulson, *Rowlandson: A New Interpretation* (New York: Oxford University Press, 1972). A broader perspective is offered by Louise Lippincott, *Selling Art in Georgian London: The Rise of Arthur Pond* (New Haven, CT: Yale University Press, 1983); and Diana Donald, *The Age of Caricature: Satirical Prints in the Reign of George III* (New Haven, CT: Yale University Press, 1996). Also useful are E. E. C. Nicholson, "Consumers and Spectators: The Public of the Political Print in Eighteenth-Century England," *History* 81 (1996), 5–21; and R. Porter, "Seeing the Past," *Past and Present* 118 (1988), 186–205.

Additional Resources: Literature

Allison, Robert J., ed., *The Interesting Narrative of the Life of Olaudah Equiano. Written by Himself.* 1995.
Atkins, Stuart, trans., *Goethe: Faust.* 2002.
Cranston, Maurice, trans., *Jean-Jacques Rousseau: The Social Contract.* 1968.
Gordon, Daniel, ed., *Voltaire: Candide.* 1999.
Heitzenrater, Richard. *John Wesley's Sermons: An Anthology.* 1991.
Hutter, Catherine, trans., *Johann Wolfgang von Goethe: Sorrows of Young Werther and Selected Writings.* 1987.
Krueger, Alan B., trans., *Adam Smith: The Wealth of Nations.* 2003.
Luvaas, Jay, trans., *Frederick the Great on the Art of War. By himself.* 1999.
Meiklejohn, J. M. D., trans., *Critique of Pure Reason.* 1990.
Roche, Daniel, trans., *Jacques Louis Ménétra: Journal of My Life.* 1986.
Schechter, Ronald, trans., *Gotthold Ephraim Lessing: Nathan the Wise.* 2004.
Scholar, Angela, trans., *Jean-Jacques Rousseau's Confessions.* 2000.

Additional Resources: Film and Video

Dangerous Liaisons (1988; VHS/DVD, 120 min.). This lush adaptation of Choderlos de Laclos's 1782 novel thoroughly captures the maliciousness and sexual depravity of the aristocracy on the eve of the French Revolution.

The Fortunes and Misfortunes of Moll Flanders (2002; DVD, 195 min.). Several cuts/versions of this 1996 miniseries are available. Adapted from Daniel Defoe's 1722 novel, the long but entertaining film examines social mores, the treatment and mistreatment of women, and the lives of the rich and poor of the period from a variety of angles.

Ridicule (1996; VHS/DVD, 103 min.). This film is set at the court of Louis XVI, where wit is prized above all other qualities. The film nicely captures the sense of decadence of the period, and is especially strong on such details as costuming and setting (in French with English subtitles).

Tom Jones (1963; VHS/DVD, 129 min.). A great deal of period detail in the film adapted from Henry Fielding's 1749 novel; the storyline is disjointed and earthy, but for a satirical look at aristocratic mores, questions of legitimacy, and urban life as well as the world of country houses, there is much here to work with.

OTHER BEDFORD/ST. MARTIN'S RESOURCES FOR CHAPTER 18

The following resources are available to accompany Chapter 18. Please refer to the Preface of this manual for detailed descriptions of all the ancillaries.

For Instructors

Transparencies

The following maps and images from Chapter 18 are available as full-color acetates.

- Map 18.1: War of the Austrian Succession, 1740–1748
- Map 18.2: The Seven Years' War, 1756–1763
- Mapping the West: Europe and the World, c. 1780
- Jean-Baptiste Greuze, *Broken Eggs* (1756), p. 570
- Neoclassical Style, p. 569

Instructor's Resources CD-ROM

The following maps and image from Chapter 18, as well as a chapter outline, are available on disc in both PowerPoint and jpeg formats.

- Map 18.1: War of the Austrian Succession, 1740–1748
- Map 18.2: The Seven Years' War, 1756–1763
- Mapping the West: Europe and the World, c. 1780
- Jean-Baptiste Greuze, *Broken Eggs* (1756), p. 570

Using the Bedford Series with The Making of the West

Available in print as well as online at **bedfordstmartins.com/usingseries,** this guide offers practical suggestions for using Margaret C. Jacob, *The Enlightenment: A Brief History with Documents*, in conjunction with chapters 17 and 18 of the textbook; *Candide* by Voltaire, translated, edited, and with an Introduction by Daniel Gordon, *The Interesting Narrative of the Life of Olaudah Equiano,* second edition, with an introduction by Robert J. Allison, and *Nathan the Wise* by Gotthold Ephraism Lessing with *Related Documents*, translated, edited, and with an Introduction by Ronald Schechter, in conjunction with Chapter 18 of the textbook.

For Students

Study Guides

The Online Study Guide at **bedfordstmartins.com/hunt** helps students synthesize the material they have learned as well as practice the skills historians use to make sense of the past. The following Map, Visual, and Document activities are available for Chapter 18.

Map Activity

- Map 18.2: The Seven Years' War, 1756–1763

Visual Activity

- Jean-Baptiste Greuze, *Broken Eggs* (1756), p. 570

Reading Historical Documents

- Denis Diderot, "Encyclopedia" (1755), p. 559
- Thomas Jefferson, Declaration of Independence (July 4, 1776), p. 582
- Contrasting Views: Women and the Enlightenment, pp. 562–563

CHAPTER

19

The Cataclysm of Revolution

1789–1799

CHAPTER RESOURCES

Main Chapter Topics

1. All across Europe and in the United States, people steeped in the Enlightenment discussed constitutions and representative government, but in Europe, only France's government succumbed to a full-fledged revolution.

2. French revolutionaries were the first to establish a constitutional monarchy based on Enlightenment principles. The failure of the National Assembly eventually gave way to the more radical National Convention and the establishment of a republic.

3. Under the pressure of war and resistance to the revolution, the National Convention centralized government to provide food, prosecute the war, and punish counterrevolutionaries, thus beginning the Terror.

4. Maximilien Robespierre, leader of the government during the Terror, tried to create a "Republic of Virtue," through a massive and often violent program of political reeducation and de-Christianization.

5. After the execution of Robespierre in July 1794, the National Convention wrote a new constitution and established the Directory. There was a popular reaction against the Terror, but the republic was maintained.

6. In the continual wars from 1792, France came to dominate Europe using new means of mobilizing soldiers and through the rise of talented officers, including the brilliant Napoleon Bonaparte. French military campaigns also spread reforms based on Enlightenment principles.

Focus Question

What was so revolutionary about the French Revolution?

1. The revolution affected every country in the west to varying degrees. The collapse of the French monarchy, supposedly the most powerful in Europe, was a shock to everyone. The revolution produced a tremendous amount of social upheaval in France, including the radical politicization of many, particularly women. Besides the execution of members of the royal family, including the king and queen, the revolution led directly and indirectly to a great deal of class conflict, as the feudal system was abolished, and the aristocrats lost all political influence and frequently their lives. Revolutionary documents such as the Declaration of the Rights of Man were important, practical efforts to establish many enlightenment principles.

2. Radical social reform during the period of the Terror attacked the Catholic church from many directions and weakened it as an institution. While the Terror killed tens of thousands, civil wars in response to the government's actions also killed thousands in France. The wars of the revolutionary era led to the spread of radical French principles and reforms across much of Europe, particularly to those areas where the armies of the revolution triumphed.

Annotated Chapter Outline

I. The Revolutionary Wave, 1787–1789

A. Protesters in the Low Countries and Poland, pp. 589–591

1. In the Dutch Republic, the Patriots wanted to reduce the powers of the *stadholder*, the Prince of Orange.
2. Patriot protest began among middle-class bankers, merchants, and writers but soon gained a wider audience by demanding political reforms, forming citizen militias called Free Corps, and forcing more open elections.
3. In 1787, a national assembly of the Free Corps joined with a group of Patriot Regents to demand a republic.

4. Although the Free Corps overpowered the Prince of Orange's troops, Frederick II of Prussia sent troops to intervene, putting an end to the rebellion.
5. The Patriots were then weakened by internal divisions between the Patriot Regents and the Free Corps, allowing the Prince of Orange to reestablish control.
6. The Austrian Netherlands was another arena for rebellion.
7. Joseph II's reforms, which included the reorganization of the administrative and judicial system, caused nobles and lawyers to organize to defend their traditional interests.
8. Democrats were attracted to the movement as well, and by late 1789, each province had declared independence and announced the federation of the United States of Belgium.
9. Class interests divided the independence movements. When urban democrats challenged noble authority, aristocratic leaders banded with the Catholic clergy and peasants, who forced the return of Austrian rule under the new emperor, Leopold II (r. 1790–1792).
10. A Patriot party emerged in Poland as well.
11. Composed of a few aristocrats, middle-class professionals, clergy who espoused Enlightenment ideas, and the king, the Patriots sought to modernize Polish politics in order to avoid a further loss of territory like that which occurred in the 1772 partition.
12. Austria and Prussia allowed the reform movement to proceed but, shortly after the new parliament enacted the reforming constitution of 1791, Catherine II of Russia intervened to put down the rebellion.

B. Origins of the French Revolution, 1787–1789, pp. 591–594

1. The French Revolution began with a fiscal crisis.
2. With half the national budget going to pay interest on the debt that had accumulated during past wars, particularly in support of the Americans in their revolution, the French crown needed to overhaul the inequitable and inefficient tax system.
3. During the Reign of Louis XVI (r. 1774–1792) and his widely disliked Austrian Queen, Marie Antoinette, the monarchy became increasingly unpopular.
4. The king was eventually forced to call a meeting of the Estates-General, a representative body that had not met since 1614.
5. Thousands of men and women (by proxy) met all over France to elect representatives to the three orders that made up the Estates-General: the First Estate represented the clergy, the Second Estate represented the nobility, and the Third Estate represented the commoners. Each group had grievances: the Third Estate denounced the traditional privileges of the nobility and called for voting by head rather than order, which would prevent the first two estates from overriding the voice of the Third Estate.
6. The process of selecting delegates led to a breakdown in censorship laws. Rapid, radical politicization of many members of the Third Estate and hard economic times increased the demands of many for radical reform.
7. The deputies arrived at Versailles in May 1789, but the actual meeting began only after weeks of stalemate over the question of whether to vote by head or by order.
8. The Third Estate finally broke away from the meeting and declared itself the National Assembly on June 17, 1789.
9. The clergy joined them two days later, and on June 20 they were forced to meet in a nearby tennis court, where the National Assembly swore not to disband until they had written a constitution.
10. Although Louis XVI publicly appeared to honor the new assembly, he had privately ordered thousands of soldiers to march on Paris.
11. When the king fired his popular finance minister Jacques Necker on July 11, rumors spread quickly through Paris and the populace began to arm themselves.
12. On July 14, Parisian crowds stormed the Bastille—a fortified prison that symbolized royal authority—in a fierce battle that left more than one hundred people dead.
13. The fall of the Bastille set an important precedent by demonstrating that the common people were willing to intervene violently at a crucial political moment.

II. From Monarchy to Republic, 1789–1793

A. The Revolution of Rights and Reason, pp. 594–598

1. Before drafting a constitution, the National Assembly had to confront growing violence in the countryside.
2. Peasants in the French countryside, who made up some 80 percent of the population, were angry at high rents, taxes,

and tithes; fearing that the presence of beggars and vagrants indicated an aristocratic plot, they attacked their landlords in a movement historians refer to as the Great Fear.

3. To restore order, on August 4 the deputies of the new National Assembly abolished seigneurial dues, special legal privileges, and serfdom.
4. Three weeks later, the assembly issued the Declaration of the Rights of Man and Citizen, which granted freedom of religion, freedom of the press, equality of taxation, and equality before the law, declaring that sovereignty rested in the nation, not the monarchy.
5. The document raised questions about the inclusion of blacks (free and enslaved), Jews, Protestants, and women.
6. Male Protestants and Jews received the right to vote, and women were declared citizens but could not vote.
7. Many women protested. In her 1791 *Declaration of the Rights of Women,* Olympe de Gouges (1748–1793) pointed out that the revolutionaries' own language implied that women should be included.
8. The Constitution of 1791 established a constitutional monarchy, but reserved voting rights to white men who had passed a test of wealth.
9. The powerful one-house legislature reformed the administrative and tax system.
10. In 1790, the deputies attempted to reform the Catholic church by confiscating all church property and issuing the Civil Constitution of the Clergy, which provided for the payment of the clergy by the state and the election of parish priests and bishops.
11. Church property was used as a guarantee for a new currency, *assignats*, which were quickly rendered less valuable as the state sold off church land.
12. In November 1790, the National Assembly required the clergy to swear an oath of loyalty, which about half the clergy refused to do.
13. Popular support for the clergy, many of whom were executed or exiled, weakened the revolutionary government.

B. The End of Monarchy, pp. 598–600

1. In June 1791, Louis XVI and his family attempted to flee France to Austria.
2. When they were captured and brought back to Paris, some now regarded them traitors.
3. Louis XVI was forced to endorse the Constitution, and a new Legislative Assembly was elected.
4. Hoping that a war would overturn the Revolution, Louis declared war on Austria on April 21, 1792. Many deputies supported the war, hoping it would lead to a republic.
5. Prussia immediately allied with Austria, and thousands of French aristocrats joined the Austrian army.
6. Early defeats of the unprepared armies weakened the Assembly in France. In Paris, the common people—also called the *sans-culottes*—discussed the news in newly organized political clubs, the most influential of which was known as the Jacobin Club.
7. On August 10, 1792, the sans-culottes attacked the Tuileries palace.
8. Under popular pressure, the Legislative Assembly agreed to new elections by universal male suffrage, and became the National Convention.
9. When the National Convention, dominated by the radical Jacobin party, met on September 22, 1792, it abolished the monarchy and declared France a republic.
10. As Prussian troops advanced into France, crowds of Parisians stormed the prisons and killed supposed traitors in the September massacres.
11. In November and December, deputies wrote a new constitution and debated the fate of the former king as the war continued.
12. The Girondins resented the growing power of the Parisian militants and favored reprimanding or exiling the king, but the Mountain, whose members were allied with the Parisian militants, favored execution.
13. The Mountain won, and Louis XVI was executed on January 21, 1793.

III. Terror and Resistance

A. Robespierre and the Committee of Public Safety, pp. 600–602

1. After the king's execution, Mountain militants called for the expulsion of the Girondins.
2. The Girondins responded by arresting Jean-Paul Marat, a Mountain leader.

3. Marat was acquitted, and on June 2, 1793 the militants organized a demonstration, invaded the National Convention, and forced the arrest of twenty-nine Girondins.
4. The Convention agreed to establish paramilitary "revolutionary armies" and the Committee of Public Safety, which under Robespierre quickly acquired almost total control of the government.
5. In September 1793, the Convention decided that emergency measures were needed and decreed the beginning of the Terror.
6. Despite Robespierre's own belief in the importance of freedom, democracy, and property rights, he became the chief proponent of the Terror, which aimed to eradicate dissent by purging unreliable officials, uncovering dissidents, confiscating property, establishing wage and price controls, and eliminating enemies of the Revolution.
7. The Terror also organized the war effort to great success, establishing the first universal draft of men in history.
8. The execution of the king caused Prussia, Great Britain, Spain, Sardinia, and the Dutch Republic to join the war against France.
9. However, with the entire country mobilized for war, the French armies stopped the advances of the allied powers by the end of 1793, and, in the summer of 1794, they invaded the Austrian Netherlands and crossed the Rhine River.

B. The Republic of Virtue, 1793–1794, pp. 602–604

1. In addition to fighting the war and eliminating domestic enemies, the Terror attempted a cultural revolution.
2. Writings deemed counterrevolutionary were censored, whereas songs, paintings, books, posters, and even chamber pots educated the population in the new revolutionary virtues.
3. Festivals were held modeled on Rousseau's plan for civic religion as the government aimed to destroy the mystique of monarchy and make the republic sacred.
4. The government also undertook a campaign of de-Christianization, closing churches and forcing clergy to forsake religious life.
5. Extremists attempted to establish a Cult of Reason to replace Christianity, but out of fear that devout rural populations would protest, the government offered an alternative: the Cult of Supreme Being.
6. The Convention attempted to set up a system of free and compulsory primary schools for boys and girls but without trained teachers, most of whom had been in Catholic religious orders, the effort failed, and school attendance dropped dramatically.
7. All citizens were urged to manifest the Revolution in everything: by flying the tricolor flag of the republic, using republican language, and no longer naming children after biblical characters and saints.
8. To create a people shaped by reason and revolutionary virtue, the government changed the various units of measurement used throughout France to the metric system and developed a new calendar—in which Year I dated from the beginning of the republic on September 22, 1792.
9. The rules governing family organization also changed.
10. Marriage became a civil contract and divorce was easy to obtain.
11. Equal inheritance replaced the previous practice of passing all of one's possessions to the eldest son.

C. Resisting the Revolution, pp. 604–605

1. The magnitude of the changes instituted by the revolutionary government brought about resistance.
2. Women expressed discontent concerning food shortages, high prices, and the persecution of the church.
3. Their complaints sometimes turned into demonstrations or riots.
4. Individuals resisted as well: Charlotte Corday, a supporter of the more moderate Girondins, murdered Jean-Paul Marat, a fervent supporter of radical and violent revolution.
5. Organized insurrection erupted in several areas when the Girondins were arrested in June 1793.
6. Resistance was greatest in the Vendée, a region in western France, and, between March and December 1793, peasants, artisans, and weavers from the countryside joined under noble leadership to attack towns where the Revolution was firmly established.

7. The peasants fought to defend Catholicism, to protest the draft, and to challenge the economic dominance of the towns.
8. In the fighting that ensued, both sides committed horrible atrocities; many thousands of republican soldiers and civilians lost their lives; rebel deaths have been estimated at 200,000–250,000 or perhaps even higher.

D. The Fall of Robespierre and the End of the Terror, 1794–1799, pp. 605–607

1. In the fall of 1793, the government began suppressing pro-revolutionary groups it could not control.
2. These included women's political clubs, in particular the Society of Revolutionary Republican Women, groups of "ultra-revolutionaries," and then more moderate "indulgents," including the deputy Georges-Jacques Danton, a former member of the Committee of Public Safety.
3. After these groups were eliminated, the Terror worsened.
4. Although the military situation improved (with a French victory over the main Austrian army), the political situation deteriorated: those accused of crimes were no longer allowed counsel, fewer jurors were necessary for conviction, the categories of political crimes were expanded, and judgments were now either acquittal or death.
5. The Terror, although not active in all parts of France, killed at least forty thousand people. As many as 300,000 were arrested. Aristocrats and clergy were particularly likely to be victims, but many peasants and ordinary working people were also executed.
6. Fearing for the safety of its members, in July 1794 (the revolutionary month of Thermidor), the Convention ended the Terror by arresting and executing Robespierre and his followers.
7. The Convention then ordered new elections and drew up a new constitution that set up a two-house legislature and gave executive powers to a Directory headed by five directors.
8. The new government released suspects and engineered a truce in the Vendée.
9. Within a year, all the Jacobin Clubs were closed.
10. Leading "Terrorists" were put to death and, during the White Terror in the southeast, paramilitary bands attacked those who had previously held power during the Jacobins' Red Terror.
11. Churches reopened, and people sought escape from the atmosphere and anxiety of the Terror in a new pursuit of pleasure.

IV. Revolution on the March

A. Arms and Conquests, pp. 607–608

1. In 1793, the French armies, although large, were weakened by disease, low morale, and lack of supplies, and could have been easily defeated.
2. But Prussia, Russia, and Austria were too preoccupied with Poland to engage France.
3. By the summer of 1794, patriotic French soldiers fought hard.
4. As they moved into the Austrian Netherlands, Mainz, Savoy, and Nice, French armies were welcomed by many, especially those of the middle class, and officers organized Jacobin Clubs that petitioned for annexation to France. The Directory created semi-independent "sister republics" as the army advanced.
5. When Prussia declared neutrality in 1795, French armies moved into the Dutch Republic, creating a new satellite called the Batavian Republic.
6. In 1796–1797, young general Napoleon Bonaparte crossed into northern Italy to create the Cisalpine Republic; in 1798, the French turned the Swiss cantons into the Helvetic Republic; and in 1798 they took over the papal states and renamed them the Roman Republic, forcing the pope to flee.
7. All over Europe, constant war caused a rising death rate and the interruption of commerce and manufacturing.

B. European Reactions to Revolutionary Change, pp. 608–612

1. The French Revolution transformed European politics and social relations.
2. In Great Britain, supporters of the Revolution joined constitutional and reform societies.
3. Pro-French feeling was strong in Ireland, where Catholics and Presbyterians, both excluded from the vote, pressed for secession from England.
4. In 1798, the Society of United Irishmen timed a rebellion to coincide with a French invasion, but it failed.
5. Although countries close to France with large middle classes generally sympathized

with French ideas, other countries resisted French occupation.
6. In the German Rhineland, gangs of bandits preyed upon the French and Jews (because the French emancipated Jews).
7. After 1793, many intellectuals in the German states turned against the Revolution because of its record of violence and military aggression.
8. These German intellectuals developed an anti-French nationalism followed by an artistic and intellectual regeneration.
9. Countries farther from France were less affected.
10. In Sweden, the assassination of King Gustavus III (r. 1771–1792) raised unfounded fears of a Jacobin plot.
11. In Russia, 278 outbreaks of peasant unrest occurred between 1796 and 1798. Many saw them as inspired by events in other parts of Europe.

C. Poland Extinguished, 1793–1795, pp. 612–613

1. The spirit of revolt was especially strong in Poland and Lithuania, both of which had lost territory and population.
2. Prussia and Russia took possession of additional portions of Polish territory in the Second Partition of Poland in 1793.
3. The Polish reform movement became more pro-French, and in the spring of 1794, Tadeusz Kosciuszko incited an uprising that spread from Cracow to Warsaw and the old Lithuanian capital, Vilnius.
4. The uprising failed, in part because Kosciuszko could not offer complete freedom to serfs without alienating the nobles.
5. Russia, Prussia, and Austria combined wiped Poland off the map in the Third Partition of 1795.

D. Revolution in the Colonies, pp. 613–615

1. Revolution reached the French Caribbean colonies, the most important of which was St. Domingue. These territories were crucial to the French economy.
2. Most French revolutionaries had not considered slavery an important issue and saw it as necessary to the economy.
3. In August 1791, slaves in northern St. Domingue organized a revolt.
4. To restore authority over the slaves, the Legislative Assembly in Paris granted civil and political rights to free blacks.
5. Angered white planters and merchants signed a treaty with Great Britain, while Spain offered freedom to slaves who joined the Spanish armies that controlled the rest of the island.
6. In August 1793, the French commissioner freed all the slaves and, following his lead, the National Convention formally abolished slavery in February 1794.
7. François Dominique Toussaint L'Ouverture (1743–1803), an ex-slave who served as a general in the Spanish army, changed sides and joined the French.
8. The vicious fighting that continued in the colony left the economy in ruins.
9. Toussaint, who had been named governor of the island, was arrested in 1802 by order of Napoleon Bonaparte, who attempted to restore slavery.
10. Toussaint died in a French prison.
11. In 1804, the remaining black generals defeated Napoleon's forces and proclaimed the Republic of Haiti.

Lecture Strategies

1. The origins of the French Revolution are worth analyzing in some detail. Contemporary historians have abandoned the Marxist approach, and now view the Revolution's origins in the politics of the 1780s, a politics deeply affected by the currents of the Enlightenment and the socioeconomic issues of that time. A good place to begin is Colin Lucas's article "Nobles, Bourgeois, and the Origins of the French Revolution," *Past and Present* 60 (August 1973), reprinted in Douglas Johnson, *French Society and the Revolution* (Cambridge: Cambridge University Press, 1976). William Doyle, *Origins of the French Revolution*, 3rd ed. (Oxford: Oxford University Press, 1999), offers in Part 2 a brief account of the origins from 1786 to the end of the summer of 1789. P. M. Jones's useful book *Reform and Revolution in France: The Politics of Transition, 1774–1791* (Cambridge: Cambridge University Press, 1995) presents the monarchy as an institution actively engaged in reform. Along these same lines, Simon Schama, *Citizens: A Chronicle of the French Revolution* (New York: Alfred A. Knopf, 1989) offers in Part 1 a more favorable picture of the France of Louis XVI than is usually the case.

Several titles are useful not only for this topic, but also for subsequent topics (and cited in following suggestions). One is William Doyle, *The Oxford History of the French Revolution*, 2nd ed. (Oxford: Oxford University Press, 2003). A second synthesis is Donald Sutherland, *France, 1789–1815: Revolution and Counterrevolution* (Oxford: Oxford University Press, 1986). A good selection of relevant documents may be found in Laura Mason and Tracey Rizzo, eds., *The French Revolution: A Document Collection* (Boston: Houghton Mifflin, 1999). The essays in François Furet and Mona Ozouf, eds., *A Critical Dictionary of the French Revolution* (Cambridge, MA: Harvard University Press, 1989) are helpful. Jacques Sole, *Questions of the French Revolution: A Historical Overview* (New York: Pantheon, 1989) is a handy compendium of questions and answers. A solid and workable shorter account of the details of the revolution can be found in Jeremy Popkin, *A Short History of the French Revolution* (New York: Prentice Hall, 1997).

2. Many nineteenth-century observers commented favorably on the moderate period of the Revolution, but decried the period of the Terror as radical, bloody, and excessive. It is important, first, to outline why the attempt at constitutional monarchy failed. Second, it is necessary to distinguish in the Terror those efforts to preserve the Revolution from the threat of war and civil war and also from the more radical efforts to create a Republic of Virtue. In addition to Vovelle, listed in suggestion 1, see Marc Bouloiseau, *The Jacobin Republic, 1792–1794* (Cambridge: Cambridge University Press, 1983). A classic account of 1793–1794 is R. R. Palmer, *Twelve Who Ruled: The Year of the Terror in the French Revolution* (Princeton, NJ: Princeton University Press, 1970), first published in 1941. Another classic account, heavily Marxist but still useful, is Albert Soboul, *The Sans-Culottes: The Popular Movement and Revolutionary Government, 1793–1794* (Princeton, NJ: Princeton University Press, 1980). Two books helpful for understanding the perspectives of the revolutionaries are Patrice Higonnet, *Goodness beyond Virtue: Jacobins during the French Revolution* (Cambridge, MA: Harvard University Press, 1998); and Lynn Hunt, *The Family Romance of the French Revolution* (Berkeley: University of California Press, 1992). See also the essays in Volume 4, "The Terror," in Keith Michael Baker, ed., *The French Revolution and the Creation of Modern Political Culture* (Oxford: Pergamon Press, 1994).

3. A good place to begin study of women in the French Revolution is Joan B. Landes, *Women and the Public Sphere in the Age of the French Revolution* (Ithaca, NY: Cornell University Press, 1988), which demonstrates that the Revolution in some ways provided less room for women in the public sphere than had the Old Regime. See also Chapter 4, "The Bad Mother," in Lynn Hunt, *The Family Romance of the French Revolution*, and her *The French Revolution and Human Rights* (cited in suggestions 2 and 1, respectively). Sara E. Melzer and Leslie W. Rabine, eds., *Rebel Daughters: Women and the French Revolution* (Oxford: Oxford University Press, 1992) contains a number of interesting essays on women and the French Revolution. Additionally, Dominique Godineau, *The Women of Paris and Their French Revolution* (Berkeley: University of California Press, 1988) is a detailed study of that topic.

4. Although the French Revolution dwarfs similar events of this period, it would be worthwhile to examine other revolutions, both those that were contemporaneous and those that occurred in response to the French Revolution. R. R. Palmer, *The Age of Democratic Revolution: A Political History of Europe and America, 1760–1800*, two volumes (Princeton, NJ: Princeton University Press, 1959, 1964), is the major work on the events of this period. Simon Schama has written an excellent study of the Dutch revolutions of this period: *Patriots and Liberators: Revolution in the Netherlands, 1780–1813* (New York: Alfred A. Knopf, 1977). The impact of the French Revolution in the Caribbean is covered in David Gaspar and David P. Geggus, eds., *A Turbulent Time: The French Revolution and the Greater Caribbean* (Bloomington: Indiana University Press, 1997); its impact in the western hemisphere is explored in Lester Langley, *The Americas in the Age of Revolution, 1750–1850* (New Haven, CT: Yale University Press, 1996). See also Joan Wallach Scott, *Only Paradoxes to Offer: French Feminists and the Rights of Man* (Cambridge, MA: Harvard University Press, 1996); and François Furet, *Revolutionary France 1770–1880* (Oxford: Blackwell, 1992). Do what you can in lecture to demonstrate connections between these movements.

Class Discussion Starters

1. Ask students to consider an event in 1789 that best marks the beginning of the French Revolution. Did it come as early as the publication of the Abbé Sieyès's incendiary pamphlet, *What Is the Third Estate?* Was it when the Third Estate declared itself the National Assembly or when the Bastille fell? Or, did it only come with the Declaration of the Rights of Man and Citizen in August? Still worth reading, although set in a Marxist framework and a little too schematic, is Georges Lefebvre, *The Coming of the French Revolution* (New York: Random House, 1947). On Sieyès, see William H. Sewell Jr., *A Rhetoric of Bourgeois Revolution: The Abbé Sieyès and What Is the Third Estate?* (Durham, NC: Duke University Press, 1994). On the Declaration of the Rights of Man and Citizen, see Lynn Hunt, *The French Revolution and Human Rights: A Brief Documentary History* (Boston: Bedford Books, 1996). In addition to the two books by Doyle listed in Lecture Strategy 1, see also Chapter 4 of Michel Vovelle, *The Fall of the French Monarchy, 1787–1792* (Cambridge: Cambridge University Press, 1984). An

important book on the development of the National Assembly in the first two years of the Revolution is Timothy Tackett, *Becoming a Revolutionary: The Deputies of the French National Assembly and the Emergence of a Revolutionary Culture (1789–1790)* (Princeton, NJ: Princeton University Press, 1996).

2. Have students consider the "anti-revolutionary" arguments of François Furet (see "Terms of History: Revolution," p. 590) and Edmund Burke, articulated in the excerpt from *Reflections on the Revolution* (see "Contrasting Views: Perspectives on the French Revolution," p. 610). Discuss similarities and differences, but be sure to have students focus on what both have to say about the limitations of politics. Do students agree? Would the revolutionary generation in the new United States have agreed? What evidence can students advance from the events of the two revolutions that would help them think about the arguments?

3. Discuss ways in which, even at its most radical, the revolution often failed to offer much to many social groups (women, slaves in the French colonies, the poor), while it raised their hopes for change. Ask students to list the ways, from the text and your lectures, that women had participated in and even helped to initiate the revolution. How did they continue to act and react politically throughout the entire period? A good source for thinking about the common people throughout the country (not just in Paris) and the dynamics of revolution is David Andress, *The French Revolution and the People* (London: Hambledon and London, 2004). How did events in Paris look from the Vendée? St. Domingue?

4. Present students with a copy of the Declaration of the Rights of Man. How do these rights reflect Enlightenment principles? How do they reflect the need for the revolutionary regime to build support from different social groups? To what extent are the particular rights listed fundamentally social, political, or economic? Are there any tensions in the document?

5. Maximilien Robespierre is a key figure of the French Revolution. Was he simply a ruthless but pragmatic dictator, or was he a fanatical revolutionary, the prototype of the totalitarian ruler who sought to control every aspect of life? Several good biographies and studies are available, including David Jordan, *The Revolutionary Career of Maximilien Robespierre* (New York: Free Press, 1986); George Rude, *Robespierre* (New York: Viking, 1975); and Colin Haydon and William Doyle, eds., *Robespierre: History, Historiography, and Literature* (Cambridge: Cambridge University Press, 1998).

6. Did the revolutionaries make an error by not compromising with the Catholic church? What factors contributed to the hostility felt by government in many radical revolutionaries toward organized religion? Make sure you discuss those elements of Enlightenment thought that led some revolutionaries to determine that France needed to be "de-Christianized." How significantly did religious opposition to the revolution weaken the government?

Reviewing the Text

Review Questions

1. How did the beginning of the French Revolution resemble the other revolutions of 1787–1789?
[model answer] • ***The Revolution was based on a desire for liberty:*** *The protests and revolutions that broke out in the Dutch Republic, the Austrian Netherlands, Poland, and France were all begun by people who wanted to protect or defend their historic rights within their governments. The notion of "liberty" had become a central one throughout the west in this era.*
• ***Revolutionary desires were fueled by Europe's long-term economic prosperity:*** *Increased wealth, increasingly widespread education, and Enlightenment ideas led to high expectations for individual achievement.*
• ***The American Revolution inspired it:*** *Political protests in the Dutch Republic and France both escalated into revolutions in part because of the financial effects of choosing sides in the American Revolution. Similarly, the American conflict arose in part when colonists opposed taxes meant to offset debts from the Seven Years' War. Beyond the financial effects, the American Revolution and its ideals served as a model for those who sought independence.*
• ***Aristocrats and the growing middle class supported it:*** *In the Dutch Republic, the protesters appealed to middle-class bankers, merchants, and writers whose support the government needed, and who could call for new elections. Wealthy merchants were involved in the revolution because of the financial involvement of the Republic in the American Revolution. In France, it was the nobles and judges of the parlement who became popular heroes for resisting the tyranny of the king.*

2. Why did the French Revolution turn in an increasingly radical direction after 1789?
[model answer] • ***Conflict with the Catholic Church:*** *The Civil Constitution of the Clergy that passed in July 1790 impounded church property, and associated legislation required a loyalty oath of clergy willing to submit to its provisions. These changes permanently divided the Catholic population and caused many to resist the government. They also offended the king and contributed to his decision to attempt to flee France.*
• ***The end of the monarchy:*** *The royal family's attempt to flee the country led to war with Austria and Prussia in 1792, their imprisonment, and eventually their execution.*
• ***War:*** *After war broke out with Austria and Prussia, the sorry state of the military led to a new, more radical*

assembly elected through universal suffrage and mob action. The ascendancy in the new assembly of the Jacobin party executed the king and queen, and instituted much more radical social and political reforms.

3. What factors can explain the Terror? To what extent was it simply a response to a national emergency or a reflection of deeper problems within the French Revolution?
[model answer] • ***The need to unite and militarize France:*** *Wars with other European countries required more money and men than France could provide. The Committee of Public Safety set up public weapons forges, a draft, and disseminated propaganda to galvanize popular sentiment and encourage a cultural revolution. Unreliable officials and perceived enemies of the revolution had to be removed so as not to hamper the war effort or dampen public morale.*
• ***Enlightenment ideas were taken to the extreme:*** *Robespierre read the classics of republicanism and modern Enlightenment authors. He wanted to apply theoretical ideas to the new French republic, to govern using reason, and whatever means necessary—to defend the new republic from those he considered enemies of liberty.*
• ***The Terror led to French military success, but became self-perpetuating:*** *The public works set up for weapons production and the mobilization of all French citizens for the war effort created an atmosphere of resistance and fueled an escalating fear of conspiracy. Robespierre, the Committee of Public Safety, and the National Convention all tightened their control over public activities and increased the crackdown on resisters.*
• ***The Terror increased societal divisions and showed that forcing reforms could backfire:*** *Ultimately, the Terror led to fear and distrust within the government itself and the overthrow of Robespierre and his followers.*

4. Why did some groups outside of France embrace the French Revolution while others resisted it?
[model answer] • ***Widespread European support for the French Revolution arose:*** *Supporters of the revolution from many countries flooded to Paris to witness events firsthand, and many British citizens joined constitutional and reform societies that sprang up in cities across that country. Pro-French feeling was especially strong in Ireland, where Catholics and Presbyterians excluded from voting were inspired to form their own reform societies, but particularly during its early phases, support for the revolution was widespread among progressive thinkers throughout Britain. Middle-class persons near the northern and eastern borders of France reacted most positively to the French revolution and the French invasions that followed, hoping to benefit from republican changes to society.*
• ***European elites opposed the French abolition of monarchy and nobility and the encouragement of popular participation in politics:*** *The British government suppressed many of the constitutional and reform societies that sprang up and charged their leaders with sedition. In places like Ireland and Poland, it is easy to see how dangerous such notions and examples could be to the established order. In many nations, elites feared that the French were actively encouraging peasant rebellions or working to overthrow their governments through assassination plots or political intrigues.*

Making Connections

1. Should the French Revolution be viewed as the origin of democracy or the origin of totalitarianism (a government in which no dissent is allowed)? Explain.
[model answer] *Elements of both democracy and totalitarianism can be found in the French Revolution. The revolutionaries intended democratic reforms, but they stalled on how to achieve them. The resulting vacuum gave strong men, such as Robespierre, the opportunity to seize control and embark on a totalitarian agenda.*

2. Why did other European rulers find the French Revolution so threatening?
[model answer] *The Revolution represented a model of government that was, in theory, more representative than in many places in Europe. The seeming success of the Revolution generated agitation for reform along similar lines in other countries. For many of these same countries, the Revolution was virtually next door, and it was feared that the conflict could easily spread beyond French borders. And the conflict had not entirely resolved pre-Revolution problems of a poor economy, social unrest, and a weak and nonresponsive government. Additionally, the killing field in France was on a scale hardly imaginable, and the aristocracy and middle classes in other countries were concerned literally for their own heads.*

Discussing the Documents

Questions from Online Study Guide with Model Answers

The Rights of Minorities, p. 597

1. What barriers does Clermont Tonnerre see to Jews being given French citizenship, and how does he propose to overcome them?
[model answer] *According to Clermont Tonnerre, adversaries of the Jews argue that Jews are not sociable, are commanded to loan money at usurious rates, cannot be joined to the French by marriage or social interchange, could not serve in the armies in the defense of the country, and have their own judges and laws. Clermont Tonnerre proposes that Jews be treated and handled as*

individuals, not as a separate nation, and that their separate judges and laws should be removed so that they can become integrated into France. If they refuse, then they should be banished.

2. How does Clermont Tonnerre's speech represent some of the ideals of the Enlightenment?
[model answer] *One of the key ideals of the Enlightenment that this speech represents is that Jews, or any other group, should not be oppressed or denied civil rights based on their religion. He argues that the only test a creed should pass in regard to the social body is that of morals. The idea that citizenship should be based on secular rather than religious qualifications is one of the hallmarks of the Enlightenment.*

Address Abolishing the Slave Trade (February 5, 1790), p. 613

1. What is the Society of the Friends of Blacks' position on slavery?
[model answer] *In the fourth paragraph the society alludes to the notion that slavery should eventually end, although not yet because an immediate end to slavery would create chaos in the colonies and the slaves themselves are not ready for their freedom. Immediate freedom would be a "deadly gift" tantamount to abandoning "without assistance children in the cradle or mutilated and impotent beings."*

2. On what grounds does the society condemn slavery and the slave trade?
[model answer] *Although the society condemns the mistreatment of black slaves on the plantations and the "prostitution" of the slave trade, it seems to be more from a concern with preserving the image of France than with the slaves themselves. The pamphlet even suggests keeping the institution of slavery, but treating slaves more kindly so that they might reproduce and make the slave trade unnecessary. According to the pamphlet, it is how slaves are mistreated rather than the institution of slavery itself that is the main problem.*

Contrasting Views: Perspectives on the French Revolution, pp. 610–611

1. Which aspect of the French Revolution most disturbed these commentators?
[model answer] *Burke is concerned about the abstract nature of the values of the French Revolution, and the difficulty of restraining and controlling liberty. The consequence of the revolution has been the lifting of constraints and "protecting" restraints on political conduct, and Burke suggests that the service of abstract, "natural" rights will end in the "gallows." Joseph de Maistre felt that the revolution was "satanic." He was particularly concerned about its connection to religious persecution, the desecration of "objects of worship," and the efforts of the revolutionaries to "install . . . the goddess of reason." The revolution, he suggests, snowballed and in the end produced a degree of evil "beyond the ordinary circle of crime." Anne-Louise-Germaine de Staël condemned revolutionary excess, and blamed the monarchy and the church for corrupting the people. The oppressive system in France before the revolution provoked and twisted the people, making it difficult to institute reform.*

2. How would you align each of these writers on a spectrum running from extreme right to extreme left in politics?
[model answer] *Paine represents the extreme left of politics. He is enthusiastic about the revolution and critical of Burke and others for denying the importance of natural rights and the authority and ability of the people to establish constitutions in accordance with them. Paine argues that the only legitimate authority is the one that secures rights. Staël, a great advocate for enlightenment principles and an opponent of monarchy, might be in basic agreement. She certainly sees that oppression, in France or in St. Domingue, sows "the seed of so many vices." The "privileges of feudal nobility" lead to social disorder and revolution. Burke and Maistre are both on the right. Burke opposed the revolution because it prioritized abstract, idealized natural rights over political structures that had been developed over time in practice as opposed to in theory. He was suspicious of the ability of people to anticipate and design moral cause and effect. Maistre, in very stark terms, criticized the revolution for attacking and destroying religious institutions and sensibility. For him, the revolution was about evil, anti-religious change.*

3. How would each of these writers judge the Enlightenment that preceded the French Revolution?
[model answer] *Burke was a critic of abstract reasoning and believed that the elevation of Enlightenment ideals such as liberty separate from established political structures was dangerous. He criticized a priori reasoning (although not necessarily reason itself) and the lack of respect for practical experience and human limitations when reforming the social order. Paine was a strong believer in the Enlightenment, and the ability of reason to secure natural rights and construct political institutions designed to protect liberty. For Paine, civil rights derive from natural rights. Maistre was a reformer, but opposed the Enlightenment because he saw it, like the revolution in France, as fundamentally hostile toward religion. Staël was a defender of the Enlightenment; she saw its reforms and principles as being vindicated by the excesses of the revolution, which were brought on by the nature of the previous irrational monarchial system.*

Other Questions for Discussing These Documents in Class

The Rights of Minorities

1. Discuss why Tonnerre argued for the extension of civil rights to Jews, but was careful to distinguish between Jews as individuals and Jews as a nation. Tonnerre argues that a nation could not exist within another nation; French citizens had to be loyal first and foremost to France since divided loyalties could be dangerous to the state. Recently, the French government banned elementary and high school students from wearing class symbols (crosses, headscarves, and so forth) that emphasize ethnic and religious separateness. The government is trying to keep issues of church and state separate in order to promote citizenship as a unifying sociopolitical force. In what ways are such tensions present in American society?

2. For Tonnerre, what is the nature of citizenship for individuals? Social groups? Discuss with students the implications of such a view of citizenship.

Address Abolishing the Slave Trade (February 5, 1790)

1. What specific appeals does the society make to the National Assembly? What is the relationship between the ideals of the revolution and ending the slave trade?

2. Discuss the interest groups that the Address suggests oppose ending the slave trade, and the reasons advanced against immediate emancipation.

3. Discuss how slaves and freed blacks in French colonies may have reacted to this document. In what ways might it have been a "dangerous" document, from the point of view of planters and those interested in maintaining the slave system?

Contrasting Views: Perspectives on the French Revolution

1. In different ways, the documents all discuss the challenges societies face when they change radically and rapidly. What are the concerns on that question from the authors? Do they offer any suggestions as to why change can move too quickly at times, or how to constrain the actions of revolutionaries once, as Staël put it, "the people were freed from their harness?"

2. Staël suggested that the privileged orders in France, particularly the church and the aristocracy, were reaping what they sowed; that the weight of oppression was what made the revolution so violent. Discuss with students, in relation to the events of the revolution, what the "cost" of the revolution was for various social groups, including women, devout Catholics, peasants, aristocrats, the urban poor, and so on.

Comparative Questions

1. What do these documents, taken together, suggest about the demands and definitions of citizenship that emerged from the events of the revolution? How was being a citizen different from being a subject?

2. Did the revolution increase or decrease the power of the state? Did it enhance or restrict liberty and freedom? What factors influenced individual and group experiences of the revolution?

For Users of *Sources of The Making of the West*

The following documents are available in Chapter 19 of the companion sourcebook by Katharine J. Lualdi, University of Southern Maine.

1. Defining the Nation: Abbé Sieyès, *What Is the Third Estate?* (1789)
2. The People under the Old Regime: *Political Cartoon* (1815)
3. Establishing Rights: National Assembly, *The Declaration of the Rights of Man and of the Citizen* (1789)
4. Defending Terror: Maximilien Robespierre, *Report on the Principles of Political Morality* (1794)
5. Dissent on Trial: Olympe de Gouges, *Letters on the Trial* (1793)
6. Liberty for All?: François Dominique Toussaint L'Ouverture, *Revolution in the Colonies* (1794–1795)

Discussion Ideas for Sources of The Making of the West, *Chapter 19*

1. What do the various documents (particularly numbers 1, 2, and 3) have to say about the grievances of the Third Estate? Which ones do students believe were most significant and why?

2. Considering Robespierre's *Report* and *The Declaration of the Rights of Man*, what power did the new governments claim over citizens, and on what grounds? Considering de Gouges as a victim of the Terror, on what grounds did the court claim the right and responsibility of prosecution? How did she defend herself and her literary productions? Together, what do these documents say about the nature of the revolutionary governments?

3. To what extent does Toussaint identify with the principles of the revolution and the policies of the revolutionary government? Was Toussaint (as revealed here) an opportunist or an idealist?

Working with Visual Sources

For this exercise, please refer to The Third Estate Awakens on p. 593 of the textbook or view the image on the book companion site's Online Study Guide under the "Visual Activity" for Chapter 19.

Students viewing the image at the Online Study Guide are asked two questions about the image. The questions and model answers (not made available to students) are below. Project this image, available on the Instructor's Resources CD-ROM, in class or ask students to look at the image in their textbooks and answer the questions.

1. This print shows three figures interacting with each other: a noble, a clergyman, and a member of the Third Estate. Judging from the gestures of the figures, which two groups in society were shown as working for the same cause?
[model answer] *The noble and the clergyman (representing the Second and First Estates respectively) are standing together, displaying similar expressions of alarm. The clergyman has his hand on the shoulder of the noble, thus reinforcing the close tie between the two.*

2. Judging from your reading of this print, was it meant to gain support for the actions of the Third Estate or to oppose them?
[model answer] *The lack of effective defense on the part of the noble and the clergyman and their slightly comic stance and expressions make them seem weak and lacking any power. The member of the Third Estate seems strong (having just broken his chains) and determined, so many viewers would likely see this positive portrayal of the Third Estate as supporting its actions. However, for those who feared what course the Revolution might take, the presence of arms in the foreground and the Bastille and National Guard in the background might raise some concern.*

Mapping Exercises

Map Activity from OSG—Model Answers for Map Activity #2

For this activity, please refer to Map 19.3: French Expansion, 1791–1799 on p. 608. Students are asked these questions:

Which territories had France annexed or occupied by 1799?
[model answer] *By 1799, France had annexed Nice, Savoy, the Austrian Netherlands, and the papal territories in southern France just north of Marseilles. France had also occupied Piedmont and Tuscany on the Italian peninsula.*

Which states had revolutionary France established by 1799?
[model answer] *By 1799, France had established the Batavian Republic by the North Sea, and a series of states on the Italian peninsula including the Neapolitan Republic, the Roman Republic, the Ligurian Republic, and the Cisalpine Republic. France had also established the Helvetic Republic in modern-day Switzerland.*

Which states would have felt threatened by the French expansion during the 1790s?
[model answer] *French expansion would have been perceived as a threat to the German states, Prussia, and the Austrian empire to the east. Great Britain would have also felt threatened, as would Spain to the south.*

Map 19.1: Revolutionary Paris, 1789, p. 594

Have the students note the locations of the various public buildings marked on the map. Which ones were targets of mob action, according to the text? Why might various buildings have been targets for crowds, whether they actually were attacked or not?

Map 19.2: Redrawing the Map of France, 1789–1791, p. 596

Have students carefully examine and compare the maps showing France in 1789 and in 1791. They should be able to discuss the differences made by the change from organization by provinces to that of organization by departments. Ask students to comment on the substitution of new names for the old. Is the redrawing of the map a project of which the philosophes would have approved? Why or why not?

Map 19.3: French Expansion, 1791–1799, p. 608

Ask students to consider this paradox: the French republic not only completed the project of Louis XIV to establish a France that had expanded to its natural frontiers (such as the Rhine River), but also accomplished the old dream of reestablishing the Roman Empire (in the form of sister republics). Was there a contradiction between extending the Revolution by liberating peoples and doing so by creating an empire (even if it was not called an empire)?

Map 19.4: The Second and Third Partitions of Poland, 1793 and 1795, p. 612

Which states acquired the most Polish territory? Which acquired the most Polish people? Which partition was most significant and why? What does the fate of Poland reveal about the ability of the great powers to cooperate? What does it reveal about the dangers of failing to form effective alliances or the likely fate of weak nations in the European state system?

Mapping the West: Europe in 1799, p. 616

Ask students to comment on the differences caused by events in the last two decades of the eighteenth century. The map of Europe and the World, c. 1780 (see chapter 18, Mapping the West, p. 583), shows a rough balance of power in Europe and British imperialism dominant outside Europe. What does the map of Europe in 1799 seem to indicate about the balance of power in Europe? How was the west changing? Ask students to think about what it does not show, that is, the balance of imperial power in the rest of the world. What was the situation of France as an imperial power at this point?

In-Class Assignments and Presentation Topics

1. Assign students to write an essay on the summer of 1789 in France based on Chapter 19 and selected documents from Mason and Rizzo (see "Lecture Strategies," number 1). This essay should be an analysis of the development of revolutionary escalation. What actions or developments constituted turning points? How did authorities respond?

2. Use Lynn Hunt's *The French Revolution and Human Rights* as the basis for a discussion on the meaning of the *Declaration of the Rights of Man and Citizen.* The discussion might range over the entire Revolution, or be confined to a particular group that did not seem to be included in the Declaration. Ask students to particularly consider the universal language employed in the Declaration and the sociopolitical implications of that language. Have students identify the parts of the document that seem to be addressing the concerns of 1) peasants, 2) the urban working class, and 3) merchants and tradesmen. To what might aristocrats and clergymen object in the document? To what might the king object? You might also encourage students to also link their thoughts about the Declaration with present-day concerns about identity politics.

3. Have students view *La Nuit de Varennes* (*The Night of Varennes* [1983]), a film that brings together Casanova, Thomas Paine, Nicolas Edme Restif de Bretonne, among other figures of the Enlightenment era. Restif, a journalist and printer, is following a coach that contains the royal family as they attempt to flee the country. The others do not realize they are involved in an event of historic importance. After viewing the film, students might write an essay on the different points of view presented by the characters in the film. It would be helpful to prepare a brief guide to the characters for the students to review before they view the film.

4. Students might base reports on the essays contained in François Furet and Mona Ozouf, *A Critical Dictionary of the French Revolution.* These essays go well beyond the simple provision of information to discuss the issues and questions involved. They might be supplemented with documents from Mason and Rizzo (see suggestion 1) or with material selected from one or more of the sources cited earlier.

5. Some of the excesses of the French royal family and aristocracy can best be understood visually. Students should analyze Fragonard's *The Swing*, painted in 1765. What is the relationship between the woman in the swing and the man on the ground? Exactly what is the man doing? Is there anything in the picture that might indicate whether this meeting is licit or illicit? What is the servant's job? Is there anything in the picture that might cause resentment among the lower classes? Another possibility might be to have the students view the recent film *Marie Antoinette* (2006). While it takes some liberties with history, it places issues of court culture and royal excess and conspicuous consumption front and center. Students should also be exposed to some revolutionary-era propaganda, widely available online, particularly material directed against the queen. How might such behavior and associated debates have contributed to popular hatred of the monarchy? How might it have contributed to the monarchy's own sense of connectedness to the French people?

Essay Questions

1. The Terror is a dramatic and critical period of the French Revolution. How one understands and evaluates the Terror often determines how one views the Revolution as a whole. Ask students to first become acquainted with the outlines of the Terror by reading William Doyle or Donald Sutherland (see "Lecture Strategies," number 1). Then have them choose a month from July 1793 to July 1794 to investigate. What were the major events that occurred in that month? Who were the most prominent leaders? What documents, images, accounts, and descriptions can they find that inform them about that month? The finished product might be a standard research paper; a mockup of a news magazine reporting on the events and personalities of that month; a diary of a fictional character who has just experienced that month; or some other approach that requires students to assimilate and make sense of the information they have assembled. See "Lecture Strategies," numbers 3 and 4, for bibliographical citations.

2. The period after the Ninth of Thermidor, the time of the Thermidorian reaction and the Directory (1794–1799), generally receives little attention. Yet, it

is a period in which the French Revolution spreads beyond France and also begins, somewhat haltingly, a process of consolidation. It is also the period when Napoleon Bonaparte first makes his mark. Have students again begin with a broad history of the Revolution, such as Doyle or Sutherland (see "Lecture Strategies," number 1), to obtain an overview of Thermidor and the Directory. Then, have students select topics and do a research project on an aspect of Thermidor and the Directory. A useful source for more detailed information is Denis Woronoff, *The Thermidorean Regime and the Directory, 1794–1799* (Cambridge: Cambridge University Press, 1984). Other good sources include Martyn Lyons, *France under the Directory* (Cambridge: Cambridge University Press, 1975); and Bronislaw Baczko, *Ending the Terror: The French Revolution After Robespierre* (Cambridge: Cambridge University Press, 1994).

Additional Resources: Literature

Brody, Miriam, ed., *A Vindication of the Rights of Women*. 1992.
Clarke, J. C. D., ed., *Reflections on the Revolution in France: A Critical Edition*. 2001.
Foner, Eric, ed., *Thomas Paine: Collected Writings*. 1995.
Lamport, F. J., trans., *Friedrich von Schiller: Robbers and Wallenstein*. 1979.
Mainland, William F., trans., *Friedrich von Schiller: Wilhelm Tell*. 1972.
Sonenscher, Michael, ed., *Sieyès: Political Writings: Including the Debate Between Sieyès and Tom Paine*. 2003.

Additional Resources: Film and Video

Danton (1990: VHS, 138 min.) Andrzej Wajda's excellent film is in Polish, but Gerard Depardieu gives a first-rate performance as Robespierre's revolutionary comrade with a conscience—a nice focus on the Terror era.

The History Channel's *French Revolution* (2005; DVD, 100 min.) is well done, mixing documents, academic perspectives, and "reenactments" to offer a rich overview of the major events of the period; excerpts might be shown in class.

Jefferson in Paris (1995; VHS/DVD, 139 min.) offers an American perspective on revolutionary France and the usual Merchant Ivory production values in a rich recreation of the era.

A Tale of Two Cities (1935: VHS/DVD, 135 min.) There are many versions of Dickens's classic tale of the revolution, but the 1935 version is often pointed to as the best of the bunch.

Other Bedford/St. Martin's Resources for Chapter 19

The following resources are available to accompany Chapter 19. Please refer to the Preface of this manual for detailed descriptions of all the ancillaries.

For Instructors

Transparencies

The following maps and images from Chapter 19 are available as full-color acetates.

- Map 19.1: Revolutionary Paris, 1789
- Map 19.2: Redrawing the Map of France, 1789–1791
- Map 19.3: French Expansion, 1791–1799
- Map 19.4: The Second and Third Partitions of Poland, 1793 and 1795
- Mapping the West: Europe in 1799
- The Third Estate Awakens, p. 593
- Fall of the Bastille, p. 593

Instructor's Resources CD-ROM

The following maps and image from Chapter 19, as well as a chapter outline, are available on disc in both PowerPoint and jpeg formats.

- Map 19.1: Revolutionary Paris, 1789
- Map 19.2: Redrawing the Map of France, 1789–1791
- Map 19.3: French Expansion, 1791–1799
- Map 19.4: The Second and Third Partitions of Poland, 1793 and 1795
- Mapping the West: Europe in 1799
- The Third Estate Awakens, p. 593

Using the Bedford Series with The Making of the West

Available in print as well as online at **bedfordstmartins.com/usingseries**, this guide offers practical suggestions for using *The French Revolution and Human Rights: A Brief Documentary History*, edited, translated, and with an Introduction by Lynn Hunt; *Napoleon, Symbol for an* Age, by Rafe Blaufarb; and *Slave Revolution in the Caribbean, 1789–1804*, by Laurent Dubois and John D. Garrigus in conjunction with Chapter 19 of the textbook.

For Students

Study Guides

The Online Study Guide at **bedfordstmartins.com/hunt** helps students synthesize the material they have learned as well as practice the skills historians use to make sense of the past. The following Map, Visual, and Document activities are available for Chapter 19.

Map Activity

- Map 19.3: French Expansion, 1791–1799

Visual Activity

- The Third Estate Awakens, p. 593

Reading Historical Documents

- The Rights of Minorities, p. 597
- Address on Abolishing the Slave Trade (February 5, 1790), p. 613
- Contrasting Views: Perspectives on the French Revolution, pp. 610–611

CHAPTER

20

Napoleon and the Revolutionary Legacy

1800–1830

Chapter Resources

Main Chapter Topics

1. Napoleon Bonaparte ended the French Revolution and created an authoritarian state. At the same time, he made many improvements in the administration of France and oversaw the making of a new civil code.

2. Napoleon's astute use of a large, enthusiastic, and highly mobile army enabled him to construct an impressive empire that did not, however, endure because he could not defeat Britain and Russia, and because he insisted on treating conquered areas as little more than colonies.

3. The Congress of Vienna (1814–1815) set the boundaries of European states and scheduled periodic meetings of major powers to oversee international affairs. Although this diplomatic system, or "concert of Europe," did not long work as planned, it did, however, help to prevent a major war until the 1850s. The congress promoted domestic stability and conservative principles but could not prevent liberal and nationalistic rebellions.

4. Although romanticism was primarily an artistic movement that glorified nature, emotion, individual genius, and imagination, it frequently supported nationalist aspirations in the first half of the nineteenth century.

5. Revolts in the 1820s and the revolutions of 1830 sought autonomy, national unity, and constitutional guarantees of individual liberties. Few succeeded except the Serbs, the Belgians, the Greeks, and the Latin American colonies.

Focus Question

How did Napoleon Bonaparte's actions force other European rulers to change their policies?

1. Bonaparte's actions forced a wide range of changes from other European rulers. His aggressive modernization of French military, education, legal and scientific institutions, and his determination to spread French power and his own influence through wars of conquest, put tremendous pressure on the rest of the west to "keep up" in order to resist French military and cultural power. In Prussia, for example, Frederick William III abolished serfdom and reformed the Prussian army in response to the French threat. By extending his Napoleonic Code to conquered states, and by consolidating states in Germany and Italy, Napoleon forced a re-drawing of the map of Europe.

2. The diplomatic system that took form after his defeats during the Congress of Vienna also reflected the influence of Napoleon, who forced new levels of cooperation and coordination on his enemies. Furthermore, his conquests and policies strengthened nationalism in much of the west, and forced the restored monarchs of Europe to adopt and adapt a range of counter-revolutionary policies in the decades after his defeat.

Annotated Chapter Outline

I. **The Rise of Napoleon Bonaparte**

A. **A General Takes Over, pp. 620–622**

1. Napoleon Bonaparte (1769–1821) rose from penniless artillery officer to supreme ruler of France in four years.
2. After his astounding military successes in the Italian campaigns of 1796–1797, he defeated the Piedmontese and the Austrians.
3. He established client republics that were dependent upon him by negotiating directly with the Austrians, while paying

his army with the cash he received as tribute to ensure its loyalty.

4. Napoleon quieted any discontent in the Directory by sending confiscated Italian art back to France.
5. In 1798 he was given command of an Egyptian invasion force, sent to cut the British trade route to India. British naval activity caused the invasion to fail.
6. Napoleon did introduce Enlightenment legal reform to Egypt, and his forces uncovered the Rosetta Stone, a slab of black basalt dating back to 196 B.C.E. that was inscribed with Egyptian hieroglyphics, Demotic, and Greek, allowing linguists to decipher hieroglyphs for the first time.
7. Bonaparte returned to France in October 1799, when France was in the midst of a series of crises.
8. Anti-Directory conspirators, including Bonaparte's brother, arranged for the overthrow of the legislature, allowing a rump assembly to abolish the Directory and establish the Consulate, a three-man executive called the Consulate that included Napoleon as First Consul.
9. A new constitution was written and submitted to the apathetic public for a vote, the results of which were falsified to show more support for the new government.

B. From Republic to Empire, pp. 622–625

1. The Constitution of 1799 installed Napoleon Bonaparte as First Consul with the right to choose the Council of State, which drew up all the laws.
2. The Council eliminated direct elections for deputies and denied independent powers to the three houses of the legislature.
3. Although he was not religious, Napoleon signed a concordat (agreement) with Pope Pius VII (r. 1800–1823) in 1801 to reconcile Catholics to the regime. Catholicism was recognized as the religion of "the great majority of French citizens," and the pope validated the sale of church lands that had occurred during the Revolution.
4. Napoleon continued to centralize state power by creating the Bank of France and appointing prefects who supervised local affairs in each department in the country. He reestablished order in France, in part by using government censors and the police to limit opposition and by censoring newspapers, operas, and plays.
5. In 1802, he named himself Consul for life and, in December of 1804, he crowned himself emperor. His actions were approved by plebiscites.
6. Napoleon worked hard to establish his authority and to cultivate his image, which was reproduced on coins, on public monuments, and in paintings.
7. His ostentatious building projects, most of which were in the neoclassical style, included the Arc de Triomphe and the Stock Exchange.
8. Napoleon's most trusted officials from past military campaigns helped him rule, and his effective bureaucracy was based on a patron–client relationship.
9. He reinstituted a social hierarchy that rewarded merit and talent regardless of birth. He also created an aristocracy based in part on wealth and installed his relatives in positions of power and influence.
10. In 1810, to establish a new dynasty, he divorced his childless wife Josephine and married an Austrian princess. He designated their son the King of Rome.

C. The New Paternalism: The Civil Code, pp. 625–627

1. One of Napoleon's first acts as emperor was the creation of the Civil, or Napoleonic Code: the first unified system of law for France.
2. The code assured property rights, guaranteed religious liberty, and established a uniform system of law for all men that provided equal treatment for all adult males and affirmed the right of men to choose their professions.
3. Napoleon's familial model of power placed men firmly in charge: The Civil Code reasserted the Old Regime's system of male domination over women and insisted on a father's control over, and responsibility for, his children.
4. The code severely curtailed women's rights, making women responsible for private virtue because Napoleon believed a woman's place was in the home.
5. The code was adopted in many European and Latin American countries, as well as in the French colony of Louisiana.
6. The government managed military-style education at the new lycées for boys but took little interest in educating girls.

7. All workers were required to carry a card attesting to their good conduct, and workers' organizations were prohibited.
8. Arbitration boards were established in 1806 to settle labor disputes, but they treated workers as minors and demanded that they be represented by foremen and shop superintendents.
9. Limitations on workers' rights won Napoleon the support of French business.

D. Patronage of Science and Intellectual Life, pp. 627–628

1. Napoleon promoted scientific inquiry, especially if it served practical purposes.
2. During his reign, experiments with balloons led to the discovery of laws about the expansion of gases, research on fossil shells prepared the way for new theories of evolutionary change later in the century, and new techniques of amputation and medical care were developed.
3. While he encouraged scientists, Napoleon considered most writers useless or dangerous.
4. Madame de Staël (1766–1817), like many of the country's talented writers, had to live in exile.
5. Her novel *Corinne* (1807) criticized the regime by focusing on a brilliant woman thwarted by the French patriarchal system.
6. Even though Napoleon restored the authority of the state and of religion, many Catholics and royalists criticized him as a usurper.
7. François-René de Chateaubriand (1768–1848) believed that Napoleon did not properly defend Christian values against the Enlightenment's emphasis on reason.
8. In his *Genius of Christianity* (1802), Chateaubriand argued that Napoleon did not understand the mystical power of faith.

II. "Europe Was at My Feet": Napoleon's Conquests

A. The Grand Army and Its Victories, 1800–1807, pp. 628–630

1. Conscription provided Napoleon with a large army, and the army also offered social mobility and appealed to French patriotism. Officers who rose through the ranks were young, ambitious, and experienced, and the French military had higher morale than the armies of other powers.
2. Napoleon also inspired an almost fanatical loyalty, fighting next to his soldiers in some sixty battles.
3. Napoleon's favorite tactic was to attack the main body of the opposing army in a lightning strike with the largest force possible, and to follow up decisive victories with relentless pursuit.
4. He served as his own operations officer, but failed to train independent subordinates. Supply was a constant problem.
5. A lack of coordination among his enemies' armies was one of his greatest advantages; he therefore maneuvered diplomatically and militarily to face them one at a time.
6. Napoleon's victories in the battles of Marengo and Hohenlinden in 1800 forced the Austrians to agree to peace.
7. This success was followed in 1802 by the Treaty of Amiens with the British, which lasted only until 1803.
8. During this temporary truce, Napoleon sent forces to St. Domingue to retake the colony, but was forced to withdraw because of the organized resistance by the black population and an epidemic of yellow fever.
9. As part of his retreat from the western hemisphere, and his especial need for funds, Napoleon sold Louisiana to the United States in 1803.
10. When war resumed, the British navy defeated the French and their Spanish allies in the battle of Trafalgar (1805).
11. That same year, Napoleon defeated the Austrians at Ulm, and the Austrians and Russians at Austerlitz.
12. Prussia entered the war and was promptly defeated at Jena and Auerstadt in 1806.
13. In 1807, Napoleon again defeated the Russians at Friedland.
14. The ensuing treaties of Tilsit—negotiated between Napoleon and Russian tsar Alexander I (r. 1801–1825)—resulted in Prussia's suffering a significant loss of territory.

B. The Impact of French Victories, pp. 630–632

1. By annexing some territories and setting up others as satellite kingdoms with little autonomy, Napoleon attempted to unite Europe.
2. He united the disparate German and Italian states to rule them more effectively and in 1806 he established the Confederation of the Rhine, which

included all the German states except Austria and Prussia.

3. Napoleon consolidated Italy by annexing the territories next to France and establishing the kingdoms of Italy and Naples.
4. Annexed territories, ruled directly from France, and satellite kingdoms, usually ruled by one of Napoleon's relatives, were subject to French laws and French-style reforms.
5. Napoleon abolished serfdom, eliminated seigneurial dues, introduced the Napoleonic Code, suppressed monasteries, subordinated church to state, and extended civil rights to Jews and other religious minorities.
6. Reactions to these innovations were mixed: real improvements in roads, public works, law codes, education, and the economy were achieved, but increased taxes and conscription to support conquests and occupations aggravated dissent.
7. Conflicts arose when Napoleon's desire to standardize and unify came up against local insistence on old customs and traditions. Such resistance led Napoleon to annex the satellite kingdom of Holland in 1810 when his brother Louis became too sympathetic to Dutch interests.
8. Napoleon's success put pressure on defeated rulers to rethink political and cultural assumptions. In Prussia, Frederick William III abolished serfdom, expanded the liberties of peasants, and reformed the army along French lines in order to compete.
9. The one power standing between Napoleon and total domination of Europe was Great Britain.
10. In 1806, Napoleon established the Continental System, which prohibited trade between Great Britain and France, its dependent states, and its allies.
11. The system at first harmed Britain's trade, but because smuggling was rampant, British industrial growth continued.
12. Resistance to the French encouraged the development of nationalism in other countries.
13. In southern Italy, gangs of bandits and a network of secret societies, the *carbonari*, harassed the French army and local officials.
14. Resistance was greatest in Spain and Portugal: the nobles feared revolutionary reforms, the Catholic church spread anti-French propaganda, and the peasants fought to defend their priests and resented French requisitions of food.
15. Assisted by the British, Portuguese, and Spanish rebels engaged Napoleon in a six-year war for national independence.

C. From Russian Winter to Final Defeat, 1812–1815, pp. 632–635

1. By 1812, only Great Britain and Russia remained independent of Napoleon.
2. Great Britain sent aid to the Portuguese and Spanish rebels, while Tsar Alexander I made peace with the Ottoman Empire and allied himself with Great Britain and Sweden.
3. In 1812, Napoleon invaded Russia with an enormous army, engaging the main Russian force at Borodino in September, which resulted in heavy casualties on both sides.
4. Napoleon took Moscow, but the departing Russians had set the city on fire, and the tsar refused to negotiate.
5. With supplies running low, Napoleon began his retreat in October; in November, the bitter Russian winter began.
6. By December, only one-sixth of Napoleon's original troops had returned to France.
7. Napoleon replenished his armies by the spring of 1813, but a coalition of Russian, Austrian, Prussian, and Swedish armies—backed by British financial support—defeated him at the Battle of the Nations, as satellite provinces revolted and joined the coalition.
8. In March 1814, the French Senate deposed and exiled Napoleon to the island of Elba off the coast of Italy.
9. Louis XVIII (r. 1814–1824) was restored to the throne.
10. The new king was caught between returning émigré nobles, who demanded restoration of their lands and powers, and those who had benefited from the Revolution or from Napoleon's reign.
11. This chaos gave Napoleon the opportunity to escape exile and return to France, which he did during the so-called Hundred Days.
12. Louis XVIII fled, and Napoleon reconstituted his army with former soldiers still loyal to him.

13. Napoleon was once again defeated by a coalition of European powers at Waterloo.
14. He abdicated and entered permanent exile on the island of St. Helena off the coast of West Africa, where he died in 1821.
15. Napoleon's wars killed 750,000 French soldiers and 400,000 soldiers from territories he controlled, but his unification of Europe, his spread of French reforms, and the national sentiment generated by resistance to him all set the agenda for modern European history.

III. The "Restoration" of Europe

A. The Congress of Vienna, 1814–1815, pp. 636–638

1. The Congress of Vienna balanced post-Napoleonic Europe by relying on the major powers to cooperate while guaranteeing the status of smaller states.
2. Boundaries were settled by representatives of the five major powers: Austria, Russia, Prussia, Britain, and France.
3. The Austrian prince Klemens von Metternich (1773–1859) took the lead in the negotiations.
4. He worked with the ambitious British prime minister Robert Castlereagh (1769–1822) to check French aggression while preserving it as a great power to counter the ambitions of Prussia and Russia.
5. Prince Charles Maurice de Talleyrand (1754–1838) represented France.
6. Where possible, the congress restored traditional rulers, as in Spain and Italy.
7. Elsewhere, it rearranged territorial boundaries to balance the competing interests of the great powers; the duchy of Warsaw thus became the kingdom of Poland ruled by the Russian tsar.
8. The Dutch Republic and Austrian Netherlands united as the new kingdom of the Netherlands under the House of Orange.
9. Austria took charge of the German Confederation, which replaced the Holy Roman Empire.
10. Sardinia was given Piedmont, Genoa, Nice, and part of Savoy.
11. Sweden acquired Norway and accepted Russian control of Finland.
12. The congress also condemned the slave trade in principle, but did not ban it.
13. Alexander I of Russia proposed a Holy Alliance to ensure divine assistance in upholding religion, peace, and justice; Prussia and Austria agreed, but Great Britain declined.
14. From that point on, the legitimacy of states depended on a treaty system, not divine right.

B. The Emergence of Conservatism, pp. 638–639

1. The French Revolution and Napoleon's domination of Europe had proved that the old order of society was subject to sudden change and disruption.
2. People needed justification to believe in restored governments, and conservatism provided that justification.
3. Conservatives believed that the Enlightenment had led to the French Revolution, which produced both the Terror and the authoritarian Napoleon.
4. The most influential spokesman of conservatism was Britain's Edmund Burke (1729–1799), who believed that any change in government should be gradual and must respect national and historical traditions.
5. Conservatives defended hereditary monarchy and the authority of the church, arguing that the "rights of man" must be balanced by the rights of the community; and that faith, sentiment, history, and tradition must fill the vacuum left by the failure of reason and the excessive belief in individual rights.
6. Not surprisingly, conservatism had its strongest appeal in ruling circles: the ascension of Louis XVIII tested conservative beliefs in France.
7. He maintained the Civil Code, guaranteed rights of ownership to church lands sold during the Revolution, and created a parliament based on restricted suffrage.
8. While the king tried to follow a moderate course of compromise, the Ultras (ultraroyalists) pushed for complete repudiation of the revolutionary past.
9. In 1816, the Ultras insisted on abolishing divorce and set up special courts to punish opponents of the regime.

C. The Revival of Religion, pp. 639–640

1. Once peace returned to Europe, many renewed their religious faith.
2. Revivalist movements, which had begun in Great Britain and Germany in the eighteenth century, sometimes challenged the status quo.
3. In England, the Methodists, or Wesleyans, attracted thousands of shopkeepers, artisans, agricultural laborers, and workers in cottage industry, often to large-scale revival meetings that went on for days.
4. Although Methodism stressed obedience to the government, the group's hostility to rigid doctrine and encouragement of popular preaching promoted a sense of democratic community and even a rudimentary sexual equality.
5. Women preachers traveled to sermonize in barns, town halls, and textile dye houses; and Sunday schools taught thousands of poor children to read and write.
6. In the United States, the second Great Awakening began around 1790, bringing together thousands of worshipers in huge camp meetings.
7. Protestant sects began missionary activity in other parts of the world in the late eighteenth century as well.
8. In India, British missionaries succeeded in getting the practice of *sati*—the burning alive of widows on the funeral pyres of their husbands—abolished in 1829.
9. Missionary activity by both Protestants and Catholics would become one of the arms of European imperialism and cultural influence later in the nineteenth century.

IV. Challenges to the Conservative Order

A. Romanticism, pp. 640–643

1. Romanticism was an artistic movement that glorified nature, emotion, genius, and imagination as antidotes to the Enlightenment's emphasis on reason, and classicism's emphasis on symmetry and ordered geometric space.
2. Romantic poets such as George Gordon Byron (1788–1824) celebrated emotion and creative imagination.
3. Byron also symbolized romanticism's idealism when he died fighting for Greek independence from the Turks.
4. William Wordsworth (1770–1850) elevated the wonders of nature to a transcendent height.
5. Mary Shelley (1797–1851) explored the nightmarish side of human genius in *Frankenstein* (1818).
6. In the same mode as Shelley, Johann Wolfgang von Goethe (1749–1832) elaborated on the destructive potential of human nature in *Faust* (1832).
7. In painting, romanticism idealized nature and often expressed anxiety about industrial changes.
8. Caspar David Friedrich (1774–1840) depicted individual figures overwhelmed by an overpowering nature, and the steadfast nature of faith.
9. Joseph M. W. Turner (1775–1851) anticipated later artists by blurring the outlines of objects in his misty seascapes.
10. Like other romantics, French painter Eugène Delacroix (1798–1863) experimented with new techniques, emphasizing light and color in medieval and contemporary scenes.
11. The German composer Ludwig van Beethoven (1770–1827) helped set the direction for romanticism in music when he transformed the symphony into a connected work with recurring and evolving musical themes, conveying the impression of organic growth.
12. If any common political thread existed among the romantics, it was the support of nationalist aspirations—especially through the search for the historical origins of national identity.
13. The enormously influential novels of Sir Walter Scott (1771–1832) were infused with romantic nationalism.

B. Political Revolts in the 1820s, pp. 644–646

1. Those who had hoped for constitutional government after Napoleon's fall were disappointed.
2. In Spain, Ferdinand VII restored the pre-revolutionary nobility, church, and monarchy, and established strict censorship.
3. Members of the middle class, disturbed by repressive policies, and army officers who had encountered and adopted French ideas, joined secret societies.
4. A revolt by soldiers demanding that Ferdinand restore the constitution was put down by French troops, and Ferdinand's absolute power was restored.
5. The Spanish revolt encouraged Italian rebellions in Naples, Piedmont, and Sardinia, all squashed by Austria in 1821.

6. Great Britain opposed Austria's actions, but the other great powers supported it.
7. In the German Confederation, student groups led by Friedrich Ludwig Jahn advocated a racially pure German nationalism. The Karlsbad Decrees (1819) suppressed the groups.
8. In Russia, a brief revolt erupted in December 1825 over Alexander I's successor.
9. His brother Nicholas was to be crowned, but a faction of rebel officers preferred another brother, Constantine, because he would favor reform and a constitution.
10. When the officers called for Constantine to take the throne, soldiers loyal to Nicholas suppressed them in the so-called Decembrist Revolt; the rebels became heroes to later generations.
11. Nicholas I (r. 1825–1855) dedicated his reign to preventing any further calls for reform.
12. Serbia revolted and gained independence from the Turks in 1817.
13. Prince Alexander Ypsilanti led a Greek revolt in 1820, but failed because he had not gained support from the great powers.
14. A second Greek revolt, led by peasants, unleashed atrocities 1821 and 1822; public opinion in Europe supported the Greeks.
15. In 1827, a combined British, French, and Russian force destroyed the Turkish fleet at Navarino Bay; and in 1828, Russia declared war on Turkey and advanced close to Istanbul.
16. The 1829 Treaty of Adrianople gave Russia a protectorate over the Danubian principalities in the Balkans and provided for an international congress that included Great Britain, Russia, and France.
17. In 1830, Greece was declared an independent kingdom.
18. This successful nationalist struggle was the first breach in Metternich's conservative system.
19. Revolt spread across the Atlantic, when colonists from Mexico to Argentina took advantage of the upheaval in Spain and Portugal.
20. Leading these revolts was Simon Bolívar, the son of a slave owner, who had been educated in Europe on the works of Voltaire and Rousseau.
21. Independent republics were formed in Latin America between 1821 and 1823.
22. In 1823, U.S. President James Monroe issued the foreign policy statement, the Monroe Doctrine, in opposition to European interference in the Americas.

C. Revolution and Reform, 1830–1832, pp. 646–649

1. In 1830, a new wave of liberal and nationalist revolts broke out throughout the European continent.
2. In France, Charles X (r. 1824–1830) passed a Law of Indemnity that compensated those nobles who had lost estates during the Revolution, and a Law of Sacrilege that imposed the death penalty for offenses such as stealing religious objects from churches.
3. Charles also dissolved the legislature, removed many wealthy and powerful voters from the rolls, and imposed strict censorship.
4. A revolution began on July 26, 1830 and, after three days of street fighting and the flight of the king, a group of moderate liberals asked Charles X's cousin, Louis-Philippe, to take the throne.
5. Although Louis-Philippe extended suffrage, only 170,000 out of a population of 30 million could vote.
6. Expressing their dissatisfaction, the indigent and working classes rebelled in Lyon in 1831, but the revolt was quickly put down.
7. Events in France inspired a revolt in Belgium, which had been annexed to the Netherlands in 1815.
8. At a congress of the great powers, Belgium was granted its independence as a constitutional monarchy in exchange for neutrality in international affairs.
9. Revolts in the Austrian Empire's Italian territories were also unsuccessful because of a lack of outside support.
10. In November 1830, Poland rebelled against Russia, and Polish aristocrats formed a provisional government.
11. Without support from the British or French, the rebels were defeated by Russian forces.
12. Nicholas I abolished the Polish constitution and ordered thousands of Poles executed or banished.
13. Great Britain pursued reform during the 1820s and 1830s.
14. Controversy over George IV's (r. 1820–1830) attempt to divorce his wife

Caroline tarnished the reputation of the monarchy and sped the reform movement.

15. In the 1820s, Sir Robert Peel (1788–1850), the secretary for home affairs, revised the criminal code and established a municipal police force.
16. In 1824, laws prohibiting unions were repealed (but the restrictions placed on strikes remained), and in 1829, Catholics were allowed to sit in Parliament and hold most public offices.
17. In 1832, Whigs in Parliament enacted the Reform Bill to extend voting rights.
18. Mass demonstrations in favor of the bill had been held in many cities, but the bill granted the vote to only one-fifth of British voters, and still only male property-owners could vote.
19. The bill, however, increased the number of voters by about 50 percent, granted representation to the new industrial centers in the north for the first time, and set a precedent for widening suffrage without revolution.

Lecture Strategies

1. Lectures on the characteristics of the new state established by Napoleon can be reinforced by looking at period paintings. A close examination of the many portraits of Napoleon produced during his lifetime immediately illustrates the essence of his character and ambition and would complement any of the topics already suggested. See, in particular, the portraits done by Jacques-Louis David (*An Unfinished Portrait* [c. 1798], *Crossing the St. Bernard* [1804], *The Coronation of Napoleon and Josephine* [1806–1807], and *Emperor in His Study* [1812]); and Jean-Auguste-Dominique Ingres (*First Consul* [1804]; and *Emperor* [1806]). For an interesting contrast, see English political cartoons of Napoleon, especially those done during the Napoleonic Wars. In these cartoons, Napoleon is at his least attractive—bow-legged, short, hawk-nosed, and generally maniacal. It would be worthwhile to present students with some of this visual evidence of the importance of image to the new regime's supporters and critics.

Napoleon (PBS, 2000), a four-hour video documentary, offers a great deal of striking visual material. The Napoleonic era is also the setting for the immensely popular and historically, extremely rich Aubrey/Maturin series of novels by Patrick O'Brian, which were also the basis for the recent film, *Master and Commander—The Far Side of the World* (2004). See also the widely popular *Horatio Hornblower* films, based on C. S. Forester's ten novels. The films feature Ioan Gruffud as a British naval officer, with storylines set against revolutionary and Napoleonic France. A recent television miniseries, available on DVD, attempted to reinvent the classic, with some success. See Additional Resources for details.

2. It is important to emphasize the drama of these years of considerable challenge to existing political systems. If the French Revolution had offered a supreme example of the power of emerging ideologies to disrupt and even destroy the most powerful of states, the military efficiency and relentless aggression of the Napoleonic regime also represented a fundamental threat to the entire European state system. Review with students the attractions of revolutionary ideas to a variety of social groups. The immediate post-war era in Britain offers a particularly vivid range of popular disturbances and political tensions. The Peterloo massacre and associated disturbances lends itself to description and analysis. An excellent range of articles surveying the impact of revolutionary thought in Britain through the Great Reform Act is Mark Philip's collection, *The French Revolution and British Popular Politics* (Cambridge: Cambridge University Press, 2004). For a recent appreciation of the evolution of British conservative and reactionary thought that also pays useful attention to popular politics, see Don Herzog, *Poisoning the Minds of the Lower Orders*, (Princeton, NJ: Princeton University Press, 2000). Overviews of the period as a whole include Charles Breunig, *The Age of Revolution and Reaction, 1789–1859* (New York: W. W. Norton, 1970); older but still useful, Eric J. Hobsbawm, *The Age of Revolution: Europe, 1789–1848* (New York: Praeger, 1969), part of a fine series; and Robert Gildea, *Barricades and Borders: Europe 1800–1914* (New York: Oxford University Press, 1987), part of *The Short Oxford History of the Modern World* series.

3. Studying the Congress of Vienna provides a good opportunity to survey the European situation between 1815 and 1848. Among other tasks, you might indicate theareas that were affected by the French Revolution (and in what ways), and the areas that would soon thereafter be affected by the Industrial Revolution. Metternich and the Congress System (the concert of Europe) must first be reviewed. To what extent was Metternich successful in making the concert of Europe work? Did his success depend on the dominant position of Austria in Germany and Italy? Did Metternich dominate European affairs in order to maintain political stability in the Austrian Empire? What were the diplomatic goals of the British Empire at the conference, and how did they see their role in the Vienna system?

In addition to the sources cited in the chapter bibliography, see Tim Chapman, *The Congress of Vienna: Origins, Processes, and Results* (New York: Routledge,

1998), which avoids being overwhelming and provides an overview of the goals and interests of the various European powers. Alan W. Palmer, *Metternich* (New York: Harper & Row, 1972) continues to be useful. Part 3 of James J. Sheehan, *German History, 1770–1866* (New York: Oxford University Press, 1989); and Part 1 of David Blackbourn, *The Long Nineteenth Century: A History of Germany, 1780–1918* (New York: Oxford University Press, 1998), provide good coverage of Austria and Germany during this period. Part 2 of Gordon Wright's classic *France in Modern Times*, 3rd ed. (New York: W. W. Norton, 1981) is an excellent source. Part 3 of W. Bruce Lincoln's *The Romanovs: Autocrats of All the Russias* (New York: Dial Press, 1981) places Nicholas I in context. See also Lincoln's full-scale biography, *Nicholas I: Emperor and Autocrat of All the Russias* (Bloomington: Indiana University Press, 1978). A classic on the foreign policy of Britain in this period, Charles Webster's *The Foreign Policy of Castlereagh, 1815–1822: Britain and the European Alliance* (London: G. Bell, 1958) still holds up and has insight to offer on the unique position of Britain in the post-war diplomatic world.

4. Perhaps in connection to number 2 above, a class session might be used to compare the French Revolution of 1830 to the British Reform Bill of 1832. Why did France turn to revolution in 1830? How different was the situation in Great Britain, where passage of the Reform Bill of 1832 ended the major urban protest movement? How might we assess the progress achieved by the European revolutionary movement at the time of the 1830s? To what extent had the labor movement developed by this time? A good place to begin is Clive H. Church, *Europe in 1830: Revolution and Political Change* (London: George Allen & Unwin, 1983). For the French Revolution, see David H. Pinkney, *The French Revolution of 1830* (Princeton, NJ: Princeton University Press, 1972); John M. Merriman, ed., *1830 in France* (New York: Franklin Watts, 1975); and Robert Bezucha, *The Lyon Uprising of 1834* (Cambridge, MA: Harvard University Press, 1976). William H. Sewell Jr., *Work and Revolution in France: The Language of Labor from the Old Regime to 1848* (Cambridge: Cambridge University Press, 1980) shows the extent to which working-class socialism in the nineteenth century derived from the guild structure of the eighteenth. Craig Calhoun, *The Question of Class Struggle: Social Foundations of Popular Radicalism during the Industrial Revolution* (Chicago: University of Chicago Press, 1982) presents evidence of the importance of artisan communities in early-nineteenth-century protest movements in England. Eric Hobsbawm and George Rude, *Captain Swing* (New York: Pantheon Books, 1968) is a fascinating discussion of the agricultural uprising of 1830. Fortunately for the British government, the agricultural unrest and the urban political protest remained largely separate phenomena.

Class Discussion Starters

1. Napoleon is, of course, the dominant figure of this period. Even after his defeat at Waterloo and exile to St. Helena, he continued to exert considerable influence through the romantic myth associated with him. A session on Napoleon should attempt to answer all or most of the following questions: Why was Napoleon successful in bringing an end to the period of revolutionary turmoil? How much credit should go to the Directory? What were Napoleon's most important contributions to the administration of France? How successful was he in his imperial ventures? What were the main factors leading to the collapse of the empire? What made a romanticized, Napoleonic myth possible? Another way of organizing this session would be to ask how best to characterize Napoleon. To what extent did his goals and accomplishments reflect Enlightenment values? Ancien Regime approaches to governing France? The values and principles of the French Revolution?

In addition to sources cited in the bibliography for Chapter 20, a rather critical biography of Napoleon is Alan Schom, *Napoleon Bonaparte* (New York: HarperCollins, 1997). Other useful studies include Louis Bergeron, *France under Napoleon* (Princeton, NJ: Princeton University Press, 1981); and Isser Woloch, *Napoleon and His Collaborators: The Making of a Dictatorship* (New York: Norton, 2001), which explores the workings of the Napoleanic regime. A useful documentary source is Somerset de Chair, ed., *Napoleon on Napoleon: The Autobiography of an Emperor* (London: Cassell, 1991). Among the many reference books available is David Nicholls, *Napoleon: A Biographical Companion* (Santa Barbara: ABC-Clio, 1999), which includes a lengthy essay on Napoleon and his importance in history and entries in alphabetical order; Owen Connelly, Harold T. Parker, Peter W. Becker, and June K. Burton, eds., *Historical Dictionary of Napoleonic France, 1799–1815* (Westport, CT: Greenwood Press, 1985); and also David G. Chandler, *Dictionary of the Napoleonic War* (New York: Simon & Schuster, 1993). Two interesting books written for a wider audience should be mentioned. First is Carollyn Erickson's biography, *Josephine: A Life of the Empress* (New York: St. Martin's Press, 1999), which stresses the more sensational aspects of Josephine's life. Second is the book by Ben Weider and David Hapgood, *The Murder of Napoleon* (iUniverse.com, 1998), guaranteed to provoke discussion.

2. Romanticism is a protean topic, but it can be made manageable by dealing primarily with its political aspects. As *The Making of the West: Peoples and Cultures* notes, romanticism was associated with conservatism, liberalism, nationalism, and revolution. A session on romanticism might begin by discussing the varying ways in which followers of the movement

viewed the world. While most Romantics emphasized nature, emotion, and genius, even this common basis might lead the discussion in different directions. The session might then focus on whether romanticism was largely a conservative or even reactionary movement in the first two decades of the nineteenth century, and a liberal or even radical movement in the following two decades. Finally, the connection between romanticism and nationalism should be given some attention. In which ways did the two movements complement one another? At some point it might, of course, be helpful to emphasize that romanticism is a far larger topic than just its connections with politics in the first half of the nineteenth century.

A comprehensive introduction to romanticism is Maurice William Cranston, *The Romantic Movement* (Cambridge, MA: Blackwell, 1994). Another broad study, written for the nonspecialist, is Howard Mumford Jones, *Revolution and Romanticism* (Cambridge, MA: Belknap Press, 1974). See also Martin Travers, *An Introduction to Modern European Literature: From Romanticism to Postmodernism* (New York: St. Martin's Press, 1998); Nicholas V. Riasanovsky, *The Emergence of Romanticism* (New York: Oxford University Press, 1992); Roy Porter and Mikulas Teich, eds., *Romanticism in National Context* (New York: Cambridge University Press, 1988); and Charles Rosen, *The Romantic Generation* (Cambridge, MA: Harvard University Press, 1995). Among the many books available on British romanticism are Laura Dabundo, ed., *The Encyclopedia of Romanticism: Culture in Britain, 1780s–1830s* (New York: Garland, 1992); Stuart Curran, ed., *The Cambridge Companion to British Romanticism* (New York: Cambridge University Press, 1993); and two edited by Duncan Wu, *Romanticism: An Anthology*, 2nd ed. (Malden, MA: Blackwell, 1998), and *A Companion to Romanticism* (Malden, MA: Blackwell, 1999). See also E. P. Thompson, *The Romantics: England in a Revolutionary Age* (New York: New Press, 1997). For France, see D. G. Charlton, ed., *The French Romantics*, 2 vols. (New York: Cambridge University Press, 1984). For Russia, see *History of Russian Literature of the Romantic Period* (Ann Arbor, MI: Ardis, 1986). More specialized but highly interesting are Ronald Paulson, *Representations of Revolution, 1789–1820* (New Haven, CT: Yale University Press, 1983); Gregory Dart, *Rousseau, Robespierre, and English Romanticism* (New York: Cambridge University Press, 1999); Emily W. Sunstein, *Mary Shelley: Romance and Reality* (Boston: Little, Brown, 1989); and John Hardman, *The Double in Nineteenth-Century Fiction: The Shadow Life* (New York: St. Martin's Press, 1991).

3. Students might also be asked to consider the political and class dimensions of the work and career of an appropriate romantic-era poet. Alphonse de Lamartine would be an excellent choice, or Lord Byron, but best in terms of accessibility and direct political references, Percy Bysshe Shelley might work best. Alternately, students could work in groups on different poets and the juncture between their artistic and political lives. For Shelley, have the students read all or parts of "Mask of Anarchy" (1819) or "The Call to Freedom" (1819). To what extent can they see the questions and tensions of this period in these literary productions?

Reviewing the Text

Review Questions

1. In what ways did Napoleon continue the French Revolution, and in what ways did he break with it?
[model answer] • ***Napoleon did not reject revolutionary progress or restore the monarchy:*** *Sometimes what matters most is what is* not *done. Napoleon was a product of the Revolution; he acted forcefully against reactionary ideas of restoring the Bourbon dynasty, the old aristocracy, and other aspects of the old regime. He fought back against Royalist conspirators.*
• ***Napoleon continued revolutionary-era efforts to centralize the state and spread French political values:*** Napoleon expanded state power and control over the regions and used the military to enforce obedience to the state in France and in conquered territories. He demanded loyalty to the state and punished opponents of the government. The French military, as it had in the revolutionary era, spread the French political system (now dominated by Napoleon) to other parts of Europe.
• ***Napoleon continued revolutionary-era efforts to introduce "rational" government and a more egalitarian social order:*** Napoleon's Civil Code attempted to reform and rationalize legal practice across France and other territories under French control. By expanding educational opportunities for some (especially the middle class) and endeavoring to create an "aristocracy of talent" dedicated to serving the state, Napoleon sought to strengthen the government by harnessing the loyalty and services of the best and the brightest from a variety of backgrounds. He undermined this principle, however, by making extensive use of family members in running his system.
• ***Napoleon severely restricted liberty and political freedoms:*** Napoleon's system was autocratic and relied on censorship and control of information. Representative institutions were subordinated or eliminated, newspapers and publications were restricted, and liberties were restricted in a variety of other ways. He governed first as a dictator and then as an emperor, undermining the revolution's republican principles.
• ***Napoleon rejected or moderated revolutionary-era anti-Catholicism and emphasized public order:*** In order to build support for his rule and to stabilize the

government, Napoleon established a concordat with Pope Pius VII and ended a decade of church–state conflict in France. He did his best to restore public order and limit popular protest and violence, often at the expense of civil liberties and freedoms.

2. Why was Napoleon able to gain control over so much of Europe's territory?
[model answer] • ***Centralization of government ensured internal order and created a new class of supportive nobility:*** *Napoleon's reforms limited political expression that could influence elections, reduced the number of newspapers to lessen dissent, banned antigovernment art and writing, and set up a new legal system to codify French law. He kept dissenters under constant surveillance and imprisoned or deported them, but did not stir up rebellions by publicly executing them.*
• ***Napoleon's military innovations encouraged loyalty, tactical success, and high morale:*** Military service became a patriotic duty as well as a means for upward social mobility. Young men were able to rise through the ranks to become officers, which yielded loyal officers. Also, unlike earlier French leaders, Napoleon fought alongside his men, and his presence and skill inspired fanatical loyalty.
• ***Napoleon benefited from the traditionalism of his opponents:*** Other powers continued to restrict their officer corps to nobility and regarded conscription as too democratic. They therefore had smaller armies and lower morale.
• ***Napoleon's annexation of conquered territories fueled military success:*** Wherever France's army conquered, Napoleon brought French-style reforms, such as public education and public works. Annexed territories and satellite kingdoms paid half of the French war expenses.

3. To what extent did the Congress of Vienna restore the old order?
[model answer] • ***A new international equilibrium to prevent war was created:*** *Monarchs allied against Napoleon hoped to nullify revolutionary and Napoleonic reforms by reinstating old regimes; the Congress restored some traditional rulers, but new kingdoms were created out of territories that belonged to monarchies before being annexed to France. This process created an international peace to protect and encourage cooperation among the great powers, thus guaranteeing the status of smaller states and allowing rulers to focus on maintaining internal stability.*
• ***Old-order rulers who had ruled by divine right now needed earthly legitimacy:*** Some Congress participants wanted to impart spiritual meaning to its political settlement. A Holy Alliance proposed by the Russian tsar swore to uphold religion, peace, and justice to win divine support. Some nations signed on, but Great Britain and the papacy refused. The former felt that it was "nonsense" and the latter thought that the pope alone interpreted Christian truth. These events separated secular authority and legitimacy from religion.
• ***Member nations spurned international competition and helped one another maintain peace:*** The decisions of the Congress disappointed revolutionary Europeans, and within a few years discontent arose again. Many powers involved in the Congress intervened to help one another stop rebels, where in the past they might have used the opportunity to begin or further international conflict.

4. Why were Austria and Russia able to thwart independence movements in Italy and Poland but not in Greece, Belgium, and Latin America?
[model answer] • ***Austria and Russia were in a position to use force to repress independence movements in Italy and Poland:*** *In the Italian states of Naples and Piedmont, Austrians, with Russian support, were able to put down independence movements by force in 1821 and arrest prominent liberals. In Poland, Russian police and military were able to arrest advocates of independence and disband the provisional government by force. In the Latin American revolutions, the new states were remote from European powers, and the United States and Britain both supported the independence movements and prevented military interventions.*
• ***Effective outside intervention by other major powers did not occur in the Polish and Italian rebellions:*** Hoped for French pressure and intervention on behalf of Italian independence movements did not occur in the 1820s and 1830s, and the influence of the pope was exercised against political independence. In Poland, Britain and France refrained from intervening on behalf of independence movements. Greek independence from Ottoman rule was supported by the major powers, including Britain and Russia, and Belgian independence, although opposed by Russia and Austria, was supported by Britain and France.

Making Connections

1. What was the long-term significance of Napoleon for Europe?
[model answer] *The Napoleonic Wars, along with the French Revolution, had demonstrated that regimes could be overturned virtually overnight. This led to the rise of conservatism, wherein the ideas of both the Enlightenment and French Revolution were rejected: monarchy was favored over republicanism, tradition over revolution, and religion over reason. But after the Napoleonic Wars, a return to authoritarianism failed to contain the*

nationalism and liberalism that periodically yielded civil conflict during the 1820s and 1830s, and finally boiled over completely in the revolutions of 1848.

The disturbances of the revolutionary and Napoleonic era contributed to the success of other movements besides conservatism. Religious revivals succeeded in France, Britain, and the United States. The romantic movement in the arts, inspired by Napoleon and the turmoil of the period, celebrated and reveled in turmoil, freedom, and individual energy, but also sometimes warned against the perils of unchecked ambition and hubris.

2. In what ways did Metternich succeed in holding back the revolutionary legacy? In what ways did he fail?
[model answer] *Metternich tried to hold back forces for change by restoring traditional rulers, returning countries to their prewar boundaries wherever possible, and, when restoration was impossible, rearranging territories in a way such as to balance the interests of the great powers without trampling on the smaller nations. He also sought to check French aggression while keeping it strong enough to balance the ambitions of Prussia and Russia. This arrangement may have prevented the outbreak of widespread European conflict until 1914, but it did not prevent smaller wars—like the Crimean War—between individual countries.*

Discussing the Documents

Questions from Online Study Guide with Model Answers

An Ordinary Soldier on Campaign with Napoleon, p. 633

1. What are some of the obstacles that Napoleon's army faced when it invaded Russia?
[model answer] *Although they defeated the Russian army when they confronted it, the march into Russia was slowed by the scorched-earth strategy employed by the retreating Russian army. The French were further slowed by the need to clear downed trees and barricades left behind by the Russians to impede the French. Napoleon's army also faced serious morale problems, as suggested in Walter's memoir. Because the countryside had been so completely devastated, the French army could not forage for food, and so was weakened by supply problems.*

2. How did the Russian campaign differ from Napoleon's preferred strategy?
[model answer] *Napoleon preferred to face the enemy in a decisive battle and then overwhelm it with superior numbers. He also recognized the importance of soldier morale. The army he brought into Russia was enormous (over 600,000) but the Russians never met him in a decisive battle. As a result, Napoleon was forced deeper and deeper into Russia, and supply problems eroded the army's morale.*

Wordsworth's Poetry, p. 642

1. What are the main themes or images of this poem?
[model answer] *Wordsworth writes a nostalgic recollection of his childhood "when first I came among these hills." He also writes about the beauty of nature with its deep rivers, lonely streams, tall rocks, and gloomy woods. He has a melancholic sense of regret for the past and the sense of union he felt with nature as a child.*

2. How does Romanticism as exemplified here differ from Enlightenment thought?
[model answer] *Wordsworth's emphasis on emotion, melancholy, and nostalgia is in sharp contrast with the Enlightenment emphasis on reason. This poem is about an escape from human society, whereas the Enlightenment sought to apply reason to solve social problems.*

Contrasting Views: Napoleon: For and Against, pp. 634–635

1. Which of these views of Napoleon has the most lasting value as opposed to immediate dramatic effect?
[model answer] *Constant's assessment is the most substantial and useful for historical analysis. It is dramatic to see Napoleon's own self-serving verdict on his rule, and Hugo's poem reveals something about how Napoleon's legacy was influential and emotionally charged. Constant's argument, however, attempts to explain the reasons why Napoleon was able to accomplish what he did, and does much to connect revolutionary and Enlightenment-era changes to his success and motivation. The indignant liberal reaction against Bonapartism and tyranny (of which Constant is a specimen) was very influential for the coming century.*

2. According to these selections, what was Napoleon's greatest accomplishment? His greatest failure?
[model answer] *Napoleon himself suggested that his legacy was his own life and accomplishments, as a great man. He pointed to his egalitarianism, military glory, and law code as examples of why he would remain famous. Constant was far more critical and suggested that "greed," "barbarism," and conflict were Napoleon's legacies. For Hugo, he is a tragic if somewhat romantic figure ("chain[ed], living, on that lonely shore"), but his ultimate legacy is, according to the final stanza, "tears" and "blood."*

3. Victor Hugo called Napoleon "the vast Colossus." Why did he pick this larger-than-life metaphor even when writing lines critical of Napoleon's legacy of tears and bloodshed?
[model answer] *Clearly Hugo saw Napoleon as a man who transformed his world and accomplished a great*

deal, even if his legacy was ultimately a tragic one. He had to be struck down from great heights before he could be humbled, and even then it took the efforts of kings (and perhaps heaven as well!) to destroy the Bonaparte.

Other Questions for Discussing These Documents in Class

An Ordinary Soldier on Campaign with Napoleon

1. What were the principle challenges of the advance described by Walter? How did the Russians make Napoleon's advance difficult?

2. Working from Walter's account, what was the state of morale in the French army as the advance continued? What were the consequences of all the difficulties they faced for the soldiers who survived them?

Wordsworth's Poetry

1. How many times does Wordsworth use the word "I"? Notice the degree to which the narrator focuses on his thoughts and feelings. What do these lines reveal about the appeal of early Romantic poetry?

2. Is there a sense of disillusionment in the poem? Given Wordsworth's life and "times," what world events might have contributed and how?

Contrasting Views: Napoleon: For and Against

1. Note what Napoleon considered his most notable achievements to have been. Do students agree? Which of his accomplishments seems most significant and why?

2. To what does Constant attribute Napoleon's success? What aspects of the revolution made his rise to power harder to resist? It is important to note Constant's sense of Napoleon as an anti-Enlightenment figure. To what Enlightenment values and virtues did Napoleon do violence? Do students agree that Napoleon was opposed to the traditions of the Enlightenment?

3. Do you get the sense that Hugo admires Napoleon? In what sense does he portray Napoleon as a remarkable or exceptional figure? What does he suggest his legacy was?

Comparative Questions

1. Consider what the documents reveal about the impact of Napoleon on nineteenth-century Europe. What aspects of his legacy do you find to be the most important? On the question of his legacy, how might an ordinary Napoleonic soldier answer Hugo, Constant, and Napoleon himself? How might a romantic poet such as Wordsworth answer it?

2. Given all of these documents, was Napoleon an Enlightenment figure, or does he represent a corruption or negation of "Enlightenment values"?

For Users of *Sources of The Making of the West*

The following documents are available in Chapter 20 of the companion sourcebook by Katharine J. Lualdi, University of Southern Maine.

1. Napoleon in Egypt: *The Chronicle of Abd al-Rahman al-Jabartî* (1798)
2. The Conservative Order: Prince Klemens von Metternich, *Results of the Congress at Laybach* (1821)
3. Challenge to Autocracy: Peter Kakhovsky, *The Decembrist Insurrection in Russia* (1825)
4. The Romantic Imagination: John Keats, *Letter to Benjamin Bailey* (1817)
5. Technology's Wrath: Mary Shelley, *Frankenstein* (1818)

Discussion Ideas for Sources of The Making of the West, *Chapter 20*

1. What aspects of the French regime trouble al-Jabartî most? Why does he mistrust Napoleon? Considering the French proclamation, to what set(s) of interest does it appeal? Who does it suggest would benefit from a French occupation? Does the document promote "nationalism" in Egypt? Enlightenment principles? Or is it, as al-Jabartî suggests, a "lie"?

2. What are the differences between Kakhovsky's understanding of revolution and Metternich's? Do they both claim to want the same things? How does Kakhovsy portray Metternich's congress system? Would Metternich agree?

3. Do you suppose Keats and Shelley would agree on the nature and value of human genius? Of boldness? To what extent do their writings here shed light on the relationship between madness and genius? Risk and reward in art and science? What do both writers have to say about the relationship between imagination and reality?

Working with Visual Sources

For this exercise, please refer to Napoleon's Coronation as Emperor on p. 625 of the textbook or view the image on the book companion site's Online Study Guide under the "Visual Activity" for Chapter 20.

Students viewing the image at the Online Study Guide are asked three questions about the image. The questions and model answers (not made available to students) are below. Project this image, available on the Instructor's Resources CD-ROM, in class or ask students to look at the image in their textbooks and answer the questions.

1. Is the scene depicted in *The Coronation of Napoleon and Josephine* one of grandeur and respectfulness, or one of disorganization and lawlessness? What in the picture leads you to describe it this way?
[model answer] *The scene depicted in* The Coronation of Napoleon and Josephine *is one of grandeur and respectfulness. The elegant and large room, the noblemen, the ladies-in-waiting, and the orderliness of the scene all suggest grandeur and solemn respect.*

2. In his diary and in the history of his reign, Napoleon argued that his rule was legitimate because it was based on popular sovereignty. Does this painting send the same message?
[model answer] *An upstart who seized power in a military coup, Napoleon was concerned with placing his rule on a continuum of the long tradition of French rulers. David's painting shows a crowd of people watching Napoleon's coronation, which could be taken as a statement regarding popular approval concerning this event. The painting shows a court scene, with richly dressed people and impressive surroundings, which give the impression that Napoleon's coronation was legitimate.*

3. Why did David choose to paint Napoleon crowning Josephine, instead of showing him crowning himself?
[model answer] *Napoleon's belief that he was the master of his destiny came across in his decision to crown himself, rather than have the pope crown him, as was traditional. Although some may have admired this act, others may have seen it as the action of an upstart with no respect for tradition or the church. It was much safer for David to depict Napoleon crowning his wife, especially because this action seemed consonant with beliefs concerning women's subordination to men that were codified in the Civil Code and widely accepted at the time.*

For this exercise, please refer to Seeing History: The Clothing Revolution: The Social Meaning of Changes in Postrevolutionary Fashion on p. 624 of the textbook or view the images on the book companion site's Online Study Guide under the "Visual Activity: Seeing History" for Chapter 20.

Students viewing the images at the Online Study Guide are asked two questions about the images. The questions and model answers (not made available to students) are below. Project these images, available on the Instructor's Resources CD-ROM, in class or ask students to look at the images in their textbooks and answer the questions.

1. Which style of dress is more "practical" and comfortable? Why? (Be sure to consider this from both the male and female points of view!)
[model answer] *Knee breeches, stockings, and buckled shoes shown in the first illustration would have been less comfortable and "practical" for men. By the 1830s, men were wearing long trousers, dressing more comfortably and practically. For women, dresses depicted in the images remained full and long, uncomfortable and impractical for moving around and working.*

2. In what ways do the fashions depicted here reflect changing political and social realities?
[model answer] *The dress in the earlier period, especially for men, reflected elaborate, sophisticated, aristocratic taste. As the events of the French Revolution and the Napoleonic period weakened the aristocracy and as the middle class became more important socially and politically, style of dress became more simplified, practical, and streamlined.*

Mapping Exercises

Map Activity from OSG—Model Answers for Map Activity #2

For this activity, please refer to Map 20.2: Europe after the Congress of Vienna, 1815, on p. 637. Students are asked these questions:

How was Europe in 1815 "restored," and in which ways was the Congress of Vienna not a restoration?
[model answer] *Wherever possible, the delegates at the Congress restored pre-Napoleonic monarchs to their thrones, such as the king of Spain. France had to surrender all the territories it had gained after 1790, but still kept its status as a major power to balance other European powers. However, not everything was returned to the way it was. The Austrian Netherlands and the Dutch Republic were united to form the kingdom of the Netherlands, the German states were made into a German Confederation, and the Grand Duchy of Warsaw became the kingdom of Poland with the Russian tsar as its ruler.*

Compare this map to Map 20.1: Napoleon's Empire at Its Height, 1812, on p. 628 of your textbook. Which territories did France lose as a result of the Congress of Vienna, and what became of the French satellite states?
[model answer] *France lost its territories in Savoy, central Italy, the Netherlands, and on the east coast of the Adriatic Sea as a result of the Congress of Vienna. Some of Napoleon's satellite states, such as Spain, returned to their pre-revolutionary rulers. The Grand Duchy of Warsaw was absorbed by Russia and Prussia. Some of the Confederation of the Rhine was given to the Austrian Empire, whereas the remainder became the*

German Confederation. Napoleon's satellite kingdoms in Italy were formed into a series of small kingdoms.

Map 20.1: Napoleon's Empire at Its Height, 1812, p. 628

Ask students to compare Napoleon's empire with previous empires they have studied. Focusing on the enemies of the French, particularly Portugal, Great Britain, and the Russian Empire, what problems does the map suggest Napoleon faced in 1812?

Map 20.2: Europe after the Congress of Vienna, 1815, p. 637

What changes have taken place in the extent of territories controlled by the Austrian Empire and Prussia? What are the possible repercussions of the transformation of the Holy Roman Empire into the Germanic Confederation? Did the new boundaries of the Russian Empire make any appreciable difference in its interactions with western Europe over following decades?

Map 20.3: Revolutionary Movements of the 1820s, p. 644

The map indicates that these revolutions occurred on the periphery of Europe. What else does it reveal about their nature? Were the disturbances urban or rural? Where were governments weaker or stronger?

Map 20.4: Latin American Independence, 1804–1830, p. 647; and Mapping the West: Europe in 1830, p. 650

Ask students to consider why revolutionary movements were almost completely successful in liberating the Latin American colonies, whereas in Europe these movements resulted in only one new state—Belgium, and one new government—in France.

In-Class Assignments and Presentation Topics

1. After discussing with students Napoleon's efforts to create a heroic image for himself, ask them to write a short essay comparing the creation of Napoleon's image with American techniques of political image-making. American politicians have immensely greater media resources, but can they do the kinds of things Napoleon did to enhance his image? What actions of Napoleon reveal his interest in "creating" an image?

2. Have students write a diary entry from a negotiator present at Vienna for one of the major or minor powers, planning the conservative settlement. What were the fears of those who sought to reestablish monarchy and state religions? Why were such leaders as successful as they were at re-establishing order? It might be profitable to revisit some of the themes of the Restoration period in Britain in considering the restored monarchies of the 1820s. How were things different a century and a half later? Students should reflect not only on the diplomatic and military considerations, but also on the difficulties of controlling the circulation of ideas and information after 1815. You may wish to assign some additional reading in either Gildea or Hobsbawm for this essay (see "Lecture Strategies," number 2), and have the students read "excerpts" from the work.

3. Assign a class presentation on conservatism. Those students involved in the presentation should first agree on a definition of conservatism (ask them to think about whether it is a single ideology or perhaps several closely related ideologies) and then select figures to present to the class. They must decide how to present these representative figures, and they should provide a short quotation for each that will help other students get a better sense of what that particular person believed.

4. Have each student find an example of romanticism that he or she can present to the class. Find out beforehand what each student plans to present because there may be some logistical problems to deal with. For example, one student may wish to play a polonaise by Chopin, which, of course, requires an instrument or tape/CD/MP3 player. Each student should find out as much as possible about his or her example and be prepared to answer questions.

Essay Questions

1. Ask students to investigate Napoleon's impact outside France. You will probably want to restrict the time frame to the period of Napoleon's greatest activity, 1800–1814, but exceptions may be made if students wish to trace Napoleon's influence during the nineteenth century. There are many possibilities in Europe itself, both in countries or areas closely associated with France, and in countries that were considered sovereignties. Outside Europe, students might investigate the failure of France to regain Haiti, the sale of the Louisiana Territory to the United States, the spread of the Napoleonic Code to other parts of the world, and various other topics. Use the bibliographic citations in "Discussion Strategies," number 1, to get started.

2. The Romantic poets did not live or write in a vacuum, and many of them were highly critical of the society in which they lived. Assign students to look at William Blake's "Holy Thursday," "The Chimney Sweeper," "Nurse's Song" in *Songs of Innocence* and compare them to their counterparts in *Songs of Experience*; or have students read Percy Bysshe Shelley's "Lines Written during the Castlereagh Administration," "Similes for Two Political Characters of 1819," "Song to the Men of England," "Sonnet: England 1819," "The Mask of Anarchy," "Ode to Liberty," "Sonnet: To the Republic of Benevento," and "Written on Hearing the News of the Death of Napoleon," all written between 1819 and 1821; or have students study William Wordsworth's "1801 (I Grieved for Buonaparté, with a vain" "London, 1802," "On the Extinction of the Venetian Republic," "The World Is Too Much With Us," and "Thought of a Briton on the Subjugation of Switzerland." The intertwined poetical and political career of Alphonse de Lamartine and Victor Hugo also offer insights into the era. How did these poets evolve politically over time? Did they stay true to Romantic ideals? To what degree does their poetry reflect their politics, and the wider political and social concerns of the era? See David V. Erdman, ed., *The Selected Poetry of Blake* (New York: Meridian, 1976; reprint, 1981); *The Complete Poetical Works of Percy Bysshe Shelley*, volume II (Blackmask Online, 2002); Jack Stillinger, ed., *Selected Poems and Prefaces by William Wordsworth* (Boston: Houghton Mifflin, Riverside Editions, 1965). Translations of some of Lamartine's and Hugo's works and biographical sketches can be found in A. M. Blackmore's *Six Nineteenth-Century French Poets* (Oxford: Oxford University Press, 2000).

Additional Resources: Literature

Ferber, Michael, ed., *European Romantic Poetry*. 2005.

Garnett, Constance, trans., *Tolstoy: War and Peace*. 1994.

Gill, Stephen, ed., *Wordsworth: The Major Works*. 2000.

Goldberger, Avriel H., trans., *Madame de Staël: Corinne, or Italy*. 1987.

Hugo, Howard E., ed., *The Romantic Reader*. 1957.

Kaufmann, Walter, trans., *Goethe: Faust*. 1962.

Marchand, Leslie A., ed., *Selected Poetry of Lord Byron*. 2002.

Penman, Bruce, trans., *Manzoni: The Betrothed*. 1984.

Shelley, Mary, *Frankenstein, or the Modern Prometheus*. 1818.

Walter Scott, *Ivanhoe*. 1791.

Waterfield, Robin, trans., *Alexandre Dumas: The Count of Monte Cristo*. 1996.

Additional Resources: Film and Video

War and Peace (1968; VHS/DVD, 6 hrs., 50 min.). This version of Tolstoy's novel (published 1863–1869), set in Russia during the Napoleonic Wars, is considered to be the most faithful of the versions made. Five years in the making, it is a lavish production and an interesting perspective on the wars.

The Count of Monte Cristo (1998; VHS/DVD, approx. 8 hrs.). Gerard Depardieu stars in this dramatization of Alexandre Dumas's 1844–1845 novel set between the years 1813 and 1838. Care has been lavished on the costumes and sets, and the details of everyday life during the period have been reasonably captured.

Napoleon, the Myths, the Battles, the Legend (2001; VHS/DVD, approx. 3 hrs.). This biographical portrait of Napoleon includes letters, diary extracts, and dramatic re-creations of important events in his life.

PBS Empires Series: Napoleon (2000; VHS/DVD, 4 hrs., 16 min.). This is a thorough PBS documentary on Napoleon.

Napoleon (2003; VHS/DVD, 9 hrs., 20 min.). This lavish series dramatizes the main events of Napoleon's life.

The Emperor's New Clothes (2001; VHS/DVD, 108 min). In a lighter vein, but still an excellent period piece, particularly on questions of Napoleon's legacy and lingering popularity, this piece of "what-if" history proposes a hypothetical second return to France by the exiled emperor.

Sharpe's Rifles (1990s; VHS/DVD). Bernard Cornwall's novels about the adventures of Richard Sharpe, an English soldier during the Napoleonic Wars, are chronicled in fourteen made-for-television movies, each lasting approximately 100 minutes each. The films are excellent for their attention to detail in costuming and setting, and for weaving an ordinary soldier's experience of the Napoleonic Wars into the narrative.

Horatio Hornblower (1990s, 2000s; VHS/DVD). C. S. Forester's novels about a young seaman's experiences as he works his way up the ranks during the Napoleonic Wars are dramatized in a series of television movies, each lasting approximately 100 minutes. Excellent on such details as costuming and setting, the plots are infused with historical detail about life in the English navy.

Films of Jane Austen's Novels

All of Jane Austen's (1775–1817) novels have been dramatized, some of them several times over. Like her novels, these films concentrate on the lives led by

Englishwomen from gentry families and the contemporary issues of inheritance, marriage, manners, and social conventions that so affected their lives. In the following list (arranged chronologically by date of publication), the date that immediately follows the title refers to the date of its first print publication.

Sense and Sensibility (1811). (1995; VHS/DVD, 136 min.)
Pride and Prejudice (1813). (1995; VHS/DVD, approx. 5 hrs.)
Mansfield Park (1814). (1999; VHS/DVD, 107 min.)
Emma (1816). (1997; VHS/DVD, 105 min.)
Northanger Abbey (1818). (1986; VHS/DVD, 90 min.)
Persuasion (1818). (1995; VHS/DVD, 104 min.)

OTHER BEDFORD/ST. MARTIN'S RESOURCES FOR CHAPTER 20

The following resources are available to accompany Chapter 20. Please refer to the Preface of this manual for detailed descriptions of all the ancillaries.

For Instructors

Transparencies

The following maps and image from Chapter 20 are available as full-color acetates.

- Map 20.1: Napoleon's Empire at Its Height, 1812
- Map 20.2: Europe after the Congress of Vienna, 1815
- Map 20.3: Revolutionary Movements of the 1820s
- Map 20.4: Latin American Independence, 1804–1830
- Mapping the West: Europe in 1830
- Napoleon's Coronation as Emperor, p. 625

Instructor's Resources CD-ROM

The following maps and image from Chapter 20, as well as a chapter outline, are available on disc in both PowerPoint and jpeg formats.

- Map 20.1: Napoleon's Empire at Its Height, 1812
- Map 20.2: Europe after the Congress of Vienna, 1815
- Map 20.3: Revolutionary Movements of the 1820s
- Map 20.4: Latin American Independence, 1804–1830
- Mapping the West: Europe in 1830
- Napoleon's Coronation as Emperor, p. 625

Using the Bedford Series with The Making of the West

Available in print as well as online at **bedfordstmartins.com/usingseries,** this guide offers practical suggestions for using *The French Revolution and Human Rights: A Brief Documentary History*, translated, edited, and with an Introduction by Lynn Hunt, and *Slave Revolution in the Caribbean, 1789-1804,* by Laurent Dubois and John D. Garrigus, in conjunction with chapters 19 and 20 of the textbook, *Crosscurrents in the Black Atlantic, 1770-1965,* by David Northrup, in conjunction with chapters 17 and 20 of the textbook, and *Napoleon: Symbol for an Age*, by Rafe Blaufarb, and *European Romanticism*, by Warren Breckman, in conjunction with chapter 20 of the textbook.

For Students

Study Guides

The Online Study Guide at **bedfordstmartins.com/hunt** helps students synthesize the material they have learned as well as practice the skills historians use to make sense of the past. The following Map, Visual, and Document activities are available for Chapter 20.

Map Activity

- Map 20.2: Europe after the Congress of Vienna, 1815, p. 637

Visual Activity

- Napoleon's Coronation as Emperor, p. 625
- Gentleman Proposing to Lady, 1778, p. 624
- Fashion for Men and Women, 1830, p. 624

Reading Historical Documents

- An Ordinary Soldier on Campaign with Napoleon, p. 633
- Wordsworth's Poetry, p. 642
- Contrasting Views: Napoleon: For and Against, pp. 634–635

CHAPTER

21

Industrialization and Social Ferment

1830–1850

Chapter Resources

Main Chapter Topics

1. The Industrial Revolution began in Great Britain in the 1770s and 1780s in textile manufacturing.

2. Population growth in Britain had increased demand for textiles. Available capital, labor, and a ready supply of cotton provided necessary resources. Opportunities for social mobility and scientific education as well as overall political stability encouraged technological advances.

3. In the 1830s and 1840s, after witnessing Great Britain's success with industrialization, and building on recent expansion of domestic forms of manufacture, European states encouraged the construction of railroads and the mechanization of manufacturing. At the same time, and due in large part to industrialization, urban growth accelerated and soon created a host of problems, some of which were unprecedented.

4. In response to new social problems, including child labor, overcrowding, inadequate sanitation, an inadequate water supply, and the consequent diseases and epidemics, some governments—particularly the British —undertook massive studies, passed ameliorative laws, and began public works. Europeans began to organize reform movements designed to alter the ways in which the lower classes lived and to target alcoholism, prostitution, and illiteracy. Similar movements attempted to deal with slavery, which was made illegal in the British and French empires. Depictions of social problems in art and literature provided an important impetus for reform.

5. Nationalism looked past the problems associated with industrialization and urbanization and toward political autonomy and self-determination for groups identified by common languages and cultures. It also sought state boundaries that reflected these group identifications.

6. Liberal reformers supported Enlightenment principles and argued in favor of limited constitutional governments, free marketplaces, and government policies that favored education and other social improvements. Liberal reform movements were strongest in Britain and urban, industrial areas of Europe.

7. All socialists in the 1830s and 1840s considered liberalism an inadequate response to the problems caused by industrialization and emphasized the importance of organizing the working classes and restructuring society. Communists called for the abolition of private property and for the institution of communal ownership.

8. During the revolutions of 1848, a series of demonstrations and uprisings toppled governments in France, Italy, Germany, and Austria, affording liberals, socialists, and nationalists opportunities to put their ideas into practice. Their inability to mutually work with one another created openings through which their rulers and armies were able to retake power.

9. The revolutions of 1848 failed and conservative governments returned, but the ideals and goals behind these revolutions were neither discredited nor eradicated. Moreover, Britain saw its slow liberalization justified; many of the German states gained constitutions; France recognized the impossibility of government without popular approval; and revolutionaries learned the importance of planning beyond the overthrow of the government in power.

Focus Question

How did the Industrial Revolution create new social and political conflicts?

1. The Industrial Revolution and its accompanying urbanization disrupted existing class structures. Urban factory workers, although representing only a small percentage of the working population, were

concentrated and organized, and contributed greatly to the creation of a more unified and politically influential working-class culture. Certainly there were growing divisions and tensions between the urban working class and the commercial and industrial managers and factory owners who comprised the middle class and the urban elite. Environmental, demographic, and economic changes associated with the Industrial Revolution also contributed to conflicts. Urban and factory living and working conditions, including long work days; strict systems of factory rules and regulations; pollution; and poor sanitation, housing, and water supplies made city life difficult and fueled working-class discontent. These conditions also served to alienate the urban, working poor from rural laborers in many ways, and divisions between peasants and urban workers featured prominently in events such as the June Days in France's 1848 revolution.

2. Meanwhile, liberal reformers bent on a range of social changes, but also supportive of the Industrial Revolution, became increasingly influential in places like England, where successful Parliamentary reform and anti-corn-law movements demonstrated the power of the rising middle class. While middle-class, often religiously inspired, reform movements thrived, they often portrayed working-class life as fundamentally degraded and corrupt. More radical political ideologies such as socialism and communism attracted a great deal of working-class support, and a real fear of revolution grew among all classes.

Annotated Chapter Outline

I. The Industrial Revolution

A. Roots of Industrialization, pp. 654–656

1. A key breakthrough in the Industrial Revolution occurred in 1776 when James Watt adapted existing steam engines to make them more efficient.
2. Combined with John Kay's flying shuttle developed in the 1730s and the spinning jenny and water frame of the 1760s, new power machinery was assembled in factories that replaced skilled weavers with semiskilled men, women, and children.
3. Factors contributing to early industrialization in England included a rapidly growing population, available capital, and access to cotton, coal, and iron. Opportunity for social mobility and access to scientific education, as well as a plentiful supply of labor, also contributed.
4. The spread of domestic manufacture throughout Europe grew dramatically in the eighteenth century.
5. Workers in the industrial and domestic textile production industry enjoyed few protections from frequent marketplace fluctuations. Weavers sometimes resisted the introduction of technology with violence.

B. Engines of Change, pp. 656–661

1. George Stephenson developed a steam engine powerful enough to pull train cars in the 1820s, leading to railroads as an effective means of transportation.
2. In the 1830s and 1840s, industrialization began to spread throughout continental Europe, as major countries built railroad systems.
3. Railroad construction and investment grew rapidly in the 1840s, particularly in Britain and the United States.
4. Governments and private investors backed railroads, as states realized that railroad construction with its demand for iron and coal pushed further industrial development.
5. Steam-powered engines made Britain the world leader in manufacturing. Other powers such as Germany tried to keep up.
6. Industrialization by British engineers and exported machinery spread slowly from key areas. By 1850, continental Europe still lagged some twenty years behind British industrial development. Eastern Europe was further behind due largely to the survival of serfdom.
7. Although they attracted much attention, factory workers were a small minority, even in England.
8. Many peasants continued to alternate seasonally between manufacturing and agriculture. Workers also continued putting-out work.
9. Cotton cloth became England's major export, and British cotton cloth exports destroyed native cloth production industry in India.
10. Industrial workers came from rural areas as an increasing birthrate in Britain fed workers into the factory system. Family wages and a grueling twelve- to seventeen-hour workday were typical.
11. As urban factories grew, workers came to constitute a new socioeconomic class holding common interests.
12. This new working class organized societies for mutual aid and political reform, from which would come the first labor unions.

13. Factories drew criticism for the pollution they created and for the pitiful working conditions.
14. As industrialism and its consequences grew, local and national governments collected information about workers' health, their living conditions, and their families.
15. Government inquiries often focused on women and children and, in Great Britain, inquiries led to the Factory Act of 1833, which outlawed the employment of children under age nine in textile mills and limited the hours of children under age eighteen, and the 1842 Mines Act, which prohibited the employment of women and girls underground. In 1847 Parliament limited the workday of women and children to ten hours.
16. The continental countries eventually followed the British lead, but most did not insist on inspection, so enforcement was therefore lax.

C. Urbanization and Its Consequences, pp. 661–663

1. Industrialization was linked with rapid urban growth.
2. Great Britain was the leader in this case also: by 1850, half the population of England and Wales lived in towns.
3. Urban populations soared all over Europe because of massive rural out-migration.
4. Agricultural improvements had increased the food supply and therefore the rural population, reducing opportunities for employment. Factories and urban life attracted the rural poor.
5. As the cities grew, they dismantled their medieval walls and incorporated parks, zoos, cemeteries, and greenways.
6. Housing expanded more slowly than urban population, and severe overcrowding fostered disease.
7. Garbage and refuse littered the streets, smog and smoke obscured the atmosphere, and water was scarce and unclean due to human and animal waste.
8. Unsanitary conditions led to cholera. From 1830 to 1832, and again from 1847 to 1852, cholera epidemics killed hundreds of thousands. Tuberculosis killed even more.
9. Middle-class persons lived in more spacious and cleaner neighborhoods, but the nearby poor were a source of anxiety.
10. Middle-class reformers, pointing to the living conditions of the poor as a cause of moral degeneracy, collected statistics on illegitimacy and infanticide.
11. Reformers also addressed prostitution, alcoholism, and crime.
12. At the same time that they drew attention to public health issues, reformers unfortunately stereotyped workers as helpless and out of control.
13. Contemporary observers saw working-class anger as a growing threat.

D. Agricultural Perils and Prosperity, pp. 663–664

1. Burgeoning populations created rising demands for food and altered rural life.
2. Peasants and farmers planted fallow land, chopped down forests, and drained marshes, but population grew faster in the first half of the nineteenth century than food production.
3. Railroads and canals improved food distribution, but much of Europe remained isolated from markets and thus vulnerable to local famines.
4. Most still lived on the land, and the upper classes still dominated rural society, although businessmen and peasants were sometimes able to buy land.
5. In France, almost two million independent peasants tended their own small properties.
6. But in England, southern Italy, Prussia, and eastern Europe, large landowners expanded their estates.
7. The survival of independent peasant families was threatened as men often migrated seasonally to earn cash in factories while women stayed behind to tend the crops.
8. To avoid further subdivision of their land to potential heirs, peasants practiced rudimentary forms of birth control.
9. Unpropertied individuals in cities began marrying earlier.
10. Population pressure also caused people to emigrate from their homelands, often to the United States.
11. Between 1816 and 1850, five million Europeans left their home countries and traveled overseas.
12. In Europe, political power remained in the hands of traditional elites. The biggest property owners controlled political assemblies and often personally selected clergy and local officials.

13. The old rural order seemed most impregnable in Russia, where troops easily suppressed serf rebellions in 1831 and 1842.

II. **Reforming the Social Order**

A. **Cultural Responses to the Social Question, pp. 664–667**

1. The social question reflected concern about social changes arising from industrialization and urbanization—a concern that pervaded all forms of art and literature.
2. The dominant artistic movement of the time, Romanticism, tended to glorify nature and deplore industrial and urban growth.
3. The English poet Elizabeth Barrett Browning decried child labor, and architects used the Gothic style, reminiscent of the Middle Ages, to glorify the preindustrial world.
4. Although romantic painters glorified the landscape as a way of calling attention to the wonders of nature, some painted landscapes reflected the power of new technologies.
5. Attention to social problems reached its greatest audience via the novel thanks to increasing literacy, the spread of reading rooms and lending libraries, and serials published in newspapers and journals.
6. Unlike the novels of the eighteenth century, which focused on individual personalities, the great novels of the 1830s and 1840s tended to portray individuals in the context of social life.
7. French novelist Honoré de Balzac (1799–1850) cataloged the social types of French society, whereas English writer Charles Dickens (1812–1870) drew attention to the negative effects of industrialization and urbanization.
8. Novels by women (usually published under a male pseudonym) often revealed the bleaker side of women's situations.
9. In *Jane Eyre* (1847), Charlotte Brontë (1816–1855) explored the difficulties that unmarried middle-class women faced when trying to earn a living.
10. French novelist George Sand (Amandine-Aurore Lucie Dupin, 1804–1876) scandalized Europe with her love affairs, her masculine dress, her novels, and her socialist political activity.
11. Just as an audience for novels grew, so too did a public for cultural events.
12. Popular theaters drew large crowds of lower- and middle-class spectators.
13. Museums opened to the public and middle-class persons began to collect art.
14. In 1839, photography offered artists a new medium for expression.
15. Whether in painting or photography, visual images heightened the public's awareness of the effects of industrialization and urbanization.

B. **The Varieties of Social Reform, pp. 667–670**

1. Religious convictions inspired many reformers, as many clergy and religious groups tried to raise working-class peoples' low level of interest in religion.
2. In Great Britain, the Sunday school movement taught working-class children to read at a time when few could attend school.
3. Women assumed a prominent role in charitable works.
4. Catholic religious orders enrolled women to run schools, hospitals, leper colonies, insane asylums, and old-age homes.
5. Protestant women established Bible, missionary, and reform societies.
6. One of their chief concerns was prostitution.
7. Both Catholics and Protestants promoted temperance.
8. Temperance advocates viewed drunkenness as immoral and a threat to social order.
9. Social reformers stressed education for the poor and working classes.
10. British churches organized to promote education, and in 1833, the French government passed a law that required every town to maintain a primary school, pay a teacher, and provide free education to poor boys.
11. In France, girls' schools were optional, but hundreds of women taught at the primary level. Only one in thirty children went to school in France.
12. Prussia had 75 percent of its children in primary school by 1835.
13. By contrast, Russian tsar Nicholas I (r. 1825–1855) blamed the Decembrist Revolt on education, and thus excluded peasants from primary schools.
14. The elite sought to impose discipline and order on working people. In Great Britain,

the Society for the Prevention of Cruelty to Animals attempted to eliminate lower-class sports such as cockfighting and bearbaiting.

15. Governments often intervened when private charities failed to meet the needs of the poor.
16. In Britain, attempts to control the costs of public welfare included workhouses with unpleasant conditions, separating those receiving relief from other family members; this so-called "Starvation Act" of 1834 prompted protests from anti-poor-law societies.
17. Many women saw public charity work as an extension of their domestic role and moral influence. According to the ideals of domesticity, women were to devote their lives to home and family.
18. Many believed that men and women had to act according to distinct roles in order to ensure social order.
19. The notion of separate spheres for women and men left most women economically dependent, preventing them from pursuing higher education, careers, or politics.
20. Gender distinctions were most noticeable among elites.
21. Boys attended school while girls lived at home; men wore practical clothing while women dressed for decorative effect.
22. Lower-class women may have considered domesticity an ideal, however, because they had to work to support their families, staying at home was rarely a reality.

C. Abuses and Reforms Overseas, pp. 670–671

1. In the first half of the nineteenth century, colonialism became imperialism. Direct rule shifted to indirect rule by European nations, and focus shifted from the Caribbean to Asia and Africa and toward more indirect forms of economic exploitation.
2. One sign of the decline of colonialism was the decline of the slave trade.
3. British religious groups took the lead in establishing abolitionist organizations and pressuring Parliament for reforms. In 1807, the British withdrew from the slave trade, and abolished slavery in 1833, whereas the French government suppressed the clandestine slave trade in the 1830s, and abolished slavery in its colonies in 1848.
4. Brazil, Cuba, and the United States continued slavery, and the slave trade in those countries reached its peak in the early 1840s.
5. In 1830, France invaded Algeria, taking control by 1850.
6. France also took over Tahiti.
7. The British granted Canada greater self-determination in 1839, but annexed Singapore in 1819, and New Zealand in 1840.
8. In addition, the British extended their control over India via the East India Company and educated a native elite as colonial administrators.
9. The East India Company pushed opium trade with China, which the Chinese government attempted to keep out.
10. When the Chinese tried to expel British merchants for importing the drug, the British bombarded Chinese coastal cities and imposed the Treaty of Nanking in 1842, which forced the Chinese to open four more ports to Europeans, and to cede the British Hong Kong with the guarantee that British merchants could continue the opium trade.

III. Ideologies and Political Movements

A. The Spell of Nationalism, pp. 672–674

1. Nationalists insisted that all peoples derived their identity from nations defined by common language, cultural traditions, and sometimes religion, and wanted nations to coincide with state boundaries.
2. Nationalism made the Austrian Empire especially volatile because it comprised so many ethnic groups.
3. In opposition to Metternich's efforts to stifle nationalism in the Italian parts of the Austrian empire, Giuseppe Mazzini (1805–1872) founded Young Italy, a secret society dedicated to an Italian-led, European-wide revolution.
4. In 1834, the German states moved toward economic unification by creating, under Prussian leadership, a customs union, the *Zollverein*, to help Germans compete economically with the rest of Europe.
5. German nationalists desired political union as well, but the question of whether to include both Prussia and Austria was difficult to resolve.
6. After the failed revolt against the Russians in 1830, ten thousand Poles fled Poland, primarily to western Europe.

7. The poet Adam Mickiewicz (1798–1855) became a hero by portraying Polish exiles as martyrs and by forming a Polish Legion to fight for restoration of Poland, but conflicts among the nationalists prevented action until 1846.
8. Galicia's revolt against the Austrian Empire collapsed when peasants slaughtered not the Austrians but their Polish masters.
9. Russian nationalism defined itself as opposition to western ideas.
10. Slavophiles ("lovers of the Slavs") argued that only a return to non-westernized religious traditions and historical principles could protect the country against the corrosive effects of rationalization and materialism.
11. Irish nationalists developed strong organizations in the 1840s.
12. The Young Ireland movement, formed in 1842, aimed to recover history and preserve the Gaelic language.
13. Irish landowner and representative to Parliament Daniel O'Connell attracted huge crowds with his call to repeal the 1801 Act of Union, which had made Ireland part of Great Britain.
14. O'Connell was arrested and convicted of conspiracy, and thereafter, he withdrew from politics and was succeeded by more radical leaders.

B. Liberalism in Economics and Politics, pp. 674–675

1. Liberalism, with its origins in the writings of John Locke, favored Enlightenment principles of personal liberty and free trade. Liberalism sought social improvement and generally applauded the social and economic changes produced by the Industrial Revolution. Liberalism was strongest among the middle class.
2. Jeremy Bentham (1748–1832) argued that government was most useful when it promoted "the greatest good for the greatest number"—a clear rejection of policies that favored the aristocratic minority.
3. British liberals advocated free markets, arguing that governments should limit their economic role to maintaining the currency, enforcing contracts, and financing major enterprises like the military and the railroads.
4. Liberals sought to repeal tariffs such as the Corn Laws, which kept the price of grain artificially high to the benefit of landowners and the detriment of the poor.
5. When their efforts to lower grain tariffs were thwarted by landowners, liberals established an Anti-Corn Law League, which published newspapers and journals, campaigned in elections, and eventually won the support of the Tory prime minister Sir Robert Peel, whose government repealed the Corn Laws in 1846.
6. On the continent, liberals, craving more political control, gave priority to constitutional reform.
7. Fearing competition from Great Britain, they did not support international free trade, although they did seek to abolish internal tariffs.
8. In France and elsewhere, governments used repression and censorship to stifle the reformers.
9. Reform organizations emerged where industrialization was most developed, as industrialists called for greater political clout.
10. In Hungary, the nationalist Lajos Kossuth (1802–1894) publicized American democracy and British political liberalism, and advocated a boycott of all non-Hungarian (and especially Austrian) goods.
11. Despite state opposition, reformers emerged even in Russia, where they discussed western ideas in informal "circles."
12. Nicholas I banned all western liberal writings and all books about the United States and exiled tens of thousands of political activists to Siberia.

C. Socialism and the Early Labor Movement, pp. 675–678

1. Socialism had many variants in the 1830s and 1840s, but all socialists considered liberalism inadequate to deal with the class inequalities caused and perpetuated by industrialization.
2. Socialists believed that society was divided into two classes: the middle-class factory owners, or capitalists, and the downtrodden working class.
3. Socialists advocated the total reorganization of society rather than reforming it.
4. Socialist Robert Owen, a Welsh-born manufacturer, established a model factory town in New Lanark, Scotland, where working hours were curtailed, and

children were sent to school rather than the factory.

5. In France, Claude Henri de Saint-Simon (1760–1825) and Charles Fourier (1772–1837) were the most influential early socialist thinkers.
6. Saint-Simon believed that work was the central element in the new society and that it should be controlled by scientists, artists, engineers, and *industrialists* (a term he coined, along with "industrialism").
7. Fourier also advocated the creation of utopian communities in which jobs would be rotated to maximize happiness, and in which women would be emancipated.
8. Many Saint-Simonistes argued that the liberation of women would lead to the liberation of workers.
9. In Great Britain, many women joined Robert Owen's movement and helped to form cooperative societies and trade unions.
10. Women's influence turned Owenism toward community experimentation and to issues of religious thought, women's rights, marriage reform, and popular education.
11. French activist Flora Tristan (1801–1844) sought to reconcile the interests of male and female workers, but most socialist groups did not welcome women.
12. French socialists Louis Blanc (1811–1882) and Pierre-Joseph Proudhon (1809–1865) both argued for the importance of working-class associations; their arguments shaped the French labor movement.
13. After 1840, some socialists, such as Étienne Cabet (1788–1856), began to call themselves communists to indicate their plan to replace private property with communal ownership. French socialist ideas circulated throughout Europe, evoking a response in areas undergoing industrialization.
14. Karl Marx (1818–1883) and Friedrich Engels (1820–1895)—both sons of prosperous German-Jewish, middle-class families—developed a form of "scientific" socialism.
15. Marx established the Communist League and, with Engels, published *The Communist Manifesto* (1848).
16. Marx and Engels embraced industrialization, believing it would bring about the inevitable proletarian revolution and thus the abolition of exploitation, private property, and social class.
17. Socialist doctrines led to working-class organizations: cooperative societies, local trade unions, and societies for mutual aid.
18. Workers became more involved in politics as well.
19. In Great Britain, workers joined the Chartist movement, which called for universal manhood suffrage, vote by secret ballot, equal electoral districts, and the payment of stipends to members of Parliament.
20. Although many women took part in the movement, leaders feared that advocating women's suffrage would alienate potential supporters.
21. The Chartists organized massive petition campaigns in 1838 and 1839, presenting the House of Commons with the People's Charter (as their list of demands was called), signed by more than a million people.
22. Because the House of Commons repeatedly refused to act, Chartists allied themselves with working-class strike movements and distanced themselves from women workers.
23. The last wave of Chartist demonstrations came in 1848.
24. Trade unions and strikes were illegal on the continent, so workers there were less organized.

IV. The Revolutions of 1848

A. The Hungry Forties, pp. 678–679

1. Beginning in 1845, an airborne blight destroyed the potato crop, a staple of peasant diets, especially in Ireland.
2. During the following year, drought in southern Europe and excessive rain in northern Europe destroyed other crops.
3. Those farmers who did produce enough to sell sold their goods at inflated prices. Marginal cultivators and farm laborers starved, while urban workers, thrown out of work by a lack of demand for manufactured goods in rural areas, faced higher food prices. The population growth of the 1830s and 1840s exacerbated the food shortage.
4. In Ireland alone, as many as one-eighth of the population died horribly of starvation and disease.
5. Hundreds of thousands emigrated from Ireland to England, the United States, and Canada.

6. Across Europe, famine led village crowds to attack bakeries, markets, and officials to prevent rumored hoarding.
7. By 1848, when harvests improved, many in rural areas had lost their land or become hopelessly indebted.
8. In the cities, unemployment and higher costs of living rendered workers' lives even more difficult.

B. Another French Revolution, pp. 679–680

1. Everywhere, hunger gave rise to voices that were critical of the government.
2. On February 22, 1848, reform demonstrations began in Paris, and students, workers, and the unemployed began to build barricades. Fighting broke out between the crowds and soldiers, and on February 24, Louis-Philippe abdicated and fled to England.
3. The leaders of the new republic issued liberal reforms and established universal manhood suffrage.
4. To further appease the lower classes, Lamartine's government set up national workshops to provide construction work for minimal wages to unemployed men (later to women as well).
5. To pay for the workshops, not popular with the middle-class to begin with, the government levied a surtax on property taxes, alienating the peasants from the landowners.
6. Simultaneously, many supported the reforms and the workshops with enthusiasm; priests blessed liberty trees, while new newspapers praised the republic, and political clubs sought to give men and women an opportunity to debate political issues.
7. This outburst of activism alarmed middle-class liberals and conservatives, and prompted the government to enlist unemployed youths in a mobile guard.
8. Concern about demonstrations led by radicals resulted in the election of a largely conservative National Assembly in April 1848, which closed the national workshops.
9. In response to the closure of the workshops, workers took to the streets on June 23 by the tens of thousands.
10. During the June Days, as the following week came to be called, the army, the National Guard, and the mobile guard were joined by provincial volunteers to put down the uprising.
11. More than ten thousand demonstrators were killed and twelve thousand were arrested.
12. Later that year, Louis-Napoleon Bonaparte, nephew of the dead emperor, won the presidential election.
13. In 1852, he declared himself Emperor Napoleon III.

C. Nationalist Revolution in Italy, pp. 680–681

1. In January 1848, a revolt against the Bourbons broke out in Palermo, Sicily.
2. When news of the revolution in Paris arrived, mass demonstrations took place throughout the Italian peninsula.
3. Nationalists hoped to unite the diverse territories of Italy, but class divisions and regional differences barred the way; nationalists found themselves in conflict with the Bourbon rulers in the south, as well as the pope and the Austrian emperor.
4. In central Italy, peasants and artisans turned against local rulers, demanding land reform and higher wages.
5. Property owners and business leaders supported liberal reforms and a conservative government, while workers and intellectuals envisioned a social democracy.
6. Charles Albert, king of Piedmont-Sardinia, the most powerful Italian state, led a military campaign against Austria that failed largely because of disagreements over tactics and goals.
7. Austria defeated the rebels in the north during the summer of 1848.
8. In the fall, the Romans drove the pope from the city and declared a republic, but Louis-Napoleon Bonaparte intervened to restore Pius IX to the papal throne.
9. Republican leaders Mazzini and Garibaldi fled; the revolution was over in Italy.

D. Revolt and Reaction in Central Europe, pp. 681–684

1. As in Italy, news of the revolt in Paris touched off demonstrations in Austria, Prussia, and the many German states of central Europe.
2. In March, revolutions in the German states brought together different social groups demanding political liberalization.
3. After violence in Berlin, the Prussian king agreed to call an assembly to draft a constitution, but the goal of German unification soon took precedence over social and political reform among the rebels.

4. In March and April, most of the German states agreed to elect delegates to a federal parliament at Frankfurt that would attempt to unite Germany.
5. But the delegates had little political experience, no access to an army, and feared demands for social reforms made by the lower classes. Disturbances and attacks on property and Jewish money-lenders persisted.
6. The Prussian king Frederick William IV (r. 1840–1860) soon recovered his confidence and crushed the revolution in Berlin in the fall of 1848.
7. His troops intervened to put down revolts in other German states during the spring of 1849.
8. In Austria, Metternich was forced to flee the country in disguise after rioting in Vienna in March 1848. The empire seemed in a state of collapse in the summer of 1848.
9. In addition to the revolts in Italy, the Austrians faced Magyar nationalists who demanded autonomy for Hungary, and revolution for political reform in Vienna itself.
10. The beleaguered Austrians granted Hungary home rule, but the Magyars alienated other ethnic groups in Hungary who preferred the Austrians.
11. Social conflicts and ethnic divisions like these would doom the diverse nationalist revolutionaries within the Austrian Empire.
12. The Austrians took advantage of these divisions and abolished serfdom to put an end to peasant discontent.
13. The continued fragmentation of revolutionary groups enabled military forces, in June 1848, to begin a counteroffensive, crushing the revolt in Prague, then Vienna, and eventually Hungary, which was placed under martial law.
14. Eighteen-year-old Francis Joseph (r. 1848–1916) ascended to the throne as the new Habsburg ruler.
15. In conjunction with a large Russian army, the Hungarian revolution was finally defeated in the spring of 1849.

E. Aftermath to 1848, pp. 684–685

1. The revolutionaries of 1848 failed to achieve most of their goals, but the revolutions did have an impact on Europe.
2. After 1848, no French government, even Louis-Napoleon's empire, could rule without extensive popular consultation.
3. Likewise, after 1850, almost all the German states had a constitution and a parliament.
4. In Italy and Germany, calls for national unity had been given widespread publicity and came to be seen as a practical reality, not just an ideal.
5. Political awareness, organization, and activity increased.
6. No revolution occurred in Great Britain, despite massive demonstrations organized by the Chartists.
7. But the middle classes, encouraged by the 1832 Reform Bill, did not support revolution as they had in other countries; and working classes were satisfied by Parliamentary reforms that regulated women's and children's work.
8. Russia, where Nicholas I kept a tight grip on education and the expression of ideas, also escaped revolution.
9. Almost everywhere, the aristocracy remained the dominant power.
10. Women's participation in revolutionary activity led to a conservative reaction against women's public roles.
11. The feminist movement in France, the most advanced in Europe, disintegrated after the conservative Republican government forbade women to form political clubs and arrested feminist leaders.
12. The revolutions of 1848 brought to the fore the profound tensions within a European society moving toward industrialization and modernization, but revolution had done little to resolve these tensions.
13. Confronted with the threat of further revolts on the scale and scope of 1848, political leaders began to search for alternatives.

Lecture Strategies

1. The causes of the Industrial Revolution in Britain are worth exploring, not only because reviewing the various possible triggers and catalysts for this change helps students understand the culture and economy of the period and to think about cause and effect in history, but also because considering the various explanations allows exploration of important questions of historical

interpretation and debate and the evolution of historical argument.

Two classics in the debate are T. S. Ashton's *The Industrial Revolution*, recently reissued with a preface by Pat Hudson (Oxford: Oxford University Press, 1997) and Phyllis Deane, *The First Industrial Revolution* (Cambridge: Cambridge University Press, 1979). Some useful overviews of the rise of industrialism and overviews of this debate can be found in Eric Hobsbawm's revised *Industry and Empire: The Birth of the Industrial Revolution* (New York: New Press, 1999) and the revised version of Joel Mokyr's *The British Industrial Revolution: An Economic Assessment* (Boulder, CO: Westview Press, 1999).

2. It is important for students to understand both the forces of change and the forces of continuity in the 1830s and 1840s. A good way to do this is by carefully analyzing the spread of the Industrial Revolution to the continent. Although the British industrial economy was still well ahead of the economies of other European nations, by the 1851 exhibition at the Crystal Palace, France, Belgium, several of the German states, and the Austrian Empire had achieved some important advances. The fact that the Russian Empire does not belong on this list is worth noting. Comment on the differences between the continent and Great Britain, especially in connection with the roles of government, finance, and tariffs versus free trade.

Two particularly good starting points for this topic are Chapter 3 of David S. Landes, *The Unbound Prometheus: Technological Change and Industrial Development in Western Europe from 1750 to the Present* (Cambridge, MA: Harvard University Press, 1969); and chapters 8 to 10 of Rondo Cameron, *A Concise Economic History of the World: From Paleolithic Times to the Present* (New York: Oxford University Press, 1989) for a comprehensive chronological and global context for this discussion as well. Cameron also provides a quite useful bibliography. There are some valuable insights and provocative assertions in Jeff Horn's *The Path Not Taken: French Industrialization in the Age of Revolution 1750–1830* (Boston: MIT Press, 2006). Peter N. Stearns and John H. Hinshaw, *The ABC-Clio World History Companion to the Industrial Revolution* (Santa Barbara, CA: ABC-Clio, 1996); and an overview by Peter N. Stearns, recently revised and reprinted a third time, *The Industrial Revolution in World History* (Boulder, CO: Westview Press, 2007) are likewise fine sources to consult. See also Mikulas Teich and Roy Porter, eds., *The Industrial Revolution in National Context* (Cambridge: Cambridge University Press, 1996) and the absorbing and original book by Wolfgang Schivelbush, *The Railway Journey: Trains and Travel in the Nineteenth Century* (New York: Urizen Books, 1979).

3. As the factory system and the mechanization of production spread to countries outside Great Britain, the composition of the working classes changed in important ways. The factory worker, or proletariat, became an increasingly large part of the workforce, but was not yet an important political force. Generally speaking, factory workers in the early industrial period were neither well organized nor politically radical. The more important changes took place among the artisans and craftspersons, many of whom found competition from machine-made goods devastating to their trade. It is important to convey to students the many different paths working-class lives might have taken during this period. Those who possessed the skills needed by industrial capitalists made up a new labor aristocracy. Others—unskilled or semiskilled—endured cyclical unemployment and the problems of illness or injury. Those who had been skilled artisans often fought a losing battle against changes in the economy. The cyclical nature of industrial employment and the business cycle, however, left all urban workers of this period vulnerable.

A good place to begin a presentation of the changing circumstances of the working classes is Peter N. Stearns and Herrick Chapman, *European Society in Upheaval: Social History Since 1750*, 3rd ed. (New York: Macmillan, 1992). The bibliography is extensive and helpful. See also John R. Gillis, *The Development of European Society, 1770–1870* (Boston: Houghton Mifflin, 1977), which takes a more topical approach. E. P. Thompson's wonderful book, *The Making of the English Working Class* (New York: Pantheon Books, 1963), offers a wealth of information for those with the time to make their way through it. William H. Sewell, Jr., *Work and Revolution in France: The Language of Labor from the Old Regime to 1848* (Cambridge: Cambridge University Press, 1980), describes the extent to which working-class socialism in the nineteenth century derived from the guild structure of the eighteenth. John M. Merriman, ed., *Consciousness and Class Experience in Nineteenth-Century Europe* (New York: Holmes & Meier, 1979), deals with the situation of the artisan. See also Gareth Stedman Jones, *Languages of Class: Studies in English Working-Class History, 1832–1982* (Cambridge: Cambridge University Press, 1983), a series of essays that looks at the development of class consciousness.

There is less material available on social conditions and living standards. One useful book is Katherine Lynch, *Family, Class, and Ideology in Early Industrial France: Social Policy and the Working-Class Family, 1815–1848* (Madison: University of Wisconsin Press, 1988). Another is Colin Heywood, *Childhood in Nineteenth-Century France: Work, Health, and Education among the "Classes Populaires"* (Cambridge: Cambridge University Press, 1988). For Britain, Kenneth Morgan's *The Birth of Industrial Britain, 1750–1850* (New York: Longman, 2004) offers a brief but thorough review of the social consequences of industrialization for the working class in particular. A useful overview is Louise Tilly and Joan W. Scott, *Women, Work, and Family* (New York: Holt, Rinehart & Winston, 1978). See also Enid Gauldie, *Cruel Habitations, A History of Working-Class Housing, 1790–1918* (New York: Barnes & Noble, 1974). One fine source that makes clear the desperate plight of many artisans by midcentury is Eileen Yeo and E. P. Thompson, eds., *The Unknown Mayhew* (New York: Schocken Books, 1972), a selection from the eighty-two letters Henry Mayhew published in the *Morning Chronicle* (1849–1850). John Burnett, ed., *Useful Toil* (New York: Routledge, 1994) offers a collection of working-class autobiographical material, which provides a very valuable collection of firsthand accounts from admittedly exceptional members of the much-condescended-to working poor of the nineteenth century.

4. Karl Marx came of age during this period, and a review of his life to age thirty (that is, 1848) is an excellent way to give students a sense of the focused discussion in this period. (Charles Darwin or Alexander Herzen could also be discussed for much the same purpose.) Marx was thoroughly familiar with the German idealist philosophers of the period, a student of the French Revolution at a time when the first great histories of that event were being written and published, and deeply interested in the Industrial Revolution and the development of capitalism. Like so many of his contemporaries, Marx was not only busy making sense of the present, he was also at work on his own grand theory of history that was meant to point the way to the future.

A recent, highly readable biography of Marx is Francis Wheen, *Karl Marx: A Life* (New York: W. W. Norton, 2000). Wheen is good on biographical information but not always very dependable in his discussion of Marx's ideas. Isaiah Berlin, *Karl Marx: His Life and Environment*, 3rd ed. (New York: Oxford University Press, 1963), is a good short study. David McLellan, *Karl Marx: His Life and Thought* (New York: Harper & Row, 1973), is probably the best book overall, but it is long. Jerrold Seigel, *Marx's Fate: The Shape of a Life* (University Park, PA: Pennsylvania State University Press, 1993), is a difficult but rewarding biographical study. The best anthology of Marx's writings (and Friedrich Engels's as well) is Robert C. Tucker, *The Marx-Engels Reader*, 2nd ed. (New York: W. W. Norton, 1978). Also useful is Eugene Kamenka, *The Portable Karl Marx* (New York: Penguin Books, 1983). Helpful editions of *The Communist Manifesto* are John E. Toews, ed., *The Communist Manifesto by Karl Marx and Frederick Engels with Related Documents* (Boston: Bedford/St. Martin's, 1999); and Frederic L. Bender, *The Communist Manifesto* (New York: W. W. Norton, 1988). The supplemental primary materials in the Bedford edition can give students a good sense of the context of this work. For a critical evaluation of Marx, see Paul Johnson, *Intellectuals* (New York: Harper & Row, 1989). For Engels in this period, see Steven Marcus, *Engels, Manchester, and the Working Class* (New York: Vintage Press, 1974).

5. Rather than attempting to cover all the revolutions, it might be better to take a closer look at the revolutions of 1848 by concentrating on one or two that deal with important issues. The revolution of 1848 in France not only refers back to the French Revolution and Napoleon, it also introduces the importance of the social issue in that France is the one location where that issue is not obscured by national aspirations. The German insurrections of 1848 call up the crucial issue of German nationalism. The "German question"—that is, who will control the German states and to what purpose—is placed on the agenda and will remain there for the next century and a half.

In addition to the excellent books cited in the chapter bibliography, see also Peter N. Stearns, *1848: The Revolutionary Tide in Europe* (New York: W. W. Norton, 1974); and the recent collection edited by Robert Evans and Hartmut Pogge von Strandmann, *The Revolutions in Europe, 1848–49* (Oxford: Oxford University Press, 2000). On France, see Maurice Agulhon, *The Republican Experiment, 1848–1852* (Cambridge: Cambridge University Press, 1983); John M. Merriman, *The Agony of the Republic: The Repression of the Left in Revolutionary France, 1848–1851* (New Haven, CT: Yale University Press, 1978); and Mark Traugott, *Armies of the Poor: Determinants of Working-Class Participation in the Parisian Insurrection of June 1848* (Princeton, NJ: Princeton University Press, 1985). For Germany, see Wolfram Siemann, *The German Revolution of 1848–1849* (New York: St. Martin's Press, 1998); and Jonathan Sperber, *Rhineland Radicals: The Democratic Movement and the Revolution of 1848–1849* (Princeton, NJ: Princeton University Press, 1991).

Class Discussion Starters

1. The appearance and development of nationalist movements is a major feature of this period. Poles, Greeks, Italians, Germans, Czechs, and other groups actively founded nations or attempted to found nations. Perhaps the most important theme unifying these movements is a blending of the romantic ideas about the past with nationalist ideas about the future. Another important theme is the strain and tension multinational empires experienced during this period. It is vital that students understand the emotional appeal of nationalist ideology, and the attractions that nationalism had to activists across class boundaries as

a potentially unifying ideology that emphasized cross-class unity. Of course, nationalism's attempts to construct an in-group, many have argued, inevitably led to greater tensions between states, and within states as minority groups were excluded from the all-important "we" that nationalists sought to establish.

One very effective way of exploring these dynamics is to distribute to the students nationalist propaganda of the period. As a mass movement, nationalism sought to convince people of their membership in a national community with particular characteristics. Poetry and anthems from a variety of national perspectives are widely available on the Web and elsewhere, as are extracts from editorials and nationalistic speeches. The Irish poetry of Tom Davis, speeches from Mazzini, and poetry and propaganda from the likes of Kossuth can be distributed and read aloud or analyzed in groups by students. Common rhetorical characteristics and aspects of identity that are emphasized by particular nationalists are well worth discussing. To what extent do the authors appeal to reason? Shared religion and language? Culture? Racial identity? History?

For general background reading on nationalism, Chapter 7 of Eric J. Hobsbawm's *The Age of Revolution, 1789–1848* is useful. See also Eric J. Hobsbawm, *Nations and Nationalism Since 1780: Programme, Myth, Reality* (New York: Cambridge University Press, 1990). The latest edition of Benedict Anderson's classic *Imagined Communities* (London: Verso, 2006) offers a fruitful starting point for thinking about nationalism as an exercise in collective conceptualization. Alan Sked, *The Decline and Fall of the Habsburg Empire, 1815–1918* (London: Longman, 1989), provides a dependable survey of the situation in central Europe. More specialized sources include George Barany, *Stephen Széchenyi and the Awakening of Hungarian Nationalism, 1791–1841* (Princeton, NJ: Princeton University Press, 1968); and Joseph Zacek, *Palacky: The Historian As Scholar and Nationalist* (The Hague: Mouton, 1970). On the Greek revolt, see Douglas Dakin, *The Greek Struggle for Independence, 1821–1833* (Berkeley: University of California Press, 1973); and Richard Clogg, ed., *The Struggle for Greek Independence* (Hamden, CT: Archon Books, 1973). For Italy, an excellent source is Denis Mack Smith, *Mazzini* (New Haven, CT: Yale University Press, 1994). For Germany, see Chapters 7 and 10 of James J. Sheehan, *German History, 1770–1866* (Oxford: Clarendon Press, 1989); and Chapter 2 of David Blackbourn, *The Long Nineteenth Century: A History of Germany, 1780–1918* (New York: Oxford University Press, 1998). D. George Boyce's *Nationalism in Ireland* (New York: Routledge, 1995) remains the classic text on Irish nationalism, but the Young Ireland movement of the 1840s offers a particularly vivid example of romantic, journalistic, poetic, and eventually revolutionary nationalism at work. See Richard Davis's *The Young Ireland Movement* (Totowa, NJ: Rowman and Littlefield, 1987) and Helen Mulvey, *Tom Davis and Ireland* (Washington: Catholic University Press, 2003).

2. In the summer of 1858, the odor emitting from the Thames River, which flowed with raw sewage, was so overwhelming that sheets soaked in disinfectant were hung over the windows of Parliament. In the following year, the situation even worsened, and Parliament was actually forced to adjourn for the summer. The problems of sanitation in London were longstanding, and measures were undertaken to improve it after major cholera epidemics killed thousands in the city in 1832 and 1849. A discussion can begin with the work of Sir Edwin Chadwick, author of the report of a parliamentary commission, *The Sanitary Condition of the Laboring Population of Britain, 1842*, which marks the beginnings of comprehensive waste-management systems in Europe. Many published histories of the "water closet" are available should a discussion lead in that direction.

3. Most women did not manage to improve their situation to any great degree during this period. Thomas Mann's novel *Buddenbrooks*, about a German merchant family, features Antonie (Tony) Buddenbrooks whose two disastrous marriages weaken the family fortunes. Yet Tony is the one who cares most about the family, its place in society, and its reputation. The only way for most women to maintain or improve their living situations was through marriages that were regarded as "successful," which more often than not meant they brought money into the family. Notwithstanding, changes in the period are worth discussing. In 1848, for example, Elizabeth Cady Stanton and Susan B. Anthony met with other women at Seneca Falls, New York, and passed the Declaration of Sentiments, which demanded equality with men, the right to vote, and full participation in civic life. Students should find it interesting to discuss the polarity of the growing cult of domesticity at one end of the spectrum of opinion, and the simultaneous efforts of a few women to open new doors on the other.

A useful point of departure is Louise Tilly, "Industrialization and Gender Inequality," in the American Historical Association's series *Essays on Global and Comparative History* (Washington, DC: American Historical Association, 1993). Tilly discusses the impact of socioeconomic changes on gender inequality through a comparison of Britain, China, France, Germany, Japan, and the United States. See also the books by Tilly and Scott, and by Stearns and Chapman, both cited previously in Lecture Strategies, number 3. Chapters 4 and 5 in Bonnie G. Smith, *Changing Lives: Women in European History Since 1700* (Lexington, MA: D. C. Heath, 1989) provide a good introduction to women and work and the cult of domesticity. Bonnie S. Anderson and Judith P. Zinsser, *A History of Their Own: Women in Europe from Prehistory to the Present*, vol. 2 (New York: Harper & Row, 1988), is organized topically. Parts 7 and 8 have much to offer, including an extensive bibliography. Books on women in the working class or the peasantry include Deborah Valenze's *The First Industrial Women* (Oxford: Oxford University Press, 1995) as well as Angela V. John, *Unequal Opportunities: Women's Employment in England 1800–1918* (New York: Blackwell, 1986); and Martine Segalen, *Love and Power in the Peasant Family: Rural France in the Nineteenth Century* (Chicago: University of Chicago Press, 1983). Other books take a national approach to this topic. Among them are Ute Frevert, *Women in German History: From Bourgeois Emancipation to Sexual Liberation* (New York: Berg, 1988); and Catherine M. Prelinger, *Charity, Challenge, and Change: Religious Dimensions of the Mid-Nineteenth Century Women's Movement in Germany* (New York: Greenwood Press, 1987). See also Martha Vicinus, ed., *Suffer and Be Still: Women in the Victorian Age* (Bloomington: Indiana University Press, 1973); Martha Vicinus, ed., *A Widening Sphere: Changing Roles of Victorian Women* (Bloomington: Indiana University Press, 1977); and David Ransel, ed., *The Family in Imperial Russia* (Urbana: University of Illinois Press, 1976). Several other important works are cited in the chapter.

Reviewing the Text

Review Questions

1. What dangers did the Industrial Revolution pose to both urban and rural life?
[model answer] • ***Factories and the jobs they provided contributed to the urban population surge:*** *The rising birthrate fed workers into the new factory system, and the new urban workers worked closely together and developed a common culture and a common set of interests.*
• ***Cities attracted massive rural emigration and absorbed settlements that sprang up and expanded outside the city limits:*** *Overcrowding and disease due to poor sanitation were serious problems and reduced urban life expectancy. Cholera was a particular problem and killed hundreds of thousands.*
• ***Class tensions and rising levels of social disorder caused widespread concern, particularly among the middle class:*** *Middle-class proximity to urban poverty led to widespread concerns about overcrowding, rising illegitimacy rates, prostitution, and drinking.*
• ***In the countryside, rising agriculture production struggled to keep up with population increase:*** *Cultivation was expanded, and land speculation increased the number of landholders.*
• ***Small farmers struggled as subdivision became more common:*** *Emigration to colonies and the Americas as well as seasonal migration became increasingly common.*
• ***The social order and the power of rural aristocratic elites persisted:*** *Social and economic elites in rural areas controlled local political assemblies and institutions, and class tensions were present in rural areas as well.*

2. How did reformers try to address the social problems created by industrialization and urbanization? In which areas did they succeed, and in which did they fail?
[model answer] • ***Concern about social problems and efforts to alleviate them were widespread:*** *Government reports, art, and novels contributed to these concerns about the "social question." Moral reform societies, Sunday schools, temperance societies, and other organizations, often led by women, aimed to make the poor "respectable."*
• ***Religiously inspired reformers struggled to improve the habits of the poor and to overcome growing working-class indifference toward religion:*** *The Sunday school movement taught many working-class children how to read, while women's religious orders and temperance and bible societies proliferated.*
• ***Education was a particular focus of reforming energy:*** *Government-sponsored education became increasingly common, but few children went to school.*
• ***The ideal of female domesticity was emphasized, although many women were forced by economic circumstances to become domestic servants and factory workers:*** *Idealized domestic roles for women were particularly influential among the upper and middle classes. Many scientists considered women to be mentally inferior to men, and female education was less formal and more centered on domestic concerns.*
• ***The anti-slavery movement spread throughout the west, and succeeded in abolishing or restricting slavery and the slave trade:*** *The anti-slavery movement mobilized millions of people in support of its goals and applied pressure to the political system to force reform.*

3. Why did ideologies have such a powerful appeal in the 1830s and 1840s?
[model answer] • ***People gathered around ideologies to find solutions to questions developing about society, political theory, and change:*** *Events of the 1790s produced enormous differences of opinion about what constituted the ideal government, while the industrial revolution led to questions about how much the new social order differed from the old, and whether governments should moderate or accelerate the pace of change. Ideologies offered frameworks for understanding change and ordering social relations between classes.*
• ***Each ideology appealed to a specific class:*** *Conservatism appealed to established elites, monarchs, and aristocrats because it explained recent revolutions as a logical progression of events, and advocated faith,*

sentiment, history, and tradition as the basis for society rather than Enlightenment theories. Liberalism emphasized constitutionalism and free trade, appealing to middle-class manufacturers, merchants, and professionals. Though spread by literate authors who had traveled widely throughout Europe, socialism and communism focused on organizing the working class.

• ***Ethnic minorities living under foreign rule found a rallying cry in nationalism:*** *Germans living under Prussians, Poles living under Russians or in exile, Irish living under English rule, and Italians living under the Austrian Empire found a new source of hope and pride with nationalism.*

4. Why did the revolutions of 1848 fail?

[model answer] • ***Many voters, particularly rural ones, were frightened by urban disturbances into supporting more conservative governments:*** *Fearing a return to a Reign of Terror after the events of 1848, voters in France elected a conservative National Assembly. The Assembly's election of Louis-Napoleon Bonaparte as president, followed by his self-declaration as Emperor Napoleon III, ended France's Second Republic.*

• ***Internal conflict among revolutionaries:*** *In the eastern Austrian Empire, class and ethnic conflict allowed the emperor to play groups against one another and regain control when violence escalated. In Italy, the nation remained divided because of different regions' needs, while in Germany, conflict increased as a result of the middle class refusing to meet the demands of the lower classes.*

• ***Revolutionaries lacked political experience or military support:*** *In Germany, the delegates sent to construct a unified government were educated, but had no political experience. They also had no military support with which to defend states that wanted parliamentary rule from the strongest German princes. In the eastern Austrian Empire, revolutionaries were overwhelmed by internal conflict and lacked military support.*

Making Connections

1. Which of the ideologies of this period had the greatest impact on political events? How can you explain this?

[model answer] *Nationalism had by far the greatest impact on political events. Nationalism looked past the problems associated with industrialization and urbanization, issues that preoccupied liberals and socialists, toward political autonomy and self-determination for groups identified by common language and culture. Nationalism was a more inclusive and unifying force than either liberalism or socialism.*

2. In what ways might industrialization be considered a force for peaceful change rather than a revolution? (Hint: Think about the situation in Great Britain.)

[model answer] *Factories became the object of public criticism as centers of pollution, noise, and human degradation. Governmental investigations found that dire conditions existed both at work and in the living quarters of the factory workers. The British led the way in passing laws intended to protect women and children from extreme exploitation. The British also undertook major public works projects, such as the construction of sewers, to help improve the lives of the poor. Real, substantive changes began to be formulated by the leadership of the country, largely because industrialization, while it created new social problems, also mobilized social classes and politicians to seek solutions.*

Discussing the Documents

Questions from Online Study Guide with Model Answers

Marx and Engels, The Communist Manifesto (1848), p. 677

1. How do Marx and Engels fit into the "new historical imagination" that was prevalent around the same time?

[model answer] *Like proponents of other political ideologies, Marx and Engels offered their own reading of history that supported their political position. They summarize all of history as a constant class struggle between "oppressor" and "oppressed." Despite the rapid changes of the nineteenth century and the fall of feudalism, class antagonisms continued.*

2. Why did Marx and Engels believe that industrialization was a positive development?

[model answer] *Marx and Engels believed that industrialization would bring about the final downfall of the bourgeoisie. By bringing together the proletariat, who were previously isolated from one another, industry would unite them as a single class that would inevitably overtake the bourgeoisie.*

Alexis de Tocqueville Describes the June Days in Paris (1848), p. 681

1. Tocqueville noted that the insurgents had no leaders or flag, and yet were unified. What united them, according to him?

[model answer] *They were united by class, and by a sense on the part of the workers of being oppressed. For Tocqueville, "greedy desires and false theories" had led the workers to believe that their poverty was caused by the wealth of others. They believed that morality, the best interests of society, and the laws of nature all vindicated their cause.*

2. In what ways were the insurgents' opponents also united, according to Tocqueville?
[model answer] *The opponents of the insurgents came from all social classes, and served "jumbled up together in the same ranks." Class unity among the workers inspired a reaction from other classes. Technology and railroads allowed opponents of the workers' rebellion to gather quickly to oppose the insurgents.*

New Sources, New Perspectives: Statistics and the Standard of Living of the Working Class, pp. 660–661

1. What is a good measure of the standard of living in the first half of the nineteenth century? How would you measure the standard of living today?
[model answer] *There is a great deal of statistical debate about the standard of living in the nineteenth century. Jeffrey Williamson's chart measures the gap between farm and nonfarm wages, and indicates a rapid rise in nonfarm wages in particular for the period between 1820 and 1851. This seems to indicate a rising standard of living for most workers, particularly nonfarm laborers. Standard of living today is measured in a variety of ways, including by calculating family income and making allowances for changes in prices for consumer goods.*

2. How do you explain the initial decline in nonfarm wages relative to farm wages and the subsequent rise?
[model answer] *The initial low level of nonfarm wages may have had to do with a ready labor supply in urban areas; as demand for nonfarm labor increased, and as migration to urban and mining areas failed to keep pace with rising demand for labor, wages for nonfarm labor increased relative to farm labor, eventually far outstripping the rates for farm labor.*

3. What are the virtues of using statistical measures to determine the standard of living? What are the defects?
[model answer] *Statistics, when accurate, can reveal a great deal about changing social conditions. Some statistical measures used to determine standard of living may also reveal other important social information, such as the relative health of workers. Statistics can be read in a variety of ways, however, and many statistics that show "average" conditions may not reveal much about underlying inequalities.*

Other Questions for Discussing These Documents in Class

Marx and Engels, The Communist Manifesto *(1848)*

1. What characterizes "Modern Industry" for Marx? It is important to assess what this excerpt reveals about how Marx saw industrialization as a crucial turning point in human history.

2. Think about why this particular piece of propaganda was historically so effective. Have students consider the rhetorical style and the attractiveness of the images and arguments Marx and Engels present in *Manifesto.*

Alexis de Tocqueville Describes the June Days in Paris (1848)

1. In what sense did Tocqueville term the "insurrection" both "great" and "strange"? What does his use of the term tell us about his perspective?

2. In what ways did Tocqueville suggest the workers were "mistaken"? What does he claim socialism had taught them to believe?

New Sources, New Perspectives: Statistics and the Standard of Living of the Working Class

1. Does historical argument produce better answers over time? If more is now known about the economic and social consequences of industrialization, how have past and present political and social divisions contributed to advancing knowledge? What else led to effective arguments on all sides?

2. What specific evidence in this segment supports the notion that the Industrial Revolution, over time, improved the well-being of average workers?

Comparative Questions

1. What evidence do these documents provide for the assertion that the nature of the working class changed significantly because of industrialization? If it did, how? Do the sources offer any insights into why the working classes were "discontented"?

2. What contributed to the revolutionary nature of the 1840s, according to these documents? What evidence do they provide for the "inevitability" of violent class conflict?

For Users of *Sources of The Making of the West*

The following documents are available in Chapter 21 of the companion sourcebook by Katharine J. Lualdi, University of Southern Maine.

1. Establishing New Work Habits: *Factory Rules in Berlin* (1844)
2. New Rules for the Middle Class: Sarah Stickney Ellis, *Characteristics of the Women of England* (1839)

3. The Division of Labor Illustrated: "Capital and Labour," *Punch* Magazine (1843)
4. What Is the Proletariat?: Friedrich Engels, *Draft of a Communist Confession of Faith* (1847)
5. The Poetry of Freedom: Sándor Petofi, "*National Song*" *of Hungary* (1848)
6. Imperialism and Opium: Commissioner Lin, *Letter to Queen Victoria* (1839)

Discussion Ideas for Sources of The Making of the West, *Chapter 21*

1. What aspects of the factory rules reflect a lack of trust between managers/owners and workers? Can any of the same kind of class tensions be seen in *Punch* Magazine's "Capital and Labour"?

2. Can Ellis's piece be read as nationalist propaganda? How might gender and idealized gender roles contribute to growing national self-consciousness?

3. According to Engels, what is new about the proletariat as a class? Why are they worse off than slaves or serfs?

4. Track the use of historical and violent themes in Petofi's poem. How prominent are they? How did they shape his (and his readers) understanding of what it meant to be Hungarian?

Working with Visual Sources

For this exercise, please refer to Joseph M. W. Turner, *The Fighting "Téméraire" Tugged to Her Last Berth to Be Broken Up* (1838) on p. 665 of the textbook or view the image on the book companion site's Online Study Guide under the "Visual Activity" for Chapter 21.

Students viewing the image at the Online Study Guide are asked two questions about the image. The questions and model answers (not made available to students) are below. Project this image, available on the Instructor's Resources CD-ROM, in class or ask students to look at the image in their textbooks and answer the questions.

1. What does this painting symbolize?
[model answer] *This painting is about change and the passing of old ways. New industrial technologies are changing the older ways of life.*

2. What elements of this painting are typical of romanticism?
[model answer] *The emphasis on nature, which takes more of the canvas than human activity, is typical for romanticism. It also conveys a sense of nostalgia for the passing of the old ways. Even on its final voyage, the Téméraire is a beautiful ship.*

Mapping Exercises

Map Activity from OSG—Model Answers for Map Activity #2

For this activity, please refer to Map 21.1 Industrialization in Europe, c. 1850 on p. 657. Students are asked these questions:

Where were the most industrialized regions in Europe by 1850?
[model answer] *Great Britain was by far the most industrialized nation in Europe by 1850, with the greatest concentration of railroads, and heavily industrialized regions around Liverpool and Manchester, Birmingham, and Glasgow. France and northern Italy also had some industrialized areas along with Belgium. There were also several pockets of industrialization in the German Confederation.*

In what ways were nonindustrialized countries still important to the Industrial Revolution?
[model answer] *Countries such as Spain, Sweden, and Norway were not very industrialized, but had important deposits of iron ore and coal. These raw materials were extremely important for the Industrial Revolution. Areas of France that were not industrialized also had large amounts of coal and iron.*

Map 21.1: Industrialization in Europe, c. 1850, p. 657

Ask students to think about industrialization and peasant emancipation. How might the two be related? Also ask them to discuss the connections between railroad construction and industrialization. What does this map indicate about the advantages possessed by the British industrial economy around 1850?

Map 21.2: The Spread of Cholera, 1826–1855, p. 662

Given the consequences of European diseases such as smallpox on the Americas, it can be interesting to think about cholera, historically based in India, and the two pandemics mapped in Map 21.2 that struck Europe so hard. What conditions in western industrial cities contributed to the scale of the pandemic? What does the spread of cholera beyond its traditional areas tell students about the changing nature of the world by this period?

Map 21.3: Languages of Nineteenth-Century Europe, p. 673

If we consider language to be one of the building blocks of separate cultural identities, how well did language groups in Europe line up with national boundaries? (Map 20.2 on p. 637 may be useful here.) It is also worth considering where, geographically, state boundaries seemed least reflective of linguistic realities.

Map 21.4: The Revolutions of 1848, p. 679

Using the map, each student should choose five sites of revolution and then rank them in importance, one through five, without revealing the basis for their ranking system. These ranks could then be tabulated for the class as a whole. After the results are in, ask students to comment on why they chose a particular site as first or second or third on the list. Should Paris be first because it was the site of a revolutionary tradition that reaches back to the French Revolution? Should Frankfurt be first because the failure there to create the basis for a united Germany led to a much different solution under Bismarck?

Mapping the West: Europe in 1850, p. 686

Which areas show the most rapid increase in population in the period between 1800 and 1850? Does there appear to be a correlation between population growth and power?

In-Class Assignments and Presentation Topics

1. Ask students to imagine that they have the opportunity to travel back in time to the 1830s and 1840s to conduct interviews for oral histories of the working class. Each student should provide an introduction to the person he or she interviews, a list of questions to be asked, and read aloud or hand in a transcript of the "interview." It may be a good idea to draw up a list of several types of workers based on primary and secondary sources readily available to students. Students could then select from the prepared list or you could assign a particular type of worker to each student. See "Lecture Strategies," number 3 and "Discussion Starters," number 3, for bibliographical citations.

2. An annotated timeline, with which students will be familiar from the Study Guide, is a useful exercise. Each student selects a country or a theme, such as the development of the railroad or romanticism in literature, and prepares a timeline that briefly identifies and discusses major events, institutions, persons, and so forth. The timeline would also make a good class presentation (if you do this assignment as a presentation, limit the number of students covering the 1830s and 1840s, and assign the others to do later periods). Students will probably need some bibliographical pointers. Introduce them to such publications as William L. Langer, ed., *An Encyclopedia of World History*, 4th ed. (Boston: Houghton Mifflin, 1968); or Richard B. Morris and Graham W. Irwin, eds., *Harper Encyclopedia of the Modern World* (New York: Harper & Row, 1970).

3. Divide the class into several groups, and ask each group to write, rehearse, and present a fifteen-minute play based on the idea of domesticity in the context of a specific family situation, such as a middle-class family or a working-class family. Each member of the group would have one major role (for example, a writer, director, actor, and/or producer). Each group's play could be based on an actual historical family (see, for example, Phyllis Rose, *Parallel Lives: Five Victorian Marriages* [New York: Vintage, 1983]) or be fictional but factually based; that is, the family might be fictional, but the experiences of the characters should be historically factual. Each student would then write a short essay discussing the experience of putting together their group's play and evaluating what he or she learned about family dynamics from the play. See "Lecture Strategies," number 2, for bibliographical citations.

4. Discuss in class the types of indices that would prove useful for comparing European nations in the 1840s. These data might include population figures, miles of railroad track, the number of steam engines used in factories, and so forth. Students should then select a country, find as many relevant statistics for it as possible, and present these in graphs or tables. Students should also write a brief essay explaining what they believe the statistics show about their chosen country. In addition to the bibliographical notations in "Lecture Strategies," number 2, students should become familiar with B. R. Mitchell, *European Historical Statistics, 1750–1970* (New York: Columbia University Press, 1975).

5. Have the students consider the revolutions of 1848 in a particular place (Paris will do) from the perspective of various social classes and individuals. Create, or have students create, brief biographies of representative types, including a peasant or small holder, a large landowner, an urban merchant, an apprentice artisan, an unemployed participant in the national workshop, a working-class member of the "mobile guard," a middle-class liberal representative to the Assembly, and so on. (This exercise can be usefully combined with number 3 above.) Then have them write a "letter to the editor" reacting to the June Days, and suggesting a course of action and an ideal outcome for France.

Essay Questions

1. In addition to Marx and Engels, many other seminal figures in European life came of age in the

1830s and 1840s. Students might be assigned to write a research essay on the formative years of one of the following persons: Charles Darwin, Alexander Herzen, John Stuart Mill, George Eliot, Florence Nightingale, or George Sand. For Darwin, see Janet Browne, *Charles Darwin: Voyaging* (Princeton, NJ: Princeton University Press, 1995), a fine biography that concentrates largely on the voyage of *HMS Beagle*, but takes the story into the 1850s. Another useful source is Philip Appleman, *Darwin: A Norton Critical Edition* (New York: W. W. Norton, 1970), which includes writings by Darwin and writings about him. For Florence Nightingale, students might begin with Nancy Boyd, *Three Victorian Women Who Changed Their World: Josephine Butler, Octavia Hill, Florence Nightingale* (New York: Oxford University Press, 1982). Another useful source is Martha Vicinus and Bea Nergaard, eds., *Ever Yours, Florence Nightingale: Selected Letters* (Cambridge, MA: Harvard University Press, 1989). Students should, of course, develop their own list of sources, but it may be useful, as with Darwin and Nightingale here, to supply them with two or three good sources to help them get started.

2. The revolutions of 1848 provide a rich and varied array of possible topics for research and writing. Students might choose to analyze the origins of a particular revolution. This analysis could range from a discussion of the events and developments of the 1840s to a more tightly focused dissection of the particular events in 1848 leading to the temporarily successful revolution in Prussia. In the latter case, of particular interest is William L. Langer, "The Pattern of Urban Revolution in 1848," in Evelyn M. Acomb and Marvin L. Brown, Jr., eds., *French Society and Culture Since the Old Regime* (New York: Holt, Rinehart & Winston, 1966). Another direction students might take would involve following an individual through 1848. Who was Louis-Napoleon Bonaparte? What role did he play in 1848? Or, what was Friedrich Engels, coauthor of *The Communist Manifesto*, doing in 1848? Students might also look at countries or areas where no revolution took place: Why was this the case? Use "Lecture Strategies," number 6, for bibliographical leads. Sperber and Stearns both have extensive bibliographies in their books.

Additional Resources: Literature

Dickens, Charles, *Oliver Twist*. 1837–1839.

Forster, Margaret, ed., *Selected Poems of Elizabeth Barrett Browning*. 1988.

Ives, George Burnham, trans., *George Sand: Indiana*. 1978.

Katz, Michael R., trans., *Ivan Turgenev: Fathers and Sons*. 1995.

Keach, William, ed., *Samuel Taylor Coleridge: The Complete Poems*. 1997.

Krailsheimer, A. J., trans., *Honoré de Balzac: Père Goriot*. 1991.

Milligan, Barry, ed., *Thomas de Quincey: Confessions of an English Opium Eater and Other Writings*. 2003.

Additional Resources: Film and Video

Middlemarch (1994; VHS/DVD, approx. 6 hrs.). This excellent dramatization of George Eliot's 1871–1872 novel explores a number of themes, including the political tensions that followed the Great Reform Bill of 1831, the hypocrisy of those who took up religion as a profession, and the restrictions placed on women in England in the 1830s.

Jane Eyre (1997; VHS/DVD, 105 min.). This excellent adaptation of Charlotte Brontë's 1847 novel tells of a young woman trying to make her way in the world as a governess. It graphically depicts the restrictions on and limited opportunities for intelligent but impoverished young women in mid-Victorian England.

Charles Dickens (2003; DVD, 8 hrs., 30 min.). This three-part series examines Dickens's life and the motivations behind his writing by interviewing actors portraying Dickens and those persons who knew him. Dickens's overwhelming concern for the poor, who suffered most from industrialization, is especially emphasized.

Films of Charles Dickens's Novels

Virtually all of Charles Dickens's novels have been dramatized, some of them several times over. Like the novels, the films capture the vagaries of fortune and the hardship of life for the poor and impoverished in the Victorian period. In the following list (arranged chronologically by date of publication), the date that immediately follows the title refers to the date of its first publication.

Oliver Twist (1837–1838). (1997; VHS, 6 hrs.)

Nicholas Nickleby (1838–1839). (2002; VHS/DVD, approx. 200 min.)

Martin Chuzzlewit (1843–1844). (1994; VHS, 288 min.)

David Copperfield (1849–1850). (2000; VHS/DVD, approx. 3 hrs.)

Bleak House (1852–1853). (1988 VHS, 6 hrs., 31 min.)

Hard Times (1854). (1994; VHS, 102 min.)

Little Dorrit (1855–1854). (1988; VHS, 6 hrs.)

Great Expectations (1860–1861). (2001; VHS, 3 hrs.)
Our Mutual Friend (1864–1865). (1998; VHS/DVD, approx. 5 hrs., 30 min.)

OTHER BEDFORD/ST. MARTIN'S RESOURCES FOR CHAPTER 21

The following resources are available to accompany Chapter 21. Please refer to the Preface of this manual for detailed descriptions of all the ancillaries.

For Instructors

Transparencies

The following maps and images from Chapter 21 are available as full-color acetates.

- Map 21.1: Industrialization in Europe, c. 1850
- Map 21.2: The Spread of Cholera, 1826–1855
- Map 21.3: Languages of Nineteenth-Century Europe
- Map 21.4: The Revolutions of 1848
- Mapping the West: Europe in 1850
- Joseph M. W. Turner, *The Fighting "Téméraire" Tugged to Her Last Berth to Be Broken Up* (1838), p. 665
- The Crystal Palace, 1851, p. 685

Instructor's Resources CD-ROM

The following maps and image from Chapter 21, as well as a chapter outline, are available on disc in both PowerPoint and jpeg formats.

- Map 21.1: Industrialization in Europe, c. 1850
- Map 21.2: The Spread of Cholera, 1826–1855
- Map 21.3: Languages of Nineteenth-Century Europe
- Map 21.4: The Revolutions of 1848
- Mapping the West: Europe in 1850
- Joseph M. W. Turner, *The Fighting "Téméraire" Tugged to Her Last Berth to Be Broken Up* (1838), p. 665

Using the Bedford Series with The Making of the West

Available in print as well as online at **bedfordstmartins.com/usingseries,** this guide offers practical suggestions for using *The Communist Manifesto* by Karl Marx and Frederick Engels, with *Related Documents*, edited with an Introduction by John E. Toews, in conjunction with Chapter 21 of the textbook.

For Students

Study Guides

The Online Study Guide at **bedfordstmartins.com/hunt** helps students synthesize the material they have learned as well as practice the skills historians use to make sense of the past. The following Map, Visual, and Document activities are available for Chapter 21.

Map Activity

- Map 21.1: Industrialization in Europe, c. 1850

Visual Activity

- Joseph M. W. Turner, *The Fighting "Téméraire" Tugged to Her Last Berth to Be Broken Up* (1838), p. 665

Reading Historical Documents

- Marx and Engels, *The Communist Manifesto,* p. 677
- Alexis de Tocqueville Describes the June Days in Paris (1848), p. 681
- New Sources, New Perspectives: Statistics and the Standard of Living of the Working Class, pp. 660–661

CHAPTER

22

Politics and Culture of the Nation-State

1850–1870

Chapter Resources

Main Chapter Topics

1. Destabilized by the revolutions of 1848, the concert of Europe dissolved in the 1850s, in part because Napoleon III worked to weaken its hold over France. Napoleon III helped to engineer the Crimean War (1853–1856), which, by splitting the alliance between Russia and Austria, shifted the distribution of European power.

2. Reforms in Russia under Alexander II, sparked by the defeat in the Crimea and a wave of peasant uprisings, led to the emancipation of Russia's serfs and extensive reforms of local administration, the judiciary, and the military. The principle of equality before the law was introduced for the first time.

3. Both the German and the Italian states used the changed circumstances of the 1850s and 1860s, combined with Realpolitik and nationalism, to unify their countries quickly through war. Austria's absolutist regime failed in many respects to modernize and was forced to concede independent power to Hungarians within the empire.

4. Political parties in Britain embraced liberal reform while preserving aristocracy and monarchy. The United States was obliged to wage a civil war to restore national unity.

5. Governments undertook urban improvements—from opera houses to sewers—to avoid revolution and epidemics by attending to the well-being of their citizens. These efforts were generally popular, yet disturbed and dislocated many of the poor, who were, of course, resentful.

6. Governmental attempts to impose order extended as well to colonial enterprises. The British, Russians, and French instituted direct rule over their colonies, expanding the colonial bureaucracies, and in some cases, providing more services.

7. Realism in both art and literature claimed to look at society objectively and to depict it starkly and accurately, claims similar to those of Realpolitik and positivism.

8. Charles Darwin revealed and extended the power of science. His ideas were misunderstood and distorted into Social Darwinism, an application of "survival of the fittest" to modern society that opposed aiding the "unfit." Marxism, with its doctrines of class struggle and the social evolution of history, was also a scion of Darwinism. Evolution was even used to justify racism and imperialism.

9. Karl Marx attacked socialists and anarchists and encouraged workers to think in terms of a revolution that would destroy bourgeois society and the nation-state.

Focus Question

How did the creation and strengthening of nation-states change European politics, society, and culture in the mid-nineteenth century?

1. By the mid-nineteenth century, politics, society and culture increasingly came to revolve around nation-states. In France, Napoleon III attempted to restore French glory and independent action in the international arena, and combined authoritarian rule with social reforms and urban renewal. In Russia, after the defeat in the Crimean War, Alexander II emancipated the serfs and reformed aspects of public life by, for example, lifting travel restrictions and revamping the military and judicial systems. But emancipated peasants remained tied to the land by debts, and reforms caused generational splits in the ruling classes and encouraged radicalism among the young. With French assistance, Italy united (under Piedmont-Sardinia's prime minister Cavour, and king, Victor Emmanuel II), largely in opposition to Austrian domination of parts of the national

territory, but struggled to create a common national culture. German unification also came through the offices of a dominant state (Prussia), a dynamic prime minister (Bismarck), and military conflict with equally ambitious neighboring states such as Austria (1866) and France (1871). In Britain (excepting Ireland) national unity was strengthened by a dedicated monarch, a cooperative aristocracy, and the willingness to embrace aspects of liberal reform, all aided by prosperity and commercial and imperial expansion. In the United States, victory over Mexico and an end (after the Civil War) to festering divisions over slavery fostered a stronger central government as well.

2. In general, across the west, governments increased their regulatory and taxing powers, their responsibility to carry out hygienic and aesthetic alterations of the landscape and, by sponsoring public education in many places, their influence over rising generations. Religion's influence was reduced, in part by state actions (such as Bismarck's *Kultukampf*) and growing state control of education, and in part by the rise of Darwinism, which offered what to many amounted to an alternate explanatory framework for the origins and development of human communities. Developments in political theory reflected tremendous interest in growing state power—Marxists imagined it currently harnessed to support narrow bourgeois interest, but one day being used to create a universal socialism; Comptians imagined it in the service of rational and reasonable social reform, while Anarchists saw it as the ultimate enemy of humanity.

Annotated Chapter Outline

I. The End of the Concert of Europe

A. Napoleon III and the Quest for French Glory, pp. 691–692

1. In France, Louis-Napoleon encouraged French grandeur and the cult of his famous uncle.
2. As emperor, Napoleon III combined economic liberalism with authoritarian rule, maintaining a lavish court while his wife, the Empress Eugénie, fulfilled the role of devoted mother and philanthropist.
3. Napoleon III also supported modernization, sponsoring the rebuilding of Paris and artistic exhibitions, while promoting economic growth, free trade, railroad construction, and innovative investment banking.
4. Following an economic downturn in the late 1850s, Napoleon III sought broader support by allowing working-class organizations and some democratic reforms.
5. Napoleon III broke the Congress of Vienna's containment of France by realigning foreign powers and engaging Russia, Austria, and Prussia in a series of wars.
6. Outside of Europe, he enforced French rule in Algeria and southeast Asia, and attempted to install Habsburg Maximilian as ruler of Mexico, a plan that ended in rebellion and Maximilian's execution in 1867. He also encouraged such projects as the Suez Canal, which connected the Mediterranean and Red seas.
7. Overall, Napoleon III's foreign policy broke down the international system of peaceful diplomacy established by the Congress of Vienna.

B. The Crimean War, 1853–1856: Turning Point in European Affairs, pp. 692–694

1. Russian tsar Nicholas I had wanted to absorb as much of the ailing Ottoman Empire as possible, and Napoleon III encouraged his aggressiveness.
2. The conflict between Russia and the Ottoman Empire upset the balance of power. Because Britain feared Russia would control British routes through the Mediterranean to East Asia, the British supported the Ottomans.
3. The Austrians, who still harbored resentment over Russia helping to put down a Hungarian revolt in 1849, remained neutral—again with encouragement from Napoleon III, ending the Russian-Austrian alliance that had checked French power.
4. Traditional enemies France and Great Britain declared war on Russia in 1854.
5. The Russian naval base at Sevastopol in the Crimea on the Black Sea was besieged for a year; both sides suffered high casualties.
6. Lacking adequate sanitation and medical care, and led by incompetent generals, three-quarters of a million men died, more than two-thirds of them from disease and starvation.
7. Upon his father's death Alexander II (r. 1855–1881) became tsar and sued for peace.
8. The 1856 Peace of Paris deprived Russia of its naval bases in the Dardanelles Straits and the Black Sea.
9. Moldavia and Walachia (which soon merged to form Romania) became

autonomous Turkish provinces, reducing Russian influence.

10. The Crimean War introduced new technologies such as the railroad, the shell-firing cannon, the breech-loading rifle, the telegraph, and the steam-powered ship.
11. It was also the first war to be subjected to extensive public scrutiny, as increased press coverage, the use of the telegraph, and the advent of photography brought the war home to Europeans in a way never before possible. Many were outraged by the way the war was conducted.

C. Reform in Russia, pp. 694–696

1. In the decade preceding the Crimean War, peasant insurrection was common in Russia.
2. Defeat in the war confronted the educated public with the poor performance of serf-conscripted armies and the intolerable liability of serf labor.
3. To avoid revolution, Tsar Alexander II launched a series of "Great Reforms," beginning with the emancipation of nearly 50 million serfs.
4. The former serfs were given land, but not as private landowners.
5. Rather, they and the land they farmed were organized into a community (*mir*) controlled by male village elders.
6. Although no individual peasants actually owned land, all were required to repay the original landowners via payments to the government.
7. Emancipated but chained to enormous debts and particular plots of land, the serfs still could not form the pool of free labor Russia needed.
8. The state also reformed local administration and the judiciary by giving all Russians access to modern civil courts.
9. Travel restrictions were lifted, allowing Russians to see how the rest of Europe was governed.
10. Military reform followed in 1874 when the government replaced the twenty-five-year period of conscription with a six-year term.
11. Attention to education, efficiency, and humane treatment of recruits created a Russian army more competitive with other European forces.
12. Reaction to the reforms often differed along generational lines. Older aristocrats resented the weakening of their personal authority.
13. Younger aristocrats emphasized the importance of practical activity over leisure and identified with workers and peasants, and younger aristocratic women sought greater independence.
14. Traditionalists pessimistically labeled these radical young people "nihilists"—those who believed that nothing exists, is knowable, or can be communicated, and who rejected all moral values.
15. The reforms also sparked resistance in Russian-dominated nations, including Poland, which sought full independence in 1863. Polish peasants were promised reforms.
16. As in the past, the Russian government responded to unrest in the Caucasus and elsewhere with military force, but also with a policy of Russification—an intense campaign to force minorities to adopt Russian language and culture.
17. Despite the Great Reforms, Alexander II only partially developed the institutions that buttressed other nation-states.
18. The reins of government were still tightly held by the tsar and his inner circle.
19. The persistence of autocracy and the abuse of large population groups suffocated the shared national identity felt so strongly elsewhere.

II. War and Nation Building

A. Cavour, Garibaldi, and the Process of Italian Unification, pp. 696–698

1. Despite failed revolutions in 1848, the idea of political unification had not disappeared in Italy.
2. The obvious leader for this Risorgimento was Piedmont-Sardinia, the most economically and militarily advanced of the Italian states, with a liberal political climate.
3. Its prime minister, Camillo di Cavour (1810–1861) attempted to liberate Austrian-held regions by encouraging economic development and allying with Napoleon III.
4. In exchange for military aid, France was promised the city of Nice and the province of Savoy.
5. Cavour provoked the Austrians to invade northern Italy in April 1859, which united nationalist Italians in support of Piedmont.
6. With the help of the French and the newly built Piedmontese railroad, the forces of

Piedmont-Sardinia won stunning victories over Austria.

7. To Cavour's dismay, Napoleon III then signed a treaty granting Lombardy to Piedmont-Sardinia, but leaving Venetia in Austrian hands.
8. Nevertheless, the Piedmontese victories had created a groundswell of nationalism, and Parma, Modena, Tuscany, and the Papal States (except Rome, which was occupied by French troops) elected to join Piedmont-Sardinia.
9. In May 1860, Giuseppe Garibaldi (1807–1882), a committed republican and inspired guerrilla fighter, raised a volunteer army, liberated Sicily from overbearing landlords and a corrupt government, and then crossed to the mainland and headed north.
10. Cavour sent his troops south and when the two armies met in Naples in the autumn of 1860, Garibaldi gave way to Cavour and, in 1861, the kingdom of Italy was proclaimed, with former Piedmont-Sardinian king Victor Emmanuel at its head.
11. Cavour died shortly thereafter, and divisions among successive political leaders and differences between the wealthy commercial north and the impoverished agricultural south kept Italy relatively weak.
12. The legend of the daring Garibaldi became more important to evolving Italian national pride than the economic and military Realpolitik of Cavour.

B. Bismarck and the Realpolitik of German Unification, pp. 699–702

1. The creation of a united Germany was the most momentous act of nation building for the future of Europe and the world.
2. The architect of a united Germany was Otto von Bismarck (1815–1898). Called by William I of Prussia (r. 1861–1871) to take the position of prime minister in 1862, Bismarck overrode liberals in parliament and rammed through programs to build up the army.
3. He then embarked on a series of wars: with Denmark in 1864, Austria in 1866, and France in 1870.
4. In the course of these wars, Bismarck united the smaller German states behind Prussia rather than Austria, thus excluding that great power from German unification.
5. This exclusion was confirmed when an overconfident Austria, laden with debt and plagued by its restless national minorities, was provoked by Bismarck into declaring war on Prussia over the administration of the provinces of Schleswig and Holstein.
6. Within seven weeks, the modernized and mobile Prussian military won a decisive victory.
7. To bring in the remaining German holdouts, Bismarck goaded France into declaring war over the choice of a new king for Spain, in part by provoking French public opinion.
8. France quickly fell to the Prussian forces, ending Napoleon III's Second Empire, on September 4, 1870.
9. France had to give Alsace and Lorraine to Germany and pay an indemnity.
10. As the crowning blow, the Germans crowned King William of Prussia kaiser of the new German Empire at the Palace of Versailles in January 1871.
11. The kaiser retained his title as the king of Prussia, and henceforth Prussia became a state of the new empire.
12. The kaiser controlled the military and appointed Bismarck chancellor of the empire.
13. The adult male population of all the states elected representatives to a new assembly, the Reichstag, which ratified budgets but had little power to initiate legislation.
14. To maintain the social hierarchy, votes from the upper classes counted more than those from the lower classes.
15. The liberals, giddy with military success, supported Bismarck's blend of economic progress, constitutionalism, and militaristic nationalism.
16. Led by Bismarck and filled with national pride, the German state was now poised to dominate continental politics.

C. Francis Joseph and the Creation of the Austro-Hungarian Monarchy, 702–703

1. Confrontations with Cavour and Bismarck confronted Austria with the need to make some changes.
2. Hardworking Emperor Francis Joseph (r. 1848–1916) attempted to enhance his authority through elaborate and formal court ceremony, but he resisted change.
3. Nonetheless, in the 1850s and 1860s, standards of honesty and efficiency improved within the government, and

the state promoted local education and respected the rights of minorities to be educated—and to communicate with officials—in their native language.

4. Most internal customs barriers were abolished, free trade with Germany was established, and much of the state railway system was sold, creating a boom in private railway construction and foreign investment.
5. Eventually, Vienna underwent extensive renovation, and more jobs opened up as industrialization progressed.
6. Francis Joseph was forced to modify his absolutism as German liberals imposed financial constraints on the military and blocked other measures that would strengthen the government.
7. In 1866, the Hungarian agrarian elites requested Magyar home rule, which was granted, creating a "dual monarchy."
8. Although Francis Joseph was crowned king of Hungary and was in charge of coordinating Austro-Hungarian foreign policy, Hungary largely ruled itself after 1867 through the restored Hungarian parliament.
9. Following the establishment of this dual monarchy, other ethnic groups within the empire increased their demands for self-rule.
10. Some turned to Russia, hoping to form a Pan-Slavism movement (a transnational alliance of all Slavic peoples) that would allow them to break away from Austria's influence.
11. Loyalty to the Hapsburgs remained, but imperial subjects had increasing difficulty relating to one another as members of a single nation.

D. Political Stability through Gradual Reform in Great Britain, pp. 703–705

1. In contrast to the upheaval in continental Europe, Great Britain, ruled by Queen Victoria (r. 1837–1901) with the aid of her husband Prince Albert, basked in domestic tranquility, morality, and middle-class virtues.
2. Parliament, dominated by the Conservatives (formerly the Tory party) and the Liberals (formerly the Whigs), enjoyed smooth decision making and liberal progress.
3. In 1867, the Conservative party, led by Benjamin Disraeli (1804–1881), passed the Second Reform Bill, which enfranchised a million new male voters.
4. Interest groups pressured both parties to support reform.
5. Under pressure from women's groups, the government addressed family and marital issues, passing the Matrimonial Causes Act of 1857, which facilitated divorce; and the Married Women's Property Act of 1870, which allowed married women to own property and keep the wages they earned. Mass demonstrations led to passage of the Second Reform Bill.
6. Plush royal ceremonies united supporters and opponents of the government, as well as members of all social classes. The monarchy promoted respectability and the family.
7. Architects adopted building styles that glorified the English past, while the term "Victorian" came to refer to anything from manners to political institutions during Victoria's reign.
8. All was not peaceful, however: Britain's politicians were as devoted to Realpolitik as Bismarck, and used violence to expand their overseas empire and to control Ireland, where little reform occurred.
9. But the violence was far removed from the sights and minds of most British citizens, who saw their nation as peaceful, advanced, and united.

E. Nation Building in the United States and Canada, p. 705

1. The United States had a more democratic political culture, including near-universal male suffrage, an independent press, and combative mass political parties that believed that sovereignty derived from the people.
2. The United States continued to expand westward; Texas was annexed in 1845, and an 1848 victory over Mexico brought in California and large portions of the southwest.
3. Although politicians and citizens agreed that Native American peoples should be banned from these lands, they disagreed over whether slavery should be allowed.
4. As the issue came to polarize the country, the election in 1860 of Abraham Lincoln led most of the slaveholding states to secede to form the Confederate States of America.
5. Although he initially fought to maintain the Union, in January 1863, Lincoln issued

the Emancipation Proclamation, which freed slaves in the Confederate states, as a wartime measure.

6. By April 1865, despite the assassination of Lincoln, the North, stronger economically and militarily, had prevailed.
7. Slavery was abolished, but the constitutional guarantee of full political rights to African American men was effectively nullified once Southern whites regained control of state politics after 1877.
8. The Union's victory opened the way to a stronger national government and economic advance not tied to the slave economy.
9. The North's victory allowed the United States to contribute to Napoleon III's defeat in Mexico in 1867.
10. In retribution for Great Britain's partiality to the Confederacy, the United States demanded the annexation of Canada.
11. To avoid this, Great Britain granted Canada the status of self-governing dominion.

III. Establishing Social Order

A. Bringing Order to the Cities, pp. 706–708

1. European cities became the backdrop for displays of state power and national solidarity, thus efforts to improve sanitation and beautify cities revitalized the state's credit.
2. In 1857, Austrian emperor Francis Joseph ordered the destruction of Vienna's medieval city walls and replaced them with boulevards lined with public buildings such as the opera house and the Reichsrat.
3. Other cities built broad boulevards that enabled crowds to observe royal pageantry and allowed troops faster access to the city and its inhabitants.
4. These renovated cities highlighted class differences: poor neighborhoods were razed, and boulevards separated the rich from the poor.
5. In London, renovation replaced slums and lower-class neighborhoods with large commercial streets, all designed to foster civic pride and stabilize the state.
6. Despite such renovation, disease still remained a problem. Poor sanitation contributed to disorder, and improving sanitation became a government priority.
7. Scientific research was increasingly conducted in government-financed universities and hospitals. Louis Pasteur discovered that bacteria and parasites were responsible for many illnesses, and he demonstrated that heating foods such as wine and milk—pasteurization—could kill these organisms.
8. Joseph Lister applied Pasteur's discovery to medical care and developed antiseptics for treating wounds.
9. At the same time, governments improved drainage and water supplies.
10. In Paris, Haussmann devised a system to pipe in water from less-contaminated sources in the countryside, a system imitated throughout Europe.
11. On the lookout for disease and sanitary dangers, people became more aware of foul odors and air that had been an accepted part of life for thousands of years.
12. Now aware of the importance of hygiene, the middle and lower classes began to bathe more often, a refinement in harmony with government concern for order.

B. Expanding the Reach of Government, pp. 708–709

1. Enacting new programs to build social order and safety and to enhance the nation expanded state bureaucracies.
2. Government authority reached further into the realm of everyday life, in part through regular census taking.
3. Details of people's lives—their ages, occupations, and marital status, for example—could be used to set quotas for military conscription or to predict the need for new prisons.
4. Sweden, in 1860, introduced an income tax, exposing its citizens' earnings to governmental scrutiny.
5. Reformers such as Florence Nightingale believed that the gathering of quantitative information made government less susceptible to corruption and inefficiency.
6. Decisions would be based on facts rather than influence-peddling or ill-informed guesses.
7. Another "intrusion" was the increase in government regulation of prostitution, designed to limit the spread of venereal disease.
8. As government increased such functions, new departments and agencies were established, providing new sources of employment.

C. Schooling and Professionalizing Society, pp. 709–710

1. Increased requirements for empirical knowledge and objective standards of evaluation elevated and altered certain professions: doctors, lawyers, managers, professors, and journalists began to influence state policy and regulate admission to their fields.
2. The middle classes successfully lobbied to make civil-service jobs merit-based rather than rewards for political loyalty or high birth.
3. Britain and other countries passed legislation requiring that these positions be earned through competitive examinations.
4. Citizens thus ordered the state to conform with their ideas of fairness, competence, and opportunity.
5. Nation building required major improvements in education.
6. Governments introduced compulsory schooling to inculcate nationalism, reduce illiteracy, and educate their growing electorates.
7. Traditionally, primary education had been religious, but after the 1850s states increasingly introduced secular and scientific instruction.
8. The economic importance of children made it difficult to enforce school attendance, but over time, among the working poor and the middle classes, education became a shared value and made traveling lecturers, public forums, reading groups, and debating societies popular.
9. Secondary and university education remained elite luxuries, but now secondary education developed along different tracks.
10. Reformers pushed for more advanced and complex courses for young women than they had been offered in the past.
11. Secondary and university-level courses for women, especially in Paris and Zurich, opened professional doors for them.
12. Some young women took advantage of new opportunities in medicine.
13. These women saw the need to protect the modesty of female patients and to bring feminine values to health care.
14. Women also entered teaching in large numbers, as primary education expanded.
15. Yet, because this work took them outside the domestic sphere, it raised a storm of controversy.

D. Spreading Western Order beyond the West, pp. 710–713

1. In an age of nation building and industrial development, colonies took on a new political dimension.
2. After mid-century, Great Britain, France, and Russia revised their colonial policy by instituting direct rule, expanding colonial bureaucracies, and providing a wide array of social and cultural services.
3. Although British colonialism in the first half of the century had been laissez-faire, British institutions and power nonetheless gradually spread through India.
4. In 1857, Hindu and Muslim troops rebelled against regulations that violated their religious beliefs.
5. This Indian mutiny coincided with a revolt in Jhansi, sparked when the East India Company tried to seize the kingdom from rani (queen) Lakshmibai (widow of Jhansi's previous ruler).
6. After putting down the revolt, the British government took direct control with the 1858 Government of India Act. In 1876 Queen Victoria was named the "Empress of India."
7. The French government pushed its dominion over Cochin China (in modern Vietnam) in the 1860s and occupied all of Algeria by 1870.
8. Local leaders in Algeria were attracted to services such as schools and to French goods, technology, and institutions, and thus cooperated in building railroads and borrowing money from French banks.
9. Direct British rule led to more cultural domination by Britian and subtle interventions in everyday life. Indians became more politically united and nationalistic over time in response.
10. France's dominion over Cochin China allowed the French to benefit economically while providing sanitation and public health improvements that led to population growth. The French were also determined to spread their culture.
11. Once the Suez Canal was opened in 1869, it offered a shorter trade route to Asia and led to a European fascination with Egypt and its culture.

12. French expansion into Algeria was aided by the attraction of locals to European goods and technology, but war and European-spread diseases led to a 20 percent population decline between 1867 and 1872.
13. China had eluded complete takeover, but Christian missionaries and traders disturbed a society that was already unsteady from exploding population, defeat in the Opium Wars, and other trade pressures from Europe.
14. Contact with the West touched off the Taiping (Heavenly Kingdom) movement, which attracted millions of followers, who wanted the end of the ruling Qing dynasty, reform, and the expulsion of foreigners.
15. By the mid 1850s, the Taiping controlled half of China.
16. A bloody civil war broke out between Taiping followers and the Qing regime.
17. When peace finally came, the Europeans had profited, gaining virtually unlimited access to the country.
18. Japan alone was able to escape domination.
19. By 1854, when Americans claimed to open Japan to trade, Dutch traders at Nagasaki had already made the Japanese keenly aware of Western industrial, military, and commercial innovations.
20. Trade agreements with the United States and others followed, leading to concerted effort for reform.
21. In 1867, Japanese reformers, after a brief civil war, pressured the ruling shogun to abdicate and then restored the emperor to full power in 1868.
22. The goal of this Meiji Restoration was to establish Japan as a modern, technologically powerful state free from Western control.

E. Confronting the Nation-State's Order at Home, pp. 713–715

1. By the close of the 1860s, the unchecked growth of the state and the ongoing process of economic change had led to palpable tensions in European society.
2. New theories of work life and politics appeared to explain political and economic changes.
3. Among the new theorists was French printer and utopian socialist Pierre-Joseph Proudhon (1809–1865), who argued that the private ownership of property robbed those without property of their share of the planet's benefits; he advocated the organization of artisans into mutualist social organizations that would bring about the end of government.
4. Russian nobleman Mikhail Bakunin (1814–1876) argued that the state should not in any way infringe upon individual freedom.
5. His ideas formed the basis of anarchism, a doctrine that advocated the destruction of all state power.
6. Particularly influential was the author of *The Communist Manifesto* (written with Friedrich Engels [1848]) and *Das Kapital* (1867–1894), Karl Marx (1818–1883).
7. From the 1870s onward, Karl Marx offered a Realpolitik for the working classes, arguing that social organization was derived from the relationships of classes to productive processes. This idea, materialism, rejected the liberal focus on individual rights and pointed toward an inevitable, class-based social revolution that would be won by the modern industrial working class. Marx believed that capitalism would give way to socialism, that a proletariat revolution would eradicate private ownership and bring about a classless society.
8. Marx and others saw the future in contemporary events, such as the Paris Commune. In the winter of 1870–1871, Paris was suffering from a harsh winter and the Prussian siege that deprived them of food.
9. Parisians demanded a local elected government to deal with the crisis.
10. In March 1871, Parisians declared themselves a self-governing commune, an act that was imitated by other French cities.
11. The Paris Commune lasted for two months; during that time, Parisians set up political clubs, local ceremonies, and cooperative workshops.
12. The Communards (members of the commune) were inspired by mutualist and socialist ideas and agreed to bring about a social revolution, one that would include women.
13. But they frequently disagreed on the path to a changed society: mutualism, anticlericalism, feminism, international socialism, and anarchism were proposed.

14. Meanwhile, the provisional government at Versailles quickly stamped out communes in other cities.
15. On May 21 of that year, the army entered the capital.
16. In a week of fighting, both the Communards and the army executed hostages and set fire to the city.
17. The commune was put down, and the army shot down tens of thousands citizens in the streets.
18. Many more were arrested and either executed or sent to penal colonies.
19. The French establishment saw all Parisians as traitors, but gradually a new "history" of the commune was promulgated: it was the fault of women—a case of women run mad, crowding the streets in a frenzy of destruction and wanton sexuality.
20. The French state struggled to recover from defeat and civil war. Conservatives saw the commune as a symptom of collapsing social order and gender relations; for Marx it represented a class rebellion, an attack on property, and a government determined to protect the wealthy.

IV. The Culture of Social Order

A. The Arts Confront Social Reality, pp. 716–718

1. The reading public devoured biographies of political leaders, and the general public attended an increasing number of artistic, scientific, and natural history exhibitions.
2. Realism dominated the novel.
3. The hugely popular novels of Charles Dickens (1812–1870) appeared in serial form in magazines and periodicals.
4. His characters came from contemporary English society and ranged from starving orphans to ruthless opportunists that drew attention to the impact on society of industrialization and civil law.
5. The widely read novels of George Eliot (Mary Ann Evans, 1819–1880) explored contemporary personal problems.
6. French writer Gustave Flaubert (1821–1880) scandalized French society with *Madame Bovary* (1857), the tale of an unhappy wife whose longing for possessions she could ill afford, and illicit affairs, ultimately led her to commit suicide.
7. The poet Charles-Pierre Baudelaire (1821–1867) also shocked the public by writing explicitly about sex, as well as drug- and wine-induced fantasies, in *Les Fleurs du mal* (Flowers of Evil [1857]).
8. Russian writers during this era of Great Reforms debated whether or not Western European values were insidiously transforming their societies.
9. Ivan Turgenev (1818–1883) captured generational conflict in *Fathers and Sons* (1862), a story of nihilistic children rejecting the older generation's Romantic spiritual values.
10. Fyodor Dostoevsky (1821–1881) created antiheroes in works such as *Notes from Underground* (1864) and *Crime and Punishment* (1866).
11. After 1848, despite their dependency on elite audiences and patronage, painters turned away from idealized portraits of workers and peasants and adopted the realist style.
12. French painter Gustave Courbet (1819–1877) depicted how backbreaking physical labor could be.
13. Édouard Manet (1823–1883) abandoned romanticism in his portrayals of women and sexuality in paintings such as *Olympia* (1865) and *Universal Exhibition* (1867).
14. Opera was a commercially profitable enterprise and accessible to most classes of society.
15. Giuseppe Verdi (1813–1901) used the genre to contrast the noble ideals of honor, love, and patriotism with the corrosive effects of power; he explored social issues as well.
16. Richard Wagner (1813–1883), the era's most flamboyant and musically innovative composer, revolutionized opera by fusing music and drama to arouse an audience's fear, awe, and engagement with his vision.
17. His cycle of four operas—*The Ring of the Nibelungen*—exploring the destructiveness of materialism and the pursuit of power, concluded that only unselfish love could redeem society.
18. Although oftentimes controversial, writers, visual artists, and composers helped create a unified cultural community.

B. Religion and National Order, pp. 718–720

1. Although organized religion provided a source of stability after 1848, some liberals and nationalists came to reject a religious worldview.

2. Bismarck attacked Catholicism in Germany as contrary to the national interest. The pope, the German bishops, and many Catholics and conservatives resisted repression of religion.
3. The Catholic church resisted growing nationalism and rationalism, which it saw as attempts to replace religious faith and loyalty.
4. In 1864, Pope Pius IX (r. 1846–1878) issued *The Syllabus of Errors*, which put the church explicitly at odds with aspects of liberalism, progress, and modern civilization.
5. In 1870, the First Vatican Council approved the doctrine of papal infallibility.
6. In 1878, a new pope, Leo XIII, encouraged the church to modernize by accepting aspects of democracy and encouraging Catholic universities to be open to up-to-date scholarship. It became easier for faithful Catholics to be patriotic citizens.
7. Religion remained a powerful influence, but religious practice changed. Church attendance declined among workers and artisans, although many in the upper and middle classes and most of the peasantry remained faithful.
8. This period saw an outburst of religious fervor, among women in particular.
9. In 1858, a peasant girl in Lourdes in southern France, Bernadette Soubirous (1844–1879), began having visions of the Virgin Mary.
10. Less than ten years later, railroad track had to be laid to Lourdes to enable millions of pilgrims to visit the shrine.
11. At the same time, Charles Darwin (1809–1882) published *On the Origin of Species* (1859), in which he stated that human beings had evolved over the course of millions of years.
12. Darwin argued that only the strongest or best adapted to the environment would find sexual partners and reproduce.
13. Darwin's theories challenged the biblical creation story and the view that nature was noble and humans essentially rational.
14. Darwin tried to explain the social hierarchy by maintaining that white European men naturally dominated the world because they were more highly evolved than men of color and all women. Social Darwinism, promoted by men such as Herbert Spencer, used its version of evolutionary theory to argue against Christian charity as a source of weakness to modern nation-states.

C. **From the Natural Sciences to Social Science, pp. 720–721**

1. Darwin's theories accelerated the search for alternatives to the religious explanation of social order.
2. Auguste Comte (1798–1857) originated the ideas for positivism, a social science that called for the careful study of facts so as to generate accurate or "positive" laws of society.
3. Because Comte promoted women's participation in reform, his ideas opened the fields of the social sciences to them.
4. English philosopher John Stuart Mill (1806–1873) was initially an enthusiastic supporter of Comte and argued for mass education and the complete enfranchisement of women.
5. His treatise *On Liberty* (1859) argued for individual liberty protected from state intrusion.
6. Mill's promotion of women's rights—an argument he developed with the help of his wife, Harriet Taylor Mill (1808–1858)—inspired him to write *The Subjection of Women* (1869), in which he stated that a woman's assigned role of love and obedience in marriage masked gross marital inequality.
7. Mill's thought, however, was submerged in a flood of Social Darwinism.

Lecture Strategies

1. The unification of Germany under Bismarck is one of the most important topics covered in Chapter 22. Besides being an excellent example of realism in politics, it also provides an opportunity for students to become acquainted with the "German question." Germany quickly became the most powerful country in Europe in military, economic, and cultural terms, with consequences that quickly became obvious to all. The German question refers to the implications for the rest of Europe of a powerful, somewhat restless Germany. Bismarck was, of course, one of the great figures of the nineteenth century. The influence of his activities in the 1860s extended well into the following century, and the implications of German unification should be explored at some length with students.

Many biographies of Bismarck are available, but three stand out: Lothar Gall, *Bismarck: The White*

Revolutionary, 2 vols. (London: Allen & Unwin, 1986); and Otto Pflanze, *Bismarck and the Development of Germany*, 3 vols. (Princeton, NJ: Princeton University Press, 1990). D. G. Williamson's *Bismarck and Germany 1862–1890* (New York: Longman, 1998) is short, but accurate and insightful. Part 4 of James J. Sheehan's *German History, 1770–1866* (Oxford: Clarendon Press, 1989) covers developments in Germany between 1848 and 1866. The initial chapter in Gordon A. Craig, *Germany, 1866–1945* (New York: Oxford University Press, 1980) deals with the unification of Germany between 1866 and 1871. John Breuilly's long view of unification is very useful, particularly on the questions the text raises about Austrian–German relations, Austria, Prussia, and the making of modern Germany (New York: Longman, 2002). A different perspective on German unification may be found in the early chapters of Patricia Kollander, *Frederick III: Germany's Liberal Emperor* (Westport, CT: Greenwood Press, 1995). Frederick, the son of Wilhelm I, did not always agree with the policies of Bismarck and his father. See also the convenient selection of primary sources in Theodore S. Hamerow, ed., *The Age of Bismarck: Documents and Interpretations* (New York: Harper & Row, 1973). A good introduction to German unification and nation-building in general can be found in Chapter 7 of Robert Gildea, *Barricades and Borders, Europe 1800–1914* (Oxford: Oxford University Press, 1987).

2. The reorganization of Russia during this period is also of great importance. Although Alexander II was a reluctant reformer, he did realize the necessity of emancipating the serfs and so also instituted several other reforms, which, under different circumstances, would have helped to create a Russian Empire far different from the one that eventually emerged. The fragmented reaction of the Russian aristocracy to reform is worth framing as well, as it contributed to the consequential radical streak in Russian political culture.

On the emancipation of the serfs, see first Gregory L. Freeze, "Reform and Counter-Reform, 1855–1890," in Gregory L. Freeze, ed., *Russia: A History* (Oxford: Oxford University Press, 1997). David Moon, *The Russian Peasantry* (New York: Longman, 1999) offers an excellent study of the peasantry in the emancipation and immediate post-emancipation era. W. Bruce Lincoln, *The Great Reforms: Autocracy, Bureaucracy, and the Politics of Change in Imperial Russia* (DeKalb, IL: Northern Illinois University Press, 1990), is the best overview. Lincoln was a prolific and highly readable writer on Russian history topics. Ben Eklof and John Bushnell, eds., *Russia's Great Reforms, 1855–1881* (Bloomington, IN: University of Indiana Press, 1994) is an important collection of essays on the reforms. Russian industrialization, critical and consequential, is treated engagingly in A. I. Fenin's memoirs, *Coal and Politics in Late Imperial Russia* (DeKalb, IL: Northern Illinois University Press, 1990). Part 2 of Gregory L. Freeze, *From Supplication to Revolution: A Documentary Social History of Imperial Russia* (New York: Oxford University Press, 1988) brings together an excellent collection of documents on Russian society in the 1860s. Finally, Ivan Turgenev's great novel *Fathers and Sons* is useful in understanding the temper of the times in Russia. The *Norton Critical Edition*, Michael R. Katz, ed. (New York: W. W. Norton, 1995) reprints the novel along with many documents and critical essays.

3. Efforts to improve public health, particularly in urban areas, extended the power of the government to intervene in the lives of citizens in important ways. This topic has not yet been fully explored, but sufficient material is available for an interesting lecture and discussion. See first a book that explores the period when Edwin Chadwick, an English pioneer in the field of public health, was active: Christopher Hamlin, *Public Health and Social Justice in the Age of Chadwick, Britain, 1800–1854* (Cambridge: Cambridge University Press, 1998). Chadwick's own book, *The Sanitary Condition of the Laboring Population of Britain* (1842), paints a grim picture of working-class life, but also proposes a solution to the important problem of waste management. In addition, see also the study by Jean-Pierre Goubert, *The Conquest of Water: The Advent of Health in the Industrial Age* (Princeton, NJ: Princeton University Press, 1989). Somewhat more specialized, but full of fascinating material, is Donald Reid, *Paris Sewers and Sewermen: Realities and Representations* (Cambridge, MA: Harvard University Press, 1993). For a broader perspective on sanitation in France, and the relationship between scientific knowledge, ideologies, and public policy, see Ann Elizabeth Fowler La Berge, *Mission and Method: The Early Nineteenth Century French Public Health Movement* (Cambridge: Cambridge University Press, 2002). Two books deal with theories about disease: Michael Worboys, *Spreading Germs: Diseases, Theories, and Medical Practice in Britain, 1865–1900* (Cambridge: Cambridge University Press, 2000); and Andrew Robert Aisenberg, *Contagion: Disease, Government, and the "Social Question" in Nineteenth-Century France* (Palo Alto, CA: Stanford University Press, 1999). See also Patrice Debre's highly useful biography of the father of the germ theory, *Louis Pasteur* (Baltimore, MD: Johns Hopkins University Press, 1998).

4. Much has been written about the British in India. A good beginning is Stanley Wolpert, *A New History of India*, 6th ed. (New York: Oxford University Press, 1999). Another good survey is one by Judith M. Brown, *Modern India: The Origins of an Asian Democracy*, 2nd ed. (Oxford: Oxford University Press, 1994). A more specialized study is David Arnold, *Colonizing*

the Body: State Medicine and Epidemic Disease in Nineteenth-Century India (Berkeley: University of California Press, 1993). Arnold discusses not only the introduction of western medicine to India, but also efforts to adjust western practices to Indian customs and expectations. Thomas R. Metcalf, *Ideologies of the Raj* (Cambridge: Cambridge University Press, 1994) covers the various attempts to justify British rule in India, and can be supplemented with Martin Moir, Douglas Peers, and Lynn Zastoupil's edited volume, *J. S. Mill's Encounter With India*, (Toronto: University of Toronto Press, 1999), which examines the intersection between progressive thinking and imperial administration. Rajnarayan Chandavarkar, *Imperial Power and Popular Politics: Class, Resistance, and the State in India, c. 1850–1950* (Cambridge: Cambridge University Press, 1998) examines an aspect of colonialism in India not often discussed: the growth of industrial capitalism and a working class.

5. The theories of Charles Darwin have, in one way or another, virtually taken over many disciplines in the past few years. Even during Darwin's lifetime, Social Darwinism was a powerful force. Students should be introduced to Darwin's life, career, and main ideas. Although his life after the voyage on the *Beagle* was one of few excitements, it held enough interesting developments, particularly after the publication of *On the Origin of Species*, to make a review of his career useful and interesting. A good place to begin is Janet Browne, *Charles Darwin: Voyaging* (Princeton, NJ: Princeton University Press, 1995), a fine biography that concentrates largely on the voyage of *HMS Beagle* but also continues the story into the 1850s. Another useful source is Philip Appleman, *Darwin: A Norton Critical Edition*, 3rd ed. (New York: W. W. Norton, 2000), which includes writings by Darwin and writings about him. Another Norton publication along these lines is Mark Ridley, ed., *The Darwin Reader*, 2nd ed. (New York: W. W. Norton, 1996). See also *The Autobiography of Charles Darwin*, reissue ed. (New York: W. W. Norton, 1993); and Frederick Burkhardt, ed., *Charles Darwin's Letters: A Selection, 1825–1859* (Cambridge: Cambridge University Press, 1998). Helpful for placing Darwin's ideas in the context of his times is Michael Ruse, *The Darwinian Revolution: Science Red in Tooth and Claw* (Chicago: University of Chicago Press, 1999). Mike Hawkins, *Social Darwinism in European and American Thought, 1860–1945: Nature as Model and Nature as Threat* (Cambridge: Cambridge University Press, 1997) will be invaluable for tracing the influence of Darwin's ideas. Also on the subject of influence, see Peter J. Bowler, *Charles Darwin: The Man and His Influence* (Cambridge: Cambridge University Press, 1996). A biography of Thomas Henry Huxley by Adrian J. Desmond, *Huxley: From Devil's Disciple to Evolution's High Priest* (Reading, MA: Addison-Wesley, 1997), is useful in tracing the spread of Darwin's ideas by one of his chief admirers.

6. Karl Marx and John Stuart Mill are perhaps the two most important political thinkers of the 1850s and 1860s. Marx has, of course, received far more attention than Mill. On Marx, see first David McLellan, *Karl Marx: His Life and Thought* (New York: Harper & Row, 1973), long, but probably the best book overall. See also Lecture Strategies number 4 for Chapter 21.

For Mill, a good place to begin is William Stafford, *John Stuart Mill* (New York: St. Martin's Press, 1999). John Skorupski, *The Cambridge Companion to Mill* (Cambridge: Cambridge University Press, 1997) has much to offer. Anthologies include Alan Ryan, ed., *Mill: Texts, Commentaries* (New York: W. W. Norton, 1996); and David Spitz, ed., *On Liberty: Annotated Text, Sources and Background, Criticism* (New York: W. W. Norton, 1975). See also John Stuart Mill, Harriet Hardy Taylor Mill, and Helen Mill, *Sexual Equality: A John Stuart Mill, Harriet Taylor Mill, and Helen Taylor Reader* (Toronto: University of Toronto Press, 1994); and Harriet Taylor Mill, *The Complete Works of Harriet Taylor Mill* (Bloomington, IN: Indiana University Press, 1998).

Class Discussion Starters

1. In connection with "Lecture Strategies," number 4, events in India in 1857–1858 are dramatic, but also serve as a good jumping-off point for a discussion considering practical aspects of the Raj and its relationship to the Indian people. The tensions between cultural reformers of one kind or another and those who wanted to manage India to produce maximum profit and minimal difficulties are worth bringing out, because the debate raises broader questions about the competing agendas of European imperialists more generally.

2. Benjamin Disraeli is a fascinating and peculiarly modern political character. His wit, novelistic career, and even fashion sense make him accessible to students, while the terms of "Tory Democracy" as it evolved in the 1860s and 1870s offer an interesting take on how conservatism in Britain adapted to democratic politics. Disraeli's willingness to use state power to interfere with "free markets" in order to build popular support is worth discussing, and his eagerness to embrace more aggressive forms of imperialism and to popularize pomp and monarchy are worth exploring with students. Excerpts from his readable public speeches can certainly spur discussion about the relationship between populism, ideological principle, and emotion in the emerging democratic

age. The canonical biography remains Robert Blake's *Disraeli* (Oxford: Oxford University Press, 1969), but other insightful books for informing a discussion might include Stanley Weintraub's *Disraeli: A Biography* (New York: Dutton, 1993), which gives exhaustive consideration to Disraeli's literary career, or Edgar Feuchtwanger's more manageable *Disraeli* (London: Arnold, 2000), and several of the essays contained in Charles Richmond and Paul Smith's collection, *The Self-Fashioning of Disraeli* (Cambridge: Cambridge University Press, 1999). Ian St. John's *Disraeli and the Art of Victorian Politics* (London: Anthem Press, 2005) offers a useful synthesis of scholarship and debates about Disraeli's life and times. It may be worth reading all or parts of his political novels of the 1840s, including *Coningsby* (1844), *Sybil* (1845), and *Tancred* (1847).

3. The relative importance of violence, statecraft, charisma, and dramatic gesture are worth discussing with students in relation to German and Italian unification. How important to both processes was the existence of an outside (or inside?) threat to the well-being of the (imagined) state? In addition to materials on German unification in "Lecture Strategies," number 1, it may be worth consulting Denis Mack Smith's classic study of the Risorgimento, *Cavour and Garibaldi 1860: A Study in Political Conflict* (new. ed.) (Cambridge: Cambridge University Press, 1985), Lucy Riall's *The Italian Risorgimento: State, Society, and National Unification* (New York: Routledge, 1994), or the thought-provoking recent work of Daniel Ziblatt, *Structuring the State: The Formation of Italy and Germany and the Puzzle of Federalism* (Princeton, NJ: Princeton University Press, 2006).

Reviewing the Text

Review Questions

1. What were the main results of the Crimean War?
[model answer] • ***New technologies were introduced to warfare:*** *The railroad, the shell-firing cannon, breech-loading rifles, and steam-powered ships all changed the way war was fought. The telegraph meant home audiences now received news from the front lines rapidly and in great detail.*
• ***New civilian attitudes toward war:*** *News from the front included reports of incompetence, poor sanitation, and the huge death toll. Civilian outrage and national pride inspired some Europeans to head for the front to help.*
• ***Russia and Austria's dominance of European politics ended:*** *Napoleon III met his goal of reducing the strength of Russia and Austria in the European political world. Afterward, the two nations were unable to contain the forces of liberalism and nationalism within the territories they controlled.*
• ***Russia was forced to reform:*** *The poor performance of conscripted serf armies indicated to educated Russians that serf labor was a liability. Tsar Alexander began the age of Great Reforms: serfs were freed from aristocrats' land, but were not given complete freedom to enter the urban workforce. The tsar created aristocratic regional councils, set up a nationwide civil judiciary system based on equality of all persons before the law, and reformed the military by shortening conscription and educating Russian troops.*

2. What role did warfare play in the various nineteenth-century nation-building efforts?
[model answer] • ***War with outsiders helped nations build nationalism and unity under one ruler:*** *In Italy, the entire peninsula eventually united in victory with Piedmont-Sardinia to oust first Austria and then France. Prussia's prime minister led it into a series of wars, boosting nationalism and convincing the German states to rally around Prussia's modern army.*
• ***War abroad to build an overseas empire provided income and maintained peace and prosperity at home:*** *Great Britain used warfare to expand its empire in places such as India, as well as to maintain control of Ireland. Because the violence was beyond the view of most British people, they were able to imagine their nation as peaceful, advanced, and united.*
• ***Internal warfare preserved national unity at the expense of regionalism:*** *In the United States, President Lincoln led a war against the southern states to force them back into the Union. Though he did not originally intend to abolish slavery, his Emancipation Proclamation freed all southern slaves from the states that had seceded and turned the war from a fight for the Union into a fight to end slavery in the United States.*
• ***The threat of warfare increased colonial independence:*** *To prevent the United States from annexing Canada following the U.S. civil war, the British government allowed Canadians to form a united, self-governing dominion, answering Canadian appeals for home rule.*

3. How did Europe's expanding nation-states attempt to impose social order within and beyond Europe and what resistance did they face?
[model answer] • ***States faced challenges to public order from economically disempowered artisans and workers:*** *Trade unionism, anarchism, socialism, and Marxism became increasingly powerful and were determined to challenge the state. In Paris, in particular, after defeat in the war with Prussia in 1870–1871, local citizens established workers' republics and attempted to promote social revolution.*
• ***The military was used to maintain order:*** *In Paris, the army of the new government suppressed the Paris*

Commune. In other countries, the military remained a source of power and stability for national governments.

• ***Centralized states promoted social order by emphasizing family virtues, fortifying religion, and maintaining the boundaries between the male political sphere and the female domestic sphere:*** *Revolutionaries often endorsed a range of social changes that dismayed many, including mutualism, anti-clericalism, feminism, socialism, and anarchy. Female revolutionaries in Paris, in particular, were blamed for the part they played in supporting the commune.*

• ***States enlisted culture in their quest for national power:*** *Museums, scientific exhibitions, and the arts were often sponsored by the state and helped to shape national heritages, by creating shared cultural experiences.*

• ***States controlled and limited the place of religion in society:*** *Although politicians often saw the value of religion in preserving public order, many nation-builders, notably Bismarck in Germany, worked hard to limit the influence of religion, particularly Catholicism.*

• ***Social scientists advocated for mass education and widespread, sweeping, state-sponsored reform:*** *John Stuart Mill, Auguste Comte, and Charles Darwin offer striking examples of systematic social reformers who influenced social development by applying reason to progress, governance, and social relationships such as the family.*

4. How did cultural expression and scientific and social thought help produce the hardheaded and realistic values of the times?

[model answer] • ***Tough-minded and realistic economic and political thought was dominant:*** *Typified by the theories of Karl Marx, who attacked romantic and utopian critiques of the social order, many thinkers rejected the Enlightenment notion that society was basically harmonious.*

• ***Realism in literature and the arts reflected disenchantment with romanticism:*** *Many novels focused on the difficulties and challenges of ordinary life and showed readers the hard realities of modern times. Painters offered graphic and realistic portrayals of people and urban environments.*

• ***Natural science, particularly as presented by Darwin and others, suggested a society based on competition and the response of life to often hostile environments:*** *Darwin and others such as Herbert Spencer used the theory of evolution to explain the dominance of European men as in keeping with the natural order. Social Darwinists argued against traditional Christian notions of charity and emphasized the value of conflict and competition in shaping nations and races.*

• ***Social scientists devised scientific systems of social organization that encouraged a statistically based, hard-headed approach to building strong, unified nations:*** *Auguste Compte, John Stuart Mill, and others advocated for social reorganization and re-prioritization to reflect factual and realistic appraisals of society and social problems.*

Making Connections

1. How did realism in social thought break with Enlightenment values?

[model answer] *Philosophes of the Enlightenment intellectualized the problems of the world, whereas realists took action and dealt with the world as they found it, whether it was the Realpolitik politician, who did what he had to do to achieve his goals (such as Bismarck and the unification); or the artist, who depicted in excruciating detail the lives of the working poor (such as Dickens in his many novels). Stimulated by the thinking of Charles Darwin, positivism grew out of the attempt to understand the world outside religious constraints. It was believed that social scientists could construct knowledge of the political order as they would an understanding of the natural world; that is, according to informed secular investigation. This idea inspired persons to believe that they could resolve the social problems spawned by economic and social change.*

2. Why did some nation-states tend toward secularism while the kingdoms that preceded them were based on religion?

[model answer] *If religion was the legitimizing force for rulers in early, modern kingdoms, nation-states of this period, such as Germany and Italy, were increasingly rooted in the secular concepts of nationalism and Realpolitik. National unity was based mainly on such things as language and culture, but also, as time progressed, on the rejection of "outside" influences and, frequently, violence.*

3. How was the Paris Commune related to earlier revolutions in France? How did it differ from them? How was it related to nation building?

[model answer] *As with previous French uprisings, the situation seemed dire prior to the establishment of the Paris Commune. Prussian forces marched on Paris and, lacking bare necessities, the citizens demanded republican reforms. The provisional government, set up after the departure of Napoleon III, reacted in a typical, traditional way: troops were dispatched to quell the unrest. The Paris Commune was declared in the face of this military threat from Prussia but, as in the past, commune leaders argued over how to proceed, which gave the provisional government time to take action. The Paris Commune was suppressed, as were those communes that had been formed in other French cities. As with earlier revolutions, a good deal of violence was involved on both sides of the conflict.*

And, as with the French Revolution, the worst of the atrocities committed during the commune were later blamed on women agitators.

Discussing the Documents

Questions from Online Study Guide with Model Answers

Mrs. Seacole: The Other Florence Nightingale, p. 694

1. How does Mary Seacole's career reflect nineteenth-century attitudes about the roles of women?
[model answer] *Mary Seacole's activities as a nurse were an extension of the domestic role of women. She talks about bringing the comforts of home to sick soldiers, and providing them with nourishing food. She performs these tasks with modesty, and not for her own reputation.*

2. What was unconventional about Mary Seacole's career?
[model answer] *Mary Seacole was performing these services at a time when medicine was becoming more professionalized, and persons without official training and certification—especially women—were being forced out. The fact that a woman of minority descent was able to participate in the Crimean War in this capacity was also unconventional.*

Bismarck Tricks the Public to Get His War, p. 701

1. How does Bismarck justify doctoring this document to trick the public into war?
[model answer] *Bismarck justifies his actions by arguing that avoiding war will cost Prussia its honor and national confidence in the state. Maintaining national honor is the highest priority, and without honor there would be no confidence in the state, which could lead to disorder.*

2. What were some of the social conditions in nineteenth-century Prussia that allowed Bismarck to pull this deception off?
[model answer] *The most important condition that allowed Bismarck to trick the public into going to war was a literate public that read newspapers. The political importance of public opinion was another condition, as were nationalist sentiments about the honor and pride of the state.*

Other Questions for Discussing These Documents in Class

Mrs. Seacole: The Other Florence Nightingale

1. What did Seacole's successes, particularly given her modest means, indicate about the standards of treatment and supply for soldiers of the period?

2. Given how Seacole describes what she did for soldiers, what aspect of her services most likely drew the soldiers to her?

Bismarck Tricks the Public to Get His War

1. Why was Bismarck reluctant to avoid war? Why did he consider the risks associated with doing so unacceptable? Who helped him make the decision?

2. What insight does the selection provide into Realpolitik in practice? How does it affect your understanding of the way politics of the period operated?

Comparative Questions

1. What do these documents together tell you about the importance of public opinion in this period? How is public opinion related to the actions of Bismarck and Mrs. Seacole?

2. Is there a connection between Bismarck's Realpolitik and Seacole's labors in the Crimea? How much concern does Bismarck seem to have for the average German soldier, based on this excerpt?

For Users of *Sources of The Making of the West*

The following documents are available in Chapter 22 of the companion sourcebook by Katharine J. Lualdi, University of Southern Maine.

1. Ending Serfdom in Russia: Peter Kropótkin, *Memoirs of a Revolutionist* (1861)
2. Fighting for Italian Nationalism: Camillo di Cavour, *Letter to King Victor Emmanuel* (July 24, 1858)
3. Realpolitik and Otto von Bismarck: Rudolf von Ihering, *Two Letters* (1866)
4. Evolutionary Principles: Charles Darwin, *The Descent of Man* (1871)
5. Social Evolution: Walter Bagehot, *Physics and Politics* (1872)

Discussion Ideas for Sources of The Making of the West, *Chapter 22*

1. Track the question of public opinion in these documents. Do rulers care about it? What sort of views of the common people do the authors have? Discuss how the place of public opinion in policy making may have been changing.

2. The first three documents all deal with the consequential political actions of "great men." What can be learned about the practice of Realpolitik? What

was (or seemed to be) effective about it? What characterized Realpolitik in practice?

3. Considering the documents together, in what ways might some people of the era see war as a good thing? In what ways can we see conflict in the readings as an agent of change and progress?

Working with Visual Sources

For this exercise, please refer to Darwin Ridiculed, c. 1860, on p. 720 of the textbook or view the image on the book companion site's Online Study Guide under the "Visual Activity" for Chapter 22.

Students viewing the image at the Online Study Guide are asked three questions about the image. The questions and model answers (not made available to students) are below. Project this image, available on the Instructor's Resources CD-ROM, in class or ask students to look at the image in their textbooks and answer the questions.

1. Why did this illustrator picture Darwin with a monkey? In what ways are Darwin and the monkey similar?
[model answer] *Darwin argued that all species developed through evolution, a process whereby species responded to their environments in ways that enhanced their ability to reproduce; as species evolved, they got stronger. The illustrator is demonstrating the principle of evolution by showing the similarities between humans and monkeys. Darwin and the monkey both have similarly shaped, hairy bodies; similar hands and feet; and both have high, bald foreheads, large ears, and long chins.*

2. In which ways do Darwin and the monkey differ?
[model answer] *Although both have human expressions on their faces, Darwin's face is more recognizably human, whereas the monkey's face still looks like that of a monkey. Darwin seems to be older than the monkey, and is more active, holding out the mirror into which they both gaze.*

3. Are Darwin and the monkey depicted as equals in the illustration? Which one has more authority, and what is used to indicate that? How does this reflect Social Darwinism?
[model answer] *Darwin seems to have more authority because he is older and active, holding out the mirror in an authoritative manner. Social Darwinists believed that evolution had created a natural social hierarchy whereby more evolved groups, viewed as superior to less evolved groups, were justified in their claims to more power and more wealth. By depicting the monkey and Darwin as similar, and yet not equal, the illustration reflects Social Darwinist assumptions about the consequences of evolution and perceived social roles.*

For this exercise, please refer to Seeing History: Photographing the Nation: Domesticity and War on p. 704 of the textbook or view the images on the book companion site's Online Study Guide under the "Visual Activity: Seeing History" for Chapter 22.

Students viewing the images at the Online Study Guide are asked two questions about the images. The questions and model answers (not made available to students) are below. Project these images, available on the Instructor's Resources CD-ROM, in class or ask students to look at the images in their textbooks and answer the questions.

1. Assuming these photographs were meant to influence how the public perceived both the monarchy and the military, what image is presented in each photograph?
[model answer] *Queen Victoria and Prince Albert are shown relaxing at home, like any other ordinary British couple of a certain class. Queen Victoria appears demure and modest, looking down as her husband instructs/reads to her. In that sense, the image would reinforce gender roles of the period, and also prevailing class structures. The monarchy here is presented as modest and rather ordinary. Roger Fenton and his companions are dressed in full uniforms, and although their tents are modest, they seem comfortable, well-fed, and even relaxed. They seem confident, well-prepared, and capable.*

2. How might these photographs affect viewers' perceptions?
[model answer] *Photography of exotic locations or important personages circulating in these ways was new in this period. Because photographs were more "realistic" than paintings, and because they were often seen as more "authentic," these types of images were both popular and influential.*

Mapping Exercises

Map Activity from OSG—Model Answers for Map Activity #2

For this activity, please refer to Map 22.1: The Crimean War, 1853–1856, on p. 692. Students are asked these questions:

What strategic interests were at stake during the Crimean War?
[model answer] *The Ottoman Empire controlled the Dardanelles Straits. These connected the Black Sea (and Russia) to the Mediterranean Sea. The weakening of the Ottoman Empire opened the possibility for Russia and the Austrian Empire to gain new territories.*

Why were France and Great Britain drawn into the Crimean War, even though it did not affect their borders?

[model answer] *France helped orchestrate the war to fracture the conservative alliance between Russia and the Austrian Empire that had kept French ambitions in check since the Congress of Vienna. Great Britain was drawn in because it needed to protect its Mediterranean trade routes to East Asia, which would have been threatened if the Russians gained dominance over that region.*

Map 22.1: The Crimean War, 1853–1856, p. 692

What is striking about this conflict in relation to Russian geography as a whole? What does the map reveal about the changing nature of warfare? What was unusual about this conflict? Emphasize the lack of borders between the Allied powers and Russia and the compartmentalized nature of the conflict. The nature of the geography of the Dardenelles is well worth underscoring.

Map 22.2: Unification of Italy, 1859–1870, p. 698

Ask students to use this map as a basis for discussing the extent to which Cavour's plans for unification succeeded. Help them understand that it was not only a matter of the territories remaining outside the new kingdom of Italy (Venetia, Rome), it was also the incorporation of southern Italy that would have to figure in any assessment of Cavour's plans and activities.

Map 22.3: Unification of Germany, 1862–1871, p. 700

Ask students to use this map as a basis for discussing Bismarck's actions and intentions during the unification process of Germany. Have students particularly discuss the differences between the outcome of the Austro-Prussian War of 1866 (that is, the North German Confederation) and the Franco-Prussian War of 1870 (the German Empire).

Map 22.4: U.S. Expansion, 1850–1870, p. 706

What does this map reveal about the nature of the expansion of the United States in these years? How was American expansion different from the processes of national aggrandizement going on in Europe? In what ways did expansion of America's territory relate to processes of industrialization and immigration/migration?

Map 22.5: The Paris Commune, 1871, p. 714

What sorts of buildings were burned by the communards? What does the map reveal about where fighting took place, and what was the relationship of the army's march to urban geography?

Mapping the West: Europe and the Mediterranean, 1871, p. 722

Ask students to consider the consequences of a Europe organized into nation-states. Is any room left for nations to expand without interfering with the interests of other nations? The only area left in Europe proper was in southeastern Europe: the Balkans. As the Ottoman Empire continued to decline, this area grew in its importance to both major and minor powers.

In-Class Assignments and Presentation Topics

1. Ask students to reflect on Bismarck's actions during the process of unifying Germany, particularly his use of war as a political tactic. What were his political objectives? How did he manage both to avoid revolution and to transform the country? Why did Bismarck decide it was necessary to create the German Empire as such? Were the opponents of growing Prussian power, as Emperor Francis-Joseph suggested, "dumb"?

You may wish to assign students short selections from one or more of the biographies and studies mentioned in "Lecture Strategies," number 1. Excerpts from primary sources, including those in the text and Katharine Lualdi's documentary supplement (see above) can be used to help students connect their judgments to evidence. See the convenient collection of material in Theodore S. Hamerow, ed., *The Age of Bismarck: Documents and Interpretations* (New York: Harper & Row, 1973).

2. Student presentations on different aspects of the 1860s in Russia offer many possibilities. Students might report on the process by which the government decided to emancipate the serfs, on the other major reforms, on the Polish revolt of 1863, and on the individuals most closely associated with the reforms. The chapter by Gregory L. Freeze mentioned in "Lecture Strategies," number 2, is a good place to begin. Students will find Joseph Wieczenski, ed., *The Modern Encyclopedia of Russian and Soviet History*, 60 vols. (Gulf Breeze, FL: Academic International Press, 1976–1996) indispensable.

3. Have students write a short essay describing the reason behind the intense interest in the 1850s and 1860s in realism in fiction or in the visual arts. It may be useful to remind students about the overwhelming influence of the idea of Realpolitik in national and international politics and the fascination with scientific and technological advances, especially after the publication of Darwin's *On the Origin of Species*. What role might the development of photography have played in the development of painting? To provide focus to the essay, students should refer to the works of

realist novelists, such as Charles Dickens and George Eliot, or examine realist paintings such as those of Manet.

4. Assign students a three-part essay in which they are to summarize the views of Marx and Mill, and in the third part point out the ways in which these two men differed. Preface the assignment with an in-class discussion of the views of Marx and Mill. During the discussion, help students understand that Marx presented a complete picture of human history moving inexorably to a predetermined end by means of revolution. Mill, by contrast, subscribed to change, reform, and progress, but presented no overarching picture or predetermined end.

Essay Questions

1. A comparative study of serfdom in Russia with slavery in the United States offers a challenging assignment. Students' studies might compare living and working conditions of serfs with those of slaves; investigate the possibilities for gaining freedom in the period before emancipation in each country; compare the impact of Harriet Beecher Stowe's *Uncle Tom's Cabin* with that of Ivan Turgenev's *A Hunter's Sketches*; or examine the realities of the period after emancipation as experienced by serfs and slaves. How were the terms of emancipation different? Similar? Published comparative works are available. Students may wish to begin with Peter Kolchin, *Unfree Labor: American Slavery and Russian Serfdom* (Cambridge, MA: Belknap Press, 1987).

2. During this period, society and government devoted much energy to achieving social order. Students might investigate efforts to eradicate venereal disease. These efforts always involved issues of gender, class, and power. A good starting point would be Bonnie Smith, *Changing Lives: Women in European History Since 1700* (Lexington, MA: D. C. Heath, 1989), Chapter 4, "The Rise of the Woman Worker: The Early Years," and the bibliography for the chapter. See also Peter Gay, *The Tender Passion*, vol. 2 of *The Bourgeois Experience: Victoria to Freud* (New York: Oxford University Press, 1986), Chapter 6, "The Price of Repression," and the relevant section of Gay's bibliographical essay. There are, of course, several other good, country-specific studies available in print.

3. Another sphere in which it was thought that order and control could be brought to bear was on the home front. Have students research the subject of domestic life in Victorian England, looking first at Mrs. Beeton's *Book of Household Management* (1861). What sort of instructions does Mrs. Beeton give to housewives? How practical would Mrs. Beeton's advice have been at that time? How do "class" and nationality figure into Mrs. Beeton's worldview? Compare these instructions to 1950s exhortations to American housewives. Are any similarities evident? Would Mrs. Beeton's instructions resonate anywhere in the world today? See Nicola Humble, ed., *Mrs. Beeton's Book of Household Management* (Oxford: Oxford University Press, 2000). In a related subject, have students research the subject of manners—especially food and table etiquette in Victorian England. How had food preparation and storage changed since the beginning of the century? How was food served and eaten at the table in the mid-Victorian period? How were idealized gender roles played out in the etiquette of high-society dinner parties? How easily can they be studied from the novels of the period? What role did science and technology play in the changes in food and how people consumed it during this period? Students can begin with Maggie Black, *Food and Cooking in Nineteenth-Century Britain: History and Recipes* (English Heritage, 1985); and Pamela A. Sambrook and Peter Brears, eds., *The Country House Kitchen 1650–1900* (Gloucestershire: Alan Sutton [in association with the National Trust], 1997).

4. Ask students to research and compare the careers of Florence Nightingale and Mrs. Seacole, the daughter of a free black Jamaican woman and a Scottish army officer. What were Nightingale's contributions to the medical field? Mrs. Seacole's contributions? Why did Mrs. Seacole, although quite well known in her own time through her medical work and her autobiography, not become the same kind of iconic figure as Florence Nightingale? Were class and race factors in their achievements and their ability to capitalize on the opportunities their service generated? How they are remembered by posterity?

5. Have students research the subject of realism in art in the 1850s and 1860s. What was meant by realism? What were John Ruskin's opinions on the subject? What role did scientific and technological advances play in artists' work? How did the pre-Raphaelite movement fit into their desire to depict realism? Compare the work of pre-Raphaelite painters such as Dante Gabriel Rossetti, John Everett Millais, and William Holman Hunt with the work of continental painters, such as Gustave Courbet and Édouard Manet.

Additional Resources: Literature

Ashton, Rosemary, ed., *George Eliot: Middlemarch.* 1994.

Bair, Lowell, trans., *Gustave Flaubert: Madame Bovary.* 1982.

Carlyle, Thomas, *A Carlyle Reader.* 2000.

Disraeli, Benjamin, *Tancred, or the New Crusade.* Various editions are in print.

Dubas, Danielle, ed., *Charles Dickens: Four Complete Novels: Great Expectations, Hard Times, A Christmas Carol, A Tale of Two Cities.* 2003.
Katz, Michael R., trans., *Ivan Turgenev: Fathers and Sons.* 1995.
Magarshack, David, trans., *Fyodor M. Dostoevsky: The Possessed.* 1954.
McGowan, James, trans., *Charles Baudelaire: "The Flowers of Evil."* 1998.
Pevear, Richard and Larissa Volokhonsky, trans., *Fyodor Dostoevsky: The Brothers Karamazov.* 2002.
Sklar, Kathryn Kish, ed., *Harriet Beecher Stowe: Three Novels: Uncle Tom's Cabin Or, Life Among the Lowly; The Minister's Wooing; Oldtown Folks.* 1982.

Additional Resources: Film and Video

Edward the King (1975; VHS, approx. 13 hrs.). This thirteen-part series (approximately 1 hour each part) chronicles the life of King Edward VII of England. It is strong on detail and the plot, costumes, and settings are vibrant and realistic.

A Tale of Two Cities (1991; VHS/DVD, 195 min.). Charles Dickens's 1857 novel diverges from his other works in that it is an epic tale of love and sacrifice during the French Revolution. It is particularly interesting for its Victorian perspective on the Revolution some sixty-five years later. This film is largely faithful to the novel.

Wives and Daughters (1999; PBS, VHS/DVD, approx. 6 hrs.) An adaptation of Elizabeth Gaskell's 1864–1866 novel about a young woman tried by her father's remarriage and initially rebuffed in love.

Victoria and Albert (2001; VHS/DVD, 200 min.). This highly entertaining and largely factual biographical dramatization shows Queen Victoria and her husband Prince Albert during their married years. Care has been lavished on the costumes and sets.

Gangs of New York (2002; VHS/DVD, 167 min.). The film overstates the violence of the era, but does capture quite vividly urban squalor and aspects of the urban immigrant experience in the United States in the middle decades of the century.

Charles Dickens (2003; DVD, 8 hrs., 30 min.). This three-part series examines Dickens's life and the motivations behind his writings. Dickens's overwhelming concern for the poor, who suffered most from industrialization, is especially emphasized.

Virtually all of Charles Dickens's novels have been dramatized, some of them several times over. Like the novels, the films capture the vagaries of fortune and the hardship of life for the Victorian poor and impoverished. In the following list (arranged chronologically by date of publication), the date that immediately follows the title refers to the date of its first publication.

Oliver Twist (1837–1838). (1997; VHS, 6 hrs.)
Nicholas Nickleby (1838–1839). (2002; VHS/DVD, approx. 200 min.)
Martin Chuzzlewit (1843–1844). (1994; VHS, 288 min.)
David Copperfield (1849–1850). (2000; VHS/DVD, approx. 3 hrs.)
Bleak House (1852–1853). (1988; VHS, 6 hrs., 31 min.)
Hard Times (1854). (1994; VHS, 102 min.)
Little Dorrit (1855–1857). (1988; VHS, 6 hrs.)
Great Expectations (1860–1861). (2001; VHS, 3 hrs.)
Our Mutual Friend (1864–1865). (1998; VHS/DVD, approx. 5 hrs., 30 min.)

OTHER BEDFORD/ST. MARTIN'S RESOURCES FOR CHAPTER 22

The following resources are available to accompany Chapter 22. Please refer to the Preface of this manual for detailed descriptions of all the ancillaries.

For Instructors

Transparencies

The following maps and images from Chapter 22 are available as full-color acetates.

- Map 22.1: The Crimean War, 1853–1856
- Map 22.2: Unification of Italy, 1859–1870
- Map 22.3: Unification of Germany, 1862–1871
- Map 22.4: U.S. Expansion, 1850–1870
- Map 22.5: The Paris Commune, 1871
- Mapping the West: Europe and the Mediterranean, 1871
- Darwin Ridiculed, c. 1860, p. 720
- Napoleon III and Eugénie Receive the Siamese Ambassadors, 1864, p. 691

Instructor's Resources CD-ROM

The following maps and image from Chapter 22, as well as a chapter outline, are available on disc in both PowerPoint and jpeg formats.

- Map 22.1: The Crimean War, 1853–1856
- Map 22.2: Unification of Italy, 1859–1870
- Map 22.3: Unification of Germany, 1862–1871
- Map 22.4: U.S. Expansion, 1850–1870
- Map 22.5: The Paris Commune, 1871

- Mapping the West: Europe and the Mediterranean, 1871
- Darwin Ridiculed, c. 1860 (chapter image, p. 720)

Using the Bedford Series with The Making of the West

Available in print as well as online at **bedfordstmartins .com/usingseries,** this guide offers practical suggestions for using *The Communist Manifesto,* with an Introduction by John E. Towes, *The Japanese Discovery of America,* by Peter Duus, and *On Liberty,* with an Introduction by Alan Kahan, in conjunction with Chapter 22 of the textbook.

For Students

Study Guides

The Online Study Guide at **bedfordstmartins.com/ hunt** helps students synthesize the material they have learned as well as practice the skills historians use to make sense of the past. The following Map, Visual, and Document activities are available for Chapter 22.

Map Activity

- Map 22.1: The Crimean War, 1853–1856

Visual Activity

- Darwin Ridiculed, c. 1860, p. 720
- Portrait of Queen Victoria and Prince Albert at Buckingham Palace, May 15, 1860, p. 704
- Roger Fenton, Officers of the 57th Regiment, 1855, p. 704

Reading Historical Documents

- Mrs. Seacole: The *Other* Florence Nightingale, p. 694
- Bismarck Tricks the Public to Get His War, p. 701

CHAPTER

23

Industry, Empire, and Everyday Life

1870–1890

CHAPTER RESOURCES

Main Chapter Topics

1. A series of downturns in business, beginning in 1873, created problems for both entrepreneurs and the working classes. Businesspersons, in search of answers, turned to innovation, new managerial techniques, and significant changes in marketing techniques, such as the department store. Advances in industry and the rise of a consumer economy changed the working lives of millions.

2. The "new imperialism," which brought direct rule by European nations to Africa and Asia, was closely connected with both industrial prosperity and the formation of national identity.

3. The upper class expanded through empire and industry, and their children were raised to support imperialism and industrial progress. The middle classes, particularly the ranks of the professionals, grew, and emphasized domesticity and useful recreations. For millions in the working class, emigration presented possibilities for a new, perhaps better, life overseas or in the city. Mostly middle-class social reformers sought to apply scientific and rational principles to the reorganization of working-class family life.

4. In the 1870s and 1880s, artists and writers explored the results of imperialism and industrialization using techniques associated with realism. These artists often adopted or responded to a gloomy Social Darwinism that focused on decline and degeneration perhaps as much as on progress.

5. The expansion of the franchise, still limited to men during this period, marked the beginnings of mass politics. Other characteristics of mass politics included extensive election campaigns, political clubs, and other organizations designed to mobilize voters, and the ready availability of inexpensive newspapers.

6. To differing extents, mass politics and the phenomena associated with it did not develop fully in Germany, Austria-Hungary, and Russia.

7. Workers organizations, often influenced by new ideologies such as Marxism, expanded and, through strikes and political action, put pressure on governments and employers to improve working conditions and raise wages.

Focus Question

How were industrial expansion and imperial conquest related, and how did they affect Western society, culture, and politics in the late nineteenth century?

1. Industrial expansion created a new economy from mid-century across much of the west. The need for raw materials such as Indian cotton and the ability of westerners to extract a variety of resources continued to increase, while the ability of non-western peoples to resist western military and economic power decreased. Manufacturers saw an international marketplace as an effective way of expanding demand, particularly as western states increased trade barriers and tariffs from the 1870s and anxieties about access to foreign markets gave added incentives to imperialism. Certain industries were particularly dependent on foreign and colonial trade and added to the interest in imperialism at all levels of society. In these senses, industrialization and imperialism went hand-in-hand during this period.

2. The social, cultural, and political consequences were extensive. The upper classes expanded and came to incorporate wealthy, new imperial and industrial elites. Members of the upper classes increasingly saw it as their duty and interest to strengthen and sustain industrialism and imperial expansion. The middle classes also increasingly saw themselves as interested in

and connected to modern industrial and imperial states, while the working classes were economically dependent in many cases on the ups and downs of industrial economies. Workers and farmers were increasingly aware of the opportunities of imperial connections as well, and patterns of migration and emigration were closely connected to imperial and industrial realities. Working-class culture was increasingly influenced by trade unionism, working-class political ideologies and activities such as suffrage expanded, and workers sought to improve their living and working conditions. Social Darwinism offered an explanation for European dominance, and also encouraged westerners to see their societies as dependent on expansion and growth for survival. Artistic movements such as realism were shaped by the new realities and the growing influence of industrial and imperial progress.

Annotated Chapter Outline

I. The Advance of Industry in an Age of Empire

A. Industrial Innovation, pp. 727–729

1. Industrial, technological, and commercial innovation characterized the late nineteenth century.
2. New products—from the telephone to the internal-combustion engine—provided proof of industrial progress.
3. Leading industrial nations mined massive quantities of coal, iron, and produced steel during the 1870s and 1880s, all necessary for the growth of industry.
4. For Great Britain, a second Industrial Revolution developed, founded this time not on steam and textiles but on heavy industrial products like iron and steel.
5. On the continent, the two industrial revolutions arrived simultaneously in many countries.
6. Industrialization transformed agriculture in the late nineteenth century, as chemical fertilizers boosted crop yields and reapers and threshers mechanized harvesting.
7. The development of refrigeration accommodated the transport of fruit and meat, diversifying and increasing the urban food supply, while the importation of tin from the colonies facilitated the large-scale commercial canning of foods.
8. Great Britain began to lose its industrial predominance to Germany and the United States, both of which rapidly industrialized during this period.
9. French industry grew, but French business establishments remained smaller than those in Germany and the United States.
10. In Spain, Austria-Hungary, and Italy, industry developed in highly concentrated areas, but the rest of these countries remained tied to nonmechanized agriculture.
11. Electricity allowed the Scandinavian countries, poor in coal and ore, to industrialize, and Sweden and Norway became leaders in the use of hydroelectric power and the development of electrical products.
12. Russian industrialization continued to lag behind.
13. Russian peasants, still tied to the *mir*, only worked in small numbers in industry when they were not needed to work the land.
14. Russian workers and peasants could not afford to buy the goods they produced.

B. Facing Economic Crisis, pp. 729–731

1. Before 1850, economic crises were usually caused by an agricultural crisis.
2. In 1873, however, a crisis of industry and finance developed on its own because entrepreneurs were facing more and more obstacles.
3. First, industry had become "capital intensive" because entrepreneurs had to invest heavily in expensive machinery to start a business.
4. Second, the distribution and consumption of goods were both inadequate to sustain growth. Slumps became common.
5. Governments responded to this crisis with new laws that limited personal liability in cases of bankruptcy, thereby increasing investor confidence.
6. Stock markets trading in a wide variety of securities raised money from larger, more international polls of capital.
7. Businesses began to band together into cartels (favored in Germany) and trusts (predominant in the United States) in order to control prices and competition.
8. Trusts and cartels also vertically integrated companies thereby enabling them to control the entire process of manufacturing from raw material to finished product.
9. Trusts and cartels restricted the free market. Governments also restricted the market by raising tariffs in response to recessions and trade deficits. All countries

except Belgium, Britain, and the Netherlands ended free trade by the 1890s.

C. **Revolution in Business Practices, pp. 731–733**

1. To minimize the effects of the economic crises, industrialists revolutionized the everyday conduct of their businesses by hiring specialized managers to run their complex operations, improving manufacturing, marketing, and worker productivity.
2. A white-collar service sector emerged simultaneously, consisting of office workers employed as secretaries, file clerks, typists, and bank tellers, all educated in state-run primary schools.
3. Women, including middle-class women, filled the majority of service-sector jobs, despite the strength of the domestic ideal that discouraged them from working.
4. Employers saved money by designating certain types of jobs as "female" and then paying women lower wages than they would have had to pay men.
5. The drive to boost consumption led to the development of merchandising.
6. The department store, developed after mid-century, sought to stimulate consumer desires, especially among female shoppers.
7. Such stores brought women out of the domestic sphere into the public, either as shoppers or as salesclerks.
8. Mail-order catalogs and the extension of the railroad system gave rural populations access to the variety of goods department stores had to offer, many of which (coffee, tea, or soap made from palm oil) were imported from the colonies.
9. Consumerism was shaped by empire and industry. New industrial goods and products from the colonies became more widespread and shaped ordinary life.

II. **The New Imperialism**

A. **Taming the Mediterranean, p. 733**

1. The European countries eyed the African and Asian shores of the Mediterranean for the chance to profit from trade.
2. Europeans invested heavily in Egyptian development and lent money at exorbitant rates of interest to Egyptian rulers.
3. In 1879, the French and British took over the Egyptian treasury to secure their investments, and Britain used the nationalist resistance that ensued as an excuse to invade Egypt in 1882.
4. The British began to run the government from behind the scenes, reshaping the Egyptian economy to meet British needs.
5. In place of a diversified and self-sufficient agricultural system, for example, British officials, working with local landowners and moneylenders, limited agricultural production to a few crops destined for export.
6. In Algeria, the French continued to extend their presence and occupied neighboring Tunisia in 1881.
7. Businessmen from Britain, France, and Germany flooded Asia Minor with cheap goods, driving artisans out from their trades and into low-paying work building railroads or processing tobacco.

B. **Scramble for Africa, pp. 733–737**

1. After the British takeover of the Egyptian government, Europeans became more involved in sub-Saharan Africa, seeking to expand trade in raw materials such as palm oil, rubber, and diamonds, and to use coastal areas as stopover ports on the route to Asia.
2. In the 1880s, one African territory after another fell to the French, Belgians, Portuguese, Italians, and Germans.
3. The competition raised European tensions and prompted German chancellor Otto von Bismarck to call a conference in Berlin.
4. During a series of meetings in 1884 and 1885, the European powers agreed that settlements along the African coast guaranteed rights to internal territory, an agreement that divided Africa into territories along straight lines that cut across indigenous boundaries.
5. Western penetration of all continents was accelerated by industrial technology. Railroads, steamships, breech-loading rifles, and the machine gun strengthened the west.
6. The discovery of quinine in South America and its use in Africa allowed Europeans to survive in areas where malaria flourished.
7. In southern Africa, farmers of European descent wrested farmland and mineral resources from native peoples.
8. Social Darwinism reshaped racism to justify conquest of African lands.
9. Europeans destroyed African economic and political systems to ensure their own profit and domination.

10. Ignoring evidence to the contrary, most Europeans considered Africans barely civilized, unlike the Chinese and Indians, whom Europeans credited with a scientific and artistic heritage, deeming Africans good only for manual labor.

C. **Acquiring Territory in Asia, pp. 737–738**
   1. European expansion was occurring around the world. Much of Asia was integrated into European empires.
   2. Discrimination drove educated elite Indians to found the Indian National Congress in 1885, which, while it accepted aspects of liberalism, challenged Britain's right to rule.
   3. To the east, Britain took control of the Malay Peninsula in 1874, and the interior of Burma in 1885, territories that provided natural resources and a trade route to China.
   4. The British viewed with mistrust Russian annexations in central Asia and France's creation (in 1887) of the Union of Indochina from Cambodia, Tonkin, Annam, and Cochin China. (Laos was added in 1893.)
   5. The French, like the British, imported their culture to their colonies; the upper classes of the Indochinese were exposed to French art and literature, and Indochinese nationalists took up western models.

D. **Japan's Imperial Agenda, pp. 738–739**
   1. Under the Meiji Restoration, the Japanese embraced foreign trade, imperialism, and industry.
   2. In the 1870s, Japanese officials traveled to Europe and the United States to study industry and technology; Western dress was adopted at the imperial court, and Western architecture was introduced in Tokyo.
   3. The government tolerated no opposition to these changes.
   4. In 1889, legal scholars drafted a constitution on the German model that emphasized state power rather than individual rights.
   5. The state also invested in economic development by building railroads and shipyards and establishing financial institutions.
   6. Japan also adopted the imperialist mentality of the West and began intervening in struggles elsewhere in Asia.

E. **The Paradoxes of Imperialism, pp. 739–740**
   1. Although imperialism was intended to stabilize great-power status, international distrust intensified as countries vied for world influence.
   2. Politicians began to question the value of colonies whose costs exceeded their profits.
   3. Yet, for certain businesses, such as French metallurgy, colonies provided crucial markets.
   4. They also provided jobs for people in European port cities, but all taxpayers shared the burden of paying for colonial armies and administration.
   5. Many believed that colonies meant national strength, but others worried that they might be a source of weakness and conflict.
   6. Europeans agreed, however, in the belief that they were superior in culture and religion to the people they colonized and also that the imperialist venture was a noble and worthwhile cause in that it converted indigenous peoples to Christianity or generally "civilized" them.
   7. Western scholars and travelers added to this notion of Western superiority, despite their claims of objectivity.
   8. Although a few believed that conquered peoples were better off than Europeans because they were less "civilized," this romantic notion ignored the realities of imperialist rule.

III. **Imperial Society and Culture**

A. **The "Best" Circles and the Expanding Middle Class, pp. 741–742**
   1. The profits from industry and empire building added new members to the upper classes, or "best" circles, as they were called.
   2. Persons in these circles often came from the aristocracy, but new millionaires from the ranks of the bourgeoisie joined, and some intermarried.
   3. The ranks of aristocrats and rich bourgeois became increasingly blurred, and millionaires without aristocratic connections made conspicuous displays of wealth and segregated themselves in suburbs or new urban areas away from the bourgeois and the indigent.
   4. Upper-class men popularized big-game hunting expeditions in Asia and Africa, which replaced the more modest fox and

bird hunting as the fashionable masculine sport of the highest class.

5. Members of the best circles maintained exclusivity by controlling their children's social lives, especially their marriages.
6. Once married, upper-class women devoted themselves to having children, directing staffs of servants, and maintaining standards of etiquette and social conduct.
7. A solid middle class was expanding in western and central Europe.
8. The lives of these businessmen and professionals remained modest; most households employed at least one servant.
9. In place of the conspicuous consumption of the very rich, the middle class proudly maintained a high level of cleanliness and polish.

B. Professional Sports and Organized Leisure, pp. 742–743

1. Organized team sports replaced village games, integrating migrants as well as the lower and higher classes in a common pastime.
2. Newspapers reported the results of sporting contests such as the Tour de France, and competitive sports began to be viewed as a sign of national strength and spirit.
3. Team sports for women emerged, such as soccer, field hockey, and rowing; but individual sports, such as horseback riding, were considered more feminine.
4. Men were encouraged to embrace team sports, fostering a sense of national unity and preparing them for cooperation in the governments and militaries of empire. Demonstrating the increased belief in physical health and strength for both sexes, schools for girls introduced gymnastics and exercise.
5. The middle classes believed that leisure pursuits should strengthen the mind and fortify the body.
6. Working-class persons adopted middle-class habits by joining clubs for pursuits such as bicycling, touring, and hiking.
7. The new emphasis on healthy recreation afforded individuals a greater sense of individual freedom and power and thereby contributed to a developing sense of citizenship based less on constitutions and rights than on an individual nation's exercise of raw power.

C. Working People's Strategies, pp. 743–746

1. Empire and industry were powerful factors in migration.
2. Parts of Europe simply could not produce enough or provide enough employment to support a growing population, so hundreds of thousands left their native lands to find work elsewhere in Europe or the United States.
3. Millions of rural eastern European Jews, Swedes, and Sicilian and Irish peasants left for economic reasons.
4. Russian Jews fled in the face of violent pogroms that destroyed Jewish homes, businesses, and lives.
5. Most emigrated to North and South America, Australia, and New Zealand to seek out new opportunities.
6. The development of railroads and steamships made the trip faster, cheaper, and more comfortable.
7. Once established in their new countries, immigrants frequently sent money home.
8. Male immigrants had to learn new languages and new civic practices in order to obtain employment, as did some female immigrants.
9. Immigrant women who stayed at home were insulated from their new environments and often preserved traditional ways and languages.
10. Urbanization accelerated, although most still resided in rural areas; many urban dwellers returned to rural areas at harvest time.
11. In cities, changes in technology and management meant that workers had to adapt to an insecure job market and changing work conditions.
12. Stepped-up productivity demanded more physical exertion, but wages were not increased accordingly.
13. Men and women resented managers, and women were often sexually harassed.
14. Many women worked at home doing outwork for which they were paid extremely low wages, forcing them to work long hours to make ends meet.
15. Notwithstanding, the urban working classes grew more informed, more visible, and more connected to the progress of industry and empire.

D. Reform Efforts for Working-Class People, pp. 746–747

1. The social problems caused by economic instability, the uneven prosperity of industrialization, and the upheaval of migration were addressed through reform organizations and charities formed by the middle and upper classes.
2. Young men and women of the middle and upper classes, some motivated by religion, turned to scientific study of the poor to find solutions to social problems.
3. Philanthropists, industrialists, schools, and governmental agencies, influenced by Social Darwinism, intervened in workers' lives to teach mothers child-care techniques and to provide health care for children.
4. They expected working-class mothers to conform to middle-class standards of housekeeping and childrearing.
5. Dutch physician Aletta Jacobs began to make birth control available.
6. Working-class women sought out these clinics, and knowledge of birth control spread by word of mouth among workers. Churches and many reformers opposed the spread of birth control.
7. Governments took a different approach, sponsoring laws that barred women from "unhealthy" night work and from trades such as pottery that were considered dangerous.
8. Laws also limited women's access to higher-paying jobs.

E. Artistic Responses to Empire and Industry, pp. 747–750

1. Darwin had theorized that strong civilizations that failed to keep up with changing conditions would perish, an idea that influenced many writers.
2. Émile Zola (1840–1902) produced a series of novels that described the effects of industrial society on individuals through the portrayal of a family plagued by alcoholism and madness.
3. Spanish writer Emilia Pardo Bazán (1859–1921) depicted a fatalistic world in which men and women faced personal deterioration and forces beyond their control.
4. Norwegian playwright Henrik Ibsen (1828–1906) and South African novelist Olive Schreiner (1855–1920) criticized the oppressive aspects of marriage on women.
5. Country people used mass-produced textiles to design "traditional" costumes and concocted ceremonies based on a mythical past.
6. Thought to be old and authentic, these quaint "traditions" attracted tourists and caught the eye of architects and industrial designers, who turned to rural styles for models.
7. English designers William Morris (1834–1896) and his daughter Mary Morris (1862–1938) designed fabrics, wallpaper, and household items with motifs found in nature, such as the silhouettes of plants, and Asian art.
8. New photographers' depictions of places and people were accessible to a wider public.
9. In response, painters altered their styles, while still maintaining their focus on the depiction of contemporary society.
10. Georges Seurat (1859–1891) depicted white-collar workers at leisure in newly created parks.
11. Artists, trying to capture a fleeting moment by focusing on the ever-changing light and color of everyday vision, experimented with a new style labeled impressionism. Impressionists Claude Monet and Vincent Van Gogh experimented with color and brush strokes.
12. Many impressionists, like the American expatriate Mary Cassatt (1845–1926), were influenced by Japanese art.

IV. The Birth of Mass Politics

A. Workers, Politics, and Protest, pp. 750–752

1. Struggling for a political voice, workers came together in unions to exert pressure on governments and businesses, marking the beginning of mass politics.
2. Despite fears of revolution, some industrialists found unions appealing because they made strikes more predictable (or even preventable) and also provided a liaison for labor-management relations.
3. From the 1880s on, the pace of collective action for more pay, lower prices, and better working conditions accelerated, and the number of strikes increased.
4. Housewives carried out their own protests against high food prices, confiscating merchants' goods and selling them at what they considered a just price.

5. Although most strikes were not revolutionary, governments increasingly responded with force.
6. Unions continued to attract skilled artisans, but a new unionism also attracted transport workers, miners, matchgirls, and dockworkers.
7. These new unions were nationwide groups that could plan massive general strikes affecting a number of trades simultaneously.
8. Like cartels and trusts, these unions increasingly influenced business practices and society's views of workers.
9. New political parties, such as the Labour Party in England, most of them inspired by Marxist theories, also addressed working-class issues.
10. In 1889, some four hundred socialists from across Europe formed the Second International.
11. This organization adopted a Marxist revolutionary program, but also advocated suffrage.
12. Members wanted to rid the organization of anarchists for whom Marxist ideology was not applicable, and who flourished in less industrial parts of Europe, notably Italy, Spain, and Russia.
13. During the 1880s, anarchists had bombed stock exchanges, parliaments, and businesses.
14. Politics were also incorporated more informally into everyday life through a range of organizations designed to forge worker solidarity through leisure activities—gymnastic and choral societies, for example.

B. Expanding Political Participation in Western Europe, pp. 752–754

1. Western European nations moved toward mass politics more rapidly than did countries to the east.
2. The rise of mass journalism after 1880 gave Europeans access to information about politics and world events.
3. Journalism created a national community of up-to-date citizens, but elites grumbled about its predilection for the sensational and the scandalous.
4. William Gladstone used journalism to his advantage when he waged a campaign for a seat in the British Parliament in 1879; newspapers reported his tour of northern England and Scotland, highlighting his speeches to thousands of working men and women.
5. This campaign exemplified the trend toward expanded participation in Britain's political life, a process begun with the Reform Act of 1832—an extension of the franchise to middle-class men—and continued with the Ballot Act of 1872, which made voting secret.
6. Then, with the Reform Act of 1884, the electorate was doubled, enfranchising many urban workers and artisans.
7. As many British men entered politics for the first time, both Liberals and Conservatives established political clubs to gain party loyalty.
8. British political reforms weakened the control of the landed aristocracy, a change that was especially revolutionary in Ireland, where Irish tenant farmers gained the right to vote and could use that vote against absentee landlords. Under the leadership of Charles Stewart Parnell, the Irish demanded their own Parliament (home rule).
9. In France, the Third Republic (established in 1874) was unstable, due to scandal and political struggle among competing factions.
10. This instability was diminished somewhat when a new constitution strengthening the Chamber of Deputies was elected in 1875, by universal manhood suffrage, at the expense of the presidency.
11. However, newspaper stories of financial scandals involving members of the Chamber of Deputies eroded confidence in the government; an aborted coup by General Georges Boulanger might have succeeded had he not bowed out at the last minute.
12. Republican leaders sought to create national unity by instituting a system of compulsory and free public education in the 1880s.
13. Spain and Belgium established universal manhood suffrage in 1890 and 1893, respectively, whereas Denmark, Sweden, Italy, and the Netherlands continued to limit political participation.

C. Power Politics in Central and Eastern Europe, pp. 754–759

1. In Germany, Austria-Hungary, and Russia, agrarian political forces remained powerful, often working to block political, social, and economic change.

2. Once Bismarck succeeded in uniting the German states, he sought stability and a respite from war.
3. In 1873, he forged an alliance called the Three Emperors' League with Austria-Hungary and Russia, both of which shared Germany's commitment to maintain the political status quo.
4. Bismarck joined with liberals at home to create financial institutions destined to further German commerce and industry. He also opposed the growth of socialist political parties and organizations, and sided with conservatives in establishing agricultural tariffs.
5. In Austria-Hungary, the liberals held power for a time in the 1870s, and the government enacted free-trade provisions, but the country remained monarchist and authoritarian.
6. In the Balkans, Slavs of Bulgaria and Bosnia-Herzegovina rebelled against Ottoman control in 1876; they were followed by Serbia and Montenegro.
7. Russian Pan-Slavic organizations sent relief to the rebels, and Russia declared war on Turkey in 1877.
8. The 1878 Treaty of San Stefano created a large, pro-Russian Bulgaria.
9. Austria-Hungary and Great Britain feared that it would become a Russian satellite enabling the tsar to dominate the Balkans.
10. An international congress held in Berlin staved off the threat of war, and rolled back the Russian victory by partitioning Bulgaria.
11. Following this congress, the European powers attempted to ensure stability through a series of alliances and treaties.
12. Germany and Austria-Hungary formed a defensive alliance in 1879 against Russia.
13. In 1882, Italy joined, turning the Dual Alliance into the Triple Alliance.
14. At the same time, Germany, Austria-Hungary, and Russia joined a revived Three Emperors' League that lasted from 1881 to 1887.
15. Although Russia achieved some international success, its internal affairs were in disarray; the era of Great Reforms had come to an end, and a dissatisfied, reform-minded youth increasingly turned to revolutionary groups for solutions to political and social problems.
16. Writers participated in the debate over Russia's future.
17. Leo Tolstoy and Fyodor Dostoevsky both opposed revolution, believing that Russia required spiritual regeneration.
18. The more radical revolutionary groups, however, saw a need for violent action.
19. In 1881, one of these groups—the People's Will—murdered Tsar Alexander II in a bomb attack.
20. In response, Alexander III (r. 1881–1894) rejected any calls for further reform, gave the secret police virtually unchecked power, and embarked on a campaign of intense Russification.
21. The five million Jews who were confined to the Pale of Settlement, an area to which they had been restricted since the eighteenth century, suffered especially severe oppression in the form of government-instigated pogroms.
22. As Russia's internal politics became more chaotic and repressive, its international alliances were altered by the decision of the new German kaiser William II (r. 1888–1918) to dismiss Bismarck and allow the alliance with Russia to lapse in favor of closer ties with Austria-Hungary.
23. The international scene was growing ever more dangerous and unpredictable.

Lecture Strategies

1. One approach to examining the changes in industry and commerce that occurred during this period would be to compare the Universal Exposition of 1889 in Paris to the Crystal Palace Exhibition of 1851 in London. To take one example, electricity, particularly in the form of electrical lighting, characterizes the 1889 exposition and sets it apart from the earlier exhibition. It might be worth consulting Jill Jonnes's compelling *Empires of Light: Edison, Tesla, Westinghouse and the Race to Electrify the World* (New York: Random House, 2004) for some inspiration. Comparing the two exhibitions offers possibilities for lecturing on new products, new technologies, new management techniques, and new patterns of consumption.

2. City life is an important topic that may be presented in interesting ways, and one that can be demonstrated wonderfully visually. Compare images from film, paintings, or photography contrasting the rabbit-warren-like character of eighteenth- and early-nineteenth-century urban environments with the grand boulevards and imposing structures of the later-nineteenth-century city. Berlin and Paris underwent rapid and extensive changes during this period in terms

of architecture and physical layout, transportation, cultural venues, and other aspects of life. Either Berlin or Paris or a comparison between the two would form a good subject for a lecture, especially one with illustrations.

An explosion of books published on Berlin include, among others, David Clay Large, *Berlin* (New York: Basic Books, 2000); Alexandra Richie, *Faust's Metropolis: A History of Berlin* (New York: Carroll & Graf, 1998); and Giles MacDonogh, *Berlin* (New York: St. Martin's Press, 1998). See also a useful study by Ronald Taylor, *Berlin and Its Culture: A Historical Portrait* (New Haven: Yale University Press, 1997).

For city life in Paris, many sources are available. A good place to begin would be with Donald J. Olson, *The City As a Work of Art: London, Paris, Vienna*, rpt. ed. (New Haven: Yale University Press, 1988). Useful overviews are Johannes Willms, *Paris, Capital of Europe: From the Revolution to the Belle Époque* (New York: Holmes & Meier, 1997); and Norma Evenson, *Paris: A Century of Change, 1878–1978* (New Haven: Yale University Press, 1979). Anthony Sutcliffe, *Paris: An Architectural History* (New Haven: Yale University Press, 1993) offers a detailed discussion. On Paris and art, see T. J. Clark, *The Painting of Modern Life: Paris in the Art of Manet and His Followers* (New York: Knopf, 1984). On the working class in Paris, see Lenard R. Berlanstein, *The Working People of Paris, 1871–1914* (Baltimore: Johns Hopkins University Press, 1984); and W. Scott Haine, *The World of the Paris Café: Sociability among the French Working Class, 1789–1914* (Baltimore: Johns Hopkins University Press, 1996). For the Bohemian world of Paris, see Jerrold Seigel, *Bohemian Paris: Culture, Politics, and the Boundaries of Bourgeois Life, 1830–1930* (New York: Viking Press, 1986). It may be worth contrasting pre- and post-fire Chicago as an example of the influence of urban planning in the later nineteenth century. See Donald L. Miller's *City of the Century: The Epic of Chicago and the Making of America* (New York: Simon and Schuster, 1997), especially Chapter 6.

3. France may serve as a good example of the problems and potential of mass politics. The Third Republic experienced a difficult birth and continued to struggle for existence in the 1880s and later. Some discussion of the self-conscious effort to forge a nation and loyalty to the republic would be useful.

Part 3 of Gordon Wright, *France in Modern Times*, 3rd ed. (New York: W. W. Norton, 1981) offers an excellent overview of the Third Republic. Eugen Weber, *Peasants into Frenchmen: The Modernization of Rural France, 1870–1914* (Stanford, CA: Stanford University Press, 1976) is a fascinating examination of the ways in which France was re-created as a nation at the end of the century. Two more specialized studies are Michael Burns, *Rural Society and French Politics: Boulangism and the Dreyfus Affair, 1886–1900* (Princeton: Princeton University Press, 1984); and Steven C. Hause and Anne R. Kenney, *Women's Suffrage and Social Politics in the French Third Republic* (Princeton: Princeton University Press, 1984). Perhaps the best survey is Jean-Marie Mayeur and Madeleine Reberioux, *The Third Republic from Its Origins to the Great War, 1871–1914* (Cambridge: Cambridge University Press, 1984). See also Maurice Agulhon, *The French Republic, 1879–1992* (Malden, MA: Blackwell Publishers date). Also useful is Patrick J. Hutton, ed., *Historical Dictionary of the Third French Republic, 1870–1940*, 2 vols. (Westport, CT: Greenwood Press, 1986).

4. Ireland richly repays separate consideration in this period, given the accessibility of primary documents, student interest in the country's history, and the ambivalent Irish relationship to many of the dominant themes of the chapter. The Irish experience of famine and mass emigration in the 1840s and 1850s was related to the subordinate and agrarian nature of the Irish economy within the British and the emerging global systems. The Irish participated disproportionately in the British Empire as soldiers, administrators, and colonists, and thus benefited from imperialism, but they also often sympathized with the non-western victims of the imperial dynamic. The Irish were proud of their "European-ness" but also understood from experience how religious, cultural, and even perceived racial differences could keep them on the margins of "civilization," even when they lived in its capital cities. Many in England in both the Conservative and Liberal parties rejected the Irish demand for a separate legislature because, it was argued, the political future and Social Darwinism (given contemporary developments in Italy, Germany, Russia, and the United States) demanded political consolidation, not devolution and fragmentation. The simultaneously subversive and assertive cultural resurgence of the 1880's and beyond, involving as it did the likes of Douglas Hyde, William Butler Yeats, Jonathan Synge, Oscar Wilde, and George Bernard Shaw, to name just a few, represents one of the truly great literary flowerings of the nineteenth century, in both the Irish and English language. Some lecture focus on the "exceptional" relationship of Ireland to chapter themes helps to illustrate the importance of perspective. It also offers an opportunity to highlight the variability of European experiences, and it could be argued that the Irish perspective was not so very different from that of Poland, Hungary, or other parts of Ottoman-, Russian-, and Austrian-dominated eastern Europe, where cultural, linguistic, and religious minorities struggled to define and assert identities and economic power within imperial, hegemonic states.

For the Irish Home Rule movement, see Alan O'Day, *Irish Home Rule* (Manchester: Manchester University Press, 1998). There has been a useful recent focus on the Irish role in the British Empire; see Kevin Kenny, ed., *Ireland and the British Empire* (Oxford: Oxford University Press, 2004). On the Gaelic revival, a good starting point is John Hutchinson, *The Dynamics of Cultural Nationalism: The Gaelic Revival and the Creation of the Irish Nation-State* (Boston: Allen and Unwin, 1987), but see also George Watson, *Irish Identity and the Literary Revival* (Washington, DC: Catholic University of America Press, 1994). Emmet Larkin's multivolume history of Irish church–state relations is daunting, but for a representative and important piece of his argument, try *The Roman Catholic Church and the Creation of the Modern Irish State, 1878–1886* (Philadelphia: American Philosophical Society, 1975). To tap into the debates within Irish studies about race, ethnicity, and the ambiguous position of the Irish within increasingly racialized western thought, see Noel Ignatiev, *How the Irish Became White* (New York: Routledge, 1996); Roy Foster, *Paddy and Mr. Punch: Connections in English and Irish History* (New York: Penguin 1996); and Michael de Nie, *The Eternal Paddy: Irish Identity and the British Press, 1798–1882* (Madison: University of Wisconsin Press, 2004).

Class Discussion Starters

1. In connection with "Lecture Strategies," number 1, have the class discuss how a young visitor to the Crystal Palace Exhibition of 1851 might feel about the pace of change upon visiting the Universal Exposition of 1889 in late middle age. What would be the major differences? What political and cultural developments of the intervening decades might have affected his/her perspective?

2. The Belgian Congo, the private property of King Leopold II, exemplifies colonialism practiced at its worst. Student response to and discussion of Joseph Conrad's (1857–1924) *Heart of Darkness*, based on his experiences in the Belgian Congo, offer a way of examining colonial practices in the Congo as well as a range of issues including imperialism, Social Darwinism, racism, sexism, and the nature of European civilization.

On the Congo itself, an excellent source is Adam Hochschild, *King Leopold's Ghost: A Story of Greed, Terror, and Heroism in Colonial Africa* (Boston: Houghton Mifflin, 1998). See also Lewis H. Gann and Peter Duigan, *The Rulers of Belgian Africa, 1884–1914* (Princeton: Princeton University Press, 1979). On Conrad, the literature is vast. Start with Adam Gillon, *Joseph Conrad* (Boston: Twayne, 1982); and Gary Adelman, *Heart of Darkness: Search for the Unconscious* (Boston: Twayne, 1987). Other good, introductory sources include Owen Knowles and Gene M. Moore, eds., *The Oxford Reader's Companion to Conrad* (Oxford: Oxford University Press, 2000); J. H. Stape, ed., *The Cambridge Companion to Joseph Conrad* (Cambridge: Cambridge University Press, 1996); and Robert Kimbrough, *Heart of Darkness: An Authoritative Text; Background and Sources; Criticism*, 3rd ed. (New York: W. W. Norton, 1988). More specialized titles include Sven Lindqvist, *Exterminate All the Brutes* (New York: New Press, 1996); Susan Jones, *Conrad and Women* (Oxford: Clarendon Press, 1999); Chris Bongie, *Exotic Memories: Literature, Colonialism, and the Fin de Siècle* (Stanford, CA: Stanford University Press, 1991); Peter Finchow, *Envisioning Africa: Racism and Imperialism in Conrad's Heart of Darkness* (Lexington: University of Kentucky Press, 2000); and John W. Griffith, *Joseph Conrad and the Anthropological Dilemma: "Bewildered Traveler"* (Oxford: Clarendon Press, 1995).

3. Themes of decline, decay, and degeneration are not limited to art and literature, but appear as well in discussions about society, politics, and economies. Why these themes should be so prevalent in an era of industrial innovation and imperial conquest should furnish the basis for a good discussion. Be sure to incorporate the challenge that Darwinism offered to notions of progress, especially in relation to the themes of charity and national competition introduced in the text.

Besides excerpts from Herbert Spencer, and Darwin's own *Descent of Man* (especially Chapters 5 and 7, which contributed to widespread anxiety about the future of the "race,") a good place to begin is Chapter 1 of Eugen Weber, *France: Fin de Siècle* (Cambridge, MA: Belknap Press, 1986). Daniel Pick, *Faces of Degeneration: A European Disorder, c. 1848–c. 1918* (Cambridge: Cambridge University Press, 1993) is the best recent study. An older but still useful study is Koenraad Wolter Swart, *The Sense of Decadence in Nineteenth-Century France* (The Hague: M. Nijhoff, 1964). See also Robert A. Nye, *Crime, Madness, and Politics in Modern France: The Medical Concept of National Decline* (Princeton: Princeton University Press, 1984). Max Simon Nordau, *Degeneration* (Lincoln: University of Nebraska Press, 1993), a reprint of the 1895 edition with an introduction by George L. Mosse, is a classic polemic from the era. Judith Walkowitz's *City of Dreadful Delight: Narratives of Sexual Danger in Late Victorian London* (Chicago: University of Chicago Press, 1992) manages to convey some sense of the seedier side of London of the era and associated social anxieties, particularly as they played out in the press. See also Carl E. Schorske, *Fin-de-Siècle Vienna: Politics and Culture* (New York: Alfred A. Knopf, 1980). Asti Hustvedt, *The Decadent Reader: Fiction, Fantasy, and Perversion from Fin-de-Siècle France* (Cambridge, MA: MIT Press, 1998) provides a convenient introduction to the literature of the times. Mike Jay and Michael Neve, eds., *1900: A*

Fin-de-Siècle Reader (New York: Penguin, 2000) is also a useful collection of sources. On the social impact of Darwinism, see Paul Crook's *Darwin's Coat Tails: Essays on Social Darwinism* (New York: Peter Lang, 2007).

Reviewing the Text

Review Questions

1. What were the major economic changes in industry and business by the end of the nineteenth century?
[model answer] • ***Governments recognized economic superiority as a key to political superiority:*** *Nations with superior systems of technical education, industrial innovations, and a high economic growth rate were willing to invest in research and education, as in Germany, or exploit the advantages they had in natural resources, as in the United States.*
• ***New business laws and practices developed to raise capital and encourage investment:*** *The development of the limited liability corporation protected investors from personal responsibility for a company's debt. Public financing via stocks helped raise capital, a practice taken from government-sponsored enterprises.*
• ***Innovative approaches to business management and production created new types of jobs:*** *Industrialists hired managers to run their factories, creating a variety of skilled jobs that did not require traditional craft abilities. New low-level office jobs were often filled by middle-class women. These became respectable professional positions for women, while businesses benefited from being able to pay them less.*
• ***A new consumer economy encouraged spending:*** *The economic success of new products and the companies that produced them required that consumers want and purchase goods. The displays and marketing techniques of the department store were intended to stimulate consumer whims rather than simply provide them with necessities.*

2. What were the goals of the new imperialism, and how did Europeans accomplish those goals?
[model answer] • ***The new imperialism aimed at direct rule and control of territories:*** *Expanding trade and gaining access to raw materials became increasingly important in an industrial era, and direct control of territory was seen to be an effective means of securing both.*
• ***Industrial and territorial expansions were seen as connected to national identity:*** *Imperial powers sought glory in expansion, and many believed that imperial expansion was an inevitable consequence of western racial superiority.*
• ***Missionaries and social reformers sought to spread what they saw as western cultural and spiritual superiority:*** *Efforts by reformers to benefit and improve non-western cultures often led instead to increased subjugation and violence.*

3. How did empire and industry influence art and everyday life?
[model answer] • ***The global marketplace influenced the development of western economies:*** *Imperial endeavors generated tremendous wealth. Success in manufacturing and foreign ventures created millionaires and encouraged the expansion of the global economy.*
• ***Travel became more common:*** *Big-game hunting, scientific expeditions, and the collection for and development of museums and exhibitions all contributed to a growing awareness of the world outside the west.*
• ***Health and diet improved:*** *Governments undertook a range of programs designed to cultivate citizens capable of sustaining imperial efforts, including health-care improvements and the development of sporting culture.*
• ***Mass migrations:*** *Poorer citizens took advantage of the opportunities that overseas empires afforded for colonization and industrial employment by migrating in millions.*
• ***Artists were critical of the new global economy and imperial efforts:*** *Writers criticized aspects of industrial society, and in the arts the rustic and rural were celebrated.*
• ***Art became more global:*** *Themes in painting and novels became more international, and the scope and scale of artistic imagination expanded by taking on "foreign" ideas.*

4. What were the major changes in political life from the 1870s to the 1890s, and which areas of Europe did they most affect?
[model answer] • ***Electorates and political participation expanded:*** *In many western states, electorates were expanded, and citizens' sense of belonging to nations increased. Politicians began to make direct appeals to mass electorates.*
• ***In authoritarian states, ethnic conflict and violence shaped political systems:*** *The need to control the people in undemocratic eastern states often led to harsh and autocratic political systems.*
• ***Workers became increasingly politicized and organized:*** *Marxist and socialist political parties expanded and gained influence. Unions became larger and more powerful, and used strikes to put pressure on governments for political and social change.*

Making Connections

1. Compare the political and social goals of the newly enfranchised male electorate with those of people from the "best circles."
[model answer] *The newly enfranchised male electorate joined unions (at both the local and national levels) to bargain for better pay, lower prices, and improved working conditions. Workers established political clubs, while new political parties formed to represent workers' interests at the highest levels of government. Political*

campaigns often focused on workers' issues. The middle classes, however, in their new prosperity, joined the upper classes, or "best" circles. The line between aristocrat and bourgeois became blurred, both by the awarding of titles to outstanding members of the middle classes and by marriages between aristocrats and the nouveau riche. The wealthiest members of the middle classes lived like the aristocracy, indulging in conspicuous consumption, and they were interested in maintaining the status quo.

2. Describe the effects of imperialism on European politics and society as a whole.
[model answer] *A direct connection was made between imperial expansion and national identity. National prestige demanded colonial expansion. Because of this, European nations became increasingly distrustful of each other's colonial ambitions. But colonization was not merely a matter of national pride. It was widely believed that colonial natives were inferior and that it was the duty of European Christians to bring Christianity and "civilization" to them. As a result of "civilizing" colonial people, the products of imperialism poured into Europe by way of Oriental carpets, Chinese porcelain, wicker furniture, rich fabrics, and exotic foods and plants. Imperialism became a part of daily life for many Europeans.*

Discussing the Documents

Questions from Online Study Guide with Model Answers

Imperialism's Popularity among the People, p. 736

1. What sort of character is Stanley, according to the song?
[model answer] *The song suggests that Stanley is adventurous, determined, and resourceful. He has access to wealth and is willing to use it in order to accomplish his goals, in this case finding Pasha. Stanley appears to be religious in that he carries "tracts" and is willing to use violence, as indicated by the Maxim gun he has taken with him.*

2. What does this song reveal about European attitudes toward imperialism?
[model answer] *The song suggests that Europeans did not have much sense of the consequences of their actions for indigenous civilization. Africa is presented as an almost empty continent where anyone with trinkets to sell and a gun could take whatever he or she wanted.*

Henrik Ibsen, From A Doll's House*, p. 748*

1. What is the central conflict in this excerpt?
[model answer] *The central conflict is a woman's duty. Helmer claims that a wife's "sacred duty" is to her husband and children. Nora claims that she has an equally sacred duty toward herself.*

2. Which contemporary social tensions are reflected in this excerpt?
[model answer] *Darwinistic anxieties about the health of the nation led many to emphasize the role of women as mothers whose primary focus was the household. This was particularly true for the middle class, where the potential for women to earn income was not as crucial. However, there were new opportunities for middle-class women to work in the service industry or in department stores. Women were also becoming more politically active, some joining workers' parties. Thus, there was a tension between what many considered to be the ideal for women and the other options available to them.*

Contrasting Views: Experiences of Migration, pp. 744–745

1. Did the vast nineteenth-century migration ultimately enrich or diminish European culture and society?
[model answer] *The Hungarian census and Kjelberg's defense of migration suggests that migration enriched culture by increasing opportunities for migrants and enriching their native communities. Borkowska's letters and the Slovak song remind readers of the personal price migrants and their families paid for these opportunities.*

2. How would you characterize the experience of migration for families and individuals?
[model answer] *As these sources reveal, migration was often hard on families, although it also could provide additional resources and income to make life easier for migrants and their families. While migration often destroyed or weakened a variety of personal, family, or civic and national ties that individuals cherished, it also provided migrants with opportunities. Of course, these hopes were often unrealized, and migrants typically lived difficult and often marginal lives.*

3. How did migration affect the national identity of both receiving countries and European countries of origin?
[model answer] *Some migrants, as the Swedish poem included in the collection indicates, embraced new opportunities and identities, and rejected the political and social systems they left behind. Patriotism could also be placed under pressure by migration and the "disloyalty" some thought it represented. Some governments, however, welcomed the social and economic consequences of emigration, as the Hungarian document reveals.*

Other Questions for Discussing These Documents in Class

Imperialism's Popularity among the People

1. Why might music hall audiences have found the song to be amusing?
2. What image of Stanley does the song offer, and what does the image tell you about imperialism?

Henrik Ibsen, From A Doll's House

1. What does Nora associate with independence? What other ideas seem to be part of independence, for her?

2. What are the contrasting perspectives on responsibility demonstrated here? How does Helmer see Nora's responsibilities? How does Nora see them?

Contrasting Views: Experiences of Migration

1. How might the contrast between the official Hungarian position on emigration and the Swedish charges against emigrants be explained?

2. To what extent were the expectations of the emigrants and those left behind fulfilled?

Comparative Questions

1. In different ways, the documents deal with individuals and their relationships to new realities—imperial adventure, emigration, and women's independence. What do they reveal about how individuals responded to these changes?

2. Do the documents indicate that people had more freedom and choice at this time in western history than they had in the past? How does class create or limit such freedom?

For Users of *Sources of The Making of the West*

The following documents are available in Chapter 23 of the companion sourcebook by Katharine J. Lualdi, University of Southern Maine.

1. Defending Conquest: Jules Ferry, *Speech before the French National Assembly* (1883)
2. Imperialism and Anti-Imperialism: Joseph Rudyard Kipling, *The White Man's Burden* and Editorial from the *San Francisco Call* (1899)
3. Global Competition: Ernest Edwin Williams, *Made in Germany* (1896)
4. The Advance of Unionism: Margaret Bondfield, *A Life's Work* (1948)
5. Artistic Expression: Edgar Degas, *Notebooks* (1863–1884)

Discussion Ideas for Sources of The Making of the West, *Chapter 23*

1. How are the views of imperialism as advanced by Ferry, Kipling, and the *San Francisco Call* different? Similar? Do they reflect the growing influence of "realism"? What do they reveal about the relationship between public opinion and empire?

2. Williams and Bondfield offer very different perspectives on industrialism of this era. How did the national and class loyalties these pieces display relate to the development of industry? Can it be argued, from these documents, that the social changes and economics provoked by industrial life became more important than ever?

3. In what ways do the notebooks of Degas reveal an anti-romantic focus on realism? To what degree did Degas's subjects and his proposed methods reflect a concern with real life? What other concerns did he apparently have, and how do they relate to trends of the era?

Working with Visual Sources

For this exercise, please refer to Mary Cassatt, *The Letter* (c. 1890) on p. 749 of the textbook or view the image on the book companion site's Online Study Guide under the "Visual Activity" for Chapter 23.

Students viewing the image at the Online Study Guide are asked two questions about the image. The questions and model answers (not made available to students) are below. Project this image, available on the Instructor's Resources CD-ROM, in class or ask students to look at the image in their textbooks and answer the questions.

1. How does this painting compare with earlier portraits such as that of Germaine de Staël on p. 627 of your textbook?
[model answer] *This painting is not as realistic as earlier artwork and shows a distorted version of reality. The subject is also different. This is not a portrait of a woman, but a glimpse of a fleeting moment of life.*

2. Which contemporary social and cultural trends are evident in this painting?
[model answer] *This is a scene of a middle-class woman at home, which reflects the emphasis on domesticity for women. The clothing she is wearing shows the influence of foreign cultures on European fashions. One could imagine that she bought them at one of the new department stores that were appearing at the time. The style, technique, and palette of the painting itself also show the impact of foreign cultures in Europe.*

Mapping Exercises

Map Activity from OSG—Model Answers for Map Activity #2

For this activity, please refer to Map 23.1 Africa, c. 1890 on p. 735. Students are asked these questions:

What were the major routes of colonial expansion into Africa?

[model answer] *Colonial expansion into Africa generally began along the coastlines in places where European powers had established colonies and then penetrated inward. The French and the British were the two main powers that expanded into the interior, with France moving from its territories in Algeria and Senegal, and the British moving into Egypt and northward from Cape Colony.*

How did the borders of the Congo Free State correspond with political and geographic boundaries?
[model answer] *The borders of the Congo Free State were rather linear and did not correspond with any natural boundaries. It encompassed parts of several different indigenous political territories, such as Tippu Tib's Domain, Msiri's Kingdom, and Chokwi Domain. In some cases, the boundaries actually divided indigenous territories and did not correspond with any indigenous political boundaries.*

Map 23.1: Africa, c. 1890, p. 735

Use this map first as the basis for a discussion of the "scramble for Africa." What set off the scramble? How did national attitudes toward colonization differ? Ask students if they know or can guess which powers eventually became the major rivals by the end of the century. Next, use this map as a basis for a discussion of how existing African kingdoms might have made conquest relatively easy, but colonial administration somewhat difficult.

Map 23.2: Expansion of Russia in Asia, 1865–1895, p. 738

Students can be brought into a discussion by reminding them of American expansion to the west and drawing some comparisons. Where was the "frontier" for Russians? Be sure to discuss what was on the periphery of areas into which the Russians expanded. Which nations might be concerned with Russian expansion? Why would Britain be concerned about it?

Map 23.3: Expansion of Berlin to 1914, p. 755

Ask students to use the information contained on this map and its caption to describe Berlin in the closing decades of the nineteenth century. In addition to the capital of the German Empire, which other labels might fit it? Draw the students' attention to the groups that comprised the growing population of Berlin and also the extensive transportation network of railroad lines and canals.

Map 23.4: The Balkans, c. 1878, p. 757

Based on changes in the Balkans approved at the Congress of Berlin in 1878, what potential problems do students see in this area? Ask them to review the status of the major powers—Austria-Hungary, Russia, and the Ottoman Empire—and also the situations in Serbia and Bulgaria.

Mapping the West: The West and the World, c. 1890, p. 760

Have students compare Russian emigration to Siberia with the overseas emigration to the Western Hemisphere. Why was the United States the destination of choice for immigrants of so many different nationalities? What would have been different about immigrant life in Siberia? Students should also examine Figure 23.1, "European Emigration, 1870–1890" (p. 746), in connection with this question.

In-Class Assignments and Presentation Topics

1. Role-playing class presentation assignments are plentiful for this period. Students could assume the role of a department store employee, an emigrant, a colonial official, or a particular person, such as King Leopold II of Belgium, Mary Cassatt, or Charles Parnell. You may wish to suggest a list of possible roles for which source material is available in your library or online. You might engage students by having different voices address the same dynamic of the period—a factory owner, an immigrant, and an urban "reformer" on migration could work well, for instance.
2. Assign students to write a short essay on arguments for and against emigration. Although most of the essay should be a review of the arguments, students should also discuss the factors that would cause them to personally consider emigration (one possibility is, of course, that they would not consider it under any circumstances). You may wish to supplement the documents in the chapter. Ask students to consider the decision to emigrate as the end result of a network of "push" and "pull" factors, with the availability of employment always playing a crucial role.
3. Give students an opportunity to present reports on French and British politics in this period. The class may be divided into two groups, one for each country. Students in each group decide what to report on and how to do the reporting. For example, they may present a TV newscast based on stories filed by reporters sent back into the past in one of H. G. Wells's time machines. Reports might cover personalities, scandals, party platforms, and other relevant topics. Why would the British oppose Irish Home Rule? How would French governments respond to the Prussian defeat and the Paris Commune's collapse?
4. Ask students to reflect on why Bismarck might be considered the greatest or at least the most important individual in nineteenth-century Europe.

The emphasis in the essay should focus not on what he accomplished (although a brief review of Bismarck's more important activities is in order), but on the significance of his acts. What was his impact on Germany and, through Germany, on the rest of Europe? What did his accomplishments change?

Essay Questions

1. Students might do a research project on one of the many innovations of the period. The typewriter, bicycle, telephone, electric light, and gasoline engine have been mentioned in the text. Other innovations, such as the sewing machine or the vacuum cleaner, might be the basis for a research project as well. The paper or presentation should focus either on the process of inventing and developing the product or on the significance of the new product in industry or the home.

2. Ask each student to select a writer, artist, or composer active during this period. Set a minimum requirement for the amount of reading, viewing, or listening each student should do for the project. It is vitally important that the student gain at least some acquaintance with some of the work of his or her subject. If an art exhibition or a concert is available at a convenient time and location, you may wish to ask all students to attend and to do further research on the artist or composer. You may find it helpful to draw up a list of people about whom research material is available in your library or, if not in the library, online.

Additional Resources: Literature

Barash, Carol, ed., *An Olive Schreiner Reader: Writings on Women and South Africa.* 1987.
Eliot, George. *Middlemarch.* 2003.
Ingham, Patricia, ed., *Thomas Hardy: Jude the Obscure.* 1996.
Parmee, Douglas, trans., *Émile Zola: The Earth.* 1980.
Sharp, R. Farquharson, trans., *Four Great Plays by Ibsen.* 1981.

Additional Resources: Film and Video

Edward the King (1975; VHS, approx. 13 hrs.). This thirteen-part series (approximately 1 hour each) chronicles the life of King Edward VII of England. It is strong on detail, plot, costumes, and settings.

The Way We Live Now (2001; VHS/DVD, 5 hrs.). Anthony Trollope's 1875 novel is dramatized in this excellent, lavish, multi-part series. A financier, who mixes with the best in society and is given a seat in parliament, turns out to be a confidence trickster, while his daughter plays a different commercial game, that of the marriage market. The series captures the commercialism of the Victorian age, and really is focused, as the novel was, on conveying the "spirit of the age."

Daniel Deronda (2003; VHS/DVD, 3 hrs., 30 min.). This film adaptation of the 1876 novel by George Eliot (Mary Ann Evans) includes as one of its themes the social and financial limits placed on women. Most interesting, however, is the window opened to view Jewish life in Victorian England.

The Mayor of Casterbridge (2003; A&E, DVD, approx. 3 hrs., 30 min.). A compelling adaptation of Thomas Hardy's 1886 novel about a man from humble origins who rises to become a prominent citizen, only to be felled by his own ambition, pride, and early unconscionable acts.

Middlemarch (1994; VHS/DVD, 420 min.). A six-part miniseries, this adaptation of George Eliot's masterpiece is brought to life with the usual BBC attention to detail. A wonderful window onto the era, the storyline is sufficiently fast-paced and offers a good range of class perspectives on industrial society.

OTHER BEDFORD/ST. MARTIN'S RESOURCES FOR CHAPTER 23

The following resources are available to accompany Chapter 23. Please refer to the Preface of this manual for detailed descriptions of all the ancillaries.

For Instructors

Transparencies

The following maps and images from Chapter 23 are available as full-color acetates.

- Map 23.1: Africa, c. 1890
- Map 23.2: Expansion of Russia in Asia, 1865–1895
- Map 23.3: Expansion of Berlin to 1914
- Map 23.4: The Balkans, c. 1878
- Mapping the West: The West and the World, c. 1890
- Mary Cassatt, *The Letter* (c. 1890), p. 749
- Interior of Au Coin de la Rue (c. 1870), p. 732

Instructor's Resources CD-ROM

The following maps and image from Chapter 23, as well as a chapter outline, are available on disc in both PowerPoint and jpeg formats.

- Map 23.1: Africa, c. 1890
- Map 23.2: Expansion of Russia in Asia, 1865–1895
- Map 23.3: Expansion of Berlin to 1914
- Map 23.4: The Balkans, c. 1878
- Mapping the West: The West and the World, c. 1890
- Mary Cassatt, *The Letter* (c. 1890), p. 749

Using the Bedford Series with The Making of the West

Available in print as well as online at **bedfordstmartins.com/usingseries,** this guide offers practical suggestions for using *Nietzsche and the Death of God*, by Peter Fritzsche, in conjunction with chapter 23 of the textbook.

For Students

Study Guides

The Online Study Guide at **bedfordstmartins.com/hunt** helps students synthesize the material they have learned as well as practice the skills historians use to make sense of the past. The following Map, Visual, and Document activities are available for Chapter 23.

Map Activity

- Map 23.1: Africa, c. 1890

Visual Activity

- Mary Cassatt, *The Letter* (c. 1890), p. 749

Reading Historical Documents

- Imperialism's Popularity among the People, p. 736
- Henrik Ibsen, From *A Doll's House,* p. 748
- Contrasting Views: Experiences of Migration, pp. 744–745

CHAPTER

24

Modernity and the Road to War

1890–1914

CHAPTER RESOURCES

Main Chapter Topics

1. In the decades preceding World War I, industrialization, the accelerated pace of life, the rise of mass politics, the decline in the rural order, and radical innovations in science, philosophy, and the arts ("modernization") resulted in increased conflicts and heightened anxiety for many Europeans. The assassination of the heir to the Austrian throne, Francis Ferdinand (June 1914), was the catalyst for the eruption of the political, cultural, and societal discord that had been simmering for decades.

2. Concurrently with modernization, population patterns began to change. Europe became more urbanized and, due to improvements in sanitation and public health, the population soared. Despite this increase, however, Social Darwinists and eugenicists feared that the rise in population growth among the "lesser" classes was outpacing that of the middle and upper classes whose birthrates were declining as birth control became more common. Efforts were made to encourage women to bear children, which included liberalizing laws governing marriage and divorce. As another inducement, politicians played on the middle and upper classes' fears of ethnic minorities and the poor, polarizing European and American societies that had only recently moved toward nationalism.

3. Radical social change and reform of domestic laws and institutions changed life considerably for women across the West, and gender roles and relations more broadly. The "new woman" emerged as educated, mostly middle-class, women took white-collar jobs, joined the workforce, and exhibited a greater degree of independence, challenging accepted notions about female behavior and social roles. Homosexuality, still widely condemned, caused more open scandals as nationalists, eugenicists, and others rejected homosexual behavior. In general, the way was paved for greater sexual openness in future generations, and sexual issues became regular weapons in politics.

4. Those scientists who examined the rapidly changing conditions of modern life became alarmed by individuals' complaints of nervousness, fatigue, and irritability. As a result, sciences of the mind—psychology and psychoanalysis—began to consider the mental health of the entire population, not just that of the insane. Sigmund Freud's conclusions, both optimistic with respect to treatment of patients and pessimistic with respect to mass psychology, were the most influential of the period.

5. Artists, scientists, and intellectuals at the turn of the century responded to and accelerated the pace of changes in ideas, values, beliefs, and artistic forms. Science flourished, gaining authority and acceptability, although some critics questioned its ability to answer the most important questions of human existence. Cubism, fauvism, expressionism, relativity, Freudianism, nihilism, feminism, socialism, anarchism, Marxism, anti-Semitism, and mass politics exacerbated the uncertainty, anxiety, and sense of decay that characterized the era.

6. The new mass politics threatened the old order, as disenfranchised groups, such as the working class and women, demanded rights and shaped political developments. Demagogues employed virulent anti-Semitism and militant nationalism to win support and elections. As a result, mass politics did not bring harmonizing rational debate and compromise, but instead simplistic, divisive, pernicious rhetoric and attitudes.

7. Heated competition for colonies, growing tensions among colonial powers, the rise of non-Western powers such as Japan, and the increasing resistance of

colonial peoples made empire-building diplomatically and financially problematic and potentially explosive.

8. Imperial competition, the arms race, militarism, ethnicity-based nationalism, a tangle of alliances, and conflicts in domestic politics set the stage for World War I. Europeans—facing revolutions, terrorism, violent repression, controversy in the arts and sciences, and industrial conflicts—had come to feel that war would set events back on course and save them from the perils of modernity.

Focus Question

How did developments in social life, art, intellectual life and politics at the turn of the century produce instability and set the backdrop for war?

1. "Modernity," understood as a series of rapid changes and widespread and sharp breaks with tradition, was broadly destabilizing to social and intellectual life and politics in the West at the end of the nineteenth century and into the twentieth. For many, war looked to offer an opportunity for certainty and progress. Population pressures combined with ongoing urbanization, and eugenic and Social Darwinist anxieties about falling birthrates among the upper orders were worrisome to many. Gender relations were clearly in a state of flux as the "new woman" emerged and many agitated for social and political reform of established roles and responsibilities. Intellectual developments, particularly those related to psychology and philosophy (typified by the appeal of Sigmund Freud's ideas about human personality and Friedrich Nietzsche's nihilism) led many to question accepted systems of morality and social organization. Scientific advances, particularly in physics, likewise disturbed existing cosmologies.

2. In politics, growing electorates and the increasing political influence of previously marginalized groups (especially the organized working class) led to a variety of efforts to transform politics by revolutionary or evolutionary means. Broadly speaking, elites often attempted to retain their influence by encouraging popular imperialism, or by portraying racial or cultural differences as threats to nationalism and the state. Elites lost political influence and control even when they retained political power as politics became more subject to public opinion, emotion, and prejudice, even in states that did not function democratically. These political differences in particular reduced the flexibility of states in responding to crisis, and increased the likelihood of conflict, even while popular arms races escalated tensions, and armies became larger and, because of technology, exponentially more capable of inflicting casualties.

Annotated Chapter Outline

I. Public Debate over Private Life

A. Population Pressure, pp. 765–766

1. The staggering population increase of the eighteenth century continued through the nineteenth century due to improvements in sanitation and public health that extended longevity and reduced infant mortality.
2. However, despite an absolute rise in the population in much of the West, the birthrate (births per thousand people), which had been decreasing in France since the eighteenth century, began declining in other countries as well.
3. As society industrialized, individuals began making the decision to limit births on their own, often practicing coitus interruptus (withdrawing before ejaculation).
4. In the 1840s, the development of the vulcanization process for rubber made diaphragms and condoms fairly reliable methods of birth control.
5. Abortion, although illegal, was also common.
6. Government officials and concerned citizens worried that declining birthrates would result in an inability to compete militarily with other European powers.
7. Activists and politicians feared that a declining birthrate among the middle and upper classes would lead to social decay as those from the "worst" classes would outnumber those from the "better."
8. Nationalism and racism also played a role because many feared that the declining birthrate would cause western European populations to be absorbed by foreigners such as Slavs and Jews.

B. Reforming Marriage, pp. 766–767

1. The pseudoscience of eugenics grew in popularity as eugenicists advocated increasing the fertility of the "fittest" and limiting the fertility of, or even sterilizing, "degenerates."
2. Some believed that the answer to the population problem resided in marriage reform.
3. The inability of women to control their wages and property, the complications and costs of divorce where permitted, and women's lack of legal control over their

children were cited as reasons why women limited their fertility.

4. In response to such complaints, and the pressure for reform exerted by feminists, women gained legal rights to their wages and their property in much of Europe.
5. Some countries legalized divorce and made it easier and cheaper to obtain.
6. By the early twentieth century, several countries had passed legislation that provided government subsidies to assist mothers among the lower classes.
7. The concern for population laid the foundation for the modern welfare state that would be concerned not just with war and diplomacy, but also with the everyday life of its citizens.
8. The extent of change in women's lives varied widely, but reform was more rapid in western Europe.

C. New Women, New Men, and the Politics of Sexual Identity, pp. 767–768

1. The increasing availability of white-collar employment meant that more European women could travel and live independently.
2. These so-called new women dressed with fewer petticoats and looser corsets, biked and hiked, lived on their own in women's clubs or apartments, supported themselves financially, and adopted new attitudes toward sexuality and reproduction.
3. Sexual identity was generally a topic of great discussion as the new field of sexology emerged.
4. Havelock Ellis (1859–1939), a British medical doctor who wanted to study sex scientifically, argued in his book *Sexual Inversion* (1894) for the existence of a new personality type: the homosexual, or "third sex."
5. Self-identified homosexuals called for recognition, while the press reported on homosexual scandals such as the trial of British playwright Oscar Wilde (1854–1900) for indecency, or the court-martials of men in German kaiser William II's entourage for transvestitism and homosexuality.
6. In the context of concern over falling birthrates, sexual identity and sexuality came to be viewed through the light of nationalism, and patriotism and sexual issues became weapons regularly employed in politics even while the way was paved for growing sexual openness in the future.

D. Sciences of the Modern Self, pp. 768–770

1. Social Darwinists also believed that nervous illness was a cause of national decline.
2. In one of the most influential of the many books written on this subject in the 1890s, Hungarian-born physician Max Nordau (1849–1923) blamed overstimulation of the senses for individual and national degeneration in a world characterized by rapid change.
3. The cure for such overstimulation, Social Darwinists claimed, was imperial adventure, renewed virility, and increased childbearing.
4. The Viennese physician Sigmund Freud (1856–1939) sought a means to understand and remedy a variety of nervous ailments.
5. In works such as *The Interpretation of Dreams* (1900), Freud argued that repressed parts of a person's personality are located in the "unconscious" and surface only indirectly via dreams, symptoms of physical illness, and abnormal behavior.
6. He also argued that the psyche was composed of three parts—the id, the superego, and the ego—and that psychic development (or the creation of a healthy ego) entailed a constant attempt on the part of the superego (the conscience) to repress the sexual urges (seated in the id) that all children possess from birth. These ideas challenged the liberal belief in a unified, rational self. Freud demanded that sexual life be regarded objectively, free from moral and religious judgments.
7. Freud, a meticulous scientist who believed in the rational examination of detailed evidence, believed that human beings were motivated by irrational drives toward death and destruction and that these drives shaped society's collective mentality.

II. Modernity and the Revolt in Ideas

A. The Opposition to Positivism, pp. 771–772

1. Late in the nineteenth century, many philosophers and social thinkers rejected positivism: the belief that in science one could discover social laws based on rationally determined principles.
2. Critics, called relativists and pragmatists declared instead that human life and

society were ever-changing and complex, forcing persons and society to react pragmatically to the immediate conditions at hand.

3. German sociologist and political theorist Max Weber (1864–1920) began to question the dependability of bureaucracy, maintaining that, as the numbers of persons involved in policymaking expanded, decisive action would become impossible, especially in times of crisis.
4. In this situation, Weber argued, a charismatic leader might usurp power.
5. German philosopher Friedrich Nietzsche (1844–1900), a "nihilist," stated that all assertions of scientific fact and theory were illusions that people clung to because they could not face the primal, irrational side of human existence.
6. Nietzsche wrote much of his work in aphorisms—short, disconnected statements of truth or opinion—a form that broke with the logical rigor of traditional philosophy and that presented his ideas as statements of individual perspective and not as universal truths.
7. One aphorism declared, "God is dead, we have killed him," meaning that dogmatic truth was on the decline, freeing people to search for new "poetries of life." Nietzsche believed that individuals should cultivate their "will to power" and become uninhibited, dynamic "supermen."

B. Revolutionizing Science, pp. 772–773

1. Scientific inquiry flourished and gained authority. Breakthroughs and progress in public hygiene earned science prestige.
2. New scientific discoveries challenged accepted knowledge about the nature of the universe, undermining the principles of time, space, matter, and energy.
3. In 1896, Antoine Becquerel (1852–1908) discovered radioactivity and suggested the mutability of elements by a rearrangement of their atoms.
4. French chemist Marie Curie (1867–1934) and her husband Pierre (1859–1906) isolated the elements polonium and radium.
5. Building on these and other discoveries, scientists concluded that atoms are largely empty space acting as an intangible electromagnetic field.
6. German physicist Max Planck (1858–1947) announced his quantum theorem in 1900, which demonstrated that energy is emitted in irregular packets, not in a steady stream.
7. In 1905, physicist Albert Einstein (1879–1955) published his special theory of relativity, which argued that space and time are not absolutes, but rather vary according to the vantage point of the observer, and that only the speed of light is constant.
8. Einstein also transformed Planck's quantum theorem by suggesting that light travels in little packets and as waves.
9. Later, Einstein proposed the blurring of mass and energy, expressed as $E = mc^2$, and postulated a fourth mathematical dimension to the universe.
10. These theories often faced resistance from the scientific community but eventually transformed the foundations of science.

C. Modern Art, pp. 773–774

1. The same conflicts between traditional values and new ideas raged in the arts, as artists distanced themselves still further from classical Western styles and from the conventions of polite society.
2. A group of Parisian artists who decided to abandon the soft colors of impressionism for intense blues, greens, reds, and oranges came to be known as the fauves (wild beasts).
3. One of the movement's leaders, Henri Matisse (1869–1954), soon struck out in a new direction, seeking to create soothing art designed for white-collar workers.
4. Paul Cézanne (1839–1906) adopted a geometric vision in his paintings, accentuating the lines and planes found in nature.
5. Spanish artist Pablo Picasso (1881–1973) followed in Cézanne's footsteps and developed cubism—a style of painting in which a radical emphasis is placed on planes and surfaces that made people and objects almost unrecognizable.
6. Picasso was influenced by African, Asian, and South American art, as well as by the anarchist sentiments that flourished in his native Barcelona.
7. In 1912, he and French painter Georges Braque (1882–1963) devised a new kind of collage that incorporated newspaper clippings (which often described battles and murders), bits of string, and other artifacts, effectively creating a canvas covered in refuse.

8. Many artists mixed political criticism with radical stylistic changes, opposing aspects of modern life.
9. Expressionism, another artistic style, broke with middle-class optimism, using geometric forms and striking colors to emphasize emotion, as is evident in Norwegian painter Edvard Munch's (1863–1944) attempt to convey the horror of modern life in *The Scream* (1895).
10. Trade in art became increasingly professionalized, and the market more complex.
11. One innovative style that was a commercial success was art nouveau ("new style").
12. Designers working in this new style created an array of beautiful things for the general public—from posters to street lamps to dishes—drawing inspiration from organic and natural elements and from Asian art.

D. The Revolt in Music and Dance, pp. 775–776

1. Modern dance and music shocked audiences.
2. Popular American dancer Isadora Duncan (1877–1927) developed the first performance of modern dance.
3. Like Duncan, the Russian ballet experimented with bodily expression in the 1913 performance of Igor Stravinsky's (1882–1971) controversial *The Rite of Spring*.
4. French composers such as Claude Debussy (1862–1918) transformed their style to reflect the influence of non-European musical patterns and themes.
5. Composers also experimented with tonality, creating sounds that jarred the listeners.
6. Richard Strauss (1864–1949) used several keys simultaneously to distort familiar harmonic patterns.
7. Austrian composer Arnold Schoenberg (1874–1951) proposed eliminating tonality altogether.
8. Modernists in music, like those in the other arts, felt that they were shattering old norms and values.
9. But new aesthetic models distanced these artists from their audiences, separating high and low culture, and creating a distinction between the artistic elite and the social elite.

III. Growing Tensions in Mass Politics

A. Labor's Expanding Power, pp. 776–777

1. European leaders watched with dismay as working-class political power increased in the late nineteenth century.
2. In many countries such as Germany, England, and France, socialists gained seats in the government.
3. The growing strength of the labor movement raised problems. Some socialists felt uncomfortable sitting in parliament with members of the upper classes, whereas others worried that electoral victories might compromise the goal of revolution.
4. Between 1900 and 1904, the Second International debated the issue of revisionism, which proposed that socialism be achieved by evolutionary rather than revolutionary means.
5. Russian socialists had little power, and most operated in exile.
6. Russian activist V. I. Lenin (1870–1924) moved to Western Europe after serving a jail term in Siberia, where he had become involved with exiled Russian Marxists and advanced the theory that a highly disciplined party elite would lead a lightly industrialized Russia into socialism.
7. His faction of Bolsheviks constantly struggled with the dominant Mensheviks.
8. Neither group, however, had as large a constituency as the Socialist Revolutionaries, whose goal was to politicize peasants rather than workers.
9. During this period, anarchists and some trade union members, known as syndicalists, resorted to terrorist acts and assassinated prominent political figures.
10. The power of working people's voices caused the upper and middle classes grave anxiety.

B. Rights for Women and the Battle for Suffrage, pp. 777–778

1. Throughout the nineteenth century, the women's movement had been committed to gaining rights for women and had worked for various causes, including women's education, the monitoring of the regulation of prostitution, and pacifism.
2. By the 1890s, however, many activists concluded that the right to vote should be the primary goal.
3. Women's rights activists were predominantly from the middle class; their

education exposed them to feminist ideas, and their greater leisure time gave them the opportunity to organize.

4. Most working-class women distrusted middle-class men and women, and believed that economic reform was more important than suffrage.
5. Influential women such as Millicent Garrett Fawcett (1847–1929) in England and Susan B. Anthony (1820–1906) in the United States emerged as leaders of the movement.
6. In 1906, suffragists achieved their first major victory when women were granted the vote in Finland.
7. But failure elsewhere prompted some women to more radical tactics.
8. The Women's Social and Political Union founded in England by Emmeline Pankhurst (1858–1928) and her daughters began a campaign of violence, property destruction, and hunger strikes in 1909.

C. Liberalism Tested, pp. 778–779

1. In 1905, the British Liberal Party won a majority in the House of Commons and passed the National Insurance Act of 1911. When Conservatives in the House of Lords resisted raising taxes to pay for this and other social programs, the Liberals threatened to demand the creation of more peers (lords) so as to dilute the power of the nobility.
2. Under this threat, the House of Lords approved the Parliament Bill of 1911, which eliminated their veto power.
3. Irish artists and nationalists promoted an "Irish way of life" revolving around language, culture, and Catholicism. Sinn Fein and other groups promoted home rule or more radical demands for complete independence.
4. In 1913, the British Parliament approved home rule for Ireland.
5. The outbreak of World War I prevented this legislation from taking effect.
6. In Italy, corruption plagued the constitutional monarchy.
7. In the 1890s, prime ministers used patriotic rhetoric, bribes to the press and imperial adventure, which culminated in the failed attempt to conquer Ethiopia (1896), to forge a national consensus.
8. These policies failed and led to riots and strikes that were repressed by armed government troops.
9. A new prime minister, Giovanni Giolitti (1842–1928), followed a policy known as *trasformismo* (Italian for "transform"), using bribes, public works programs, and other benefits to localities to influence their deputies in parliament in the absence of well-developed political parties.
10. Giolitti's policies met with unrest in the rapidly industrializing cities of Turin and Milan and in the depressed agrarian south.
11. Urban and rural workers demanded change, especially a widening of the suffrage.
12. Giolitti appeased the protesters by instituting social welfare programs, and in 1912, virtually complete male suffrage.

D. Anti-Semitism, Nationalism, and Zionism in Mass Politics, pp. 779–783

1. Anti-Semitism and nationalism offered pat answers to complex questions, and leaders invoked these concepts in order to maintain interest-group support, to direct hostility away from themselves, and to win elections.
2. Russian tsar Nicholas II supported the Russian orthodox religion, autocratic politics, and anti-Semitic social values. Jews were blamed for any failure in Russian policy. Pogroms became a regular threat to Russian Jews, and Nicholas II increasingly limited where Jews could live and how they could earn a living.
3. In France, widespread prejudice against Jews was exploited to weaken the republican government they were said to control.
4. A Jewish army officer, Alfred Dreyfus (1859–1935), was convicted of spying for Germany in 1894.
5. As evidence came to light regarding his innocence, novelist Émile Zola (1840–1902) accused governmental officials of a list of lies and cover-ups in the affair, and Dreyfus was eventually pardoned in 1899.
6. In Germany, ruling elites used anti-Semitism as a political weapon to gain support from those who feared the consequences of Germany's rapid industrialization.
7. These elites based their power and wealth on agriculture.
8. As agriculture came to comprise a smaller percentage of the gross national product,

these elites came to loathe industry and the working class.

9. In Austria-Hungary, nationalism and anti-Semitism were also used to win votes, but the presence of many ethnic groups and competing nationalisms made the politics of hate more complex.
10. While Hungarians demanded more autonomy for themselves, they forcibly imposed their own language and culture on other, smaller ethnic groups (a policy called Magyarization).
11. Unrest in Hungary fueled unrest elsewhere in the empire, as Croats, Serbs, and other Slavic groups in the south called for equality with the Hungarians.
12. The central government granted the Czechs more privileges because the heightened development of industry in their region gave them more influence.
13. This increase in Czech influence outraged ethnic Germans and politicians in Vienna, like mayor Karl Lueger (1844–1910), who linked the growing power of Hungarian and Czech politicians with the Jews.
14. The rise of nationalism and anti-Semitism further destabilized politics in the Dual Monarchy.
15. Jews in Western Europe had responded to legal emancipation with assimilation, adopting liberal political and cultural values, intermarrying with Christians, and sometimes converting to Christianity.
16. By contrast, Jews in Russia and Romania were increasingly singled out for persecution, legally disadvantaged, and forced to live in ghettos.
17. In the 1880s, Ukrainian physician Leon Pinsker (1821–1891) advocated the migration of Jews to Palestine.
18. In 1896, Hungarian journalist Theodor Herzl (1860–1904) published *The Jewish State*, which called for the creation of a Jewish nation-state.
19. With the support of poor eastern European Jews, Herzl succeeded in calling the first International Zionist Congress in 1897, which endorsed settlement in Palestine.
20. By 1914, some eighty-five thousand Jews had resettled in Palestine.

IV. European Imperialism Challenged

A. The Trials of Empire, pp. 784–787

1. As the twentieth century opened, imperial adventure soured for Britain and France, while Italy and Germany found it difficult to establish themselves as imperial powers.
2. In 1896, the British experienced a bloody defeat when Cecil Rhodes (1853–1902), prime minister of the Cape Colony in southern Africa, ordered a raid into Boer territory.
3. Not willing to accept defeat, Britain went to war with the Boers and succeeded in annexing the Transvaal and the Orange Free State in 1902.
4. The brutality of the war horrified Britons, and many more people began to criticize imperialism.
5. At almost the same time, Spain lost Cuba, Puerto Rico, and the Philippines as a result of rebellions and the defeat in the Spanish-American war of 1898.
6. Subsequently, the United States waged a bloody war against the Filipinos who were demanding independence, further disillusioning the European public about the "civilizing" aspect of imperialism.
7. Italy and Germany still remained interested in imperial expansion.
8. European confidence fell further as Japan emerged as a power.
9. In 1894, Japan sparked the Sino-Japanese War, which forced China to end its domination of Korea.
10. As Russia expanded east and south into Asia, the Japanese became anxious, and attacked Russian forces (1904).
11. The complete destruction of Russia's ineptly led Baltic fleet in the battle of Tsushima Straits (1905) was the first victory of a non-European power over a European power in modern history.

B. The Russian Empire Threatened, pp. 787–788

1. Although the Russian Empire had expanded during the nineteenth century, internally the threat of revolution was constant.
2. In January 1905, a crowd gathered outside the tsar's palace in St. Petersburg to make Nicholas II aware of industry's brutal working conditions.
3. Soldiers fired on the crowd, killing hundreds and wounding thousands, an event that came to be known as Bloody Sunday.
4. The quashing of this demonstration spurred other workers to rebel.
5. During the following year, workers struck over wages, hours, and working conditions, and demanded political representation.

6. In response to the continuing violence, Nicholas II created a representative body: the Duma.
7. The Duma convened in 1907, and revolutionary activity abated.
8. Although very few citizens had voting privileges, the Duma's existence—coupled with the right of public political debate—liberalized government.
9. However, when the tsar disliked its recommendations, he disbanded the Duma.
10. Prime Minister Pyotr Stolypin (1863–1911) resolved to eliminate sources of discontent by ending the mir system, canceling land redemption payments, and making governmental loans available to peasants.
11. These reforms allowed more persons to move to the cities and created a larger group of independent peasants.
12. At the same time, Stolypin clamped down on revolutionary organizations, urged more pogroms, and stepped up Russification.
13. Despite these measures, rebels continued to assassinate government officials, including Stolypin himself, who was killed in 1911.
14. Without curbing unrest, the reforms created a larger industrial workforce and a more assertive peasantry.

C. **Growing Resistance to Colonial Domination, pp. 788–790**

1. China's 1895 defeat by Japan forced the ruling Qing dynasty to grant economic concessions to the Western powers.
2. Consequently, peasants organized into secret societies to restore Chinese integrity.
3. One such group, the Society of the Righteous and Harmonious Fists (or Boxers) rebelled in 1900, killing missionaries and Chinese Christians. Colonial powers, after putting down the rebellion, forced the Chinese government to pay a huge indemnity and to allow more extensive foreign military occupation.
4. In 1911, the Qing dynasty was overthrown, and the following year China was declared a republic.
5. Sun Yat-Sen (1866–1925), the leader of the revolutionaries, used Western concepts to promote Chinese values while pursuing a cluster of Western programs.
6. In India, the Japanese victory over Russia and the Russian Revolution of 1905 stimulated politicians to take a more radical course than that offered by the Indian National Congress.
7. A Hindu leader, B. G. Tilak (1856–1920), preached complete noncooperation with the British and promoted Hindu customs, while inspiring violent rebellion in his followers.
8. In an attempt to stop Tilak, the British sponsored the Muslim League, a rival nationalist group, but also conceded some political power to Indian elites.
9. Nationalism was also weakening the Ottoman Empire.
10. When Sultan Abdul Hamid II (r. 1876–1909) attempted to promote a pan-Islamic solution to nationalist discontent, he provoked Turkish nationalism in Constantinople.
11. Turkish nationalists emphasized their distinct history, culture, and language.
12. In 1908, a group of nationalists, called the Young Turks, took control of Constantinople.
13. Their victory motivated other groups in the Middle East and the Balkans to assert their independence from the Ottomans and economic dependence on the West.
14. In German East Africa, colonial forces responded to native rebellion with a scorched-earth policy, while in Indochina the French closed the University of Hanoi, executed Indo-Chinese intellectuals, and deported thousands of suspected nationalists.

V. **Roads to War**

A. **Competing Alliances and Clashing Ambitions, pp. 790–792**

1. At the beginning of the twentieth century, the Triple Alliance between Germany, Austria-Hungary, and Italy faced the alliance forged by France and Russia in the 1890s.
2. France and Great Britain also strengthened ties with a series of secret agreements concerning French claims in Morocco and British claims in Egypt.
3. These agreements became a British–French alliance called the "Entente Cordiale."
4. Germany unwittingly strengthened this alliance in a series of challenges to French predominance in Morocco in 1905 and 1911, known respectively as the first and second Moroccan Crises.

5. However, they were disappointed in their expectations for more colonial power.
6. Frustrated in the colonies, German statesmen turned their hopes to the creation of a Mitteleuropa that would include central Europe, the Balkans, and Turkey.
7. The Habsburgs, backed by Germany, wished to expand into the Balkans, believing the resulting addition of more ethnic groups would weaken those already present in the Dual Monarchy.
8. Promoting itself as protector of the Slavs, Russia was outraged at Austria-Hungary's 1908 annexation of Bosnia-Hungary, where many Serbian Slavs resided.
9. Among the Balkan states themselves, Greece, Serbia, Bulgaria, Romania, and Montenegro all wanted to incorporate territories in Austria-Hungary and the Ottoman Empire in which members of their ethnic groups lived.
10. In 1912, the First Balkan War broke out.
11. Greece, Serbia, Bulgaria, and Montenegro joined forces to take Macedonia and Albania from the Ottomans.
12. In a second war in 1913, Greece, Serbia, and Montenegro won a quick victory over Bulgaria.
13. Strategists began to think that a quick war in the Balkans could resolve the multiple tensions that existed.

B. The Race to Arms, pp. 792–793

1. Rivalries, territorial ambitions, and aspirations for greatness made constant readiness for war seem increasingly necessary.
2. During the nineteenth century, governments began to draft ordinary citizens for periods of two to six years in large standing armies.
3. Between 1890 and 1914, as competition in the colonies and in Europe increased the threat of war, the rates of conscription and military expenditure rose.
4. At the same time, the modernization of weaponry had a huge impact.
5. Swedish arms manufacturer Alfred Nobel (1833–1896) patented dynamite and developed a type of gunpowder that improved the accuracy of firearms.
6. Military leaders began to devise strategies to protect their armies, such as the trenches used by Russia during the Russo-Japanese War.
7. Arms manufacturers throughout Europe increased production as governments stockpiled weapons.
8. The modernization of weaponry also affected navies; battleships began to be constructed out of metal rather than wood.
9. William II, following naval theorist Alfred Thayer Mahan (1840–1914), thought that command of the seas determined international power, and sought to increase and modernize Germany's fleet.
10. German ambitions caused France and Great Britain to increase naval spending and to draw even closer together in the Entente Cordiale.
11. Military buildup was a response to a possible threat of war; however, it also added to economic and social stability by creating jobs.
12. Public relations campaigns created support for an arms race that had external and internal benefits.
13. By 1914, most of the general public believed that war was imminent and necessary to settle lingering international tensions.

C. 1914: War Erupts, pp. 793–794

1. On June 28, 1914, Bosnian nationalist Gavrilo Princip (1895–1918) assassinated Archduke Francis Ferdinand (1863–1914), heir to the Habsburg throne, and his wife, Sophie, when they were on a state visit to Bosnia.
2. Evidence showed that Princip had received arms and information from Serbian officials who hoped, like Princip, to join Bosnia to Serbia.
3. Austria, backed by Germany, presented Serbia with a harsh ultimatum.
4. Serbia agreed to every condition except Austrian participation in the investigation. Austria-Hungary, confident of Germany's backing, declared war on Serbia on July 28.
5. As the tsar and the kaiser corresponded, each asked the other to avoid starting a European war; British foreign secretary unsuccessfully proposed an international conference.
6. The German military leadership was fixed on fighting a short war that could provide territorial gains leading toward the goal of Mitteleuropa, and hoped that martial law would justify arresting the leaders of the Social Democratic Party.

7. While the press fanned war fever, military leaders prepared for an attack.
8. The Austrians mobilized on July 31.
9. In response, Nicholas II ordered Russian mobilization to aid her ally, Serbia.
10. The Germans mobilized on August 1, and France declared war on Germany.
11. German military strategy was based on the plan drawn up by Alfred von Schlieffen, which anticipated a two-front war and thus called for a rapid strike through Belgium against France and a subsequent campaign against Russia.
12. When Belgium refused Germany uncontested passage, the Germans entered anyway, triggering a British war declaration.
13. As war broke out, celebrations erupted throughout Europe.
14. Europeans believed the conflict would be short, and that it would resolve tensions ranging from the rise of the working class to imperial competition.

Lecture Strategies

1. One of the significant developments of this period was the explosive growth of the modern city. A good way to frame a lecture or discussion on the changes in daily life is to look at how cities evolved and transformed, and how architectural styles changed during the latter part of the nineteenth and the early twentieth centuries. Slides of buildings and cityscapes would add greatly to the presentation. Good sources for this topic are Donald J. Olsen, *The City As Work of Art: London, Paris, Vienna* (New Haven: Yale University Press, 1986); Franco Borsi, *Vienna 1900* (New York: Rizzoli, 1986); William Johnston, *Vienna: The Golden Age, 1815–1914* (New York: Clarkson N. Potter, 1981); François Loyer, *Paris, Nineteenth Century: Architecture and Urbanism* (New York: Abbeville Press, 1988); Alastair Service, *London 1900* (New York: Rizzoli, 1979); and Mark Girouard, *Cities and People: A Social and Architectural History* (New Haven: Yale University Press, 1985). A comprehensive overview is provided in Thomas Hall's *Planning Europe's Capital Cities: Aspects of Nineteenth Century Urban Development* (New York: Routledge, 1997).

2. The lives of European women and the suffrage movement are important topics for understanding some of the social transformations that occurred during this period. What was everyday life like for women? What ideas were common about marriage and family? What role did women play in European society? How was that role changing? What motivated women to take part in the suffrage movement? What were the results of the women's movements throughout the countries of Europe? A good introduction on European women's history is Bonnie G. Smith, *Changing Lives: Women in European History Since 1700* (Lexington, MA: D. C. Heath, 1989); Karen Offen, *European Feminisms, 1700–1950: A Political History* (Stanford: Stanford University Press, 2000), especially Part II; and Deborah Simonton, ed., *The Routledge History of Women in Europe, 1700–the Present* (New York: Routledge, 2007). Other useful sources include Ute Frevert, *Women in German History: From Bourgeois Emancipation to Sexual Liberation* (Washington, DC: Berg, 1990); Ann Taylor Allen, *Feminism and Motherhood in Germany, 1800–1914* (New Brunswick: Rutgers University Press, 1991); Nancy Reagin, *A German Women's Movement: Class and Gender in Hanover, 1880–1933* (Chapel Hill, NC: University of North Carolina Press, 1995); Richard Stites, *The Women's Liberation Movement in Russia: Feminism, Nihilism, and Bolshevism, 1860–1930* (Princeton, NJ: Princeton University Press, 1978); Barbara Engel, *Women in Russia 1700–2000* (Cambridge: Cambridge University Press, 2003); Rose Glickman, *Russian Factory Women: Workplace and Society, 1880–1914* (Berkeley, CA: University of California Press, 1984); and Philippa Levine, *Victorian Feminism, 1850–1900* (London: Hutchinson Education, 1987). Ellen Ross's *Love and Toil: Motherhood in Outcast London, 1870–1918* (New York: Oxford University Press, 1993) is excellent on gender roles and working-class life. For a biographical approach, try June Purvis, *Emmeline Pankhurst: A Biography* (New York: Routledge, 2004), who may have been the era's indispensable feminist, or, more broadly, Valerie Sanders, *The Private Lives of Victorian Women: Autobiography in 19th* Century England (Hemel Hempstead: Harvester Wheatsheaf, 1989).

3. Slides comparing various examples of modern art with more traditional academic art are a good way to demonstrate how radical these art movements were at the time. Briefly explain the origins and philosophy of each movement and then show the images. In class, ask students to describe the content and style of traditional art and then compare these to examples from a variety of modern movements (for example, fauvism, cubism, and expressionism). Of the innumerable books published on artists and art movements from this period, a good introductory text on modern art movements is Nikos Stangos, ed., *Concepts of Modern Art: From Fauvism to Postmodernism*, 3rd ed. (New York: Thames and Hudson, 1994).

4. In order for students to understand the motivations for the various revolutionary movements in Russia during this period, discuss in some detail the

conditions in Russia in the years just prior to World War I. For evidence of everyday life, good sources include Olga Semyonova Tian-Sahnskaia, *Village Life in Late Tsarist Russia* (Bloomington: Indiana University Press, 1993); and Victoria E. Bonnell, ed., *The Russian Worker: Life and Labor under the Tsarist Regime* (Berkeley: University of California Press, 1983). For sources on Russian women, see suggestion 2. Sources on the Revolution of 1905 include Abraham Ascher, *The Revolution of 1905*, 2 vols. (Stanford, CA: Stanford University Press, 1988, 1992); Laura Engelstein, *Moscow 1905: Working Class Organization and Political Conflict* (Stanford, CA: Stanford University Press, 1982); Shmuel Galai, *The Liberation Movement in Russia, 1900–1905* (New York: Cambridge University Press, 1973); and Walter Sablinsky, *The Road to Bloody Sunday: Father Gapon and the St. Petersburg Massacre of 1905* (Princeton, NJ: Princeton University Press, 1976). A good documentary film that will help contrast the conditions of everyday life for the common people with that of the royal family is *Last of the Czars*; a classic, silent Russian film on an episode of the Revolution of 1905 is Sergei Eisenstein's *Battleship Potemkin*.

Class Discussion Starters

1. In order to deepen students' understanding of how ordinary Europeans lived, develop a discussion on the lives of the urban working class. One way to approach this topic is to have students read autobiographical accounts written by individuals who lived during this period. Two excellent sources from which readings could be assigned are David Kelly, *The German Worker: Working-Class Autobiographies from the Age of Industrialization* (Berkeley: University of California Press, 1987); and Mark Traugott, *The French Worker: Autobiographies from the Early Industrial Era* (Berkeley: University of California Press, 1993). Also try Proffes Burnett, *Useful Toil: Autobiographies of Working People from the 1820s to the 1920s* (New York: Routledge, 1994). For an intriguing overview of some of the junctures between class, gender, and social change, see Seth Koven's *Slumming: Sexual and Social Politics in Victorian London* (Princeton: Princeton University Press, 2006), which is quite focused on working-class life.

2. To help students understand how deeply rooted and heinous anti-Semitism was (and still is in some places), it would be useful to explore the most infamous case of the era. Discuss in some detail the Dreyfus Affair in France and how it demonstrated both divisions within France—especially in the military—and the wider problem of anti-Semitism in Europe. Sources on this topic include Jean Denis Bredin, *The Affair: The Case of Alfred Dreyfus* (New York: George Braziller, 1986); Martin Phillip Johnson, *The Dreyfus Affair: Honor and Politics in the Belle Époque* (New York: St. Martin's Press, 1999); and Michael Burns, *France and the Dreyfus Affair: A Documentary History* (Boston: Bedford/St. Martin's, 1999).

3. Along with discussing the process of European colonization, you should examine how colonization affected the subjugated peoples and how treatment differed according to the colonial power and the region colonized. Good sources for this include Muriel Evelyn Chamberlain, *The Scramble for Africa*, 2nd ed. (New York: Longman, 1999); Thomas Pakenham, *The Scramble for Africa: White Man's Conquest of the Dark Continent from 1876 to 1912* (New York: Random House, 1991); Adam Hochschild, *King Leopold's Ghost: The Story of Greed, Terror, and Heroism in Colonial Africa* (Boston: Houghton Mifflin, 1998); Winfried Baumgart, *Imperialism: The Idea and Reality of British and French Colonial Explosion, 1880–1914* (New York: Oxford University Press, 1989); and Raymond F. Betts, *The False Dawn: European Imperialism in the Nineteenth Century* (Lexington, MA: D. C. Heath, 1975).

4. The many forces at work within European society made a coming conflict seem, in retrospect, inevitable. Discuss in some detail the foreign and domestic politics of the great powers in order to demonstrate how Europe wound up fighting a world war over events in the Balkans. It may be useful for students to prepare in groups before class to articulate the reasons European nations fought for nations (and why they allied with those nations) that became embroiled in the Great War. General sources on the situation in Europe on the eve of the war include John Keegan, *The First World War* (New York: Alfred A. Knopf, 1999); Martin Gilbert, *The First World War: A Complete History* (New York: Henry Holt, 1994); Hew Strachan, *The Outbreak of the First World War* (Oxford: Oxford University Press, 2004); Laurence Lafore, *The Long Fuse: An Interpretation of the Origins of World War I*, 2nd ed. (New York: J. B. Lippincott, 1971); and Robert K. Massie, *Dreadnought: Britain, Germany, and the Coming of the Great War* (New York: Random House, 1991). An overview of the debate on the war's origins can be found in Richard Hamilton's *Decisions for War, 1914–1917* (Cambridge: Cambridge University Press, 2004). More detailed studies of individual countries include Mark Hewitson, *Germany and the Causes of the First World War* (New York: Berg, 2004); D. C. B. Lieven, *Russia and the Origins of the First World War* (New York: St. Martin's Press, 1983); John Keiger, *France and the Origins of the First World War* (New York: St. Martin's Press, 1983); Samuel R. Williamson, *Austria-Hungary and the Origins of the First World War* (New York: St. Martin's Press, 1990); and Zara

S. Steiner, *Britain and the Origins of the First World War* (New York: St. Martin's Press, 1977).

Reviewing the Text

Review Questions

1. How did ideas about the self and about personal life change at the beginning of the twentieth century?
[model answer] • ***Public debate about, and widespread private practice of, birth control and family planning reflected changes in personal life and ideas about the self:*** *Declining birth rates across much of the West by the early twentieth century reflected growing practice of a variety of birth control and family planning methods. Religious and political authorities fretted about "selfishness" and "birth strikes," and the social effects of declining middle- and upper-class birthrates.*
• ***Human sexuality and gender relations and roles became the topic of wider secular discussion:*** *The rights and roles of women were widely debated, and a variety of legal reforms gave more freedom to many women. Freud and others demanded that sexual life be studied scientifically, free from religious and moral judgments. For the first time scientists defined homosexuality as a personality type rather than as a form of sin. Amid growing concern over population and traditional family values, homosexuality was portrayed by the press as a lifestyle harmful to the nation, and homosexuals were portrayed as unpatriotic.*
• ***Psychoanalysis and the scientific study of personality became pervasive:*** *Influenced by Freud's ideas, the study of human consciousness and the development of theories about the causes of mental disorders expanded.*
• ***The idea that no absolute truth exists became more accepted:*** *Relativist and pragmatist social thinkers such as Max Weber and Friedrich Nietzsche rejected positivism, thus denying the belief that knowledge of fundamental social laws could be used to perfect society.*

2. How did modernism transform the arts and the world of ideas?
[model answer] *Modernism gave birth to new aesthetic approaches. Artists, writers, choreographers, and musicians turned away from Western classical realism, traditional forms of dance, and theories of musical composition. They accepted new influences such as scientific and psychological theories, political ideas, and foreign styles, often in hopes of encouraging debate and dissent among viewers.*

3. What were the points of tension in European political life at the beginning of the twentieth century?
[model answer] • ***The working class gained political power:*** *A new sense of solidarity arose, translating into a greater voice in society. Socialist parties attracted many workers and won elections throughout Europe. However, divisions developed between workers who favored violent revolution and those who preferred political reform.*
• ***Voting rights and activism among the working class forced politicians to appeal to a wider voting audience:*** *Politicians gave speeches in favor of self-determination and middle-class values, or played on hatred of other groups. Daily newspapers focused on political and global issues, which helped to disseminate political ideas.*
• ***The fight for women's rights and suffrage became a highly public movement:*** *Activists concluded that only women's right to vote would correct all the problems caused by male privilege. Major suffrage organizations with hundreds of members and vocal leaders developed out of single-issue reform groups, and held marches and parades.*
• ***Governments veered away from liberal values:*** *Governments sought to control social conflicts with policies that struck at liberalism's foundations. Anti-Semitism and nationalism were used to combat the radical left of social democracy. Governments ended laissez-faire trade policies and expanded social welfare legislation. Politicians used patriotic rhetoric, bribes, and imperialist enterprises to maintain support.*

4. How and why did events in overseas empires from the 1890s on challenge Western faith in imperialism?
[model answer] • ***The British fought the difficult Boer War in South Africa:*** *The British military performed poorly in the conflict and suffered heavy casualties. The government was criticized for the expense of the campaign, and for adopting brutal and repressive measures in order to achieve some measure of success.*
• ***Newer imperial powers faced challenges in building empires:*** *Resistance by native peoples in the Philippines against the United States, in Ethiopia against the Italians, and in the German African colonies raised questions about the cost and morality of imperialism.*
• ***Japanese expansion challenged notions of Western superiority:*** *Japanese expansion into China and Korea, and their military successes against Russia in 1904, raised questions about the supposed superiority of European culture.*

5. What were the major factors leading to the outbreak of World War I?
[model answer] • ***Imperial competition led to delicate diplomacy and new alliances:*** *Europe's peace could be easily disrupted by rivalries or by a single nation's desire for more power on the continent or in distant colonies. Alliances based on binding agreements between nations to deploy forces to help one another in case of war were meant to protect their members and lessen the aggression of outsiders, but easily drove international relations into chaos.*
• ***Arms race:*** *Global rivalries made constant readiness for war seem increasingly necessary. Technological advances revolutionized the instruments of warfare and stimulated*

the economy as growing numbers of European munitions factories provided jobs. Politicians and political parties used military construction as a rallying point, arguing that armament production and large navies benefited trade and industry, and used pro-armament arguments to pull citizens' support away from political enemies' liberal programs.

Making Connections

1. How did changes in society at the turn of the century affect the development of mass politics?
[model answer] *Fear of the working class and women's movements, which sometimes embraced violence as a means to an end, was not assuaged by mass politics. It was hoped that mass politics would bring more harmonious debate and compromise, but further conflict often resulted. In the two decades before WWI, many politicians deliberately inflamed anti-Semitism to gain support from certain constituencies and win elections. State-sponsored anti-Jewish pogroms in Russia; the rise of radical nationalism and anti-Semitic groups in Germany, Italy, and Austria-Hungary; and the Dreyfus Affair in France are all examples of "the politics of the irrational." Indeed, throughout Europe, statesmen used hate-filled slogans blaming the Jews for social, economic, and political problems.*

2. How was culture connected to the world of politics in the years 1890–1914?
[model answer] *Across Europe, artists mixed political criticism with radical stylistic changes in their work. Some artists tried to use their creations to comfort urbanites caught up in the rush of modern life; others sought to shock people out of complacent acceptance of the state of the world. Viewers were intended to reflect on the horrors of modern life and its causes. For example, Picasso and Braque made a collage using newspaper clippings that described battles and murders, thus suggesting the shallowness of Western pretensions to high civilization. In eastern and central Europe, artists criticized the growing nationalism that determined which sculptures or paintings would be officially purchased. These purchases tended to be traditional in form and subject matter, rather than reflections of contemporary society. Even music could have a political edge. Béla Bartók used folk melodies to promote Hungarian ethnicity over the Habsburg Empire's multinationalism.*

3. How had nationalism changed since the French Revolution?
[model answer] • ***Nationalism spread beyond Europe:*** *Many non-Western peoples, notably in Japan, China, Turkey, and India, developed national movements that asserted independence and challenged Western power and colonialism.*
• ***In the West, nationalism became more militant in some quarters:*** *The rise of militancy, in the form of arms races and more widespread military training and service, contributed to the development of strains of nationalism that emphasized power, conflict, and violent struggles between nations as natural and possibly even beneficial.*

Discussing the Documents

Questions from Online Study Guide with Model Answers

Leon Pinsker Calls for a Jewish State, p. 783

1. What arguments does Leon Pinsker present for why European Jews should have their own nation?
[model answer] *Pinsker begins by saying that Jews are a "distinctive element" within the nations they live in, and that they cannot be assimilated into any nation. He also mentions the long history of hostility toward Jews, arguing that because Jews have no nation, they are defenseless against aggression. A Jewish nation would allow Jews to live in security.*

2. What contemporary social trends are evident in this excerpt?
[model answer] *Pinsker is much aware of the mounting anti-Semitism that was spreading throughout Europe at the time and led to great violence perpetrated against the Jews—particularly in Russia—where Pinsker was from. Another trend is nationalism, both in the sense that nationalism contributed to the exclusion of Jews in European society, and in the sense among Jews that they themselves comprised a nation.*

A Historian Promotes Militant Nationalism, p. 795

1. Why, according to Heinrich von Treitschke, was war a necessity?
[model answer] *Von Treitschke argues that the protection of its members is a state's primary task. As long as there are multiple states, each with the duty of protecting its members, there will be war. War is a natural part of the human psyche that cannot be changed.*

2. What scientific and historical evidence does he use to support his claims?
[model answer] *Von Treitschke argues that every state in history has come into being through war. He also speaks of the "laws of human thought and of human nature."*

New Sources, New Perspectives: Psychohistory and Its Lessons, p. 770

1. What are the advantages and disadvantages of psychohistory?
[model answer] *Psychohistory draws attention to the way in which individuals and groups are motivated by fears, desires, and perceptions that may not always appear rational, but that may be rooted in emotional traumas or a*

feeling of being threatened. Psychohistory emphasizes the way in which events take on form and meaning for human beings in unexpected ways, and teaches that emotions, fears, and anxieties, however irrational they may appear, should be taken into account when studying the past. Critics of psychohistory claim that it can be formulaic because it fits the behavior of historical individuals into Freud's schema, which is in itself controversial. Other critics find psychohistory to be too imprecise because it is more theoretical and not based on the same kinds of documentary evidence that historians usually use.

2. How would you set out to investigate the psychological reasons for the actions of William II, Emmeline Pankhurst, Marie Curie, or Gavrilo Princip? Would you look at their character, their childhood, their social background, or other parts of their lives?
[model answer] *Any information that could be gathered on all of these subjects would be important. Personal and preferably private sources that might reveal details of personal conduct, human relationships, and the thought processes of the subject would be particularly important—diaries, letters to intimate friends, and private or honest accounts of the person's conduct from knowledgeable sources would be of great use. A historian using this approach might make much use of previously neglected sources, particularly ones that date from the subject's childhood. Family life in particular would need to be closely examined for clues that it might provide about the subject's conduct, motivations, and worldview.*

3. Can we write history without talking about the emotions, mental habits, and human relationships of major figures? Should we avoid psychologizing when thinking about the past?
[model answer] *Psychologists understand how complex human behaviors often are. There are limitations to how much evidence a historian can have in analyzing the psychological causes of the actions and decisions of historical figures. But it is also important that historians take human behavior, personality, upbringing, prejudices and similar considerations into account when they study historical figures of any kind. Thinking in terms of human psychology not only can help historians engage with why "major figures" did what they did, but also why certain kinds of social and political changes occur when and how they do, or why particular leaders or policies may have been popular or unpopular. In that sense, "psychologizing when thinking about the past" is valuable.*

Other Questions for Discussing These Documents in Class

Leon Pinsker Calls for a Jewish State

1. Why might someone like Pinsker have been frustrated by the problems Jews faced in the West in the closing decades of the nineteenth century?

2. How should the Jewish community respond to "Judeophobia"?

A Historian Promotes Militant Nationalism

1. What absolutes does Treitschke offer his readers? Why is war essential?

2. What role should value judgments play in the writing of history?

New Sources, New Perspectives: Psychohistory and Its Lessons

1. What arguments were advanced by advocates of psychohistory?

2. What practical challenges do historians face in attempting to practice psychohistory?

Comparative Questions

1. How do the documents reflect "modern" society and its discontents, as defined in the "Terms of History" text feature?

2. For Pinsker and Treitschke, in particular, what are the attractions or uses of the nation? How important is security to their conception of what nations are for?

For Users of *Sources of The Making of the West*

The following documents are available in Chapter 24 of the companion sourcebook by Katharine J. Lualdi, University of Southern Maine.

1. "God Is Dead": Friedrich Nietzsche, *The Gay Science* (1882)
2. The Dreyfuss Affair: Émile Zola, "J'Accuse!" (January 13, 1898)
3. Rising Up Against Western Imperialism: The I-ho-ch'uan (Boxers), *The Boxers Demand Death for All "Foreign Devils"* (1900)
4. Militant Suffrage: Emmeline Pankhurst, *Speech from the Dock* (1908)
5. Tapping the Human Psyche: Sigmund Freud, *The Interpretation of Dreams* (1900)
6. The Idealized Family: Eugenics Education Society of London, *Eugenics for Citizens: Aim of Eugenics* (c. 1907)

Discussion Ideas for Sources of The Making of the West, *Chapter 24*

1. Do the documents provide evidence that gender roles and traditional senses of male and female "spheres" were being challenged or were under pressure?

2. To what extent can the documents be seen as attacks on established power structures more generally? Consider their implications for the legal and political systems in particular.

Working with Visual Sources

For this exercise, please refer to The Foreign Pig Is Put to Death on p. 789 of the textbook or view the image on the book companion site's Online Study Guide under the "Visual Activity" for Chapter 24.

Students viewing the image at the Online Study Guide are asked two questions about the image. The questions and model answers (not made available to students) are below. Project this image, available on the Instructor's Resources CD-ROM, in class or ask students to look at the image in their textbooks and answer the questions.

1. How are foreigners and those who adopt foreign ways portrayed in this image?
[model answer] *Both foreigners and those who adopt foreign ways are portrayed as animals and less than human. The foreign missionary is portrayed as a pig; the Chinese converts are depicted as goats. The foreigner suffers a worse fate, being killed with arrows; the Chinese converts are beheaded. Because the Chinese converts are depicted as goats, which are passive animals and easily led astray, they are considered less guilty than the missionary pig.*

2. How does this image legitimize the Boxer's actions?
[model answer] *The depiction of the Boxers in traditional Chinese garb, and the depiction of the cross, a symbol of foreign religion, presents the Boxers as upholding Chinese culture and protecting it from foreign influence. The violence they are committing is not random, but is being carried out in an orderly fashion by the man behind the desk. His magisterial appearance suggests that the killings are even lawful, and that the Boxers were, in fact, encouraged by the Qing Dowager Empress Tz'u-hsi.*

Mapping Exercises

Map Activity from OSG—Model Answers for Map Activity #2

For this activity, please refer to Map 24.2: Africa in 1914 on p. 784. Students are asked these questions:

Look at the territory controlled by Great Britain and France. What might be Britain's goals for expansion? French goals for expansion?
[model answer] *The British controlled territory stretching from Egypt in the northeast, to southern Africa, to portions of the eastern coast. They wished to create a united north-south block encompassing most of eastern and central Africa. The French controlled much of the northwestern corner of Africa as well as portions of central Africa and French Somaliland on the eastern coast. They wished to push eastward from central Africa to unite the western and central territories to French Somaliland.*

Judging from the map of Africa, why might Germany have felt insecure about its position as an imperial power?
[model answer] *France and Great Britain control large portions of Africa; Germany controls relatively little territory. Because the possession of colonies was increasingly considered necessary for great power status, Germany's lack of possessions fueled the country's feelings of insecurity. Germany's desire for colonies at any cost led to the 1905 and 1911 Moroccan crises in which Germany unsuccessfully challenged France for control of Morocco.*

Which patterns are evident in the uprisings against Europeans, and what might explain the timing of the uprisings?
[model answer] *With the exception of the insurrection in German East Africa, the uprisings were located along the central and southern western coast of Africa, suggesting that each was influenced by the other. The uprisings on the Gold Coast and in German southwest Africa occurred during or immediately following the Boer War, whereas most other rebellions occurred following the Russo-Japanese War. In both cases, outside conflicts kept the Europeans occupied, which encouraged opponents of colonialism to resist their European conquerors.*

Map 24.1: Jewish Migrations in the Late Nineteenth Century, p. 782

Ask students to locate and identify centers of Jewish population in late-nineteenth-century Europe. Where were Jews emigrating to? What were their reasons?

Map 24.2: Africa in 1914, p. 784

Ask students to locate and identify the few independent African states on the eve of World War I. Compare this map to a current map of Africa and have students note the tremendous political transformation of the African continent over the past century. How might other methods of mapping the continent (language, religion) affect ideas about borders and boundaries?

Map 24.3: Imperialism in Asia, 1894–1914, p. 786

Ask students to consider where the interests of various imperial powers (including Japan) might be likely to clash, or were clashing. How did China's geography contribute to its difficulties in this era?

Map 24.4: The Balkans, 1908–1914, p. 791

Ask students to locate and identify the major and minor powers on this map. Given the geography, what potential sources of conflict existed in this region? How might other methods of mapping the same region (language, religion) affect ideas about borders and boundaries?

Mapping the West: Europe at the Outbreak of World War I, August 1914, p. 796

Ask students to identify Germany on this map. Where are Germany's potential enemies located? How were Germany's political developments and worldview in the late nineteenth and early twentieth centuries affected by these geographical relationships?

In-Class Assignments and Presentation Topics

1. In order to explore how far-reaching anti-Semitism was during this period, have students a) research the Dreyfus Affair for a written essay and then reenact one of Captain Dreyfus's trials in class or b) research the problems of eastern European Jewish peasants, and write a creative, first-hand account of a pogrom.

2. Divide the class into groups and have each group research the various domestic and foreign policy concerns of the individual great powers before World War I. Each student in the group should write on one reason for their group's assigned great power to seek war, and one reason to avoid it. Have each group present the cumulative pressures experienced by their assigned country and its motivations for preparing for war. Beyond the books listed in "Class Discussion Starters," number 4, short works that can be assigned on the debates surrounding the outbreak of the war include David Stevenson, *The Outbreak of the First World War: 1914 in Perspective* (New York: St. Martin's Press, 1997); and Holger H. Herwig, *The Outbreak of World War I*, 5th ed. (Lexington, MA: D. C. Heath, 1991).

3. Ask students to write an essay comparing independence movements against European domination. Movements may include those of the Irish, the Boxers in China, the nationalists in India, Filipino resistance of the 1890s, or the Young Turks in the Ottoman Empire. Ask students to explain how the colonized people were treated by the colonial power(s), the origins of the independence movements, and the results of the movements by 1914. Good sources are listed in the chapter bibliography.

4. Have each student research and write an essay or give an in-class presentation about an artist of the period. Students should provide images of the artist's work and discuss his or her style, philosophy, and relationship to the concept "modern" as articulated in the "Terms of History" text feature.

Essay Questions

1. The women's suffrage movement was a significant element of international politics before the outbreak of World War I. Ask students to do a research project exploring the origins of the suffrage movement, the membership, the obstacles faced, and the level of success prior to World War I. They may elect to focus on the movement in one country. Sources besides those listed in "Lecture Strategies," number 2, include Leila J. Rupp, *World of Women: The Making of an International Women's Movement* (Princeton: Princeton University Press, 1999); Richard J. Evans, *The Feminists: Women's Emancipation Movements in Europe, America, and Australasia, 1840–1920* (London: Croom Helm, 1977); Sandra Stanley Holton, *Feminism and Democracy: Women's Suffrage and Reform Politics in Britain, 1900–1918* (New York: Cambridge University Press, 1986); Claire Eustance, Joan Ryan, and Laura Ugolini, eds., *A Suffrage Reader: Charting Directions in British Suffrage History* (Leicester: Leicester University Press, 2000); Angela V. John and Claire Eustance, eds., *The Men's Share?: Masculinities, Male Support, and Women's Suffrage in Britain, 1890–1920* (New York: Routledge, 1997); Sophia A. van Wingerden, *The Women's Suffrage Movement in Britain, 1866–1938* (New York: St. Martin's Press, 1999); Patricia Greenwood Harrison, *Connecting Links: The British and American Woman Suffrage Movements, 1900–1914* (Westport, CT: Greenwood Press, 2000); Cliona Murphy, *The Women's Suffrage Movement and Irish Society in the Early Twentieth Century* (Philadelphia: Temple University Press, 1989); Steven Hause, *Hubertine Auclert: The French Suffragette* (New Haven: Yale University Press, 1987); and Steven Hause and Anne Kenney, *Women's Suffrage and Social Politics in the French Third Republic* (Princeton: Princeton University Press, 1984).

2. Anti-Semitism emerged as a major issue in turn-of-the-century European culture and politics. In a research project, ask students to explore the impact of anti-Semitism in a particular European country. Topics include pogroms in Russia, the Dreyfus Affair in France, and the emergence of anti-Semitic parties and organizations in Austria-Hungary. Another topic would be the Jewish response to these developments and the emergence of the Zionist movement. Beyond the works on the Dreyfus Affair listed in "Class Discussion Starters," number 2, other sources include Albert S. Lindemann, *The Jew Accused: Three Anti-Semitic Affairs (Dreyfus, Beilis, Frank), 1894–1915*

(New York: Cambridge University Press, 1991); George L. Mosse, *Toward the Final Solution: A History of European Racism* (Madison: University of Wisconsin Press, 1978); John Doyle Klier and Shlomo Lambroza, eds., *Pogroms: Anti-Jewish Violence in Modern Russian History* (New York: Cambridge University Press, 1992); Heinz-Dietrich Lowe, *The Tsars and the Jews: Reform, Reaction, and Anti-Semitism in Imperial Russia, 1772–1917* (New York: Harwood, 1992); Brigitte Hamann, *Hitler's Vienna: A Dictator's Apprenticeship* (New York: Oxford University Press, 1999); Carl E. Schorske, *Fin-de-Siècle Vienna: Politics and Culture* (New York: Alfred A. Knopf, 1980); and Walter Laqueur, *A History of Zionism* (New York: Schocken Books), 1972.

3. Many people, including the monarchs themselves, believed that the family relationships existing between the main royal houses of Europe (Britain, Russia, and Germany) would prevent all-out war. Have students research exactly what those relationships were, beginning first by sorting out who was related to whom. Then see Robert K. Massie, *Dreadnought: Britain, Germany, and the Great War* (New York: Random House, 1992). See also biographies of the main ruling figures of the period. For Nicholas II, see Robert K. Massie, *Nicholas and Alexandra* (New York: Atheneum, 1967; rpt. 2000); and D. C. B. Lieven, *Nicholas II: Twilight of the Empire* (New York: St. Martin's Press, 1996). For Kaiser Wilhelm, see Giles MacDonogh, *The Last Kaiser: The Life of Wilhelm II* (New York: St. Martin's Press, 2000). For George V, see Kenneth Rose, *King George V* (London: Phoenix Press, 2000).

Additional Resources: Literature

Eugenides, Jeffrey, ed., *Oscar Wilde: The Picture of Dorian Gray*. 1998.
Hingley, Ronald, trans., *Five Plays by Chekhov*. 1998.
Joyce, James, *Dubliners*. 2001. Especially "The Dead."
Kaufmann, Walter, trans., *The Portable Nietzsche*. 1977.
Nunally, Tiina, trans., *The Unknown Sigrid Undset: Jenny and Other Works*. 2001.
Pruitt, Ida. *A Daughter of Han: The Autobiography of a Chinese Working Woman*. 1945.
Woods, John E., trans., *Thomas Mann: Buddenbrooks, The Decline of a Family*. 1994.

Additional Resources: Film and Video

Edward the King (1975; VHS, approx. 13 hrs.). This thirteen-part series (each part approximately 1 hour) chronicles the life of King Edward VII of England. It is accurate on detail, plot, costumes, and settings.

Howard's End (1992; DVD/VHS, 2 hrs., 16 min.). This film adaptation of E. M. Forster's 1910 novel nicely captures what life was like for upper-middle-class Edwardians, especially women. Stultifying Edwardian moral and social conventions are essential elements of the plot.

1900 House (2002; VHS/DVD, 4 hrs.) and *Manor House* (2003; VHS/DVD, 6 hrs.). In these two series, contemporary English people find out firsthand what life was like in the early twentieth century. For several months, they live as people would have done more than one hundred years ago: they wear authentic clothing of the period, live in accommodations true to the period, and perform the jobs appropriate to their class and position in society. In *1900 House*, the focus is on a family of six. In *Manor House*, the division between the upstairs family and downstairs staff makes for an interesting and volatile contrast. Although slightly voyeuristic, these series do highlight in an immediate way what life was like in the early twentieth century.

The Forsyte Saga, Series I (2002; VHS/DVD, 4 hrs., 20 min.). John Galsworthy's early novels about the Forsyte family are dramatized in this excellent series. Eight episodes of approximately 50 minutes each graphically depict the reality of marriage and extramarital relationships in late-Victorian society and the plight of women trapped in a patriarchal world of stultifying manners and loveless marriages. Lavish costumes and sets help re-create the late-Victorian period.

The Lost Prince (2005; VHS/DVD, 3 hrs.). Haunting and evocative of pre-war Britain and anxieties of the era (dynastic and otherwise), Stephen Poliakoff's beautiful film explores the life of Prince John, the learning-disabled youngest child of George V. This work could inspire discussion about themes advanced in the text—decay, eugenics, and dynastic politics.

Other Bedford/St. Martin's Resources for Chapter 24

The following resources are available to accompany Chapter 24. Please refer to the Preface of this manual for detailed descriptions of all the ancillaries.

For Instructors

Transparencies

The following maps and images from Chapter 24 are available as full-color acetates.

- Map 24.1: Jewish Migrations in the Late Nineteenth Century
- Map 24.2: Africa in 1914
- Map 24.3: Imperialism in Asia, 1894–1914
- Map 24.4: The Balkans, 1908–1914
- Mapping the West: Europe at the Outbreak of World War I, August 1914
- The Foreign Pig Is Put to Death, p. 789
- Pablo Picasso, *Les Demoiselles d'Avignon* (1907), p. 774

Instructor's Resources CD-ROM

The following maps and image from Chapter 24, as well as a chapter outline, are available on disc in both PowerPoint and jpeg formats.

- Map 24.1: Jewish Migrations in the Late Nineteenth Century
- Map 24.2: Africa in 1914
- Map 24.3: Imperialism in Asia, 1894–1914
- Map 24.4: The Balkans, 1908–1914
- Mapping the West: Europe at the Outbreak of World War I, August 1914
- The Foreign Pig Is Put to Death, p. 789

Using the Bedford Series with The Making of the West

Available in print as well as online at **bedfordstmartins.com/usingseries,** this guide offers practical suggestions for using *France and the Dreyfus Affair: A Brief Documentary History* by Michael Burns in conjunction with Chapter 24 of the textbook, and *July 1914: Soldiers, Statesmen, and the Coming of the Great War, A Brief Documentary History* by Samuel R. Williamson Jr. and Russel Van Wyk, in conjunction with Chapters 24 and 25 of the textbook.

For Students

Study Guides

The Online Study Guide at **bedfordstmartins.com/hunt** helps students synthesize the material they have learned as well as practice the skills historians use to make sense of the past. The following Map, Visual, and Document activities are available for Chapter 24.

Map Activity

- Map 24.2: Africa in 1914

Visual Activity

- The Foreign Pig Is Put to Death, p. 789

Reading Historical Documents

- Leon Pinsker Calls for a Jewish State, p. 783
- A Historian Promotes Militant Nationalism, p. 795
- New Sources, New Perspectives: Psychohistory and Its Lessons, p. 770

CHAPTER

25

World War I and Its Aftermath

1914–1929

Chapter Resources

Main Chapter Topics

1. When war erupted in August 1914, long-standing alliances formed into the Central Powers (Germany and Austria-Hungary, and later the Ottoman Empire) on the one side, and the Allied forces (Britain, France, and Russia, and later Japan and the United States) on the other. Both sides of the conflict utilized modern military technologies such as heavy artillery, machine guns, and airplanes, but clung to obsolete strategies and tactics, notably the Schlieffen Plan and the "cult of the offensive." Looking to earlier, rapid victories by Prussia and Japan, a short, decisive conflict was predicted by all. But the four-year war would be a total war, mobilizing entire societies and causing unprecedented mass slaughter and horror.

2. Ordinary soldiers in World War I were not automatons. Some battalions went for long periods with low casualties. These low casualty rates stemmed from fraternization between opposing troops who fought in fairly close proximity to each other. Throughout the war, soldiers across the trenches agreed to avoid fighting. New male camaraderie alleviated misery, aided survival, and weakened traditional class distinctions. Positive memories of this front-line community survived the war and influenced postwar politics.

3. Initially, nearly all set aside their differences, but divisions reemerged when citizens faced shortages, runaway inflation, and staggering casualties. The populace's relentless suffering pushed Russia into revolution. In March 1917, Tsar Nicholas II abdicated. Bolshevik leader Vladimir Lenin returned to Russia and began calling for the spontaneously elected soviets to overturn the democratic Provisional Government, nationalize all privately held lands, and end the war. Lenin took over the soviets, formed a Communist government, and won a civil war against antirevolutionary forces by 1922.

4. In November 1918, revolutionaries in Germany declared a republic and forced Kaiser William II to abdicate. Although Germany's revolutions—from both the left and right—failed, the Weimar Republic set the dangerous precedent of relying on street violence, paramilitary groups, and protests to resolve problems.

5. At the Paris Peace Conference (1919), Woodrow Wilson presented his Fourteen Points for a new international order and a nonvindictive peace settlement. The Fourteen Points did not, however, suit the European victors. The Peace of Paris (1919–1920), a cluster of individual treaties, shocked the defeated countries and some farseeing experts: it destabilized eastern and central Europe through the formation of states consisting of multiple ethnic groups, such as Czechoslovakia, Yugoslavia, and Poland; broke apart the Ottoman Empire; and treated Germany severely with impossible reparations and a "guilt clause" that placed the blame for the war directly on Germany.

6. During World War I, Europe had lost many of its international markets to overseas competitors, including Japan, which grew even stronger during the 1920s. Although Europe overcame economic problems and enjoyed renewed prosperity by the late 1920s, the United States had become the trendsetter of economic modernization. Adopting some methods and ideas from the United States, European economies modernized, as both the managerial class and the union movement continued to grow.

7. Postwar society had to deal with millions of brutalized, incapacitated, shell-shocked, often resentful veterans who returned to a changed world. Fearful of the threat of widespread discontent, governments wanted to integrate these men back into society as quickly as possible. Pensions for veterans, benefits for the unemployed, and housing for the returning soldiers

and seamen were all designed to alleviate the people's problems and pent-up anger, which had resulted from the war.

8. Cultural leaders in the 1920s were either obsessed by the horrendous experiences of war or, like the prewar modernists, held high hopes for creating a fresh, utopian future that would have little relation to the past. In both cases, the art produced broke with tradition, thereby continuing the prewar cultural debates about traditional versus modern art.

9. Despite the hopes of many Europeans for a more democratic world, by the end of the 1920s, political strongmen (such as Joseph Stalin and Benito Mussolini) had risen to power in several European states. Using mass communications, these despotic, tyrannical leaders promoted mass politics that were antidemocratic, brutal, and totalitarian. These leaders and their systems would be perceived by many as a precursor of the future—particularly after the stock market crash (1929) and the resulting global economic depression.

Focus Question

What political, social, and economic impact did World War I have during the conflict, immediately after it, and through the 1920s?

1. World War I was a transformative event. The length and severity of the conflict placed political systems and governments under severe pressure; the experience of conflict and casualties changed soldiers and those who contributed in other ways to the total war effort. Politically, the need to dedicate the entire social system to the war effort ended traditional political parties and divisions in many nations at war. Unity and mobilization in support of the war effort changed politics and restricted liberties, freedoms, and dissent, even while it strengthened nationalism. Increasingly desperate and difficult conditions led to political crises in the long run in many countries, most notably in Russia where the system broke down completely in revolution in 1917, but serious disturbances and growing popular frustration with casualties and wartime conditions occurred nearly everywhere. After the war, revolutions broke out across the west, and cynicism about politics and demands for radical change were in the ascendancy. The breakup of long-established polities (Russia, the Ottoman and Austrian empires) produced new nations and political dynamics. There was pressure to admit women into the democratic process, and also to establish international bodies such as the League of Nations, which would manage conflict, limit the power of the nation-state, and produce peace.

2. Socially and economically, the war was equally transformative and a great catalyst for change. The total war effort involved the bulk of the citizenry of belligerent powers in wartime production or military service. Established gender and class relations were disrupted by military service and new responsibilities. The difficult experiences of soldiers at the front created bonds of comradeship but also alienation and anger among many. Demobilization and reintegration into "normal" life was difficult for soldiers, and also for women and other workers who had assumed new roles in the workplace and in family life. Wartime transformations of dating and social interaction transformed gender relations. Economically, the war was tremendously disruptive and expensive. The war weakened the economies of most participants through war debts and reparations payments, although the United States prospered and became more central to the western economic system as a result of the war.

Annotated Chapter Outline

I. The Great War, 1914–1918

A. Blueprints for War, pp. 800–803

1. World War I pitted the Central Powers—Germany, Austria-Hungary, and Turkey, against the Allies—Great Britain, France, and Russia.
2. In late August 1914, Japan joined the Allies and, in the fall, Turkey joined the Central Powers.
3. Italy joined the Allies in 1915 in exchange for a promise of territorial gains after the war (agreed to in the Treaty of London).
4. Germany's goal in entering the war was to create a Central European empire formed by annexing Russian territory and parts of Belgium, France, and Luxembourg.
5. Austria-Hungary wanted to retain its great power status, whereas Russia wanted to reassert its status as a great power *and* as the protector of the Slavs by annexing a reunified Poland and the Austro-Hungarian territory peopled by Ukrainians, and reorganizing Austria-Hungary into a Triple Monarchy that would recognize the Slavs.
6. Colonial powers enlisted millions of soldiers to help fight the conflict, and the war was global in scope, with fighting occurring in Africa, the Middle East, the Caucasus, and China.
7. Machinery and technology influenced the war. Rail and motorized transportation

were important. All the powers used recently developed, more powerful weaponry; and the new technologies that had emerged: chlorine gas, bombs, and tanks.
8. On both sides of the conflict, officers originally believed in a "cult of the offensive," which called for spirited attacks and a reliance on old-fashioned weaponry—sabers, lances, and bayonets—because, at the opening of the war, such Napoleonic weaponry and strategy seemed crucial to victory. In the face of modern technology, such tactics cost millions of lives.

B. The Battlefronts, pp. 803–806

1. The major armies mobilized rapidly and hoped for quick victory. Germany's Schlieffen Plan required the invasion of Belgium and the rapid defeat of France.
2. The Belgians put up spirited resistance, which afforded the British and French forces time to engage the Germans along the Marne River.
3. Casualties were shocking, as defensive military technology ended expectations of a war of movement. In the first three months of the war, 1.5 million men fell on the western front alone.
4. During the following four years, the two sides faced off along a deep trench line that stretched from the North Sea in Belgium and northern France to Switzerland, as both sides dug in.
5. On the eastern front, the Russians advanced more quickly than expected, driving into East Prussia and parts of Austria-Hungary by mid-August, but Germany crushed the invading Russian forces. The fighting, however, diverted soldiers from the western front and undermined the Schlieffen Plan.
6. War at sea proved equally indecisive.
7. The Allies blockaded the entries to the Mediterranean and North seas to prevent supplies from reaching Germany and Austria-Hungary.
8. William II retaliated with a massive U-boat (submarine) campaign against Allied and neutral shipping around Britain and France.
9. In May 1915, the Germans sank a British passenger ship, the *Lusitania*, killing 1,198 people, including 124 Americans.
10. Not wanting to provoke U.S. president Woodrow Wilson further, the Germans called off unrestricted submarine warfare.
11. In May 1916, the navies of Germany and Great Britain clashed in the battle of Jutland, which, although inconclusive, proved that the German fleet could not defeat the British.
12. On both sides, governments rejected the idea of a negotiated peace, and maintained the cult of the offensive.
13. Each attack opened with troops going "over the top" to charge the enemy's trenches, usually to be confronted with round upon round of machine-gun fire.
14. In 1916, the Germans assaulted the forts of Verdun, hoping to crush French morale by its loss. Although French and German losses were close to a million men, the French held Verdun.
15. In June 1916, the British launched an offensive in the Somme region; over several months of battle, 1.25 million men were killed or wounded, with no decisive victory won by either side.
16. On the eastern front, in 1915 Russian advances were turned back and German forces pushed toward St. Petersburg. The Austrians routed the Serbs only to have to face the newly mobilized Italian army. In 1916, Russian offensives into Austria were stopped by the German army. The Germans took over Austrian military operations, weakening that state's sovereignty.
17. Whereas governments and officers saw the war as a "kill or be killed" situation, some battalions on the front lines often went long stretches with hardly a casualty as both sides' troops mutually agreed to avoid battles.
18. Soldiers on both fronts fraternized, and sometimes came to feel more warmly toward their "enemies" in the trenches than toward civilians back home who did not share their experiences.
19. Male camaraderie alleviated some of the misery of trench life and aided survival.
20. Living, fighting, and dying together weakened traditional class distinctions, and sometimes even racial barriers.
21. Most troops of colonized soldiers, however, experienced the front differently from that experienced by their European comrades.

22. Colonials were often placed in the immediate front ranks where the risks were greatest, and endured unfamiliar climates and strange foods.
23. Apart from their suffering, colonial troops gained a new perspective on Europeans, whom they observed exhibiting completely "uncivilized" behavior.

C. The Home Front, pp. 806–809

1. World War I was a "total war," meaning that committed civilian involvement was indispensable to the war effort.
2. Civilians were needed to manufacture the weapons that were the backbone of technological warfare, as well as the crutches, wheelchairs, and coffins needed after an assault.
3. The war effort depended on extensive government direction.
4. When hostilities broke out in 1914, most of the population—including the socialists—put aside their differences to support the war. National leaders urged an end to political and social divisions.
5. Feminists were divided over whether to continue traditional pacifism, but many did participate in war work and philanthropic efforts.
6. Governments mobilized the home front with varying degrees of success. After the first heavy losses occurred, all involved countries were caught without replacement military equipment.
7. War ministries were established to allocate labor on the home and military fronts, and to ensure the steady production of armaments and other necessities.
8. Industrialists were offered incentives to encourage productivity, and all citizens—both men and women—were increasingly expected to perform some sort of war work.
9. Governments passed laws that made it a crime to criticize official policies, and created propaganda agencies that presented the war as a patriotic mission and demonized the enemy.
10. Open opposition to the war did, however, exist.
11. In 1915, activists in the international women's movement met in The Hague, determined to end the war. They failed to inspire negotiations.
12. Others indirectly hampered the war effort, such as nationalist groups in Austria-Hungary, whose agitation for independence detracted from an all-out focus on the war.
13. The Allies encouraged independence movements as part of their strategy to defeat the Habsburgs.
14. In addition to increasing nationalist agitation, the war restructured the workforce: women took over higher paying jobs vacated by men who left for the trenches.
15. The press praised women's patriotism, but others were concerned that the war would destroy women's femininity and that, once the war was over, women would refuse to give up their jobs to men.
16. Class conflict continued as the poor suffered even more under wartime conditions.
17. While workers endured longer hours on less food (because rationing had begun), the wealthier classes were able to afford food and fashionable clothing, paying large amounts of money for products only available on the black market that operated outside the official system of rationing.
18. Governments also allowed many businesses to reap high profits, a policy that brought about increases in the cost of living as shortages of staples like bread and meat worsened during the brutal winter of 1916–1917 (called the turnip winter because turnips were often the only food available).
19. Civilians in occupied areas and the colonies suffered the worst conditions.
20. Combatants were deported or able-bodied persons were conscripted in occupied territories, and inhabitants of the colonies were forced to work for the war effort at home or in Europe.
21. Colonized peoples also experienced increased taxes and elevated prices.

II. Protest, Revolution, and War's End, 1917–1918

A. War Protest, p. 810

1. On February 1, 1917, hard-pressed by public clamor over mounting casualties, the German government resumed unrestricted submarine warfare.
2. The British responded by mining harbors and the seas and by developing depth charges—antisubmarine weapons dropped or catapulted from ships' decks that exploded underwater.

3. Unrestricted submarine warfare brought the United States into the war in April 1917 after the Germans had sunk several American ships.
4. As living conditions deteriorated, political opposition took the form of outright revolt by civilians. In Ireland, on Easter Monday 1916, republican rebels tried to seize power but were defeated.
5. Food shortages in Italy, Russia, Germany, and Austria-Hungary provoked women to riot and, as inflation mounted, tenants conducted rent strikes and factory and white-collar workers went on strike.
6. By 1917, the war had also strengthened nationalist movements, and the new emperor of Austria-Hungary secretly asked the Allies for a negotiated peace.
7. The German Reichstag also announced its desire for peace, and American president Woodrow Wilson issued his Fourteen Points in January 1918, promising a nonvindictive peace settlement.

B. Revolution in Russia, pp. 810–814

1. Of all the warring nations, Russia had sustained the greatest number of casualties: 7.5 million by 1917.
2. The government's incompetence during the war and the failure to unite the people behind the war effort created a highly unstable situation.
3. When riots erupted in March 1917, Nicholas II abdicated and politicians from the old Duma formed a new Provisional Government.
4. However, continuing hardships made governing difficult.
5. Spontaneously elected soviets—councils of workers and soldiers—competed with the government for political support and often challenged its policies.
6. The peasantry began to confiscate the gentry's estates and withheld produce from the market, which intensified urban food shortages.
7. In April 1917, the Germans provided safe rail transportation for Lenin and other prominent Bolsheviks to return from exile to Petrograd.
8. Upon his return, Lenin issued the April Theses, a radical document that called for Russia to withdraw from the war, for the soviets to seize power on behalf of workers and poor peasants, and for all private lands to be nationalized.
9. After another Russian defeat to the Austrians, groups of workers, soldiers, and sailors agitated for the soviets to replace the Provisional Government.
10. As Bolshevik popularity rose, the Provisional Government led by Aleksandr Kerensky (1881–1970) was thoroughly discredited by continued military defeats.
11. In November 1917, the Bolshevik leadership, urged on by Lenin, staged an uprising and the Bolsheviks seized power in the event called the Bolshevik Revolution.
12. In January 1918, elections were finally held and, when the Bolsheviks did not fare well, they forcibly took control of the government. They abolished private property and nationalized production, limiting candidates in elections to members of the Communist Party.
13. Soon after, the Bolsheviks sued Germany for peace. The resulting Treaty of Brest-Litovsk (March 1918) placed vast regions of the old Russian Empire under German occupation.
14. Because the loss of territory placed Petrograd at risk, the Bolsheviks relocated the capital to Moscow.
15. Lenin had agreed to this catastrophic treaty because he had promised to bring peace, but also because he believed that the rest of Europe would soon rebel and overthrow the capitalist order.
16. Resistance to Bolshevik policies, especially those that nationalized private property, soon mushroomed into full-fledged civil war between the pro-Bolshevik "Reds" and antirevolutionary "Whites." Many of Russia's former allies landed troops to block German advances and fight the Bolsheviks.
17. Some fought to restore the old government, but others—especially non-Russian nationality groups—fought for independence.
18. However, without a common goal, the counterrevolutionaries could not win.
19. The civil war shaped communism; Leon Trotsky (1879–1940), Bolshevik commissar of war, built a highly disciplined army by ending democratic procedures that had originally attracted soldiers to Bolshevism.
20. Lenin and Trotsky also introduced war communism, whereby urban workers and

troops confiscated grain from the peasantry.

21. The Cheka (secret police) set up detention camps for political opponents and black marketers and often shot them without trial. The government became more authoritarian.
22. The Bolsheviks also founded the Third International, known as the Comintern (Communist International) to distinguish it from its predecessors.
23. By mid-1921, the Red Army had successfully consolidated Bolshevism in Russia and secured the Crimea, the Caucasus, and the Muslim borderlands.
24. When the Japanese withdrew from Siberia in 1922, the civil war ended in Central and East Asia.
25. Although revolution had removed the tsar and the privileged aristocracy, the oppression meted out by the Bolsheviks ushered in a brutal political style far different from that which had been hoped for by earlier socialists.

C. Ending the War, 1918, pp. 814–815

1. In the spring of 1918, using new tactics and troops from the eastern front, the Germans made a final attempt to smash through Allied lines, but by then the British and French had begun to make effective use of tanks supported by airplanes.
2. The fighting halted and, in the summer of 1918, the Allies—fortified with American troops—pushed back the Germans all along the western front and inflicted huge numbers of casualties.
3. By October 1918, the German high command helped create a new civilian government, saddling it with the responsibility for defeat; the military insisted that it was not losing the war and that, by suing for peace, the civilian government had "stabbed Germany in the back."
4. On November 9, 1918, Kaiser William II fled.
5. By the fall of 1918, unrest had reached unmanageable proportions in Austria-Hungary as well, where Czechs and Slovaks declared an independent state, as did Croatians.
6. Finally, on November 11, 1918, an armistice was signed.
7. Conservative figures put the battlefield toll at a minimum of 10 million dead, 30 million wounded, and of the latter, some would eventually die from their wounds.
8. In Europe, food supplies for civilians had often fallen below subsistence levels, and the impact of Europe's declining production was felt worldwide.
9. From 1918 to 1919, the weakened global population was hit by an influenza epidemic that killed at least 100 million more.
10. In addition to the physical costs, war provoked tremendous moral questioning, as soldiers returning home published memoirs in order to try to come to terms with their experiences.
11. While some maintained that the Great War had been a heroic endeavor, others insisted that the fighting had been absolutely meaningless.

III. The Search for Peace in an Era of Revolution

A. Europe in Turmoil, pp. 815–816

1. Until 1921, the triumph of socialism seemed plausible across Europe, particularly in urban areas as angry soldiers returned from the front. Many of the newly independent peoples of Eastern and Central Europe supported socialist principles, and workers and peasants in Germany were in a revolutionary frame of mind.
2. Germany was particularly unstable in November 1918, partly because of the shock of defeat.
3. By December, independent socialist groups and workers' councils were vying with the dominant Social Democrats for control of the government.
4. Demonstrators demanded economic policies that would assuage workers' misery and remit the veterans' back pay.
5. Some were inspired by one of the most radical socialist factions—the Spartacists—led by cofounders Karl Liebknecht (1871–1919) and Rosa Luxemburg (1870–1919).
6. The Spartacists favored direct worker control of institutions.
7. Social Democratic leader Friedrich Ebert (1871–1925), who headed the new government, believed that parliamentary politics would best realize his party's objectives.
8. He called on the German army and the Freikorps— a paramilitary band of students, demobilized soldiers, and others—to suppress the workers' councils and demonstrators.

9. Members of the Freikorps hunted down and killed Luxemburg and Liebknecht.
10. In February 1919, a constituent assembly met in the city of Weimar, where it approved a constitution and founded a parliamentary republic.
11. When the military command refused to crush the Freikorps' coup, Ebert called for a general strike.
12. Although coups from the right and left failed, the Weimar Republic's grip on power was tenuous, and it had set the precedent of relying on extraparliamentary means to resolve political conflict.
13. In Bavaria and Hungary, leftists proclaimed soviet republics in late winter 1919, both of which were overthrown.
14. The Bolsheviks attempted to establish a Marxist regime in Poland, but the Poles resisted the advancing Red Army and the Allies rushed supplies and advisers to Warsaw.

B. The Paris Peace Conference, 1919–1920, pp. 816–820

1. The Paris Peace Conference opened in January 1919, with fears of communism spreading westward.
2. But the desperation of war-ravaged citizens, the status of Germany, and the reconstruction of a secure Europe topped the agenda.
3. French premier Georges Clemenceau (1841–1929) had to satisfy angry French citizens who demanded revenge, or at least compensation.
4. British prime minister, David Lloyd George (1863–1945), also supported the harsh treatment of Germany, whereas Italy wanted the territory promised to it in the Treaty of London.
5. The presence of Woodrow Wilson (1856–1924) indicated a realignment of power away from any single European country.
6. Wilson hoped for a conciliatory peace, one that would incorporate his Fourteen Points, which called for open diplomacy, arms reduction, and the self-determination of peoples.
7. However, while the Germans refused to admit that their army had lost the war, the Allies campaigned to make Wilson appear naive and deluded.
8. In fact, Wilson's commitment to settlement as opposed to surrender recognized the need to avoid humiliating Germany and to balance the various European powers.
9. After six months, the statesmen produced the Peace of Paris, composed of a cluster of individual treaties.
10. The treaties shocked the countries that had to accept them.
11. Austria and Hungary were separated, Hungary was enormously reduced, and the Ottoman Empire was broken up.
12. A series of small, weak states were created as a result: Czechoslovakia; Poland; and the Kingdom of the Serbs, Croats, and Slovenes, later renamed Yugoslavia.
13. Many Austrians wanted to join Germany, but that was forbidden.
14. Poland was reconstructed from parts of Russia, Germany, and Austria-Hungary, with one-third of its population ethnically non-Polish.
15. The treaties also called for a Polish corridor that connected Poland to the Baltic Sea and separated East Prussia from the rest of Germany.
16. The Treaty of Versailles with Germany returned Alsace and Lorraine to France, which would also temporarily occupy the western bank of the Rhine and the coal-bearing Saar basin.
17. Germany was to pay reparations set in 1921 in the amount of 132 billion gold marks.
18. Additionally, Germany was to surrender the largest ships of its merchant marine, reduce its army, almost eliminate its navy, cease manufacturing offensive weapons, deliver a large amount of free coal each year to Belgium and France, eliminate its air force, and give up its colonies.
19. The Peace of Paris also set up a League of Nations, which was henceforth to be responsible for maintaining peace, a principle called "collective security."
20. The effectiveness of the league was limited, however, when the United States Senate failed to ratify the peace settlement and refused to join.
21. Further, Germany and Russia were initially excluded from the league.
22. The charter of the league called for Germany and the Ottoman Empire's former colonies to be ruled through a system of mandates in which European powers would exercise political control over mandated territory, but local leaders would retain limited authority.

23. However, the war had depleted the financial resources and mental resolve of the European powers, and colonized peoples began to challenge the claims of their European masters.

C. Economic and Diplomatic Consequences of the Peace, pp. 820–821

1. In the aftermath of the World War I, Western leaders were deeply concerned about economic recovery and an enduring peace.
2. France, the hardest hit by wartime destruction, was billions of dollars in debt to the United States and therefore in dire need of collecting German reparations.
3. The British worried about maintaining their empire and restoring trade with Germany, but still wanted some form of financial redress to pay war debts back to the United States.
4. Germany claimed that the demand for reparations further strained its already unstable political system.
5. As early as 1919, economists predicted that placing a heavy financial burden on Germany would have disastrous repercussions.
6. Because the kaiser had refused to increase taxes to pay for the war, inflation was a serious problem; this, along with war debt and reparations, created a serious economic situation in Germany.
7. Only after France occupied parts of the Ruhr did Germany agree to a payment plan.
8. Embroiled in conflict in the west, Germany turned east and reached an agreement to foster economic ties with Russia in the Treaty of Rapallo (1922).
9. In 1923, after Germany defaulted on coal deliveries, the French and Belgians sent troops into the Ruhr basin.
10. Ruhr citizens refused to work, and the German government issued trillions of worthless marks to support them.
11. Germany was soon suffering from a staggering inflation that wiped out people's savings and ruined those individuals living on fixed incomes.
12. The Dawes Plan (1924) and Young Plan (1929) restored economic stability by reducing reparation payments, restoring the value of German currency, and balancing Germany's trade between east and west.
13. Still, inflation and the difficulties of the postwar economy in Germany led many to reject democratic institutions.
14. Even before the economic question was settled, statesmen concluded that ensuring a lasting peace meant disarmament.
15. At the 1921 Washington Conference, the United States, Great Britain, Japan, France, and Italy agreed to reduce the number of their existing battleships and cease constructing new ones for ten years.
16. In 1925, at a meeting of the great powers in Locarno, Switzerland, German diplomat Gustav Stresemann (1878–1929) negotiated a treaty that provided Germany a seat in the League of Nations (as of 1926) in return for a promise not to violate the borders of France and Belgium and to keep troops out of the Rhineland.
17. To prevent German expansion to the east, Czechoslovakia, Yugoslavia, and Romania formed the Little Entente in 1920–1921.
18. Between 1924 and 1927, France allied itself with the Little Entente and with Poland.
19. In 1928, the major European powers, Japan, and the United States signed the Kellogg-Briand Pact, which formally condemned international violence.
20. The nations did not, however, commit themselves to concrete action to prevent its outbreak.
21. The new openness among the great powers suggested a diplomatic revolution and promised a peaceful age.
22. However, open diplomacy also exposed the negotiating process to nationalist demagogues who could rekindle political hatreds.

IV. The Aftermath of War: Europe in the 1920s

A. Changes in the Political Landscape, pp. 822–824

1. After the war, many governments (except France and Italy) extended the vote to women, claiming it was to reward them for their war work and to make revolution less tempting and help to contribute to a sense of democratic rebirth.
2. Governments also continued to build welfare states by expanding insurance programs for workers and payments to families with dependent children.
3. New governments believed that economic democracy—more evenly distributed wealth—would contribute to maintaining social stability.

4. The reemergence of cycles of boom and bust made it difficult to maintain the trend toward economic democracy.
5. A short postwar boom gave way to a severe economic downturn in 1920.
6. Women in particular lost many of the economic opportunities they had gained by the mid-1920s.
7. Skyrocketing unemployment led some to question governmental policies.
8. Hard times corroded the new republics of Eastern Europe, especially because of refugee and migration crises, and because none but Czechoslovakia had a mature industrial sector.
9. Poland exemplified the postwar political landscape in Eastern Europe.
10. Polish reunification occurred without a common currency, political structure, or language, and with virtually no support from the Allies, economic or otherwise. Notwithstanding, a government was formed under a constitution that professed equal rights for all ethnic and religious groups.
11. Economic conditions made it difficult for the Sejm (parliament) to redistribute large estates to the peasantry, and urban workers were worse off than other laborers across Europe.
12. Strikes and violence began in 1922, and the inability of coalition governments to bring about economic prosperity led to a coup (1926) by Jozef Pilsudski (1867–1935).
13. In Germany, although the economy had improved, political life remained precarious because so many people felt nostalgia for the empire and associated defeat with the new Weimar Republic.
14. Contempt for parliamentary politics was widespread, and right-wing parties favored violence rather than consensus building.
15. Support for the far right came from wealthy landowners and businessmen, white-collar workers whose standard of living had declined during the war; and members of the lower and middle classes hurt by inflation.
16. Bands of disaffected youths and veterans proliferated.
17. One group, the Brown Shirts, led by Adolf Hitler (1889–1945), participated in a failed coup in Munich in 1923.
18. Hitler spent less than a year in jail, while his co-conspirator, Erich Ludendorff (1865–1937), was acquitted. He became a national hero to many.
19. After the mid-1920s, however, the economy improved and extreme political movements lost some of their appeal.
20. In France and Britain, right-wing parties had less of an effect because parliamentary politics were better established and the upper classes were not plotting to restore an authoritarian monarchy.
21. Politicians in France formed coalitions to rally support for reconstruction and the pursuit of reparations.
22. The French parliament also focused on increasing the birthrate, making the distribution of birth-control information illegal and abortion a severely punished crime.
23. In Britain, the election of the first Labour prime minister, Ramsay MacDonald, in 1924, was a sign of the growing political ambitions of the working class.
24. Much of British industry was obsolete or in poor condition, as in the ailing coal industry when, in May 1926, workers conducted a nine-day general strike against wage cuts and dangerous conditions in the mines.
25. The strike provoked unprecedented middle-class resistance, with individuals from all walks of life stepping in to drive trains, work on docks, and replace workers in other sorts of jobs.
26. Ireland also continued to be a problem.
27. In January 1919, republican leaders announced Ireland's independence from Britain and established a separate parliament.
28. The British refused to recognize the parliament, and sent in a volunteer army—the Black and Tans—who waged guerrilla warfare in Ireland.
29. By 1921, public outrage forced the British to negotiate.
30. A treaty created the Irish Free State, a self-governing dominion owing an oath of allegiance to the British crown.
31. Ulster, a group of six northern counties, was self-governing but had representation in the British Parliament. The settlement left a great deal of bitterness, and violence in Ireland persisted.
32. European powers also encountered rebellion in overseas colonies, as colonized peoples who had served in the war

expected increased rights, if not outright independence.

33. The British massacred protesters at Amritsar, India, in 1919, and put down revolts against the mandate system in Egypt and Iran in the early 1920s.
34. The Dutch jailed political leaders in Indonesia, while the French punished Indochinese nationalists.
35. Europeans wanted to hold on to their empires because any hint of declining prestige abroad would feed antidemocratic forces at home.
36. Japanese economic and imperial power expanded during and after the war. Japan resented its treatment in the crafting of the peace and in postwar naval conferences.

B. Reconstructing the Economy, pp. 824–825

1. Although the European economy had lost many of its international markets to other countries, the war had forced manufacturing to become more efficient.
2. Mergers and the formation of cartels continued after the war, and owners of large manufacturing conglomerates came to wield extensive financial and political power.
3. By the late 1920s, Europe was enjoying economic prosperity.
4. The United States was the trendsetter in modernization, and Europeans visited Henry Ford's auto plant to study his high productivity.
5. Scientific management also aimed to increase productivity by ridding the work process of superfluous movements.
6. European industrialists balanced this focus on Frederick Taylor's management methods with a belief that workers also needed time for leisure.
7. However, although union leaders promoted these benefits of the "cult of efficiency," many workers felt that the emphasis on efficiency turned them into human automatons.
8. Management expanded during the war and continued to do so afterward, but workers were perceived as uncreative and lacking in innovation, and women received lower wages to stem male competition.
9. Union bureaucracy also continued to expand after the war, with unions mobilizing masses of people and playing a key role in mass politics.

C. Restoring Society, pp. 825–827

1. Many returning veterans were hostile toward civilians who, they believed, had overly complained about wartime conditions instead of patriotically and stoically enduring them.
2. Veterans returned to a world that was markedly different from the one they left to serve in the war, while military service had eroded class distinctions for many soldiers.
3. Veterans felt particularly alienated from women who had bobbed their hair and now smoked, held jobs, and sometimes found other men to replace them while they were overseas performing their patriotic duty.
4. Among the working classes, the flapper became a new symbol of womanhood.
5. Although patriotic at the beginning of the war, many women felt estranged from the returning soldiers who had survived different and brutalizing experiences.
6. Many suffragists embraced the gender segregation that they had fought so hard to dismantle before the war, and focused their attention now on aiding women and their families.
7. Governments wanted to reintegrate veterans so as to avoid the spread of Bolshevism.
8. They created programs granting pension plans for veterans, stipends for war widows, benefits for unemployed men, and housing for veterans.
9. Despite governmental efforts to restore traditional family values, war had dissolved many middle-class conventions. Freer, more open discussions of sex and sexuality occurred, and unmarried men and women now socialized without chaperones.
10. Still, most discussions of sexuality placed it within the context of marriage, where greater attention to sexual pleasure was advocated by authors such as Theodoor van de Velde (1873–1937) in his 1927 *Ideal Marriage: Its Physiology and Technique.*
11. Male sexual prowess was examined by authors such as D. H. Lawrence (1885–1930) in *Women in Love* (1920) and Ernest Hemingway (1899–1961) in *The Sun Also Rises* (1926).
12. As images of men and women changed, greater attention was paid to physical appearance and hygiene.

13. Ordinary women began "painting" their faces—something only prostitutes had done previously, and a multibillion-dollar cosmetics industry emerged.
14. Exercise also became more important because the consumer focus on personal health coincided with modern industry's need for a physically fit workforce.
15. As prosperity returned, people could buy more consumer goods.
16. Modern conveniences became standard household items, sometimes purchased on the new installment plans that were popularized in the 1920s.
17. Housework became more mechanized, and family intimacy came to revolve around radios, phonographs, and automobiles.

V. **Mass Culture and the Rise of Modern Dictators**

A. **Culture for the Masses, p. 828**

1. The instruments of mass culture—primarily radio, film, and newspapers—expanded their influence in the 1920s.
2. Media had received a big boost from the war.
3. Bulletins from the battlefront whetted the public's appetite for new, real-life stories and sales of practical nonfiction books soared.
4. In the 1920s, filmmaking became an international business, with a star system that turned film personalities into international celebrities.
5. Films incorporated familiar elements from everyday life: the piano accompaniment for silent films was derived from music halls and familiar classical compositions; while comic characters, farcical plots, and slapstick humor had their origins in street or burlesque shows.
6. Movies attracted some one hundred million weekly viewers, the majority of them women, and crossed national borders easily.
7. Filmmakers touched upon postwar fantasies and fears.
8. The German film *The Cabinet of Dr. Caligari* (1919) depicted events and inmates in an insane asylum as symbols of state power.
9. English comedian Charlie Chaplin (1889–1977) won international popularity with his character of the Little Tramp, the anonymous modern man.
10. Radio broadcasts also gained in popularity.
11. In the first half of the 1920s, mass audiences listened to radio broadcasts in public halls but, when radio receivers became inexpensive, people could listen to the broadcasts in their homes.
12. By the 1930s, radio was used as a powerful tool for politicians.

B. **Cultural Debates over the Future, pp. 828–831**

1. Many cultural leaders were obsessed by the horrendous experiences of war.
2. German artist Kaethe Köllwitz (1867–1945) portrayed heart-wrenching, anti-war images of bereaved parents and starving children.
3. George Grosz (1893–1959) joined Dada, an artistic and literary movement that had emerged during World War I.
4. His paintings and political cartoons depicted maimed soldiers and brutally murdered women.
5. Dadaists produced works punctuated by nonsense, incongruity, and shrieking expressions of alienation.
6. Portrayals of seedy scenes from everyday life flourished in theaters and reinforced the veterans' beliefs in civilian decadence.
7. A controversy erupted in postwar Germany over what the proper attitude should be toward the war, as popular writers such as Ernst Jünger (1895–1998) glorified life in the trenches and called for the militarization of society.
8. On the side of the controversy, Erich Maria Remarque's (1898–1970) *All Quiet on the Western Front* was a powerful anti-war statement.
9. Poets throughout Europe also reflected on postwar conditions, often using innovative styles. T. S. Eliot (1888–1965) portrayed postwar life as petty and futile in "The Waste Land" (1922) and "The Hollow Men" (1925), while William Butler Yeats (1865–1939) bemoaned the end of traditional society.
10. In the arts, dystopia, a utopian fantasy turned upside down, became an important theme.
11. Franz Kafka (1883–1924) depicted the world as a vast, impersonal machine in novels such as *The Trial* (1925) and *The Castle* (1926).
12. James Joyce (1882–1941) and Virginia Woolf (1882–1941) also focused on the interior life and the power of memories and sensations in *Ulysses* (1922) and *Mrs. Dalloway* (1925), respectively.

13. Other artists looked to the future and celebrated the promise of technology.
14. Many worked in large collectives, such as the Bauhaus led by Walter Gropius (1883–1969).
15. This group of German artists created streamlined office buildings and designed functional furniture, utensils, and decorative objects.
16. Russian artists optimistically wrote novels about cement factories and created ballets about steel.
17. Artists, fascinated by technology and machinery, were drawn to the United States, the most modern of all countries, and were especially attracted to jazz.
18. American performers such as Josephine Baker (1906–1975) and Louis Armstrong (1901–1971) became international sensations.

C. The Communist Utopia, pp. 831–833

1. Communism promised a modern, technological culture and a shining future.
2. But Bolsheviks encountered significant obstacles to consolidating their rule and became increasingly ruthless and authoritarian.
3. In the early 1920s, peasant bands, called "Green Armies" revolted against war communism.
4. Further, industrial production stood at only 13 percent of its pre-war output.
5. The civil war had produced massive casualties, housing shortages that affected the entire population, and refugees who clogged the cities and roamed the countryside.
6. In the early spring of 1921, workers in Petrograd and seamen at the naval base at Kronstadt revolted, calling for "soviets without Communists."
7. Lenin was enraged by the rebels, and Trotsky had many of them shot, but the rebellion did force Lenin to realize that reform was needed.
8. He instituted the New Economic Policy (NEP), which returned portions of the economy to the free market; consumer goods and more food soon became available.
9. This change led to the rise of "NEPmen" who lived in splendid homes and practiced conspicuous consumption.
10. Protest over this change erupted among the Communists, and Lenin responded by setting up procedures for purging dissidents.
11. Bolshevik leaders also attempted to create a cultural revolution, setting up classes in the countryside on various social and political subjects.
12. They also made birth control, abortion, and divorce readily available, and Alexandra Kollontai (1872–1952) promoted birth-control education and day-care programs.
13. Hygiene and efficiency became the focus of a swelling bureaucracy.
14. The Zhenotdel (Women's Bureau) sought to educate the masses about the changes taking place.
15. Officials promoted the use of Henry Ford and Frederick Taylor's methods in the factories, the army, the arts, and everyday life to increase efficiency.
16. Russian artists experimented with blending high art, technology, and mass culture.
17. The government's agency, Proletkult, aimed at developing proletarian culture.
18. As with war communism, many resisted the reshaping of culture to "modern" or "Western" standards, as Bolshevik policies undermined traditional ways of life and belief systems and provoked resistance, particularly from peasants and in Islamic regions of central Asia.
19. Lenin suffered a debilitating stroke in 1922 and died in 1924.
20. The party congress declared the day of his death a permanent holiday, his funeral was celebrated with elaborate pomp, and no one was allowed to criticize anything associated with his name.
21. The general secretary of the Communist Party, Joseph Stalin (1879–1953) led the deification of Lenin.
22. He also discredited his chief rival, Trotsky, and expanded the Party so as to achieve virtually complete dictatorship by 1928–1929.

D. Fascism on the March in Italy, p. 833–834

1. Postwar discontent in Italy began when the Allies refused to honor the promises made in the Treaty of London (1915).
2. To make matters worse, peasants, who had made great sacrifices during the war, protested their serf-like status, and workers seized factories to draw attention to their economic plight.

3. Many Italians blamed parliament for their problems.
4. In the midst of this chaos, Benito Mussolini (1883–1945), a socialist journalist who joined the radical right, built a personal army of veterans and unemployed men called the "Black Shirts."
5. In 1922, Mussolini's supporters, known as Fascists, staged a march to Rome and threatened a coup.
6. To save his throne, King Victor Emmanuel III (r. 1900–1946) "invited" Mussolini to become prime minister.
7. The Fascist movement attracted many who opposed socialism and parliament, and who felt cheated by the postwar settlement.
8. Mussolini placed himself at the head of governmental departments, made criticism of the state a criminal offense, and used force—even murder—to silence his opponents.
9. Despite this brutality, many saw his Black Shirts as restorers of order.
10. Large landowners and businessmen approved the tough tactics the Fascists had taken against socialists, and supported them financially.
11. Mussolini used mass propaganda and the media to gain support, while hiring the unemployed to work for the state or on massive building projects.
12. Mussolini recognized the importance of maintaining traditional values, signing the Lateran Agreement with the Vatican (1929), which recognized the Vatican as a state under papal sovereignty and the church's right to determine family doctrine and to assume a role in education.
13. Mussolini also introduced the "corporate" state that denied individual rights in favor of duty to the state, organizing employers, workers, and professionals into groups that could settle grievances through state-controlled channels.
14. Mussolini also gained favor by reducing women's wages and barring them from certain professions.
15. Mussolini had many admirers, including Adolf Hitler, who had been occupied during the 1920s with building a paramilitary group and a political organization called the National Socialist German Workers' Party (Nazis).
16. But, to Hitler's chagrin, the austere conditions that had allowed Mussolini's rise to power in 1922 no longer existed in Germany by the late 1920s.
17. During his brief imprisonment, after a failed coup, Hitler wrote *Mein Kampf* (1925), a political plan calling for vicious anti-Semitism and political manipulation of the masses.

Lecture Strategies

1. In order to help explain why World War I traumatized Europe, ask students to discuss the conditions of life on the front lines, and the sheer size of draftee armies of the period. What did the men and women at the front witness? How were they forever changed by the experience? A good way to explore these questions is to have students read the writings of those who lived through the war. Two excellent contemporary novels on the war are Erich Maria Remarque's classic *All Quiet on the Western Front* (Boston: Little, Brown, 1929); and Helen Zenna Smith's answer from a woman's perspective, *Not So Quiet . . . Stepdaughters of War* (New York: The Feminist Press, 1930, 1989). As an alternative to assigning both books, the 1930 film version of *All Quiet on the Western Front* can serve in lieu of the novel. Two excellent collections of World War I poetry are Candace Ward, ed., *World War One British Poets: Brooke, Owen, Sassoon, Rosenberg and Others* (Mineola, NY: Dover, 1997); and Jon Silkin, ed., *First World War Poetry* (New York: Viking Press, 1997). Also, the video set *The Great War and the Shaping of the Twentieth Century* (Alexandria, VA: PBS Home Video, 1996); R. C. Sherriff's play *Journey's End*; and Ernest Hemingway's *In Our Time* (1925) will further illuminate the war for students. Works on the battlefield experience include John Elis, *Eye-Deep in Hell: Trench Warfare in World War I* (Baltimore: Johns Hopkins University Press, 1989); Denis Winter, *Death's Men: Soldiers of the Great War* (London: Allen Unwin, 1978); Lyn Macdonald, *1915: The Death of Innocence* (Baltimore: Johns Hopkins University Press, 2000); Lyn Macdonald, *Somme* (London: Michael Joseph, 1983); Robert Graves's autobiography, *Goodbye to All That* (New York: Doubleday, 1929, 1985); Eric J. Leed, *No Man's Land: Combat and Identity in World War I* (New York: Cambridge University Press, 1979); John Keegan, *The Face of Battle: a Study of Agincourt, Waterloo, and the Somme* (New York: Random House, 1967); and Alistair Horne, *The Price of Glory: Verdun 1916* (New York: Penguin, 1993). Works on the cultural impact and memory of the war include Modris Eksteins, *Rites of Spring: The Great War and the Birth of the Modern Age* (Boston: Houghton Mifflin, 1989); Paul Fussell, *The Great War and Modern Memory* (New York: Oxford University Press, 1975); George L. Mosse, *Fallen*

Soldiers: Reshaping the Memory of the World Wars (New York: Oxford University Press, 1990); Jay Winter, *Sites of Memory, Sites of Mourning: The Great War in European Cultural Memory* (New York: Cambridge University Press, 1995); and Robert Wohl, *The Generation of 1914* (Cambridge, MA: Harvard University Press, 1979).

2. Another way for students to explore the experience of war is to examine the visual arts of the period. Works by artists such as Otto Dix, Max Beckmann, Kaethe Köllwitz, Ernst Ludwig Kirschner, and George Grosz contain many, often brutal and violent, images of the war and its aftermath. In class, show slides of artworks that depict the war and discuss the artists' imagery. By exploring this art, students will gain a deeper understanding of how and why the war continued to haunt the participants and how it shaped the culture of the following decades and beyond. An excellent source for images and information on these artists is Richard Cork, *A Bitter Truth: Avant-Garde Art and the Great War* (New Haven, CT: Yale University Press, 1994). In addition, Cork's book has an extensive bibliography of works on artists and World War I. A video on Otto Dix that examines his images of the war in some detail is *Otto Dix: The Painter Is the Eyes of the World*. Another excellent source on Otto Dix is "The Work of the Devil," Chapter 1, vol. 4, *The Great War and the Shaping of the Twentieth Century*.

3. A good way to gain some insight into the popular images of the changing status of women and the debate over modernity is to show film clips that depict the modern "new woman" of the 1920s. How is the new woman depicted? Is she shown in a positive light? A negative light? A neutral light? How do the depictions compare among the film clips? How does she differ from "traditional" women? What makes her "modern"? Films that portray the new woman include *Sunrise* (1927), *Pandora's Box* (1928), *Metropolis* (1926), and *The Blue Angel* (1930). See also the many films of the German silent screen actress Louise Brooks.

4. One of the most important events of the era was the Russian Revolution. Discuss in some detail the origins of the revolution, its course, and how the Communists solidified their power during this era. In addition, it would be useful to detail the society—both the reality and the ideal—that emerged in the Soviet Union during the 1920s. An excellent book to assign on the Russian Revolution and its aftermath is Sheila Fitzpatrick, *The Russian Revolution*, 2nd ed. (New York: Oxford University Press, 1994). Other books on the revolution and the developments of the 1920s include Katerina Clark, *Petersburg: Crucible of Cultural Revolution* (Cambridge, MA: Harvard University Press, 1995); Orlando Figes, *A People's Tragedy: A History of the Russian Revolution* (New York: Viking, 1996); Peter Kenez, *The Birth of the Propaganda State: Soviet Methods of Mass Mobilization, 1917–1929* (Cambridge: Cambridge University Press, 1985); W. Bruce Lincoln, *Red Victory: A History of the Russian Civil War* (New York: Da Capo Press, 1999); Richard Pipes, *A Concise History of the Russian Revolution* (New York: Alfred A. Knopf, 1995); Alexander Rabinowitch, *The Bolsheviks Come to Power: The Revolution of 1917 in Petrograd* (New York: W. W. Norton, 1976); Richard Stites, *Revolutionary Dreams: Utopian Vision and Experimental Life in the Russian Revolution* (New York: Oxford University Press, 1989); and John M. Thompson, *Revolutionary Russia, 1917* (New York: Charles Scribner's Sons, 1981).

Class Discussion Starters

1. After the horrors of World War I, many Europeans rejected traditional culture and the political systems that were seen to be responsible for the war. As a result, the United States fascinated many Europeans during the 1920s. Why might America have appeared attractive? Discuss the impact of Americanization on Europe and how Europeans adopted and adapted "America" during this decade. What impact did Americanization have on European culture? Did this impact last? Good sources on this issue include Frank Costigliola, *Awkward Dominion: American Political, Economic, and Cultural Relations with Europe, 1919–1933* (Ithaca, NY: Cornell University Press, 1984); Mary Nolan, *Visions of Modernity: American Business and the Modernization of Germany* (New York: Oxford University Press, 1994); and Thomas J. Saunders, *Hollywood in Berlin: American Cinema and Weimar Germany* (Berkeley, CA: University of California Press, 1994).

2. The 1920s were a great era of social change that was connected to emergent technologies. Have students working in groups brainstorm a wide range of social, cultural, and economic consequences that might stem from: 1) widespread use of the automobile; 2) the spread of film, moviegoing, and Hollywood culture; or 3) the widespread commercial use of radio. In various ways, all of these technologies came of age during this period. Students could be urged to argue for reasons why the development they have been assigned was particularly decisive. Students could be prepped for their discussion with appropriate statistics, and also by reviewing the text and considering the major social and economic changes of the era. There are a number of excellent websites on all of these technologies; texts to consider and review might include Michele Hiles, *Only Connect: A Cultural History of Broadcasting in the United States* (Belmont, CA: Wadsworth, 2002) and Nathan Miller, *New World Coming: The 1930s and the Making of Modern America* (New York: Scribner, 2003).

3. Use the information presented in "Lecture Strategies," number 2, to explore some of the connections between postwar social alienation and energy and political movements of the time. You might begin by further exposing the students to futurist art and manifestos from postwar Italy, available on the Web and in books such as Apollonio Umbro, ed., Robert Brain, trans., *Futurist Manifestos* (Boston: MFA Publications, 2001); Willard Bohn, ed. and trans., *Italian Futurist Poetry* (Toronto: University of Toronto Press, 2005); and Marjorie Perloff's *The Futurist Moment* (Chicago: University of Chicago Press, 2003). How do these works compare to those of Otto Dix or Kaethe Köllwitz? What connections do students see between political movements such as fascism as it developed in Italy and elsewhere, and the futurist movement? How might support for peace societies and the League of Nations have drawn from some of the same cultural sources?

4. Women's roles changed enormously during the war, but after hostilities had ceased, a debate ensued over women's "proper" role in European society. Discuss how women's status changed during the 1920s. What roles did women play in the Great War? What was the impact of suffrage? Which issues surrounded women's entry into the workforce? How were women depicted differently in the mass media? A good introduction on European women's history is Bonnie G. Smith, *Changing Lives: Women in European History Since 1700* (Lexington, MA: D. C. Heath, 1989). Primary sources include Vera Brittain's classic memoir of the British home front, *Testament of Youth: An Autobiographical Study of the Years 1900–1925* (New York: Penguin Books, 1933, 1989), a text which also serves well as an intellectual coming of age story. The deaths of Vera's brother, fiancé, and others at the front, as well as her own wartime college and nursing experiences, are vividly considered. Excerpts from the text on a variety of subjects, from college life during the war, to nursing the wounded, to postwar alienation and social activism, can be used profitably to provoke discussion. Other useful sources on women's wartime experiences include Ute Daniel, *The War from Within: German Women in the First World War* (New York: Berg, 1997); Susan R. Grayzel, *Women's Identities at War: Gender, Motherhood, and Politics in Britain and France During the First World War* (Chapel Hill, NC: University of North Carolina Press, 1999); Margaret Randolph Higonnet and Jane Jenson, eds., *Behind the Lines: Gender and the Two World Wars* (New Haven: Yale University Press, 1987); and Angela Woollacott, *On Her Their Lives Depend: Munitions Workers in the Great War* (Berkeley, CA: University of California Press, 1994). Works on the changing status and roles of women during the 1920s include Katharina von Ankum, ed., *Women in the Metropolis: Gender and Modernity in Weimar Culture* (Berkeley: University of California Press, 1997); Victoria de Grazia, *How Fascism Ruled Women: Italy, 1922–1945* (Berkeley, CA: University of California Press, 1992); Mary Louise Roberts, *Civilization without Sexes: Reconstructing Gender in Postwar France, 1917–1927* (Chicago: University of Chicago Press, 1994); and Elizabeth A. Wood, *The Baba and the Comrade: Gender and Politics in Revolutionary Russia* (Bloomington: Indiana University Press, 1997).

Reviewing the Text

Review Questions

1. In what ways was World War I a total war?

[model answer] • ***Full mobilization of civilian labor:*** *Civilians manufactured the weapons and machines that were the backbone of technological warfare, as well as increased production of coffins and prosthetics for soldiers. Many countries drafted both men and women for military and industrial service, blurring the distinctions between military and civilian life.*

• ***Huge numbers of troops drawn from European nations and their colonies globalized the war:*** *Europe's large armies grew through conscription to replace huge numbers of casualties. Millions of colonial Africans, Arabs, Indians, and others became troops and conscripted laborers. European colonies also became battlegrounds as nations fought for each other's possessions around the world.*

• ***Output capacity increases in the most industrialized nations:*** *Unprecedented use of machinery determined the course of the war. Machine guns and rifles, airplanes, battleships, submarines, and motorized transport were at the military's disposal, along with new technologies such as chlorine gas, tanks, and bombs.*

• ***Political and social issues overshadowed:*** *Political parties put aside their differences concerning gender, economics, and class to support the war; minority social groups who suffered discrimination believed the war would lead to a new day of unity. Government control of industries and daily life, laws against sedition, and factory working conditions that might normally appall liberals were accepted and deemed necessary.*

2. Why did people rebel during World War I, and what turned rebellion into outright revolution in Russia?

[model answer] • ***Poor living conditions and continued military failures:*** *Citizens revolted against high prices and food shortages, and even on the front lines, troops sometimes mutinied rather than participate in fruitless* *and bloody offensives. Citizens believed their leaders had failed them.*

• ***Russia sustained the greatest number of casualties; slaughter on the eastern front forced thousands of peasants into the interior:*** *Economic underdevelopment made shortages more acute than elsewhere, and people rioted in the streets. Russian peasants had been ready for political change since their last revolution in 1905 and were provoked further by economic hardship.*

• ***Continued peasant riots, elite incompetence, and German support of Russian revolutionaries:*** *Unlike other European leaders, Tsar Nicholas II had failed to unify his people in a concerted war effort, and at the same time, he received harsh criticism for allowing questionable advisors to influence his decisions. Many prominent and educated Russian leaders withdrew their support from him, so that when riots reached their peak in March 1917, the tsar was forced to abdicate.*

3. What were the major outcomes of the postwar peacemaking process?

[model answer] • ***Political destabilization of Eastern and east-central Europe:*** *The cluster of individual treaties that comprised the Peace of Paris created new states out of Austria-Hungary and the Ottoman Empire. Politically and economically weak, and typically ethnically diverse, these new states formed political alliances among themselves and with their powerful neighbors.*

• ***Ostracism of Germany:*** *The Allies, seeking retribution for their suffering, humiliated Germany by forcing it into a treaty to accept responsibility and guilt for the war, and to pay huge reparations in currency and matériel. Germany was initially excluded from the League of Nations as well.*

• ***Economic upheaval across Europe:*** *Many nations depended on German reparations and/or restored trade with Germany to remain solvent. Germany was in the tightest financial bind of all due to its inability to raise taxes for war-related expenses and the need to pay reparations. The government attempted to solve its financial problems by printing trillions of marks, destroying Germany's currency and threatening global economy.*

• ***The League of Nations fostered diplomatic openness but did not actually solve international problems:*** *The league's principle of collective security was intended to replace secretive and divisive prewar power politics. The new openness in international relations was used by politicians to harness public sentiment, but it did not solve problems or prevent international violence.*

• ***Mandate system kept imperialism alive, but the colonial war experience encouraged resistance:*** *The League of Nations exercised political control over former German colonies and Ottoman territories through a system of mandates, while local rulers retained limited authority. But the colonized began to challenge European claims of superiority through increased political movements and revolts, and European colonial powers were weakened politically and economically by the war.*

4. What were the major political, social, and economic problems facing postwar Europe, and how did governments attempt to address them?

[model answer] • ***Governments had to build new democracies, cease internal and external violence, and prevent revolts:*** *Governments tried to follow voters' demands by holding rallies to build consensus and arresting dissidents. Maintaining empires abroad was crucial to national prestige; rebellions, therefore, elicited strong reprisals and military responses.*

• ***Industrialists and governments had to respond to widespread unemployment and global economic competition:*** *Unemployment skyrocketed when jobs in military factories disappeared and veterans returned home seeking work. Governments provided pensions for veterans, and unions agreed to hold down women's wages or make them ineligible for certain jobs. Worldwide economic competition was a huge challenge to economic recovery because many European factories had lost their international customers to companies in nations untouched by war. Efficiency had improved during the war, and demand for some goods had expanded. By the late 1920s Europe had overcome wild economic swings and was enjoying renewed prosperity.*

• ***Many leaders introduced strong social programs:*** *Governments tried to improve civilian life to reintegrate men into society and reduce the appeal of Bolshevism. Housing for the working class improved. Politicians believed in the stabilizing effect of traditional family values.*

5. How did the postwar atmosphere influence cultural expression and encourage the trend toward dictatorship?

[model answer] • ***Many expressed optimism for a better future through technology, organization, and efficiency:*** *Europeans felt driven to achieve material success after years of war-related and postwar deprivation, and to participate in the technological, literary, and artistic achievements. Wartime experience broke down rigid class boundaries.*

• ***Dictatorships developed where populations remained severely dissatisfied:*** *Many nations were unable to achieve prosperity, efficiency, and organization through either technology or their current governments. In nations where domestic unrest continued after the war, dictators used citizens' intense desires for unity and organization to their advantage, easily setting up their own armies and limiting freedoms, for the benefit of the state, with people's approval. New technological developments such as radio and film provided dictators with tools for propaganda to gain support.*

Making Connections

1. How did the experience of war shape postwar mass politics?
[model answer] *After World War I, returning soldiers found economic depression and social unrest. German soldiers had the added burden of wounded national pride. Democracies seemed unable to deal effectively with these challenges, while totalitarian figures such as Mussolini in Italy and Hitler in Germany, who blamed Jews for their problems, offered authoritarian solutions that seemed to work and promised action and change. Germans and Italians seemed ready and willing to give up individual freedoms in exchange for a restoration of their national dignity and promises of economic progress. Through a strategic use of mass media and public displays of power, Mussolini and Hitler promoted mass politics that were antidemocratic, brutal, and totalitarian.*

2. What social changes from the war carried over into the postwar years and why?
[model answer] *During the war, soldiers from every class had fought side by side, which served to end rigid class distinctions that had been so entrenched just a few years before. As prosperity returned in the postwar period, the middle and upper classes resumed their consumption of innovative consumer goods. But the greatest social change that carried over into the postwar years concerned women. During the war, women had gone to work to support themselves or their families, and had become independent in the process. Whereas some women returned to their traditional roles, many remained in the workforce.*

Discussing the Documents

Questions from Online Study Guide with Model Answers

Outbreak of the Russian Revolution, p. 813

1. What was the mood of the crowd on this first day of the revolution?
[model answer] *The crowd was in an almost "festive" mood, and strangers embraced and kissed in the streets. The mood was relatively peaceful, and there was no mob violence.*

2. Where did the crowd go?
[model answer] *The crowd marched out in the streets, to military barracks at several locations, including Krutitskie and the Red Gates, urging soldiers to join them in overthrowing the state.*

Battlefield Tourism, p. 830

1. Where exactly does Vera Brittain go and why?
[model answer] *Brittain went to the mountain area of Northern Italy, to the site of the British front lines during the war. She wanted to find the grave of her brother, and see the area where he died.*

2. What was her dominant response to her experience?
[model answer] *The experience was painful for her. She had a melancholy reaction to finding the grave, and it led her to wonder about the meaning of her own life since the war, and her efforts to "improve civilization." She felt as if she wanted to stay up with him at the gravesite.*

Contrasting Views: Arguing with the Victors, pp. 818–819

1. Describe the various contending claims beyond those of the official combatant powers. Did the victorious powers heed these voices when forging the peace?
[model answer] *Arab nationalists in the document sought a unified Arab state that would reflect their aspirations for independence from Ottoman or European rule. Pan-Africanists asked for many things, including better treatment of Africans by colonial powers and more access to national resources, especially land, and political independence. The Congress of Women demanded more attention to the need for peace, and for international institutions and economic reforms that would ensure cooperation and the peaceful resolution of differences. In Poland and elsewhere, anti-Semites demanded that the power of Jewish minorities be curbed. In general, the peace was drawn up along lines that the major victorious belligerent powers approved of, and the lobbying efforts of various interest groups did not by themselves shape the nature of the peace.*

2. How were the various demands at the peace conference related to the politics and conditions of World War I?
[model answer] *Several of the demands related, directly and indirectly, to the politics and conditions of World War I. Arab nationalist demands reflected the push for self-determination and a proliferation of nation-states similar to the conditions in the Balkans that had triggered the conflict. The demands of pacifists for limitations of the power of nation-states, on the other hand, was a reaction to the problems of alliances, secret treaty provisions, and other causes and effects of the war that related to the strength of nationalism of the era. The demands of Pan-Africanists reflected the problems associated with colonial empires, from the native point of view.*

3. Do any of the demands seem more justifiable in addressing the peacetime needs of Europe and the world?
[model answer] *The demands for greater international cooperation on economic and social reforms resonated for many. The part that nationalism and unfettered state power and ambition had played in causing and prolonging the war was clear to many. Arab and African reformers also brought forward demands that reflected the problem*

of European dominance and expansion, and the need for a reordering of the relationships of western states to each other and the rest of the world.

Other Questions for Discussing These Documents in Class

Outbreak of the Russian Revolution

1. In what way was the revolution an emotional experience? What does the emotional reaction described by Dune reveal about the revolution?

2. What does the document reveal about who participated in the revolution and who did not?

Battlefield Tourism

1. Why did Brittain want to visit the place her brother died?

2. How did the experience of finding his grave make her think about the present?

Contrasting Views: Arguing with the Victors

1. What do the appeals presented have in common?

2. What do they tell you about perceptions of western power in the postwar era?

Comparative Questions

1. What do the documents indicate about the transformative nature of the First World War? Consider the question in relation to personal, social, and political realities.

2. To what extent do the documents make it easier to understand postwar anxiety, angst, and even anger? What aspects of the documents demonstrate discontent?

For Users of *Sources of The Making of the West*

The following documents are available in Chapter 25 of the companion sourcebook by Katharine J. Lualdi, University of Southern Maine.

1. Two Soldiers' Views of the Horrors of War: Fritz Franke and Siegfried Sassoon (1914–1918)
2. Mobilizing for Total War: L. Doriat, *Women on the Home Front* (1917)
3. Revolutionary Marxism Defended: Vladimir Ilich Lenin, *Letter to Nikolai Aleksandrovich Rozhkov* (January 29, 1919)
4. Establishing Fascism in Italy: Benito Mussolini, *The Doctrine of Fascism* (1932)
5. A New Form of Anti-Semitism: Adolf Hitler, *Mein Kampf* (1925)

Discussion Ideas for Sources of The Making of the West, *Chapter 25*

1. What role did patriotism seem to play for soldiers and workers? Discuss what these voices have to say about how wartime provided insight into the character of others.

2. Consider the visions of the state offered by Hitler, Mussolini, and Lenin. How are they similar and different? Focus on two dimensions in particular: the place of the individual in the state, and the groups, attitudes, or forms of behavior that are dangerous to the new forms of politics on offered.

Working with Visual Sources

For this exercise, please refer to Inflation in Germany (1923) on p. 820 of the textbook or view the image on the book companion site's Online Study Guide under the "Visual Activity" for Chapter 25.

Students viewing the image at the Online Study Guide are asked two questions about the image. The questions and model answers (not made available to students) are below. Project this image, available on the Instructor's Resources CD-ROM, in class or ask students to look at the image in their textbooks and answer the questions.

1. What does this image say about the state of the German economy in 1923?
[model answer] *This picture suggests that the economy was in such poor shape that German currency had become a plaything during the 1920s. However, the fact that these children are obviously not living in poverty suggests that at least some people were able to manage. The worthlessness of the German mark at this time did, however, ruin many people's life savings.*

2. What type of response might images such as this have solicited from the German people?
[model answer] *Images such as this might have stirred up resentment among the German people toward the countries they were being forced to pay reparations to, as well as toward their own government's leaders. Germans might have become more willing to listen to leaders who presented themselves as strong enough to stand up for their nation.*

For this exercise, please refer to Seeing History: Demonizing the Enemy: Italian Propaganda Posters from World War I on p. 808 of the textbook or to the images on the book companion site's Online Study Guide under the "Visual Activity: Seeing History" for Chapter 25.

Students viewing the images at the Online Study Guide are asked two questions about the images. The questions and model answers (not made available to students) are below. Project these images, available on the Instructor's Resources CD, in class or ask students to look at the images in their textbooks and answer the questions.

1. How do these Allied images depict Germany differently?
[model answer] *The "Bond Program" poster looks operatic. Germany is depicted as a fierce, bearded man wielding a flaming torch and a club, but he is checked in his assault on the female Italian figure by her sword. In "The Prussian Squid," Prussia (and Austria) is depicted as an aggressive octopus with human-looking eyes, greedily grabbing neighboring territories. This poster has an extended textual explanation.*

2. Which poster offers the more "emotional" appeal? How might the purpose of the posters be related to the nature of their appeal?
[model answer] *The "Bond Program" poster, with its depiction of an aggressive, personified Germany attacking Italy depicted as a woman, makes a more emotional appeal. The "Prussian Squid" image, with its lengthy explanation and its depiction of the expansion of Prussia into a united Germany, offers more detail and a more reasoned appeal. The "Bond Program" poster, because it was meant to inspire viewers to support the war effort by sacrificing financially, may have used an emotional appeal to help motivate citizens to respond.*

Mapping Exercises

Map Activity from OSG—Model Answers for Map Activity #2

For this activity, please refer to the map on p. 817. Students are asked these questions:

Look at the territory ceded by Austria-Hungary. What happened to this multiethnic empire?
[model answer] *Austria-Hungary was divided into several separate countries, ending the empire. Austria-Hungary contributed territory to the new states of Hungary, Austria, Poland, Czechoslovakia, and Yugoslavia.*

What effect did the treaties have on Germany's national territory?
[model answer] *In the west, Germany lost the provinces of Alsace and Lorraine, which were returned to France. Because of French security concerns, a demilitarized zone was also established on the French border. In the east, Germany lost considerable territory to newly created states, primarily to Poland.*

How was the map of postwar Europe different?
[model answer] *The peace settlement took territory from the Central Powers and created more and smaller states. In general, in eastern Europe the fragmentation of Austria-Hungary created smaller and weaker states sandwiched between Russia and Germany.*

Map 25.1: The Fronts of World War I, 1914–1918, p. 802

Where was the war fought? Be clear on which states participated in the conflict from front to front. Note the core German difficulty of the war: the need to fight and deploy large numbers of troops on multiple fronts. In what sense was the war a "world war," according to the map?

Map 25.2: The Western Front, p. 804

Note the points of furthest advance, by both sets of armies. Where was most of the war fought? Where was fighting most intense? Does the map help you to understand the frustrations and difficulties soldiers faced on the western front?

Map 25.3: The Russian Civil War, 1917–1922, p. 814

Where was this conflict fought? Did either side have a "geographical advantage?" Who controlled the major cities?

Map 25.4: Europe and the Middle East after the Peace Settlements of 1919–1920, p. 817

Ask students to compare this map to the map of Europe at the Outbreak of World War I (p. 796). Which empires have been dissolved? Which new states have emerged? What potential problems and conflicts could arise from this geopolitical transformation of Europe?

Mapping the West: Europe and the World in 1929, p. 836

Ask students to locate and identify the major powers that were not members of the League of Nations as of 1929. What potential problems could arise from these states not being members of the league?

In-Class Assignments and Presentation Topics

1. Have students research and write an essay on the so-called war guilt debate. By exploring this issue and then debating it in class, students will not only deepen their understanding of the war, but will also get an insight into issues concerning evidence and interpretation. Sources should include works by Fritz Fischer, whose first book presented a controversial

account of war guilt that sparked the debate that still reverberates today. Fischer's books are *Germany's Aims in the First World War* (New York: W. W. Norton, 1967); *World Power or Decline: The Controversy over Germany's Aims in the First World War* (New York: W. W. Norton, 1974); and *War of Illusions: German Politics from 1911 to 1914* (New York: W. W. Norton, 1975). Other sources include Holger H. Herwig, *The Outbreak of World War I*, 5th ed. (Lexington, MA: D. C. Heath, 1991); John Anthony Moses, *The Politics of Illusion: The Fischer Controversy in German Historiography* (New York: Barnes & Noble, 1975); and Gregor Schollen, ed., *Escape into War?: The Foreign Policy of Imperial Germany* (New York: Berg, 1990). See the sources from "Class Discussion Starters," number 4, in the Instructor's Resource Manual for textbook Chapter 24 for additional information.

2. One of the significant developments in the wake of World War I was the dissolution of the Austro-Hungarian Empire. Have the students divide into groups and research one of the successor states from independence through the late 1920s. What challenges did these newly independent states encounter? How did they deal with them? Focus particularly on Poland and Czechoslovakia, and the Russo-Polish War. It may be helpful to consult Norman Davies, *White Eagle, Red Star: The Polish-Soviet War, 1919–1920* (London: Pimlico Press, 2003). Class presentations will help students understand the issues facing these new states and the problems that continued to plague them through World War II.

3. World War I was one of the first heavily photographed wars. Send students to any or several of the wonderful web-based repositories of wartime photographs and have them return with one, two, or several images. Perhaps these can be e-mailed or shared electronically. There are textual options as well, including Richard Holmes, *The First World War in Photographs* (London: Carleton Books, 2001) or John Keegan's *The First World War: An Illustrated History* (London: Pimlico, 2002), or the more reflective Jane Carmichael's *First World War Photographers* (London: Routledge, 1989). Students should discuss and/or write about their reactions to these photographs, but should also be encouraged to explore the social and political consequences of the availability of such images. How might they have changed attitudes toward war?

4. Ask students to write an essay comparing the propaganda of two of the combatant nations of World War I. Have them address the following questions: What kinds of appeals, messages, and imagery are used? How, for example, are the enemy and the home front depicted? How do the depictions compare from country to country? Which propaganda messages and images are more effective and why? Sources for World War I posters include Joseph Darracott, *The First World War in Posters* (New York: Dover, 1974); and Peter Paret, Beth Irwin Lewis, and Paul Paret, *Persuasive Images: Posters of War and Revolution* (Princeton, NJ: Princeton University Press, 1992).

5. To further students' understanding of the peace settlement and its flaws, divide the class into groups and have each group research and then represent individual countries at the Paris Peace Conference. Have students reenact the conference, arguing territorial or reparation issues from their country's unique perspective. Make sure to include representation from groups whose nationalist ambitions were frustrated in connection with the peace talks (such as pan-Arab nationalists, Irish nationalists). It may be worth consulting several of the essays in Manfred Boemeke, Gerlad Feldman, and Elisabeth Glaser, eds., *The Treaty of Versailles: A Reassessment After 75 Years* (Cambridge: Cambridge University Press, 1998) or Margaret MacMillan, *Paris 1919: Six Months That Changed the World* (New York: Random House, 2002), perhaps balanced by Allen Sharp's *The Versailles Settlement: Peacemaking in Paris, 1919* (Basingstoke, UK: Macmillan, 1991).

6. Comparative studies are a good way to develop understanding of historical events. Have students write essays comparing Fascist Italy to Nazi Germany. Ask students to investigate the origins of the movements, their agendas, their members, their use of propaganda, and the role of their leader. Three good sources that examine these regimes are Richard Bessel, ed., *Fascist Italy and Nazi Germany: Comparisons and Contrasts* (New York: Cambridge University Press, 1996); Alexander J. De Grand, *Fascist Italy and Nazi Germany: The "Fascist" Style of Rule* (New York: Routledge, 1995); and Bruce F. Pauley, *Hitler, Stalin, and Mussolini: Totalitarianism in the Twentieth Century* (Wheeling, IL: Harlan Davidson, 1997).

Essay Questions

1. During the 1920s, an unprecedented explosion of artistic creativity emerged from the cafés, cabarets, and studios of Paris and Berlin. By exploring the output of painters, sculptors, writers, architects, and filmmakers, students can better understand why this era witnessed a cultural flowering that directly challenged centuries-old ideas and conceptions. Have students write research papers on an artist or a movement of the period or focus on the developments in either Paris or Berlin. Examples of topics are Dada, surrealism, futurism, postwar literature, film, Art Deco, and the Bauhaus. Sources on general cultural developments in Paris during the 1920s include Charles Rearick, *The*

French in Love and War: Popular Culture in the Era of the World Wars (New Haven, CT: Yale University Press, 1997); and William Wiser, *The Crazy Years: Paris in the Twenties* (New York: Thames and Hudson, 1983). Sources on general developments in Berlin include Otto Friedrich, *Before the Deluge: A Portrait of Berlin in the 1920s* (New York: Harper & Row, 1972); Peter Gay, *Weimar Culture: The Insider As Outsider* (New York: Harper & Row, 1968); and John Willett, *Art and Politics in the Weimar Period: The New Sobriety 1917–1933* (New York: Da Capo Press, 1978). Works on Dada and surrealism include Matthew Gale, *Dada and Surrealism* (London: Phaidon Press, 1997); and such primary sources as André Breton, *Manifestoes of Surrealism* (Ann Arbor: University of Michigan Press, 1969) and Robert Motherwell, ed., *The Dada Painters and Poets: An Anthology*, 2nd ed. (Boston: G. K. Hall, 1981). Sources on the Bauhaus include Barbara Miller Lane, *Architecture and Politics in Germany, 1918–1945* (Cambridge, MA: Harvard University Press, 1968); and Frank Whitford, *Bauhaus* (New York: Thames and Hudson, 1984). See also the sources on futurism in "Class Discussion Starters," number 3.

2. During the 1920s, Paris became the home of a truly unique international community of American expatriate artists and writers who sought the artistic freedom and inspiration that they found lacking in their homelands. Have students write research papers that discuss why a particular artist or group of artists sought refuge in Paris, what they found there, and the art or literature they produced. Examples of subjects are Ernest Hemingway, F. Scott Fitzgerald, Henry Miller, Man Ray, Gertrude Stein, Djuna Barnes, and Janet Flanner. Important literary works from the period include Ernest Hemingway, *In Our Time*, *The Sun Also Rises*, and *A Farewell to Arms*; Henry Miller, *Tropic of Cancer*; and Gertrude Stein, *The Autobiography of Alice B. Toklas*. Sources for this topic include Shari Benstock, *Women of the Left Bank: Paris, 1900–1940* (Austin: University of Texas Press, 1986); Malcolm Cowley, *A Second Flowering: Works and Days of the Lost Generation* (New York: Viking Press, 1973); Tyler Stoval, *Paris Noir: African Americans in the City of Light* (New York; Mariner Books, 1996); Andrea Weiss, *Paris Was a Woman: Portraits from the Left Bank* (San Francisco: Harper San Francisco, 1995); and George Wickes, *Americans in Paris* (Garden City, NY: Doubleday, 1969).

3. As a "total war," World War I had a direct and lasting impact on the home front. Ask students to choose one European country and write research papers that explore the political, economic, social, and cultural changes that took place in their chosen nation during the war. Sources include Jean-Jacques Becker, *The Great War and the French People* (New York: St. Martin's, 1986); Brian Bond, *War and Society in Europe, 1870–1970* (New York: St. Martin's, 1983); Jürgen Kocka, *Facing Total War: German Society, 1914–1918* (New York: Berg, 1984); Arthur Marwick, *The Deluge: British Society and the First World War* (Boston: Little, Brown, 1965); John Williams, *The Other Battleground: The Home Fronts: Britain, France and Germany, 1914–1918* (Chicago: Henry Regency, 1972); and J. M. Winter, *The Great War and the British People* (Cambridge, MA: Harvard University Press, 1986).

Additional Resources: Literature

Bloom, Harold, ed., *Ernest Hemingway: The Sun Also Rises*. 1996.
Clark, David, and Rosalind Clark, eds., *The Collected Works of W. B. Yeats*. 1999–2001.
Fitzgerald, F. Scott, *The Great Gatsby*. 1925.
Graves, Robert, *Goodbye to All That*. 1929.
Joyce, James, *Ulysses* (amended and reprinted). 1961.
Kilmartin, Terence, ed., *Marcel Proust*. 1871–1922.
Kollontai, Alexsandra, *Love of Worker Bees*. 1923.
Lawrence, D. H., *Women in Love*. 1920.
Moncrieff, C. K. Scott, and Terence Kilmartin, trans., *Marcel Proust: Remembrance of Things Past*. 1981.
Muir, Willa, and Edwin Muir, trans., *Franz Kafka: The Trial*. 1956.
Murdoch, Brian, trans., *Erich Maria Remarque: All Quiet on the Western Front*. 1994.
North, Michael, ed., *"The Waste Land," by T. S. Eliot*. 2000.
Proust, Marcel, *Remembrance of Things Past*.
Waugh, Evelyn, *A Handful of Dust*. 1934.
Woolf, Virginia, *Mrs. Dalloway*. 1925.

Additional Resources: Film and Video

Johnny Got His Gun (1971; VHS, 106 min.). Evocative and stylized adaptation of Dalton Trumbo's novel, this film focuses on the life of a horribly wounded World War I soldier: a classic anti-war film.

Testament of Youth (1979; VHS, 3 hrs., 20 min.). This series dramatizes Vera Brittain's 1933 novel of the same name and chronicles her real-life struggle to get an education at Oxford and her work as a battlefield nurse in World War I.

All Quiet on the Western Front (1979; DVD, 2 hrs., 11 min.). This dramatization of Erich Maria Remarque's 1929 novel shows the disillusionment of a German soldier during World War I as he experiences the horror of warfare.

Brideshead Revisited (1981; VHS/DVD, approx. 11 hrs.). Based on Evelyn Waugh's 1945 novel, this miniseries charts the relationships a middle-class artist has with a fading aristocratic family in the decadent pre-World War II period.

Gallipoli (1981; VHS/DVD, 111 min.). This film, although weak on the particular details of the disastrous Gallipoli campaign in Turkey, offers a good general portrayal of the horrors of combat in the era, as well as a "colonial" perspective on World War I in its depictions of the war from the point of view of initially enthusiastic Australian soldiers. It provides a unique perspective on the global dimensions of the conflict.

Out of Africa (1985; VHS/DVD, 2 hrs., 41 min.). This film is based on Danish writer Karen Blixen's (Isak Dinesen) 1937 autobiographical book of the same name. Her relationship with the native peoples and her efforts to set up and run a plantation in Africa in 1914 has been romanticized to some extent, but the film does capture the dichotomy between the white owners and the indigenous people.

Orlando (1992; VHS/DVD, 1 hr., 33 min). This excellent dramatization of Virginia Woolf's 1928 novel shows about the limits society has placed on women throughout history. Orlando begins life as a man at Elizabeth I's court and is periodically reincarnated. During one of those reincarnations, he becomes a woman, and faces firsthand the discrimination of society.

Remains of the Day (1993; VHS/DVD, 2 hrs., 14 min.). This film, set in an English country manor house on the eve of World War II, focuses on the relationship between the household's butler and housekeeper, and the minutia of everyday life for people "in service" is brilliantly captured. The film portrays quite literally the end of an era, as large households such as those depicted disappeared forever with the coming of war.

The Great War and the Shaping of the Twentieth Century (1996; VHS, 8 hrs.). This exhaustive documentary examines World War I.

Gosford Park (2001; VHS/DVD, 2 hrs., 18 min.). Although this film is a murder mystery in the tradition of Agatha Christie, it captures to perfection the decadence of life for the upper classes between the war years. Life "below stairs" for servants in an English manor house is meticulously re-created and highly illuminating.

Lost Battalion (2001; VHS/DVD, 133 min.). This film focuses on a minor wartime disaster, the isolation and near annihilation of an American battalion in one of the war's final offensives in the Argonne forest. It provides an excellent depiction of the nature of World War I combat, and an American perspective on the tragedy of the war.

Dr. Zhivago (2003; VHS/DVD, 3 hrs., 45 min.). This two-part adaptation of Boris Pasternak's 1957 novel about two lovers in the midst of the Russian Revolution is lavish in every respect.

The Forsyte Saga, Series II (2003; VHS/DVD, 4 hrs., 45 min.). John Galsworthy's novel, *To Let*, is dramatized in three episodes of approximately 90 minutes each and continues the Forsyte story in 1920, as the family continues to struggle with issues of social and moral convention in a world much changed after World War I.

OTHER BEDFORD/ST. MARTIN'S RESOURCES FOR CHAPTER 25

The following resources are available to accompany Chapter 25. Please refer to the Preface of this manual for detailed descriptions of all the ancillaries.

For Instructors

Transparencies

The following maps and images from Chapter 25 are available as full-color acetates.

- Map 25.1: The Fronts of World War I, 1914–1918
- Map 25.2: The Western Front
- Map 25.3: The Russian Civil War, 1917–1922
- Map 25.4: Europe and the Middle East after the Peace Settlements of 1919–1920
- Mapping the West: Europe and the World in 1929
- Inflation in Germany (1923), p. 820
- The Flapper, p. 827

Instructor's Resources CD-ROM

The following maps and image from Chapter 25, as well as a chapter outline, are available on disc in both PowerPoint and jpeg formats.

- Map 25.1: The Fronts of World War I, 1914–1918
- Map 25.2: The Western Front
- Map 25.3: The Russian Civil War, 1917–1922
- Map 25.4: Europe and the Middle East after the Peace Settlements of 1919–1920
- Mapping the West: Europe and the World in 1929
- Inflation in Germany (1923), p. 820

Using the Bedford Series with The Making of the West

Available in print as well as online at **bedfordstmartins.com/usingseries,** this guide offers practical suggestions for using Samuel R. Williamson Jr. and Russel Van Wyk, *July 1914: Soldiers, Statesmen, and the Coming of the Great War, A Brief Documentary History,* and *Lenin and the Making of the Soviet State,* by Jeffrey Brooks and Georgiy Chernyavskey, in conjunction with Chapter 25 of the textbook.

For Students

Study Guides

The Online Study Guide at **bedfordstmartins.com/hunt** helps students synthesize the material they have learned as well as practice the skills historians use to make sense of the past. The following Map, Visual, and Document activities are available for Chapter 25.

Map Activity

- Map 25.4: Europe and the Middle East after the Peace Settlements of 1919–1920

Visual Activity

- Inflation in Germany (1923), p. 820
- "Subscribe to the Bond Program," 1914–1918, p. 808
- "The Prussian Squid or 'Sea Demon,'" 1916, p. 808

Reading Historical Documents

- Outbreak of the Russian Revolution, p. 813
- Battlefield Tourism, p. 830
- Contrasting Views: Arguing with the Victors, pp. 818–819

CHAPTER

26

The Great Depression and World War II

1929–1945

Chapter Resources

Main Chapter Topics

1. The Great Depression, set off by a collapse of the U.S. stock market, presented a global challenge to existing economic, social, and political institutions.

2. Some nations turned to totalitarian regimes in their attempts to remedy the problems connected with the depression and other difficulties faced by nation-states during this period.

3. Although FDR's New Deal was an aggressive effort to bolster democracy and respond to economic crisis, democratic countries often made cautious and largely ineffective efforts to combat both the depression and the menace of fascism.

4. World War II began largely because of the fascist powers' aggressions—especially Nazi Germany—and also because of the weakness displayed by the democratic powers.

5. Germany and Japan were initially highly successful in World War II, but, by 1943, the superior productive power of the Allies—particularly that of the United States—made the defeat of the Axis powers inevitable.

6. The Depression and the war produced horrific suffering. An estimated one hundred million were killed, fifty million refugees were created, and the Holocaust, Japanese slaughters in China, and wartime efforts directed against civilian populations amounted to one of the most abominable moral legacies in human history.

7. Efforts displayed at the international conferences of Yalta and Potsdam (1945) to put the world back together faced both a growing cold-war antagonism and national liberation movements in the colonies.

Focus Question

What were the main economic, social, and political challenges of the years 1929–1945, and how did governments and individuals respond to them?

1. The Great Depression, brought on by the collapse of the American stock market and economy after the crash of 1929, posed a fundamental challenge to the global economic system. In the United States, democratic values were preserved by the aggressive, constructive response of Franklin Delano Roosevelt. The American economy remained in dire straits, however. While bright spots remained in the western economy and modernization continued in countries such as Sweden, in general western democracies faltered, introducing measures such as tariffs that deepened the crisis and failing to form strong, effective governments that could forge an effective consensus. In Germany, of course, economic crisis combined with simmering resentment led to the rise of anti-democratic forces in the form of the Nazis and the Communists. Hitler's Nazi party used vicious, aggressive, and racist tactics to seize political power by 1933. Stalin's economic and social policies during this same period turned Russia into an industrial power, but at tremendous human cost and only by devastating the agricultural sector of the economy.

2. Individuals suffered in the west as well, as unemployment and economic privatization gave way to military conflict with the outbreak of the Second World War in September 1939. The failure of other states to control Japanese, Italian, and especially German aggression led directly to a catastrophic war that culminated in concerted efforts to destroy racial "enemies" and attack civilian populations. While in the end the Axis powers were defeated, an estimated one hundred million died along the way, and in many ways the events of these years must be counted among the darkest in history.

Annotated Chapter Outline

I. **The Great Depression**

A. **Economic Disaster Strikes, pp. 840–841**

1. In the 1920s, U.S. corporations, banks, and millions of individuals borrowed money on margin to invest in the stock market, which had experienced a long, upward trend.
2. In order to stabilize the market, the nation's central bank—the Federal Reserve Bank—tightened the availability of credit, forcing anxious brokerage firms to send margin calls demanding that clients immediately pay back the money they had borrowed to buy stock.
3. As more and more individuals and institutions sold their stocks to pay back their margin debts to brokers, the market collapsed between October and mid-November 1929.
4. In response to the crisis, the United States cut back on loans to Europe and called in short-term, international debts, which caused a financial crisis in Europe.
5. This worldwide crisis was worsened by rising unemployment, budget cuts, and tariff increases. Industry closed down, and agricultural price declines led to a rural debt crisis.
6. This worldwide economic crisis is called the Great Depression.

B. **Social Effects of the Depression, pp. 842–843**

1. The situation was not, however, uniformly bleak, and modernization proceeded during the 1930s in some industries and countries.
2. Municipal and national governments continued road construction and sanitation projects and running water, electricity, and sewage pipes were installed in many homes for the first time.
3. Despite high rates of unemployment, the majority of Europeans and Americans were employed throughout the 1930s, and some even enjoyed considerable prosperity as prices declined.
4. Even those who held jobs, however, felt the threat of unemployment, which created a mood of fear and resentment throughout the West.
5. Economic catastrophe upset social life and strained gender relations.
6. Women accepted low-paying jobs, such as housecleaning or doing laundry, to make ends meet, and men often had to assume housekeeping chores at home.
7. Men could be observed on street corners begging while women worked to support their families. Young men in cities faced severe unemployment and were receptive to political radicalism.
8. As the percentage of farm workers decreased, patriarchal authority continued to decline in rural areas.
9. Demagogues blamed democracy for the economy's failings. Nazi and fascist politicians promised to create jobs.
10. The falling birthrate also concerned politicians.
11. Tough economic times led couples to have fewer children, and mandatory education caused parents extra expense and prevented children of working-class families from bringing in wages. Birth control was more acceptable and widely available.
12. The population crisis reinvigorated racist politics and rhetoric with the argument that, while "superior" peoples were failing to breed, "inferior" peoples were ready to take their place. Anti-Semitism was often featured in critiques of the economic crisis and relief efforts.

C. **The Great Depression beyond the West, pp. 843–844**

1. The effects of declining purchasing power and unavailability of ready credit extended beyond the West, reducing the demand for copper, tin, and other raw materials and for the finished products manufactured in urban factories.
2. The depression also drove down the price of foodstuffs such as rice and coffee, which proved disastrous to those persons who had been forced to grow a single, cash crop.
3. The economic picture was also uneven in the colonies; established industrial sectors of the Indian economy, such as textiles, gained strength, with India achieving virtual independence from British cloth.
4. Economic distress added to smoldering grievances and contributed to colonial independence movements.
5. In India, Mohandas (Mahatma or "great-souled") Gandhi (1869–1948) emerged as the charismatic leader for Indian independence by advocating civil

disobedience: the peaceful but deliberate breaking of the law.

6. In the Middle East, westernizer Mustafa Kemal (1881–1938) or Atatürk ("first among Turks") took advantage of Europe's vulnerability both after World War I and during the depression to found an independent Turkish republic (1923).
7. Persia also loosened Europe's grip by forcing the negotiation of oil contracts and, in 1935, changed its name to Iran.
8. In 1936, Britain agreed to end its military occupation of Egypt (but *not* the Suez Canal).
9. The French made fewer concessions because their trade with the colonies increased as trade with Europe lagged; they viewed the population growth in Africa and Asia in an optimistic light.
10. When, in 1930, Western-educated leader Ho Chi Minh (1890–1969), the founder of the Indochinese Communist Party, led a peasant uprising against French rule, the French responded with force.
11. British and French military forces were needed in their empires to control resistance movements, leaving totalitarianism to spread unchecked throughout Europe.

II. Totalitarian Triumph

A. The Rise of Stalinism, pp. 844–847

1. When Joseph Stalin (1879–1953) took control of the Soviet Union, he ended Lenin's New Economic Policy (NEP) and announced (spring of 1929) the first of several five-year plans to radically industrialize the Soviet economy.
2. This first plan called for massive increases in the output of coal, iron ore, steel, and industrial goods as an emergency measure to end Soviet backwardness and prevent the west from crushing communism.
3. Such central planning, which had its precedent in World War I, helped create a new elite of bureaucrats and industrial officials, especially managers who dominated the workers by limiting their ability to change jobs or move from place to place. Heavy industry grew some 500 percent from 1929–1935.
4. Workers often lacked the technical education and the tools necessary to accomplish the goals set out in the five-year plan, so almost everyone falsified records to protect their jobs.
5. To feed this workforce, Stalin demanded more grain from peasants, grain that could also be exported to finance this forced industrialization.
6. When peasants resisted these demands by reducing production or withholding produce from the market, Stalin called for the liquidation of the kulaks ("prosperous peasants").
7. Kulaks and their associates were evicted, imprisoned, exiled, or murdered.
8. Confiscated kulak land formed the basis of the *kolkhoz* ("collective farm").
9. Collectivization was a disaster, and Soviet citizens starved as the grain harvest declined.
10. Because work life was politicized, economic failure took on political meaning; Stalin blamed the failure on "wreckers," saboteurs of communism.
11. He instituted purges—state violence in the form of widespread arrests, imprisonment in labor camps, show trials, and executions—to rid society of these traitors.
12. To accommodate detaining those caught in the purges, Stalin's government developed an extensive system of brutal prison camps, known as the Gulag, that stretched from Moscow to Siberia. Some one million died in them annually from overwork, starvation, beatings, and murder.
13. In the midst of the anxiety caused by the purges, cultural and social life retreated from its earlier emphasis on experimentation.
14. Modernism in the arts and creativity in urban planning were curtailed; the falling birthrate led to a restriction of birth-control information, the encouragement of marriage, and the criminalization of homosexuality.
15. Propaganda now referred to the family unit as a "school for socialism"—a miniature Soviet state.

B. Hitler's Rise to Power, pp. 847–848

1. When the Great Depression hit Germany, the National Socialist German Workers' Party (Nazi Party), led by Adolf Hitler, began to outstrip its rivals in elections.
2. The Nazi Party gained the support of prominent businessmen and media tycoons who viewed it as a preferable alternative to communism, which also enjoyed widespread support.

3. As parliamentary government was virtually halted over their inability to reach an accord on economic measures, Hitler's followers made the government appear even less effective by rampaging through the streets, wrecking stores owned by Jews, and beating up Social Democrats and Communists.
4. The Nazis' attack on the left won them the approval of the middle classes who feared Russian-style revolution and the loss of their property.
5. Most of Hitler's strongest supporters were young and idealistic, the vast majority of Nazi Party members being under age forty, but the party also found support in every class.
6. In the elections of 1930 and 1932, both the Nazis and the Communists made huge gains.
7. Effective propaganda in the media garnered further support for Hitler.
8. To stop the Communists, the political and social elite persuaded President Paul von Hindenburg (1847–1934) to invite Hitler to become chancellor in January 1933.

C. The Nazification of German Politics, pp. 848–849

1. When the Reichstag building was destroyed by fire in February 1933, Hitler blamed the Communists and suspended civil rights, declared censorship of the press, prohibited meetings of opposition writers and artists, and disrupted the work of other political parties.
2. Intimidated delegates of the Reichstag passed the Enabling Act the following March, which suspended the constitution for four years and allowed subsequent Nazi law to take effect without parliamentary approval.
3. The Nazis then began suppressing individual rights in the name of what they called a *Volksgemeinschaft* ("people's community") composed of like-minded, racially pure Germans ("Aryans," in Nazi terminology), and organizations with vast powers to arrest, execute, or imprison people in the newly built concentration camps.
4. The Nazis filled these camps with socialists, homosexuals, Jews, and other so-called non-Aryans.
5. Hitler, although he purged the party of those seeking a leveling of social privilege, continued his drastic reform of Germany via social and economic programs.
6. Needing to reduce the rate of unemployment, he stimulated the economy through government spending.
7. Hitler also announced a four-year plan in 1936, with the secret aim of preparing Germany for war by 1940.
8. Defense spending soared to 50 percent of Germany's budget but, although huge deficits were created, Hitler believed the spoils of future conquest would eliminate these.
9. Hitler also enacted legislation designed to increase the birthrate and reinforce traditional gender roles.
10. Censorship and social control through a system of informers characterized Nazi Germany.

D. Nazi Racism, pp. 849–852

1. The Nazis defined Jews as an "inferior" race and held them responsible for most of Germany's problems.
2. The 1935 Nuremberg Laws deprived Jews of citizenship, assigned "Jewishness" according to a person's ancestry, ended special consideration for Jewish war veterans, and prohibited marriage between Jews and other "Aryan" Germans.
3. Nazi doctors helped organize the T4 project, which used carbon monoxide and other means to exterminate large numbers of elderly and handicapped persons.
4. Jews were forced into slave labor and harshly discriminated against. By the outbreak of World War II in 1939, more than 50 percent of Germany's half a million Jews had emigrated, often leaving behind all their possessions and paying huge fees to the government for exit visas.

III. Democracies on the Defensive

A. Confronting the Economic Crisis, pp. 852–854

1. As the rate of unemployment in the United States rose to 15 million persons, Franklin Delano Roosevelt (FDR [1882–1945]), promising relief and recovery, defeated Herbert Hoover (1874–1964) in the 1932 presidential election.
2. Roosevelt pushed through legislation known as the "New Deal." It included relief for businesses and instructions for how firms could cooperate in stabilizing prices,

price supports for farmers, and public works projects.

3. The Social Security Act of 1935 established a fund for retirement, unemployment, and payments to mothers with dependent children and the disabled.
4. Roosevelt and his wife Eleanor were experts at using mass media to promote democratic values, and although the depression remained severe, the new programs and the media success kept most Americans committed to democracy.
5. Sweden likewise developed a coherent program for resolving economic and population problems.
6. Under Sweden's program, central planning of the economy and social welfare programs were instituted, and its currency was devalued to make exports appear more attractive to international buyers.
7. Sweden used pump-priming programs of public works to maintain consumer spending and encourage modernization. Support and subsidies for families built widespread approval for the welfare state.
8. Britain and France also sought ways to escape economic crisis.
9. Declining government revenue forced cuts in unemployment insurance payments in Britain. In 1933, the British government took effective steps: a massive program of slum clearance and new housing projects provided employment and infused money into the economy.
10. Shocked into action by the spread of fascism, French members of the Liberal, Socialist, and Communist parties rallied in support of democracy and established a coalition known as the Popular Front, which established Socialist leader Léon Blum (1872–1950) as premier.
11. Blum extended family subsidies, state services, and welfare benefits, and appointed women to his government.
12. In June 1936, the government of France guaranteed workers two weeks' paid vacations, a forty-hour work week, and the right to collective bargaining.
13. Blum's government was politically weak, and investors, bankers, and industrialists undermined his policies. The government fell when it failed to aid republican Spanish forces.
14. Fledging democracies in central Europe created by the Peace of Paris, including Austria, Hungary, and Czechoslovakia, were hard hit by the depression, which led to simmering ethnic tensions and an increase in the appeal of fascism.

B. Cultural Visions in Hard Times, pp. 854–856

1. Instead of turning away from public life, writers, filmmakers, and artists of the 1930s responded vigorously to the depression.
2. In 1931, French director René Clair's (1898–1981) *À nous la liberté* (Give Us Liberty) depicted prison life as an analogy to work on a factory assembly line.
3. Charlie Chaplin's film *Modern Times* (1936) showed his character, the Little Tramp, as a worker in a modern factory, his job so ingrained that he assumed everything he could see needed mechanical adjustment.
4. Women were portrayed alternately as the cause of or the cure for society's problems.
5. *The Blue Angel* (1930), a German film starring Marlene Dietrich (1901–1992), showed how a modern woman could destroy civilization.
6. In comedies and musicals, however, women pulled men out of debt and set things right, smiling all the while.
7. Art became increasingly politicized because some writers found it crucial to reaffirm their belief in Western values such as rationalism, rights, and concern for the poor.
8. German writer Thomas Mann (1875–1955) went into self-imposed exile when Hitler came to power and began a series of novels based on the Old Testament that commented on the struggle between humanist values and barbarism.
9. In her nonfiction work *Three Guineas* (1938), Virginia Woolf (1882–1941) also rejected experimental forms for a direct attack on militarism, poverty, and the oppression of women.
10. Scientists continued to point out limits to human understanding and turn away from the certainties that science and technology once boasted of.
11. In California, astronomer Edwin Hubble (1889–1953) determined, in the early 1930s, that the universe is an expanding entity.
12. German physicist Werner Heisenberg (1901–1976) developed the "uncertainty" or "indeterminacy" principle in physics.

13. Scientific observation of atomic behavior, according to this theory, actually disturbs the atom, thereby making precise formulations impossible.
14. The Swiss theologian Karl Barth (1886–1968) encouraged rebellion against the Nazis.
15. In his 1931 address to the world on social issues, Pope Pius XI (1922–1939) condemned the failure of modern societies to provide their citizens with a decent life and supported governmental intervention to create better moral and material conditions.

IV. The Road to Global War

A. A Surge in Global Imperialism, pp. 856–859

1. Global imperialism of the 1930s led to global war.
2. European Jews continued to go to Palestine and claim the area as theirs; pan-Arabism intensified; and Japan, Germany, and Italy entered into competition with other nations for land and resources.
3. Japan's military leaders dominated the young Emperor Hirohito and sought greater control of Asia and saw China, Russia, and other powers as obstacles to their empire's prosperity and the fulfillment of its racial destiny.
4. In September 1931, Japan invaded Manchuria and set up a puppet government.
5. The League of Nations formally condemned the invasion, but imposed no sanctions.
6. The condemnation nonetheless outraged the Japanese public and goaded the government into an alliance with Hitler and Mussolini.
7. In 1937, Japan again attacked China, justifying its offensive as the first step in a "new order" that would liberate East Asia from Western imperialism.
8. Hundreds of thousands of Chinese were massacred in the "Rape of Nanjing."
9. President Roosevelt immediately announced an embargo on the U.S. export of airplane parts to Japan and later enforced stringent economic sanctions on the crucial raw materials that drove Japanese industry.
10. However, the actions by Western powers and the Soviet Union did not effectively curtail Japan's territorial expansion in Asia and the Pacific.
11. Hitler's agenda included reestablishing control over the Rhineland, breaking free from the Versailles Treaty's military restrictions, and bringing Germans living in other nations into the Third Reich's orbit.
12. Superior "Aryans," Hitler believed, needed more Lebensraum ("living space") to thrive, space that would be taken from "inferior" Slavic peoples and Bolsheviks.
13. In 1935 Hitler rejected the Versailles Treaty and began rearming. In March 1936, Hitler ordered his troops into the demilitarized Rhineland.
14. Instead of countering with an invasion as they had in the Ruhr in 1923, the French protested to the League of Nations.
15. In 1935, Mussolini invaded Ethiopia, taking the capital, Addis Ababa, in the spring of 1936.
16. The League of Nations voted in favor of imposing sanctions against Italy, but British and French opposition to a serious oil embargo, kept the sanctions from having an affect.
17. The imposition of sanctions, notwithstanding, drove Mussolini into Hitler's camp.
18. Hitler and Mussolini formed a Rome-Berlin Axis, which appeared powerful next to the seemingly timid democracies of France and Great Britain.

B. The Spanish Civil War, 1936–1939, pp. 859–860

1. In what seemed like an exception to the trend toward authoritarian government, Spanish republicans overthrew their king in 1931.
2. Although the republicans hoped to modernize Spain's economy, they failed to build an effective political program or enact land redistribution, which would have won them popular endorsement and loyalty.
3. Antimonarchist forces included an array of competing and thus divided groups, whereas fascists, monarchists, large landowners, and clergy acted in unison and drew on their substantial, collective, financial resources.
4. In 1936, pro-republican forces temporarily banded together in a Popular Front coalition to win elections and to prevent the republic from collapsing under the weight of growing monarchist opposition.

5. The right-wingers, however, revolted under the leadership of General Francisco Franco (1892–1975).
6. This military uprising led to the Spanish Civil War, which pitted the republicans, or Loyalists, against the fascist Falangists and the authoritarian right.
7. The struggle became a rehearsal for World War II when Hitler and Mussolini sent military personnel in support of Franco and the right to test new weapons and to practice new tactics, particularly terror bombing civilians.
8. The Spanish republican government appealed everywhere for assistance, but only the Soviet Union answered.
9. Stalin sent troops and tanks, but withdrew in 1938 as the government's ranks floundered.
10. Despite the outpouring of popular support for the cause of democracy, Britain and France refused to send aid.
11. Instead, a few thousand volunteers from several countries fought for the republic.
12. Franco defeated the republicans in 1939 and established a dictatorship, generating thousands of refugees.

C. Hitler's Conquest of Central Europe, 1938–1939, pp. 860–861

1. In March 1938, Hitler ordered an invasion and annexed Austria.
2. This action, known as the Anschluss—a unification between Austria and Germany—was the first step in Germany's taking over the resources of Central and Eastern Europe.
3. Hitler next turned his focus toward Czechoslovakia.
4. His task was more difficult here because Czechoslovakia had a large army, formidable border defenses, and armament factories, and most Czechs were prepared to defend their country.
5. German propaganda accused Czechoslovakia of persecuting its German minority and demanded that it grant autonomy to the German-populated region of the Sudetenland.
6. British prime minister Neville Chamberlain (1869–1940), French premier Edouard Daladier (1884–1970), and Mussolini met with Hitler in Munich and agreed not to oppose Hitler's claim to the Sudetenland.
7. Appeasement, the strategy of preventing war by making concessions, was, at that time, perceived as a positive act.
8. Despite the decision taken at the conference, Hitler, in March 1939, invaded Czechoslovakia anyway.
9. In August, to the shock of many, Germany and the USSR signed a non-aggression pact with secret provisions to partition Poland and the Baltic States between them. Hitler prepared to attack Poland.

V. World War II, 1939–1945

A. The German Onslaught, pp. 862–863

1. Hitler's Blitzkrieg ("lightning war") tactics in which airplanes, tanks, and motorized infantry encircled defenders, assured Germans that the human cost of conquest would be light.
2. After successfully using this strategy first in Poland, then in Denmark and Norway, the Germans attacked Belgium, the Netherlands, and France in May and June 1940.
3. When the French surrendered on June 22, 1940, Germany ruled the northern half of the country.
4. The southern part was named Vichy France, after the spa town where the government sat, and the aged World War I hero Henri Philippe Pétain (1856–1951) was allowed to govern.
5. Stalin used the diversion of war in the west to annex the Baltic States and to seize Bessarabia and Bukovina from Romania.
6. Britain, now alone in its fight against Hitler's Germany, elected Winston Churchill (1874–1965) as prime minister.
7. In the battle of Britain, which the British called the Blitz, the German air force (Luftwaffe) bombed public buildings and monuments, harbors, weapons depots, military bases, and industry.
8. The British government poured its resources into antiaircraft weapons, its code-breaking group Ultra, and the development of radar.
9. By the fall of 1940, German air losses over England forced Hitler to abandon his plan for a naval invasion of that country.
10. In June 1941, Hitler began the invasion of the Soviet Union.
11. Although German troops quickly penetrated Soviet territory and inflicted immense casualties, they were slowed down by Hitler's insistence on attacking several regions simultaneously.

12. This strategy cost the Germans time because they got bogged down by the autumnal Soviet rains.
13. In the winter, the Soviets began to fight back, and Hitler's ill-supplied troops succumbed to weather and disease.

B. War Expands: The Pacific and Beyond, p. 864

1. With the outbreak of war in Europe, Japan took control of parts of the British Empire, bullied the Dutch in Indonesia, and invaded parts of Indochina to procure raw materials for industrial production.
2. In December 1941, Japanese launched airplanes from aircraft carriers and bombed American naval and air bases at Pearl Harbor in Hawaii, then decimated a fleet of U.S. airplanes based in the Philippines.
3. The U.S. Congress declared war on Japan.
4. By spring 1942, as the United States prepared to intervene actively in the war, Japan had conquered Guam, the Philippines, Malaya, Burma, Indonesia, Singapore, and much of the southwestern Pacific.
5. Hitler declared war on the United States, which was unprepared for war, and Mussolini followed suit.
6. Hitler's four enemies—Great Britain, the Free French, the Soviet Union, and the United States—came together in the Grand Alliance, and with a coalition that included twenty other countries, these Allies worked hard to subdue the Axis powers who were fanatically committed to global conquest.

C. The War against Civilians, pp. 864–866

1. Everyone was a target in World War II, and the war killed far more civilians than soldiers.
2. Both sides bombed cities to destroy the civilian will to survive; conversely, this tactic often seemed to inspire defiance.
3. As the German army moved through Eastern Europe, it slaughtered racial "inferiors," including Jews, Communists, and Slavs. Japanese forces behaved similarly in China and elsewhere, killing some thirty million in China alone.
4. In Poland, the SS (Hitler's elite military force) murdered nobility, clergy, and intellectuals, and transported hundreds of thousands of Polish citizens to forced labor camps.
5. The extermination of Jews during the war became a special mission of the Nazis.
6. As German troops gained control of much of Europe, vast numbers of Jews were confined to ghettoes, or massacred en masse.
7. In addition to the massacres, a bureaucratically organized and efficient technological system for rounding up Jews and sending them to extermination camps had taken shape by the fall of 1941.
8. Six camps in Poland were developed specifically for the singular purpose of mass murder.
9. About 60 percent of new arrivals—particularly children, women, and the elderly—were directly selected to be mass murdered in Nazi gas chambers.
10. The remaining 40 percent labored until they too were sent to their deaths.
11. Effective resistance was nearly impossible; starvation and disease weakened Jews in the ghettos and, because men and young women had emigrated, ghettos were more likely to be populated by middle-aged women and the elderly.
12. Resistance, as in the uprising at the Warsaw ghetto in 1943, meant certain death.
13. The Nazis went to great lengths to hide what they were doing in the extermination camps.
14. They had bands playing when the trains arrived at the camps, and sometimes gave people cheery postcards to send home.
15. Those not immediately killed in the camps experienced harsh conditions of forced labor, which killed most of the internees more slowly.
16. By the end of the war, six million Jews—the vast majority from eastern Europe—along with an estimated five–six million gypsies, homosexuals, Slavs, and others were murdered by the Nazis.

D. Societies at War, pp. 866–868

1. Even more than World War I, World War II depended on industrial productivity geared totally toward war and mass murder.
2. Neither Japan nor Germany took the resources and morale of its enemies into full account.
3. Allied governments were overwhelmingly successful in generating civilian participation, especially among women.

4. In the Axis, women followed the fascist doctrine of separate spheres, even though they were desperately needed in offices and factories.
5. In the Soviet Union, women constituted more than half the workforce by war's end.
6. Stalin encouraged a revival of Russian nationalism and religion.
7. Propaganda was used everywhere to boost morale. People were glued to their radios for war news; and films, monitored by governmental agencies, depicted aviation heroes, infantry men, and the working women and wives left behind.
8. Governments organized many aspects of ordinary life during the war, and mass mobilization and the standardization of many items contributed to the development of mass society in which people lived and thought in identical ways.
9. Anti-Semitic, anti-Slav, and anti-gypsy sentiment was a hallmark of Nazism, whereas Allied propaganda depicted Germans as sadists and perverts and Japanese as uncivilized, insect-like fanatics.

E. From Resistance to Allied Victory, pp. 868–873

1. The combined efforts of the military ultimately defeated the Axis powers, but civilian resistance in Nazi-occupied areas, such as the *maquis* in France also contributed to the Allied victory.
2. A major turning point came for the Allied forces in August 1942, when the German army began its siege of Stalingrad, a Russian city that would provide access to Soviet oil.
3. Stalin's successful defense of Stalingrad marked the beginning of the Soviet's drive westward.
4. Meanwhile, the British army in North Africa stood firm against the Germans in Egypt and Libya and, together with U.S. forces, invaded Morocco and Algeria in the autumn of 1942.
5. The Allies invaded North Africa and Europe and pounded German cities with strategic bombing to demoralize civilians and destroy the enemy's war industry.
6. On June 6, 1944, the combined Allied forces under the command of U.S. General Dwight D. Eisenhower (1890–1969) invaded the Normandy coast of France.
7. In late July, Allied forces broke through German defenses and, in August, helped liberate Paris, where rebellion had erupted against the occupiers.
8. British, Canadian, U.S., and other Allied forces then fought their way eastward to join the Soviets.
9. When the Soviet army entered and took the city of Berlin, Hitler and his wife, Eva Braun, committed suicide.
10. Germany surrendered on May 8, 1945.
11. The German surrender allowed the Allies to shift their focus on Japan.
12. Three years earlier, in May 1942, the U.S. forces had stopped the Japanese in the battle of the Coral Sea.
13. In battles at Midway Island and Guadalcanal later that year, the Allies turned the tide, destroying some of Japan's formidable naval power.
14. Japan had far less resources and manpower than the United States alone.
15. The Allies, at great personnel loss, took one Pacific island after another, but the Japanese refused to surrender.
16. Instead, they adopted *kamikaze* tactics, in which pilots deliberately crashed their planes into American ships, killing themselves in the process.
17. More than one hundred thousand scientists, technicians, and others were, meanwhile, developing the atomic bomb.
18. Fearing that defeating Japan might take too long, cost too many lives, and allow the Soviet Union the opportunity to seize territory in the East, the United States dropped atomic bombs on Hiroshima and Nagasaki on August 6 and 9, 1945.
19. One hundred forty thousand people were killed instantly; tens of thousands died later of burns and wounds.
20. On August 14, 1945, Japan surrendered.

F. An Uneasy Postwar Settlement, pp. 873–875

1. The Grand Alliance was composed of nations with vastly different political and economic systems and agendas, and wartime agreements reflected continuing differences concerning the shape of postwar Europe.
2. In 1941, Roosevelt and Churchill forged the Atlantic Charter, which condemned aggression, reaffirmed the idea of collective security, and endorsed the right of all peoples to choose their governments.
3. In October 1944, Churchill and Stalin planned the postwar distribution and occupation of territories.

4. In an agreement that went against Roosevelt's faith in collective security and threatened the principle of self-determination, Churchill and Stalin decided that the Soviets would control Romania and Bulgaria, while Britain would control Greece and, together, they would oversee Hungary and Yugoslavia.
5. Roosevelt, Churchill, and Stalin met in the Crimean town of Yalta in February 1945, where Roosevelt advocated the establishment of the United Nations, and supported Soviet influence in Korea, Manchuria, and the Sakhalin and Kurile islands in exchange for Stalin's promise of help against any future Japanese aggression.
6. At the final meeting in Potsdam, Germany, in the summer of 1945, the leaders of the Soviet Union and the Allied leaders agreed to give the Soviets control of eastern Poland, to cede a large stretch of eastern Germany to Poland, and to adopt a temporary four-way occupation of Germany that included France among the supervising nations.
7. The Second World War killed an estimated 100 million people and left fifty million refugees. It finished non-European deference toward the West and weakened democracy.
8. As victory unfolded, the Allies scrambled to outmaneuver each other in what became the Cold War.

Lecture Strategies

1. It is difficult to deal with the Great Depression in class, but the effort is worth making. The events of these years provide a good opportunity to demonstrate the growing interrelatedness of the global economy as well as to illustrate the potentially devastating consequences for individuals and societies of meltdowns in economic equilibrium. The fact that the Depression offered a fundamental (if varied) challenge to political leadership across national boundaries offers comparative opportunities, in terms of both the experiences of individuals and the decisions of governments and leaders. A few overviews that will help in framing the subject include Maury Klein's close study of the U.S. stock market and the Depression, *Rainbow's End: The Crash* (Oxford: Oxford University Press, 2001); Gilbert Ziebura, *World Economy and World Politics, 1924–1931*, trans. by Bruce Little (New York: St. Martin's Press, 1990); and Charles Kindleberger, *The World in Depression, 1929–1939* (Berkeley, CA: University of California Press, 1986).

2. The successes of the dictators of the interwar period offer rich subject matter for lectures. For Adolf Hitler and Nazi Germany, 1933 and 1934 are crucially important years. A review of Hitler's efforts to consolidate power, including the drama of the Night of the Long Knives, and end with the pageantry and propaganda of the Nuremberg Rally of 1934, could be based on the discussion in Chapter 9, "Hitler's Revolution," of Alan Bullock, *Hitler and Stalin: Parallel Lives* (New York: Random House, 1993). It should also consider Conan Fischer's *The Rise of the Nazis* (Manchester, UK: Manchester University Press, 2002, 2nd ed.). See also "Night of the Long Knives," in David Large's *Between Two Fires* (New York: W. W. Norton, 1991). At least a few scenes from Leni Riefenstahl's brilliant documentary *Triumph of the Will* (Embassy Home Entertainment, 1986) should be shown to demonstrate the Nazi Party's amalgam of youth, dynamism, power, and nationalism. This film also illustrates the early use of propaganda by the Nazi Party.

For Stalin, in addition to a class on the five-year plan or the purges, an interesting session might be based on Victoria E. Bonnell's *Iconography of Power: Soviet Political Posters under Lenin and Stalin* (Berkeley, CA: University of California Press, 1997), especially Chapter 3, "Peasant Women in Political Posters of the 1930s," and Chapter 4, "The Leader's Two Bodies: Iconography of the Vozhd." For example, plate 4 of *Iconography of Power*, "Every Collective Farm Peasant or Individual Farmer Now Has the Opportunity to Live Like a Human Being," offers a useful starting point for a discussion. The poster shows an electric light bulb; a phonograph; a happy, well-dressed peasant family; books by Maxim Gorky, Vladimir Lenin, and Stalin; and a poster with Stalin's silhouette superimposed on Lenin's silhouette. It is meant to portray how people will live in the new Soviet Union, while also subtly glorifying Stalin by association with Lenin and Gorky. Sheila Fitzpatrick, *Everyday Stalinism: Ordinary Life in Extraordinary Times: Soviet Russia in the 1930s* (New York and Oxford: Oxford University Press, 1999) details in chapters 3 and 4 the gap between the realities of Soviet life and the promise. A particularly interesting section of Chapter 3 discusses the Soviet government's attempts to find heroes: Stalin and also polar explorers, aviators, and "shockworkers" were made larger than life in order to inspire—and also divert—the masses. For deeper background, see David Priestland, *Stalinism and the Politics of Mobilization: Ideas, Power and Terror in Inter-War Russia* (Oxford: Oxford University Press, 2007).

3. One approach to talking about the dilemmas new democracies faced in the 1930s is to focus on Czechoslovakia. As an industrialized country with

a large urban population, Czechoslovakia maintained a functioning democracy when all other successor states in central Europe had resorted to dictatorships. The particular problems the Czechs faced in regard to the Sudetenland are worth exploring, and some sense of the ethnic geography of the country will help students understand why the likes of Chamberlain were reluctant to fight to maintain the country's territorial integrity. Joseph Rothschild offers a good discussion of Czech affairs in the 1930s in *East Central Europe between the Two World Wars* (Seattle: University of Washington Press, 1993).

4. Stalingrad is the site of the most important battle of the European Theater in World War II. The intensity and brutality of the long months of combat in the city were unmatched during the war. A major book on this battle is Anthony Beevor, *Stalingrad: The Fateful Siege, 1942–1943* (New York: Viking Penguin, 1998). A useful overview may be found in Gerhard L. Weinberg, *A World at Arms: A Global History of World War II* (Cambridge: Cambridge University Press, 1994). The German view of Stalingrad is vividly portrayed in *Stalingrad*, a film by Joseph Vilsmaier (Fox Lorber Home Video, 1986). Timothy W. Ryback, in "Stalingrad: Letters from the Dead," *The New Yorker* (February 1, 1993), provides another German perspective on Stalingrad based on letters by German soldiers describing conditions there. Finally, Donovan Webster, in Chapter 2 of *Aftermath: The Remnants of War* (New York: Pantheon Books, 1996), looks at recent efforts to identify and bury many thousands of nameless dead left without proper burial in the decades after the battle.

D-Day is, of course, more familiar to American students. Stephen E. Ambrose, *D-Day, June 6, 1944: The Climactic Battle of World War II* (New York: Simon & Schuster, 1994), based on fourteen hundred oral histories, is a useful source. See also Ambrose's comments on the television show *Booknotes* on the Web. Again, Weinberg's *A World at Arms* provides a dependable overview.

Class Discussion Starters

1. One way to engage students on the subject of the Depression is to ask them to compare the responses of two different countries. As the basis for a discussion, try using Chapter 5, "'Red Ellen' Wilkinson and the Jarrow Crusade: Great Britain in the Great Slump," in David Clay Large, *Between Two Fires: Europe's Path in the 1930s* (New York: W. W. Norton, 1991). This essay uses a dramatic event—a march on London by the unemployed citizens of Jarrow—to give an impression of how ordinary people experienced the Depression, before opening up the topic to include all who were affected throughout Great Britain.

France, because it is atypical of the Depression experience, also makes an interesting choice for discussion and should illustrate just how widespread the Depression was. Chapters 2 and 3 in Eugene Weber, *The Hollow Years: France in the 1930s* (New York: W. W. Norton, 1994), set the Depression in the context of the interwar economy. These chapters also provide a fascinating look at how people lived during this period. Another useful source would be Anthony Adamthwaite, *Grandeur and Misery: France's Bid for Power in Europe, 1914–1940* (New York: Arnold, 1995).

2. Most students will already be familiar with Anne Frank, and many will have read *The Diary of a Young Girl*. This autobiography can be used to build discussion; comparisons can be drawn between Anne Frank and Etty Hillesum, whose story opens the chapter. Their different yet related experiences make it possible to begin to present the Holocaust in a compelling way. Their experiences also raise questions about gender issues in the 1930s and 1940s, and the two stories will draw students' attention to the use of autobiography. Finally, the class might consider how Anne Frank's experiences can be used to support various perspectives on the Holocaust (in connection with this, see "New Sources, New Perspectives: Museums and Memory" [p. 867]).

In addition to Anne Frank, *The Diary of a Young Girl: The Definitive Edition* (New York: Doubleday, 1995), a great deal of useful material can be found in *The Diary of Anne Frank: The Critical Edition* (Garden City, NY: Doubleday, 1989). Also helpful are Ruud van der Rol and Rian Verhoeven, *Anne Frank: Beyond the Diary* (New York: Viking, 1993); Willy Lindwer, *The Last Seven Months of Anne Frank* (New York: Anchor Books, 1992); Hyman A. Enzer and Sandra Solotaroff-Enzer, eds., *Anne Frank: Reflections on Her Life and Legacy* (Champaign: University of Illinois Press, 1999); and the film *Anne Frank Remembered* (Columbia Tristar Home Video, 1996).

Etty Hillesum's diary and letters are conveniently bound together in *An Interrupted Life: The Diaries, 1941–1943 and Letters from Westerbork* (New York: Henry Holt, 1996). Rachel F. Brenner, *Writing As Resistance: Four Women Confronting the Holocaust: Edith Stein, Simone Weil, Anne Frank, Etty Hillesum* (University Park, PA: Pennsylvania State University Press, 1997); and Denise de Costa, *Anne Frank and Etty Hillesum: Inscribing Spirituality and Sexuality* (New Brunswick, NJ: Rutgers University Press, 1998) may also be helpful.

3. In conjunction with "Lecture Strategies," number 2, a class on the Munich Conference presents the possibility of a role-playing exercise. Using the chapter

in Large's *Between Two Fires* (see "Lecture Strategies," number 2), students could be assigned to role-play Hitler, Mussolini, Daladier, Chamberlain, Benes, and Stalin in a historical simulation. Other students could act as radio reporters and commentators. The idea would be to present the positions of the leaders and their countries and to explore contemporary reactions to events. Students should be cautioned against the temptation to use the hindsight they have looking back on events from the vantage point of the twenty-first century.

The Nazi-Soviet Pact is also a compelling and important event. First, the pact itself, the secret protocol, and a conversation held after the signing are all available on the Web site of The Avalon Project at the Yale Law School—a repository for a large number of documents connected with treaty-making. Bullock places the Nazi-Soviet Pact in its full diplomatic context and examines the motives of Stalin and Hitler in Chapter 14, "The Nazi-Soviet Pact," in *Hitler and Stalin* (see "Lecture Strategies," number 2). Robert C. Tucker places the pact in the context of Soviet history in the last two chapters of *Stalin in Power: The Revolution from Above, 1928–1941* (New York: W. W. Norton, 1990).

Reviewing the Text

Review Questions

1. How did the Great Depression affect society and politics?
[model answer] • ***Social relations and gender roles altered:*** *Unemployed men often had little to do with their time. Many took on the care of the household because their wives could find low-paying jobs working for the wealthy; others loitered in public places. Social discontent was fueled by both activities.*
• ***Politicians used crises to gain votes:*** *Politicians of all political persuasions forecast national collapse as a result of economic decline and falling birthrates. Politicians used nationalist, racist, and anti-Semitic platforms to appeal to the dissatisfied.*
• ***Colonial exploitation fueled rebellion:*** *The effects of the depression extended beyond the West, as the prices of imports were driven down. Colonial powers worsened the situation by insisting that taxes and loans be paid in full and by manipulating currency exchange rates in favor of their home country's currency. Imperialist nations had to confront both civil disobedience and outright revolt, but managed to maintain control.*
• ***Life was not uniformly bleak:*** *Despite the U.S. stock market crash and unemployment as high as 50 percent, modernization continued in some areas and those with jobs benefited from a drastic drop in prices. Some economies advanced despite the Depression.*

2. What role did violence play in the Soviet and Nazi regimes?
[model answer] • ***Soviet violence ensured political conformity and deflected blame away from the government:*** *Stalin used and encouraged violence against those who threatened the social and political order or resisted government demands, including former Bolsheviks, military leaders, prosperous peasants, and government bureaucrats and engineers who failed to achieve quotas. Millions were arrested and put on trial, sent to prison camps, or condemned to death without trial, officially or through public violence. Stalin created a climate of fear in which people were willing to denounce their neighbors or confess to crimes in hopes of avoiding danger.*
• ***The Nazis used violence to publicly display power and limit opposition:*** *Before the Nazi Party ever came to power, Hitler's followers took to the streets attacking Communists and Jews to show the ineffectuality of the parliamentary government. After being elected, Hitler used his storm troopers to publicly display the strength of the Nazi Party. After the Reichstag parliament was forced to agree to the suspension of the constitution, Hitler used violence within the party and against outsiders to reduce threats to his and the party's power.*

3. How did the democracies' responses to the twin challenges of economic depression and the rise of fascism differ from those of totalitarian regimes?
[model answer] • ***Democracy backed away from principles of limited interference in the marketplace:*** *In the United States, New Deal legislation ushered in and provided economic relief in what came to be called "the welfare state." Sweden went further in assisting mothers and large families in order to boost population. Economic reforms helped the poorest workers and the unemployed, those most likely to blame the government for their problems and turn to nondemocratic solutions.*
• ***Parties united in Popular Front:*** *In France, liberals, socialists, and communists came together to establish an antifascist coalition called the Popular Front, which created a government, made reforms that extended welfare benefits, protected working people's rights, and celebrated democracy. The elite did not approve of proworker reforms, however, and the movement eventually collapsed.*
• ***Political leaders used propaganda:*** *All successful politicians of the 1930s used mass media for propaganda. Unlike fascist leaders, the American president FDR used radio broadcasts and public speeches to sustain faith in democratic rights, popular government, and justice. Cultural leaders also produced films, novels, and art to celebrate freedom and oppose state-controlled expression. Many films and novels also portrayed "poor but happy" individuals not turning to fascism to solve their problems.*

4. How did the aggression of Japan, Germany, and Italy create the conditions for global war?

[model answer] • ***Western powers did nothing about imperialist expansion:*** *Japan, Germany, and Italy all believed that their nations deserved larger territories by virtue of their racial superiority. The League of Nations attempted to impose sanctions, but these drove Japan to greater opposition and proved economically unenforceable in the cases of Germany and Italy.*

• ***Appeasement was a reaction to World War I and the turbulent 1930s:*** *British and French leaders agreed not to oppose Germany's claims to the Sudetenland in order to avoid war. At the time, this policy was praised as a path to peace, but some historians have criticized it, saying it gave Hitler time to build his army and sent the wrong message, condoning further aggression. Other historians counter that appeasement actually gave Western powers time to build their own armies and prepare their citizens for war.*

• ***New alliances involved all of Europe:*** *Hitler and Mussolini forged first a "Rome-Berlin Axis" to control Europe and colonies abroad, and later signed the "Pact of Steel" to offer each other offensive and defensive support. The Pact of Steel was signed to counter a pledge made by Britain and France to provide military support to Poland, Romania, Greece, and Turkey in case of Nazi invasion.*

5. How and where was World War II fought and won, and what were its major consequences?

[model answer] • ***World War II was a global conflict, and combat occurred on land and sea across much of the world, particularly across Europe and North Africa, in China, and among the islands of the South Pacific:*** *Initial German and Italian offensives led to the conquest or annexations, in addition to Austria, Czechoslovakia, and Poland, of Denmark, Norway, France, Greece, Yugoslavia, much of the Soviet Union's European territory, and North Africa. Japanese offensives led to the conquest of much of Southern Asia, including Singapore, Burma, the Philippine Islands, and vast portions of China in Manchuria and beyond.*

• ***"Blitzkrieg," or lightning war, characterized military combat on land, and civilian populations were directly targeted by all sides as part of the total war effort aimed at breaking the enemy's will to resist:*** *Combat on land depended on coordinated attacks by tanks, aircraft, and motorized infantry to create and exploit "breaks" in enemy lines and encircle enemy forces. Civilian populations were targets for organized and systematic violence in many ways—through the use of death camps to control and shape the racial and ideological makeup of populations, and aerial bombing assaults designed to destroy industrial infrastructure and the will of populations to support the war effort. Forced civilian slave labor was widely practiced by the Germans.*

• ***German defeats from 1942–1944 were crucial in determining the outcome of the war in Europe:*** *The successful defense of Stalingrad in 1942–1943 and allied offensives in North Africa and Italy checked German expansion. Relentless Soviet pressure in the east and the Anglo-American invasion of Normandy in 1944 were critical in turning the tide against Hitler.*

• ***Military production was the key to victory:*** *The combined resources of the allied powers and the superior productive capacity of their industrial economies, resources, and willing workforces allowed the allied powers to eventually overwhelm and defeat Germany, Japan, and their allies. The major consequences of World War II included:*

• ***Postwar division of Europe and Germany:*** *Roosevelt, Churchill, and Stalin met repeatedly to divide control of nations formerly under Nazi control. Much of Eastern Europe was placed under control of the Soviet Union, while some small nations in Western Europe were placed under the oversight of Western nations. Allied leaders also agreed to a temporary four-way occupation of Germany. Despite these agreements, however, the Soviet Union and Allied powers were soon scrambling for more territory in a cold war.*

• ***Creation of the United Nations:*** *Roosevelt advocated the formation of the United Nations to replace the dysfunctional League of Nations as a global peace mechanism, hoping for collective security, self-determination, and open-door international trade.*

• ***Atomic weapons:*** *A U.S.-based international team of more than 100,000 scientists, technicians, and other workers had developed the atomic bomb as an offensive weapon to counter Japanese kamikaze tactics and end the war more quickly. In the hands of the United States and the Soviet Union, these new weapons figured prominently in threats of another war.*

Making Connections

1. Compare fascist ideas of the individual with the idea of individual rights that inspired the American and French revolutions.

[model answer] *Fascist nations promised a superior society based on unity and obedience rather than on the freedom and rights of the individual citizen. The duty of the individual was first and foremost to serve the needs of the state as the state directed, and the purpose and meaning of life could only be found within the state. These ideas were in sharp contrast to the American and French revolutions, where individual rights were considered to be so precious and inviolable that they were enshrined in key documents: the Declaration of Independence and the Declaration of the Rights of Man and Citizen. The citizen–government relationship was overseen by a social contract rooted in nature. When a government violates that contract through tyranny, citizens have a right to overthrow it. Such a concept would have been anathema to the fascists.*

2. What are the major differences between World War I and World War II?
[model answer] *World War I was a war of attrition, where defensive technologies and tactics were far more effective than offensive ones. In the west, in particular, armies used similar tactics and were similarly equipped for most of the war. Machine guns, long-range artillery, and a lack of mobility tended to produce static warfare and inconclusive battles with huge casualty figures. Germany had been secretly rearming for years before World War II and was in a much stronger military position than Britain or France at the beginning of the war. Technology, particularly tanks, and more effective tactical aircraft and Blitzkrieg tactics made maneuver and offensive warfare much more effective. And, whereas World War I had begun more or less accidentally with the assassination of Archduke Franz Ferdinand, Hitler had planned a European war since the early 1930s, and deliberately provoked Britain and France in 1939. Deliberate attacks on civilian population centers, strategic bombing, and genocidal treatment of Jews and others were also a marked feature of World War II.*

Discussing the Documents

Questions from Online Study Guide with Model Answers

A Family Copes with Unemployment, p. 842

1. How does the father seem to be coping with his circumstances?
[model answer] *The father is attempting to remain "useful" by repairing hopelessly worn-out shoes. The interviewer suggests that he answered questions "with embarrassment." He admits that the situation is getting worse and seems to be defeated by his circumstances.*

2. What indications are there that the family is ashamed of their condition?
[model answer] *The father answers the questions with "embarrassment." He expresses his frustration with the children's appearance, and the fact that the condition of their shoes makes them unable to function as respectable members of society. The mother is crying, and the family is unable to afford doctor or hospital visits for a sick child.*

The Greater East Asia Co-Prosperity Sphere, p. 858

1. What does this document reveal about Japan's ambitions?
[model answer] *This document shows that Japan had intended to occupy or "emancipate" Siberia, China, Indochina, Australia, the South Seas, and India. Japan also planned to eliminate any competing influences from the region and create a single state under totalitarian rule.*

2. How did the Japanese government portray itself and its goals?
[model answer] *The Japanese government portrayed itself as a liberator that would rescue the region from aggressive British, American, and Russian influences. It also viewed itself as bringing superior values to the region.*

Contrasting Views: Stalin and Hitler: For and Against, pp. 850–851

1. What are the positive qualities that supporters attribute to Hitler and Stalin?
[model answer] *Muller-Otfried sees Hitler as a "steel-hardened" leader for difficult times and a great source of hope. Children were encouraged to pray to him as a man sent by God and a provider of "daily bread." Russian patriotic poetry portrayed Stalin as a heroic creator and inspirer for all Soviet citizens, a "masterful" parent figure who would provide and help his people. Dramatist Afinogenov came to see Stalin doing the necessary work of cutting away all that would impede progress toward the perfect Communist state.*

2. What are the major criticisms of Hitler's and Stalin's opponents?
[model answer] *For Klemperer, Hitler was a self-righteous, agitated whiner, full of disorganized passion and false conviction. The poet Akhmotova saw Stalin's Russia as a joyless, dangerous place where "only the dead wore smiles." Even Afinogenov's positive portrayal of Stalin concedes that he is "merciless."*

3. To what do you attribute the different opinions about these dictators?
[model answer] *The readings emphasize how difficult times were, particularly in Germany. All the opinions shown reflect an understanding of how tough and demanding the dictators were. Some clearly worried that they sought to enslave the people, but others believed that the sacrifices and challenges would in the long run save the nation and its citizens. Some people saw the human and moral costs of these systems and their leaders as unreasonable and disastrous; for others, the need for hope was so strong that they embraced the leaders as saviors.*

New Sources, New Perspectives: Museums and Memory, p. 867

1. What is the difference between a historical textbook and a historical monument?
[model answer] *Monuments and memorials spring from the emotional and human need to remember. They have a relationship to human participation in and connection to specific historical events and places. They are, in that sense, meant to be emotional and evocative. Textbooks are meant to relate the facts of what happened, and are also meant to provide a broad, reasonable representation of the past in measured terms.*

2. Do you trust a history book more than you trust a museum? How do people compare and evaluate the presentation of the past in either one?
[model answer] *Both books and museums reflect interpretation and emphasize what their authors decide is important about the past, but museums seek to incorporate and express bias, memories, and political sensibilities about events in ways that textbooks, at least, often strive to transcend. Both sources are used by people to learn about the past, and with both the evidence they offer must be compared to other sources (particularly "primary sources" that add to our knowledge about how events were understood by those who experienced them) and evaluated to determine their fairness and accuracy. The emotional power of museum exhibitions in particular can be very valuable in helping to understand historical experiences, but the power of their vivid appeal must be assessed in conjunction with other sources.*

3. Why do museums and public exhibitions of art and artifacts arouse more debate than do history books?
[model answer] *The emotional and evocative power of museum exhibitions and their ability to make history feel more "real" or "come to life" often inspires debate, particularly when material is presented in a way that seems to at least some people to reflect bias of one sort or another on the part of the authors of the exhibit. Museum exhibits are representations of the past and of memory, and are often designed to be provocative or to suggest and "interpret" historical events in ways that some find to be manipulative or to lack objectivity.*

Other Questions for Discussing These Documents in Class

A Family Copes with Unemployment

1. How had the children in the family been affected by unemployment?
2. What emotional consequences seem to be connected to the family's difficult economic circumstances?

The Greater East Asia Co-Prosperity Sphere

1. How far was Japanese expansion going to reach, according to the document?
2. What was the preferred order in which the plans and goals would be accomplished? How central was war to the plan?

Contrasting Views: Stalin and Hitler: For and Against

1. In what way do views of both leaders see them as products of their times?
2. How are the leaders seen to be similar by both critics and supporters?

New Sources, New Perspectives: Museums and Memory

1. In what ways have the victims of Nazi atrocities and mass murder been remembered?
2. In what ways is memory "repackaged" according to the article, and why?

Comparative Questions

1. What evidence do these documents provide to indicate that these years were traumatic and transformative?
2. What motivation for popular support for the radical political action described in the second and fourth documents (radical state expansion; mass murder of undesirables) can be found in the first document?

For Users of *Sources of The Making of the West*

The following documents are available in Chapter 26 of the companion sourcebook by Katharine J. Lualdi, University of Southern Maine.

1. Socialist Nationalism: Joseph Goebbels, *Nazi Propaganda Pamphlet* (1930)
2. Seeking a Diplomatic Solution: Neville Chamberlain, *Speech on the Munich Crisis* (1938)
3. The Spanish Civil War: Isidora Dolores Ibárruri Gómez, *La Pasionaria's Farewell Address* (November 1, 1938)
4. Memories of the Holocaust: Sam Bankhalter and Hinda Kibort (1938–1945)
5. Atomic Catastrophe: Michihiko Hachiya, *Hiroshima Diary* (August 7, 1945)

Discussion Ideas for Sources of The Making of the West, *Chapter 26*

1. Contrast the tone of Goebbels with those of Gómez and Chamberlain. If both the speeches and the pamphlet are propaganda, how are they different? Ideas contained aside, which one is most effective and why?
2. What do the words and experiences of Bankhalter, Kibort, and Hachiya reveal about how humans experience such extreme circumstances? What do you learn from these documents about human nature?

Working with Visual Sources

For this exercise, please refer to Nazis on Parade on p. 838 of the textbook or view the image on the book companion site's Online Study Guide under the "Visual Activity" for Chapter 26.

Students viewing the image at the Online Study Guide are asked three questions about the image. The questions and model answers (not made available to students) are below. Project this image, available on the Instructor's Resources CD-ROM, in class or ask students to look at the image in their textbooks and answer the questions.

1. At first glance, what is happening in this picture? What might be the symbolic significance of these orderly troops?
[model answer] *The picture seems to show a military parade with crowds of people watching and Nazi flags flying. The Nazi troops, with their military bearing and uniforms, signify a restoration of Germany's military might—a historical reversal of fortunes because one of the great complaints of the Nazis and their supporters was that the German military had been betrayed following World War I. One of the promises the Nazis made was to restore order, and the troops certainly give the impression of order and masculine power.*

2. Why did the Nazis fly so many flags and include so many swastikas? Wouldn't one have been sufficient, or was there a message they were trying to send?
[model answer] *The endless flags, banners, and other insignia serve to place the Nazi icon anywhere one might look. The Nazis wanted to create a total reality, in which all aspects of each function would be controlled and defined by the Nazis. From whatever angle one observed this parade, one could not miss that this was a Nazi event.*

3. The Nazis retained power through coercion and fear. Do any aspects of this picture appear menacing to you? Might it have seemed menacing to a German citizen in 1933?
[model answer] *The towering Nazi eagle and the profusion of black flags and black uniforms seem to give this photo a menacing air. However, our hindsight of what occurred in Germany under the Nazis allows us to interpret this photo in a way that most German citizens in 1933 would not have. They would have seen the large crowd, the impressive decorations, and the strong military presence, and perhaps believed that Germany was on the road to recovery, and that politics could be effective and consequential.*

Mapping Exercises

Map Activity from OSG—Model Answers for Map Activity #2

For this activity, please refer to the Map 26.3: The Growth of Nazi Germany, 1933–1939 on p. 862. Students are asked these questions:

Why did Hitler need to enter into an agreement with the Soviet Union to continue his eastward expansion?
[model answer] *Hitler was conquering and annexing territories in the east, and was thus coming dangerously close to the Soviet Union. Only by signing an agreement with the Soviets could Hitler hope to continue his eastward expansion without provoking a war on Germany's eastern front during the initial phases of his expansion.*

Looking at the map of Germany as it was in 1933, and paying special attention to its shape, why do you think Hitler might have targeted the territories he did?
[model answer] *Germany in 1933 looked as if it has been carved up: it has a slice taken off its western border, a big hole cut out of its southeastern corner, and its northeastern corner is divided from the rest of the country. Issues of territorial integrity were certainly a motivation in Hitler's expansion plan. The larger Germany created by 1939 is a far more unified geographical entity, a nation well on its way to achieving Lebensraum ("living space") in Central Europe.*

Map 26.1: The Expansion of Japan, 1931–1941, p. 857

Which powers lost territory to Japan? Where did most of the expansion occur? How does the map relate to the "plan" for the "Greater East Asia Co-Prosperity Sphere" discussed in the chapter document on p. 858?

Map 26.2: The Spanish Civil War, 1936–1939, p. 860

Where were the "front lines" for this conflict? Does the map tell you anything about the nature of the Spanish Civil War?

Map 26.3: The Growth of Nazi Germany, 1933–1939, p. 862

Ask students to review the enlargement of Nazi Germany from 1935 to the start of World War II in September 1939. How were the territorial changes different, and which were easiest to justify? Which changes would the students consider the most important in causing World War II? Have them explain why.

Map 26.4: Concentration Camps and Extermination Sites in Europe, p. 865

Which concentration camps were specifically established as "death camps," that is, camps in which the systematic murder of Jews and others took place (Auschwitz-Birkenau, Belzec, Chelmno, Majdanek, Sobibor, and Treblinka)? Ask students to discuss the differences between death camps and other camps. What do they know about some of the other camps, such as Dachau, Buchenwald, or Ravensbrück?

Map 26.5: World War II in Europe and Africa, p. 869

To what extent was World War II an African conflict? Why was Africa strategically important to both sides? In what ways was African geography conducive to "modern" warfare?

Map 26.6: World War II in the Pacific, p. 872

Have the students focus on the distances involved in the Pacific Theatre of the war. What do they reveal about the nature of modern warfare? The growing military power of the United States?

Mapping the West: Europe at War's End, 1945, p. 876

Why was the human toll in the Soviet Union so great? Ask students to discuss the implications that Soviet losses may have had for the postwar period. What were the circumstances leading to high casualty figures in Poland and Yugoslavia? Why are civilian casualties so much higher than military casualties in Poland?

In-Class Assignments and Presentation Topics

1. Assign students selected passages from the diaries of Anne Frank and Etty Hillesum to read. Ask students to compare and contrast these passages, allowing for the differences in age, background, and experience between the two authors. Students might consider whether the writing of one author or the other is more powerful, more poignant, or bears a better witness to events. It may be helpful to use the selected passages as a basis for an in-class discussion before students write their essays. You will have to be careful, however, to avoid giving the impression that you favor one approach to the material.

2. Divide the class into several groups and assign each group a country to investigate its experiences during the period from 1929 to 1939. Each of these investigations should result in a timeline, capsule biographies of major figures, and a summary of major events. It should directly address the severity of the Depression, responses to it, and what happened in this country in the period before World War II as sides were drawn up. Within a particular group, each student should have a definite assignment to fulfill as his or her contribution to the group effort. Each student should also write a brief essay on how the group worked together and his or her role within the group. The group should jointly present a report to the entire class when finished with their individual research and write-ups. Students might wish to use a series of images and comments in the tradition of *Let Us Now Praise Famous Men: Three Tenant Families* by James Agee and Walker Evans (Boston: Houghton Mifflin, 1980), first published in 1941. Or, students could write and present a series of radio news broadcasts, as they would have been broadcast in the 1930s. The chapter bibliography offers a number of books that may also be used as starting points. Rondo Cameron, *A Concise Economic History of the World: From Paleolithic Times to the Present* (New York: Oxford University Press, 1989), presents an overview of the Depression that you may wish to assign as background reading, and it also contains an extensive bibliography.

3. Sometimes counterfactual history can be instructive. Ask students to imagine that the Munich Conference never took place and, instead, war broke out in the fall of 1938. What do they think the outcome would have been in this case? Would, for example, determined resistance by the Czech army have caused the German generals to lose their nerve and stage a coup against Hitler? What does the historical evidence they are aware of indicate might have happened? Would the Soviet Union and France have come to the aid of Czechoslovakia? What would Great Britain or the United States have done? Ask students to describe what they conjecture would have happened from the fall of 1938 to the fall of 1939 and to provide evidence for the plausibility of their scenarios. You may wish to assign "'Peace for Our Time': Appeasement and the Munich Conference," in David Clay Large, *Between Two Fires: Europe's Path in the 1930s* (New York: W. W. Norton, 1991), as background reading.

4. Was Stalingrad the single most important battle in World War II? Ask students to respond to this question in an essay; the essay should not be a retelling of the story of Stalingrad. Students may summarize the major aspects of the battle, but their essays should focus on analyses of the battle's outcome that either support or refute the proposition that it was the most important battle in World War II. Students may wish to compare the battle of Stalingrad to another battle—the D-Day invasion, for example, or the Battle of Midway—as a way of supporting their positions. Call students' attention to Gerhard Weinberg's *A World at Arms*, cited in "Lecture Strategies," number 4, as a good source for information.

Essay Questions

1. Investigating what life was like in the Soviet Union or Nazi Germany in the 1930s is an obvious, although unwieldy, research assignment. Because it is such a big subject, students should be encouraged to focus on a particular group, such as peasants in the Soviet Union, German Jews in Nazi Germany, or factory workers or women in either country. Require students to read primary sources (you may wish to set a minimum number of pages) as well as the better

secondary sources. Alan Bullock, *Hitler and Stalin: Parallel Lives* (New York: Random House, 1993) is a good place to start. For the Soviet Union, a good introduction is Lewis Siegelbaum's essay "Building Stalinism, 1929–1941," in Gregory L. Freeze, ed., Russia: *A History* (Oxford: Oxford University Press, 1997). Sheila Fitzpatrick, *Everyday Stalinism: Ordinary Life in Extraordinary Times, Soviet Russia in the 1930s* (Oxford: Oxford University Press, 1999), is filled with information. For Nazi Germany, a good overview is "The Brown Revolution: National Socialism, 1933–1939," in Holger H. Herwig, *Hammer or Anvil?: Modern Germany, 1648–Present* (Lexington, MA: D. C. Heath, 1994). See also Detlev Peukert, *Inside Nazi Germany: Conformity, Opposition, and Racism in Everyday Life* (New Haven, CT: Yale University Press, 1987).

2. The wealth of material available on the Holocaust offers many possibilities for research projects. Students may wish to use the essays in Raul Hilberg, *Perpetrators, Victims, Bystanders: The Jewish Catastrophe, 1933–1945* (New York: HarperCollins, 1992), as a beginning point. Another book that would be useful for this purpose is Michael R. Marrus, *The Holocaust in History* (Hanover, NH: University Press of New England, 1987). Marrus's bibliography, now a little dated, is nonetheless useful. Students should also be encouraged to investigate the Holocaust Museum Web site listed in the chapter bibliography. Abundant memoir and documentary materials are also available once students have selected specific topics. Students may also wish to research resistance to the Holocaust. Many fact-based films document collective and individual acts of heroism in this regard: *The Scarlet and the Black* (1983), *The Assisi Underground* (1984), *Escape from Sobibor* (1987), *Schindler's List* (1993), and *The Pianist* (2002), to name but a few. Additionally, students can look at the career of Raoul Wallenberg, a Swedish diplomat who lived in Hungary and who is credited with saving as many as one hundred thousand Hungarian Jews before his disappearance. Or, students can read Edith H. Beer, *The Nazi Officer's Wife: How One Jewish Woman Survived the Holocaust* (New York: HarperCollins, 2000).

Additional Resources: Literature

Frank and Pressler, eds., Massotty, trans., *Anne Frank, The Diary of a Young Girl: The Definitive Edition*. 1995.

Hersley, John, ed., *Hiroshima*. 1946.

Keeley, Edmund, and Philip Sherrard, trans., *Seferis: Collected Poems*. 1995.

Lyell, William, trans., *Diary of a Madman and Other Stories by Lu Xun*. 1990.

Orwell, George, *1984*. 1949.

Orwell, George, *Down and Out in Paris and London*. 1933.

Pomerans, Arnold J., trans., *Etty Hillesum: An Interrupted Life*. 1983.

Steinbeck, John, *Grapes of Wrath*. 1939.

Thomas, D. M., trans., *Anna Akhmatova: Selected Poems*. 1992.

Ward, Matthew, trans., *Albert Camus: The Stranger*. 1988.

Wiesel, Elie, *Night*. 2001.

Additional Resources: Film and Video

Olympia (1938; VHS, 2 hrs., 40 min.). German filmmaker Leni Riefenstahl was commissioned by the German government to make this film about the 1936 Berlin Olympics. It glorified German athletes and was used by the government for propaganda purposes.

The World at War (1974; VHS/DVD, 26 hrs.). This multipart series is an expansive examination of World War II and includes rare film footage and interviews with soldiers, housewives, and Holocaust survivors.

The Holocaust (1978). This award-winning miniseries, first televised in 1978, follows two German families between 1935 and 1945. The Jewish family struggles simply to survive, while a member of the non-Jewish family rises in the Nazi regime. This series revitalized Holocaust studies, brought discussion about the Holocaust into the mainstream media, and inspired other important films on the subject.

The Jewel in the Crown (1984; VHS/DVD, 12 hrs., 30 min.). An adaptation of Paul Scott's *The Raj Quartet*, this series follows the lives of the Layton family and their connections who are touched in varying ways by India's struggle for independence during and immediately following World War II.

Good Evening, Mr. Wallenberg (1990; VHS/DVD, 1 hr., 55 min.). Excellent dramatic retelling of the true story of Swedish diplomat Raoul Wallenberg who saved thousands of Hungarian Jews during World War II, only to disappear into the hands of the Soviets who invaded Hungary at the end of the war. The film is in Swedish with English subtitles.

The Complete Churchill (1991; VHS, 6 hrs., 40 min.). Martin Gilbert is considered by many to be the definitive biographer of Winston Churchill. In this multipart series, Gilbert examines Churchill's life using archival footage, new documentary material, and interviews with individuals who knew the prime minister.

The Eye of Vichy (1993; VHS/DVD, 1 hr., 50 min.). Claude Chabrol's film consists of official newsreel footage shot during the German occupation of

France. This material, shown in France between 1940 and 1944, is a sobering look at Nazi manipulation of propaganda and the power of mass media.

The Wannsee Conference (1984; VHS, 1 hr., 27 min.). A chilling dramatization of the 1942 meeting held by leading Nazi officials at Wannsee to determine a plan to exterminate the Jews. Based on notes of the meeting, the dramatization unsettlingly runs about as long as the original meeting.

The Final Solution (1999; VHS, 3 hrs., 28 min.). This multipart series is an examination of Hitler's systematic extermination of the Jews through the use of period film and firsthand accounts.

Charlotte Gray (2001; VHS/DVD, approx. 1 hr.). Cate Blanchett stars in this film about the French resistance during World War II. The film well captures the danger that resistance fighters faced during the war.

World War II in Color: The British Story (2001; VHS/DVD, 3 hrs.). Archival film story of Britain and World War II in recently restored color footage.

1940s House (2003; VHS/DVD, 3 hrs.). In this series, a contemporary English family finds out firsthand what life was like during World War II. Although slightly voyeuristic, this series highlights in an immediate way what life was like during the war as the family copes with the rationing of food and clothing, mock air raids in the middle of the night, and women entering the workforce.

Bonhoeffer (2003; DVD, 1 hr., 30 min.). Archival material, on-location shooting, and interviews with individuals who knew him help tell the story of Dietrich Bonhoeffer, a Protestant theologian who openly criticized Hitler and the Nazi regime and participated in a plot to assassinate the Führer.

Cambridge Spies (2003; DVD, 4 hrs.). This short but excellent series focuses on Guy Burgess, Anthony Blunt, Kim Philby, and Donald Maclean, all Cambridge students in the 1930s who became double agents, spying for the Soviet Union. In time, they rose to the highest levels of the English establishment.

The Gathering Storm (2002; DVD approx. 3 hrs.). This film focuses on the relationship between Winston Churchill and his wife Clementine during the 1930s when Churchill was out of office and warning all who would listen about a coming war with Germany.

Foyle's War, Series I and II (2003, 2004; VHS/DVD, approx. 3 hrs. each episode). The Foyle's War series are detective stories set during World War II. Although the stories are fiction, the production staff has been careful to correctly show the costuming and setting and to weave details about everyday life during the war years seamlessly into the narrative. The episodes are self-contained.

Films and World War II

Many of the films made during the 1930s and World War II years were, to some extent, propaganda pieces, and their use in the classroom can add an interesting dimension to any study of this period. Students can be asked to research films of this period and perhaps select one for individual review. The following lists some of the better-known films.

The Great Dictator (1940; VHS/DVD, 2 hrs.). A Jewish barber in World War I saves a German officer and, when their paths cross again twenty years later, the officer tries to protect his old friend in the face of a Hitleresque dictator and a repressive government. This is a scathing satire of Hitler and the Nazi regime.

In Which We Serve (1942; DVD, 1 hr., 54 min.). This semibiographical account of Lord Louis Mountbatten describes his experiences aboard the HMS *Kelly*, which was torpedoed by the Germans. The film emphasizes courage, teamwork, and resilience in the face of wartime hardship.

Mrs. Miniver (1942; DVD, 2 hrs., 13 min.). Mrs. Miniver is an upper-middle-class English housewife who bravely looks after her family during World War II. Her husband and his small boat are used to help evacuate Dunkirk, her son becomes an RAF pilot, her daughter-in-law (a civilian) is killed in an air raid, and the community where she resides comes to terms with their wartime losses. In terms of propaganda, Winston Churchill reputedly said this film was worth a dozen battleships.

Casablanca (1942; VHS/DVD, 1 hr., 42 min.). Humphrey Bogart plays an American expatriate nightclub owner who struggles with a decision to help an old flame, Ingrid Bergman, and her husband as the Germans solidify their control over this Moroccan outpost.

The Fighting Seabees (1944; DVD, 1 hr., 40 min.). This film highlights a civilian construction company that is drafted into the Navy to help form the U.S. Navy's Construction Battalions (CB). The CBs (Seabees) built, among other things, runways in inhospitable territory for U.S. fighter planes.

The Fighting Sullivans (1944; VHS/DVD, 1 hr., 51 min.). This is the true story of five brothers who served on the same ship in the Pacific theater and who died together when their vessel was sunk. Although the film concentrates on the brothers' transition from boys into men, audiences were shocked by the tragedy, and a law was subsequently passed disallowing brothers from serving on the same ship.

The Story of G. I. Joe (1945; VHS/DVD, 1 hr., 45 min.). This film is based on the columns of wartime correspondent Ernie Pyle who reported home on the experiences of everyday soldiers. Infantrymen who fought in the war thought the film was remarkably accurate in its depictions of soldiers' lives.

Why We Fight (2000; VHS/DVD, 6 hrs., 55 min.). Originally produced as a seven-part motion picture by Frank Capra in the United States between 1942 and 1945, in conjunction with the Army Signal Corps, this film is well worth looking at to see how the war was presented to Americans.

Many more films about World War II were made after the war. Some were highly critical of certain aspects of the war; some waxed nostalgic, clearly embracing the camaraderie and patriotism of the period; and some merely used the war as a backdrop for comedy pieces. Again, students can be asked to research post–World War II films and perhaps select one for viewing. The following lists a few of the better-known films.

The Best Years of Our Lives (1946; VHS/DVD, 2 hrs., 52 min.). This film focuses on the difficult readjustments to family and civilian life made by three servicemen returning from the war.

Twelve O'Clock High (1949; VHS/DVD, 2 hrs., 12 min.). This film is about the mental and emotional stresses faced by air force fighter pilots during World War II.

Judgment at Nuremberg (1961; VHS/DVD, 1 hr., 58 min.). This fictional drama about Germans on trial for war crimes harkens back to the war crimes trials of 1948.

In Harm's Way (1965; VHS/DVD, 2 hrs., 47 min.). This realistic film is about the war in the Pacific. It captures the tensions that existed between military commanders, the difficulties facing women who served as nurses, and the sheer horror and destruction of World War II naval battles.

Patton (1970; VHS/DVD, 2 hrs., 51 min.). This biographical film concentrates on the career of General George Patton between the years 1943 and 1945.

Das Boot (1981; VHS/DVD, 1 hr., 25 min.). This film is based on Lothar-Günther Buchheim's autobiographical novel about his wartime experiences. The film focuses on a German U-boat and its crew as it seeks out, and hides from, the enemy. The film is in German with English subtitles.

Schindler's List (1993; DVD, 3 hrs., 16 min.). Based on the true story of Oskar Schindler, who, during World War II, personally saved more than one thousand Jews from certain death. This film is a chillingly accurate look at how the Jews were maltreated by the Nazis.

Stalingrad (1993; VHS/DVD, 2 hrs., 18 min.). This film follows the nightmarish experiences of German soldiers in this battle. It presents very much a "grunt's-eye" view of the war.

Saving Private Ryan (1998; VHS/DVD, 2 hrs., 50 min.). A combat unit is sent from the D-Day beaches to seek out Private Ryan who is behind enemy lines. Ryan's three brothers have already been killed, and the U.S. government wants to ensure his safe return. The film is notable for its realistic depiction of the carnage of war.

Band of Brothers (2001; VHS/DVD, 11 hrs., 45 min. [including additional features]). This ten-part miniseries, based on Stephen Ambrose's novel of the same name, focuses on the real-life soldiers of Easy Company, an elite paratrooper unit of the First Airborne division. The series follows the unit from basic training to the end of the World War II.

Enemy at the Gates (2001; VHS/DVD, 2 hrs., 11 min.). This film presents a gritty and at times gripping take on the fighting at Stalingrad, from a Soviet perspective.

OTHER BEDFORD/ST. MARTIN'S RESOURCES FOR CHAPTER 26

The following resources are available to accompany Chapter 26. Please refer to the Preface of this manual for detailed descriptions of all the ancillaries.

For Instructors

Transparencies

The following maps and images from Chapter 26 are available as full-color acetates.

- Map 26.1: The Expansion of Japan, 1931–1941
- Map 26.2: The Spanish Civil War, 1936–1939
- Map 26.3: The Growth of Nazi Germany, 1933–1939
- Map 26.4: Concentration Camps and Extermination Sites in Europe
- Map 26.5: World War II in Europe and Africa
- Map 26.6: World War II in the Pacific
- Mapping the West: Europe at War's End, 1945
- Unemployed in Germany (1932), p. 841
- N. J. Altman, *Anna Akhmatova*, p. 851

Instructor's Resources CD-ROM

The following maps and image from Chapter 26, as well as a chapter outline, are available on disc in both PowerPoint and jpeg formats.

- Map 26.1: The Expansion of Japan, 1931–1941
- Map 26.2: The Spanish Civil War, 1936–1939

- Map 26.3: The Growth of Nazi Germany, 1933–1939
- Map 26.4: Concentration Camps and Extermination Sites in Europe
- Map 26.5: World War II in Europe and Africa
- Map 26.6: World War II in the Pacific
- Mapping the West: Europe at War's End, 1945
- Nazis on Parade (chapter image, p. 838)

Using the Bedford Series with The Making of the West

Available in print as well as online at **bedfordstmartins.com/usingseries,** this guide offers practical suggestions for using Timothy Cheek, *Mao Zedong and China's Revolutions,* and *Pearl Harbor and the Coming of the Pacific War: A Brief History with Documents and Essays* by Akira Iriye, in conjunction with Chapters 26 and 27 of the textbook.

For Students

Study Guides

The Online Study Guide at **bedfordstmartins.com/hunt** helps students synthesize the material they have learned as well as practice the skills historians use to make sense of the past. The following Map, Visual, and Document activities are available for Chapter 26.

Map Activity

- Map 26.3: The Growth of Nazi Germany, 1933–1939

Visual Activity

- Nazis on Parade, p. 838

Reading Historical Documents

- A Family Copes with Unemployment, p. 842
- Contrasting Views: Stalin and Hitler: For and Against, pp. 850–851
- New Sources, New Perspectives: Museums and Memory, p. 867
- The Greater East Asia Co-Prosperity Sphere, p. 858

CHAPTER

27

The Cold War and the Remaking of Europe

c. 1945–1965

CHAPTER RESOURCES

Main Chapter Topics

1. After World War II, Europe, in essence, surrendered global leadership to the United States and the Soviet Union. These two superpowers divided Europe between them, the Soviet Union imposing Communist rule in the East and the United States exercising a powerful if somewhat benign influence in the West.

2. The breakdown of the agreement that was reached at Yalta and Potsdam led to a divided Germany (and Europe) and to the creation of two large military blocs. Mutual mistrust and the determination to protect perceived interests contributed to the growing tensions. The Marshall Plan and the Berlin Airlift were peaceful measures, but they still communicated resolve on the part of the United States not to allow further Soviet expansion into Western Europe.

3. Collective security agreements such as NATO (North Atlantic Treaty Organization) in the west and the Warsaw Pact in the east characterized the Cold War world. Western European countries created the European Economic Community (EEC) or Common Market, which was part of a highly productive postwar economy. The United Nations offered a framework for collective global security and development. Eastern European countries endured repressive political systems; they could industrialize their economies, but they could not match the productivity or prosperity occurring in the West.

4. Colonized peoples expected independence because of their service in the war and because they were certain Western values should apply to them. Frequently disappointed by the powers bent on retaining their empires, colonials willingly used violence to obtain their liberation.

5. Growing affluence and Americanization contrasted with the horrors of the Holocaust and the menace of the cold war in shaping European culture.

6. The cold war came closest to becoming a nuclear war in the confrontation between the United States and the Soviet Union over nuclear Soviet missiles based in Cuba in October 1962. Thereafter, the two powers avoided direct confrontation, while still continuing the cold war.

Focus Question

How did the cold war shape the politics, economy, social life, and culture of post–World War II Europe?

1. The cold war was the dominant political reality of the postwar world in Europe. The division of Europe (and even nations such as Germany) reflected the ideological split between the political and social systems of east and west. The Berlin Wall stood as a physical reminder of the divided nature of postwar Europe. Aid from the United States, as well the desire to form a united front against communism and ensure continued economic recovery and prosperity, led to the development of shared pan-European organizations and institutions in the west, most notably the European Community.

2. Atomic rivalries and threat of war colored social and cultural life. Film and other art forms often reflected or commented on the rivalry between the communist bloc and Western Europe and the United States. Prosperity in the west brought with it consumerism. The political and economic realities of the post-war world led to European decolonization, but ironically prosperity in the west attracted millions of non-western immigrants and migrant workers to Europe, and in the long run contributed to diversity and social transformation.

Annotated Chapter Outline

I. **World Politics Transformed**

A. **Chaos in Europe, pp. 881–883**

1. In contrast to World War I, armies in World War II fought a war that leveled thousands of square miles of territory, leaving cities in shambles and millions of people suffering.
2. People were so exhausted by the struggle for bare survival that, unlike after World War I, there were no uprisings.
3. The tens of millions of refugees suffered the most.
4. Many had been inmates of prisons and death camps; others, especially ethnic Germans, had fled westward to escape the Soviet Red Army as it pushed toward Berlin.
5. Survivors of the concentration camps continued to suffer after the war.
6. Many had no home to return to because property had been confiscated and entire communities destroyed. Anti-Semitism continued in Europe.
7. Many Jews eventually went to Palestine.

B. **New Superpowers: The United States and the Soviet Union, p. 883**

1. Only two powerful countries remained in 1945: the United States and the Soviet Union.
2. The United States was now the richest country in the world, and a confident mood swept throughout the country.
3. A wave of suburban housing developments and high consumer spending kept the economy buoyant.
4. Population soared with the "baby boom" that lasted from the late 1940s to the early 1960s.
5. In a departure from U.S. isolationist attitudes before the war, increasingly internationalized Americans embraced their country's position as a global leader.
6. The Soviets also came out of the war with a sense of accomplishment, and, after their sacrifices in the war, expected equality in decision making with the United States rather than the imposed international isolation of the prewar period.
7. Citizens of the USSR expected hardship to end because they believed that the defeat of Hitler proved that goals concerning industrialization and defense had been met.
8. Stalin, however, increased repression in order to increase his control; mobilization for total war had encouraged individual responsibility while relaxing Communist oversight.
9. Stalin announced a new five-year plan (1946) that set increased production goals and mandated stricter collectivization of agriculture.
10. To increase the birthrate, Stalin intensified propaganda emphasizing that working women should also fulfill their true nature by having many children.
11. Soviet citizens were taught that enemies threatened the state. Jews in particular were targeted in a growing atmosphere of fear.

C. **Origins of the Cold War, pp. 883–886**

1. Because no peace treaty officially ended the conflict with Germany, the origins of the cold war remain a matter of debate.
2. After the war, Churchill sought to limit Soviet expansion and maintain Britain's imperial power. Truman was tougher on the Soviets than Roosevelt, and cut off aid to them as soon as the war ended.
3. Stalin wanted a buffer zone of friendly states to prevent what he perceived as aggression from Western Europe.
4. To create this buffer zone, the USSR repressed democratic government in Central and Eastern Europe between 1945 and 1948, imposing Communist rule in Bulgaria, Romania, Hungary, Czechoslovakia, and Poland.
5. As Western leaders witnessed the Soviets intervening in Eastern Europe, they worried about further Communist expansion.
6. In March 1947, Truman reacted to the threat by announcing economic and military aid to regions threatened by communism, a policy that came to be known as the Truman Doctrine.
7. Citing the deterioration of economic exchange during World War II as a threat to political stability, the United States also announced the Marshall Plan, a program of massive economic aid to Europe, under which the United States sent more than $12 billion in food, equipment, and services to Europe by the early 1950s.
8. Stalin considered the Marshall Plan a political ploy that found him unable to supply similar economic aid to Eastern

Europe, and his reaction was to suppress the remaining democracies in Central and Eastern Europe.

9. The only exception to the imposition of Soviet control came in Yugoslavia, ruled by the Communist leader Tito (Josip Broz, 1892–1980).
10. Tito wished to see Yugoslavia develop industrially independent of the Soviet Union.
11. Under Tito's strong leadership, the various ethnic groups that made up Yugoslavia's federation of six republics and two independent provinces remained at peace.

D. The Division of Germany, pp. 886–888

1. The agreements reached at Yalta provided for Germany's occupation by troops divided into four zones, each of which was controlled by one of the four principal victors of the war: the United States, the Soviet Union, Great Britain, and France.
2. American leaders hoped for economic coordination among the four zones that would benefit the occupying countries and also support Germany, whereas the Soviets planned to use the economic output of their zone to help repair the Soviet economy.
3. Amidst these tensions, the three Western allies agreed to merge their zones into a West German state instead of continuing to curtail German power as wartime agreements had stated.
4. The United States began an economic buildup under the Marshall Plan to make the western zone a buffer against the Soviets.
5. Stalin struck back at the Marshall Plan on July 24, 1948, when Soviet troops blockaded Germany's capital, Berlin.
6. Although the city was deep in Soviet territory, it too had been divided into four occupation zones.
7. The Soviets refused to allow vehicles from the west to travel through their zone.
8. The United States responded by air shipping millions of tons of provisions to Berlin during the winter of 1948–1949, an operation known as the Berlin airlift.
9. With this crisis, many Westerners began to view the conflict as a moral crusade.
10. By the time the Soviet blockade ended (May 12, 1949), a divided Berlin had become the symbol of the cold war; this conflict created competing military alliances.
11. The United States, Canada, and their European allies formed the North Atlantic Treaty Organization (NATO).
12. The Soviet Union in turn established a military organization known as the Warsaw Pact, which included Albania, Bulgaria, Czechoslovakia, East Germany, Hungary, Poland, and Romania.

II. Political and Economic Recovery in Europe

A. Dealing with Nazism, pp. 888–889

1. Confusion reigned in May 1945, because Europeans were living under a complex system of political jurisdictions that included those of local resistance leaders, Allied armies of the occupation, international relief workers, and the remnants of bureaucracies.
2. Occupying armies often operated independent of any law.
3. While some helped by distributing food and clothing, others—particularly the Soviet army—raped and robbed.
4. With the discovery of the death camps, desire for revenge against the Nazis grew.
5. Civilians perpetrated vigilante justice, shaving the heads of women suspected of collaborating or associating with Germans and making them parade naked through the streets.
6. Members of the resistance conducted on-the-spot executions of tens of thousands of Nazi officers and collaborators.
7. Governmental officials and Allied representatives undertook a more systematic "denazification."
8. In the trials conducted at Nuremberg, Germany (fall of 1945), the Allies used Nazi documents to provide a horrifying image of Nazi crimes.
9. Nuremberg established the precedent of international war crimes trials for crimes against humanity.
10. As hardship continued in Germany, the Germans began to believe that they were the main victims of the war.
11. Allied officials themselves often relied on high-ranking fascists and Nazis whose expertise was necessary for restoring governmental services, and many Nazi bureaucrats kept their jobs in the new West Germany to help wage the cold war more effectively.

B. Rebirth of the West, pp. 889–893

1. Resistance leaders had the first claim to offices in post-fascist Western Europe.
2. The French approved a constitution in 1946 that established the Fourth Republic and finally granted women the vote.
3. Italy replaced its constitutional monarchy with a full parliamentary system that allowed women the vote for the first time as well.
4. Throughout Western Europe, although Christian Democratic parties with leaders from the former resistance were influential, the Communist Party also attracted the vocal loyalty of a consistently large sector of the population.
5. People still remembered the common man's plight in the 1930s, and the Communists advocated his welfare most forcefully.
6. In flourishing West Germany, however, communism had no appeal.
7. In 1949, centrist politicians helped create a new state: the German Federal Republic.
8. Its first chancellor was Catholic, anti-Communist Konrad Adenauer (1876–1967).
9. In the United States, democracy and individual freedom were threatened after the war.
10. In 1949, fear caused by the detonation of a Soviet-built atomic bomb and a Communist revolution in China brought to the fore Joseph McCarthy (1908–1957), a senator from Wisconsin, who announced that Communists were infiltrating American institutions. Anticommunism dominated public life.
11. Economic conditions across Europe after the war required massive investment in infrastructure and frustrated hard-working, hard-pressed ordinary people.
12. As Marshall Plan funds began to have an impact, food and consumer goods became more plentiful, and demand for automobiles, washing machines, and vacuum cleaners boosted economies.
13. The postwar recovery also featured continued military spending and the adaptation of wartime technology to consumer industry.
14. In 1951, Italy, France, Germany, Belgium, Luxembourg, and the Netherlands formed the European Coal and Steel Community (ECSC).
15. This organization would manage coal and steel production and prices, and, through creating common economic interests, prevent France and Germany from going to war.
16. In 1957, ECSC members signed the Treaty of Rome, which provided for the sharing of atomic resources through a commission called EUROCOM and created a trading partnership called the European Economic Community (EEC), known as the Common Market.
17. The EEC reduced tariffs among its members that led to increased cooperation and produced great economic rewards.
18. Britain initially refused to join, fearing an end to trade arrangements with Commonwealth partners.
19. Government experts, called "technocrats" after 1945, based decisions regarding economic policy on expertise rather than political interest, while those working for the Common Market were to disregard the self-interest of any one nation.

C. The Welfare State: Common Ground East and West, pp. 893–894

1. On both sides of the cold war, governments intervened forcefully to ameliorate social conditions.
2. This policy of intervention became known as the welfare state, something that had been gradually building for almost a century.
3. The welfare state encouraged population growth with direct financial aid, imitating the Swedish programs of the 1930s that had created family allowances, health care and medical benefits, and programs for pregnant women and new mothers. Some policies were designed to keep women out of the workforce.
4. Nearly everywhere except the United States, state-funded medical insurance and subsidized medical care covered healthcare needs.
5. The combination of better material conditions and state provision of health care dramatically extended life expectancy and lowered rates of infant mortality.
6. Vaccines for diseases such as tuberculosis, diphtheria, measles, and polio made an enormous difference.
7. Governments sponsored a postwar housing boom; in Western Europe, governments provided incentives

to private builders as well as sponsored building projects.

8. New cities arose around the edges of major urban areas in both East and West.

D. Recovery in the East, pp. 894–897

1. As he had done in the Soviet Union before the war, Stalin collectivized agriculture and industrialized Eastern European countries by nationalizing private property.
2. The Soviet Union formed regional organizations, instituting the Council for Mutual Economic Assistance (COMECON) to coordinate economic relations among the satellite countries and Moscow.
3. The terms of the COMECON relationship thwarted development in the satellite states because the USSR was allowed to buy goods from its clients at bargain prices and reap profits by selling these goods at exorbitant prices.
4. These formerly peasant states did, however, become oriented toward technology and bureaucratically directed industrial economies.
5. People moved to cities where they received better education, health care, and jobs.
6. Repression against religion and the social elites accompanied the drive for modernization, and the Soviet Union dominated its alliances through physical coercion along with state-instituted programs to build loyalty to the regime.
7. After Stalin's death in 1953, Nikita Khrushchev (1894–1971) emerged as the undisputed leader of the Soviet Union in 1955.
8. Khrushchev denounced the "cult of personality" that Stalin had surrounded himself with, and announced that Stalinism did *not* equal communism.
9. In this climate of uncertainty, protest erupted in the summer of 1956, most notably in Poland and Hungary.
10. When these rebellions were brutally suppressed, the United States refused to intervene, demonstrating that it would not risk another world war by militarily challenging the Soviets in their sphere of influence.
11. The failure of Eastern European uprisings overshadowed significant changes in Soviet policy.
12. Khrushchev ended the Stalinist purges, reformed the courts, and set a policy of more limited sentences for political offenders and criminals.
13. In 1957, the Soviets successfully launched the first artificial Earth satellite, *Sputnik* and, in 1961, sent the first cosmonaut, Yuri Gagarin (1934–1968), into orbit around earth.
14. The Soviets' edge in space technology shocked the Western bloc and motivated the creation of the U.S. National Aeronautics and Space Administration (NASA).

III. Decolonization in a Cold War Climate

A. The End of Empire in Asia, pp. 897–899

1. By the end of World War II, leaders in Asia had begun to mobilize the mass discontent that had intensified during the war.
2. The British had promised to grant India its independence in the 1930s, but postponed it when war broke out.
3. After the war, the British Labour government, presiding over the end of the British Empire in India, decreed that because distrust was so great between the Indian National Congress and the Muslim League, two countries should be created.
4. Hundreds of thousands died in violence, and Gandhi was assassinated in the partition of India and Pakistan that followed.
5. China experienced a Communist takeover (1949) led by Mao Zedong (1893–1976).
6. Mao instituted social reforms such as civil equality for women, but also copied Soviet collectivization, rapid industrialization, and the brutal repression of the privileged classes.
7. The Communist victory in China spurred both the United States and the USSR to increase their involvement in Asian politics.
8. In 1950, the North Koreans, supported by the Soviet Union, invaded U.S.-backed South Korea.
9. The United States maneuvered the UN Security Council into approving a "police action" against North Korea but, after two and a half years of stalemate, the opposing sides agreed to a settlement (1953) that reestablished the border between North Korea and South Korea at the thirty-eighth parallel.
10. The conflict led to the formation in 1954 of the U.S.-backed Southeast Asia Treaty Organization and a huge increase in U.S. defense spending.
11. The cold war spread to Indochina after the war as well, where nationalists had been

struggling against the renewal of French imperialism.

12. The French fought all efforts at independence, but peasant guerrillas forced them to withdraw after the bloody battle of Dien Bien Phu (1954).
13. The Geneva Convention of 1954 carved out an independent Laos and divided Vietnam into North Vietnam and South Vietnam, each free from French control.

B. The Struggle for Identity in the Middle East, pp. 899–900

1. Middle Eastern peoples also renewed their commitment to independence and resisted attempts by the major powers to regain imperial control.
2. The cold war gave Middle Eastern leaders an opening to bargain with the superpowers, playing them off one another, especially over resources (such as oil) to repair war-torn economies.
3. The Western powers' commitment to secure a Jewish homeland in the Middle East made Arabs more determined to regain economic and political control of the region.
4. Great Britain ceded Palestine to the United Nations, in 1947, to work out a settlement between the Jews and the Arabs.
5. The UN voted to partition Palestine into an Arab region and a Jewish region.
6. Conflicting claims led to war, and the Jewish military forces prevailed; Israel was established on May 14, 1948.
7. Egypt had gained its independence from Britain at the end of the war.
8. However, Britain retained its control of the Suez Canal, which was owned by a British-run company.
9. In 1952, Colonel Gamal Abdel Nasser (1918–1970) became Egypt's president and, in July 1956, he nationalized the canal.
10. The British called on the United States, which refused to help in order to avoid military conflict with the Soviet Union.
11. American opposition to their plans caused the British to back down; Nasser's triumph inspired confidence that the Middle East could confront the West and win.

C. New Nations in Africa, pp. 900–901

1. In sub-Saharan Africa, nationalist leaders roused their people to challenge Europe's increasing demands for resources and labor, which resulted in poverty for African peoples.
2. Kwame Nkrumah (1909–1972) led the diverse inhabitants of the relatively prosperous, British-controlled West African Gold Coast in passive resistance, in imitation of Gandhian methods.
3. After years of such resistance, the British withdrew, allowing the state of Ghana to come into being in 1957.
4. Nigeria, the most populous African region, became independent in 1960.
5. The eastern coast and southern and central areas of Africa, particularly in British East Africa, contained numerous European settlers who violently resisted independence movements.
6. France easily granted certain demands for independence, such as those of Tunisia, Morocco, and West Africa, where there were fewer settlers, more limited economic stakes, and less military involvement.
7. When Algerian nationalists rebelled against the restoration of French rule in the final days of World War II, the French army massacred tens of thousands of protesters.
8. The Algerian Front for National Liberation, formed in 1954, attacked European settlers and their Arab supporters.
9. The French fought back savagely, sending in more than 400,000 soldiers.
10. The Algerian war threatened French stability as protests in Paris greeted reports of the army's barbarous practices, and the Fourth Republic eventually collapsed over the issue.
11. In 1958, Charles de Gaulle, supported by the army and approved by the Chamber of Deputies, returned to power.
12. In return for leading France out of its Algerian quagmire, de Gaulle demanded the creation of the Fifth Republic, a new republican government with a strong president who could exercise emergency power.
13. As these new nations emerged, the United Nations was formed as a mechanism to promote international security.
14. Both the United States and the Soviet Union were active members of the United Nations from its beginning.
15. The charter of the UN outlined a collective, global authority that would adjudicate conflicts, provide military protection, and oversee the fate of emerging states.

D. Newcomers Arrive in Europe, pp. 901–902

1. In a reversal of the nineteenth-century trend of emigration out of Europe, people from former colonies began immigrating to Europe after the war.
2. As European economies recovered, labor was in short supply, so immigrants were invited as temporary residents who would work in Europe as "guest workers" for a fixed period and then return home.
3. Initially, immigrants were housed in barracks-like dormitories where they formed their own enclaves rather than assimilate into the population.
4. These guest workers were welcomed because they availed themselves of few social services and, because they came as adults, they did not even require public education.
5. Most worked in less desirable jobs such as collecting garbage, building roads, and cleaning homes.
6. Former colonials came to view Europe as a land of opportunity and illegal immigration increased.
7. As empires collapsed, the composition of the European population in terms of race, religion, ethnicity, and social life began to change, becoming more multicultural and diverse than ever before in modern times.

IV. Daily Life and Culture in the Shadow of Nuclear War

A. Restoring "Western" Values, pp. 903–905

1. After the depravity and inhumanity of fascism, cultural currents in Europe and the United States reemphasized universal values, spiritual renewal, and political choice.
2. Some saw the churches as central to the restoration of values, and the Catholic church in particular, under the leadership of Pope John XXIII, underwent reform and promoted cooperation between faiths after the Second Vatican Council.
3. Their success was only partial, however, as the trend toward a more secular culture continued.
4. Instead, people emphasized the triumph of a Western heritage, a Western civilization, and Western values over fascism.
5. Literature called for a new commitment to tolerance and pluralism.
6. Governments erected permanent plaques at locations where resisters had been killed; their biographies filled magazines and bookstalls; organizations of resisters commemorated their role in winning the war.
7. By the end of the 1940s, existential philosophy became the rage among the cultural elite and students.
8. It explored the meaning of human existence in a world where evil flourished, and attempted to define *being* in the absence of God and in the midst of the breakdown of morality.
9. In 1949, Simone de Beauvoir (1908–1986) published *The Second Sex*, in which she argues that most women failed to take the kind of action necessary to create an authentic "self" through considered action.
10. In the 1950s and 1960s, the immensely influential writings of Frantz Fanon (1925–1961), a black psychiatrist from the French colony of Martinique, began analyzing liberation movements.
11. Fanon wrote that the mental functioning of the colonized person was "traumatized" by the violence and the brutal imposition of another culture as the only standard of value.
12. Ruled by guns, the colonized person would decolonize through violence.
13. In the United States, African Americans, who had fought in the war to defeat the Nazi idea of white racial supremacy, intensified their commitment to the civil rights culture, advancing the cause of such long-standing organizations as the National Association for the Advancement of Colored People (NAACP, founded 1909).
14. In 1954, the U.S. Supreme Court declared segregated education to be unconstitutional in *Brown v. Board of Education*, a case initiated by the NAACP.
15. Foremost among the many talented leaders of civil rights groups that emerged was Martin Luther King, Jr. (1929–1968), a pastor who promoted nonviolent resistance to racism.

B. Consumerism and Shifting Gender Norms, pp. 905–908

1. Governmental spending on reconstruction, productivity, and welfare helped prevent the kind of social, political, and economic upheaval that had followed World War I.

2. Nonetheless, the war affected men's roles and their sense of themselves.
3. Young men who had missed World War II adopted the violent style of soldiers.
4. Young men also took cues from pop culture.
5. The leader of rock-and-roll style and substance was the American singer Elvis Presley (1935–1977), while film stars James Dean (1931–1955) in *Rebel Without a Cause* and Marlon Brando (1924–2004) in *The Wild One* inspired American and European youths alike.
6. The rebellious and rough masculine style also appeared in literature.
7. The American "beat" poets critiqued traditional ideals of the upright and rational male achiever.
8. In 1953, the inaugural issue of *Playboy* magazine ushered in a widely imitated depiction of a changed male identity.
9. The new man was depicted as sexually aggressive and independent of dull, domestic life—just as he had been during the war.
10. The notion of men's liberty had come to include not just political and economic rights but also freedom of sexual expression.
11. In contrast, postwar women were made to symbolize a return to normalcy by returning to the domestic sphere and no longer working outside the home.
12. In the late 1940s, the fashion house of Christian Dior (1905–1957) launched a clothing style called the "new look," which was essentially a return to the nineteenth-century female silhouette.
13. New look propaganda did not, however, mesh with reality.
14. European women continued to work outside the home after the war; indeed, mature women and mothers were working more than ever before.
15. The advertising business presided over the creation of new cultural messages.
16. Guided by marketing experts, Western Europeans were imitating Americans, driving some forty million motorized vehicles, including motorbikes, cars, buses, and trucks.

C. The Culture of Cold War, pp. 908–909

1. Films, books, and other cultural productions promoted the cold war at the same time that they conveyed antiwar messages.
2. Ray Bradbury's (b. 1920) popular *Fahrenheit 451*, whose title indicated the temperature at which books would burn, condemned the cold war curtailment of intellectual freedom.
3. Consumer culture as a whole came under the cold war banner, as people debated the "Americanization" they witnessed taking place in Europe.
4. The Communist Party in France led a successful campaign to ban Coca-Cola for a time in the 1950s.
5. Leadership of the art world passed to the United States when art became part of the cold war.
6. Abstract expressionism, practiced by American artists such as Jackson Pollock (1912–1956), departed completely from realism.
7. Abstract expressionism spoke of the artist's self-discovery, spiritual growth, and physical sensations in the process of painting.
8. Their canvases were said to exemplify Western "freedom."
9. In Italy, the neorealist technique was developed by filmmakers such as Roberto Rossellini (1906–1977) in *Open City* (1945) and Vittorio De Sica (1902–1974) in *The Bicycle Thief* (1948).
10. Such works challenged Hollywood-style sets and costumes by using ordinary characters living in devastated, impoverished cities.

D. The Atomic Brink, pp. 909–911

1. Radio broadcasts were at the center of the cold war.
2. During the late 1940s and early 1950s, the Voice of America, with its main studio in Washington, D.C., broadcast in thirty-eight languages from one hundred transmitters and provided an alternative source of news for peoples in Eastern Europe.
3. The Soviet counterpart broadcast in Russian around the clock, although it initially spent much of its wattage jamming U.S. programming.
4. News reports also kept the cold war alive, featuring stories about nuclear testing, military buildups, and hostile diplomatic incidents.
5. In school, children rehearsed for nuclear war, and some families built personal bomb shelters.

6. John Fitzgerald Kennedy (1917–1963) became president of the United States in 1960.
7. A war hero, and early fan of the fictional cold-war spy James Bond, Kennedy intensified the arms race and escalated the cold war.
8. In 1959, a revolution in Cuba brought Fidel Castro (b. 1927) to power, and he allied his government with the Soviet Union.
9. In the spring of 1961, Kennedy, assured by the Central Intelligence Agency (CIA) of success, launched an invasion of Cuba at the Bay of Pigs to overthrow Castro.
10. The invasion failed miserably.
11. Cold war rivalries continued to escalate over the continuing U.S. presence in Berlin.
12. In the summer of 1961, East German workers, supervised by police, began construction of a wall on the city's east-west border.
13. The wall blocked movement between east and west, and increased superpower tensions.
14. The matter came to a head when the CIA reported, in October 1962, that the Soviets were installing medium-range missiles in Cuba.
15. Kennedy called for a blockade of ships headed for Cuba and threatened nuclear war.
16. After a few tense days, the two leaders negotiated an end to the crisis.
17. Following this scare, both Kennedy and Khrushchev worked to improve nuclear diplomacy.

Lecture Strategies

1. How and why the cold war began is a crucial topic. There are many aspects that might be examined, including what was agreed to at the Yalta and Potsdam conferences, the illness and death of Roosevelt and American perceptions of Soviet behavior in 1946, and the announcement of the Truman Doctrine in 1947. The Marshall Plan should be closely examined. When General George C. Marshall spoke about his ideas at Harvard in June 1947, and even when Europeans gathered later that summer in Paris to discuss possibilities, there was suspicion on both sides but no cold war as such. By the time Congress passed the European Recovery Act in 1948, which funded the Marshall Plan, the cold war was rapidly taking shape. Questions to use as a basis for a lecture or as a theme for discussion are: What was the true nature of the Marshall Plan? Was it primarily a humanitarian gesture? Was it a rather disingenuous attempt by American businesses to gain control of the global economy? Was it merely another device in the developing cold war competition with the Soviet Union?

In addition to books on the cold war listed in the chapter's bibliography, Melvyn P. Leffler, *The Specter of Communism: The United States and the Origins of the Cold War, 1917–1953* (New York: Hill & Wang, 1994), is an excellent introduction to the topic. George F. Kennan, *Memoirs 1925–1950* (New York: Pantheon, 1967), devotes a chapter to his part in the origins of the Marshall Plan. George C. Marshall, "Against Hunger, Poverty, Desperation, and Chaos," *Foreign Affairs* 76, no. 3 (May/June 1997), is a convenient source for the speech Marshall gave at Harvard. (This issue contains a useful special section, "The Marshall Plan and Its Legacy.") See also Michael J. Hogan, *The Marshall Plan: America, Britain, and the Reconstruction of Western Europe* (New York: Cambridge University Press, 1987); and Charles S. Maier and Günter Bischof, eds., *The Marshall Plan and Germany* (New York: Berg, 1991). *The Marshall Plan: Against All Odds* is an interesting and well-informed documentary film on the topic.

On the cold war in general, see Leffler's *For the Soul of Mankind: The United States, the Soviet Union, and the Cold War* (New York: Hill and Wang, 2007); and, for a closer look at the Soviet perspective, Gladiola Uzbek's *A Failed Empire: The Soviet Union in the Cold War from Stalin to Gorbachev* (Chapel Hill, NC: University of North Carolina Press, 2007). A broad perspective is offered by Odd Arne Westar's recent Bancroft Prize winner, *The Global Cold: Third World Interventions and the Making of Our Times* (Cambridge: Cambridge University Press, 2005); see also Jessie M. Hanhimaki and Odd Arne Westad, eds., *The Cold War: A History in Documents and Eyewitness Accounts* (Oxford: Oxford University Press, 2004); Michael Kort, *The Columbia Guide to the Cold War* (New York: Columbia University Press, 1998); and Thomas S. Arms, ed., *Encyclopedia of the Cold War* (New York: Facts on File, 1994).

2. The Berlin blockade and airlift in 1948–1949 is another good vantage point from which to observe the development of the cold war. Neither the United States nor the Soviet Union understood the other's intentions in Germany after the war. One possible interpretation is that the United States had a German policy that it followed consistently, whereas the Soviet Union lacked one. In this view, the American effort to create a Germany that could pay its own expenses and also help to restart the European economy led directly to the Soviet challenge in the Berlin blockade. The success of the Berlin airlift caused the Soviets to give up the blockade and resulted in the division of

Germany into East Germany and West Germany in 1949. The cold war also played a role in the formation of NATO that same year. Berlin remained a flash point, at least through the building of the Berlin Wall in 1961, and the two Germanys remained a major focus of the cold war until 1989.

In addition to titles cited in the chapter's bibliography and Leffler's book noted in suggestion 1, see also the special commemorative section, "The Berlin Airlift and the City's Future," *Foreign Affairs* 77, no. 4, (July/August 1998), 147–194. Recent studies include Michael D. Haydock, *City under Siege: The Berlin Blockade and Airlift, 1948–49* (Dulles, VA: Brassey's, 1999); and Thomas Parrish, *Berlin in the Balance, 1945–1949: The Blockade, the Airlift, the First Major Battle of the Cold War* (Reading, MA: Addison Wesley Longman, 1998). Avi Shlaim, *The United States and the Berlin Blockade, 1948–49* (Berkeley, CA: University of California Press, 1983) is probably the leading study of the Berlin blockade. Paul Steege's *Black Market, Cold War: Everyday Life in Berlin 1946–1949* (Cambridge: Cambridge University Press, 2007) does an excellent job providing a broader background and also telling the story of life in Berlin for ordinary Germans. In addition, the Public Broadcasting System, *The Berlin Airlift* (distr. Unapix/Miramar, 1998) is a fascinating account of the Berlin airlift featuring contemporary footage and interviews with some of the participants.

3. The new, prosperous Europe that was created in the 1950s and 1960s and the role of the European Economic Community (EEC) in that process are linked topics well worth investigating. One good approach would be presenting the life of Jean Monnet, whose vision of a united and peaceful Europe was most responsible first for the European Coal and Steel Community and then for the EEC. A good place to start is Monnet's *Memoirs* (Garden City, NY: Doubleday, 1978), especially Part 2, chapters 13–16. Two good biographies of Monnet are those by Douglas Brinkley and Clifford P. Hackett, *Jean Monnet: The Path to European Unity* (New York: St. Martin's Press, 1991); and François Duchêne, *Jean Monnet: The First Statesman of Interdependence* (New York: W. W. Norton, 1994). Probably the most useful single source is Sherrill B. Wells, *Jean Monnet: Visionary and Architect of European Union: A Brief Biography and Documents* (Boston: Bedford/St. Martin's, 2000). Derek W. Urwin, *The Community of Europe: A History of European Integration Since 1945*, 2nd ed. (London: Longman, 1995) is an excellent introduction. Two authoritative surveys are Rondo Cameron, *A Concise Economic History of the World: From Paleolithic Times to the Present*, 3rd ed. (Oxford: Oxford University Press, 1997); and David S. Landes, *The Unbound Prometheus: Technological Change and Industrial Development in Western Europe from 1750 to the Present* (Cambridge: Cambridge University Press, 1969). In Landes, Chapter 7 provides a good summary of the founding of the EEC.

For insights into life in Western Europe in the 1950s and 1960s, see Laurence Wylie's fascinating *Village in the Vaucluse*, 3rd ed. (Cambridge, MA: Harvard University Press, 1977). See also the first book by one of the best American journalists reporting on Europe, Jane Kramer, *Unsettling Europe* (New York: Random House, 1980). Kramer presents the stories of four groups of outsiders in Europe in the 1960s and 1970s, Italian Communists in their own country, Yugoslav guest workers in Sweden, Indians from Uganda in England, and colons from Algeria in France.

4. The Cuban missile crisis is, first of all, a moment of high drama in which the entire world was at risk. It also offers the possibility of looking carefully at the conduct of politics in the Soviet Union and the United States. Finally, it provides an opportunity to examine American, European, and Soviet reactions to the crisis at the time. The motives and responses of the main players in the crisis would also form a good basis for discussion on leadership and crisis management.

A wealth of material is available. Chapter 9 of John Lewis Gaddis, *We Now Know: Rethinking Cold War History* (Oxford: Clarendon Press, 1997) offers a thoughtful review of scholarship on several major issues connected with the crisis. Aleksandr Fursenko and Timothy Naftali, *One Hell of a Gamble: Khrushchev, Kennedy, and Castro, 1958–1964* (New York: W. W. Norton, 1998) is, to a large extent, based on Soviet archival sources and provides a good picture of the Soviet side of the crisis. Laurence Chang and Peter Kornbluh, *The Cuban Missile Crisis, 1962: A National Security Archive Documents Reader* (New York: The New Press, 1992) contains an excellent selection of documents combined with an extensive chronology and other helpful material. See also Robert Kennedy, *Thirteen Days: A Memoir of the Cuban Missile Crisis* (New York: W. W. Norton, 1969); Ernest R. May and Philip D. Zelikow, *The Kennedy Tapes: Inside the White House During the Cuban Missile Crisis* (Cambridge, MA: Belknap Press, 1997); and Michael R. Beschloss, *The Crisis Years: Kennedy and Khrushchev, 1960–1963* (New York: Edward Burlingame Books, 1991). You might consider showing all or part of the Roger Donaldson film, *Thirteen Days* (2001), which makes an effort to recreate both the atmosphere and history of the crisis.

Class Discussion Starters

1. Consider focusing a discussion session on American strategic thinking in the early postwar era. A session dealing with the Korean War might discuss the differences between the concept of "containment"

voiced in the late 1940s and the idea of "rollback" that came to be dominant after 1950. A helpful book in terms of background for the Korean War is Sergei N. Goncharov, John W. Lewis, and Xue Litai, *Uncertain Partners: Stalin, Mao, and the Korean War* (Stanford, CA: Stanford University Press, 1993). *Uncertain Partners* makes a case that Kim Il-sung, the North Korean leader, had the most to do with starting the war. It also points up the complicated and delicate relationships between Stalin and Mao and the Soviet Union and the People's Republic of China. There are some excellent essays and an excellent introduction in William Stuek, ed., *The Korean War in World History* (Lexington, KY: University of Kentucky Press, 2004). What makes the Korean War such a fateful event is that it broke out just as American officials were considering a major policy statement, NSC 68, a document that helped turn the cold war into a series of military confrontations. On NSC 68, see the useful book by Ernest R. May, *American Cold War Strategy: Interpreting NSC 68* (Boston: Bedford/St. Martin's, 1993). On the Korean War itself, useful sources are James I. Matray, *Historical Dictionary of the Korean War* (Westport, CT: Greenwood Press, 1991); James I. Matray, *The Uncivil War: Korea, 1945–1953* (Armonk, NY: M. E. Sharpe, 1999); and Stanley Sandler, *The Korean War: No Victors, No Vanquished* (Louisville, KY: University Press of Kentucky, 1999).

2. Another possibility is a session focused on a particular crisis in decolonization. Students should debate the process of colonial disengagement, and the initial challenges faced by newly independent nations to build viable independent economic and political systems. Consider dividing students into groups to present the perspectives of the colonial power (often divided itself between those who favored various degrees of engagement/disengagement), various national factions in the former colony, and perhaps even the United Nations. One possibility would be to relate to France and the Algerian revolution. Because the French considered Algeria an integral part of France, the attempt by the Algerian rebels to liberate their country had a definitive impact on domestic affairs in France. In addition to the books cited in the chapter's bibliography, see also Alistair Horne, *A Savage War of Peace: Algeria 1954–1962* (New York: Viking Press, 1978), an excellent if long account. See also Charles S. Maier and Dan S. White, eds., *The Thirteenth of May: The Advent of de Gaulle's Republic* (New York: Oxford University Press, 1968), a useful collection of documents about the end of the Fourth Republic and beginnings of the Fifth Republic in 1958. De Gaulle's account of 1958 and his successful efforts to end the war in Algeria are contained in his *Memoirs of Hope: Renewal and Endeavor* (New York: Simon & Schuster, 1971). A convenient short biography is Andrew Shennan, *De Gaulle* (London: Longman, 1993). See also Matthew Connelly, *A Diplomatic Revolution: Algeria's Fight for Independence and the Origins of the Post-Cold War Era* (Oxford: Oxford University Press, 2002) for an excellent contextualization of the Algerian events. A session might also focus on the tremendously complex but very teachable disaster that unfolded in South Asia as Britain withdrew from India. For an overview, see Jeff Hay's brief and evenhanded *The Partition of British India* (New York: Chelsea House, 2006), or Patrick French, *Liberty or Death: India's Journey to Independence and Division* (London: HarperCollins, 1997). For a variety of perspectives on partition see Mushirul Hasan, ed., *Inventing Boundaries: Gender, Politics, and the Partition of India* (New York: Oxford University Press, 2000). Sukeshi Kamra offers a range of first-hand experiences of, and reactions to, the partition in *Bearing Witness: Partition, Independence, and the End of the Raj* (Calgary: University of Calgary Press, 2002).

3. Students will probably be curious about what it was like to live during the 1950s and early 1960s when the threat of nuclear war seemed all too real. One possibility is to show the film *Dr. Strangelove or: How I Learned to Stop Worrying and Love the Bomb*, Stanley Kubrick's masterpiece from 1964 (Burbank, CA: RCA/Columbia Pictures Home Video, 1987). Ninety-three minutes long, it will not fit conveniently into most class periods, but it would be worth the trouble to arrange an evening showing with an in-class discussion the following day. The screenplay was written by Kubrick, Terry Southern, and Peter George. Peter Sellers plays most of the major parts, including Dr. Strangelove.

Several books may be helpful in dealing with *Dr. Strangelove* and American culture in the nuclear age. One by Margot A. Henriksen, *Dr. Strangelove's America: Society and Culture in the Atomic Age* (Berkeley, CA: University of California Press, 1997), is a readable and interesting discussion of films, novels, and other cultural artifacts from that period. Another direction is taken by Tom Engelhart, *The End of Victory Culture: Cold War America and the Disillusioning of a Generation*, 2nd ed. (Amherst, MA: University of Massachusetts Press, 1998). Engelhart believes the idea that America was always on the side of the good became increasingly difficult to sustain in the nuclear age. See also Philip Jenkins, *The Cold War at Home: The Red Scare in Pennsylvania* (Chapel Hill, NC: University of North Carolina Press, 1999), a case study that is set in the national context; Lisle A. Rose, *The Cold War Comes to Main Street: America in 1950* (Lawrence, KS: University of Kansas Press, 1999); Stephen J. Whitfield, *The Culture of the Cold War* (Baltimore: Johns Hopkins University Press, 1991); and Richard Alan Schwartz, ed., *Cold War Culture: Media and the*

Arts, 1945–1990 (New York: Facts on File, 1998). Many of the titles listed in "Lecture Strategies," number 1, may also be helpful.

A different approach, which depends to some extent on your familiarity with 1950s rock and roll, is a focus on Elvis Presley. Why was Presley so enormously popular? What did his popularity say about America in the 1950s? Peter Guralnick, *Last Train to Memphis: The Rise of Elvis Presley* (Boston: Little, Brown, 1994), a longish but fascinating book, is the best source. Guralnick charts Presley's downfall in *Careless Love: The Unmaking of Elvis Presley* (Boston: Little, Brown, 1999). See also Karal Ann Marling, *Graceland: Going Home with Elvis* (Cambridge, MA: Harvard University Press, 1996). Other useful sources include Lee Cotton, *All Shook Up: Elvis Day-by-Day, 1954–1977* (Ann Arbor, MI: Pierian Press, 1985); Ernst Jorgensen, *Reconsider Baby: The Definitive Elvis Session-ography, 1954–1977* (Ann Arbor, MI: Pierian Press, 1986); and Erika Doss, *Elvis Culture: Fans, Faith, & Image* (Lawrence, KS: University of Kansas Press, 1999).

Reviewing the Text

Review Questions

1. What were the major events in the development of the cold war?

[model answer] • ***Economic pressure:*** *The United States wanted to stop the spread of communism and used economic and military aid as a way of keeping countries democratic. The Marshall Plan was designed to alleviate the hardships in Western Europe that might make communism seem attractive. Stalin viewed U.S. aid as a political ploy and, unable to offer similar aid to his client countries, clamped down on their governments to remove any democratic elements and ensure obedience.*

• ***The partitioning of Germany:*** *The Soviet Union disagreed with its allies regarding the political and economic system adopted to govern Germany. Tensions escalated as the western Allies merged their zones into a unified West German state and built it up under the Marshall Plan. Stalin then blockaded Berlin to claim it for the USSR. Even after the blockade was lifted, the divided city was considered a symbol of the cold war.*

• ***Military alliances:*** *The United States, Canada, and their allies in Western Europe and Scandinavia formed the North Atlantic Treaty Organization (NATO) to provide a unified military force for its member countries. After the United States invited France and Britain to join, the Soviet Union retaliated by establishing an organization with its satellite countries, the Warsaw Pact. These two alliances created a system of mutual defense treaties as a way of deterring conflict, and the model was later extended by the United States to Asia (SEATO).*

2. What factors drove recovery in Western Europe? In Eastern Europe?

[model answer] • ***Civilian-oriented governments, cooperation, and economic specialists in the West:*** *Governments diverted labor and capital into rebuilding infrastructure. International cooperation, through the Marshall Plan, boosted recovery with American dollars and products, and eventually inspired the creation of the European Economic Community (EEC). Countries that joined the EEC experienced soaring economic growth as a result of reduced tariffs, common trade policies, and a larger number of consumers. Wartime technology was adapted to consumer industry, providing the market with new products. Spending on weapons and the military continued, providing jobs throughout the cold war. Western democracies increased state involvement in the economy by expanding social support systems and government-provided services such as healthcare, known collectively as the "welfare state."*

• ***Harsh policies and political pressure in the East:*** *Stalin's vision of recovery through industrialization required the transformation of peasant economies. Peasants were dispossessed of land and pushed into cooperative farming, causing many to move to urban areas. Rural productivity continued to be hampered by a lack of motivation and government investment. Many farmers who did remain in rural areas felt their lives had improved. Stalin prodded his allies to match U.S. productivity, and formed regional market associations similar to those in the West. The Council for Mutual Economic Assistance (COMECON), however, worked for the benefit of the USSR and to the detriment, economically, of its satellite states.*

3. What were the results of decolonization?

[model answer] • ***Independent nations were established out of former colonies and territories:*** *The British Labour government, presiding over the end of the British Empire in India, decreed that because distrust was so great between the Indian National Congress and the Muslim League, two countries should be created. Hundreds of thousands died in violence, and Gandhi was assassinated in the partition of India and Pakistan that followed. The Geneva Convention of 1954 carved out an independent Laos and divided Vietnam into North Vietnam and South Vietnam, each free from French control. Great Britain ceded Palestine to the United Nations, in 1947, to work out a settlement between the Jews and the Arabs. The UN voted to partition Palestine into an Arab region and a Jewish region. Conflicting claims led to war, and the Jewish military forces prevailed; Israel was established on May 14, 1948. Egypt gained its independence from Britain at the end of the war. Kwame Nkrumah (1909–1972) led the diverse inhabitants of the relatively prosperous, British-controlled West African Gold Coast in passive resistance, in imitation of*

Gandhian methods. After years of such resistance, the British withdrew, allowing the state of Ghana to come into being in 1957. Nigeria, the most populous African region, became independent in 1960.

• ***Cold War conflict developed in many formerly colonized states and regions:*** *Korea and Vietnam, both partitioned after World War II, became focal points of conflict between the superpowers.*

• ***In the Middle East, oil and competing nationalist visions complicated political development:*** *Western states competed for access to oil in the Middle East, and the establishment of Israel after the war and the Holocaust led to conflict between that state and much of the Arab world. Egyptian leader Nasser offered a model of independent nationalism that inspired much imitation.*

• ***Africans established independent states but struggled to find order and prosperity:*** *Decolonization was complicated in Africa by the continuing interest of the West in extracting resources, and by the problems of European settlement in some areas, particularly in Kenya and Algeria.*

• ***Structures arose in the postwar world to promote global cooperation and development:*** *The UN benefited from the involvement of both superpowers and newly independent states. It began to address issues of human rights and inequality.*

• ***Immigration to Europe from former colonies became widespread:*** *By the 1980s, 8 percent of the European population was foreign born. Immigrants were attracted by security, relative prosperity, and jobs.*

4. How did the cold war affect everyday culture and social life?

[model answer] • ***Radio propaganda proliferated over the airwaves:*** *Radio was at the center of the cold war, disseminating propaganda just as it had in wartime. The Soviet Union and the United States each demonstrated its own national, ideological values.*

• ***Nuclear threat permeated everyday life:*** *Cold-war media messages featured news of nuclear buildup. Along with the usual fire drills held in schools, children practiced what to do in the event of a nuclear attack. On the home front, families built backyard or basement bomb shelters.*

• ***Books with cold war themes rose in popularity:*** *Books that condemned cold war curtailment of freedom were popular, such as Orwell's* 1984 *and Bradbury's* Fahrenheit 451. *Books that told of the aftermath of a nuclear event were also published and filmed, such as* On the Beach. *Spy stories abounded in the East. Authors in both the East and West topped best-seller lists with novels set in the culture of international distrust and espionage; radio, TV shows, and film soon followed.*

• ***Use of consumerism as an ideological tool:*** *While many Europeans admired American innovation, the Communist Party in France successfully banned Coca-Cola for a time. Soviet magazines carried fashion photos intended to combat appreciation of garments from the West, considered too highly sexualized. In the West, the proliferation of consumer goods of all types was seen as a symbol of success and prosperity, for individuals and also for the Western economic system.*

• ***Art was another cold war battleground:*** *In the United States, abstract expressionism's nonrepresentational works were said to exemplify Western freedom, and the government supported abstract artists. Meanwhile, the Soviets condemned American art while Italian neo-realist filmmakers challenged Hollywood's dominance in film. By portraying stark conditions, these filmmakers conveyed their distance from both middle-class prosperity and fascism, identifying with communism in their concern for the poor.*

Making Connections

1. What was the political climate after World War II, and how did it differ from the political climate after World War I?

[model answer] *After World War I, no single, dominant power in Europe existed until the rise of the fascists in the 1930s. But, after World War II, both the Soviet Union and the United States emerged as strong powers and embraced their new role as world leaders. Indeed, the standoff between these two nations after World War II seemed to suggest that further conflict was imminent. After World War I, Europe had been divided into independent nations under the protection of varying countries. But, after World War II, Europe was divided into two distinct blocs: many Eastern and Central European countries allied with the Soviet Union, and Western European countries allied with the United States. Colonial peoples had been denied their independence after the first world war, but after the second world war, these colonials demanded and sometimes fought to achieve independence. They were sometimes in a position, particularly when they controlled valuable resources, to bargain for the support of both the Soviet Union and the United States.*

2. What were the relative strengths of the two European blocs in the cold war?

[model answer] *Western European economies recovered quickly after the introduction of the Marshall Plan in 1947. The EEC, formed in 1957, became an economic success. Politically, economically, socially, and militarily, Europe had a strong ally in the United States, which helped to counter the power of the Soviet Union and Soviet-bloc countries. However, the Soviet Union was heavily industrialized, had full employment, and had geared every aspect of life toward cold war competition. It also possessed tremendous resources by way of its satellite countries. It prided itself on technological innovation, and had a thriving space program to prove it. Both sides, of course, built up nuclear arsenals capable of delivering unprecedented destruction.*

3. What were the main developments of postwar cultural life?
[model answer] *Although life in postwar Europe was hard and reconstruction took time, people felt a general sense of release after World War II. Young people embraced rock and roll, and some young men adopted a rebellious anti-establishment stance in music and film. The beat poets critiqued traditional ideals of the upright and* rational *male achiever, while the American magazine* Playboy *reflected a changed male identity, where men were independent of domestic life just as they had been in the war. The ideal for women was complete domesticity, but the reality was that across most of the west women had to continue to work to support their families, just as they had done during the war. The thriftiness of the war years was abandoned in favor of spending on new consumer goods. The United States had played a decisive role in the war and continued to do so as Western Europe was being rebuilt, which had the effect of Americanizing Western European culture.*

4. Why did decolonization follow the war so immediately?
[model answer] *Decolonization happened swiftly in part because colonials remembered what had occurred after World War I. After helping to fight the war through various means, colonial peoples expected they would be given their independence. When independence did not occur, resentment grew until it erupted at the end of World War II. With leaders steeped in Western values and experienced in military and manufacturing technology, people in Asia, Africa, and the Middle East embraced the cause of independence. Exhausted economically and militarily, most European countries were in no position to fight independence movements. Some countries, such as Ghana, achieved independence peacefully; others, like Algeria, clashed directly in bloody combat with Western powers.*

Discussing the Documents

Questions from Online Study Guide with Model Answers

The Schuman Plan on European Unity (1950), p. 893

1. How did Schuman propose to end the long-standing rivalry between Germany and France?
[model answer] *Schuman appealed to the economic interests of these two countries by proposing an economic union between the two so that war would be "not only unthinkable, but materially impossible." Such a union would counter nationalist impulses, and create interdependence among member nations so that war would be counterproductive and against their interests.*

2. Why can unions such as the one Schuman was proposing be considered products of the postwar era?
[model answer] *The destruction wrought by World War II made clear the importance of avoiding another catastrophic war and maintaining world peace. Such unions were also important for the recovery of Europe, and for maintaining independence from the superpowers that had emerged after the war.*

Consumerism, Youth, and the Birth of the Generation Gap, p. 905

1. What types of cultural changes and tensions are described here?
[model answer] *This woman's description of her youth shows that new styles of clothing, hairdos, and music were coming into fashion among Austria's youth. Sex and sexuality also appears to have been talked about more openly among the young, although, as the woman explains, they never discussed these topics among their elders. These changes in values and fashion created tensions between the young and the old, and the woman describes her mother's opposition to her choice in clothing, and her boss's opposition to her hairstyle.*

2. What were some of the important changes in Western society that contributed to these changes?
[model answer] *American culture was being introduced into Europe at the time, both as a result of America's increased participation in world affairs, and of the expansion of the consumer market after World War II. More young people were working outside the home, especially after Europe's dramatic economic recovery from the war, and would have had more of their own money to spend on items such as records and fashionable clothing.*

New Sources, New Perspectives: Government Archives and the Truth about the Cold War, p. 885

1. Are archives overseen by government officials more or less likely to be biased than other sources? How can we know the extent to which archives contain the truth?
[model answer] *Archived materials, while they can reflect the biases of the authors of their documents and the collecting practices of sponsoring states, are protected from tampering. Access to them, however, is often limited for political reasons. The existence of an "official" set of documents on some subjects can privilege some kinds of evidence, and limit or constrain historical inquiry. Archival sources must be supplemented by other materials.*

2. What are the most reliable sources for discovering historical truth? Make a list and provide reasons for your counting these sources as reliable.
[model answer] *Reliable sources are related to the historical questions a historian asks. Valuable sources*

often include archival material from official sources, but other kinds of evidence that offer first-hand information about a topic should be evaluated and used as well, such as newspapers, account books, letters, diaries, oral testimony, novels, paintings, and photographs. Architecture, monuments, and other physical evidence can also provide reliable and useful information about the past.

Other Questions for Discussing These Documents in Class

The Schuman Plan on European Unity (1950)

1. Discuss with students how this response to the Second World War compared to dominant reactions after the First World War. Has anything changed?

2. Why was coal chosen as a link between the two states? Did it have any symbolic importance? Particular economic importance?

Consumerism, Youth, and the Birth of the Generation Gap

1. What specifically puts this young woman in opposition to her parents?

2. Discuss with students the question of a contemporary youth gap. Does it exist? Does it come from the same kind of sources that made up the one described in the document?

New Sources, New Perspectives: Government Archives and the Truth about the Cold War

1. Discuss with students (ideally from your own experiences) the nature of national and state archives. How do such institutional frameworks limit historical inquiry?

2. How have recent archival discoveries described in the document "made a difference" in our understanding of history? Focus on the Cuban missile crisis, for example.

Comparative Questions

1. Was the cold-war era a time when the West pulled together (encourage students to think broadly about this) or a time when divisions were deepened? How do the documents speak to the question?

2. What challenges face historians working on this era? Consider questions of bias, availability of sources, and lack of "distance" from the events, in light of these documents. How is it different from working on, say, the first world-war era?

For Users of *Sources of The Making of the West*

The following documents are available in Chapter 27 of the companion sourcebook by Katharine J. Lualdi, University of Southern Maine.

1. Stalin and the Western Threat: *The Formation of the Communist Information Bureau (Cominform)* (1947)
2. Truman and the Soviet Threat: National Security Council, *Paper Number 68* (1950)
3. Throwing Off Colonialism: Ho Chi Minh, *Declaration of Independence of the Republic of Vietnam* (1945)
4. The Condition of Modern Women: Simone de Beauvoir, *The Second Sex* (1949)
5. The Hungarian Uprising: Béla Lipták, *Birth of MEFESZ* (1956)

Discussion Ideas for Sources of The Making of the West, *Chapter 27*

1. Examine and discuss what documents 1 and 2 reveal about the origins of cold-war tensions. How "defensive" did both sides see their actions as being? What did they identify as the most important thing for their side to recognize?

2. Taking the idea of "liberation" as it appears in documents 3, 4, and 5, what can we say about this era as a time of liberation? How important was the idea of liberty/freedom to these authors? Especially note how they defined freedom differently. What causes oppression?

Working with Visual Sources

For this exercise, please refer to Women Clearing Berlin on p. 890 of the textbook or view the image on the book companion site's Online Study Guide under the "Visual Activity" for Chapter 27.

Students viewing the image at the Online Study Guide are asked three questions about the image. The questions and model answers (not made available to students) are below. Project this image, available on the Instructor's Resources CD-ROM, in class or ask students to look at the image in their textbooks and answer the questions.

1. During World War II, Allied propaganda was designed to strengthen American resolve to defeat Germany. Following the war and as the cold war began, propaganda had to convince Americans to protect Germany from the Soviet Union. How might

this photograph contribute to making Americans more willing to aid Germany?
[model answer] *The photograph shows the tremendous devastation of Berlin from Allied bombing attacks. We see the enormous task facing these women as they try to clean up the rubble. The viewer identifies with the hardship these women are facing and feels sympathy toward them. If wartime propaganda had often attempted to dehumanize Germans, it was now necessary to make them human again.*

2. How are these women dressed? Does their dress contribute to the impact of the photograph?
[model answer] *These women are dressed in everyday clothing: simple dresses and skirts. They lack gloves or any other sort of protective clothing. Their simple attire helps the viewers identify these women as ordinary women, while their lack of protective clothing makes them appear more vulnerable. They are clearly civilians and victims of war.*

3. The women are shown carrying something as a group. Would the photograph have been as effective if they had been shown picking through the rubble individually?
[model answer] *The fact that these women are all carrying something as a group draws our attention to the differences between them (e.g., the age differences) and underscores the significance of their united effort for recovery. This effort implies the existence of a united society, able to overcome its differences and work together to clear the devastation left by World War II. Americans, who considered themselves part of a "melting pot" society, may have been reassured by the impression that divisions among differing groups in society seemed unlikely to cause the conflicts they had in the past. Also, the image may have inspired confidence that Europeans were not simply looking for handouts. They were working and pulling together and deserved help.*

Mapping Exercises

Map Activity from OSG—Model Answers for Map Activity #2

For this activity, please refer to Map 27.2: Divided Germany and the Berlin Airlift, 1946–1949 on p. 887. Students are asked these questions:

Why did cold war tensions center on Germany?
[model answer] *After World War II, Germany was divided by the Allies into East and West. With the exception of the border between West Germany and Czechoslovakia, the border within Germany was the only place where East and West met in Europe. For both superpowers, the future of this historically powerful country seemed vital to ensure their national security and international interests.*

Why did Stalin let Yugoslavia avoid Soviet control, but not Hungary or Poland?
[model answer] *One of Stalin's primary concerns after World War II, along with bringing about the economic recovery of the Soviet Union, was creating a buffer zone of states that could protect the Soviet Union from future Western aggression. Whereas the inclusion of Yugoslavia in the Warsaw Pact would have increased the size of that buffer zone, its borders do not touch those of the Soviet Union. Hungary and Poland's borders, on the other hand, touch directly to the Soviet Union; they could not therefore be allowed to leave the Soviet sphere.*

Map 27.1: The Impact of World War II on Europe, p. 882

Discuss with students the reasons that various groups of refugees were on the move. In particular, review the situations many Germans found themselves in after the war ended. Ask students to explain why and how the Soviet Union acquired the various areas along its western borders between 1940 and 1956. Consider refugee movements in light of the immediate events of the postwar era.

Map 27.2: Divided Germany and the Berlin Airlift, 1946–1949, p. 887

Point out to students that the British also participated in the Berlin airlift. Ask students if they know which airfields in Berlin were used by the Americans and British (the Americans used Tempelhof and the British used Gatow; Tegel, the current Berlin airport, was built during the airlift in the French sector). This is a useful opportunity to point out how important it was for the United States to have allies if it sought to limit Soviet/Communist expansion.

Map 27.3: European NATO Members and the Warsaw Pact in the 1950s, p. 888

Be certain to discuss the shared border between these two alliance systems. Where would a war have been fought? Which countries tried to stay out of the system?

Map 27.4: The Partition of Palestine and the Creation of Israel, 1947–1948, p. 899

What does the map reveal about the difficulties of creating Israel where it was done? What were some of the strategic problems Israel confronted due to its geography?

Map 27.5: The Decolonization of Africa (1951–1990), p. 900

Note how quickly decolonization progressed. Pay particular attention to what happened to state boundaries in relation to colonial borders, and explore with students what sort of difficulties might have resulted.

Map 27.6: The Cuban Missile Crisis, 1962, p. 911

Underscore the proximity of Cuba to the United States, and consider why American leaders may have been inclined to see Russian actions as aggression. From the Cuban government's perspective, why might the missiles have been useful?

Mapping the West: The Cold War World, c. 1960, p. 912

Ask students to point out which states beyond those in NATO or the WTO might be counted as supporters of the United States or of the Soviet Union in 1960. What was the situation of Cuba? Examining this map might be a good opportunity to discuss the Nonaligned Movement that began at the Bandung Conference in 1955. Various nations, among them India, Indonesia, and Yugoslavia, tried to avoid siding with either the United States or the Soviet Union. Ask students to discuss why this effort was unsuccessful.

In-Class Assignments and Presentation Topics

1. Ask students to write an essay on the cold war as it developed in 1947. In addition to material in the chapter, you may wish to assign some of the documents in Judge and Langdon and perhaps Chapter 3 of Powaski's *The Cold War*, both cited in "Lecture Strategies," number 1. In the essay, students should not merely recount what happened in 1947 but try to sort out the more important from the less important events. What caused President Truman to proclaim the Truman Doctrine? What was the connection between the Truman Doctrine and the Marshall Plan? What led to the formation of the COMINFORM (Communist Information Bureau)? Finally, did 1947 mark the beginning of the cold war? Explain why. Emphasize that precise chronology becomes very important in discussing how an event like the cold war unfolds.

2. Assign teams of students the task of presenting one of the following cold war events: the Berlin blockade and airlift, the formation of NATO, the victory of the Chinese Communist Party and the founding of the People's Republic of China, the Korean War, or the Geneva Conference of 1954. Some additional reading will be necessary, but the material cited at the end of "Lectures Strategies," number 1, should be adequate. Each student should, in addition to his or her team assignment, write a short essay on the presentation and the experience of working with the team.

3. Have students compare and contrast the experience of two European countries, one from the West and the other from the East, in the 1950s. One rather obvious possibility is West Germany and East Germany. The discussion will most likely center on the politics of the two countries, but students should also try to ascertain the quality of life in the two countries. For this assignment, you may want to assign students a chapter or two in surveys such as Gordon Wright, *France in Modern Times*, 3rd ed. (New York: W. W. Norton, 1981); or Dietrich Orlow, *A History of Modern Germany: 1871 to Present* (Englewood Cliffs, NJ: Prentice Hall, 1995). For statistics and other material, alert students to publications such as the *Statesman's Year Book* (New York: St. Martin's Press, annual). Another approach to this assignment might be to consider the cold war from the perspective of non-aligned western states, such as Austria, Switzerland, Finland, or Ireland. What aspects of these countries' history or geography may have contributed to their neutrality?

4. As part of a 1950s day or week, present students with a selection of possible topics on which they may give five-minute reports. Topics might include political figures such as Konrad Adenauer, Nikita Khrushchev, or Martin Luther King, Jr.; events such as the coronation of Queen Elizabeth II, the launching of *Sputnik*, or the opening of the first McDonald's; rock-and-roll songs, stars, or dances; or movies, magazines, and other cultural phenomena. Students should be encouraged to be creative. For example, someone might decide to come to class wearing the attire of the 1950s. His or her report should be a brief description of the clothing, hairdo, accessories, and functionality—if any—of the way the person was dressed. David Halberstam, *The Fifties* (New York: Villard Books, 1993) would be a good resource to put on reserve.

Essay Questions

1. In addition to the topics in "In-Class Assignments and Presentation Topics," number 2, several other cold war topics from the 1950s and 1960s would serve as a basis for interesting research assignments. They might include the East German uprising in 1953, the Hungarian Revolution of 1956, the Suez Canal crisis of 1956, the Berlin crisis of 1958 to 1962, the building of the Berlin Wall in 1961, the Bay of Pigs invasion of Cuba in 1961, and the Cuban missile crisis of 1962.

Sources listed at the end of "Lecture Strategies," number 1 should be sufficient to get students started.

2. Assign students a research project on the process of liberation in a country in Africa or Asia. You may wish to limit the possibilities available. Some areas—the Indian subcontinent, for example—form too large and complicated a topic for a research paper unless it is to be the major paper for the term. Also consider whether you will be able to refer students to available sources in many different areas. Ask students to define a problem or present a tentative thesis. The paper should not simply retell the story of the liberation of a particular country, but should focus on the major challenges the country faces, and the various legacies of its colonial experience and history.

In addition to the titles by Vadney, Hargreaves, and McIntyre cited in the chapter's bibliography, see Franz Ansprenger, *The Dissolution of the Colonial Empires* (London: Routledge, 1989). Also useful is the encyclopedic book by J. A. S. Grenville, *A History of the World in the Twentieth Century*, enlarged ed. (Cambridge, MA: Belknap Press, 2000).

Additional Resources: Literature

Beauvoir, Simone de, *The Mandarins*. 1956.
Beckett, Samuel, *Waiting for Godot*. 1954.
Bradbury, Ray, *Fahrenheit 451*. 1953.
Farrington, Constance, trans., *Frantz Faron: The Wretched of the Earth*. 1986.
Hayward, Max, and Manya Harari, trans., *Boris Pasternak: Doctor Zhivago*. 1958.
Orwell, George, *1984*. 1949.
Orwell, George, *Animal Farm*. 1945.
Parshley, H. M., trans., *Simone de Beauvoir: The Second Sex*. 1993.
Sidhwa, Bapsi, *Cracking India: A Novel*. 1992.
Vannewitz, Leila, trans., *Heinrich Böll: The Clown*. 1994.

Additional Resources: Film and Video

Dr. Strangelove or: How I Learned to Stop Worrying and Love the Bomb (1964; VHS/DVD, 1 hr., 33 min.). Stanley Kubrick's cold-war classic is the ultimate satire of the nuclear age.

The Cold War (1998; VHS, 28 hrs.). The ambitious, twelve-part documentary by CNN presents perspectives on the cold war from 1917–1990.

Thirteen Days (2001; VHS/DVD, 2 hrs, 22 min.). This film presents a solid recreation in detail of the events of the Cuban missile crisis.

There are a countless cold war propaganda films (that may or may not have been entertaining as well!) that are worth viewing alongside of a critical film like *Dr. Strangelove*. They might include:

Red Menace (1949; VHS, 1 hr., 27 min.).
Kiss Me Deadly (1955; VHS/DVD, 1 hr., 45 min.).
Jet Pilot (1959, VHS/DVD, 1 hr., 55 min.).
The Manchurian Candidate (1962; VHS/DVD, 2 hrs., 6 min.).

OTHER BEDFORD/ST. MARTIN'S RESOURCES FOR CHAPTER 27

The following resources are available to accompany Chapter 27. Please refer to the Preface of this manual for detailed descriptions of all the ancillaries.

For Instructors

Transparencies

The following maps and images from Chapter 27 are available as full-color acetates.

- Map 27.1: The Impact of World War II on Europe
- Map 27.2: Divided Germany and the Berlin Airlift, 1946–1949
- Map 27.3: European NATO Members and the Warsaw Pact in the 1950s
- Map 27.4: The Partition of Palestine and the Creation of Israel, 1947–1948
- Map 27.5: The Decolonization of Africa (1951–1990)
- Map 27.6: The Cuban Missile Crisis, 1962
- Mapping the West: The Cold War World, c. 1960
- Women Clearing Berlin, p. 890
- Re-creating Hungarian Youth, p. 895

Instructor's Resources CD-ROM

The following maps and image from Chapter 27, as well as a chapter outline, are available on disc in both PowerPoint and jpeg formats.

- Map 27.1: The Impact of World War II on Europe
- Map 27.2: Divided Germany and the Berlin Airlift, 1946–1949

- Map 27.3: European NATO Members and the Warsaw Pact in the 1950s
- Map 27.4: The Partition of Palestine and the Creation of Israel, 1947–1948
- Map 27.5: The Decolonization of Africa (1951–1990)
- Map 27.6: The Cuban Missile Crisis, 1962
- Mapping the West: The Cold War World, c. 1960
- Women Clearing Berlin, p. 890

Using the Bedford Series with The Making of the West

Available in print as well as online at **bedfordstmartins.com/usingseries,** this guide offers practical suggestions for using Akira Iriye, *Pearl Harbor and the Coming of the Pacific War: A Brief History with Documents and Essays*, in conjunction with chapters 26 and 27 of the textbook; Charles G. Cogaan, *Charles de Gaulle: A Brief Biography with Documents* in conjunction with chapters 27 and 28 of the textbook; Sherrill Brown Wells, *Pioneers of European Integration and Peace*, and Michael Marrus, *The Nuremberg War Crimes Trial, 1945–46: A Documentary History* in conjunction with Chapter 27 of the textbook.

For Students

Study Guides

The Online Study Guide at **bedfordstmartins.com/hunt** helps students synthesize the material they have learned as well as practice the skills historians use to make sense of the past. The following Map, Visual, and Document activities are available for Chapter 27.

Map Activity

- Map 27.3: European NATO Members and the Warsaw Pact in the 1950s

Visual Activity

- Women Clearing Berlin, p. 890

Reading Historical Documents

- The Schuman Plan on European Unity (1950), p. 893
- Consumerism, Youth, and the Birth of the Generation Gap, p. 905
- New Sources, New Perspectives: Government Archives and the Truth about the Cold War, p. 885

CHAPTER

28

Postindustrial Society and the End of the Cold War Order

1965–1989

Chapter Resources

Main Chapter Topics

1. Humans were, by the 1970s, highly dependent upon machines, even for ordinary daily life, because of the technological advances achieved in increasingly prosperous industrialized countries. Living conditions and workplaces were particularly changed by the introduction of television receivers and personal and mainframe computers. Information technologies revolutionized economies in the post-industrial age, and knowledge, culture, and political information came to be shared and transmitted globally. The "space age" and the "nuclear age" and associated complex systems created new venues and technologies for cold-war competition as well as global development and cooperation. The advances in the biological sciences—especially in the area of reproduction—raised difficult ethical questions.

2. Postindustrial society moved from an economy based on manufacturing to one that emphasized the service sectors. This new economy depended on multinational corporations and large numbers of highly educated professionals and technical experts to gather and analyze data. Changes in the family, the arts, and politics appeared as products of and responses to the economic transformations taking place.

3. Protests against the status quo—domestic and foreign—exploded in the United States, Western Europe, and in other locations globally, prompting a wide range of reactions. In the United States, the civil rights movement achieved some progress for African Americans and came to be broadened to include the rights of other minority groups and women. The women's movement exploded across the political spectrum in the West and pushed for changes everywhere. The Soviet Union dealt harshly with dissent and failed to respond adequately to the problems that caused it. In 1968, in France and Czechoslovakia, protests escalated toward revolution but were defused.

4. The 1970s brought dramatic changes to international politics. In addition to an era of détente, which included negotiations to limit the nuclear arms race, other players—the oil-producing states organized in OPEC and loosely connected bands of terrorists—challenged the two superpowers and their allies.

5. Beginning in the late 1970s, Margaret Thatcher's neoliberalism became the standard Western tactic for dealing with "stagflation." Ronald Reagan built upon Thatcher's policies and applied them in the United States; Sweden and France persisted in welfare-state programs with equal success.

6. By the early 1980s, wars in Vietnam and Afghanistan, the power of oil-producing states, and the growing political force of Islam had weakened superpower preeminence. Yet, the largely peaceful collapse of communism in the Soviet satellite countries—Poland, Hungary, Germany, Czechoslovakia, and Romania—was an utter surprise, even though Gorbachev had introduced glasnost and perestroika to respond to the USSR's multiple problems.

Focus Question

How did technological, economic, and social change contribute to increased activism, and what were the political results of that activism?

1. Technological, economic and social change contributed to activism across the West in several ways. The increasing technological progress in the West led to greater prosperity but also to people's expectations of change and better lives. The complex systems and economies of the modern West made university and

technical training a necessity; more students in universities for longer periods of time created a new atmosphere of social protest and discontent with the status quo across the West, as youth culture changed fashion, lifestyle, and entertainment. Student-led movements at times rejected the values and expectations of mass culture, even while economic and social changes made advertisers, marketers, and corporations more adept at melding aspects of youth and consumer culture. Just as importantly, the transformation of communication through new technologies—television, computers, satellites, etc.—made the global transmission and sharing of information easier, and aided in the ability of the media and protesters across the West to publicize and popularize new ideas and social movements.

2. The results of the activism of the period were considerable, even if the development of mass culture continued and social systems became more homogenous in the long run. In the United States, despite setback, the civil rights campaigners expanded liberty and made society more inclusive. Women's rights made broad advances across Western societies, and women expanded their economic and social opportunities. Change was most significant in the Soviet bloc, where protest movements in the Soviet Union and throughout Eastern Europe, sustained by improved communication and support from the West, led in the long run to dramatic political change and the collapse of the communist system.

Annotated Chapter Outline

I. **The Revolution in Technology**

A. The Information Age: Television and Computers, pp. 916–918

1. Information technology catalyzed social change, as television, computers, and telecommunications increased the speed and range for conveying knowledge, culture, and politics globally.
2. These media continued the trend begun by mass journalism, film, and radio, of forming a more homogeneous society.
3. Between the mid-1950s and mid-1970s, Europeans rapidly adopted television.
4. As with radio, European governments owned and controlled television stations and their programming, which they funded with tax revenues.
5. In the belief that this medium should be used to preserve and enhance the humanist tradition, programming featured drama, ballet, concerts, variety shows, and news.
6. The emergence of communications satellites and video recorders in the 1960s introduced competition to state-sponsored television because sports broadcasts could be diffused globally and television stations could purchase feature films on videocassette.
7. News and educational programming were staples; travel shows were popular with an audience for whom travel was either impossible or forbidden.
8. In both East and West, heads of state could and did preempt regular programming.
9. In the West, electoral success increasingly depended on cultivating a successful media image.
10. Computers were another important innovation.
11. From the size of a gymnasium in the 1940s, computers shrank to the size of a briefcase by the 1980s and changed the pace and procedures of work by speeding up and easing tasks. Prices declined and computers became commonplace.
12. Computers also made possible a revival of "cottage industry," allowing individuals to work from their homes.

B. The Space Age, pp. 918–919

1. In 1957, the Soviet Union launched the world's first satellite, *Sputnik*, into orbit, beginning a competition with the United States that was quickly labeled the "space race."
2. In July 1969, a global audience watched on television as America put a man on the moon. Astronauts and cosmonauts were the era's most admired heroes.
3. The space race spawned a new fantasy world in the West, influencing children's toys and games, and popularizing science-fiction novels and films such as Stanley Kubrick's (1928–1999) *2001: A Space Odyssey* (1968).
4. Similarly, Polish writer Stanislaw Lem's (b. 1921) novel *Solaris* (1961) portrayed space-age individuals engaged in personal quests.
5. An international consortium headed by the United States launched the first commercial communications satellite, *Intelsat I*, in 1965, and by the 1970s, global satellite communication was a reality.
6. Space exploration advanced pure science, as data regarding cosmic radiation,

magnetic fields, and infrared sources were gathered by unmanned spacecraft.
7. This information reinforced the "big bang" theory of the universe's origins, first posited in the 1930s by American astronomer Edwin Hubble (1889–1953).

C. The Nuclear Age, p. 919

1. The economic use of the atom in the form of nuclear power boosted available energy and supported continued economic expansion.
2. The first nuclear power plant to produce electricity was built in Obinsk in the USSR in 1954.
3. Nuclear power for industrial, household, and military use multiplied a hundredfold during the 1960s and 1970s.
4. A new function for the modern state was technological development through the funding of projects such as nuclear reactors.

D. Revolutions in Biology and Reproductive Technology, pp. 919–921

1. In 1952, scientists Francis Crick (b. 1916) and James Watson (b. 1928) discovered the configuration of deoxyribonucleic acid (DNA), the material in a cell's chromosomes that carries hereditary information.
2. Beginning in the 1960s, genetics and the new field of molecular biology progressed rapidly, and a broader understanding of nucleic acids and proteins made possible new vaccines to combat polio and other deadly diseases.
3. Understanding how DNA worked allowed scientists to bypass natural reproduction through a process called "cloning."
4. Cloning and science's growing ability to genetically alter or even create new species raised ethical questions for many.
5. As Western societies industrialized and urbanized, traditional constraints on sexuality began to weaken.
6. By 1970, the widespread distribution of a new birth-control device, "the pill," provided the most reliable, temporary means of preventing pregnancy.
7. Popular use of birth control led people to separate sexuality from reproduction; young people began sexual relations earlier with less risk of pregnancy.
8. Pregnancy and childbirth were also transformed, as new medical procedures and equipment allowed closer monitoring of mother and child and childbirth increasingly took place in hospitals.
9. New technologies, such as in vitro fertilization, also allowed couples who might otherwise be childless to reproduce.

II. Postindustrial Society and Culture

A. Multinational Corporations, pp. 921–922

1. One aspect of this postindustrial society was the rise of multinational corporations.
2. These companies produced for a global market and conducted business worldwide but, unlike older international firms, they also established major factories in countries other than their home base.
3. The United States led the way in establishing such companies, but European and Japanese industries followed.
4. Some multinational corporations had revenues greater than entire nations, and their interests reached beyond a national or local outlook.
5. In the 1960s, to minimize labor costs and taxes, multinationals repositioned more of their operations from Europe to the emerging economies of formerly colonized states or third world countries.
6. Although these corporations provided jobs to third world inhabitants, profits mostly enriched foreign stockholders. The companies had little concern for localities and nations where they did business.
7. Critics initially denounced multinationals as a new form of imperialism; however, multinational firms believed global expansion was necessary to remain competitive.
8. In Europe, huge conglomerates were formed in sectors such as construction, and contributed to Europe's continuing economic growth.
9. European firms were often closely tied to their nations' governments.

B. The New Worker, pp. 922–924

1. In both Eastern-bloc and Western countries, a new working class emerged, consisting of white-collar, service personnel. Industrial labor and unions declined in numbers and influence.
2. The relationship of workers to their bosses shifted as workers adopted attitudes and gained responsibilities that had once been managerial prerogatives.
3. Economic distinctions based on the way one worked were also undermined.

4. By the 1970s, service-sector workers were a majority in several industrial countries.
5. In the Eastern bloc in the 1960s, huge differences remained between professional occupations and those involving physical work because of lower investment in advanced machinery and cleaner work processes.
6. In both the Western and Eastern-bloc countries, gender shaped the workforce.
7. In the East, women held less prestigious, lower-paying jobs than men.
8. In the West, farm life was modernized and became "agribusiness."
9. To run a modern farm, one needed the newest technology and chemical products, and producers tailored their crops to global markets.
10. Governments, farmers' cooperatives, and planning agencies took over decision making from the individual farmer, setting production quotas and handling market transactions.

C. The Boom in Education and Research, p. 924

1. Because research was necessary to economic growth and military power, the United States funneled more than 20 percent of its gross national product (GNP) into research in the 1960s, siphoning off many of Europe's leading intellectuals and technicians in what came to be known as the "brain drain."
2. In Eastern-bloc countries, on the other hand, having to navigate through enormous bureaucratic red tape often meant that scientific findings became obsolete before they received governmental approval and be applied to technology.
3. In the West, the new criteria for success fostered an unprecedented growth in education, especially in universities and scientific institutes.
4. Great Britain established a new network of polytechnics and universities to encourage technical research; France set up administrative schools to train future high-level bureaucrats.
5. Institutions of higher learning, in the West especially, added courses in business management and information technology to educate postindustrial workers.

D. Changing Family Life and the Generation Gap, pp. 924–925

1. In the 1960s, the family appeared in many forms: single-parent households; "blended" households of two previously married persons, each with their own children; unmarried couples of the same sex or opposite sexes cohabiting; and traditionally married couples with fewer children.
2. As the marriage rate was falling, the divorce rate was rising and, by the mid-1960s, the birthrate was falling as well.
3. At the same time, however, the percentage of out-of-wedlock children soared.
4. Daily life within the family changed, as radio and television filled a family's leisure time.
5. Household appliances made housework less taxing, but also raised standards of cleanliness.
6. More women worked outside the home, in part because children were going on to schools of higher education, which meant they stayed in school longer and therefore cost couples more money for their education.
7. Whereas the early modern family organized labor, taught craft skills, and monitored reproductive behavior, the modern family seemed to have a primarily psychological function: to nurture the child while he or she learned intellectual skills in school.
8. Psychologists, social workers, and social service agencies offered additional aid, if necessary, in providing this emotional support, while television programs about family life gave viewers the opportunity to observe how others—even fictitious others—dealt with the tensions of modern life.
9. Even though young people stayed in school longer and were thus more financially dependent upon their parents than before, the development of a youth culture gave them an alternative emotional focus.
10. This youth culture was characterized by rebelliousness expressed through the music of heavily marketed and wildly successful bands such as the Beatles.
11. The cultural divide between parents and their children gave rise to a "generation gap" during the 1960s.

E. Art, Ideas, and Religion in a Technocratic Society, pp. 925–927

1. A new artistic movement, "pop art," featured images from everyday life and employed the glossy techniques and products of a mass-consumer society, what its practitioners called "admass."
2. Artists parodied modern commercialism and depicted grotesque aspects of ordinary consumer products, as in Swedish-born artist Claes Oldenburg's (b. 1929) *Giant Hamburger with Pickle Attached* (1962).
3. Artists also drew on other sources such as folk traditions of the Caribbean and Africa for inspiration.
4. In music, American composer John Cage (1912–1992) added sounds produced by everyday items to his musical scores.
5. Other composers, called "minimalists," simplified music by scoring repeated and sustained notes.
6. Some, such as Karlheinz Stockhausen (b. 1928), emphasized modern technology and introduced electronic music into classical compositions in 1953.
7. The social sciences were at the peak of their prestige during these decades, often because of social scientists' increasing use of statistical models and predictions made possible by advanced, electronic computations.
8. The social sciences often undermined faith in the Enlightenment ideal of individual agency and freedom. In anthropology, Claude Lévi-Strauss (b. 1908) developed structuralism, a theory that maintained that all societies functioned within controlling structures (such as kinship or exchange) that operated according to coercive rules.
9. Amidst rapid social change, the Catholic church rejected birth control and voiced concerns over the crisis of faith caused by affluence and secularism, but it also engaged in a new global vision implementing the ideals of Vatican II.
10. In the United States, Protestant revivalism drew many people to join sects that believed in the literal truth of the Scriptures.
11. In Western Europe, churchgoing remained low, and the Soviet bloc promoted an antireligious culture.
12. Throughout the West, the religious landscape became more diverse as Muslims, Hindus, and Jews emigrated in search of economic opportunity and an escape from the hardships of decolonization.

III. Protesting Cold War Conditions

A. Cracks in the Cold War Order, pp. 927–930

1. Across the social and political spectrum, calls for softening the effects of the cold war were heard, and many nations struck out on their own political course that was independent from the superpowers.
2. Willy Brandt (1913–1992), the Socialist mayor of West Berlin, became foreign minister (1966) and pursued a policy of reconciliation and trade with Communist East Germany known as Ostpolitik.
3. In France, President Charles de Gaulle (1890–1970) steered a middle course between the United States and the Soviet Union, pulling France out of NATO, and signing trade agreements with Soviet-bloc countries.
4. Following de Gaulle's lead, Western Europe began to reassert itself.
5. In the Soviet Union, reform continued under new leaders: Leonid Brezhnev (1906–1982) and Alexei Kosygin (1904–1980), who tried to reduce discontent by producing more consumer goods.
6. In the arts, Ukrainian poet Yevgeny Yevtushenko (b. 1933) exposed Soviet complicity in the Holocaust in *Babi Yar* (1961).
7. In East Berlin, Christa Wolf (b. 1929) wrote about a couple tragically divided by the Berlin Wall in *Divided Heaven* (1965).
8. Repression returned later in the 1960s, and visual artists began holding secret exhibitions while writers circulated uncensored publications by hand.
9. In the United States, violent racism was a weak link in the American claim to moral superiority in the cold war.
10. Lyndon B. Johnson (1908–1973; president 1963–1969), who became president when Kennedy was assassinated, steered the Civil Rights Act through Congress in 1964.
11. This legislation forbade segregation in public facilities and created the Equal Employment Opportunity Commission (EEOC) to fight job discrimination.
12. Johnson's Great Society program attempted to improve the lives of the poorest Americans.

13. At the same time, the United States was becoming increasingly embroiled beyond its borders in Vietnam, where it supported non-Communist South Vietnamese leaders against a Communist uprising backed by the Soviet Union and China.
14. The seemingly endless conflict created domestic tension and led to Johnson's decision in 1968 not to seek the presidency in the next election.

B. **The Growth of Citizen Activism, pp. 930–933**

1. In the midst of continued conflict, a new social activism emerged in the West. A broad cross-section of Americans embraced the civil rights movement in the United States and transformed it.
2. In 1965, César Chávez (1927–1993) led Mexican American migrant workers in the California grape agribusiness in a strike for better wages and working conditions.
3. Meanwhile, the African American civil rights movement took a dramatic turn when riots erupted across the United States in 1965, and in subsequent summers.
4. Some activists transformed their struggle into a militant affirmation of racial differences.
5. They argued that blacks should celebrate their African heritage and work for "black power" by asserting and claiming the rights they were constitutionally entitled to instead of begging for them nonviolently.
6. As the emphasis shifted in the civil rights movement, white, American university students who had participated in the early stages of the civil rights movement found themselves excluded from leadership positions among black activists.
7. Many turned instead to the growing protest against technological change, consumerism, sexual repression, the educational establishment, and the Vietnam War.
8. European youths also rebelled in Rome, Prague, and Poland.
9. Students attacked the traditional university curriculum, and turned the defiant rebelliousness of 1950s youth culture into a politically activist style.
10. In their personal lives, they rejected middle-class values concerning fashion, personal hygiene, living arrangements, drug use, and sexuality.
11. Businesses made billions of dollars selling blue jeans, dolls dressed as hippies, natural foods, and drugs, as well as packaging and managing the superstars of the counterculture.
12. Women's activism exploded across the political spectrum.
13. Many middle-class women responded positively to the international best-seller *The Feminine Mystique* (1963), written by American journalist Betty Friedan (b. 1921).
14. In the United States, the National Organization for Women (NOW) was formed in 1966 to bring about full female participation in American society.
15. Activist women came to resent sex discrimination within the civil rights and student movements, and some women demanded abortion rights or the decriminalization of homosexuality.
16. Many women of color went further, speaking out against the "double jeopardy" of being both black and female.
17. Demands for equal pay, job opportunities, and protection from physical and sexual violence framed the major legal struggles of the women's movement of the 1970s.

C. **1968: Year of Crisis, pp. 933–936**

1. In January 1968, on the first day of the Vietnamese New Year, or Tet, the Vietcong and the North Vietnamese attacked more than one hundred South Vietnamese towns and American bases, inflicting heavy casualties and causing many Americans to conclude that the war might be unwinnable.
2. The antiwar movement gained crucial momentum, and protest escalated.
3. Adding to the unstable situation was the assassination of Martin Luther King, Jr. on April 4, 1968.
4. More than a hundred cities across the United States erupted in violence as a result.
5. In France, students at Nanterre University had gone on strike in January, demanding a say in university governance.
6. Students at the Sorbonne showed solidarity, and the police responded by assaulting and arresting student demonstrators.
7. The Parisian middle classes were sympathetic to the students, horrified by

police violence and sharing the students' resentment of bureaucracy.

8. By May, the protests had become outright revolt, and workers joined in.
9. In June, President Charles de Gaulle announced a pay raise for workers, and businesses offered them a stronger voice in decision making.
10. De Gaulle then sent tanks into Paris, and shut down the student movement.
11. Protest erupted in Czechoslovakia as well. In autumn 1967, at a Czechoslovak Communist Party congress, Alexander Dubček (1921–1992), head of the Slovak branch of the party, called for more social and political openness, beginning the "Prague Spring."
12. As the Czechs and Slovaks experimented with their newfound freedom of expression, Poland, East Germany, and the Soviet Union threatened Dubček's government daily.
13. When Dubček failed to attend a meeting of Warsaw Pact leaders, Soviet threats intensified.
14. On the night of August 20–21, 1968, Soviet tanks rolled into Prague and despite Czechoslovak resistance put an end to the reform movement.
15. Soviet determination to retain control over its Eastern-bloc countries was expressed in the Brezhnev Doctrine, announced in November 1968, which made clear that further moves toward change would meet similar repression.
16. Repression of artists and intellectuals as well as anti-Semitism in Russia increased, and Jews were subject to educational restrictions, severe job discrimination, and constant assault on their religious practice.
17. As attacks intensified in the 1970s, Soviet Jews protested and sought to emigrate to Israel or the United States, but the government severely restricted emigration.
18. Repression increased the "brain drain" from the East, and the presence of these exiles and escapees in the United States and Western Europe helped erode any lingering support for communism.
19. In the United States, the newly elected president Richard Nixon ordered the invasion of Cambodia in the Vietnam War, which instigated further student protests and ultimately resulted in the shooting of students at Kent State University by the National Guard.
20. Mired in turmoil, the United States and North Vietnam continued to support hostilities until, in 1975, South Vietnam collapsed under a determined North Vietnamese offensive, and Vietnam was forcibly reunified.
21. In the aftermath of the war, the United States experienced a crisis of confidence, and many blamed protesters and activists rather than the government for the country's perceived decline.

IV. The Testing of Superpower Domination and the End of the Cold War

A. A Changing Balance of World Power, pp. 936–939

1. After being tested by protest at home, the great powers confronted the world.
2. In 1972, the United States pulled off a foreign policy triumph over the USSR when it opened relations with China, the other Communist giant.
3. The Soviet Union reacted to this possible rapprochement between China and the United States by making overtures to the West.
4. In 1972, the superpowers signed the Strategic Arms Limitation Treaty (SALT I), which set a cap on the number of antimissile and antiballistic weapons each country could own and position.
5. In 1975, in the Helsinki accords on human rights, the Western nations officially acknowledged Soviet territorial gains in World War II in exchange for the Soviet-bloc countries' guarantee of basic human rights.
6. Despite these successes, rising purchases of military and imported goods made the United States a debtor nation that owed billions of U.S. dollars to other countries. The United States was forced to share leadership in the global economic system with the Common Market countries.
7. In the meantime, U.S. president Richard Nixon's (1913–1994; president, 1969–1974) administration was rocked by the Watergate scandal, and he resigned in disgrace in the summer of 1974.
8. The Middle East provided a new challenge to Western global dominance.
9. In June 1967, Israeli forces responded to Palestinian guerrilla attacks by seizing Gaza and the Sinai Peninsula from Egypt, the Golan Heights from Syria, and the West Bank from Jordan.

10. In 1973, Egypt and Syria attacked Israel on Yom Kippur and, with military assistance from the United States, Israel successfully turned back the invasion.
11. After their defeat, the Arab nations established in the Organization of Petroleum Exporting Countries (OPEC), quadrupled the price of oil, and imposed an embargo on oil exports to the United States in retaliation for its support of Israel.
12. The oil embargo caused unemployment to rise by more than 50 percent in Europe and the United States.
13. Whereas previous recessions had brought falling prices because goods remained unsold, the oil shortage created a recession that was accompanied by inflation, while rising interest rates discouraged industrial investment and consumer buying.
14. The simultaneous rise in prices, unemployment, and interest rates was dubbed "stagflation."
15. Encouraged by OPEC's successful stand against the West, many ordinary persons in the Middle East called for reform and, at the end of the 1970s, an uprising in Iran overthrew the U.S.-backed government and created an Islamic society.

B. The Western Bloc Meets Challenges with Reform, pp. 939–942

1. In Europe in the 1970s, the restoration of political order was met with terrorism as disaffected youths perpetrated kidnappings, bank robberies, bombings, and assassinations in West Germany and Italy.
2. In Ireland, nationalist and religious violence pitted Catholics against Protestants in the north.
3. In Britain, Margaret Thatcher's (b. 1925) Conservative Party came to power amidst stagflation and violence in Ireland, and instituted a package of economic policies known as "neoliberalism," based on the monetarist or supply-side economic theory, that the only way to ensure prosperity was in a business-friendly environment with a reduced role for government and a dismantled welfare state.
4. Thatcher's mix of income tax cuts, privatization, and budget cuts shocked the British economy and reduced her popularity.
5. War against Argentina in 1982 over the Falkland Islands revived her popularity, and the economy strengthened.
6. Thatcher's example was followed by Ronald Reagan (1911–2004) in the United States, who served as president from 1981–1989.
7. Reagan vowed to promote the values of the "moral majority," cutting taxes and reducing government support for the welfare state.
8. Reagan increased military spending and budget deficits, warning repeatedly of the Communist threat.
9. Helmut Kohl (b. 1930) in West Germany also froze government spending and reduced taxes.
10. In France, president François Mitterrand (1916–1996) took a different approach by increasing wages and social spending to stimulate the economy, although his successor Jacques Chirac (b. 1932) adopted neoliberal policies.
11. Some smaller European countries, such as Spain and Ireland, thrived by combining Common Market membership with investment in education and neoliberal economic policies.
12. Only Sweden maintained a full array of social programs for everyone, although high taxes and a huge influx of immigrants caused many to wonder whether the welfare state had become too extreme.

C. Collapse of Communism in the Soviet Bloc, pp. 942–947

1. Reform was also begun in the Soviet Union but, instead of strengthening the economy, it provoked further rebellion and the eventual collapse of Communist rule in the USSR.
2. A deteriorating economy, a corrupt system of political and economic management, and a deteriorating standard of living brought the need for reform to the forefront.
3. In 1985, Mikhail Gorbachev (b. 1931) opened an era of change with a program of economic reform called "perestroika," and a policy of greater freedom of speech and openness in government called "glasnost."
4. Glasnost brought many of the Soviet Union's social and economic problems into the public arena and fostered increasing dissent.

5. The explosion of the nuclear reactor at Chernobyl in 1986 highlighted the shortcomings of the system and increased criticism in the Soviet press.
6. In the fall of 1987 a Gorbachev ally, Boris Yeltsin, quit the government and demanded more radical reform. He inspired political opposition to the regime.
7. In Poland, Lech Walesa (b. 1943) and Anna Walentynowicz (b. 1929) formed the independent labor movement called "Solidarity," which rivaled the influence of the Communist Party.
8. In a reversal of the Brezhnev Doctrine, Gorbachev refused to interfere in the political course of another nation, and Walesa became president of Poland in 1990.
9. Chinese Communists struggled to control dissident students, whose inspirational protest movement was crushed by military force.
10. Communism next collapsed in Hungary.
11. In the summer of 1989, the Berlin Wall—the most potent and obvious symbol of a divided Europe—fell as crowds of East Germans flooded the borders of the crumbling Soviet bloc.
12. In the "velvet revolution" of Czechoslovakia, dissident playwright Václav Havel was elected to the presidency.
13. In Romania, the brutal Communist dictator Nicolae Ceauşescu (1918–1989) was tried by a military court in 1989, and executed.
14. His death signaled that the very worst of communism was over.

Lecture Strategies

1. Many instructors in Western Civilization courses are not comfortable with discussions of technology. Nevertheless, too many extraordinary technological developments occurred in the postwar period to simply ignore them. To make presentations manageable, you may want to focus part of a lecture on just one aspect of technological change, perhaps following the lecture up with some reading for students or a discussion (a few ideas are offered below). One good place to start would be the technological innovation of the modern era that may have sparked the most cultural and political change, and one that was ubiquitous by the 1960s—the television.

In addition to titles cited in the chapter's bibliography, you may wish to consult some of the following titles: David E. Fisher and Marshall Jon Fisher, *Tube: The Invention of Television* (Washington, DC: Counterpoint, 1996), offers a solid, readable history of the invention of television. Although it concentrates mostly on the 1920s and 1930s, it carries the story into the 1960s and 1970s and also features a useful bibliography. It is a part of the Sloan Technology series, a highly recommended series of books on technology and science for laypersons. Anthony Smith, ed., *Television: An International History* (Oxford: Oxford University Press, 1995), provides a wide-ranging and authoritative collection of essays. Also useful is Jeff Kisseloff, ed., *The Box: An Oral History of Television (1920–1961)* (New York: Viking Press, 1995), which deals largely with television broadcasting. Ellen Mickiewicz offers an interesting and thorough account of the influence of television on Soviet culture in *Changing Channels: Television and the Struggle for Power in Russia* (New York: Oxford University Press, 1997). Although not directly relevant, "Big Dream, Small Screen," part of *The American Experience* series (PBS, 1997), provides a fine biography of Philo Farnsworth, a self-taught inventor who played a highly important role in the development of television in the 1930s. It should be useful to consult Elana Levine, *Wallowing in Sex: The New Sexual Culture of 1970s American Television* (Durham, NC: Duke University Press, 2007) for some insight into the juncture between feminism, pop culture, and television in that era.

The development and popularization of computers and their rapid development in the 1960s and 1970s was equally consequential, and cannot be separated from the political events of this period. Students may know little or nothing about the history of computing, and a brief side lecture on the topic would provide a different angle on history for some students, and will make it clear how technology, politics, and social change are all interconnected. The following are a few good sources with which to begin. Paul Cerruzi, *A History of Modern Computing* (Cambridge, MA: MIT Press, 2003), is an excellent introduction and features an extensive bibliography. Scott McCartney, *ENIAC: The Triumphs and Tragedies of the World's First Computer* (New York: Walker & Co., 1999) is useful mostly for background. McCartney offers a careful study of the development of ENIAC in the 1940s and examines the problems the developers faced in marketing their invention. Arthur L. Norberg and Judy E. O'Neill, *Transforming Computing: The Pentagon's Role, 1962–1987* (Baltimore: Johns Hopkins University Press, 1996), discusses the impact of the cold war and defense contracts on computing.

Although intended for college and high school students in survey courses, Michael D. Richards and Philip F. Riley, *Term Paper Resource Guide to Twentieth-Century World History* (Westport, CT: Greenwood

Press, 2000), will probably be of use to instructors as well. A large number of the entries concern topics on technology and science. Each entry contains an extensive bibliography of primary and secondary sources.

2. The space race has many possibilities as a lecture topic. It can be used as an alternative means for approaching cold-war history and for helping students contemplate the competitive dimension of the conflict as a spur to human activity. It lends itself to any number of comparative topics, such as exploration and discovery, the search for heroes, new ways of doing science, or even of exploring the effects of cold-war competition on other areas of human endeavor, such as athletics. Enthralling as the story of the space race is, it is important to emphasize the military imperative behind it. Whatever else it might have been, it was first and foremost a component of the arms race. Ronald Reagan's "star wars" initiative can be brought into the story to drive this point home.

The best starting place for the space race is Walter A. McDougall, *The Heavens and the Earth: A Political History of the Space Age* (New York: Basic Books, 1985). Other useful sources include David Baker, *Conquest: A History of Space Achievements from Science Fiction to the Shuttle* (Salem, NH: Salem House, 1984); and Phillip Clark, *The Soviet Manned Space Program: An Illustrated History of the Men, the Missions, and the Spacecraft* (New York: Orion Books, 1988). To emphasize that the Soviet Union hoped to land a man on the moon before the United States, you might show the fascinating documentary *Secret Soviet Moon Mission* (PBS Home Video, 1999, 1 hr.). It covers the career of Sergei Pavlovich Korolev and focuses on his efforts to land a Soviet cosmonaut on the moon. James Harford, *Korolev: How One Man Masterminded the Soviet Drive to Beat America to the Moon* (New York: John Wiley & Sons, 1997), uses Russian sources and is the best biography in English of this important figure. Frances Fitzgerald provides a lively but well-sourced look at the "star wars" initiative and the Reagan presidency in *Way Out There in the Blue: Reagan, Star Wars, and the End of the Cold War* (New York: Simon and Schuster, 2000). For a somewhat broader view, see Nigel Hey, *The Star Wars Enigma: Behind the Scenes of the Cold War Race for Missile Defense* (Washington D.C.: Potomac Books, 2006).

3. Basic sources on the many important developments in biology include, first, these books on the discovery of the structure of DNA: Francis Crick, *What Mad Pursuit: A Personal View of Scientific Discovery* (New York: Basic Books, 1988); James Watson, *The Double Helix: A Personal Account of the Discovery of the Structure of DNA* (New York: Athenaeum, 1968), which has also been published as a Norton Critical Edition (1980); and John Gribbin, *In Search of the Double Helix* (New York: McGraw-Hill, 1985).

Among the many books on reproductive technology, Roger Gosden, *Designing Babies: The Brave New World of Reproductive Technology* (New York: W. H. Freeman, 1999), presents the latest information on reproductive technology in nontechnical language. A good discussion from a historical perspective is that of Margaret Marsh and Wanda Ronner, *The Empty Cradle: Infertility in America from Colonial Times to the Present* (Baltimore: Johns Hopkins University Press, 1996). See also R. G. Edwards and Patrick Steptoe, *A Matter of Life, the Story of a Medical Breakthrough* (New York: William Morrow, 1980), an account of the first "test-tube" baby from the perspective of the doctors. Robin Henig, *Pandora's Baby: How the First Test Tube Babies Sparked the Reproductive Revolution* (Boston: Houghton-Mifflin, 2004), offers a longer-term perspective on the same events. The best book on the birth control pill is Elizabeth Siegel Watkins, *On the Pill: A Social History of Oral Contraceptives, 1950–1970* (Baltimore: Johns Hopkins University Press, 1998).

4. Social change is an important topic, but also one that is sometimes elusive. Two chapters in J. Robert Wegs and Robert Ladrech, *Europe Since 1945: A Concise History*, 4th ed. (New York: St. Martin's Press, 1996), provide a useful introduction to the topic: Chapter 9, "Postwar European Society: The Managed"; and Chapter 10, "Postwar European Society: The Managers." Each chapter features a good deal of statistical information and an extensive bibliography. Another useful source is Chapter 10, "The Social Revolution, 1945–1990," in Eric Hobsbawm, *The Age of Extremes: A History of the World, 1914–1991* (New York: Pantheon Books, 1994). Arthur Marwick, in *Class in the Twentieth Century* (New York: St. Martin's Press, 1986), offers a general survey.

A quite different approach involves using the Beatles as a focus for an examination of popular culture, much as the suggestion in Chapter 27 for using Elvis as a focus. In this case, the questions to ask might be: Why were the Beatles so popular? And, what does their popularity say about Europe and the United States (and, to a considerable extent, much of the rest of the world) in the 1960s? Using the Beatles for this purpose is more complicated than using Elvis, in that the Beatles—and especially their manager, Brian Epstein—were quite astute in playing off existing trends and determining what would set the Beatles apart and set new trends.

From the embarrassment of riches on the Beatles, here are a few of the most basic sources: The best place to start may be James Miller, *Flowers in the Dustbin: The Rise of Rock and Roll, 1947–1977* (New York: Simon & Schuster, 1999). Miller, a well-known rock critic, devotes five chapters to the Beatles, placing them in the context of the development of rock and roll. Also useful for this purpose is Ian MacDonald, *Revolution in the Head: The Beatles' Records and the Sixties*, 2nd ed. (London: Fourth Estate, 1997). In the way of primary sources, the massive 1995 ABC network television production is available on videocassettes as *The Beatles Anthology* (Turner Home Entertainment, 1996; 8 videocassettes, 10 hrs., 28 min). The Beatles's first film is available on CD-ROM: *A Hard Day's Night* (Voyager Co., 1993). John Lennon, *Lennon Remembers: The Rolling Stone Interviews* (New York: Popular Library, 1971), presents Lennon on the Beatles just as they were breaking up. Brian Epstein and Martin Lewis, *A Cellarful of Noise: The Autobiography of the Man Who Made the Beatles, with a New Companion Narrative* (Los Angeles, CA: Byron Press Multimedia Books, 1998), provide some insights into Epstein's highly successful efforts to create and market the Beatles. Also useful is Charles Neises, ed., *The Beatles Reader: A Selection of Contemporary Views, News, & Reviews of the Beatles in Their Heyday* (Ann Arbor, MI: Popular Culture, Ink., 1991).

A number of good biographies are also available. Perhaps the best is Philip Norman, *Shout!: The Beatles in Their Generation*, 2nd ed. (New York: Simon & Schuster, 1996); also highly regarded is Mark Hertsgaard, *A Day in the Life: The Music and Artistry of the Beatles* (New York: Delacorte Press, 1995). Two books that view the Beatles as serious musicians are Walter Everett, *The Beatles as Musicians: Revolver through the Anthology* (New York: Oxford University Press, 1999); and Allan Kozinn, *The Beatles* (New York: Chronicle Books, 1995).

For more general background, see Arthur Marwick, *The Sixties: Cultural Revolution in Britain, France, Italy, and the United States, c. 1958–c. 1974* (Oxford: Oxford University Press, 1998). See also CNN's *Cold War*, Episode 13, "Make Love, Not War: 1960s"; and Neil A. Hamilton, ed., *The ABC-CLIO Companion to the 1960s Counterculture in America* (Santa Barbara, CA: ABC-CLIO, 1997). A good recent general history of the era in America is Mark Lytle, *America's Uncivil Wars: The Sixties Era, From Elvis to the Fall of Nixon* (New York: Oxford University Press, 2006).

5. Domestic politics in the 1960s is a fascinating but also large topic. Because it would be difficult to ignore the United States in this period (in itself a huge topic), you might consider a discussion of the 1960s in America based on the lives of Martin Luther King, Jr. and Lyndon B. Johnson, fellow southerners who were similar in their heroic struggles to recall America to its fundamental values. The Great Society program of Johnson is well worth lecturing on in detail, as emblematic of a large-scale, practical political effort to harness American idealism and respond to the volatile social circumstances of the era. The difficulties and challenges of the efforts to extend the welfare state will make the success of Thatcher- and Reagan-style neoliberalism more understandable to students. Fortunately, several fine books with which to work are available. A basic text is James T. Patterson, *Grand Expectations: The United States, 1945–1974* (New York: Oxford University Press, 1996). Chapter 15, "The Polarized Sixties: An Overview," is indispensable. Chapters 16 to 21 carry the story to 1968. A good short account is John A. Salmond, *My Mind Set on Freedom: A History of the Civil Rights Movement, 1954–1968* (Chicago: Ivan R. Dee, 1997). On King, see Taylor Branch, *Parting the Waters: America in the King Years, 1954–1963* (New York: Simon & Schuster, 1988); and Taylor Branch, *Pillar of Fire: America in the King Years, 1963–1965* (New York: Simon & Schuster, 1998). Clayborne Carson, ed., *The Papers of Martin Luther King, Jr.* (Berkeley, CA: University of California Press, 1992) has thus far reached the end of 1958 in four volumes. *The Eyes on the Prize* series consists of two parts, the first with six episodes (Alexandria, VA: PBS Video, 1986), and the second with eight (Alexandria, VA: PBS Video, 1989–1992). See also David Bradley and Shelley Fisher Fishkin, eds., *The Encyclopedia of Civil Rights in America*, 3 vols. (Armonk, NY: Sharpe Reference, 1998). On Johnson, see Robert Dallek, *Flawed Giant: Lyndon Johnson and His Times, 1961–1973* (New York: Oxford University Press, 1998). The literature on Johnson and Vietnam is vast and controversial. David Kaiser, *American Tragedy: Kennedy, Johnson, and the Origins of the Vietnam War* (Cambridge, MA: The Belknap Press, 2000), offers a thorough and careful examination of an important aspect of the topic. An excellent guide to the history of the war is Marilyn B. Young, *The Vietnam Wars, 1945–1990* (New York: HarperCollins, 1991). The best reference source is Spencer Tucker, ed., *Encyclopedia of the Vietnam War: A Political, Social, and Military History*, 3 vols. (Santa Barbara, CA: ABC-CLIO, 1998). *Vietnam: A Television History* (New York: Sony Corporation of America, 1987, 13 episodes, 780 min.) is an extraordinarily useful resource. A good overview of the Great Society is John Andrew, *Lyndon Johnson and the Great Society* (Chicago: I.R. Dee, 1998).

6. It may be best to approach 1968 as a series of reports followed by a class discussion. For this possibility, see the "In-Class Assignments and Presentation Topics," number 3. If you wish to concentrate on a single, crucial development, a lecture on the Prague Spring is suggested, a turning point that was not allowed to turn. Or, as some wit put it 21 years later, "'89 is just '68 turned upside down."

Joseph Rothschild, *Return to Diversity: A Political History of East Central Europe Since World War II*, 2nd ed. (New York: Oxford University Press, 1993) is the best book with which to begin. Kieran Williams, *The Prague Spring and Its Aftermath: Czechoslovak Politics,*

1968–1970 (Cambridge: Cambridge University Press, 1997) is a comprehensive analysis of the reform movement and its suppression by the Soviet Union that makes use of the archival sources available since the events of 1989. Jaromir Navratil, ed., *The Prague Spring '68* (Budapest: Central European University Press, 1998), is a good collection of documents. Two excellent studies are William Shawcross, *Dubček: Dubček and Czechoslovakia, 1918–1990* (London: Weidenfeld and Nicolson, 1991); and Jiri Valenta, *Soviet Intervention in Czechoslovakia, 1968: Anatomy of a Decision* (Baltimore: Johns Hopkins University Press, 1979 [rev. ed., 1991]), is a useful effort to explain the Soviet decision to invade. Also useful is Alexander Dubček with Jiri Hochman, *Hope Dies Last: The Autobiography of Alexander Dubček* (London: HarperCollins, 1993), which covers 1968 from Dubček's point of view; and Milan Kundera, *The Unbearable Lightness of Being* (New York: Harper & Row, 1984), a brilliant novel that, among many other things, explores aspects of 1968.

France in 1968 is another possibility. It would be worth considering why May 1968 in France came as close as it did to toppling de Gaulle's government. An in-depth analysis of events would show a nation undergoing the stresses of incomplete social and economic change, as well as revealing the unusual degree to which cultural, intellectual, and political affairs were concentrated in Paris. It also might contrast the attractive, even charismatic, anarchy of the student movement with the fumbling and uncertain but brutal response of the government. All of these elements created a crisis that seemed to be far more momentous than it was.

A good place to start is Chapter 12 of J. Robert Wegs and Robert Ladrech, *Europe Since 1945: A Concise History*, 4th ed. (New York: St. Martin's Press, 1996). See Keith A. Reader and Khursheed Wadia, *The May 1968 Events in France: Reproductions and Interpretations* (New York: St. Martin's Press, 1993). Two useful books on de Gaulle are Charles Cogan, *Charles de Gaulle: A Brief Biography with Documents* (Boston: Bedford/St. Martin's, 1996); and Jean Lacouture, *De Gaulle: The Ruler, 1945–1970* (New York: W. W. Norton, 1992). In addition to David Caute's book cited in the chapter's bibliography, see an oral history put together by Ronald Fraser, ed., *1968: A Student Generation in Revolt* (New York: Pantheon, 1988); Carole Fink, Philipp Gassert, and Detlef Junker, *1968: The World Transformed* (Washington, DC: German Historical Institute and Cambridge University Press, 1998); and Michael Seidman, *Imaginary Revolution: Parisian Students and Workers in 1968* (New York: Berghahn Books, 2004). For a more Teutonic focus, refer to the detailed and entertaining Nick Thomas, *Protest Movements in 1960s West Germany*, (New York: Berg, 2003).

7. The 1970s feature many developments in international politics, of which probably the most important are steps taken to reinforce détente and the impact of OPEC. The two are related in that the increasingly interconnected world economy made it difficult for the two superpowers to conduct the cold war without regard to the rest of the world. In addition, the Soviet Union, which in the 1970s was becoming a "gerontocracy" (government by old men), showed serious signs of social strain. Its aging leaders seemed to respond to domestic difficulties by a kind of international adventurism, including intervention in Afghanistan.

On SALT I, see, first, the memoirs by Henry Kissinger, *White House Years* (Boston: Little, Brown, 1979); Richard M. Nixon, *RN: The Memoirs of Richard Nixon* (New York: Grosset & Dunlap, 1978); and Gerald Smith, *Doubletalk: The Untold Story of SALT* (Garden City, NY: Doubleday, 1981). Smith was the chief American delegate and views Nixon's SALT diplomacy rather critically. See also Anatoly Dobrynin, *In Confidence: Moscow's Ambassador to America's Six Cold War Presidents* (New York: Times Books, 1995). John Morton Blum, *Years of Discord: American Politics and Society, 1961–1974* (New York: W. W. Norton, 1991) is good on the domestic considerations of SALT. William Bundy, *A Tangled Web: The Making of Foreign Policy in the Nixon Presidency* (New York: Hill & Wang, 1998), is a highly critical examination of American foreign policy as practiced by Kissinger and Nixon. Adam Ulam, *Dangerous Relations: The Soviet Union in World Politics, 1970–1982* (New York: Oxford University Press, 1983), provides an overview of Soviet activities in the international arena. John W. Young, ed., *The Longman Companion to Cold War and Détente, 1941–1991* (London: Longman, 1993), is a useful reference work. See also CNN's *Cold War*, Episode 16, "Détente, 1969–1975."

The Helsinki Accords of 1975, which were a notable and promising step at the time, would also be worth discussion. On Helsinki, see Michael B. Froman, *The Development of the Idea of Détente: Coming to Terms* (New York: St. Martin's Press, 1991); and Vojtech Mastny, ed., *Helsinki, Human Rights, and European Security* (Durham, NC: Duke University Press, 1986). See also the books by Bundy, Dobrynin, and Ulam listed in the preceding paragraph.

For OPEC, see Daniel Yergin, *The Prize: The Epic Quest for Oil, Money, and Power* (New York: Touchstone, 1993), a long but fascinating and informative book. See also Terry Lynn Karl, *The Paradox of Plenty: Oil Booms and Petro-States* (Berkeley, CA: University of California Press, 1997); and Morris Adelmen, *Genie Out of the Bottle: World Oil Since 1970* (Cambridge, MA: MIT Press, 1995).

The Soviet Union in the 1970s appeared headed toward serious crises on the domestic front. Begin with Gregory L. Freeze, "From Stalinism to

Stagnation, 1953–1985," in his *Russia: A History* (Oxford: Oxford University Press, 1997). A highly critical discussion is found in Chapter 10 of Martin Malia, *The Soviet Tragedy: A History of Socialism in Russia, 1917–1991* (New York: The Free Press, 1994). See also Seweryn Bialer, *The Soviet Paradox: External Expansion, Internal Decline* (New York: Alfred A. Knopf, 1986). More specialized titles include Marshall I. Goldman, *U.S.S.R. in Crisis: The Failure of an Economic System* (New York: W. W. Norton, 1983); and Murray Feshbach, *The Soviet Union: Population, Trends, and Dilemmas* (Washington, D.C.: Population Reference Bureau, 1982). See also Ulam, listed earlier.

Class Discussion Starters

1. Students will know a great deal about television as popular culture and will have opinions about its sociological and economic importance. Many are also fascinated by television as a technology and astounded to learn that some television programming was already happening in the 1930s. Television offers a way to discuss technological change in this period and also to chart the many repercussions in various aspects of life and work. A discussion focused on brainstorming changes related to television, or possibly tracking how the widespread use of television changed the way events like the fall of the Berlin wall or the Vietnam War were responded to by the public, would be useful and instructive.

2. The developments in biology (see "Lecture Strategies," number 3) obviously lend themselves to a class discussion about the cultural consequences of the separation of reproduction and sex, or the moral dilemmas associated with the advance of biological science in particular. Such a discussion will work best if it is rooted in lecture or textbook material about how and when these changes occurred, and some appreciation by students of the varieties of responses to them from various religious traditions, scientific organizations, and governments.

3. A particularly effective way to approach the Beatles or rock-and-roll culture in general is by connecting changes in pop culture to their relationship to broader developments relating to gender relations/roles, and/or consumer culture. See "Lecture Strategies," number 4, for a few sources, but students will have their own opinions as well about the relationship between male and female gender roles and pop music (make sure to keep the discussion historically focused) and the relationship between youth and consumer culture. Tom Frank's *The Conquest of Cool: Business Culture, Counterculture, and the Rise of Hip Consumerism* (Chicago: University of Chicago Press, 1997), may prove to be inspirational.

4. Margaret Thatcher and her policies are at the heart of attempts to revise the welfare state and jump-start the economy. There may be more distance between students and British politics than might be found in a similar discussion on the legacy of Ronald Reagan. After familiarizing students with the basics of Thatcher's approach, try a class discussion on the challenges her policies presented to her society. Students might usefully be assigned perspectives to critique or defend Thatcher as Labor party representatives, Liberal Democrats, or representatives of such broad social interests as unemployed workers, entrepreneurs, etc.

In addition to books listed in the chapter's bibliography, Thatcher's own views on her term in office are worth reading. See Margaret Thatcher, *The Downing Street Years* (London: HarperCollins, 1993). David Cannadine, *History in Our Time* (New Haven: Yale University Press, 1998), has an excellent chapter on Margaret Thatcher and her politics. Eric J. Evans, *Thatcher and Thatcherism* (New York: Routledge, 1997) provides a solid introduction to the former British prime minister's conservative revolution. Paul Pierson, *Dismantling the Welfare State: Reagan, Thatcher, and the Politics of Retrenchment* (New York: Cambridge University Press, 1996), is useful in showing the ideological connections between the two leaders. Several other titles may also be useful for background, including Thomas Janoski and Alexander Hicks, *The Comparative Political Economy of the Welfare State* (New York: Cambridge University Press, 1993); Monica Prasad's comparative and interestingly counterintuitive *The Politics of Free Markets: The Rise of Neoliberal Economic Policies in Britain, France, Germany and the United States* (Chicago: University of Chicago Press, 2006); and Theda Skocpol, *Social Policy in the United States: Future Possibilities in Historical Perspective* (Princeton, NJ: Princeton University Press, 1995).

5. Consider a class discussion where students construct, articulate, and defend their own explanations for why the Soviet bloc collapsed how and when it did. Consider the impact of communications, consumer culture, religion, pop culture, economic difficulties, and political leadership in West and East.

Reviewing the Text

Review Questions

1. What were the technological and scientific advances of the 1960s and 1970s, and how did they change human life and society?

[model answer] • ***Medical technology transformed treatments and outcomes:*** *Genetics and the new field of* *molecular biology progressed rapidly beginning in the 1960s. Growing understanding of nucleic acids effectively ended the ravages of polio, tetanus, syphilis, tuberculosis, and dangerous childhood diseases (mumps and measles) in the West. Heart transplants began in the late 1960s.*

• ***Ethical responsibility:*** *The possibility of genetically altering species or creating new ones led to concerns about affecting the balance of nature. Similarly, the development of expensive, lifesaving medical procedures led to debate about whether the enormous cost of medical technology to save a few lives would be better spent on helping the many who lacked basic health care.*

• ***Procreation and birth control:*** *Conception, pregnancy, and childbirth came to be classified as medical processes; in vitro fertilization and techniques to monitor labor and delivery developed. The availability of reliable birth control devices and techniques for safe abortions and sterilization procedures permitted young people to begin sexual relations earlier and separated sexuality from reproduction. In 1978, the first "test-tube" baby was born as treatments for infertility advanced.*

• ***A "sexual revolution":*** *Global media made public discussion of sexual matters explicit, technical, and widespread. The advent of the birth control pill meant that sexuality and reproduction no longer had to be directly connected. Western music, literature, and journalism became saturated with sexuality and in the climate of increased sexual awareness, homosexual behavior became more open.*

2. How did Western society and culture change in the postindustrial age?

[model answer] • ***The innovation of multinational corporations began:*** *These companies produced goods and services for a global market and conducted business worldwide but, unlike older kinds of international firms, these multinational corporations established major factories in countries other than their home base.*

• ***Workers shifted rank:*** *Postindustrial economic strength moved away from blue-collar work and toward the distribution of services, leading to a swelling of service workers.*

• ***Factories and rural labor became streamlined:*** *The relationship of factory workers to bosses shifted as workers were given more responsibility for production, causing a decline in union membership. In rural areas, individual farmers gave way to agribusinesses that improved productivity.*

• ***Criteria for success fostered growth in education:*** *The need for more scientists and bureaucrats fostered this increase. Education made the avenues to success more democratic by basing them on talent instead of wealth, but societal leveling did not occur in most Western universities, and instruction often remained rigid and old-fashioned.*

• ***Family dynamics were redefined and altered:*** *Media such as radio and television became a household's common social life. More women worked outside the home, but were still responsible for traditional household chores and child care. Young people remained dependent longer because of increased education requirements, but gained new roles as consumers. Advertisers and industrialists wooed the teenage market with consumer items associated with rock music, which fueled a unique youth culture and a growing generation gap.*

• ***Shifts in religious practice:*** *The Catholic church tried to accommodate the interest in toleration and democracy through Vatican II reforms. Religious fervor increased among many Protestants, who joined sects stressing literal Scriptural truth. In many Western European countries, churchgoing remained at a low ebb. Most striking was the changing composition of the Western religious public.*

3. What were the main issues for protestors in the 1960s, and how did governments address them?

[model answer] • ***Social equality:*** *Groups within society that felt exploited or not permitted equal economic, political, or social opportunities began to demand equality or cultural separation and independence.*

• ***Geopolitics:*** *Young people protested the superpowers' competition for dominance, which included the Vietnam War, consumerism, and technological advance. Communist countries faced increasing anticommunist activism in violent student demonstrations and even local Communist party leaders' efforts for change.*

• ***Education:*** *European university students protested high student-teacher ratios, outdated curriculums, and the lack of university funds. In many cases students were able to build coalitions with workers or antibureaucracy members of the middle class.*

• ***Nations worked to restore order:*** *In the United States and Europe, police and the military were used to maintain order in cities and on college campuses. The war in Vietnam eventually ended with a U.S. defeat, but public opinion was that activists, not the war or government corruption, had dealt the harshest blow to the United States' image. In the East, the Soviets developed the Brezhnev Doctrine, which stated that reform movements were a "common problem" of all socialist countries and would face swift repression.*

4. How and why did the balance of world power change during the 1980s?

[model answer] • ***Conservative leaders in the West, particularly Margaret Thatcher in Britain and Ronald Reagan in the United States, engaged in military buildups and warned electorates of the dangers of communism:*** *Thatcher and Reagan were determined to end "stagflation" and to adopt a more assertive foreign policy. As Western economies revived* *and military spending increased, the Soviet Union was subject to new pressures.*

• ***Reform in the Soviet Union led to the collapse of the communist system in the West:*** *As Gorbachev tried to loosen censorship and invigorate the Soviet economy; he also attempted to increase Soviet military spending to keep pace with the West. The Soviet system became less and less able to provide necessities and luxuries to its citizens.*

• ***Beginning in 1985, the relationship between Gorbachev and Reagan began to thaw:*** *Meetings between these leaders reduced tensions, and the Soviet withdrawal from Afghanistan also helped defuse the Cold War.*

Making Connections

1. What were the differences between industrial society of the late nineteenth century and postindustrial society of the late twentieth century?
[model answer] *Heavy industrialization was a feature of the late nineteenth century, but in the postindustrial period, society moved from an economy based on manufacturing to one that emphasized services. This new economy depended on large numbers of highly educated professional and technical experts to gather and analyze data, and to establish and maintain complex systems. And yet, white-collar workers did not necessarily enjoy better pay than blue-collar workers, even though they made up the majority of the workforce. Even though many jobs in the late nineteenth century demanded some degree of education, the need was less pronounced for factory work. There was also a significant social and economic divide between white-collar and blue-collar jobs. In the post-industrial society, computers simultaneously were smaller built, more powerful, and cheaper throughout the period, both increasing the pace of work and making it less labor intensive. In some cases, computers transformed the way work was performed. Communication technologies in particular proliferated and changed the way work was done. New technological improvements reduced the size of computers, which enabled individuals who owned a PC to perform their jobs at home for the first time since the eighteenth century.*

2. Why were there so many protests, acts of terrorism, and uprisings across the West in the decades between 1960 and 1990?
[model answer] *Prosperity and the rising benefits of a postindustrial, service-oriented economy made people ever more eager for peace. Communication technologies such as television also seemed to make it easier for protest movements and demonstrators to get their messages across and coordinate campaigns and demonstrations. Growing numbers of university students, after years of study, did not want to end their lives on some far away battlefield fighting a war that probably could not be won. Still other activists—including women and minorities—simply wanted a fair (or equal) chance at education, jobs, and political influence. Students, blacks, and other racial minorities, Soviet-bloc citizens, women, environmentalists, and homosexuals sometimes brought their societies to the brink of revolution during what became increasingly angry protests. Most were against the cold-war order and wanted to share equally in postindustrial prosperity. When they felt their voices had not been heard, many resorted to violence to get their message across.*

3. What have been the long-term consequences of Communist rule between 1917 and 1989?
[model answer] *For most of its existence, the Soviet Union relied on heavy industrialization, which was tied to its military programs. With so much of its resources committed to the military, spending on consumer production and other government services fell and standards of living slowly declined. Communism stifled creativity and motivation, while a corrupt economic and political system caused many to experience despair. Technologically, the Soviet Union lagged behind other European countries in bringing new technological know-how to bear on economic challenges, making Eastern Europe's transition from a Communist to a capitalist-based postmodern service economy all the more difficult.*

Discussing the Documents

Questions from Online Study Guide with Model Answers

Margaret Thatcher's Economic Vision, p. 941

1. What were Margaret Thatcher's economic policies and what did she hope to accomplish with them?
[model answer] *Thatcher's economic policies were to cut back on government spending, particularly in social programs, and then use the savings to reduce taxes for businesses. She hoped to stimulate the economy by easing the pressure on businesses, which would consequently create more jobs for the unemployed. Greater employment would in turn contribute to a more prosperous, "independent" Great Britain.*

2. What were the prevailing economic and social conditions in Great Britain when this document was produced?
[model answer] *When this document was produced, Great Britain, like most of Western Europe, was deep in a recession that had been largely brought about by the dramatic increase in oil prices. The days of prosperity and economic confidence were over, and Great Britain was faced with high inflation and high unemployment, as well as the revolt in Northern Ireland.*

Criticizing Gorbachev, p. 944

1. Why does the author suggest Gorbachev's reforms failed?
[model answer] *Tolstoya suggests that the logical outcome of Gorbachev's moves toward economic and political democracy was his own destruction. She suggests that because he was a creature of the party system, he had little appreciation for the likely consequences of liberalization, and that eventually he became much more interested in preventing reform than encouraging it.*

2. Why does she seem to have little respect for Gorbachev as a reformer?
[model answer] *Tolstoya sees Gorbachev as a privileged member of the elite, bent on maintaining his and the party's position and perks. The goal of Perestroika, she suggests, was to entrench and enhance the position of the party and its leaders, so Gorbachev was acting in the interests of the few, not the people as a whole.*

Contrasting Views: Feminist Debates, pp. 932–933

1. Was the feminist movement of the 1960s and 1970s primarily an offshoot of other reform movements of the day, or did it have a character of its own?
[model answer] *The Combahee River statement suggests that feminism, at least for some participants, was closely linked to other campaigns for rights and justice. Mamonova indicated that, within socialism, problems of gender equity remained and may even have worsened. The Italian feminists cited here saw gender inequality as fundamental to other forms of social and economic exploitation, while the "Green" feminists cited the connected nature of environmental difficulties and gender inequality. Taken as a whole, the documents indicate that feminism and its concern for gender equality, while it was connected to a variety of other reform causes, remained a fundamental concern for many.*

2. In what ways was feminism in these decades a unified movement, and in what ways was it a set of multiple movements?
[model answer] *Clearly from the documents, concern about gender equality could be found within a variety of movements for change and reform, and were often put forward as integral to achieving other goals as well. The documents indicate that feminism was fragmented in that many feminists were connected to other reform movements, but also that they were united by a sense that addressing questions of gender inequality was integral to achieving progress on other issues.*

3. What issues do these activists raise?
[model answer] *The Combahee River Statement demonstrates the issue of the difficulty of raising the question of gender inequality without addressing the question of racial inequality first. The statement suggests that gender equality is best attained by racial groups acting for themselves. Mamanova raises the problem of the persistence of gender inequality within socialist economic systems. The Feminists Movement of Rome suggests that "sexual liberation" has produced more gender inequality and exploitation of women by men, and that patriarchy continues as the dominant social model. The "Green" women point out the particular vulnerabilities women face in relation to environmental concerns, and the critical importance of environmental issues for men and women alike.*

Other Questions for Discussing These Documents in Class

Margaret Thatcher's Economic Vision

1. In what ways did Thatcher's vision place pressure on the Enlightenment ideal that government should benefit the governed?
2. How does Thatcher argue that public-sector spending hurts the unemployed and small businesses?

Criticizing Gorbachev

1. In what way does Tolstaya claim Gorbachev's ability to innovate was limited?
2. What was her view of the nature of the Communist Party, and how did it line up with the understanding Karl Marx would have had?

Contrasting Views: Feminist Debates

1. How do these feminist voices describe the marginalization of women in their societies? Are their stories similar?
2. In what ways did these women argue that the oppression of women was symptomatic of broader social problems? What were identified as serious underlying problems that women's disempowerment was related to?

Comparative Questions

1. These readings all reflect discontent with various views of established power and entrenched systems. Taken together, what do they reveal about the nature and extent of discontent in the East and West?
2. What do the documents reveal about the growing assertiveness and activism of women?

For Users of *Sources of The Making of the West*

The following documents are available in Chapter 28 of the companion sourcebook by Katharine J. Lualdi, University of Southern Maine.

1. Prague Spring: Josef Smrkovský, *What Lies Ahead* (February 9, 1968)
2. A Revolutionary Time: *Student Voices of Protest* (1968)
3. Children Fleeing from a Napalm Attack in South Vietnam: A Photograph by Nick Ut (June 8, 1972)
4. The Rising Power of OPEC: U.S. Embassy, Saudi Arabia, *Saudi Ban on Oil Shipments to the United States* (October 23, 1973)
5. Facing Terrorism: *Jacques Chirac on New French Antiterrorist Laws* (September 14, 1986)
6. Debating Change in the Soviet Union: *Glasnost and the Soviet Press* (1988)

Discussion Ideas for Sources of The Making of the West, *Chapter 28*

1. What do these documents reveal about how and why social reform was both exciting and frightening for people involved in the process?

2. In what ways do these documents reveal the limitations of state power? What limitations and constraints were there on their influence and ability to control circumstances?

Working with Visual Sources

For this exercise, please refer to Thalidomide Children on p. 920 of the textbook or view the image on the book companion site's Online Study Guide under the "Visual Activity" for Chapter 28.

Students viewing the image at the Online Study Guide are asked three questions about the image. The questions and model answers (not made available to students) are below. Project this image, available on the Instructor's Resources CD-ROM, in class or ask students to look at the image in their textbooks and answer the questions.

1. These children were born with birth defects because their mothers took a drug called thalidomide while pregnant. What are the most noticeable birth defects? Do the children seem to be aware of their birth defects?
[model answer] *The children have either drastically shrunken or missing arms. The children are playing and seem very happy. Even the boy in the front, who appears pensive, is smiling slightly.*

2. We neither know what the purpose of this photograph is, nor do we know how it was used. How might this photograph have been part of a message to condemn the use of thalidomide?
[model answer] *The photograph is heart-wrenching in its depiction of these children with birth defects. Although they look happy, one might assume that they have faced, and will continue to face, numerous difficulties in life. In a way, their happiness adds to their appeal and increases our sympathy for their situation. The juxtaposition of the trees and the tire-like objects could be seen as emphasizing the way in which science and technology encroach on natural environments and processes, like the womb or childbirth, respectively.*

3. Assuming that the photograph was presented in defense of the companies and physicians that distributed thalidomide to pregnant women, what might their message be?
[model answer] *Despite the birth defects, the children are smiling. The companies might wish to send a message that they care about the children affected by the drug, and that even though the drug had terrible consequences, the children still appear to be able to live normal lives.*

For this exercise, please refer to Seeing History: Critiquing the Soviet System: Dissident Art in the 1960s and 1970s on p. 929 of the textbook or view the images on the book companion site's Online Study Guide under the "Visual Activity" for Chapter 28.

Students viewing the images at the Online Study Guide are asked two questions about the image. The questions and model answers (not made available to students) are below. Project this image, available on the Instructor's Resources CD-ROM, in class or ask students to look at the image in their textbooks and answer the questions.

1. In what ways can these images both be seen as criticisms of the Soviet regime?
[model answer] *Bulatov's image shows ordinary citizens, dressed in modern clothing, walking in the opposite direction from the striding, dapper image of Lenin. They also seem to be busily ignoring the poster, and the image has an air of unreality about it. Orlov's work is clearly a parody of a portrait bust, and the puffed-out chest of the general with his dizzying array of meaningless medals was not designed to inspire admiration for a hero of the state.*

2. What do these works suggest about the place of art in Soviet culture?
[model answer] *The images both suggest that art could be used to criticize the state and its pretensions, or to underscore the disconnect between the official self-image of the state, as depicted in Orlov's general or Bulatov's image of Lenin, and the perceptions of ordinary citizens, who might be inclined to mock or ignore official portrayals of authority. Art was an important aspect of Soviet state building and propaganda, but clearly it could also be used to weaken the state, or to reflect ambivalence about it.*

Mapping Exercises

Map Activity from OSG—Model Answers for Map Activity #2

For this activity, please refer to Mapping the West: The Collapse of Communism in Europe, 1989–1990 on p. 947. Students are asked these questions:

What aspects of post-war German geography may have led to the fall of the Berlin Wall in November 1989?
[model answer] *East Germany's border with Hungary and other Eastern European states allowed easy travel into East Germany from the rest of the Soviet bloc. The location of West Berlin, meanwhile, deep inside East Germany, the divided nature of that city, and the willingness of West Germany to take immigrants from East Germany meant that it required a determined effort of the East German and Soviet governments to prevent transit within Berlin and across the German border. If that determination wavered, as it did in 1989, the fall of the wall was likely.*

What do the countries here colored in orange have in common?
[model answer] *These countries served as an effective border between the USSR and Western Europe. Following Russia's terrible losses during World War II, losing some 25 million of its citizens, Stalin believed he had much to fear from the West. Truman, the new American president, fearing Soviet expansionism, immediately cut off aid to Russia at the end of the war. Stalin, ever more suspicious, engineered not just a temporary military occupation, but a permanent "buffer zone" of European states loyal to the USSR. Russia imposed Communist rule on Bulgaria and Romania, as well as provided support to the communist regimes in Hungary, Poland, and elsewhere. The countries colored here in orange are part of that "buffer zone."*

Map 28.1, The Airbus Production System, p. 922

Ask students to discuss the advantages and disadvantages of having components of the Airbus manufactured in four different countries. What difference does it make that all four countries are members of the European Union (EU)? Ask students to compare and contrast this production system with what they may know of the production system used by many multinational corporations.

Map 28.2, The Vietnam War, 1954–1975, p. 930

Use the map to discuss the Tet offensive with students. Ask them to locate and describe what happened at Hue, Da Nang, Saigon, and My Lai in 1968, and relate why these events were important. Through which countries does the Ho Chi Minh Trail run? What did the United States do to try to stop the North Vietnamese from using the trail?

Mapping the West: The Collapse of Communism in Europe, 1989–1990, p. 948

Use the map to review the sequence and locations of anticommunist movements in Eastern Europe. Why might Poland and Czechoslovakia have been early sites of activity? What characteristics of German geography may have aided the pace of communism's collapse there?

In-Class Assignments and Presentation Topics

1. Require students to interview at least two individuals about their most vivid memories of such things as the cold war in the 1950s and 1960s, television in the 1960s and 1970s, and, if possible, someone living in Europe during 1989 when communism fell. The subjects should have been at least 10 years old during the period being investigated. This assignment would be an opportunity to talk with students about oral history. You may wish to provide them with an article describing how an oral history is collected or make up a brief guide for them. Before they start the project, talk with students about questions they might ask, background knowledge they might need, and so on. It would certainly be useful to talk with them afterward concerning their experiences of interviewing individuals. Schoolchildren crouching in the hallways, practicing for a nuclear event, is often a prominent memory of those who were young in the 1950s and 1960s. You may want to mention your own vivid memories, if you were at least age ten in 1960. For the record, I remember quite well John F. Kennedy's inauguration in 1961, both his speech and Robert Frost's attempt to read a poem he had written for the occasion in the bright sunlight and finally reciting one from memory. I also remember the Beatles' first appearance on the *Ed Sullivan Show* in 1964 and the excitement in 1969 surrounding the report of the first men on the moon. The fall of communism in 1989 was a far more electrifying experience for Europeans than it was for those living in the United States, and interviewing persons who were there would bring an interesting perspective to the subject.

2. The space race in the 1960s should work well as a source for class presentations. These presentations might be relatively brief and focus on the

pioneering astronauts and cosmonauts, the various missions, spacecraft, and the technology involved. What were the critical technical problems involved? Reports could make use of material from video documentaries and from Web sites. At the end of the reports, the class might reflect on the meaning of the space race and on its accomplishments. Was it merely an extension of the cold war, or did it speak to larger purposes? Was it money well spent and time and energy used wisely? Does humanity somehow need this kind of enterprise periodically? Explain why or why not.

3. The year 1968 was such a protean year that it might be best to approach it through a series of class presentations. You may wish to limit the possible topics by drawing up a list of those you are already familiar with. Remind students of the vast amount of material available through recordings, video documentaries, and Web sites (see "Lecture Strategies," number 6). In this case, combining the class presentation with an essay in which the student reflects on his or her topic and discusses how it might be placed in the context of the 1960s. For example, someone giving a report on the assassination of Martin Luther King, Jr. could use television news footage of King at the Memphis sanitation workers' strike and a recording of the speech he gave the night before he was killed. The report could also refer to newspaper or newsmagazine accounts of the riots that followed King's assassination and the eventual capture of the man accused of killing King, James Earl Ray. The paper, however, would reflect on King's role in the 1960s and perhaps at least note the turn toward black power that the civil rights movement took.

4. Assign students a paper on détente between 1969 and 1975. You may wish to have them view Episode 16, "Détente, 1969–1975," of CNN's *Cold War*. (They should at least view the Web site for that episode.) Another possibility is to assign students a relatively brief reading, such as Chapter 24, "Nixon, Vietnam, and the World," in James T. Patterson, *Grand Expectations* (see "Lecture Strategies," number 5).

5. The Russian sense of humor can offer rich insights into the failings of the Soviet political system. Joke-telling was one way to soften criticism and avoid direct responsibility for it, and anti-Soviet jokes proliferated and are widely available on the Web in collected form (or pull a few from Algis Ruksensas, *Is That You Laughing, Comrade? The World's Best Russian (Underground) Jokes* (Secaucus, N.J.: Citadel, 1986). Choose a few of the richer or more telling anecdotes and have students make written or oral attempts to "explain" the jokes. What do they reveal about the system that produced them? How serious a problem was it for the system that such jokes were so widespread? How was humor deployed in attacking power structures in the United States and Western Europe? It might be worthwhile showing/playing a little Lenny Bruce or George Carlin, and have students analyze for political and social criticisms.

Essay Questions

1. Ask students to imagine that they have been given a contract to compile an encyclopedia on the 1970s: *The Seventies in Europe and North America.* Students may wish to see how an actual encyclopedia covering similar ground is laid out. See Carl Singleton, ed., *The Sixties in America*, 3 vols. (Pasadena, CA: Salem Press, 1999). Divide the students into groups and have each group deal with a different European country or with a single category such as painting or sports. Each group then draws up a list of topics to be covered and the number of words to be devoted to each topic. Then assign each individual in the group one or more topics so that each person is writing about 2,000 words. For West Germany, for example, topics might include Willy Brandt, Hans Schmidt, the Baader-Meinhof gang, Heinrich Böll, Rainer Werner Fassbinder, and so forth. Students should copyedit each other's work and revise as required. Each entry should have a short bibliography of important sources and be cross-referenced as appropriate. Two books on the 1970s may be useful: Peter Carroll, *It Seemed Like Nothing Happened: The Tragedy and Promise of America in the 1970s* (New York: Holt, Rinehart & Winston, 1982); and David Frum, *How We Got Here: The 70s, the Decade that Brought You Modern Life (for Better or Worse)* (New York: Basic Books, 2000).

2. Have students investigate the lives of prominent figures from the 1960s and 1970s and either write a biographical essay or do a class presentation. You may want to compile a list of names for students to select from. While some background information might be necessary, the essay or presentation should focus on what that person was doing during the period and what its significance was. For example, an essay on Betty Friedan would certainly include a discussion of *The Feminine Mystique* (1963) and her work in the National Organization for Women (NOW). It should not mention, except perhaps in passing, her book on aging, *The Fountain of Age* (1993). It probably should mention *Life So Far: A Memoir* (2000) but note that this book is a reflection long after the fact on events of the 1960s and 1970s and therefore a source to be used with care. Ask students to relate the lives of these individuals to major themes in this chapter of the text.

Additional Resources: Literature

Emecheta, Buchi, *The Joys of Motherhood.* 1980.
Grossman, Edith, trans., *Gabriel García Márquez: Love in the Time of Cholera.* 1999.
Irving, John, *The World According to Garp.* 1978.
Kundera, Milan, *The Unbearable Lightness of Being.* 1984.
Middleton, Christopher, trans., *Christa Wolf: The Quest for Christa T.* 1979.
Rushdie, Salman, *The Satanic Verses.* 1989.
Smith, Zadie, *White Teeth.* 2000.
Thompson, Hunter S., *Fear and Loathing on the Campaign Trail.* 1973.
Todd, Albert C., and James Ragan, eds., *Yevgeny Yevtushenko: The Collected Poems, 1952–1990.* 1992.
Whitney, Thomas P., and Harry Willetts, trans., *Aleksandr Solzhenitsyn: Gulag Archipelago.* 1973–1974.

Additional Resources: Film and Video

A Hard Day's Night (1964; VHS/DVD, 1 hr., 48 min.). This popular satire on the Beatles, starring themselves, presents a fictionalized day in the life of the Beatles as they give a performance on a live television show.

All the President's Men (1976, VHS/DVD, 2 hrs., 18 min.). This Oscar-winning 1976 film is about Carl Bernstein and Bob Woodward, the two *Washington Post* reporters who broke the biggest story of the 1970s—that of the Watergate scandal. It originally seemed like a small story, a break-in at the Democratic headquarters, but because of these two young men doggedly going after the facts, it brought down a president.

The Right Stuff (1983; VHS/DVD, 3 hrs., 13 min.). Philip Kaufman's intimate epic about the *Mercury* astronauts (based on Tom Wolfe's book) was one of the most ambitious and spectacularly exciting movies of the 1980s.

Mississippi Burning (1988; VHS/DVD, 2 hrs., 7 min.) An atmospheric account of civil-rights era murders, this film offers an overly optimistic account of the Federal government's role in investigating the crimes.

Malcolm X (1992; VHS/DVD, 3 hrs., 19 min.). Filmmaker Spike Lee, star Denzel Washington, and other talents vividly portray the life and times of the visionary leader.

Quiz Show (1994; VHS/DVD, 2 hrs., 10 min.). This vigorously entertaining film is based on the game-show scandals of the 1950s, when TV quiz shows were rigged to attract higher ratings and lucrative sponsorships.

Bloody Sunday (2002; VHS/DVD, 1 hr., 50 min.). A stunning re-creation of events that took place in 1972 in Londonderry, Northern Ireland, when British paratroopers, trying to restore order after a particularly unruly period, opened fire on a peaceful demonstration, and fourteen Irish Catholic civil-rights protesters died.

Other Bedford/St. Martin's Resources for Chapter 28

The following resources are available to accompany Chapter 28. Please refer to the Preface of this manual for detailed descriptions of all the ancillaries.

For Instructors

Transparencies

The following maps and images from Chapter 28 are available as full-color acetates.

- Map 28.1: The Airbus Production System
- Map 28.2: The Vietnam War, 1954–1975
- Mapping the West: The Collapse of Communism in Europe, 1989–1990
- Thalidomide Children, p. 920
- Reunited Berliners Welcome the New Year, p. 946

Instructor's Resources CD-ROM

The following maps and image from Chapter 28, as well as a chapter outline, are available on disc in both PowerPoint and jpeg formats.

- Map 28.1: The Airbus Production System
- Map 28.2: The Vietnam War, 1954–1975
- Mapping the West: The Collapse of Communism in Europe, 1989–1990
- Thalidomide Children, p. 920

Using the Bedford Series with The Making of the West

Available in print as well as online at **bedfordstmartins.com/usingseries,** this guide offers practical suggestions for using Charles G. Cogan, *Charles de Gaulle: A Brief Biography with Documents,* in conjunction with Chapters 27 and 28 of the textbook, and *My Lai,* by James S. Olson and Randy Roberts, in conjunction with Chapter 28 of the textbook.

For Students

Study Guides

The Online Study Guide at **bedfordstmartins.com/hunt** helps students synthesize the material they have learned as well as practice the skills historians use to make sense of the past. The following Map, Visual, and Document activities are available for Chapter 28.

Map Activity

- Mapping the West: The Collapse of Communism in Europe, 1989–1990

Visual Activity

- Thalidomide Children (chapter image, p. 920)
- Eric Bulatov, *Krasikov Street,* 1977, p. 929
- Boris Orlov, *The General,* 1970, p. 929

Reading Historical Documents

- Margaret Thatcher's Economic Vision, p. 941
- Criticizing Gorbachev, p. 944
- Contrasting Views: Feminist Debates, pp. 932–933

CHAPTER

29

A New Globalism

1989 to the Present

Chapter Resources

Main Chapter Topics

1. The introduction of the Euro in 2002 and the admittance of former Soviet-bloc countries to the European Union (EU) were reflections of the globalization that had occurred in the preceding twenty years. Globalization raised hopes and opportunities, but it also presented new challenges.

2. The fall of communism in Europe led to a revival of ethnic tensions in former Communist countries. Serbia attempted to dominate the Yugoslav federation by force, resulting in a wave of "ethnic cleansing," or genocide, not seen since World War II. The global response to the violence was delayed and largely ineffective.

3. The transition from a command economy to a free market economy was difficult and painful for most former Communist countries, especially Russia, owing to widespread corruption and shortages of essential necessities. The war in Chechnya bogged down and caused further problems for Russia, and Eastern European economies have struggled with a brain drain to the west as they attempt to establish prosperity at home.

4. The trend toward the establishment of regional associations of nations has continued, and the successes of the European Community inspired the establishment of the North American Free Trade Agreement. European countries prospered and forged closer ties through the introduction of a common currency (the Euro) and the opening of the EU to new members, some of which were former Communist countries. Efforts to strengthen further EU ties have run into some difficulties as concern has deepened about disconnect between the EC bureaucracy and ordinary people. The European Community's prosperity has attracted immigrants to European cities, arousing resistance from traditionalists who worry about the loss of local ways of life.

5. Global organizations such as the World Bank, the International Monetary Fund (IMF), and the World Trade Organization (WTO), along with nongovernmental organizations (NGOs), exercised considerable power and influence over developing nations. The intervention of the global organizations in world affairs was considered highly controversial and undemocratic.

6. Globalization contributed to an increase in pollution levels, and environmentalists urged a list of remedies: conservation, alternative means of transportation, reductions in greenhouse gases, and recycling. Many countries embraced these "green" programs, but the United States and Russia lagged behind other countries in promoting environmentalism. The spread of disease became a world issue. Health care improved in the West for those who were financially better off, but the poor and unemployed were often deprived of such services. Health care became especially dire in African countries where AIDS created a demographic crisis. While global population continued to rise sharply due to longer life expectancies across much of the world, Europe faced a demographic challenge as fertility rates fell well below replacement levels across the west, threatening the viability of the welfare state.

7. Western countries clashed with Islam and international terrorism increased. The United States broke off diplomatic relations with Iran after the hostage crisis (1979), and the Soviet Union went to war with Afghanistan. Saddam Hussein's invasion of Kuwait sparked the first war in the Persian Gulf (1990). After the destruction of the World Trade Center and damage to the Pentagon (2001) was caused by hijacked planes piloted by militant Muslims, the United States invaded Afghanistan and routed the

Taliban government, which had been responsible for training the hijackers. In 2003, in a hugely unpopular move, the United States and Britain went to war against Iraq because these countries feared it possessed weapons of mass destruction (WMDs).

8. The global economy was transformed by increasing prosperity in parts of Asia, although working conditions remained poor even in many places where investors and capitalists prospered. Unprecedented levels of global migrations to labor markets continue to transform host cultures. The Internet created a virtual global community and marketplace, although such developments disadvantage the poor who lack access. The spread of post-industrial skills has led to the increasing "outsourcing" of technology-related jobs to countries with lower labor costs.

9. Globalization blurred cultural and national identities. Although Western culture predominated—especially in film, television, and music—foreign films and literature became widely popular. Music from former Communist-bloc countries was listened to for the first time and the works of dissident writers were reappraised. Postmodernism, where no one particular style predominated, was reflected in architecture. But postmodernism also referred to a movement away from cherished eighteenth-century ideas regarding individual freedoms and the nation-state. The global age has not resulted in the triumph of Western civilization; rather, such factors as international migration; the information revolution; and the sharing of a global, popular culture have all created a climate in which nationalism paradoxically has been both weakened and strengthened.

Focus Question

How has globalization been both a unifying and a divisive influence on the West in the twenty-first century?

1. Globalization, particularly in its economic dimension, has produced new forms of unity. The European Community, NAFTA, and other supranational institutions integrate nation-states in webs of commerce, and encourage global cooperation on a wide range of issues. Culturally, new information technologies have continued to speed and aid the effectiveness of communication across national boundaries. The Internet has led to the creation of a "virtual" global community for those who have access to it, although predominantly to date these have been westerners. These new technologies and structures have already promoted massive unifications—of currencies, of culture and ideas, of political and social movements, and of people, as migrations to global urban centers in particular have brought people together in new ways. Shared challenges, particularly environmental ones, do not respect national boundaries and require global solutions in the long run.

2. At the same time, globalization in some of its aspects, has promoted division as well. Reactions against migrations and job losses associated with globalizing economies have fueled national and regional movements for greater autonomy and independence. Global institutions are increasingly criticized for their lack of accountability, and for their reliance on bureaucracy and markets rather than public opinion. Likewise, many blame the dynamics of globalization for weakening local identities and, indeed, human communities. People are increasingly dislocated and out of touch with locality and community in ways that are disturbing to many.

Annotated Chapter Outline

I. Collapse of the Soviet Union and Its Aftermath

A. The Breakup of Yugoslavia, pp. 953–956

1. Tensions erupted in Yugoslavia in 1990 when a Serb Communist, Slobodan Milosevic (b. 1941), won the presidency of Serbia and began to assert Serb ascendancy instead of communism in the Yugoslav federation.
2. Other ethnic groups in Yugoslavia resisted Milosevic's pro-Serb nationalism and called for secession.
3. In 1991, when Slovenia seceded followed by Croatia, the Serb-dominated Yugoslav army invaded.
4. An even worse civil war engulfed Bosnia-Herzegovina where the Muslim majority attempted to create a multiethnic state and Bosnian Serbs formed a guerrilla army supported by Milosevic.
5. Tens of thousands perished and countless atrocities were committed under Milosevic's policy of genocide called "ethnic cleansing."
6. This campaign was followed by attacks in the Albanian region of Kosovo.
7. After several years of violence, NATO and UN peacekeeping forces intervened.
8. Milosevic was captured and handed over to a world tribunal for crimes against humanity.
9. His moderate successor was assassinated by pro-Milosevic loyalists in 2003.

B. The Soviet Union Comes Apart, pp. 956–958

1. The total collapse of the Soviet Union (1992) launched a string of secessions with

the potential for widespread regional and perhaps even global destabilization.

2. Mikhail Gorbachev's (b. 1931) policy of perestroika had, by 1990, failed to revitalize the Soviet economy.
3. In 1991, Boris Yeltsin (b. 1931) was elected president of the Russian parliament over the Communist candidate.
4. In response, a group of hard-liners who opposed reform launched an unsuccessful coup that fell apart when hundreds of thousands of civilians took to the streets in favor or reform, and military units defected to protect Yeltsin.
5. The Soviet Union disintegrated after the failed coup as one republic after another that had made up the USSR declared their independence.
6. These secessions were often followed by bloody, ethnic violence, and the Russian economy fell into further crisis as corrupt officials sold state property for personal profit.
7. In an attempt to consolidate support after the disastrous failure of many of his policies, Yeltsin launched military action against Muslim dissenters in the province of Chechnya.
8. Political order, social disarray, and a corruption scandal involving Yeltsin and his family forced him to resign on December 31, 1999, and he appointed his protégé Vladimir Putin (b. 1952) as interim president.
9. Although Putin was himself associated with the Yeltsin corruption scandal, he was a strong leader, committed to the "dictatorship of law," and drove corrupt politicians from office, restored strong government, and ended the influence of billionaires.
10. But Putin also continued the destructive war in Chechnya, and some felt he merely transferred assets to his own cronies.

C. Toward a Market Economy, pp. 958–960

1. The attempt to develop a free market and a republican government brought misery to Russia and the rest of Eastern Europe.
2. As salaries went unpaid, particularly for the army and state employees, desperate measures to survive were sought, such as prostitution or selling household possessions.
3. Many persons, such as members of collective farms, opposed the introduction of the new market-oriented measures because these eroded what little economic security they possessed.
4. Countries such as Hungary and Poland, where administers had earlier introduced elements of free trade, emerged from the transition less strained, whereas other countries continued to be mired in political corruption, tax evasion, and black markets.
5. "Privatization" of worthless, outdated industries often resulted in their closing, and the transition to a market economy was more difficult than many imagined.
6. The former Soviet Union also suffered from a "brain drain" because the newly opened borders permitted talented workers with marketable skills to emigrate in search of better opportunities and living conditions.

D. International Politics and the New Russia, pp. 960–961

1. In the fall of 1991, the National Congress of the Chechen people took control of the government of the oil-rich Chechen region of the USSR in a move toward independence similar to that of the Baltic nations and other states within the Soviet Union.
2. After the collapse of the Soviet Union (1992), Chechen rebels seized massive stores of Russian weapons.
3. In December 1994, the Russian government sealed the Chechen borders and invaded, in part, to bolster Yeltsin's sagging presidency with what it thought would be a small, victorious war.
4. The war dragged on, however, with high civilian casualties, many of which were retaliatory terrorist attacks committed by Chechens in Russian cities.
5. The war only compounded Russia's problems of establishing a sound economy and a credible post-Communist government.

II. The Nation-State in a Global Age

A. Europe Looks beyond the Nation-State, pp. 961–964

1. The European Common Market opened the pathway to supranational, unified policy in economic matters, and its evolution into the European Union expanded cooperation into political and cultural matters.
2. In 1992, the twelve countries of the Common Market ended nationalistic

distinctions in the spheres of business activity, border controls, and transportation, effectively ending passport controls at the borders between most Common Market countries.

3. Citizens of the European Community (EC) carried a common passport, and municipal governments agreed to treat all member nations' firms the same.
4. In 1994, the EC became the European Union (EU) under the terms of the Maastricht Treaty.
5. In 1999, the euro came into being and entirely replaced the national currency of EU members in 2002.
6. The EU parliament convened regularly in Strasbourg, France; subgroups met to negotiate cultural, economic, and social policies.
7. One of the advantages of the EU was the pacifist role it played in Europe, as traditional enemies became supportive of each other.
8. Among its drawbacks were the facts that the EU did not enforce any common regulatory practices, and the common policies demanding economic cooperation among members were not always observed.
9. The benefits of EU membership were made clear to nations in Eastern Europe, as economic cooperation and the infusion of EU funds bolstered the economies of early members such as Greece.
10. The collapse of the Soviet Union had brought Eastern European nations closer to the West, especially as industries became privatized and purchased by Western firms.
11. Lower wages and business costs in Eastern Europe attracted foreign investment.
12. Ten new members, mostly from Central and Eastern Europe, joined the EU in 2004, and two more in 2007.
13. Although the standards of living in many of these countries had risen in the late 1990s, there were large discrepancies between the thriving cities and the ailing countrysides.
14. As the purchasing power of many Eastern countries grew, sales of consumer items—automobiles, computers, portable phones, and freezers—also rose.
15. Opportunities for well-educated Eastern Europeans increased. Consumption assumed symbolic importance for many as a sign that isolation and communist poverty had ended.

B. Globalizing Cities and Fragmenting Nations, pp. 964–965

1. During this transitional period, the West fragmented into more nation-states and consolidated new forms, most notably the global city.
2. Global cities were urban areas whose institutions, functions, and visions were overwhelmingly global rather than regional or national.
3. These cities contained stock markets, legal firms, insurance companies, financial service organizations, and other enterprises that operated across local and national borders.
4. The high-powered and high-priced nature of such enterprises made the cost of living in global cities highly expensive, which drove mid-level managers to seek lower-priced housing in the suburbs and the lowest-paid service providers into poorer living conditions.
5. Global cities became centers of migration with the many opportunities they offered, although they also drew criticism as centers of concentrated wealth, which was often observed to be taken at the expense of poorer, southern countries.
6. There were more nations in Europe in 2000 than there had been in 1945, as individual nation-states fragmented under the rising tide of ethnicity.
7. In 1993, Czechoslovakia split into the Czech Republic and Slovakia.
8. Activists in the Breton and Corsican region of France, and the Basque region of Spain pushed for autonomy, at times resorting to terrorism.

C. Global Organizations, p. 965

1. Globalization spawned the proliferation of supranational organizations to regulate international finance and address social issues.
2. The World Bank and International Monetary Fund (IMF) had been around for several decades, but gained new importance as national economies began to interact more closely.
3. Raising money from individual governments, the IMF granted loans to developing countries on condition that they restructure their economies according to neoliberal principles.

4. Other supranational organizations were charitable foundations, many of which were based in Europe and the United States.
5. Some of these nongovernmental organizations (NGOs) controlled vast sums of money and possessed considerable international power.
6. After the fall of the USSR, NGOs shaped economic and social policy and the course of political reform.
7. Not everyone supported globalization, such as the Association for the Benefit of Citizens (ATTAC), which worked to block the control of globalization by the forces of high finance.

III. Challenges from an Interconnected World

A. The Problems of Pollution, pp. 966–968

1. Technological development and expansion of technology's use continued to threaten the environment.
2. In 1986, the nuclear plant at Chernobyl in the Soviet Union exploded during a test of reactor No. 4 and spewed radioactive dust into the atmosphere.
3. Many locals (about 15,000) perished over a period of time from the effects of radiation.
4. Numerous lakes, rivers, and seas across Asia were filled with toxic wastes from nuclear testing and the dumping of nuclear fuel, making them completely uninhabitable.
5. In industrial areas, fossil-fuel pollutants from natural gas, coal, and oil mixed with atmospheric moisture to produce acid rain, a poisonous brew that destroyed forests.
6. In less industrial areas, the clearing of forests for farming depleted the global oxygen supply and threatened the biological diversity of the entire planet.
7. The use of chlorofluorocarbons (CFCs), chemicals contained in or released by aerosols, refrigeration products, and automobile and industrial emissions damaged Earth's atmosphere.
8. Many worried that the ensuing dramatic weather changes were the product of global warming and its resultant "greenhouse effect."
9. Rising activity to protect the environment took decades to develop.
10. In West Germany, the Green Party was founded (1979) and was successful in promoting political awareness on environmental issues across Europe.
11. Europeans confronted environmental problems on both the local and global level, with many cities adopting more environmentally sound policies, and many countries implementing alternatives to fossil fuel.
12. Many European countries signed the Kyoto Protocol (1997), an international treaty aimed at reducing pollution levels around the world.
13. The refusal of the United States—the worlds' biggest polluter—to participate made cooperation on environmental protection a symbol of a potential fragmenting of the West.

B. Population, Health, and Disease, pp. 968–969

1. Nations with less developed economies struggled with the pressing problem of surging populations, while the global public health establishment confronted the spread of deadly diseases.
2. By late 1999, Earth's population reached six billion, and is expected to double by the year 2045.
3. Declining fertility across Europe led to population declines, particularly in Russia.
4. Western medicine and better health found their way into the less-developed world in the form of vaccines and pharmaceuticals to treat diseases; however, many individuals living in these regions still did not have access to basic necessities, such as safe drinking water.
5. Many critics pointed to the disparity between the extent of expensive, high-tech health services supplied to the wealthy in industrialized nations, and that which the poor received even though they suffered more from chronic illnesses.
6. In the early 1980s, Western values and technological expertise were challenged by the global spread of AIDS, which causes the body's immune system to shut down; the disease is primarily passed by men to and through women.
7. This disease started in central Africa and was later found among Haitian immigrants to the United States.
8. Within a decade, AIDS had become pandemic.
9. Negative interconnectedness again became apparent in 2003, when Severe Acute

Respiratory Syndrome (SARS) caused worldwide panic, affected travel, and interfered with economic activity in Asia.

C. North Versus South?, p. 969

1. With Australians and New Zealanders as the exceptions, people in the southern hemisphere generally suffered lower living standards and measures of health.
2. Inexperienced governments in southern regions struggled to provide welfare services and education. Aid money from northern countries and international institutions came with conditions, such as cutting government spending.
3. Latin-American nations grappled with governmental corruption, multibillion-dollar debt, widespread crime, and poverty.
4. Sub-Saharan Africa suffered from drought, famine, and eventually civil war.
5. Rwanda and Somalia experienced genocide in the 1990s and beyond, and millions of Africans died or were left starving and homeless as global economic advance was uneven on the continent.

D. Islam Meets the West, pp. 969–973

1. The charismatic Middle Eastern leaders of the 1980s—Iran's Ayatollah Ruhollah Khomeini, Libya's Muammar Qaddafi, Iraq's Saddam Hussein, and al-Qaeda leader Osama bin Laden—variously promoted a pan-Arabic or pan-Islamic world order.
2. They argued that Muslims should confront the superpowers, a sentiment that had wide appeal.
3. In Iran, the government rejected Westernization, required women to cover their heads and bodies in special clothing, restricted their right to divorce, and eliminated other rights.
4. Despite the call for a pan-Islamic front, power in the Middle East remained fragmented.
5. In September 1980, Iraq's president Saddam Hussein, fearful that the Shi'ite minority in his country might be inspired by Shi'ite success in Iran, launched an attack on Iran.
6. After eight years of fighting, no conclusive victory was attained by either side.
7. The Soviet Union became embroiled in 1979 in a losing war in Afghanistan, where the United States, China, Saudi Arabia, and Pakistan all supported the resistance. The Soviets withdrew in 1989, and Afghanistan was controlled by the militantly Islamic Taliban.
8. At the end of the Iran war, Iraq's debt had risen greatly; in 1990, Hussein decided to annex the wealthy neighboring country of Kuwait.
9. International resistance was galvanized, and multinational UN force led by the United States defeated the Iraqi army.
10. The Middle East remained in turmoil as conflict between Palestinians and Israelis continued. As Israeli settlers took more Palestinian land, suicide bombings murdered Israeli citizens. An Israeli invasion of Lebanon in 2006 damaged cities and infrastructure.
11. Terrorism became one of the most frightening global challenges of the twenty-first century, particularly after a band of Muslim militants hijacked several planes and flew them into the World Trade Center in New York and the Pentagon in Washington, D.C., in September 2001.
12. After an initial period of cooperation, as an international coalition drove the Taliban from Afghanistan and European countries rounded up terrorists and successfully prosecuted them, the West ultimately fragmented when the United States and other nations invaded Iraq (March 2003) claiming that Saddam Hussein had been behind the attack on the World Trade Center, and several European nations refused to support the invasion.
13. Mutual antagonism over the issue engendered a sense that the West was coming apart.

E. World Economies on the Rise, pp. 973–974

1. Just as economic changes in the early modern period had redirected the European economy from the Mediterranean to the Atlantic, so too the emergence of powerful Asian economies began to spread economic power to the Pacific.
2. South Korea, Taiwan, Singapore, Hong Kong, and China were called Pacific tigers because of the ferocity of their growth.
3. Japan led the charge, exporting high-tech consumer goods throughout the world.
4. The Japanese and other Asians also purchased U.S. government bonds, thereby effectively financing America's ballooning national debt while the United States

poured mounting sums into its cold war military budget.

5. Working conditions in emerging Asian economies were often difficult.
6. Other emerging economies in the Southern Hemisphere continued to increase their share of world GDP. Newly democratic South Africa benefited, like Russia, Brazil, Iran, Saudi Arabia, Nigeria, and Chile, from growing demand for raw materials.
7. Despite political turmoil, India's economy soared in the early twenty-first century, taking business from Western firms.

IV. **Global Culture and Society in the Twenty-first Century**

A. **Redefining the West: The Impact of Global Migration, pp. 974–975**

1. Uneven economic development, political persecution, and warfare left tens of millions of people homeless refugees.
2. By 2001, many of the approximately 120 million migrants worldwide were headed to the West.
3. Money sent home from immigrant workers contributed a significant portion of the national economies of many countries.
4. Foreign workers were a convenient scapegoat in difficult economic times.
5. In Europe, political parties with racist agendas attracted support as unemployment rose.
6. The children of immigrants often faced problems of identity, as did citizens of immigrant descent who struggled to be accepted in the face of anti-immigration and white supremacist politicians and government officials.
7. Whether the migration was coerced (as in international sex rings) or voluntary (those seeking a better life), the West remained a place of opportunity. Employers remained eager for low-wage immigrant labor.

B. **Global Networks and the Economy, pp. 975–977**

1. Rapid technological changes—especially the development of the Internet—made national borders permeable.
2. Conducting business and communicating via computer allowed individuals to escape state regulations such as censorship, and a global marketplace in goods and services was also formed.
3. Enthusiasts claimed that the Internet would promote democracy, but critics argued that those without computer skills or the money to buy a computer were marginalized; although, in many countries, individuals' computer skills advanced at a rapid pace.
4. The Internet allowed the outsourcing and subcontracting of service work, such as call centers and help desks, to countries with lower wage scales and business costs.
5. This outsourcing threatened the jobs of ordinary Western service workers.
6. Globalization thus redistributed jobs, and reworked economic networks.

C. **A Global Culture?, pp. 977–981**

1. In the postwar period, new forms of transportation and communication facilitated cultural exchange.
2. Tourism soared, and videotapes and satellite-beamed telecasts transported movies and television shows worldwide.
3. Although many countries absorbed Western culture, the West in turn continued to absorb material from other cultures.
4. Publishers marketed the written works of non-Western artists and intellectuals.
5. Nobel Prize-winning Egyptian writer Naguib Mahfouz (b. 1911) drew large Western audiences even as he was accused of adopting a European style aimed at appealing to Western audiences.
6. Gao Xingjian, a Chinese author, was harassed in China because of his "intellectual pollution," and finished his Nobel Prize–winning novel *Soul Mountain* (1990) in exile in Paris.
7. Immigrants to Europe wrote about their personal experiences of Western culture.
8. Buchi Emecheta's (b. 1944) novels describe her life as a newcomer to Great Britain.
9. The experiences of minorities living in the West drew increasing attention, much to the chagrin of politicians who saw such multiculturalism as a sign of deterioration.
10. Toni Morrison (b. 1931), the first African American woman to win the Nobel Prize in literature, describes the experiences and dreams of the descendants of slaves.
11. Many artists from the former Soviet Union who had worked underground during Communist rule gained newfound attention in the West after the collapse of communism.

12. Authors Andrei Makine and Victor Pelevin gave expression to postcommunist Russian culture, and "secret" unpublished musical compositions from the communist period emerged.
13. U.S. cultural dominance continued, particularly in the widespread use of English and in film, even while American cultural tastes became more global and diverse.
14. Some called such a mixing of influences "postmodernism."
15. By this definition, postmodernism meant multiplicity without a unifying theme.
16. Architects designed buildings that mixed materials, forms, and perspectives that did not traditionally go together.
17. Postmodernism can also be defined in political terms as an outgrowth of the demise of eighteenth-century ideals of individuality, human rights, personal freedom, and the nation-state.
18. A third definition of postmodernism involved investigating the irrationality, tied to a lack of freedom that shaped human lives.
19. The issues raised by postmodernism—whether in architecture, ideas, or the popular media—focused on the basic ingredients of Western identity as it had been defined over the past two hundred years.
20. Postmodernism was part of a great enterprise of rethinking and questioning that accompanied globalization.

Lecture Strategies

1. The challenges of the global age offer opportunities as well as potentials for disasters. A workable approach might involve a review of several of the general trends covered by Paul Kennedy in Part 1 of *Preparing for the Twenty-first Century* (New York: Random House, 1992). Kennedy discusses demographics, the rise of multinational corporations, agriculture and the biotechnology revolutions, and a new industrial revolution, among other topics. Students could also read Kennedy's final chapter, "Preparing for the Twenty-first Century," which asserts that the key elements of the new century are "the role of education, the place of women, and the need for political leadership" (p. 339). This source should produce a good discussion of what issues students see facing the world today. Something similar might be done with Chapter 17, "Goods and Values," and the Epilogue of David Reynolds, *One World Divisible: A Global History Since 1945* (New York: W. W. Norton, 2000). Also useful is T. E. Vadney, *The World Since 1945: The Complete History of Global Change from 1945 to the End of the Twentieth Century* (New York: Penguin, 1999).

A different approach emphasizes the history of the environment over the past few decades. J. R. McNeill, *Something New Under the Sun: An Environmental History of the Twentieth-Century World* (New York: W. W. Norton, 2000), argues that the past century was unusual both for the intensity of environmental change and the role of humans in causing it. He points out the extent to which Western civilization depends on circumstances in the natural world that may be in danger of changing drastically. In this case, you might survey some of the ways in which humanity has altered or is in the process of altering the environment and the resultant repercussions of these alterations. McNeill discusses the different parts of the environment, for example, the atmosphere and the hydrosphere, in Part 1, "The Music of the Spheres." Examining one or two chapters of Part 1 will give students an entirely different perspective on the history of the past few decades and present them with a different context into which to fit European or world history. Lester R. Brown, Christopher Flavin, and Hilary French, eds., *State of the World 2007* (New York: W. W. Norton, 2000), may be used for a somewhat similar purpose. Students could be asked to read and discuss one or more of the chapters. A good overview is "Challenges of the New Century" by Lester R. Brown, whereas "Creating Jobs, Preserving the Environment" by Michael Renner introduces the crucial issue of whether environmental concerns may harm the economy. Several other chapters might furnish the basis for a lecture or a lively discussion, or students could be exposed to some of the introductory and later material in Roy Woodbridge, *The Next World War: Tribes, Cities, Nations and Ecological Decline* (Toronto: University of Toronto Press, 2004), which offers a historical perspective on contemporary concerns about environmental degradation and its historical effects on human communities. This could be especially useful in framing a discussion about how insights from history courses might help in anticipating or thinking about future developments.

2. A major shift in thinking over the past two decades has resulted in a different approach to the welfare state. Essentially, most countries have ceased expanding the welfare state and, instead, have turned large parts of the public sector over to private investors or managers. Opinions vary as to what this shift produced: a generally prosperous economy that provides opportunity for nearly everyone, or an economy that favors the wealthy and influential at the expense of the poor. It is also unclear whether governmental policies

have caused the economic developments in question; prosperity might have come into being regardless of what governments of various countries did or tried to do. One source for thinking about this in a European perspective is the articles in Stephan Leibfried, *Welfare State Futures* (Cambridge: Cambridge University Press, 2001), or, more narrowly, Rodney Lowe's *The Welfare State in Britain Since 1945*, 3rd ed. (New York: Palgrave Macmillan, 2005).

3. If time permits, there is real value in reviewing the denouncement of armed conflict in Northern Ireland, and something of the tangled web of the peace process underway since the mid-1990s. Scholars disagree about the relative weight to assign to factors of leadership and statecraft, European and American economic incentives, successful counter-terrorism strategies, or simple war fatigue, but there can be no doubt that the apparent end to the seemingly endless "troubles" in Northern Ireland has transformed politics within the British Isles. Moreover, because the conflict was actively addressed by internal factions—the United States, multiple nation-states, and the European Community—the peace process itself has become a model of sorts for conflict resolution and offers an interesting case study in managing terrorism and stubborn and debilitating ethnic/religious disputes that threaten global development and cooperation. One focus for the lecture might be just that—to what extent does the end to conflict in Northern Ireland offer hope for the future?

A good recent overview of the troubles would be Joseph Ruane and Jennifer Todd, *The Dynamics of Conflict in Northern Ireland: Power, Conflict and Emancipation* (Cambridge: Cambridge University Press, 2007) or David McKittrick and David McVea, *Making Sense of the Troubles: The Story of the Conflict in Northern Ireland* (Chicago: New Amsterdam Books, 2002). McKittrick is a journalist who has closely covered events in Northern Ireland for a long time. Thomas Hennesey's *The Northern Ireland Peace Process* (New York: Palgrave, 2001) is valuable, although students might also want to try the University of Ulster's CAIN website for a remarkable range of up-to-the-minute information on Northern Ireland and the peace process. Former Senator George Mitchell offers a firsthand account of negotiations in *Making Peace* (New York: Random House, 1999). More comparative studies are emerging—a good place to start is John McGarry, *Northern Ireland and the Divided World: The Northern Ireland Conflict and the Good Friday Agreement in Comparative Perspective* (New York: Oxford University Press, 2001).

4. Similarly, the disintegration of Yugoslavia may seem a specialized topic, but it involves issues central to the meaning of the twentieth century and even to history in general. For example, what is the price of political ambition? The power wielded by Slobodan Milosevic and Franjo Tudjman in the 1990s resulted from events that recalled the Holocaust in their cruelty and brutality. What role should the great powers play in the affairs of a sovereign nation? How did the reluctance to intervene in Yugoslavia compare with the decision to intervene against Saddam Hussein? Even deeper issues might include questions about human nature and about the impact of historical experience on different groups of people.

A good place to begin would be Carole Rogel, *The Breakup of Yugoslavia and War in Bosnia* (Westport, CT: Greenwood Press, 1998), a solid introduction with some documents and other features. Probably the best overall discussion is that of Sabrina P. Ramet, *Balkan Babel: The Disintegration of Yugoslavia from the Death of Tito to the War for Kosovo*, 3rd ed. (Boulder, CO: Westview Press, 1999). Another good book, although not quite as comprehensive, is Laura Silber and Allan Little, *Yugoslavia: Death of a Nation*, revised and updated (New York: Penguin, 1997). Daoud Sarhandi, *Evil Doesn't Live Here: Posters of the Bosnian War* (New York: Princeton Architectural Press, 2001) may provide some useful visuals. Timothy Judah, *The Serbs: History, Myth, and the Destruction of Yugoslavia* (New Haven: Yale University Press, 1998), provides a close look at the Serbian part of the Yugoslavian tangle. Also useful in this regard is Dusko Doder and Louise Branson, *Milosevic: Portrait of a Tyrant* (New York: Simon & Schuster, 1999), a critical biography by two seasoned journalists. See also the recent scholarly study, Robert Thomas, *The Politics of Serbia in the 1990s* (New York: Columbia University Press, 1999). Franjo Tudjman, the president of Croatia until his recent death, was also responsible for much of the horror of the 1990s. Marcus Tanner, *Croatia: A Nation Forged in War* (New Haven: Yale University Press, 1997), offers a useful discussion of Tudjman's role in the making of Croatia and unmaking of Yugoslavia. For Bosnia, see first Noel Malcolm, *Bosnia: A Short History*, updated edition (New York: New York University Press, 1996). Useful for a discussion of the war is Steven L. Burg and Paul S. Shoup, *The War in Bosnia-Herzegovina: Ethnic Conflict and International Intervention* (Armonk, NY: M. E. Sharpe, 1999). Michael A. Sells, *The Bridge Betrayed: Religion and Genocide in Bosnia* (Berkeley, CA: University of California Press, 1998), argues against the idea of ethnic hostility over the centuries. On Kosovo, see first Tim Judah, *Kosovo: War and Revenge* (New Haven: Yale University Press, 2000). A valuable study of the Kosovar experience and human rights is Julie A. Mertus, *Kosovo: How Myths and Truths Started a War* (Berkeley, CA: University of California Press, 1999). You may also want to review Adam LeBor, *Milosevik: A Biography* (London: Bloomsbury, 2003).

5. As Putin's Russia assumes an increasingly assertive role on the world stage, and Russia's control of energy supplies and transit lines becomes increasingly strategically consequential, the collapse of the Soviet Union (1991) and the struggles of the Russian Republic under Boris Yeltsin and Putin are topics that deserve to be looked at in more detail. Some historical assessment of Gorbachev's role in the collapse would also be useful. Still intensely disliked in Russia, Gorbachev was nonetheless one of the major figures of the latter part of the twentieth century due to his contribution to the end of the cold war and his attempt to reform communism.

In addition to books cited in the chapter's bibliography, a wealth of memoirs, reportage, and scholarly studies is available. First, Boris Yeltsin has written several autobiographical works: *Against the Grain: An Autobiography* (New York: Summit Books, 1990); *The Struggle for Russia* (New York: Random House, 1994); and *Midnight Diaries* (New York: Public Affairs, 2000). See also the somewhat uncritical biography by Leon Aron, *Yeltsin: A Revolutionary Life* (New York: St. Martin's Press, 2000). Talented and perceptive reporters have provided us with brilliant reports on the Soviet Union and its successors. Among the best is David Remnick, whose books include *Lenin's Tomb: The Last Days of the Soviet Empire* (New York: Random House, 1993); and *Resurrection: The Struggle for a New Russia* (New York: Vintage Books, 1998). J. F. Matlock Jr., *Autopsy on an Empire: The American Ambassador's Account of the Collapse of the Soviet Union* (New York: Random House, 1995), provides a massive, well-informed account. Two books that cover the Yeltsin era are Stephen M. Fish, *Democracy from Scratch: Opposition and Regime in the New Russian Revolution* (Princeton, NJ: Princeton University Press, 1995); and Michael Urban, with Vyacheslav Igrunov and Sergei Mitrokhin, *The Rebirth of Politics in Russia* (Cambridge and New York: Cambridge University Press, 1997). See also Graeme J. Gill and Roger D. Markwich, *Russia's Stillborn Democracy?: From Gorbachev to Yeltsin* (Oxford: Oxford University Press, 2000); and Thane Gustafson, *Capitalism Russian-Style* (Cambridge: Cambridge University Press, 2000). A solid recent study of Putin's Russia is Richard Sakwa, *Putin: Russia's Choice* (New York: Routledge, 2007).

Class Discussion Starters

1. In connection with "Lecture Strategies," number 4, students (individually or assigned to groups) could discuss the applicability of the Northern Ireland process to other contemporary trouble spots, presenting and discussing findings from Internet research. Possible sites for comparison are, unfortunately, easy enough to find. Besides Iraq's sectarian conflict, Palestine offers obvious parallels, as do events in the former Yugoslavia, Darfur, Chiapas, the Basque region, and elsewhere. Are these hotspots more different then alike? Ask students to specifically address the role of history and historical understanding in dividing some communities.

2. It is a bit daunting to suggest a closer look at the last chapter in the book—in effect, the last session of what will have been for some a year-long process. Look at two topics: the Internet, a mostly positive subject, albeit not without its downside; and AIDS, a dark subject to be sure, but one with some potential for thinking about international cooperation as well as persistent global inequalities. On the Internet, simply listen to what your students have to say. Some suggestions follow for resources. For AIDS, lay out a few lines of inquiry and then lead the class in a discussion.

It seems only fitting to begin with an Internet source. "A Brief History of the Internet," http://www.isoc.org/internet-history/#Origins, is at times a little technical, but it is nevertheless a useful overview of the Internet's history, written in many cases by persons who played prominent roles in that history. Probably a better place to start, though, is the last part of Martin Campbell-Kelly and William Aspray, *Computer: A History of the Information Machine* (New York: Basic Books, 1996). Books on the origins of the Internet include Janet Abbate, *Inventing the Internet* (Cambridge, MA: MIT Press, 1999); and Katie Hafner and Matthew Lyon, *Where Wizards Stay Up Late: The Origins of the Internet* (New York: Simon & Schuster, 1998). *Nerds 2.0.1: A Brief History of the Internet* (PBS Home Video, 1999; 3 hrs.) is a good documentary. It does require some prior familiarity with the topic, however. For some ideas about the social consequences of the Internet, try Sarah Oates, Diana Owen and Rachel Gibson (eds.), *The Internet and Politics: Citizens, Voters and Activists* (New York: Routledge, 2006), particularly the introduction. Student response to the chapter on American youth, politics, and the Internet would be interesting.

There is no shortage of information on AIDS. "AEGIS" at http://www.aegis.com is a huge Web site filled with information on AIDS. It includes links to documents and reports of all kinds. Three print sources of information are Raymond A. Smith, ed., *Encyclopedia of AIDS: A Social, Political, Cultural, and Scientific Record of the HIV Epidemic* (Chicago: Fitzroy Dearborn, 1998); Darrell E. Ward, *The AmFAR AIDS Handbook* (New York: W. W. Norton, 1998); and Sarah Barbara Watstein with Karen Chandler, *AIDS Dictionary* (New York: Facts on File, 1998). See also Douglas A. Feldman and Julia Wang Miller, eds., *AIDS Crisis: A Documentary History* (Westport, CT: Greenwood Press, 1998). Edward Hooper and Bill Hamilton, *The*

River: A Journey to the Source of HIV and AIDS (Boston: Little, Brown, 1999), is a long, compelling, but also controversial book. Its premise is that HIV jumped from simians to humans through the administration of the oral polio vaccine in Africa in the 1950s. Douglas Starr, *Blood: An Epic History of Medicine and Commerce* (New York: Alfred A. Knopf, 1998), while not focused on AIDS, includes the scandals connected with HIV-tainted blood. After the international AIDS conference in Durban, South Africa, in the summer of 2000, it is clear that AIDS in Europe and North America is a different problem with different possible solutions from the AIDS in developing countries in Africa and Asia. In the developing countries, the challenges are many: the need for better health care and better preventive measures for what will surely be a demographic disaster of mammoth proportions, even in the best of circumstances. See Helen Epstein's recent *Invisible Cure: Africa and the West, and the Fight Against AIDS* (New York: Farrar, Straus and Giroux, 2007) for a firsthand account of many of these challenges.

3. At the center of events in Europe during the last decade of the twentieth century were the German revolution of 1989 and the subsequent unification of the two Germanys. Students should have some sense of how the German Democratic Republic (GDR) could go from being a success story in the 1970s and then, seemingly overnight, turn into a regime doomed to fall apart in the late 1980s. With some framing, the drama of the fall of 1989 is certainly worth discussing as are the intricate maneuvers leading to the unification of Germany. Some consideration of the career of Helmut Kohl, whose great moment was the unification process, would be helpful in dealing with the crucial role of Germany in European affairs, and it would be appropriate to encourage a student discussion of the centrality of the German experience to the modern history of the west. To what extent does reunification offer hope for the future? What were the central problems that needed to be overcome? What does reunification say about the persistence of national identity, or the power of new collective identities, such as the European Community, to influence events?

In addition to books cited in the chapter's bibliography, see Mary Fulbrook, *Anatomy of a Dictatorship: Inside the GDR, 1949–1989* (Oxford: Oxford University Press, 1995), for excellent coverage of the history of the GDR. Charles S. Maier, *Dissolution: The Crisis of Communism and the End of East Germany* (Princeton, NJ: Princeton University Press, 1997), is the best book on the events of 1989. Philip Zelikow and Condoleezza Rice, *Germany Unified and Europe Transformed: A Study in Statecraft* (Cambridge, MA: Harvard University Press, 1995), is an authoritative study of the diplomacy involved in the unification of Germany. Unfortunately, no good biography of Helmut Kohl is available. Peter E. Quint, *The Imperfect Union* (Princeton, NJ: Princeton University Press, 1997), discusses the impact of the unification process on East Germany. Andreas M. Glaeser, *Divided in Unity: Identity, Germany, and the Berlin Police* (Chicago: University of Chicago Press, 1999), offers a unique perspective on unification by looking at East and West Berliners working together in the Berlin police force. Jonathan P. G. Bach, *Between Sovereignty and Integration: German Foreign Policy and National Identity After 1989* (New York: St. Martin's Press, 1999), surveys the effort by Kohl and others to connect German unification to integration in transnational bodies. Two collections of documents will be useful: Richard T. Gray and Sabine Wilke, eds., *German Unification and Its Discontents: Documents from the Peaceful Revolution* (Seattle: University of Washington Press, 1996); and Konrad H. Jarausch and Volker Gransow, *Uniting Germany: Documents and Debates, 1944–1993* (Providence, RI: Berghann Books, 1994). Tina Rosenberg, *The Haunted Land: Facing Europe's Ghosts After Communism* (New York: Random House, 1995), offers fascinating reports on the aftermath of 1989 in Germany, and also in Czechoslovakia and Poland.

Reviewing the Text

Review Questions

1. What were the major issues facing the former Soviet bloc in the 1990s and early 2000s?
[model answer] • ***Loss of population:*** *Hundreds of thousands of Russians who had been sent to satellite nations as colonizers returned to Russia as refugees, depopulating the former satellites and putting more stress on the Russian economy. Many young, educated Russians emigrated to more prosperous parts of the world, causing a regional brain drain.*
• ***Racial, ethnic, and religious hatred:*** *Ethnic nationalism came to replace communism in movements for independence and as people sought scapegoats for their problems. Ethnic cleansing was used to eradicate minorities and their cultural heritage, military actions were launched against Muslims to lessen political opposition, and economic problems were blamed on Jews.*
• ***Economic chaos and corruption:*** *Members of the government bought natural resources, weapons, and goods and sold them out of the country for personal profit. The conditions of everyday life grew increasingly dire as salaries went unpaid, food remained in short supply, and essential services disintegrated. Organized crime was rampant and unemployment increased as out-of-date factories closed for lack of funds to invest in modernization.*

2. What trends suggest that the nation-state was a declining institution at the beginning of the twenty-first century?
[model answer] • ***The twelve countries of the Common Market formed the European Union (EU) and developed a common currency:*** *Common policies were developed to govern social, environmental, and health issues that concerned all member nations. Countries clamored to join the EU in order to have disputes adjudicated by the larger body of European states and so that they could reduce their defense budgets.*
• ***Globalization of cities:*** *Western cities with the best transportation and communications facilities developed institutions, functions, and visions that were global rather than regional or national. High-level decision makers met in these cities to set global economic policy and enact global business. Globalized cities also became centers of migration for immigrant workers.*
• ***Supranational organizations that loaned money to nations developed greater influence as national economies interacted more closely:*** *Raising money from individual governments, the International Monetary Fund (IMF) made loans to developing countries on condition that they restructure their economies according to neoliberal principles. Other supranational organizations included nongovernmental charity organizations (NGOs), which wielded considerable power to shape policies and political reform because of the resources they controlled.*

3. What were the principal challenges facing the West at the beginning of the twenty-first century?
[model answer] • ***Pollution:*** *Political and economic fragmentation between Europe and the former superpowers made a global solution to environmental concerns difficult. When the United States refused to sign the Kyoto Protocol, it in essence refused to reduce its emissions of pollutants.*
• ***Population, health care, and disease:*** *While the population in the less-developed world was increasing, birthrates across Europe fell, and life expectancy also declined among the former superpowers. Lowered life expectancy in the West was attributed to the uneven distribution of health services between the rich and poor. New global epidemics developed and traveled quickly; treatment was expensive or, in the case of AIDS, not successful.*
• ***Terrorism:*** *The open borders, economic globalization, and cultural exchange of the new millennium allowed terrorists to operate on a global scale.*
• ***Downturns in global financial markets:*** *When financial scandals, currency speculation, and corruption destabilized Japan and other Pacific economies, the downturn spread to the West, drawing attention to similar corruption in business and worsening with low levels of investment in economic growth.*

4. What social and cultural questions has globalization raised?
[model answer] • ***Complaints about cultural imperialism from non-Western observers:*** *Migration, media, and economic exchange made products, entertainment, and communication fully global. Despite exchanges of ideas and consumer tastes with other cultures, the West continues to exercise global economic and cultural influence, raising concerns that non-Western artists and writers needed to abandon native traditions to attract Western audiences.*
• ***Redistribution of work and wages:*** *Workers in outsourcing enterprises were more likely than those in domestic firms to participate in the global consumer economy and purchase Western goods. Many Western workers found their jobs threatened as a result of economic incentives for businesses to move to countries with lower operating costs. Immigrants searching for work have faced exploitation and unstable work and living conditions.*
• ***Conflicts over multiculturalism:*** *Some critics objected to the inclusion of minorities' works among the classics of the West, arguing that these works represent only a partial vision. In both the United States and Europe, politicians on the right saw multiculturalism as a sign of deterioration.*
• ***Postmodernist critique of the West:*** *Intellectuals have used postmodern political, philosophical, and psychological theories to critique global culture. Commentators have pointed to the demise of Enlightenment ideals because of the demise of their guarantor, the Western nation-state. The West's conviction that it has achieved freedom has also been critiqued, with the argument that many aspects of Western culture and human nature are themselves constraining.*

Making Connections

1. In what ways were global connections at the beginning of the twenty-first century different from the global connections at the beginning of the twentieth century?
[model answer] *At the beginning of the twentieth century, many, perhaps most, people traveled short distances by horse and buggy. Railroads were faster, but these were land-locked. For continental travel, slow-moving boats were the only transportation available. There were, however, trade and cultural exchanges between countries, although not instantaneous as they virtually are today. New forms of transportation and communication truly have made the world "smaller." International cities are cosmopolitan, and are more economically connected with each other and the outside world than they are with their own national economies. Up-to-date, foreign-based television programs, newspapers, and magazines are*

widely available in many parts of the world. People listen to the popular music of different countries by way of radio programs and CDs. Dissident voices from repressive regimes can be heard around the world. In this global economic environment, consumer goods are often made in faraway countries, while economic downturns tend to affect all countries.

2. How did the Western nation-state of the early twenty-first century differ from the Western nation-state at the opening of the twentieth century?
[model answer] *The Western nation-state of the early twentieth century thought mainly in terms of its own country's interests. Today, nations sometimes band together on issues that concern everyone, such as global pollution. The early-twentieth-century nation-state probably actively pursued imperialism, although today Western nations publicly eschew imperial ambitions, even when they find it necessary to invade sovereign states. The economies of nation-states are today bound much more closely together than they have been in the past. Western countries today embrace the principle of representation for its citizens, regardless of gender or race. As Western countries face growing immigrant populations, and the world economy generates millions of migrants, economic downturns, and neofascist groups, care must be taken not to fall prey to the kind of racist nationalism that prompted World War II.*

Discussing the Documents

Questions from Online Study Guide with Model Answers

Václav Havel, "Czechoslovakia Is Returning to Europe," p. 963

1. What argument does Václav Havel make against claims that the lack of prosperity in Czechoslovakia would drag the European Union down?
[model answer] *Havel argues that Czechoslovakia's unsuitability for the European Union is not due to its innate inadequacies, but is a legacy of Soviet subjugation. He also argues that Czechoslovakians are like "wayward children" of Europe who were unnaturally cut off during Soviet rule.*

2. What special insight does Czechoslovakia possess that Havel believes would be beneficial to the European Union?
[model answer] *Havel argues that years of living under Soviet rule have given Czechoslovakia a special introspection into human nature and moral responsibility. He claims that people are still unable "to put morality ahead of politics, science, and economics." Czechoslovakia's experience living under an oppressive regime has taught it the importance of moral responsibility that would benefit the European Union.*

The European Green Party Becomes Transnational (2006), p. 967

1. What "caused" the emergence of Green Parties?
[model answer] *The document claims that the Green Parties were caused by the cold war and the energy crisis of the 1970s. Environmental, social, and economic dangers led to a variety of social movements on a range of issues, from environmental and antinuclear campaigns to feminism and antidictatorial political movements. These movements coalesced and allied into Green Parties.*

2. What do Green Parties want?
[model answer] *Because of their roots in a variety of social movements, they have diverse goals. Overall they claim to stand for the sustainable development of humanity and development modes that respect human rights and build upon values of environmental responsibility, freedom, justice, diversity, and non-violence. They are consciously transnational.*

Contrasting Views: Muslim Immigrants and Turkey in the EU: The Dutch Debate Globalization, pp. 976–977

1. What are the main points of view in the debate over immigration and the admission of Turkey to the European Union?
[model answer] *Politicians such as Pim Fortuyn suggested that "Holland is full," and argued that European nations did not need or want immigrants. "Leon" worried about the loss of Dutch identity and an overwhelming number of foreigners arriving who "did not want to work." Others worried about the Islamic culture of many immigrants, particularly as it became more visible and assertive. Geert Wilders, a member of Dutch Parliament, expressed similar opinions when he argued that there was too much Turkish immigration already, and that recent immigrants could not be assimilated, and they contributed to crime and unemployment. Prime Minister Jan Peter Balkenende suggested that fear of Islam might be behind resistance to Turkey's admission to the European Union, and others such as actress Funda Müjde felt that there was a great deal of intolerance in Dutch culture.*

2. How do you evaluate the strength of each position?
[model answer] *Clearly, concern about the impact and nature of likely emigration is a critical part of the debate about Turkey's admission. Immigrants are widely seen as a "problem" of one sort or another, and even those who urge more acceptance and tolerance acknowledge the prevalence of anti-immigrant sentiment, perhaps rooted*

in anti-Islamic sentiments. Balkenende's position, coming from the prime minister, might be assumed to represent a powerful and influential perspective, however, urging greater toleration and a more open-minded approach to considering expanding the EU to include Turkey.

3. Given that globalization brought about a wide variety of changes, why would immigration and Turkish EU membership become such heated issues?
[model answer] *Immigration questions put the changes associated with globalization right on people's doorsteps. Concerns about competition for jobs, dealing with cultural differences, and absorbing or including poor migrants into communities are particularly challenging for societies, as the readings show, and offer opportunities for politicians to exploit divisions and animosities. In addition, given the cultural heritage of Europe, it is easy to see how the question of including a primarily Islamic country would raise important questions about identity and globalization.*

Other Questions for Discussing These Documents in Class

Václav Havel, "Czechoslovakia Is Returning to Europe"

1. What legacies does Havel see communism having, good and bad?
2. Is Havel right that history has accelerated? Discuss what that might mean.

The European Green Party Becomes Transnational (2006)

1. Why did the Federation of Green Parties develop? What was its historical context?
2. To what twentieth-century experiences would students connect the Green Party? Are they reactive or proactive?

Contrasting Views: Muslim Immigrants and Turkey in the EU: The Dutch Debate Globalization

1. What challenges do Muslim migrants in particular present to countries such as the Netherlands?
2. What historical experiences of the Dutch covered in the text might be useful in thinking about the problems of immigration and diversity? How might historical awareness make the problem better/worse?

Comparative Questions

1. What do the readings have to say about diversity in the contemporary world? In what ways does it seem to provide or offer hope? In what ways can it be dysfunctional or a threat?
2. How do Havel's words speak to the ideas in the other documents? What insights might they offer to our understanding of the Green political movement, or the problem of immigration to the Netherlands?

For Users of *Sources of The Making of the West*

The following documents are available in Chapter 29 of the companion sourcebook by Katharine J. Lualdi, University of Southern Maine.

1. A Child's Life in Sarajevo: *The Diary of Zlata Filipović* (October 6, 1991–June 29, 1992)
2. Critiquing the European Union: Lief Zetterling, Klasskamrater *(Classmates) Cartoon* (January 22, 2001)
3. Doctors Without Borders: Joelle Tanguy and Fiona Terry, *Médecins Sans Frontières*, "On Humanitarian Responsibility" (December 12, 1999)
4. The African National Congress: *Introductory Statement to the Truth and Reconciliation Commission* (August 19, 1996)
5. China in the Global Age: Beijing Organizing Committee for the Games of the XXIX Olympiad, *Announcements on Preparations for the 2008 Summer Olympic Games* (2004–2007)
6. The Post-9/11 Era: Amartya Sen, *A World Not Neatly Divided* (November 23, 2001)

Discussion Ideas for Sources of The Making of the West, *Chapter 29*

1. Do Sen's points make sense in relation to the other documents? How are they relevant to the point that the world community is increasingly intertwined?
2. What is the relationship of historians and history to these documents? What challenges do historians face in assessing their significance?

Working with Visual Sources

For this exercise, please refer to Europeans React to 9/11 Terror on p. 970 of the textbook or view the image on the book companion site's Online Study Guide under the "Visual Activity" for Chapter 28.

Students viewing the image at the Online Study Guide are asked two questions about the image. The questions and model answers (not made available to students) are below. Project this image, available on the Instructor's Resources CD-ROM, in class or ask students to look at the image in their textbooks and answer the questions.

1. What elements of a global culture are apparent in this picture?
[model answer] *This person is reading a British newspaper in Italy about an event that took place in the United States. The availability of foreign-language newspapers in Italy attests to a more global marketplace, while the fact that a British newspaper has this headline shows that news such as this had international implications. Presumably, the person reading this newspaper is not Italian, which shows that people travel a lot, either as tourists or for business.*

2. In what ways are terrorist attacks, such as the one depicted here, challenges unique to the late twentieth and early twenty-first century?
[model answer] *Terrorist attacks such as those on September 11 were motivated by a desire to wreak retribution on the West for its role in geopolitical affairs. The nature of the attacks themselves had an international aspect because the hijackers were trained in Afghanistan in camps established by a wealthy Saudi Arabian. The destruction of the World Trade Center had an important symbolic value for the hijackers, while their method was made possible through modern technology and the commonality of air travel.*

Mapping Exercises

Map Activity from OSG—Model Answers for Map Activity #2

For this activity, please refer to Map 29.3: Countries of the Former Soviet Union, c. 2000 on p. 957. Students are asked these questions:

Why are the areas where violent ethnic conflicts occurred located in areas that broke away from the Soviet Union, and not, for example, within Russia itself?
[model answer] *When these territories broke away from the Soviet Union, they were free to establish their own identities and create their own political, social, and cultural systems. Without the uniformity imposed by communism and Russian domination, ethnic and national differences became more important, as diverse groups struggled to make their voices heard. In some places, this resulted in the establishment of multiple states.*

Why was the capital of the CIS placed in Minsk, a city in Belarus, and not in Moscow?
[model answer] *Moscow was the capital of the Soviet Union. By locating the capital elsewhere, the CIS demonstrated its desire to break its ties with the Soviet past. At the same time, Minsk is relatively close to Moscow, which retains enormous economic, cultural, and political clout in the region.*

Map 29.1: Eastern Europe in the 1990s, p. 954

Compare this map to *Mapping the West: The Collapse of Communism in Europe, 1989–1990* (Chapter 28, p. 948). What has changed? Pay particular attention to the fates of Germany, Czechoslovakia, and the former Yugoslavia. What does the map suggest about nationalism in the 1990s? Does our assessment change when we consider that these countries sought EC and even NATO membership?

Map 29.2: The Former Yugoslavia, c. 2000, p. 955

As with the previous one, this map may be used in discussing the disintegration of Yugoslavia. Ask students to comment on the effect Slovenia's geographic location had on its experiences in the 1990s. Call students' attention to the fact that Serbia, Montenegro, and the province of Kosovo technically constitute the Federal Republic of Yugoslavia. What role did Croatia's geographic location play in its experiences in the 1990s? How does Bosnia-Herzegovina differ from Slovenia? Croatia? Serbia? Macedonia? Note the location of Kosovo and Macedonia, and ask students to comment on Macedonia's role during the expulsion of the Albanian Kosovars and the NATO bombing campaign in 1999.

Map 29.3: Countries of the Former Soviet Union, c. 2000, p. 957

Again, students should consider the meaning of this map for those who now live within these new borders. Consider in particular the effects on Russians, and how their perspective on the map might be quite different from inhabitants of new states. What concerns might the wider global community, the United Nations, or the European Union have about this map?

Map 29.4, The European Union in 2007, p. 962

Have students use the map as a basis for a discussion of the concepts of "widening" and "deepening" the EU. Ask students to discuss the reasons why various countries joined when they did. Which countries among those applying for membership were more likely to fit in immediately? Why might some observers have reservations about admitting Turkey into the EU?

Map 29.5: The Middle East in the Twenty-first Century, p. 971

The geographical relationship between Iran and Iraq are worth considering, as well as the geographic details of the very small area of Palestine. Ask students to discuss the extent to which these boundaries reflect identities. What events covered in the textbook chapter (including the Iran/Iraq War, the conflict in Palestine, the Kuwait invasion, the breakup of the Soviet Union, and the invasion of Iraq by the United States and coalition forces) might have influenced or even changed the significance of these national borders?

Mapping the West: The World in the New Millennium, p. 983

To what extent is the North–South division a useful concept? Does it oversimplify the complexity of the division of wealth among nations? Is there any correlation between wealth and Internet diffusion? Ask students to comment on any connections they note.

In-Class Assignments and Presentation Topics

1. Ask students to reflect on one event they believe is likely to happen in the next decade, based on historical trends. It may be something fairly specific, such as a forceful international intervention into Darfur, or something far more general, such as the end of the Gutenberg era in the face of electronic books. Ask students to support their predictions on the basis of historical evidence, such as growing concern about the failure of the international community to respond effectively to earlier crises in Bosnia and Rwanda, or the increasing number of experiments with publishing on the Internet after the fashion of Stephen King. In effect, they have to show how they extrapolated from known facts to what is not yet known.

2. Organize students into several groups and assign each group the task of presenting to the rest of the class the events of 1989 in a particular country. You will need to set some parameters. Should they deal only with what happened in 1989? Should they be allowed or encouraged to choose an earlier starting date and perhaps also to take the presentation past the end of 1989? What kinds of sources do you want them to examine? Encourage students to use, whenever possible, visual material, primary sources, and material objects (a piece of the asbestos-laced Berlin Wall, for example). Each group should organize itself so that every student has a definite assignment. Every student should write a brief essay critiquing his or her experience.

3. Require students to keep a journal on events in a particular country over a period of at least three or four weeks. Decide whether you wish to receive the journal in paper format or as an attachment to an e-mail. Ideally, each student would put her or his journal on a personal Web site or a course Web site. (This option would, however, necessitate that everyone have these skills already or acquire these skills as part of the work for the course.) Set minimum numbers for this journal; for example, students might be required to read or view at least two items each week and write a minimum of two pages of commentary; or students may have four items one week and only one item the following week. Encourage students to cast as wide a net as possible, using not only print sources or Web sites but also art, music, documentaries, and items from the material culture of the country.

4. Present students with a case study of the expansion of NATO or the widening and deepening of the EU (other topics are, of course, possible; these are suggested because they involve transnational questions). Include in the case study a few pages of narrative, mostly to set the scene, and some primary sources. Give students a question to consider; for example, ask them to work through a case study on the euro and then comment on whether it was a good thing to introduce the euro at this juncture. Good places to begin putting together a case study are the following Web sites: for NATO, North Atlantic Treaty Organization at http://www.nato.int; for the EU, Europe at http://europa.eu.int.

Essay Questions

1. The journal mentioned in "In-Class Assignments and Presentation Topics," number 3, could serve as preparation for a larger research project on a country in the 1990s. Of course, students might simply be assigned a research paper on a specific aspect of the politics and economics of a particular country in the 1990s. It may be useful, if you have not already done so, to invite a reference librarian from your college to demonstrate methods for finding information on recent historical events. Many useful Web resources are available, particularly if students know a few techniques for more sophisticated searching, as well as annual publications, compilations, and indexes, that make it possible to find information and analysis.

2. Arrange the students into two groups and assign each group the task of designing a magazine (or e-zine if they have the requisite skills) on the twenty-first century. The magazine/e-zine is meant to deal not only with current events but also with past events that have a bearing on the present and, to a more limited extent, with what people might expect in the future given existing lines of development. Each group should collectively choose a title, determine departments that will continue from issue to issue, such as "Technology and the Twenty-First Century," and draw up a list of articles and essays for the first issue. The groups should then work together to write one or more of the articles and essays, with some students serving as researchers, some as authors, others as editors, picture editors, and so forth.

Present students with a partial model or an outline of such a magazine/e-zine. For example, introductory text might include the following:

> Clemenceau noted in World War I that "war is too important to be left to the generals." We would change that slightly to note that recent history is too important to be left to the social scientists. *20/20 Vision* covers in each issue significant topics in world history in a manner designed to provide the reader with an introduction, together with suggestions on the best Web sites, videos, books, articles, and other sources of information and analysis. The following topics will be covered in the initial issue.
>
> Russia: A Funny Thing Happened on the Way to Democracy and Free Enterprise
>
> Nelson Mandela, the End of Apartheid, and the Rainbow Nation
>
> Water
>
> Energy
>
> AIDS
>
> Another WTO to Worry About: The World Trade Organization

Discuss with them what sorts of illustrations and additional information might be relevant for these topics.

3. Alternately, have students compose an essay or a Web page on the legacy of twentieth-century Western history for the increasingly "global" twenty-first century on any of the following topics:

- the rights of women and/or minority groups
- nationalism
- international organizations
- environmental/resource issues
- demographics/reproduction

Common questions could include: What were the significant events/developments of the last century on this topic? Where do we stand today? What might the future hold for this issue, and what major challenges does the west/world face for the future?

Additional Resources: Literature

Carson, Rachel, *Silent Spring*. 1962.
Emecheta, Buchi, *The Joys of Motherhood*. 1979.
Grossman, Edith, trans., *Gabriel García Márquez: Love in the Time of Cholera*. 1999.
Heaney, Seamus, *Opened Ground: Selected Poems, 1966–1996*. 1996.
Hosseini, Khaled, *The Kite Runner*. 2003.
Kundera, Milan, *The Unbearable Lightness of Being*. 1984.
Morrison, Toni, *Paradise*. 1998.
Rushdie, Salman, *The Satanic Verses*. 1989.
Schumacher, E.F., *Small is Beautiful*. 1973.
Todd, Albert C., and James Ragan, eds., *Yevgeny Yevtushenko: The Collected Poems, 1952–1990*. 1992.

Additional Resources: Film and Video

The Gods Must Be Crazy (1981; VHS/DVD, 1 hr., 49 min.). This film presents a classic take on "early" globalization from a non-Western perspective.

Salaam Bombay (1988; VHS/DVD, 1 hr., 54 min.). This film offers an inside look at migration and urban life in 1980s India.

The Fourth World War (2004; DVD, 1 hr., 15 min.). Taken from a speech by Marcos calling the war against globalization "the Fourth World War," this film is a brief, slightly glamorized documentary of radical resistance to global capitalism.

An Inconvenient Truth (2006; DVD, 1 hr., 36 min.). Director Davis Guggenheim eloquently weaves the science of global warming with Al Gore's personal history and lifelong commitment to reversing the effects of global climate change in this audience and critical favorite. This film could be shown perhaps in conjunction with connecting students up with Internet debates on the film from a variety of perspectives.

Blood Diamond (2006; DVD, 2 hrs., 23 min.). Amid the explosive civil war overtaking 1999 Sierra Leone, two men join for two desperate missions: recovering a rare pink diamond of immense value and rescuing one man's son, conscripted as a child soldier into the brutal rebel forces ripping a swath of torture and bloodshed across the alternately beautiful and ravaged countryside.

The Take (2006; DVD, 1 hr., 27 min.). This film gives an Argentinean take on the sometimes disruptive dynamics of the global economy.

OTHER BEDFORD/ST. MARTIN'S RESOURCES FOR CHAPTER 29

The following resources are available to accompany Chapter 29. Please refer to the Preface of this manual for detailed descriptions of all the ancillaries.

For Instructors

Transparencies

The following maps and image from Chapter 29 are available as full-color acetates.

- Map 29.1: Eastern Europe in the 1990s
- Map 29.2: The Former Yugoslavia, c. 2000
- Map 29.3: Countries of the Former Soviet Union, c. 2000
- Map 29.4: The European Union in 2007
- Map 29.5: The Middle East in the Twenty-first Century
- Mapping the West: The World in the New Millennium
- Aftermath of Communism's Collapse, p. 958
- Europeans React to 9/11 Terror, p. 970

Instructor's Resources CD-ROM

The following maps and image from Chapter 29, as well as a chapter outline, are available on disc in both PowerPoint and jpeg formats.

- Map 29.1: Eastern Europe in the 1990s
- Map 29.2: The Former Yugoslavia, c. 2000
- Map 29.3: Countries of the Former Soviet Union, c. 2000
- Map 29.4: The European Union in 2007
- Map 29.5: The Middle East in the Twenty-first Century
- Mapping the West: The World in the New Millennium
- Europeans React to 9/11 Terror, p. 970

For Students

Study Guides

The Online Study Guide at **bedfordstmartins.com/hunt** helps students synthesize the material they have learned as well as practice the skills historians use to make sense of the past. The following Map, Visual, and Document activities are available for Chapter 29.

Map Activity

- Map 29.3: Countries of the Former Soviet Union, c. 2000

Visual Activity

- Europeans React to 9/11 Terror, p. 970

Reading Historical Documents

- Václav Havel, "Czechoslovakia Is Returning to Europe," p. 963
- The European Green Party Becomes Transnational (2006), p. 967
- Contrasting Views: Muslim Immigrants and Turkey in the EU: The Dutch Debate Globalization, pp. 976–977

Appendix: Essays

What Is "The West"?

Michael D. Richards

Sweet Briar College

Edward Said, in his classic study *Orientalism* (1978), asserts that "as much as the West itself, the Orient is an idea that has a history and a tradition of thought, imagery, and vocabulary that have given it reality and presence. . . ." Can it be that "the West" or even "Western civilization" is only an idea that has taken different forms at various times and places? Rather than try to answer the question immediately and directly, it might be helpful to look at several possibilities that allow us to approach it in more indirect ways. First, perhaps we can establish a geographical basis for the notion of "the West." Immediately, we land in difficulties. A large part of Western civilization, the Judeo-Christian heritage, Greek civilization, and Roman civilization, is "southern," that is, Mediterranean. Even if we ignore this conundrum, we still find little agreement on the question of what, in terms of geography, the West is. Martin W. Lewis and Kären E. Wigen suggest in *The Myth of Continents* (1997) seven different geographical interpretations of the West. The most extreme limits the West to Britain, as in "The Wogs begin at Calais." The second interpretation is a slightly more expansive but still minimal West, confined to the northwest of Europe and including only Britain, France, the Low Countries, and Switzerland. A third possibility is the historical West of medieval Christendom, expanding slowly over time. By the twentieth century, a fourth version is derived from the West of the cold war or, alternatively, Europe and its white settler colonies (both versions often include Japan). The fifth version is a cultural West, a West defined by language, religion, and high culture. This version takes in those parts of Latin America that otherwise would not be included. The penultimate version is the maximum West and includes all areas with a Christian or Islamic heritage. Finally, there is the West as defined by the idea of modernization—those areas with a high concentration of urbanism and industrial capitalism.

Geographical interpretations, as it turns out, do not provide a clear-cut answer. We can see that, at different times and places, the spatial extent of the West has been variously understood. Perhaps we might get closer to a definition if we examine certain processes and institutions that are the common property of different groups. Supposedly, the West is characterized by reason and its chief product, science; by democracy and representative government; and by capitalism. David Gress gives the West (Britain and the Netherlands in particular) credit for "inventing" what he calls "the three pillars of modernity." It may be more accurate to say here that the West developed particularly dynamic and effective versions of these processes, aided in no small way by borrowings from the Islamic and Chinese cultures. In any case, Gress believes these processes are not necessarily connected to European culture, but are universal and can be adopted without having to adopt

European culture at the same time. Here, at least, he avoids the triumphalism of recent years in which history is reduced to the story of Western civilization becoming the model the rest of the world will follow in the future. J. M. Roberts's video series, *The Triumph of the West*, the last episode of which is entitled "Capitulation," is a sophisticated version of this latter view.

Perhaps it is not the large processes of science, capitalism, and democracy that set the West apart but smaller items, certain cultural artifacts. We could point to, for example, the Greek and Roman classical sources, which served as a basis for the Renaissance and, later, as one of the inspirations for the Enlightenment. There is additionally the literary canon, today much modified and enlarged, but nonetheless still viable. Similarly, there are the great and beloved bodies of European art and music. Finally, there exist the long philosophical and epistemological traditions that stand behind the large processes discussed above. All of these are familiar elements of something we might call Western civilization. William McNeill puts it this way: "A shared literary canon, and expectations about human behavior framed by that canon, are probably central to what we mean by a civilization" (8).

In the twentieth century, of course, the concept of ideas and values from the past serving as guidelines for behavior has been attacked, first by the Futurists, then by many other movements. Yet, for all those attacks, it is striking that we continue to examine and think about the great body of art and ideas we call Western culture. And while there will always be argument about what to include in that body, there is a rough if continually evolving consensus.

This brings us back to Said's formulation: the West, like the Orient, is an idea that changes from place to place and from one time to another. It built on the Greco-Roman and Judeo-Christian traditions, but only slowly and with great difficulty. The first version of the West was medieval Christendom. It depended heavily on the existence of something different from itself in order to define itself. One important "other" was Islam. When Charles Martel supposedly stopped the advance of Islam in Europe at Tours in about 732, the idea that the West was not Islam began to take hold. The Crusades played a vital role in defining what the West was by the process of clarifying what it was not. Other events, the centuries-long process of the *reconquista*, in which Spaniards took Spain back from the Moors, and the defense of Vienna against the Ottoman Empire in the late seventeenth century, helped as well to consolidate the idea of Europe as Christendom.

By the seventeenth century, however, Europeans began to use the word Europe in a positive sense, and Europeans viewed the world in terms of Europe by the start of the eighteenth century. Denys Hay illustrates the shift by pointing to the terminology used in two similar documents. When the king of England issued Cabot a patent in 1496, he commissioned him to explore lands hitherto "unknown to all Christians." Two and a half centuries later, Commodore John Byron was ordered to search for "lands and islands of great extent hitherto invisited by an European power" (Hay 117).

In the process, Europeans had come to see themselves as superior to the people they encountered. This view may have originated in Christianity, in that Christians believed they possessed the keys to salvation, while pagans did not. The Drang nach Osten by the Teutonic Order, which by definition created a West, is one example. In the seventeenth and eighteenth centuries, advanced technology associated with military matters and commerce reinforced this attitude. The Enlightenment, while critical of aspects of Western civilization, set up a process involving the use of human reason that was supposed to lead to greater and greater progress in the future. It was, in a very real way, a secular version of the promise of Christianity.

It is probably in the nineteenth century that the idea of the West and Western civilization became fully developed. One major factor was the Industrial Revolution(s), the several quantum jumps in productivity, beginning in Britain with the production of textiles, continuing with the development of the iron and steel industries, railroads, and steamships, and reaching a temporary plateau at the end of the century with the advent of the electrical and chemical industries and the great expansion of the production of consumer goods. Another factor was the overall success enjoyed by Europeans in dealing with the ancient Chinese empire. Yet another is probably the visibility of the British Empire, with India as its jewel in the crown. Additionally, the "scramble for Africa" contributed to the sense that the West had triumphed. The West now included Europe and its many colonies, several white settler colonies that formed the British Commonwealth, and one former colony, the United States, now an independent and increasingly powerful country. Social Darwinism and eugenics attributed the very real power and seeming superiority to what was believed to be a scientifically justified racial basis.

In the twentieth century, the support of German National Socialism for a racial interpretation of history, and the horrendous policies that came out of that approach, called into question any racial basis for alleged superiority. Marxism, in the form of Soviet communism, actually challenged the idea of the West much more effectively than National Socialism. It also helped to redefine the idea of the West, in that the West and Western civilization became everything that communism was not.

We are left now in a post-Communist, postcolonial world in which many countries seem to be more or less western. David Gress may be correct: these countries may be simply modern and only superficially western. It complicates matters even further when writers from the former colonies win major literary prizes and are well received by the guardians of the Western literary tradition. It is probably simply too early to locate an adequate replacement for the older anti-Communist idea of the West. However, the consensus that exists among historians and other interpreters of Western civilization is striking: certain items are seen as essential to any understanding of the West and Western civilization.

These include the Golden Age of Athens; Hellenism; the Jewish faith; the Roman Republic and Empire; medieval Christianity and the beginnings of artistic, musical, and literary traditions; the Renaissance; the Reformation; the scientific revolution; the Enlightenment; the French Revolution, the Industrial Revolution; nationalism; imperialism; war; revolution; and the cold war, among others. We may approach these topics differently, emphasizing the role of women, for example, or looking at mass culture as well as high culture, but we nonetheless believe we see in them the outlines of something we call the West or Western civilization.

That there would be at any given time several distinct ideas about what is the "West" should not be a problem. Americans will have a different sense of what the West is than Poles or Czechs, who may see themselves on the frontiers of the West instead of at its powerful, confident center. Certainly across time there have been different ideas about the West and Western civilization—and this is an important idea to convey to students. We not only have to construct an understanding for ourselves of what the West and Western civilization are, we also have to be aware of the many times in the past when people put together their ideas of the West and Western civilization. This awareness is, of course, fundamental to historical understanding. Every era writes its own history. However, to paraphrase Marx in *The Eighteenth Brumaire of Louis Bonaparte*, each era is not free to write history just as it pleases. The past comes with various aspects already in place that cannot simply be ignored. The West and Western civilization are works in progress. There is no guarantee they will continue to dominate the world as they have for the past two centuries. In fact, it is very likely that the locus of power and development will shift from the Atlantic to the Pacific Rim in the next few decades. Even if this were to happen, however, examining the idea of the West and the reality of Western civilization would still be useful, as it is the only way for large numbers of people to gain true orientation as to their present circumstances and a useful perspective on the future. The West is, as Edward Said states, only an idea with a history, but it has been and continues to be a powerful and significant idea.

Bibliography

Gress, David. *From Plato to NATO: The Idea of the West and Its Critics*. New York: Free Press, 1998.

Hay, Denys. *Europe: The Emergence of an Idea*. 1957.

Lewis, Martin W., and Kären E. Wigen. *The Myth of Continents*. Berkeley: University of California Press, 1997.

McNeill, William. "The Rise of the West after Twenty-five Years." *Journal of World History* 1.1 (1990):8.

Roberts, J. M. *History of the World*. 1993. ———. *The Triumph of the West*. Chicago, IL: Public Media, 1987.

Said, Edward. *Orientalism*. New York: Pantheon Books, 1978.

Active Learning Strategies for the Western Classroom

Dakota Hamilton

Humboldt State University

Two challenges often face instructors of the Western Civilization survey: compulsion and high enrollment. Because many college and university students *must* take Western Civilization courses for their program of study or to fulfill general education requirements, enrollment caps are often set at ridiculously high levels. As a result, instructors often face large classes filled with students who *have to*, rather than *want to*, be there.

From the instructor's point of view, traditional lectures can be the easiest method of instruction for these kinds of classes. These can work well, especially when the instructor has real enthusiasm for the subject matter. During our course of study, we probably all have been the students of brilliant lecturers who enthralled, inspired, thrilled, amused, and moved us deeply. But structuring classes solely around lectures can be problematic from the students' perspective. Studies have shown that attention spans average between ten and twenty minutes for most students, which means that student restlessness, or even sleep, may set in before a class is half over. As opposed to passive learning, which is typically epitomized by the traditional lecture format, active learning has to be part of the classroom, whatever its size. Probably few instructors are scintillating lecturers all of the time or even want to spend every class lecturing. Fortunately, there are many active learning strategies that can complement traditional lectures.

Active learning strategies are activities designed to elicit direct student participation. Rather than being passive receptors of information, students are encouraged to become active participants in the learning process through carefully designed assignments. Such assignments can be either straightforward—intended to recapture students' wandering attention; or more complex—intended to stimulate critical thinking about a particular issue or subject. Group work is often emphasized because active learning assignments are meant to generate thought provoking discussions. Instructors wishing to explore the theoretical basis and practical applications of active learning strategies might read John C. Bean, *Engaging Ideas: The Professor's Guide to Integrating Writing, Critical Thinking, and Active Learning in the Classroom* (San Francisco: Jossey-Bass Publishers, 2001).

This is not to say that lectures should be abandoned outright because the traditional lecture format can be transformed into an active learning situation. After lecturing for ten or twenty minutes, instructors could do a number of things to reengage student attention. For example, an instructor could give a quiz on the material presented up to that point, with students referring back to their notes. Or, an instructor could ask students to write a short summary of what has just been presented or to devise true/false or multiple-choice questions for an upcoming exam based on that same material. It is also possible to introduce analysis or critical thinking with a carefully designed question, based on the lecture material that asks students to argue a particular position, either in writing or in a small discussion group or as part of a wider class discussion.

In-class interviews can also be an effective approach to keeping students active and involved. Students can select or be assigned the roles of specific historical figures and be interviewed by the rest of the class at appropriate times during the course. A pair or group of historical figures could take opposing sides of a historical issue. To ensure full participation by the entire class, every student might be asked to contribute by preparing questions a week in advance, which the instructor could then review; or by submitting a short, written report on their historical figure(s). This way, the instructor can review the questions in advance to be sure they are relevant and will give voice to students who might otherwise simply sit quietly in class. Using the Spanish Armada as an example, students might ask "King Philip II of Spain" a mix of factual and speculative questions, such as how many

Spaniards made it home after the defeat of the Armada or whether he still believes God is on his side in the conflict between Catholics and Protestants. "Queen Elizabeth I" then might join the discussion, and students could ask whether England was militarily prepared to meet the Armada because it was clearly over a year before the attack that Spain was mobilizing, or whether "Elizabeth" would have executed her cousin if she had known the Armada would have been the result. Other appropriate historical figures for this kind of activity include Pericles, Augustus, Mohammed, Charlemagne, a survivor of the fourteenth-century plague, a medieval monk or nun, Dante, and Joan of Arc. Pairings or groupings of historical figures and issues might include a manorial lord and a peasant discussing medieval justice, Charles I and Oliver Cromwell discussing the tensions between monarchy and parliamentary rule, and Louis XVI and Robespierre discussing the French Revolution. What is particularly engaging about this kind of assignment is that individual interests can be accommodated to some degree because students could work within their own areas of interest. For example, a student studying the natural sciences might choose Newton or Darwin; a student majoring in literature might select Dante or Dickens; an art student might prefer Leonardo or Hogarth; an education major might want Locke or Rousseau; and a musician might select Bach or Mozart. Having students present material and answer questions in front of their peers keeps the classroom lively—the presenters have to know the material well, as do the students asking the questions.

Film assignments are another good way to stimulate interesting active learning situations. Students could all view the same film, or each student could select a historically based film from the list of film suggestions provided with each chapter of this Instructor's Resource Manual. Students often feel comfortable critiquing films in a way that they do not feel about other kinds of material. In their reviews, students might consider issues of historical accuracy: Are the characters, whether fictional or based on real figures, appropriately drawn? How close is the plot to real events? If the plot is fictionalized, does the storyline still seem plausible? Does the setting have the right look and feel? Did the researchers working on the film get the details correct? Once the particulars of a film or films have been considered, students could move on to the overarching question of whether films should be as historically accurate as possible. After the instructor has collected the essays, students might then post their reviews on the course Web site, so that they can discuss each other's essays online before bringing the discussion into the classroom. The instructor has the choice of reviewing the online postings for grades, monitoring the discussion but staying out of it, or prompting a new line of analysis at appropriate points. Under the guidance of an instructor, such online postings can really enhance the discussion that takes place in the classroom.

Appropriate visual material could also be introduced after lecturing for ten or fifteen minutes, perhaps with a short, in-class writing assignment based on that material prior to a larger, class discussion. Such assignments have the additional advantages of offering students the opportunity to work with visual material as primary sources and to practice the responses that might be expected of them on an examination. Visual activities could last for ten minutes, followed by a concluding lecture segment, or even for the remainder of the class period.

Visual images or literary texts can also be introduced into the classroom by having students select or perhaps draw by lottery for significant works of art or literature. Rather than writing and presenting a "review" style essay, students might be asked to take a position on a particular work or several related works. For example, the Renaissance artist Albrecht Dürer produced no less than seven portraits of himself between the ages of 13 and 37, including *The Martyrdom of the 10,000* (1508), in which Dürer places himself in the center of the work. Students might be asked to trace Dürer's changing sense of self through these paintings, to compare it with shifting notions of the artist during the Renaissance, and to indicate how Dürer visually signaled his changed view of himself. Alternatively, students might be asked to support or refute the idea that Charles Dickens exaggerated the situation of the working classes in his novels. Because Dickens's novels were initially serialized, many sections actually stand on their own and might serve as appropriate examples, or students might refer to *A Christmas Carol*, which is relatively short. Again, after instructors have collected their essays, students might then post them on the course Web site before an in-class discussion.

Other writing assignments lend themselves to both individual and group work. An instructor might give students contradictory quotations on various historical issues and ask them to wrestle with them, either in an individual essay or as part of a group assignment. Similarly, an instructor might frame a thesis and ask students, either individually or in groups, to take opposing sides and to debate the issue in front of the class, with the remaining students not directly involved serving as judges.

In addition to eliciting student participation, critical thinking and writing are other important elements of active learning. These elements are intimately connected because it is during the writing process that ideas are thought through and organized into coherent analyses and arguments. If students start writing early in their academic careers, instructors can start them on the journey to becoming sophisticated, critical thinkers. Assignments that are intended merely to elicit data or information do little to help students either remember the information or think critically about it. Students have become all too good at searching the Internet and piecing together papers that are chock full of information but containing little or no analysis. Although these papers may be informative and well organized, this does not make up for the lack of critical thinking. Instead, instructors should construct writing assignments that force students to think critically about an issue and to understand and weigh opposing viewpoints in order to arrive at some personal conclusion. It is important for instructors to structure questions in a way such that there are no "right" or "wrong" answers, and for students to understand that the assignment will be evaluated on the quality of its argument rather than on getting the "right" result.

Instructors of large Western Civilization survey courses should not balk at making such writing assignments because they can be managed even in large classrooms as long as the assignments are carefully thought out. Some fruitful assignments can be made using the primary sources in *The Making of the West: Peoples and Cultures* or its accompanying reader, *Sources of* THE MAKING OF THE WEST by Katharine J. Lualdi. Such an assignment might ask students to consider whether they could successfully make the "negative confession" contained in the Egyptian Book of the Dead, or to propose an alternative confession that reflects contemporary culture and values; to write a letter to a friend about why they should or should not enter into public service in today's world after reading Giovanni Rucellai's advice to his sons; to "update" John Milton's *Areopagitica* (1644) by finding more contemporary arguments for a free press, including Thomas Jefferson's *Declaration of Independence* (1776); to rewrite a print document, such as *The Funeral Oration of Pericles* (429 B.C.E.) by Thucydides, or *The Accomplishments of Augustus* (14 C.E.), in the barest of modern-day English; to take the opposite view of that expressed in a primary source, such as writing a letter home from the perspective of the factory worker in contrast to *Factory Rules in Berlin* (1844); or to write "diary" entries for historical figures during a controversial time in their figures' lives, or playing the role of a courtier-chronicler in the mode of Saint-Simon in his *Memoirs* (1694–1723), or Montesquieu in his *Persian Letters: Letter 37* (1721). All of these sample assignments could later be read aloud in small groups or even to the whole class, thus stimulating discussions of related issues. Such assignments require students to have a thorough understanding of the original sources, as well as of their historical context. However, they would also be short (probably no longer than one page), so they would be appropriate for a large class. These kinds of assignments would therefore encourage students to think critically beyond the original source, and yet still be manageable for an instructor of a large class.

Asking students to work with other original documents in their original script can also make for a stimulating exercise. Students may be used to reading primary documents that have been translated or transcribed and then neatly typed into English in their textbooks and readers. However, it is an entirely different experience for them to look at sixteenth-century English documents in their original form. An instructor might begin with a brief overview of the kinds of documents that have survived from this period before moving on to related subjects, such as the production of paper and ink. With a bit of coaching, students might then look at and try to transcribe a few lines from several different kinds of documents, some written in italic form, some in the more difficult "secretary hand."

Students might then be asked, by themselves, to transcribe a carefully selected letter, such as the letter by Henry VIII to Cardinal Wolsey in about 1521 concerning the king's fears over the loyalty of several noblemen, including the duke of Buckingham, who was shortly to be executed on charges of treason. The instructor could conclude the lecture by discussing how one might interpret the documents based first on internal evidence and then through context. In addition to engaging students in examining primary source material, this type of exercise helps students to understand that history involves looking at original material, making informed judgments about it, and only then writing a historical narrative.

Studies have shown that groups consisting of no more than five students work best, but group work can still be successfully incorporated into large classrooms. Instructors might assign questions or problems such that each group defends a position or renders an opinion. To combat the difficulties associated with determining the individual contribution of each student, each group member might be required to keep a journal of his or her research on the topic, including a possible thesis statement, which would then be shared with group members. Based on the independent research notes, thesis statements, and rough drafts, the group would then collectively formulate and write a paper for presentation. Ultimately, instructors could review the individual journals to determine if a student had participated fully in their group and could be assigned credit for his or her individual contribution, as well as for their final papers. A peer review, where groups read each other's papers for content, argument, and flow, might also be incorporated into this process, but this might depend on how much class time is available to devote to such a project.

Although most students ultimately find it to be a rewarding experience, instructors should be prepared for some degree of resistance when turning a classroom into an active learning environment. Asking students to *think* about what they are doing in a critical way is inherently more challenging than listening to a long lecture. In addition, students are often reluctant to voice an opinion for fear of being "wrong." One further complication is that students tend to be very trusting of what they see in print and asking them to challenge or test what they have read can be unsettling. However, after engaging in some of these active learning activities, most classes appreciate the stimulation, the challenge, and the break from the traditional lecture format.

Working Primary Sources into the Western Civilization Syllabus

Katharine J. Lualdi

University of Southern Maine

Teaching the history of Western civilization at the survey level poses an array of exciting but difficult challenges for instructors. While it is important to construct a narrative that is coherent and engaging, instructors must also fit their coverage of vast expanses of time, place, and culture within the typical one-semester survey format. A textbook can provide a chronological and thematic framework for surmounting this challenge, yet neither it nor any other work alone can adequately elucidate the many dimensions of the past. Primary sources fill this gap with the voices of people who shaped and were shaped by history as it unfolded around them. Documents thus provide an invaluable means of enlivening and deepening the major issues, ideas, and events addressed in the survey narrative while allowing students to see that history is not a static compilation of facts and dates, but rather an ongoing process of discovery and interpretation.

The value of including primary source materials in the Western civilization survey extends beyond their ability to illuminate specific topics and points of view through first-person accounts. They also reveal historians' broad appreciation of the multitude of peoples and societies both within and outside Europe that shaped Western values, institutions, and traditions. Using a collection of documents to place the development of the West on both the European and world stage can thereby enhance students' understanding of the past and its relationship to the present in today's global age.

Compiled specifically to accompany *The Making of the West: Peoples and Cultures,* the documents included in *Sources of* THE MAKING OF THE WEST were selected with these goals in mind. The collection is organized into individual chapters, comprised of four documents each, which speak to key events and opinions of a specific historical era in important, and often surprising, ways. Traditional political documents are included alongside less conventional sources that elucidate Europe's social and cultural life as well as its increasing interconnectedness with the world at large. The voices of women and minorities were also granted a special place in the selection process because of their crucial yet often undervalued impact on the course of Western history.

Each chapter of *Sources of* THE MAKING OF THE WEST includes several editorial features to facilitate the use of the documents in a classroom setting. A summary situating the documents within the broader historical context and addressing their relationship to each other prefaces every chapter. An explanatory headnote accompanies each document to provide fundamental background information on the author and the source while highlighting its significance. Discussion questions are also included to help students examine the fundamental points and issues in greater depth. Finally, all chapters close with comparative questions to encourage students to see both the harmony and discordance among the document sets.

Together, these editorial features strengthen the coherency of each chapter as a pedagogical unit while still allowing instructors the freedom to choose documents and questions that best suit their own teaching goals and methods. The editorial apparatus is also geared toward strengthening students' analytical skills by encouraging them to consider the connections between the content of each document to a specific author, time, place, and audience. In this way, students learn that all primary sources are unique products of human enterprise and are often colored by personal concerns, biases, and objectives. It is the job of the historian, whether a professional or novice, to sift through such nuances to uncover what they reveal about the past.

Thus, both the content and format of *Sources of* THE MAKING OF THE WEST make it a valuable resource for teaching students not only about the formation of Western civilization but also about the process of historical inquiry. As such, the collection is also intended to be a springboard for more advanced work with primary sources.

The Western and world history titles in the Bedford Series in History and Culture are ideally suited for this purpose. The French Revolution and the Dreyfus Affair, for example, are both treated in the textbook and document reader, but the series volumes on these subjects delve into greater detail and from many more angles. By incorporating these and other relevant titles from the series into a Western civilization survey course, instructors can further engage students in unraveling the historical record in all of its diversity and complexity.

Visual Literacy: The Image in the Western Civilization Classroom

Paul R. Deslandes

Texas Tech University

We often hear that, for good or bad, the current generation of traditional college-aged students is a group used to digesting (or at least ingesting) a diversity of visual stimuli ranging from fast-paced and remarkably intricate computer games to the music videos offered up to them on MTV and VH1.While some within the academy decry this development as the "dumbing of America," others view it as fertile ground for both research and teaching. Historians who teach general Western civilization surveys can use this reality to their advantage by thinking about their courses as opportunities to promote an understanding of the past through visual as well as written means. By employing a range of visual materials (including films, traditional slides and overheads, and high-tech computer simulations) in new and innovative ways, instructors can move beyond the tendency to use images as "illustrations" alone. The Western civilization classroom needs to be viewed as an ideal environment within which historians can actively promote visual literacy among college students by encouraging them to "read" and analyze images with a critical eye that will broaden their interpretive skills while possibly turning them on to the study of history in a way that document-based exercises alone cannot.

Naturally, resistant instructors might consider such a pedagogical approach as the active encouragement of a dangerous and worrying trend—the tendency on the part of students to avoid serious reading at all costs. What I am proposing in this brief examination of visual media in the Western civilization classroom is not an abandonment of the traditional document study but, rather, a broadened conception of what constitutes a valuable, or even an essential, source. The skills that we hope our students will acquire by reading Jean-Jacques Rousseau's *The New Heloise*, Mary Wollstonecraft's *Vindication of the Rights of Woman*, or Friedrich Engels's *The Condition of the Working Class in England* are nicely complemented by those that are honed by having them examine Sergei Eisenstein's *Battleship Potemkin*, images of the industrial landscape, or photographs of the Victorian family. Indeed, as university and college history departments rethink the utility of teaching Western civilization (by examining, for example, the various ways in which we might incorporate non-Western perspectives and histories into more standard history surveys), we need to consider very seriously a broadening of the parameters of what we define as valid sources.

By encouraging students to read images, films, photographs, and other types of evidence critically, we can go some way toward establishing what is often labeled, by art historians and others, as "visual literacy."[1] While this concept has multiple meanings, it is used here to convey several key points. First, visual literacy in the western civilization classroom is not exclusively about allowing students to further acquire the so-called cultural capital often associated with higher education by teaching them about the great artists in Western history. Rather, it is about encouraging an active and integrative approach to learning that allows students to conceptualize, in the broadest possible sense, what constitutes the material of history. In this way, the use of images, be they static or moving, forces students to think actively about the process of "doing history." Questions about authenticity, motive, intention, and selectivity naturally emerge from a consideration of these sources and thus improve dramatically the Western civilization student's critical capacities. It is the active promotion of the student's ability to ask these sorts of questions that constitutes the first cornerstone of an education in visual literacy.

The second major advantage of this particular form of literacy is that it allows students to actually visualize the past. Images that help to set a context, allow students to attach a human face to social movements, or illustrate clearly the discrepancies in wealth in the European past enrich students' overall understanding of history and, quite possibly, ensure that some of the big themes of our classes actually stay with them beyond the final examination.

Finally, developing visual literacy in the Western civilization classroom renders what we do in these general surveys—which are often populated by history majors and nonmajors in nearly equal numbers—relevant to other departments. By actively encouraging students to "read" images critically in our classroom, we are able to make broader claims about the validity of the Western civilization survey in universities and colleges increasingly under pressure to illustrate the utility of certain courses. Visually literate students are better able to pursue not only the further study of history but degree courses in business, mass communications, fine arts, and the sciences. In this way, the encouragement of this type of learning in our classrooms serves a broader and very important educative function.

Methods of the Presentation of Visuals

Two central questions emerge for any instructor who chooses to pursue a visually oriented approach to the teaching of Western civilization. First, what are the best methods for presenting images to students in classes that may range in size from twenty to five hundred? Second, how does one present images in a fashion that goes beyond the merely illustrative function toward the goal of encouraging visual literacy? While many of the answers to these questions will only be worked out during the course of teaching a Western civilization survey, there are several key issues to consider beforehand.

The way in which instructors might present images is largely dependent upon the types of technologies available to them at their respective institutions. Ranging from the simple and usually ubiquitous overhead projector to the most sophisticated of wired classrooms, the options are indeed numerous. Each method has its own advantages and disadvantages. In the case of the low-tech overhead projector, its chief virtue is its versatility and flexibility. This device, which projects transparencies that can be made professionally or manually by the instructor, allows for any image from a textbook or monograph to be reproduced quickly and easily on a photocopier for classroom presentation. This method facilitates the ability of the instructor to decide on a visual presentation at the very last minute and enables quick additions and shifts in focus. It also has the added benefit of allowing for the integration of visual evidence from recently published books and articles, thus encouraging Western civilization professors to include up-to-date scholarship in their lectures.

Another highly utilized method is the slide projector, the favored device of most art historians even in this age of increasingly sophisticated computer-generated images. Slides, which must be produced in a photographic laboratory, require a little more advanced planning than do overheads. They do, however, provide the Western civilization instructor with some flexibility by allowing for nearly any image from a wide variety of sources to be reproduced cheaply. Slides also allow the instructor to take photographs of historic sites, buildings, and museum exhibits that might then be useful for classroom instruction. Also, while there are some mass-produced overhead sets (usually of maps), there are far more invaluable and highly varied slide collections (generally sold through textbook publishing companies) that focus exclusively on Western civilization images ranging from paintings by the Great Masters to political cartoons to contemporary photography.[2] The equipment required for this sort of image is fairly inexpensive and low-tech. While a little more prone to mechanical problems (such as burnt-out lamps or defective remotes) than the overhead, the slide projector also has the advantage of being highly portable and generally hassle-free.

Of course, at a point in time when discussions of technology and the teaching of history are increasingly frequent, Western civilization instructors must also consider a range of high-tech options when making the decision to "go visual." There are now available a number of computer presentation programs that enable instructors to generate images freely and easily in their classrooms. Most people who choose to pursue this route use PowerPoint, part of the Microsoft Office package found on most university and college computers. This software has been adapted by many instructors to construct user-friendly and visually stimulating lectures. Rather than engaging in a full-scale discussion of the merits and disadvantages of this particular type of transmission of knowledge, I would like to focus here briefly on how one might use this sort of software to produce clear and crisp images for classroom discussion. Software of this sort allows instructors to store images that have been either scanned from books and other sources or downloaded from one of several Western civilization image Web sites or CD-ROMs on a computer's hard drive. These images are thus saved permanently and easily used time and again in multimedia lectures. While somewhat problematic in terms of the amount of disk space required, programs of this sort also allow for short video clips to be stored in a computer for classroom use.

Once mastered, these high-tech options can be quite simple to work with, cost-effective, and enjoyable. These newer forms of technology also have the very clear advantage of efficiency. Instead of searching in overcrowded offices for storage space for multiple boxes of slides and files of transparencies, Western civilization instructors can simply have these images scanned (there are, in fact, slide scanners available on the market and in many university computer labs) and stored, centrally and in a far more organized fashion, on the hard drive of a laptop computer.

While undoubtedly useful, this technique is not without its problems. First, there is the expense of the equipment. At the very minimum, the instructor who chooses this option will need to have a laptop computer and portable LCD projector. Increasingly, universities and colleges are creating wired classrooms in which this equipment is permanently installed. Depending on the financial health of an institution, equipment of this sort may or may not be made readily available. Second, there are the problems of time associated with scanning images and familiarizing the instructor with the software and the methods of presentation. Unless one can hire a graduate or undergraduate assistant to help with the scanning and organization of images, work of this type will divert the attention of the instructor away from other valuable activities, such as research or administration. Finally, there is always the possibility of complete equipment failure in which key files are erased or hard drives crashed, effectively negating all of this time-consuming work. Although the possibility of total failure is remote, it is worthwhile thinking about the relative security of the tangible transparency and slide. Even though projectors might also break down, it is far easier to run down the hall to the audio-visual closet than it is to embark once again on a time-consuming scanning project.

One other method of presentation and storage, also of the high-tech variety, merits some consideration here. Instructors used to working with computers might wish to construct a Western civilization Web site to which images, short video clips, and a whole array of primary sources can be posted. The site can be used to store all of the images drawn upon for lectures and classroom exercises, thus providing a permanent record of visual material that students can consult easily and conveniently for research and study purposes. An individual Web site also enables the instructor to establish direct links to other relevant image Web sites as well as various repositories of primary source materials.

Interpretation of Visuals

While decisions about the method of presentation are indeed crucial, more serious pedagogical questions must also be considered as the instructor decides how to proceed in promoting visual literacy among Western civilization students. There are several approaches to the teaching of images that are worthwhile to think about.

Image presentation and interpretation in the classroom might be divided into two distinct categories, loosely characterized as either freestanding or complementary exercises. Freestanding exercises are best conceived as entire (or partial) class sessions devoted to the interpretation and discussion of selected images. This sort of format works best in considering topics such as "Fascist Propaganda" or "Everyday Life in the Eighteenth Century." In pursuing such an exercise, the instructor would have students read appropriate textbook chapters and various supplementary background materials. With a solid base, students would then be expected to interpret, in the case of the exercise on fascist propaganda, images of posters and photographs reflecting Fascist and Nazi efforts to organize daily life in Italy and Germany during the 1920s and 1930s. These might include posters produced for the Mussolini-inspired Mothers' and Infants' Day in Italy and pictures of various Nazi youth organizations that encouraged and actively enforced uniformity, physical fitness, and loyalty to the state.[3] Another immensely powerful source that might be used in this particular exercise is Leni Riefenstahl's documentary of the 1934 Nazi Party rally at Nuremberg. As an example of how Hitler attempted to forge a sense of unity in the aftermath of the purges of the SA in June of 1934, *Triumph of the Will* serves as a powerful example of how the moving image could be used to very explicit political ends. Perhaps most striking for students is the extent to which the film conveys ostensible mass support for enormous party spectacles as well as the orchestrated and choreographed nature of the rally.

Complementary exercises often take on the same form as freestanding exercises, but with a slightly different intent. Rather than asking students to simply acquire background information by reading a textbook, the complementary exercise uses images to broaden and enliven discussions of printed primary source materials. The focus then is on encouraging students to consider the full range of sources at the disposal of the historian in learning about, for example, the social and cultural impact of the Industrial Revolution. An exploration of this particular theme can be effectively accomplished by pairing several different types of sources. An instructor might, for example, provide students with excerpts from several different reports on working conditions in England from the early to mid-nineteenth century, which they would be asked to read in preparation for a class meeting. During the meeting, students could discuss the content of these sources and their historiographical significance by considering them alongside a range of images depicting the industrial landscape, factory conditions, and working-class housing. On its most basic level, this technique tends to serve as a catalyst for discussion by prompting responses to the images that are informed by the student's careful reading of the printed material. On a more sophisticated level, this type of exercise provides students and instructors alike with an opportunity to discuss issues related to veracity, authorial or artistic intent, and the complementary nature of different types of historical sources. It also serves another vital function by ensuring that the images of working-class life and the industrial landscape formulated in students' minds have a tangible relationship to "reality" that transcends what are often excessively romanticized or overdramatized film portrayals.

Substantial planning and advanced thinking is required to execute these sorts of exercises effectively. Any instructor intending to work extensively with visual evidence in the Western civilization classroom should construct a checklist of questions and issues—which should be distributed to students in printed form—to consider when interpreting visual evidence. Robert Levine, a prominent historian of Latin America, has offered some general guidelines for interpreting photographs as historical evidence that can, with some manipulation, be applied to the analysis of a whole range of visual evidence including paintings, films, and political cartoons. Levine states in his book, *Images of History: Nineteenth and Early Twentieth Century Latin American Photographs as Documents*, that there are ten themes to consider when "reading" photographs as historical evidence. These include, among others, the need for students of history to ask the same sorts of questions of visual images as they might of printed material. Levine argues that issues related to attribution as well as questions of time, place, bias, intentions, and audience should emerge as foremost in any consideration of this sort of Evidence.[4]

Other questions that should appear on any checklist to be used by students when considering historic images might include:

What does the image tell us about a given society's values, mores, and social norms?
How have these norms changed over time?
How do images demarcate social divisions in a given society or time period?
How are rural and urban scenes portrayed?
What do visual portrayals of a point in the past tell us about material culture in that era?
And, what is revealed about customs, dress, religious beliefs, family organization, and gender roles in historic images?

While the list of questions that can be posed is potentially enormous, instructors should tailor their own checklists to both the demands and abilities of their students and the specific goals of the course. Those intent on integrating visual material into written assignments (such as exams or formal essays) will need to think more seriously about what sorts of "objective" information about each image or set of images they want students to master for the purposes of assessment. This will necessitate a uniform "viewing sheet" which students should be required to complete, for each interpretive exercise, as a component of the class participation grade. While this degree of integration may be preferred, instructors interested in making the transition to a visual classroom more slowly may require a less substantial or formal checklist.

For those students not used to approaching history through visual sources, instructors will also need to impress upon them, from the very beginning, the seriousness of this pursuit. It must be stressed that adequate preparation is as essential for visual exercises as it is for more traditional discussions of course readings. To remind students of this, instructors may find it necessary to build into their syllabi periodic quizzes, graded viewing exercises, and other assignments that will encourage students to take seriously this style of learning about the past. Furthermore, instructors need to be absolutely comfortable with visual analysis in order for this type of learning experience to be effective. Thus, extensive reading will be required in the fields of art history, cultural studies, film studies, and visual theory, all of which have dealt more precisely and explicitly with the promotion of visual literacy in the university and college classroom.

Suggested Exercises for the Visually Oriented Western Civilization Classroom

While there are, quite literally, dozens of possible exercises, the approach taken by any instructor of Western civilization will largely depend on her or his methodological and intellectual interests and predispositions. What follows are three basic exercises that might be adapted to any classroom setting. Each of these exercises could be presented to a class as either complementary or freestanding, depending on the needs of the instructor.

1. The Iconography of the French Revolution

This exercise draws on the numerous political cartoons, prints, and various material artifacts generated during the years of the French Revolution to encourage students to think about the ways in which political ideas could be expressed visually through artistic metaphors and caricatures. Following Lynn Hunt's lead in her book *The Family Romance of the French Revolution*, this exercise might present students with an opportunity to examine how the French Revolution was conceived of, at least by some, as a form of family rebellion and patricide, in which the king, as the symbolic head of the French "family," was ritually executed. The iconography of the French Revolution opens up all sorts of other possibilities. An instructor might ask students, in the classroom, to examine images of "Liberty" in discussing not only revolutionary ideology but also gender roles and ideals in the late eighteenth century.

Possible sources for images, primary documents, and interpretive approaches include: Lynn Hunt, *The Family Romance of the French Revolution* (Berkeley: University of California Press, 1992), and Emmet Kennedy, *A Cultural History of the French Revolution* (New Haven, CT: Yale University Press, 1989). An impressive collection of images and sources has been gathered for a new CD-ROM to be produced by Pennsylvania State University Press. See Jack Censer and Lynn Hunt, *Liberty, Equality, Fraternity: Exploring the French Revolution* (forthcoming). For further information on this CD-ROM, consult the Web site of the Center for History and New Media at George Mason University at <http://chnm.gmu.edu>.

2. Colonialism and Popular Culture

This particular exercise asks students to analyze a series of images (c. 1880–1920) that help to illuminate ideas about race, cultural superiority, and the civilizing mission in the age of new imperialism. Drawing primarily on examples from European popular culture, these images might consist of the highly evocative advertisements created in Great Britain for Pears' Soap, which drew on ideas about the civilizing nature of European products as well as stereotyped images of the unenlightened (particularly with respect to the emerging consumer ethos) "dark savage." Complementary documentary sources might include the poetry of Rudyard Kipling and other writings by various advocates of empire.

Possible sources for images and interpretive approaches include: Anne McClintock, *Imperial Leather: Race, Gender and Sexuality in the Colonial Context* (London and New York: Routledge, 1995) and Thomas Richards, *The Commodity Culture of Victorian England: Advertising and Spectacle, 1851–1914* (Stanford, CA: Stanford University Press, 1990).

3. Ideology and Film in the Early Soviet Union

This exercise focuses on an interpretation of Sergei Eisenstein's 1925 film, *Battleship Potemkin*, about a revolutionary mutiny that occurred aboard a Russian navy vessel in 1905. By analyzing the film, students are able to examine the impact of the Russian Revolution and communist ideology upon the visual arts. Themes to be covered in analyzing this film might include the filmmaker's portrayal of class antagonism in the relationship between ordinary soldiers and naval officers, the infusion of revolutionary ideology into the plotline, and the power of images in conveying political messages. An exercise of this sort also provides a wonderful opportunity to initiate discussions on the techniques of filmmaking (especially Eisenstein's use of separate and titled acts and alternating close-ups and long shots), encouraging students in the process to think about the method as well as the message of presentation.

Possible sources for film suggestions, primary documents, and interpretive approaches include: Sergei Eisenstein, *Selected Works, Vol. I: Writings, 1922–34*, edited and translated by Richard Taylor (London: British Film Institute, 1988) and Peter Kenez, *Cinema and Soviet Society, 1917–1953* (Cambridge: Cambridge University Press, 1992).

Conclusion

The degree to which it is possible to integrate visual learning into the Western civilization classroom will depend largely on the predilections and predispositions of the individual instructor. For those interested in departing from the "stand and deliver" lecture format, this style of teaching provides invaluable opportunities for integrative and participatory learning. Adding a visual dimension to the standard Western civilization survey enhances the learning experience by encouraging students to broaden their understanding of how historians learn about the past while giving them a sense of what that past (an often abstract concept reflected only in awkward sounding and occasionally confusing documents) "actually" looked like. By expanding the routes through which Western civilization students learn about the past, instructors can actively improve upon the skills of analytical thought, interpretation, and creative and accurate expression that every university and college professor tries to facilitate.

The benefits to the instructor of this sort of approach are equally important. By integrating visual material, new instructors might discover a style of teaching that they will be able to adapt to different situations throughout their academic careers. Similarly, experienced teachers might find that this new approach breathes fresh life into stale lectures, encourages new avenues of inquiry and fields of exploration, and reinvigorates a waning or possibly lost enthusiasm for teaching. While instructors will certainly differ in their opinions on the utility of such an approach, it is certainly one worthy of at least a period of trial and experimentation. The possibilities are endless and the rewards considerable.

Suggested Sources

Readings

Allen, Robert C. "Historiography and the Teaching of Film History." *Film and History* 10–2 (1980).

Carnes, Mark C. "Beyond Words: Reviewing Moving Pictures." *Perspectives* 34.5 (May/June 1996).

Herman, Gerald. "History through Film: Making Multi-Media Lectures for Classroom Use." *Film and History* 2.4 (1972).

Hiley, Michael. *Seeing through Photographs.* London: Gordon Fraser, 1983.
Levine, Robert M. *Images of History: Nineteenth and Early Twentieth Century Latin American Photographs as Documents.* Durham and London: Duke University Press, 1989.
Margolis, Eric. "Mining Photographs: Unearthing the Meaning of Historical Photos." *Radical History Review* 40 (1985).
O'Connor, John. "Special Report: The Moving-Image Media in the History Classroom." *Film and History* 16.3 (1986). ———. *Teaching History with Film and Television.* Washington, DC: American Historical Association, 1987.
Rosenstone, Robert. *Visions of the Past: The Challenge of Film to Our Idea of History.* Cambridge, MA: Harvard University Press, 1995.
Schulkin, Carl. "The Challenge of Integration." *Perspectives* 37.2 (February 1999).
Susman, Warren I. "History and Film: Artifact and Experience." *Film and History* 15.2 (1985).
Trinkle, Dennis A. "Computers and the Practice of History: Where Are We? Where Are We Headed?" *Perspectives* 37.2 (February 1999).
Zukas, Alex. "Different Drummers: Using Music to Teach History." *Perspectives* 34.6 (September 1996).

Web Sites

Center for History and New Media. <http://chnm.gmu.edu/>.
Modern History Sourcebook. <http://www.fordham.edu/halsall/mod/modsbook.html>.
Western Culture: Links and Online Book. <http://www.westernculture.com/>.

Notes

[1] The term implies that literacy is acquired through a reading of images and other forms of communication as well as written texts. Visual literacy is, in fact, a specific field of academic study that ranges in focus from reception theory to pedagogic examinations of visual media in the classroom. The diversity of issues that are dealt with by scholars working in this area is reflected in the contents of the *Journal of Visual Literacy*, published by the International Visual Literacy Association. For additional information, see their Web site at <http://www.ivla.org/>.
[2] For one example of these collections see "The Western Civilization Slide Collection" produced by the Instructional Resources Corporation of Annapolis, Maryland.
[3] I have drawn material for this particular type of exercise from Victoria de Grazia, *How Fascism Ruled Women: Italy, 1922–1945* (Berkeley: University of California Press, 1992), and Claudia Koonz, *Mothers in the Fatherland: Women, Family Life and Nazi Politics* (New York: St. Martin's Press, 1987).
[4] For a discussion of these issues, see Robert M. Levine, *Images of History: Nineteenth and Early Twentieth Century Latin American Photographs as Documents* (Durham and London: Duke University Press, 1989).

Literature and the Western Civilization Classroom

Michael D. Richards

Sweet Briar College

Every time I teach the Western civilization survey, I make it a point to introduce students to at least one classic of Western literature. Even if the students do not remember much about the course, perhaps they will remember reading and enjoying *Candide* or *Madame Bovary* or *One Day in the Life of Ivan Denisovich.* There are times, too, when a novel or play can help students understand a historical issue or situation in ways that the textbook or a historical monograph cannot. And there is probably nothing better than fiction or poetry for drawing students into a consideration of the big historiographical questions: what is right or wrong in a given circumstance, what has or does not have significance, and whether there is purpose or meaning to the history of humanity.

In the next few pages, I will take up some of the problems and also some of the joys of using literature in Western civilization courses. Overall, I mean to encourage anyone who has not tried using literature to utilize this important resource. I also want to reassure those who have used literature in the past that this is a direction they should continue to take. Much of teaching is a process of trial and error, and you must discover what you are comfortable doing and make your own creative mistakes. Nonetheless, I will include a few practical applications for you to consider.

The Colossal Responsibility of Teaching Great Literature

Historians are sometimes daunted by what they see as the huge responsibility associated with the teaching of a novel or a play. My approach to this is roughly that of Georges Clemenceau during World War I when he remarked that "war is too important to be left to the generals."

Literature is a vital part of Western civilization, and it also helps us understand better many other aspects of Western civilization. We have an obligation to take a novel or a poem seriously as a source of history and to communicate this significance to our students. We must do the best we can in this regard, but we are not charged with explicating a particular work from a literary point of view. The most crucial piece of advice I can give is simply to read the novel or play or poem carefully. Ideally, you should read it at least twice, once to get a sense of the piece and a second time to take notes. A couple of examples may be helpful at this point.

Heart of Darkness *by Joseph Conrad*

A few years back, I tried to summarize Conrad's novel in an introduction I was writing for a text on twentieth-century Europe. I contended the book was not so much about the Belgian Congo as it was about the fragility and precariousness of Western civilization. The heart of darkness was not upriver but in every man and woman. When I showed this summary to a good friend, who is a gifted teacher of English literature, she warned me that critical opinion of Conrad was rather unfavorable and that many considered him a racist and a misogynist. Did this mean, I wondered, that I ought not to teach Conrad any longer? If I chose to continue, how much of the new criticism did I need to read and how much did I need to pass on to my students? The answer to the first question is I still teach Conrad. The answers to the second question are "some" and "very little."

The second question is important, and I want to outline here what "some" and "very little" actually meant in this case. I was fortunate in that one of the main feminist critics of Conrad, Marianna Torgovnick, was then teaching at the university where I did my graduate work. About the time I became aware of the new interpretations of Conrad, the alumni magazine featured an excellent article about her. Not too long after that, David Denby wrote about Conrad and the new interpretations in *The New Yorker* ("Jungle Fever," 6 November 1995, pp. 118–129). All this was perhaps serendipitous, but serendipity happens most often to those whose minds are prepared for it. Beyond serendipity, there were many other sources available. For example, there was the Norton Critical Edition of *Heart of Darkness* (New York: W. W. Norton, 1988), third edition, edited by Robert Kimbrough. For most authors or titles, a number of resources are available in libraries or on Web sites. Time and interest will limit what you realistically should do. There is no need to pursue the study of a novel to the point of publishing a critical analysis of the book, although this did happen to me once.

In the case of Conrad, students will have to know there are controversies, quite important ones. I discuss the controversies briefly, making a case for Conrad and against him. I also indicate that my reading of the book may be incorrect. Since the students have read the book themselves, it is up to them to arrive at their own conclusions. The most important reason for reading *Heart of Darkness* or any piece of fiction in a history course is that students attempt to form and defend some opinions about the work itself and attempt to use it to understand history more fully—in this case, the history of late nineteenth-century imperialism. It gives them practice in what should be a lifelong effort to arrive at and articulate informed opinions.

Madame Bovary *by Gustave Flaubert*

That Flaubert is famous for his great effort to find "le mot juste" makes *Madame Bovary* a little daunting. The book is, however, also an extraordinary resource for social history. It has much to say about the practice of medicine in France in the first part of the nineteenth century, the pretensions of small-town intellectuals, the impact of romanticism, and life in provincial France generally. But shouldn't you discuss the wonderful writing? Yes, but only to the extent you can. If you can't, don't try to fake it. In my case, a friend who taught French literature casually mentioned one day the wonderful passage in which Rodolphe begins his seduction of Emma during the agricultural show. Flaubert sets off their romantic blather against speeches about the importance of agriculture and announcements of awards for the best sheep or pig. While I had noted Rodolphe's smooth insincerity, I had overlooked this example of Flaubert's art. Now that this ironic juxtaposition has been pointed out to me, I can mention to students both the literary aspects and the pathetic story of the old servant. While it is certainly advantageous to be alert to the literary aspects, and even to seek out colleagues who may be able to help expand on them, comprehension of these should not be the major goal of the presentation or discussion of the novel.

Teachable Sources versus Unwieldy Novels

After many valiant efforts, I have stopped trying to teach *The Magic Mountain* in a history course. I still spend a portion of a class talking about Thomas Mann and *The Magic Mountain* when we examine Weimar Germany and the rise of Hitler. But the novel itself is much too long and complicated and includes many pages written in French. Rather than the novel, I might have students read "Mario and the Magician," a short story by Mann that lends itself to a discussion of fascism in the interwar period.

It is philistine not to use a novel because it is longer than three hundred pages. Still, a little pragmatism is in order when teaching the Western civilization survey. A novella, a short story, a play, perhaps a few poems, or excerpts from a long novel will generally work better than a lengthy novel, no matter how wonderful the novel. So, try Aleksandr Solzhenitsyn's *One Day in the Life of Ivan Denisovich* instead of *First Circle* or Charles Dickens's *Hard Times* rather than *Our Mutual Friend.*

One Day in the Life of Ivan Denisovich *by Aleksandr Solzhenitsyn*

Solzhenitsyn's novella works almost perfectly in a Western civilization survey. One drawback is that it is now often read in high school; therefore, it may not be new to many students. An additional problem is that there is no longer quite the same interest in the Soviet Union as there once was when the cold war had just ended. In its favor, this book is not only a quick read but is also an absorbing tale. It is also a part of Nikita Khrushchev's efforts to contend with the Stalinist legacy (he personally intervened to allow it to be published in the Soviet literary periodical *Novy Mir*), and therefore it stands as a part of the larger political history. Lastly, it effectively introduces students to the Gulag Archipelago, the vast system of prisons and labor camps created by the secret police in the 1920s and 1930s, and to the disturbing questions this system raises about humanity in the twentieth century.

Anthologies

Anthologies are a staple of Western civilization courses, but the kind of anthology we might use to bring fiction or poetry into our course is not available. Most anthologies for history courses contain documents having to do with politics, economics, and society. Only one that I am aware of departs very far from the familiar mix, and that is *Movements, Currents, Trends: Aspects of European Thought in the Nineteenth and Twentieth Centuries* by Eugen Weber. Some may be familiar with the original version of the book: *Paths to the Present.* This very interesting anthology is a collection of documents about major cultural movements beginning with romanticism. It leans toward prefaces, manifestos, and critical essays. Other anthologies designed for humanities courses cover art and music as well as literature, but they are generally less useful for Western civilization courses.

One series of anthologies, while still not quite what we might wish for, should be mentioned here. I first became acquainted with the series published by Viking Press through *The Portable Twentieth-Century Russian Reader*, edited by Clarence Brown, and, later, *The Portable Nineteenth-Century Russian Reader*, edited by George Gibian. Most volumes are devoted to particular authors, but there is *The Portable Greek Reader*, edited by W. H. Auden; *The Portable Roman Reader*, edited by Basil Davenport; *The Portable Medieval Reader*, edited by James Bruce Ross and Mary Martin McLaughlin; *The Portable Renaissance Reader*, also edited by Ross and McLaughlin; *The Portable Romantic Poets*, edited by Auden and Norman Holmes Pearson; and *The Portable Victorian Reader*, edited by Gordon S. Haight.

There are often anthologies available for a particular national literary tradition. For example, anthologies of Russian literature include *Twentieth Century Russian Plays: An Anthology*, edited by F. D. Reeve (New York: W. W. Norton, 1963), and *The Penguin Book of Russian Short Stories*, edited by David Richards (New York: Penguin, 1981). There are also anthologies devoted to a particular period or event. Two examples are *The Penguin Book of First World War Poetry*, second edition, edited by Jon Silkin (New York: Penguin, 1981), and *Against Forgetting: Twentieth Century Poetry of Witness*, edited by Carolyn Forché (New York: W. W. Norton, 1993).

To the best of my knowledge, there is nothing comparable to the Viking series of portable readers for all of Western civilization. There are anthologies of western literature such as *The Norton Anthology of World Masterpieces*, seventh edition, edited by Sarah Lawall, but they are designed for a course on comparative literature. *The Norton Anthology of World Masterpieces*, for example, consists of two volumes, each 2,350 pages in length. Given the extraordinary amount of material covered in a Western civilization course, it is more practical for you to choose one novel or perhaps to put together a short reader of your own (in this day of desktop publishing that is relatively easy to do).

Other Possibilities

You should also keep in mind essays, autobiographies, memoirs, and diaries. I have frequently used Eugenia Semyanovna Ginzburg's *Journey into the Whirlwind*, her account of her experiences in the purges in the Soviet Union in the 1930s, with considerable success. This is more familiar ground for historians in that these genres frequently form the documentary basis for our work.

Resources

You may wish to use one or more of a number of very useful resources to help in dealing with a particular novel or author. One such outstanding resource is the Cambridge Companion series. This series includes, for example, *The Cambridge Companion to Renaissance Humanism*, edited by Jill Kraye, and *The Cambridge Companion to the Eighteenth-Century Novel*, edited by John Richetti. Most of the titles in the series center on individual authors, but a few cover national literary traditions. Other series that generally focus on one book or a single theme or personality include the Oxford Reader's Companion series, the Norton

Critical Editions, and the Bedford Series in History and Culture. Twayne Publishers offers both short biographies and critical studies of individual titles. Collections of critical essays on particular authors or titles are also published by Garland Press, Greenwood Publishers, G. K. Hall, and Prentice-Hall. Web sites are very important. One excellent site is the GaleNet Literature Resource Center at <http://www.galenet.com/servlet/LitRC?&u= LRC&u=CA&u=ClC&u>. This Web site combines the resources of various Gale Group publications: Contemporary Authors, Contemporary Literary Criticism Select, and Dictionary of Literary Biography. (Note: GaleNet access is only available through libraries; you must see your librarian to obtain a username and password.) The Lycos search engine is also a good way to find information on the Web for a particular author or title. Here, however, you will quickly come upon material that is not relevant, not useful, or simply incorrect. Your students will likely use this resource as well. A discussion of Web sites, and their advantages and disadvantages, early in the course is highly recommended.

Practical Ways to Use Literature in the Western Civilization Classroom

Heart of Darkness by Joseph Conrad

There is a plethora of resources for work on *Heart of Darkness*. In addition to the Norton Critical Edition, there are *The Cambridge Companion to Joseph Conrad*, ed. J. H. Stape (Cambridge: Cambridge University Press, 1996), and *The Oxford Reader's Companion to Conrad*, ed. by Owen Knowles and Gene Moore (Oxford: Oxford University Press, 2000). Gary Adelman has published *Heart of Darkness: Search for the Unconscious* (Boston: Twayne, 1987). Marianna Torgovnick's *Gone Primitive: Savage Intellects, Modern Lives* (Chicago: University of Chicago Press, 1990) includes an informative section on the novel. There is also a great deal of useful information on the GaleNet Literature Resource Center. A search on Lycos turned up some interesting and helpful sites as well. If anything, there is almost too much in the way of resources.

One approach is to set the novel in the context of a larger issue or problem. In this case, we can set Conrad's novel in the context of imperialism at the end of the nineteenth century. This gives us more questions to ask and helps to de-emphasize the literary aspects. Before talking about the novel, take a few minutes to tell the class who Conrad was and to make a few comments on the novel itself. In this case, we would need to mention the controversies surrounding the novel, the accusations that Conrad was a racist and a misogynist. You may want to provide students with a few ideas to ponder before they begin reading. For example, you might ask them to consider why the opening of the novel is set on the Thames, or what implicit comparison Conrad makes between the Thames and the Congo. A one-page guide asking students to consider a few basic questions and providing some background will be helpful.

There are two basic ways to deal with the book. One is a discussion of some of the main themes set beforehand. These might include the following questions: What is imperialism? How did Europeans view themselves at the end of the century? How did European men view European women? What was their attitude toward the people that they colonized? How did people deal with power in this period? What was Western civilization to Marlow? What was the "heart of darkness"? If possible, tie the discussion to the text by quoting from the novel.

The other basic approach is an explication of the text, a specialized lecture that takes the students through the book in pursuit of one or more themes. I might wish, for instance, to assert that Conrad believed that civilization was fragile. Unfortunately, in his observation, the lure of power was immensely strong. *Heart of Darkness* is full of stories of Europeans succumbing to the lure of power. By way of contrast, Conrad introduces the plight of the native crew on the steamboat Marlow is taking up the river. They have all but used up their food supply, which is separate from that of the Europeans, and it may be some time before they find a village on the river where they can trade for food. They are also cannibals, and Marlow wonders why they don't simply take over the boat and have the

Europeans for dinner. Something restrains them. He can't name it, but it impresses him that these so-called savages had not given in to hunger (Conrad 114–117). In contrast to the natives' restraint, Marlow describes how the helmsman, whom he liked, lacked restraint and got himself killed as a result. When people on the shore attack the boat, the helmsman throws open the shutter that protected him from the arrows and shoots a rifle at the attackers. The boat is close to the shore, and the helmsman is speared through the open window and dies (Conrad 120–122). Then Marlow identifies the helmsman with Kurtz, the person everyone in the company thought would go far: " 'Poor fool! If he had only left that shutter alone. He had no restraint, no restraint—just like Kurtz—a tree swayed by the wind' " (Conrad 129). Speaking of Kurtz directly, Marlow says, " 'the wilderness had found him out early . . . I think it had whispered to him things about himself which he did not know, things of which he had no conception till he took counsel with this great solitude—and the whisper had proved irresistibly fascinating' " (Conrad 138).

The third way to approach the novel is simply to let the discussion go where it will, but be prepared to step in occasionally with relevant passages for the students to consider. In the case of such free-form discussion, you would resist the temptation to lay things out to students and only guide them toward the kinds of insights you hope they will take away from the material. You may be surprised at what your student readers will find and point out. This method gives you the opportunity to make what points you might wish to make but allows for the possibility that others will have different insights to contribute. Such an approach actually takes more preparation than the first two methods (and requires you to be quick on your feet), but may well bring greater rewards.

Reference

Conrad, Joseph. *Heart of Darkness*. 1950. Signet Classics Edition. (New York: Penguin, 1997).